A NEW DICTIONARY OF SAINTS:
EAST AND WEST

A NEW DICTIONARY
OF SAINTS:
EAST AND WEST

Michael Walsh

LITURGICAL PRESS
Collegeville, Minnesota

www.litpress.org

Published in the United States and Canada by:
LITURGICAL PRESS
Saint John's Abbey
Collegeville, MN 56321
www.litpress.org

First published 2007

ISBN 978-0-8146-3186-7

Library of Congress Cataloging-in-Publication Data
Walsh, Michael J., 1937-
   A new dictionary of saints : east and west / Michael Walsh.
   p. cm.
   Includes bibliographical references.
   ISBN-13: 978-0-8146-3186-7
   1. Christian saints–Dictionaries. I. Title.
   BR1710.W35 2007
   270.092'2–dc22
   [B]

                                                        2007017729

Typeset by YHT Ltd, London
Printed and bound in England by
Antony Rowe Ltd, Chippenham, Wiltshire

CONTENTS

INTRODUCTION

There have been many dictionaries of saints, many collections of lives of saints who have been soldiers, or young when they died, or founders of religious orders, or great sinners who converted and became great evangelists of the gospel, or missionaries, or people who died for their faith, sometimes in lands far away from where they were born. In the Christian tradition the first saints seem to have been precisely that, men and women who died as witnesses for their faith. They were called 'martyrs', because *martyr* is the Greek for 'witness'. This book contains the lives of people who fall into each of these categories. In that sense it is no different from many other publications. But it is different, and to the best of my knowledge it is in fact unique, because it attempts to list in one volume saints who are revered in each of the major Christian traditions, whether of the East or of the West. Only the Churches of the sixteenth-century Reform turned their back on the cult of saints, and are therefore omitted from this collection.

Most, if not all, world religions have saints. They have holy men and women, and the word 'saint' simply comes from the Latin *sanctus*, meaning holy. These are people whose lives have often been recognized as displaying great holiness even during their lifetimes, and are now, after their deaths, held up for our admiration and emulation. Occasionally, however, this holiness is recognized only after the death of the saint, but is then confirmed by the saint's apparent ability to work miracles.

That at least is the theory. The reality is frequently rather different. For instance, in a great number of cases little or nothing is known about the life of a saint beyond the bare fact of their existence and the day on which their 'feast' is celebrated. They were, presumably, once admired and venerated, but although their names were somehow preserved in liturgical celebrations, we no longer know why they were so renowned in their day. In the case of the English scholar Alcuin, we know quite a lot about his life, which seems to have been a holy one, and he is mentioned as a 'blessed' in a list of the saints of the early Frankish Church, but there is no evidence of a cult of Alcuin. On the other hand, there is some evidence of a cult of Charlemagne, at whose court Alcuin worked, 'despite the emperor's immoral private life and his unsoundness concerning the dogmatic validity of icons', as *The Book of Saints* (see Bibliography below) says rather censoriously. What is true of Charlemagne in the West is equally true of the fourth-century Emperor Constantine in the East, revered in the Russian and Greek Churches for his care both towards his people and towards the Church.

In other words, although most hagiography (that is, the lives of saints) is written as if the saint is being held up for our emulation, that is in practice only one reason, and perhaps the least common reason, why people are venerated. The monk Paisius of Chlendar, who lived in the middle of the eighteenth century, is venerated in Bulgaria not because of the holiness of his life – next to nothing is known of him – but because his vast history of the Bulgarian Church and people was first published in the mid-nineteenth century, on the high tide of Bulgarian nationalism. He is celebrated as a national hero rather than as a holy man. He may very well also have been the latter, of course, but we simply do not know. In the Churches of Greece and – especially – Russia, there is a group of saints who were 'fools for Christ', living evidently eccentric lives, perhaps to humiliate themselves before others as an act of abasement and a form of mortification, or perhaps because they were indeed personally highly eccentric. Such people occur not only among the saints of Russia or Greece: the popular figure of the French nomad Benedict Joseph Labré also falls into this category.

For members of religious orders, it is important that their founder be declared a saint, because this is evidence that their manner of life, and more particularly the special inspiration or 'charism' which the founder imparted to his or her followers, enjoys official approval. As many of the new congregations which have come into being have, in their day, been controversial – including even such major ones as the Dominicans and the Jesuits – the process of canonization provides a final seal that the 'charism' is an authentic interpretation of the Christian message.

Canonization, the process by which someone is declared a saint, varies from Church to Church. Perhaps none is as cumbersome as that in the Roman Catholic Church, which even has a special department of the Vatican, the Congregation for the Causes of Saints, to handle it. A candidate is called 'Venerable' when his or her cause is officially accepted by the Vatican, then 'Blessed', a status which allows public veneration to be given to the person so recognized, and finally 'Saint'. Nowadays there is little difference between the rank of 'Saint' and that of 'Blessed', and the latter status tends to be looked upon as a halfway house. But when it was first introduced, in the seventeenth century, beatification (as the process of declaring a candidate 'Blessed' is called) was meant to permit veneration but only in a local area. In the Churches of the Orthodox tradition the process is simpler: a person is declared to be a saint by a decision of the Church's synod, that is, by a gathering of its bishops.

Saints are normally commemorated annually on the anniversary of the day of their death. This is their 'birth day', the *dies natalis*, the day of birth into heaven. This is the common, even though not the absolutely invariable, practice: some Russian saints, for example, are commemorated on more than one day, and their 'feasts' can be attached to the Church's year, to Lent or to Easter, for example, rather than to a fixed day in the calendar. But for the most part it is possible to draw up a 'calendar of saints', to list them by the day of their feast. There has been a calendar such as this in existence for the Church of Rome since the middle of the fourth century, and from the fifth century there has existed the *Martyrologium Hieronymianum*, or 'Martyrology of Jerome', named after St Jerome quite erroneously and based on an earlier version from Asia Minor. This is again arranged in date order, but as well as assigning feast days, it says a little – usually a very little – about the life of the saint, particularly the place of death and sometimes a rough indication of the date: 'in the persecution of Diocletian', for example.

The Roman Church has recently brought out a new version of the martyrology (see the Bibliography), but the Orthodox Churches have something very similar in the *Menologion*, a book of lives of the saints, again arranged according to date order. There is also the *Synaxarion*, a book which contains a brief life of the saint for each day, which is read out during the morning service in the Eastern Churches. It is from books such as these that lists of saints can be compiled, but we know of saints by other means, from chronicles, from surviving lives of early saints which mention them, from church dedications and so on. But often enough, information is minimal: the name of a saint is known, and the feast day, as indicated above, yet with no indication of place, or even century, though sometimes both can be guessed at. And of course, there are the entirely legendary saints, saints who have come into being perhaps through a genuine mistake, a misreading of a text, or a misinterpretation of a piece of archaeological data, or simply as heroes and heroines of a good story – the popular figure of St Christopher falls into the latter category, although happily Santa Claus, St Nicholas of Myra, was a real person who can be placed and dated.

BIBLIOGRAPHY

A large number of books have been used in the preparation of this list of saints of the Churches of East and West. For the Western Church there is a vast range of encyclopaedias and dictionaries available. The fundamental work is the *Martyrologium Romanum*, published by the Vatican in 2001 with a second edition in 2004. This contains nearly 700 pages of text, with another 150 pages or so of index, in double columns. This volume lists all the saints and blessed who can be venerated publicly, and indicates the day on which the feast is celebrated.

The Book of Saints published in London by A. & C. Black in 2002 declares itself to be, in the subtitle, 'A Comprehensive Biographical Dictionary'. It has been appearing at intervals since the 1920s. The latest edition, edited by Dom Basil Watkins on behalf of the Benedictine monks of St Augustine's Abbey, Ramsgate, is invaluable for quick reference: the entries are short, but for the most part to the point.

David Farmer's *Oxford Dictionary of Saints*, has also been regularly reprinted since it first appeared in 1978. It is particularly strong on the English saints, but it is also to be valued for the way in which Dr Farmer recounts the history of a saint's cult, as well as his or her life.

Between 1756 and 1759 there appeared, in theory in four volumes but in practice in rather more parts, *The Lives of the Fathers, Martyrs and other Principal Saints*. It was written by Father Alban Butler, and has since become known as *Butler's Lives of the Saints*. This book has been published in many different guises, but in the late 1990s a new edition appeared, published by Burns and Oates, a volume a month of saints. It has been edited by different hands, and is of somewhat uneven quality, but is on the whole a most useful guide to the lives of the major (Western) saints, and has been used extensively in this book.

The *Liber Pontificalis*, or *Book of the Popes*, referred to in the text, is a collection of lives of the popes, first compiled in the first half of the sixth century, and added to throughout the middle ages.

For the Eastern saints the major source has been *Enciclopedia dei Santi: Le Chiese Orientali* (Rome: Città Nuova, 1998). This two-volume work has been indispensable. Without it, the present book could not have been written. In fact, its existence was to some extent the inspiration for it. Again, it is written by many different hands, and the variation in the approach of various scholars can at times be disconcerting.

Central though this *Enciclopedia* has been, it was very helpful to be able to turn to Otto Meinardus's *The Saints of Greece* (Athens: George Scouras, 1970), as well as, for the saints of the first few hundred years of Christian history, Angelo Di Berardino's *Encyclopedia of the Early Church* (Cambridge: James Clarke, 1992).

Finally, though this book was inspired in great part by the *Enciclopedia dei Santi*, it also had its origins in a book I edited, the *Dictionary of Christian Biography* (London: Continuum, 2001). This book contained saints' lives, as well as many more lives of Christians who were not saints (or at least, not recognized as such). These lives have been extracted from the original and added to this volume, in almost all cases lightly edited. The *Dictionary of Christian Biography* was the work of many hands, and I would again like to thank them all for their help.

ACKNOWLEDGEMENTS

As I remarked above, the *Dictionary of Christian Biography* was the work of many hands. This current volume has been produced by far fewer. Kate Walsh went through the *Dictionary of Christian Biography* and constructed a list of all the saints and blesseds to be found in it. Anne-Marie Sharman worked away meticulously on several volumes of *Butler's Lives of the Saints*, and Clare Walsh did likewise, speedily, for one of the volumes. A number of people gave me advice from time to time, perhaps without realizing it. I would like to make mention of two in particular, Professor Andrew Louth of Durham University, and Dr Richard Price of Heythrop College, University of London. I am deeply grateful to all, and especially to those who undertook some of the writing.

CONVENTIONS

Most entries in this volume are, obviously, of saints, so the term is not used. If, however, the person listed is a 'blessed' or a 'venerable', this status is indicated after their name by the insertion of 'bl.' or 'ven.' respectively. Saints mentioned in the Bible have not been included.

The (Roman) Catholic Church has the largest number of entries, so an individual's membership of the Catholic Church is not indicated. Membership of other Churches is given: the conventions for this usage are described in the Appendix (see pp. 643–646). A good many saints, of course, and especially those of the early centuries, are venerated by most Churches, East and West.

As has been remarked, feast days mainly fall on the day of a saint's death. When this is the case – and obviously it can only be the case when the day of death is known precisely – no date for a feast day is given. There are occasionally multiple feast days: usually only the day judged to be the main one is recorded.

Names run in strict alphabetical order, the order itself being determined strictly by the elements of the name which have been displayed in bold type. However, dealing with so many different languages has given rise to a large number of problems. Names are sometimes given in the appropriate language. Most, however, are given in an English form whenever possible – thus Basil for Vasili, or Charles for Carlo. Otherwise, names are given in the nearest approximation the Roman alphabet can achieve. Often, to keep them in sequence, a Latin form is used – thus Pius for the popular figure of Padre Pio. Medieval Latin names, on the other hand, have been rendered into modern English equivalents, where these exist. The convention that saints are known by their first, Christian, or given names has been strictly applied – so Thomas More, for example, is filed in that form, not as More, Thomas.

Finally, I have tried for the most part to follow a formula. The standard entry, therefore, will begin in this manner:

Paisius Grigorevic Moskot, martyr, born Peski Radkovskie, 8 December 1869, died Char'kov, 15 December 1937. Ukrainian Church, Moscow Patriarchate.

The name is given in bold, followed by his/her status (martyr, bl. [for 'blessed'], etc.), followed by place and date of birth, then place and date of death. The last element, here 'Ukrainian Church', indicates the branch of Christianity which venerates the saint. If any of these elements is missing, then at the time of completing this book I did not know it. However, if no branch of Christianity is mentioned, it is either because the saint is venerated in the Western, i.e. Roman Catholic, Church, or, especially in the case of first-millennium saints, by several, or possibly most, Churches.

Aaron and **Julius**, martyrs, died Caerleon, Wales, 304. If historical, they were probably traders. Feast 1 July.

Aba, catholicos of the Assyrian Church, born 504, died Ctesiphon, 552. He was a royal official, originally a Zoroastrian, who was converted to Christianity after a conversation with a young Christian whom he had ordered off a ferry over the Tigris, but had to allow back on board when the ferry would not cross the river. He studied at the school of Nisibis, then travelled in the Eastern Roman Empire. From 523 there was a schism in the Church which was only resolved in 540 on Aba's election as catholicos. He then embarked on a visitation of the Church to repair the damage done by the schism. Although something of a favourite of King Chosroes I, he was sent into exile in Azerbaijan after converting some Zoroastrian priests to Christianity. Because of further problems in his Church, he returned illegally to Persia, where for a few months in 550–1 he was imprisoned in the royal palace, and survived further attempts to incriminate him in the rebellion of Chosroes's Christian son. Feast (1) the sixth Friday after Epiphany, (2) the second Friday of Lent, the day of his death.

Aba, bishop of Nineveh in the Assyrian Church, end of sixth century. He was an excellent pastor, but was exiled by King Hormisdas IV and went into exile in Byzantine territory, where he was treated as a prisoner of war. He seems to have acted for Chosroes as part of the peace delegation attempting to end the war between Byzantium and Persia. The conflict ended in the winter of 589–90,

and Aba was able to return to Nineveh in the summer of 591. Feast 17 December.

Ababio, monk in the Coptic Church in the second half of the fourth century. The son of devout parents of Memphis, and the youngest of seven children, he went into the desert of Scete after the death of his father and a revelation to his mother. He lived on dry bread and a little salt, kept silence, and taught his disciples a love of solitude. Feast 8 July, the day of his death.

Abamun, martyr, born Tuh in the Nile delta, fourth century. Coptic Church. After a vision of the Archangel Michael, he went to Antinoë to witness to his faith before the Roman governor. He was subjected to many tortures, and was then decapitated. Feast 7 July, the day of his martyrdom.

Abbo of Fleury, abbot, born near Orleans, *c.* 945, died Fleury sur Loire, 13 November 1004, from a wound received while trying to resolve a monastic dispute in Gascony. He was renowned for learning and sanctity, having studied philosophy, mathematics and astronomy. He calmed those who foresaw the end of the world in the millennium year 1000. He served for two years in England from 965 as director of the newly founded Ramsey monastery school in Huntingdon. Gerbert (later Pope Sylvester II) intervened when his election as abbot of Fleury was contested.

Abd Al-Malak, abbot, born Asyut, *c.* 1728, died in the monastery of al-Muharraq, 25 October 1808. Coptic Church. He joined the monastery at 15 and was cook for many years before becoming abbot in 1772.

Abd Al-Masih, martyr, seventh or eighth century (?), died 17 July. Coptic Church.

Abda, bishop of Edessa. Syriac Church. Feast 16 February.

Abdas (Audas) and Companions, martyrs, died Ledan, Persia, 420. Abdas was bishop of Kascar and was killed with seven priests, nine deacons and seven young women. Their deaths were the beginning of renewed widespread persecution of Christians in the country. Feast 16 May.

Abdias of Babylon, supposed first bishop of Babylon appointed by Ss Simon and Jude.

Abdiso, hermit, fourth century. Assyrian Church. His family originally came from Hazza near Arbil, but had moved north to Tamanun on the Tigris. He entered a monastery, but then established a hermitage near Erbil. He determined to convert the governor of Erbil, **Qardag**, but Qardag, after failing to get the better of him in debate, threw him into prison, then was eventually converted by him. Abdiso and two of his disciples are buried in a church dedicated to his memory at Tal, near Thuman in Turkey.

Abdon and Sennen, martyrs, died *c.* 303. According to tradition, Abdon and Sennen lived in Persia during the reign of Decius, ministering to people who suffered persecution and burying the bodies of martyrs. However, it is more likely that they suffered under Diocletian. They were thrown to the wild beasts when they refused to make sacrifices to the gods, but the beasts would not harm them, and so they were murdered and cut to pieces. The Roman Christians buried their bodies in secret, but when Constantine became emperor their relics were moved to the burial place of Pontian. Feast 30 July.

Abel of Rheims, born England or Ireland, died abbey of Lobbes, in modern Belgium, *c.* 750. He was a missionary with **Boniface** and in 744 he was appointed archbishop of Rheims. The see was, however, occupied by an intruder, so he went to Lobbes, where he became abbot. Feast 5 August.

Abercius of Hieropolis, bishop, died Hieropolis, *c.* 200. When he was 72 he made a pilgrimage to Rome, which is recorded on his tomb – he wrote it himself. Feast 22 October.

Abiatar and **Sidonia**, lived and died in Mzcheta, the ancient capital of Georgia, fourth century. Georgian Church. They were Jews, father and son, converted to Christianity by St **Nina**. Sidonia was the first of the two to be baptized. Feast 1 October.

Abiba, see **Philotheus**.

Abibo of Nekresi, bishop and martyr, died Rechi, second half of the sixth century. Georgian Church. Abibo was very active in spreading Christianity, which brought him into conflict with the Zoroastrians who were very influential in Eastern Georgia. He was imprisoned, and offered his life were he to convert to Zoroastrianism, but he refused and was stoned to death. He is buried in the cathedral of the ancient Georgian capital Mzcheta.

Abibus, martyr, born Edessa, died there, *c.* 320. He was burned to death during the persecution of Licinius. Feast 15 November.

Abimelech, monk and founder, born Qardi on the Tigris, died Nisibis, *c.* 575. Assyrian Church. He became a monk near Nisibis and was a disciple of **Abraham of Kaskar**. He taught at Mosul, but *c.* 550 was called back to Nisibis to teach there – though not in the famous academy. He founded a monastic house in Nisibis, and was renowned as a miracle worker. He was buried in the house he founded.

Abiya Egzi, monk, end of thirteenth, beginning of fourteenth centuries. Ethiopian Church. He began life as a shepherd, but entered the monastery of Saqual before becoming a hermit. Later, however, he returned to the monastic life. He was famous for miracles. He died in the monastery of Dabra Madhanit on 14 May, but his feast is celebrated on 27 April.

Abo of Tiis (Tbilisi), martyr, born Baghdad, Iraq, died Tbilisi, Georgia, 6 January 786. Converting from Islam, he was a 'closet' Christian in an area under Muslim rule until he was denounced. He was beheaded, his body burned and thrown in the river Kura.

Abraham (Abraamios), bishop, died Telman, Persia, c. 345. He was bishop of Arbela in Assyria, killed under Shapur II, king of Persia. Feast 5 February.

Abraham and **Coprio**, monks, second half of the fourteenth century. Russian Church. Of unknown origin, they settled on the banks of the river Pecenga, where they built a church dedicated to the Saviour, and in 1485 founded the monastery of the Transfiguration. Feast 4 February.

Abraham, Andrew, John, Athanasius, Neonila, Gliceria and Companions, martyrs, seventeenth century. Old Believers. Abraham and Andrew were brothers who suffered alongside some of their relatives and friends in the persecution against the Old Believers. Feast 7 February.

Abraham Kenski, abbot, born Priluki, died monastery of Kozeezerski, near the lake of Kozezero, 7 June 1634. Russian Church. He ruled the monastery from 1611 until his death. Feast 7 June.

Abraham Kidunaia, hermit, sixth century. Born of a wealthy family living near Edessa, he left home on the day of his arranged marriage to become for 50 years a hermit in the desert near the town of Beth Kiduna. However, at the request of his bishop, he spent three years preaching to a settlement close by until the villagers were converted to Christianity. There is a story that he rescued his orphaned niece from a brothel. She had lived in a hermitage beside his own, but had run away in shame after a visiting monk raped her. Abraham discovered where she was and went there, disguised as a customer. He persuaded her that, whatever her supposed sins, God loved her and she returned with him. Abraham died when he was some 70 years old. Feast 16 March.

Abraham Kurilose, bishop, born Kattumangat, died Thozhiyur, 10 July 1802. Mar Thoma Church.

He came from a Christian family, but little is known of him before his election as bishop in 1768. He was caught up in disputes in the Mar Thoma Church which were not of his doing, and the local maharajah was turned against him. He had to flee, first to Vettical and then, when that hiding place was discovered, to Anjur, a village in Malabar. He lived there in a cabin with a few disciples, and gained fame as a miracle worker. The maharajah of Punnathoor then gave him land and funds to build a church at Thozhiyur, where he lived for the rest of his life.

Abraham, martyr, born Kazan, Russia, and died there, 1 April 1229. Bulgarian Church. A convert from Islam, he rejected attempts to reconvert him, and was killed. His relics were buried in the city of Vladimir.

Abraham Mirozski, monk, died monastery of the Most Holy Saviour at Pskov, 24 September 1158 (?). Russian Church. He was the first hegumenos of this monastery.

Abraham, monk and martyr, born Novgorod, died Moscow, in the spring of 1672. Church of the Old Believers. Originally called Athanasius, he became for a time a fool for Christ's sake, wandering about dressed only in a shirt. He was then persuaded to preach in defence of the Old Faith, and abandoned his vagrant life, changed his name, moved to Moscow, and undertook a life of writing. He was arrested in February 1670, imprisoned and tortured for his beliefs. He was finally burned alive.

Abraham, monk (?). Syriac Church. Apparently born near Mosul. Feast 15 November.

Abraham, monk, born c. 613, died Scete, 693, Coptic Church. After the conquest of Egypt, his mother was taken as a captive to Persia. There she had a vision of her release, which occurred in 628. About 642 Abraham entered the monastery of St Macarios, and became a disciple of **John of Scete**. With another monk, George, he established a cell near that of John, where he remained for the rest of his life. It became a place of pilgrimage.

Abraham of Alexandria I, patriarch, born Syria, died Alexandria, 978. Coptic Church. Originally a

Syrian trader with Egypt, he was elected patriarch though still a layman in 975. He was a reformer, suppressing simony among the clergy (he refused any payment for ordinations to the priesthood) and concubinage among the laity. He was renowned for working a miracle which, it was said, converted the caliph, who resigned, but not before giving him permission to restore a number of churches.

Abraham of al-Fayyum, bishop, born Dalga, 1829, died al-Fayyum, 10 June 1914. Coptic Church. He entered a monastery of the Virgin in the province of Asyut aged 19, changing his name from Joseph to Abraham, and stayed there for 11 years before being asked to assist the local bishop. This he did for three years, eventually being ordained priest and returning to the monastery to become abbot in 1866. He was deposed at the request of some discontented monks who complained of his distributing the goods of the monastery to the poor. He and four companions then moved to a monastery in Cairo, and shortly after to another at Wadi al-Natrun. When the Negus of Ethiopia asked the Coptic patriarch for bishops, Joseph's four companions were consecrated; he himself, however, at first refused the episcopacy, then became bishop of al-Fayyum in mid-1881. As bishop he was renowned for his care of the poor, his humility and his dedication to prayer. His tomb, just outside al-Fayyum, became a place of pilgrimage. He was declared a saint in 1963.

Abraham of Dabra Seyon, monk and founder, fourteenth to fifteenth centuries. Ethiopian Church. Founder of the monastery of Dabra Seyon.

Abraham of Farsut, abbot, sixth century, died Farsut, 19 January. Coptic Church. When young, he entered a monastery in Farsut in Upper Egypt, of which he became abbot. He was summoned by the Emperor Justinian to Constantinople to accede to the Chalcedonian definition, but refused and went into exile. He then entered the monastery of **Senute of Atripe**, whose Rule he copied – against the monks' wishes – and, when he returned to Farsut, imposed it on the two monasteries, one for men, the other for women, which he founded there.

Abraham of Galic, mid-fourteenth century. Russian Church. He was a monk of Sergius of Radonez's monastery of the Most Holy Trinity, and was ordained priest there. Seeking silence, he went into the region of Galic, where he discovered an icon of the Virgin and received an apparition of her. He founded a monastery in honour of the Virgin, but was persuaded by Prince Dimitri of Galic to bring the icon to the city of Galic itself. Dimitri helped him to found both a church and a monastery at Cuchloma, the site of the apparition, but he preferred the solitary life and withdrew from the monastery he had built. Eventually, with his disciples, he founded four monasteries in all, each in honour of the Virgin. He and his monasteries helped to spread Christianity among the Finns of the region. Feast 2 July.

Abraham of Jaroslav, monk, eighteenth century. Russian Church. Although nothing is known of him, his feast is celebrated either on the second Sunday after Pentecost, or on 23 May.

Abraham of Kaskar, also known as 'the Great', founder, sixth century. Assyrian Church. He was a student of the school at Nisibis, then, already known as a miracle worker, he went to the desert of Scete, then to Mount Sinai. On his return to Nisibis he set up a monastery on Mount Izla, the 'great monastery' from which sprang monastic reform through the many disciples Abraham gathered. In 571 he drew up a Rule for his monks, which was later translated from Syriac into Persian and became the Rule of the monasteries of his reform. He lived to the age of 85. Feast 2 May.

Abraham of Nethpar, hermit, born and died at Nethpar in the north-west of Iraq, sixth century. Assyrian Church. He first lived in a cave near his native village before visiting hermits in the desert of Scete and the Holy Places in Palestine. He also spent some time evangelizing in Azerbaijan. He was a disciple of **Abraham of Kaskar**, and a writer, including the work *The Paradise of the Fathers*. He returned to his cave towards the end of his life, and died there. A monastery was built over it.

Abraham of Qata, monk. Ethiopian Church. A native of Tigre.

Abraham of Rostov, monk, born Cuchlov in the mid-eleventh century, died Rostov, 29 October, perhaps early twelfth century. Russian Church. Some sources say he was of non-Christian parents, others that he came to the monastery of Valaam, where he took the name Abraham, as a Christian but after an illness. After some years as a monk, he left the monastery and evangelized in the region around Rostov. He is said to have received directly from John the Evangelist the staff with which he destroyed idols.

Abraham of Smolensk, monk, born 1172, died Smolensk, *c.* 1220. Russian Church. He came from a rich and devout family, and was attracted to the liturgy from an early age. After his parents' death he gave away his wealth and entered the monastery of Selisce, near Smolensk. He was a student of the Fathers of the Church, and spiritual father of the monastery. He was ordained priest and after 30 years in the monastery became its hegumenos. However, the jealousy of some of the other monks led him to retire to the monastery of the Holy Cross in Smolensk, but the complaints followed him and the bishop suspended him from his priesthood, sending him back to Selisce. However, the bishop later reinstated him, and made him archimandrite of a monastery which the bishop had founded.

Abraham Paleostrovski, monk, either twelfth or fifteenth century. Russian Church. Nothing is known of him except that he was a disciple of the founder of the monastery of the Nativity of the Mother of God on the island of Pali on the lake Onega. His feast is celebrated on the third Sunday of Pentecost.

Abraham Pinezski, monk. Russian Church. Nothing is known about him, although his feast was celebrated on 21 June.

Abraham Spasski, monk, sixteenth or seventeenth centuries. Russian Church. Hegumenos of the Most Merciful Saviour at Korjazemski. Feast on second Sunday of Pentecost.

Abraham the Bulgar, martyr, born Veilie Bolgary, died there, early thirteenth century. Russian Church. He was a merchant who converted to Islam, and was decapitated for doing so. His remains were taken to Vladimir, and entombed in the convent of the Dormition. Feast 1 April.

Abraham the Hegumenos, abbot, fourteenth century. Coptic Church. Abbot of the monastery of St Anthony near the Red Sea.

Abraham the Penitent, monk and founder, second half of the sixth century. Assyrian Church. Founded a small monastery in Northern Iraq. Feast last Friday of October.

Abraham the Recluse and **Abraham the Lover of Good Works**, monks, twelfth or thirteenth centuries, died in Kiev. Russian Church.

Abranyos, monk, born Kanat, Ethiopia, February 1633, died Serae, 1718. Coptic Church. At the age of 12 he became a monk at Dabra Dabsan and was in due course ordained priest. With some companions, attracted by the fame of a hermit, he established another monastery near his spiritual father. He was imprisoned for not mentioning the king in the prayers of the mass, but was rehabilitated and offered a place at court, which he refused and returned to the monastery of Serae. During his lifetime the Church in Ethiopia was torn by Christological debates, in the course of which the king himself took a hand, imprisoning many monks for a time, among them Abranyos.

Abreha and **Asbeha**, monks, mid-fourth century. Ethiopian Church. They were brothers, but otherwise little is known of them. Feast 14/15 October.

Abrunculus of Auvergne, bishop, died 490. Feast 4 January.

Absadi, monk, died 28 October 1380/1381 (?). Ethiopian Church. Son of a noble family, he early showed signs of great holiness of life, and put himself under the direction of **Gabra Masqual**, who, when he went on pilgrimage to Jerusalem, entrusted his community to the young monk. He later lived an eremetical life of prayer and penance and, in the manner of St **Anthony**, was much tempted in his faith and in his purity. By the end of his life he had over a thousand disciples.

Absadi of Azazo, monk. Ethiopian Church. Founder of the monastery of Zoz Amba in Salasa.

Absolon, martyr, deacon of Alexandria, died 311. Feast 15 January.

Abundius, see also **Irenaeus and Abundius**.

Abundius and Companions, martyrs, died Rome, 16 September c. 304. Abundius was a priest, executed on the via Flaminia, outside Rome. His 'companions', including a deacon called Abundantius and two other Christians, Marcian and Marcian's son John, come from very doubtful accounts of Abundius's martyrdom.

Abundius of Córdoba, martyr, died Córdoba, 11 July 854. One of the martyrs of Córdoba who suffered during the anti-Christian persecution by the Moors between 850 and 859. The martyrs are also venerated as a group on 11 March.

Acacius, martyr, born Cappadocia, died Byzantium, 303. A Roman centurion, stationed in Thrace, he was scourged and beheaded. Constantine built him a church in Byzantium (i.e., Constantinople) around the walnut tree on which he was hanged to be scourged. Venerated as Agario in Calabria and Acato in parts of Spain. Feast 8 May.

Acacius, bishop of Tver, died Moscow, 14 January 1567. Russian Church. Known as Alexander in his monastery, he was bishop from 1522. Feast 29 June.

Acacius, martyr, born Neochori, Thessalonika, decapitated Constantinople, 1 May 1816. Byzantine Church. His birth name was Athanasius. With his family he left his home town to earn a living at Serre. He was apprenticed to a shoemaker who treated him so badly he decided to become a Muslim, on doing which he was adopted by the Turkish overlord of the district. When he was 18 the overlord's wife accused him of trying to seduce her, and he fled back to the family home in Thessalonika. But fearing his conversion to Islam would be held against him, he went to the monastery of Timios Podromos on Mount Athos, putting himself under the guidance of an ancient monk. After a long period of preparation, and accompanied by a monk called Gregory, he went to Constantinople (Istanbul) and there confessed to the Turkish vizier that he had renounced Islam. Gregory took his body back to Athos.

Acacius and Irenarchus, martyrs, died Sebaste, Armenia, 305 (?). Acacius, a priest, was martyred with seven women and two children, his converts. Irenarchus was converted by their constancy and died with them. Feast 27 November.

Acacius the Young Kapsokalivita, monk, born Golitsa (now St Acacius), c. 1630, died Mount Athos, 12 April 1730. Byzantine Church. After being converted to a life of asceticism through reading the lives of saints, he first joined the monastery of the Most Holy Trinity at Survia, then moved to Mount Athos where he lived in various houses before taking up residence in a cave. He was renowned for both the purity of his life and his wisdom.

Acca, monk, died 556. He was from Syria and was a founder of monasteries. Feast 25 January.

Acca, bishop of Hexham, born c. 660, died Whithorn, Galloway, 20 October 742. A disciple of **Wilfrid**, he was made abbot of St Andrew's monastery, Hexham, when Wilfrid was reinstated bishop. He eventually succeeded Wilfrid in 709. He built up the church materially, liturgically and in learning. He brought to the north a famous cantor named Maban, encouraged Eddius to write the life of Wilfrid and was patron of St **Bede** for some biblical works. Honoured as a saint after his death, two high stone crosses were erected at the ends of his grave.

Achard of Saint-Victor, bl., bishop, born English or of a noble Norman family, died Avranches, France, March 1172. After studies in England he entered the Canons Regular at Saint-Victor, Paris, and in 1155 became second abbot (on the death of Gilduin). Elected bishop to Seez in 1157, he did not obtain royal approval, but the Plantagenet Henry II allowed him to become bishop of Avranches in 1162. Achard met **Thomas Becket** in Tours in 1163 and supported him in his persecution. He is known for a treatise entitled *De Trinitate*.

Achilles, monk, died Kiev, fourteenth century. Russian Church. Achilles was a deacon and a monk of the Laura of the Caves of Kiev, renowned for his extreme asceticism, especially in fasting. After some years his body was found to be incorrupt, and he was popularly regarded as a saint. Feast 4 January.

Achilleus (Achilles), bishop, died *c.* 330. He was bishop of Larissa in Thessaly. He is said to have been at the first council of Nicaea. Feast 15 May.

Achilleus, see **Nereus**.

Acisclus, martyr, born Cordoba, died there, *c.* 303 (?). Imprisoned with his sister **Victoria**, according to some stories, he and she were executed possibly under Diocletian. Feast 17 November.

Adalar, priest and martyr, martyred at Dokkum, Netherlands (with St **Boniface**), 5 June 754. Listed as a companion of St Boniface and fellow martyr, he is known only as a priest. However, there is an unsubstantiated tradition that he was bishop of Erfurt, where his remains are in the cathedral. He was consecrated by St Boniface in 741.

Adalard, abbot, born *c.* 751, died Corbie Abbey, 2 January 827. After education at the court of **Charlemagne**, of whom he was a relation, he entered the Benedictines at Corbie in Picardy. After a spell in Monte Cassino, he was elected abbot at Corbie, and appointed by Charlemagne prime minister to Pepin, who was half-brother to Adalard's father. Exiled for suspected involvement in Pepin's son Bernard's bid to be emperor, he was later reinstated and helped to found the monastery at Corvey in Westphalia.

Adalbald of Ostrevant, nobleman, assassinated near Perigueux, Aquitaine, by antagonistic in-laws, *c.* 652. Husband of **Rictrude**, whose ninth-century life exists, he met his future wife on an expedition sent by King Dagobert against the Gascons. Their four children were all monastic saints. He helped his fellow Fleming St **Amandus** to set up the monastery of Marchiennes. His maternal grandmother was St **Gertrude of Hamage**. Feast 2 February.

Adalbero of Augsburg, bl., bishop, died 28 April 909. Bishop of Augsburg from 887 to his death, he is buried in the church of St Afra in Augsburg. Monk (850) and afterwards abbot of Ellwanger, abbot restorer of Lorsch, he is known for his scientific knowledge and musical ability. He helped to educate Louis the Child; he later served as his adviser. He kept a close spiritual connection with the monastery of Sankt Gallen, and encouraged the monastic discipline at the abbey of Borsch. Feast 9 October.

Adalbero of Metz II, bl., bishop, monastic reformer, born between 955 and 962, died Metz, 14 December 1005. A nephew of Adalbero I, he became bishop of Metz in 984 after a short time in Verdun, under pressure of his mother Beatrice on the empress Adelaide. He avoided political activity, but still defended Church rights. Against the canons, however, he is known to have ordained sons of secular priests. He pushed the Cluniac reforms in the monasteries, and founded two monasteries at Metz.

Adalbero of Würzburg, bishop, born *c.* 1010, died Lambach Abbey, 6 October 1090. The son of Count Arnold of Lambach-Wells, Austria, he studied at Paris with St **Altmann of Passau**, and became a canon of Würzburg Cathedral. Emperor Henry II named him bishop and he was consecrated on 30 June 1045. He at first sided with the emperor Henry IV when in dispute with Pope **Gregory VII**, but broke with him when Henry 'excommunicated' the Pope (1076). An anti-bishop Meginhard took his see so he retired to Lambach, a Benedictine monastery in his ancestral home which he had helped to found. Feast 5 October.

Adalbert of Egmond, born Northumbria, England, died Egmond (modern Alkmaar, Holland), *c.* 710. He was a follower of **Willibrord**, and a deacon. He possibly studied in Ireland before going to Friesland. He was for a time archdeacon of Utrecht. Feast 25 June.

Adalbert of Magdeburg, bishop, born Lorraine, *c.* 910, died Merseburg, 20 June 981. A monk of the abbey of St Maxim at Trier, he was sent by Emperor Otto III to evangelize Kievan Rus. Many of his band of missionaries were killed by pagans, and he returned to Mainz, then becoming abbot of Weissenburg before being appointed, in 968, first archbishop of Magdeburg. He founded a number of other dioceses, including that of Merseburg where he died, and was metropolitan of the Slavs. His work inspired **Adalbert of Prague**.

Adalbert of Prague, bishop, 'Apostle of Prussia', born 956 of a noble Bohemian family, died 997, murdered near Gdansk at the instigation of a pagan priest. From Magdeburg, centre for the apostolate to the Slavs, he went to Prague, Hungary, Poland and Prussia, inspired by **Adalbert of Magdeburg** whose name he assumed. He met resistance both within and without the Christian fold, and spent some time in Rome, where he was prior of a monastery.

Adalbert the Deacon, monk, missionary, born Northumberland, England, died Egmond, Netherlands, 25 June 705. Possibly a grandson of King Oswald of Deira, Adalbert became a monk at Rathmelgisi and in 690 accompanied St **Willibrord** in the evangelization of the Frisians. Assigned to the northern Netherlands in 702, he preached in Kennemaria as archdeacon of Utrecht. He built the church at Egmond where he is buried.

Adaldag, archbishop, born 900, died in Bremen, Germany, 28 or 29 April 988. In 937, when the emperor Otto succeeded Unni as archbishop of Bremen, Adaldag was elected his chancellor and in 964, when Otto removed Pope Benedict III from office, he was appointed his guardian. Fulfilling his role as archbishop of Bremen-Hamburg, Adaldag was particularly known for his missionary activity, especially in founding the sees of Schleswig, Ribe, Aarhus and Odense in Denmark. He was also directly responsible for resisting the archbishop of Cologne's assertion of leadership over Bremen. Feast 28 April.

Adalgar of Bremen, archbishop, died in Bremen, 9 May 909. A monk and deacon at Corvey, Adalgar was appointed assistant to archbishop Rembert of Bremen-Hamburg in 865. His subsequent succession of Rembert was confirmed by King Louis II, his two sons, the emperor Arnulf and the abbot and community of Corvey by means of a local synod. Although wars restricted his missionary activity, Adalgar travelled throughout his see and assisted the royal court. Following the synod of Tribur (895), archbishop Herman of Cologne reduced Bremen to the rank of suffragan see, a decision which was only revoked at Adalgar's death.

Adalgis of Novara, bishop, died Novara 849/50. Appointed bishop of Novara *c.* 830. He is thought to have been related to the last Lombard king, Desiderius, and it is unclear whether his appointment was due to personal qualities or family connections. He is named in various imperial and ecclesiastical documents of his time, indicating his particular concern in such matters. He is especially believed to have been Lotario's councillor. This is evinced in correspondence to Lotario in 840 urging him to react against ongoing violence to the Church, and in a document in which Lotario gave over St Michael in Lucedio and St Genuario's Abbey to the church of Novara. Feast 6 October.

Adalgott I, abbot, died Disentis, 1 November 1031. Originally a monk of Einsiedeln, he was appointed abbot of Disentis in 1016. He concerned himself primarily with the promotion of monastic reform and the liturgy. Feast 26 October.

Adalgott II, abbot and bishop, died Disentis, 3 October 1160. Originally a monk of Clairvaux, he was appointed abbot of Disentis and bishop of Chur in 1150 and appears to have been very dedicated to both these offices. He is particularly remembered for his generous financial support to Münster and Schannis's religious communities and it seems he was closely connected with emperor Frederic I Barbarossa and Pope Stephen III, with the latter of whom he was a co-student.

Adam Chmielowski (Brother Albert), Polish saint and well-known artist, especially for his painting of the 'Ecce Homo', born Krakow, 20 August 1845, died there, 25 December 1916. He was a student of engineering both in Poland and Belgium, then of art in Paris and Munich. As a politically active student he took part in the 1863 uprising against Russia, in which he lost a leg. He decided to adopt a form of religious life, and founded the Congregation of the Brothers of the Third Order of St

Francis Servants of the Poor (the Albertines), and a similar Congregation of Albertine nuns. He devoted his life to work with the sick, the poor, orphans (he had himself been orphaned at an early age) and the homeless. Karol Wojtyla wrote a play around his life entitled *Our God's Brother*. As Pope John Paul II, Wojtyla canonized him on 12 November 1989.

Adam of Ebrach, bl., abbot, born near Cologne, 1100, died Ebrach, 20 November 1166. Adam was an associate of **Bernard of Clairvaux**, who addressed two extant letters to a certain Adam of Morimond, commonly acknowledged to be the same. Initially a monk of Marmoutier, Adam joined the Cistercian community at Foligny in 1121 and went on to become abbot at Morimond. In 1125 with other monks he left the abbey (the reason for this is unclear) and returned only under pressure from Bernard. Successful and popular in living out the monastic life, Adam founded and became abbot of Ebrad abbey in 1127 and went on to found at Reim (1129), Heilsbronn and Langheim (1133), Nepomuk (1145), Alderspach (1146) and Bildhausen (1158). Adam's holiness and wise council is also evinced in his correspondence with the great mystic **Hildegard of Bingen**. He also proved a firm supporter of the Crusades. Feast 25 February.

Adam of Kratia, bishop, born Emesa, 474, died Palestine, *c.* 558. He became a monk at Emesa, but fled to Constantinople when his community was dispersed by invaders. He joined a community in Constantinople, but then was made abbot of Kratia in Bithynia. After ten years in that office he fled to Palestine seeking solitude, but was found and brought back to his monastery, and shortly afterwards he was made bishop of Kratia. After serving for 13 years, he was permitted to return to solitude in Palestine. Feast 6 December.

Adam of Loccum, bl., monk, died Loccum, Hanover, *c.* 1210. A Cistercian monk, he was, according to Caesarius of Heisterbach, the recipient of visions, and was particularly devout to Mary. Feast 22 December.

Adamnan of Coldingham, born Ireland, died Berwick on Tweed, *c.* 680, cult confirmed 1898. A

monk at the double monastery at Coldingham, Berwick upon Tweed, under **Ebba the Elder**, **Bede** records that he correctly prophesied the monastery later burning down because of the laxity of the monks and nuns. Feast 31 January.

Adamnan of Iona, abbot, born Drumhome, Co. Donegal, Ireland, 625, died Iona, Scotland, 23 September 704. Having moved to the island of Iona, Adamnan succeeded **Columba**, becoming the ninth abbot of the abbey there in 679. On a mission to help the cause of Irish captives held in England in 685, he was converted to the Roman position regarding the date of Easter and to the Roman tonsure. Back in Scotland, Adamnan did much work to ensure the application of this and in many places – although not on Iona – succeeded. A deeply pastoral man, he expressed his concern that women should have no part in fighting (Synod of Tara, 697). The 'Canon of Adamnan' ('Cain Adamnain') is ascribed to him and he wrote the first biography of **Columba** of Iona.

Adauctus, see **Felix and Adauctus**.

Addai (also known as **Thaddeus**), first century. According to Christian tradition, he was one of Jesus's 72 disciples and, along with St **Mari**, brought Christianity to Syria and Persia, founding the churches there. Addai is mentioned in Eusebius's *History of the Church*, which contains the *Acta Eddesa*. This document recounts some of the Doctrine of Addai, a fourth-century apocryphal work describing how Christianity reached Edessa. The Nestorians claimed that Ss Addai and Mari were the source of their liturgy. Feast 5 August.

Adela, princess and abbess, born England, died Pfalzel, near Trier, *c.* 724. A daughter of **Dagobert II**, she married and had a son, but after the death of her husband she became a nun, founding the abbey at Pfalzel. Feast 24 December.

Adelaide of Burgundy, born Burgundy, *c.* 931, died abbey of Seltz, Alsace, 999. At the age of two she was betrothed to Lothair, the future king of Italy, and married him at 16. After Lothair's early death, Berengarius of Ivrea tried to force her to marry his son and, when she refused, had her imprisoned. From that imprisonment she was rescued by (the future emperor) Otto I of Germany, whom she married in 951. Otto died in 973, and Otto II, their son, succeeded to the throne, but he was dominated by his Byzantine wife who was hostile to Adelaide. Adelaide therefore left the court, until she was eventually reconciled to her son. But his wife Theophano became regent for her son Otto III after Otto II's untimely death, and once more Adelaide had to leave the court. However, Theophano died relatively young, and Adelaide herself became regent. She was a devout woman and a friend of a number of future saints. She restored monasteries and convents, and retired to one, her own foundation at Seltz, for the last few years of her life. Feast 16 December.

Adelaide of Vilich, abbess, born 960, died Cologne, 5 February 1015. Adelaide's father was Count Megingoz of Gelder. Generous and devout by nature, she entered St Ursula's convent. Here she introduced the Benedictine Rule, as more fitting and demanding than the previous one of St **Jerome**. Her love of prayer led her to urge her community to learn Latin in order that they might better understand the Breviary. She became abbess both of Vilich (which her own parents had founded) and of St Marie im Kapitol, Cologne, where she succeeded her sister Bertrande. A confidante of Herbert, archbishop of Cologne, Adelaide was renowned for her generosity towards the poor in times of famine.

Adelelm of Burgos (or Lesmes), abbot, born probably near Poitiers, died Burgos, 30 January 1097. Patron saint of Burgos and one of the four eleventh-century Benedictine abbots in Castile, he gave up great wealth and the military life to pursue his religious calling. He was famed as a miracleworker, especially miracles involving the use of bread or water blessed by him. He successfully rid the Queen of England (Matilda of Flanders) of her lethargy when she ate blessed bread sent by him. He is also believed to have crossed the river Tagus without getting wet.

Adelhelm, bl., abbot, died Engelberg, 25 February 1131. Originally a Benedictine of the community of Sankt Blasien, he was appointed *c.* 1112 the first abbot of Engelberg, Switzerland (founded by Conrad of Switzerland). Adelhelm strove to obtain complete autonomy of the abbey from external influences. In 1124 he received papal and royal confirmation of this. Renowned for his prayerful nature, miracles are reputed to have occurred at his tomb. He became the object of popular veneration from the mid-twelfth century.

Adelphus of Metz, bishop, died Metz, 29 August 460. It is believed that he succeeded St Rufus as archbishop of Metz, a position which he held for some 17 years.

Adeodatus, pope, see also **Deusdedit**.

Adeotatus II, pope, elected 7 April 672, died Rome, 17 June 676. When the church was confronted with the threat of monothelitism, Adeodatus appears to have had a role in ridding the Church of this heresy. Originally a monk, during his papacy he contributed greatly to the refurbishment of St Erasmus's monastery. A religious at heart, he wrote two letters in which he expressed his wish that monasteries be permitted to rely on internal jurisdiction only. He initiated the papal tradition of dating events according to his reign. Feast 26 June.

Adhani, monk, mid-fourteenth century. Ethiopian Church. A disciple of **Takla Haymanot**, he evangelized the Damit region.

Adjustor, monk, died Tiron, France, 30 April 1131. A devout young man, he was one of the first Normans involved in the 1095 crusade. The best known of his miracles was his own miraculous flight from Muslim captivity during the first crusade. He was deeply affected by his experience of the Crusades, and on his return to France he entered Torin abbey. In his latter years he lived as a hermit. Feast 20 April.

Ado of Vienne, archbishop and chronicler, born Sens, near Paris, 800, died Vienne, 16 November 875. After entering a monastery and receiving his formation from abbots Lupus of Ferrieres and Markward, Ado went to Italy for five years. On his return he was made parish priest at Lyon and then archbishop of Vienne. He remained in office from 6 July 859 to 22 October 860. He was well respected by Popes Nicholas I and Adrian II, King Charles the Bald and Louis the German. A great pastor, Ado was particularly concerned to promote fervour among the clergy and was an enthusiast of the Divine Office. His writings include a history of the world (*Chronicum sive Breviarium de sex mundi aetatibus ab Adamo usque ad annum 869*) and the disputed martyrology *Passionum codices undecumque collecti*. Most of this latter was taken from the writings of Florus of Lyon and the remainder is also thought to be largely plagiarized.

Adolf Kolping, bl., priest and pioneer of Catholic social work in Germany, born Kerpen, near Cologne, 8 December 1813, died Cologne, 4 December 1865. A shoemaker, spare time learning enabled him at 28 to study at the universities of Münich and Bonn (1841–4). He was ordained in 1845 and sent to Eberfeld, where he came across an organization for young workers which gave him the key to his life's work. He moved to Cologne in 1849, and partly as an antidote to rationalist socialism he founded a Catholic association of young journeymen with the aim of enabling them to become trustworthy, responsible members of society. He required the men to be efficient at their work, provided them with opportunities for self-improvement, and based everything on down-to-earth Christianity. At his death there were 26,000 members in Germany and the USA.

Adorhomizd, martyr, born Bet Lashpar, decapitated Yatre, 25 April 447. Syriac Church. Originally a Zoroastrian, he converted to Christianity after his daughter was healed by a Christian monk. The king sent someone to convert him back, but when that failed he was martyred.

Adrian, martyr, died Nicomedia, third century. Said to have been a pagan solider, married to a Christian (Natalia), who was converted by the constancy of Christians under persecution. Feast 26 August.

Adrian, martyred Caesarea, Palestine, 308, with **Eubulus**. Feast 5 March.

Adrian, martyr and bishop, possibly born Ireland, died Scotland, 875. According to legend, Adrian was of royal blood, and born in Hungary. After his appointment as bishop in Hungary, Adrian went to Scotland where he preached to the Fifeshire Picts. Adrian built a monastery on the Isle of May and was martyred with some monks on Holy Thursday 875 during fighting between Danes and Scots that took place on the Firth of Forth. Feast 4 March.

Adrian III, pope, born Rome, died near Modena, Italy, some time in 885. Adrian's pontificate lasted only 16 months, from 17 May 884 to *c.* September 885. During this time he implemented the policies of Pope John III rather than those of his predecessor, Marinus I. An exceptionally severe character, he is known to have had an official of the Lateran palace blinded. Adrian died while on the way to Germany to speak to Emperor Charles III regarding a possible successor (Charles had no legitimate heir). Feast 8 July.

Adrian and Bogolep of Uglic, monks, died Uglic, late fifteenth century. Russian Church. Two disciples of **Paisio of Uglic** who helped him to spread devotion to The Protection of the Mother of God, which devotion had come to Paisio and Adrian in a vision. It was Bogolep, who had been a baker before entering the monastery and continued in that trade as a monk, who found the icon of the Protection in a river.

Adrian Fortescue, bl., martyr, born Punsborne, Hertfordshire, *c.* 1476 and died Tower Hill, London, 9 July 1539. A country gentleman and a Knight of St John, he was present at the Field of the Cloth of Gold in 1520. Second cousin to Anne Boleyn, he was arrested and released in 1534, and arrested and imprisoned in the Tower in 1539. He was not accused of any specific act of treason, but of 'sedition and refusing allegiance', and was beheaded.

Adrian Monzenski, monk, born Kostroma, died near there, 5 May 1619. Russian Church. His baptismal name was Amos. As a result of a dream while recovering from illness, he left home and entered the monastery of Tolga near Jaroslav, where he took the name Adrian. He moved between monasteries, however, seeking the church which he had seen in his dream. Eventually he settled on the banks of the river Monza, at its confluence with the river Kostroma. His Rule for the monks stressed manual labour in the fields, and in times of famine they were able to supply the surrounding area. The founding of his monastery was accompanied by many miracles.

Adrian of Nicomedia, martyr, born Nicomedia, c. 270, died there, 304 (?). Said to have been a pagan officer who, with his wife **Natalia**, assisted the Christians persecuted in Nicomedia. He was arrested and put to death with them. Feast 8 September.

Adrian of Posechon'e, monk and martyr, died near Posechon'e, 5 March 1550. Russian Church. In miraculous circumstances he and a disciple founded a monastery in the forest near the town of Posechon'e in 1540. Then years later it was attacked by bandits, and Adrian was killed, his body being recovered some 75 years later, after the place where it was hidden became famous for miracles.

Adrian of Solovki, hermit, early seventeenth century. Russian Church. Commemorated on 9 August along with all the other saints of the island of Solovki.

Adrian Ondrusovski, monk, born Moscow, died near Obza, 26 August 1549/50. Russian Church. Of a noble family, Andrew Zavalisim (his baptismal and family name) encountered the hermit **Alexander Svirski** while out hunting, was instructed by him, and entered the monastery of Valaam on lake Ladoga, where he took the name Adrian. Seeking greater solitude, he left the monastery and established a hermitage on the eastern bank of the lake, at a place called Ondrusov. There disciples gathered around him, and he founded the monastery of St **Nicholas**. The rulers of this territory were at first hostile to Adrian, but he eventually converted them. Although he had abandoned his riches, Adrian's noble birth attracted donations to his monastery from the local nobility, and in 1549 he was godfather to the daughter of the Tsar. On his way home from Moscow he was set upon by bandits and killed, his body lying in a swamp for two years before its location was revealed in a vision, whereupon it was recovered and buried in his monastic church.

Adrio, martyr, died Alexandria, fourth century. It is not clear whether Arians or pagans killed him. He is commemorated with two companions, **Victor** and **Basilea**. Feast 17 May.

Aedesius, born Tyre, Palestine, died there, fourth century. He was a companion to **Frumentius**, and supplied the information upon which accounts of Frumentius's life are based. Unlike his companion, he did not stay in Ethiopia, but returned to Palestine. Feast 27 October.

Aedh, bishop, born Offaly (?), Ireland, died West Meath (?), 589. His brothers deprived him of his inheritance, and Aedh intended to take vengeance until dissuaded by St Illand of Rathlihen. Instead he established a monastery, and became a bishop in West Meath. Feast 10 November.

Aelfric of Canterbury, archbishop, died Canterbury, 16 November 1005. Originally a monk of Abingdon, Aelfric became abbot of St Albans and bishop of Ramsbury and Wilton (c. 990). On Easter Sunday 995 he received his appointment as bishop of Canterbury and in 997 he received the pallium from Gregory V. Either Sigeric (Aelfric's predecessor) or Aelfric himself was responsible for removing diocesan clergy from Canterbury cathedral in favour of monks.

Aelfryth, died Croyland, 834. Aelfryth (also known as Elfrieda, Etheldreda, Etheldritha) was one of King Offa of Mercia's daughters. It is commonly believed that she was to be married to St **Ethelbert**, king of East Anglia. He was killed, under King Offa's orders, c. 790. Aelfryth took to the solitary life at Croyland. She outlived her father by some 38 years and is sometimes mistaken for her sister Aelfreda, who was assassinated. Feast 2 August.

Aelred (Ailred), abbot, spiritual writer and historian, born Hexham, the son of a Saxon priest, 1109, died Rievaulx, 12 January 1166. He lived at the court of King David, son of St **Margaret of Scotland**, joined the Cistercians at the recently founded abbey of Rievaulx, Yorkshire about 1133 and took charge of the abbey of Revesby, Lincolnshire in 1143. He became abbot of Rievaulx in 1147, in which capacity he not only had charge of some 300 monks in the abbey, but was head of all the Cistercian abbots in England and had to travel to visit them. He attended the general chapter of his order in France and was present at the translation of the remains of **Edward the Confessor** in Westminster Abbey in 1163. He wrote a life of David of Scotland and of Edward. He also left many eloquent sermons, similar in style and spirit to those of **Bernard of Clairvaux**, at whose invitation he wrote his *Speculum Caritatis*. He suffered much physical pain in his own life and showed a devotion to the suffering humanity of Christ. His *De Spiritali Amicitia*, following Cicero's work, is a detailed discussion on friendship.

Aemilius, see **Castus**.

Aeonius of Arles, bishop, died *c.* 500. Appointed bishop and metropolitan of the diocese of Arles on 23 August 494, Aeonius remained in office for six years. On 29 September 500 he was, at his own request, succeeded by **Caesarius of Arles**. While Aeonius was bishop, he defined the diocese's boundary with Vienne and asserted its superiority. A great enthusiast of the monastic movement, Aeonius founded Chalon-sur-Saône with Caesarius and did much to help the spread of monasticism in France. Among his correspondents were Popes Anastasius III and Symmachus and also Ruricuis I of Limoges. Feast 18 August.

Aethirius, see **Basil, Eugene**, et al.

Afan, bishop, born Wales, died Llanafan Fawr, Powys, sixth century (?). Nothing is known of him, apart from an inscription on a gravestone.

Affonio of Novgorod, bishop, died Chutynski, 6 April 1653. Russian Church. Hegumenos of the monastery at Perejaslav-Zalesk, he become bishop of Novgorod in 1635, but in 1649, because of age and illness, resigned the post and retired to the monastery of Chutynski.

Afra, martyr, born Augsburg, died there, 302. She was, according to legend, originally a prostitute, who repented and converted to Christianity after hiding a bishop during Diocletian's persecution. Feast 7 August.

Afse, monk, fifth/sixth century. Ethiopian Church. A pious Christian from Asia Minor who was forced by a famine to leave his homeland. In Constantinople he met **Garima**, with whom – plus seven others – he travelled to Ethiopia. There, guided by the Archangel Uriel, they each established a monastery. Afse and Garima first settled by the river Geba, but later separated, Afse settling at Yeha. There he received the king and healed his wife, who was to become the mother of **Gabra Masqal**. In gratitude the king gave him the village of Baray, where he spent the rest of his life. Feast 5 June.

Agapa, martyred at Antioch, Syria, fourth century. Feast 11 March.

Agape, Chionia and **Irene of Thessalonika**, martyrs, died Saloniki, Macedonia, 304. Sisters arrested for keeping copies of the Scriptures, a capital offence, they refused under torture to reveal who else had copies. Two were burned alive; the youngest, **Irene** (cult suppressed), was incarcerated in a military brothel and killed when the soldiers refused to molest her. Feast 1 April.

Agapitus, bishop, fourth century. He was bishop of Sinai. Feast 18 February.

Agapitus, martyr, died Palestrina, Italy, 274 (?). Said to have been a boy of 15. Feast 18 August.

Agapitus I, pope, born Rome, died Constantinople, 22 April 536. Agapitus was of a noble family, his father being Gordianus, a priest assassinated in 502. Agapitus's great love of the intellectual life led him to erect a Christian university in Rome. He was elected pope 13 May 535. A firm supporter of Chalcedonian faith, he would not allow penitent Arians to rise to clerical office, even against the wishes of Emperor Justinian. He was also responsible for approving Pope John II's document stating that the Theopaschite formula was orthodox, himself adding that laypersons were not to be allowed to preach. Agapitus was especially popular in the East and was involved in anathematizing many monophysites.

Agapitus, Felicissimus and Agapitus, martyrs, died Rome, 258. Deacons of the Roman Church, they were martyred under Valerian with Pope Sixtus II, and buried in the cemetery of Praetextatus. Feast 6 August.

Agapitus Markuevski, monk and martyr, died near the village of Kalinin, 21 May 1584. Russian Church. A monk of the monastery of Ss Boris and Gleb at Sol'vycegodsk, he was cured of a serious illness in 1576 by an icon of St **Nicholas** and instructed in return to found a monastery beside the river Markusa. This he did, and some years later he sought from the Tsar permission to build a mill on the river Lochta to supply the monastery with food. The local people, fearing that he would take their land from them, had him killed, pushed between the grinding stones of the mill, his body then thrown into the river, whence it was recovered and buried in the monastery church.

Agapitus of the Kievan Cave Monastery, monk, eleventh century. Russian Church. A skilled doctor, he healed among others Prince Vladimir Vsevolodovic, who eventually became the Grand Prince of Kiev. Feast 1 June.

Agapius, martyr, died Caesarea, Palestine, 306. He was thrown into the sea and drowned for his faith. Feast 19 August.

Agapius, martyred Cirta, Numidia, North Africa, c. 259. He and **Secundinus** were Spanish bishops or priests exiled to Cirta, where they were executed with a small group of women. Feast 4 May.

Agapius, see also **Thecla of Gaza**.

Agatha, martyr, born Catania or Palermo, died Catania, possibly 250. According to legend, she was sent to a brothel to induce her to renounce her faith. She was tortured by rods, rack and fire; her breasts were cut off, but she was miraculously healed by a vision of St Peter; she died of new cruelties the next day. She is credited with preserving Catania from successive eruptions of Mount Etna and is patron of wet-nurses, bell-founders and jewellers. In art, her emblem is usually a dish on which her severed breasts repose, and a knife, or shears, in her hand. Feast 5 February.

Agatha, died Carinthia (now Austria), 1024. The wife of Count Paul of Carinthia, she bore the ill-treatment of her jealous husband with patience and eventually converted him. Feast 5 February.

Agatha Kim, see **Augustine Yi and Companions**.

Agatha Kouen, see **Augustine Pak**.

Agatha Lin-Tchao, bl., martyred China, 1858. She was a school teacher who was beheaded. She is commemorated with **Jerome Lou-Tin-Mey** and **Laurence Ouang-Pin** – see **Martyrs of China**. Feast 28 January.

Agatha Ni, see **Augustine Pak**.

Agatha Phutta, martyr, born Sonkong, 1881, died there, 26 December 1940. She was an unmarried woman, and a kitchen help at the mission. She and several others (see **Martyrs of Thailand**) were marched to the cemetery and shot. Feast 16 December.

Agatha Yi, martyred Korea, 1840, commemorated with **Teresa Kim**. Feast 9 January.

Agathangelus, see also **Clement of Ancyra**.

Agathangelus, bl., martyr, born Vendôme, France, 1598, died Gandar, Ethiopia, 1638. Baptized Francis Noury, he became a Capuchin friar, being ordained in 1625. He went to Aleppo, where he learned Arabic, and in 1633 to Cairo, where he was joined by **Cassian** and others. They worked, with some success, for reconciliation between the Roman Catholic and Coptic Churches, even being well received by Coptic monks. But when the formal suggestion of reconciliation was made, the Coptic patriarch's advisers warned against it, on the ground of the immorality of Catholics in Cairo. Agathangelus and Cassian then went to Ethiopia, but were there arrested and taken to Gandar. They were asked to abjure their Christianity, but when they refused they were executed by stoning. Feast 7 August.

Agatho, pope, born Palermo, Sicily, c. 577, elected 27 June 678, died Rome, 10 January 681. He had been a monk, and spoke Greek as well as Latin. His election to the papacy was speedily ratified by the imperial exarch at Ravenna; he supported the Sixth General Council convened by Constantine IV Pogonatus in 680 against the Monothelites, at which was asserted, in explicit agreement with Agatho's letters, the orthodox doctrine of two wills and operations in Christ. His short reign was thus important for the abandonment of monothelitism by the Byzantine government and the resultant reopening of amicable relations between the Holy See and Constantinople. He upheld Bishop Wilfrid of York's appeal to Rome against the unexpected division by Theodore, Archbishop of Canterbury, of his see, and restored him to York. He also furthered the spread of the Roman liturgy in England. A kindly man, cheerful and good humoured, and generous to his clergy even though desperately short of funds. Buried in St Peter's, he came to be venerated in the Eastern as well as the Western Church.

Agathodorus, see **Basil, Euguene**, et al.

Agathonice, see **Carpus**.

Agathonicus, Zoticus and Companions, martyrs, died in or near Byzantium, the future Constantinople, fourth century (?). Feast 21 August.

Agaton, monk and stylite, born Tinnis, seventh century, died Saha, 11 September, eighth century. Coptic Church. An only son, he could not become a priest until he was 30, or realize his ambition to be a monk until 40, when he joined a monastery at Mareote. Three years later he entered the community of **John of Scete**, where he lived for seven years. A great admirer of **Simon Stylites**, he then decided to imitate Simon, and occupied a column at Saha until he died, aged 100. He was famed for miracles and especially the casting out of demons.

Agaton, patriarch of Alexandria, born Mareote, died Alexandria, 13 October 677. Coptic Church. A priest in Alexandria during the Muslim conquest, he dressed as a workman so that he might still visit Christian homes. He became patriarch in 661, and was renowned for his good works, especially the redemption of slaves brought from Sicily to Egypt by the Arabs.

Agaton of the Kievan Cave Monastery, fourteenth century. Russian church. Renowned for his miracles of healing and prophecy, and for the fact that he knew long before the date he would die. When exhumed a few years after his death, his body was incorrupt. Canonized in 1643. Feast 20 February.

Agericus, bishop, born bear Verdun, c. 521, died there, 588. He had the king of Austrasia as his godfather, and was appointed bishop of Verdun aged 33. He enjoyed the confidence of successive kings. Feast 1 December.

Agibeus, martyred, c. 300. Feast 25 January.

Agil(e) (or Aile, Aygul), abbot and missionary, born Franche-Comte, c. 583, died Rebais, c. 650. He received in infancy the blessing of St **Columbanus**, after which he became, in 590, an oblate at the abbey of Luxeuil. He remained there and accompanied St **Eustace**, successor to Columban, to Bavaria in 612. He was designated bishop of Langres in 628, but must have refused the dignity since no record of the election remains. He became first abbot of Rebais, and was consecrated in the presence of Dagobert I at Clichy in 636, at which time the king granted the abbey a charter of immunity conceding the privilege of following the Rule of St Benedict and of St Columbanus in the manner of Luxeuil, i.e., the compromise rule practised by St **Waldebert** since 629. Feast 30 August.

Agilbert, bishop, France, died Paris, c. 690. He went to Ireland to study, then became bishop at Dorchester. He attended the synod of Whitby. He fell out with the king of Wessex, however, when the king decided to divide the diocese without asking Agilbert's advice (also, perhaps, because he could not speak English). He returned to France, where in 668 he became bishop of Paris. He retained links with England, sending his nephew in his place when the king of Wessex asked him to return, and consecrating **Wilfrid**. **Theodore** visited him on his way to take up his office in Canterbury. Feast 11 October.

Agilulf of Cologne, bishop of Cologne, died Cologne, c. 750. Bishop of Cologne after 745, he supported the reforms of St **Boniface** and attended the Frankish synod of 747. There has been some confusion with others named Agilulf. He may have been wrongly identified with the martyr Agilulf (died March 716), and with the Benedictine monk Agilulf, said to have been abbot of Stavelot-Malmedy and bishop of Cologne after 745. Feast 9 July.

Agnellus of Pisa, bl., founder of the English Franciscan province. Born Pisa, *c.* 1194, died Oxford, 3 March 1232. He was received into the Friars Minor at Pisa by St **Francis of Assisi** himself, who sent him to Paris *c.* 1217 to found a convent. Although he was still a deacon, Francis despatched him to England in 1224. He established friaries at Canterbury and Oxford and was ordained priest before 1229 at the urging of his superior. The friars were received everywhere with enthusiasm and Matthew Paris says that Agnellus was on familiar terms with Henry III, who built churches for the Franciscans and granted them land in aid of their foundation at Oxford. There he engaged Robert Grosseteste to teach, and this helped to raise Oxford rapidly to a position the equal of Paris as a centre of learning. He was politically influential in the conflict between Henry and the Earl Marshal. Feast 13 March.

Agnes, virgin and martyr, born Rome, *c.* 290, died there, *c.* 305. One of the most celebrated Roman martyrs at the end of the persecution of Diocletian. Her name figured already in the *Deposito Martyrium* of 354. The basilica erected in her honour in the via Nomentana *c.* 350 is counted among the Constantinian foundations and was embellished or restored by successive popes. Pope Damasus had engraved for her *c.* 385 an inscription of which the original marble is still extant. St Ambrose and the poet Prudentius both sang her praises. Her name occurs in the first eucharistic prayer, and, as a special patroness of chastity, she is one of the most popular saints. Early legends of her martyrdom vary considerably, and nothing certain can be deduced as to the manner of her death. We do know, however, that she was a young girl of 12 or 13 when decapitated, after refusing marriage and resisting all attempts to make her lose her virginity. Her head, brought to the Lateran in the ninth century, is preserved in the Sancta Sanctorum of the pontifical palace. In art she is represented with

a lamb, and the archiepiscopal pallium is made from the wool of two lambs, blessed each year in her basilica, on her feast. Feast 21 January.

Agnes of Assisi, abbess, born Assisi, 1197 and died there, 27 August 1253. Younger sister of St **Clare**, whom she joined, aged 16, at the Benedictine convent of San Angelo di Panzo, and where she heroically resisted family opposition. St **Francis** gave Agnes the habit, as she desired, and sent her and Clare to San Damiano. When the Benedictines of Montecelli at Florence asked to become Poor Clares, Francis sent her to them as abbess, *c.* 1219. From there she opened houses at Padua, Venice and Mantua. Agnes firmly upheld her sister in her long struggle for the privilege of complete poverty. She returned to San Damiano in 1253, where she witnessed the death of Clare, dying herself three months later. Feast 16 November.

Agnes of Bagno, bl., died *c.* 1105. She was a Camaldolese nun at Santa Lucia near Bagno di Roma, Tuscany and her relics are in the church of the village of Pereto. Feast 29 January.

Agnes of Bohemia, bl., abbess, born Prague, 1205, died there, 1282. Of royal blood, descendant of **Wenceslas** the Holy ('Good King Wenceslas'), daughter of Ottokar, king of Bohemia, and Constantia of Hungary (St **Elizabeth of Hungary** was her first cousin), she was educated by Cistercian nuns at Trebnitz in Silesia. She was betrothed as a child, but resisted strongly and, with help from Gregory IX, was able subsequently to appeal against the marriages proposed for her to, among others, Henry III of England and Emperor Frederich II of Austria. Having established her right to freedom, Agnes consecrated herself and her possessions wholly to God. She built a convent in Prague for the Friars Minor, she endowed a great hospital for the poor staffed by the Brothers of the Cross, and a convent for Poor Clares; she herself received the veil in 1236. Gregory IX induced her, with great difficulty, to become abbess and she obtained the same concession as St **Clare** to embrace absolute poverty. Feast 2 March.

Agnes of Montepulciano, born near Montepulciano, *c.* 1270, died there, 20 April 1317, canonized 1726. She joined the Sisters of the Sack (a name describing their rough clothes), becoming superior, aged 15, of their new convent near Viterbo. She became known for ecstasies and miracles and later opened a convent in Montepulciano.

Agnes of Poitiers, abbess, died Poitiers, *c.* 588. She was brought up as the adopted daughter of St **Radegund**, whom she followed into her monastery, where the foundress designated her first abbess. She was consecrated in that office by St **Germanus** of Paris in 561. Around 570, she accompanied Radegund to Arles to study, before adopting the rule of St **Caesarius**. In 573, Radegund, seeking from several bishops confirmation of her institution, insisted that authority should rest with Agnes alone. She was replaced in 589 following a revolt by some of the nuns. Her saintly character is commemorated by the poet Venantius Fortunatus, who called her his 'sister', and who was also a correspondent of her mother. Agnes died shortly after Radegund. Feast 13 May.

Agnes Phila, born Ban, 1909, died Sonkong, Thailand, 26 December 1940. She was a member of the Congregation of the Lovers of the Cross, and in charge of the school in Sonkong. She and several others (see **Martyrs of Thailand**) were marched to the cemetery and shot. Feast 16 December.

Agobard of Lyon, archbishop and reformer, born Spain, 769, died Lyon, 840. Consecrated coadjutor to Leidrad in 813, he succeeded to the see in 816. Little is known of his early life. He pursued the same rigorous policy as his predecessor, who had been one of Charlemagne's most active agents in the reformation of the Church. His opposition to the schemes of the Empress Judith, and his support for Lothair and Pippin against their father Louis I, led to his deposition at the Council of Thionville and to his exile in Italy in 835. His position was given to his opponent, Analarius of Metz, but he was reconciled to Louis and reinstated in 837. Agobard was a versatile scholar whose works were marked by much originality. He attacked the excessive veneration of images, trial by ordeal, belief in witchcraft and 'the absurd opinion of the vulgar concerning hail and thunder' that it was due to magic. His theological writings include a treatise against the Adoptionist heresy of Felix of Urgel,

and *De insolentia Judaeorum*, against the Jews. Agobard was one of the greatest prelates of his day; he played an important role in the Carolingian Renaissance and, although ignored during the Middle Ages, his works were rediscovered in 1605. Feast 6 June.

Agricius of Trier, bishop, died Trier, 329. He probably succeeded St **Paternus** as bishop of Trier. He is known to have taken part in the Council of Arles in 314, with the exorcist Felix. Feast 13 January.

Agricola, martyr, died Bologna. He was the slave of a Christian master, **Vitalis**, and both were put to death for their faith. Agricola was the first to die, thrown to the wild beasts in the hope that his fate would lead his master to deny his faith. It had the opposite effect. His body was discovered in the Jewish cemetery in 392. Feast 4 November.

Agricola (Arègle, Agrèle), bishop, died 580. Bishop of Châlon sur Saône, he was described by contemporaries as living an extremely austere life. Feast 17 March.

Agricola, died *c.* 594. He is said to have been bishop of Nevers from 570. Feast 26 February.

Agricolus of Avignon, bishop, born Avignon, *c.* 630, died there, 2 September 700. His father, a senator, became a monk at Lérins, and Agricolus followed him. When his father became bishop of Avignon he came as archdeacon, was ordained bishop in 660, and became bishop of Avignon in 670.

Agrippa and Companions, martyrs, fourth century. Feast 22 May.

Agrippinus of Autun, bishop, died *c.* 538. He was bishop of Autun and ordained **Germanus of Paris**. Feast 1 January.

Agustin Coloca, martyr, born Teul, Mexico, 5 May 1898, died Totalice, 25 May 1927. Ordained in 1923, he was assistant priest to **Christopher Magallanes**, and suffered with him.

Ahha the Egyptian, monk, fourth century. Syriac Church. A disciple of **Awgen**, 'the father of monks'. Evangelized the region of Qardu, to the west of Tigri, where he helped found a monastery. Feast 1 November.

Ahmet Kalhas, martyr, died Constantinople, 3 May 1682. Byzantine Church. A scribe in the Turkish administration in Constantinople, he had a Christian Russian slave who introduced him to Christianity. When he went to a service held by the patriarch he saw a heavenly light over the congregation, and was converted. He was subsequently hanged for apostasy. Feast 25 December.

Ahudemmeh, catholicos, born Balad, north-west of Mosul, died 575. Syriac Church. He became bishop of the West Syriac Church at Bet Arabaye, now Giazira. He was appointed 'Grand Metropolitan of the East' in 559, probably residing in Tikrit. He was imprisoned for converting some Zoroastrian priests and a member of the royal family, and died there. He was buried near Tikrit. Feast 2 August.

Aichard, abbot, born Poitiers (?), died Jumièges, Normandy, c. 687. He studied in a monastery at Poitiers, then entered one at Ansion, Poitou, rather against the wishes of his father. After nearly 40 years there he moved to Quinçay for reasons that are unclear. He served there over a small community as its prior, then was nominated as abbot of Jumièges by **Philibert** when he retired, and remained there, despite initial hostility from some of the monks, until his death. Feast 15 September.

Aichard of Clairvaux, bl., died Clairvaux, c. 1170. For a time he was in charge of novices. Feast 15 September.

Aidan of Ferns, see **Maedoc of Ferns**.

Aidan of Lindisfarne, monk and bishop, born Ireland, died Bamburgh, 651. At the request of St **Oswald**, king of Northumbria, he was sent to revive the missionary work of **Paulinus** and was consecrated bishop in 635. Oswald bestowed on him the episcopal seat of Lindisfarne (Holy Island) in the North Sea, accessible to the shore at low tide, facing the royal residence at Bamburgh. The Christian practices taught by Aidan were those of the Celtic Church, and his see was referred to as the English Iona. He carefully educated a group of 12 English boys to be the future leaders of their people, among them St **Chad**. According to **Bede**, almost the sole source of knowledge about the saint, Aidan's asceticism and gentleness won rapid success for his mission, exhibiting such apostolic activity and having such great influence as to be referred to as 'the apostle of Northumbria'. Feast 31 August.

Aigulf of Lérins (Aygulphe), abbot, born Blois, c. 630; died Capri, c. 674. At 20 he joined the recently founded abbey of Fleury-sur-Loire (St Benoit-sur-Loire). Abbot Mummolus is reported to have sent him, in 652, to Monte Cassino, ravaged by the Lombards, to bring back the remains of St **Benedict**. Having benefited from a miraculous indication as to the whereabouts of Benedict and his sister **Scholastica**, Aigulf and his companions took charge of the bodies and returned quickly to France with their precious cargo, to avoid soldiers sent by the Pope to apprehend them. The monks at Fleury are said to have kept the body of Benedict while pilgrims from Mano took that of Scholastica to their diocese. Aigulf was made abbot of Lérins in 671, and his strict reform of the Rule led to his abduction and martyrdom. Feast 3 September.

Ailbe, bishop, born Ireland, died there, c. 526. Possibly made a bishop while on a visit to Rome. Little is known of him except that it is said he preached right around Ireland. Feast 12 September.

Ailred, see **Aelred**.

Aimon Taparelli, bl., born Savigliano, Piedmont, 1395, died there, 1495. He was of noble birth and after he had become a Dominican he was appointed chaplain to Duke **Amadeus of Savoy**. He also served as an inquisitor. Feast 15 August.

Airaldus of Maurienne, bl., bishop, died c. 1156. He was Carthusian prior of Portes and bishop of St John of Maurienne, Savoy, 1132–56. Feast 2 January.

Akala Krestos, monk, fourteenth/fifteenth centuries. Ethiopian Church. A disciple of **Zena Marqos**, and founder of the monastery of Dabra Mahew at Zoga.

Alan de la Roche (also **Alanus de Rupe**), bl., born Brittany, *c.* 1428, died Zwolle, Holland, 18 September 1475. He entered the Order of Preachers at Dinan in the diocese of St Malo and studied at St Jacques in Paris, distinguishing himself in philosophy and theology. He taught at Paris, Lille, Douai, Ghent and Rostock, where, in 1473, he was made Master of Sacred Theology. He saw it as his special mission to preach and re-establish devotion to the rosary, which he did with success throughout northern France, Flanders and the Netherlands. At his death Alan left numerous writings which have occasioned much controversy among scholars.

Alaniqos, monk, born Axum (?), died near Axum (?), early fourteenth century. Ethiopian Church. Son of a king (Yekuno Amlak, d. 1285) and brother of a king (Wedem Ar'ad, d. 1314), he was renowned for a collection of 12 miracles attributed to him.

Alban, martyr, died St Albans, 303. A non-Christian, possibly a soldier, living in Britain under Roman rule, he sheltered a priest escaping persecution. Impressed by his guest's faith, Alban was baptized before helping the priest to escape by exchanging clothes with him. He was arrested in this disguise and, when his true identity was discovered, condemned to death in place of the priest. His courage so impressed his executioner that he also declared himself a Christian and asked to be put to death. Feast 20 June.

Alban-Bartholomew Roe, martyr, born Bury St Edmunds, England, 1583; died Tyburn, London, 21 January 1642. Roe converted to Catholicism and enrolled at the English College, Douai in 1608, but was dismissed for insubordination. Undaunted, he joined the Benedictines at Dieulouard (later Ampleforth Abbey, Yorkshire), and after ordination in 1615 went to Paris to help found the community of St Edmund. He returned to the English mission in 1618, was caught the same year and imprisoned in New Prison, Maiden Lane until

1623. Banished to Douai (later Downside Abbey near Bath), he returned after two years, was again apprehended, imprisoned in St Alban's, and subsequently in the Fleet Prison, London, where he ministered to fellow Catholics. Transferred to Newgate Prison in 1642, but this time tried as a priest and seducer of the people, Roe was condemned to be hanged, drawn and quartered. Feast 31 January.

Alberic, died Citeaux, France, 26 January 1109. He founded the Cistercian Order with **Robert of Molesme** and **Stephen Harding**. He was a hermit, then in a community under Robert. Seeking a more austere monastic life, these three founded Citeaux in 1098, where Alberic became the second abbot.

Alberic Crescitelli, bl., born near Naples, Italy, 1863, martyred Shansi, China, 22 July 1900, beatified 1951. Ordained 1887, a missionary in China from 1888, he had preached and set up schools in the areas near the Han River. He was tortured for 24 hours, then hacked to death. See also **Martyrs of China**. Feast 9 July.

Alberic of Utrecht, monk and bishop, died Utrecht, 21 August 784. Nephew of an earlier bishop of Utrecht, St **Gregory**, the successor of St **Boniface**. He was a friend of intellectual leaders of the Carolingian Renaissance, such as Alcuin and Ludger of Munster. He was consecrated bishop in 780 at Cologne. As bishop of Utrecht he reorganized the cathedral school, dividing the teaching under four masters. Alberic participated in the mission to convert the pagan Frisians, directing Ludger's activity there. Feast 14 November.

Albert Chmielowski, founder, born Iglomia, near Krakow, 20 August 1845, died Krakow, 25 December 1916. Adam Chmielowski was born into Russian-occupied Poland, studied in Warsaw and St Petersburg, and lost a leg in an uprising against Russia in 1863. He then went to Paris to study painting, returning to Poland in 1874. Six years later he entered the Society of Jesus, but had to leave through ill-health. He then joined the secular Franciscans, gathered a group of like-minded men, and founded the Brothers of the Third Order of St Francis, Servants of the Poor (or the Albertine

Brothers). He also founded a similar group for women. They opened refuges for the homeless poor throughout Poland, and it was in one of these that he died.

Albert Hurtado Cruchaga, born Viña del Mar, Chile, 22 January 1901, died Santiago de Chile, 18 August 1952. Born into a poor family, he was educated by the Jesuits, and became one in 1923, being ordained priest ten years later. He taught, then became chaplain to the Catholic youth movement in Chile. He started the 'Hogar de Cristo', an organization to provide homes for the poor. He also started a periodical, *Mensaje*, to spread the Christian message. He produced a number of books on Catholic social doctrine.

Albert of Ancona, monk, 1350. Feast 7 August.

Albert of Cashel, born Ireland, died Regensburg, possibly eighth century. Venerated in Ireland. Accounts conflict. He may have been English and been elected bishop of Cashel, Ireland, by popular acclaim, later renouncing his position to make the pilgrimage to Jerusalem. He died on the return journey. Feast 8 January.

Albert of Cremona (or Bergamo), bl., born Ogna, near Bergamo, died Cremona, 1279. He was a married farmer, a Dominican tertiary, and a great supporter of the poor in his region. He went on pilgrimage to Santiago de Compostela in Spain, to Rome and to Jerusalem. On his return he settled at Cremona, where he is said to have worked miracles. Feast 11 May.

Albert of Jerusalem, bishop and martyr, born Castel Gualtieri, Parma, died Acre, Palestine, 14 September 1214. Born into a distiguished family, he entered the canons regular at Mortara, near Pavia. In 1134 he became bishop of Bobbio, and then, almost immediately, bishop of Vercelli. He played a considerable part in papal policy as a diplomat, but then was appointed bishop of Jerusalem – although, as Jerusalem was controlled by Saladin, he resided at Acre. In his first years there he produced a Rule for the Carmelites at the request of **Brocard**. He was stabbed to death during a procession by a man whom he had

dismissed from his post as Master of the Order of the Holy Spirit.

Albert of Louvain, bishop and martyr, born Louvain, c. 1166, died Rheims, 24 November 1192. The son of the Duke of Brabant, he was made a canon of Liège when only 12, but a decade later became a knight in the entourage of the Count of Hainault. Soon afterwards, however, he reverted to his clerical state, and became a subdeacon and archdeacon of Brabant. In 1191 he was elected bishop of Liège, but the appointment was contested and the emperor chose someone else. Albert appealed to Rome, and set off there in disguise. His election was declared valid by the Pope, and on his return he was consecrated bishop by the archbishop of Rheims. Because the emperor was in Liège, Albert decided to remain in Rheims, but was murdered there by some of the emperor's followers as he was on his way outside the city walls to visit the monastery of St Rémi. Feast 21 November.

Albert of Trapani, born Trapani, Sicily, died near Messina, c. 1387. He became a Carmelite, was sent to Messina, and spent the last years of his life as a hermit. Feast 7 August.

Albert the Great, philosopher, theologian and scientist, born Lauingen, near Ulm, c. 1200, died Cologne, 15 November 1280. Of a noble family, he attended the University of Padua, which is where he joined the Dominican order, despite the opposition of his family who tried to remove him by force, in 1222. By 1228 he was teaching in Cologne, and then taught at a number of German houses and held one of the Dominican chairs of theology at Paris (1245–8), before being sent back to Cologne where he became the teacher of St **Thomas Aquinas**, and a proponent of Aristotelianism. Always keen on the natural sciences, he went out of his way to observe natural phenomena, and combined this with proficiency in all branches of philosophy and theology. Albert commented on almost the whole corpus of Aristotle presented in the Latin translations and notes of Averroës, and other Arabic commentators, including the *Liber de Causis*, which Albert believed to be the crown of peripatetic philosophy. His own scientific observations allowed him considerably to expand on Aristotle's *Naturalia*; he also wrote on mathematics, and several biblical commentaries. His principal theological works are a commentary in three volumes on the *Books of the Sentences* of Peter Lombard, and the *Summa Theologiae* in two volumes; his contemporaries bestowed on him the honourable surnames 'The Great' and 'Doctor Universalis'. In 1254 he became prior provincial of Germany, and in 1260, at the express instruction of Pope Alexander IV he became bishop of Regensburg in an unsuccessful effort to restore order in that diocese. He resigned after two years and returned to Cologne. In 1274 he went to the Council of Lyons, and in 1277 he went to Paris to defend the teachings of his former pupil Thomas Aquinas. In 1278 his memory suddenly failed him in the middle of a lecture, and he suffered from an increasing loss of memory. Canonized and declared a Doctor of the Church by **Pius XI** in 1931, **Pius XII** proclaimed him patron of natural scientists in 1941. Feast 15 November.

Albinus (Aubin), bishop, from Vannes, died *c.* 554. Abbot of Tincillac and bishop of Angers from *c.* 529, he participated in the third council of Orleans in 538. Feast 1 March.

Albinus, bishop, died 1005. Bishop of Brixen in the Tyrol, commemorated with **Genuinus**. Feast 5 February.

Alcmund (Alchmund), martyred Lilleshall, Shropshire, *c.* 800. A prince from Northumbria, he was exiled in Scotland. The circumstances of his death led to him being venerated as a martyr, first at Lilleshall, then, after the translation of his relics, at Derby. Feast 19 March.

Alcmund, bishop, died Hexham, 7 September 781. He was bishop of Hexham from 767.

Alcuin, bl., Anglo-Saxon contributor to the Carolingian Renaissance. Born York, *c.* 735; died Tours, 19 May 804. He was educated in the episcopal school at York and succeeded Aelbert in its headship in 767 when Aelbert became archbishop. On a journey to Rome in 780 he met **Charlemagne** at Parma, who persuaded him to join his court, where he systematized the educational programme, his principal subjects of academic concern being **Boethius**, **Augustine** and the grammarians. France

became his residence until his death. His extant literary works include a quantity of biblical exegesis; a major work on the Trinity; treatises directed against the Adoptionism of Felix of Urgel, whom he opposed in person at the Council of Aachen; moral and philosophical writings; the *Lives* of Ss **Willibrord** and **Martin of Tours**; manuals of grammar, rhetoric, dialectic, orthography and mathematics. He wrote numerous poems and letters (311 are extant), above all to Charlemagne. They are a mine of information as to the literary, political and social conditions of the time, and the most reliable authority for the history of humanism in the Carolingian age. He has been listed as a 'blessed', but there is no evidence of a cult to him.

Aldebrandus, bishop, born Sorrivoli, near Cesena, 1119, died Fossombrone, 1219. He was provost of Rimini, where his courageous preaching against immorality led to an attempt on his life. In 1170, he became bishop of Fossombrone and is now the town's patron. Feast 1 May.

Aldegund, abbess, born 630, died 684. She founded and was first abbess of Maubeuge and was a daughter of **Waldebert** and **Bertilia** and sister of **Waldetrude**. Feast 30 January.

Aldemar, abbot, born Capua, died *c.* 1080. A Benedictine at Monte Cassino, he was a director of nuns at Capua, where he became known for his miracles. Recalled because of the publicity, he then founded and ruled over several abbeys including Bocchignano in the Abruzzi. Feast 24 March.

Aldetrude (Adeltrude), died Maubeuge, 526. She was the daughter of **Vincent Madelgarius** and **Waldetrude**. Her aunt, **Aldegund**, abbess of Maubeuge, took care of her there and she became second abbess. Her grandparents **Waldebert** and **Bertilla** and her siblings **Landericus (Landry)**, **Dentelin** and **Madelberta** are all saints. Feast 25 February.

Aldhelm, bishop, born Wessex, *c.* 640, died Doulting, Somerset, 709. Related to Ine, king of Wessex, and educated at the church school of Canterbury, Aldhelm became abbot of Malmesbury *c.* 675, then bishop of Sherborne in 705, and bequeathed to the Church a mixed Roman and

Celtic tradition. Much of his Latin writing has survived: held in high repute as a poet, and esteemed by **Bede**, Aldhelm's learning and piety inspired many scholars. Feast 25 May.

Aldric, born *c.* 800, died Le Mans, 7 January 856. He left **Charlemagne**'s court for the priesthood, but was recalled as chaplain by Louis le Pieux. Bishop of Le Mans from 832, a great organizer, he has been suspected, probably unjustly, of involvement in the forgery called the 'Decretals of pseudo-Isidore'.

Aldric, monk, died 1200. He was a Praemonstratensian monk in the Rhineland. Feast 6 February.

Aled, martyr, died Slwch Hill, near Brecon, Wales, sixth century. Her story is almost identical with that of St **Winifred**. The daughter of a Welsh king, she had consecrated herself to God, but had to flee princely suitors, first to Llandew, then to Llanfillo, next to Llechfaen, and finally to Slwch Tump, where her frustrated suitor found her and cut off her head. Where the head landed, a spring gushed out. Feast 1 August.

Alef, monk, late fifth, early sixth century. Ethiopian Church. Founded a monastery at Ahseya. Feast 20 March.

Alexander, martyr, died Bergamo, third/fourth century. A member of the **Theban Legion**. Feast 26 August.

Alexander, martyred at Pidna, Macedonia, *c.* 390. An evangelist for Christianity. Feast 14 March.

Alexander, see also **Antonina**.

Alexander, see also **Eventius**.

Alexander, see also **Gaius**.

Alexander Briant, martyr, born Somerset, England, 1556, died Tyburn, London, 1 December 1581. He was educated at Oxford and converted to the Roman Catholic faith. He went to Douai to study for ordination. In 1579 he was sent back to England. Two years later he was captured in London and taken to the Tower, where he was tortured to compel him to reveal the hiding place of Father Persons. Whilst imprisoned, he became a Jesuit. He was hanged, drawn and quartered along with **Edmund Campion** and **Ralph Sherwin**.

Alexander Chotovicki, archpriest, martyr, born Kremence, 11 February 1872, died Moscow, November (?) 1937. Russian Church. His father was rector of the seminary of Volinia, where Alexander studied before taking a doctorate in St Petersburg in 1895. He was sent to the USA, appointed to a parish in New York. He was in charge of the finances of the Russian Orthodox Church in New York before being sent in 1914 for three years to Helsinki, and then in 1917 to the Cathedral of Christ the Saviour in Moscow as treasurer. After the 1917 revolution he was active in distributing alms to the poor of Moscow, and teaching religion to children, for which he was imprisoned in 1922. He only served a year of his ten-year sentence, but in 1924 he was sentenced to three years internal exile. He returned to Moscow, but was arrested again in the autumn of 1937 and executed. He was canonized in 1994. Feast 29 November.

Alexander Crow, bl., martyr, born Howden, Yorkshire, died York, 30 November 1587. He had worked in York as a shoemaker, but went to Rheims in 1581 to become a priest. He was ordained in December 1583, and the following February returned to England. He was arrested in South Duffield and sent to York Castle. He was condemned to be hanged, drawn and quartered.

Alexander Guttoeva, martyr, died Novgorod, seventeenth century. Church of the Old Believers. Originally from Olonec, he was sent to Novgorod to be instructed in the new reforms. When he refused to be persuaded, an official hit him so hard with a heavy liturgical book that he had to be taken to hospital. He escaped, and remained hidden for a time, but was so inflamed by zeal after hearing of the fate of his companion **Gabriel** that he left his hiding place, was arrested and executed by being burned alive. Gabriel himself was from Karelia, and did not speak Russian. He did not escape from captivity as did Alexander when he had the chance, was tortured and eventually executed. Their other companion, **Mark**, was also from Olonec; he escaped from prison and lived freely for seven years, but was then arrested, tortured and, as with his other companions, burned alive. Feast 22 February.

Alexander, Joachim and Isaiah, monks, sixteenth century. Russian Church. Companions of St **Anthony**, founder of the monastery of the Most Holy Trinity on the river Sija.

Alexander Kerzenski, monk and martyr, born Kostroma, 1674, died Nizni Novgorod, February 1720. Church of the Old Believers. Deacon of the church dedicated to the icon of the Mother of God of Vladimir, he celebrated the liturgy according to the rite introduced by Nikon, but at the age of 28 became convinced that he ought to join the Old Believers, and in 1703 established a monastery near Nizni Novgorod, of which he was elected superior. He was imprisoned for about a year for his beliefs, but he was forced to abjure them, an act of which Alexander and his companions swiftly repented. He was then denounced to the Tsar, Peter the Great, on 12 February 1720, and was questioned by him in St Petersburg before being executed.

Alexander Kustski, monk, born Vologda 1371, died 9 June 1439. Russian Church. He became a monk of a monastery on an island on Lake Kuben. He lived an austere life, but in search of greater solitude left the monastery and wandered for a time until he encountered the monk **Eutimius** who had built a hermitage at the mouth of the river Kusta. Although Eutimius moved on, Alexander sought from the archbishop of Rostov approval for a church, dedicated to the Dormition, and a monastery. He lived there until his death, renowned for holiness and miracles.

Alexander Nevski, prince, born Perejaslav-Zalesski, 30 May 1220, died Gorodec, 14 November 1263. Russian Church. His father was ruler of the city of his birth, and he was invested as prince in the city's cathedral by **Simon of Suzdal**. In 1235 he took part in the battle of the river Emajygi in Estonia, where his father's troops routed the Teutonic Knights. The following year Alexander became ruler of Novgorod. In 1239 he married Alexandra, the daughter of the prince of Polock Brjacislav. He was a defender of the integrity of Russia, against

the Swedish army at the battle of the river Neva (hence his name Nevski) in 1240, then against the Knights, whom he decisively defeated in the battle on the ice of Lake Cudskoe on 5 April 1242, then against the Mongols who were attacking from the East and with whom he concluded an alliance. He rejected a proposal from the Pope to make an alliance against the Mongols, which he also saw as an opportunity for converting the pagan East. By 1253 he was prince of Kiev, Novgorod and Vladimir. He maintained peace on the Eastern border only with great difficulty and by journeys to the capital of the Khan. It was in the course of his return for the fourth time from the Golden Horde that he died, having taken shelter in a monastery. Before he died he received the monastic tonsure and took the name Alexis. Feast 30 August.

Alexander of Alexandria, patriarch from 312, born c. 250, died Alexandria, 18 April 328. He vigorously attacked Arianism and convened a synod of all Egyptian bishops, which condemned and excommunicated Arius in 321. Arius received support from Eusebius, bishop of Caesarea, and Eusebius of Nicomedia, but Alexander defended his action, adhering to the doctrine of Origen and insisting on the natural, eternal generation of the Son and his perfect likeness to the Father. He allied himself with Hosius of Cordoba and, together with his deacon, St **Athanasius**, attended the Council of Nicaea in 325, where the term *homoousias* was included in the Nicene Creed. The Council determined that Melitius, who had founded a schismatic church with clergy of his own ordination, would be allowed to remain a bishop, though subordinated to Alexander, but this arrangement broke down when Athanasius succeeded him. Feast 26 February.

Alexander of Alexandria II, patriarch, died Alexandria, 1 February 730. Coptic Church. He was a monk of the monastery of Enaton, gentle and humble, elected patriarch of Alexandria after a three-year vacancy in 705. Although his first years were peaceful, a new governor demanded that all, including for the first time monks and bishops, pay a levy, a charge which led to much apostasy. The situation changed with governors of Egypt, but rarely improved, and churches and monasteries fell into ruins.

Alexander of Caesarea, bishop and martyr, born Cappadocia, died Caesarea, c. 250. A pagan convert, bishop of Cappadocia, he succeeded the bishop of Jerusalem after being named coadjutor and successor, the first known example. When very old he was thrown to the beasts. They refused to harm him, and he died in chains. Feast 16 May.

Alexander of Char'kov, archbishop, martyr, born Luck, 1851, died Char'kov, 24 May 1940. Ukrainian Church. Alexander Teofanic Petrovski first studied law and lived a dissolute life, but was converted after a dream he had of his deceased mother and entered a monastery, becoming an archimandrite. After the 1917 revolution he and other priests whose churches had been closed founded a monastery on the river Psel. It was also later closed. He became bishop of Umansk in 1932, then of Vinnica, and in 1937 archbishop of Char'kov. His zeal, however, led to his imprisonment in July 1938, and he was condemned to ten years in prison for 'counter-revolutionary propaganda'. He died in prison. His cult was approved in 1993. Feast 11 May.

Alexander of Constantinople, patriarch, died Constantinople, 340. He was patriarch from 317, elected when he was already 73 years old, it is claimed. When in 336 Arius, whom Alexander had vigorously opposed, arrived in the imperial city, Alexander refused Arius communion, although commanded to receive him by the emperor, and locked himself in his church. Arius died suddenly, before the matter could be forced on the patriarch. Feast 28 August.

Alexander of Jerusalem, bishop and martyr, died Caesarea, Palestine, c. 250. One of the great bishops of the early Church, and a pupil of Origen. Bishop of a see in Cappadocia c. 200, imprisoned c. 204 in the Severan persecution, he became bishop of Jerusalem in 222, and founded the library later used by Eusebius of Caesarea in preparing his history of the early Church. When Origen was condemned by the bishop of Alexandria, he took refuge at Jerusalem where Alexander ordained him, and appointed him to teach Scripture and theology in the diocese. Alexander died in prison at Caesarea during the persecution of Decius. Feast 18 March.

Alexander of Methymna, bishop, fifth century. Byzantine Church.

Alexander of Moscow, monk, died Moscow, after 1427. Russian Church. A disciple of **Sergius of Radonez**, he became the third hegumenos of the monastery of the Saviour in Moscow, where he is buried. Feast 13 June.

Alexander of Oseven, monk, born near Beloozero, 17 March 1427, died Oseven, 20 April 1479. Russian Church. Baptized Alexis, he was the youngest of eight children of a wealthy farming family. Before his marriage he went to spend some time in prayer in the monastery of St Cyril at Beloozero. The hegumenos suggested he become a monk. He at first refused, but remained studying theology for seven years before taking the habit, and his new name. His father meanwhile had founded a new village, called Oseven, on the river Cur'juga. Alexander went there on leaving his monastery to seek more solitude, and his father asked him to stay, promising to help with building a hermitage. Before doing so, however, Alexander returned to the monastery of St Cyril, and spent some time there in various tasks before getting the superior's blessing to found his own monastery, for which he laid down a very strict Rule. He remained in his foundation for 27 years, much in demand as a spiritual guide, and also as a miracle worker. Feast 20 April.

Alexander of Perejaslav, bishop. Russian Church. Feast 23 May.

Alexander of Svir, monk, born Mandera, near Novgorod, 15 June 1448, died Svirski, 30 August 1533. Russian Church. Baptized Amos, he met a monk from the monastery of Valaam one day and confided his desire to become a monk, although his pious parents wished him to marry. He entered the monastery of Valaam, taking the name Alexander, without his parents' consent. Three years after he had entered the monastery, his parents discovered where he was and his father, Stephen, came to try to persuade him to return home. Instead Alexander persuaded his father and mother both to enter religious life. He then retired to a hermitage on an island for 13 years. However, many people came to learn of his whereabouts, and with the permission of St **Serapion**, who ordained him priest, he built a monastery and a church.

Alexander of Thessalonika, bishop, beginning of the fourth century. Byzantine Church. Took part in the Council of Nicaea.

Alexander of Tver, bishop, died Tver, 1492 (?). Russian Church. Renowned as a miracle worker.

Alexander Okropiridze, bishop, born Kulbithi in Eastern Georgia, 1824, died Sciomgvime, 1907. Georgian Church. Baptized Alexis, he studied at Gori, then Tbilisi, then in the academy at Kazan. After teaching for a time, he became a monk and in 1862 a bishop, first of Abchazia then of a number of different dioceses, because the Tsarist government would not allow any individual bishop to stay long in one see. He was a protagonist of Georgian language and culture, as a result of which he was forced to spend the last four years of his life in the monastery of Sciomgvime. Canonized in September 1995.

Alexander Rawlins (alias Alexander Neam or Francis Feriman), bl., born Oxford, 1560, martyred York, 7 April 1595, beatified 1929. First arrested and exiled as a recusant, he was ordained in Soissons in 1590 and worked in Yorkshire and Durham until arrested on Christmas Day 1594. He was hanged, drawn and quartered with **Henry Walpole**.

Alexander Sauli, bishop, born Milan, 1534, died Calosso, 11 October 1592. He was a page at the court of the Emperor Charles V, but at 17 entered the Barnabites. He was ordained in 1556, and then taught philosophy and theology at the university. He came to be head of his order, and successfully fought off attempts to merge it with another, dying order. In 1570 he was appointed bishop of Aleria in Corsica, which he set out to reform. So impressed with his efforts was the Pope that in 1591 he was made bishop of Pavia, although he did not live to visit it, dying on the way. He wrote a number of books, and was a leading member of the reform group of prelates after the Council of Trent.

Alexander the Charcoal Burner, bishop and martyr, born Comana (modern Gumenek, Turkey), died there, 275. An educated man who had given away all his possessions and pursued life as a charcoal burner in order to be closer to God. He was elected bishop of Comana on the advice of **Gregory the Wonderworker**. Feast 11 August.

Alexander the Dervish, martyr, born Thessalonika, died Smyrna (Izmir), 26 May 1794. Byzantine Church. He was sent to Smyrna by his parents for safety, but there converted to Islam. He made a pilgrimage to Mecca and entered the order of Dervishes. He travelled about the Ottoman Empire teaching, but increasingly criticized the Turks for their treatment of Christians. Eventually he returned to Smyrna, where he turned back to Christianity, and was beheaded.

Alexander Vockski, monk, fifteenth/sixteenth centuries, died near Soligalic. Feast 27 March.

Alexander II Michailovic, prince of Tver, martyr, born Tver, 1301, died 28 October 1338. Russian Church. He was driven from his throne by an alliance of the prince of Moscow and the Mongols, and had to take refuge in Lithuania. Eighteen months later he was able to return and occupied the throne of Pskov, and ten years after that attempted to recover Tver for his son Theodore by going to see the Khan. The prince of Moscow, however, now accused Alexander of fomenting rebellion against the Khan, and the Mongol ruler had father and son decapitated.

Alexander I, pope, c. 109 – c. 116. Early accounts have him succeeding Evaristus as fifth in line from St Peter, but later convention reckoned him as sixth pope. According to Eusebius, his reign lasted ten years, but this is uncertain. The *Liber Pontificalis* reports him as being a Roman, the son of a man also called Alexander. The Roman tradition that he died a martyr, decapitated on the via Nomentana, apparently confused him with an actual martyr bearing the same name, whose tomb was discovered in 1855.

Alexandra the Recluse, born Alexandria, died there, 14 February, end of fourth century. Coptic Church. To reject the unwelcome advances of a man, she enclosed herself in a tomb with only a single window through which food was brought to her. She was visited by **Melania the Elder**, who left an account of her life. She lived in the tomb for ten (or, according to other sources, 12) years.

Alexis Elnatski, martyr, born Alexis Ivanovic Vorosin, in the village of Kaurcicha, where his father was parish priest, *c.* 1890, died Kinesma, 1937. Russian Church. He tried his vocation as a monk, but returned to his village and lived a life of prayer and strict asceticism even after, in the aftermath of the revolution, he was elected head of the village soviet. In 1928, however, he abandoned his life in the village and became a 'fool for Christ's sake', wandering naked through the fields and villages. For this he was sent to a psychiatric hospital. In 1937 he was arrested and imprisoned, and died in the prison hospital. His cult was authorized by the patriarch of Moscow in 1993. Feast 12 September.

Alexis Falconeri, founder, born Florence, died Monte Sennario, 17 February 1310. The son of a wealthy Florentine merchant, he joined the Confraternity of the Blessed Virgin in 1225, and became one of the Seven Founders of the Servite Order – although the only one to remain a lay brother, and the only one to survive to see it formally approved in 1304. He was canonized in 1887.

Alexis Nikolaevic Tatarinov, martyr, born Kune, 4 January 1878, died Char'kov, 16 December 1937. Ukrainian Church, Moscow patriarchate. He had served as a priest in the village of Gnidovka, on the outskirts of Izjum. Feast 19 May.

Alexis of Goloseevo, born Vladimir Ivanovic Sepelev in Kiev, 14 April 1840, died in the hermitage of Goloseevo, in the Cave Monasteries of Kiev, 11 March 1917. Ukrainian Church. Of a noble family, he was dumb until 12 years old, when he was miraculously healed by bishop **Philaret** of Kiev. He then went to the Cave Monasteries of Kiev, and in 1857 officially joined the Laura, being ordained priest in 1875. After being accused of theft, he was transferred in 1891 to the hermitage of the Transfiguration, and four years later to that of Goloseevo. His fame for sanctity drew the faithful not only from the Ukraine, but from across Russia as well, and he was greatly in demand as a

spiritual guide. He was canonized in 1993 by the Synod of the Ukrainian Church.

Alexis of Moscow, metropolitan, born Moscow, 1300, died there, 12 February 1378. Russian Church. Born Eleutherius, of parents who were refugees in Moscow from the Tartars, he displayed a great love of spiritual things from his early years and entered the monastery of the Theophany when he was 20. There he displayed a particular love of the Scriptures, and learned Greek to read the New Testament in the original language: he translated it into Slavonic. He was asked to served as an official of the diocese, which he did for 12 years before being ordained bishop of Vladimir. In 1354, after the death of the metropolitan through plague, the patriarch of Constantinople appointed Alexis metropolitan of Kiev and all Russia, and he chose, as had his predecessor, to live in Moscow. He was an active intermediary with the Golden Horde, on one occasion being summoned by the Khan, who had heard of his miraculous powers, to heal his wife's blindness – which he did. He returned again to the Khan when, as regent during the minority of Prince **Dimitri**, he sought his approval for Dimitri's accession to the throne. He also used his authority to persuade other Russian princes to accept Dimitri, creating an alliance which was eventually able to free Russia from the stranglehold of the Horde. He was equally active on strictly Church matters, founding monasteries, establishing a new rule of life for women and making women's monasteries independent of those of men, building churches, training pastors, and caring for the needy. His cult stems from 1431 when his body was discovered incorrupt. His relics are now in the patriarchal cathedral of the Theophany in Moscow. The day of the discovery of his relics, 20 May, is celebrated as a feast of Alexis, along with the day of his death.

Alexis the Recluse, monk, thirteenth century. Russian Church. Lived in ascetical seclusion near the Laura of the Kievan Caves. His relics were discovered in 1675 after an earthquake.

Alexis Toth, priest and missionary, born Szepes, Hungary (now Slovakia), 18 March 1854, died Pennsylvania, USA, 7 May 1909. Russian Orthodox Church in America. Son of a Greek Catholic (uniate) priest, he was ordained and emigrated to America to care for the many Carpatho-Russians there. Rejected by the local Catholic bishop, he eventually united himself and his parish to the Russian Orthodox bishop in San Francisco. Thus began the mass return of the uniates to Orthodoxy, involving about 30,000 people. He worked tirelessly among his poor immigrants and was a great temperance promoter. He was canonized by the Orthodox in America, 30 May 1994. Feast day 7 May.

Aleydis, born Scharembeke, near Brussels, died there, 1250. She was educated in a convent just outside the city, but contracted leprosy, a disease which she bore bravely, including the segregation from the nuns of the convent. Feast 15 June.

Alfred the Great, king of Wessex from 871, born Wantage, 849, died Winchester, 26 October 899. The son of King Aethelwulf and Osburh, he defeated the Danes in 878 and 885, and united the English, which contributed materially to the maintenance of Christianity in England. Alfred is remembered for the care he brought to ecclesiastical reform and the revival of learning. A man of deep piety and considerable learning, he gathered about him scholars from England, Wales and the continent. With them he developed an educational plan for clergy and laity based on translations of the most popular Latin works of the time, of which he himself was largely responsible for 'Pastoral Care' by **Gregory the Great**, the 'Consolation of Philosophy' of **Boethius**, the 'Soliloquies' of St **Augustine**, and the first 50 psalms of the Psalter. These and other works mark the beginnings of English prose through which Alfred hoped to give to his people an education at once practical and liberal, and so to rebuild the once flourishing Christian civilization ruined by the Danish invasions. He promoted the interests of the Church, and founded monastic communities at Shaftesbury and Athelny. He is remembered as having done his utmost for the education of his clergy and monks and, in his own life, as the model of a Christian king. Feast 26 October.

Alice, see **Aleydis**.

Alipius, bishop, born Tagaste, Africa (Algeria), c. 360, died there, after 429. A close student friend of St **Augustine**, both deviated into Manichaeism in Carthage. He joined Augustine at Rome in 384, and went with him to Milan where they were baptized by **Ambrose** that year. He afterwards participated in the dialogues organized by Augustine at Cassiciacum, and followed him back to Africa in 388, where they lived in a quasi-monastic community at Hippo; after three years he was ordained a priest. On a pilgrimage to the Holy Land, c. 393, he met **Jerome** and helped to foster a relationship between him and Augustine. In 394 he was elected bishop of Tagaste, where he remained for the rest of his life, taking part in the same councils as Augustine, and in struggles against the Pelagians and the Donatists. Feast 15 August.

Alipius the Icon Painter, monk, died in the Laura of the Kievan Cave monasteries, c. 1114. Russian Church. He studied the Greek art of icon painting, and was in 1084 employed in the Laura, first as an apprentice, but later as a master of the art. He entered the monastery in 1087, but continued to paint icons which are now to be found in several churches across Russia, including that of the Dormition in the Kremlin.

Alix le Clerq, bl., born Lorraine, 1576, died 1622, beatified 1947. After early years of frivolity she converted and, directed by **Peter Fourier**, founded the Congregation of Canonesses of St Augustine to teach poor children. She was both an energetic person and a mystic. Feast 9 January.

Allowin, see **Bavo**.

Alodia, see **Nunilo and Alodia**.

Alonso Briceno, philosopher and theologian, born Santiago, Chile, in 1587, died Trujillo, Venezuela, 15 November 1668. In 1605 he entered the Franciscans, and quickly gained a reputation as a teacher. Greatly interested in **John Duns Scotus**, he published works on him which reveal his clarity of mind and brilliance as a scholar. After holding a number of important ecclesiastical offices in Chile, Briceno was appointed bishop of Nicaragua in 1646. In 1649 he was transferred to Caracas.

Alonso Rodriguez, Jesuit martyr, born Segovia, 1598. See **Roque González**.

Aloysius Gonzaga, patron of youth, born Castiglione, 9 March 1568, died Rome, 21 June 1591. Of noble descent, and destined for a military career, he made a vow of virginity at the age of seven; at 12 he became devoted to the Eucharist after receiving his first communion from **Charles Borromeo**; at 13, influenced by reading Louis of Granada, he practised mental prayer as much as five hours a day, while also studying philosophy at Alcala. He renounced his inheritance in favour of a younger brother in 1585, entered the Society of Jesus, despite his father's objections, and studied at the Roman College, under the spiritual direction of **Robert Bellarmine**. Humble and obedient as a novice, he laboured among the sick and was himself a victim of the plague among the stricken of Rome.

Aloysius Rabata, bl., born Sicily, *c.* 1430, died there, 1490. He was a Carmelite friar who refused to bring his attacker to justice. He died from the effects of the blow he had received to the head. Feast 8 May.

Aloysius (Luigi) **Scrosoppi**, bl., born Udine, Italy, 4 August 1804, died there, 3 April 1884, beatified 1981. Ordained an Oratorian in 1828, he worked in a refuge for orphan girls, founding the Sisters of Providence to help him. He undertook much social work, including starting a foundation to support poor older priests.

Aloysius Stepinac, bl., archbishop, born Brezaric, now Croatia, 8 May 1898, died there, 10 February 1960. Born into a large family, he served in the Austro-Hungarian army during World War I, and was briefly imprisoned at the end of it. He studied agriculture in Zagreb, but in 1924 went to Rome to study for the priesthood. After ordination in 1930 he worked in a parish in Zagreb, and was appointed archbishop of the city in 1937. In 1946 he was put on trial, ostensibly because of collaboration, but in reality because he had been attacking the Communist government. In 1951, because of his ill-health, he was moved to house arrest in Brezaric. He was made a cardinal in 1953.

Alpais, bl., born Cudot, near Orleans, *c.* 1150, died there, 3 November 1211. Of a peasant family, she worked in the fields until struck down by an illness – possibly leprosy. She was partially cured by a vision of the Virgin in 1170, but had to remain in her bed. She reportedly lived on nothing but the sacred host, and knowledge of this spread widely so that Cudot became a place of pilgrimage. The bishop had a church built next to her house, so that through her window she could participate in the liturgy.

Alphaeus, martyr, born Eleutheropolis, died Palestine, 303. He was a lector in the church in Caesarea, who encouraged other Christians to remain constant during Diocletian's persecution. After being beaten, he was thrown into the same cell as, and was beheaded with, **Zachaeus**. Feast 17 November.

Alphege of Canterbury, archbishop and martyr, born *c.* 954, died Greenwich, 19 April 1012. He left the monastery at Deerhurst, or possibly Glastonbury, to become an anchorite near Bath, and later abbot, until St **Dunstan** called him to succeed Athelwold at Winchester in 984; translated to Canterbury, he went to Rome in 1006 for his pallium. Five years later the Danes sacked Canterbury and held him to ransom, which at first he agreed to pay, but his captors murdered him during a drunken feast when he refused to ransom himself at the expense of his poor tenants.

Alphege the Elder, bishop, died *c.* 951. A Benedictine, bishop of Winchester from 935, he won many over to the religious life, including **Dunstan** and **Ethelwold**, whom he ordained on the same day. Little is known of him, except that he was nicknamed 'the bald'. Feast 12 March.

Alphius and Companions, martyrs, born Vaste, near Otranto, south-east Italy, died Lentini, near Catania, Sicily, *c.* 251. Nothing is known except that he was killed with his brothers Cyrinus and Philadelpus. They rapidly became popular locally and are venerated as patrons of Vaste and Lentini. Feast 10 May.

Alphonsa Muttathupadathu, bl., born Kudamaloor, Kerala, India, 1910, died Bharananganam,

India, 28 July 1946. Anna Muttathupadathu was orphaned at a young age and raised by her aunt, who arranged a marriage for her when she was 13. To avoid the marriage she deliberately burned her feet. She joined the Poor Clare convent, Bharananganam, in 1927, taking the name Alphonsa of the Immaculate Conception, and took her vows in 1930. She became a teacher, but suffered so badly from ill-health that she soon had to give this up. She accepted her pain, saying, 'I believe the Lord has chosen me to be an oblation, a sacrifice of suffering.' Many miracles of healing are said to take place at her tomb.

Alphonsus Liguori, founder, Doctor of the Church, born Marianella, 27 September 1696, died Pagani, near Salerno, 1 August 1787. Of an ancient Neapolitan family, he founded in Naples an association of mission preachers, approved by Benedict XIV in 1749 as the Congregation of the Holy Redeemer (Redemptorists); elected superior general for life, and Bishop of San't Agata dei Soti in 1762, he resigned his see in 1775 on the plea of ill-health and retired to Nocera, but lived another 12 years, a period taken up in much controversy arising from the affairs of his Congregation. He dedicated himself to the devotion and working morality of the Church. He sought to commend the gospel to a sceptical age. He preached simply and to the heart, believing that the largely Jansenist influence on the rigorism of the sacrament of penance repelled rather than reconciled the sinful. It is as a moral theologian that he is chiefly celebrated, and his *Theologia Moralis* (1753–5), for the use of religious and priests engaged in pastoral work, especially the confessional, stresses the search for the will of God in all circumstances. Many of the manuals of moral theology used in seminaries throughout the world either belong to his school, or are strongly marked by his influence, and the practical direction traced by him has been substantially adopted by the Church.

Alphonsus of Orozco, born Oropesa, near Avila, 17 October 1500, died Madrid, 19 September 1591. He studied in Toledo and Salamanca, and in the latter heard **Thomas of Villanova** preach, which decided him to become an Augustinian at the end of his studies. He served in a number of houses in Spain, and once set off for Mexico, but had to turn back because of ill-health. He served for a time in Valladolid, which was then the capital city, and was appointed court preacher to King Philip II. When Philip moved the capital to Madrid he went too, but worked with the poor and with prisoners as well as with courtiers. Towards the end of his life he was asked to write an account of his mystical experiences.

Alphonsus Rodriguez, Spanish Jesuit mystic, born Segovia, 25 July 1532, died Majorca, 31 October 1617. Rodriguez married, but on the death of his wife and family sought admission to the Society. Accepted in 1571 as a lay brother and sent to the college of Montesione, he served as house porter for 46 years, being remembered for his humility, obedience, patience and mystical absorption in prayer. Leo XIII canonized him in 1888. Feast 30 October.

Altfridus of Hildesheim, bishop, died 874. He had been a monk of Corvey. Feast 15 August.

Altmann of Passau, bishop and reformer, born Westphalia, c. 1015, died Zeiselmauer, near Vienna, 8 August 1091. He became canon and teacher at Paderborn, provost at Aachen, chaplain to Empress Agnes, and bishop of Passau in 1065. Concerned for the spiritual well-being of his clergy, he imposed the Rule of St **Augustine** in several churches, and founded Augustinian houses at Rothenbuch and Reichersberg. He supported papal decrees against married priests in 1094, and in 1076 was the first to announce Emperor Henry IV's excommunication in Germany. Exiled from his diocese by the imperial party in 1077, he fled to Rome, but continued his pastoral and political duties, in spite of Henry's persecution until his death, under the protection of Margrave Leopold II.

Alvarez de Córdoba, bl., preacher and reformer, born Córdoba, 1360, died there, 19 February 1430. A Dominican, he preached throughout Andalusia and in Italy, swung Castile against the antipope Pedro de Luna (Benedict XIII), acted as confessor and counsellor to Queen Catherine and King John II, and retired to Córdoba in 1423, where he founded the Scala Coeli priory. He developed a great devotion to the passion of Christ during a pilgrimage to Palestine in 1405, and this moved him to erect in the priory gardens tableaux of the passion that were forerunners of the Way of the Cross.

Al-Wadih ibn Raga, monk, tenth/eleventh centuries, died Sundufa, *c.* 1010. Coptic Church. The son of a Muslim judge in Cairo, he was greatly impressed by a young Christian convert who was about to be burned at the stake. His father sent him on a pilgrimage to Mecca, but on his journey home he lost his way and was rescued by a mysterious figure on a horse, who was later recognized as St Mercurius. This figure brought him to the church of St Mercurius in Cairo, where he became a Christian, taking the name Paul. He then fled to the desert of Scete, where he became a monk, but later returned to Cairo to confess his faith. Paul had a son, and his father the judge threatened to drown him before Paul's eyes if he did not renounce Christianity. The caliph, however, sympathized with Paul and set him free. He returned to Scete and was ordained in the monastery of St Macarius. His father sent some Bedouin to kill him. He lived for two years in hiding in the village of Sundufa on the Delta before he was recognized. After his death his tomb was hidden so that the Muslims would not burn his body.

Amadeus of Savoy IX, bl., Duke of Savoy, born Thonen, 1 February 1435, died Vercelli, 30 March 1472. The husband of Yolanda, daughter of Charles VII of France, he succeeded to the throne in 1456. Austere and devout, generous to the poor, he readily forgave his enemies; an able and wise administrator, but tolerant of troublemakers, he showed great forbearance and forgiveness towards his adversaries, the Sforzas, and some of his many brothers, which appears to have encouraged strife. He suffered from epilepsy, which eventually wore him down, and he relinquished authority to his wife.

Amadeus of Lausanne, abbot of Hautecombe and bishop of Lausanne, born Chateau de Chatte, Dauphine, 21 January 1110, died Lausanne, 27 August 1159. He quit his noble rank for the anonymity of the Cistercians in 1125, but his abbot, **Bernard of Clairvaux**, urged him to undertake positions of leadership as counsellor to

the counts of Savoy and envoy to the papal court. As bishop he practised the monastic ideals of personal piety and devotion to communal peace.

Amalberga, the lives of two saints of this name, one seventh century and the other eighth century, have become intertwined to the point where they are indistinguishable. It seems, however, that the first, a widow, became the wife of count Witger and had two daughters, **Gudule**, patroness of Brussels, and Remilde, and a son, Emebert, later to become bishop of Cambrai. After the birth of Gudule, the parents entered religion and Amalberga, having received the veil from St **Aubert**, entered the convent at Maubeuge, where she died *c.* 690. Her body was transferred to the abbey at Lobbes, where Witger had become a monk. The second Amalberga was born in the Ardennes (Belgium) and introduced to a holy life by St **Landrade**, abbess of Bilsen, possibly sent there by St **Willibrord**. She led a pious life at a retreat in Flanders, which she owned, and where she died *c.* 772. It has been said that her beauty was such that Pepin III wished her to marry his son **Charlemagne**, but that she escaped his attentions by taking the veil, although not his brutality – she broke an arm while fending him off. Feast 10 July.

Amand, apostle of Flanders, born south of Nantes, *c.* 584, died 6 February, after 675. He is not well known partly because of confusion with other saints with more or less similar names. Essentially a missionary going from country to country, he stopped only to found church or monastery, returning to the search for other souls to be gained for Christ. Consecrated bishop in 628, he began active missionary work in Flanders and Carintha; in 633 he founded two monasteries at Ghent under the patronage of St Peter, and later a large monastery at Elmon near Tournai, of which he was abbot in his last years. He is said to have been bishop of Tongres, Maastricht, from 649 to 652, which is referred to in a letter of 649 from Martin I, dissuading him from resigning his see.

Amand of Bordeaux, bishop, born Bordeaux, died there, *c.* 431. He was a priest of Bordeaux and was elected bishop there. After a good number of years he had a vision suggesting to him that **Severinus** should succeed him: he retired, and Severinus was elected, but died soon after and Amand had to take over once again. He prepared **Paulinus of Nola** for baptism. Feast 18 June.

Amasius of Teano, bishop, died *c.* 356. A Greek who left the East to escape the Arians, he was the second bishop of Teano, central Italy, from 346. Feast 23 January.

Amator of Auxerre (Amatre), bishop, from Burgundy, died Auxerre, 418. Possibly married earlier in life, he was for many years bishop of Auxerre, predecessor to **Germanus of Auxerre**. He built churches, converted country people from paganism and is credited with healing miracles. Feast 1 May.

Amatus, abbot, born Grenoble, *c.* 570, died Remiremont, eastern France, *c.* 630. As a boy he was sent to a monastery to study, and eventually entered the community, although he spent some years near his monastery as a hermit. He then went to the monastery of Luxueil in eastern France and from there founded the monastery at Remiremont, on the Moselle, of which he became abbot, possibly returning to an eremitical existence in the last years of his life. Feast 13 September.

Amatus, bishop, died Breuil, Flanders, *c.* 690. He was bishop of Sion – now Sitten in Switzerland – but was banished by the king to the abbey of Péronne. He later moved to the abbey of Breuil, where he lived a humble life in a separate cell near the abbey church. Feast 13 September.

Amatus of Musco, bishop and abbot, born Musco, *c.* 1104, died 1193. Of noble parents, he became a Benedictine. He founded the abbey of Fontignano, near Orvieto, in 1142, and was made bishop of Musco in 1154. Feast 31 August.

Amatus Ronconi, bl., born near Rimini, died there, 1292. He travelled four times to Santiago de Compostela and then became a Benedictine lay brother at San Giuliano abbey near Rimini. Feast 8 May.

Ambrose, metropolitan, born near Enos (Greece), 1791, died Cilli, 30 October 1863. Church of the Old Believers. The son of a priest – the twenty-second in the family – he was married in 1811 and immediately ordained priest, although his wife died only three years later, leaving him with a son, George. In 1817 he become a monk, in 1823 he became superior of a monastery on the island of Halki in the Sea of Marmara, and in 1835 he was consecrated metropolitan of Bosnia. He was recalled to Constantinople in 1840 because of his support for Bosnian rebels against the Turkish occupation. In 1846, however, he was recruited by Russian Old Believers in an attempt to reconstitute their hierarchy after a severe persecution. He took up residence in the monastery of Belaja Krinica until in December the following year he was removed under pressure from Tsar Nicholas I and went to live in Cilli with his family. He considered returning to his original spiritual allegiance, but decided to remain with the Old Believers, living according to the monastic rule. He was canonized by the Old Believers in 1996.

Ambrose (Edward) Barlow, Benedictine monk and martyr, born Barlow Hall, England, 1585, executed Lancaster, 10 September 1641. Despite his Catholic background he, with many others, conformed to the Protestant Church during his youth. At 22 he joined the English seminary at Douai. In 1613 he was imprisoned during a visit to England but released after a few months. He then entered the English Benedictine monks at St Gregory's, Douai, and changed his name to Ambrose. Professed in 1614 and ordained in 1617, he returned to England. He spent 24 years working amongst the poor in the districts of Manchester and Liverpool. A stroke in 1641 left him partially paralysed, and on Easter Day in the same year he was arrested while in Lancashire. On 8 September he was condemned to death.

Ambrose Chelaia, patriarch, born Martvili, western Georgia, 1861, died 27 March 1927. Georgian Church. The son of a priest, and originally called Bessarion, he studied in the seminary of Tbilisi and was ordained in 1887. He worked in a parish in the city of Soci, today in Russia, and in 1892 was transferred to the cathedral at Suchumi. Five years later he enrolled in the ecclesiastical academy of Kazan, and in 1888 he became a monk, being named archimandrite of the monastery of Celisci in western Georgia in 1902. Four years later he was made hegumenos of the monastery of St John the Baptist, and became a member of the synod of western Georgia. He was an active protagonist in the campaign for an autocephalous Church for Georgia, which led to his exile in Russia, being imprisoned for a time and then becoming hegumenos of a monastery in the eparchy of Novgorod. In 1917 he became metropolitan of Cqondidi in western Georgia, two years later of Suchumi and in 1921, after the Church had achieved autocephalous status, patriarch-catholicos of all Georgia. He was a severe critic of the Society regime, for which he was put in prison, where he died. Canonized by the Georgian Church in 1995. Feast 2 March.

Ambrose Fernández, bl., born Sisto, Portugal, 1551, martyred Japan, 1620, beatified 1867. He went to Japan looking for a career and there became a Jesuit lay brother. He died of apoplexy in Suzota prison, Omura, where conditions were appalling. Feast 7 January.

Ambrose of Cahors, bishop, died near Bourges, *c.* 770. Named bishop of Cahors, under Pepin the Short, it seems that despite his works of charity he was unpopular with the faithful, so he gave up his see and lived in a cave for three years near the river Lot. He went to Rome on pilgrimage and died on the return journey. Feast 16 October.

Ambrose of Massa, ven., born Massa Maritima, Tuscany, died Orvieto, 17 April 1240. A parish priest in the Tuscan Maremma, when he was led to reform his life by the preaching of Moricus, an early companion of St **Francis**. He joined the Franciscans in 1225. For the last 15 years of his life he devoted himself to penance and works of charity. The Franciscans honour him with the title of 'blessed'.

Ambrose of Milan, born Trier, 340, died Milan, 4 April 397. Of a distinguished family (his father had been Praetorian Prefect of Gaul), he studied in Rome and became consul of Liguria and Aemilia, administered from Milan. He became bishop of Milan in 373 or 374, elected by the people of the city although he was not yet a baptized Christian. He was an outstanding preacher, a staunch opponent of Arianism, and a powerful influence on the Roman emperors who lived in Milan. He

wrote *De Sacramentis*, and a study of ethics, with particular reference to the clergy, entitled *De Officiis Ministorum*. He is sometimes known as the founder of Latin hymnody. His name is given to a specific liturgy and thereby a set of chants. He is one of the four ancient doctors of the Western Church. Feast 7 December.

Ambrose of Optina Pustyn, hieromonk, born in the region of Tambov, 5 October 1812, died in the monastery of Optina Pustyn, 22 October 1891. Russian Church. Born Alexander Grenkov, he studied in the seminary at Tambov. After being struck by a serious illness, he vowed to become a monk should God spare him, a vow which he did not immediately fulfil after leaving the seminary, instead becoming a teacher of Greek in the seminary of Lipeck. He eventually became a monk in 1839 in the monastery of Optina. He took the name Ambrose when donning the monastic habit in 1842, in due course being ordained priest. The monastery was active in translating and publishing texts of the Church Fathers and other spiritual writers, and his skill with languages was put to good use despite a long period of illness. He was particularly skilful in transmitting Slav spiritual writings, which were widely read. He was much sought out as a spiritual guide, including by Dostoevski who portrayed him as the starets Zosima in *The Brothers Karamazov*. Despite his importance as a literary figure, his first concern was always the care of souls. Canonized 1988. Feast 10 June.

Ambrose Sansedoni, bl., born Siena, 1220, died there, 1287, cult confirmed 1622. Joining the Dominicans in 1237, he studied with **Thomas Aquinas** before a life of preaching during which he travelled through France, Germany and Italy. Feast 20 March.

Ambrose Traversari, bl., monk and early Christian humanist, born Portico, 16 September 1386, died Fontebuono, 17 November 1439. In 1400 he entered the Camaldolese monastery at Florence. During the Quattrocento, there were few intellectual and spiritual centres more open or active, Ambrose being one of its more endearing figures. Of a modest family, a model of discipline and work, he had an excellent knowledge of Greek and translated numerous works of the Greek Fathers, notably **John Chrysostom** (his preferred author), **Basil** and **Athanasius**. A renowned professor and of a comprehensive charity, he established relations with the greatest names of the age, and Florentine humanists such as Niccoli, Strozzi and Cosimo de Medici visited him to discuss classical and patristic literature, philosophy and theology. Eugene IV, who regarded him highly, named him general of his order in 1431 and supported his movement for reform. He represented Eugene at the Council of Basle, defended the primacy of the papacy, and opposed all schism in the Church. At Ferrara and Florence, in 1438, he negotiated with Byzantine representatives in discussions leading to reunion.

Amda Mika'el, fifteenth century. Coptic Church. A royal minister and governor of a province, he was renowned for his virtues and his care for the poor and for religion. He was falsely accused, and exiled for a time, but then assassinated.

Amenawag of Derjan, martyr, born in Karnberdak, south-central Anatolia, died there, 10 March 1335. Armenian Church. He was wrongly believed by Muslim neighbours to have undertaken to become a convert to Islam. He at first fled his village, but later returned, was arrested and tortured, but refused to apostatize.

Amicus, hermit, born Camerino, near Ancona, Italy, died abbey of Fonteavellana, 1045. Originally a priest in Camerino, he entered a monastery and persuaded many of his family to do likewise. He did not find monastic discipline sufficiently strict, and became a hermit in the Abruzzi, although in later life he joined the monastery of Fonteavellana. Feast 3 November.

Amlakawi, monk. Ethiopian Church. A monk in Eritrea.

Ammi, bishop and martyr, born Hah, Tur'Abdin, fifth century. Syriac Church. A disciple of **Simeon of Qartmin** and first bishop of Tur'Abdin. He was martyred at Tanazi (modern Tanzi). Feast 3 September.

Ammon, monk, born Egypt, c. 285, died Kellia, c. 350. Despite being attracted to a hermit's life, Ammon was obliged to marry by his parents. He

and his wife, however, lived as celibate for 18 years, at which point he was able to retreat to Nitria, while his wife formed a community of women in their house. Ammon went to a place which came to be known as the Kellia, on the edge of the desert, to create a more ordered community of hermits, who came together occasionally and were governed by a council of senior members. Ammon himself was renowned for the severity of his asceticism, and for his miracles. Feast 4 October.

Ammon and Companions, martyrs, died Alexandria, 250. Ammon, Zeno, Ptolemy, Ingenes and Theophilus were soldiers attending the execution of Christians in the persecution of Decius. When the Christians appeared to waver in their faith, Ammon and his companions encouraged them to persevere, revealing themselves to be Christians also, and were martyred. Feast 20 December.

Ammonas, bishop, monk, died c. 403. Coptic Church. Lived for 40 years in the desert of Scete and was visited by St **Anthony** in 350. After Anthony's death he was the spiritual guide of the monks of Pispir, on the left bank of the Nile. He was consecrated bishop by St **Athanasius**, and in 373, during the persecution of Lucius, he had to go into hiding. Feast 26 January.

Ammone the Recluse, monk. Russian Church. A monk of the Laura of the Kievan Cave monasteries, he went on a pilgrimage to Mount Athos and to the Holy Land. On his return he lived a life of exemplary holiness, the record says.

Ammonius, see also **Moseus**.

Ammonius of Tunhah, fourth century. Coptic Church. After a vision of St **Anthony** he became a monk and went eventually to live in a cave in the mountains of Tunhah, where he was tempted by the devil in the form of a nun. When this failed, the devil spread calumnies about him that he had married a nun, but a group of monks came to reveal his innocence. Feast 15 May, the day of his death.

Amphilochius, born 1487, died in the monastery of Moldovita, northern Moldavia, 7 September 1570. Romanian Church. He entered the monastery of

Moldovita at a young age, and after some years entered a hermitage with a disciple in the valley of Pangarati, where he lived for the next 50 years. He became renowned as a healer, and for his gift of prophecy. More disciples gathered, and in 1560 a monastery was established there with Amphilochius as hegumenos. In 1566, however, he retired back to the monastery of Moldovita, and lived there in strict asceticism for the rest of his life. He was venerated as a saint during his life, and immediately after his death his monastery named 8 September as his feast day. Canonized 1992.

Amphilochius, Macarius, Tarasius and Theodosius, monks and ascetics, fifteenth century. Russian Church. Amphilochius entered the monastery of Glusica in 1427. He became the principal assistant to the hegumenos, and was concerned with the observance of the rule by the monks. He himself was particularly devoted to poverty. Ten years after entering he became hegumenos, and died in 1452. Macarius, baptized Matthew, entered Glusica when 12 years old. He was remarkable for the holiness of his life, and died in 1478. Tarasius was originally the hegumenos of a monastery in Perm, committed to spreading the gospel in that region, but decided to enter Glusica also in 1427, attracted by the holiness of its hegumenos Dionisius. He had the gift of tears, and died in 1440 at a great age. Theodosius was also a disciple of Dionisius. They are commemorated together on 12 October.

Amphilochius of Iconium, bishop, born Caesarea, c. 340, died Iconium, after 394. A cousin of St **Gregory Nazianzus** and a friend of St **Basil**, he became bishop of Iconium in 373, having retired from public life in 370, after a decade of teaching law. As metropolitan of Lycaonia, he supported the cause of orthodoxy and played an important role at the Council of Constantinople I (381). He presided at the Council of Side (390), which condemned the Messalians, and he campaigned against puritanical and extremist cults. Among his extant works are a synodal letter in defence of the Holy Spirit issued after a council at Iconium (376), and a poem entitled 'Iambi ad Seleucum', preserved among the works of St Gregory Nazianzus. He earned great esteem as a source of patristic teaching in the fifth century. Feast 23 November.

Anabasa, monk, sixteenth century. Ethiopian Church. Founder of the monastery of Dabra Hazalo. Feast 13/14 September.

Anacletus (Cletus), bishop of Rome, c. 79 – c. 91. His name is correctly Anencletus, a Greek adjective meaning 'blameless', and is probably to be identified with 'Cletus', a shortened form of the full name. He followed St **Linus** (the successor of St Peter), but preceded St **Clement of Rome**, and is commemorated as Cletus in the canon of the mass.

Anania, martyr. Coptic Church. Martyred on 12 December, possibly in Ahmin in Upper Egypt.

Anania, monk, martyr, born Maraguz, died Gabala, sixteenth century. Ethiopian Church. Entered the monastery of Dabra Sarabi at a very early age, where he became abbot despite some opposition from his community. His life was full of miracles, and he even knew the time of his death. When that time came he went to the spot he had foreseen, where he was attacked by pagans and pierced with a lance. His corpse continued to work miracles.

Anania of Novgorod, icon painter and monk, sixteenth century. Russian Church. Monk of the monastery of St Anthony the Roman at Novgorod. He never left the monastery. Feast 17 June.

Ananias, priest, martyred Phoenicia, c. 298. Imprisoned under Diocletian, he converted the gaoler, **Peter**, and seven soldiers of the guard. They were all killed together. Feast 27 January.

Anastasia, martyr, died Sirmium, Pannonia, c. 305. Feast 25 December.

Anastasia, hegumena of Uglic, and 35 companions, martyrs, died Uglic, 1609. Head of the convent of the Theophany, she was slaughtered by Polish soldiers with her nuns. Feast 23 May.

Anastasius, see also **Astrick**.

Anastasius, see also **Julian**.

Anastasius, monk, died 19 December. Coptic Church. Known only through the story of one of his monks who was miraculously transported to Jerusalem.

Anastasius, bishop, died *c.* 680. He was bishop of Brescia in Lombardy. He was one of those who helped to convert the Arian Lombards to Christian orthodoxy. Feast 20 May.

Anastasius, bishop, died *c.* 600. He was a converted Arian who became bishop of Pavia, Lombardy from 668. Feast 30 May.

Anastasius, archbishop, born Germany (?), died Esztergom, 12 November *c.* 1036. A disciple of Adalbert, bishop of Prague, he became abbot of his newly founded monasteries at Brevnov, near Prague, in 993, and then in Poland. He later went as apostle to the Magyars, at the request of King **Stephen I** of Hungary, and became Hungary's first prelate, abbot of St Stephen's foundation at Pannonkalma, and later archbishop of Esztergom.

Anastasius I, pope from 399, born Rome, died there, 19 December 402. He plunged immediately on his election into the controversy over Origen and his writings, particularly a whitewashing translation of his 'First Principles' by Rufinus of Aquileia, which had greatly offended **Jerome** in Bethlehem, and his influential circle of friends in Rome. Although Origen was only a name to Anastasius, and he had little grasp of the issues at stake, he condemned a number of Origen's doctrines on the strength of a letter, received in 400 from Theophilus, the powerful patriarch of Alexandria, dwelling on the evils caused by Origen's works and reporting their recent condemnation in Egypt. Rufinus then defended his translation and his own theological position, and Anastasius, although sceptical about the motive behind Rufinus's notorious translation, left him to God's judgement. Anastasius thereby earned the praise of Jerome and **Paulinus of Nola** for his blameless life and apostolic solicitude. In other matters, Anastasius did not commend himself to the African bishops who, because of a shortage of clergy, wanted a relaxation of the ban on Donatist clergy returning to the Church. Anastasius told them to continue the struggle against Donatism, advice the Africans tactfully ignored.

Anastasius Hartman, ven., Capuchin bishop, missionary to India, born Altwis, Lucerne Canton, Switzerland, 20 February 1803, died Patna, Bihar, India, 24 April 1886. He entered the Capuchins at Baden, Germany in 1821 and was ordained four years later. Hartman taught theology and philosophy for a while before leaving for India as a missionary. He was appointed first vicar apostolic of Patna. He recruited missionaries to Patna and engaged in an extensive school building programme. He was transferred to Bombay, but then returned to Rome as an adviser on India for the Vatican's Congregation of Propaganda. He promoted the establishment of Capuchins in the USA and from 1858 to 1860 was the director of the missions of his order. He returned to Patna in 1860 as vicar apostolic. Hartman wrote a Hindustani Catechism (1853) and two books on psychology. The cause for his beatification was introduced in 1906.

Anastasius of Alexandria, patriarch, died 18 December 616. Coptic Church. Of an influential family in Alexandria, he was involved in government administration before becoming a priest. After the death of **Damian** he was chosen as patriarch. He built up the Church of Alexandria, but had difficulties with extreme monophysites on the one hand, and on the other with the emperor who was trying to impose the Chalcedonian formula. He was forced to retire to a monastery, but he had the support of the patriarch of Antioch who, in 609–10, came to visit him accompanied by five bishops.

Anastasius of Ancyra, martyr, born Ancyra (modern Ankara), died there, 1777. Byzantine Church. Martyred by Muslims.

Anastasius of Antioch I, patriarch of Antioch from 559, born Palestine, died Antioch, *c.* 599. A monk of Sinai and 'Apokisianios' of Alexandria before his election to the see of Antioch, he suffered banishment to Jerusalem for his strenuous opposition to Justinian I's edict on 'Aphtharto-docetism'. **Gregory the Great** befriended him and requested Emperor Maurice to restore him to his see. As a Neo-Chalcedonian, Anastasius strongly defended Orthodoxy, and staunchly defended the creed of Chalcedon, although he attempted to close the gap with the monophysites. His works greatly influenced later Greek theologians, such as **Maximus the Confessor** and **John of Damascus**. Five important treatises on Christological and trinitarian questions have survived in Latin translations, in addition to a compendium of Christian doctrine in Greek. Feast 21 April.

Anastasius of Antioch II, patriarch of Antioch from 599, died there, *c.* 609. He succeeded **Anastasius I** at Antioch, and **Gregory the Great**'s letter acknowledging him as patriarch and accepting his profession of faith has survived. He translated Gregory's *Liber regulae pastoralis* into Greek. He met his death during an insurrection of the Jews against the emperor Phocas, who had attempted to convert them by force. Feast 20 April.

Anastasius of Bulgaria, born Radovis, Bulgaria, martyred Thessalonika, 6 August 1794. He moved to Thessalonika as a young man and worked making armaments. He was asked by the owner of the workshop to smuggle out of the city some valued Turkish clothing, but was stopped and challenged over his religion. He refused to abandon his faith, was imprisoned, tortured, and finally martyred.

Anastasius of Cluny, monk, born Venice, died Doydes, *c.* 1085. He first became a monk at Mont St Michel, but left when the abbot was accused of simony. He then lived as a hermit on an island off the Normandy coast until he was persuaded by **Hugh of Cluny** to join the monastery at Cluny. He stayed at Cluny for some time, but then was sent on a papal mission to Spain. When he returned he spent time again as a hermit, then returned to the monastery, and once again became a hermit near Toulouse. He was recalled to Cluny in 1085, but died on the return journey. Feast 16 October.

Anastasius of Giannina, martyr, born Vlasio near Giannina, died Constantinople, 8 July 1743. Byzantine Church. He was parish priest in Constantinople, put to death for evangelizing among the Muslims of the city.

Anastasius of Nauplia, martyr, born Nauplia, died there, 1 February 1655. Byzantine Church. He was decapitated for evangelizing, according to one account, or because he refused to convert to Islam, according to another.

Anastasius of Paramythia, martyr, born Paramythia, Epirus, died there, 18 November 1750. Byzantine Church. He was working in the fields with his sister when the son of the local Turkish pasha passed by. The young man was taken by the beauty of Anastasius's sister, but Anastasius would not let him approach her. He then reported Anastasius to the pasha, accusing him falsely of having undertaken to convert to Islam. Anastasius was imprisoned, but the young Turk, having been impressed by his constancy, visited him there and eventually himself became a Christian and became a monk in Corfu. Anastasius was beheaded.

Anastasius of Peristerona, twelfth century. Church of Cyprus. One of the 300 holy men who fled from Palestine to Cyprus after the occupation of Palestine by the Turks. Feast 17 September.

Anastasius of Sinai, abbot, seventh century, born Palestine, died St Catherine's Monastery, Mount Sinai. Abbot of St Catherine's, he was a champion of orthodoxy against all forms of heresy, and became known as the New Moses. He attacked, as early as 640, the Egyptian and Syrian monophysites at Alexandria, against whom his most important treatise, the *Hodegos*, or 'Guide', is primarily directed. He also published an allegorical exegesis of the *Hexaemeron*, as well as a collection of 154 'Questions and Answers' on various theological themes. Feast 21 April.

Anastasius of the Kievan Cave Monastery, monk and martyr, twelfth century. Russian Church. A companion of **Titus**. Feast 22 January.

Anastasius Paneras, martyr, born Lesbos, *c.* 1795, died Kasaba, Asia Minor, 11 August 1816 or 1819. Byzantine Church. Martyred together with **Demetrius Bejazis** for teaching Christianity.

Anastasius the Fuller, martyr, born Aquileia, Italy, died Salona (Split), Dalmatia, *c.* 304. He painted a cross on his door during the persecution of Diocletian. Feast 26 August.

Anastasius the Persian, martyr, born Persia, died Palestine, 628. A soldier, he converted and became a monk near Jerusalem. Arrested by the Persian rulers for openly denouncing their religion, he was tortured and strangled with about 70 other Christians. His relics are in Rome. **Bede** wrote about him. Feast 22 January.

Anatolianus (Antholian), martyred Auvergne, *c.* 265. Feast 6 February.

Anatolius, monk and martyr, died near Suchumi, *c.* 1920. Russian Church. He was a monk of the hermitage of Glina, near Kursk, but was sent to Kazakhstan. He was a good singer, and director of the choir, and by 1916 was in charge of the music in the cathedral at Alma Ata. He was shot after moving to the Caucasus.

Anatolius, monks. Russian Church. The name of two monks, or hermits, of the Kievan Cave monasteries, one of the twelfth and the other of the thirteenth century, whose relics were found in 1675 after an earthquake. Feasts 3 July and 31 October respectively.

Anatolius of Constantinople, patriarch, born Alexandria, *c.* 400, died Constantinople, 3 July 458. A disciple of St **Cyril**, who sent him to Constantinople, he succeeded the deposed Flavian as bishop. Pope **Leo I** challenged his good faith, and demanded that he rehabilitate the bishops deposed at Ephesus in 449, explicitly condemn Eutyches and Nestorius, and subscribe to Leo's 'Tome to Flavian'. On the accession of Marcian and Pulcheria as emperors in 450, Anatolius accepted Leo's terms and exhumed the body of Flavian for burial in the Church of the Holy Apostles. He seems to have encouraged Marcian to summon the Council of Chalcedon in 451, and helped to convince the Illyrian and Egyptian bishops of the orthodoxy of the 'Tome to Flavian'; he played a part in formulating the Definition of Chalcedon. He also promoted the famous Canon 28 of the Council, which declared the see of Constantinople second after Rome, but this led to acrimony; in general, however, he and Leo co-operated in pursuing an anti-monophysite policy.

Anatolius of Laodicea, bishop, born Alexandria, died there, *c.* 283. He founded a school of Aristotelian philosophy, and achieved the honour of a seat in the senate. Consecrated coadjutor bishop by Theotecnus, bishop of Caesarea, he became bishop of Laodicea in 268, on his way to the Synod at Antioch to deal with Paul of Samosata. A man of great learning, Eusebius and **Jerome** held him in high esteem. His writings were few, but include a treatise on the date of Easter, based on the 19-year cycle still in use, and a work on the elements of arithmetic. Feast 30 July.

Anatolius of Odessa, bishop and martyr, born Kovel, Volinia, 20 August 1880, died in the concentration camp of Uchto-Pecorski, northern Russia, 23 January 1938. Ukrainian Church. The son of a clerk, Andrew Grigorevic Grisjuk entered the theological academy of Kiev, three years later becoming a monk and a priest. He continued his studies, specializing in the history of Syrian monasticism before the Arab conquest. He became a professor in 1912, and inspector of the theological academy of Moscow. A year later he was consecrated bishop of Cistopol and rector of the theological academy of Kazan. He was arrested in 1921 and sentenced to a year's hard labour. On his release he became bishop of Samara. He was arrested again in 1923, but released the same year and named an archbishop. In 1923, however, he was accused of disseminating anti-Soviet literature and imprisoned for three years in Krasnovodsk. He returned to Moscow in 1927, subscribing to the declaration of submission to the state drawn up by the patriarchal vicar of Moscow, and became bishop of Odessa. He was, however, active in defending the rights of the faithful and in 1936 he was again arrested, sent to Kiev and imprisoned there, later being transferred to Moscow. The following year he was sentenced to five years' hard labour but, already ill, he died soon after arriving at the camp. Canonized in 1997.

Anatolius of Optina the Elder, monk, born Bobyli, Kaluga, 6 August 1824, died Optina, 25 January 1894. Alexis Moisevic Kopev was the son of a deacon. In 1836 he entered the seminary at Kaluga. In 1855 he joined the monastery of Optina, in 1862 taking the name of Anatolius. He became a priest in 1870. He served as a spiritual guide to pilgrims who came to the monastery, and in 1874 was named superior of the hermitage of Optina and confessor to the community. After **Ambrose of Optina** founded the convent of Samordino, he became confessor to the nuns. He was a devotee and propagator of the Jesus Prayer.

Anatolius of Optina the Younger, monk, born Moscow, 1855, died Optina, 30 July 1922. Russian Church. Alexander Alexis Potapov, as he was named before taking the name Anatolius on entering the monastery, worked for a time as a clerk in Kaluga. He entered Optina in 1855 after the death of his mother, became assistant to **Ambrose of Optina** and, after Ambrose's death, of **Joseph of Optina**. He lived in a hermitage attached to the monastery, where he received many visitors for spiritual direction. He was ordained priest in 1906 and became confessor to a convent founded by Ambrose. Two years later he moved back to the monastery as confessor to pilgrims, hearing confessions for 24 hours a day. He was also famous for miracles of healing, and for prophecy. In 1921 he became seriously ill. A year later the political police came to interrogate him, but, having spent the night in prayer, he died the day after they came to arrest him. Feast 11 October.

Andeolus of Viviers, from Smyrna, martyred near Viviers, on the Rhone, *c.* 208. He was a subdeacon whom **Polycarp** is supposed to have sent to France, where he was knifed in the head. Feast 1 May.

Andrew, monk, born Sanhur, Upper Egypt, sixth century, died near Danfiq, seventh century. Coptic Church. Worked first as a shepherd, becoming a monk when 20 years old at the monastery of St Samuel. He was ordained by bishop **Pisenzius**. He later moved to the Monastery of the Cross, where he became abbot. Pisenzius built another monastery around his tomb.

Andrew, died Florence, *c.* 407. He was bishop of Florence and was either the predecessor or the successor of **Zenobius** as bishop there. Feast 26 February.

Andrew, see also **Peter**.

Andrew Abellon, bl., reformer and artist, born St Maximin-la-Sainte-Baume, *c.* 1375, died Aix-en-Provence, 15 May 1450. He joined the Dominicans at an early age and taught philosophy and theology in various priories until 1408, when he was sent to Montpellier. There he became master of theology, despite his course having been interrupted by the plague, during which he ministered to the population. In October 1419, Andrew was named prior of the monastery in his native village, where he applied three principal directives: to restore the traditional discipline, to assure the resources necessary for the life of the religious, and to rebuild and complete the cloister buildings. In 1432 he was sent to Arles to restore discipline there, and then to Aix, as prior, in 1438. He spent several years in Marseilles, and was appointed prior at Aix-en-Provence, but refused the office, going instead as a simple religious. He fell ill there and died among his brothers in religion.

Andrew Avellino, preacher and reformer, born Castronuovo, Naples, 1521, died Naples, 10 November 1608. Of noble birth, he became a priest in 1545, studied canon and civil law, but abandoned that in 1548 after making the spiritual exercises under the Jesuit Lainez and devoted himself to the care of souls. He joined the Theatines in 1556, after recovering from a beating by enemies of his reform of a convent in Baiano, and became superior of the community in Naples. **Charles Borromeo** asked him to found a house in Milan in 1570, and he acted as spiritual director of several institutions in Milan and Piacenza (1570–82). He left some 3,000 letters of spiritual direction, some of which were published after his canonization.

Andrew Bessette, bl., born Saint-Grégoire d'Iberville, Canada, 9 August 1845, died Montreal, 6 January 1937, beatified 1982. Joining the Brothers of the Holy Cross, he performed humble manual tasks with them all his life. As infirmarian, he gained a reputation as a healer, ascribing this to St Joseph's intercession.

Andrew Bobola, martyr, born Sandomir, Poland, 1591, died Pinsk, 16 May 1657. After becoming a Jesuit in 1609 he worked as a parish priest in Vilna, Lithuania, and was superior at Bobrinsk. Despite strong anti-Catholic opposition he was a successful preacher. In 1652, with the support of Prince Radziwill, he founded a Jesuit centre at Pinsk and invited other Jesuits to leave their places of hiding and join him. In 1657 the Cossacks attacked Pinsk, capturing Bobola. He was killed slowly and cruelly. Canonized 1938, he is a patron of Poland. Feast 31 May.

Andrew Caccioli, bl., preacher, born Spello, near Assisi, 1194, died there, 3 June 1254. He received the habit from St Francis himself and was among the first, if not the first, to join the group. Francis commissioned Andrew to preach, and he was present at Francis's death in 1226. Like many of the saint's early companions, Andrew interpreted the Rule strictly, even rigidly, and for this he was twice imprisoned under the administration of Elias of Cortona; released by Gregory IX, the first time on the intercession of **Anthony of Padua**, and on the second by John of Parma. He attended the general chapter held at Soria in 1233.

Andrew Corsini, bishop, born Florence, 30 November 1302, died Fiesole, 6 January 1373. Repenting his misspent youth, he joined the Carmelite order c. 1317. He studied at the University of Paris, 1329 and was named provincial of the order in Tuscany in 1348. He was active in this office during the plague, and in rebuilding the hard-hit religious communities to restore their spiritual fervour and monastic discipline. Consecrated bishop of Fiesole in 1360, he was a wise and able administrator, sought everywhere as a peacemaker; at Bologna he made peace between the nobility and the people. Feast 4 February.

Andrew de Comitibus, bl., lay brother, born Anagni, c. 1240, died convent of San Lorenzo al Piglio, 1 February 1302. Of the noble family of the Conti, he was a close relative of Popes Innocent III, Gregory IX, Alexander IV and Boniface VIII. He entered the Franciscans and was known for his humility and holiness of life. This led him to refuse the dignity of the cardinalate proffered by Boniface, although some chronicles suggest he was created cardinal but renounced the office. In any event, he lived the life of a simple friar. Feast 17 February.

Andrew de' Gallerani, bl., founder, died Siena, Tuscany, 1251. A soldier, he was exiled from Siena after accidentally killing a blasphemer and lived a life of penance. Allowed back, he founded the Brothers of Mercy, which lasted until 1308. Feast 19 March.

Andrew Denisov, founder, born Povenec, 1674, died Vyg, 1730. Church of the Old Believers. At the age of 17 he left home, and for a time lived as a hermit and nomad before founding, with **Daniel Vikulin**, the Old Believer monastery on the river Vyg. He became its superior after the retirement of Daniel. He was a considerable scholar and wrote a number of works, upholding his belief that the sacraments of the majority Church were invalid, and that it had no validly ordained clergy. Feast 19 August.

Andrew Dotti, bl., preacher, born San Sepulcro, Tuscany, 1256, died Vallucola, 31 August 1315. Of noble parentage, he entered the Servite order in 1278 at Florence, where **Alexis Falconeri**, one of the seven founders, was superior. He progressed rapidly in religious virtue and occupied various positions of honour in the order. He joined a group of hermits at Vallucola, and united them with the Servites in 1294. After the death of Alexis Falconeri, he returned to the hermitage at Vallucola, where he led a life of charity, mortification and contemplation.

Andrew Fardeau, bl., martyr, died 1794. A **Martyr of the French Revolution**. Feast 24 August.

Andrew Franchi, bl., bishop, born Pistoia, 1335, died there, 26 May 1401. He was of the noble family Franchi-Boccagni, became a Dominican c. 1351 and earned a doctorate in theology at Rome. He was prior at Pistoia, Orvieto, and twice at Lucca, between 1370 and 1375, and distinguished himself as a preacher, teacher and spiritual director. He was made bishop of Pistoia c. 1380, but resigned his see in 1400, having lived as a religious; he preached, spent his income on the poor and on pious causes, converted many sinners and healed factional strife.

Andrew Hubert Fournet, co-founder of the Daughters of the Holy Cross of St Andrew, born

Maillé, near Poitiers, France, 6 December 1752, died La Puye, near Poitiers, 13 May 1834. Ordained in 1776, he was amongst those who, during the revolution, refused to take the oath required under the Civil Constitution of the Clergy. For a number of years he continued to say mass in his former parish – often in secret. During the time of Napoleon, he took on greater responsibility for the churches in the Maillé area. In 1797 he met St **Jeanne Elizabeth Bichier des Ages**, encouraging her to form a religious community dedicated to the care and education of the poor and sick (the Daughters of the Holy Cross of St Andrew), for which Fournet wrote the Rule.

Andrew Ibernón, bl., born near Murcia, Spain, *c*. 1534, died Gandia, 1602, beatified 1791. From a poor family, he became a Franciscan lay brother, moving to a stricter house *c*. 1563. He was honoured as a saint during his life, credited with miracles and the gift of prophecy. Feast 18 April.

Andrew Kaggwa, martyr, born Bunyoro, Uganda, died Munyonyo, 26 May 1866, canonized 1964. He was the royal bandmaster of King Mwanga of Uganda. Converted by the Missionaries of Africa and baptized in 1881, his right arm was cut from his body before he was beheaded. See **Martyrs of Uganda**.

Andrew Kim, priest and martyr, born in Tchoung-Echeng Province, Korea, 21 August 1821, died Seoul, 16 September 1846. The son of Korean converts to Catholicism (his father was martyred in 1839), in 1836 he trained for the priesthood in China, returning to Korea in 1842. In 1844 he was ordained deacon, and in 1845 he was ordained priest in Shanghai. He was the first native Korean priest. Following his ordination he returned once more to Korea, where he had been given the task of arranging for more missionaries. He was arrested, tortured and then beheaded. In 1925 he was beatified, along with a further 78 Korean martyrs, and canonized in 1984. In 1949 Pope Pius XII designated him the principal patron of the clergy in Korea. Feast of the **Martyrs of Korea** 20 September.

Andrew Konstantinovic, prince of Suzdal, died Novgorod, 2 June 1365. Russian Church. Offered the throne of Vladimir, but gave it up in favour of his younger brother.

Andrew Nikitovic Miscenko, martyr, born Char'kov, 30 October 1893, died there, 25 May 1938. Ukrainian Church, Moscow Patriarchate. Before the revolution he had worked as a teacher, and became director of the choir in Santa Sophia in Char'kov. He was arrested on 25 May 1938 and shot.

Andrew of Antioch, bl., born Antioch, *c*. 1268, died Annecy, *c*. 1348. He became a member of the Augustinian canons, and served the Latin patriarch of Jerusalem as the keybearer of the Church of the Holy Sepulchre – an entirely honorary office as the keys were held by two Muslim families. He was sent to Europe to raise funds for the Holy Places, travelling widely to do so, and it was during this journey that he died. Feast 30 November.

Andrew of Bogolyubovo, prince, born southern Russia, 1110, died Bogolyubovo, 30 June 1174. Russian Church. His father was the prince of Rostov and Suzdal, later grand prince of Kiev. Andrew and his father founded several cities, including Moscow, and built many churches. In 1154 he became prince of Vysegorod, and in the summer of the following year he took an icon of the Mother of God secretly from Vysegorod to Rostov. That at least was his intention, but he had a vision of the Virgin which instructed him to take it instead to Vladimir. In memory of this event he had an icon painted which was called the Bogojubskaja, which was also famous for miracles. Where the Virgin had indicated he founded in 1159 a city called Bogolyubovo and a stone church. During his principate he founded 30 churches in all, one of them the Cathedral of the Dormition in Vladimir where he placed the icon of the Mother of God which he had brought from Vysegorod. He sometimes took that, or other, icons into battle with him as he fought to defend Russia, especially from the Bulgars, and to establish control of the river Volga. By the end of 1170 all of Russia was in his hands. Andrew had attempted to persuade the patriarch of Constantinople to raise the bishop of Vladimir to the rank of a metropolitan, but the patriarch refused, insisting that the bishop of Vladimir be subject to the metropolitan of Kiev:

the seat of the metropolitan was transferred to Vladimir only in 1330. Andrew was assassinated by conspirators who included in their number some members of his own family. Feast 4 July.

Andrew of Constantinople, martyr, born Chiusa, Italian Alps, died Constantinople, 1465. Accused of having abandoned Islam, he declared always to have been a Christian. He was then tortured, scourged, flayed, his limbs broken, until at last he was beheaded. Feast 29 May.

Andrew of Crete, monk, born Damascus, c. 660, died Erissos, 4 July 740. He was a monk in Jerusalem (678), became a deacon in Constantinople (c. 685) and head of a refuge for orphans and the aged. He became archbishop of Gortyna in Crete (692). He subscribed to the repudiation of 'two wills' in Christ, defined at Constantinople III; in 713 he retracted, explaining his doctrine in a metrical confession, and participated in the quarrels over iconoclasm. He was remarkable as an orator. He was the author of many scriptural discourses, but is principally interesting as the inventor of the 'Greek Canon', a form of hymnology previously unknown, which earned him respect as one of the principal hymnographers of the Oriental Church.

Andrew of Crete, martyr, died Constantinople, 766. A monk in Crete, he went to Constantinople to defend the veneration of images during the iconoclast controversy. He publicly protested at the harsh treatment of those who supported the veneration of images, and was himself arrested. As he was being taken along a street he was killed by someone in the crowd and his body thrown into a cess pit. His body was recovered, and a monastery dedicated to St Andrew was built on the site. Feast 20 October.

Andrew of Dabra Libanos, abbot, died 1462. Ethiopian Church. Enjoyed the favour for a time of the king, who kept two of the monks of the monastery of Dabra Libanos at court to advise him on religious affairs. He also endowed the monastery. Andrew was, however, later falsely accused and imprisoned. He died in prison. Feast 11 July.

Andrew of Fiesole, archdeacon of Fiesole, near Florence, born Scotland or Ireland, died Fiesole, c. 876. A tradition has it that Andrew accompanied St **Donatus** to Fiesole on his return from Rome, just when the local bishop's see was vacant and the local people were assembled in prayer for a new and worthy replacement. There was much ringing of bells and lighting of candles, considered miraculous by the assembly, who inferred that Donatus was to be their new bishop. He ordained Andrew as his archdeacon. There is some doubt he existed. Feast 22 August.

Andrew of Novgorod, monk, twelfth century. Russian Church. Second hegumenos of the Monastery of the Nativity of the Mother of God, founded in 1106 by **Anthony the Roman**.

Andrew of Peschiera, bl., preacher, born Peschiera, Lake Garda, 1400, died Morbegno, Switzerland, 18 January 1485. Of Greek origin, Andrew Grego became a Dominican at Brescia and was sent to Florence for his studies. He was attracted especially to the life of obedience. His career was spent in the evangelization of Vatellina and neighbouring districts. He was not well received, but nonetheless preached tirelessly and won many converts by his words, by his humble and austere way of life and his great charity for the poor. He assisted in the foundation of two Dominican houses, and at times acted as inquisitor at Como. Feast 19 January.

Andrew of Rafailovo, monk, born 1746, died Moscow, 14 March 1820. Russian Church. Originally hegumenos of the Monastery of the Holy Trinity at Rafailovo, in 1811 he moved to the Monastery of St Simon in Moscow, where he was known for the holiness of his life.

Andrew of Rinn, bl., martyr, born 16 November 1459, died Rinn, near Innsbruck, 12 July 1462. When his father died, his mother entrusted him to his uncle's care. At the age of three his mother found his body hanging from a tree in a nearby wood. The uncle claimed he had sold the child to Jews returning from a fair, who, he said, cruelly put him to death through hatred of the faith. He was beatified by Benedict XIV in 1752, but was refused canonization. Feast 12 July.

Andrew of Saffea, fifteenth century. Ethiopian Church. A disciple of **Gabra Krestos**, he was a monk at Dabra Salida, but then took to an itinerant life as an evangelist, especially in the region of Eritrea. Feast 8/9 February.

Andrew of Smolensk, prince, born mid-thirteenth century, died Perejasvl-Zalesski, fourteenth century. Russian Church. In 1360 he gave up his claim to his princedom to avoid quarrelling with his brothers and lived for 30 years a secret life as sacristan to the Church of St Nicholas in Perejasvl-Zalesski. His noble birth was discovered only after his death. Many miracles were worked at his tomb. He was canonized in 1749. Feast 27 October.

Andrew of Solovki, hermit, sixteenth/seventeenth centuries. Originally from the monastery of Solovki, he lived a solitary life in a cave for some 60 years. Feast 9 August.

Andrew of Strumi, bl., abbot and reformer, born Parma, died there, 10 March, 1097. A disciple of Arialdo, a deacon of the church in Milan, who battled against abuses, attacking especially married priests and those in concubinage, numerous in north Italy. Arialdo was tortured and killed in 1066 by partisans of the simoniacal archbishop Guido of Velate, who favoured the abuses. At great personal risk Andrew recovered Arialdo's body. Andrew entered the Vallambrosans around 1069 and became abbot of Strumi c.1085, when they replaced the Benedictines there. Andrew wrote a life of Arialdo and also one of **John Gualbert**.

Andrew of Totma, born near Vologda, died Totma, seventeenth century. Russian Church. He entered the monastery of Galic, but became a 'fool for Christ's sake' and moved to Totma where he was unknown and lived near the church of the Resurrection. He spent the nights in prayer and by day collected alms to give to the poor. He was recognized as a saint immediately on his death. Feast 10 October.

Andrew of Uglic, prince, born Uglic, 13 August 1446, died 6 November 1494. Russian Church. Named Andrew Vasilevic Bolson, in 1462 he inherited the cities of Uglic, Zvenigorod and Bedeck, but a decade later clashed with his eldest brother Ivan Vasilevic III over territory, and again some years later, this time allied with Novgorod and King Casimir of Poland. Ivan had him arrested in 1492, and he died in prison two years later.

Andrew Rublev, monk and icon painter, born c. 1360, died Moscow (?), c. 1430. Russian Church. As a young man he joined the monastery of the Trinity at Radonez, although he trained as a monk at the monastery of Sepuchov, and was ordained priest there. Back at Radonez he studied the art of icon painting, especially under the guidance of **Daniel the Black**, of whom he became a close friend. He made frequent visits to Moscow and became well known there, being invited in 1405 to help decorate the Cathedral of the Annunciation in the Kremlin. Three years later he was in Vladimir decorating the Cathedral of the Dormition, possibly his masterwork. About 1420, again with Daniel, he was ordered to decorate the cathedral within his own monastery at Radonez. It was for this that he painted the famous icon of the three angels, representing the Trinity, meeting Abraham at the tree of Mambre. His final work was in the monastery of Spaso-Andronikov at Moscow, where he is buried. Feast 4 July.

Andrew-Svorad, see **Zoerardus and Benedict**.

Andrew the Hermit, born Monodendron, thirteenth century. Byzantine Church. Left his family to live as a hermit in a cave on Mount Kalang in Greece. His death was marked by a heavenly light, and the Empress Theodora had him buried in the cave in which his body was found, and built a church at the site. Feast 15 May.

Andrew the Tribune, martyr, died Taurus Mountains, c. 300. Said to have been a captain in the Roman army, and when fighting the Persians he called upon the Christian God for help, having heard he was a powerful protector. He and those in his section survived, and decided to become Christians, being baptized by Peter, bishop of Caesarea in Cappadocia. They were then threatened with execution, and fled into the Taurus Mountains, where they were caught and executed. Feast 19 August.

Andronicus of Alexandria, patriarch, born Alexandria, died there, 3 January 622. Coptic Church. Andronicus was from an aristocratic family and was in civil government before being elected to succeed the patriarch **Anastasius** in 616. He was faced with difficulties not only from the Chalcedonian patriarch, but also from the Persians, who captured the city in 619, slaughtering many monks on the way.

Andronicus of Moscow, hegumenos, born Rostov, died Moscow, 13 June 1404 (?). Russian Church. A monk of the monastery of the Holy Trinity at Radonez, he was sent to oversee the beginning of the monastery of the Face of the Saviour at Moscow, and was named its hegumenos in 1361.

Angadrisma, abbess, born northern France, died Beauvais, *c.* 695. Her father wished her to marry, but she wanted to become a nun. She prayed that she might become repulsive – and was afflicted with leprosy, which miraculously cleared up when she entered a convent. She became abbess of a convent at Beauvais. Feast 14 October.

Angela Chigi, bl., died 1400. A member of the influential Chigi family, she belonged to a congregation of hermits of St Augustine, living a holy life in Siena, where she died. She was never officially beatified.

Angela de' Merici, foundress, born Desenzano, Lombardy, 21 March 1474, died Brescia, 27 January 1540. In 1533 Angela trained 12 young women to assist her in the teaching of girls, and by 1535 the group had become the Company of St Ursula, dedicated to re-Christianizing family life, and thus society, through the education of future wives and mothers. There were no formal vows, but Angela's rule prescribed virginity, poverty and obedience; after her death St **Charles Borromeo** adapted the structure to conform to the decisions of the Council of Trent, and Paul III formally recognized the Company in 1544. The people of Brescia honoured Angela as a saint when she died, and Pius VII canonized her in 1807.

Angela Maria of the Immaculate Conception, ven., reformer, born Cantalapiedra, diocese of Salamanca, 1 March 1649, died El Toboso (Toledo), 13 April 1690. She entered the Discalced Carmelites, against the opposition of her devout and prosperous family, at the age of 21, but left before her profession. She then entered the order of the Holy Trinity at Medina del Campo, Valladolid, where she was professed. In 1681 she founded, with some young companions, a Trinitarian convent under a reformed rule, approved by Innocent XI as Trinitarians of the Primitive Observance. She was gifted with a high degree of intelligence and knowledge; her theological learning astounded the theologians of her time; she was favoured with discernment of souls and had extraordinary administrative ability. She published in 1691 an autobiography, *Vida de la Venerable Madre Sor Angela de la Concepcion*, and, in the same year, *Riego espiritual para nuevas plantas*, a treatise on perfection by way of meditation and contemplation.

Angela of Foligno, bl., penitent and mystic, born Foligno, *c.* 1248, died there, 4 January 1309. She was married and lived a worldly, even sinful, life until nearly 40, when she suddenly converted, for reasons unknown, and established a community at Foligno of the Third Order of St Francis. She desired an austere life of chastity away from the world, but as this could not be fulfilled as a wife and mother, she is reported to have prayed for her family's deaths. Her *Book of Visions and Instructions* records the history of her conversion and, in a penetrating analysis, Angela traces the 'twenty steps of penitence' which brought her to the threshold of the mystical life.

Angeles of Argos, martyr, born Argos, died Vunaki, 3 December 1813. Byzantine Church. He worked as a doctor in Kusadasi, where he once challenged a French atheist to a duel, intending only to defend himself by prayer. Before the duel took place, however, the Frenchman, overcome by fear, fled the town. In 1813 Angeles suddenly renounced Christianity and embraced Islam. His remarkable conversion surprised the Turks, who sent him to Chios. Six months later he announced that he had repudiated his new-found faith and returned to Christianity. For this he was imprisoned for a time and decapitated, thus achieving the martyrdom which may have been the motive for his actions all along. His body was thrown into the sea.

Angeles of Constantinople, martyr, born Constantinople, died there, 1 September 1680. Byzantine Church. A married man, he worked as a goldsmith in Constantinople. The day after the Feast of the Dormition of the Virgin he was accused by some Turks of having undertaken, in the midst of the previous day's festivities, to become a Muslim. He denied having done so, but was taken before the vizier and condemned to death.

Angeles of Retimno, martyr, born Melampus, Crete, died Retimno, 28 October 1824. Byzantine Church. With his brother Manuel and his cousins **George** and **Nicholas**, in 1821 Angeles decided to live openly as a Christian – hitherto his family had kept their faith secret. They then joined the unsuccessful revolt of the Greeks against the Turks, after which, in 1824, they returned home, living openly as Christians. They refused, however, to pay the tax on Christians. The Turks then tried to persuade them to convert to Islam, but when they refused the four were taken before the pasha at Retimno, and condemned to be decapitated. They were interred in the church of the Four Martyrs in Retimno, although some relics were taken to the monastery of St Constantine at Arkadi, where there were many miracles.

Angelina, princess and despot of Serbia, died Frusha Gora, Yugoslavia, *c.* 1510. A daughter, or relative, of Ivan Tornoievic, prince of the independent state of Zeta, she married Stephen Branovic, who became despot of Serbia in 1458 on the death of his brother. Her husband died in 1477 and, after the death of Vanuk, who succeedeed him, Angelina herself assumed the title of despot, ruled the Zetans 1497–9 and repulsed the Turks to preserve Zetan independence. She was a devout woman and became a heroine to the Serbians, to whom she was known as the mother and queen of Montenegro. She is still venerated for her piety and patriotism in Serbia and Montenegro, and commemorated there in folk poems and songs. She is buried in the monastery of Krusedol in the Frusha Gora mountains. Feast 30 June.

Angelina of Marsciano (Angelina of Corbara and of Foligno), bl., foundress of the Franciscan Third Order Regular for women. Born 1377; died Foligno, 14 July, 1435. She was the daughter of Jacques Angioballi, Count of Marsciano, near Orvieto, and Anne Corbara. She was forced to marry Jean de Thermis, Count of Civitella, at the age of 15. It was agreed with him that she would conserve her virginity and dedicate herself to works of charity and piety. After his death two years later, she took the habit of the Third Order of St Francis and, with some other young girls, converted her household in the Abruzzi into a kind of religious community. Persecuted by her family and by King Ladislaus, who accused her of sorcery and heresy for encouraging young girls to a life of virginity, she was finally banished from the kingdom. Following a visit to Assisi, she founded at Foligno in 1397 the convent of St Anne, according to the Franciscan Rule, followed by other foundations in Italy. Pope Martin V assembled the 16 houses existing in 1450 into one congregation, making Angelina superior general of what became the Third Order Regular for women. After a life of action and ecstasy, she died in the odour of sanctity. Her body was found incorrupt in 1492 and Leo XII approved her cult in 1825. Feast 21 July.

Angelo, see **Angelus**.

Angelus, martyr, died Sicily, 1220. A Carmelite account describes him as one of twins, sons of converted Jews, who became Carmelites aged 18. After five years as a hermit on Mount Carmel, he went to Sicily, where thugs murdered him. Many, including 200 Jews, were converted by his teachings and miracles. Feast 5 May.

Angelus Augustine of Florence, bl., born Florence, 1377, died there, 16 August 1438. Baptized Angelo Agostino Mazzinghi, he came from a wealthy family. He joined the Carmelites, and held a number of important offices in various friaries. He was renowned for his ability as a preacher, and also for the reform of his order.

Angelus Carletti di Chivasso, bl., moral theologian and canonist, born Chivasso, 1411, died Coni, 12 April 1495. Of a wealthy and distinguished family, he obtained a doctorate in civil and canon law, gave up worldly pursuits at the age of 30, and became a Franciscan of the Cismontane Observance. He was four times chosen vicar-general of his order. He was appointed apostolic nuncio by Sixtus IV to preach a holy war against the invading Turks at Otranto, and by Innocent VIII to prevent the spread of the Waldensian heresy. Angelo's reputation as a moralist rests chiefly on his *Cases of Conscience*, a dictionary of moral theology, originally printed at Venice by himself in 1486.

Angelus of Acri, bl., preacher, born Luke Anthony Falcone, Acri, 19 October 1669, died there, 30 October 1739. Of poor parents in southern Italy, he was successful, on his third attempt, in joining the Capuchin Order in 1690. He won fame in southern Italy for his preaching at home missions and at 40 Hours devotions, talks which were simple and void of all ornate rhetoric. He was elected provincial for the province of Cosenze in 1717, and founded a convent of Capuchinesses in 1725, for whom he wrote a book of prayers on Christ's sufferings.

Angelus of Foligno, bl., born Foligno, 1226, died there, 1312. Angelo Conti joined the Augustinians at about the age of 20 and founded three houses of the order in Umbria. Feast 27 August.

Angelo of Gualdo, bl., born Gualdo, Nocera, died there, 25 January 1325. A Camaldolese lay brother, before he had entered the order he had made a barefoot pilgrimage to Compostela. Feast 15 January.

Angelus of Massaccio, bl., martyr, died 1548. A Benedictine Calmadolese at Santa Maria di Serra, Marches of Ancona, he was a passionate preacher. Heretics known as Fraticelli or Bertolani killed him because of this. Feast 8 May.

Angelus Scarpetti, bl., born Borgo San Sepolcro, Umbria, died there, *c.* 1306. He became a missionary, taking the Augustinian habit, *c.* 1254, and is supposed to have been sent to England, where he preached and built many monasteries. Feast 1 October.

Angelus the Hermit, bl., died Ancona, 1373. Feast 19 August.

Angilbert, poet and courtier, abbot, born *c.* 750, died 18 February 814. Of a Frankish family, he was an early, and remained always, friend of **Charlemagne**; a figure in the Carolingian Renaissance, a student of Alcuin and tutor to young Pepin the Short, made king of Italy in 781. Angilbert was a member of the court and the Palatine Academy under the name of Homer, being held in great esteem as a poet. Angilbert had not received holy orders, but was none the less chaplain and counsellor to the king. Against the advice of his friend Alcuin, he led a worldly life and had, with Bertha, daughter of Charles, two sons out of wedlock. Angilbert was appointed in 781 as lay abbot of Saint-Riquier, which he restored; he took part in three embassies to Rome between 792 and 796, taking the *Livres carolins* to Adrian I in 794, and was present at Charlemagne's coronation in 800. He was touched by the spirit of monastic life and his last years were spent in edifying penance.

Anianus and Marinus, seventh-century hermits. Anianus, deacon, and Marinus, a bishop, established a hermitage at Wilparting in the Bavarian Alps. Of either Irish or West Frankish origin, they were martyred by a band of Vandals, or Wends. Feast 15 November.

Anianus of Chartres, bishop. He was fifth bishop of Chartres in the early years of the fifth century. Feast 7 December.

Anianus of Orleans, bishop, born Vienna, died Orleans, *c.* 453. Feast 17 November.

Aniceto Adolfo Gutierrez, martyr, born Celada Marlantes, Santander, 4 October 1912, died Turon, Asturias, 9 October 1934. Baptized Manuel, he entered the de la Salle Brothers on 6 September 1928. He was arrested with the other **Martyrs of Asterias** by a group of rebel soldiers and was executed by firing squad.

Anicetus, pope and martyr, born Emesa, Syria, died Rome, 168. The *Book of the Popes* records that he was a martyr and that he was the eleventh pope. According to Eusebius, he ruled 11 years, placing his death in 168. It was probably Anicetus who built a sepulchral monument to St Peter on Vatican Hill that was familiar to visitors *c.* 200. Feast 20 April.

Anicetus and Photius, martyrs, died Nicomedia, 305. Feast 12 August.

Anna Kasinskaya, princess, born Rostov, thirteenth century, died Kasin, fourteenth century. Russian Church. She was the daughter of Dimitri Borisovic, prince of Rostov, and in 1294 married Michael Jaroslovic, prince of Tver, martyred (by the Golden Horde) in 1318. She then entered a convent at Tver, taking the name Sophia, but later moved to Kasin at the request of her younger son Basil, who was prince of that city. There she entered the convent of the Dormition, now taking the name Euphosyne. The day of her death is variously given as 2 or 12 October – the year is even more uncertain. She was canonized in 1649. Feast 12 June.

Anna Maria Lapini (née Fiorelli), founder, born Florence, Italy, 27 May 1809, died there, 15 April 1860. Her desire to enter religious life was thwarted due to family pressure and in 1835 she married Giovanni Lapini, a situation which caused her much heartache and disappointment. Her husband, however, died in 1844. In 1848 she founded the Order of the Poor Daughters of the Holy Stigmata of St Francis, which followed the Rule of the Third Order of the saint. Anna and her companions received their habits in 1850 and their order, whilst steadily increasing in numbers, was finally approved by the Holy See in 1888. By 1961 there were 123 houses, mostly in Italy. Anna's life of great poverty and suffering through ill-health was recognized when her cause for beatification was introduced in 1918.

Anna of Kiev, princess, born Kiev, died there, 3 November 1112 or 18 May 1116. Russian Church. Daughter of Prince Vsevolod Jaroslavic, she entered St Andrew's convent at Kiev in 1087, and remained there except for a journey to Constantinople in 1090. She encouraged learning among the nuns, as well as their spiritual life. Feast 3 November.

Anna of Novgorod, princess, eleventh century, born Sweden, died Novgorod. Russian Church. She was baptized c. 1000, and was well educated for the time. In 1016 she married grand prince Jaroslav the Wise of Kiev, changing her name to Irina. She had ten children, several of whom became princes in their own right, while three daughters married kings, one in France, one in Hungary and the third in Norway. She was a devout woman, concerned for the welfare of the poor. She founded the first convent for nuns in Kiev. She died in Novgorod while visiting her son Vladimir. Feast 10 October.

Annabilis, parish priest in the Auvergne, born Riom, c. 397, died there, 1 November c. 475. Feast 11 June.

Anne Line, martyr, born Dunmow, late 1560s, hanged Tyburn, London, 27 February 1601. From a Calvinist family, Anne Heigham became a Catholic and married Roger Line, also a convert. After his death in exile in Flanders in 1594, Anne managed a household established in London by the Jesuit John Gerard as a refuge for priests. When Gerard escaped from the Tower in 1597, she came under suspicion and moved to another location, but she and others were arrested after mass in 1601. Tried and executed for harbouring a priest, even though the charge could not be proved because the celebrant escaped, Anne was canonized in 1970.

Anne Mary Javouhey, bl., religious, born Jallanges, France, 10 November 1779, died Paris, 15 July 1851. During the French Revolution she helped her family to house many non-juring priests, one of whom encouraged her religious vocation. In 1800 she spent a short time in the novitiate at the convent of the Sisters of Charity of St Joan Antida at Besancon, and then later (1803) with the Trappistines in Switzerland. In 1806, with her three sisters, she founded a school and Association of St Joseph in Chalon-sur-Saône, and in 1807 founded the Sisters of St Joseph of Cluny to conduct schools and orphanages and to aid the sick and elderly. In 1817 she travelled to Senegal in an attempt to encourage boys into the priesthood. Having little success, she later set up hospitals in Gambia and Sierra Leone. In 1828 she established a colony of enfranchised slaves. She spent much of her time visiting the many foundations which had grown up. At her death, there were 118 houses with 700 sisters in France alone, with 300 sisters in Africa, and sisters in India, Tahiti and South America.

Anne Mary Taigi, bl., born Siena, 29 May 1769, died Rome, 9 June 1837. Her family name was Gianetti, and her father was a pharmacist, until his business failed and he took the family to Rome, where he and his wife worked as domestic servants. In 1789 Anne married Domenico Taigi, who worked as a servant in the Chigi palace. For the first years of marriage she led a somewhat dissolute life, but then underwent a conversion experience while in St Peter's. She reformed both herself and her husband. She gave what she could to the poor, and worked with the sick and dying. She sought out spiritual directors, and received many mystical experiences. Domenico survived her, to give evidence in the process for her beatification.

Anne of Jesus, ven., nun, born Medina del Campo, Leon, 25 November 1545, died Brussels, 4 March 1621. Of a prominent Spanish family, she rejected marriage because of a vow of chastity, sought admission to the reformed Carmel at Salamanca, and was professed in October 1571. She aided **Teresa of Avila** to found convents in Andalusia in 1575, where she was prioress for three years, and in Granada in 1581. After Teresa's death she became prioress in Madrid, edited Teresa's works and wrote her biography. At the invitation of Cardinal Pierre de Benille, with **Anne of St Bartholomew** and four other nuns, she founded the reformed Carmelite houses at Paris, Pointoise and Brussels (1604–7). She returned to Spain and approved of foundations at Krakow, Galicia and Antwerp. She translated Teresa's works into Latin and Flemish.

Anne (Ana) of Monteagudo, bl., born Arequipa, Peru, 1606, died there, 1686, beatified 1985. She joined the local Dominican convent of Santa Catalina and lived a life of strict enclosure. She was said to have gifts of counsel and prophecy that benefited the whole town. Feast 10 January.

Anne of St Bartholomew, bl., nun, born Almendral, near Avila, 1 October 1549, died Antwerp, 7 June 1626. Although from the lowly peasantry, Anne Garcia was very advanced in the way of prayer. She entered the Carmelite convent of St Joseph at Avila as a lay sister, the first to be received under the Reform, and was professed in 1572. Very faithful to **Teresa**, whom she served personally night and day, she accompanied her on her travels and held her in her arms as she was dying. She was much in demand in the Spanish Carmels as the inheritor of the Teresian tradition, and in this capacity accompanied **Anne of Jesus** to France, there to establish the Carmelite reform. In 1605 she replaced Anne of Jesus as prioress at Paris, and shared with her an inflexible desire to submit only to the authority of the Discalced Carmelites. In 1612 she founded the Carmel at Antwerp. She left various writings: an autobiography and other works of spiritual value, which were all the more remarkable in that Anne could not write when she entered the Carmel, and only learned to do so on the order of Teresa.

Annemund, bishop, born Lyon (?), died Macon, 29 September 658. He was brought up at the court of Dagobert I, and became adviser to Clovis II. At some unknown date he became bishop of Lyon, and there welcomed **Benedict Biscop** and **Wilfrid** as they passed through on their way to Rome. Wilfrid returned via Lyons, stayed there three years, and was with Annemund when he was killed during the unrest which followed Clovis's death. Feast 28 September.

Anno (Hanno, Anno II), archbishop, born Swabia c. 1010, died Abbey of Siegburg, 4 December 1075. Of a noble Swabian family and educated at Bambury, he became confessor to Henry III, who appointed him archbishop of Cologne, and chancellor of the Empire in 1056. He was prominent in the government of Germany and led the party which, in 1063, seized Henry IV, still a minor, deprived his mother, the empress Agnes, of power, and made himself guardian and regent of the boy. Anno settled, in 1064, the dispute between the antipope Cadalus, bishop of Parma, and Alexander II, declaring the latter to be the rightful pope at a synod held at Mantua in May 1064. Returning to Germany, he found that Adalbert of Bremen had usurped his place, and he was dismissed by Henry who disliked his severe discipline. He was reinstated in 1066, however, on the fall of Adalbert, put down a rising against his authority in Cologne in 1074, and retired to the monastery of Siegburg, where he died; he was canonized in 1183 by Pope Lucius III. He was a founder of monasteries and a builder of churches, advocated clerical celibacy and was a strict disciplinarian.

Annunziata Cochetti, bl., born Roveta, Italy, 9 May 1800, died Cemmo, 23 March 1882, beatified 1991. After several years working as a teacher, she founded the Institute of the Sisters of St Dorothy of Cemmo in 1843 for the education of girls.

Anonymous Anchorite of the Desert. Coptic Church. An anchorite was told by an angel in a vision that there was a merchant who was perfect. He sought this man out, and imitated his prayer, humility and almsgiving. Feast 5 November.

Anonymous of Crete, martyr, born Crete, died Alexandria, July 1810 or 1811, Byzantine Church. Attacked by a Turk whose servant he was, the young Cretan killed him with a sword. He fled, but was discovered and confessed to the murder. The judge offered him the alternatives of being executed or denying his faith. He refused to deny Christianity and was put to death.

Anonymous of the Desert. Coptic Church. A monk whose married brother died. He returned home to organize his brother's affairs, but while there the widow attempted to persuade him to marry her. He escaped by pretending madness. Feast 14 December.

Anonymous of Upper Egypt. Coptic Church. The son of a pagan priest who was converted by a vision of demons tempting Christians. Feast 15 November.

Anonymous Three of the Peloponnese, martyrs, died Vrachori, 1786. Byzantine Church. Three merchants who tried to evade the duties imposed on Christians by posing as Turks were discovered, and required to abjure Christianity. They refused and were executed.

Ansbald, abbot, died Prum, 12 July 886. Elected abbot of Prum in 860, under his leadership the abbey gained great renown for its flourishing religious observance. He was a close friend of Lupus of Ferrieres, whose correspondence reveals Ansbald's concern to collate the monastery's manuscripts of classical authors, especially those of the letters of Cicero. Ansbald worked actively to increase the goods and privileges of his monastery, as indicated by the numerous diplomas, donations, exchanges, concessions of rights and immunities accorded to him. In 861 King Lothair allowed him to coin money and to establish a market. In 882 the monastery was burned by the Normans, but Ansbald was able rapidly to restore it with the help of Charles the Fat.

Ansbert of Rouen, archbishop, born Chaussy, died Hautmont, 9 February 693. Son of a distinguished nobleman, Siwin, he received an excellent education. He was brilliant at court and became chancellor, but abandoned the worldly life and fled to the abbey of Fontenelle, founded by St **Wandrille**. He received holy orders from St **Ouen**, became abbot, founded three hospitals, or hospices, for the poor and established wise Rules. On the death of **Ouen**, he was elected archbishop of Rouen (683) and consecrated by St **Lambert**. His zeal was not well received, however, and his austere life caused offence. He was banished by Pepin of Heristal to a monastery at Hautmont, but was later authorized to return to Rouen, although he died before he could do so.

Ansegis, abbot, born Lyonnais *c.* 770, died Fontenelle, 20 July 833. He became a monk at Fontenelle in Normandy, and met **Charlemagne**, who entrusted him with various political missions. Named abbot of Saint-Germer-de-Flay, he restored the abbey, both spiritually and materially. The emperor called him to the imperial court at Aachen, and sent him to the Spanish March. Louis the Pious made him abbot of Luxueil in 817, and of Fontenelle in 823, where he restored discipline, observance of the Rule and a dedication to learning, as evidenced in Fontenelle's famous library and scriptorium. He undertook a collection of Carolingian laws from 789 to 826, divided into four capitularies, which became the great authority on ecclesiastical law (books 1–2) and civil law (books 3–4) in the Frankish Empire.

Ansegisus, see **Ansegis**.

Anselm of Canterbury, archbishop, born Aosta, Val d'Aosta, *c.* 1033, died Canterbury (probably), 21 April 1109. He entered the monastic school of Bec in 1059, where he succeeded Lanfranc as prior in 1063 and Herluin as abbot in 1078. Lanfranc became archbishop of Canterbury in 1070, and

Anselm succeeded him in 1089, although a dispute with King William II (Rufus) over lay investiture delayed his assumption until 1093. Conflict arose again in 1097 over church independence, and while Anselm was in Rome seeking support, the king seized the properties of his see. In 1100 William was killed and Henry I recalled Anselm, who demanded that he should again receive, from him in person, investiture in his office of archbishop, and that he should consecrate all bishops and abbots nominated by himself. Anselm again went to Rome for support and Henry then surrendered the right of lay investiture, establishing supremacy of the papacy over the English Church. Anselm is generally considered the outstanding theologian between St **Augustine** and St **Thomas Aquinas**. He asserted the harmony between faith and reason, contending that faith preceded reason, but could be demonstrated by reason, and did not rely solely on the authority of Scripture and tradition. He was the first successfully to incorporate dialectics into theology. In his greatest work, *Cur Deus Homo*, Anselm undertakes to make plain, even to infidels, the rational necessity of the Christian mystery of the atonement. The theory rests on three positions: that satisfaction is necessary on account of God's honour and justice; that such satisfaction can only be given by the peculiar personality of the God-man; that such satisfaction is really given by the voluntary death of this infinitely valuable person. This theory has had immense influence on the form of Church doctrine and, in contrast with the subjective theory of Abelard and others, asserts the necessity of an objective act of atonement for man's sin. Anselm's speculations did not receive in the Middle Ages the respect and attention they deserved, perhaps because of their unsystematic character. He differed from most of his predecessors in preferring to defend the faith by intellectual reasoning, instead of employing scriptural and patristic authorities. Canonized in 1163, Clement XI declared him a doctor of the Church in 1720.

Anselm of Lucca, bishop, born Mantua, *c.* 1035, died there, 18 March 1086. His uncle, Pope Alexander II, also Bishop Anselm of Lucca, nominated his nephew to the see in 1073. He resigned the bishopric and retired to a monastery, but resumed it in 1075 at the insistence of Gregory VII, whom

he firmly supported in his movement to reform the Church. He lived an austere life and sought to impose strict discipline on an unwilling chapter; he opposed the antipope Clement III, and Emperor Henry IV, whose partisans expelled him from Lucca in 1080, and became Gregory's standing legate in Lombardy. He made a collection of canons, *c.* 1083, and wrote a polemical treatise in support of Gregory against Clement.

Anselm of Nonantola, Lombard duke and abbot, born modern Friuli, died Nonantola, 3 March 803. Duke of Friuli, he founded the abbey of Fanano in 750, and of Nonantola *c.* 752, which included a hospital and a hospice for pilgrims. King Desiderius banished him to Monte Cassino for several years, but **Charlemagne** restored him to his flourishing monastery.

Ansfrid (Anfrid, Anfroi), duke of Brabant, bishop, died Heiligen, 3 May 1010. Educated at the imperial school at Cologne, he supported Emperor Otto III and strove to suppress brigandage. In 992 he became a monk, founded a convent at Thorn, which his wife and daughter entered, and, persuaded by the emperor, agreed to be bishop of Utrecht, where he served until he lost his sight in 1006, at which point he retired to Heiligen, a monastery he had founded.

Ansgar (Anskar, Anschar, Scharies), 'Apostle of the North', born Picardie, near Corbie, *c.* 801, died Bremen, 3 February 865. He became a monk at Corbie, taught and preached at Corvey, and thence went to Denmark, where King Harold had recently converted to Christianity. He founded a school at Schleswig but, expelled by the local heathen, he returned to Corvey in 829 without having achieved any missionary success. In response to the request of a Swedish embassy, he set out with another monk and after great hardship reached Bjorko, where King Bjorn received them well, and there built the first Christian church. Among his converts was Heriger, governor and councillor to the king. Louis I, the Pious, named him abbot of Corvey, and Gregory IV appointed him bishop of Hamburg and papal legate to Scandinavia; Nicholas I named him bishop of Bremen in 848. In 854, again in Denmark, he converted Haavik, King of Jutland, and then King Olaf of Sweden. He did much to alleviate the horrors of the slave trade. The Scandinavian countries relapsed into paganism after his death.

Anstrudis, abbess, born *c.* 645, died Laon, before 709. Her parents were probably Ss **Blandinus** and **Salaberga**. She entered while very young the monastery of Notre-Dame de Laon, founded by her mother, and became abbess at the age of 20. One of her brothers, Baldwin, deacon of Laon *c.* 679, was treacherously murdered by Ebroim, mayor of the palace, and she nearly suffered the same fate, having been accused of acting against the mayor's interests. Feast 17 October.

Ansuerus, abbot and martyr, born Mechlenburg, *c.* 1040, died Ratzeburg, 15 July 1066. He became a monk, and an early missionary among the pagan Slavic tribes still living around Ratzeburg. He and about 30 companions were stoned to death by pagan Wends, or Obotrites, at Ratzeburg, during which ordeal he beseeched his executioners to kill him last so that his companions would not apostatize, and so that he could comfort them in their sufferings.

Anterus, pope from 23 November 235 to 3 January 236. He succeeded Pontian and was of Greek extraction. He briefly reigned during the persecution of Emperor Maximus Thrax, and although he has been represented as a martyr, this is improbable. The first to be buried in the new papal crypt in the catacomb of Callistus.

Anthelm of Chignin, reformer and bishop, born Chignin (Savoy), 1107, died Belley, 26 June 1178. A Carthusian at Portes in 1136, he rebuilt the recently damaged La Grande-Chartreuse and became its seventh prior in 1139, after the resignation of Hugh, and the first minister general of the Order in 1142. He supported Alexander III against antipope Victor IV, who rewarded him with the see of Belley in 1163, and was consecrated by Alexander himself. Alexander named him legate to England in the hope of reconciling Henry II with **Thomas Becket**, but Anthelm could not go. In 1175 Frederick Barbarossa conferred on him and his successors the title of Prince of the Holy Roman Empire.

Anthemius of Poitiers (also Anthemus, Attenius, Aptemius). He is named as thirteenth in the episcopal list, which suggests his being bishop around the year 400, but the authority for the list at this time is to be treated with great caution. Feast 3 December.

Anthimus, bishop of Nicomedia (Izmit, Turkey), beheaded in the Diocletian persecution of 302. He declined an offer of pagan priesthood and relief from torture before he was beheaded. Feast 27 April.

Anthimus, martyr, died Rome, second/third century. He is said to have been a priest who converted a pagan prefect married to a Christian well known for her charity to imprisoned Christians. He was thrown into the Tiber, rescued by an angel, and then beheaded. Feast 11 May.

Anthimus, hymnographer, born Constantinople (?), died there, fifth century. He belonged to the imperial guard and to a group of lay ascetics called the 'Spondaioi', who kept vigils in the church of St Irene in Constantinople. As a priest (after 457) and leader of the Chalcedonian party, he wrote strophes, hymns and psalmody for choirs of men and women. Feast 7 June.

Anthimus of Uvaria, bishop and martyr, born Ivaria (in modern Georgia), *c.* 1650, died Adrianople, 22 September 1716. Romanian Church. Baptized Andrew, he became a slave and was taken to Istanbul, learning Greek, Turkish and Arabic, and the arts of carving and painting. When he had been freed he went, *c.* 1690, to Wallacia, to work in the royal printing press at Bucharest, of which he became director, producing religious books. He had become a monk at some point, and from 1695 to 1701 was superior of a monastery to the north of Bucharest, where he founded another printing press. In March 1705 he was elected bishop of Ramnic and in 1708 metropolitan of the Church in Wallacia. He continued to create new printing presses, producing spiritual and liturgical books. One of his achievements was to introduce the Romanian language into worship. He also founded the monastery of All Saints in Bucharest, now named after him. He was in favour of allying his Church with the Western Church in an attempt to shake off Turkish domination, and for this he was arrested and imprisoned in 1716. The patriarch of Constantinople was induced to strip him of his clerical state and he was condemned to exile in St Catherine's monastery on Mount Sinai. The sultan ordered his escort to kill him in the course of the journey into exile. He was canonized in 1992. Feast 27 September.

Anthimus the New Ascetic, born Cefalonia, died there, 1782. Byzantine Church.

Anthony, see also **Julian**.

Anthony. Byzantine Church. A monk of the monastery of Pieria, but transferred to a cave near Veroia, in Macedonia, where he gained a reputation for holiness. Feast 17 January.

Anthony, monk, born Serae, fourteenth century. Ethiopian Church. Despite the hostility of his father, Amanky Egzi received a Christian education and was eventually ordained. He married, but his wife was seized in a raid, and he became a monk, taking the name Anthony. He founded the first monastery, and a convent of nuns, in his region. His life was marked by miracles and the gift of foresight.

Anthony and John, bl., martyrs, born Tizatlan, Mexico, 1516/1517, died Cuauhtinchan, Mexico, 1529. Anthony was of a noble family and attended the Franciscan school at Tlaxcala; John also attended the school, but seems to have been Anthony's servant. Both were recruited by Dominican missionaries in 1529 as helpers. On one occasion, when John went into an empty house to destroy idols, as was the practice, he was ambushed and beaten to death. Anthony also died when he went to John's help. They were beatified with **Christopher**.

Anthony and Theodosius Pechersky, abbots, died Kiev, 1073 and 1074. Their name comes from the monastery of the Caves of Kiev, Kiev-Pecierskaya Laura, of which they were both abbot. They are not related. Antipa was born at Lubech, near Tchernigov, in 983. He went on a pilgrimage to Mount Athos, Greece, and spent some time there, changing his name to Anthony. On his return he joined one of the Russian monasteries, but it did not provide the solitude and austerity he wanted. He moved to a cave in a cliff above the river Dnieper at Kiev. As disciples came to him more caves were hollowed out, including larger caves to be used as a chapel and a refectory. A church and monastery were also built on the hill above the caves. Anthony retired to Tchernigov, where he founded another monastery, but came back to Pecierskaya-Laura and died in his cave. Theodosius was an original disciple of Anthony. Born near Kiev in about 1002, he escaped to the caves in 1032 when his mother tried to stop him becoming a monk. He became abbot of the caves in 1063, and built a hospital and a hostel for travellers. He helped prisoners, and sent monks to help evangelize the surrounding area. He died in 1074, and in accordance with his wishes was buried in one of the original caves. Feast 10 July.

Anthony Artemovic Gorban, martyr, born Gorban, 22 January 1866, died Char'kov, 22 December 1937. Ukrainian Church, Moscow Patriarchate. A monk before the Revolution, after the closure of his monastery he worked in various churches in Char'kov. He was arrested in November 1937.

Anthony Baldinucci, bl., Jesuit preacher, born Florence, Italy, 19 June 1665, died Pofio, 7 November 1717. Joined the Society of Jesus in 1681 and was ordained in 1695. In 1697 he was sent to Abruzzi and the Romagna as a missionary. He spent the rest of his life travelling from town to town, often barefoot, to preach, and would beat himself publicly to convert his hearers. He had tremendous success. He died after collapsing while ministering to the sick in his parish. Beatified in 1893. Feast 7 November.

Anthony Bonfadini, bl., missionary, born Ferrara, c. 1422, died Cotignola, 1 December 1482. Of a noble family, he became a Franciscan at the Friary of the Holy Spirit, Ferrara, in 1439, and a missionary in the Holy Land. He was a renowned preacher there and, when he returned to Italy, at Cotignola.

Anthony Chevrier, founder, born Lyons, 16 April 1826, died there, 2 October 1879. He studied in Lyons and was ordained priest there in 1850. After the Rhone flooded, he became chaplain to a house to accommodate those who had been left homeless. In 1860 he bought a ballroom called The Prado, which he turned into a refuge. A number of priests worked with him, and he founded the Society of Priests of the Prado, following the Franciscan Rule, although remaining diocesan clergy. He also founded an order of nuns to teach catechism and care for the sick. He published a number of books, particularly on the spiritual formation of the clergy.

Anthony Daniel, martyr, born Dieppe, 27 May 1601, died Teaneoste, Ontario, 4 July 1648. He joined the Jesuits in 1621 and was ordained eight years later. In 1632 he went to Canada, where he worked among the Huron, and founded the first boys' college in North America, in Quebec. He died when his chapel was burned down by Hurons as he ended mass. Feast, with **John de Brébeuf**, 19 October.

Anthony della Chiesa, bl., born near Vercelli, Italy, died there, 1459. A nobleman, he became a Dominican, and was given charge of several Dominican houses. He assisted **Bernardine of Siena**. Feast 22 January.

Anthony Fatati, bl., bishop, born Ancona c.1410, died 1484. He held church positions in Ancona, Siena and at the Vatican, and was bishop of Teramao and Ancona. Feast 9 January.

Anthony Fournier, bl., martyred France, 1794, see **Martyrs of the French Revolution**. Feast 12 January.

Anthony Frederick Ozanam, bl., Catholic writer, lecturer and founder of the Society of St Vincent de Paul, born Milan, 23 April 1813, died of tuberculosis and exhaustion at Marseilles, 8 September 1853. Studied law and literature at Paris. A leader in the nineteenth-century Roman Catholic revival in France. His society, formed in 1833, consisted of lay men to carry out spiritual and charitable work among the poor. In 1844 he was appointed professor in foreign literature at the Sorbonne. In 1848 he co-edited the *Ere nouvelle*, a periodical expressing Catholic Socialism. His writings include *La Civilisation chrétienne chez les Francs* (1849).

Anthony Gianelli, founder and bishop, born Cereta, Italy, 12 April 1789, died Piacenza, Italy, 7 June 1846. He was ordained in 1812 following an education in Genoa, and taught rhetoric until 1823. He was appointed archpriest at Chiavari in 1826 and consecrated bishop of Bobbio in 1838. He acquired a great reputation as a preacher, a retreat conductor, a writer of tracts and discourses, and a correspondent. He founded the Daughters of Our Lady of the Garden and the Oblates of St Alfonsus for Clerical Formation.

Anthony Grassi, bl., provost of Fermo Oratory, born Fermo, Italy, 13 November 1592, died there 13 December 1671. A native of Fermo, Grassi joined the local Oratory, founded by St **Philip Neri,** when he was 18 and remained a member until his death. In 1625, three years after Philip Neri was canonized, Grassi made pilgrimage to honour him and devoted his life to imitating him. He was elected provost of the Oratory in 1635 and was re-elected to the post 12 times, despite his continued protestations, holding the office until his death. He was personally known for his mortified life, for hearing confessions (up to five hours a day), and for guiding the Oratory into being an example of the Rule of St Philip Neri.

Anthony Ixida and Companions, bl., martyrs, died Nagasaki, 3 September 1632. Anthony was born in 1570 at Shimbara, near Nagasaki, into a Christian family. He studied with the Jesuits and entered the Society, being ordained priest in 1608, after which he was sent to Hiroshima. He was imprisoned, presumably for his faith, in 1616, and when released continued working secretly. In 1629 he was again arrested and tortured, in an effort to make him abjure the faith. In 1631 he managed to return to Nagasaki, but was rearrested, and burned at the stake. With him died John Jerome Jo, a Japanese priest, Bartholomew Guttierrez, Vincenzo Carvalho and Francis of Jesus, Augustinians, and Gabriel della Maddalena, who was a Franciscan.

Anthony, John and Eustace, fourteenth century. Russian Church. Born of noble families (Anthony and John were brothers) as Nezilo, Kume and

Kruglec, they received their names as among the first Christians of Lithuania. They were executed for refusing to sacrifice to idols. Canonized 1549. Feast 14 April.

Anthony Kustski, monk. Russian Church. Possibly a disciple of **Alexander Kustski**.

Anthony Lucci, bl., bishop, born Agnone del Sannio (Abruzzo), Italy, August 1681, died Bovino, Italy, July 1752. He joined the Conventual Franciscans and was ordained in 1705. A dedicated teacher, he was a professor in Agnone and Naples, and in 1718 became rector of the college of St Bonaventure in Rome. He was a consultor of the Holy Office and an official theologian at two Roman synods, and in 1729 was appointed bishop of Bovino by Pope Benedict XIII. He was nicknamed the 'angel of charity' due to his life of poverty and simplicity, as well as his work for the poor. He set up free elementary schools and a seminary in his see. Miracles were reported at his tomb soon after his death. Feast 25 July.

Anthony Margil, ven., Franciscan missionary and promoter of missionary colleges in Spanish America, born Valencia, Spain, 18 August 1657, died Mexico City, 6 August 1726. He entered the order in 1673 and was ordained in 1682, arriving with 22 fellow friars in Veracruz, Mexico in 1683. Margil is linked with the institution of missionary colleges under the general title of Propagation of the Faith. He took over the first college, Santa Cruz de Querétaro, in 1684, a year after its foundation, and guided it through its formative years. He developed two more, Cristo Crucificado in Guatemala City in 1701, and Our Lady of Guadalupe in 1708, and his missionary work extended beyond Mexico to Central America, and to present-day Louisiana and Texas.

Anthony Mary Claret, founder of the Missionary Sons of the Immaculate Heart of Mary, also known as Claretians, born Sallent, Spain, 23 December 1807, died in the Cistercian monastery of Narbonne, 24 October 1870. He was ordained priest at Vich in 1835. Ill-health caused him to leave a Jesuit novitiate in Rome. He returned to pastoral work in Sallent, conducting missions and retreats in Catalonia. At Vich he founded the Missionary Sons

dedicated to preaching missions. He was appointed archbishop of Santiago, Cuba in 1850 and made many enemies in his attempts at reform. He resigned his see in 1858 and became director of the Escorial and confessor to Queen Isabella II. He attended Vatican Council I in 1869/70. He retired to Prades in France, but had to flee to a Cistercian monastery when the Spanish ambassador demanded his arrest. An important figure in the revival of Catholicism in Spain, he was canonized in 1950.

Anthony Mary Pucci, born near Florence, 1819, ordained 1843, died Viareggio, 12 January 1892, beatified 1952, canonized 1962. A Servite in Florence, he was the much-loved parish priest at Viareggio from 1847 and prior provincial in Tuscany 1883–90. An innovator, he started a seaside nursing home for sick children.

Anthony Middleton, bl., born Middleton Tyas, Yorkshire, martyred Clerkenwell, London, 1590, beatified 1929. Ordained at Rheims in 1586, he looked young and worked for some years before being discovered by spies. Commemorated with **Edward Jones**, he was hanged, drawn and quartered. Feast 6 May.

Anthony Neyrot, bl., martyr, born Tivoli, c. 1432, died Tunis, 10 April 1460. After entering the Dominican order he went to Sicily to preach, contrary to the advice of St **Antoninus**, Dominican archbishop of Florence, but he then took ship to Naples in August 1458. The ship was captured by pirates, who imprisoned him in Tunis. While waiting to be ransomed, he succumbed to temptation, publicly denied Christ, became a Muslim and in 1459 married. Some months later he repented and was reconciled to the Church. On Palm Sunday 1460 he publicly abjured Islam, renounced his apostasy and preached before the sultan, who had him executed by stoning.

Anthony of Amandola, bl., born Amandola, in the Marches of Ancona, c. 1355, died 1450. He joined the Augustinian Hermits and followed the example of **Nicholas of Tolentino**. He is mainly venerated at Ancona. Feast 25 January.

Anthony of Cqondidi, died Nacharebou, 1815. Georgian Church. The son of a grand duke, he entered the monastery of Martvili. He became interested in Western Christian theology, which he studied with French missionaries. He went in 1757 to Tbilisi, continuing his studies, and in 1761 he returned to Samegrelo, where his father had been grand duke, as bishop of Zagheri, becoming metropolitan of Cqondidi in western Georgia in 1777. He gave up his see in 1788 and returned to the monastic life at the monastery of Nacharebou, which he had founded a few years before. Feast 13 October.

Anthony of Cudov, monk and martyr, died Moscow, July 1451. Russian Church. A monk of the Cudov monastery in Moscow, he was killed when the Tartars laid siege to the city.

Anthony of Dymsk, born Novgorod, 1206, died Dymskoe, Russian Church. After a number of years as a monk, he became a hermit at Lake Dymskoe, near Novgorod, where he lived a life of great penance, wearing an iron cap. He gathered numerous disciples, and eventually founded a monastery dedicated to St **Anthony of Egypt (the Great)**. Feast 24 June.

Anthony of Egypt (the Great), hermit and father of anchoritic monasticism, born Kome, Upper Egypt, *c*. 251, died Pispir, 356. The son of a prosperous Coptic family, he gave away all his possessions (*c*. 269) and withdrew from society to lead an ascetical life near his home. In 285 he retired into complete isolation in an abandoned fort near Pispir, where he suffered his famous 'temptations', and began to attract followers. In 305 he emerged to give the disciples a Rule, the first of anchoritic life. He retired into solitude again five years later, but re-emerged during the Arian conflict to support St **Athanasius**, who is credited with the *Vita Antonii*, the evidence for his life that has influenced the whole Christian world. In it, Anthony is depicted as the perfect man who follows moderate ascetic practices, supports the Church hierarchy, and performs miracles with divine assistance. Anthony died in his 'Inner Mountain', his refuge (still called Der Mar Antonios), near the Red Sea at the age of 105. Feast 17 January.

Anthony of Kiev, hermit, died Kiev, 1073. Feast 7 May.

Anthony of Krasnocholmsk, monk, died Krasnocholmsk, 1481/2. Russian Church. Already a monk, he was staying with a wealthy boyar when he was taken ill. He decided to remain in the region where he found himself, and with the aid of the boyar established a cell on the left bank of the river Mologa, a tributary of the Volga. Disciples gathered, and again with the help of the boyar, he built at Krasnocholmsk a church and a monastery dedicated to St Nicholas. Feast 17 January.

Anthony of Leochnovo, monk, born Tver, died Novgorod, *c*. 1611. Russian Church. Of noble parents, he ran away from home to take up the life of a solitary, but in a vision he was told to travel to Leochnovo on the river Ilmen near Novgorod, where he founded a monastery and became renowned for miracles and prophecy. During the Swedish invasion of 1611 he was called to Novgorod for his own safety. Feast 17 October.

Anthony of Lérins, monk, born Valeria, Pannonia, died Lérins, *c*. 520. After the death of his father he became the ward of **Boethius**, and after him of the bishop of Lorch. He set up a hermitage near lake Como, but troubled by visitors, he finally settled at Lérins. Feast 28 December.

Anthony of Milan, bl., see **Monaldus of Ancona**.

Anthony of Novgorod, archbishop, died Chutynski, 8 October 1231 or 1232. Russian Church. Born Dobryna Andrejkovic, he came from a wealthy family and, before becoming a monk, made a pilgrimage to Constantinople of which he left an account. He joined the monastery of Chutynski *c*. 1190, and became archbishop of Novgorod probably in 1211 when his predecessor was banished, but in 1219 returned the see to him when he was allowed to return. Anthony again succeeded him in 1225, but in 1228 retired to his monastery because of his ill-health. Feast 10 February.

Anthony of Optina, monk, born Romanov, 9 March 1795, died Optina, 7 August 1865. Russian Church. Born Alexander Ivanovic Putilov, the brother of **Moses of Optina**, from 1809 to 1812 he was working in Moscow, then until 1816 in Rostov, but then went to join his brother in a hermitage in the forest of Roslavl. He became a monk in 1820, taking the name Anthony, and with his brother moved to Optina the following year. There he held various offices, being ordained priest in 1827, and despite prolonged ill-health in 1839 he was appointed superior of St Nicholas in Malojaroslavec. On the grounds of ill-health he resigned the office in 1853 and returned to Optina. Canonized 1996. Feast day 11 October.

Anthony of Padua, theologian, preacher, doctor of the Church, born Lisbon, 15 August 1195, died Arcella, near Padua, 13 June 1231. The son of noble parents, and given the name Ferdinand at baptism, he joined the Canons Regular of St Augustine at 15, and for eight years practised piety and studied Scripture at Coimbra. Deeply moved by the relics of some Franciscan missionaries killed in Morocco and brought to Coimbra in 1220, a desire seized him to become a Franciscan, to preach the gospel in Africa, and to suffer a martyr's death. Accepted by the order, he changed his name to Anthony and went to Morocco within the year. Serious illness, however, obliged him to return, but his ship was blown off course and carried him to Sicily. He proceeded to Assisi, where St **Francis** had convoked a general chapter in 1221. His reputation for preaching and learning having been established in the Romagna province, and against the heretics in France, Francis approved his appointment as lector in theology to the order, the first to hold the post, and he taught at Montpellier, Bologna, Padua and Toulouse. He led the rigorous party in the Franciscan Order against the mitigations introduced by the general, Elias.

Anthony of Radonez, monk, born Lyskovo, near Novgorod, 6 October 1792, died Radonez, 12 May 1877. Russian Church. Born Andrew Gavrilovic Medvedev, his father was a cook in the service of a Georgian prince. (According to some, he was the prince's illegitimate son.) After working as a doctor, he entered the monastery of the Dormition of the Mother of God of Sarov, there taking the name Anthony. He was ordained in 1822 and four years later became superior of the monastery of Vysokogorski at Arzamas. Because of his fame as a spiritual guide, the patriarch **Philaret** made him superior of the monastery of the Most Holy Trinity at Radonez in 1831, a post he held until his death.

Anthony of Raifskaia Pustyn, martyr, born Cistopol, 1860, died near Raifskaia Pustyn, 7 April 1930. Russian Church. His family name was Cirkov. He entered the monastery of Raifskaia Pustyn in 1890. He was ordained priest after the revolution and when the monastery was closed worked nearby as a carpenter. He was arrested in January 1930, along with many others, after the liturgy, and was later shot. Feast 14 January.

Anthony of Solovki, monk, died Moscow, 22 March 1612. Russian Church. Hegumenos of the monastery of the Solovki from 1603 or 1605, he was a skilled diplomat, especially in defending the interests of his monastery, to which he attracted many donations. Feast 9 August.

Anthony of Stroncone, bl., lay brother, born Stroncone, Umbria, 1381, died Assisi, 7 February 1461. He joined the Observant Friars Minor at the age of 12 and, like St **Francis**, refused the dignity of priesthood and remained a lay brother. He served as assistant novice master at Fiesole (1411–20), under the saintly Thomas Bellacci, whom he helped to repress and convert the Fraticelli in Tuscany and Corsica (1420–35). He spent the last 25 years of his life at the Carceri hermitage above Assisi, and was revered for his humility, mortification, prophesies and contemplative prayer. Feast 8 February.

Anthony of Tobolsk, bishop, born Cernigov, c. 1670, died Tobolsk, 27 March 1740. Russian Church. Born Andrew Stachovski, his father was a priest. He studied in Kiev. He taught rhetoric and dialectic in the college at Cernigov, as well as being superior of the monastery there. In 1709 he became an archimandrite and in 1713 bishop of Cernigov. He clashed with Peter the Great over the Tsar's treatment of the Cossacks, and in 1721 was transferred to the see of Tobolsk in Siberia as metropolitan, where he was a promoter of missionary work. Feast 10 June.

Anthony of Vologda, born c. 1526, died Vologda, 26 October 1588. Russian Church. A monk of the monastery of Bolding, where he became hegumenos, he became bishop of Vologda in November 1586. Feast 17 January.

Anthony Page, bl., born Harrow, Middlesex, c. 1563, martyred York, 20 April 1563, beatified 1987. He studied at Rheims and was ordained in 1591. Although suffering greatly in prison after his arrest, he engaged in theological arguments with Protestant ministers. He was hanged, drawn and quartered.

Anthony Patrizi, bl., born near Amandula, in Piceno, died Monticiano, c. 1311. He was an Augustinian priest, living most of his life in the Augustinian house at Lecceto. He died in the Augustinian house at Moniciano while on his way to visit a friend. Feast 9 October.

Anthony Pavoni, bl., inquisitor and martyr, born Savigliano, c. 1326, died Bricherasio, 9 April 1374. He entered the Dominicans at Savigliano in 1341, became a master in theology in 1365, and was appointed inquisitor general for Liguria and upper Lombardy, where his opponents were chiefly the Waldensians, whose numbers he much reduced through his preaching and official duties. He was murdered as he left the church after preaching.

Anthony Primaldi and Companions, bl., martyrs, died Otranto, Italy, 1480. They were put to death for refusing to abjure Christianity when the Turks captured their city. Anthony, an old man at the time and a devout Christian, was the spokesman for the 800 or so said to have been massacred. Feast 14 August.

Anthony Rawah, martyred eighth century. He was beheaded. Feast 19 January.

Anthony Sihustral, born Alcea, died 1714. Romanian Church. Joined the hermitage of Iezeru in the province of Alcea, but left there c. 1690 to seek silence in a cave in the mountains where he built a small chapel, descending from his cave only to attend the liturgy. His holiness attracted many disciples. Feast 23 November.

Anthony Sijski, monk, born Knecht, near Archangel, 1477 or 1478, died Michajlov, 7 December 1556. Russian Church. Baptized Andrew, as a child he learned to read and write, and also how to paint icons. After his parents' death, when he was 25, he moved to Novgorod to work for a noble family,

marrying a daughter of the house. After a year of marriage, however, he decided to enter the monastery of the Transfiguration on the river Kena, near Olonec. In 1508 he received the monastic tonsure. In 1513, seeking real solitude, with two other monks he left his monastery and established a hermitage dedicated to St Nicholas near the rivers Enca and Seleksna. After seven years, however, the hostility of the local population forced him to abandon the hermitage, and he moved to an uninhabited region beside Lake Michajlov. The Grand Prince Basil III Ivanovic asked him to establish a monastery, providing him with the lands for that purpose. The monastery of the Most Holy Trinity grew to be a community of some 70 monks living by a strict rule of life with an emphasis on the performance of the liturgy. In the final years of his life he returned to a solitary existence, moving to a hermitage on a nearby island. Canonized 1579.

Anthony Schwartz, bl., born Baden, near Vienna, 28 February 1852, died Vienna, 15 September 1929. He was a choirboy at the Cistercian abbey of Heiligenkreuz, and was then educated by the Benedictines in Vienna. In 1869 he joined the Piarists, but left and instead went to the diocesan seminary. Ordained in 1875, he worked first as a curate not far from Vienna, then as chaplain to the hospital in Sechshaus. He was struck by the poverty in which apprentices had to work and in 1886 founded the Catholic Apprentices' Association, and created a residence for them in Vienna. In 1889 he founded the Congregation for the Devout Workers of St **Joseph Calasanz**, Calasanz being the founder of the Piarists whom he had originally joined. He built a church in Vienna, from which he not only looked after apprentices, but preached against the exploitation of workers and backed the efforts of the workers to obtain their rights.

Anthony the Athenian, born Athens 1754, died Constantinople, 5 February 1774. Byzantine Church. He entered as a slave into an Albanian-Turkish family in Athens, but the family moved to the Peloponnese and he was sold to a Turkish family who tried to convert him to Islam. When he refused he was sold on to another household, something which happened several times. Eventually he was bought by a Christian silk merchant of Constantinople, but he was denounced by one of his former masters as having once converted to Islam but then reverted to Christianity. When he was taken to court the judge believed Anthony's story, that the accusation was false, and sent him to the vizier. The vizier also believed him, but put him in prison. The vizier himself, however, was accused of too great a leniency, and Anthony was eventually decapitated.

Anthony the Quraisite, martyr, died al-Rafiqa on the Euphrates, 29 October 799. Syriac Church. Called Ruhi or Abu Ruh before his conversion, he became a Christian and took the name Anthony after a vision of an angel during the Eucharist. He was put to death as an apostate from Islam.

Anthony the Roman, born Rome, 1067, died Novgorod. Russian Church. According to legend, he was born into a wealthy Greek family at Rome, and was brought up in the Orthodox faith. When he was 17 he left Rome to become a monk. He gave much of his wealth to the poor, the rest he threw into the sea, then he visited several monasteries before spending 20 years as a hermit by the sea. In September 1106, however, he was swept away in a great storm and carried by the sea to the neighbourhood of Novgorod, where he was delighted to discover the Orthodox liturgy being celebrated. He was welcomed by the bishop **Nicetas**, and with his blessing built a monastery dedicated to the Nativity of the Mother of God on the rock where the sea had left him. The box in which he had put his valuables to throw them in the sea was found by some local fishermen, who returned it to Anthony, and with the money inside it he was able to buy land around his monastery. This account, it should be remarked, appears only some four centuries after his death. Feast 3 August.

Anthony Zaccaria, founder of the Barnabite order and the Angelicals of St Paul, born Cremona, 1502, died there, 5 July 1539. He studied medicine at Padua and practised among the poor in his home town, where he began teaching catechism in the church of St Vitale, and became a priest in 1528, having felt called to exercise spiritual as well as physical compassion. At his first mass, angels are reported to have appeared at the altar. In 1530 he was transferred to Milan where he, with two

friends, founded the Congregation of Clerks Regular of St Paul, known generally as Barnabites, approved by Clement VII in 1533. They were bound by vows 'to regenerate and revive the love of divine worship and a properly Christian way of life, by frequent preaching and faithful ministry of the sacraments'. The teaching of St Paul and emphasis on the Eucharist were two characteristic devotions. He also instituted, with Countess Ludovica Torelli, the Angelicals of St Paul for religious women. Their joint ambition was to reform the decadent society of the sixteenth century, beginning with the clergy, and including a renewal of spiritual life in monasteries of women and men in Italy at a time of notorious abuses. His body rests at Milan in the crypt of St Barnabas.

Anthusa of Constantinople, born Constantinople, died there, 811. Said to have been the daughter of the Emperor Constantine V Copronymus, but opposed to his iconoclasm. She became a nun in a convent in Constantinople. Feast 27 July.

Anthusa the Younger, martyr, died Persia. Feast 27 August.

Antiochus, monk, died c. 630. He was in **Sabas**'s monastery in the Judean desert. Feast 22 January.

Antiochus of Lyons, bishop, died c. 500. He was sent to Egypt to persuade the bishop of Lyons to return home, after he had gone to become a monk. He failed in his mission, and instead became bishop himself. Feast 13 August.

Antipa of Calapodesti, born Calapodesti, 1816, died Alamo, 10 January 1882. Romanian Church. The son of a deacon and baptized Alexandru, he entered the monastery of Caldarusani, north of Bucharest, when aged about 20. There he was given the name Alipius. Two years later he went to the Romanian monastery on Mount Athos. He stayed there for 15 years, but then moved to a Moldavian monastery, where he was given the name Antipa. In 1860 he was sent to Moldavia itself to found the monastery of the Precursor. In 1865, however, he settled in the monastery on the island of Alamo, not far from Finland. Feast 10 January.

Antonia Messina, bl., born Orogosolo, Sardinia, 21 June 1919, died there, 17 May 1935, beatified 1987. She was from a poor peasant family. Like **Maria Goretti**, she was killed with stones while resisting a violent sexual assault. Her family forgave the attacker, who repented, admitted his crime and was executed.

Antonia of Florence, bl., nun, died Aquila, 29 February 1472. A Florentine widow, she entered the Franciscan Third Order Regular in 1429, became prioress at Foligno, and at Aquila for 13 years where, on the advice of St **John Capistran**, she founded a monastery under the first rule of the Poor Clares. An example of patience under the trials of a long, painful illness and of family difficulties caused by a spendthrift son and other relatives. Feast 28 February.

Antonina, martyr, died Nicaea (Iznik, Turkey), 304. Nothing is known of her, except that she was burned to death after torture. The pre-1970 Roman Martyrology said that **Alexander**, a soldier, freed her, taking her place in prison by changing clothes with her, but that then both were tortured and burned together. Feast 4 May.

Antoninus and Moseus, hermits, Antioch, Syria, fifth century. Feast 23 February.

Antoninus of Alexandra, Feast 9 August.

Antoninus of Florence (Antonio Pierozzi, also, de Forciglioni), archbishop, born Florence, 1 March 1389, died there, 2 May 1459. He entered the Dominican Order at 15, and was soon entrusted, in spite of his youth, with the government of houses at Cortona, Rome, Naples and Florence, which he laboured zealously to reform. Consecrated archbishop of Florence by Eugenius IV in 1446, it is said on the advice of **Fra Angelico**, he became a counsellor of popes and statesmen, and won the esteem and love of his people by his energy and resource in combating the effects of plague and earthquake in 1448 and 1453. Of his various theological works, the best known are the *Summa theologica* (1477) and the *Summa confessionalis* (1472); also a general history of the world, *Chronicon* (1440–59), illustrating from the past how men should live in this world, and

drawing on the Scriptures, lives of the saints and the Fathers and doctors of the Church, decrees of popes and councils. He also wrote on economic questions, adapted Catholic traditions to modern conditions, maintaining that money invested in business was true capital, and that it is not therefore necessarily wrong to receive interest on it. Feast 10 May.

Anuarite Nengapeta, bl., martyr, born Wamba, in the (then) Belgian Congo, died Isiro, 1 December 1964. A member of the Congregation of the Holy Family, and a teacher, she was at Bafwabakka near the border with Uganda when they were collected by a group of soldiers, it was claimed for their own safety, and taken to the local military headquarters. There the nun's youth attracted the attention of some of the men. She was killed resisting sexual advances from the soldiers.

Anysius, bishop, died Thessalonika (?), c. 410. Little is known of him. He became bishop in 383, and was appointed patriarchal vicar in Illyricum by Pope **Damasus**. He was a strong supporter of **John Chrysostom**, and went to Constantinople to plead his cause. Feast 30 December.

Apaiule and Ptolemy, third/fourth century. Coptic Church. Ptolemy was a soldier who refused to sacrifice to the emperor in the persecution of Diocletian. He was imprisoned, where he was visited by the monk Apaiule. Both were executed. Feast 16 January.

Aper of Toul, bishop, born Trancault, Troyes, died c. 507. The seventh bishop of Toul, a late account of his life states that he served seven years. Aper built a basilica at the gates of Toul, where he is buried, and which bore his name early in the seventh century, later becoming better known as the Abbey of St Aper. Feast 15 September.

Aphraates (a Greek form of the Persian name Aphrahat, or Pharhadh), died Persia, 378 (?). The earliest of the Syriac Fathers, called 'The Persian Sage', he lived through the persecution of the Sasanid king Shapur II (310–79). What is known about him comes mainly from his 23 treatises, or 'Demonstrations' (not homilies), the first ten of which, on faith, love, fasting, prayer, the resurrection and humility, were completed in 337; the next 12, almost all directed against the Jews and their religious practices, in 344, and the final one in 345. The first 22 are arranged as an acrostic, each beginning with a different letter of the alphabet, and give 'a full and ordered exposition of the Christian faith', with a strong emphasis on ascetical practice – he was himself an ascetic. His grasp of Scripture is remarkable, but the absence of contemporary Western influence, such as the Nicene theology, would seem to indicate the isolation of the Persian Church, because of both persecution and differences of language, and the Bible may well have been his only written source. It is possible he was a bishop. Feast 29 January.

Aphrodisius and Companions, martyrs, died Palestine, third/fourth century. He may have been a priest, martyred with about 30 of his flock. Feast 4 May.

Apollinaris Claudius, bishop, Christian apologist. He received his see of Hierapolis during the reign of Marcus Aurelius (161–80), and is known as an outstanding champion of orthodoxy in the early days of Montanism. His writings include a 'Defence of the Faith', presented to Marcus Aurelius in 172, five treatises 'Against the Pagans', two 'On the Truth', and two 'Against the Jews'. His refutations of the early Montanists were highly esteemed by Serapion of Antioch. Apart from a few fragments , all his writings are lost. Feast 8 January.

Apollinaris of Monte Cassino, abbot, died Monte Cassino, 27 November, 828. Entrusted to the abbey as a young child and eventually ordained priest, he succeeded Abbot Gisulfus in 817. During his reign the abbey reached a high point of development, both materially and spiritually.

Apollinaris of Ravenna, bishop and martyr. Traditionally, Apollinaris was a disciple of St Peter, and was appointed as the first bishop of Ravenna by him. This tradition dates from the seventh century, however, and although Apollinaris is mentioned in the writings of **Peter Chrysologus**, as well as in the fifth-century *Hieronymianum*, there are no reliable accounts of his life. Feast 23 July.

Apollinaris of Valence, bishop, born Vienne, *c.* 453, died Valence, *c.* 520. The son of St **Hosychius** (Isicius) and brother of St **Avitus**. When he became bishop *c.* 490, he laboured to renew discipline in his diocese, vacant for some years, and to restore the Burgundians, who had fallen into Arianism, to the Catholic faith. Exiled by King Sigismund following the Synod of Epaon in 517, he returned the following year. Feast 5 October.

Apollo, died *c.* 395. The story of his life is one of a hermit who became leader of a community near Heliopolis, Egypt. Unusually, he apparently remained a hermit until past 80 years old and died in extreme old age. **Petronius** may have visited him. Feast 25 January.

Apollo the Shepherd, monk, Coptic Church. As a shepherd he had led a dissolute life, but having killed a pregnant woman he was overcome with remorse, abandoned his flock, and lived as a solitary in Scete. After 40 years he heard a heavenly voice tell him all his sins were forgiven save that of killing the woman. A year later he was told that even that sin had been forgiven. He received communion and died immediately. Feast 30 January.

Apollonia of Alexandria, martyr, born Alexandria, died there, *c.* 249. A victim of the anti-Christian disturbances in Alexandria towards the end of the reign of Emperor Philip the Arabian, her martyrdom is described in a letter of Dionysius, bishop of Alexandria, to Fabius, bishop of Antioch, according to which, a mob seized 'the marvellous aged virgin Apollonia', broke her teeth and threatened to burn her alive, whereupon she leapt into a fire and was consumed. Although usually pictured as a young maiden, she was in fact an elderly deaconess at the time of her death, and is honoured as the patron saint of dentists. Feast 9 February.

Apollonius, born Greece or Asia Minor, martyred 21 April 185. A Roman senator, denounced by his servant, Eusebius and **Jerome** describe his speech defending the moral superiority of Christianity, which his fellow senators listened to with respect. He was put to death, either after torture or, more probably, by beheading.

Apollonius, see also **Proculus**. Feast 14 February.

Apostolos the Young Man, born Thessaly, died Constantinople, 16 August 1686. Byzantine Church. He was orphaned as a young man and left his city for Constantinople when he was 15. When some of his compatriots came to Constantinople to seek relief from the tax they had to pay as Christians, and were imprisoned, Apostolos went to seek their liberty, and was himself imprisoned. He escaped, but was recaptured and tortured. He refused to deny his faith, and was executed.

Apphian, born Lycia, now Turkey, martyred Caesarea, Palestine, 2 April 306. When he was thrown into the sea weighed with stones for refusing to sacrifice to the gods, there was an immediate earthquake and his body returned to the shore (wrote Eusebius). He is commemorated with **Theodosia**.

Appianus, born Liguria, died Commachio on the Adriatic coast, c. 800. He was a monk at the Benedictine abbey at St Peter of Ciel d'Oro, Pavia, and then a recluse at Commachio, evangelizing the region. Feast 4 March.

Aprunculus, bishop of Langres, died 488. Feast 14 May.

Apsada, priest, martyred fourth century. Feast 19 January.

Aptimaran, monk, born Kirkuk, seventh century. Assyrian Church. Aptimaran the Great received the monastic tonsure between 626 and 636 at the monastery of Bet Awe, now in northern Iraq. After some years he left the monastery to live a hermit's life, but after being accused of Messalianism he broke his links with Bet Awe and lived in a number of other monasteries, eventually settling in a hermitage on the mountain of Gabal Behayr, still in northern Iraq. He died there, 100 years old, after having founded a monastery on the spot for his numerous disciples.

Aquila, see also **Eugenius**. Feast 20 January.

Aquila, see also **Severinus**. Feast 23 January.

Aquilina, born Zagliveri, near Thessalonika, 1745, died there, 27 September 1764. Her father had converted to Islam, and tried to persuade Aquilina to do likewise. When she refused she was taken in chains before a judge, but supported by her mother she remained faithful.

Aquilinus, martyr, born Wurzburg, c. 970, died Milan, c. 1015. He studied at Cologne, but left there when his fellow canons chose him as successor to the bishop; he went to Paris and left there, for the same reason. He crossed the Alps to Pavia and from there went to the church of San Lorenzo in Milan. Feast 29 January.

Aquilinus of Evreux, bishop, born Bayeux, c. 620, died Evreux, c. 690. He was a soldier, and married, but when he was about 40 he and his wife both decided to take a vow of chastity and devote their lives to the poor. They went to live at Evreux, where Aquilinus was, after some ten years in the town, elected its bishop. Even as a bishop he tried to live as a hermit, in a cell attached to the cathedral. Feast 19 October.

Arayanna Saggahu, monk, thirteenth/fourteenth centuries. Ethiopian Church. A disciple of **Takla Haymanot**, who had raised him from the dead.

Arbogast of Strasbourg, bishop, born Aquitaine, died near Strasbourg, mid-sixth century. He lived as a hermit in a forest in Alsace, and became bishop of Strasbourg c. 673, through the influence of King Dagobert II of Austrasia, who seems to have been his patron. Known for his humility, he wanted to be buried in a cemetery with criminals. Feast 21 July.

Arcadius, see **Basil, Eugene**, et al.

Arcadius, see also **Xenophon**.

Arcadius, emperor, born 377, died 408. Byzantine Church. Arcadius became emperor of the East in 395, with his capital at Constantinople. He was a gentle man, who had to suffer much from the barbarian invasions, including a siege of Constantinople itself. His wife, Eudocia, led him into conflict with **John Chrysostom**. Feast 27 August.

Arcadius, martyr, died *c.* 304, possibly at Caesaria, Mauritania, then a Roman province. The story is that, during the persecutions of Valerian or Diocletian, he surrendered to free a relative held hostage, was chopped into pieces and local Christians buried the parts. Feast 12 January.

Arcadius, bishop, died Bourges, France, *c.* 540. Bishop of Bourges. Feast 1 August.

Arcadius and Companions, martyrs, died Africa (Tunisia?), 437. Arcadius, Paschasius, Probus and Eutychian were put to death under the Arian King Gaiseric for rejecting his version of Christianity. Feast 13 November.

Arcadius and Constantine, born in the Urals, died there, near the river Sylvy, 18 January 1857. Church of the Old Believers. Ordained priests, they lived in the woods in the Urals where they were murdered by brigands.

Arcadius of Dorogobuz, monk and recluse, died Dorogobuz, between 1582 and 1592. Russian Church. A disciple of **Gerasimus**, founder of the monastery of the Most Holy Trinity at Boldino, near Dorogobuz, close to Smolensk.

Arcadius of Novgorod, bishop, died Novgorod, 19 September 1163. Russian Church. Of humble origins, he became a monk in Novgorod, but later left it and moved. Sometime between 1134 and 1148 he moved to the monastery of St Pantaleon founded by Prince Izjaslav. For a time he led a solitary life, but then himself founded a monastery of which he was hegumenos. He was elected bishop in 1156. Feast 18 September.

Arcadius of Vjaz'ma, monk, born Vjaz'ma near Solensk, died 1053. Russian Church. He decided after reading the lives of some Greek saints to become 'a fool for Christ'. He lived in silence for much of his life in a wood just outside the city, but gained fame for sanctity and miracles. However, when he met by chance **Ephrem of Novotorzok** who had decided to build a monastery, Arcadius came to live there, although he continued his practice of spending the night in prayer and maintaining silence. Feast 14 August.

Arcadius of Vjaznikov, monk, died Dorogobuz, 1592. Russian Church. Frequently confused with **Arcadius of Vjaz'ma**, he was a recluse in the monastery of **Gerasimus** of Dorogobuz. Feast 26 January.

Archangela Girlani, bl., nun, born Eleanora at Trino, 1460, died Mantua, 15 January 1494. Her desire to lead a strict religious life was at first thwarted by her father, who finally allowed her to enter a Benedictine convent of relaxed observance, but she later joined the Carmelites at Parma in 1477, where she became prioress. Shortly afterwards, the influential Gonzaga family requested that she found a new convent at Mantua. Renowned for her austerity, charity and spirit of prayer, she had a reputation for mystical experiences. Feast 13 February.

Archangelo of Calatami, bl., hermit, born Archangelo Placenza, at Calatafimi, *c.* 1390, died Alcamo, 10 April 1460. His reputation for sanctity and the miracles attributed to him attracted so many that he could no longer continue his solitary life at Calatafimi, so he fled to Alcamo, where he organized a hospice for the poor. When Martin V required all hermits in Sicily to accept religious life under a rule, he became a Franciscan of the Observance at Palermo; he returned to Alcamo to make his hospice a Franciscan foundation, and later became provincial of the Sicilian Observants. Feast 30 July.

Archelais, martyred Salerno, Campagna, 293. She and two other Christian girls, **Thecla** and **Susanna**, all from the Romagna, took refuge in Nola, in the Campagna, to avoid death. They were still arrested, tortured and beheaded. Feast 19 January.

Archelaus, Cyril and Photius, martyrs, died Nicomedia, third century. Nothing further is known. Feast 4 March.

Arc'il, martyred Notkore, Georgia, 786. He was a king. Feast 20 March.

Arcontius of Viviers, bishop, martyred *c.* 745. He was killed by a mob for defending the rights of the Church in a local matter. Feast 10 January.

Ardanus (Ardagnus, Ardaing, Ardan), died 1058. A Benedictine, he was abbot of Tournus in Burgundy, and is remembered for caring for the local people during the famine of 1030–33. Feast 11 February.

Ardo, abbot, born Smaragdus in the Languedoc, died Aniane, 843. A Benedictine in the abbey of Aniane, he directed the abbey's schools and was **Benedict**'s secretary. He succeeded him as abbot and became his biographer. Feast 7 March.

Arduin, hermit, died Rimini, 1009. A priest, he became a hermit and then at the end of his life went to live in a monastery. Feast 15 August.

Aredius (also Aridius, Arigius, Yrieix), abbot, born Limoges, died Abbey of St Yriex, 25 August 591. Son of an important family, he grew up in the court of Theudebert I. Attracted by his sanctity and eloquence, Bishop Nicetius made him a member of his clergy; he then used his patrimony to build churches, in particular the Abbey of Attane, later named St Yrieix, of which he became first abbot, and followed the teachings of **Basil** and **John Cassian**. His friend Fortunatus celebrates Aredius in his poems, and St **Gregory of Tours** reports that many miracles were performed through his intercession.

Aretas and Companions, martyrs, died Najran, Yemen, 523. After the kingdom of Axum had imposed its (Christian) rule on the Yemen, there was an uprising led by Dunaan, a member of the ruling family which had been deposed by the Ethiopians. He massacred all the inhabitants of the Christian stronghold of Najran. The leader of those in Najran was Banu Harith, whose name became Arestas. He was beheaded, as were his wife and daughters. Four thousand people died in all. Feast 24 October.

Aretas of Verchotur'e, monk, born Orlov, 1865, died Verchotur'e, 15 May 1903. Russian Church. Born into a large family, Athanasius Tichonovic Katargin became a monk of the monastery of the Transfiguration at Salaam in 1893, but when one of his fellow monks became hegumenos of the monastery of St Nicholas at Verchotur'e, in the diocese of Ekaterinburg, he asked Aretas to accompany him. Aretas became archimandrite in 1900 and revived the religious spirit of the community. Feast 10 June.

Aretas the Recluse, bishop, born Tver, died 1409. Russian Church. A monk of the Kievan Cave monasteries, he came to know the metropolitan **Cyprian**, who lived in the Cave monasteries for three years between being deposed from a southern Russian diocese and appointed metropolitan of Moscow. He took Aretas with him to Moscow as his archdeacon and later, at the request of the prince of Tver, he was made bishop of that city, although he continued to live a monastic style of life as far as he could. He founded a monastery near Tver, at Zeltikovo, on the river Tamanka, where he would retire to pray. Feast 29 June.

Argentea of Córdoba, martyr, died Córdoba, 931. She was the daughter of a Christian Mozarabic family who resisted Muslim incursion into their territory for 50 years. In Córdoba, when **Wulfram** started preaching and was arrested, she then publicly declared her faith. They were executed and are commemorated together. Feast 13 May.

Argeus, martyred Tomi, Pontus, 320. He is commemorated with his brothers **Narcissus** and **Marcellinus**, all soldiers. Marcellinus was imprisoned, flogged and thrown into the sea; the others were beheaded. Feast 2 January.

Argimir, martyr, born Cabra, died Córdoba, 28 June 856. He held the office of 'censor' in the administration of justice, in the Muslim government of Córdoba, from which he retired to a monastery. Certain Muslims accused him of scurrilous derision of the prophet of Allah, and of having professed the divinity of Christ. Argimir admitted the charges before the cadi, who sentenced him to death. Feast 7 July.

Argiris of Constantinople, born Presa, 1688, died there, 1721 or 1725. Byzantine Church. Of a devout family, she had not been long married when a Turk tried to win her over. When she refused, he accused her before a judge of having reneged on her promise to become a Muslim. She was imprisoned for 17 years, even refusing one opportunity of freedom so she might suffer for her faith. Feast 30 April.

Argiros of Thessalonika, born Apanone (now Epanome), Macedonia, 1788, died Thessalonika, 11 May 1806. Byzantine Church. He moved to Thessalonika to work with a tailor. There he met a Christian who had denied his faith, and Argiros attempted to show him his error. He was overheard, arrested and eventually hanged, although the judge at first insisted he had committed no crime.

Argretius (Agnitius, Agrecius) of Trier, bishop, died *c.* 320. The known fact is that he attended the Council of Arles in 314. His (unhistorical) story recounts that he re-evangelized his German diocese and was given some of the relics of the cross by St **Helen**. Feast 13 January.

Ariadne, empress, born 442, died 515. Byzantine Church. Ruled the Eastern empire first as regent for her son, and after his death with her husband Zeno. After Zeno's death in 491, Ariadne proposed the election as emperor of the senator Anastasius, whom she married, after he had first given a written commitment to abide by the decisions of Chalcedon – which Zeno had not always done.

Arigius, bishop, born 535, died Gap, France, 604. He was bishop of Gap for 20 years, with a reputation as a great pastor. Feast 1 May.

Arigius of Lyon, bishop, seventh century. Feast 10 August.

Aristides, born Athens, died there (?), second century. He wrote a defence of the Christian faith to the Emperor Hadrian in 125. Feast 31 August.

Arkaledes, monk, fourteenth century. Ethiopian Church. After the death of his parents he became a shepherd, but was then taken in by his uncle, who was a monk. He, too, became a monk, and after his uncle's death retreated to the solitude of Mount Guonay'eba. He was joined by many disciples.

Armand Chapt de Rastignac, bl., theologian, born Périgot, France, 2 October 1729, died Paris, 3–5 September 1792. As vicar-general of the diocese of Arles, he attempted at the Estates-General meetings in 1789 to prevent Church properties being taken over, published *Question sur la propriété des biens ecclésiastiques* (Paris, 1789) and signed protests against the anti-clerical laws of the Constituent Assembly. He was arrested, imprisoned and killed in the massacres of September 1792. He was beatified in 1926. Feast 2 September.

Armel (Erme, Armagilus), born south Wales, died Ploërmel, Brittany, sixth century. Said to have been a missionary in Cornwall before moving to Brittany and founding monasteries at Plouarmel and Ploërmel. Feast 16 August.

Armentarius of Pavia, bishop, died *c.* 731. While he was bishop of Pavia, the see was moved from the jurisdiction of Milan to that of Rome. Feast 30 January.

Arnold Janssen, bl., born Goch, Lower Rhine, 5 November 1837, ordained 1861, died Steyl, Holland, 15 January 1909, beatified 1975. Founder of the Divine Word Missionaries, he also founded women's orders – missionary and contemplative – and created the magazine *Stadt Gottes* (*City of God*), still existing in Germany.

Arnold of Hiltensweiler, bl., founder, died 1127. A lay man, he founded a convent at Langnan, near Berne. He appears to have been a member of the First Crusade, 1099–1100. Married, but childless, in 1122 he formally bequeathed all his property to the house of All Saints at Schaffhausen on the Rhine; he is buried at the oratory he founded at Hiltensweiler. Feast 1 May.

Arnold (Arnald, Arnaud) **of Padua**, bl., born Padua, *c.* 1184, died Asolo, 1254. A Benedictine at St Justina, Padua, and then abbot there, he was persecuted by Ezzelino da Romano and died after eight years in prison. Feast 10 February.

Arnold Rèche, bl., born Landruff, near Metz, 12 September 1838, died Courlancy, 23 October 1890. Baptized Nicholas Jules, at 21 he became a coachman, then a mule driver for a builder. He became increasingly devout, saying his rosary as he went about his business, and started working in Sunday school classes with the Brothers of the

Christian Schools (the de la Salle Brothers). He joined the order in 1862, and until 1877 worked as a teacher in a school in Rheims. He was not a great success, but was much valued as the novice master he became in 1877 at Thjillois. In 1890 he became superior of the Brothers' house at Courlancy.

Arnulf, martyred eighth century. He was a soldier. Feast 29 January.

Arnulf of Gap, bishop, born Vendome, died Gap, 19 September 1070/79. A Benedictine monk at Sainte Trinite, Vendome, he went to Rome in 1061 to secure for Sainte Trinite papal confirmation of the church of St Priscia, and, for its abbot, the dignity of cardinal priest. Alexander II detained Arnulf and consecrated him bishop of Gap in 1063, where he became a zealous supporter of the Gregorian reform movement.

Arnulf of Metz (also Arnoul), bishop, born near Nancy, c. 582, died Remiremont, 18 July c. 641. Of a noble family, he rose rapidly in the court of Theodebert II, King of Austrasia (595–612), and took an active part in securing the accession of Clothar II in 613. Consecrated bishop of Metz c. 614, he helped Clothar's son Dagobert to govern his kingdom in the Ardennes. He took part in the Councils of Clichy (626–7) and Rheims (627). After 15 years of service to Church and state, he resigned his see and joined his friend St **Romanic** in a deserted place near Remiremont in the Vosges, where he spent his last years in meditation and prayer. He had been married before becoming a bishop, and had two sons, of whom Ansegis married (St) **Begga**, daughter of Pepin of Landeu, and became the father of Pepin of Heristal; Arnulf is thus the progenitor of the Carolingian dynasty.

Arnulf of Soissons, monastic reformer, bishop, born Brabant, c. 1040, died Oudenbourg, 15 August 1087. He had a brief military career, and then became a monk at St Medard (Soissons), where his rigorous asceticism so impressed his fellow monks that they elected him abbot to replace Raymond, a worldly man and guilty of simony. In 1080 he became bishop of Soissons, again to replace a man of ill repute, Ursio, but his efforts to reform the diocesan clergy there were thoroughly repulsed and he had to leave the diocese. He founded a Benedictine monastery at Oudenbourg in Flanders, where he died.

Arsenius, hermit in Egypt, fourth/fifth century. Feast 8 May.

Arsenius, born Rome, c. 360, died Troë, Egypt, c. 450. He was the tutor of the sons of Emperor Theodosius I for about ten years. In 394 he retired to Alexandria and joined the monastery of Scetis in Lower Egypt. He became a hermit, living in solitude near Petra. When the settlement at Scetis was destroyed by barbarians about 40 years later, Arsenius went to Troë (now Truah, near Cairo), where he died sometime between 440 and 450. Feast 19 July.

Arsenius of Cappadocia, born Farasa, Cappadocia, c. 1840, died Corfu, 10 November 1924. Byzantine Church. He was brought up by two uncles in Smyrna and entered the monastic life, when he took the name Arsenius in place of his baptismal name of Theodore, at the monastery of Timios Podromos in Caesarea. Illness forced him to leave, at which point he was ordained deacon by the metropolitan of Caesarea. He then worked as a teacher at Farasa until, aged 30, he was ordained priest, and was given the rank of archimandrite. After a pilgrimage to the Holy Land he returned to work in Farasa, where he taught the Orthodox faith and gained fame as a healer and visionary. When the Greek and Turkish governments arranged an exchange of populations, he migrated in August 1924 to Corfu. Beatified 11 February 1986.

Arsenius of Corfu, bishop, from Constantinople, died Corfu, c. 959. Originally Jewish, he became the first bishop of Corfu and is venerated as the island's patron. Feast 19 January.

Arsenius of Elassona-Suzdal, born Kalopiano, near Thessalonika, c. 1550, died Suzdal, 13 April 1626. Russian Church. Born into the family of a priest – four of his brothers were monks, two of whom became bishops – he entered the monastery at Larissa where he became a hieromonk. In 1572 the metropolitan of Larissa, Jeremias, became patriarch of Constantinople and Arsenius went with him, soon afterwards being appointed bishop of Elassona-Dimoniki. In 1585 he was sent as part of a delegation to Moscow, and on his return he was asked by the bishop of L'vov to remain there, teaching Greek and Church Slavonic. In 1588 Patriarch Jeremias went to Moscow and Arsenius, still in L'vov, joined his entourage. In Moscow in January 1589 Jeremias elevated the Moscow metropolitan to the title of Patriarch of Moscow and All Russia, Arsenius taking part in the proceedings and writing an account of it. Arsenius remained in Moscow, being appointed archbishop of the cathedral of the Archangel in the Kremlin. He took a major part in the affairs of the Russian Church, and was one of those who signed the decree of the election of Boris Godunov to the throne of Russia. He endured with the citizens of Moscow the occupation by the Polish army and the sacking of his palace. He continued to live in Moscow even when made bishop of the cathedrals of Tver and Kasin, and also when he was given the title of Archbishop of Suzdal and Tarusa. However, in 1621 he moved to Suzdal, where he spent his last years. Feast 29 April.

Arsenius of Iqaltho, born Iqaltho, died early twelfth century. Georgian Church. Probably of an aristocratic family, he moved to Constantinople to study, and then to the monastery of St Simeon on Mount Sinai, where he began to translate Greek lives of the saints into Georgian. Returning to Georgia at the beginning of the twelfth century, he assisted the king, and played a considerable part in the Church council of 1105, of which he wrote an account, thereby founding Georgian canon law. He settled at the monastery of Sciomgvine.

Arsenius of Komel, monk, born Moscow, died Komel, 24 August 1550. Russian Church. He was of a boyar family, and joined the monastery of the Most Holy Trinity founded by **Sergius of Radonez**, where in 1525 he was elected hegumenos. He made unsuccessful attempts to retire from the office, but in 1527 he fled the monastery and established a hermitage, first near Vologda, and then near the confluence of the rivers Leza and Kochtys. There the people proved hostile, killing a disciple of Arsenius, and he moved again, to the forest of Silegon, near the river Singor. However, because of the Tartar invasions, the local inhabitants took refuge in the forest, and he therefore returned to the hermitage he had abandoned in the forest of Komel. Here he founded a monastery in which he died.

Arsenius of Konevec, monk, born Novgorod, died Konevec, 12 June 1444. Russian Church. Apprenticed to a potter, he entered the monastery of Lisica at Novgorod, but after 12 years went to Mount Athos, where he was put to work making crockery for his own and other monasteries. He stayed for three years, and on his return settled on the island of Konevec on lake Ladoga. He lived there for five years, founding a monastery in which he installed an icon of the Mother of God which he had brought from Mount Athos.

Arsenius of Latmo, monk, born Constantinople, tenth century, died Mount Latro, eleventh century. Byzantine Church. Of a Constantinopolitan family, he was a general in the imperial army, but when the fleet he was commanding sank in a storm, and he was saved, as he believed, miraculously, he decided to become a monk. He lived in his monastery in great asceticism, wearing a goatskin habit with an iron belt around his wait, and eating only wild herbs. After a time he went to the monastery of Kellivaron on Mount Latro in Asia Minor, and although after a time he left there to live in solitude, he eventually returned there for the rest of his life.

Arsenius of Ninozminda, monk, died Mount Athos, *c.* 1018. Georgian Church. Although bishop of Ninozminda, he abandoned his see and asked the king's permission to enter a monastery. The king agreed. He entered the monastery of Otchta, where he met John Grdzelidze, and after some years the two left Otchta for the monastery of Iviron on Mount Athos, where they translated Greek theological and liturgical works into Georgian. Feast 31 July.

Arsenius of Novgorod, hegumenos, born Rzev Vladimirski, died there, 12 July 1570. Russian Church. Baptized Ambrose, he married at the insistence of his parents, but after six months of marriage went to Novgorod, where he became a worker in leather. He took the name Arsenius when becoming a monk in 1556. He founded a small monastery on the river Volchov outside Novgorod, where he was visited by Ivan the

Terrible who had just destroyed the city. Arsenius rebuked him: the Tsar asked his blessing. Feast 12 May.

Arsenius of Parios, monk, born Giannini, 1800, died Parios, 31 January 1877. Byzantine Church. Baptized Athanasius, he went aged nine to Sidonia in Asia Minor, and at 15 went to a monastery on Mount Athos, where he took the name Arsenius. After six years there he moved again, to a monastery near Athens. He moved finally to the island of Parios, where he taught, gaining a great reputation for holiness. Canonized 1970.

Arsenius of the Kievan Cave Monasteries, monk, fourteenth century. Known only from the inscription on his reliquary, Arsenius was known for his great asceticism, in particular for not eating until after sundown.

Arsenius of Tver, bishop, died Tver, early fifteenth century. Russian Church. Of a rich family, after the death of his parents he gave away his wealth to the poor and entered the cave monasteries at Kiev. In 1391 he was elected bishop of Tver, where he continued his life of strict asceticism, and founded the monastery of the Dormition at Zeltikovo. Canonized 1547. Feast 2 March.

Arsenius of Veroia, metropolitan, martyr, died Veroia. Byzantine Church. Thought to be the first bishop martyred by the Turks, he was imprisoned for his defence of the faith of his flock, had his right hand cut off because it was with this he had written his sermons, and was eventually executed.

Arsenius the Great, patriarch, born c. 839, died 887. Georgian Church. Youngest son of the Grand Duke Mirian of Samzche, his parents dedicated him to the monastic life when he was six at the monastery of Chanztha, and in 860 appointed him catholicos of Karthli, eastern Georgia. This caused considerable disturbance, and a council was called, almost all of the participants being against Arsenius. Thanks, however, to the intervention of **Gregory of Khandztha**, he was confirmed in his office.

Arsinius of Chur, bishop, died c. 450. Feast 19 January.

Artaldus, monk and bishop, born Savoy, c. 1101, died monastery of Arvières, 1206. He joined the Carthusians at Portes, then became prior at Val Romey near Geneva. He had a great reputation for holiness, and despite his protests was appointed, when already over 80, to the bishopric of Belley. He lasted there only two years before returning to the monastery at Arvières, which had replaced the one at Val Romey, destroyed in a fire. He died there when 105 years old. Feast 7 October.

Artemis of Verkola, born Verkola, 1532, died there, 1545. Russian Church. A pious youth who, when 12 or 13, was killed by lightning while working with his father in the fields. His body remained unburied for 28 years, but was then miraculously discovered and taken to the church of St Nicholas, where it worked miracles. Feast 23 June.

Artemius, martyr, died Alexandria (?), 363. Said to have been a soldier, who was appointed the imperial representative in Egypt. He was, however, an Arian heretic, and an opponent of **Athanasius** whom he vigorously pursued. He was accused of being a Christian under Julian the Apostate, and beheaded. He has been regarded as a saint despite his heretical views. Feast 20 October.

Artemon, bishop, second century. He was bishop of Seleucia, Pisidia. Feast 24 March.

Arthellais of Benevento (Arthelais), born Constantinople, 544, died of fever at Benevento, c. 560. She fled to Benevento, apparently escaping the attentions of Emperor Justinian. Supposed to have been miraculously freed from kidnappers, she is a patron saint of kidnap victims and of Benevento. Feast 3 March.

Asaph, bishop, born Wales, died at what is now St Asaph, c. 610. He took over from **Kentigern** at his monastery of Llanelwy (now St Asaph) in north Wales, then became a bishop c. 590. He mainly worked in Flintshire. Feast 1 May.

Asclas, martyred c. 300. He was killed by being thrown in the Nile. Feast 20 January.

Asicus, bishop, born Ireland, died Ballintra, Ireland, c. 470. Described as an early disciple of **Patrick**, he is venerated as Elphin's first bishop. Unsuccessful or unhappy, he retired to an island in Donegal Bay, remaining for seven years until found by monks from Elphin. He died while returning to his diocese. Feast 27 April.

Asclepiodotus, see **Maximus**. Feast 19 February.

Ascolius of Thessalonika, bishop, died c. 383. Feast 23 January.

Ascot Kuropalati, grand duke, ninth century, died Artanugi. Georgian Church. He and his sons were devout Christians who founded many monasteries and churches. He was killed by Arabs. Feast 27 January.

Aser of Bali, martyr, sixteenth century. Ethiopian Church. Killed during a pilgrimage to Jerusalem.

Asot I Bagratuni, king, 819–90. Armenian Church. Son of **Smbat II** and father of **Smbat the Martyr**, he began the Bagratuni dynasty in Armenia, gaining recognition of his sovereignty both from the Arabs and the Byzantine Empire. Feast 27 and 28 May.

Asot III the Merciful, king, died 977. Armenian Church. King of Armenia from c. 952 until his death, he was renowned for his acts of piety, including bringing the poor to his own table, and for building churches and monasteries.

Asprenatis of Naples, bishop and martyr, died Naples, second century. Said to have been the first bishop of Naples. Feast 3 August.

Asterius, see also **Marinus**.

Asterius of Amasia, bishop, born Cappadocia, c. 350, died Amasia, c. 410. Little is known of his life except that he abandoned the law to enter the clergy, and became a bishop around 385. His fame rests chiefly on his 'Homilies', much esteemed in the Eastern Church, most of which have been lost, but 21 survive in full and there are fragments of others. Feast 30 October.

Astrick (Anastasius), bishop, born Bohemia (?), died Kalocsa (?), Hungary, c. 1040. His original name seems to have been Radla, and he was a close friend of **Adalbert of Prague**. He presumably took the name Astrick (or, in its Latinized version, Anastasius) when he became a monk, possibly in Rome or more likely at the monastery of Brevnov in Bohemia. He went as a missionary to the Magyars. **Stephen of Hungary** sent him to Rome shortly before he was crowned king, and on his return he became bishop, apparently, over the whole Hungarian Church. He spent the rest of his life working to convert the Magyars. Feast 12 November.

Athala of Bobbio, abbot, born Burgundy, c. 570, died 10 March 627. He spent some years in the monastery of Lérins, and in the stricter observance of Luxeuil. Nominated to replace Columban, exiled by Brunhilde in 610, he instead followed him into northern Italy, where they established the monastery of Bobbio, and there he succeeded Columban as abbot, c. 615. He combated Arianism among the Lombards and supported the papacy in the controversy of the 'Three Chapters'.

Athanasia, born island of Aegina, died Timia, c. 860. She married a soldier who was killed in battle only 16 days after their wedding. Her second marriage was to a devout man who after a while said he wanted to become a monk. As Athanasia had long wanted to be a nun, she readily agreed, and turned her own house into a convent, over which she presided. After a time, as the community grew, the convent moved to Timia. Athanasia had attracted a reputation as a wonder worker, and was invited to Constantinople as an adviser to the empress. She stayed at the court – although living in a cell – for seven years, after which she returned to Timia, where she died shortly afterwards. Feast 15 August.

Athanasius, abbot, born Constantinople, died c. 826. He was abbot of Ss Peter and Paul monastery near Nicomedia in Bithynia, and was exiled for defending images under the iconoclast emperor Leo the Armenian. Feast 22 February.

Athanasius, monk, Syriac Church. Feast 11 July.

Athanasius Bazzekuketta, martyr, died Uganda, 1886, canonized 1964. He was a page of King Mwanga of Uganda and Keeper of the Royal Treasury. He was converted by the Missionaries of Africa and baptized in 1885. He is commemorated with **Gonzaga Gonza** – see **Martyrs of Uganda**. Feast 27 May.

Athanasius of Alexandria I, bishop, born Alexandria, *c.* 295, died there, 2 May 373. One of the most illustrious defenders of the Christian faith, a Father and doctor of the Church, defender of the Nicene faith, friend of St **Anthony of Egypt**, he attended the Council of Nicaea (325) as deacon and secretary to Bishop Alexander, and succeeded him in 328. Constantine banished Athanasius to Trier because of the intrigues against him of Eusebius of Nicomedia, the Arians, and partisans of the Miletian schism, but he returned after a successful appeal to Julius I. His enemies forced Athanasius from his see four more times between 335 and 366. His writings are (a) dogmatic: 'Discourses against the Arians' being the most important; (b) historical-polemical: three apologies, of which 'Apology against the Arians' is valuable; (c) ascetical: the principal work is his 'Life of Anthony', which profoundly influenced subsequent Greek and Latin hagiography; (d) his correspondence is of prime importance for the history of Arianism and the development of Christian doctrine in the fourth century, amongst which are of note: the 'Festal Letters', annual messages to the bishops of Egypt; the 'Synodal Letters' explain the Nicene faith and warn against Arian errors; four 'Letters to Serapion of Thmuis', a unified dogmatic treatise setting forth the correct doctrine of the Holy Spirit. His most famous work, 'De Incarnatione', is the second of two closely linked treatises (the other is 'Contra Gentiles'), and the 'locus classicus' for the teaching of the ancient Church on the subject of salvation. In it God himself, the Word (logos), has entered into humanity and restored fallen man to the image of God in which he had been created (Gen. 1.27); by his death and resurrection he met and overcame death, the consequence of sin, thus leading mankind back to God. Athanasius's writings are occasional pieces, born of controversy and intended for controversial ends, the abstract exposition of theological ideas being everywhere subordinated to the polemical purpose. Inspired

with an enthusiastic devotion to Christ, his main distinction was his zealous advocacy of the essential divinity of Jesus; he has been called 'The Father of Orthodoxy'.

Athanasius of Alexandra II, patriarch, died Alexandria, 17 September 494. Coptic Church.

Athanasius of Attalia, martyr, born Attalia, died Smyrna, 7 January 1700. Byzantine Church. Moved to Smyrna, where he was accused of having given up Islam, because he had used Turkish when saying 'Glory be to God'. He was decapitated.

Athanasius of Brest, martyr, born Brest, end of sixteenth century, died there, 4 September 1648. Russian Church. An opponent of the Union of Brest, he received a good theological education and worked as tutor in a noble family for seven years before entering the monastery of the Holy Spirit at Vilno, although he spent time afterwards at a number of different monasteries before returning to Vilno, where he became a hieromonk. He later transferred to the monastery at Kupjati, near Minsk, where there was a miraculous image of the Mother of God, and he was sent in 1637 to collect alms for the restoration of the monastic church, a journey which was accompanied by visions and miraculous signs, as well as physical dangers. In 1640 he was invited by the monks of the monastery of St Simeon at Brest to become their hegumenos. During his stay there he studied the history of Orthodoxy, and came out openly opposed to the Union. At the Diet held in Warsaw in 1643 he spoke out so passionately in favour of Orthodoxy that he was declared insane and put under arrest. He therefore pretended to be mad, 'a fool for Christ's sake', and escaped from prison and, dressed only in a monk's habit, he walked the streets of Warsaw crying out, 'Woe to the excommunicated and the faithless!' He was once more imprisoned, and stripped of his priestly and monastic rank by the bishop of Warsaw. He was sent then to the metropolitan of Kiev, **Peter Mogila**, where his punishment was rescinded, and Peter sent him back to Brest. He still continued to protest, however, and in 1664 was once again arrested and taken to Warsaw. The king of Poland released him a year later and sent him back to Peter Mogila. He went to live in the Laura of the

Kievan cave monasteries. After the death of Mogila he was able once again to return to Brest, only to be arrested again and accused this time of having links to rebel Cossacks. This time he was sentenced to be executed. Feast 5 September.

Athanasius of Cerepovec, and Theodosius of Cerepovec, monks, fourteenth century. Russian Church. Founders of the monastery at Cerepovec, possibly disciples of **Sergius of Radonez**. Feast 26 November.

Athanasius of Constantinople III, Patelario, patriarch, born Regileni, Crete, 1580, died Lubny, 5 April 1654. Russian Church. Baptized Alexis, he went to Mount Athos after the death of his parents, where he became known both for his learning and his preaching. He went on to become metropolitan of Thessalonika, but in that position clashed with the Patriarch Cyril I Lukaris, whom he believed to hold strongly Protestant opinions. After Cyril was arrested in 1633 he was elected patriarch, but little more than a month later he went to Ancona, where the Pope gave him the title of Patriarch of Constantinople of the Greek Catholics. At the last moment, however, he decided he could not abandon the Orthodox faith for Catholicism, and took refuge in Moldavia. In 1634, when Cyril was once again deposed, he returned to Constantinople. His Catholic sympathies alienated him from his flock. He was deposed and sent to Rhodes. In 1651 he was again nominated to the see of Constantinople, but the metropolitans refused to acknowledge him, and he was forced once more to leave, going back to Moldavia, and then, in 1653, to Moscow. In Moscow he supported the right of the Tsar to occupy the throne of Byzantium, and of the right of the Moscow patriarch to the see of Constantinople. Because of his stance he was given many gifts of money for his monastery in Moldavia. He also inspired the Moscow patriarch to undertake the liturgical reforms which eventually led to the schism of the Old Believers. He died on his way back to his monastery. Feast 2 May.

Athanasius of Cristianoupolis, archbishop, born Corfu 1665, died Cristianoupolis, 1735. Byzantine Church. Baptized Anastasius, his father was an official of the Venetian administration in the Peloponnese. In 1648 the family moved to Caritene, and Anastasius studied there and in Venice. His parents wished him to marry, but he instead went to Constantinople where he was ordained deaon, and later priest. In 1711 he was consecrated archbishop of Cristianoupolis, with the name Athanasius, when the person proposed by the Venetians refused the office. As archbishop he was concerned with both the spiritual and the cultural health of his flock, especially in preparing them to resist the influence of the Latin Church, favoured by Venice. Feast 17 May.

Athanasius of Jerusalem, martyr, died 451. A deacon in the church of the Resurrection in Jerusalem, he denounced Theodosius, who had deposed the bishop of Jerusalem, Juvenal, during the council of Chalcedon. Theodosius saw Athanasius as an obstacle to his leadership and had him murdered, or possibly even murdered him himself. Athanasius was added to the Roman Martyrology in the sixteenth century as a champion of orthodoxy. Feast 5 July.

Athanasius of Khios, born Khios, died Parmak-Capi, 24 July 1670. Byzantine Church. It is unclear whether Athanasius was from the Greek island of Khios (Chios), or from Khios in Asia Minor. It seems he was a high official who decided to move from his place of residence because of the heavy burden of tax levied against Christians. The people of the region, fearing they were going to have to bear the subsequent burden of taxation, denounced him to the vizier, who condemned him to death when he refused to give up his faith.

Athanasius of Koliakiote, martyr, born Koliakiote (now Chalastra, near Thessalonika), 1749, died Thessalonika, 8 September 1774. Byzantine Church. He went to Thessalonika to study, thence to Mount Athos and afterwards to Constantinople, where he came to know Philemon who became patriarch of Antioch. He spent two years with Philemon, returned to Athos, and eventually went back to Koliakiote. There, when once engaged in a religious debate with the emir, he pronounced the Muslim profession of faith. The emir claimed that he had thereby renounced Christianity, and when Athanasius protested he had not, he sent him before a judge in Thessalonika who, although first disposed to free him, was finally obliged to sentence him to death.

Athanasius of Lemnos, born Lemnos, died there, 1846. Byzantine Church. As a very young man he visited the Great Laura on Mount Athos, and was taken prisoner there in 1821 during the Greek uprising. He was sold to a rich Egyptian, who had him circumcized and then married him to a Christian prisoner. For a time in Egypt he lived a dissolute life, but repented and, having ensured that his wife had all she needed, he returned to Mount Athos. After a short time there he went back to Lemnos. There he was arrested for denying Islam, and was thrown into the sea.

Athanasius of Murmansk, hegumenos, fifteenth century. Russian Church. Hegumenos of the monastery of the Dormition at Murmansk, founded by **Lazarus of Murmansk**. He was famous for the degree of his bodily mortification. Feast 8 March.

Athanasius of Naples, bishop, born Naples, 832, died Veroli, 872. His father was Sergius, duke of Naples, and he was elected bishop of Naples when 18. He was renowned for personal austerity and compassion for others, especially the poor, orphans and Saracen prisoners. He rebuilt churches, reunited communities of priests and monks and championed their interests before the emperor. After his father's death he was imprisoned by his nephew, the young Duke Sergius, who then drove him from his see. He lived for five years from 867 with his brother Stephen, Bishop of Sorrento. Feast 15 July.

Athanasius of Navolock, born Kargopol, northern Russia, died Vercholed, province of Archangel, sixteenth/seventeenth centuries. Russian Church.

Athanasius of Novye Krupcy, monk, died Novye Krupcy, Poland, *c.* 1858. Church of the Old Believers. Born into a noble but impoverished family, he entered the Old Believer monastery at Novye Krupcy, established by **Vincent of Novye Krupcy**, and lived there for 70 years in great holiness.

Athanasius of Qennesrin, bishop, died 644. Syriac Church. Originally from the monastery of Qennesrin on the Euphrates.

Athanasius of Rostov, a 'fool for Christ', died Rostov, seventeenth century. Russian Church. Feast 23 May.

Athanasius of Sjandemki, monk, born Zavalisin, sixteenth century. Russian Church. Baptized Andrew, and born into a noble family, he joined the monastery of Salaam and put himself under the guidance of **Alexander of Svir**, whom he followed to his monastery on the Svir, but after Alexander's death he and other disciples set up a monastery between the lakes Sjandemki and Roscanki, near Olonec. He was forced to return for a time to the monastery of Svir because of local hostility, and was elected its superior. He returned to Sjandemki in 1577. He spent his final years in strict solitude, on an island on lake Sjandemki. Feast 18 January.

Athanasius of Sorrento, bishop, possibly sixth/seventh century. He is venerated at Sorrento, but nothing is known about him and he may be the same as **Athanasius of Naples**. Feast 26 January.

Athanasius of Sparta in Piscidia, martyr, died Mudania, Bithynia, 29 October 1653. Byzantine Church.

Athanasius of the Meteora, born New Patrasso (modern Hypati), 1310, died 1383. Byzantine Church. Baptized Andronicus, he was brought up by an uncle and, after being imprisoned by the Catalans, fled their city for Thessalonika, where he studied philosophy, and then went to Mount Athos, although because of his youth he was not allowed to remain. He then went to Crete, but in 1340 returned to Athos. There he took the name Anthony, but later changed it to Athanasius. Because of pirates, he fled finally to western Macedonia, to a rocky area called Kalampaka where he settled. He attracted many disciples, and a monastery was established dedicated to the Transfiguration, for which he wrote the Rule. Feast 20 April.

Athanasius of Tours, deacon in Tours, died 1198. Feast 5 May.

Athanasius of Vysock the Elder, hegumenos, born Obonezskoe, died Vysock, early fifteenth century. Russian Church. The son of a priest, and baptized Andrew, he entered the monastery of the Most Holy Trinity, founded by St **Sergius** at Radonez. He later founded a monastery on the river Nara, near Okra, and became the hegumenos. He was friendly with the metropolitan Cyprian, whom he followed from Moscow to Kiev in 1383 and shortly afterwards to Constantinople, where he settled in a Russian monastery. He later returned to his monastery at Vysock, for which he wrote a Rule of life. He died after 1401. Feast 12 September.

Athanasius of Vysock the Younger, hegumenos, born Jaroslavl, died Vysock, 1395. Russian Church. Baptized Amos, and of noble birth, he entered the monastery founded by St **Sergius** at Radonez, and became a disciple of **Athanasius of Vysock the Elder** and went with him to Vysock. When Athanasius the Elder left the monastery, he became hegumenos. Feast 12 September.

Athanasius Sandalaya, metropolitan, died Harran, 11 June 758. Syriac Church. A monk of Qartmin, he became metropolitan of Mayperqat. He was strangled for reasons that are unclear.

Athanasius the Athonite, abbot, born Trebizond, c. 920, died c. 1003. He studied at Constantinople, where he became friends with St Michael Maleinos and the future emperor, Nicephorus Phocas. He was born Abraham but took the name Athanasius when he became a monk at St Michael's monastery at Kymina, Bithynia. Worried that he was going to be appointed as abbot, he fled to Mount Athos in about 958, and lived there as a hermit, hiding his identity. He was sought out by Phocas, who wanted his help to organize an expedition against the Saracens. Athanasius reluctantly gave his assistance, and Phocas gave him part of the money raised to found a monastery on Mount Athos. He died in 1003 when the cupola of a church collapsed on him. Feast 5 July.

Athanasius the Camel Driver, patriarch. Syriac Church. Patriarch of Antioch, 595–630.

Athanasius the Recluse, monk, died Kiev, c. 1176. Russian Church. He lived in the Kievan cave

monasteries, and died there after a long illness. Three days after his death, however, he was found alive, weeping bitterly because he had seen life after death, although he told no one what he had seen. He lived a life of ever greater asceticism, and died 12 years later. Feast 2 December.

Athenogenes, bishop and martyr, died Sebaste, Armenia, c. 305. He was murdered along with ten disciples during the persecution under the emperor Diocletian. Feast 16 July.

Athonites, The Twelve, martyrs, thirteenth century, Byzantine Church. Twelve monks of the Vatopedi monastery on Mount Athos who condemned Patriarch Michael Palaeologus for his Latin Catholic sympathies, and the union with Rome following the Council of Lyons of 1274. They were hanged by imperial decree. Feast 4 January.

Atilano Cruz Alvarado, martyr, born Mexico, 1901, died Cuquio, 1 July 1928. He was ordained in 1927, and had only just arrived to assist **Justino Orona Madrigal** when they were taken and executed during the Mexican persecution. Feast 25 May.

Atom and Companions, martyrs, died Duin, 853. Armenian Church. A number of young Christians were imprisoned by Bugha al-Kabir with the intention of forcing them to convert to Islam, and were eventually executed. Feast 3 March.

Atom, Nerseh, Varaiavor and Manachir, martyrs, died 421. Feast 4 August.

Atqen of Sis, founder, seventh century. Assyrian Church. He had fled north to somewhere near Kirkuk in front of the Islamic invasion. He lived first on Mount Izla near Nisibis, then moved further north to the monastery of Rabban Saliba at Berestek, where he became the superior. After a while he moved on again to what is now the Iraq/Turkish border, where he founded a monastery at Sis.

Atticus of Constantinople, patriarch of Constantinople, born Sebaste, Armenia, died Constantinople, 10 October 425. He testified against

John Chrysostom at the Synod of the Oak in 403, and later persecuted his followers. However, as patriarch from 406, he restored Chrysostom's name to the diptychs in 421. He pained **Augustine of Hippo** with his references to the latter's Manichaean attitude to sex. Feast 11 October.

Attilanus, patron and first bishop of Zamora, died there, 916. A disciple of **Froilan**, and his colleague in the organization of monastic life in northern Spain, he became bishop of Zamora in 900. Feast 5 October.

Atto (Atho), bishop, born Bajadoz, Spain, died Pistoia, Italy, 1153. He was a Benedictine at Vallumbrosa monastery, near Fiesole, who became abbot-general of the order and bishop of Pistoia, near Florence. He wrote books on **John Gualbert** and **Bernard of Parma** and on Santiago de Compostela. Feast 22 May.

Auberon, see **Adalbero of Metz II**.

Aubert of Avranches, bishop, died Avranches, 725. According to tradition, Aubert was told in a dream to build a church on the site of what became Mont St Michel, dedicated to St Michael the Archangel. The church was duly erected and dedicated in 709, and entrusted to a chapter of canons. Feast 10 September.

Aubert of Cambrai, bishop, born Cambrai, died there, *c.* 669. He became bishop of Cambrai *c.* 633. Feast 13 December.

Auctor of Metz, flourished *c.* 451, a contemporary of Attila the Hun who ravaged the region at that time. Feast 10 August.

Audas, see **Abdas**.

Audomarus, see **Omer of Thérouanne**.

Augustina Pietrantoni, bl., martyr, born Pozzaglia Sabina, near Rieti, 27 March 1864, died Rome, 13 November 1894. Baptized Livia, and from a peasant family, she took the name Augustina when she joined the Sisters of Charity. She worked in Rome with tubercular patients, and contracted the disease. She was, however, killed by one of the patients she had cared for, who had been put out of the hospital because of his violent behaviour, and who blamed Sister Augustina for this. He stabbed her to death.

Augustine (Aurelius Augustinus), bishop of Hippo Regius, born Tagaste (Souk-Ahras, Algeria), 13 November 354, died Hippo, 28 August 430. His first years, up to his conversion (354–6), are recounted at length in his *Confessions*, with the added charm of personal disclosure; the *Retractiones* (426–7), at the end of his life, constitutes an exacting examination of conscience by a writer, in which he seeks to correct what was erroneous, and to make clear what was doubtful in his literary activity. His other writings, especially his sermons and letters (more than 200 have survived), are filled with traits of his character and biographical details. Finally, one of his disciples, Possidius of Calama, wrote, shortly after his death, an account of his life that is rich in information and of great historical value. Professor of rhetoric (Carthage, Rome, Milan), Augustine adhered to Manichaeism (373–83), but converted to Christianity after discovering Neo-Platonic philosophy, and responding to the influence of his mother (**Monica**), and of **Ambrose of Milan** (386). Returning to Africa in 388, he lived a monastic life, was ordained priest at Hippo in 391, and acclaimed bishop there in 395. A dedicated and effective pastor, he engaged fully in the affairs of his diocese. Abroad he became one of the principal personalities of the Christian West, affirming his doctrine in the face of heresies: against the Donatists he proclaimed the universal vocation of the Church; against the Pelagians he affirmed, at the same time, the inability of man to merit his salvation and the powerful effect of grace; against the Manichaeans, finally, he argued that absolute evil and absolute good constitute an error. The good and the evil are bound, at the level of action, in the manner of obscurity and light. However, the evil is subordinate to the good, which alone proceeds from the divine power; evil is thus efficient only by the good that it harbours. Against their pessimism, he affirms the goodness of creation, the work of God. Among Augustine's other principal works are: the *Soliloquies* (386–7), written when he was at Cassisiacum at the time of his conversion, on the significance of evil in the world; *De magistro* (389), in which, as in other treatises, is apparent the influence of the Neo-Platonic thought. *De doctrina christiana* (396–426) and *Enchiridion* (421), two summaries of Catholic doctrine; *De Trinitate* (399–422), a systematic treatise, unlike most of his dogmatic writings, not provoked by any special controversial emergency; *The City of God* (413–24), the occasion for which was the sack of Rome in 410, by Alaric, written as a reply to the pagans who attributed the catastrophe to the anger of the old gods against Christianity. The influence of St Augustine has dominated Western theology, and he continues also to occupy an important place in the history of philosophy, notably in the theory of knowledge.

Augustine, see also **Flavius**.

Augustine Kazotoic, bl., bishop, born Trogir, Dalmatia, *c.* 1260, died Lucera, Apulia, 3 August 1323. He entered the Order of Preachers and studied at the University of Paris. On returning to Dalmatia he founded several convents, and undertook missions in Italy, Bosnia and Hungary. Benedict XI consecrated him bishop of Zagreb in 1303; he restored discipline in the diocese and fostered learning, particularly in biblical studies. Miladin, governor of Dalmatia, whose tyranny he opposed, persecuted him until John XXII transferred him to the see of Lucera in Apulia, where he died in a convent he had founded. Feast 8 August.

Augustine Novellus, bl., jurist, born Tarano, Sabina, date unknown, died near Siena, 19 May 1309. He studied law at Bologna, became chancellor to King Manfred of Sicily, and entered the Augustinians, where his reputation as a jurist preceded him. Confessor to Nicholas IV, he went to Siena as papal legate under Boniface VIII. He helped to revise the constitutions of the order and became prior general in 1298. He resigned in 1300 and retired to Siena.

Augustine of Biella, bl., born Biella, Piedmont, 1430, died Venice, 22 July 1493. He joined the Dominicans, and although he suffered from long-term illness, accepted his pain with patience. He was prior of several friaries and became known as a preacher and confessor, as well as for working miracles. To escape this fame he retired to the friary in Venice in about 1483, and lived there for the rest of his life. His body was found to be incorrupt when his tomb was opened three years after his death.

Augustine of Canterbury, apostle of England and first archbishop of Canterbury, died 26 May *c.* 604. **Gregory I (the Great)**, consecrated him bishop, and in 596 sent him from Rome, with 30 monks, to evangelize the Anglo-Saxons. He landed at Ebbsfleet in 597, where the king, Ethelbert of Kent, married to a Christian, Bertha, allowed the monks to preach, giving them an old house in Canterbury. His preaching converted many, including the king, and he established his cathedral seat, with a monastic chapter, at Canterbury – contrary to Gregory's wish that it be at London, with another at York – and consecrated bishops for London and Rochester. His attempts at co-operation with Christian Britons and Celtic bishops in the west of Britain failed, because of their attachment to their own traditions and customs, such as their own date, not the Roman, for the observance of Easter.

Augustine of Lucera, bl., bishop, born Trogir, Dalmatia, *c.* 1260, died Lucera, Italy, 3 August 1322. His family name was Gazotich. He became a Dominican and went to study in Paris before returning to Bosnia and to Italy to preach. While working in Hungary he met the future Pope Benedict XI, who appointed him bishop of Zagreb. He worked there for 14 years, reforming the diocese and the clergy, despite the opposition of the governor of Dalmatia. He was then sent as bishop to Lucera, where he worked for five years also to achieve reform in his diocese.

Augustine Ota, bl., martyr, born island of Hirado-Jima, died Iki, Japan, 1622. A catechist, he entered the Society of Jesus while in prison. He was beheaded. Feast 10 August.

Augustine Pak, martyred Korea, 1840. He is commemorated with **Peter Hong**, Agatha Kouen, **Agatha Ni** and **Magdalen Son** – see **Martyrs of Korea**. Feast 31 January.

Augustine Schöfer (Scoeffler), born Mittelbronn, Moselle, France, 22 November 1822, martyred Ha Tây, Vietnam, 1 May 1851, beatified 1900, canonized 1988. A priest of the Paris Foreign Missions

Society, he had arrived in Tonkin in 1848 – see **Martyrs of Vietnam**.

Augustine Thevarparampil, bl., born Ramapuram, Kerala, 1 April 1891, died there, 16 October 1973. He was ordained priest in 1921, and two years later went as assistant priest to Kadanad, but ill-health forced him to return to his native village in 1926. During his convalescence, he became aware of the miserable living conditions of the 'untouchables', the Dalits, those belonging to the lowest caste of Indian society. He rose at four each morning, then went with a catechist to the families in the surrounding villages. He was very short, and was known as Kunjchan, 'little priest'. He baptized almost 6,000 people during his ministry. Although he wanted a simple funeral, in derelict ground, his parishioners insisted that he be buried within the village church, and his tomb has become a centre of pilgrimage.

Augustine Yi and Companions, martyrs, died Korea, 1839. He is one of a group of martyrs that includes **Agatha Kim** – see **Martyrs of Korea**. Feast 24 May.

Augusto Andres Fernández, martyr, born Santander, 6 May 1910, died Turon, Asturias, 9 October 1934. Baptized Román Martín, entered the de la Salle Brothers on 3 February 1926. He had arrived in Turon a year or so before his death, after his previous school had been closed by anti-religious forces. He was arrested with the other **Martyrs of Asturias** by a group of rebel soldiers, and executed by firing squad.

Aunarius of Auxerre (Aunacharius), bishop of Auxerre, born Orleans, died Auxerre, 25 September 601. He spent his youth at the royal court of Burgundy, became a priest, and a bishop in 561, participating in councils at Paris (573) and Macon (583, 585). He is famous for the 45 canons issuing from a diocesan synod *c.* 588, some of which discuss marriage and superstitions, and shed interesting light on the mode of living, when pagan abuse of Christian practices still persisted. He arranged for a transcription (592) of the martyrology attributed to St Jerome, from which all extant copies are derived. He provided vitae of his two distinguished predecessors, St Amator and St Germain, and organized liturgical prayer in the diocese. His relics, transferred to the crypt of the abbatial church of St Germain, were seized by the Calvinists in 1567, but retrieved, and are recognized as authentic.

Aunemund of Lyon, bishop, died Macon, 28 September 658. Brought up at the court of Dagobert I and Clovis II, he became bishop of Lyon. **Bede** recounts in his *Ecclesiastical History* that in 653 **Benedict Biscop** and **Wilfrid** were hospitably received at Lyon by Aunemund, who is called Dalfinus in Bede's narrative, during their journey to Rome; very impressed by Wilfrid, he offered him 'the government of a large part of France', and his niece as wife. Wilfrid declined, however, and continued to Rome, but returned to Lyon, and stayed three years, received the tonsure from Aunemund, and was present when Queen Bathildis sent soldiers and 'commanded that the bishop be put to death'. However, most scholars say that Aunemund was murdered by Ebroin, mayor of the palace of Neustria.

Auraeus, bishop and martyr, died Mainz, fifth century. He was bishop of Mainz. Rabanus Maurus, and the oldest sources, place his martyrdom, and that of his sister **Justina**, in the time of Attila, *c.* 451. More recent research suggests martyrdom by the vandals in 406, when they destroyed Mainz. Feast 16 June.

Aurea, martyr, died Ostia, *c.* 270. She is said to have been thrown into the sea to drown. Feast 24 August.

Aurea of Córdoba, martyr, born Córdoba, *c.* 810, died there, 19 July 856. An Arab of noble descent, her father had been a Muslim and after the martyrdom of her brothers, Adolphe and John, in 825, she went for 30 years to live in the monastery of Cuteclara with her mother. When her relatives from Seville denounced her to the cadi, also a relative, she abandoned Christianity, but immediately returned to the faith. Denounced a second time, she remained constant and suffered death by decree of the emir. Her body was thrown into the Guadalquivir and never recovered.

Aurelian of Arles, archbishop, died Lyon, 16 June 551. Elected bishop of Arles to succeed Auxanius, and named papal vicar for Gaul by Pope Vigilius in 546, he founded a monastery and a convent for women, the Rule for the men being a modified form of that of **Benedict**, and that for the nuns of St Mary of Arles modelled on the monks. He exchanged letters with Vigilius regarding the 'Three Chapters', a matter that caused concern in the West, since by agreeing with Emperor Justinian I that three bishops should be condemned by papal approval, the authority of the Council of Chalcedon might be weakened. Vigilius was not disposed to agree with the emperor and replied to him in noncommittal terms in 558. Aurelian is interred in the basilica of the Holy Apostles (Saint-Nizier), where his epitaph was discovered in 1308.

Aurelius and Natalia, martyrs, died 27 July 852. They were husband and wife and lived in Spain during the Moorish occupation and persecution of Christians. Natalia had been born Sabigotho, and changed her name when she converted and was baptized. They had two children, and partly for their sake kept their faith a secret until Aurelius saw a man being publicly beaten for being a Christian. They put their children into the care of the widow of a martyred Christian and began to visit Christian prisoners and publicly declare their faith. They were arrested along with a number of other Christians who were attending mass in Aurelius's house, and condemned to death.

Aurelius and Sabigotona, martyrs, born Córdoba, *c.* 820; died there, 27 July 852. Of a noble Muslim father and a Christian mother, Aurelius was brought up by a Christian aunt. He married Sabigotona, also a Christian, and they lived secretly as such, but, inspired by the courage of the Christians they saw suffering under Moorish persecution, they let their faith be known publicly. With another couple, Felix and Liliose, and a monk named George from Jerusalem, they were beheaded, on orders from the cadi.

Aurelius of Armenia, bishop in Armenia, died Milan, 475. Nothing is known of his early life, but a ninth-century account, now lost, stated that he brought from Cappadocia to Milan the relics of St Dionysius, bishop in 335, who had died in exile. Feast 9 November.

Aurelius of Carthage, died Carthage, 430. Bishop of Carthage from 391 and a close friend of **Augustine** who praised him for the measures he took to advance the cause of Christianity in his city. As leader of the African bishops, he presided over a long series of ecclesiastical councils, mostly at Carthage, the most important being in 411, which condemned Donatism, and in 418, which condemned Pelagius and Celestius. Some of the letters addressed to him by Augustine survive. Feast 20 July.

Ausentius, born Vellas, Epirus, 1690, died Constantinople, 25 January 1720. Byzantine Church. He moved to Constantinople as a young man, and became a Muslim when he joined the navy. However, when accused of abandoning Christianity out of fear, he fled his ship, repented his past actions and sought martyrdom. His confessor, fearing he would not have the strength for martyrdom, advised him to enter a monastery, but instead he went back to work, giving away his money to the poor. He was arrested, charged with abandoning Islam, and decapitated.

Ausentius of Cyprus, born Germany, died Carpaso, Cyprus. Church of Cyprus. A soldier, he came to Cyprus with 300 soldiers of his command. After landing they all went their separate ways, but Ausentius lived in a cave at Iuzio, where he practised a strict asceticism and became famous for his powers of healing. (There are a number of saints with the same name and similar stories.)

Ausentius of Vologda and **Onuphrius of Vologda**, hermits, died sixteenth century. Russian Church. Founded a hermitage near Vologda. Feast 12 June.

Ausilius, martyr, died *c.* 483. Feast 26 January.

Ausonius, bishop, third century. He is traditionally seen as a disciple of **Martial** of Limoges and the first bishop of Angoulême. Feast 22 May.

Auspicius, bishop of Apt, Provence, third century (?). Feast 2 August.

Austreberta, abbess, born Therousanne, *c.* 635, died Abbey of Pavilly, 10 February 704. Her father was apparently a member of the Merovingian royal family, her mother of German royal blood, and later honoured as a saint at the Abbey of Sainte Austreberta at Montreuil-sur-Mer. Betrothed while still a young girl, she instead took the veil in 655, and entered the Abbey of Port-le-Grand, Ponthieu, where for 14 years she was prioress, and then abbess of the newly founded Pavilly *c.* 670. Her rule combined those of **Benedict** and **Columban**.

Austregisilus, abbot and bishop, born Bourges, 29 November 551, died 20 May 624. Of noble parents, he lived at the court of King Guntram from about the age of 24, until he became a priest, then abbot of St Nicetius and bishop of Bourges in 612. He attended a synod at Paris in 614, and his name appears eighth in the list of 79 bishops who signed the decrees. He is reported to have granted a hermitage at Bourges to **Amand**, the apostle of Belgium.

Austremonius, bishop, born Rome (?), died in the Auvergne, France, fourth century (?). A missionary bishop, claimed to have been the first bishop of Clermont.

Auxibius of Soli, bishop, Cyprus, probably after the sixth century. It was formerly claimed he lived in the first century, was baptized by **Mark** and ordained by **Paul** as first bishop of Soli. Feast 17 February.

Aventinus, bishop, died Chartres, *c.* 520. He was bishop of Chartres, succeeding his brother **Solemnis** to this see. Feast 4 February.

Aventinus of Troyes, born central France, died *c.* 538. He was almoner to **Lupus**, bishop of Troyes, then a hermit, living in a place now called Saint-Aventin. Feast 4 February.

Avertanus, born Limoges, died Lucca, Tuscany, *c.* 1386. He was a Carmelite lay brother who died on his way to Palestine as a pilgrim. Feast 25 February.

Avitus, abbot, born Auvergne, mid-fifth century, died Chateaudun, 17 June *c.* 530. He left the abbey of Menat to live as a hermit at the abbey of Micy in the Loire. When Abbot Maximus died in 520, the monks made him their abbot. **Gregory of Tours** relates that Avitus pleaded unsuccessfully with King Clodinus to spare the lives of Sigismund of Burgundy and his family, who had been captured in war.

Avitus of Vienne, bishop, born in the Auvergne, *c.* 450, died Vienne, *c.* 519. Alcinus Ecdidius Avitus succeeded his father **Hesychius** as bishop of Vienne, from *c.* 490. Of a Roman senatorial family, he became leader of the Gallo-Roman episcopate, and exercised enduring influence on the ecclesiastical life of Burgundy. A strong advocate of closer union of Gaul with Rome, and an ardent defender of the primacy of Rome. Praised by his contemporaries for his charity and literary achievement, Clovis, then still a pagan, was greatly impressed by his reputation for learning. He converted the Arian Burgundian prince, Sigismund, to the Catholic faith. Of his many works some 90 letters, as well as homilies and poems, survive. Feast 5 February.

Avvakum, martyr, born Zakudem, near Niznij Novgorod, 1620, died Pustozersk, 1682. Church of the Old Believers. His father was a drunkard, but his mother was devout, and entered a convent. When 17 he married a local girl aged 14. He was ordained deacon when he was 21 and in 1644 he became a priest, serving the village of Lopatisci. He was renowned for his religious zeal and his conformity to the Church's canons. For his radical preaching and views, he was driven from his village and went to Moscow, but later returned to his parish only to be driven out again in 1648. In 1652 he was named archpriest of the city of Jur'evec, but was driven out after two months because of the liturgical changes he attempted to impose, and went back to Msocow. He was a severe critic of the liturgical innovations introduced by Patriarch Nikon, and was arrested, imprisoned, then exiled with his family to Tobolsk in Siberia. In 1661 he was allowed to return to Moscow, but continued his opposition to the changes and condemned the council of 1666 which approved the new rites. In 1667 he was imprisoned at Pustozersk, although he was still able to direct the Church of the Old

Believers from the jail. He was executed on Good Friday. He was canonized in 1916. Feast 14 April.

Awag, martyr, born Bales, near Lake Van, died 1390. Armenian Church. As a young man he was apprenticed to a Persian in Salmast, southern Iran. When he returned to Bales 30 years later he was accused of abandoning Islam, and executed.

Awgen, born island of Kom al-Qulzum, near Suez, died Nisibis, fourth century. Assyrian Church. A pearl fisher for 25 years, but won great renown for the ability to foretell the weather. He joined the monastery of St **Pachomius**, where his reputation as a miracle worker grew, and he gained many disciples. He went with his disciples to Nisibis, living for 30 years on Mount Izla. He is known as the 'father of monasticism in the East' because his 70 (or 28) disciples spread throughout the East founding monasteries. Feast 12 October.

Aymard, bl., abbot, died Cluny, 5 October 965. He succeeded Odo in 942, whose work in the Cluniac Reform he continued. In 948 Pope Agapitus confirmed the direct dependence of Cluny and its dependencies on the apostolic see. Aymard resigned his office in 948 because of blindness, having provided for the election of Majolus as fourth abbot. In 1063 **Peter Damian** collected the oral testimony of Aymard's patience, simplicity and humility.

Azalia the Faster, monk. Russian Church. A monk of the Laura of the Kievan Cave monasteries.

Aziza, monk, died 394. Syriac Church. Son of a pagan Egyptian, he became one of the disciples of **Awgen**. From Mount Izla he went to Hims, then to Jerusalem with two disciples. He went back to Gazarta (Cizre, on the Tigris), where he established a monastery on Mount Dorak.

Azizail, martyr, born Samosata (?), died Rome, 304. Syriac Church. Of a distinguished family, he was taken to Rome when he was 14. Under the Emperor Maximianus he was offered a life of luxury should he deny his faith, but he refused to do so. He was executed on the via Aurelia. Feast 12 May.

B

Babi, catholicos, born Tella, north of Seleucia-Ctesiphon, died 484. Assyrian Church. A convert probably from Zoroastrianism under the influence of monks, he became a monk himself, and was elected catholicos in 457. He clashed with Barsauma, bishop of Nisibis, over the latter's propagation of Nestorianism, and was imprisoned for two years. He attempted to impose a stricter morality on Christians, and in this was also opposed by Barsauma. After writing a letter to the Byzantine Emperor Zeno, seeking his protection for the Church, he was accused of treason and executed.

Babnu, martyr, died 15 January. Coptic Church. Nothing else is known of him.

Babylas and Companions, martyrs, died Antioch, *c.* 250. Babylas was bishop of Antioch. He refused an emperor (possibly Philip the Arab, who may have been a Christian) entrance to his cathedral. He was executed with three young men – perhaps his sons – during the persecution of Decius. Feast 24 January.

Bacchus, see **Sergius and Bacchus**.

Bachtiesus, martyr, died Persia, fourth century, with Isaac and Symeon. Feast 15 May.

Baggeu of Manana Hayq, monk, thirteenth century. Coptic Church. A brigand who was persuaded to become a monk, which he did at Dabra Hayq, where he chained himself into his cell and spent the rest of his life in fasting, prayer and penance. Feast 5 January.

Bahaila Maryam, martyr. Ethiopian Church. A monk of Dabra Metmaq, whose martyrdom is commemorated on 29 January, although nothing else is known of him.

Bakimos of Sarabi, monk, fourteenth century. Ethiopian Church. A disciple of **Eustace** and his successor as abbot of Dabra Sarabi, he was exiled with some other monks to the Holy Land *c.* 1338. He later went on to Cyprus and then to Armenia, eventually settling in Anatolia, but returned to Egypt on the death of Eustace *c.* 1352.

Baldomerus, died in or near Lyon, France, *c.* 660. Apparently a devout and charitable locksmith, he was invited to live at the monastery of Saint-Just and was ordained subdeacon. He was sometimes venerated as patron saint of locksmiths. Feast 27 February.

Balthasar Ravaschieri, Franciscan, born Chiaveri, 1419, died Briasco, 17 October 1492. Of a noble family, Ravaschieri's aunts, both Franciscan tertiaries, provided a sense of piety and morality in his life after his father's death. He entered a friary of Franciscan observants, and in 1478 met Bernardine of Feltre, whose friend and associate he became, until afflicted with a crippling case of gout, which he saw as a means of drawing closer to God, but continued to preach and hear confessions. A cult, begun at his death, was confirmed in 1930, for the Franciscans, Pavia and Genoa. Feast 25 October.

Banadlewos, monk, born Tigre, 1303, died Mareb, 18 April 1400. Ethiopian Church. He was of a noble family. He married, but with the consent of his wife Orni he became a monk at Dabra Mahago, soon afterwards retreating to the hermitage of Baraka. He was attacked there by robbers and left for dead, but revived and moved near to Mareb where he started an orchard and built a church, getting permission from the patriarch to celebrate mass with only two priests instead of the customary five.

Bandaricus, bishop, died Soissons, 566. Bishop of Soissons from 540. He also founded the abbey of Crépin. He was banished for seven years by the king, and tradition has it that he worked as a gardener in an abbey in Britain. Feast 9 August.

Baptist of Mantua, bl., Carmelite and poet, born Mantua, 17 April 1447, died there, 22 March 1516. Baptized John Baptist Spagnuolo, his father was a Spanish nobleman at the court of Mantua. He studied at Pavia and, having fallen out with his father, went to Venice and Ferrara, where he joined the Carmelites. He taught philosophy and divinity at Bologna before becoming reconciled with his father, when he became tutor to the duke of Mantua's children. A distinguished, prolific Renaissance poet, much of his work was inspired by the duke's family, but he was criticized for drawing too much on pagan mythology. In 1513 he was made general of the Carmelite order. Beatified in 1890. Feast 23 March.

Baptista Varani, bl., born Camerino, Macerato, Italy, 9 April 1458, died there, 31 May 1524. Baptized Camilla Varani, she was the daughter of the commander of the papal army. She received the education proper to her status, but instead of marriage, she decided to become a Poor Clare. Her family was opposed, but eventually reluctantly granted her wish and she became a nun in Urbino, although her father then founded a convent for her in her home town. At the request of Pope Julius II she established a Poor Clare convent at Fermo, but returned to Camerino as superior until her death.

Barachisius, see **Jonas**.

Barbara, tradition places her in the third century, the beautiful daughter of a pagan, Dioscorus. Her father kept her in a tower to discourage suitors. Before he went on a journey, her father had a bath house erected for her. She had three windows inserted in it to symbolize the Trinity, and on his return told her father she was a Christian. He took her before the prefect of the province, Martinianus. She was tortured and condemned to be beheaded at the hand of her father. On his way home following the execution, her father was struck dead by lightning. Various accounts are set in Egypt, Rome, Tuscany and elsewhere. The place of martyrdom is attributed to Heliopolis in Egypt or Nicodemia. Because of the circumstances of her father's death, Barbara was regarded as the patron saint of those beset by thunder or fire, and later of soldiers in the artillery and of miners. She is also regarded as the advocate for ensuring believers are able to receive the sacraments of penance and holy communion at death. Her feast day, originally 4 December, was suppressed in 1969.

Barbara Jakovleva, born *c.* 1883, died Alapaevsk, 19 July 1918. Russian Church. A disciple of (Princess) **Elizabeth Fedorovna**, she joined her monastery of Martha and Mary, founded in Moscow in 1910. The nuns ran a school for girls, fed the poor and opened a free clinic, in all of which Barbara was closely involved. She was close to her superior, whom she regularly accompanied on pilgrimage to the shrines of Russia. Early in 1918 the two nuns were arrested, but Barbara was freed while Elizabeth was sent to a prison at Alapaevsk, near Ekaterinburg. Fearing that Elizabeth would be put to death, Barbara determined to share her fate and made her way to Alapaevsk, where she too was confined, in her case in a school. While she was there she helped Elizabeth and other members of the imperial family who were with her. On 18 July 1918, however, she and other prisoners, including Elizabeth Fedorovna, were taken outside the city and thrown into a well. Many of the prisoners died in the fall, but Barbara and the princess fell on a ledge, and survived. They spent the night singing hymns and praying, but the following day the soldiers returned and threw grenades down the well. Their bodies were eventually recovered, and their remains reburied in Jerusalem in December 1920. Barbara was declared blessed by the Russian Church on 1 November 1981, and canonized in 1992. Feast 18 July.

Barbara Kim, martyr, died Korea, 1839. She is commemorated with **Barbara Yi**, **Teresa Yi**, **Martha Kim** and **Lucy Kim** – see **Martyrs of Korea**. Feast 27 May.

Barbara Yi, see **Barbara Kim**, see also **Martyrs of Korea**.

Barbasymas (Barbascemin), bishop, martyred Persia, 346, with 16 companions. He was bishop of Seleucia-Ctesiphon. The group was imprisoned under Shapur II, and all were tortured and killed after 11 months. Feast 9 January.

Barbatus, bishop, patron of Benevento, born Cerreto Sannita, Italy, early seventh century, died Benevento, Italy, 19 February 682. A relative unknown until his succession to Hildebrand as bishop of Benevento in 663. He attended the sixth general council, Constantinople III, but died not long after his return.

Barbea, see **Bebais**.

Bardo of Oppershofen, archbishop, born Oppershofen, Germany, 980, died Dornloh, 10 June 1051. In his youth he studied at the monastery of Fulda, where later he became a monk and director of the monastic school. He became abbot of Werden in 1029 and in 1031 of the monastery of Hersfield. In the same year he was consecrated as archbishop of Mainz and worked on the construction of the cathedral, consecrated in 1036 in the presence of Emperor Conrad II.

Bar'Eta, founder, born Rusafa, on the Euphrates, died Marga, 612. Assyrian Church. He spent 23 years in a monastery on Mount Izla as a disciple of **Abraham of Kaskar**, who finally sent him out to preach around Nineveh with nine other monks. In 562 he founded another monastery in Marga, and the following year one nearby for women, where his sister lived.

Barhadbsabba of Qartmin, monk, fifth century. Syriac Church. A disciple of **Samuel**. Feast 8 March.

Barlaam, martyr, died Antioch, fourth century (?). Apparently a man of little or no learning, and mocked for his lack of it by the judge who condemned him to death for refusing to sacrifice to idols. Feast 19 November.

Barlaam of Khutyn, abbot, born Novgorod, died Khutyn, 6 November 1193. Baptized Alexis, he gave away his substantial wealth to the poor, and went to live at Khutyn on the Volga river. A monastic community gathered around him.

Barlaam of Raifskaia Pustyn, martyr, born Porpurovcy, 1870, died near Raifskaia Pustyn, 7 April 1930. Russian Church. He was ordained, and served in the diocese of Kazan before becoming a monk at the monastery of Raifskaia Pustyn in 1912. He then became parish priest nearby. He was arrested in January 1930 along with many others, and was later shot. Feast 14 January.

Barlamio, bishop of Suzdal, died Suzdal, 1585/7. Russian Church. Hegumenos of the monastery of the Trinity at Machrisca from *c.* 1550 to 1570, then bishop of Suzdal, where in 1577 he built the church of the Presentation of the Mother of God in the Temple. He was buried at Machrisca. Feast 19 November.

Barlamio, hegumenos of the Laura of the Kievan Cave monasteries, born Kiev, died Volinia, 1065. Russian Church. Born John, of a leading noble family of Kiev, he became a monk *c.* 1055 against his parents' wishes, and he built the first of the monasteries at the Kievan Caves. He was hegumenos there, and was sent to a nearby monastery in the same capacity. He twice visited the Holy Land and Constantinople, and it was on the way back to the Kievan Caves from Constantinople that he died. Feast 19 November.

Barlamio, monk, born Morezovo, 1774, died Kjachta, 23 January 1846. Russian Church. Born Basilio Nadezin into a peasant family, he married and, being childless, he and his wife adopted an orphan. However, seeking solitude, he abandoned his family and in 1811 came to the Kievan Cave monasteries, where he lived as a pilgrim. He was arrested as a vagabond and sent to Siberia, settling near lake Baikal, where he stayed for seven years. After this he established a hermitage in woods near the river Cikoj, where he lived for five years, binding himself in chains to overcome temptations. Eventually he built a chapel, and cells for other hermits, but he was again arrested. This time he was defended by the people of the nearby town of Kjachta and the police sent him to the archbishop at Irkutsk. To regularize the situation, the archbishop proposed that he become a monk and evangelize the region in which he lived. He was tonsured on 5 October 1833, at which point he changed his name, was ordained priest, and began missionary work among the Tartars and Old Believers in his locality. In 1839 he became hegumenos. He built a school, to which many Old Believers sent their children, and he converted many to Orthodoxy.

Barlamio Kereckij, hieromonk, born near Keret on the White Sea, sixteenth century. Russian Church. He was a village priest in Kola, and, becoming suspicious of his wife's faithfulness, he killed her. He was then filled with remorse – his wife was wholly innocent – and he lived a life of great penance. But thinking that not enough, he put his wife's incorrupt body on a boat and sailed down the river towards the White Sea, praying all the time. He attributed his safety on the journey to God's miraculous intervention, which he took as a sign that he had been pardoned. He then became a monk and lived in solitude near Keret, but he felt it was not solitary enough and moved to the bay of Cupskij, where he died, although his body was brought back to Keret. Feast 6 November.

Barlamio of Sepuchov, monk, died Sepuchov, 1377. Russian Church. Sent by **Alexis of Moscow** to choose a spot for the monastery the metropolitan wished to found, according to tradition he was guided by a dream to the city of Sepuchov, and specifically to a hill beside the rivers Oka and Nara, where there was established the monastery of the Presentation of the Mother of God in the Temple. The first church was built there in 1362. Barlamio became the first superior of the monastery. He was accompanied in his mission by another monk, **Gideon**. Feast 5 May.

Barlamio of Tobolsk, bishop, born Moscow, 1729, died Tobolsk, 27 December 1802. Russian Church. Baptized Petrov, his father was a priest, and he entered the monastery of Alexander Nevski at St Petersburg, although he became archimandrite of the monastery of Ss Boris and Gleb at Novotorzok. He was made bishop of Tobolsk in 1768. He was gentle and humble, lived an ascetic life, and was generous to the poor, the sick and the imprisoned of his diocese. He was made an archbishop in 1792. He opposed Tsar Paul II's transfer of the Order of Malta to Russia. Feast 10 June.

Barlamio of Ulejma of Uglic, monk, born Rostov, fifteenth century. Russian Church. A disciple of **Paisio of Uglic**, he established himself in a cell, with a small chapel dedicated to St Nicholas, on the river Ulejma, near Uglic, in 1460. Feast 23 May.

Barlamio of Vaga and of Senkursk, monk, died 19 June 1467. Russian Church. Vasilij Stepanovic Svoezemcev belonged to a noble family of Novgorod. The family had extensive possessions on the river Vaga, near Archangel, where he attempted to win over the pagans to Christianity, and he engaged in treaty negotiations on behalf of Novgorod with Moscow. After these affairs of state he became a monk, and settled at the confluence of the rivers Vaga and Pinea: it was at this time that he took his new name. He lived the ascetic life for many years and built a number of churches in nearby villages, as well as endowing the monastery he founded. Canonized in 1631.

Barnabas and **Hilarion**, possibly eighth/ninth century. Church of Cyprus.

Barnabas of Gethsemane, monk, born Prudisci, 24 January 1831, died Kiev, 17 February 1906. Russian Church. By birth Vasilij Ilic Merkulov, he came from a peasant family, but trained as a blacksmith. He was very devout, and felt called to the monastic life. In 1851 he entered the Laura of the Kievan Cave monasteries, and went to live in the hermitage of Gethsemane. He took the name Barnabas in 1851, was ordained deacon in 1871 and priest the following year. He was appointed chaplain to the pilgrims who came to Gethsemane, and was in great demand as a confessor. He was credited with the miraculous gift of healing. In 1864 he founded a house for pious women which in 1887 became a monastery. He was canonized in 1995.

Barnabas of Vassa of Kilanion, monk, thirteenth/ fourteenth centuries. Church of Cyprus. According to tradition, Barnabas lived in a cave to the west of Vassa. Feast 11 June.

Barnabas of Vetluga, monk, born Velikij Ustjug, died Mount Krasnaja, 11 June 1445. Russian Church. He was a priest in his native city before becoming a monk in 1417 and establishing his hermitage on Mount Krasnaja, beside the river Vetluga. He lived there in solitude for 28 years, gaining a great reputation for sanctity.

Barnard of Vienne, monk, founder of the monastery at Ambronay, archbishop, born near Lyon, *c.* 778, died Valence, 22 January 842. He was married and a soldier, but gave up both for the spiritual life, becoming a monk in 803 and archbishop of Vienne in 810. He became embroiled in the politics of the time and was forced to flee to Italy because he had sided with Lothair against the latter's victorious father, Louis I the Pious. He was allowed to return to France and founded the Abbey of Saints-Severin-Exupère-et-Félicien, where he spent his last years.

Barontius, monk, birth date and place unknown, died Pistoia, Italy, *c.* 695. Coming from a wealthy family, Barontius distributed his wealth to the poor, although he secretly withheld some of it. With his son he joined the Abbey of Lonray (Berry, France). A series of visions on hell and purgatory during an illness caused him to give away the remainder of his wealth, make a pilgrimage to Peter's tomb in Rome, and become a hermit at Monte Cavo near Pistoia, where he (presumably) died. Feast 25 March.

Barsauma the Naked, hermit, born Cairo, *c.* 1257, died Sahran, 28 August 1317. Coptic Church. Born into a wealthy and influential family. After his parents' death he was brought up by a maternal uncle, but abandoned his wealth to live outside the city dressed only in a coarse cloak. After five years of this, he moved to a cave near a church in Old Cairo (having first tamed the snake that had made its home there). After another 20 years he moved for a further 15 years to the church itself. During the persecution of Christians which broke out in 1301, he continued to wear a white turban,

although Christians were obliged to wear blue. He was imprisoned, but only for a week. On his release, still wearing white, he went to the monastery of Sahran, south of Cairo, where he stayed for the remainder of his life, although he never became a monk.

Barsimaeus, bishop, possibly third century. He was a bishop of Edessa, Syria, who converted many people. He was thought to have been martyred under Trajan, but this is now rejected. Feast 30 January.

Barsonuphia, nun, first half of the sixteenth century. Russian Church. Barbara Kolycova was the mother of **Philip**, metropolitan of Moscow. Late in life she became a nun of strict observance, taking the name Barsonuphia.

Barsonuphius, hermit, born Egypt, died Palestine, *c.* 550. He was renowned for his holiness and wisdom, writing his advice to avoid contact with outsiders. About 850 letters from him and a neighbouring hermit, John the Prophet, survive. These were influential then, and now clarify the spirituality of that time. Feast 11 April.

Barsonuphius, martyr, born St Petersburg, died Char'kov, 18 January 1938. Ukrainian Church, Moscow Patriarchate. Baptized Valentine Michailovic Mamcic, he became a monk of the monastery of Tolga, but later moved to Char'kov, in the Ukraine. When his monastery was closed after the Russian Revolution, he continued to work in various parishes in Char'kov until he was arrested and shot. Feast 19 May.

Barsonuphius of Optina, monk, born 5 July 1845, died 1 April 1913. Russian Church. Pavel Invanovic Plichankov came from a wealthy family, studied at a military academy and was promoted to the rank of colonel. He decided, however, to enter a monastery and entered Optina in 1892, taking the name of Barsonuphius in 1900. He was ordained deacon in 1902 and priest the following year. In 1904 he was sent to China as a chaplain to the forces, returning the following year and becoming hegumenos in 1907. He had a reputation as a confessor, as a mystic and as a miracle worker. He went to see the dying Tolstoy, but the writer's relatives and friends would not allow Barsonuphius to see him. Barsonuphius had opponents in the monastery, and the bishops set up an enquiry into its running in 1911–12, at the end of which he was moved away, to the monastery of the Theophany of Stao-Golutvin as its superior, with the rank of archimandrite. Although he deeply regretted the move, he nonetheless dedicated himself to the reform of his new monastery. He was, however, buried at Optina.

Barsonuphius of Tver, bishop, born Serpuchov, 1495, died Kazan, 11 April 1576. Russian Church. He was the son of a priest, and was originally named Vasilij, or possibly John. In 1512 he was taken prisoner by the Crimean Tartars, but spent the time in prison in prayer and in the study of Islam, with the intention of eventually becoming a missionary. He returned home in 1515 and entered the monastery of the Saviour of St Andronicus at Moscow, although he immediately became ierodeacon to the bishop of Tver. In 1544 he became superior of the monastery of St Nicholas at Pesna. After Ivan IV's conquest of Kazan, Barsonuphius was sent there as the archimandrite of the first monastery to be founded in that city, that of the Transfiguration, and he engaged in missionary work among both the Muslims and the pagans of the region. He was made bishop of Tver in 1567. In 1571, however, he returned to his monastery, where he died.

Barsonuphius of Tver II, and **Saba**, monks, fifteenth century. Russian Church. They founded the monastery of the Presentation of the Lord in the Temple at Tver in 1397. The first had a considerable knowledge of Scripture, the second was renowned for his works of charity, especially among the sick – he died in 1467. Feasts 2 March.

Bartholomew 'Aiutami-Cristo', bl., born Pisa, died there, 1224. He became a Camaldolese lay brother at San Frediano monastery in Pisa and was given his surname, meaning 'Christ help me', because he always prayed this invocation. Feast 28 January.

Bartholomew Diez Laurel, bl., Franciscan martyr, born Puerto de Santa Maria, Spain, died Nagasaki, Japan, 17 August 1627. His real name was Diaz Laruel. He was a sailor, and while living in Acapulco, Mexico, he requested permission to enter the Franciscan Order. He took the habit of a lay brother on 13 May 1615 in Valladolid (Morelia), Mexico, but he did not persevere. He again took the habit on 17 October 1616 in the same convent, where this time he was professed – on 18 October 1617 – as a lay brother. At the end of 1618 he was in the convent of San Francisco del Monte in Manila. There he learned and practised medicine in a hospital. In 1623 he went to work as a missionary in Japan, where he disguised himself as a physician. At Pentecost in 1627 he was imprisoned in Nagasaki, and in August of the same year he was martyred.

Bartholomew Ferrari, ven., co-founder of the Barnabites, born Milan, 1499, died there, 25 November 1544. He founded this order with a friend, **Anthony Zaccaria**, with a mission to defend the Catholic faith against heresy and to work for moral reform. Helped by his brother, who worked at the papal court, he was able to obtain approval for his project from Pope **Clement VII** in 1533, with the bull *Vota per quae vos*. Ordained around 1532, he became general of his order in 1542. He was declared venerable by Pope **Urban VIII** in 1634.

Bartholomew Gutiérrez, bl., Augustinian missionary and martyr, born Mexico City, *c.* 1580, burned alive, Nagasaki, Japan, 3 September 1632. He became an Augustinian friar in 1596, was ordained, and went to the Philippines in 1606 before going to Japan in 1612 and becoming prior of Ukusi. Temporarily exiled 1614–18, he was seized in 1639, imprisoned for three years and tortured before being put to death along with six fellow victims. He was beatified in 1867. Feast 28 September.

Bartholomew, John and Ignatius of Simonov, monks, fourteenth/fifteenth centuries. Russian Church. All three were members of the monastery of Simonov in Moscow, renowned for their undeviating observance of the monastic rule. Bartholomew was superior, John the monastic treasurer, and Ignatius an icon painter.

Bartholomew Longo, bl., founder, born Latiano, 10 February 1841, died 5 October 1926. He studied law in Naples, and was reconverted to Christianity under Dominican influence, becoming a Dominican tertiary. He returned to Latiano and practised law for a time, but then decided to live as a celibate, and to give up his work as a solicitor. He became tutor to children of the Countess Maria Anna de Fusco, and lived in her house. This caused much gossip, so, on the advice of the pope, they decided to marry, while still living celibate lives. Bartholomew spread devotion to Mary and to the rosary on the countess's estates around Pompeii, and eventually founded a shrine which opened in 1887. He founded a congregation called the Daughters of the Rosary of Pompeii to run an orphanage. He also worked with criminals, and set up a school for the children of criminals. He ran the shrine to Our Lady of Pompeii until 1906, when he retired through ill-health.

Bartholomew of Braga, ven., Dominican archbishop and theologian, born Lisbon, 3 May 1514, died Viana, 16 July 1590. In 1528 he became a Dominican and taught philosophy and theology for 20 years. In 1558 he became archbishop of Braga, despite his doubts. In the Council of Trent sessions from 1562 to 1563 Bartholomew was very influential in the discussions about reform. During his time as archbishop of Braga he began a seminary in his palace, visited and preached in his 1,300 parishes, instituted chairs of moral theology in Braga and Viana do Castelo and created a catechism. Amongst his works are *Stimulus pastorum* (1565) and *Compendium spiritualis doctrinae* (1582). He resigned in 1582.

Bartholomew of Cervere, bl., born Savigliano, Piedmont, martyred 1466. A Dominican at Savigliano priory, he became an inquisitor after his brilliant theological studies in Turin. He was murdered on his way to take up his post in Cervere and is said to have foretold his death. Feast 21 April.

Bartholomew of Farne, hermit, born Whitby, died Inner Farne, 1193. He was originally called Tostig, but changed his name to William, and then to Bartholomew on becoming a monk at Durham. Before that he had travelled in Norway – perhaps becuase his family was of Scandinavian origin (hence his name). He was ordained priest at what

is now Trondheim, and was then under pressure to marry, but instead returned to England to become a monk. He finally became a monk on the island of Inner Farne, where he was joined by the prior of the community at Durham, with whom he did not at first get along. He was buried on the island. Feast 24 June.

Bartholomew of Grottaferrata, abbot, born Rossano, Calabria, Italy, *c.* 980, died Grottaferrata, *c.* 1050. Aged 12, he became a companion of St **Nilus**, and was with him when he decided to found a Greek-rite monastery at Grottaferrata. Little is known of Bartholomew, who went on to become abbot, except that he completed the building of the abbey, and that he fostered scholarship among the monks. Feast 11 November.

Bartholomew of Grottaferrata, abbot, died Grottaferrata, Calabria, 1130. Feast 19 August.

Bartholomew of Mantua, bl., born Mantua, 1443, died there, 5 December 1495. He joined the Carmelites in his native city, became a priest and won renown as a preacher and a healer.

Bartholomew of Marmoutier, Benedictine abbot, died Marmoutier, near Tours, 24 February 1084. He was abbot of the monastery at Marmoutier from 1063 and resisted Geoffrey the Bearded's attempts to claim dominion over it. The monks under Bartholomew's rule were so well disciplined they were highly sought after to reform old monasteries and found new ones. Even William the Conqueror asked for (and received) Bartholomew's monks when he founded the Battle Abbey near Hastings to give thanks for his victory. Bartholomew has never had an official cult.

Bartholomew of Monte, bl., founder, born Bologna, 3 November 1726, died there, 24 December 1778. The son of a banker of Bologna, he first tried to follow his father's career, but was attracted to the priesthood, especially after hearing a mission preached by **Leonard of Port Maurice**. He decided to become a missioner himself, and was ordained in 1749. From then on he toured Italy – and Italian communities elsewhere – attempting to convert people to a more holy way of life. He was much in demand, and he founded a small institute whose purpose was regularly to provide missions to each of the parishes in Bologna.

Bartholomew of Montepulciano, bl., died Montepulciano at an advanced age, 1330, cult confirmed 1880. He became a Franciscan priest after many years of marriage, with his wife also taking vows of chastity. He was reported to have visions of Our Lady and the angels. Feast 6 May.

Bartholomew of San Gimignano, bl., born Mucchio, died Celloli, 12 December 1300. Bartolomeo (Bartolo) Buonpedoni was the heir to the count of Mucchio, but rather than continue the family line he believed he had a vocation to the priesthood. He went to live as a servant in a Benedictine house in Pisa, but although he was invited to become a monk he decided instead to become a diocesan priest, and was sent to serve in the parish of Peccioli, becoming also a Franciscan tertiary. In 1280 he contracted leprosy, and retired to the leper house of Celloli, not far from San Gimignano, where he remained as chaplain until his death.

Bartholomew of Simeri, Basilian abbot, born Simeri, Calabria, Italy, died Rossano, 19 August 1130. In his youth Bartholomew joined the hermit Cyril in his ascetic lifestyle. Before the end of the eleventh century he had founded the monastery of Santa Maria Odigitria in the mountains near Rossano. After 1104 he was ordained and in 1105 travelled to Rome to confirm from the pope immunity for his monastery. During this time he appears to have paid a visit to Constantinople, where he collected gifts of icons, sacred vessels and liturgical books from the emperor and the high officials of the empire. On return to Italy, Bartholomew organized another monastery, San Salvatore de Messina.

Bartholomew of Vicenza, bl., Dominican preacher and bishop, born 1200, died Vicenza, Italy, 1270. In 1223 Bartholomew was responsible for the founding of the military order Militia of Jesus Christ. In 1252 he was ordained as bishop of Limassol, Cyprus, after having been the regent of the theological faculty at the papal Curia. In 1255 he was transferred to Vicenza and served as the papal envoy to England and France. At this time

Louis IX sent him a thorn from the alleged crown of thorns. His main works were *An Exposition of the Canticle of Canticles* and *The Search for Divine Love*. Bartholomew seems to have been, before his episcopal career began, active as a preacher and an opponent of heretics. His cult received approval in 1793.

Bartolomea Capitanio, religious co-founder, born Lovere, Lombardy, 13 January 1807, died there, 26 July 1833. She joined the Poor Clares in Lovere when she was 11, but returned home in 1824 and opened a school in her house. Two years later she started a hospital in Lovere and acted as counsellor to many young people, as well as writing devotional works, prayers and guides to the spiritual life. In 1832 she and **Vincenza Gerosa** dedicated themselves to God and founded the Sisters of Charity of Lovere.

Barunak of Amid, martyr, born Marala, died Amid (modern Diarbekir), 1524/5. Armenian Church. Originally from Persia, he moved with his parents to Amid, where he worked as a blacksmith. A devout man, he talked to the Muslims who frequented his smithy, and converted many to Christianity. For this he was eventually imprisoned, tortured, and finally burned alive.

Baselios Yaldo, catholicos, born Tigri, Persia, died Kothamangalam, India, 1685. Syrian Orthodox Church of India (Malankara). He lived for some years in India as a member of the Malankara rite, and had a great influence on his contemporaries. His reliquary is still an important centre of pilgrimage in Berala. Canonized 1947.

Basil, died Caesarea, Cappadocia, *c.* 370. He was the son of **Macrina the Elder**. With his wife **Emmelia**, commemorated with him, he was exiled for a time. They were the parents of **Basil the Great, Gregory of Nyssa, Peter of Sebaste** and **Macrina the Younger**. Feast 30 May.

Basil, monk, born Hamasen, Eritrea. Ethiopian Church.

Basil, martyr, died Ancyra, Galatia (modern Ankara), 362. He was a priest opposed to Arianism and was killed under Julian the Apostate. The Acts of his life seems to be genuine. Feast 22 March.

Basil, poet and hymn writer, first half of the eleventh century. Georgian Church. The son of Bagrat III, he was a monk at the monastery of Chachuli. He composed the first sung canon, written probably on Mount Athos. Feast 27 May.

Basil and Procopius, died *c.* 750. They were monks who defended the veneration of images against the Emperor Leo the Isaurian. Feast 27 February.

Basil I and Basil II, see also **Boris, James, Theodore I, Silvanus, Theodore II, Basil I, Demetrius, Michael, John, Basil II**.

Basil, Eugene, Agathodorus, Elpidius, Aethirius, Gapito, Ephrem, Nestor and Arcadius, bishops and martyrs, died fourth century. They were missionary bishops. The first seven preached and were martyred in the Crimea or Russia, the last two in Cyprus. Feast 7 March.

Basil Kadomski, born *c.* 1775, died Rjazan, 2 May 1848. He came from a noble but very poor family. In the Napoleonic wars he served in the army, although he did not directly take part in battle. After this he determined to become 'a fool for Christ's sake', and wandered from place to place uttering strange sayings, which gave him a reputation as a prophet.

Basil of Caesarea, bishop and theologian, born Pontus, 330, died Caesarea, 379. He was educated in Pontus and Athens before becoming a teacher of rhetoric in 356. In 357 he was baptized and became a hermit on his family land. It was during his time as a hermit that he began to write against the various heresies that were challenging orthodoxy. His life's works include *De Spiritu Sancto*, in which he defends the deity of the Holy Spirit, and the *Adversus Eunomium* in which he predicts the Council of Constantinople (381) in understanding the Trinity as one substance (*ousia*), three persons (*hypostaseis*). In 364 he was encouraged to leave his hermitage by Eusebius of Caesarea, who made him a presbyter, and Basil became bishop of Caesarea in 370. He also developed the Rule of St Basil,

which is today still the structure for Eastern monasticism. Feast 1 January.

Basil of Jaroslavl, prince, died Vladimir, 1249, **and Constantine of Jaroslavl**, prince, died Jaroslavl, 1275. Russian Church. After their father, the prince of Jaroslavl, had been killed in 1238 fighting the Tartars, the brothers inherited the principality. Basil wore himself out both defending his territory and restoring the churches that had been destroyed by the invasions of the Tartars. He died a natural death, and his body was brought back to Jaroslavl. Constantine then became sole ruler. He was killed leading a force against the Tartars, then at the gates of his city. He was buried beside his brother.

Basil of Kamena, monk, fifteenth century. Russian Church. A monk of the the monastery of Christ the Saviour on the island of Kamena on lake Kubenskoe. Feast 3 August.

Basil of Kasino and **Irene of Kasino**, husband and wife, died Kasino, *c.* 1420. Russian Church. The parents of **Macarius of Kaljazin**. Feast 1 July.

Basil of Kinesma, bishop, born Kinesma, 1875, died Kranojarsk, 13 August 1945. Russian Church. Born Benjamin Sergeevic Preobrazenski, the son of a priest, he lived a very sheltered, almost monastic, life in his childhood. In 1901 he completed his theology doctorate in Kiev, taught until 1910 in the seminary of Veronez, went to London for further studies, then returned to Russia to teach at Morgorod and Moscow. On one occasion he nearly drowned crossing a river, and promised to commit himself to the service of the Church should he be saved, which he was. He then returned to Kinesma, where he went about preaching. He was ordained priest in 1920 and became a monk, changing his name to Basil. The following year he became bishop of Kinesma. He immediately gave away all he had and lived a life of strict asceticism allied to apostolic activity. His popularity among the people led to his arrest and two-year exile to Siberia in 1923. He returned in 1925, but was again forced to leave the city and live in an isolated village. In 1926 he was appointed bishop of Vjazniki, but after the success of a published collection of his homilies he was required to return to Kinesma. He was arrested several times and exiled, eventually being sent to a concentration camp near Ryinsk, where he was put to work on constructing a canal. Freed in 1938, he went to Kostrova near Jaroslavl, were he built a secret chapel. This was discovered in 1943 and he was again arrested and sent to Moscow, where he was sentenced to five years of exile in Siberia, where he died. Feast 3 July.

Basil of Mangazeja, martyr, born Jaroslavl, 1583, died Mangazeja, 4 April 1602. Russian Church. Born Theodore, he worked as a merchant, and moved in 1602 to the Siberian city of Mangazeja, beyond the Arctic Circle. He was very devout. One day, while he was in church at prayer, his master's shop was broken into. He did not respond immediately to his master's calls, and when he eventually returned from the church his master accused him of complicity in the robbery. He was handed over to the military, but remained silent, even under torture. When he was released, his master killed him in a fit of temper, then secretly buried his body. When his grave was discovered, miracles began to occur through his intercession. Feast 6 June.

Basil of Moldovita, miracle worker, born Bucovina, 1370–75, died Moldovita, c. 1455. Romanian Church. He was hegumenos of the monastery of Moldovita between 1445 and 1455, and organized the monks into three groups who took it in turns to pray, work and celebrate the liturgy. He had the gift of healing.

Basil of Moscow, 'fool for Christ', born Elochov, near Moscow, 1468, died Moscow, 2 August 1552. Russian Church. Born into a farming family, he was apprenticed to a shoemaker. One day a client asked him to make some shoes which would last for several years. He laughed. When asked why he had laughed, Basil reluctantly replied that the man would die the following day, which proved to be the case. He then fled the shop, and lived the rest of his life on the streets of Moscow, wearing scarcely any clothes no matter what the time of the year. His bizarre behaviour won him many admirers among the people of Moscow, including among them Ivan the Terrible. Despite the harsh asceticism of his life, he lived to a considerable age, and at his death was immediately venerated as a saint. The Cathedral of St Basil in Red Square is named after him.

Basil of Novgorod, archbishop, born Novgorod, died Pskov, 3 July 1352. Russian Church. Georgia Kalika became bishop in 1329, having already travelled to the Holy Land on pilgrimage. He played a large part in the life of the city, including averting a clash with King Magnus of Sweden. He was also made bishop of Pskov, and died there after visiting the city to bless it against the plague.

Basil of Novgorod, prince, died 1218. Russian Church.

Basil of Ostrog, metropolitan, born Herzegovina, died Ostrog. Serbian Church. He entered the monastery of the Assumption at Trebinje in Montenegro, and from 1639 to 1671 was metropolitan of Zahumia and Skenderia. He was, however, driven out by the Turks, and spent the remainder of his life at Ostrog. He made two journeys to Rome to visit the pope. Feast 29 April.

Basil of Poiana Marului, monk, born Ukraine, 1692, died Poiana Marului, 25 April 1767. Romanian Church. He came with two other monks to what is now Romania in 1713, first to Dalhauti and then, 20 years later, to Poiana Marului where he built a church. He became a hieromonk, and was held in high regard for his teaching and his practice of hesychasm, the method of mystical prayer associated with Mount Athos, whence Basil also drew his monastic Rule. A synod held at Bucharest in 1749 approved his teaching as being in conformity with the Scriptures and the Fathers of the Church.

Basil of Priluki, bishop, born Zimoarovo, 1870, died Irkutsk, February 1930. Ukrainian Church, Moscow Patriarchate. Born Vasili Ivanovic Zelecov, he studied law and theology at St Petersburg, becoming a priest at Poltava in 1920. Despite a brief period in schism, in 1924 he became bishop of Priluki. He was arrested the following year and condemned to death, but then freed. Arrested again in 1926, he was imprisoned for three years on the island of Solovki. In 1927 he opposed Metropolitan Sergi as too sympathetic to the state, was again arrested and sent to Irkutsk, where he was shot.

Basil of Rjazan, bishop, thirteenth/fourteenth centuries. Russian Church. According to legend, the bishop of Murom, who had to flee Murom when falsely accused of fornication. He took with him a miraculous icon of the Mother of God, went down to the river Oka and sailed up it on his episcopal cloak. Arriving near the city of Rjazan, he met that city's prince, and moved his episcopal see to that place. Feast 3 July.

Basil of Rostov, prince, born Rostov, 7 December 1209, died Serensk, March 1238. Russian Church. The eldest son of the prince of Rostov. His father became grand prince of Vladimir in 1216, but died two years later, when Basil became prince of Rostov. He took part in a number of military expeditions, and in 1227 married, and had two sons. In March 1238 he was defeated and taken prisoner by the Mongols. He refused to go over to their side, saying that the oaths required of him would be a blasphemy, and he was killed in the forest of Serensk. His body was later taken back to Rostov for burial.

Basil of Solovki, monk, born Novgorod, died Solovki, fifteenth century. Russian Church. Of a boyar family, and famous for his strength, he became a brigand, but then repented and became a monk. He briefly returned to his old ways, however, and fled to another island where he fell into a deep sleep. In a dream he was rebuked by his former master **Zosimus**, and returned to the monastery to do penance.

Basil of Surat, bishop, twelfth (?) century. Russian Church.

Basil the Gentle, archbishop, thirteenth century. Byzantine Church. The archbishop of Thessalonika.

Basil the Macedonian (Basil I), emperor, born Chariopoli, Thracia, 837, died Constantinople, 29 August 886. Byzantine Church. From a family of peasants, in 856 he joined the imperial staff of Emperor Michael III. He was of imposing build, a good soldier and administrator, and the emperor made him first co-emperor and then, on Michael's assassination in September 867, he became sole emperor. Although not able to save Syracuse from the Arabs, he otherwise successfully defended Byzantium against them, and established good relations with other neighbouring states. He backed the patriarch Ignatius against Photius, held two councils, the first of which (Constantinople IV, 869) is regarded by Rome as ecumenical and was ecclesiastically generally pro-Rome. When Ignatius died, he permitted Photius, to whom he had entrusted the education of his children, to become patriarch. He died in a hunting accident.

Basil the Monk, born eighteenth century, died Kabeni, early nineteenth century. Georgian Church. A famous miracle worker of the monastery of Kabeni.

Basilea, see **Adrio**.

Basiliscus, bishop and martyr, died near Nicomedia, 312. Bishop of Comana, Pontus, Asia Minor, now Turkey, he was beheaded and thrown into a river. Feast 22 May.

Basilissa, see **Callinica and Basilissa**.

Basilissa, martyred, fourth century, married to **Julian**. She is commemorated with him, but was not martyred with him. Feast 6 January.

Basilissa, empress, fourth century. Byzantine Church. The wife of Maxentius, she was martyred for her faith. Feast 25 November.

Basilla of Smyrna, martyr. Smyrna is now Izmir, in Turkey, but it may be a mistake for Sirmium, now Srem Mitrovica, Serbia. Feast 29 August.

Basinus, bishop, died St Maximin, Trier, *c.* 705. He was abbot of the Benedictine abbey of St Maximin, then bishop of Trier, and helped English missionaries, including **Willibrord**. Feast 4 March.

Basolus, hermit, born Limoges, died near Rheims, *c.* 620. Originally a soldier, he eventually entered the monastery of Verzy, near Rheims, and then became a hermit, settling at the top of a nearby hill. Feast 26 November.

Bassa, Theogonius, Agapius and Fidelis, martyrs, died Larissa, Greece, 304. Bassa was the wife of a pagan priest, the others her sons. Feast 21 August.

Bassalota Mikael, thirteenth/fourteenth centuries. Ethiopian Church. Born after a vision of Michael the Archangel, he studied Scripture from an early age and wanted to join a monastery, although his parents wished him to marry. He fled to a monastery, but was forced to return to his family by the king, who was related to his mother. They even attempted to have him seduced by the widow of his brother, but he resisted the temptation and fled to Dabra Gol, where he was ordained priest. He then moved for a time to Tigre, where he lived in various monasteries, studying Scripture. He denounced the metropolitan John for having taken bribes to ordain men, but John managed to convince the king of his innocence, and had Bassalota Mikael sent into exile back to Tigre and imprisoned there for three years. After his release he denounced King Amda Seyon for an illicit marriage. The king had him flogged and sent into exile in Dara, where he converted many Muslims. He was becoming increasingly famous for his miracles, so the king sent him and his disciples to an island on lake Zeway and later on, after a further clash with the king, to Gelo Makada, where he lived out his final days in a cave. Feast 28 July.

Bassianus of Kasin, monk. Russian Church. Founder of the monastery of the Most Holy Trinity at Kasin, near Tver.

Bassianus of Krestimirov, monk, fourteenth century. Russian Church. Founder of the monastery of the Transfiguration at Krestimirov, on the river Onega, at the White Sea. Feast 3 July.

Bassianus of Lodi, bishop, from Sicily, died 409. He was bishop of Lodi, Lombardy and a great friend of **Ambrose of Milan**, with whom he attended the council of Aquileia in 381 and whom he attended at his death. Feast 19 January.

Bassianus of Marom, monk, died Pskov, 20 February 1570. Russian Church. A disciple of **Cornelius of the Cave of Pskov**, and martyred with him by Ivan the Terrible.

Bassianus of Pertoma and Jonah of Pertoma, monks, died on the river Dvina, c. 1561. Russian Church. Monks of the monastery of the Solovki, they were drowned during a storm on the river as they were attempting to find materials to build a church.

Bassianus of Rostov I, bishop, born Rylovo, died Rostov, 23 March 1481. Russian Church. Became hegumenos of the monastery of the Trinity of St Sergius in 1455, and with another monk travelled three years later in western Russia, to persuade – without much success – the local clergy to submit to the rule of the metropolitan of Moscow. As hegumenos he brought several works of art to the monastery. In 1466 he became archimandrite of the monastery of Novspasski in Moscow, and a year later was appointed bishop of Rostov, although he remained a councillor of Prince Ivan III in Moscow. He opposed paying tribute to the Khan of the Golden Horde, Ahmet, who was threatening Moscow. He called Ivan a coward for considering this, and offered to take command of the Russian troops himself.

Bassianus of Rostov II, bishop, died Moscow, 25 January 1516. Russian Church. The brother of **Joseph of Volokamsk**, and a monk of the monastery of St Paphnutius at Borovsk, he became bishop of Rostov in 1506, and supported his brother Joseph in his clash with **Serapion**, the archbishop of Novgorod.

Bassianus of Strokin, monk, sixteenth century. Russian Church. Founder of the monastery of the Transfiguration at Strokin, near lake Onega.

Bassianus of the Laura of the Kievan Cave Monasteries, monk. Russian Church.

Bassianus of Tiksna, monk, born Burcevo (or Strelica), near Tooma, died Tksna, 12 September 1624 or 1633. Russian Church. Basil was a tailor, married with two children. Very devout, he decided to leave his family for the monastic life at the monastery of the Saviour at Tooma – which was at first hesitant about admitting him, given the fact that he had abandoned his wife and children. He was eventually admitted, and took the name Bassianus. In 1594, with the blessing of the hegumenos, he left the monastery for a hermitage beside the river Tiksna, where he lived a life of great asceticism and bodily mortification, speaking to few, and then only through the window of his bare cell, where he slept on the ground. A cult of Bassianus developed quickly after his death, particularly so because of the plague of 1647, during which his heavenly protection was much sought.

Bassianus of Uglic, monk, born Rozalov, died near Uglic, 12 February 1509. Russian Church. He was of a princely but impoverished family, and did not become a monk, under the hegumenos **Paisius of Uglic**, until he was 33. In 1492 he decided to live the remainder of his life in complete silence. He left the monastery, and established a hermitage some distance south of Uglic. People came to him for counsel, and with their gifts to him he acquired land on which to build a church, and a group of disciples gathered about him, determined to imitate his life.

Bata of Persia, hermit, martyr, died third century. Feast 1 May.

Batergela Maryam, prince, sixteenth century. Ethiopic Church. Little is known about him, except that he appears to have been unjustly condemned by his father, possibly falsely accused of pagan practices. Although he twice passed through a region infected by the plague, he himself remained unaffected.

Bathilde, wife of Clovis II, king of France. Born possibly in England, she died near Paris in January 680. Bathilde was a slave in the palace of Neustria, but Clovis was so impressed by her beauty and goodness that he freed her and in 649 married her. She became known for her humility, prayerfulness and generosity. Clovis II died in 656. His son, Clothaire III, aged five, became king and Bathilde regent. She abolished Christian slavery and repressed the custom among clergy of buying and selling promotion in the Church. She founded religious institutions, such as hospitals and monasteries, including the abbeys of Corbie and Chelles. When her children were grown up she withdrew to Chelles. Feast 26 January.

Batra Maryam, monk, sixteenth/seventeenth centuries, born Sablo, 29 May, died Zage, 24 July. Ethiopic Church. Baptized Baston of Maria, at the age of six he was given by his parents to a monk for instruction. He then decided, against his parents' wishes, to become a monk himself – they gave in after he recounted that he had been granted a vision of two angels. They, however, died soon afterwards, and he gave away his inheritance and put himself under the direction of abbot John of Dabra Sabla, becoming both a monk and a priest. After their monastery was attacked, the remaining community moved to Damot, where there was a famine. To pay for food, Batra became a slave. His master's daughter became ill and died, accusing Batra of working magic on her. He then raised her to life by blessing her with holy water. This act revealed his true identity, and he was freed. Many came to him seeking healing. He travelled across Ethiopia, performing miracles, settling finally at Zage, where he gathered disciples and built a church dedicated to St George, remaining there for 23 years. He died at the age of 89.

Baudelius of Nîmes, martyr, born Orléans, died Nîmes, third century. He was a fervent and active Christian and a married man. He was executed at Nîmes and his cult spread in France and northern Spain. Feast 20 May.

Bavon (also called Allowin), patron saint of Ghent and of the diocese of Haarlem, Holland, died c. 653. Born into a noble family in Hesbaye, Brabant, he married but was then widowed. He converted to a life of Christian poverty after hearing a sermon preached by **Armand** and entered the monastery at Ghent. He travelled with Armand to France and Flanders, but then lived the life of a hermit near to the monastery. Feast 1 October.

Beatrice da Silva, founder, born Ceuta, Portugal, 1424, died Toledo, 1 September 1490. Brites da Silva Menses was brought up at the Portuguese court, but when a Portuguese princess married the king of Castile she journeyed to Toledo in her entourage. After a time she went to the Dominican convent in Toledo and lived there for 30 years, but in 1484 she set up the Congregation of the Immaculate Conception of the Blessed Virgin Mary. Feast 16 August.

Beatrice d'Este, bl., Benedictine nun, born *c.* 1191, died Gemolo, Italy, 10 May 1226. She secretly left home aged 14 and entered the convent of St Margaret at Solarola. The community later moved to the empty monastery of St John the Baptist near Gemolo, where they adopted the Benedictine rule.

Beatrice d'Este, bl., Benedictine nun and niece of the above, born 1230, died Ferrara, 18 January 1262. She had been promised in marriage by her parents, but she herself wanted to follow the religious life. Following the death of the man to whom she was espoused, she joined the convent at St Lazarus and her family later had a new convent built for the community at Ferrara.

Beatus of Lungern, hermit and saint, died *c.* 112. He lived in a cave on what became Mount St Beatenberg, Switzerland. According to a tenth-century legend, he was of Gallic origin, was baptized in England by St Barnabas, ordained at Rome by St Peter, and commissioned to be the apostle to the Swiss. His cave, where he was said to have fought and slain a dragon, became a place of pilgrimage. Patron of central Switzerland, he is invoked against various illnesses. Feast 9 May.

Bebais, see **Sarbellius**.

Bede the Venerable, monk and doctor of the Church, born near Sunderland, England, *c.* 673, died in the monastery of Jarrow, *c.* 735. He entered the monastery at Wearmouth as a boy, and was educated there by **Benedict Biscop**, but later moved to Jarrow, where he was ordained *c.* 703. He wrote Scripture commentaries which display a thorough knowledge of the Fathers of the Church, both Latin and to some extent Greek: he may well also have known some Hebrew. He wrote homilies, letters, a study of chronology, a history of his own monastery. It is, however, mainly in his *Ecclesiastical History of the English People*, completed some four years before his death, that his fame rests. Although he probably never travelled beyond the borders of the kingdom of Northumbria, he took great care to establish facts, and wrote vividly about the figures of the early Church in England, as well as about the political events which went to shape it. In his own day he was admired for his learning, and his writings were widely known in the Middle Ages. Feast 25 May.

Be'ese Salam, monk. Ethiopic Church. Founder of a monastery located between Taltal and Azabo.

Begga, abbess, born Landen, died Andenne, 693. The daughter of Pepin I, mayor of the palace at Landen, she married the son of **Arnulf of Metz**, but after his death in a hunting accident she established a monastery at Andenne, on the river Meuse, where she spent the remainder of her days. Feast 17 December.

Begu, died Hackness, north Yorksire, seventh century. Feast 31 October.

Bendinian, hermit in Bithynia, fifth century. Feast 1 February.

Benedict, monastic founder, born Norcia, Italy, 480, died Monte Cassino, *c.* 550. He studied in Rome, was influenced by the developments in Byzantine monasticism, and his journey in faith began when he became a hermit, living in caves, probably near Subiaco. He was gradually joined by others, many like himself from influential families. They built basic monastic accommodation, but Benedict conceived the need for a grander and more organized structure, and in about 529 the community moved to Monte Cassino where they set about the new construction, and where the Rule of St Benedict, which was soon to become the guiding norm for Western monasticism, is thought to have been drawn up. There is strong claim to this being the site of Benedict's death and burial and the resting place of his relics, although much controversy surrounds this question. Benedict was in touch with many of the monastic and ecclesiastical leaders of his day and the community developed to the extent that another foundation, St Stephen's, was established in the diocese of Terracina. Most of what we know of his life comes from the *Dialogues* of **Gregory the Great**, written in 593 and 594 and told to Gregory by the confrères and disciples of Benedict. Feast, in the West, 11 July, which is thought to be the date his relics were taken to St-Benoit-sur-Loire; in addition, 21 March is kept within the order, as the transitus, or date of death, and in the East 14 March.

Benedict II, pope, born Rome, died there, 8 March 685. He became a Scripture scholar and an expert in sacred chants. Elected in 683, his consecration was delayed almost a year until 26 June 684, awaiting the emperor's confirmation. During his term, he amended the process to speed approval of papal elections by having the exarch of Ravenna confirm the election, rather than the emperor, thus eliminating long delays. Benedict was greatly respected by Emperor Constantine the Bearded, who sent him locks of his sons' hair, making them the pope's spiritual sons. Benedict brought back to orthodoxy Macarius, the ex-patriarch of Antioch, and restored several Roman churches. He upheld the cause of **Wilfrid** of York, who sought the return of his see from which he had been deposed by Theodore.

Benedict XI, bl., pope, born Niccolò Boccasino at Treviso, Italy, 1240; elected 22 October 1303, died Perugia, 7 July 1304. He entered the Dominican Order at the age of 14. In 1296 he was elected master general of the order. Hostility to Boniface VIII was becoming more pronounced, and he issued an ordinance forbidding his Dominican brethren to favour the opponents of the reigning pontiff. When Boniface died, he was unanimously elected pope. The principal event of his pontificate was the restoration of peace with the French court. After a pontificate of eight months, Benedict died suddenly. He was beatified in 1773. He is the author of a volume of sermons and commentaries on a part of the Gospel of St Matthew, on the Psalms, the book of Job and the Apocalypse.

Benedict Biscop, abbot, born Northumbria, England, *c.* 628, died Wearmouth, 12 January *c.* 690. He is also known as Benet Biscop and Biscop Baducing. In 674, at the mouth of the river Wear (Wearmouth), he built a church and monastery dedicated to St Peter. He is acknowledged as the founder of the joint monasteries of Ss Peter and Paul at Wearmouth and Jarrow. He was the first to introduce glass into England. He organized the scriptorium in which was written the manuscript that his successor **Ceolfrid** took with him in 716 as a present to Pope **Gregory II**, the Codex Amiatinus. **Bede**, whose work was made possible by Benedict's library, says that the civilization and

learning of the eighth century rested in the monastery founded by Benedict.

Benedict Caneld, see **William Fitch**.

Benedict Crispus, bishop, died 725. He was bishop of Milan for 45 years and composed the epitaph for **Caedwalla**, king of Wessex, buried in Rome. Feast 11 March.

Benedict Joseph Labré, 'the Beggar of Rome', born Amettes, France, 25 March 1748, died Rome, 16 April 1783. Rejected as unsuitable by the religious orders to whom he applied, he found his vocation in pilgrimage. In 1770 he began a pilgrimage on foot to Rome, living on alms. On the way he decided to go to all the principal places of pilgrimage in Europe, always walking, sleeping rough and taking nothing except a cloak and a few books, and sharing what he was given with other beggars. He reached Rome in 1776, spent his nights in the Colosseum and his days in different churches, particularly those which celebrated the 40 Hours devotion, which he loved and did what he could to promote. He died in Holy Week 1743 and was popularly proclaimed to be a saint.

Benedict Menni, born Milan, 11 March 1841, died France, 24 April 1914, beatified 1985, canonized 1999. A Brother Hospitaller of St John of God, he was sent to re-establish the order in Spain. He set up hospitals for men, notably psychiatric ones. In 1881 he founded the Hospitaller Sisters to care for women, opening 13 hospitals.

Benedict of Aniane, abbot, born in Languedoc, France, 750, died Aachen, 11 February 821. In 774 he became a monk at St-Seine near Dijon, France. When Bishop Felix of Urgel proposed that Christ was only the adoptive son of the eternal Father (adoptionism), Benedict opposed this heresy and assisted in the Council (synod) of Frankfurt in 794. He also refuted this heresy in four treatises, which were published in the miscellanies of Balusius. He and Emperor Louis the Pious co-operated with each other to mutual benefit. The emperor made Benedict director of all the monasteries in the empire. He compiled the *Codex regularum*, a collection of all monastic regulations, and *Concordia regularum*.

Benedict of Arezzo, bl., born Arezzo, died 1281. One of the earliest followers of **Francis of Assisi**, and appointed by him to the post of provincial. He travelled to the Holy Land and to Constantinople. Feast 31 August.

Benedict of Benevento, missionary and martyr, born Benevento, died 12 November 1005, along with his four brothers and fellow missionaries John, Matthew, Isaac and Christian, near Miedzyrxec, Poland. He and his brothers followed **Adalbert of Prague** in the mission among the Slavs, and were massacred at their hermitage by robbers acting on a rumour that Duke Boleslav I, who built the hermitage, had given them a great treasure. The five were buried at their hermitage, which soon became a pilgrimage centre.

Benedict of Cluse II, ven., abbot, reformer, born Toulouse, *c.* 1030, died Cluse, 31 May 1091. When very young he was entrusted by his father to the Abbey of Saint-Hilaire at Carcassone in France. He later entered the monastery of San Michele della Chiusa (Cluse), becoming abbot in 1066, and was consecrated by Pope Alexander II. Benedict then began a reform of the abbey insisting on asceticism, humility and manual labour. When **Gregory VII** became pope, Benedict's bishop, Cunibert of Turin, devastated the property at Cluse and put the abbey under interdict. Benedict was forced to flee. For the remainder of his life he struggled with William, Cunibert's successor.

Benedict of Urbino, bl., born Urbino, Italy, 13 September 1560, died Fossombrone, 30 April 1625, beatified 1867. After a short legal career, he defied his family to become a Capuchin at Fano in 1584. A successful preacher, he spent some years travelling with **Laurence of Brindisi** in Austria and Bohemia.

Benedict Revelli, died *c.* 900, cult confirmed by Pope Gregory XVI. He is said to have been a Benedictine at Santa Maria dei Fonti, then a hermit on Gallinaria island in the Gulf of Genoa, and bishop of Albenga in Liguria from 870. Feast 12 February.

Benedict Ricasoli, bl., born Coltiboni, near Fiesole, died *c.* 1107, cult confirmed 1907. He joined the Benedictine monastery at Vallumbrosa near Fiesole founded by **John Gualbert**. He then lived as a hermit, returning to the community at major feasts. Reported miracles led to a persisting local cult. Feast 20 January.

Benedict the Moor, also known as Benedict the Black, Franciscan, born near Messina, Italy, 1526, died Palermo, 4 April 1589, beatified 1743, canonized 1807. He was the son of freed slaves brought to Sicily from Africa. He was about 21 when he was publicly insulted on account of his race. The leader of a group of Franciscan hermits observed his dignified demeanour on that occasion and Benedict was invited to join the group at Montepellegrino. In 1578 Benedict was appointed superior, although he was an illiterate lay brother. After serving as superior, he became novice master, but asked to be relieved of this post and returned to his former position as cook. Benedict is the patron of African-Americans in the USA.

Benedicta and Cecilia, abbesses, died Susteren, Germany, tenth century. Sisters, and successive abbesses of the convent founded for them by their father at Susteren. Feast 17 August.

Benedicta Frassinello, bl., founder, born in Liguria, Italy, 2 October 1791, died Ronco, 21 March 1858, beatified 1987. Forced to marry in 1816, the couple chose a celibate marriage and Benedicta's husband Giovanni supported her work throughout. In 1825 she joined the Ursulines and her husband the Somaschi, but when she had to leave because of ill-health, he did likewise. She dedicated herself to working with poor young girls, to protect them from prostitution, founding an order, the Benedictines of Providence.

Benen, see **Benignus**.

Benezet, born near St Jean-de-Maurienne, Savoy, 1163, died Avignon, 14 April 1184. While a shepherd in the south of France, he received a divine commission to build a bridge over the Rhône at Avignon. The bridge was never completed, however. He is supposed to have founded the Lay Brotherhood of Bridgebuilders (Fratres Pontifices), who were particularly active in the south of France building bridges, bridge chapels, streets and pilgrim hostels. Canonized in 1233, he is patron saint of Avignon, bridge builders and shepherds.

Benicasa of La Cava, bl., abbot, died Sicily, 1194, cult confirmed 1928. A Benedictine, he was abbot of La Cava from 1171. He helped found a monastery at Monreale, Sicily, sending over hundreds of monks. Feast 10 January.

Benignus (Benen), bishop, born Meath, Ireland, c. 420, died 467 (?). He was the son of a chieftain and was given the name Benignus by St **Patrick**, whom he went on to accompany in his missionary activity, and whom he eventually succeeded. He is said to have evangelized counties Clare and Kerry, and to have spent 20 years looking after the church at Drumlease, in Kilmore, which Patrick had founded. He was particularly noted for his musical ability. The place and date of his death are only recorded in unreliable sources. Feast 9 November.

Benignus of Dijon, patron saint of Dijon, early martyr, thought to have died under Marcus Aurelius, possibly a native of Asia Minor, a disciple of **Polycarp** and a missionary to Burgundy. The basilica and abbey in Dijon are built over his tomb. Feast 1 November.

Benignus of Todi, martyr, died c. 303. He was priest at Todi in Umbria, killed under Diocletian. Feast 13 February.

Benildus, born Thuret, France, 13 June 1805, died Saugues, Haute-Loire, 13 August 1862. Baptized Peter Romançon, he studied at Riom with the Brothers of the Christian Schools and entered the noviceship in 1820. He trained as a teacher at Riom, then went to Billom to be in charge of the school there. In 1841 he was sent to open a school at Saugues. He was particularly effective as a teacher of religion.

Benito de Jesús Saèz, martyr, born Buenos Aires, Argentina, 31 October 1910, died Turon, Asturias, 9 October 1934. He was baptized Hector Validivieso, and entered the de la Salle Brothers on 7 August 1926. He was talented as an author, and had been involved in the Eucharistic Crusade in Spain. He was arrested with the other **Martyrs of Asturias** by a group of rebel soldiers, and executed by firing squad.

Benjamin, martyr, died Argos, Persia, c. 420. He was a deacon who refused to stop preaching the gospel and was tortured to death. Feast 31 March.

Benjamin Julian Andres, martyr, born Jamarillo de la Fuente, near Burgos, 27 October 1908, died Turon, Asturias, 9 October 1934. Baptized Vicente Alonso, he entered the de la Salle Brothers on 24 August 1924. He was considered by his superiors to be a man of sound political sense, which was why he had been sent to Turon a year or so before his martyrdom. He was arrested with the other **Martyrs of Asturias** by a group of rebel soldiers, and executed by firing squad.

Benjamin of Alexandria, patriarch, born Barsut, 590, died Alexandria, 3 January 661. Coptic Church. From a well-off family, he did not become a monk until he was 30, entering the monastery of Canopo near Alexandria. After a dream in which he learned that he would become shepherd of Christ's flock, he became secretary to the patriarch **Andronicus**, who ordained him priest and named him as his successor. He succeeded in 622, under the Persian occupation. When, however, the Byzantine Emperor Heraclius put the Persians to flight in 629, he also brought back the anti-monophysite bishops, including the patriarch. Benjamin fled into the desert and urged all his bishops to do likewise. The subsequent invasion of Islam was seen by many monophysites as God's punishment on the Byzantines. The Muslim leader invited Benjamin to return to his city after a 13-year exile. He then set to work restoring the cathedral and the many churches which had been destroyed during the Arab invasion.

Benjamin of Dara, hermit and martyr, died Dara, c. 371. Syriac Church. Ordained in Edessa, he converted Ma'in, a general of King Shapur II, for which he was executed.

Benjamin of Kazan, metropolitan and martyr, born diocese of Olonec, 1874, died St Petersburg, 13 August 1922. Russian Church. Vasilii Pavlovic Kazanski was the son of a country priest. He studied at the seminary in Olonec, then at the ecclesiastical academy in St Petersburg. As a seminarian he worked among the poor people of the city, but then followed an academic career, returning to St Petersburg as rector of the seminary in 1905, by which time he was already an archimandrite with a reputation for holiness of life. In 1910 he became bishop of Gdov and seven years later was unanimously elected metropolitan of St Petersburg. In that capacity he protested, after the October Revolution, at the separation of Church and state and the confiscation of Church property. To help relieve the famine which followed the revolution, he set up a society in St Petersburg under the presidency of Jurii Petrovickii, professor of law at the university. A canonist from the Laura of St Alexander Nevski, Giovanni (Ivan) Michailovic Kovarov, was also an active member of the society. They were arrested in June 1922, along with over 80 others. They were defended by the archimandrite **Sergius Sein**, who had been a member of the duma and of the All-Russia Council. He too was condemned with the others, and the four were shot. Feast 31 July.

Benjamin of the Laura of the Caves of Kiev, monk, died Kiev, fourteenth century. Russian Church. A wealthy merchant before becoming a monk, he was suddenly converted by hearing the words, 'It is difficult for a rich man to enter heaven' (Mt. 19.23). He gave away all his property and lived a holy life in the Cave monastery until his death. Feast 28 August.

Benno of Einsiedeln, bl., bishop, born Strasbourg, died Einsiedeln, Switzerland, 940. Originally a priest in Strasbourg, he became a hermit in Switzerland and founded the abbey of Einsiedeln. He then became bishop of Metz, but was unpopular because of his reforms and was attacked and blinded. He retired back to Einsiedeln. Feast 3 August.

Benno of Meissen, bishop, born Hildesheim, *c.* 1010, died Meissen, 16 June 1106. He was the son of the count of Bultenberg. He entered the monastery at Hildesheim, and was then appointed by Henry III to Goslar, and in 1066 was made bishop of Meissen. He was of the Gregorian reform party, which brought him into conflict with Henry IV, and he was imprisoned and deposed in 1085 by

the other German bishops at the synod of Mainz. He spent his time in exile as a missionary, but regained his see in the last decade of his life.

Benno of Osnabrück, bl., bishop, born Lohningen, Swabia, died Iburg, 1088. A master architect, he was builder-in-chief to Emperor Henry III (1039–56). He was appointed bishop of Osnabrück by the emperor in 1068. Benno was one of the signatories of the attempted deposition of Pope **Gregory VII** at Worms in 1075, but when the pope excommunicated all those involved he went to Italy with the other German bishops to ask for forgiveness and absolution. Benno acted as envoy of Emperor Henry IV to the pope on several occasions, but after Henry was excommunicated in 1080, Benno went into hiding to avoid taking sides. He went to Iburg, where he founded a monastery, and lived there until his death in 1088. Feast 28 July.

Bentivoglio de Bonis, Franciscan, born San Severino, 1188, died there, 25 December 1232. One of the first disciples of **Francis of Assisi**, he was remarkable for the depth of his prayer life and his ecstasies.

Benvenuta Boiani, bl., born Cividale, Friuli, 1254, died there, 30 October 1292. Of a wealthy family, she was very devout and joined the Dominican Third Order. She subjected herself to a rigorous ascetical regime, and had frequent visions.

Benvenutus of Gubbio, bl., born Gubbio, died Corneto, Apulia, 1232. He was a soldier and became a Franciscan lay brother. He devoted himself to the care of lepers. Feast 27 June.

Benvenutus of Recanati (Mareni), bl., born Recanati, near Loreto, died 1289. He was a Franciscan lay brother, working mainly in the kitchens, who experienced visions and ecstasies. Feast 9 May.

Benvenutus Scotivoli, bishop, born Ancona, died Osimo, 1282, canonized 1283. A Franciscan, he studied law at Bologna and later became bishop of Osimo, Piceno. Feast 22 March.

Berach, born Ireland, died Kilberry (?), sixth century. A descendant of Brian, prince of Connaught, brought up by his uncle Froch, he was a disciple of

Kevin and became abbot of Kilberry (Cill Beraigh). He is patron of Killardy. Feast 15 February.

Bercharius, martyr, died Moutier-en-Der, Champagne, c. 896. The first abbot of the Benedictine monastery of Hautvilliers, he founded two other Benedictine houses and travelled to Rome and Palestine. He died after being stabbed at night by a young monk whom he had chastised. He forgave him before he died. Feast 26 March.

Berengarius, monk in Narbonne, died 1093. Feast 26 May.

Berlinda (Berlindis, Bellaude), died Meerbeke, Belgium, c. 702. A niece of **Amandus**, she was a Benedictine nun at Moorsel, near Alost, then a recluse at Meerbeke. Feast 3 February.

Bernard Beaulieu, see **Simeon**.

Bernard Lichtenberg, bl., born Ohlau, Germany (now in Poland), 5 December 1875, died Hof, Germany, 5 November 1943. He came from a middle-class family, studied in Innsbruck and was ordained aged 24. Rather conservative in outlook, he was an active member of the Catholic Centre Party. After the advent of Hitler he came to the defence of the Jews. He was imprisoned, then sent to Dachau. He died in a cattle truck on his way to the concentration camp.

Bernard, Mary and Grace, martyrs, died Valencia, c. 1180. They were a brother and two sisters, named Ahmed, Zoraida and Zaida, the children of the emir of Lerida. Ahmed converted to Christianity and became a Cistercian monk at Poblet, taking the name Bernard, and then converted his two sisters. They were executed as renegades from Islam by their brother. Feast 21 August.

Bernard Meccati, bl., born Villamagna, Tuscany, c. 1194, died possibly 1276 (or 1242), cult confirmed 1833. He may have been in the Holy Land, either fighting a crusade or as a pilgrim. He returned home and lived as a hermit until his death, possibly becoming a Franciscan tertiary. Feast 13 May.

Bernard of Aosta (Menton, Mont Joux), archdeacon, patron of mountain climbers, born probably in Italy, died Novara, 15 June 1081. He was archdeacon of Aosta for about 40 years, respected for his preaching and loved for his goodness. He is known to all as the restorer and patron of the hospices for travellers in the Alps, under the care of the community that eventually became the Canons Regular of St Augustine.

Bernard of Baden, bl., born Baden, 1428, died Moncalieri, 1458. Son of Margrave James I of Baden, and succeeded him in 1453 as Bernard II. He was sent by Emperor Frederick III to raise funds for a crusade against the Turks, and became so involved with this work that he give up his position as margrave to his brother Charles. In 1458 he left for Rome, to meet Pope Callistus III, but on the journey he caught the plague and died in the Franciscan monastery at Moncalieri. Feast 15 July.

Bernard of Carinola, bishop, born Capua, died Carinola, Campania, 1109. He became bishop of Forum-Claudii in 1087, then of Carinola in 1100, dying at a very old age. He is patron of Carinola. Feast 12 March.

Bernard of Clairvaux, abbot, born near Dijon, 1090, died Clairvaux, 20 August 1153. The well-educated son of a noble family, he entered the (Cistercian) abbey of Citeaux in 1111 with 31 companions, thereby saving it from probable extinction. Three years later he became abbot of Clairvaux, a new foundation, and was ordained in 1115. By the time of Bernard's death there were over 700 monks in the monastery, and the Cistercians had made some 500 new foundations. He was so convinced of the superiority of the Cistercian way of life that he was critical of other forms, particularly that of Cluny, and a lively correspondence on the matter developed between Bernard and Cluny's abbot, Peter the Venerable. He was much involved in Church politics, backing Innocent II against the antipope, and giving vigorous support (and advice) to Eugenius III who had been one of his disciples. He gave equally vigorous support through his preaching to the disastrous second crusade. He engaged in theological debate with Peter Abelard and Gilbert de la

Porrée. Much of his writing is on prayer and spiritual subjects, and he fostered devotion to the person of Christ and to the Virgin Mary. His *Liber de diligendo dei* ('On how to love God') is a classic, and so are his sermons on the Song of Songs. He was canonized in 1174, and declared a doctor of the Church in 1830.

Bernard of Corleone, born Philip Latini, Corleone, Sicily, 1605, died Palermo, 1667. A shoemaker and a noted swordsman, he took sanctuary with the Capuchins in Palermo after wounding an opponent. He became a lay brother in 1632 and was a noted penitent henceforth. He was canonized in 2001. Feast 12 January.

Bernard of Parma, bishop, born Florence, died Parma, 4 December 1133. A member of the Uberti family, he entered the recently founded abbey of Vallombrosa. He later became abbot of San Salvio, then general of the order. He was made a cardinal by **Urban II** and subsequently became bishop of Parma. He was an ardent follower of the reforms set in train by **Gregory VII**, but was opposed by many in his diocese and for a time lived in exile.

Bernard of Tiron, abbot, born Abbeville, *c.* 1046, died Fontaine-Gehard, 14 or 25 April 1117. He was a wandering preacher, a hermit in the forest of Craon in Britanny, monk, then prior, at Saint-Savin-sur-Gartempe, before founding his own monastery at Tiron, near Chartres. This became the mother house of a small, reformed monastic order, with houses in France, Wales and Scotland. By the thirteenth century its Scottish daughter houses had managed to secure their independence from Tiron, and the houses on the continent of Europe became indistinguishable from other Benedictine monasteries. Feast 14 April.

Bernard Peroni, bl., born Ancona, 1604, died Offida, 1694. A Franciscan lay brother, he joined the Capuchins at Offida, worked at Fermo, then returned to Offida where he had a reputation as a miracle worker. Feast 22 August.

Bernard Scammacca, bl., monk, from Catania, Sicily, died *c.* 1487. After a riotous youth, he changed his way of life after being seriously wounded in a duel. He became a Dominican and henceforth lived a life of penance. Feast 11 January.

Bernard Silvestrelli, bl., born Rome, 7 November 1831, died Moricone, 9 December 1911. He was born into the noble Silvestrelli-Gozani family, and joined the novitiate of the Congregation of the Passion in 1854, changing his name from Cesare to Bernard Mary. He held many offices in the Congregation, including – twice – that of superior general. After he had resigned this post, the pope gave him the title of 'Honorary General for Life'.

Bernard the Penitent, bl., born Provence, died Saint-Bertin, near Saint-Omer, north-east France. In 1170 his bishop imposed seven years of strict penance for unspecified crimes. He became a wandering penitent, apparently doing more than required, for a longer period. He became a monk at Saint-Bertin shortly before his death. Feast 19 April.

Bernard Tolomei, bl., abbot, born Siena, 1272, died Mount Oliveto, near Siena, 20 August 1348. Baptized John (Giovanni), he studied at Siena and began to teach there, but in 1312 he went off to a solitary spot called Chiusuri and lived there as a hermit. He was joined by two others from Siena, but when they were suspected of heresy they agreed to follow a traditional monastic rule. They took the Rule of St **Benedict**, and renamed their hermitage Mount Oliveto. The Olivetans followed a strict interpretation of the Rule, with some additional mortifications, and they wore a white habit. A second monastery was opened in Siena in Bernard's own lifetime. When plague broke out in Siena, Bernard and the other monks cared for the sick. Bernard himself died of plague.

Bernardette Soubirous, visionary, born Lourdes, France, 7 January 1844, died Nevers, 16 April 1879. She was born into a very poor family and was uneducated. While gathering wood beside the river Gave on 11 February 1858, she had the first of 18 visions – they lasted until 16 July that year – of the Virgin Mary, who identified herself, in the local patois, under the recently defined title of 'The Immaculate Conception'. Although she was not at first believed, the visions came eventually to be accepted as authentic, and Lourdes became a major shrine. Bernardette was then received into the school of the Sisters of Charity of Nevers, who had a house in Lourdes, and in 1866 she joined the order at Nevers.

Bernardine of Feltre, bl., born Feltre, near Venice, 1439, died Pavia, 28 September 1494. Baptized Martino Tomitano, he went to study law and philosophy in Padua in 1456, but encountered **James of the Marches**, as a result of which he joined the Friars Minor of the Observance, taking the name Bernardine after **Bernardine of Siena**. He was ordained in 1463, and six years later was appointed one of the order's preachers. For the next quarter of a century he travelled around Italy preaching against the abuses of society to enormous effect. He was particularly concerned about usury, and in 1484 started the first of his *mibtes di pietà*, foundations in the form of pawn shops to lend money to the poor. He was not the first to have had the idea, but he developed a viable system, administered by a committee of friars and lay people, and charging a very low rate of interest.

Bernardine of Fossa, bl., born Fossa in the Abruzzi, 1420, died near Aquila, 27 November 1503. Having studied at Aquila and Perugia, he joined the Observant Franciscans after hearing a sermon by **James of the Marches**, and went on himself to become a successful preacher. He was sent to the Balkans as a peacemaker among warring Franciscans, in which he was successful. He avoided being made a bishop, and produced a number of books, among which were a life of **Bernardine of Siena** and a history of his order.

Bernardine of Siena, preacher, born near Siena, 8 September 1380, died Aquila, 20 May 1444. An orphan, he was brought up by relatives in Siena, attended school, studied humanities and philosophy and later canon law at the university. He finished in 1400 and worked with plague victims in the hospital and himself became ill. In 1402 he joined the Franciscans and was ordained in 1404. He preached, studied and wrote and in 1414 became vicar provincial of the Observants of Tuscany. From 1417 to 1429 he preached throughout central and northern Italy, sometimes to crowds of about 30,000 people. He was a gifted speaker, intelligent, holy, sensitive to individuals

and to political situations, full of human warmth and joy. He continued preaching until his death, but combined this with writing and with administrative office. He was one of the leading proponents of devotion to the Holy Name, and the creator of the often used 'yhs' (or 'ihs') trigram, set in the middle of a radiant sun. His writings consist mainly of his sermons, but he also wrote more systematic theological works.

Bernardine Realino, Jesuit and humanist, born Carpi, near Modena, 1 December 1530, died Lecce, 2 July 1616. Realino was named master of novices by **Francis Borgia**, the general of the Jesuits. Assigned to Lecce in Apulia, he remained there for 42 years, founding a college, building a baroque church and gaining a reputation for sanctity in the direction of souls. Numerous miraculous cures and prophecies were attributed to him, as well as several visions of Our Lady and the crucified Jesus. He agreed on his deathbed to be the protector of Lecce in heaven. Pius XII canonized him in 1947.

Berno, bl., first abbot of Cluny, born Burgundy, *c.* 850, died Cluny, 13 January 927. He joined the Benedictines at St Martin of Autun, was at the abbey of Baume-les-Messieres, and in about 890 he founded Gigny, becoming its superior. In 909 he was given the territory of Cluny by the duke of Aquitaine and built a new abbey dedicated to Ss Peter and Paul. Under the Cluniac reforms it was placed under the immediate authority of the Holy See. The houses of Deols and Sauvigny were also put in Berno's charge.

Bernulf of Utrecht, bishop, died Utrecht, 19 July 1054. He was appointed bishop of Utrecht by the emperor, Conrad II, and probably took part in an expedition against the Hungarians led by his successor, Henry III. He was a reformer, promoting Clunaic reform in the monasteries in his diocese.

Bernward, bishop, born Utrecht, *c.* 960, died 20 November 1022. He was brought up by his uncle, the bishop of Utrecht, and educated in the cathedral school at Hildesheim. He studied at Mainz and became a priest. He was imperial chaplain and tutor to the future Emperor Henry III. In 993 he became bishop of Hildesheim. He reorganized the diocese, built many new churches (as a result of which he became patron saint of builders and of the skills related to building). In addition he was himself a distinguished worker in metal. He resigned his bishopric in 1020, and for the last two years of his life entered a Benedictine monastery.

Bertha de' Alberti, bl., born Florence, died Tuscany, 1163. A nun in the Vallombrosan convent in Florence, her superior, **Qualdo Galli**, sent her to be abbess of Cavriglia in the Valdardo. Feast 24 March.

Bertha of Blangy, abbess, born Arras, died Blangy, *c.* 725. She founded the monastery of Blangy in about 686, and went to live there with two of her daughters. Feast 4 July.

Bertha of Val d'Or, founder and abbess, died Aenay, *c.* 690. She lived a celibate life with Gombert, the founder of the convent of St Peter in Rheims. He was murdered and Bertha founded a convent at Avenay, previously Val d'Or, and was its first abbess. It is thought that she herself was murdered by her husband's relatives. Feast 1 May.

Bertharius, abbot and martyr, born in Lombardy, died at the hands of the Saracens in Teano, Campania, 22 October 884. Joined the monastery at Monte Cassino and became abbot there in 848. He entertained the Emperor Louis II in 866, gained many privileges for the monastery and secured its exemption from episcopal jurisdiction from Pope John VIII. He encouraged the development of sacred studies and many of those who studied in the monastery became bishops. His extant writings include a homily on **Scholastica**, the sister of **Benedict**, who was buried at Monte Cassino, and a poem on the life, death and miracles of Benedict himself. Feast 22 October.

Berthold, born France, died Palestine, *c.* 1195. A Crusader, he either joined, or established, a group of hermits living on Mount Carmel and became their first superior-general. He is considered the founder of the Carmelite Order, although he did not write their first Rule. Feast 29 March.

Berthold of Garsten, bl., Benedictine abbot and reformer, born Constance, died Garsten, Austria, 27 July 1142 . Became a monk at Sankt Blasien and

later its subprior; appointed prior at Götweig in 1107 and later made abbot of Garsten, which flourished as a centre for reform during his reign as abbot.

Bertilia of Mareuil, died France, early eighth century. As a married woman in the Frankish aristocracy, she devoted herself to the poor and sick. As a widow, she lived as a solitary in a cell adjoining the church of St Amand that she had had built at Mareuil in north-eastern France. Feast 3 January.

Bertilla of Chelles, abbess, born near Soisson, died Chelles, *c.* 705. She joined the monastery of Jouarre, near Meaux, but headed a small group to form the community of Chelles, a monastery refounded by **Bathilde**, the English wife of King Clovis II. Bathilde herself joined the community, as did **Hereswitha**, the widow of a king of the East Angles. Bertilla is said to have ruled the community for 46 years. Feast 5 November.

Bertinus, Benedictine abbot, born Orval, near Coutances, France, *c.* 615, died Sithiu, France, 5 September 709. Following his training at Luxeuil, he was called to Morinia (modern Pas-de-Calais) where he succeeded Momelin as abbot of Ss Peter and Paul on the island of Sithiu. As abbot, Bertinus oversaw both the abbey and the church of Sainte-Marie on the hill. He built a small monastery at Wormhout on property he received from a Flemish noble for four men whom he received as monks: Quadanoc, Ingenoc, Madoc and St Winnoc. At his request, Rigobert built the church of Saint-Martin on Sithiu.

Bertrand of Aquileia, bl., patriarch of Aquileia, born probably Montcuq, France, *c.* 1260, died near Spilimbergo, Italy, 6 June 1350. After training in both canon and civil law at the university of Toulouse and holding a professorship there, Bertrand became a pontifical chaplain in 1318. In 1334 he was made patriarch of Aquileia, which he then set about reconquering and restoring. His success alarmed the leaders of Florence, who allied with the pope and Venice to regain what Bertrand had conquered. In response, Bertrand called a synod at Aquileia (1339) to affirm the protection of Church officials from secular rulers. This failed, however, and Bertrand's travelling party was attacked by forces of the count of Goritz after the Synod of Padua in 1350, leaving Bertrand mortally wounded. Feast 6 June.

Bertrand of Comminges, bishop, born Isle-Jourdain, France, c. 1050, died probably Comminges, France, 16 October 1123. Nobly born, Bertrand studied in the Abbey of La Chaise-Dieu before being made canon and archdeacon of Toulouse. He was elected bishop of Comminges in 1073. He visited every corner of his diocese during his 50-year tenure. In his diocese, 2 May is commemorated as the 'Great Pardon of Comminges', remembering a time when Bertrand delivered from Moorish exile a dishonest noble who once opposed him. Feast 16 October.

Bertrand of Garrigues, bl., born Garrigues, southern France, c. 1172, died Toulouse, France, after 1230. Bertrand was a friend and follower of St **Dominic**, joining the Dominican Order in 1215. He frequently accompanied his mentor on his many travels, or else was placed in charge of the fledgling organization in Dominic's absence. In 1217 he went to Paris, returning to Toulouse as prior of St Romanus in 1218, a post he held until his death. He was made provincial of Provence in 1221 and had a reputation for prayer and piety. Feast 3 September.

Bertrand of Le Mans, bishop, born c. 550, died Le Mans, 623. Little or nothing is known about his early life. He was educated in the cathedral school at Paris, became an archdeacon and, in 573, bishop of Le Mans. It was a difficult time, and he was more than once driven from his see, but occupied permanently from 605 thanks to the support of King Clothaire II. He founded an abbey to serve as a hospice for pilgrims, but is best remembered for encouraging the planting of vineyards. Feast 30 June.

Bertulf, bishop and martyr, died Mondovi, Liguria, c. 800. Feast 24 March.

Bertulf of Bobbio, abbot, died 639 or 640. From a noble pagan family in Austrasia, he converted to Christianity, becoming a monk in 620. He later transferred to the monastery of Bobbio, Italy, where he was elected abbot in 627. He preached against Arianism, which had spread to Italy. He also fought against attempts at episcopal control, persuading Pope Honorius to grant his monastery exemption from the jurisdiction of the bishop of Tortona. Feast 19 August.

Bertulf (or Bertoul) of Renty, born in Germany, died in the monastery of Renty, Flanders, c. 705. Travelled to Flanders, where he became a Christian and steward to Count Wamba and his wife, with whom he made a pilgrimage to Rome. At the death of the count and his wife, Bertulf entered the monastery of Renty, which he had himself founded. Feast 5 February.

Besamone, martyr, third/fourth centuries. Coptic Church. The son of a royal official called Basilides, and a soldier. He confessed himself to be a Christian and was martyred, possibly during the reign of Diocletian.

Bessarion of Egypt, hermit and saint, died 425. A native of Egypt, he became a hermit under **Anthony** and then **Macarius**, and established a pilgrim shelter in Jerusalem and a monastery at Sinai. He was famed for his severe asceticism and, as with his mentors, many miracles were attributed to him. Feast 17 June.

Bessarion of Larissa I, bishop, fourteenth/fifteenth centuries. Byzantine Church. Elected bishop in 1490.

Bessarion of Larissa II, bishop, born Porta Panaghia, c. 1490, died Trikala, 13 September 1540. Byzantine Church. He was ordained deacon at Trikala – where the bishop of Larissa resided because of problems in his own city – c. 1516. He was consecrated bishop of Elassona when he was about 27, but he was unpopular with the people and had to return to Trikala. Four years later he became bishop of Stagona. In 1527 he returned to Trikala as metropolitan of Larissa. He reconstructed and reformed monasteries, cared for the poor and built bridges. Feast 15 September.

Bessarion of Smolen, bishop, martyr, died Smolen, 29 July 1670. Bulgarian Church. His theological college and cathedral having been demolished during a persecution, he fled to the village of Raikovo. From there he travelled around the region with a bodyguard, encouraging people to resist attempts to convert them to Islam. He was finally captured and beaten to death.

Bessarion (Saray) of Romania, Orthodox martyr, born Bosnia, 1714, died Kufstein, *c.* 1760. Romanian Church. He was a monk and wandering preacher in Transylvania at a time when the Empress Maria Teresa was attempting to unite the Orthodox under Rome. Like a number of other Serbian and Romanian priests and monks of the time, he was arrested and imprisoned at Kufstein in the Tyrol. The exact date of his death there is unknown. His name was entered into the Romanian Church calendar in 1950 and he was solemnly canonized with other martyrs in June 1992. Feast 21 October.

Bestawros, monk, died Gondar, early eighteenth century. Coptic Church. Abbot of Dabra Hayq, he was accused of teaching theology opposed by the king. He was summoned to Gondar and imprisoned. The king, however, came to think him a holy man, released him, and gave him a senior position at court.

Besu'a Amlak, founder, died Tanfe, Eritrea, *c.* 1505. Ethiopic Church. His family were refugees from persecution, and were hospitably received by monks. Besu'a Amlak (then called Besu' Zamaharo) decided himself to become a monk, changing his name in the process. He became a priest at Danba, but continued to wander for some years, eventually founding a monastery, Dabra Sellase. He died aged 75 on 18 March.

Betharius, bishop. Bishop of Chartres from 595. Feast 2 August.

Beuno, abbot, born Herefordshire, died Clynnog Fawr, north Wales, sixth/seventh century. He founded several monasteries in Wales, including Clynnog Fawr in present-day Gwynedd and on Anglesey Island. He is best remembered in connection with **Winefride**, apparently his niece, whose head he restored after her beheading. Feast 21 April.

Bibiana Khamphai, born Sonkong, 1925, died there, 26 December 1940. She was a helper on the mission station. She and several others (see **Martyrs of Thailand**) were marched to the cemetery and shot. Feast 16 December.

Bidzina, Scialva and Elisbar, princes, martyrs, died Persia, 1661. Georgian Church. The three were leaders of the Georgian army attempting to free eastern Georgia from the Persians. The shah demanded their heads, threatening otherwise to devastate the whole of Georgia. They voluntarily gave themselves up, which impressed the shah, who offered them their freedom were they to convert, but they refused and were executed. Feast 18 September.

Bifam, martyr, born Cairo, died there, 3 July, eleventh century. Coptic Church. The son of a rich family of Old Cairo, he became a Muslim, for which he was told to leave home. Soon afterwards he repented and decided to become a monk. He was, however, arrested and condemned to be decapitated for renouncing Islam. The governor, a friend of his family, would have released him if he had simulated lunacy, but this he refused to do, encouraged by a monk of his monastery.

Bilhild, abbess, early eighth century. Details of her life are only known from legends written in the twelfth century, which describe her as a noblewoman from Veitshöchheim near Würzburg who, at the age of 17, married Duke Hetan I of Thuringia. After his death she fled to her uncle, Bishop Rigibert of Mainz, became a nun and founded the monastery of Altmünster, near Mainz. Feast 27 November.

Birgitta, patron of Sweden and religious founder, born Upland, Sweden, 1302/3, died Rome, 23 July 1373. A daughter of the governor of Upland, Birgitta was the mother of eight children, including St **Catherine of Sweden**. Upon the death of her husband in 1344, she retired to a Cistercian monastery, where she experienced visions leading her to establish a contemplative order at Vadstena in 1346. In 1349 she moved to Rome to secure confirmation of her order. She is known for her charitable works, urging Church reform and pleading for the restoration of the papacy to Rome from Avignon. Her order was confirmed by the pope in 1370, and she was canonized in 1391.

Birinus, bishop of Dorchester, died Dorchester, 649 or 650, although his relics were later moved to Winchester. Birinus was possibly of German ancestry, although he was a priest in Rome. He came to England with the encouragement of Pope Honorius I and was consecrated bishop in Genoa. He arrived in England in 634, intending, it seems, to travel to the furthest parts of the island, but settled in Dorchester, where he converted the king of the West Saxons. Feast 5 December.

Bisus, monk, eleventh century. Coptic Church. A monk of **John Kama's** monastery in Wadi al-Natrun, he was renowned for miracles. On the death of the patriarch **Cristodolus** he was asked to become patriarch himself, but refused.

Bladulph (Blidulph) of Bobbio, monk, died c. 630. He was a disciple of **Columbanus**, a monk at Bobbio, Italy. He denounced the king of the Lombards, Arioald, for heresy and sought to reform the court. Feast 2 January.

Blaise (Blasius), abbot, died Constantinople, 911. Feast 31 March.

Blaise (Blasius), bishop of Sebaste and martyr, died c. 316. According to a late legend, he was martyred under Licinius, after being caught hiding in a cave. He is said to have performed numerous miracles, such as saving the life of a child who was almost choked by a fish bone, and he is invoked against throat diseases. He is also invoked for the cure of diseases in cattle, and is the patron saint of wool-combers. One of the 14 'auxiliary saints' or 'Holy Helpers'. Feast 3 February.

Blaithmaic, see **Blathmac**.

Blandina, virgin martyr, died Lyons, 177. A young slave girl arrested together with her mistress, she was martyred alongside **Pothinus**, the bishop of Lyons, and a number of others. She is said to have died tied to a stake as to a cross, a Christlike victim, sending her companions on ahead of her to God, and making a great impression on pagan onlookers. Feast 2 June.

Blandina Merten, bl., born Duppenweiler, Germany, 1883, died 1918, beatified 1987. From a devout family, she joined the Ursulines and was devoted to the children for whom she cared. She suffered greatly and died young. She is commemorated for accomplishing her ordinary duty extraordinarily well. Feast 18 May.

Blane (Blaan), bishop, born Bute, Scotland, died Kingarth, Bute, sixth century. He apparently became a monk in Ireland, and returned to evangelize Scotland. The cathedral at Dunblane is built on the site of his monastery. Feast 10 August.

Blathmac (Blaithmaic), abbot, martyred Iona, c. 793. From Ireland, he travelled to England, looking for martyrdom, and was killed by pagan Danes on the altar steps of the abbey church. Feast 19 January.

Blitmund of Saint-Valery, abbot, died c. 650. A monk at Bobbio under **Attalas**, he went with **Walaricus** (Valéry) to France. They founded the abbey of Leucone, later Saint-Valéry, where Blitmund was second abbot after Walaricus. Feast 3 January.

Bodo, bishop, born Laon, died Toul, c. 670. The brother of **Sadalberga**, it is possible that he joined the community of the monastery she founded at Laon – although in some versions of his life he is married to **Odile**, and they both entered the monastery. As bishop of Toul he founded three monasteries.

Boethius, Anicius Manlius Severinus, philosopher and martyr, born Rome, c. 480, died Pavia, c. 524. A member of the Anicia family, he was brought up by Q. Aurelius Symmachus and married his daughter, Rusticiana. He translated into Latin many of the works of Greek philosophers, including Plato, Aristotle and Pythagoras, and wrote treaties on logic, mathematics, geometry and music. His best-known theological treatise is *De Trinitate*. His philosophical work *De consolatione philosophiae*, written while he was in prison, was especially influential in medieval thought. Often considered the last Roman philosopher and first scholastic theologian, he was also involved in the politics of the day, being appointed consul in 510 and later master of offices. He was executed for defending an ex-consul against charges of treason. Canonized 1883. Feast 23 October.

Bogolep of Ceryi Jar, monk, seventeenth century. Russian Church. Of a noble family. Little is known of him for certain, but he is said to have become a monk after having been saved from drowning in the Volga. Feast 29 July.

Bogolep of Uglic, *see* **Adrian and Bogolep of Uglic**.

Bogumil, bishop, born Dobrow, Poland, died Uniejow, 1182. He and his twin brother Boguphalus were both educated in Paris. On their return to Poland, Boguphalus became a Cistercian monk and Bogumil founded a church in his home town, which he then served as a priest. His uncle was archbishop of Gniezno, and Bogumil succeeded him. He ran the diocese for five years, but not to his own high standards, so he resigned and, despite the fact that he had, as archbishop, founded a Cistercian monastery at Coronowa, became a Camaldolese monk at Uniejow. Feast 10 June.

Bohtizad of Kurhe, monk. Syriac Church. Feast 15 November.

Bojan, prince, martyr, died early ninth century. Bulgarian Church. Decapitated for releasing Christian prisoners, which was taken as a sign that he had converted to Christianity himself. Feast 28 March.

Boleslawa Maria Lament, foundress, born Lowicz, Poland, 3 July 1862, died Bialystok, 29 January 1946. She joined the Congregation of the Family of Mary when she was 22 and was sent to work in Mogilev, Russia, among the Orthodox. She founded a Congregation, the Missionary Sisters of the Holy Family, precisely to work for the reunion with Rome of the Orthodox, and set up the mother house in St Petersburg. At the Russian Revolution she and her sisters returned to Poland, and continued to work among the Orthodox in northern Poland. She set up her mother house at Bialystok.

Bona, patron of travel hostesses, born Pisa, Italy, *c*. 1156, died there, 29 May 1207. Bona joined the Canons Regular of St Augustine as a young woman, serving St Martin's church in Pisa. She had a vision that instructed her to make a trip to the Holy Land, which she did, and there she met a hermit who told her what other places to go to and when to return home. Returning to Pisa, she was attacked by Saracens and molested by highwaymen. For the rest of her life she lived in seclusion, except for pilgrimages to Santiago de Compostela and Peter's tomb in Rome.

Bonaventure, cardinal and doctor of the Church, born Verterbo, Italy, 1221, died Lyons, 15 July 1274. A Franciscan who both studied and taught in Paris. His book *The Poverty of Christ* arose from attacks on mendicant friars by other professors at Paris. Between 1257 and 1274 he was minister general of the Friars Minor, seeking a middle way in the tensions between radicals and moderates. In 1264 he established one of the earliest Marian confraternities, the Society of Gonfalone. In 1273 he became cardinal-bishop of Albano. He prepared the programme for the fourteenth Ecumenical Council of Lyons which brought union with the Greeks. His works include *Commentary on the Sentences of Peter Lombard*, *Perfection of Life*, *Soliloquy* and many biblical commentaries, sermons, a life of St **Francis** and a commentary on the Franciscan Rule. Canonized in 1482 and made doctor of the Church in 1588.

Bonaventure Baduario, bl., cardinal, born Peraga, near Padua, died Rome, 1386. Of a noble family, he became an Augustinian friar and studied in Paris. He wrote a number of theological works and was a friend of Petrarch, at whose funeral he preached. He became superior of his order in 1377, and the following year a cardinal. He was killed by an arrow while on his way to the Vatican, an assassination thought to have been commissioned by the ruler of Padua, a relative whom he had angered. Feast 10 June.

Bonaventure Buonaccorsi, bl., born Pistoia, *c*. 1240, died Orvieto, 14 December 1315. Of a noble family, and something of a troublemaker in his city, he was converted by the preaching of the Servite **Philip Benizi**, and himself joined the order. He remained as an assistant to St Philip for many years, but was also used as a peacemaker among warring states in central Italy. In 1328 he became prior in Orvieto, then prior at Montepulciano, before being sent back to Pistoia to restore peace there.

Bonaventure of Barcelona, bl., born Riudoms, Tarragona, 24 November 1620, died Rome, 1684. Baptized Miguel Bautista Grau, he worked as a shepherd, then married, but after the death of his wife two years later he joined the Franciscans. In 1658 he went to Rome, where he worked as doorkeeper of a friary. Himself much given to mystical experiences, he established retreat houses for the Reformed Franciscans, serving as guardian of one of them although he never became a priest. Feast 11 September.

Bonaventure of Forli, born Forli, died Udine, 1491, cult confirmed 1911. Joining the Servites in his thirties, he became a successful preacher, credited with bringing many people back to the faith. Vicar general of his order from 1488, he is venerated in Venice. Feast 31 March.

Bonaventure of Potenza, born Potenza, 1651, died Ravello, 26 October 1711. Baptized Carlo Antonio Lavagna, he became a Franciscan Conventual, taking the name Bonaventure. He worked for some time at Amalfi and because of his holiness of life and strict observance of the Rule, was made master of novices.

Boniface (Wynfrith), archbishop, missionary to Germany, born Crediton, Devon, 680, martyred Dokkum, Frisia, eve of Pentecost, 5 June 754. Went to Frisia in 716 to work under **Willibrord**. He was given papal authority for his mission in 719 and worked in Bavaria and Thuringia. He cut down the Oak of Thor near Fritzlar. From 741 he was given authority to reform the Frankish Church, which he did by holding a number of councils. He founded an abbey at Fulda *c.* 743 and became archbishop of Mainz *c.* 747. His influence extended papal authority. In 752 he resigned his see to return to evangelistic work in Frisia.

Boniface I, pope, born Rome, died there, 4 September 422. Having been the papal representative in Constantinople, he was elected to the papacy on 28 December 418 in a disputed election, when he was already quite old and frail. Boniface was ordered out of Rome by the Emperor Honorius because the prefect of the city supported the other candidate for the papacy, but his rival succeeded in infuriating the imperial government and Boniface was recognized on 3 April 419. He was indefatigable in promoting the authority of the papacy, and supported **Augustine** and the other north African bishops in the controversy with the Pelagians.

Boniface IV, pope, the son of a doctor from Valeria, Italy, he became a deacon under Pope **Gregory I** and in 591 is mentioned as papal treasurer. He was elected to the papacy on 15 September 608 and died 8 May 615, after a pontificate in which he in many ways tried to emulate Pope Gregory. Like Gregory, he turned his home into a monastery. He also held a synod in Rome to regulate monastic life. This synod was attended by the bishop of London, to whom he gave letters for the English, for the king of Kent and the archbishop of Canterbury. He received a letter of criticism from **Columbanus** over his predecessor's behaviour in a doctrinal dispute, and received permission to turn the Pantheon into a church dedicated to the Virgin Mary.

Boniface of Lausanne, born Brussels, died there, 1260, canonized 1702. He taught in Paris and Cologne, then became bishop of Lausanne. Unpopular because he criticized people, including the emperor – who had him physically attacked – he retired to La Cambre, a Cistercian monastery, continuing as a peripatetic bishop. Feast 19 February.

Boniface of Querfurt, see **Bruno of Querfurt**.

Boniface of Savoy, bl., monk and archbishop of Canterbury, born Savoy, *c.* 1207, son of Thomas I, count of Savoy, died there, 14 July 1270. He joined the Carthusian Order whilst still a boy and in 1234 was elected bishop of Belley in Burgundy. In 1241 he was elected to succeed **Edmund of Abingdon** at Canterbury, but because of a delay in confirmation of this office, he did not arrive until 1244. He attended the Council of Lyons in 1245 and only returned to Canterbury in 1249, when he was enthroned. During his tenure he carried through a number of financial reforms. He also made two visitations of his province – once before going to the Council and once afterwards – which met with a degree of hostility among his clergy.

Boniface of Tarsus, martyr, born Rome, died Tarsus, Cilicia, *c.* 307. His employer apparently sent him from Rome to collect some relics of martyrs. In Tarsus he saw Christians being tortured and demanded to join them. He was tortured and executed and his body returned to Rome. Feast 14 May (suppressed).

Bonitus of Clermont, bishop, died Lyons, 706. He had been chancellor to Sigebert III, king of Austrasia, and was recommended for the see of Clermont by his brother, who died in that post in 689. Bonitus was duly consecrated, but he came to doubt the legality of the procedure, resigned the see and retired to the Abbey of Manglieu. He died returning from a pilgrimage to Rome. Feast 15 January.

Bononius, abbot, born Bologna, Italy, mid-900s, died Lucedio, Italy, 30 August 1026. A Benedictine monk of St Stephen's in Bologna, he became a disciple of St **Romuald**, who sent him to preach in Syria and Egypt. He wished to become a hermit on Mount Sinai in 990, but his bishop recalled him in order to make him the abbot of Lucedio. As abbot, his major concern was monastic reform.

Bonosus, died *c.* 373. He was bishop of Trèves and a disciple of **Hilary of Poitiers**. Feast 17 February.

Boris and Gleb, princes of Kiev, died 1015. They were the sons of **Vladimir of Kiev** and his wife Anne of Constantinople who, on the death of their father, shared with other brothers their father's dominions, as was the custom. Their half-brother Svyatopolk, who wished to reunite the country, made war on his two brothers. Boris refused to fight against his brother, and was murdered beside the river Alta, calling on the passion of Christ. Gleb was subsequently assassinated on a boat travelling down the Dnieper to Kiev. When in 1020 Svyatopolk was himself overthrown by another brother, **Jaroslav** of Novgorod, the two murdered brothers were reburied in the church of St Basil at Vyshgorod, where their tomb became a centre of pilgrimage and miracles. They were regarded as martyrs in the Russian Church, and in 1724 Pope

Benedict XII approved their cult for the Western Church. Feast 24 July.

Boris, James, Theodore I, Silvanus, Theodore II, Basil I, Demetrius, Michael, John, Basil II, martyrs, died sixteenth century. Russian Church. Soldiers who died in the wars against the Muslims of Khazan, which was regarded as a holy war by the Orthodox.

Boris of Bulgaria, king, born 827, died 7 May 907. In the face of military pressure, Boris's decision to accept baptism from the Byzantine Church in 864 introduced Christianity among the Slavs and Bulgars of his kingdom. He thus became the first Christian ruler of Bulgaria. The refusal of the Byzantine Church to grant autonomy to his Church compelled Boris to turn to Rome for missionaries and bishops in 866. The Bulgarian Church returned to the Byzantine fold in 870, but in 880 Rome and Constantinople reached an agreement that placed Bulgarians under Roman jurisdiction. Political factors and distance prevented Rome from significant oversight, however, and the Church remained largely influenced by Constantinople. In 885 Boris accepted refugee clergy of the Slavonic rite who fled from Moravia after the death of **Methodius**, and their work was particularly successful amongst the Bulgarian Slavs. Upon his retirement in 889 Boris appointed his son Vladimir to the throne and became a monk. Vladimir's relapse into paganism caused Boris to resume power for a brief period while he established his son Symeon as the favoured successor, but he then went back to his monastery, where he died. Feast 2 May.

Boris of Turov, prince, died Turov, 2 May 1159. Feast 23 June.

Botulf, or Botolph, abbot, born England or possibly Ireland, died possibly Boston, Lincolnshire, *c.* 680. The earliest life comes from four centuries after his death, from which it seems he travelled for a time with his brother Adulf in Germany, before returning to England to found a monastery in 654 which is generally identified as having been at Boston, although all trace of it was destroyed during the Danish invasions. Feast 17 June.

Botvid, saint and lay evangelist, born Sweden, date unknown, died there, c. 1100. A pious layman, concerned with promoting Christianity in Sweden, he was killed by a slave he had freed. Little else is known of his life. He is portrayed in iconography with an axe and a fish. Feast 28 July.

Bova, abbess, seventh century. The place and date of Bova's birth are unknown, although according to Flodoard of Rheims, her father was Sigebert, king of Austrasia, and her sister was St **Baudry** of Montraucon. Bova was the first abbess of Saint-Pierre, Rheims, to which she introduced the Benedictine Rule. Her feast day, shared with her niece and probable successor **Doda**, is 14 April.

Braulio, bishop, born possibly Seville, died Saragossa, 651. He was a disciple of **Isidore**, and was elected bishop of Saragossa in 631. He attended the fourth, fifth and sixth councils of Toledo, and was zealous in imposing discipline upon the clergy. He was renowned for his personal asceticism. He wrote a life of, and a poem to, St **Emilian**, and he is also said to have completed some works of Isidore. Feast 26 March.

Brendan of Birr, Irish abbot, sixth century. Little is known of Brendan's life except that he was associated with **Brendan of Clonfert**. He appears only as a figure in accounts of other saints, but was referred to as 'the chief of the prophets of Ireland'. His primary monastery was located at Birr, County Offaly. Feast November 29.

Brendan of Clonfert, abbot, born perhaps near Tralee, Ireland, c. 486, died Clonfert, Ireland, c. 578. Little is known about his life, although his father's name is given as Findlugh, and it is claimed that as a child he was for some years in the charge of St **Ita**. He became a monk, and possibly the founder of the monastery at Clonfert c. 559, to which he gave a Rule of life. He founded Annadown, Inishadroun and Ardfert abbeys. There is a well-known story told in the ninth-century *Navigation of St Brendan* of him setting off with some 60 monks in coracles to find the 'Islands off the Blessed'. These are usually discounted as legends, but he may well have travelled to Scotland. Feast 16 May.

Bretannion of Tomi, bishop, died c. 380. The Arian emperor Valens exiled him from his see of Tomi, in Scythia, near the Danube's mouth, because the bishop insisted on Christ's divinity, but he was forced by the people to let him return. Feast 25 January.

Brian Lacey, bl., martyr, born Yorkshire, died Tyburn, London, 10 December 1591. He was arrested for giving help to priests, having been betrayed as a Catholic by his own brother.

Brice, bishop, died Tours, 444. He studied in Marmoutier under **Martin of Tours**. He was ordained but was an ambitious priest, envious of his tutor. In 397, after Martin's death, he was consecrated bishop of Tours and ministered with little care for those in his see. In 430 he was evicted from his diocese and spent seven years in exile in Rome, during which time his character was reformed. When he returned to Tours c. 437, his ministry had been so transformed that he was proclaimed a saint on his death. Feast 13 November.

Bridget, see also **Birgitta, Brigid**.

Brieuc, or Briocus, abbot, born possibly Cardiganshire, Wales, died Saint-Brieuc, Brittany, some time in the fifth or perhaps sixth century. He is said to have been miraculously converted from paganism, educated in France and, after his return to England, summoned back to France by a dream. He founded a monastery near Tréguier on the Brittany coast, and a second one at Saint-Brieuc. He is said to have lived almost 100 years.

Brigid, abbess, born Offaly, Ireland, c. 460, died Kildare, c. 528. After making her religious profession, Brigid founded a church on the Liffey plain called Cill Dara (Kildare), or 'the church of the oak'. Nearby lived a hermit named Conleth, who ruled a community of men as bishop and abbot. Conleth's monks shared a church with Brigid's nuns, thus forming the only double monastery to have developed in Ireland. In addition to ruling her community, Brigid was remembered for her acts of charity. She was known as the 'Mary of Gael' and devotion to her spread with the work of the Irish missionaries and pilgrims to the continent. Brigid is recognized as one of the three patron saints of Ireland. Feast 1 February.

Brihtwald, see **Brithwald**.

Brinolf Algotsson, bishop, died 1317. He was bishop of Scara, Sweden. Feast 6 February.

Brithwald, abbot and bishop, died probably Glastonbury, England, 22 April 1045. Brithwald (or Beorhtweald) was a monk at the abbey of Glastonbury before being made abbot of the same and bishop of Ramsbury, Wiltshire in 995. Even though his episcopate lasted 50 years, there is no record of his life or activity. He was remembered as a benefactor of Glastonbury, where his tomb lies, and for a vision in which he foresaw the succession of Edward the Confessor to the English throne. Feast 22 January.

Britta, see **Maura**.

Brittonius (Britto), bishop, died Trier, 386. He was a bishop of Trier who opposed the Priscillians, but always refused to hand them over to the state for condemnation. Feast 5 May.

Brocard, born France, died Mount Carmel, Palestine, c. 1230. He succeeded **Berthold** as superior of the hermits on Mount Carmel, and was responsible for negotiating and imposing upon them what became the Carmelite Rule. Feast 2 September.

Bronislawa, bl., nun, born Kamien, Silesia, Poland, 1203, died near Krakow, Poland, 29 August 1259. Of a noble birth and related to both St **Hyacinth** and Bl. **Ceslaus of Silesia**, Bronislawa entered the Premonstratensian convent near Krakow at 16. She was reportedly a model of mortification, virtue and the contemplative life. She had a vision in which she saw St Hyacinth being carried to heaven by Mary, after which she devoted almost all her time to contemplative prayer. Feast 30 August.

Bruno, founder of the Carthusian Order, born Cologne, c. 1032, died La Torre, Calabria, 6 October 1101. He studied at Rheims, Tours, and theology at Cologne c. 1048, probably being ordained c. 1055. His working life started as canon

of St Cunibert's, Cologne, and then he taught at the cathedral school of Rheims where the future Pope **Urban II** was one of his pupils. He rose through the ranks of the cathedral clergy, but, scandalized by the life of the bishop, Manasses, he decided to enter religious life. Initially this was as a hermit under the guidance of **Robert of Molesme**, who founded Citeaux, then under the protection of Bishop St Hugh of Grenoble he founded a community in the mountains near Grenoble. This was to be the Grande Chartreuse. The (Carthusian) monks lived a quasi-eremitical life, but in a monastery, a Rule of life with more in common with the early Egyptian monks than with the Benedictines of the Carthusian order. In 1090 Urban summoned him to Rome, where he lived in a hermitage he established in the baths of Diocletian. When Urban fled south, Bruno went too, and was offered the bishopric of Reggio, which he refused. Instead he founded a hermitage in La Torre.

Bruno, bishop, died Bosenburg, on the Danube, 1045. Bishop of Würzburg, Franconia, now Bavaria, from 1033, he spent all his private fortune on building churches in his diocese. A gallery gave way as he was eating with the Emperor Henry III, accidentally killing him. Feast 27 May.

Bruno of Cologne ('the Great'), archbishop, born c. 925, died Cologne, 11 October 965. He was of royal birth, son of Emperor Henry I, The Fowler, and became abbot of monasteries at Lorsch, near Worms, and Corvei on the Weser. He was ordained in 950 and travelled with his brother Henry II to Italy the following year. His appointment to the archbishopric of Cologne in 953 enabled him to further the ecclesiastical and temporal policy of his brother Emperor Otto, which led to a greater degree of peace in his domains.

Bruno of Querfurt, bishop, monk and martyr, born Saxony, c. 970, died Prussia, 14 February 1009. During the early part of his life he became a canon at Magdeburg cathedral and was attached to the court of Emperor Otto III. He travelled widely with Otto and dedicated his life to missionary work among the Slavs and Baltic peoples, emulating **Adalbert of Prague**, his educator in childhood. He entered monastic life under **Romuald**, founder of the Camaldolese at Pereum, near Ravenna. His name in religion was Boniface. In 1008 he went to Poland with colleagues and attempted to bring peace between the Poles and Germans. He was martyred with 18 companions after crossing from Poland into Prussia. His main works are a life of Adalbert of Prague and an account of the martyrdom of the Five Polish Brothers. Feast 19 June.

Bruno of Segni, bishop and abbot, born Asti of a noble family, 1049, died Segni, 18 July 1123. He studied at Bologna and Siena, where he became a canon. He was a friend of Pope **Gregory VII**, who made him bishop of Segni in 1079, and a counsellor to **Urban II** and Paschal II. He accompanied Urban to the Council of Clermont in 1095. On his return he was thrown into prison by the count of Segni. He became a monk at Monte Cassino and was elected abbot in November 1107, while retaining his bishopric. He publicly condemned the Concordat of Sutri (1111) between Paschal II and Henry V of Germany, which brought him into conflict with the pope, who forced his return to his bishopric. He was eminent in the field of exegesis and theology, and judged by some as a great liturgist.

Bruno of Würzburg, bishop and imperial counsellor, born c. 1005, died Persenbeug, near Linz, 27 May 1045. He was of royal blood, a member of the Royal Chapel and imperial chancellor of Italy (1027–34). He was elected bishop of Würzburg (1034), where he rebuilt the cathedral and contributed to improving education. During his tenure, the cathedral school expanded. He died suddenly on the way to Hungary and is buried at Würzburg. Feast 17 May.

Budoc, abbot, sixth century. Linked both with Cornwall and Brittany, but nothing reliable is known of his life. Feast 8 December.

Buithe, abbot, died 521. It is unclear whether he was Scottish or Irish. He may have studied in Italy, although more likely Wales, and is associated with Monasterboice, a monastery near Drogheda. Feast 7 December.

Bulus al-Habis, monk, martyr, died 1267. Coptic Church. He had been a senior official in the government of Egypt, but decided to become a hermit, living in the mountains south of Cairo. There, it was said, he found a great treasure hidden in a cave, with which he helped the poor. The treasure was claimed by the ruler of Egypt. When Bulus refused to hand it over, he was executed.

Buqayrah, eleventh century. Coptic Church. A government administrator and a wealthy man, during the rule of al-Hakim (996–1021) he decided to declare himself a Christian and put a cross around his neck. For this he was imprisoned, but later released. For the rest of his life he helped Christians who had suffered for their faith. He was one of the electors of the patriarch after the death of **Zaccarias**, but turned against the new patriarch because of the patriarch's acts of simony. With other rich Copts, he put his money at the service of the Church to pay off debts. His actions were not approved of by the patriarch, who on one occasion threw him out of a synod.

Burchard of Würzburg, bishop, born Wessex, died Germany, c. 754. He became a monk and followed St **Boniface** to Germany c. 732 as a disciple and collaborator. He was made the first bishop of Würzburg in 741 or 742. He travelled to Rome, attended synods in Germany and Franconia, and was entrusted with ambassadorial duties by Pepin III. Buried in the cathedral at Würzburg, his relics were translated to the monastery of St Andrew which he had founded. Feast 14 October.

Buruk Amlak, monk, martyr, fourteenth century. Ethiopic Church. His family were from Constantinople, and he was baptized Amda Mikael, but he changed his name at the age of 12 on becoming a monk in Ethiopia. There he had become the disciple of **Eustacius** and **Absadi**. He was ordained priest by the metroplitan of Scioa. His fame for sanctity reached his family, and he was joined by three brothers and a sister. They all went to live in the village of Ad Haywa in Serawe. Buruk and two of his brothers were killed by a band of rebels.

Buya, monk, seventh century. Syriac Church. With some companions, including his sister, he lived a hermit's life in a cave near the village of Saqlawa in eastern Iraq.

Cadfan, abbot, born Brittany, died Tywyn, Wales, sixth century. He came with his cousin **Padarn**, whom he left at what is now Aberystwyth, and founded a monastery at Tywyn. He is also said to have founded a monastery on Bardsey Island. Bardsey competes with Tywyn as the place of his death and burial. Feast 1 November.

Cadoc, abbot, died Llansannor, Wales, *c.* 575. The son of a Welsh chieftain, he seems to have been educated by an Irishman before founding a monastery at Llancarfan. He left Llancarfan to undertake further study, including in Ireland. Because of his reputation both for holiness and learning, the monastery flourished. There is a story that he went to Benevento in Italy, where he was elected bishop and died a martyr's death, but this seems highly unlikely. Feast 20 September.

Cadroe, abbot, born Scotland, died Metz, 976. Educated in Armagh, he went to England, then France, where he became a Benedicitine at Fleury, at Saint-Benoit-sur-Loire. He was abbot of Waulsort, Ardennes, and then went to Metz to restore St Clement's. Feast 6 March.

Caedwalla, king of Wessex, born *c.* 659, died Rome, 20 April 689 (feast suppressed). He had a very brief, but bloody, reign, during which he brought a number of surrounding kingdoms under his dominion, with the result that Wessex became very powerful. He was a friend of **Wilfrid**, who is said to have tamed his violence. He was the first Anglo-Saxon king to make a pilgrimage to Rome, where he was baptized by the pope and where, several days later, he died, still wearing his white baptismal clothes – which may account for the fact that he was regarded as a saint. The first of four Anglo-Saxon kings to die in Rome, he was buried in St Peter's.

Caesaria, first abbess of the convent in Arles, established *c.* 512 by her brother, **Caesarius of Arles**, who also wrote the Rule. Born Chalon-sur-Saône, *c.* 465, died *c.* 530. The nuns worked with the poor and sick, in girls' education and in dressmaking for themselves and for others outside the convent. They also transcribed books and engaged in daily study, and were enjoined to bathe regularly (although not in Lent) for the sake of their health. Her community also enjoyed the privilege of being exempt from episcopal authority, holding within the community the power to make all decisions concerning the community. Feast 12 January.

Caesaria, second abbess of the convent at Arles and possibly a relative of the first abbess, died Arles, *c.* 559. She commissioned Cyprian of Toulon to write the biography of **Caesarius of Arles**, the founder of the convent. She also had the sermons of Caesarius, as well as the works of **Augustine**, transcribed and sent to various parts of Gaul. Feast 12 January.

Caesarius and Julian, martyrs, died Terracina, third century (?). Caesarius is recorded as being a deacon from Africa. He was martyred in Terracina when he criticized a pagan practice. He was imprisoned for two years, and then put to death with a priest called Julian. Feast 1 November.

Caesarius of Arles, monk of Lérins and archbishop of Arles, France, born Chalon-sur-Saône, Burgundy, *c.* 470, died Arles, 27 August 543. He became bishop *c.* 503 and did much to reform laws affecting both Church and state and helped to establish Arles as the primatial see in Gaul. At the Council of Orange in 529 he played a leading role in ensuring that semipelagianism was condemned. He was an acclaimed preacher and wrote two monastic Rules, one each for monks and nuns. The latter was written for the convent which he started and which was headed by his sister, **Caesaria**. Both Rules were later taken on by other orders. His biography was written by Cyprian of Toulon.

Caesarius of Nazianzus, physician, born probably Arianzum, Cappadocia, *c.* 330, died Bithynia, 369. Younger brother of **Gregory of Nazianzus**, he studied at Alexandria and held various offices at the imperial court in Constantinople, including that of court physician. He survived the Constantinople earthquake of 368, and resolved to adopt a spiritual life. He was baptized, but died, in debt, not long afterwards. Gregory wrote a funeral panegyric for him, which is the source of most of our information. There also exists a set of four dialogues with Gregory attributed to Caesarius, but they are clearly inauthentic, deriving from a much later period. Feast 25 February.

Caimin (Cammin) of Inniskeltra, born Ireland, died there, 653. He was first a recluse on an island in Lough Derg, before founding a monastery on the island of the Seven Churches. He worked with **Senan**. Feast 24 March.

Cajetan (Gaetano), founder of the Theatines, born Vicenza, October 1480, died Naples, 7 August 1547. He was educated at Padua University and graduated as a doctor of laws. He served the papal court and founded a pious confraternity in Rome, the Oratory of Divine Love, gathering about him many of the devout of the city. He was ordained priest in Rome in 1516. He returned home to Vicenza two years later, but returned to Rome in 1523 where he determined to establish a congregation of priests who would reform the standards of religious life. One of his co-founders of this congregation was Caraffa, then Bishop of Theate, but later to become Pope Paul IV: it was

from the title of his see that the organization took its name, 'the Theatines'. The members were bound by vow, but living in common and engaged in preaching and pastoral work, mainly among the poor and sick. A number of houses were founded in Italy, including one at Naples where he died. Cajetan also founded pawnshops to help, not to exploit, their users. He was canonized in 1671.

Callinica and Basilissa, martyrs, died Galatia, Asia Minor, *c.* 250, Two wealthy women, they were put to death for helping Christians in prison for their faith. Feast 22 March.

Callinicus, see also **Thyrsus**.

Callinicus of Cernica, monk, born Bucharest, 7 October 1787, died Cernica, 11 April 1868. Romanian Church. Born Constantine Antonescu, he joined the monastery of Cernica when aged 20, formally becoming a monk in November 1808 and a priest in 1813. He was appointed confessor of the monastery, a role which he also played for many others in the region. He spent a year on Mount Athos, and on his return was made superior of the community, becoming archimandrite in April 1820. He fulfilled this role for 31 years, establishing an important library, building a church and founding other monastic houses, including one for women. During his time in office the number of monks increased to some 350. In 1850 he became bishop of Rimnicul Valcea, where he renewed the churches and monasteries of the diocese and took particular care of the training of clergy. When he became ill he retired back to his monastery, where he died.

Callistus, pope, see **Callixtus**.

Callistus Caravario, born Italy, 1903, martyred China, 25 February 1930. A Salesian, he was sent to China in 1924, was ordained priest in Shanghai in 1929 by **Aloysius Versaglia**, and died with him. See also **Martyrs of China**.

Callixtus I, pope 217–22, died 222. Originally, it seems, a Roman slave, he was then (according to **Hippolytus**) involved in some kind of fraudulent banking activity and was sent to the mines in Sardinia. Released at the request of Marcia, consort of Commodus, he was ordained by Victor I and subsequently became chief minister and successor to Pope **Zephyrinus**. He was attacked (unfairly) by Hippolytus for being a patripassian (i.e., believing that God the Father suffered in the sufferings of Christ), and for too lightly readmitting to communion those found guilty of sexual misdemeanours. He was in charge of the catacombs on the Appian Way which came to be named after him. He himself was probably martyred. His tomb in Trastevere, excavated in 1960, is still venerated. Feast 14 October.

Calocerus, martyr, born Armenia, died Rome, *c*. 250. He and his brother **Parthenius** were possibly Armenian eunuchs in the household of Tryphonia, wife of the Emperor Decius. As Christians they refused to make sacrifice to the gods and were beaten on the head until they died. Feast 19 May.

Calupannus, hermit, died Auvergne, *c*. 575. He was first a monk at Meallet, Auvergne, then a hermit living in a cave. Feast 3 March.

Camillus of Lellis, patron of the sick and of nurses, founder of the Ministers of the Sick, born in Bacchianico, Naples, 1550, died Rome, 14 July 1614. He was a soldier and a gambler in his youth, but from about 1575 began to live a reformed life. He made several attempts to join a religious order without success, partly because of infirmities which lasted throughout his life. He took an interest in the plight of the sick, and his experience as a nurse in the hospital of St Giacomo in Rome made him determined to improve their care. He was ordained priest in 1584 and set about founding a congregation which, in addition to the vows of poverty, chastity and obedience, would take a fourth vow to care for the sick and especially those with the plague. The congregation spread quickly and Camillus became its first superior-general. He introduced several reforms, including isolation of those with infectious and contagious diseases and the importance of fresh air, cleanliness and diet. He also stressed the need for spiritual as well as physical care for the dying, and his brothers were the first such to accompany soldiers into battle.

Cammin of Inniskeltra, see **Caimin**.

Canidius, see **Eugenius**.

Canion, bishop, martyr, third/fourth century. He was a bishop in North Africa. Feast 25 May.

Cantianella, see **Cantius**.

Cantianus, see **Cantius**.

Cantius, martyr, born Rome, died Aquilea, northern Italy, 304. He and his brother Cantianus and sister Cantianella were orphans, educated by a Christian tutor, **Protus**. When Diocletian's persecutions began, they all left Rome but were executed by the sword when they refused to sacrifice to the gods. Feast 31 May.

Canute (Cnut) IV, king of Denmark, martyr, born *c*. 1043, died Odense, 10 July 1086. Canute was the third son of Sweyn II (Estridsen) and father of Charles the Good, elected king *c*. 1080. He defended the interests of the Church in his reign, defeated and converted to Christianity the pagans of Courlund and Livonia, and had a reputation for stern justice. He led expeditions to England in 1075 and supported the Saxons against William the Conqueror in 1085, only to be foiled by his brother Olaf's treachery. He was assassinated in Denmark by rebels and canonized by Pope Paschal II in 1100. Feast 19 January.

Canute Lavard, patron of the Danish guilds, nobleman, born Roskilde, *c*. 1096, died by assassination Haraldsted, near Ringsted, Denmark, 7 January 1131. He was educated at court and in about 1115 became prince of the Wends in eastern Holstein and tried to convert them to Christianity. He was killed by supporters of Magnus, son of King Kniels, to whose succession to the throne he posed a threat. Civil war ensued and following reports of miracles at Canute's tomb, a chapel was built on the spot where he had been killed. He was canonized in 1169. Feast 7 January or 25 June.

Caprasius, martyr, died Agen (?), third century (?). Said to have been bishop of Agen in south-west France, but nothing is known about him. Feast 20 October.

Caprasius of Lérins, abbot, died Lérins, 430. He went to live as a hermit on Lérins, an island off the Mediterranean coast of what is now France, and there he was joined by **Honoratus** and his brother Venantius, who became his disciples. The three then went to the East, where they learned about coenobitic monasticism, and they came back (Venantius died in Greece on the return journey) to found a monastery on Lérins. Feast 1 June.

Caradoc, monk, born Brycheiniog, probably now Brecon or Brecknock, Wales, died Wales, 1124. First a monk, then a hermit in Gower, he was ordained and lived with companions on a remote island. Forced to leave by Norse raiders, he lived at St Ismael's cell, now St Issell's, Haroldstone. Feast 13 April.

Carantoc (Carannog), bishop, born Wales, died Britany (?), sixth/seventh century. A monk who became abbot and bishop of Cardigan, he is said to be the founder of churches in Llangranog in Wales, Crantock in Cornwall, Carhampton in Somerset and Caranted in Britany. Feast 16 May.

Caraunus of Chartres, martyred near Chartres, fifth century. He was of Roman descent and preached the gospel in Gaul. After he was killed by robbers, a church and monastery were built over his tomb. Feast 28 May.

Carileffus, bishop and hermit, born Aquitaine, died Anisole, Maine, *c.* 540. A monk of either the abbey of Ménat or that of Micy, after ordination he became a solitary by the river Anille in the diocese of Le Mans. The abbey of Anille (later St-Calais) was built in commemoration of him. He was buried in St-Calais, and after a period in Blois, his bones were returned there in 1663. Feast 1 July.

Cariton, monk, died Sjanzema, 11 April 1509. Russian Church. A companion of **Euthymius of Sjanzema**, whom he succeeded as head of the monastery. Feast 11 April.

Carlampius, monk, died Novye Krupcy, Poland, eighteenth century. Church of the Old Believers. He entered the monastery established by **Lawrence** at Novye Krupcy, but then left it to become a hermit, returning to the monastery only once a week. He lived in great austerity. He was thought to be a saint even during his lifetime.

Carlo Carafa II, ven., priest, born Mariglianella (Naples), 1561, died there, 8 September 1633. Of the noble Neapolitan dynasty that had produced Pope Paul IV, he was ordained in 1599 after time spent with the Jesuits and the Spanish military. He gave all his possessions to the poor and helped to organize missions for the people in 1601. He opened a house for his *Pii Operarii* in Naples in 1606, a congregation which has survived to the present. Miracles were attributed to him following his death.

Carloman, king, born 755, died Vienne, 755. The son of Charles Martel, he became king of Austrasia. He founded monasteries and assisted the efforts of **Boniface**. In 747 he became a monk at Monte Cassino. He was sent on a political mission in 755 to negotiate with his brother Pepin, but died on the way. Feast 17 August.

Carmelite Martyrs of Compiègne, bl., died Paris, 17 July 1794, during the French Revolution, beatified 1906 with Mulot de la Ménardière, a layman arrested for helping them. Discalced Carmelites, expelled from their convent in 1789 and made to wear civilian dress, they were accused of continuing their religious life in secret and plotting against the state. The 16 nuns guillotined were Marie-Madeleine-Claudine Lidoine/Sr Thérèse de Saint-Augustin (prioress), Marie-Anne Françoise Brideau/Sr Saint-Louis (subprioress), Marie-Anne Piedcourt/Sr de Jésus-Crucifié, Anne-Marie Madeleine Thouret/Sr Charlotte de la Résurrection, Marie-Claude Brard/Sr Euphrasie de l'Immaculée Conception, Marie-Françoise de Croissy/Mère Henriette de Jésus, Marie-Anne Hanisset/Sr Thérèse du Coeur de Marie, Marie-Gabrielle Trézel/Sr de Saint-Ignace, Rose Chrétien de Neuville/Sr Julie-Louise de Jésus, Marie Annette Pelras/Sr Marie-Henriette de la Providence, Angélique Roussel/Sr Marie du Saint-Esprit, Marie Dufour/Sr Sainte-Marthe, Elisabeth Juliette Vérolot/Sr Saint-François-Xavier, Marie-Geneviève Meunier/Sr Constance (novice), and two externs, sisters Catherine and Thérèse Soiron. See also **Martyrs of the French Revolution**.

Carol Lucas, bl., see **Felicity Pricet**.

Caroline Kozka, bl., martyr, born Wal-Ruda, near Tarnow, Poland, 2 August 1898, died there, 18 November 1914. She grew up in a devout, agricultural family, and died defending her virginity from the advances of a Russian soldier.

Carpo of Medusi, seventeenth century (?). Russian Church. Feast 3 June.

Carpo of Moscow, monk, seventeenth century. Russian Church.

Carpus, bishop, martyr, born Gurdos, Lydia (Anatolia), died Pergamum, now in Turkey, 170 or 250. He was tortured and burned by the Roman governor with **Papylus**, a deacon. They are commemorated with **Agathonice**, a mother, possibly Papylus's sister, burned about the same time. Feast 13 April.

Carthach, bishop, born Castle Maine, Kerry, Ireland, died Lismore, 637, cult confirmed 1903. A monk and priest, he founded Rahan monastery (Offaly) c. 495. Expelled c. 636, he moved with everyone to the banks of the river Blackwater, rebuilding his see, his monastery and his leper hospital at Lismore. Feast 14 May.

Casilda, born Toledo, died near Burgos, possibly eleventh century. Daughter of the emir of Toledo, she became a Christian after being cured at **Vincent of Briviesca**'s shrine near Burgos. She lived as a solitary near his spring, and is said to have died aged 100, the shrine later being called after both saints. Feast 9 April.

Casimir, patron saint of Poland and Lithuania, born Krakow, 1458, died of phthisis at Hrodno, 4 March 1484. A member of the Polish royal family who, to the disappointment of his relatives, led a life of prayer, philanthropy and penance, despite being offered the throne of Hungary. He was canonized in 1522. Feast 4 March.

Caspar de Bono, bl., born Valencia, Spain, 1530, died there, 14 July 1604. He joined the Dominicans but had to leave in order to support his family, and enrolled in the army of the Emperor Charles V. He served in Italy until he was badly injured in battle in 1560. He returned to Spain and joined the Minims, a branch of the Franciscans. He took his vows in 1565 and was ordained priest the following year. He was made prior of Valencia, and became provincial of the order in Spain c. 1580.

Caspar Stanggassinger, born Berchtesgaden, Bavaria, 12 January 1871, died Gars, 26 September 1899. Aged ten, he joined the junior seminary at Freising, then entered the major seminary in 1892. After a pilgrimage to the shrine of Altötting, he decided to enter the Redemptorist Congregation. He was ordained as a Redemptorist priest in 1895. He was sent to teach missionaries in the Redemptorist seminary at Dùrrnberg, and in 1899 to a new seminary at Gars as its director. He died suddenly of peritonitis soon after arriving there.

Caspar, see also **Gaspar**.

Cassian, bishop, fourth century. Feast 5 August.

Cassian and Lawrence, monks, died Komel, 1548. Russian Church. Disciples of **Cornelius of Komel**, they succeeded him as spiritual guides of the monastery. Feast 16 May.

Cassian Bosoj, monk, died Voloklmansk, 11 February 1532. Russian Church. Also known as 'the barefooted'.

Cassian of Autun, bishop, born Egypt, died Autun, c. 350. Bishop from 314. Feast 5 August.

Cassian of Avnega, martyr, died Avnega, 1392. Russian Church. Baptized Constantine Dimitrievic, he took the name Cassian when he entered the monastery founded by **Stephen of Machrisca**. He was martyred, alongside **Gregory of Avnega** during an attack by Tartars.

Cassian of Imola, martyr, died Imola. Said to have been a teacher who was condemned to die by having his pupils stab him with their pens. Feast 13 August.

Cassian of Kamensk, monk, died Kamensk, c. 1470. Russian Church. Became hegumenos of the monastery, then was used by Prince Vasilii Vasilevic as legate on church affairs to the patriarch of Constantinople, but eventually returned to his monastery and took up again the status of hegumenos.

Cassian of Muezero, monk, possibly sixteenth century. Russian Church.

Cassian of Nantes, bl., Capuchin missionary and martyr, born Nantes, France, 15 January 1607, died Condar, Ethiopia, 7 August 1638. He entered the Capuchin novitiate in 1623 and in 1633 was sent to their mission in Cairo where he joined Fr **Agathangelus**. The behaviour of local Catholics obstructed their labours and, intending to work for the reunion of Copts with Rome, they entered Ethiopia in 1637, disguised as Coptic monks. They were discovered and sent to Condar for trial. Given the choice of conversion to the Coptic faith or hanging, they chose death. Pius X beatified them on 23 October 1904.

Cassian of Tangier, martyr, died Tangier, 298 (?). The secretary at the trial of St **Marcellus**, he protested when Marcellus was sentenced to death, and was himself imprisoned and then executed. Feast 3 December.

Cassian of Uglic, died Uglic, 2 October 1504. Russian Church. Constantine Mancutius, a relative by marriage of the last Byzantine emperor, was in the service of the archbishop of Rostov and when, in 1489, the archbishop decided to retire to the monastery of Ferapont, Constantine accompanied him. One night he had a vision in which he was threatened with a beating if he himself did not enter the monastery, so he did so, taking the name Cassian. In 1492 he withdrew to a hermitage on the river Ucma, near Uglic.

Cassian the Cypriot, monk, third/fourth centuries. Cypriot Church. Probably to be identified with **John Cassian**. Feast 16 September.

Cassian the Recluse, monk. Russian Church. A monk of the Kievan Cave monasteries. Feast 8 May.

Cassius, bishop, died Rome, 538. He was bishop of Narni in Tuscany, Italy. He died on a visit to Rome. Feast 28 June.

Cassius and Companions, martyrs, died Clermont, Auvergne, c. 264. This was a group killed by the chief of invading Teutonic pagans. Two among the others are **Victorinus** and **Maximus**. Feast 15 May.

Castor, fourth century. He was a hermit in Moselle. Feast 13 February.

Castor, martyr, died Tarsus, Cilicia, in one of the early persecutions, with **Dorotheus**, no known date. Feast 28 March.

Castrensis, see **Priscus**, the saint by this name is now thought to be a description of **Priscus**, who was bishop of Castra. Feast 11 February.

Castulus, martyr, died Rome, 288. A military officer under Diocletian, married to **Irene**, he was denounced for sheltering Christians and buried alive on the via Labicana. Feast 26 March.

Castus, martyred proconsular Africa, c. 250. He and **Aemilius**, also commemorated on this day, gave way under severe torture, but later repented, were arrested again and burned. Their contemporary **Cyprian** praised them, as did **Augustine** later. Feast 22 May.

Cataldus of Rachau, bishop and patron of Taranto, born Munster, Ireland, early seventh century, died Taranto, Italy, c. 671. His life story comes from legends of the twelfth century. He is said to have become a monk at Lismore, and later, when bishop of Rachau, while returning from a pilgrimage to the Holy Land, to have been wrecked off Taranto. Here he became bishop, reformer and builder of churches. He is venerated for his miracles in Italy and in Sens and Auxerre in France. Feast 10 May.

Catherine de' Ricci, Dominican contemplative of the Counter-Reformation, born Florence, 23 April 1522, died Prato, 2 February 1590. She was professed at 14 in the Dominican convent of San Vicenzio, Prato, of which she was prioress from 1560 to 1590. From Holy Week 1542 and thereafter for 12 years she relived Christ's passion from Thursday noon to Friday at four in the afternoon. People of all classes, including many religious leaders, drawn by her ecstatic experience and (Savonarolan) spirituality, came to her for advice and help. She was beatified in 1732 and canonized in 1746.

Catherine Labouré, nun, born Fain-les-Moutiers, 2 May 1806, died Enghien-Reuilly, 31 December 1876. Her baptismal name was Zoë. Her sister joined the Sisters of Charity, but her father refused to let Catherine do likewise. Instead he sent her to Paris to work as a waitress, but relented in 1830, and she joined the Sisters of Charity of St Vincent de Paul at Châtillon-sur-Seine. Almost immediately she started to receive visions of Mary, in one of which she received instructions to have a medal struck in honour of Mary, which came to be known as the Miraculous Medal. In 1831 she moved to a convent at Enghien, where she fulfilled various roles in the community, but shunned all public activity. Feast 28 November.

Catherine of Alexandria, martyr. Legends coming from a number of tenth-century sources say that as a result of protesting to the Emperor Maxentius about the persecution of Christians, she was tortured on the wheel and decapitated in 305. Her cult became popular, especially in Italy. Feast 25 November (suppressed 1969).

Catherine of Bologna, also known as Catherine de Vigri, patron saint of artists, born Bologna, 8 September 1413, died there, 9 March 1463. Educated at the royal court at Ferrara, Italy. Became a nun in 1432. In 1456 she founded a convent of Poor Clares at Bologna, later becoming its abbess. Throughout her time at the convent she experienced visions and revelations. She also revealed a talent for calligraphy. Her main work is *The Spiritual Armour* (1438). Canonized in 1712.

Catherine of Genoa, mystic, born Genoa, 1447, died there, 15 September 1510. Catherine Fieschi married Julian Adorno at 16. He was dissolute and unfaithful, but after Catherine experienced a religious conversion she attempted to convert him to a holier way of life. After he had become bankrupt, she succeeded. They spent the rest of their lives caring for the sick and needy. From 1490 to 1496 she was matron of a hospital caring for victims of the plague. Her works include the *Trattato del Purgatorio* and the *Dialogo*. Canonized in 1737.

Catherine of Pallanza, bl., born Pallanza, northern Italy, *c.*1453, died Varese, 1478, cult approved 1769. She was an austere hermit for 15 years on the mountains of Varese, near Milan, attracted followers and eventually founded the convent of Our Lady of the Mountain, becoming its first abbess. She was credited with the gift of prophecy. Feast 6 April

Catherine of Racconigi, bl., born Racconigi, Piedmont, Italy, 24? June 1486, died Caramagna, Piedmont, 4 September 1547. A weaver, she gave her wages to the poor, vowed virginity and received the habit of a Dominican tertiary from her Dominican confessor in 1513. She received the stigmata, prophesied, and at Caramagna offered herself as a victim for sinners and the maintenance of peace. Pius VII authorized her mass and office on 9 April 1808 and she is commemorated in the Order of Preachers.

Catherine of Siena, Caterina Benincasa, mystic, born Siena, 1347, died of exhaustion Rome, 29 April 1380. Experienced visions from the age of seven and the pain, but not the manifestation, of the stigmata. In 1360 became a tertiary of the Dominican Order at Siena and soon gathered around her a group of followers or 'Caterinati'. In 1376 she visited Pope Gregory XI at Avignon as a mediator between the papacy and Florence. In 1378 went to Rome to aid Pope Urban VI in the reform of the Church. Her works include the *Dialogo*, which contains descriptions of her ecstatic experiences, and her dictated *Letters*. Canonized in 1461. Declared patron saint of Italy in 1939, and in 1970 became the first woman doctor of the Church.

Catherine of Sweden, Katarina Ulfsdotter, born 1331, died Vadstena, 24 March 1381. The daughter of St **Birgitta of Sweden**. In 1373 she succeeded her mother as superior of the Brigettines. She spent most of her life gaining recognition for her mother and the Brigettines. A supporter of Pope Urban VI against the antipope. Recognized as a saint, but never formally canonized.

Catherine (Kateri) Tekakwitha, bl., born probably at what is now Auriesville in New York State, 1656, died Caughnawaga, Canada, 17 April 1680. She was brought up by an anti-Christian uncle after surviving an outbreak of smallpox which killed the rest of her family. After encountering a group of Jesuit missionaries when she was 11, she began to live an ascetic form of life, and at the age of 20 was baptized. Because she was persecuted for her beliefs, she fled to the St Francis Xavier mission at Sault Saint-Louis, near Montreal, where she took a vow of virginity and lived an exemplary life, becoming known as 'the lily of the Mohawks'. She was beatified on 22 June 1980. Feast 17 April.

Catherine Thomas, Canoness Regular of St Augustine, born Valdemuzza, Majorca, 1533, died Palma, Majorca, 5 April 1574. An orphan, at 16 she entered the convent of St Mary Magdalene in Palma at her confessor's insistence, as she had no dowry. She was aware of her spiritual gifts, but tried to hide them as they involved her in controversy; she was said to have the gift of prophecy, to converse with angels, to suffer attacks from devils, and to have foretold the day of her death. She was beatified in 1792 and canonized in 1930.

Caul, martyred fourth century. Feast 23 January.

Cecilia (probably legendary), martyr, patroness of music, second or third century. Many poetical, prose and musical works were written in her honour. Among authors were Dryden and Auden, among composers Purcell and Britten. Feast 22 November.

Cecilia, see also **Benedicta and Cecilia**.

Cecilia and Amata, bl., born Rome, died Bologna, 1290. Cecilia Cesarini and her companion Amata – about whom nothing is known – were originally members of a community of nuns in Rome, first in Trastevere, then in San Sisto, where the community, at Cecilia's suggestion, submitted to the Dominican Rule. She and Amata were then sent to the convent of St Agnes at Bologna to help form a new Dominican community there. Feast 4 August.

Cecilia Butsi, martyr, born Sonkong, 1924, died there, 26 December 1940. She had openly challenged the police who had come to attack the mission in Sonkong. She and several others (see

Martyrs of Thailand) were marched to the cemetery and shot. Feast 16 December.

Cecilia Romana, bl., Dominican nun, born Rome, c.1200, died Bologna, c. 1290. A member of the noble Cesarini family, she became a nun at the age of 17. She moved with her community from the monastery of St Maria in Tempulo, Rome, in 1221 to the reformed monastery of St Sisto, founded that year by St **Dominic**, where they renewed their vows. He sent three of them to the newly formed monastery of St Agnes at Bologna, founded by the father of **Diana** d'Andalo, where in 1237 Cecilia became prioress. Her eyewitness recollections of St Dominic were preserved in writing by another nun in 1280. Feast 9 June.

Cecilian, priest, born Carthage, died there, c. 248 (?). The priest of Carthage who converted St **Cyprian**. Feast 3 June.

Cedda, or Cedd, bishop, brother of St **Chad**, date of birth unknown, died of the plague Lastingham, Yorkshire, 26 October 664. He was raised at Lindisfarne, where he was instructed by St **Aidan**, and was sent by Bishop Finan in 653 to convert the Mercians. He also went as a missionary to preach to the East Saxons and was made bishop of the East Saxons in 654. He founded the abbey of Lastingham, and monasteries at Bradwell-on-Sea and Tilbury.

Ceferino Jiménez Malla, bl., martyr, born Benavent de Segria, Lerida, Spain, 1861, died Barbastro, 2 August 1936. A gypsy, and probably illiterate, he converted to Catholicism as an adult. He was executed for helping a priest.

Celadion, patriarch, died Alexandria, 3 July 167. Unanimously elected patriarch of Alexandria in 157.

Celerinus, born Carthage, died there (?), third century. He is deemed a martyr, although he was not executed, because of the sufferings he endured under Decius while in Rome. He later returned to Carthage, was ordained deacon by **Cyprian** and had a church dedicated to him there. Feast 3 February.

Celestine I, pope, born in the Roman Campagna, date unknown, elected to the papacy 10 September 422, died Rome, 27 July 432. He was active in reconstructing Rome's churches after the devastation of 410, and he also suppressed Novatianism in the city as far as he could. He was active in asserting the authority of the papacy and sent St **Germain of Auxerre** to Britain in 429 to convert the followers of Pelagius, and reputedly sent Palladius as the first bishop in Ireland. He became involved in the Nestorian controversy, condemning Nestorius after a Synod of Rome in 430 and giving his support to the decisions of the Council of Ephesus (431) where Nestorius was excommunicated. Feast 6 April (suppressed 1969).

Celestine V, pope, born Pietro da Morrone, Isernia, Italy, *c.* 1215, elected pope 5 July 1294, resigned 13 December the same year, died 19 May 1296. He became a Benedictine monk *c.* 1232, later living a solitary life in the Abruzzi mountains and founding a religious order, originally called the Hermits of St Damian, but changing to the Celestines on his election as pope. However, being 80 years of age, and politically and administratively naive, he resigned in the same year (an act known as 'the great refusal'). His successor, Boniface VIII, who had pressured him into the resignation, then held him prisoner in the castle of Monte Fumone until his death. He was canonized in 1313 under pressure from the king of France, a vigorous opponent of Boniface.

Celsus, bishop (Gaelic: Ceallach mac Aedha, Cellach mac Aodh), born 1079, died Ard Patrick, 1129. Elected archbishop of Armagh as a layman in 1105, then ordained, he became a keen reformer. He and his successor at Armagh, **Malachy**, were important figures in the Gregorian reform movement. Feast 11 April.

Centolla and Helen, martyrs, died Burgos, *c.* 303. Feast 2 August.

Ceolfrid of Wearmouth, monk, born Northumbria, *c.* 642, died Langres, France, 25 September 716. An Anglo-Saxon nobleman, he entered the monastery at Gilling at 18, moved to the monastery of Ripon in 664, and was ordained under the Roman rite. **Benedict Biscop** asked him to help build the abbey of St Peter at Wearmouth in 672, and in 678 he accompanied Benedict to Rome for ideas and supplies, and returned with John the arch-chanter who taught the monks to sing the Roman liturgy. Benedict asked Ceolfrid to establish a second abbey at Jarrow, which was dedicated in 685. With their splendid libraries, the two foundations were foremost in England for their transcriptions of the Gospels. Ceolfrid died at Langres on his way to Rome with a copy, the *Codex Amiatinus* (the oldest extant manuscript of the Vulgate), in 716. **Bede** said that Ceolfrid brought him up.

Ceratius, bishop, died Grenoble, *c.* 455. He was certainly bishop of Grenoble in the mid-fifth century, but there appears to have been a bishop of the same name at Eause (modern Auch) around the same time. It is unclear whether there are two, or whether Ceratius moved to Auch from Grenoble. Feast 6 June.

Cerbonius, bishop of Populonia, died Isle of Elba, *c.* 580. When the Vandals drove the bishops out of Africa, he went with St **Regulus** (died 542) to Tuscany and was made bishop of Populonia. When Totila, king of the Ostrogoths (died 552), exposed him to a bear in punishment for sheltering Roman soldiers, it failed to attack him and he was freed, but the Lombards exiled him to Elba, where he lived out the 30 years until his death. Feast 10 October.

Cerioli, Costanza, see **Paula Cerioli**.

Cesar de Bus, bl., founder, born Cavaillon, Comtat Venaissin, 3 February 1544, died Avignon, 15 April 1607. Spent his youth as a soldier fighting the Huguenots, as an artist and a poet, and then led a life of pleasure in Paris for some years before returning to Cavaillon and his studies. He was ordained priest in 1582, and became known for his work in preachng, teaching and charitable activity. In 1592 he set up the Priests of Christian Doctrine, known as the Doctrinaires, a congregation devoted, as the name suggests, to preaching and teaching Christian doctrine. He later established a similar congregation for women, the Daughters of Christian Doctrine. His *Instructions for the Family* *on the Four Parts of the Roman Catechism* was published in five volumes.

Cesidius Giacomantonio, bl., born Fossa, L'Aquila, Italy, 30 August 1873, martyred Hengzhou, China, 4 July 1900, beatified 1846. A Franciscan priest, he was the first Catholic victim of the Boxer Rebellion, being wrapped in a cloth soaked in oil and burned. See **Franciscan Martyrs of China**.

Ceslaus of Breslau, bl., born *c.* 1180, died Wroclaw, Poland, 1242. According to tradition, Ceslaus (or Czeslao) was born into the family of the counts of Odrowatz in Silesia. He was a canon at Krakow and provost of St Mary's in Sanddomir, and went with the bishop of Krakow to Rome in 1220, where he was impressed by St **Dominic** and became a Dominican friar. He returned to Poland to preach and founded Dominican houses in Prague and Krakow. He moved to Wroclaw, and in 1232 he became Polish provincial. He was renowned for being a spiritual adviser. Feast 15 July.

Cessator of Limoges, eighth century. Feast 15 March.

Chad, Anglo-Saxon monk, bishop, died 2 March 672. A disciple of **Aidan** at Lindisfarne. Succeeded his brother **Cedda** as abbot of Lastingham. In the absence of **Wilfrid**, he was appointed bishop of York by King Oswy in 665. Theodore of Tarsus, on becoming archbishop, challenged Chad's consecration, and in 669 Chad retired to Lastingham, later becoming bishop of Lichfield. Feast 2 March.

Chaerymon, bishop and martyr, died *c.* 250. The bishop of Nilopolis in Egypt, he and his wife fled during the persecution of Decius. They went to the mountains of Arabia and disappeared. Feast 22 December.

Chantal, see **Jane Frances Fremiot de Chantal**.

Charalampias, Porphyry, Dauctus, and Three Women Companions, martyrs, died Magnesia, Asia Minor, 203. Charalampias was a priest, the other men soldiers, and they died in the persecution under Septimus Severus. Feast 10 February.

Charbel Makhlouf, born Beqaa-Kafra, Lebanon, 8 May 1828, died Annaya, Lebanon, 24 December 1898. Baptized Joseph, he was the son of a mule-driver but became a shepherd. He was very devout, and was attracted by the life of a group of hermits whom he visited. He entered the monastery at Maifouk in 1851, but moved on to the monastery of St Maro at Annaya. He studied theology at the monastery of St Cyprian, was ordained, and returned to Annaya for 15 years, after which he became a hermit, although his hermitage was not far from his monastery. He was renowned for his austerity and his devotion to the Eucharist. Many came to seek his advice. After his death his grave became a centre of pilgrimage.

Charitina, Lithuanian princess, died Novgorod, end of either the twelfth or the thirteenth century. Russian Church. She moved to Novgorod for a dynastic marriage to Prince Theodore Jaroslav, and after his death entered the nearby monastery of Ss Peter and Paul. Because of her virtues she was elected superior. Feast 5 October.

Charlemagne, bl., king of the Franks and emperor of the Romans, born Aachen (Aix-la-Chapelle), 2 April 742, died there, 28 January 814. On the death of his father Pepin he ruled the realms of the Franks jointly with his brother Carloman. In 771, on the death of his brother, he took possession of the whole inheritance and commenced extending Frankish rule, bringing large parts of Western and Central Europe not only under his own control, but under the authority of the Roman Church. In 773 he began a campaign to conquer and Christianize the Saxons and Frisians in the north of France and the Lombards of northern Italy. He also fought in Spain, and in 796 conquered the Aars in modern-day Hungary. On Christmas Day 800, Pope Leo III crowned him Roman Emperor. In the management of the empire he gathered scholars from all over Europe, including **Alcuin** of York, built churches and monasteries and strengthened the Church.

Charles Borromeo, cardinal, born Arona, Italy, 2 October 1538, died Milan, Italy, 1584. Of aristocratic parentage, he had his first benefice aged 12. From 1552 he studied canon and civil law at Pavia. In 1560 he was made cardinal and archbishop of

Milan by his uncle, Pius IV. A leader in the Catholic Reformation, he was very influential in the third and last group of sessions of the Council of Trent. He reformed the see of Milan by insisting on higher morals and discipline, introducing a more effective structure and establishing seminaries for the training of clergy. He also founded an Order of Oblates, reorganized a Confraternity of Christian Doctrine for educating children and showed concern for the poor and sick. His reforms were not always popular, but they were adopted elsewhere in Europe. He was canonized in 1610. Feast 4 November.

Charles Garnier, martyr, born Paris, 1605, died Fort St Jean, Canada, 7 December 1649. He was the son of wealthy parents and studied at a Jesuit college. He joined the Society of Jesus in 1624, was ordained ten years later, and two years after that was sent as a missionary to the Hurons. The fort he was in was attacked by the Iroquois, and he spent his last hours ministering to those wounded and dying before he himself was killed by a tomahawk. Feast, with **John de Brébeuf**, 19 October.

Charles Joseph Eugène de Mazenod, bishop and founder, born Aix-en-Provence, 2 August 1782, died Marseilles, 21 May 1861. Ordained in 1811, de Mazenod then began a lifelong apostolate to the poor. He succeeded his uncle as bishop of Marseilles in 1837. In 1816 he founded the Missionary Oblates of Mary Immaculate, whose members he sent to Canada, Ceylon, USA and South Africa, in all of which the Oblate apostolate achieved remarkable results. An ardent ultramontanist, he nevertheless supported Robert de Lamennais in controversies covering the classics, liturgy and liberalism, although he remained intransigent on educational freedom and the Roman question.

Charles Lwanga, martyr, born Buddu County, Uganda, c. 1860, died Namugongo, 3 June 1886. The chieftain of the Kabaka of Buganda, Mwanga, launched a fierce persecution of Christians in 1886, following reproaches by Joseph Mukasa, a Catholic, for sexually abusing the pages of his court. Charles Lwanga was in charge of the boys kept by Mwanga, many of whom had converted to Catholicism, and 15 of them chose death rather than abjure their faith. They were immolated on a huge

funeral pyre, and the executions greatly increased the converts to Catholicism. Charles and 21 others were canonized in 1964, and Pope Pius XI declared him patron of youth and Catholic action for sub-Saharan Africa.

Charles Meehan, bl., martyr, born Ireland, died Ruthin, Wales, 1679. An Irish Franciscan who had taken refuge from persecution in Bavaria. He was on his way back to Ireland when he was shipwrecked on the Welsh coast and executed as a Catholic priest, although he had never worked either in Wales or in England. Feast 12 August.

Charles of Blois, Franciscan tertiary, born c. 1319, died in battle Auray, France, 29 September 1364. Greatly respected as a saint and wonderworker, he fought the English de Montforts for his family territory which had been claimed by them from 1341, and was their captive 1347–56. The Franciscans propagated his cult, which Urban V condemned. Investigations of it were held up by the Great Schism and it was not authorized until 1904.

Charles of St Andrew, see **John Andrew Houben**.

Charles of Sezze, Franciscan lay brother and ascetical writer, born Sezze, Italy, 19 October 1613, died Rome, 6 January 1670. He joined the reformed Franciscan province in Rome in 1635 and after ten years of intense self-abnegation he experienced ecstatic union. He wrote at length on the spiritual life, and his autobiography has been compared with that of St **Teresa of Avila**. He was beatified in 1882 and canonized in 1959. Feast 18 January.

Charles of Villers, bl., abbot, born Cologne, died Hocht, near Maastricht, Netherlands, c. 1215. He entered the Cistercian abbey of Himmerod in 1184 or 1185, was prior at Heisterbach in 1191 and abbot of Villers 1197–1209, when he resigned and returned to Himmerod, but was later summoned to organize a foundation at Hocht. Feast 29 January.

Charles Spinola, bl., martyr, born Genoa, 1564, died Nagasaki, Japan, 10 September 1622. The son of a nobleman, he was first educated by his cardinal uncle Philip Spinola, then by the Jesuits at

Nola, whom he joined in 1584. He was ordained ten years later, then set off for Japan, a journey full of mishaps (including being imprisoned in England) which took him six years. He arrived in 1602, and worked in the college at Miyako (modern Kyoto) before moving to Nagasaki. He was arrested in 1618 in a renewed persecution of Christians, and spent four years in cages open to the elements, before being burned to death over a slow fire, just outside Nagasaki.

Charles Steeb, founder, born Tübingen, Germany, 18 December 1773, died Verona, Italy, 15 December 1856. He belonged to a wealthy Lutheran family, but studied in Verona, where in 1792 he became a Catholic and four years later a priest. He worked in hospitals and as a military chaplain, and was sought after for spiritual direction. He was co-founder of the Institute of the Sisters of Mercy.

Charles the Good, bl., martyr, born 1081, died Flanders, 2 March 1127, cult approved 1883. The son of **Canute**, he lived with his maternal relations, succeeding his cousin as count of Flanders. Always concerned for the poor, he was killed in church by vassals whom he wanted to punish for their misdeeds.

Cheledonius, see **Hemiterius**.

Chelidonia, anchoress, died Subiaco, Italy, 13 October 1152. Anything known about her comes from the history of the monastery of Subiaco written by Guglielmo Capisacchi, who was professed there in 1525 and completed the work in 1573. He claimed to have used an anonymous life of the saint, who had been abbess of a nearby convent before becoming a recluse distinguished for prophecies and miracles, and whose remains were buried under the altar of Subiaco in 1578.

Cherubino of Avigliana, bl., born Avigliana, 1451, died there, 17 September 1479. An Augustinian friar from Piedmont whose family name was Tosta, he was noted for his piety, obedience and ardent devotion to the crucifixion. Reports of his life make particular mention of his angelic purity. According to a local tradition in Avigliana, after his death the sound of celestial bells announced his

soul's arrival in heaven, and for some time afterwards his body gave off the fragrance of lilies. His cult was confirmed by Pius IX in 1865. Feast 20 February.

Chionia, see **Agape**.

Chionia, see **Irene of Thessalonika**.

Chlodulf of Metz, bishop, died *c*. 663 or 696. Son of **Arnulf of Metz** and brother-in-law of St **Begga**, he became bishop of Metz in either 652 or 656. A ninth- or tenth-century catalogue accords him a 40-year episcopate, but it is not clear if his death should be placed as late as 696, since his successor's signature is on a charter of 667. His bones are in the former Benedictine church of Lay-Saint-Christophe, near Nancy, and in St Arnulf's, Metz. Feast 8 June.

Chrisante of Senofonte, bl., died Constantinople, 10 April 1821. Byzantine Church. A monk of the Senofonte monastery, he was killed for his faith by a Turk.

Chrisi, died Slatina, 13 October 1795. Byzantine Church. A young woman of Slatina, then in Bulgaria but now in Romania, who attracted the attention of a Turk. When she refused his advances and remained constant in her faith, against the advice of her family, she was stabbed to death, tied to a tree, after three months of torture.

Christiana, see also **Nino**.

Christiana Menabuoi, bl., died 1310, founded an Augustinian convent. Feast 4 January.

Christiana of Lucca, bl., born Santa Croce sull' Arno, Italy, 1240, died there, 4 January 1310. After a pilgrimage to Monte Gargano and Assisi, she founded an Augustinian convent at Santa Croce in 1279. Acclaimed for her holy life, she was known for her devotion to the Eucharist and to the Blessed Virgin Mary. Her cult was officially recognized in 1776. Feast 18 February.

Christina (or Iazado), martyred Persia, possibly sixth century, she was a Persian girl apparently scourged to death. Feast 13 March.

Christina of Aquila, bl., died Aquila, southern Italy, 1543, local cult confirmed 1841. Entering the convent of Augustinian hermitesses in Aquila, she was popular and considered holy during her life because of her austerity, generosity to the poor and the time she gave to prayer. Feast 18 January.

Christina of Hamm, bl., mystic, born in Westphalia, Germany, died there, 1490. Little is known of her life. She is mentioned in *Fasciculus temporum* (1482), where it is stated that she bore the signs of the stigmata on her hands, feet and side. This was said to have occurred shortly after her baptism in 1464 as a young girl. Her name at the time was Stine. A popular cult grew up around her. Feast 22 June.

Christina of Markyate, bl., recluse, born Huntingdon, to a noble English family, died Markyate, near St Albans, *c.* 1155. She secretly took a private vow of virginity on a visit to St Albans as a child, which was challenged at the age of 16 by the advances of Ralph Flambard, bishop of Durham. Thereafter followed a difficult time for Christina in maintaining her vow in opposition to the wishes of her parents. She was locked up, but when she discovered she was supported by Ralph d'Escures, the archbishop of Canterbury, she arranged to escape with the help of a local hermit. She fled to Flamstead, where she hid for two years with the hermit Alwen, and then moved to Markyate where a cell was built for her. She afterwards had to put herself under the protection of Thurstan, the archbishop of York, but she returned to Markyate in 1123. She had come to know the abbot of St Albans, where her brother was a monk, and he persuaded her to make her profession as a nun, after which she was left in comparative peace. She became a spiritual adviser to the abbot. In 1145 the abbot established a convent of nuns at Markyate, with her as prioress, and ten years later she sent a gift of embroidery to the English pope, Hadrian IV. Feast 5 December.

Christina of Spoleto, bl. Augustinian nun, born Porlezza, Lugano, *c.* 1435, died Spoleto, Italy, 13 February 1456. She was born Augustina Camozzi, the daughter of a respected doctor. She married and was widowed young. This part of her life was lived in a worldly way, but she converted and entered the Third Order Regular of St Augustine at Verona, where she was given the name Christina. She led an ascetic and penitential life of such severity that she easily became the subject of veneration and had to move frequently to avoid this. Her remains are held at St Gregorio Maggiore, Spoleto. Feast 13 February.

Christina of Stommeln, bl., Beguine, born Stommeln, Cologne, 1242, died there, 6 November 1312. With origins in a well-off peasant family, she became a Beguine at Cologne. She aroused opposition in her community because of her austere and pious life and she returned to Stommeln, where in 1267 she acquired the Dominican Peter of Dacia as her spiritual director. Her spiritual experiences were recorded by him and later by her parish priest, but were of a nature to attract doubt and hostility. Despite this, she remained steadfast in faith. Her relics, kept today at Jülich, are still venerated.

Christina the Astonishing, bl., born Brusthem, near Liège, Belgium, 1150, died Trond, 24 July 1224. She was an orphan who, at the age of 21, had some form of fit which made her appear dead. During her funeral mass she awoke, and apparently levitated to the roof of the church before being ordered to come down by the priest, landing on the altar. She said that in the course of her seizure she had been to purgatory, heaven and hell, and therefore dedicated the rest of her life to save souls from purgatory. She embarked on a life of curious asceticism and was given to frequent fits, during which she said she had again visited purgatory to lead souls to heaven. She took extraordinary measures to avoid human contact – climbing trees, or even again levitating. Although she was thought very odd by some who knew her, others, including saints, sought her advice. Despite her eccentric behaviour, she was always obedient to the prioress of St Catherine's convent in Trond, where she lived and finally died. She has been the object of a continuous cult, although there has never been formal beatification.

Christodoulos, patriarch, died Alexandria, 10 December 1077. Coptic Church. As a monk of the monastery of Enaton, near Alexandria, he was named Theodore, but then went to the desert of

Scete. He became patriarch of Alexandria in December 1047 and was renowned for miracles. He was buried in the monastery of St Macarius.

Christodoulos, founder, born Nicaea, 1020, died Patmos, 1111. He became a hermit on Mount Olympus, then went to Rome and Jerusalem. He became an archimandrite with charge of monasteries on Mount Latmos, but when these were destroyed he founded a monastery on the island of Patmos. Feast 16 March.

Christodoulos of Cassandra, born Cassandra, died Thessalonika, 28 July 1777. Byzantine Church. He moved to Thessalonika as a young man, and there worked as a tailor. He was executed by the Turks when he tried to prevent a Bulgarian from converting to Islam.

Christodoulos the Monk, twelfth century. Georgian Church. Known as a polemicist, he succeeded in converting some of the Muslim authorities in Tbilisi to Christianity. Feast 18 August.

Christopher, lived in Asia Minor, third century. Western tradition has continued the legend of a giant of a man, earning his living by carrying people across a river. On one occasion he carried a child who, on becoming almost too heavy to bear, revealed that he was Jesus Christ, and that the saint was carrying the entire world upon his shoulders. He was later martyred for his faith during the Decian persecution. He is the patron saint of travellers. Feast 25 July (suppressed).

Christopher, bl., monk and martyr, born Adrianople, c. 1795, died there, 18 April 1818. Byzantine Church. Originally called Christodoulos, he took the name Christopher when he became a monk on Mount Athos, in penitence for having converted to Islam as a young man. He then returned to Adrianople, where he confessed his faith and was executed.

Christopher, bl., martyr, born Atlihetzia, Mexico, 1514/15, died there, 1527. The son of a chieftain, he was sent to a Franciscan school and decided to become a Christian when aged about 12. After failing to persuade his father to convert, he destroyed the family idols. His father beat him

practically to death, then had him held over a slow fire. He was beatified with **Anthony and John**. Feast 23 September.

Christopher, see also **Leovigild and Christopher**.

Christopher Bales (or Bayles, Mallett, or Evers), bl., martyr, born (or baptized) Coniscliffe, Durham, 12 March 1564, died London, 4 March 1590, beatified 1929. Trained in France and Rome, ordained at Laon in 1587, he returned to England in 1588, where he was arrested in 1589 and hanged, drawn and quartered. **Alexander Blake** and **Nicholas Horner**, laymen who had helped him, were hanged on the same day.

Christopher Maccassoli, bl., Franciscan, born Milan between 1415 and 1420, died Vigevano, Italy, 1485. He joined the Observants, the stricter branch of the Franciscans, in 1435, was ordained and assigned to preaching. He reformed and enlarged the priory at Vigevano. In 1890 Leo XIII authorized a mass in his honour in the diocese of Vigevano and among the Franciscans. Feast 11 March.

Christopher Magallanes, born 1869, died Colotitlan, Jalisco, Mexico, 25 May 1927. Born into a poor family, in his youth he worked as a shepherd. He entered the seminary at Guadalajara, was ordained in 1899, and became parish priest at Totatiche in 1919. He combined an active pastorate of evangelization with one of social action on behalf of the poor. In May 1927 he was arrested by government troops on the charge that he supported the Cristero rebellion, and was shot without trial. Commemorated on the same day, 25 May, are other Mexican martyrs, **David Galvan Bermudez, Luis Batiz Sainz, David Roldan Lara, Salvador Lara Puente, Manuel Morales, Jenaro Sanchez, Mateo Correa, Julio Alvarez Mendoza, David Uribe Velasco, Sabas Reyes Salazar, Roman Adame Rosales, Agustin Coloca, Jose Isabel Flores, Jose Maria Robles, Miguel de la Mora, Rodrigo Aguilar Aleman, Margarito Flores, Pedro Esqueda Ramirez, Jesus Mendez Montoya, Toribio Romo Gonzalez, Justino Orona Madrigal, Atilano Cruz Alvarado, Tranquilino Ubiarco** and **Pedro de Jesus Maldonado**.

Christopher of Guria, monk, born Guria, western Georgia, died Syria, fifteenth century. Georgian Church. He became a monk in Palestine, and after a decade living in the Jordan desert he went to Syria to evangelize, and was martyred there. Feast 16 August.

Christopher of Milan, bl., died Taggia, Liguria, 1484, cult confirmed 1875. A Dominican priest who joined the order in Milan, he is called the apostle of Liguria because of his success as a preacher. He became prior of a house built for him by the people of Taggia. Feast 1 March.

Christopher of Romandiola (also called Christopher of Cahors), bl., companion of St **Francis**, born Romandiola, Italy, *c.* 1172, died Cahors, France, 31 October 1272. When he was parish priest of Romandiola, he joined Francis and was one of the first Franciscans sent to work in Aquitaine. Not a preacher, he led a life of prayer and service to the sick and outcast. His cult was confirmed by Pius X in 1905. Feast 25 October.

Christopher Robinson, bl., martyr, born Woodside, near Carlisle, died Carlisle, April 1597, beatified 1987. He was ordained at Rheims in 1592, and was sent to England in the same year to work in Cumberland. He was hanged (so ineptly the rope broke twice), drawn and quartered. The Protestants claimed his sufferings frightened the recusants; the Catholics maintained these led to conversions. Feast 5 April.

Christopher the Monk, born Megrelia, eastern Georgia, died monastery of St John the Baptist, western Georgia, 1871. Georgian Church. Known as Christesia before becoming a monk, he was a peasant, and married, when some tragedy made him leave his family and enter the monastery, where for a long time he lived as a layman, renowned for his humility and modesty. He took the name Christopher on eventually becoming a monk. He established a refuge for pilgrims and begged money for them in the surrounding villages, where he became well known. He lived in a very narrow cell, sleeping on a plank of wood covered in sheepskin.

Christopher Wharton, bl., born Middleton, West Riding, Yorkshire, died York, 28 March 1600. He attended Trinity College, Oxford, and was briefly a Fellow before leaving for the English College at Rheims, where he was ordained priest in March 1584. He returned to England two years later. He was arrested in Nidderdale, at the house of Mrs Eleanor Hunt, who was arrested with him but reprieved. He was imprisoned in York castle before his martyrdom. Feast 28 November.

Christos of Pereza, born Pereza, Epiros, died Coo, 5 August 1668. Byzantine Church. He was a sailor, who, leaving his ship to go to confession, encountered some Janissaries. They insulted his faith, beat him and tortured him and, eventually taking him outside the town, burned him to death.

Christos the Vegetable Seller, born near the river Genousos, *c.* 1708, died Constantinople, 12 February 1748. Byzantine Church. When he was about 40, he went to Constantinople to ply his trade. He had an argument with a Turk, who then claimed he had promised to convert to Islam. When he refused to do so, he was decapitated.

Chrodegang, bishop, born Liège, Brabant, 712, died Metz, 6 March 766. A relative of King Pepin, he became a chief minister to Charles Martel and to his successor, Pepin III. In 742 he was appointed bishop of Metz, but continued to hold political office. In 748 he founded the abbey of Gorze, near Metz. A leading ecclesiastical reformer, he drew up a communal Rule (*c.* 755) which promoted a common life while allowing clerics to retain property and maintain links with diocesan officials. He also introduced Roman chant and liturgy at Metz.

Chromatius, bishop, born Aquileia, died there, *c.* 407. He was a prominent priest of the city and was elected its bishop in 388. He was a friend of a number of leading Christians, including Rufinus and **Jerome**, as well as a supporter of **John Chrysostom**. He was himself a commentator on the New Testament. Feast 2 December.

Chrysanthus and Daria, martyrs, died *c.* 300. Their stories derive from sixth- or seventh-century Roman legends, which are confused. Evidently born of an Egyptian patrician father, Chrysanthus was baptized at Rome in the reign of Numerian. Resisting his father's attempts to arrange a marriage for him, he married Daria, a former Greek priestess of Minerva, whom he converted and persuaded to live with him in chastity. Denounced as a Christian, he so impressed under torture that the tribune Claudius, his wife, two sons and a company of soldiers were all converted (whereupon they were summarily executed). Chrysanthus and Daria are said to have been buried alive. In some versions, Daria was first sent to a brothel, where she was said to have been protected by a lion. Feast 25 October.

Chrysogonus, martyr, died 304. Little is known of his life, but according to Roman legend he was arrested during Diocletian's persecution, and his martyrdom probably took place at Aquileia. From the sixth century, he is associated with St **Anastasia** of Rome as a spiritual mentor and correspondent. In the eighth century, the Frankish king Pepin the Short considered him his personal protector. His name is mentioned in the Canon of the Roman mass. He is venerated particularly in northern Italy. Feast 24 November.

Ciaran of Saighir, born Ossory (?), Ireland, where he is patron saint, died Birr, Offaly, fifth century. He founded a monastery at Saighir (Saigher), near Birr in Offaly, and may have been a bishop. Stories describe the animals coming to his cell when he was a hermit. He pre-dates **Patrick**. Feast 5 March.

Ciranna, born Ossa, near Thessalonika, died Thessalonika, 1751. Byzantine Church. She was the object of a Janissary's attentions, but refused to deny her faith and marry him. He therefore falsely accused her of reneging on her promise to convert, and brought her before a judge in Thessalonika. She was imprisoned, where the Janissary continued to visit her, contrary to the law. The Christian in charge of the prison reported the prison guard for allowing this infringement, and the guard took out his anger on the girl, who died.

Ciwa (Ciwg, Cwick, Kigwe or Kewe), fifth to seventh centuries, venerated in Gwent, Wales. She may have been an abbess. Feast 8 February.

Clare, founder of the Poor Clares, born Assisi, 1194, died there, 11 August 1253. She was born into a well-to-do family, but gave up her possessions and joined St **Francis** of Assisi, being clothed by him in the Franciscan habit in the church of the Portiuncula in March 12. As other women, including her sister **Agnes**, were attracted to the Franciscan way of life, a community was founded at San Damiano, of which Clare was abbess. Her mother and another sister also joined. The Rule she drew up was approved by the pope just two days before her death. Her remains are in the St Chiara in Assisi. She was canonized in 1255.

Clare Gambacorta, bl., Dominican reformer, born Pisa, 1362, died there, 17 April 1419. Born into a ruling family, she was married for political convenience at the age of 12 and widowed three years later. The following year she joined the Poor Clares, but met opposition from her family. Eventually her family conceded and she joined the Dominicans, founding her own community, and in 1382 the convent of St Domenico. The way the convent was run attracted vocations of quality and she exerted reforming influence on the Dominicans. She was remembered for pardoning the murderers of her father and brothers, for the fragrance which accompanied her in life and death, and for the fact of her incorrupt tongue, when her body was exhumed after 13 years.

Clare of Montefalco, Augustinian nun, born Montefalco, Umbria, c. 1275, died there, 17 August 1308. Initially Clare followed the Franciscan Rule, but in 1290 joined her sister Joan at the Augustinian convent at Montefalco. She succeeded her sister as abbess and encouraged the community away from quietism and towards penitential works. She was known for ecstasies and the gifts of miracles and the discernment of spirits. Her body is preserved intact and it is claimed that her heart displays instruments of the passion.

Clare of Pisa, bl., born Venice or Florence, 1362, died Venice, 1419. Widowed young, she became a Poor Clare and worked to re-establish the order's Rule. **John Dominici** took her and other nuns to Venice to reform his convent of Corpus Domini. Feast 17 April.

Clare of Rimini, bl., Franciscan tertiary and mystic, born Rimini, 1262 or 1282, died there, 10 February 1320 or 1346. She was born into a well-to-do family, married young and lived a worldly life until her conversion at the age of 34. She joined the Third Order of St Francis and lived a life of penance, prayer and service of the poor after the death of her husband. She lived with companions near the Poor Clare convent, but was not enclosed.

Claritus Voglia, bl., monastic founder, born Florence, c. 1300, died Convent of Chiarito, Florence, 25 May 1348. Although he delighted in the divine services of Florence cathedral, Claritus married rather than take orders; he engaged in public affairs and in charitable works, assisting young women to enter the religious life. To this end he founded a convent under the rule of St Augustine, known as Chiarito (Regina Coeli). His wife Nicolosia and their daughter joined the community, the former becoming its first abbess. Claritus ministered to their needs until his death. His tomb is in the convent and his body in the church of the Dominican sisters, Al Sodo. Feast 6 May.

Clarus, abbot, born near Vienne, died there, 1 January 660. A monk of St Ferreol Abbey, he also served as spiritual director of St Blandina convent, where his mother and sister were nuns, before becoming abbot of the monastery of St Marcellus at Vienne c. 625. Numerous miracles are attributed to him; his cult was officially confirmed by **Pius X** in 1903. He is the patron saint of tailors. Feast 1 January.

Clarus, martyr, born Rochester, England, died Naqueville, near Rouen, eighth century. He travelled from England to Normandy, where he evangelized. He then became a hermit near Naqueville. He was assassinated by two men, sent by a woman whose advances he had repulsed. Feast 4 November.

Claude Chevrier, martyr, born Saint-Jodard (now Saint-Etienne), Loire, France, died Tianjin, Hebei, China, 20 June 1870. See **Martyrs of China**.

Claudia Thévenet, born Lyons, 1774, died there, 3 February 1837, beatified 1981, canonized 1993. Deeply affected by the revolution, she devoted herself to the education of girls, orphans and street children as well as daughters of good families. She founded the Congregation of the Sacred Hearts of Jesus and Mary in 1818.

Claudius, monk, died 13 February, fifth century. Coptic Church. A monk of Senute's White Monastery. A church was dedicated to him after his death.

Claudius, see also **Galawdewos**.

Claudius and Companions, martyrs and saints, died Aegeae, Cilicia, c. 285. The history behind the legends is very difficult to access, but the three brothers Claudius, Asterius and Neon, and two women, Domnina and Theonilla, together with Domnina's child, were martyred for their Christian confession. Feast 23 August.

Claudius of Condat, bishop and abbot, born perhaps Franche-Comte, died Condat, 6 June 693. The accounts of his life are legendary, but he was apparently already elderly when he was appointed to Condat. He was then called to be bishop of Besançon, but he later resigned this see and retired to monastic life at Condat. The abbey there was dedicated to his memory, and its church became a pilgrimage site. His relics were discovered in 1213, but were lost during the French Revolution.

Clelia Barbieri, bl., foundress, born Le Budrie, Bologna, 1847, died 13 July 1870. As a child she helped in her parish church, teaching other children catechism and forming a prayer group with her friends. In 1868 she and three other young women moved into a house next to the church and dedicated themselves to Our Lady of the Seven Dolours and St Francis of Paola. This community became the Congregation of the Minims of the Addolorata. The Congregation was involved in education, parish work and care of the elderly and sick. Clelia died of tuberculosis at the age of 23.

Clement, monk of the Studion monastery, ninth century. Feast 27 May.

Clement Hofbauer, originally John, Redemptorist priest, born Tasswitz, Moravia, 26 December 1751, died Vienna, 15 March 1820. He entered Vienna

University and was later ordained. He lived in Warsaw, and set up Redemptorist houses in Switzerland and Germany. Napoleon ordered the closure of the Redemptorist community in Warsaw, so Hofbauer moved to Vienna, continuing his work in establishing Redemptorist houses in Europe. He was canonized in 1909 and named patron saint of Vienna.

Clement Marchisio, bl., founder, born Racconigi, 1 March 1833, died Rivalta, Turin, 16 December 1903. The son of a cobbler, he became a priest in 1856 and then vicar of Cambiano. Four years later he moved to Rivalta, a suburb of Turin. He was renowned for his holiness of life, and especially for his devotion to the Eucharist. He founded the Institute of the Daughters of St Joseph.

Clement of Ancyra (Ankara), bishop, martyred 309. He was a prisoner in Rome for a time, where he met and baptized **Agathangelus**, with whom he is commemorated. Both were martyred under Diocletian at Ancyra, Galatia. Feast 23 January.

Clement of Bennaque, monk, born Egypt, fifteenth century. Ethiopian Church. Came to Ethiopia to found a monastery at Bennaque.

Clement of Ireland, born Ireland, died France, after 828. He succeeded **Alcuin** as head of **Charlemagne**'s palace school, and although Theodulf of Orléans, Alcuin and Einhard all opposed his methods of instruction, Clement retained his position until *c.* 826. Among his students were Modestus of Fulda and the future Emperor Lothair I. Clement is the author of *Ars Grammatica*, in three parts: *De philosophia*, *De mentis* and *De barbarismo*, a valuable text for its extensive quotations from earlier authors. Feast 20 March.

Clement of Ochridia, see **Clement the Bulgarian**.

Clement of Rome, bishop, Church Father, *c.* 96. Early sources name Clement as the second or third bishop of Rome, although the exact connotation of that title at this early date is unclear. Numerous early Christian writings were once attributed to him, although now only the epistle known as I Clement is regarded as genuine. This is valuable for the light it sheds on the nature of early Christian

ministry and Church organization, and the early history of the Church in Rome. Little else is known of the author, and later accounts of his life are too obviously embellished with legends to be reliable. Feast 23 November.

Clement the Bulgarian (Clement of Ochridia), born Thessalonika, died Ochridia, Macedonia, 17 July 916. A pupil of **Cyril** and **Methodius**, Clement accompanied the latter to Moravia. The German bishops expelled him after Methodius's death, and he found refuge in western Bulgaria and became bishop of Velitsa (*c.* 893). He founded the monastery of St **Panteleimon**, where he is buried, and three churches. He is the father of Slavonic literature and his works include liturgical texts translated from the Greek, homilies and lives of the saints, e.g., the *Life and Enconium of St Cyril.* Feast 17 July.

Clement the Stylite, born Athens, twelfth century. Byzantine Church. Spent his monastic life on Mount Sagmata in Boecia. Feast 27 January.

Clemente Ignacio Delgado Cebrián, born Villafeliche, Saragossa, Spain, 23 November 1761, died a prisoner from hunger and thirst before he could be executed, Vietnam, 12 July 1838, beatified 1909, canonized 1988. He was a Spanish Dominican bishop and vicar apostolic of East Tonkin. See **Martyrs of Vietnam**.

Cleonicus, Eutropius and Basilicus, martyrs, died Amaseia (modern Amasya, Turkey), Pontus, Asia Minor, *c.* 303. They were part of a group of about 50 martyrs, some of whom were soldiers and others possibly slaves. Feast 3 March.

Clotilde, Frankish queen, born Lyons or Vienne, *c.* 474, died Tours, 3 June 545. A Burgundian princess, she married Clovis, king of the Franks, *c.* 492/3, and was instrumental in his conversion to Christianity. After his death in 511, she witnessed bitter internecine strife in her own household. She retired to the abbey of St Martin at Tours, where she devoted herself to a life of piety and good works which became much celebrated in legend. She was buried beside her husband in Paris, in the Basilica of the Holy Apostles. Her body was cremated in 1793 to avoid profanation; her ashes were kept in Paris. Feast 3 June.

Cloud (Clodoald, Clou), hermit, born 524, died Nogent, near Paris, *c.* 560. Grandson of King Clovis of the Franks, he lost his own father, King Clodomir of Orléans, in a family feud, and saw his two brothers murdered by an uncle. Protected by his grandmother, St **Clotilde**, he was sent to Provence. He became a hermit and disciple of St **Severinus**, revoked his claim to the Frankish throne, and later built a hermitage at Nogent. By 811 it was known as St Cloud. Feast 7 September.

Cnut, see **Canute**.

Colette, Franciscan, born Calcye, Picardy, 13 January 1381, died Ghent, 6 March 1447. In 1398, after the deaths of her parents, she became a Franciscan tertiary and lived as a hermit near the abbey church at Corbie, where her father had been a carpenter. On the foundation of her holiness and austerity was built a conviction, inspired by visions, that her mission was to recall communities of Franciscan nuns, Poor Clares, to the purity of their original Rule. In addition to reforming existing houses, she founded 17 new ones of so-called Colettines, mostly in Flanders, France and Savoy. She was canonized in 1807.

Colluthi, martyr, died Egypt, fourth century. Feast 19 May.

Colman of Cloyne, bishop, born Munster, Ireland, 530, died 606. He became a poet and royal bard at Cashel. At the age of 50, he was baptized by St **Brendan** and given the name Colman. He was ordained and worked in Limerick and Cork, where he became the first bishop and patron of Cloyne. He is said to have taught St **Columba**. He built the first church at Cloyne, and another at Kilmaclenine. Feast 24 November.

Colman of Dromore, bishop, born Cashel, Ireland, died Dromore, sixth century. He belonged to the royal house of Cashel, and in about 514 founded a monastery on the river Lagan, near Dromore. Feast 7 June.

Colman of Kilmacduagh, born Kiltartan, County Clare, seventh century. Apparently made an unwilling bishop, Colman lived as a hermit in the Burren district, and founded a great monastery at Kilmacduagh. Feast 29 October.

Colman of Lindisfarne, bishop, born Ireland, died Innisboffin, 676. A native of Ireland, he became a monk at Iona before going to Northumberland, where he became bishop of Lindisfarne in 661. As bishop he supported King Oswy's defence of the Celtic tradition against Romanizing trends. At the Synod of Whitby in 664 he pleaded unsuccessfully for the retention of the Celtic date of Easter, and for other traditions, including the Celtic tonsure. He left Lindisfarne for Iona, then Ireland, and spent the rest of his life at the monastery of Innisboffin, County Mayo. Feast 18 February.

Colman of Lynally (also known as Colman Macusailni), abbot and bishop, born Glenelly, Tyrone, *c.* 555, died Lynally, 26 September 611. The nephew of St **Columba**, who greatly influenced him. Around 590 he built a monastery at Offaly called Lann Elo (Lynally); he also founded and became first abbot of Muckamore, then bishop of Connor. He was probably the author of a work entitled *Alphabet of Devotion*.

Coloman, pilgrim, born Ireland, died Stockerau, near Vienna, 17 July 1012. While travelling to the Holy Land he had the misfortune to be mistaken for a spy, and was tortured and hanged from a tree. Miracles were reported at the place of his execution, and his cult spread through south Germany, Austria and Hungary. He is invoked by young women looking for a good husband, by farmers, and for protection against pestilence. He is a patron saint of Austria. Feast 13 October.

Columba (sometimes Colum or Columcille), born Gartan, Donegal, Ireland, 7 December 521, died Iona, Scotland, 8 June 597. He studied in schools at Moville and Clonard, became a priest and founded churches in Ireland. He set out on missionary work, and in 563 settled on the island of Iona, off the west coast of Scotland, where he arrived on the eve of Pentecost and founded a monastery. It may be that political reasons drove him to leave Ireland. It seems there was a dispute between Columba's clan and King Diarmid, the king-overlord, which ended in a battle (Cuil Dremne) in which, it was claimed, 3,000 were killed. He was censured by the Church for his involvement, and may have decided to leave the country as a result. The 12 who set off with him were all relatives. Eventually, it is sometimes alleged, he converted the whole of northern Scotland: certainly monks from Iona evangelized the Picts, the Scots and the northern English. Columba continued, however, to maintain contact with Ireland, and may even have been partly responsible for yet another battle. He died in the abbey church, just after naming a relative as his successor. His name is attached to a traditional Irish hymn tune, which was first published in the Irish Church Hymnal (1874) and is often sung to the words 'The King Of Love My Shepherd Is'. Feast 9 June.

Columba and Pomposa, Spanish virgin martyrs, born Córdoba, c. 830 and c. 840, died there, 17 and 19 September 853. The sisters built the monastery of Tabanos. The Muslim authorities martyred Columba, who had witnessed to Christ and renounced belief in the prophet Mohammed; Pomposa repeated Columba's profession of faith before the cadi, and likewise suffered death. Christians recovered their bodies from the Guadalquivir river, and buried them in a basilica outside Córdoba. Both are included in the Roman martyrology. Feasts 17 and 19 September.

Columba of Rieti, bl., Dominican tertiary, born Angelella Guadagnoli at Rieti, Italy, 2 February 1467, died Perugia, 20 May 1501. Having vowed virginity, Columba lived as a recluse, but left her seclusion aged 19 and travelled to Perugia, where she founded the convent of St Catherine (1490). Civic rulers and members of the hierarchy sought her advice, and she had remarkable influence as a peacemaker.

Columba of Sens, died near Meaux, France, c. 270. Supposedly Spanish, but baptized at Vienne and martyred in the persecution of Aurelian. Feast 31 December.

Columbanus, monk and missionary, born Leinster, Ireland, c. 543, died Bobbio, Italy, 23 November 615. In c. 590 Columbanus left the monastic

community in Ireland of which he was a member, and with a small group of followers commenced an itinerant preaching ministry. Sailing to Gaul, he revitalized the moribund Church there, although his adherence to the traditions of the Celtic Church proved unpopular with local bishops. He was eventually forced to leave Gaul and moved on to evangelize the heathen Alemanni people, before finally settling in Bobbio, which later developed into an important monastic centre.

Comgall, abbot, born Dalriada, Antrim, Ireland, c. 520, died Bangor, 10 May 602. He is said to have undertaken military service, then studied at Clonard and Clonmacnoise. He spent some time on an island in Lough Erne, where he was ordained and began zealously to promote monasticism. He founded the abbey of Bangor in the late 550s, imposing a strict Rule. **Columbanus** was his most prominent student. He made missionary journeys to Iona and elsewhere in Scotland, and his name became known also on the continent, probably as a result of the activities of Columbanus's disciples.

Comgan, abbot, born Leinster, Ireland, died Lochalsh, Scotland, eighth century. He was a king who was defeated in battle and had to flee to Scotland, where he established a monastery at Lochalsh. Feast 13 October.

Conan, bishop, died 648. He is traditionally said to have educated **Fiacre**, to have been a bishop and to have worked in the Hebrides and the Isle of Man, continuing the work of **Patrick**. Feast 26 January.

Concordia, martyr, died Rome, third century. Nothing about her is known. Feast 22 February.

Condedus, hermit, born England (?), died near Caudebec, c. 685. He went to France in search of solitude, but after a while entered the monastery of Fontenelle. He left the monastery after a few years, and established himself as a hermit on an island in the river Seine, where he died. Feast 21 October.

Congar, abbot, born Wales, died there (?), sixth century. He seems to have come from Wales to evangelize south-west England, founding a monastery perhaps at Congresbury in Somerset. He is then said to have returned to Wales, although other versions of his life have him going to Ireland, or to France. Feast 27 November.

Conindrius, see **Rumilus and Conindrius**.

Conleth of Kildare, Ireland, died c. 520. He was a hermit at Old Connell, County Kildare, known through the Lives of **Brigid**. A skilled metalworker, he is reputed to have crafted the still existing crozier of **Finbar**. One story makes him a bishop, but this is unlikely. Feast 3 May.

Conon, bl., abbot, died 1236. He was a Basilian monk, a hermit and abbot of the Greek monastery of Nesi, Sicily. Feast 28 March.

Conon, martyr, born Nazareth, Palestine, died Magydos, Pamphylia (now in southern Turkey), c. 250. He was a gardener living in poverty. Feast 5 March.

Conon the Elder, martyr, born Iconium (Konya, Turkey), died there, 275. With his son, he was accused of treason because he was a Christian, and executed. Feast (of father and son) 29 May.

Conon the Younger, martyr, son of **Conon the Elder**.

Conrad, bl., died 1154. He was a hermit at Molfetta, Apulia. Feast 17 March.

Conrad Bosinlother, bl., Benedictine abbot and reformer, born near Trier, Germany, died Oberwang, near Mondsee, 15 January 1145. When Abbot Conrad of Siegburg became bishop of Regensburg in 1126, he chose Conrad Bosinlother – a monk of Siegburg – to reform the small episcopal abbey of Mondsee. He was perhaps too successful in his reforms, for when he placed his abbey directly under the Holy See (with his bishop's permission) in order to secure his reforms, he was clubbed to death by some of the abbey's tithe-payers.

Conrad Naantwein, bl., martyr, died Wolfrathshausen, near Munich, 1286. He was on a pilgrimage to Rome when he was set upon and burned at the stake. Feast 1 August.

Conrad of Ascoli Piceno, bl., born Ascoli Piceno, Italian Marche region, 1234, died there, 1289. A Franciscan, he first preached in Rome, then went to Libya as a missionary, where it is said he converted many thousands. In later life he taught theology in Paris. Feast 19 April (suppressed).

Conrad of Bavaria, bl., Cistercian monk, born Italy, c.1105, died Modugno, 17 March 1154. The son of Henry the Black, Conrad spent some years at Clairvaux under St **Bernard**'s tutelage before going to the Holy Land to live as a hermit. Towards the end of his life he set out for Clairvaux hoping to die with Bernard, but the saint predeceased him, and Conrad ended his days as an anchorite in Modugno. Feast 14 February.

Conrad of Constance, bishop, born Germany, died Constance, 26 November 975. Educated at the cathedral school of Constance, Conrad became bishop there and, although he abstained from any political activity, Emperor Otto I held him in great esteem. His name is associated with churches in Einsiedeln, Rheingau and St Trudpert, and with the chapel of St Maurice in Constance.

Conrad of Ofda, bl., Franciscan, founder of the Celestines, born Offida, near Ancona, Italy, c. 1241, died Bastia, Umbria, 12 December 1306. At Ascoli he entered the order of Friars Minor, was ordained and became an impressive preacher. He modelled himself on St **Francis** and lived in poverty, always walking barefoot. When Brother Leo, St Francis's companion, was dying, he bequeathed his writings to Conrad. Pope **Celestine V** gave Conrad permission to separate from the main body of Franciscans and to found the Celestine congregation. Pope Boniface VIII suppressed the Celestines and Conrad returned to the main order. Conrad was giving missions at Bastia when he died. Later his remains were reburied in Perugia cathedral. In 1817 he was declared blessed. Feast 19 December.

Conrad of Ottobeuren, bl., Benedictine abbot, died 27 July 1227. Elected abbot of Ottobeuren in 1191, he was twice forced to rebuild his monastery during his 34-year reign.

Conrad of Parzham, Capuchin lay brother, born Parzham, Bavaria, 22 December 1818, died

Altötting, 21 April 1894. Born into a farming family, Conrad pronounced his solemn vows in 1852 and served, 'through devotion to the Mother of God and the Blessed Sacrament', the friary at Altötting as doorkeeper for 41 years, attending to a constant stream of pilgrims, and to the poor, with charity, meekness and patience. He had a particular concern for abandoned children. Canonized 40 years after his death, his relics are enshrined in the church of St Anne close by the monastery.

Conrad of Piacenza, from Piacenza, northern Italy, born 1290, died Sicily, 1351. To save a man wrongly accused of starting a fire and condemned to death for it, Conrad admitted that it was he who had ordered it. He thereupon became a Franciscan tertiary and hermit and his wife a Poor Clare. His fame for holiness and healing meant that his final dwelling became a popular shrine. Feast 19 February.

Conrad of Seldenbüren, bl., born Seldenbüren castle, c. 1070, martyred Zurich, 1126. From a royal family, he founded Engelbert Benedictine abbey at Unterwalden, Switzerland, where he became a lay brother. Opponents murdered him without provocation when he went to defend the abbey's right to the property he had gifted. Feast 2 May.

Constans the Russian, born Russia or the Ukraine, died Constantinople, September 1742. Byzantine Church. He was ordained in 1730 and served in the cathedral at Kiev before being sent to the Russian embassy in Constantinople in 1733. Two years later the embassy was closed. He went to Mount Athos, and then to Jerusalem. He returned to Constantinople when the embassy was reopened in 1740, but then suddenly, in 1742, converted to Islam. He repented almost immediately, and was beheaded. Feast 26 December.

Constantine, see also **Arcadius and Constantine**.

Constantine, born Cornwall, England, or possibly in Scotland, sixth century (?). One story, with little evidence, is that he was a king of Cornwall martyred in Scotland. Or he was a local chieftain who became a monk in Cornwall, where two places bear his name. Feast 11 March.

Constantine, Roman emperor, born Naissos (Nis, Serbia), c. 273, died Nicomedia (now Izmit, Turkey), 22 May 337. While in Britain in 306 Constantine was declared Cæsar of the western Roman Empire in succession to his father, Augustus Constantius. In Rome his position was usurped by Maxentius, but Constantine was not able to challenge him until 312. Prior to their crucial battle Constantine apparently had a vision of the cross, which convinced him that he should fight under its sign. He proceeded to win a decisive victory at the Battle of the Milvian Bridge, which he duly attributed to the Christian God, and in the Edict of Milan of 313 jointly decreed with the eastern emperor Licinius that within the Roman Empire Christianity would no longer be an outlawed religion. In 324 Constantine became emperor over both east and west, and established a new imperial capital at Byzantium, subsequently renamed Constantinople. During his reign he enacted legislation which positively discriminated in favour of the Church and reflected Christian ethical principles. Taking a keen interest in ecclesiastical affairs, he convened the first ecumenical council of bishops at Nicaea in 325, and his numerous endowments stimulated the building of churches throughout the empire. There has been much argument over the exact nature of Constantine's commitment to Christianity, but the evidence suggests that it was genuine, although his understanding of it could be confused or even syncretistic. In keeping with a common practice of the time, he deferred his baptism until near death. He is regarded as a saint in several parts of the Orthodox Church. Feast 21 May.

Constantine, martyr, born Ipsilometopo, Lesbos, died Constantinople, 2 June 1819 (possibly 1820). Byzantine Church. A Muslim by birth, he was cured of an illness, apparently miraculously, as a child, and became interested in religion. He met a Christian priest, and decided to visit Mount Athos, where he asked for baptism. He went back to Magnesia where his parents now lived, and he was recognized as an apostate from Islam. He was sent to Constantinople and hanged.

Constantine VI, emperor, born Constantinople, 771, died there, 797. Byzantine Church. The son of the Emperor Leo IV and Irene of Athens, he was made co-emperor in 779, the year before his father died. His mother chose for him as a bride Rotrude, daughter of **Charlemagne**, but the marriage never took place. Instead he married Maria, daughter of **Philaret the Almsgiver**, by whom he had two daughters. His mother would not cede power to her son even when he came of age, and it was only the Arab threat in the summer of 790 which led to a successful uprising against her. He proved, however, to be an unsuccessful military leader. In 795 he forced his wife and their chldren to enter a convent, so that he might marry Theodora. This led to an uprising against him. He was imprisoned and blinded on 19 August 797. He is believed to have died shortly afterwards. He and Maria are remembered as saints in the Byzantine Church because he was responsible for summoning the eighth ecumenical council in 787.

Constantine Brancoveanu, prince of Wallachia, martyr, born 15 August 1646, died 15 August 1714. Romanian Church. In a long reign of 27 years he established good relations with neigbouring countries, including with the Russia of Peter the Great and with the Ottoman emperor. The Ottoman emperor, however, was told by some conspirators against Constantine that he had been entering a treaty against them with Vienna. He and his family were arrested and taken to Constantinople, where they were imprisoned and tortured, but offered their freedom were they to convert to Islam. He and his sons refused, and they were decapitated, their bodies being thrown into the sea. Their bodies were, however, recovered by Christians, buried in a monastery, and in 1720 transferred to a church in Bucharest. He was canonized in 1992.

Constantine of Asyut, bishop, sixth century. Coptic Church. Vicar of the patriarch Damian for Upper Egypt and the author of lives of the saints. Buried in the monastery of Hanadah.

Constantine of Bogorod, martyr, born Baranovka, 1852, died 1918. Russian Church. Constantine Alexis Golubev studied at the seminary at Saratov, entered the community there, and then returned to his native village, which had embraced the sect of the Old Believers. His success in converting them back to orthodoxy led to him being given a wider

missionary responsibility. He was ordained priest in 1895 when he was made archpriest to the metropolitan Sergius. He started schools, both for boys and for girls. He himself had seven children, for whom he had to care after his wife died in 1913. In 1918 he was condemned to death by the Bolsheviks, who buried him alive. The exact date of his death is unknown. Feast 19 September.

Constantine of Edessa, bishop. Syriac Church. Unclear which of the several Constantines this is. Feast 25 July.

Constantine of Idra, martyr, born Idra, died Rhodes, 14 November 1800. Byzantine Church. He and his family left their native Idra for Rhodes, where Constantine entered the service of the Turkish governor, who converted him to Islam. Uncomfortable with his new faith, he left for the Crimea, where he reconverted to Christianity. He went to Constantinople, then spent some time at the monastery of Iviron on Mount Athos. He then returned to Rhodes, where he confessed his Christianity before the governor, who had him hanged. His body was later taken back to Idra.

Constantine of Jaroslavl, see **Basil of Jaroslavl and Constantine of Jaroslavl**.

Constantine of Kiev, bishop, born Kiev, 21 May 1871, died there, 9 or 10 November 1937. Ukrainian Church. The son of a priest, Constantine Grigor'evic D'jakov studied at Char'kov, was ordained, and became a parish priest in Char'kov. His wife died in 1924 and he became a monk. The same year he was consecrated bishop of Sumy by the patriarch of Moscow, and in 1927 became archbishop of Char'kov and patriarchal exarch for the Ukraine. In 1932 he became metropolitan, and two years later was transferred to Kiev cathedral He had been arrested several times. In October 1937 he was again taken, and died under interrogation.

Constantine of Kiev, metropolitan, died Cernigov, 1159. Russian Church. He became a bishop in 1155 and metropolitan of Kiev and all Russia the following year. He was driven out of the city in 1158 when another candidate was imposed on the see. At his death he left a wish that his body be left to dogs in the fields, because he had been the cause of discord in the Church. This was done, but after three days his remains were interred in a church. Feast 5 June.

Constantine of Kosinsk, and Cosmas, founders, Constantine died Kosinsk, 29 July 1240. Russian Church. They founded the monastery of St Nicholas at Kosinsk, near Novgorod, which later became a convent of nuns.

Constantine of Murom, and his sons Michael and Theodore, princes, born Murom, thirteenth century. Russian Church. The son of Svjatoslav Jaroslavic, he became a Christian and governor of Murom with the intention of evangelizing it. He first sent his son Michael, but the populace threw him from the walls, so Constantine took the city by force. The people then besieged him in his fortress, but when he came out carrying an icon of the Annunciation they suddenly accepted baptism. Constantine's wife Irene is also venerated at Murom, along with his other son Theodore, who joined him in evangelizing the city.

Constantine of Novotorzok, 'fool for Christ', sixteenth century. Russian Church. Buried in the cathedral square of Torzok. Feast 21 May.

Constantine of Novotorzok and Companions, martyrs, died Novotorzok, 25 January 1609. Russian Church. The archimandrite Constantine, his monks and some lay people died when Polish troops set fire to their church.

Constantine of Perugia, bishop, third century. Feast 29 January.

Constantine of Pskov, martyr, died Pskov, 4 March 1299. Russian Church. With **Joseph of Pskov**, he was killed during an attack by the Livonian Order.

Constantine the Soldier, martyr, died Ormidia, Cyprus, fourth century. Church of Cyprus. According to legend, he had been a soldier and was one of a number of pilgrims to the Holy Land. He then became an ascetic in the desert around the river Jordan, but later took a ship to Cyprus where, with three companions, he preached the gospel and was beheaded at the command of the prince.

Constantius of Fabriano, bl., Italian Dominican. Born Fabriano, 1410, died Ascoli, 24 February 1481. A man of exceptional holiness, Constantius became prior of the Dominican congregation of the strict observance, professor of theology at Bologna and Florence, and prior of the convents at Fabriano, Perugia and Ascoli (1470), where he died. Pius VIII approved his cult in 1814.

Contardo Ferrini, bl., Italian university professor and writer, born Milan, Italy, 4 April 1859, died Suna (Novara), 17 October 1902. In 1881 he became a Franciscan tertiary and took a vow of celibacy. Having studied ancient classics and ancient law, he became professor of Roman law at Messina University (1887), moving on to Modena and Pavia. He published a number of legal studies, notably on private and penal law in ancient Rome, as well as biographical reconstructions of the lives and work of several lawyers of that time. Feast 27 October.

Contestus of Bayeux, bishop, died c. 513. He was bishop of Bayeux, Normandy, from 480. Feast 19 January.

Conwoion of Brittany, died 868, venerated locally, cult confirmed 1866. He founded St Saviour Benedictine monastery near Redon. He went to Rome to defend local bishops accused of simony, returning with relics of Pope **Marcellus I**, but was later forced away by Norsemen. Feast 5 January.

Corbinian of Freising, bishop, born Chartres, near Melun, France, 670, died Obermais, 8 September 725. Baptized Waldegiso, his mother changed his name to Corbinian. He lived as a solitary at Chartres, and organized his own community of disciples. On a visit to Rome (possibly by then as a bishop), he was commissioned by Pope Gregory II to evangelize Germany. He settled at Freising, Upper Bavaria, but had to flee to Meran after denouncing the prospective marriage of his patron, Duke Grimoald, to his brother's widow. On the death of Grimoald, he returned to Bavaria and founded a monastery at Obermais, where he spent the rest of his days. His emblem of the bear derives from the legend that he compelled a bear who had killed his pack-horse to take over the horse's job.

Corentin, bishop, died Lizard Peninsula, Cornwall, 453 (?). He lived as a hermit both in Brittany and in Cornwall, gathered disciples, and so impressed the people of Cornwall that they asked him to serve as their bishop. Feast 12 December.

Cornelius, pope, elected March 251, a Roman by birth, died Civitavecchia (?), June 253. After the martyrdom of **Fabian** under Decius in 250, the see of Rome was vacant for 14 months, prior to his election. Cornelius faced strong opposition from the supporters of Novatian, who had directed the Church in the meantime. The Novatianists objected to his fairly lenient policy towards those who had lapsed during the persecution; however, the majority of bishops supported him. Several of his letters survive, including two to **Cyprian**. Exiled under Gallus's persecution, he is said to have been martyred at Centumcellae (Civitavecchia). He was buried in Rome. Feast 16 September.

Cornelius of Aleksandrov, monk, died Aleksandrov, 1681. Russian Church. A co-founder with **Lucian** of a convent of nuns at Aleksandrov. Feast 25 June.

Cornelius of Komel, monk, born Rostov, c. 1455, died Komel, 19 May 1537 or 1538. Russian Church. Born into a wealthy family, his uncle Lucian was secretary to the wife of the grand prince, and gained for Cornelius a place at court. When Cornelius was 20, however, Lucian entered the monastery of St Cyril at Beloozero, and Cornelius followed him. He lived a life of great asceticism, but became discontented because of the great number of visitors to the monastery which interfered with the silence he wished for. He travelled first to Novgorod, where he was welcomed by Archbishop Gennadius, and then retreated to a remote spot on the river Orsa, a tributary of the Volga. But people also came to visit him there, so he moved on again to the forest of Komel, on the river Nurma. Once again people came to see him, but this time he realized that solitude was not God's will for him, so he built some cells for monks, and a wooden church, and sought ordination. He also drew up a monastic Rule for his disciples, and became known as a wonderworker, especially for his dealings with the poor of the region. Some of his monks, however, became

discontented with the severity of his Rule, and he moved again, with his disciple **Gennadius**, to a monastery beside the river Kostroma, on lake Surskoe. In 1526 he was visited by Grand Prince Basil Ioannovic, who asked him to return to Komel. Cornelius refused, but in 1531, when Cornelius had to visit Moscow, the prince repeated his request, and Cornelius, taking this as a sign of the divine will, agreed to return, although he would not take on the role of hegumenos. He was canonized in 1600.

Cornelius of Olonec, monk, sixteenth century. Russian Church. A disciple of **Alexander of Svirsk**, he founded a hermitage near Olonec.

Cornelius of Paleostrovo, monk, born Pskov, died island of Pal'e, c. 1420. Russian Church. He became a monk when he was already quite old, living first in the monastery of Valaam on Lake Ladoga, but then he went to Finland and preached Christianity along the White Sea coast. He visited many monasteries, urging a strict ascetical discipline, but then, in search of solitude, settled on lake Onega, on the island of Pal'e. Many came to seek his spiritual advice, and a monastery developed, that of Paleostrovo, but he himself entrusted the monastery to his disciple **Abram** and lived in a nearby hermitage. Feast 19 May.

Cornelius of Perejaslavl, monk, died Perejaslavl, 22 July 1693. Russian Church. Conon was the son of a rich merchant of Rjazan, but when still young he left his family and became a monk, first at St Lucian's monastery, then at that of Boris and Gleb at Perejaslavl, changing his name to Cornelius.

Cornelius of the Cave of Pskov, monk and martyr, born Pskov, 1501, died there, 20 February 1570. Russian Church. Of a rich family, he entered the Cave monastery of Pskov in 1523, and became hegumenos six years later. Under his rule the monastery grew in size, established a famous library and became a centre of missionary activity for south-west Estonia. Cornelius was also responsible for the building of several churches. He supported the troops of Ivan the Terrible in their battles against the Livonians. This support was exercised through his friendship with Ivan's counsellor and commander Andrew Kurbskij.

Kurbskij, however, left the service of the Tsar for that of King Sigismund of Poland, accusing the Tsar of tyranny and criticizing Cornelius's monastery for its support of Ivan. Cornelius, however, remained loyal to the Tsar, who repaid this loyalty by imprisoning and then killing him.

Cornelius of Vyg, monk, born Tot'ma, *c.* 1570, died 30 March 1695. Church of the Old Believers. Conon's father was a smallholder, who died when Conon was about 15, at which point he decided to become a monk, eventually in the monastery of St Cornelius, receiving the tonsure when he was 18 and changing his name. He moved to Moscow, where he came to know the patriarch Philaret, whom he served, and who wanted to ordain him priest, although Cornelius refused. At the reform he left Moscow, but later returned to settle for 12 years at the monastery of St Nilus. On one occasion, having failed to prevent a priest celebrating according to the new liturgy, he hit him on the head with a thurible. He fled the monastery, and lived for some time by the river Vodla, finally settling at Vyg.

Cosconius, martyred third/fourth century with **Zeno** and **Melanippus**.

Cosmas, martyr, died Prusa, Bythinia, fifteenth century. Byzantine Church.

Cosmas, priest, born Moscow (?), died Koseeckaja, Poland, 1691. Church of the Old Believers. He was a parish priest in Moscow, but after the renewed condemnation of the Old Rites in 1667 he retired to Staodube with his family and 12 families from his parish. Others joined him, but after the persecution of Old Believers intensified from 1685 onwards, they moved to Poland where they built the village of Vetka. As the community grew, other villages were established and it was in one of these that he died.

Cosmas and Damian, martyrs and patron saints of physicians, perhaps died Cyrrhus, *c.* 302. Their lives are very obscure; legend suggests they were Arabs who practised medicine without charge, and became known as the 'silverless' ones. Both are said to have been martyred under Diocletian. Their cult was already strong in the fifth century. A church

was constructed in their honour by Felix IV in the 520s; other Roman churches have also commemorated them. They are mentioned in the Canon of the Roman mass. Feast 26 September.

Cosmas Aitolos, monk, martyr, born Taxiarchis, 1714, died 1779. Byzantine Church. Constantine Anifantis studied on Mount Athos, becoming a monk there and taking the name Cosmas. He moved to Constantinople, then became an itinerant preacher, although making regular visits back to his base on Mount Athos. In 1779 he was accused by the Turkish authorities in Albania of fomenting revolt among the Greek population and was executed, his body being thrown into a river. He was canonized in 1961.

Cosmas Hieromonk, martyr, eighteenth century. Georgian Church. Before becoming a monk he had been a royal councillor. He achieved fame through his life of **Ketevan**, martyred in 1624 by the Persians, and by the fact that he knew the Psalter by heart. He was killed by a Muslim when he left the monastery on one occasion. Feast 18 July.

Cosmas of Alexandria I, patriarch, born Bana on the Delta, died Alexandria, 24 June 731. Coptic Church. He had been a monk in the desert of Scete, and was elected patriarch in 730.

Cosmas of Alexandria II, patriarch, born Sammannud on the Delta, died Danusar on the Delta, 17 November 859. Coptic Church. He had been a monk of the monastery of St Macarius before his election, which took place on 8 July 851. He ran into trouble when he was by chance present at a fight in which one man was killed. He was held responsible and put under house arrrest until rescued by two influential Christians. Soon afterwards the caliph launched a persecution of Christians, many of whom denied their faith. The patriarch himself was spared the humiliations heaped on Christians. It only declined when a new governor was appointed in Egypt, not long before Cosmas's death.

Cosmas of Alexandria III, patriarch, died Alexandria, 27 February 932. Coptic Church.

Cosmas of Jachroma, monk, born near Vladimir, died Jachroma, 18 February 1492. Russian Church. Of a boyar family, he was in the service of a sick neighbour, with whom he travelled widely looking for a cure. In 1482, beside the river Jachroma, he had a vision of the Virgin Mary, who told him to found a monastery and heal his master. He entered the Kievan Cave monastery, but an angel in a vision told him to return to Jachroma, where he built a church. Feast 18 February.

Cosmas of Taha and Companions, martyrs. Coptic Church. Only the day of their martyrdom is known, 26 May.

Cosmas of Verchotur'e, 'fool for Christ', died Verchotur'e, 1680. Russian Church. The son of a rich merchant called Nemtinov, he showed an extraordinary devotion early in life, spending much of his day in the church. He walked barefoot, dressed in a long robe, and was renowned as a miracle worker.

Cosmas of Zografou, bl., fifteenth century. Byzantine Church. Bulgarian by origin, he was a monk of Zagrafou. Feast 22 September.

Cosmas the Melodian, Greek liturgical hymn writer, born Jerusalem, c. 706, died c. 760. Also called Hagiopolites. Adopted by the father of **John Damascene**, he and John studied with an Italian monk. Around 732, he entered the Laura (or Lavra) of St Sabas, near Jerusalem. In 743 he became bishop of Maiuma, near Gaza. His poetry is well known, and especially valued are the 14 canons (chants) for Easter, Christmas and the Exaltation of the Holy Cross, which form parts of the Byzantine liturgy. Feast 14 October in the Eastern Church.

Cosroes of Ganjak, martyr, born Ganjak (Albania), died there, 10 January 1167. Armenian Church. Accused of fathering a child with a neighbour's wife, he was told to convert or die, but he refused to convert and was stoned to death.

Credan, abbot, eighth century. Abbot of the monastery of Evesham. Nothing is known of his life. Feast 19 August.

Crescentia Hoss, Franciscan mystic, born Kaufbeuren, Germany, 20 October 1682, died there, 5 April 1744. Hoss demonstrated a sense of piety from childhood. She entered the Kaufbeuren Franciscan convent, where she eventually became mistress of novices and superior. Her reputation for sanctity and devotion was enhanced by her claims to a number of visions and other mystical experiences.

Crescentia, see also **Vitus**.

Crete, Ten Martyrs of, see **Ten Martyrs of Crete**.

Crispin and Crispinian, martyrs, died c. 285. Traditionally said to have come from a noble Roman family, they fled to Soissons, where they set up as shoemakers, and took only such money as was offered to them for their work. They are regarded as the patron saints of shoemakers, cobblers and other leather-workers. Other legend suggests (probably wrongly) that they were martyred in Rome, and their bones were taken to Soissons and elsewhere. Yet another tradition associates them with Faversham in Kent. Feast 25 October.

Crispin of Pavia, bishop, died 467. He subscribed to the acts of the Council of Milan in 451. There is another saint by the same name, a third-century bishop of Pavia. Feast 7 January.

Crispin of Viterbo, Capuchin lay brother, born Viterbo, Italy, 13 November 1678, died Rome, 19 May 1750. Born Pietro Fioretti, he was educated by the Jesuits and worked as a shoemaker until 1693 when he joined the Capuchins, taking the name Brother Crispin. He worked in the kitchen, the garden and the infirmary. He was devoted to Mary Immaculate. He was known for his unfailingly happy disposition and work on behalf of the poor. He was also believed to be capable of miracles and people on all levels went to him for help. He was beatified in 1806, and the canonization process began in 1923, and is still under way.

Crispina, martyr, born Thagara, Africa, died Thebeste, 304. She was a wealthy matron who was arrested during Diocletian's persecution and tried at Thebeste. On refusing to sacrifice to the gods, she was beheaded, probably with other martyrs. She is often mentioned by St **Augustine**, who preached a panegyric in her honour. Feast 5 December.

Cronan, abbot, born Ireland, died Roscrea (?), 665. He created monastic foundations at Tullyroe (Red Hill) and at Lusmagh, County Galway. He moved to Roscrea, County Tipperary, first living by Lough Cree but then moving to a more accessible place in order to be able to welcome the poor. Feast 28 April.

Csenia Jurevna, born Novgorod, died Tver, 1312. Russian Church. The daughter of the boyar George Michailovic Oksin'e, she married Jaroslav Jaroslavic, prince of Tver and prince of Vladimir. They had three children, two daughters and a son who was born after the death of his father. She acted as regent for a time, and was involved in the construction of the cathedral of Tver, the first stone building in north-east Russia after the Tartar invasions. Shortly before her death she entered a convent, taking the name Mary.

Csenia of Petersburg, bl., 'fool for Christ', born Petersburg, c. 1720, died c. 1790. Russian Church. Born of a noble family, she married Andrea Petrov, who died suddenly. He was presumably in a state of sin, because his widow decided to expiate his sinfulness by living the life of an ascetic wanderer. She sold all her possessions and gave the money to the poor, abandoning even her own name and adopting that of her husband. She became a well-known figure on the streets of the city, known for miracles and the gift of prophecy – although her prophecies were difficult to interpret. Feast 24 January.

Csenofonte of Tutan, monk, sixteenth to seventeenth centuries. Russian Church. The founder of the monastery of Tutan, near Tver. Feast 26 January.

Cumian, abbot, born West Munster, Ireland, c. 590, died c. 665. The son of a king, he became a monk, then abbot and bishop. It is possibly Cumian who brought the Roman way of fixing the date of Easter into Ireland. Feast 12 November.

Cunegund of Poland, bl., born c. 1224, died 24 July 1292. Cunegund, or Kinga, was the daughter of

King Bela IV of Hungary. At 16 she married King Boleslaus IV of Poland. According to tradition, she wanted to remain celibate, a request to which her husband agreed, and they both took a vow of celibacy before the bishop of Krakow a year after their marriage. Cunegund cared for the poor and sick, and although she was queen lived a simple life. After her husband's death in 1279 she declined to rule in his place. She became a Poor Clare in the convent at Stary Sacz, which she had founded, and later became prioress. Many miracles occurred during the last years of her life, including an apparition of St **Francis of Assisi**.

Cunibert of Cologne, bishop, died Cologne, c. 663. Brought up at the court of Clotaire II, he was ordained and became archdeacon of the church at Trier. He was appointed bishop of Cologne c. 625. An important royal counsellor, he was appointed as one of the two guardians of Dagobert I's son, Sigebert, as king of Austrasia. He attended several synods, and promoted the evangelization of the Frisians. Feast 12 November.

Cuthberga, queen and abbess, born Wessex, died Wimborne, Dorset, 31 August c. 725. She was the sister of the king of Wessex and was married to the king of Northumberland. They separated, and she became a nun at Barking, then, with her sister, she founded a nunnery at Wimborne.

Cuthbert Mayne, martyr, born near Barnstaple, Devon, 1544 (baptized 20 March), executed Launceston, 30 November 1577. After ordination into the Church of England and education at Oxford, he was appointed chaplain of St John's College. Latterly he was converted to Roman Catholicism and in 1573 moved to an English seminary at Douai. Ordained as priest in 1575, he returned to England in 1578 and settled on the estate of Francis Tregian near Truro in Cornwall. He secretly carried out his work as a priest until his arrest in 1577 and subsequent execution in the marketplace at Launceston. Cuthbert was canonized as one of the **Forty Martyrs** in 1970 by Pope Paul VI.

Cuthbert of Lindisfarne, bishop, born possibly near Melrose, Scotland, c. 636, died Farne Island, 20 March 687. A monk at Melrose, he accompanied his abbot, Eata, to Ripon, where they established a monastery. Refusing to conform to Roman practices, the two were expelled and returned north, although they opted to obey the Roman position at the Synod of Whitby (664). Cuthbert became prior of Melrose in 661, then prior of Lindisfarne. After a time on Farne Island, he was elected bishop of Hexham in 684, and was consecrated bishop of Lindisfarne at Easter 685. His tenure was short but active. He retired again to Farne, where he died. Buried on Lindisfarne, his body was moved several times, before being interred in Durham in 995. A large cult grew up around him. His shrine was destroyed in 1539–40. His tomb was opened in Durham Cathedral in 1827.

Cuthman, born probably near Bosham, England, *c.* 681, died Steyning. First a travelling hermit, begging for himself and his paralysed mother – this is the story in Christopher Fry's play *The Boy with a Cart* – he is supposed to have built the first, wooden, church at Steyning with his own hands. Feast 8 February.

Cybi (Kebi), abbot, born Cornwall, died Holyhead, Anglesey, sixth century. Born probably in eastern Cornwall, and belonging to the royal house – his father is said to have been commander of the king's army – he went away to study, although it is not revealed where, and then to Jerusalem, and after that to St **Hilary** at Poitiers. There apparently he was consecrated bishop, and returned to Cornwall, where there was an effort made to crown him king. He rejected the throne, went first to south Wales, then over to Ireland, and finally back to Wales, settling in Holyhead. He died on 8 November, but the year is not recorded.

Cyneburg (Kyneburg), abbess, died *c.* 680. Daughter of Penda, the pagan king of Mercia, she was wife of Alcfrith, son of Oswy of Northumbria. Possibly on his death in *c.* 664, she became abbess of the convent at Castor, Northamptonshire. Along with her sister St Cyneswide and another relative, St Tibia, she was venerated at Peterborough abbey, to which her relics were taken in the tenth century. Feast 6 March.

Cyprian, bishop, martyr, born probably Carthage, *c.* 200, died Carthage, 14 September 258. Elected bishop of Carthage in 248, he fled during the Decian persecution, but governed his Church by letter from exile. On his return in 251, he dealt strictly with those who had lapsed. He took a high view of the Church as the sole place of salvation, and argued, against Pope Stephen I, for the rebaptism of schismatics. Banished under Valerian, he tried to hide, but was eventually caught and put to death. His writings include *On the Unity of the Catholic Church*, a series of ascetical and pastoral treatises, and a highly important collection of practical letters, which constitute a major historical resource. Feast 16 September.

Cyprian, bishop, died Toulon, by 549. Consecrated bishop of Toulon before 517, he participated in various synods and was a vigorous opponent of so-called 'semi-Pelagianism' at the Council of Orange in 529. He was himself criticized for holding theopaschite views, a charge on which he defended himself in a still-extant epistle to Maximus of Geneva. He is the main author of a part of a life of his friend, **Caesarius of Arles**. Feast 3 October.

Cyprian, martyr, born Char'kov, Ukraine, 31 October 1897, died there, 26 March 1938. Ukrainian Church, Moscow Patriarchate. Baptized Leo Nikolaevic Jankovski, he became an archimandrite before the Revolution, and afterwards continued to work in Char'kov until he was arrested and shot. Feast 19 May.

Cyprian, monk, born Klitzos, died Constantinople, 5 July 1679. Byzantine Church. He left his home as a young man and became a monk on Mount Athos, dedicating himself to prayer, penance and abstinence. After a time, however, he decided he wished to embrace martyrdom. Although fellow monks tried to dissuade him, he went to Thessalonika, where he declared himself a Christian in front of a Turkish judge. The judge, however, thinking he had lost his mind, simply punished him and let him go. He then went to Constantinople, where he wrote to letter to the vizier, attacking the errors of Islam. An apostate Christian in the palace intercepted the letter and tried, unsuccessfully, to prevent him seeing the vizier. The vizier admired his courage and attempted to convert him to Islam. When Cyrpian remained constant, his execution was ordered. He was decapitated in the Fanar, the Christian quarter, as a warning to his fellow Christians.

Cyprian, see also **Felix and Cyprian**.

Cyprian Michael Iwene Tansi, bl., born Aguleri, near Onitsha, Nigeria, September 1903, died Leicester, England, 20 January 1964. His parents were pagan, and gave him the name Iwene: Michael was added when he was baptized at the age of nine. He worked as a catechist and teacher, but when he was 22 he entered the seminary for the Onitsha diocese, and was ordained in 1937. He worked in the diocese for 13 years, but then felt the call to a more contemplative life and with the permission of his bishop entered the Cistercian monastery of Mount St Bernard's, Charnwood Forest, Leicestershire. He had hoped to return to Nigeria to found a monastery, with another Nigerian priest in the monastery. A monastery was indeed opened, not in Nigeria but in Cameroon, but Cyprian – as he had become on entering the abbey – was too ill to travel. In Nigeria he had a reputation for great personal holiness, and visitors from Nigeria came frequently to the monastery. His remains were eventually taken back to Nigeria.

Cyprian of Karacev. Russian Church. He lived as a 'fool for Christ's sake' in the city of Karacev.

Cyprian of Kiev, patriarch, born Bulgaria, c. 1330, died Moscow, 16 September 1406. Russian Church. He entered the monastery of Kelifarevo on Mount Athos, where he became deeply imbued with the spirituality of hesychasm. In 1373 he was entrusted by the patriarch of Constantinople with reconciling the prince of Lithuania with Prince Dimitri Ivanovic of Moscow and his metropolitan **Alexis of Moscow**, in which he was successful. As a consequence, in December 1375 he was created metropolitan of Kiev, Rus and Lithuania. After the death of Alexis in 1378, Cyprian went to Moscow where he was arrested and briefly imprisoned. He returned to Constantinople, but was invited back by Prince **Dimitri Donskoj**, whom he aided in creating an alliance against the Golden Horde. He fled Moscow in 1382 after an attack on it, probably to Tver. His place in Moscow was seized by a 'pretender' metropolitan, Pimen, but Pimen was deposed by the patriarch Anthony in 1389, and Cyprian was restored. He returned to Moscow in March 1390. His first task was to establish his authority through the whole of Rus, including Novgorod, and then to launch a reform of the liturgy (which brought him into conflict with Prince Basil of Moscow because the emperor in Constantinople was mentioned before local princes). He continued his role as a mediator, establishing good relations with the new kingdom of Poland-Lithuania, ruled by a king newly converted to Roman Catholicism. Cyprian proposed an ecumenical council to re-establish religious unity in the region, but it never met.

Cyprian of Moscow, died Pustozerk, 7 July 1675. Church of the Old Believers. He campaigned against the liturgical reforms of Patriarch Nikon, was arrested and exiled to Pustozerk, where he continued to resist the changes. He was condemned and decapitated.

Cyprian of Storozka, monk, died Storozka, c. 1598. Russian Church. According to tradition, the leader of a band of brigands who had hindered the work of **Adrian** in establishing his own monastery near lake Ladoga, but was eventually converted and himself built a monastery near the lake. Feast 2 November.

Cyprian of Suzdal, died Voskresenskoe, 22 July 1622. Russian Church. He lived as a hermit on a small island on the river Uvod. He lived naked, and only ate what he was given in alms.

Cyprian of Tropski, monk, sixteenth century. Russian Church.

Cyprian of Ustjug, monk, born in the Dvina region, died Ustjug, 29 September 1276. Russian Church. A rich landowner, he became a monk at the monastery at Gleden. But at the time Gleden was threatened by flooding from the river Jug, and it was decided to move the town to a spot on the river Suchona. Cyprian was chosen to establish a monastery. Construction began in 1212 and lasted for four years, and Cyprian bestowed on it all his wealth. Cyprian chose to remain a monk, and refused the priesthood.

Cyran, see **Sigiramnus**.

Cyriac. Syriac Church. A disciple of **Yaret**. Feast 12 November.

Cyriac, patriarch, died 817. Syriac Church. A monk of the monastery of Bizona, on the left bank of the Euphrates, he became patriarch in 793. Feast 13 August.

Cyriac and Julietta, early fourth century, died Tarsus (?). Assyrian Church; Syriac Church. Julietta was arrested as a Christian, and tortured. Seeing this, her three-year-old son Cyriac wished to share his mother's torments and said that he, too, was a Christian. The judge grasped him by the feet and dashed out his brains. His mother gave thanks for his martyrdom, and was then decapitated.

Cyriac Chavata, bl., born Kainakary, India, 10 February 1805, ordained 1829, died Kerala, 3 January 1871, beatified 1986. First superior of the Congregation of Carmelite Brothers of Mary Immaculate, vicar general of the Syro-Malabar Church in the 1860s, he worked hard to prevent a threatened schism, not resolved until 1930.

Cyriac, Largus, Smaragdus and Companions, martyrs, died Rome, c. 303 (?). Feast 8 August.

Cyriac, Maximus, Archelaus and Companions, martyrs, died Ostia, 235 or c. 250. Said to have been a bishop, priest and deacon, martyred together with some Christian soldiers. Feast 23 August.

Cyriac of Amed, bishop, died 623. Syriac Church. A monk of the monastery of Mar Zakka, near Edessa, he became bishop of Amed in 578. Feast 3 August.

Cyriac of Bisericani, monk, born Vadul Bistreti, c. 1570, died c. 1650. Romanian Church. A monk of the monastery of Bisericani where he learned hesychasm, he spent much of his life as a hermit in a cave in a forest, speaking only to passing shepherds. Feast 31 December.

Cyriac of Solovki, monk, mid-seventeenth century. Russian Church. He served both as cellarer and infirmarian of the monastery of Solovki, and when he left with **Diodorus**, those in the infirmary complained and asked for him to be brought back.

Cyriac of Syrinsk, see **Cyril of Syrinsk**.

Cyriac of Tazlau, monk, died Tazlau, c. 1660. Romanian Church. A hesychast who lived a solitary life on the mountain of Magura Tazlaului, coming down to attend the liturgy at the monastery of Tazlau. Cyriac was well known as a holy man and a confessor. He gathered about him some 30 disciples, and was venerated as a wonderworker. Feast 31 December.

Cyriaca, martyr, died Rome, 249. A wealthy widow who gave refuge to persecuted Christians. Feast 21 August.

Cyriacus, see also **Hesperus**.

Cyricus (St Cyr), see **Quiricus**.

Cyril, bishop and martyr, died Beroa, Thrace, third century. Feast 8 March.

Cyril, martyr, born Heliopolis, Phoenicia (now Lebanon), died there, 362. He was a deacon persecuted under Julian the Apostate. Feast 28 March.

Cyril, born Thessalonika (Saloniki), Greece, 826 or 827, died Rome, Italy, 14 February 869. He is the younger brother of St **Methodius**; together they are 'the apostles of the Slavs'. He was a scholar, linguist and theologian. He was born Constantine, and took the name Cyril when he became a monk. When young he had a reputation as a philosopher. In 860 he was part of a mission to the Khazars. In 862 he went to Moravia, where he taught in the vernacular. In preparation, he devised the Glagolitic alphabet. Copies of the Scriptures were produced in this script. In 867 he returned to Rome, where he saw the new Slavonic liturgy celebrated. He died only 50 days after becoming a monk. He was buried in San Clemente in Rome. Together with Methodius, he was canonized by the Eastern Church soon after his death; Rome followed only in 1880.

Cyril, see also **Archelaus**.

Cyril and Companions, martyrs, died Axiopolis (Cernavoda, Romania), *c.* 200. Feast 12 May.

Cyril and Maria of Radonez, born Varnicy, died Radonez, *c.* 1337. Russian Church. The pious parents of **Sergius of Radonez**, they had in all three sons, of whom Bartholomew (Sergius's baptismal name) was the second. They were wealthy, of the boyar class, but were eventually impoverished by the incursions of the Tartars and tributes which had to be paid to the Khan. As a consequence they moved *c.* 1330 from Varnicy, near Rostov, to Radonez, near Moscow. There both entered the same double (i.e., for men and women) of the Protection of the Mother of God, where they died.

Cyril Bertrand Tejecdor, martyr, born Lerma, Spain, 20 March 1888, died Turon, Asturia, 9 October 1934. Baptized José Sanz, he joined the (de la Salle) Brothers of the Christian Schools. He served in a number of schools before becoming superior of the Brothers in Santander. In 1933 he went to Turon in charge of a school for the children of miners. He was arrested with the other **Martyrs of Asturia** by a group of rebel soldiers, and executed by firing squad.

Cyril of Alexandria, patriarch, theologian, born Alexandria, 375, died there, 27 June 444. He succeeded his uncle Theophilus as patriarch of Alexandria in 412, despite strong opposition. He prosecuted a vigorous campaign against various pagan, Novatianist and Jewish opponents, and may have been complicit in the murder of Hypatia, a distinguished Neoplatonist philosopher. He is chiefly famous for his fierce opposition to Nestorius on the person of Christ, 430–31. A theologian of considerable acumen, his emphasis on Christ's divinity fostered what would become the monophysite view that Christ had only one nature. A gifted writer, he left many letters, homilies and commentaries, and a number of anti-heretical dogmatic tracts. Feast 27 June.

Cyril of Alexandria II, patriarch, born Aflaqah, died Cairo, 6 June 1092. Coptic Church. He was born in a village in the Delta, and entered the monastery of St Macarius, taking the name George. He was consecrated patriarch on 18 March 1078, and was cordially received by the caliph and his family. He was not well educated, and as patriarch began to study, becoming skilled especially in Scripture. He held a synod, on the instructions of the vizier, in an attempt to bring order among the bishops, but the canons of the synod were not well received in Upper Egypt.

Cyril of Astrakhan, archimandrite, died Astrakhan, 1592. Russian Church. Sent to Astrachan after that city had united with the principate of Moscow in 1554. He built churches and a monastery, and evangelized the surrounding area. Feast 18 March.

Cyril of Beloozero, monk, born Moscow, *c.* 1337, died Beloozero, 9 June 1427. Russian Church. Baptized Cosmas and of a well-to-do family, he wished from an early age to become a monk, but his tutor, who came from a powerful, political family, obliged him to involve himself in affairs of state. He was only able to enter a monastery after being secretly tonsured when he was 31. Even then his tutor objected, but was won over by his wife. Cosmas, now Cyril, gave all his wealth to the poor and entered the monastery of Simonovo at Moscow. He worked for nine years in the monastery's bakery before he was allowed to become a copyist of manuscripts. He became archimandrite of the monastery in 1389, having gained a high reputation for his holiness of life. However, his fame aroused the envy of another archimandrite, Sergio Azakov, creating tension in the monastery. Cyril therefore retired to the former monastery (it had been moved in 1379). He had long wanted to become a hermit, and one evening in 1397 while at prayer he heard a voice telling him to go to the 'white lake' – Beloozero – and saw a vision of the spot. He consulted another monk, **Teraponte**, and both decided to go together. Travelling north, Cyril eventually recognized the place he had seen in his vision, on the bank of lake Silversk. There the two settled, but because of differences in the style of their lives – Teraponte was less severe in his penances – they separated and Teraponte moved 15 kilometres away. Cyril was, however, joined by other monks from his former monastery, and they built a church dedicated to the Dormition of the Virgin, as was the church at Simonovo. The style of monasticism which Cyril taught his monks – strict observance of the Rule, silence, spiritual reading and the copying of manuscripts – had a great influence on other monastic foundations, several of which were made by his disciples. Because of his service to the prince, he kept his ties with Moscow, and wrote letters of spiritual guidance to the prince, showing a clear understanding of the political role of monks.

Cyril of Jerusalem, bishop, born perhaps Jerusalem, c. 315, died 18 March 386. Little is known of his early years. Bishop of Jerusalem from c. 348, he found himself exiled several times for offending his Arian superior in Caesarea, Acacius. His orthodoxy was investigated by **Gregory of Nyssa** in 379, but proved satisfactory. He is famous for a series of *Catechetical Lectures* which were published in his name (although some scholars attribute them to his successor, John). They offer a valuable insight into the liturgy of the Palestinian Church, and place a strong emphasis on the eucharistic real presence and on the efficacy of baptism for the remission of sins.

Cyril of Kiev III, metropolitan, died Perejaslavl-Zalesski, 6 December 1281. Russian Church. Chosen in 1242 as metropolitan of Kiev, probably by Prince Daniel of Galic, after the death two years earlier of Metropolitan Joseph, presumably at the hands of the Mongols. He was almost certainly the archimandrite of some monastery in Galicia. He travelled to Nicaea for confirmation of his elevation by the patriarch of Constantinople (that city being then in the hands of Latin Christians), and returned to Kiev c. 1249. However, he spent most of his 30-year reign in the cities to the north of Russia, especially Vladimir, rarely in Kiev itself. He was eventually able to establish good relations with the Mongols, and sent a bishop to the court of the Khan. As the threat from the Mongols decreased, he visited the dioceses of Russia to improve both liturgy and the discipline of the clergy, circulated a code of law, and in 1274 held a meeting with the bishops of the five most important sees. This produced a code of discipline which was sent to all dioceses. Within Russia he brought about peace among the warring princes, and became a confidant of **Alexander Nevski**. The exact date of his death is uncertain: it was almost certainly in December, but it may have been 1280. He was buried in Santa Sophia, the cathedral of Kiev. Feast 19 December.

Cyril of Mount Celma, monk, born 1286, died Mount Celma, 8 December 1368. Russian Church. Cyril became a monk when he was 12 years old, entering the monastery of **Anthony the Roman** at Novgorod. Seven years later he went on pilgrimage, but when in 1316 he arrived at Mount Celma, near Kargopol, he decided to settle there, living at first in a cave, where he was joined by his brother Cornelius, although three years later Cornelius, seeking greater solitude, moved away. Although many came to see Cyril, it was only after his death that a monastery was established.

Cyril of Novgorod, hegumenos, died c. 1196 (?). Russian Church.

Cyril of Novoezersk, hegumenos, born Galic, c. 1480, died 1537. Russian Church. Of a noble family, Cyril fled his home aged 15 to become a monk in the monastery of **Cornelius of Komel**. Twelve years later his father discovered where he was, and came to attempt to bring him home. Cyril at first refused to see him, but when he did so at the request of the hegumenos, his father was so moved that he, too, entered the monastery and his wife became a nun. In 1512 Cyril left the monastery with the approval of his superior, and lived a hermit's life for five years in the forests of southern Russia. He had a dream in which the Virgin Mary instructed him to go to the New Lake, some 40 kilometres from Belozersk, where he established himself on an island on the lake. He was eventually joined by other monks, and he built a monastery, naming it Novoezersk. Feast 4 February.

Cyril of Rostov, bishop, died Rostov, 1384. Russian Church. Feast 23 May.

Cyril of Rostov II, bishop, died 12 March 1262. Russian Church. Formerly hegumenos of the monastery of the Nativity of the Mother of God at Vladimir, he was consecrated bishop of Rostov in the cathedral of Kiev on 6 April 1231, having been elected the previous year. His episcopate coincided with Mongol domination of the region, and he worked to restore churches that had been destroyed by the invasion. In all this he copied the pastoral and political approach of the metropolitan of Kiev, **Cyril III**. His wisdom and his holiness attracted the attention of the Khan, who invited him to his court at Saraj where, on his second visit, he so impressed **Peter Zarevic**, a nephew of the Khan, that he secretly returned with Cyril to Rostov and was baptized. Cyril retired from his see a year or so before his death.

Cyril of Syrinsk, monk, died Syrinsk 1402. Russian Church. Founder of the monastery of Uspensk Syrinsk, near Olonec. He is probably the same person as Cyriac of Syrinsk. Feast 28 April.

Cyril of Thessalonika, bl., born Thessalonika, died there, 6 July 1566. Byzantine Church. Baptized Cyriac, he was brought up by two uncles, one of whom was a Muslim who pressured him to convert. Instead, when aged 14, he joined two monks who were passing through Thessalonika and entered the monastery of Chelandar on Mount Athos, taking the name Cyril. For some eight years he remained on Athos, but then returned to Thessalonika where he was recognized by his Muslim uncle and brought before a judge, accused of apostatizing from Islam. The judge attempted to persuade him to deny his faith, but when he refused, ordered him to be burned alive in the hippodrome, near the church of St Constantine. When the church was demolished in 1972, Cyril's funerary urn was discovered.

Cyril of Turov, bishop, born Turov, now in Belarus, died there, 1183. Of a rich family, he was well educated and learned Greek. He entered the monastery of Boris and Gleb at Turov, and for a time was a stylite. He was renowned both for the sanctity of his life and for his sermons and writings, which included poems and moral treatises. For his rhetorical skills he was called 'the Russian Chrysostom', and his influence spread far beyond Turov, especially among the southern Slavs. Bishop from 1174, he resigned his see in 1179, and was buried in the monastery of Ss Boris and Gleb. Feast 28 April.

Cyril of Velsk, wonderworker, fifteenth century. Russian Church. He drowned in the river Vaga while fleeing from his master, and was buried in the cemetery of the village of Velsk. Miracles occurred at his tomb, and the parish priest in 1587 moved Cyril's remains into the church. Feast 9 June.

Cyril, Spiridon and Faustus of Vologda, hermits. Russian Church. Little is known of them, although Cyril is said to have lived in a wood near Lake Kubenskoe, and was buried in the monastery of Spaso-Kamenny.

Cyrinus, martyred Cyzicus, Hellespont, 320. He was killed with **Primus** and **Theogenes**, all soldiers, under Emperor Licinus. Feast 3 January.

Cyrion and Companions, martyrs, died Alexandria, third century. Commemorated together, although probably not killed together, some died by the sword, some by drowning, some by burning. Cyrion was a priest, others were a lector, Bassian, an exorcist, Agatho, and lay people listed as Ammonius, Dionysus, Luke, Moses, Protus and Tonion. Feast 14 February.

Cyrus, martyr, died Canopus, Egypt, *c.* 303. He and **John**, both doctors, went to Canopus to support Athanasia and her daughters who were being persecuted under Diocletian. All were arrested, tortured and beheaded. The Aboukir, of Nelson's victory, is derived from 'Father Cyrus' in Coptic. Feast 31 January.

Cyrus of Constantinople, bishop, died 714. Feast 7 January.

Dado, Syriac Church. Apparently a disciple of St **Awgen**, he is venerated at Tur Abdin. Feast 3 June.

Dagobert II, king, died forest of Woëuvre, Lorraine, 23 December 679. He succeeded to the throne of Austrasia in 656, but was unseated and fled to England, where he was educated by St **Wilfrid**. He married an English princess, with whom he had two children, **Irmina** and **Adela**. With Wilfrid's assistance he was restored to the throne in 675, but then was killed, either assassinated or in a hunting accident. It was, however, popularly believed he had been murdered, and he was treated as a martyr. Feast 24 December.

Daig, bishop, died 587. Daig mac Cairill is said to have been a pupil of **Finnian of Clonard**. Early legends say he had been a scribe or a metal-worker. He was probably not consecrated as a bishop; nor, contrary to legend, was his patron **Kieran of Clonmacnois**. He is the patron of Iniskeen, on the borders of Louth and Monaghan. Feast 18 August.

Dalmatius and Faustus, feast 3 August.

Dalmatius Moner, bl., born Santa Colona de Farnes, Catalonia, 1291, died Gerona, 24 September 1341. He studied at Montpellier, then joined the Dominican Order in Gerona. He taught and served as master of novices. He was somewhat eccentric, talking to women only over his shoulder, and for the last few years of his life occupied a cave which he scooped out for himself in the priory's grounds.

Dalmatius of Perm, monk, born Tobolsk, died Belagorodisca, 1697. Russian Church. Dimitri Ivanovic Mokrin came from a Cossack family, served in the army with distinction (he was ennobled for his services), married and had children. He then suddenly abandoned his family and career and entered the monastery of the Theophany at Nev'jan in the Urals, taking the name Dalmatius. He became hegumenos, but, apparently seeking a more ascetic life, left the monastery carrying an icon of the Dormition. He found a cave near the confluence of the rivers Iseta and Teca, on a hill called Belagorodisca. His renown attracted others, and a monastery was established, receiving formal approval in 1644. The local Tartar lord was opposed, but when he arrived to destroy the community he was dissuaded by a vision of the Virgin. In 1651 the community was again attacked by a mob, and this time only Dalmatius escaped with his life. But again he rebuilt his community, which in 1682 was fortified by the Tsar. Feast 15 February.

Damascene, monk, born Tirnovo, died 16 January 1771. He became a monk on Mount Athos, but was sent to Bulgaria to collect some money. While doing so he clashed with some Turks who would not return the money lent to them. They secretly introduced a woman into the monk's cell, and then accused him of impurity. He was condemned to death by hanging.

Damascene of Constantiople, born Galata (a quarter of Constantinople), died Constantinople, 1681. Byzantine Church. His name before he became a monk was Diamantis, and he was a tailor. After his parents' death he became a Muslim, but, repenting his decision, he later became a monk at the Grand Laura on Mount Athos. After 12 years he determined to confess his faith publicly, and went about Constantinople dressed as a sailor, proclaiming his Christianity. The Muslims, however, at first left him alone, and he went back to Galata. He entered a mosque and announced that he had once been a Muslim but had returned to his Christian faith. He was then taken before the vizier, who ordered him to be hanged. Feast 13 November.

Damasus I, pope, elected 1 October 366, born Rome, of Spanish descent, c. 304, died there, 11 December 384. He became a deacon and was ordained priest under Pope Liberius, whose successor he became. He was elected by a majority of the Roman clergy, despite violent opposition from a rival, Ursinus, and his supporters. He was a staunch opponent of heresy, especially Arianism; he also did much to consolidate the strength of the Church of Rome, promoting local martyr cults and building churches. In his old age, he commissioned Jerome to commence a revision of the Latin Bible, a project which laid the foundations of the Vulgate version.

Damian, bishop, died Pavia, c. 4 April 715. Son of a noble family, he became a priest and was present at the Synod of Milan in 680, where he opposed the monothelite theology that in the incarnate Christ there was only one will. He composed a letter in the name of the synod's bishop, Mansuetus, to the emperor, which was read at the third Council of Constantinople in the same year. Elected bishop of Pavia c. 685, he sought to mediate between the Byzantine emperor and the Lombards. He had a reputation for his learning and his sanctity. He visited Constantinople not long before his death. Feast 12 April.

Damian, bl., monk, died Mount Salmaria, 23 February 1280. Byzantine Church. He became a monk on Mount Athos, but then, seeking greater asceticism, he went to a hermitage on Mount Salmaria.

Damian, bl., monk, born Richovo, died Larissa, 14 February 1568. Byzantine Church. He became a monk on Mount Athos, but in a vision was instructed to abandon the monastic life for a pastoral one. He was, however, accused of being a swindler in his ministry, and eventually gave it up to construct a monastery near Kissavo. He was then accused of spreading Christianity, which he admitted, and was hanged.

Damian, monk, fourteenth century. Coptic Church. A disciple of Aronne of Daret.

Damian, see **Cosmos and Damian**.

Damian of Alexandria, patriarch, sixth century. Syriac Church. He was Syrian by birth, and had spent some time in the monastery of John the Swarf. His brother had been governor of Edessa.

Damian of Alexandria, patriarch, born Syria (?), died Alexandria, 12 June 605. Coptic Church. A monk of the monastery of St John in the desert of Scete, he was ordained deacon before moving to the monastery of Enaton. He became assistant to the patriarch Peter, and succeeded him in 569. He campaigned against heresies, but his chief difficulty arose because of the rupture of communion with the patriarch of Antioch, whom he judged to be a monophysite.

Damian of Fulchieri, bl., died Reggio, 1484. There is no known detailed contemporary record of the life of this Dominican. However, 19 years after his death at Reggio, there appeared the first manifestations of his cult and the citizens declared him to be one of their patrons. The Dominican order obtained official confirmation of the cult in 1848.

Damian of Molokai (Joseph De Veuster), missionary to the Hawaiian leper colony on Molokai, born Tremelo, Belgium, 3 January 1840, died Molokai, 15 April 1889. He joined the Congregation of the Sacred Hearts of Jesus and Mary ('Picpus Fathers') in 1859, taking the name Damien. Arriving in Honolulu in March 1864, he was ordained priest on 21 May that year. In 1873 he volunteered to serve the asylum on Molokai Island. Out of a chaos of neglect he brought order, hope and support for the community, and built houses, churches, an orphanage and a hospital. He was resented for his success, and vilified: Robert Louis Stevenson wrote a letter in his defence. By

1885 he himself had contracted leprosy, but he continued his ministry with the help of others from his congregation and the Franciscan Sisters of Syracuse. His remains were removed to Louvain in 1936 and he was beatified in 199.

Damian the Monk, died 1156. Georgian Church. The name in religion of Dimitri I, king of Georgia, who became a monk after a struggle with his eldest son David (King David V). David V reigned less than a year, however, and Damian (who as a monk had displayed a skill in poetry, including a popular verse to the Mother of God) again took over the government, together with his younger son George.

Damiana, died *c.* 303. Coptic Church. The daughter of a provincial governor, she refused marriage and wished to enter a convent. Her father built a palace outside the city for her and other women. During the persecution of Diocletian, her father lapsed back into paganism, but Damiana persuaded him to return to the faith, and he was martyred. She, too, was then martyred with her 40 (or 400?) companions.

Danact, lector, martyred second/third century. Feast 16 January.

Daniel, monk, died Syria, 439. Feast 2 May.

Daniel and Moses, monks, born al-Aris, near Armant, Upper Egypt, died Qus. Coptic Church. Two brothers who first lived a monastic life and then became hermits.

Daniel and Verda, martyrs, died Persia, 344. A priest and a woman, they were killed under Shapor II and are greatly revered in the East. Feast 25 February.

Daniel Brottier, bl., born La Ferté Saint-Cyr, France, 1876, ordained 1889, died Auteuil, 28 February 1936, beatified 1984. A missionary in Senegal, returned because of ill-health, he was a volunteer army chaplain throughout World War I. From 1923 he worked with orphaned and abandoned children, directing the still ongoing Orphan-Apprentices of Auteuil.

Daniel of Acinsk, hermit, born Novye Senzary, 12 September 1784, died Acinsk, 15 April 1843. Russian Church. Daniel Kornilevic Delie came from a Cossack family and joined the army to fight against Napoleon: he was one of the Russian troops who entered Moscow. He learned to read and write in the army, and began to read the Scriptures. He abandoned the army and went to live in a cave as an ascetic, but was arrested for desertion and sent to Siberia. He irritated his captors and fellow captives by constant prayer. When released he again established an underground hermitage at Acinsk, and practised severe fasting and other mortifications. Although neither a monk nor a priest, his fame as a miracle worker spread, and many came to speak to him.

Daniel of Belvedere, Friar Minor, martyr, died 10 October 1227. Inspired by the missionary martyrdom of St **Berard** (1219), five Friars Minor left Tuscany as missionaries to Morocco. Daniel, who became their superior, joined them in Spain. Immediately upon their arrival in the Moroccan city of Ceuta they loudly began to preach Christianity and to denounce Islam. Soon they were captured and brought before the sultan, who ordered them to be held in prison for a week. After that, since they continued their refusals to deny Christianity, they were condemned and beheaded. Feast 13 October.

Daniel of Dabra Maryam, monk, thirteenth to fourteenth centuries. Coptic Church. Founder of the monastery of Dabra Maryam.

Daniel of Edessa, bishop, died Edessa, 684. Syriac Church. Bishop of Edessa from 665, he wrote the story of his monastery of Qennesre, of which only fragments survive. Feast 11 January.

Daniel of Kostroma, priest and martyr, died Astrakhan. Church of the Old Believers. In 1653 he wrote to the Tsar complaining that the Patriarch Nikon had abandoned the old traditions of the Church and was misinterpreting Orthodoxy. Nikon dismissed him from the priesthood and imprisoned him first in the monastery at Cudov, then in an underground cell in Astrakhan, where he died.

Daniel of Moscow, prince, born Moscow, 1261, died there, 4 March 1303. Russian Church. The son of **Alexander Nevski**. He became prince of Moscow in 1271, administering it through his uncle. He built the first stone church in the Moscow Kremlin, and established a monastery dedicated to Daniel the Stylite (the Danilov monastery, the official residence of the patriarch). Much of his reign was taken up by conflict with his brothers for control of Novgorod, in the course of which Moscow itself was put to the torch.

Daniel of Padua, deacon, martyred Italy, *c.* 168. Possibly of Jewish extraction, he had worked with **Prosdocimus**, first bishop of Padua. His remains were discovered and enshrined on 3 January 1064. Feast 3 January.

Daniel of Perejaslav, monk, born Perejaslav, *c.* 1460, died there, 7 April 1540. Russian Church. Daniel was put into the care of a relative at the monastery of Nikitsk at Perejaslav for his education, but he became attracted to the ascetic life and, afraid that his parents would not let him become a monk, he secretly fled with his brother to the monastery of St Paphnutius at Borovsk, where he lived for ten years. He spent two years as a hermit *c.* 1491 before returning to Perejaslav, and to the monastery of Gorick, where a relative was the archimandrite. He was renowned not only for his asceticism, but for his care of pilgrims and the poor. He would bury the poor who had died, celebrating the funeral rites over their bodies. Once, while doing so, he had a vision and felt called to build a chapel over the place where the graveyard was located: the money to do so came from two boyars whom he had freed from captivity by his prayers. When the archimandrite of Gorick withdrew to another monastery, Daniel was chosen to take his place, introducing a stricter Rule for the monks.

Daniel of Scete, monk, born 485, died Scete, 3 May 570. Coptic Church/Syriac Church. As a young man he went into the desert of Scete, and there three times fell into the hands of barbarians. Each time he managed to escape, but the third time only by killing the man who had enslaved him. He was full of remorse, and sought a penance from his religious superiors, but no one thought he had done wrong. After a fourth barbarian invasion he fled to Tambok, where he founded a monastery, but returned to Scete when it was again safe to do so. The Syriac Church appears to venerate the same man, an Egyptian, on 2 or 5 May.

Daniel of Suzgor, born Moscow, died Belozersk, sixteenth century. He lived as a hermit attached to a monastery near Vologda, but, seeking greater solitude, he moved to a forest near Belozersk, where he eventually founded his own monastery, and died. Feast 21 September.

Daniel of Tambien, monk. Ethiopian Church. The apostle of the Tambien region, he also founded a monastery in Tigre.

Daniel of the Kievan Cave Monastery, and his Companions, Eulogius and Isidore, monks, thirteenth century. Russian Church.

Daniel of Uglic and Companions, martyrs, died Uglic, 1 October 1608. Russian Church. Hegumenos Daniel, with 30 monks and some 200 lay people, was massacred during the Russo-Polish war.

Daniel of Waqen, monk. Ethiopian Church. Originally from Scioa, he founded the monastery of Dabra Tehugan.

Daniel Sihastrul, born Bucovina, died Voronet, *c.* 1482. Romanian Church. Baptized Dumitru, he was given the name David when he entered the cathedral monastery of Radauti. Desiring a more eremitical life, he moved to St Laurence's monastery in what is today Vicovul de Sus, where he became Daniel. However, he left there for a cave hermitage in the mountains, where many came for confession and spiritual guidance. One who came was the young prince **Stephen the Great**, who on Daniel's advice began a monastery nearby. However, when Stephen wished to make Daniel the metropolitan, the monk fled to Voronet. In 1476, when Stephen was on the point of ceding the region to the Turks to avoid more bloodshed, Daniel prophesied that he would eventually be victorious – which proved to be the case. In 1488 Stephen built a monastery at Voronet, although by this time Daniel had died.

Daniel the Black, died Moscow, *c.* 1426. Russian Church. A monk and iconographer at the monastery of Andronikov at Moscow, and a teacher of Rublev. Feast 6 July.

Daniel the Doctor, hermit, fourth century, died Nhuhadra, Assyrian Church. Sacristan of the monastery of St Pachomius, he moved to the monastery of Awgen, then to Nuhadra, near Duhok, where he lived as a hermit for over 20 years, making friends with, talking to and healing wild animals of the region. Renowned as a healer, he cured the son of the governor of the city of Tell Hess, and as a result converted the city. He died aged 95. Feast 15 June.

Daniel the Stylite, born Maratha, near Samosata, 409, died Constantinople, 493. Of pious parents, at the age of 12 he entered the nearby monastery. Some years later, with his abbot, he visited **Simon Stylites** and climbed a ladder to join him on his column. He returned to his monastery, but when the monks wished to elect him abbot he fled, intending to become a hermit in the Holy Land. Because of unrest in the region, however, he went instead to Constantinople, where he established a hermitage. After the death of Simon Stylites in 459 Daniel inherited his cloak, and this made him resolve to become a stylite himself. He lived for the rest of his life on a pillar, said to have been the height of two men, near Constantinople. He was reported to have descended only once, to rebuke a usurper on the imperial throne who favoured heretics. Feast 11 December.

Daniel Vikulin, founder, born Novgorod (?), 1653, died Vyg, 12 October 1733. He was a minor church official first at Novgorod, then at Suj, near Olonec. He converted to the Old Believer faith and became a hermit before, with **Andrew Denisov**, founding the Old Believer monastery on the river Vyg. Feast 31 December.

Danilo II, archbishop, born *c.* 1270, died 19 December 1337. Of a noble family, he was called to the court of King Milutin, but left for the monastery of St Nicholas at Koncul, where he became known to the archbishop and entered his service. Soon afterwards he was elected the hegumenos of the Serbian monastery Chilandar on Mount Athos,

where he showed unexpected skill as a soldier, organizing the defence of the Holy Mountain against invaders for more than three years. In 1311 he went to the monastery of San Saba at Karyes to live an eremitical life, but the king summoned him back to Serbia, as bishop of Banjska and keeper of the royal treasury. In that capacity he was able to bring a peace settlement between the king and his brother before returning, with Milutin's agreement, to Chilandar, where he gave himself to prayer and to writing the lives of the Serbian saints. He was the king's preferred candidate as archbishop, but was not elected, becoming instead bishop of Hum. He returned once more to Mount Athos for a short time, but on 14 September 1324 he was elected archbishop, in which capacity he had once more to mediate in a dynastic dispute between King Stephen, the son of Milutin, and Stephen's own son Dusan – whom he eventually crowned. Feast 20 December.

Daria of Sezenovo, born Pikovo, 1772, died Sezenovo, 28 July 1858. Russian Church. Daria Dmitrevna Kutukova came from a peasant family. Rejecting the idea of marriage, in 1796 she entered a convent, but after six years returned home. Her stay was short. She soon went off to the convent at Tambov, then spent a year at Rostov the Great, then another year in the monastery of Murom, after which she again returned to her native region, occupying a cell in the village of Golovscino beside the church. She remained there for 12 years, attracting many visitors. In 1817 she met John of Sezenovo, whom she held in high esteem as a spiritual director. He settled in the village of Sezenovo, and Daria also went there in 1828. When John died in 1839 he was engaged in building a church, and Daria took over the task – the church was consecrated in 1849, the same year that the convent of St John of Sezenovo opened with Daria as mother superior, a position she held until 1853.

Dasius, martyr, died Silistria, Bulgaria, 303 (?). A Roman soldier, he was executed as a Christian after refusing to take part in the pagan rites of Saturnalia. Feast 20 November.

Datius, bishop, born Milan, died Constantinople, *c.* 552. After failing as bishop of Milan to save his town from the Goths, he went to Constantinople. There he became embroiled in the long-running theological and political disputes between orthodox and monophysites, which eventually led to a schism of Western bishops. Feast 14 January.

Dativus, see **Saturninus**.

Dauctus, see **Charalampias**.

David and Gurgen, born Gnunik, died 917. Armenian Church. Of noble birth, the two brothers were beheaded for refusing to renounce Christianity.

David, bl., monk, born Gardinitsa, end of fifteenth century, died Rovies. Byzantine Church. The son of a priest, he studied on Corfu before deciding to become a monk. He became the disciple of a certain Acacius who belonged to a monastery at Komninio, where David was ordained deacon, but then moved, with David, to Mount Athos. He was, however, elected metropolitan of Lepanto from 1516 to 1520. Again David went with him, and Acacius wanted to ordain him bishop, but instead David became hegumenos of the monastery of Varnakova, a position he held until the 1530s, but he then left for the Parnassus, where he lived a life of great holiness, attracting followers. He and they were not popular in the region, and David again moved on, to the Euboea, where he founded a church and a monastery and where he died, after a life of great holiness, given to preaching and hearing confessions. Feast 1 November.

David, monk. Russian Church. A monk of the Kievan Cave Monastery.

David, prince, thirteenth century, died Brodarevo. Serbian Church. Demetrios Nemanidi, son of Vukan of Zeta in what is today Montenegro. He became a monk and took the name David at the monastery of Brodarevo, which he had founded. Feast 24 September.

David I, king of Scotland, born *c.* 24 May 1080, died Carlisle, 24 May 1153. The sixth son of Malcolm III and Margaret of Scotland, he became king in 1124. He continued his mother's policy of establishing Anglo-Norman religious communities in his kingdom. A just and saintly ruler – and something of a collector of monasteries – he founded at least 12 of the major Scottish monastic houses and reorganized six Scottish dioceses.

David Galvan Bermudez, martyr, born Guadalajara, Mexico, 29 January 1881, died there, 30 January 1915. Ordained in 1909, he taught in the diocesan seminary. He was arrested and shot when tending the wounded during a street battle between government troops and those of Pancho Vilar. Feast 25 May.

David Gonson (Gunston), martyr, died Southwark, 12 July 1541. He was a knight of the Order of St John of Jerusalem (the Knights of Malta), having been received into the order in Malta in 1533. He served in the navy of the order until 1540, when he returned to England and was arrested and imprisoned in the Tower of London for refusing to acknowledge the supremacy of the king. He was executed the following year at St Thomas Waterings in Southwark.

David Lewis, martyr, born Abergavenny, Monmouth, 1617, died Usk, 27 August 1679. Brought up a Protestant, Lewis became a Catholic in Paris in 1632, studied at the English College, Rome, joined the Society of Jesus in 1644, and returned to south Wales in 1648, where he served as parish priest for 28 years. During the Titus Oates plot, his apostate servant James and his wife betrayed Lewis, who was tried and condemned for his priesthood, then hanged, drawn and quartered. He was canonized in 1970, among the **Forty Martyrs of England and Wales**.

David of Cidonia, bl., monk, born Cidonia, died Thessalonika, 1813. Byzantine Church. A monk of the monastery of St Anne on Mount Athos, he undertook to restore a church on the Holy Mountain, travelling to Smyrna to raise the money. He was later in Magnesia, where he sought martyrdom for his faith by arguing with Muslims. He was, however, martyred in Thessalonika after attempting to dissuade a monk from converting to Islam. Feast 26 June.

David of Dwin, martyred Dwin, Armenia, 694. Feast 24 January.

David of Georgia, king, died 1130. Feast 24 January.

David of Himmerod, Cistercian mystic, born Florence, *c.* 1100, died Himmerod Eifel, Germany, 11 December 1179. After his studies in Paris, David entered the monastery of Clairvaux in 1131, but in 1134 went to the abbey of Himmerod in obedience to St **Bernard**. He was renowned for his mysticism and miracles, and was venerated from the time of his death, becoming the patron saint of mothers. His biography was written by Peter of Trier (*c.* 1204), emphasizing his inner holiness rather than miracles.

David of Munktorp, see **David of Västmanland**.

David of Serpuchov, died Serpuchov, 18 October 1520. Russian Church. Originally a monk of St Paphnutius's monastery at Borovsk, he chose the eremitical life not far from Serpuchov, where in 1515 he built a church.

David of the Kievan Caves Monastery, monk. Russian Church.

David of Västmanland (of Munktorp), monk, missionary, believed bishop, died *c.* 1080. David was an English monk who went to Sweden as a missionary. Bishop Sigfrid of Vaxio sent him to Västmanland, where he founded a monastery at Munktorp. He is thought to have been the first bishop of Vasteras, and to have been a successful missionary, a holy man and a performer of miracles. Feast 15 July.

David of Wales, bishop, patron of Wales, died 601. According to the tenth-century *Annales Cambriae*, he was bishop of Mynyw or Menevia, now St David's. David took part in the Synod of Brefi *c.* 560. Much of the written information concerning him is legend.

David Roldan Lara, martyr, born Chalchihuites, Mexico, 2 March 1907, died near Zacatecas, 14 August 1926. A former seminarian, he was a prominent member of the League for the Defence of Religious Freedom, and was arrested with **Louis Batiz Sainz**, and similarly shot. Feast 25 May.

David Svjatoslavic, prince, born Smolensk, died there, 1123. Russian Church. He was driven from the throne of Smolensk, but given that of Novgorod, which he retained for only two years. He then became ruler of Rostov Mstislav. He was remembered as a meek, humble and honest man. Feast 1 August.

David the New, monk, died 15 April 1383. Coptic Church. Son of Gabriel of Barg, and monk of St Anthony's monastery.

David Uribe Velasco, martyr, born Buenavista de Cuellar, Guerrero, Mexico, 29 December 1888, died San Jose Vidal, Morales, 12 April 1927. A priest since 1913, he had been an assistant to the bishop of Tabasco. Feast 25 May.

Declan, bishop, born Desi, Waterford, Ireland, died Ardmore, fifth century. He went to the continent to study and become a priest, and was possibly consecrated as a bishop. He returned to Ireland and founded his centre at Ardmore. From this base he evangelized the area around Waterford and Lismore, and was working in Ireland before St **Patrick** arrived there. In the last years of his life he lived in a hermit's cell, but he returned to Ardmore to die. Feast 24 July.

Decorosus, bishop, died *c.* 695. He was bishop of Capua in Campania for 30 years and a bishop at the Council of Rome in 680 under Pope **Agatho**. Feast 15 February.

Deicolus of Lure, born Ireland, died valley of Orignon, France, *c.* 625. Deicolus is one of the famous Irish *peregrini minores*. He accompanied **Columban** to Luxeuil in France, and journeyed with him – until ill-health forced him to stop – when Columban was expelled in 610. Deicolus built a hermitage in the vale of Orignon, and was eventually joined by others. This became the abbey of Lure. Feast 18 January.

Deiniol, bishop, born northern Britain, died Bangor, north Wales, *c.* 584. Said to have been a disciple of **Cadoc** at Llancarfan before going to found the monastery of Bangor Iscoed on the river Dee. He also founded the monastery of Bangor Fawr on the Menai Strait. He was the first bishop of Bangor. Feast 11 September.

Delphina of Signe, bl., Franciscan tertiary, born Provence, France, 1283 or 1284, died Apt, France, 26 November 1358 or 1360. In 1299 Delphina, daughter of Count William of Glandèves, was married to **Elzéar of Sabran**, with whom she lived in continence. In 1317 Elzéar was summoned to the court of King Robert of Naples, where Delphina formed a lifelong friendship with Queen Sanchia. After the death of her husband (1323), she returned to Provence and lived as a recluse in absolute poverty, devoting herself to works of mercy. She was buried beside her husband in Apt. In 1694 Innocent XII confirmed her cult, which had been introduced under Urban V.

Delphinus, bishop, died Bordeaux, 403. He was closely linked to a number of saints of the period, including **Ambrose** and **Paulinus of Nola**. Feast 24 December.

Demetrian of Khytri, monk, bishop, died *c.* 912. Demetrian was born at Sika, Cyprus, the son of a priest. Upon the death of his wife he became a monk at St Anthony's monastery, later being elected abbot and serving for 40 years. Against his will he was made bishop of Khytri (Cerca) and ruled for 25 years. Once, when Saracens raided Cyprus during his episcopate, he succeeded in persuading them to set their Christian captives free, rather than selling them into slavery. Feast 6 November.

Demetrius, see also **Boris, James, Theodore I, Silvanus, Theodore II, Basil I, Demetrius, Michael, John, Basil II**.

Demetrius, deacon, eighth century. Feast 25 January.

Demetrius Bejazis, born Hagiasos, *c.* 1800, died Kasaba, 11 August 1816 or 1819. Byzantine Church. Born on Lesbos, he worked as a baker at Kasaba in Asia Minor. He was accused of preaching Christianity, and was executed when he refused to renounce his faith. He was 18 years old.

Demetrius Donskoi, prince of Moscow, born Moscow, 1350, died there, 19 May 1389. Russian Church. The son of Ivan Ivanovic, who died in 1359, and of Ivan's second wife Alexandra. He had to seek investiture as prince of Moscow from the head of the Golden Horde. This he received, although the Khan Murat refused the same to Demetrius Konstantinovic, who was prince of Suzdal, settled at Vladimir. Conflict broke out between the two princes, settled when Demetrius married the daughter of his rival. He then set his sights on the principality of Tver. His younger brother married the daughter of the prince. When the Tartars invaded Russian territory Demetrius gathered a league of princes and decisively defeated the Khan Mamaj at Kulikovo on 8 September 1380. Mamaj died during his retreat, to be succeeded by Tochtamys. Tochtamys promptly invaded Russia and sacked Moscow, forcing Demetrius to take refuge in Kostroma, becoming a tributary of the Golden Horde. He was canonized by the Moscow synod of 1988, not only for his concern for the safety of his people, but for his care for the Orthodox Church, especially in Moscow. Feast 9 May.

Demetrius Jurevic, prince of Galic, called 'the Handsome', born 1421, died Galic, 22 September 1440. Russian Church. The grandson of **Demetrius Donskoi**, engaged in dynastic struggles with his brothers for the throne of Moscow and in opposing the Tartars, in fact he preferred religious life, building a church at Belek, not far from his palace. His death at the age of 20 was remarkable because, although he appeared to have died, he suddenly started singing hymns, which he continued for three days before expiring. His body was taken to Moscow for burial, and his tomb was marked by miracles.

Demetrius Michailovic, prince of Tver, born Tver, 1299, died Moscow, 15 September 1326. Russian Church. When only 13 he led an attack against Moscow, a few years later against Novgorod, and in 1317 against the Tartars, whom he defeated at the battle of Vartenovo. In the battle he captured the Khan's sister, who was married to George, prince of Moscow. She was about to be restored to her father when she unexpectedly died. The Khan believed she had been poisoned and threatened to attack Tver, but Michael, Demetrius's father and ruler of Tver, handed himself over to the Khan, and was executed at Moscow, leaving Demetrius as ruler. Demetrius married a Lithuanian princess after his father's death. Tver was attacked by George of Moscow, and Demetrius now offered to pay him tribute – but, in the continuing conflict between the two princes, Demetrius avenged his father's death by killing George with a dagger. He was arrested and executed.

Demetrius of Alexandria, bishop, died Alexandria, 232. Demetrius was ordained bishop of Alexandria in 189, and governed for 43 years. Coptic sources mention his peasant origin. He appointed Origen head of the catechetical school in Alexandria, but subsequently condemned him for his (alleged) self-castration after Origen was ordained by extraneous bishops. His act of deposing Origen from the priesthood is usually held to be one of jealousy, although there is evidence that doctrinal matters also contributed. Feast 9 October.

Demetrius of Chios, born Paleocastro, *c.* 1780, died Constantinople, 29 January 1802. Byzantine Church. He left the island of Chios and, with his elder brother Zanni, he became a merchant in Constantinople. They fell out, and Demetrius was reduced to poverty. He borrowed money from a Turk, but was then unable to pay him back. To rescue himself from this he undertook to marry a Turkish woman, and converted to Islam to do so. After only a couple of months he repented of his action, and determined to seek martyrdom to atone – although his confessor tried to dissuade him. Having prepared himself by prayer and fasting, he went before a Turkish judge, who first tried to reconvert him to Islam, even offering a bribe. He was, however, finally executed, and his body thrown into the sea. It was recovered by Christians and buried in a monastery.

Demetrius of Chutyn, monk. Russian Church. Hegumenos of the monastery of Chutyn, near Novgorod.

Demetrius of Cilibin, monk, died early fifteenth century. Russian Church. Founder of a ·monastery on the river Vycegda, not far from Jarensk. Feast 26 October.

Demetrius of Constantinople, born Constantinople (?), *c.* 1760, died there, 27 January 1785 (?). Byzantine Church. He worked in a wine shop, much frequented by Turks. One day a fight broke out in his shop, and he ejected the contestants, one of whom had been wounded. The following day the Turks went to the vizier and blamed Demetrius for the injury which had been sustained. He was brought before the vizier, declaring his innocence, but the vizier ordered him either to deny his faith or be decapitated. He refused to deny his faith, and was executed in front of his shop.

Demetrius of Jurev, see **Svatoslav of Jurev**.

Demetrius of Larissa, martyr, born Larissa, died Mitylene, 8 April 1809. Byzantine Church.

Demetrius of Nizegorod, monk, Russian Church.

Demetrius of Perejaslav, prince, died Perejaslav, 1294. Russian Church. The son of **Alexander Nevski**, he took over the city of Novgorod from his father, but after the death of Alexander he was driven out, taking over instead the city of Perejaslav-Zalesk. He was, however, later invited back to Novgorod. He became the grand prince of Vladimir. A war among Demetrius's brothers deprived him for a while of Perejaslav. In 1284 he summoned the sixth council of Kiev.

Demetrius of Philadelphia, born Philadelphia (Asia Minor), *c.* 1630, died there, 2 June 1657. Byzantine Church. The son of a priest, he became a Muslim at the age of 13, married the most beautiful woman in Philadelphia, and was in charge of the city's army by the time he was 25. However, he was then assailed by his conscience and declared his intention of returning to Christianity. He was first imprisoned, but then released, continuing to proclaim publicly his rejection of Islam. The Turks then condemned him to death by burning. On his way to the place of execution they beat him repeatedly, but not fatally, until his legs were cut off. When they tried to burn his body, the flames would not destroy it, and eventually his body was pulled to pieces by the crowd.

Demetrius of Priluckij, monk, born Perejaslavl-Zalesk, died Spaso-Priluckij, 11 February 1392.

Russian Church. The devout son of a rich merchant, he joined his father's business for a time, but after a short while joined a local monastery. After a number of years there he conceived the idea of establishing a coenobitic abbey nearby, close to the city, which he did, dedicating it to St Nicholas. He became the hegumenos and spiritual guide, both by his teaching and by his example. He became a close friend of **Sergius of Radonez**, and also of **Demetrius Donskoi**, who summoned him to Moscow and asked him to baptize one of his children. Demetrius found such fame disturbing, so with a number of companions he set out to establish a new monastery in a more remote region. Eventually they settled near the village of Priluckij, where the local peasants helped them to build their monastery and a church. Demetrius Donskoi himself gave money. The monastery was on a major highway to the White Sea, and Demetrius and his monks spent themselves in looking after the travellers. His brother was one such traveller. He had fallen heavily into debt, and he went to the monastery to seek Demetrius's blessing on his new trading enterprise. He did exceedingly well, and returned the following year again for a blessing, which he was given. But the third year Demetrius told his brother he was rich enough, and refused to bless the enterprise. He went nonetheless, but did not return. Demetrius himself dressed always in the same sheepskin tunic, summer and winter, and wore iron chains to subjugate his body. After his death his tomb was famous for its miracles.

Demetrius of Rostov, metropolitan, born Makaravo, near Kiev, December 1651, died Rostov, 28 October 1709. Russian Church. Baptized Danjil Savvic Tuptalo, the son of a Cossack captain, but when he was nine his father retired from the army and worked at the monastery of St Cyril, in Kiev, to which city they moved. When he was 11 he went to the monastic school founded by Metropolitan Peter Mogila, and at 17 he entered the monastery of St Cyril, taking the name Demetrius. After his ordination some seven years later he remained for a time as preacher in the cathedral. He then went to Vilnius, where he ministered to the Polish community, and on his return became hegumenos of several Ukrainian monasteries. There he undertook, under obedience, the chief work for the

next 20 years, writing the lives of saints in four volumes, according to the Church's calendar. His work was interrupted by his successive appointment as hegumenos in different monasteries, and then, having attracted the attention of the young Peter the Great, he was ordained bishop with the title of Tobolsk and of all Siberia on 23 March 1701. However, when Demetrius protested that in Siberia he would never be able to finish his work on the saints, he was instead sent as metropolitan to Rostov and Jaroslavl, entering his new diocese just a year later. He threw himself into pastoral work with great success, although he had difficulties from the Old Believers in the region, against whom he wrote polemical works. Feast 21 September.

Demetrius of Samarina, bl., born Samarina, southern Greece, died there, 18 (?) August 1808. Byzantine Church. Although he entered a monastery in Samarina as a young man, after the repression of the revolt against Ali Pasha he left the monastery and preached throughout the region. He was arrested and accused of fomenting revolt, but insisted, despite torture, that he was doing nothing political. One Muslim, seeing his steadfastness, was himself converted and condemned to death. Demetrius was buried alive.

Demetrius of Sirmium, soldier and martyr, died 304. Patron saint of Belgrade. Demetrius has many churches in the Balkans dedicated to him. Suffered in the early fourth century under Maximian. He became especially popular in the East, where he was called the 'Great Martyr'. Feast 8 October.

Demetrius (or Dimos) of Smyrna, born Ontzu-Kiopru, near Adrianopolis, c. 1738, died Smyrna, 10 April 1763. Byzantine Church. He moved from his home village to Smyrna to ply his trade as a fisherman, working for a Turk. The Turk, however, failed to pay him before selling his business to another Turk, who also refused to pay. This led to an argument, and the Turk accused Demetrius of having undertaken to convert to Islam then failing to do so. He was thrown into prison and tortured, but remained steadfast. He was then decapitated.

Demetrius of the Peloponnese, born Peloponnese, died Mistra, 28 May 1794. Byzantine Church. At the age of 11 he took the name Mustafa and became a Muslim. He was very successful, holding high ofice, but gradually began to regret that he had abandoned his faith. He tried to live secretly as a Christian, but the change to his lifestyle attracted the attention of the Turks and he was condemned to death and beheaded.

Demetrius of the Peloponnese, born Ligudista, died Tripoli, 14 April 1803. Byzantine Church. He moved with his brother to Tripoli, where he followed the career of a mason for a time, before entering the service of a Turkish barber who persuaded him to abandon Christianity. He soon repented of his apostasy – into which he had also led his brother – and he returned home. He confessed his sin and was reconciled, living a life of strict asceticism as penance, but while on Chios he decided to present himself to the Turks as having returned to Christianity. He travelled to Tripoli, where he resumed the trade of a barber. He admitted to the Turks that he had returned to Christianity, and he was beheaded.

Demetrius of Uglic, prince, born Perejaslav, *c*. 1480, died Vologda. Russian Church. He was imprisoned with one of his brothers – a third became a monk – because they rebelled against their faith. He spent his time in prayer before an icon of the Mother of God. He was moved first to Belozersk and then to Vologda, where his elder brother was living. He died still a prisoner. Feast 25 May.

Demetrius of Uglic and Moscow, prince, born Moscow, 19 October 1581, died Uglic, 15 May 1591. Russian Church. On the death of his father Ivan the Terrible, he was sent to Uglic with his mother by his brother Theodore Jovannovic, who had succeeded to the throne, and who was afraid that Demetrius might be used as a figurehead in a palace revolt against his rule. It was, however, Boris Godunov, the intended heir to Theodore, who arranged Demetrius's assassination. His remains were eventually buried in the cathedral of Michael the Archangel in the Kremlin.

Demetrius of Zaozer, and his wife **Maria**, prince, fifteenth century. Russian Church. After his father's death in the first half of the fifteenth

century, Demetrius, son of Prince Basil Vasilevic, was much involved in the struggles for control of Russia on the side of Demetrius Semjaka. When the Tartars unexpectedly attacked he went to the defence of his territory, and died in battle. Both he and his wife, who survived him, were renowned for their religious devotion, and especially for their devotion to the monk St Alexander Kust, supporting his monastery with gifts. Their son Andrew gave up his princely state and became a monk.

Demetrius the New, born Basarabi, died there, thirteenth century. Romanian Church. He came from a poor family, and from his earliest years he worked as a shepherd. In the course of his work he encountered some monks, and was attracted to their way of life. He began to live in a cave alongside the river Lom, not far from his home village, apart from the world. When he felt himself about to die, he lay upon two stone slabs. Sometime after his death torrential rains carried his body on these slabs along the river Lom. This event was accompanied by miracles, and the people of Basarabi took his incorrupt body and built a church for it. Towards the end of the eighteenth century his remains were removed to Bucharest. He was declared a saint by the Holy Synod of the Romanian Church in 1950. Feast 27 October.

Demetrius Tornaras, died 19 March 1564. Byzantine Church. After repeatedly refusing to become a Muslim, he was accused of offending against Islam, and was decapitated.

Denha, metropolitan, seventh century. Syriac Church. Possibly vicar for the patriarch of Antioch in Persian territory. Feast 2 October.

Denha, monk. Syriac Church. Feast 25 September.

Denis, see also **Dionysius**.

Denis, or Dionysius of Paris, patron saint of France, died *c*. 250. According to **Gregory of Tours** in the sixth century, he was one of seven bishops sent to convert Gaul, and was subsequently martyred. Denis was once considered to have been the author of the Pseudo-Dionysian writings. Feast 9 October.

Denis Ssebuggwawo, martyred Uganda, 1885, canonized 1964. He was a servant of King Mwanga of Uganda, converted by the Missionaries of Africa. The king thrust a lance through him when he found him teaching the catechism, making him the first victim of the ensuing persecution – see **Martyrs of Uganda**. Feast 25 May.

Deochar (Theocar, Dietker, Gottlieb), Benedictine abbot, died c. 832. Deochar, a monk at Fulda, then a follower of **Alcuin** at **Charlemagne**'s court, became the first abbot of the monastery at Haserode (Herrieden) in Franconia which Charlemagne built (c. 795). Deochar was 'missus regis' in Regensburg, the first of the signatories to the Synod of Mainz, and died at a very old age. Feast June 7.

Deodatus of Nevers, bishop, died 18 June 679. Deodatus was the founder of the monastery of Jointures. He obtained land for the monastery from King Childeric, also obtaining exemption from the jurisdiction of the bishop of Toul. Both the monastery and the town that grew around it bear his name. His 'life', written in 1048, contains some extra legendary material.

Deodatus of Rodez, see **Nicholas of Sibenik**.

Deogratias, bishop, died Carthage, 457. Bishop of Carthage under the Vandals when they sacked Rome, he sold church gold and silver and opened his churches to ransom and care for the captives. He was buried secretly to prevent people tearing his body to pieces to obtain relics. Feast 5 January.

Desideratus of Bourges, bishop, born Soissons, died Bourges, 550. Desideratus was a councillor of King Clotaire I and a keeper of his seal. He gave up the monastic life at the request of the king, eventually succeeding Archadius to become bishop of Bourges in 543. Desideratus was present at the Synod of Orléans in 558. He is held to be the founder of the church of St Symphorien (later St Ursin) at Bourges.

Desiderius, see also **Barontius**.

Desiderius of Langres, bishop, martyr, died 407 or 411. Desiderius suffered martyrdom with many of his people at the hands of the Vandals in either 407 or 411, although his death during an earlier invasion cannot be ruled out. Desiderius is the patron saint of St Dizier. Feast 23 May.

Desiderius of Rhodonensis, bishop, martyr, died 17 September 690. Desiderius was martyred while returning from a pilgrimage to Rome, by order of King Childeris II. He was buried at the place of his murder in an oratory. This chapel was later known as St-Dezier-l'Evêque.

Desiderius of Vienne (Didier), died at the place now called St-Didier-sur-Chalaronne, c. 606. Desiderius was born of Christian parents and educated in grammar and religious studies. He refused a number of bishoprics before accepting the position of bishop of Vienne in 595. He was deposed on a morals charge at the instigation of Queen Brunhilde. After four years he was restored, but because he continued to reprove the queen and her son Theodoric II, he was arrested and assassinated. Feast 23 May.

Deusdedit, bishop, born southern England, died Canterbury, 664. Named Frithona, or Frithuwine, he took the name Deusdedit (the name of a recent pope) when he became archbishop of Canterbury. He was the first native Anglo-Saxon to be made archbishop, and was consecrated in March 655 by **Ithamar**, bishop of Rochester. He died of the plague in 664. Feast 14 July.

Deusdedit I, pope, born Rome, elected 19 October 615, died 8 November 618. He had previously served as a priest in Rome for 40 years. Deusdedit was pope during the turbulent Lombard wars, but he remained loyal to the Emperor Heraclius. During his reign he had to contend with earthquakes and plague. Deusdedit was known for his care towards diocesan clergy as opposed to the monks.

Deusdedit of Monte Cassino, abbot and martyr, died 834. Elected abbot of Monte Cassino in 828, Deusdedit was captured by Prince Sicard of Benevento, who wanted to appropriate the abbey's property, and died in captivity. Feast 9 October.

Devota, from Corsica, martyred *c*. 300. She died on the rack under Diocletian. Her relics are at Monaco and she is patron of both Corsica and Monaco. Feast 27 January.

Diana, bl., born Bologna, 1201, died there, 1236. Diana d'Andalo belonged to a powerful Bolognese family, who had originally opposed St **Dominic's** wish to establish a Dominican house in the city. Diana was determined to become a nun, despite her family's opposition. She entered the Augustinians at Ronzano, but her father brought her home. Eventually **Jordan of Saxony** succeeded in convincing the family to allow her to become a Dominican nun, and her father established a convent of the order which she entered, together with **Cecilia** Cesarini, who was sent from Rome. Feast 9 June.

Didacus Carvalho, bl., born Coimbra, Portugal, 1578, martyred Sendai, Japan, 1624, beatified 1867. A Jesuit from 1594, he went to India and was ordained in 1600. He moved to Japan in 1609 and was killed with many of his flock. See **Martyrs of Japan**. Feast 22 February.

Didacus of Alcala, Franciscan lay brother and ascetic, born near Seville, Spain, died at advanced age in Alcalá, Spain, 12 November 1463. He was at first a mendicant hermit, but he later entered the monastery of Arizafa in Córdoba and was an exemplar of virtue, especially of humility and simplicity. He was sent to the Canaries (1441–9) and became guardian of the Franciscan mission and converted many. In 1450, while in Rome for the canonization of **Bernardine of Siena**, he served the sick in the convent of Aracoeli. In 1456 he was sent from Salicetum in Castile to a new monastery in Alcalá, where he was revered for penances, miracles and a divinely infused knowledge of theology. After death his severely mortified body did not suffer rigor mortis or corruption. Miraculous cures were reported immediately. In 1562 his body was taken to the bedside of Carlos, son of Philip II, to effect his cure. His canonization, requested by Philip in 1564, was obtained in 1588. Feast 16 November.

Didacus of Azevedo, bl., bishop of Osma, died 30 December 1207. As prior, Didacus (Diego de Acebes) collaborated with Bishop Martin Bazan in transforming the cathedral chapter of Osma into a chapter of canons regular. St **Dominic** was elected his subprior. Didacus was chosen as bishop of Osma in 1201. In 1203, and again in 1205, with Dominic as companion, he went to Denmark to negotiate the marriage of Ferdinand, son of Alphonsus VIII. In 1206, after Innocent III had refused him permission to resign his bishopric to preach to the Cumans, he reorganized the preaching against the Albigenses on the pattern of Christ and the apostles, a plan that was later fully realized in the Order of Preachers. He established a community of women at Prouille, which later became the order's first monastery. Feast 5 February.

Didier of Cahors, bishop, born near Albi, died there, 655. A member of the court of King Claire, he was elected bishop of Cahors on the assassination of his brother, who was bishop of that see, in 630. He proved a zealous bishop, although at the time of his election he was still a layman. He was greatly concerned for the welfare of his flock, and for the education of his clergy. He also encouraged monasticism in his diocese. Feast 15 November.

Diego de San Vitores, bl., born Burgos, Spain, 1627, martyred Tumon, Marianas Islands, 2 April 1672, beatified 1985. Ordained a Jesuit in 1651, sent to Mexico and the Philippines, from 1668 he worked on Guam Island, south of Japan. A lapsed Christian killed Diego when he went to baptize his child.

Diego of Cadiz, bl., Spanish Capuchin preacher, born Cadiz, Spain, 30 March 1743, died Ronda (Malaga, Spain), 24 March 1801. José Francisco Lopez Camoño took the name Diego after joining the Capuchins (1759). After ordination (1766) he dedicated his religious life largely to preaching missions in Spain, Portugal and the Levant, but he won his greatest renown in Andalusia. He delivered more than 20,000 sermons, sometimes as many as 15 a day to audiences that often numbered between 15,000 and 20,000. His most common themes were the Holy Trinity and the Blessed Virgin under the title of Shepherdess of Souls and of Peace. Diego was in great demand as a confessor and impressed people as much by his asceticism as by his eloquence. Diego led the resistance to the influence of French Enlightenment in the Spanish court, but he met opposition there. When the armies of the French Revolution invaded Spain, Diego crusaded for national independence. A valuable source for knowledge of his life and spirituality is contained in his published correspondence. Diego was beatified 23 April 1894.

Dinar, queen of Herethi, tenth century. Georgian Church. Queen in eastern Georgia, she is said to have converted the Christians from monophysitism to the Orthodox faith. Feast 30 June.

Diocles, see **Zoëllus**.

Diodorus of Mount Jur, born in a village on the river Onega, died Kargopol, 27 November 1633. Russian Church. Christened by his peasant parents as Diomedes, at 15 he went on pilgrimage to the monastery of Solovki and stayed there as a monk, changing his name to Diodorus. He later lived as a hermit on an island on lake Vodla, but then decided to found a monastery on Mount Jur, receiving money for the purpose from the Tsar Michael Fedorovic's mother. He died while away from his monastery of the Most Holy Trinity on business, but his remains were eventually returned there. Feast 20 November.

Dionysia, Majoricus and Companions, martyrs, died north Africa, 484. Majoricus was the son of Dionysia. They died in the persecution of the Arian king Huneric. Feast 6 December.

Dionysia, see also **Peter**.

Dionysius, pope, 259/60? – c. 267/8, died Rome, c. 267. Dionysius is considered one of the most important popes of the third century. He reorganized the community at Rome, and called a synod which condemned both the Sabellian and Marcionite tendencies of breaking up the Trinity into three hypostases. Dionysius also helped the Cappadocian communities which had been devastated by foreign invasions. Feast 26 December.

Dionysius (Denis), bishop, third century or possibly fourth century. He is supposed to have been sent to Gaul in the third century with **Peregrinus**,

traditionally but unreliably bishop of Auxerre, and to have become bishop of Vienne, near Lyon. Feast 9 May.

Dionysius, see also **Denis**.

Dionysius Andreevic Cagovec, martyr, born Dergaci, died Char'kov, 28 November 1937. Ukrainian Church, Moscow Patriarchate. He worked as a priest until he was arrested in the village of Andreevka. Feast 19 May.

Dionysius of Alexandria (the Great), bishop, died Alexandria, 265/6. Little is known of Dionysius before he was made bishop in 248, although it is suggested he was of a wealthy background. During the Decian persecution in 249 Dionysius left Alexandria to hide in Mareotis, and later the Libyan desert, for which he was subsequently rebuked. In 251 Dionysius supported **Cornelius** against Novatian in the contest for the bishopric at Rome. Dionysius intervened in the trinitarian controversy in Libyian Pentapolis, siding against the incumbent bishop of Ptolemais. Dionysius vindicated his actions in his work *Refutation and Apologia*, fragments of which are cited by **Athanasius**. Feast 17 November.

Dionysius of Corinth, bishop, died Corinth, 180. The only chronological certainty concerning him is a letter written to Bishop **Soter** of Rome, pope 166–75, traditionally – in which he defends his actions concerning a judgement given to the bishops of Pontus. The letter reveals that Dionysius was consulted by the bishops of Pontus as to whether they should receive into the Church 'all those who are converted from every kind of sin'. Dionysius judged that they should admit them. Feast 8 April.

Dionysius of Glusic, born c. 1362, died Sosonovec, 1 June 1437. Russian Church. At baptism he received the name Demetrius, which he changed to Dionysius when he entered the monastery of Spaso-Kammennyj, on lake Kubenskoe, c. 1386. His severely ascetical life won him many followers, but, wanting a solitary life, he and a disciple called Pachomius left the monastery to find a more remote spot. They settled first at a place called St Luke, and dedicated the chapel they built to St

Luke, but the place proved too remote for Pachomius, and they moved to the eastern part of lake Kubenskoe, near the river Glusic, where they returned to their strict discipline. By the beginning of the fifteenth century there was a growing community there, which received the encouragement of the bishop of Rostov. Dionysius, however, seeking more solitude, left the monastery and established himself in a small hermitage at Sosonovec. His monks at Glusic kept insisting that he should return and live with them, and eventually, *c.* 1420, a small community was also begun at Sosonovec. Dionysius settled there in 1422.

Dionysius of Milan, bishop, died Cappadocia, *c.* 360. Bishop of Milan from 351, he was one of only three bishops who refused to endorse the condemnation of **Athanasius** by Constantius, the Aryan emperor. He was banished and died in exile. Feast 25 May.

Dionysius of Obnora, see **Ephraim of Obnora, with Dionysius, Jerome and Isaac**.

Dionysius of Olympus, born Sklatena, *c.* 1500, died Mount Olympus, 23 January 1541. Byzantine Church. Orphaned when still very young, he went for his education to a monastery in the Meteora, and then, having entered as a monk, went to Mount Athos. On a visit to Jerusalem the patriarch wanted to make him his successor, but Dionysius refused and returned to Athos, where he became hegumenos of the Filoteou monastery. His reorganization of the monastic life there aroused much opposition, and for a time he was in fear for his life. Because local people wanted to make him metropolitan, he went to Mount Olympus, where he founded a monastery dedicated to the Most Holy Trinity, although this was destroyed in a Turkish raid and he had to take refuge elsewhere before returning to rebuild the monastery.

Dionysius of Perejaslavl, monk, died Perejaslavl, 15 April 1645. Russian Church. A monk of the monastery at Perejaslavl, he rebuilt it after a Polish invasion and an epidemic of the plague which led to its abandonment.

Dionysius of Polock, bishop. Russian Church. Bishop of Polock, *c.* 1182.

Dionysius of Radonez, archimandrite, born Rzev, *c.* 1570, died Radonez, 10 May 1633. Russian Church. Born David Zebninov, he was devout as a youth and, after marrying, was ordained. But within six years his wife and children died, and he entered the monastery of Starica, where he had studied, taking the name Dionysius. Because of his fame for holiness of life, he was nominated superior of the monastery of the Most Holy Trinity at Radonez. During a Polish invasion his monastery was besieged for 15 months, but nonetheless served as a refuge for those fleeing the invaders. Dionysius looked after all these pilgrims with great solicitude, while praying passionately that the foreign forces would withdraw from Russia. He wrote to other cities and monasteries begging that assistance be sent to the resistance around Moscow. While this was going on, he also found time to examine and correct a number of texts, especially liturgical ones, issued by the Moscow patriarch. He found them full of inaccuracies, but after correcting these he was accused of corrupting the texts and embracing heresy. He was summoned to a synod in Moscow, now liberated, and was imprisoned for a year, being subject to humiliating punishments. A visit to Moscow of the patriarch of Jerusalem, who pleaded for Dionysius's rehabilitation, led to an amelioration of his punishment, and then a chance to defend himself before the Tsar, as a result of which he was acquitted of all charges. Some of his monks, however, remained hostile for a long time, all of which suffering he bore with patience.

Dionysius of Rostov ('the Greek'), born Greece, died Rostov, 18 October 1425. Russian Church. A monk of Mount Athos, he came to Moscow in the late fourteenth century, and then for a time was hegumenos at the monastery of Spaso-Kammennyj, on lake Kubenskoe. He introduced Greek spirituality and practices into the monastery. He was created metropolitan of Rostov in 1418.

Dionysius of Suzdal, archbishop, died Kiev, 15 October 1385. Russian Church. Probably originally a monk of the Kievan Cave monasteries, he became a hermit near Novgorod. His strict asceticism attracted many followers, and he founded several monasteries – including monasteries for women, after Princess Basilissa-Theodora, widow of the prince of Novgorod, became a nun – in the coenobitic tradition. In 1374 he was ordained bishop of Novgorod and Suzdal. In 1378 he was imprisoned after opposing (with **Sergius of Radonez**) the choice of the prince of Moscow as metropolitan of Kiev. On his release, thanks to Sergius's intervention, he went to Constantinople and in 1380 was present when the archimandrite Pimen was ordained as metropolitan of Kiev and of Greater Russia. While in Constantinople Dionysius impressed the Greek bishops, especially by his knowledge of Scripture, and was raised by the patriarch to the rank of archbishop. The conflict over the see of Kiev was not resolved by the ordination of Pimen – who was imprisoned for a time on his return to Russia. In 1383 Dionysius again returned to Constantinople and, according to some accounts, was there ordained metropolitan of Kiev, the two other contenders having been declared deposed. When Dionysius attempted to return to Russia he was arrested and imprisoned in Kiev, where he died after a year and a half of incarceration. Feast 26 June.

Dionysius of the Nativity (Pierre Berthelot), bl., missionary and protomartyr of the Discalced Carmelite reform, born Honfleur, France, 12 December 1600, died Sumatra, 27 November 1638. He was a professional navigator and cartographer, captured by Dutch pirates and imprisoned at Java on his first expedition to the Indies. After his release he settled in Malacca and worked for the Portuguese, assuming command of a ship. His voyages brought him into contact with the recently founded Discalced Carmelite monastery at Goa, and in 1634 he entered the order. After his ordination in 1638, his superiors assigned him as the chaplain of an expedition to Sumatra and appointed a lay brother, Bl. **Redemptus of the Cross**, as his companion. When the expedition arrived at Sumatra, both men were captured by the natives and martyred when they refused to apostatize to Islam. Leo XIII beatified them in 1900. Some of Dionysius's cartographic work is in the British Museum. Feast 29 November.

Dionysius of Zante, bishop, born Zante, 1547, died there, 17 December 1622. Byzantine Church. Of a rich family called Siguros from the island of Zante, he was originally called Draganigo. He was well educated, but was left an orphan when still fairly young. At 21 he entered a monastery on Zante, taking the name Daniel. He was eventually ordained priest. In 1577 he visited the Holy Land, and on his return was made bishop of Egina, at which point he took the name Dionysius. Two years later, however, he left Egina and returned to Zante, where he was made bishop of the island, causing conflict with the bishop of Cephalonia in whose diocese Zante lay. The doge of Venice decided in favour of the bishop of Cephalonia, and Dionysius resigned his office, seeking re-election when the bishop of Cephalonia died. He was not chosen, and remained in his monastery on Zante, teaching and living a life of prayer. In a feud between his own relatives and another family, Dionysius's brother was assassinated, and the murderer sought refuge in the monastery, where Dionysius received him.

Dionysius the Areopagite, first century. Converted by St Paul's preaching on the Areopagus in Athens, as recounted in the Acts of the Apostles. Nothing else is known about him, but he is sometimes claimed as the first bishop of Athens. To him were later attributed a number of writings produced c. 500, which are now attributed to 'the Pseudo Denis/Dionysius'. Feast 9 October.

Dionysius the Athonite, born Korissos, 1316, died Trebizond, 25 June 1388. Byzantine Church. At 19 he entered a monastery on Mount Athos where his brother was hegumenos, and was ordained priest in 1346. As his fame for sanctity spread, he retreated to the south of Antiathos in 1347, but many disciples came to settle near him. To find a more suitable spot for a monastery, he moved further west. Later he travelled to Trebizond, where his brother was now metropolitan, to seek funds for his monastery. On his return he discovered that all his monks had been taken prisoner by a party of invading Turks, and he had to ransom them. He therefore decided to re-establish his monks in the safety of Mount Athos, founding Timios Podromos, a monastery for which he received funds from the Byzantine emperor.

Dionysius the Rhetor, bl., died Mount Athos, 9 July 1606. Byzantine Church. A man of considerable education, he entered the Studite monastery in Constantinople before moving to Mount Athos.

Dioscoris, martyr, died Mara, second/third century. Feast 10 May.

Dioscorus, martyr, born Alexandria, died Fayyum. Coptic Church. He had converted to Islam, but after receiving a letter from his sister upbraiding him, he returned to Christianity, proclaimed his renewed faith, and was executed by burning.

Dioscorus, martyr, died Egypt, *c.* 305. He was a reader at the church of Kynopolis who died under torture as he was being burned with hot irons. Feast 18 May.

Dioscorus of Alexandria, patriarch, died 4 September *c.* 454. Coptic Church. Chosen in 444 to succeed St **Cyril**, he wrote to Pope **Leo the Great** announcing his election, but was rebuked by the pope because the usages of Alexandria did not coincide with those of Rome. He was later chosen to preside at the Council of Ephesus of 449 (the 'Robber Council') which supported the archimandrite Eutyches – the last council to be regarded as ecumenical by the Copts. After the death of Theodosius II, however, his sister Pulcheria came to the throne of Byzantium together with her husband Marcianus. They wanted Eutyches condemned, and another council was called at Chalcedon in 451, in the course of which, as Coptic accounts allege, Dioscorus was physically attacked for his championing of Eutyches. (Some sources allege that it was Pulcheria herself who launched this attack, in the course of which Dioscorus lost two teeth.) He was then deposed and exiled from his see, although not, according to the records of the council, for heresy, but for disciplinary reasons. During this time of exile, Coptic accounts say that he was rewarded with the gift of miracles.

Dioscorus of Alexandria II (or 'the New'), patriarch, died Alexandria, 14 October 517. Coptic Church. Secretary of John II, he was elected in 1515 on the instructions of the Emperor Anastasius, but the people of the city objected and rioted, in the course of which riot the imperial prefect was killed.

Disibod, bishop, born Ireland, died Germany, *c.* 674. He was born and brought up in Ireland, and became a bishop there, but was unsuccessful as a preacher. He moved to Germany in the middle of the seventh century, and founded a monastery in the hills overlooking the Nahe valley, near Bingen, which would become known as Disidodenberg or Diessenberg. Feast 8 July.

Dodo Garegeli, monk, born Kacheti, eastern Georgia, sixth century. Georgian Church. A disciple of David Garegeli, he was sent to found the monastery of Dodorka.

Dodo of Asch, bl., Premonstratensian hermit, died Asch, Friesland, 30 March 1231. After several years of a marriage reluctantly contracted, he became a Premonstratensian canon of Mariengaard, and his wife entered a convent. Permitted to live as a hermit in a cell at Bakkeveen, Dodo practised extraordinary austerities for many years. About five years before his death he moved to a sanctuary at Asch. His reputation for sanctity and wonder-working attracted the sick of every kind and many were cured. Stigmata were found on his body when he died, but they may have been caused by the fall that killed him. His feast has been celebrated by the Premonstratensians in Spain at least since 1636.

Dogmael, born Wales, died Britanny (?), sixth century (?). Nothing is known of him, although dedications suggest he worked in Pembrokeshire, and then moved to Britanny. Feast 14 June.

Dominic, founder of the Order of Preachers, or Dominican friars, and the Dominican sisterhoods, born Calaruega, into the Castilian family of Guzmán, *c.* 1170, died Bologna, 6 August 1221. Little is known about his early life. He was educated at the university of Palencia and began his priestly life as a canon of the cathedral at Osma, becoming prior of the chapter there *c.* 1201. In that year he went with his bishop to Denmark on a diplomatic mission and, passing through the Languedoc, encountered Albigensianism. On their way home, both Dominic and his bishop visited Rome to ask permission to evangelize in Russia, but Innocent III encouraged them to combat heresy nearer home. A visit to Citeaux, whose monks were charged with combating Albigensianism, persuaded him that they were adopting the wrong approach. Dominic became convinced that there was a need in the Church for a body of trained preachers to safeguard and spread divine truth. He also established a convent at Prouille of nuns who were mostly converts from heresy, and devised for them a Rule of life based on enclosure, prayer and penance. Pope Innocent III gave his blessing to the new order and the bishop of Toulouse employed Dominic's preachers throughout his diocese. The order was officially licensed by Pope Honorius III in 1216 and its members were to live on alms. In organization Dominic imprinted an indelibly democratic character on the order, of regular consultations and elections to offices. He spent his years establishing houses throughout Italy, France and Spain. Feast 8 August.

Dominic Barberi, bl., priest and lecturer, born near Viterbo, Italy, 22 June 1792, died Reading, England, 27 August 1849. Despite his lack of training he was accepted into the Passionists in 1814 and made his profession the next year. In 1818 he was ordained at Rome and between 1821 and 1831 he took a post as lecturer of philosophy and theology to Passionist clerics. He spent some time as the superior of the new monastery at Lucca in Italy (1831–3) and became provincial for southern Italy (1833). He moved to England in 1841 and opened the first British Passionist monastery in Aston, Staffordshire, a year later. His holy life brought many to conversion, despite the fact that he was mocked and persecuted by Catholics and Protestants alike because he was an odd-looking man. He was beatified on 27 October 1963.

Dominic Henárez, born Baena, Córdoba, Spain, 19 December 1765, martyred Vietnam, 25 June 1838, beatified 1909, canonized 1988. A Dominican bishop, auxiliary apostolic vicar of East Tonkin, he was beheaded with his Vietnamese catechist François Chien – see **Martyrs of Vietnam**.

Dominic Ibañez de Erquicia and Francis Shoyemon, bl., martyrs, died Japan 1633. Feast 14 August.

Dominic Iturrate Zubero, bl., born Dina, Basque region, Spain, 11 May 1901, died Belmonte, Spain, 7 April 1927, beatified 1983. A Trinitarian from the age of 16, he studied for the priesthood in Rome, but died soon after his ordination. He led a life of prayer and penance and vowed never to refuse God anything.

Dominic Kahm (or Cam), martyred Hung-Yen, 1859, canonized 1988. A Dominican tertiary working clandestinely in what is now Vietnam, at a time of anti-Christian persecution, he was denounced and arrested. He refused to trample on the cross and was beheaded – see also **Martyrs of Vietnam**. Feast 13 January.

Dominic Loricatus, Benedictine hermit and follower of **Peter Damian**, died 14 October 1060. After his parents made a gift which he considered to be simoniacal to the bishop who ordained him, Dominic became a hermit and lived a life of heroic penance. He gained the name 'Loricatus' – 'the armoured one' – after his ascetical practice of wearing a metal breastplate over his bare skin. Sometime around 1040, he went to Fonte Avellana to join Peter Damian, who described his penitential practices in a letter to Pope Alexander III.

Dominic Mogoshichi, see **Martyrs of Omura**.

Dominic Nguyen Van Hanh and Bernard Guyen Vu Van Due, martyrs, died 1838, see **Martyrs of Vietnam**.

Dominic of Silos, abbot, born Canas, Navarre, Spain, c. 1000, died 20 December 1076. Dominic was born into a peasant family. He was a shepherd as a youth, later becoming a Benedictine monk and then prior at San **Millan** de Cogolla monastery. When Garcia III of Navarre claimed some of the monastery's land, he refused to surrender it, instead becoming abbot at San Sebastian monastery at Silos. His reforms at San Sebastian transformed it into a great spiritual centre famous for its scriptorium and art. Dominic is also known for rescuing Christian slaves from the Moors and is credited with miracles of healing. St **Dominic**, founder of the Order of Preachers, was named after Dominic of Silos because, it was claimed, his mother had a vision of the earlier St Dominic, who promised she would bear a son.

Dominic of Sora, monk, born Foligno, Etruria, Italy, *c.* 951, died *c.* 1031. As a Benedictine monk, he is known for his work in building many monasteries across Italy. St Dominic died at Sora, one of his foundations. He was invoked as a protection against thunderstorms. Feast 22 January.

Dominic of the Causeway, hermit and builder, born Villoria, Spain, died Calzada, *c.* 1109. Dominic wanted to become a Benedictine, but was refused several times and so lived as a hermit. For a while he followed St **Gregory of Ostia** (although dates make this unlikely), but after his death returned to the life of a hermit. As he lived on the road to Santiago de Compostela, he tried to help the many pilgrims by building a highway, a bridge and a hospice. Feast 12 May.

Dominic Saraceni, martyred Córdoba, 984. He and his companions were killed while the area was under Muslim rule. Feast 31 January.

Dominic Savio, born Riva di Chieri, Italy, 2 April 1842, died Mondonio, 9 March 1857, canonized 1954. One of ten children of a blacksmith and a seamstress, he wanted to become a priest and was a pupil in Turin of **John Bosco**, who wrote up his life. He died in the family home – they had moved from Riva – but is buried in the cathedral in Turin. He is the youngest canonized non-martyr. He displayed an intense spiritual life and complete commitment to Bosco's apostolic work with street boys. Feast 9 March.

Dominic Uy, martyr, died Vietnam, 1839. He was a Dominican tertiary. Feast 19 December.

Dominica (Drusa), see **Indract**.

Domitian of Maastricht, bishop, born France, died Maastricht, 560. Domitian was bishop of Tongeren, but was transferred to Maastricht. He was present at the Councils of Clermont (535) and Orléans (549). Domitian was an evangelist who converted the Valley of the Meuse, founding both churches and hospitals, and was renowned for his generosity and his great fundraising skills at a time of famine. He is the patron saint of Huy, Belgium. According to legend he killed a dragon. Feast 7 May.

Domitian of Melitene, bishop, died *c.* 602. He became bishop at the age of 30 and was sent by the Byzantine Emperor Maurice to preach in Persia, where his success was both political and religious. He was renowned for his generosity to the poor. Feast 10 January.

Domitian of Melitene, monk, died 473. Feast 27 January.

Domna of Tomsk, born 1804, died Tomsk, 16 October 1872. Russian Church. Of noble birth, Domna fled her home to avoid marriage. She eventually travelled to Tomsk, after being several times arrested – police interest in her lasted until she was quite old. She lived as a 'fool for Christ', taking particular care of cats and dogs. Feast 10 June.

Domnolus of Le Mans, abbot and bishop, died 581. Domnolus was abbot of St Laurent in Paris. He declined the bishopric of Avignon, but in 539 he was appointed bishop of Le Mans. He attended the Synod of Tours in 567. Domnolus was responsible for the building of several churches and a hospice for pilgrims on the Sarthe river. Reputedly a man who worked many miracles.

Donald, born Scotland, died Abernethy, Scotland, eighth century. He lived at Oglivy in Forfarshire, and had nine daughters. After his wife died he lived with his daughters as a religious community, and on his death his daughters joined a monastery at Abernethy. Feast 15 July.

Donatian, bishop, died Châlons-sur-Marne, fourth century. He was bishop of Châlons-sur-Marne. Feast 7 August.

Donatian, martyr, died Nantes, Brittany, *c.* 304. He was accused of being a Christian and imprisoned. His elder brother, **Rogatian**, not yet baptized, joined him in prison. They were put to the rack and killed by the sword. Rogatian is seen as an example of 'baptism by blood'. Feast 24 May.

Donatian and Companions, bishops and martyrs, died north Africa, *c.* 484. Bishops of the province of Byzacene, they were driven out into the desert by the Vandal King Huneric, when he seized all

Church property for the Arians. They died of thirst and starvation. Feast 6 September.

Donatus, died *c.* 811. He was bishop in Dalmatia. Feast 25 February.

Donatus, monk, born Ripacandida, near Rapallo, Italy, died Petina, 1198. A monk of Montevergine. Feast 17 August.

Donatus, see also **Polyeuctus**.

Donatus of Besançon, monk, born Upper Burgundy, *c.* 590, died before 660. Donatus took to the monastic life at an early age at Luxeuil, under the guidance of **Columbanus**. Whilst bishop of Besançon in 624 Donatus founded a monastery, to which he gave a Rule combining those of St Columbanus and St **Benedict**. He also founded a monastery for women, giving it a Rule based on Columbanus, Benedict and **Caesarius of Arles**. Feast 7 August.

Donatus of Fiesole, bishop, born Ireland, died Fiesole, Italy, *c.* 876. An Irish monk, he went on pilgrimage to Rome, but he arrived, so the story has it, in Fiesole *c.* 829 just at the moment when the people were electing a new bishop, and they chose him. He wrote poetry and a number of books, including a life of St **Brigid**. He opened a hospice in Piacenza for Irish pilgrims under the patronage of St Brigid, and once led an army into battle against the Saracens. He was highy regarded by both popes and kings, and had a reputation for learning. Feast 22 October.

Donatus, Secundian, Romulus and Companions, martyrs, died Porto Gruaro (Concordia), near Venice, fourth century. A group of 89 martyrs in all, they were killed under Diocletian. Feast 17 February.

Donnan (Donan), abbot, and Companions, martyrs, died Eigg, Inner Hebrides, 618. Donnan was an Irish monk who followed **Columba** to Scotland *c.* 580, he founded a monastery on the island of Eigg. He and his companions were killed by raiders, possibly Vikings, either burned alive in their church or beheaded. Feast 17 April.

Dorotheus, see also **Castor**.

Dorotheus of Jug, monk, born Niznij Nikulski, died 1622. Russian Church. A monk of the cave monasteries of Pskov, when the Swedish army approached in 1615, as a consequence of a dream he carried off an icon of the Virgin for safety, and eventually reached his home region, stopping at the confluence of two tributaries of the river Jug. He put the icon in a pine tree, but when he wished to travel on he found he could not move it. He therefore settled where he was, and established a monastery.

Dorotheus of Pskov, monk, sixteenth century. Russian Church. When old and blind, and sitting in his cell in the monastery of Pokrov, he had a vision of Mary, and of a number of saints associated with the city of Pskov, in which he was promised that Mary would show mercy on the city, then besieged by King Stefan Batory. The siege only lasted from 7 to 8 September.

Dorothy, martyr, died *c.* 305. Dorothy (also Dorothea) lived in Alexandria and suffered martyrdom in the Diocletian persecution. Mentioned by both **Eusebius** and **Rufinus**. According to legend, as Dorothy was being taken to martyrdom she was mocked by a lawyer named Theophilus, who asked her to send him fruits from the garden to which she was going. At the time of her execution an angel appeared to her with a basket of fruit, which she sent to **Theophilus**, who became a Christian and was martyred with her. She is shown crowned or holding roses. Feast 6 February (suppressed 1969).

Dosithea of the Kiev Caves, Russian Orthodox saint and recluse, born near Riazan, 1721, died Kiev, 25 September 1776. She entered the St Sergius monastery disguised as a boy. As her parents were searching for her she moved to Kiev, living under the name Dositheus the Hermit, at the great Kievan Caves monastery. Thousands visited her for advice, including the empress Elizabeth and the future St **Seraphim of Sarov**. She is therefore regarded as a precursor of the hesychast and monastic revival in Russia. Only after her death did the monks find that she was a woman. Canonized in Ukraine as a local saint 1994. See also Dositheus of Kiev.

Dositheus, monk, seventeenth century. Church of the Old Believers. Originally hegumenos of the monastery of St Nicholas in Tichvin, when the persecution of Old Believers began he travelled around Russia bringing encouragement and spiritual comfort. He settled for a time in a monastery on the river Don, and later at Kerzenc. When a new persecution broke out, he left the church he had established at Kerzenc and travelled to the Caspian Sea, where he built a church near the river Kuma. It is there that he died.

Dositheus of Kiev, monk, born Rjazan, 1721, died Kiev, 24 September 1776. Ukrainian Orthodox Church (Moscow Patriarchate). Born Daria Tjapkina of a noble family, she lived during her early years with her grandmother, who was a nun in the monastery of the Ascension in the Kremlin. Daria, however, lived an extremely rigorous ascetical life, and in 1736 she left her home, to which she had returned, and, dressed as a man, entered the monastery of the Kievan Caves. Three years later she was found there and forcibly removed by her parents, but she once again abandoned her family and walked back to Kiev where, again dressed as a man and calling herself Dositheus, she tried to enter the Cave monastery. The bishop, however, fearing that she was a fleeing peasant seeking refuge, refused to accept her. She therefore set herself up in a hermitage on Mount Kitaj, in the suburbs of Kiev. In 1744 the Empress Elizabeth visited her, and at the empress's request she was allowed to become a novice. Many people came to her hermitage for spiritual guidance – one of them her own sister, who did not recognize her. So as to avoid being ordained, she became 'a fool for Christ's sake', wandering the streets of Kiev. At her death she left instructions that her body was not to be examined, and it was only her sister, returning to Kiev, who recognized her from a portrait. However, she continued to be venerated under her assumed name, and as a monk. She was canonized in 1993.

Dositheus of Solovki, monk, fifteenth/sixteenth centuries. Russian Church. A monk of the monastery of the Transfiguration on the Solovki islands in the White Sea.

Dositheus of Tbilisi, martyr, died Tbilisi, 1795. Georgian Church. Metropolitan of the Georgian capital, and killed by Persian troops during the sack of Tbilisi. Feast 12 September.

Dositheus of Verchneostrovo, monk, died 1482. Russian Church. Founded in 1470 the monastery whose name he bears on the lake of Pskov.

Dovmont of Pskov, prince, born Lithuania, died Pskov, 1299. Russian Church. With some 300 families he left Lithuania in 1265 because of the constant warfare there, and settled at Pskov. He ruled the region for the next 33 years, governing with justice, concern for the poor and, after his conversion (he took the name **Timothy**), with deep devotion to the Church. He took as a wife Princess Maria, daughter of the Grand Prince Demetrius, who was himself a nephew of **Alexander Nevski**. Maria entered a convent after her husband's death, changing her name to Martha. He fortified Pskov, vigorously defending his city and the north-west frontiers of Russia against attacks from the Danes and the Germans, including from the Livonian Order. Feast 20 May.

Drausius of Soissons (Drausinus), bishop, died Soissons, c. 680. As bishop of Soissons he made many religious foundations, and in medieval times soldiers camped at his tomb before battle, as this was meant to make them invincible. **Thomas Becket** prayed at his tomb for protection. Feast 5 March.

Drithelm, monk, born Northumbria, died Melrose, c. 700. He was a married man in Northumbria who fell ill and was thought to have died. He suddenly awoke, and announced that henceforth he would change his life. He divided his property between his wife, his children and the poor, and became a monk at Melrose Abbey, where he lived a rigorously ascetical life, standing in an icy river to say his prayers. The vision which inspired him to this kind of life was of a journey to the gates of hell and the gates of heaven. Feast 1 September.

Droctovius (Drotté), abbot, born Auxerre, France, died Paris (?), *c.* 580. He was abbot of St Symphorium at Autun and of St Germain des Prés in Paris. Feast 10 March.

Drogo (Dreux, Druon), born Epinoy, Artois, Flanders, *c.* 1118, died Sebourg, near Valenciennes, France, 1189. He was a penitential pilgrim, a shepherd and, disabled by a painful hernia, became a walled-up hermit in Sebourg. He is said to have been able to bilocate and is a patron of shepherds. Feast 16 April.

Droside, martyr, died Antioch, second century (?).

Drostan, abbot, born Scotland, died there, *c.* 610. He was the first abbot of the monastery at Deer, near Peterhead in Aberdeenshire. According to some sources, he moved to Glenesk in Angus to live as a hermit. While he was still alive, miracles were attributed to his intercession. Feast 11 July.

Druthmar, bl., monk and abbot, died 15 February 1046. He entered a community at Lorsch and was made abbot at Corvey, Westphalia, in 1014. His reputation for learning and observance of the monastic discipline enabled him to bring the monks to a greater degree of observance. His body and that of Unsdorf of Corvey (died 983) were exhumed in 1100, after which a cult developed. A seventeenth-century statue at Corvey gives him the title 'Blessed'. Feast 13 August.

Dubricius (also known as Dyfrig or Devereux), monk and bishop. It is claimed that he was born near Madely in Herefordshire and died Bardsey Island, *c.* 550. He was one of the earliest and most important saints of south Wales. There is little verifiable information about his life, but he became the subject of many medieval legends and was mentioned in *The Book of Llandaff* and *The Life of Benedict*. Geoffrey of Monmouth cites him as archbishop of Caerleon and claims that he crowned King Arthur. He is also said to have been bishop of Llandaff and to have had his headquarters at Henllan near Ross on Wye and at Moccas. He is credited with having set up many monastic establishments, and a number of churches in Wales are dedicated to him. He is said to

have died as a hermit on Bardsey Island. Feast 14 November.

Ducas of Mitilene, martyr, born Mitilene, died Constantinople, 24 April 1564. Byzantine Church. He worked as a tailor in Constantinople. A Muslim woman fell in love with him, but when he refused to accept her, she accused him of having attempted to rape her. He was ordered to be flayed alive.

Dula, see **Theodula**.

Dunstan, archbishop of Canterbury, abbot and ascetic, born near Glastonbury, 909, died Canterbury, 19 May 988. He came from a noble family and was educated at Glastonbury Abbey, then in the household of his uncle, who was archbishop of Canterbury. From there he went to the court of King Athelstan, was professed at Glastonbury and made abbot *c.* 940. Under his guidance, the full observance of the Rule of St **Benedict** was reinstated. Between 945 and 955 he was minister and treasurer to King Eadred. He had to go into exile after he had criticized the conduct of King Edwig, which gave him the opportunity to see for himself the style of reformed monasticism on the continent. He was recalled from exile by King Edgar in 959 and with him began the reform of Church and state. In 970, at a meeting at Winchester, there was promulgated the *Regularis Concordia*, establishing the norms by which monastic life should be observed. It reflected many of the practices Dunstan had encountered on the continent. A number of monasteries were reformed under Dunstan's influence. He was made archbishop of Canterbury in 960, and showed the same determination to reform the lives of the secular clergy. He was also known as a musician, illuminator and metalworker.

Duthac, bishop, born Scotland, died Ross, Scotland, *c.* 1065. He was bishop of Ross, where he had mainly worked after his student days in Ireland. Feast 8 March.

Dyfrig, see **Dubricius**.

Dympna (Dimpna), martyr, seventh century. There is very little historical information. The legend is said to be largely folklore. She was said to be of royal birth and escaped her father's incestuous infatuation by fleeing to her confessor St **Gerebernus** at Antwerp. Her father traced them to Gheel and found them living as solitaries. They were both killed immediately and the bodies translated in the thirteenth century. This event was accompanied by many cures of epileptics and the mentally ill, whose patron saint she became. Gheel has become well known for its progressive work with mentally ill people. Feast 15 May.

E

Eanswyth, abbess, born Kent, died near Folkestone, *c*. 640. The daughter of the second Christian king of Kent, she refused to marry a pagan prince from Northumbria and instead became a nun at a convent founded near Folkestone. It was probably the first nunnery in England. She had encountered religious life during a stay in France. Feast 31 August.

Eata, bishop, died Hexham, 686. A disciple of **Aidan**, he became abbot of Melrose, to which **Cuthbert** came as a novice. Eata was given land at Ripon and he moved there, with Cuthbert, to found a new monastery, but did not stay because of a dispute over the date of Easter. After the Synod of Whitby, however, he accepted the Roman method of calculation, and became abbot of Lindisfarne in place of **Colman**, who would not accept the change and returned to Ireland. He eventually became bishop of Lindisfarne, although he resigned this to **Cuthbert** and moved to Hexham just a year before his death. Feast 26 October.

Ebbe (Aebbe, Ebba), abbess, born Northumbria, died Coldingham, 683. She was the daughter of King Ethelfirth. On his death Edwin conquered Northumbria and Ebbe fled to Scotland. She took profession at Coldingham and later became abbess. She had a reputation for wisdom and holiness. In later life she was warned by the priest Adaman that her community needed reform under threat of dire punishment. Reforms were instituted for a short time, but lapsed. After her death the monastery burned down, but Ebbe's reputation remained and revived in the twelfth century after her relics were discovered. They are now held at Durham and Coldingham. Her name is remembered in St Abb's Head. Feast 25 August.

Ebbo, abbot and hermit, born Tonnerre, towards the end of the seventh century, died Arce, near Sens, *c*. 750. His early life as a district administrator was distasteful to him and he professed at St Pierre Le Vif near Sens, where he later became abbot. He is credited with having saved the city of Sens from the Saracens' siege by the power of prayer. His later years were spent in solitude and meditation. He was buried at St Pierre.

Eberhard of Einsiedeln, bl., abbot, died Einsiedeln, 14 August 958. He was of noble birth and became provost of Strasbourg cathedral early in his life. He developed a reputation for piety and gave up this office in 934 in order to establish the hermitage of Einsiedeln with Berno of Metz. The community here thrived and Eberhard gave family money to establish a monastery, of which he was the first abbot. The monastery prospered and had a reputation for generosity, which came to the fore during the great famine of 942. Pilgrimages took place to his tomb until his relics were lost around 1789 during the French Revolution.

Eberhard of Rohrdorf, bl., abbot and statesman, born *c*. 1160, died Salem, 10 June 1245. He was of noble birth, entering a Cistercian monastery at the Abbey of Salem and becoming abbot in 1191. He gained a reputation for humility as well as competence, and was highly regarded by his contemporaries. His abbacy was one of the most famous, and he was in office between the death of Frederick I Barbarossa and the end of the

Hohenstaufen regime. He was appointed by Innocent III to investigate some difficult questions of ecclesiastical politics, including negotiating a peace between Philip of Swabia and Pope Innocent III. He resigned office in 1240 due to advanced age and was written into the Cistercian martyrology following his death. Feast 14 April.

Eberhard of Salzburg, bishop, born Nuremberg, *c.* 1085, died Rein, 1164. Of a noble family, he became a canon of Bamberg, but resigned it to enter a monastery. The bishop of Bamberg wanted him for his diocese, and persuaded him to leave the monastery and go to Paris to study. After this, however, he returned to a monastery – at Prüf-ening near Regensberg. His family had themselves founded an abbey at Biburg, and he was sent to become superior there. In 1146 he was appointed bishop of Salzburg. A significant political figure through his family, he was one of the few German prelates who refused to back Frederick Barbarossa in the latter's conflict with the papacy. He died at the Cistercian abbey at Rein on his way back to Salzburg after mediating in a dispute between his brother Conrad, who was bishop of Passau, and the duke of Austria. Feast 22 June.

Eberhard of Tüntenhausen, shepherd, born Freis-ing, died Tüntenhausen, *c.* 1370. He is a folk saint, not canonized, and is buried under the altar at Tüntenhausen in Bavaria. He is the patron saint of shepherds and domestic animals, and is invoked in cases of cattle sickness and for good weather. His cult is first mentioned in a letter in 1428 and according to testimony given at a hearing in 1729–34, it is said that the earth taken from his grave and used as medicine for sick animals never dimin-ished. Iron and wooden figures of animals were left at his grave. Feast 12 September.

Ebrulf, see **Evroul**.

Ecgwine, bishop, died Worcester, 717 (?). He was bishop of Worcester, but otherwise nothing is known about him. He signed charters (although these may not be authentic) between 692 and 717. Feast 30 December.

Edburga, princess, born Winchester (?), died there, 960. She was the daughter of Edward the Elder,

king of Wessex, and entered the convent at Winchester, St Mary's Abbey, founded by her grandmother, the wife of King Alfred. She was remarkable for her humility. Feast 15 June.

Edigio Maria of St Joseph, bl., Franciscan lay brother, born near Taranto, Italy, 16 November 1729, died Naples, 7 February 1812. He entered the monastery in 1754 at Taranto after working as a ropemaker to support the family. A spiritual experience of note led him to a devout life of simplicity and serenity. He was drawn to the activities of the Sodality of Our Lady of the Rosary, and to devotion to Mary and Joseph, and he was held in high esteem by the sick and poor of Naples.

Edigna, bl., patron against theft, died Puch, near Fürstenfeldbruck, Bavaria, 26 February 1109. She is said to have taken a vow of virginity. Her father, a French king, instructed her to marry and as a consequence she escaped to Bavaria. Legend says that she lived in a hollow tree. This was the site of a miraculous flow of holy oil after her death. The flow ceased when merchants tried to sell it for gain. She is buried at Puch and still honoured there. Feast 26 February.

Edith, born Kemsing, Kent, 961, died Wilton Abbey, 16 September 984. Edith was the daughter of King Edgar of Wessex and Wulfrida, who may already have been a nun at Wilton Abbey – Wilton being the capital of Wessex – or went there immediately after the birth. Edith was brought up in the abbey, and proved very talented. Her father attempted to persuade her to leave the abbey, but she refused, and again refused to become queen of Wessex after the murder of her half-brother.

Edith of Polesworth, born England, died Poles-worth (?), *c.* 925 (?). Little is known about her for certain, as reports are confused. She may have been the daughter of King Egbert, and founder and abbess at an abbey at Polesworth. According to another tradition, she was the sister of King Athelstan and married the Viking leader Sihtric. Feast 15 July.

Edith Stein (Teresa Benedicta of the Cross), nun, philosopher and contemplative, born Wroclaw

(Breslau), Poland, 12 October 1891, died Auschwitz, Poland, 9 August 1942. She was born into a devout Jewish family, but lost her faith in her youth and became interested in philosophy. She went to the University of Gottingen, where she studied under, and became assistant to, Husserl, the father of phenomenology. She also came into contact with Catholicism there, through Max Scheler, and became interested in the answers it provided. She was finally converted through reading the autobiography of **Teresa of Avila**, and was baptized on 1 January 1922. She left the university and went to teach at a girls' school at Speyer in the Rhineland, run by Third Order Dominican sisters. Here she translated the treatise *On Truth* by **Thomas Aquinas**. In 1932 she was appointed lecturer at the Education Institute at Munster in Westphalia, but had to leave this post because of Nazi anti-Semitic legislation. She joined the Carmelite sisters at Cologne, and took the name Teresa Benedicta of the Cross. At Cologne she completed *Finite and Eternal Being*, in which she attempted to synthesize the philosophy of St Thomas with modern thought, especially with phenomenology. When, at the end of 1938, the Nazi persecution of the Jews became increasingly intense, she went into the Carmel at Echt, Holland, and it was here that she wrote *The Science of the Cross*, a presentation of the life and teaching of St **John of the Cross**. When the Dutch bishops condemned Hitler's anti-Semitic excesses, she was one of a number of priests and other religious of Jewish origin who were arrested as a reprisal. She was taken to the concentration camp at Auschwitz, where she died in the gas chamber. She was beatified in 1987 and canonized in 1998.

Edmund, king and martyr, born 840, died near Norwich, 20 November 869. Although the son of a king of Saxony, he was adopted by the East Angles as their king and succeeded to the throne in 865. His rule ended with the invasion of the Danes, when as a Christian he refused to share his kingdom with the Dane Ingwar. He was shot with arrows and beheaded. A cult grew up quickly and his eventual burial place in the tenth century at Bury St Edmunds became a place of pilgrimage.

Edmund Arrowsmith, martyr, born Haydock, near St Helens, Lancashire, 1585, died Lancaster, 28 August 1628. Both his parents had been imprisoned for their faith. After ordination at the English College, Douai, in 1612, he returned the following year to labour in his native Lancashire. Fearless in his apostolate, his forthright speech put him at risk. Having been arrested and examined, however, he was released by the bishop of Chester. He joined the Society of Jesus at the London novitiate of Clerkenwell, and, betrayed on his return to Lancashire, appeared before Sir Henry Yelverton, who condemned him to death. On the way to execution in Lancaster castle, St **John Southworth**, also a prisoner, gave him absolution. He refused until the end to renounce his faith: 'Tempt me no more. I will not do it, in no case, on no condition.' Canonized in 1970, his hand is preserved in the church of St Oswald at Ashton-in-Makerfield, Wigan, and has been the source of miraculous cures.

Edmund Barber, alias of **Edward Stransham**.

Edmund Campion, Jesuit priest and martyr, born London, England, 1540, died London, 1 December 1581. An Anglican deacon, Campion was received into the Roman Catholic Church at Douai after doubts concerning Protestantism led him to study at the English College. In 1573 he joined the Society of Jesus, was ordained priest, and in 1580 taught in Prague and participated in the first Jesuit mission to England. On arrival he publicized his mission in a pamphlet popularly known as *Campion's Brag*. He subsequently disseminated further pamphlets intended to encourage dispirited English Catholics, and challenging Protestants to debate. Campion was eventually arrested in 1581 and tried for high treason, resulting in his execution at Tyburn. He was canonized in 1970.

Edmund Catherick, bl., martyr, from Yorkshire, born *c.* 1605, died York, 13 April 1642, beatified 1929. Ordained at Douai, he worked in England from 1635. He was hanged, drawn and quartered with **John Lockwood**, with whom he is commemorated.

Edmund Drake and Companions, bl., martyrs, died Durham, 27 May 1590, beatified 1987. Edmund was born in Kent, 1563, and was a Protestant convert ordained in Rome in 1598. He landed near Tynemouth with three other priests, **Richard Hill**, **John Hogg** and **Richard Holiday**. They were betrayed and hanged, drawn and quartered.

Edmund Gennings, priest and martyr, born Lichfield, 1567, died London, 10 December 1591. He studied for the priesthood at the English college at Rheims, then returned to England, using the alias Ironmonger. He was captured while saying mass at the house of **Swithin Wells**. He was hanged, drawn and quartered at Grays Inn Fields, near Wells's house. His martyrdom converted his brother John, who had hitherto been a convinced Puritan.

Edmund Ignatius Rice, bl., founder of the Irish Christian Brothers and the Presentation Brothers, born near Callan, Kilkenny, 1 June 1762, died Waterford, 29 August 1844. Rice sought permission from Pius VI to establish a society to provide free education to poor boys; he opened a school in Waterford in 1803, forming a religious society in the Rule of the Presentation Sisters of Cork. Rice later asked Pius VII for permission to adopt the Rule of the Christian Brothers, founded by St **John Baptist de la Salle**, himself becoming Brother Ignatius in 1821, and superior general until he retired in 1838. At his death the Brothers had some 100 houses in Ireland, with 300 attached schools and over 30,000 pupils, as well as branches in Australia, Canada, India and Gibraltar.

Edmund of Abingdon (Edmund Rich), archbishop, born Abingdon, Berkshire, 1180, died in self-imposed exile, Pontigny, 16 November 1240. He studied at Oxford and then at Paris, taught the new logic at Oxford *c.* 1194–1200, then returned to Paris for theological studies. He was treasurer at Salisbury Cathedral by 1222, and was appointed to Canterbury in 1233. He failed in his efforts to prevent royal interference in the management of ecclesiastical affairs, and was on his way to visit the papal Curia when he died. He was canonized by Innocent IV in 1247. Feast 16 November.

Edmund Sykes, bl., born Leeds, *c.* 1550, ordained Rheims, 1581, martyred York, 23 March 1587, beatified 1987. Imprisoned and ill, he agreed to attend a Protestant church and was sentenced to banishment. Regretting his weakness, he went on

pilgrimage to Rome and, returning to England, was arrested again and hanged.

Edna, martyr. Syriac Church. Invoked for inflammation of the ear, otherwise nothing is known. Feast 18 August.

Edward, king and martyr, born 963, died by stabbing, Corfe, Dorset, 18 March 978. He succeeded to the English throne in 975 on the death of his father Edgar the Peaceful, against the wishes of his stepmother Queen Elfrida. He was murdered three years later, allegedly on the instructions of Queen Elfrida. He was first buried at Wareham and then translated to Shaftesbury. Miracles were reported at his tomb and he was officially pronounced martyr in 1001.

Edward Bamber, bl., martyr, born Poulton-le-Fylde, Lancashire, died Lancaster, 7 August 1646. He studied at Seville and was ordained in Cadiz in 1626. He was arrested on his return to England that same year, and seems to have abjured his Catholicism under threat of death. He was released, repented his apostasy, and a few years later was working as a priest in Lancashire, where he was arrested in 1643. He was kept prisoner in Lancaster Castle until his trial in 1646.

Edward Coleman, bl., born Suffolk, died Tyburn, London, 3 December 1678. He was the son of a clergyman, and became a Catholic after graduating from Cambridge. He was taken into the service of the duchess of York, sister-in-law of the king. In an outburst of anti-Catholic feeling after the mysterious death of Sir Edmund Berry Godfrey, a magistrate, he was arrested, found guilty of corresponding with a foreign power, and was executed.

Edward Jones, bl., born north Wales, martyred Fleet Street, London, 1590, beatified 1929. Ordained at Rheims in 1588, he was quickly arrested and tortured. Commemorated with **Anthony Middleton**, he was hanged, drawn and quartered. Feast 6 May.

Edward Oldcorne (alias Hall), bl., martyr, born York, 1561, died Redhill, 7 April 1606, beatified 1929. Becoming a Jesuit a year after ordination in

1587, he worked in Worcestershire and was unjustly implicated in the Gunpowder Plot. He was hanged, drawn and quartered with **Ralph Ashley**, a lay brother arrested with him.

Edward Osbaldestone, bl., martyr, born near Blackburn, Lancashire, died York, 16 November 1594. He studied at the English College at Douai, was ordained priest in 1585, and returned to England in 1589.

Edward Powell, bl., martyr, born Wales, c. 1478, died Smithfield, London, 30 July 1540. Educated at Oriel College, Oxford, he became a fellow there and received a doctorate in theology in 1506. He was a canon of both Lincoln and Salisbury. He was appointed as a canon lawyer to act as counsel for Catherine of Aragon during Henry VIII's claim for an annulment. In 1534 he was imprisoned in the Tower of London for refusing to take the Oath of Succession, which declared Catherine's and Henry's wedding null and void. He was convicted of high treason in July 1540 for denying the king's supremacy over the Church, and was sentenced to be hanged, drawn and quartered. He was beatified in 1886, along with **Richard Fetherston** and **Thomas Abel**, who were martyred on the same day.

Edward Shelley, bl., martyr, born Warminghurst, Sussex (?), died Tyburn, London, 30 August 1588. He was condemned for sheltering **William Dean**.

Edward Stransham (or Transham, or Edmund Barber, an alias), bl., born near Oxford, c. 1544, martyred with **Nicholas Woodfen** at Tyburn, London, 21 January 1586, beatified 1929. After ordination in Soissons, France, in 1580, he returned with Woodfen to England and brought 12 converts to France as potential priests. He was hanged, drawn and quartered.

Edward the Confessor, king, born Islip, 1003, died Westminster, 5 January 1066. He was educated at Ely and in Normandy, succeeding to the throne on the death of his half-brother. He had a reputation for piety and his reign was peaceful, although interspersed with internal struggles between his Saxon supporters and the Norman advisers Edward had brought with him. On his death this disunity and disputed succession resulted in hostilities. He is known for the building of the abbey of St Peter at Westminster. He was a popular saint in the Middle Ages and at one time was considered to be England's patron. He was canonized in 1161. Feast 13 October.

Edward Thwing, bl., martyr, born Heworth, York, 1565, died Lancaster, 26 July 1600. He went to the English College in Rheims in 1582, and to Rome in 1587. He returned to Rheims in 1590 and was ordained that year at Laon. He taught at the college for four years before returning to England. He was arrested in 1600 and imprisoned in Lancaster Castle. He was tried in July along with **Robert Nutter**. Both were condemned for being seminary priests working in England, and were hanged, drawn and quartered.

Edward Waterson, bl., martyr, born London, died Newcastle upon Tyne, 7 January 1593, beatified 1929. He became a Catholic while visiting Rome. After ordination in Rheims, France, in 1592, he came to England but was soon arrested. It was said that the horses harnessed to his hurdle refused to drag him to the scaffold.

Edwin, king, born Northumbria, 585, died at the battle of Heathfield, 6 October 633. He was banished from his kingdom early in life by the king of Bernicia, who conquered his realm, but he regained it in 617 and later became the most powerful monarch in England. He married **Ethelburga**, the Christian daughter of the Kentish King Eadbald in 627, and was converted to Christianity by her chaplain **Paulinus**. Paulinus was made bishop of York, where Edwin began the building of a church. This was interrupted by further invasion of his kingdom by Mercian and Welsh kings, by whom he was defeated. Feast 12 October.

Egbert, monk and hermit, born 639, died Iona, 24 April 729. His early life was spent as a monk at Lindisfarne. He travelled to Ireland to seek learning and to further his spiritual life, and was ordained priest. At this time he vowed never to return to Northumbria and was also instrumental in sending St **Willibrord** and others to evangelize Germany. Following a vision, the last 13 years of his life were highly devotional and he lived as a hermit on Iona. Whilst there he introduced the Roman method of calculating Easter, which had been resisted by the monks. He died on Easter Sunday, on the first occasion of the new observance.

Egino, bl., abbot, born Augsburg, died Pisa, 15 July 1120. He was banished from his monastery in Augsburg in 1098 owing to political opposition and fled to Switzerland. From here he was sent on a mission to Pope Paschal II. He was able to return to Augsburg in 1106 and in 1109 became abbot. He was a noted reformer and preacher, but came into conflict with his bishop, the simoniacal Hermann. He fled again in 1118 and died at the Camaldolese monastery of San Michele at Pisa, where he is buried.

Egyptian Monks of Qartmin, Syriac Church. Said to have come from Egypt to Qartmin to see the monastery there, and became monks. But nothing is known for certain. Feast 7 August.

Eheta Krestos, nun, died 2 April 1670/71. Ethiopian Church. Although she was married and had a son, she became a nun at Dabra Sina. After some time she was sent to Robt to be near **Walatta Petros**. The two were indefatigable campaigners for monophysitism, against the spread of the 'Latin' faith, and for a time they were separated by the pro-Latin king. After the persecution finished, Walatta Petros created a community in which both lived. After he died in 1644 by falling from a window, Eheta Krestos became the superior until her own death.

Eheta Petros, nun, seventeenth century. Ethiopian Church. A disciple of **Walatta Petros**.

Ehewa Krestos, Ethiopian Church. A shepherd, he married but lived with his wife in a state of virginity. The two of them provided for pilgrims, feeding them and washing their feet.

Eight London Martyrs, bl., died London, August 1588. They are **Henry Webley, Hugh More, James Claxton, Robert Morton, Thomas Felton, Thomas Holford, William Dean** and **William Gunter**,

all executed in the aftermath of the Armada. Feast 28 August.

Eighty-Five Martyrs of England, Scotland and Wales, bl., see **Alexander Blake, Alexander Crow, Anthony Page, Arthur Bell, Charles Meehan, Christopher Robinson, Christopher Wharton, Edmund Duke, Edmund Syke, Edward Bamber, Edward Burden, Edward Osbaldeston, Edward Thwing, Francis Ingleby, George Beesley, George Douglas, George Errington, George Haydock, George Nichols, Henry Heath, Henry Webley, Hugh Taylor, John Adams, John Bretton, John Fingley, John Hambley, John Hogg, John Lowe, John Norton, John Sandys, John Sugar, John Talbot, John Thules, John Woodcock, Joseph Lambton, Matthew Flathers, Marmaduke Bowes, Montford Scott, Nicholas Garlick, Nicholas Horner, Nicholas Woodfen, Peter Snow, Ralph Grimstone, Richard Flower, Richard Hill, Richard Holiday, Richard Sargeant, Richard Simpson, Richard Yaxley, Robert Bickerdike, Robert Dibdale, Robert Drury, Robert Grissold, Robert Hardesty, Robert Ludlum, Robert Middleton, Robert Nutter, Robert Sutton, Robert Thorpe, Roger Cadwallader, Roger Filcock, Roger Wrenno, Stephen Rowsham, Thomas Atkinson, Thomas Belson, Thomas Bullaker, Thomas Hunt, Thomas Palaster, Thomas Pilcher, Thomas Sprott, Thomas Watkinson, Thomas Whitaker, Thurstan Hunt, William Carter, William Davies, William Gibson, William Knight, William Lampley, William Pike, William Southerne, William Spenser, William Thomson.** Feast 22 November.

Elaphius, bishop, died c. 580. Bishop of Châlons from 572. He died on a journey to Spain. Feast 19 August.

Eldrad (Heldrade, Hildradus), abbot, born near Aix, Provence, died Novalese, 13 March between 840 and 845. He was born into a noble family and entered the Benedictine monastery of Ss Peter and Andrew at Novalese, Turin, after a lengthy pilgrimage in Spain and Italy. He was elected abbot c. 826. The abbey was already known as a cultural centre and for its library. During his abbacy it developed as a hospice for pilgrims crossing the

Alps. It is also recorded that as abbot he was given the monastery of Appagni by Lothar I in 825.

Eleazar Lazzaro, martyr, born Vazensk, died Olonec, eighteenth century. Church of the Old Believers. As a cleric, he preached adhesion to the ancient rites, and was imprisoned. Under torture he renounced his beliefs, but on his release he repented, did penance, and once again returned to preaching the old ways. He was again arrested, and burned at the stake. Feast 17 May.

Eleazar of Anzer, monk, born Kozelsk, died Anzer, 13 January 1656. Russian Church. Born into a pious merchant family, he became a monk with his parents' approval at the monastery of the Transfiguration on the Solovki islands. In 1612, however, seeking greater solitude, he went with the blessing of the hegumenos to an isolated island called Anzer. His holiness of life attracted others, and a community grew about him. One of its members, Nicholas, later changed his name to Nikon and was elected patriarch of Moscow. The Rule he drew up, based on that of the early Egyptian monks, was very strict. His monks lived in separate cells, a fair distance from one another, coming together for communal worship only on Saturday evenings and the vigils of great feasts. Otherwise they lived in silence. Eleazar himself wore iron chains bound around his body. His fame reached Moscow, and the Tsarina gave money to build a church on Anzer, and for vestments. Somewhat later Eleazar was summoned to Moscow by the Tsar. He and his wife had not produced an heir to the throne: Eleazar prophesied that the Tsarina would give birth, which she did. In gratitude the Tsar offered the monk to be prior of any monastery in Moscow, but he refused, and returned to Anzer. Twenty years later the son, by now himself the Tsar, called Eleazar to Moscow, and gave him the means to establish a fully brick-built monastery on Anzer. When he went back to his original monastery with this news, however, the monks refused to allow his foundation its independence, and accused him of subverting the proper hierarchy of the Church. Such was his meekness, however, that the monks eventually gave way. Eleazar died before he could see the building completed.

Eleazar of Murmansk, with Nazarius and Eumenius, monks, born Greece, died Murmansk, fifteenth century. Russian Church. Possibly the founders of the monastery of St John the Forerunner at Murmansk, and apostles to the Lap people of that region.

Eleda, abbess, born Northumbria, 653, died Whitby, 8 February 714. She was consecrated in infancy to the religious life by her father King Oswin of Northumbria and her mother Enfleda, in thanksgiving for the successful outcome of a battle. She spent her early life with **Hilda**, who was then abbess of Hartlepool. Later, at Whitby Abbey, both she and her mother became abbesses, during which time the *Life of Gregory the Great* was written there. She was a friend of **Cuthbert** and **Wilfrid**. As a skilled mediator, she effected the reconciliation of Wilfrid of Canterbury and the Church in Northumbria at the synod of the river Nidd (705). Her relics were discovered and translated at Whitby *c.* 1125.

Elena Guerra, bl., founder of the Oblate Sisters of the Holy Spirit, born Lucca, Italy, 23 June 1835, died there, 11 April 1914. Elena was born of a well-to-do, pious family, and was educated by a tutor. She was active in works of charity from an early age and eventually organized a number of young girls into an association following a common life and called the Pious Union of Spiritual Friendship. From these disciples she chose the first members of her congregation, founded in 1872 in honour of St **Zita**, to spread devotion to the Holy Spirit. The institution received the approval of the Holy See in 1911 as the Oblate Sisters of the Holy Spirit, but it is more commonly known as the Sisters of St Zita. In her efforts to promote devotion to the Holy Spirit, Elena wrote frequently to Pope Leo XIII, whose encyclical *Divinum Illud Munus* (1897) rewarded her efforts. She wrote some short devotional works, and was the teacher of St **Gemma Galgani**.

Elesbaan, king of Ethiopia, born Axum, died there (?), sixth century. He was urged by the patriarch of Alexandria to avenge the massacre at Najran which resulted in the death in 523 of **Aretas** and some 4,000 others, which he did. Feast 24 October.

Elessa, bl., martyr, born in the Peloponnese, died Citera, 375. The daughter of a pagan father and Christian mother, she was baptized and wanted to become a hermit. After her mother's death, however, her father wanted to marry her to a rich man, but she fled with two of her servants to the island of Citera. When her father returned from a long journey and discovered her missing, he went in search of her and tried to persuade her to return. She remained determined, and her father beheaded her.

Eleuchadius, second century. A Greek converted by **Apollinaris of Ravenna**, he governed the church there in his absence and eventually succeeded **Adheritus** as third bishop of Ravenna. Feast 14 February.

Eleutherius, pope, born Nicopolis, in the Epirus, Greece, pope from 174, died Rome, 189. He had been a deacon to pope **Anicetus**. Feast 26 May (suppressed 1969).

Eleutherius of Auxerre, bishop, died Auxerre, 562. He was bishop from 532. Feast 26 July.

Eleutherius of Nicomedia, martyr, died Nicomedia, c. 300. Said to have been a Roman soldier executed for trying to burn down the palace of the Emperor Diocletian. Feast 2 October.

Eleutherius of Tournai, bishop, born Tournai, c. 456, died there, c. 531. Information about Eleutherius comes from the *Vita S. Medardi* (c. 600), where he was said to have spent his early life at court. He was of Gallo-Roman birth and became both count and bishop of Tournai. He is said to have developed a thriving Christian community there. His first *Vita* was written in about 900, thus factual information about him is unreliable. Events credited to him such as the diocesan synod of 520 and certain writings are not definitely credited. Feast 20 February.

Elias, monk, fifteenth/sixteenth centuries. Ethiopian Church. The grandson of King Zara Ya'qob.

Elias Ardunis, born Calamata, died there, 31 January 1686. Byzantine Church. He was highly thought of in his own region as an authority in dealing with the Turks, but then suddenly he announced he was going to become a Muslim. He soon afterwards repented of his apostasy, and became a monk on Mount Athos. After eight years there he returned home and publicly declared his faith. He was arrested and tortured, but refused to renounce Christianity. He was burned alive.

Elias Facchini, born near Ferrara, Italy, 2 July 1839, martyred Taiyuan, Shanxi, China, 9 July 1900, beatified 1946, canonized 2000. Ordained in 1864, he had been training young clergy in Shanxi for 30 years. He was killed with **Gregory Grassi**'s group during the Boxer Rebellion – see **Franciscan Martyrs of China** and **Martyrs of Shanxi**. Feast 8 July.

Elias of Antioch, patriarch, died 723. Syriac Church. A monk of Gubba Baraya, he was originally a Melkite, but became a member of the Syriac Church through the writings of **Severus of Antioch**. He became bishop of Apamea in 691 and patriarch in 709. He enjoyed the high esteem of the caliph, but could not live in his patriarchal see because of the opposition of the Greeks.

Elias of Borovsk, monk, died Borovsk, fifteenth century. Russian Church. A monk of the monastery founded by **Paphnutius** at Borovsk.

Elias of Caesarea, martyr, born Egypt, died Caesarea, Palestine, 310. He died with several companions – Jeremias, Isaias, Samuel and Daniel. Eusebius describes how the Palestine governor Firmilian tortured and beheaded this group of Egyptian converts on their return from a visit to other converts condemned to the mines in Cilicia. Feast 16 February.

Elias of Hims, died Hims, 283/4. Syriac Church. A doctor who was betrayed by his father, he was martyred by having nails hammered into his head, hands and feet. Feast 6 February.

Elias of Hira, born Hira, died c. 585. Assyrian Church. He came from what is now south-west Iraq, but became a monk on Mount Izla, near Nisibis. He left there with his nephew and settled at Aburaya, on the right bank of the Tigris, not far from modern Mosul, where he founded a monastery before dying at the age of 100.

Elias of Jerusalem, patriarch and theologian, born 430, died Aila, 518. He lived as an anchorite in early life, but on the uprising of the monophysite persecution fled to Palestine and lived at the Laura in Sahel. He became patriarch of Jerusalem in 494. His life was marked by the controversies and allegiances surrounding monophysitism. His position was complex: he adhered to the Council of Chalcedon and entered into communion with Constantinopolitan patriarchs, but suffered from a misrepresentation of his position by Emperor Anastasius I, to whom he had made a profession of faith. He was exiled to Aila in 516 when he refused to sign a monophysite formula. Feast 4 July.

Elias of Murom, born Karacarovo, near Murom, died Kiev, 1188. Russian Church. Something of a mythical figure, he is said to have been a heroic soldier in the army of Prince Vladimir before becoming a monk.

Elias of Reggio (Spelaiotes), hermit, born Reggio di Calabria, *c.* 865, died Meluccà, Calabria, 11 September *c.* 960. His name, Spelaiotes, means 'cave-dweller', and he ended his life as a hermit in a cave near Meluccà. He entered monastic life at the age of 19, and lived as a hermit near Rome. He then lived with a companion called Arsenios at Armo. They both then spent some eight years at a hermitage at Patras, but Elias returned to the monastery of Saline in Calabria. He returned to eremitic life, where he stayed until his death. A group of disciples joined him at the hermitage.

Elias of Solovki, died on the Solovki islands, 1 June (July?) 1659. Church of the Old Believers. Born Pestrikov, he became hegumenos of his monastery in 1645 and archimandrite in 1651. His monastery served as a refuge for those opposed to the reforms of Patriarch Nikon, and when the new liturgical books arrived at the monastery Elias went to Moscow to protest.

Elias of Thessalonika ('the Less'), monk, born Enna, Sicily, 823, died Thessalonika, Greece, 17 August 903. Baptized as John, he was sold into slavery in 838 following the Saracen invasion of

Sicily, but was redeemed a few years later. As an act of thanksgiving he undertook a pilgrimage to the Holy Land, changing his name to Elias in honour of the patriarch of Jerusalem. When eventually he returned to Sicily, he established a monastery before setting out on a second pilgrimage, and was later received by the pope. Subsequently Elias was summoned to appear at the court of the Eastern Emperor at Byzantium, but died at Thessalonika en route.

Elias of Trebizond, martyr, born near Trebizond, died there, 1749. Byzantine Church. The son of a priest, he was arrested by the Turks for unknown reasons, ordered to renounce his faith and, when he refused, hanged.

Eligius of Noyon (Tournai), bishop, born Limousin, *c.* 588, died Noyon, 30 November 660. Eligius was from an old Gallo-Roman family, apprenticed as a goldsmith under the king's treasurer in the mint of Limoges. While still a layman, he founded the monastery of Solignac, and another for women at Paris. Eligius entered the clergy in 639 and was appointed bishop of Noyon in 641. At Noyon he founded a monastery and discovered the relics of St Quentin and St Paitus. He re-evangelized areas of his diocese that had reverted to paganism under the influence of Barbarian invasions. Feast 1 December.

Elinandus (Helinand), bl., from Pronleroy near Beauvais, died Froidemont, Franche-Comté, 1237. He was a court singer who became a Cistercian monk at Froidemont abbey. The Cistercians venerate him as a saint. Feast 3 February.

Elisbar, see **Bidzina, Scialva and Elisbar**.

Eliseus of Sumy, monk, fifteenth/sixteenth centuries. Russian Church. Nothing is known of his life except that he was a monk of the Solovki monastery who wished before he died to receive the habit of a monk of strict observance. There was no monk with the authority to invest him in his own monastery, so he was taken by river to Sumy, where such a monk lived. The journey proved very dangerous, but he remained calm, comforting his companions. When they eventually reached Sumy, Eliseus appeared to be dead, but the monks prayed to their founder St **Zosimus**, and Eliseus revived for long enough to receive the habit. Feast 14 June.

Eliseus of Tanhir, Syriac Church. Feast 24 October.

Eliseus of the Kievan Cave Monastery, monk

Elisha of St Clement, bl., nun, born Bari, 17 January 1901, died there, 25 December 1927. Baptized Theodora Fracasso, one of five children (four died as infants) of a painter and decorator. Exceptionally pious as a child, she had a vision interpreted by her mother as one of the Virgin. She joined the Third Order of the Dominicans in 1914, despite her young age, taking the name Agnes, but later left and in 1920 became a Carmelite with the name of Elisha of St Clement. In January 1927 she contracted influenza, and never fully recovered.

Elizabeth, died *c.* 1543. Serbian Church. The religious name of Princess Helena, wife of the despot Stefan Stiljanovic of Serbia, who became a nun after her husband's death. Feast 4 October.

Elizabeth Ann Seton, born New York City, 28 August 1774, died Emmitsburg, USA, 4 January 1821, beatified 1963, canonized 1975. Widowed young with small children, she became Catholic in 1805 and started a school in Boston to help pay the way for her family. This developed into the first US-founded congregation, the Daughters of Charity of St Joseph, who work with children, older people and the sick. She also founded a congregation, the Sisters of Charity, for native Americans. She is credited with paving the way for the parochial school system in the USA.

Elizabeth Bartholomea Picenardi, bl., born Mantua, 1428, died there, 1468, beatified 1804. She joined the third order of Servites, and girls from good families joined together to live under her direction. Feast 19 February.

Elizabeth Bichier des Ages, see **Jeanne Elizabeth Bichier des Ages**.

Elizabeth Fedorovna, princess, martyr, born Hesse, 1 November 1864, died Alapaevsk, 18 July 1918. Russian Church. A Lutheran by birth, she became Russian Orthodox in 1891 on her marriage to

Serge Aleksandrovic, a member of the Russian imperial family and, shortly after his marriage, governor of Moscow. He was assassinated in 1905, and the princess decided to found a convent of nuns at Moscow, dedicated to Ss Martha and Mary. The nuns were to be active as well as contemplative, and having trained in basic health care they opened a hospital. They continued their efforts during World War I, despite the princess being accused of spying for Germany. Shortly after the 1917 Revolution, at Easter, the princess, having refused to take refuge in the German embassy, was arrested and deported to Alapaevsk in Siberia, where she and other prisoners, including **Barbara Jakovleva**, a nun from her convent, were kept in an abandoned school. A year later they were thrown into a well. She did not fall the whole way, however, but was caught on a projection, and continued to sing hymns. She even bound the hand of one of the other victims who had fallen beside her. The executioners left them for the night but returned the following day, throwing in a grenade and blocking up the well. Their bodies were recovered by the White Russian Army and the body of the princess, together with that of Barbara, was eventually buried in the Garden of Gethsemane in Jerusalem. Elizabeth and Barbara were canonized in 1992. Feast 15 January.

Elizabeth of Hungary, princess, born Bratislava, 1207, died of exhaustion, Marburg, 1231. Following the death of her husband while on crusade in 1227, she and her three children were exiled from court. She lived as a Franciscan tertiary at Marburg. She sold her jewellery and clothes, and used the proceeds to build a hospital. Carrying out various works of charity, she had a concern for the poor, particularly lepers, whose sores she often washed. Believed to have performed miracles, she was canonized by Pope Gregory IX in 1235. Feast 17 November.

Elizabeth of Portugal, queen, born 1271, daughter of Peter III of Aragon, died Estremoz, Portugal, 4 July 1336. At the age of 12 she married the king of Portugal, who allowed her to continue with the many pious devotions she was accustomed to observe. She established a hospital and an orphanage. She acted as a peacemaker, successfully resolving disputes between rival royal factions.

During her later years she retired to a house she had built beside a convent of Poor Clares which she had founded near Coimbra.

Elizabeth of Ranfaing, ven., foundress, born Remiremont, 30 October 1592, died Nancy, 14 January 1649. Elizabeth had been coerced into marriage with an aged nobleman who maltreated her and, a widow at 24, she opened a refuge in Nancy, with her three daughters, for fallen women. Her congregation became Our Lady of Refuge, was approved by the Holy See in 1634 and attracted other houses of refuge, under the patronage of St **Ignatius** and with the Rule of St **Augustine** as a guide. Members were classified according to the moral status of their lives, and the rule specified that penitents proper should always constitute at least two-thirds of the community, so as to ensure the apostolic nature of the congregation.

Elizabeth of Schönau, Benedictine, born *c.* 1129, died 18 June 1165. She was professed at Schönau in 1147 and became superior in 1157. She was the subject of ecstasies and visions of many kinds, but feared that she may have been deceived. She was instructed by abbot Hildelin to report them to her brother Egbert, priest at Bonn. He put them in writing and they were published in three books of visions. She and her brother were certain of the authenticity of her visions, but doubt was cast on them by Eusebius Amort, who claimed they were imaginary or illusions of the devil, as they sometimes conflicted with history or other revelations.

Elizabeth of the Trinity, bl., Carmelite, born Elizabeth Catez, near Bourges, France, 1880, died of Addison's disease, 8 November 1906. Emphasizing holiness of life, in her writings she taught the possibility of the individual believer attaining the image of God by reliving the mysteries of the incarnate Word.

Elizabeth Renzi, bl., born Saludecio, near Rimini, 19 November 1786, died Coriani, Emilia, 14 August 1859. She came from a devout family and entered the Augustinians in 1807. Three years later, however, religious orders were dissolved. In 1818 she became a teacher at a school for poor girls at Coriani, and eventually founded, a new order, in

1839, the Sisters of Our Lady of Sorrows, for teaching the poor and destitute.

Elizabeth the Good, bl., mystic, born Waldsee, Würtemberg, 25 November 1386, died Reute, 25 November 1420. She came from a relatively poor family called Achler. She was always devout, and her confessor recommended that she become a Franciscan tertiary. She first learned weaving, but after entering a community at Reute she became the cook. She experienced visions, the stigmata from time to time, and occasionally apparently possession by the devil. Feast 17 November.

Elladius the Recluse, died Kiev, twelfth/thirteenth centuries. A monk of the Kievan Cave monastery. Feast 4 October.

Ellenus or **Ellinus**, abbot, sixth century. Feast 23 January.

Ellerius, abbot in Tuscany, died 558. Feast 15 May.

Elmo, or Erasmus, bishop of Formiae, Campania, Italy, martyred *c.* 303. According to legend he was tortured during the Diocletian persecutions and died of his wounds. Another legend states that he died by having his intestines wound out of his body on a windlass. He became the patron saint of sailors, and the blue electrical discharge seen in the rigging of ships was known as St Elmo's fire – a sign of his protection. Feast 2 June.

Elmo, see also **Peter Gonzalez**, bl., this name given to Peter Gonzalez by Portuguese and Spanish sailors arises from a confusion with **Elmo or Erasmus**.

Elpidius, see **Basil, Eugene**, et al.

Elpidius, Marcellus Eustace and Companions, martyrs, died 362. Elpidius was a member of the court of the Arian Emperor Constantius, and was then martyred with his companions under the pagan Emperor Julian by being tortured, then burned alive. Feast 16 November.

Elpidius of Aversa, bishop, possibly fifth century. Feast 15 January.

Elzéar of Sabran, count of Ariano, born in the castle of Saint-Jean, Provence, 1285, died Paris, 27 September 1325. He studied in the abbey of St Victor at Marseilles, and although he married (blessed) **Delphina** of the house of Glandèves in 1299, they both took vows of chastity. At the death of his father he returned home to claim his inheritance, was met by hostility from his vassals, but won them over. In 1312 he led an army to aid the pope against the Emperor Henry VII, and in 1324 he was sent as the king of Naples's ambassador to Paris, which is where he died. He was a Franciscan tertiary, and was buried in the Franciscan habit. He had a reputation for generosity and kindliness and Urban V, Elzéar's own godchild, formally recognized his sanctity, although the proclamation of it took place under Gregory XI. Feast 26 November.

Emebert of Cambrai, bishop, died before 645. Identification of Emebert is problematic. He is held to have been bishop of Cambrai-Arras after 627 and before 645, and could possibly have been chorbishop of Brabant. No other certain life details are available. Feast 15 January.

Emerentiana, martyred Rome, c. 304. According to her ancient (and now local) cult, she was the foster sister of **Agnes**, and was stoned by the pagan mob when found praying at the tomb of the recently martyred Agnes. Feast 23 January.

Emeric de Quart, bl., bishop, died Aosta, 1313. Bishop of Aosta from 1301. Feast 1 August.

Emeric (Imre) of Hungary, bl., prince, died 1031. Son of St **Stephen**, first king of Hungary, Emeric had been his father's choice for successor, but died in a hunting accident. Feast 4 November.

Emeterius, see **Hemiterius**.

Emilian(us), see also **Millán**.

Emilian of Cyzicus, bishop, died c. 820. He was bishop of Cyzicus on the Sea of Marmara, but was exiled for his opposition to iconoclasm, and died in exile. Feast 8 August.

Emilian of Grevena, metropolitan, martyr, born Iconium, 1871, died near Schinovo, 1 October 1911. Byzantine Church. Born Emilianus Lazaridis, he studied at the seminary of Chalki, then became deacon at a church in Pelagonija before becoming bishop of Petra and then metropolitan of Grevena. Although outstanding because of the holiness of his life, he was also a fervent (Macedonian) patriot, and it was because of this that he was assassinated. He was buried in his cathedral church.

Emily (Emilia) Bicchieri, bl., born Vercelli, Italy, 1238, died there, 3 May 1314. With the money she inherited from her father she established in Vercelli a Dominican convent, dedicated to St Margaret, which she entered, and which she served several times as prioress.

Emily de Rodat, born Druelle, near Rodez, 6 April 1787, died Villefranche-de-Romergue, 19 December 1852. Always concerned for the needs of the poor, Emily tried her vocation in various religious congregations before opening a school for poor girls in Villefranche, where she founded, with Abbé Antoine Marty, the Sisters of the Holy Family of Villefranche, dedicated to educational and charitable works among the poor. Her own sanctification included many spiritual trials against the temptation to abandon her faith. Pius XII canonized her in 1950.

Emily de Vialar, foundress, born Gaillac (Tarn), 12 September 1797, died Marseilles, 24 August 1856. Of the minor nobility, she refused to marry, took a private vow of chastity and devoted herself to the sick and the poor. In 1832, with an inheritance, she established a house in Gaillac and founded the Sisters of St Joseph of the Apparition, which received episcopal approval in 1835. The Sisters were devoted to educating children and caring for the sick, and were distinguished in Algeria for their heroic care of the afflicted during a cholera epidemic. When, in 1840, Bishop Dupuch of Algiers tried to submit the congregation totally to his aims, Emily opposed him and the Sisters were excommunicated and dismissed from the diocese. The Sisters encountered many obstacles in France in pursuit of their apostolate, and finally settled the mother house in Marseilles. By Emily's own vigorous leadership, the Congregation grew by the time of her death to more than 40 houses in France, the Near East and also Burma and Australia. She was canonized in 1951.

Emma, see **Hemma**.

Emmanuel, bishop, martyred Bulgaria, *c.* 813. He is commemorated with **George** and **Leo**, also bishops, and **Peter**, a priest, and 37 companions. Feast 22 January.

Emmanuel Domingo y Sol, bl., born Tarragona, Spain, 1 April 1836, died Tortosa, 25 January 1909, beatified 1987. Ordained in 1860, he was a parish priest, then theology lecturer at the diocesan seminary. He founded the Spanish College in Rome. He was a friend and relative of **Henry (Enrique) de Ossó y Cervelló**.

Emmanuel Ruiz and Companions, bl., martyrs of Damascus, died 1860. The resentment felt by many Muslims in the aftermath of the Crimean War in part caused the massacre of Christians in Syria in 1860. The Druse, a Syrian Muslim sect, were unhappy about the spread of Christianity into traditionally Muslim areas, and a number of minor attacks led to open conflict in the spring of that year. The Christians had been disarmed and so were unable to defend themselves, and about 14,000 Christians were murdered. About 2,000 of these were in Damascus, where there was a large Christian population. Eleven of those murdered were beatified in 1926, eight Franciscan friars and three Maronite lay people. The Franciscans were Emmanuel Ruiz, Carmel Volta, Nicanor Ascanio, Nicolás Alberca, Francisco Pinazo, Juan Jaime and Engelbert Kolland. The lay people were three brothers who had been sheltering in the friary: Francis, Abdul-Muti and Raphael Masabki. Feast 10 July.

Emmelia, see **Basil**.

Emmerham, or Emmeram, martyr, preacher, possibly a bishop, died *c.* 660. Emmerham's original name was Hainhramm. He was patron of the monastery at Sankt Emmeram, where he was buried, in 737. He was honoured as a martyr. No other facts are known about his life. In art he is shown in bishop's robes, either pierced by a lance or bound to a ladder and mutilated.

Emygdius of Ancona, bishop, martyr, died Ancona, 5 August 303/4. According to legend, Emygdius was a Barbarian from Trier who converted to Christianity there. At an early age he went to Rome and undertook vigorous missionary activity under the guidance of Pope **Marcellus I**. He was beheaded at Ancora under the Diocletian persecution of 303/4, with saints Eupolus, Germanus and Valentinius. In his cult he is considered an effective protector against earthquakes.

Enbaqom, monk, born Yemen, *c.* 1470, died Dabra Libanos, Ethiopia, *c.* 1565. Ethiopian Church. Originally called Abu'lfath, he left the Yemen when still a young man to travel to Ethiopia, where after a few years he became a member of the court of King Eskender. After the king's death, on deciding to become a Christian, he entered the monastery of Dabra Libanos, where he received his new name in baptism and became a monk. He became a priest and eventually, after some 20 years, head of the monastery, but then, because of some calumnies, he was driven into exile. After the Islamic invasion he was called back as a counsellor to the royal court. Finally the king of the day sent him back as head of the monastery of Dabra Libanos, where he died a year later.

Eneco, abbot, born Aragon, died Oña, Spain, 1057. He was a monk of the abbey of San Juan de la Peña before becoming a hermit. He was asked by the king of Castile to take charge of the monastery at Oña, to which he agreed, after much initial hesitation. Under his rule the abbey flourished. He was renowned for his tolerance. Feast 1 June.

Eneda, abbess, born York, 626 (?), died Whitby, *c.* 704. The daughter of King Edwin of Northumbria, she went to her mother's family in Kent after her father was killed in battle in 633, but returned to Northumbria to marry King Oswiu of Bernicia. She was an active supporter of the Roman tradition, rather than of the Celtic one in which she had been brought up. Her husband remained for a time in the Celtic tradition, leading to two celebrations of Easter on different days. It was this which led to the Synod of Whitby, which came down in favour of Roman practices. After the death of her husband in 670, she entered the abbey at Whitby and eventually succeeded **Hilda** as abbess. Feast 24 November.

Engelbert of Cologne, bishop, born Berg, 1185, assassinated near Schwelm, 7 November 1225. Due mainly to family connections, he quickly ascended the ecclesiastical hierarchy, becoming archbishop of Cologne in 1217. He spent most of his life as a statesman, being guardian of King Henry VII, son of Emperor Frederick II, and was murdered by political opponents. The immediate cause of his death, however, which he himself had expected and had prepared for, was his defence of a convent of nuns against the oppression of their supposed protector. He was therefore honoured as a martyr.

Engelmund, abbot, born England, died Velsen, near Haarlem, Holland, 720. He was a missionary to Friesland, born in England, but having lived in Friesland with his parents, so he spoke the language. He was an abbot before he went, so presumably a monk of some English abbey, but it is not known which one. Feast 21 June.

Ennodius of Pavia, bishop, born Arles, *c.* 473, died 521. He became bishop of Pavia in 514 and was already involved in controversy, having written a defence of Pope St **Symmachus** against the antipope Laurence. He was twice sent by Pope St **Hormisdas** to meet the patriarch of Constantinople, to try to reconcile the two Churches, but was not successful. He is best known as a prolific writer, and his works are particularly useful today as a reflection of the culture and events of his time. Feast 17 July.

Eoban, bishop, died Dokkum, 5 June 754. Eoban was an Anglo-Saxon missionary and bishop in the Netherlands. Originally a messenger for St **Boniface**, he later became his amanuensis. He was sent to England by Boniface and elevated to chorbishop. He accompanied Boniface on his last mission amongst the Frisians, and was martyred with him at Dokkum.

Eoglodius (Eucadius), abbot, seventh century. He was a disciple of **Columba**. Feast 25 January.

Eonius, bishop, died Arles, 520. Bishop of Arles. Feast 18 August.

Epaphroditus, bishop, first century. Said to be one of the Gospel's 72 disciples, St Paul sent him to Philippi, Macedonia, where he is identified as first bishop. Two other first-century saints named Epaphroditus, one considered to be the first bishop of Andriacia, Lycia, and the other the first bishop of Terracina, Italy, are probably the same person. Feast 18 May.

Eparchius, monk, born Perigord, France, *c.* 504, died Angoulême, France, 1 July 581. Eparchius entered the monastic life despite parental opposition, while he was still young. He served there under abbot Martin, gaining a reputation for virtue and the gift of miracles. He left the monastery to live in solitude at Angoulême, but the bishop of the area obliged him to receive ordination to the priesthood. Eparchius accepted disciples, but required them to live completely dependent upon providence, and to be devoted to prayer.

Ephebus, bishop in Campania, fourth century. Feast 23 May.

Ephebus, see also **Proculus**.

Ephraim, bl., martyr, born 14 September 1384, died 5 May 1426. Byzantine Church. An orphan, at 14 he entered the monastery of the Annunciation on Mount Amomon in Attica. In 1425, when returning to his monastery, he discovered all the monks killed and the monastery itself destroyed by a raiding party of Turks. He was himself taken prisoner, tortured and eventually executed.

Ephraim, patriarch, born not far from present-day Sofia, 1311, died Pec, 15 June 1399/1400. Serbian Church. He was born into the family of a priest, who wished him to marry. However, he fled to Mount Athos where he entered the Serbian monastery of Chilandar. When Mount Athos was attacked by Turks, he fled first to an island in the Aegean, then returned to Serbia. In 1375 he was elected the first legitimate patriarch of the Serbian Church, after the rift with Constantinople had been healed. In 1380 he was succeeded by the patriarch Spiridion, but once again became patriarch after the battle of Kosovo in 1389, and remained in office until his death.

Ephraim Mazqvereli ('the Great'), born Kartli, died Azuri, 885. Georgian Church. The son of the prince of Kartli, he became a monk, and then in 845 bishop of Azuri. He was given permission by the patriarch of Jerusalem to consecrate chrism for his own use – hitherto it had been brought from Jerusalem. This is taken as marking the beginning of the independent Georgian Church. Feast 17 April.

Ephraim Mzire, monk, ninth century. Georgian Church. After a theological education in Constantinople, in 1097 he was elected hegumenos of the monastery of Kalipos in Syria, where he began his life's work as a translator, contributing greatly to Georgian spiritual literature. Feast 18 January.

Ephraim of Novotorz, monk, born Hungary, died Torzok, 28 January 1053. Russian Church. With his brothers **George** and Moses he entered the service of the prince of Rostov. In 1015 the prince was assassinated, and George with him, beside the river Alt. Moses managed to escape, and became a monk at the Kievan Cave monastery. Ephraim, who was in Rostov at the time of the murder, became a hermit not far from Torzok, but in 1038 he founded a monastery, dedicated to Ss Boris and Gleb, of which he was elected hegumenos.

Ephraim of Obnora, with Dionysius, Jerome and Isaac, monks, died Obnora, January 1538. Monks of the monastery of the Most Holy Trinity in the forest of Komel near Vologda, they were killed in a raid by Tartars, being too old to flee into the woods. The monastery itself was set alight and destroyed.

Ephraim of Perejaslavl, monk, born 1615, died Perejaslavl, 1 July 1701. Russian Church. By birth Prince Ivan Petrovic Borjatinski, and married, he was an extremely generous benefactor of the monastery of Troick Danilov in Perejaslavl. In 1697 he himself entered the monastery.

Ephraim of Perekom, hegumenos, born Kasina, 1412, died near Novgorod, 1492. Russian Church. He entered a monastery in his home town, but

after three years moved to the monastery of St Saba at Viserskoe, near Novgorod, taking the name Ephraim in place of Eustace, with which he had been baptized. He lived there up to the age of 50, but then, seeking greater solitude, he established a hermitage near lake Ilmen, which in time attracted other monks, becoming a monastery with Ephraim as hegumenos. To provide the monastery with water he constructed a canal from the lake, and it is from the Russian for 'canal' that his name is derived.

Ephraim of Rostov, archbishop, died 1454. Russian Church. He became archbishop of Rostov on 13 April 1427, a founder and protector of monasteries, and supporter of the prince of Moscow against the ambitions of the prince of Galic. He also took part in the council of 1440/1 which condemned the metropolitan Isidore of Moscow for having agreed to the union of the Churches East and West at the Council of Ferrara-Florence. He presided at a council in Moscow in 1448 which chose a new metropolitan for Moscow independently of the patriarch of Constantinople, the first time this happened. After the new metropolitan had been consecrated, he raised Ephraim to the rank of archbishop. Feast 29 March.

Ephraim of Smolensk, monk, died Smolensk, c. 1237 (?). Russian Church. Known only as the author of a life of St **Abraham of Smolensk**.

Ephraim of the Kievan Cave Monastery, born Kiev, died there, 1098. Russian Church. Before entering the monastery he had been treasurer to the grand prince of Kiev, Izjaslav, who was opposed to him entering the monastery and threatened to attack it until dissuaded by his wife. It was considered safer, however, if Ephraim left his monastery, and he went to Constantinople, where he transcribed the Studite Rule, which was then adopted in the Kievan Cave monastery. In 1072 he became metropolitan of Perejaslavl, where he built a hospital for the poor and fortified the city.

Ephraim of the Kievan Cave Monastery, monk, thirteenth century. Russian Church. Venerated in the monastery, nothing is known of him except that he was a priest.

Ephraim the Syrian, poet, theologian, born Nisibis, *c.* 306, died Edessa, *c.* 373. Ephraim is the most important Syrian Church Father, and the greatest poet of the patristic period. Born of Christian parents, he grew up under the tutelage of Bishop Jacob, with whom he founded the theological school of Nisibis. Ephraim was a 'son of the covenant' (rather than a 'monk'), living in abstinence and virginity within the Christian community. Many legends arose concerning his life through monastic circles. Ephraim's works are many and include hymns and poems. Feast 9 June.

Ephrem, see **Basil, Eugene**, et al.

Epimachus of Arwat, monk, seventh century. Ethiopian Church.

Epimachus of Alexandria, martyr, died Alexandria, *c.* 250. His relics were translated to Rome and he is commemorated with **Gordian**, who was later buried in his tomb in Rome. Feast 10 May.

Epiphanius, martyr, died Pustozersk, 14 April 1682. Church of the Old Believers. After the death of his parents in 1638, he left his native village and settled in a city before going in 1645 to the Solovki monastery, where he became a monk. Unwilling to accept the liturgical reforms, he left the monastery and lived in various hermitages. In 1666–7, however, he went to Moscow and accused Patriarch Nikon and the Tsar of betraying Orthodoxy. He was arrested, tortured and sent into exile to Pustozersk. He continued to teach until, in April 1670, his tongue was torn out and his right arm amputated. His speech was miraculously restored, but he was eventually burned to death.

Epiphanius of Constantia (modern Salamis), bishop, born near Eleutheropolis, Palestine, *c.* 315, died at sea, May 402. A native of Syria and a convert from Judaism, Epiphanius studied classics in Egypt and also knew Coptic and Hebrew. He founded a monastery at Eleutheropolis and remained there for 30 years before his ordination. In 367 he was selected for the see of Constantia. A strong supporter of **Athanasius**'s doctrine, he opposed the Arians and Origenists. Epiphanius broke allegiance with Meletius over *homoousios*, and opposed philosophy. His *Ancoratus* (374)

deals with the Trinity and opposes Apollinarianism. His *Panarion* (374, 376) is a tract against heretics. He also produced *De mensuris et ponderibus* and *De duodecim gemmis*. Feast 12 May.

Epiphanius of Pavia, bishop, born Pavia, 438, died there, 496. Epiphanius became bishop of Pavia in 466 after a rapidly rising ecclesiastical career. He worked towards peace during a time of strife and intervened in disputes between various Germanic kings. He contributed to the rebuilding of Pavia, and obtained its exemption from tribute. Feast 21 January.

Epiphanius the Wise, monk, died Zagorsk, fourteenth/fifteenth centuries. Russian Church. Little is known about him. He was a monk in a monastery at Rostov, where he acquired great learning. He visited Constantinople, Mount Athos and the Holy Land, and eventually settled in the monastery of St **Sergius of Radonez**, at Zagorsk, near Moscow, where he studied and wrote the lives of the saints. Feast 12 May.

Eptadius, born Autun, France, *c.* 490, died Montelon, France, 550. Eptadius was married at 20, and shortly after was struck by a fever. He received a vision of three holy women, which rekindled his faith. He recovered from his fever and led a life of austerity and penance. Bishop Flavian tried to ordain him, but Eptadius fled. He was appointed a bishop by King Clovis, but refused the dignity. As a compromise he accepted priesthood, withdrawing to a monastic community in Cervon. He was noted for his charity. Feast 24 August.

Equba Egzi, monk. Ethiopian Church.

Equitius, abbot, born in the Abruzzi, Italy, died Pescara (?), *c.* 560 (?). Originally a hermit, he founded a monastery at Terni as well as other communities, both for men and for women. Feast 11 August.

Erasmus, see **Elmo**.

Erasmus of the Kievan Cave Monastery, died Kiev, 1160. Russian Church. He spent all his money on icons and adorning churches, then felt that he ought to have given his wealth to the poor. He was assured of his salvation in a vision of the Virgin Mary, and of Ss **Theodosius** and **Anthony**. Feast 24 February.

Erastus, bishop, born Corinth (?), died Philippi (?), first century. The city treasurer of Corinth and a convert of St Paul.

Erblon, see **Hermeland**.

Ercongota (Earcongota, Earcongotha, or Erkongota), born Kent, England, died near Meaux, France, c. 660. Descended from **Ethelbert of Kent**, she was daughter to Erconbert and **Sexburga** of Kent, sister of **Ermengild** and niece to **Ethelburga** and **Ethelreda**. She joined her two aunts at the monastery of Faremoûtiers-en-Brie and died relatively young. Feast 23 February.

Erconwald of London, bishop, monk, born Lindsey, c. 630 of royal blood, died Barking Abbey, 30 April c. 693. Erconwald was attracted to the monastic life and founded a community at Cherts, and an abbey at Barking under the direction of his sister **Ethelburga**. In 675 he was appointed bishop of London. He enlarged his cathedral and diocese. He worked for the reconciliation of **Wilfrid** of York and **Theodore**. After 11 years as bishop he retired to Barking. He was buried at St Paul's Cathedral.

Erembert, born Villiolicourt, Seine-et-Oise, c. 615, died Fontenelle, Normandy, 14 May 672. He served King Clotaire II, who appointed him bishop of Toulouse in 656. Leaving in 661 due to political difficulties, he retired home where he founded a small monastery. He later joined Fontenelle Abbey under **Lambert**.

Erhard, bishop, missionary, born Narbonne, France, died Regensburg, Germany. Details of Erhard's life are unclear, the main information coming from a mid-eleventh-century monk. Erhard is reputed to have been a zealous missionary and the founder of seven monasteries. He was also a regional missionary bishop with a great reputation for sanctity. Feast 8 January.

Eric of Sweden, king, died Uppsala, 18 May 1161. On becoming king of Sweden in 1150, he aimed with the help of **Henry of Uppsala** at converting the Finns to Christianity. However, he was killed when Uppsala was attacked by a Danish prince. Due mainly to the efforts of Eric's son Cnut to present his father as a martyr, Eric became the national saint of the Swedes until the Reformation.

Erkomodo, bishop, abbot, died Thérouanne, 12 April 734. He was accepted into the abbey of Ss Peter and Paul before 709, and became fourth abbot of the monastery in 717. Erkomodo developed the abbey's liturgical practices and intensified its life of prayer. He also bought neighbouring lands to increase the property of the monastery. In 720 he became bishop of Thérouanne, and became the object of a popular cult.

Erlembald, Milanese reformer, died Milan, Italy, 28 June 1075. After the death of his brother Landulf, Erlembald, a knight and a member of the influential Cotta family, led the military forces supporting the ecclesiastical reform of Milan. The opposition to the reform, led by Archbishop Guido Velate (died 1071), had the support of Emperor Henry IV and was ascendent until the election of Pope **Gregory VII** in 1073. Erlembald was killed in a street battle against the anti-reformers in 1075 and was canonized by Pope Urban II 20 years later. Feast 27 June.

Ermelinde, died Meldaert, near Brussels, 29 October, end of the sixth century. Ermelinde belonged to a rich family in Brabant, which had connections with the Carolingian family of Pepin I. According to legend, Ermelinde left home to avoid an arranged marriage, taking up a life of asceticism in a hermitage, first at Beauvechan, and later at Meldaert, Belgium. It was alleged that she founded a monastery at Meldaert.

Ermenburga, Anglo-Saxon queen, died Thanet, c. 695. Also known as Domna Ebba, or Domneva. Married when young to Mereweld, son of Penda, by whom she had three daughters and one son. She was given estates on Thanet as compensation for the death of her brothers in battle. Ermenburga retired there on the death of her husband, and founded the abbey of Thanet. She was succeeded as abbess by her daughter. Feast 19 November.

Ermengard, bl., abbess, born *c.* 832, died 16 July 866. Daughter of King Louis the German, and granddaughter of **Charlemagne**. She was appointed abbess of the monastery of Buchau by her father, and later she was made abbess of the royal abbey of Chiemsee, Bavaria. She was known for her virtue and good works, and for her care of the members of her houses.

Ermengild, born Kent, died Ely, *c.* 700. Descended from **Ethelbert of Kent**, daughter of Erconbert, king of Kent, and of **Sexburga**, sister of **Ercongota**, niece of **Ethelburga** and **Ethelreda**, wife of Wulfhere, king of Mercia and mother of **Werburga**. She converted her husband and, after his death, became a nun, eventually becoming abbess at Ely abbey after her aunt and her mother. Feast 13 February.

Ermin, abbot, born Herly, France, late seventh century, died Lobbes, Belgium. Ermin was born of a noble family and became chaplain and confessor to Madelgar, bishop of Laon. He entered the monastery of Lobbes, after befriending Abbot **Ursmar**. On Ursmar's resignation Ermin became abbot in 711/12. Together with Ursmar, he is patron saint of Lobbes.

Erminfrid, monk, seventh century, died monastery of Luxeuil. Of noble stock, Erminfrid spent part of his youth at the court of Clothair II. In 625 he retired (with his brother) to the area of Cusance for a life of piety. In 627 Erminfrid entered the Celtic monastic life at Luxeuil. He inherited the empty nunnery at Isalia in Cusance and restored it, to re-establish monastic life there for men, under the guidance of Eustace of Luxeuil. Feast 25 September.

Ernest of Zwiefalten, abbot and martyr, died Mecca, 1148. Not much is known of Ernest's early life. He was abbot of Zwiefalten in Swabia for five years. Because of disruptive factions at the monastery, he abdicated and set off on pilgrimage to the Holy Land together with Bishop Otto of Friesing, who accompanied Conrad III to the Crusades. Ernest, according to legend, was tortured and killed in Mecca by Saracens. Ernest is regarded as a saint at Zwiefalten, but has not been officially recognized. Feast 7 November.

Eskil, bishop and martyr, born possibly in England, died Strängnäs, Sweden, *c.* 1080. According to tradition he accompanied **Sigfrid** on an evangelistic mission to Sweden, the Swedes having relapsed into paganism after the first missionary journeys of St **Ansgar** in the ninth century. He was consecrated bishop at Strängnäs, and it was there that he was stoned to death at a pagan gathering. Feast 6 September.

Estenfasa Krestos, monk. Ethiopian Church. Founder of the monastery of Asgaj, at Dawent.

Esterwine, abbot, from Northumbria, died Wearmouth, *c.* 688. He succeeded **Benedict Biscop** as abbot of the Benedictine abbey of Wearmouth. Feast 7 March.

Ethbin, hermit, born Britain, died Ireland, sixth century. Of noble parents, he was brought up by **Samson** after his father died. He then went to Brittany, where he entered a monastery. The monastery was, however, destroyed during the Frankish invasion, and he moved to Ireland, where he became a hermit. Feast 19 October.

Ethelbert of East Anglia, king and martyr, assassinated Sutton Wells, near Hereford, England, on the orders of Offa II of Mercia, 749. Ethelbert is described as a pious youth disposed to celibacy, although he wanted to marry Elfthryth, Offa's daughter. Ethelbert became patron saint of Hereford. Feast 20 May.

Ethelbert of Kent, born 550, died Canterbury, 24 February 616. Ethelbert was head of the confederation of Anglo-Saxon kingdoms south of the Humber, and was the first Christian king of England. He was married to Bertha, a Christian princess, wife of a Frankish king who ruled in Paris. He welcomed **Augustine of Canterbury** as missionary and allowed him freedom of action and a place to stay at Canterbury. Ethelbert was baptized *c.* 601, and built several churches. There is also a code of law attributed to him. He is thought to have reigned for 56 years.

Ethelburga, abbess, died Lyming, 644. Ethelburga (also known as Tata) was the daughter of King Albert and Bertha. Ethelburga married the pagan king Edwin of Northumbria, and travelled to meet him accompanied by Bishop **Paulinus**, who became the first bishop of York. Together with Paulinus, Ethelburga spread Christianity to the north. After she gave birth to a daughter, Edwin converted to Christianity. On his death (in battle) Ethelburga returned to Lyming (Lymynge) and founded an abbey.

Ethelburga, abbess, died Barking 676. Ethelburga was the sister of Bishop **Erconwald of London**, and the first abbess of the double monastery at Barking. Feast 12 October.

Ethelburga, abbess, died Faremoûtiers-en-Brie, 695. Ethelburga was the sister of **Ethelreda**, and was the abbess of Faremoûtiers when she died. Feast 7 July.

Ethelnot (Aethelnoth) of Canterbury, archbishop, died Canterbury, 29 October 1038. Ethelnot served as a monk of Glastonbury and dean of Christ Church, Canterbury before **Wulfstan** of Worcester, the archbishop of York, consecrated him as archbishop of Canterbury in 1020. Benedict VIII gave him the pallium during a visit to Rome in 1022. He served King Canute as chief adviser. The king bestowed upon Ethelnot the earliest known writ of judicial and financial authority given to an English prelate. He arranged for the removal of the martyr **Alphege of Canterbury**'s relics from London to Canterbury in 1023.

Ethelreda of Northumbria, queen, abbess, born Suffolk, *c.* 630, died from the plague, Ely, 23 June 679. Ethelreda was the daughter of Anna, king of East Anglia. She was married to Tonbert, a prince of the Gyrvii. Tonbert endowed to her what is now known as Ely. Ethelreda lived in virginity with him, entering a convent after his death. She was married again, for diplomatic reasons, to Egfrid, once more living in virginity. She returned to the convent after 12 years, eventually becoming abbess at Ely.

Ethelwald (Oidilwald), died Farne Island, *c.* 700. He was a Benedictine at Ripon abbey who succeeded **Cuthbert** as a hermit on Farne, where he lived for 12 years. Feast 23 March.

Ethelwold of Winchester, bishop and reformer, born 908, died Beddington, Surrey, 1 August 984. Trained at Glastonbury under St **Dunstan**. In *c.* 954 he was given the task of re-establishing Abingdon abbey and in 963 he was consecrated bishop of Winchester. With St **Oswald** he helped to reform English monasticism, expelling the secular clerks from Winchester, Chertsey and other establishments. He founded several monasteries, including Peterborough and Ely. He translated the Rule of St **Benedict** and the *Regularis concordia* into English.

Eubulus, born Rome, died there (?), first century. A disciple of St Paul.

Eubulus, martyr, died Caesarea, Palestine, 7 March 308, with **Adrian**, while visiting Christians there.

Eucherius of Lyon, bishop, born Lyon (?), died there, *c.* 449. He came from a wealthy family, married and had two sons, both of whom became bishops. He entered the monastery of Lérins, but went off to the island of Ste Marguerite to become a hermit, where, among other writings, he composed a book in praise of the life of a hermit. He was elected bishop of Lyon *c.* 434, an office he served with distinction. Feast 16 November.

Eucherius of Orléans, bishop, died monastery of Saint-Trond, 738. Eucherius was born into an influential Merovingian family and was destined for the monastic life from an early age. He was professed at the Benedictine abbey of Jumièges *c.* 709. Seven years later he was elected bishop of Orléans, against his will. He was arrested due to family allegiances in 732, by Charles Martel, and sent into exile in Cologne. Eucherius was subsequently allowed to return to the abbey of Saint-Trond.

Eudaimos I Diasamidze, patriarch, martyr, died Kartli, eastern Georgia, 1643. Georgian Church. From bishop of Bodbe he was raised to the rank of patriarch/catholicos of Kartli in 1639. A supporter of King Teimuraz I, the patriarch conspired against the Muslim usurper of Teimuraz's throne, and was assassinated when the plot was discovered. Feast 14 October.

Eudochimus, Gregory, and Companions, born Caransk, died there, seventeenth century. Church of the Old Believers. They were tortured, imprisoned and in some cases killed for their adherence to the traditional liturgy. Feast 9 August.

Euchochimus of Vataopedi, bl., died monastery of Vatopedi, Mount Athos. Byzantine Church. His relics were discovered in 1841. Nothing is known of his life. Feast 5 October.

Eudocia, martyr, died Vernyj, 1918. Russian Church. She was a nun of the monastery in Vernyj, with **Seraphim** as her spiritual director. She was shot when the Red Army visited the monastery looking for the superior, who was the daughter of a general.

Eudocia of Heliopolis, martyr, born Samaria, died Heliopolis, c. 105. Said to have been a converted prostitute, who died in the persecution of Trajan. Feast 1 March.

Eudoxia of Suzdal, died Suzdal, 22 September 1776. Russian Church. Little is known about her, except that for 20 years she wandered around Suzdal as a 'fool for Christ', beating herself about the head with sticks and stones.

Eudoxia of Vladimir, princess, thirteenth century. Russian Church. A daughter of **Alexander Nevski**. Feast 29 June.

Eudoxius, Zeno, Macarius and Companions, martyrs, died Melitene, c. 311. A group of soldiers, martyred in Armenia. Feast 5 September.

Eugendus of Condat, abbot, born c. 450, died Condat, 1 January 510 or 517. Eugendus was entrusted to Ss Romanus and Lipicinus as a child, who had earlier founded the monastery of Condat (today Saint-Claude). Eugendus stayed there until his death, esteemed for humility and learning. He was renowned for his knowledge of Greek, which was unusual for his day. Eugendus rebuilt the monastery, patterning its life on the Eastern monasticism of **Basil of Caesarea** and **John Cassian**.

Eugene Bossilkov, bl., bishop and martyr, born Belene, northern Bulgaria, 16 November 1900, died Sofia, 11 November 1952. He was baptized a Latin-rite Catholic with the name Vincent. He studied with the Passionists and entered the Congregation, being ordained in July 1926, having studied in Holland as well as at Ruse in Bulgaria. He then studied in Rome before beginning work as a parish priest in Bardaski-Gheran. He became bishop of Nikopol in 1947. He was arrested for alleged anti-Communist activities in July 1952, and was either shot or died in prison.

Eugene, see also **Eugenius**.

Eugenia, abbess, died 735. Eugenia succeeded her aunt (St **Odilia**) as abbess of Odilienberg in 722, leading the community until her death in 735. Her father was Duke Adalbert of Alsace. She had two sisters, Attala and Gunlid. Eugenia was revered for her holy life and wise government. Feast 16 September.

Eugenia of Rome, martyr, died Rome, 250 (?). Nothing is known of her, although a basilica was built at her grave on the via Latina. There was a folk tale that she disguised herself as a monk, and lived in a monastery in Rome. Feast 25 December.

Eugenia, Philip, Claudia and Companions, martyrs, born Alexandria, died Rome, second century. Eugenia was the daughter of Philip and Claudia. According to tradition, she dressed as a man and became a monk, and was eventually martyred in Rome. Feast 24 December.

Eugénie Smet, see **Mary of Providence**.

Eugenius, martyred fourth century, commemorated with **Canidius**, **Valerian** and **Aquila**. Feast 20 January.

Eugenius, bishop, born Ireland, died Ardstraw, County Tyrone (?), sixth century. The see of Ardstraw was the predecessor to that of Derry. Feast 23 August.

Eugenius, see **Basil, Eugene**, et al.

Eugenius, see also **Vindemialis**.

Eugenius I, pope, born Rome, elected to the papacy 10 August 654, died Rome, 2 June 657. Eugenius was brought up in the Church's ministry from childhood. As an elderly presbyter he was elected pope after the deposition of **Martin I**, by Emperor Constans II. The main theological issue of his reign concerned the nature of the will of Christ. Eugenius had the reputation of a conciliatory pope, dispatching envoys to Patriarch Peter (654–66) at Constantinople. In 655 they agreed a new communion, affirming two natures in Christ, each having one will, yet also affirming that when Christ was a person he possessed only one will. The Roman people rejected the theological compromise and schism once again broke out.

Eugenius III, bl., pope and reformer, born Pisa as Bernardo Pignatelli, elected to the papacy 15 February 1145, died Tivoli, 8 July 1153. Possibly prior of a house in Pisa, he met and was much influenced by **Bernard of Clairvaux**, and subsequently became a Cistercian monk at Clairvaux and then abbot of Ss Vincent and Anastasius. In 1145 he became the first Cistercian to be elected as pope. Between 1146 and 1148 he was forced into exile due to his refusal to accept certain political reforms in Rome. He promoted the second Crusade and authorized Bernard of Clairvaux to preach it. He reformed clerical morality and monastic observance. In 1872 his cult was approved by **Pius IX**. Feast 8 July.

Eugenius and Macarius, martyrs, fourth century. They were exiled to Mauritania during the reign of Julian the Apostate (died 363). Feast 19 February.

Eugenius of Carthage, bishop, born Carthage (?), died near Albi, France, 505. He became bishop of Carthage in 481, the year that Huneric succeeded Genseric as king of the Arian Vandals. While at first granting Catholics some freedoms, Huneric soon started another wave of persecution. In 484 Huneric ordered the Catholic bishops to meet with their Arian counterparts, and they were given four months to apostatize. Eugenius refused, and was exiled, but was allowed to return to Carthage in 487 when the persecution was lessening, three years after the death of Huneric. However, the persecution began again when Trasimund became king in 500, and Eugenius was condemned to death. The sentence was not carried out, however, and Eugenius went into exile again, dying five years later at a monastery near Albi. Feast 13 July.

Eugenius of Toledo, monk, archbishop, born Toledo, died there, 13 November 657. He was from a royal Visigothic family of Spain, and became a cleric in the cathedral of Toledo and a monk at Saragossa. Eugenius studied theology and literature. He was appointed an archdeacon by his uncle (Bishop **Braulio**). In 645 he became archbishop of Toledo, being appointed by King Chindswinth. He was a small man in frail health, but well known for his spiritual and intellectual activity. Eugenius was active in the councils of Toledo from 646 to 656. His writings include a volume of prose and a treatise *De Trinitate* (both lost), as well as a collection of short poems.

Eulalia of Barcelona, martyr, died early fourth century. Venerated in Catalonia, where she is called Aulaire, Aulazie, Olalla, etc., she is probably the same as **Eulalia of Mérida**. Feast 12 February.

Eulampius and Eulampia, died Nicomedia, 310. Brother and sister, their martyrdom is said to have inspired many converts to Christianity. Feast 10 October.

Eulogius, monk. Syriac Church. A disciple of **Awgen**.

Eulogius, martyr, died Palestine, possibly third century. Feast 5 March.

Eulogius of Alexandria, theologian, monk, patriarch, born Antioch, died Alexandria, 607. Eulogius was a monk who became a priest and abbot of the Deipara monastery at Antioch. In 580 he became patriarch of Alexandria. He was a Chalcedonian who followed the doctrine of St **Basil of Caesarea** via John the Grammarian. He denied ignorance in Christ, a doctrine which became part of the ordinary magisterium of the Church through Pope **Gregory I**. Eulogius corresponded with the pope between 595 and 600, concerning the patriarch of Constantinople. Eulogius also wrote against Novatianism and Severian monophysites. Feast 13 September.

Eulogius of Córdoba, martyr, died Córdoba, 859. During a period of persecution carried out by occupying African Muslims, Eulogius was imprisoned. During his incarceration he wrote letters of encouragement to saints Flora and Mary, also in prison. He wrote the *Memorandum of the Saints*, an account of the sufferings of the Church during that period of persecution. He was appointed as archbishop of Toledo in 859, but was arrested again before he could be consecrated. Refusing to deny his faith, he was beheaded. Feast 11 March.

Eulogius of Edessa, bishop, died Edessa, *c.* 381. Banished for his opposition to Arianism, he was recalled as bishop *c.* 375. Feast 5 May.

Eulogius Salos, monk, died *c.* 1210 (?). Georgian Church. A 'fool for Christ', he foresaw the victory of the Georgian army over the Turks.

Eumenes of Gortina, born Gortina (Crete), died Thebaid (Egypt), seventh century. Bishop of Gortina, he also taught in Rome. Feast 18 September.

Eumenius of Murmansk, see **Eleazar of Murmansk, with Nazarius and Eumenius**.

Euphemia of Chalcedon, martyr, died 16 September 303. Possibly of wealthy parents, but nothing apart from her martyrdom is known for certain. A large cult grew concerning Euphemia, and she was the object of Asterius's and Amasea's panegyric *c.* 400. The Council of Chalcedon was held in her basilica, and gave her cult a decisive impetus.

Euphrasia, ascetic, born Constantinople, 380, died there, *c.* 410. Euphrasia was the daughter of Antigonus, a senator of Constantinople, who died shortly after her birth. She was related to Emperor **Theodosius I** (379–95), who arranged a betrothal to the son of a wealthy senator when she was five years old. Two years later she left Constantinople when her mother moved to Egypt, settling near a convent of nuns. At the age of seven she insisted on joining the nuns, declining her betrothal at the age of 12. She transferred her fortune to Emperor Arcadius (395–408) to be used for charity. Feast 13 March.

Euphrasia of Nicomedia, born Nicomedia, *c.* 290, died there, *c.* 307. Imprisoned under the Emperor Maximian, she chose execution rather than rape. Feast 19 January.

Euphrasia of Pskov, princess, born Polock, died Medvezej Golova, 1245. Russian Church. She was the daughter of Rogvolod, a Lithuanian prince, and married the prince of Pskov, Jaroslav Vladimirovic. In 1243 she founded a monastery at Pskov, of which she became hegumena, changing her name from Eudoxia, but was soon afterwards killed by her stepdaughter. Feast 16 October.

Euphrasius (or Eucrathius?) of the Auvergne, bishop, died 515. Feast 14 January.

Euphronius, bishop, died Autun, France, *c.* 475. Bishop of Autun from 460. Feast 3 August.

Euphronius, bishop, born Tours (?), 530, died there, 573. Bishop of Tours from 556, and responsible for rebuilding the city after a fire. He was a nephew of **Gregory of Langres**. Feast 4 August.

Euphronius of Tver, monk, died 1460. Russian Church. A disciple of **Sabasius of Tver**, he enjoyed a great reputation among the royal family. Feast 2 March.

Euphrosyne, nun, died Harat Zuwaylah, 3 February 1307. Coptic Church. Her parents died when she was young, and she was brought up by a childless couple. They wished her to marry, but she wanted to become a nun and cut off all her hair to deter her suitor. She entered the convent of St George at Harat Zuwaylah, eventually becoming abbess. She was ill for many years, suffering she bore with great patience.

Euphrosyne, nun, died Lesbos, 11 May 1235. Byzantine Church. According to legend, she was burned to death by pirates.

Euphrosyne of Moscow, princess, died Moscow, 7 July 1407. Russian Church. She was the daughter of the prince of Suzdal, Demetrius Konstantinovic, and in 1367 married prince **Demetrius Donskoi** of Moscow. She proved a great support for her husband during the conflict with the Tartars, although for a time they had to flee Moscow when it was captured by the Tartars, taking refuge in Rostov and then Kostroma. When they were able to return they found the city desolate, and Euphrosyne showed great care for the poor and the weak. She was also a builder of churches and monasteries, and was founder of the convent of the Ascension inside the Kremlin. Forewarned in a vision of her approaching death, she became a nun in this convent, changing her name from Eudoxia. She was buried in the crypt of the convent.

Euphrosyne of Polock, princess, born Polock, *c.* 1105, died Jerusalem, 23/4 May 1173. Russian Church. Daughter of a prince of Polock, at the age of 12, rather than marry, she determined to become a nun in a convent founded by an aunt. She was, however, given a church and founded a convent beside it, which she entered with her sister and a cousin – at which time she changed her name from Predislava. She also later established a monastery for men. For failing to come to the aid of Prince Mstislav of Moscow, in 1131 her whole family was exiled to Constantinople, where they were welcomed by the Emperor Emmanuel Commenus – one of Euphrosyne's sisters marrying a son of the emperor. At Mstislav's death they were able to return, carrying many gifts from the emperor. On their return, Euphrosyne was able to complete in stone the church she had begun, and it was consecrated in 1160. Towards the end of her life she went with her brother to the Holy Land, and died there in the Russian monastery.

Euphrosyne of Suzdal, princess, born Suzdal, *c.* 1165, died there, 25 September 1250. Russian Church. Born Elena Prebrana, she was the eldest daughter of Prince Michele Jurevic of Suzdal. In 1178 she married a former ally of her deceased father, Vladimir of Cernigov, and went to live at Cernigov, but returned to her mother at Suzdal after the death of her husband in 1201. At Suzdal she built a convent which was ready by 1207, and which she entered, leading a life of strict asceticism. When the monastery was approached by the Tartar army, thanks to the prayers of the nuns it was hidden in cloud and was left untouched, but the nuns went about the streets of Suzdal helping those who were suffering from the destruction of their city. After destroying Suzdal, the Tartars moved on to Cernigov. Prince Michele of Cernigov fled to Hungary, but returned after all other Russian princes had submitted to the Tartars. The Khan demanded that Michele apostatize, which he seemed ready to do, until Euphrosyne sent him a letter encouraging him to remain true to his faith. He was executed.

Euphrosynus of Kurzesk, hermit, died near Kargopol, *c.* 1650. Russian Church.

Euphrosynus of Pskov, born Videlebe, *c.* 1386, died Pskov, 15 May 1481. Russian Church. His parents wanted him to marry, but instead he entered the monastery of Snjatnogorski, at Pskov, where he changed his name from Eleazar, with which he had been baptized. In *c.* 1425 he set himself up in a hermitage, where he had visions, especially of the great doctors of the Church. Other monks joined him, and in 1477 he built a church to serve them. He refused, however, to take on the role of hegumenos, which instead he entrusted to his disciple Ignatius, although he drew up a form of rule for the community.

Euphrosynus of Sinoezer, monk, born Carelia, died Sinoezer, 20 March 1612. Russian Church. Baptized Ephraim, he was educated at the monastery of Valaam and then in Novgorod, eventually becoming sacristan in the village of Dolock, not far from Novgorod. He entered the monastery of the Dormition at Tichvin, where he took his new name. In 1600 he decided to embrace the eremitical life, and settled in a cave near lake Sinice. After only three years there the number of monks who wished for his counsel was such that he built a monastery, dedicated to the Annunciation. In 1612, however, because of the Polish and Lithuanian incursions, he called his followers together, telling the lay people to seek refuge wherever they could. The monks took an oath to remain where they were. The following day the Polish troops arrived. Finding Euphrosynus at prayer, they demanded to know where the monastery's treasure was hidden. He indicated the church, whereupon one of the soldiers cut his throat.

Euplus, born Catania, Sicily, died there, 304. Martyred after being found in possession of a book of the Gospels – he was a deacon – and refusing to apostatize. Feast 12 August.

Eupraxia, born Constantinople, died Thebaid, *c.* 420. She was of the imperial family. When her father died, her mother entered a convent at Tabennesis, in Egypt, taking her daughter (then aged seven) with her. After her mother's death, Eupraxia refused the emperor's suggestion that she marry and, giving all her money to the poor, remained in the convent until her death. Feast 13 March.

Eupraxia of Moscow, and Julia, nuns, born Moscow, died there, fourteenth century. The sisters of the metropolitan **Alexis**, they built a small monastery on a hill just outside Moscow, where they were joined by some 30 other nuns, thus establishing the first formal monastery for women in the city. Julia died in 1397 as hegumena of the monastery, by which time the number of nuns had apparently tripled.

Euprepia, born and died Mitilene (?). Byzantine Church. Nothing is known of her life.

Euprepius, bishop, third century. Said to have been the first bishop of Verona. Feast 21 August.

Eupsychius of Caesarea, born (?) Caesarea, Cappadocia, died there, *c.* 130. Feast 7 September.

Eupsychius of Caesarea, born (?) Caesarea, Cappadocia, died there, 362. A nobleman, he was accused by Julian the Apostate of destroying pagan temples, and was martyred. Feast 7 April.

Eurosia, see **Orosia**.

Euschemon of Lampsacos, bishop, ninth century. He was imprisoned, then exiled from his see for his opposition to iconoclasm, and had a reputation for miracle workimg.

Eusebia of Hamay, abbess, died convent of Hamay, 16 March 680/89. Eusebia was elected abbess of Hamay at the age of 12 (some records say 23). This enabled the abbey to gain the patronage of a powerful family. When the abbess of Hamay, St **Adalbald**, was murdered, Eusebia's mother

Rictrude transferred the community to Marchiennes. Eusebia eventually returned the community to Hamay, where she ruled until her death.

Eusebia of Saint-Cyr, abbess, died Marseilles, France, 838. Little is known of Eusebia's life. She may have lived as early as the fifth or sixth centuries, although her traditional death date is recognised as 838. She was a Benedictine nun who served as abbess of Saint-Cyr in Marseilles. According to her epitaph, she was martyred at the hands of the Saracens with 39 other nuns. Her tomb is located in the church of Saint-Victor in Marseilles. Feast 20 September.

Eusebius, pope, born Greece (?), elected 18 April 310, died Sicily, 21 October 310. Eusebius succeeded **Marcellus I** and immediately became embroiled with Heraclius in the controversy regarding the *lapsi*, who claimed the right to be received back into ecclesiastical communion without submitting to penance. Emperor Maxentius exiled both Eusebius and Heraclius to Sicily. Feast 17 August.

Eusebius, bishop of Saint-Paul-Trois-Châteaux, Burgundy, died *c.* 660. Feast 23 March.

Eusebius, monk, died fourth century. He was a Syrian hermit who lived on Mount Coryphe, near Antioch. Feast 23 January.

Eusebius, fifteenth century. Ethiopian Church. A disciple of **Samuel of Waldeba**.

Eusebius, Neon, Leontius, Longinus and Companions, martyrs, died Lydda, *c.* 300. Said to have been converted to Christianity by witnessing the martyrdom of St **George**, and then were themselves executed. Feast 24 April.

Eusebius, Nestabus and Companions, died Gaza, 362. Put to death by a pagan mob after they had destroyed the temple at Gaza. Feast 8 September.

Eusebius of Asicha, hermit, died Asicha, Syria, *c.* 400.

Eusebius of Milan, bishop, died *c.* 462. Bishop of Milan from 450. Feast 8 August.

Eusebius of Pilis, founder, died Pilis, Hungary, 1270. He was a canon of Esztergom, then a hermit before founding the Pauline Order of Hermits, named after **Paul the Hermit**, with a constitution written by **Thomas Aquinas**. Feast 20 January.

Eusebius of Rome, born Rome (?), died there, fourth/fifth century. He founded a church in Rome – possibly his own house. Feast 14 August.

Eusebius of Saint Gall, born Ireland, died Switzerland, 884. He was one of the *peregrini*, Irish monks who wandered Western Europe over the course of 200 years. A hermit living on Mount St Victor, venerated in his lifetime, he was killed by a peasant angry at being upbraided. Feast 31 January.

Eusebius of Samosata, died Dolichium, Syria, *c*. 380. Bishop of Samosata in Syria from 361, he was exiled by the Emperor Valens for his stand against Arianism, but on his return he was killed by a stone thrown by an Arian woman. Feast 21 June.

Eusebius of Vercelli, bishop, born Sardinia, died 1 August 371. Eusebius moved to Rome and was a strong supporter of orthodoxy in the Arian conflict. He was bishop of Vercelli from 340. After the Synod of Milan (355) he was exiled to the east, returning in 362, in the reign of the Emperor Julian. Eusebius lived with his clergy at Vercelli under monastic rule. Three written works survive. He also made a Latin translation of Eusebius of Caesarea's *Commentary on the Psalms*. Feast 2 August.

Eustace, martyr in Lithuania, see **Anthony, John and Eustace**.

Eustace, martyr, died Rome. A wholly legendary saint, supposedly a Roman general under the Emperor Trajan, who was converted to Christianity by seeing, while hunting, a crucifix between the antlers of a stag (the identical story is told of the rather less fictitious St **Hubert**). He changed his name from Placidas to Eustace. Because of his conversion, he lost his position and all contact with his wife and family, but was reunited when his military expertise was called upon in a crisis. He was, however, later martyred with all his now Christian family, **Theopista**, his wife, and his children, Agapitus and Theopistus. Feast 20 September (suppressed in 1969).

Eustace, bishop of Naples, third century. Feast 29 March.

Eustace of Abgar, the Wonderworker, monk, born Tarsus, 808, died Abgar. Byzantine Church.

Eustace of Antioch, bishop, born Side, died Thrace, 336. He was bishop of Beroea before being translated to Antioch, where he took the see from 324 to 327. Eustace attended the Council of Nicaea, being given a position of honour. When he returned to his diocese after the council he banished many of his clergy, accusing them of Arianism. He was uncompromising in his support of the Nicene position. This brought conflict with Eusebius of Caesarea. Eustace was subsequently accused of Sabellianism, and was deposed at a council at Antioch. He was banished to Thrace by **Constantine**. His work survives in fragments. Feast 16 July.

Eustace of Luxeuil, abbot, born Burgundy, *c*. 560, died Luxeuil, France, 2 April 629. Eustace became a monk at Luxeuil towards the end of the sixth century and was eventually placed in charge of the monastic school there. He followed his abbot, **Columban**, into exile *c*. 610, but was sent back to take up the leadership of the monastery *c*. 612. Eustace was in conflict with Agrestius over the latter's support for the Three Chapters. Agrestius was condemned at the Synod of Macon 626–7 on Eustace's instigation. Feast 29 March.

Eustace of Sarabi, born near Dabra Sarabi, 15 July 1273, died Sebinkarahisar, 15 September 1352. Ethiopian Church. Of a noble family, he studied under his hermit uncle **Daniel**, and aged 15 he became a monk, changing his name from Ma'qaba Egzi. He remained with his uncle in all for 19 years, spending time in a number of villages, before he established his own community at Sarabi. Among his early followers were a group known as 'the seven sons of Eustace', who played an important role in the religious development of Eritrea, as did

Eustace's Rule. One unusual feature of the Rule was the weekly celebration of two Sabbaths, that of the Jews (i.e., Saturday) and that of the Christians, a practice which was highly controversial and led to conflict – an attempt was made on Eustace's life. Sometime around 1338 Eustace left for a journey to the Holy Land, via Ethiopia and Egypt. He spent nine days visiting the holy places before deciding to visit the patriarch of Armenia who, he said, was being persecuted for upholding the law of the apostles. He went first to Cyprus, and then on to Armenia, where he died, probably in a town which is today Sebinkarahisar in central Anatolia.

Eustace of Serbia II, archbishop, died 16 August 1309. Serbian Church. Archbishop of Serbia from 1292, renowned for his asceticism.

Eustace of the Crimea, martyr, born 1745, died Feodosiya, Ukraine, 10 May 1759. Russian Church. Decapitated for refusing to deny his faith.

Eustace of Thessalonika, bishop, born Constantinople, *c.* 1125, died *c.* 1195. Byzantine Church. As a young man he entered the monastery of St Eufemia in Constantinople, and was ordained deacon in 1150. He studied, and then taught, at the university in the city before being nominated bishop of Mira in 1174. Before he could take up his see, however, he was proposed by Emperor Manuel I Commenus as metropolitan of Thessalonika. In 1178 the emperor asked that the condemnation of Mohammed's teaching be withdrawn, because it was proving a barrier to the conversion of Muslims. A synod was called, and Eustace led the opposition to the proposed change, arguing the case before the emperor himself. In Thessalonika, when it was attacked by Normans, he persuaded their leader not to suppress the Orthodox hierarchy. He was imprisoned for a few days, and wrote about the destruction of the city. In 1191, despite his general popularity among the people, a small group managed to campaign against him to such an extent that he left the city to meet the Emperor Isaac II at Philopolis, who supported him. Eustace returned to Thessalonika two and a half years later. He wrote a great number of books, including one on Thessalonika, another on classical literature, and lives of saints, as well as publishing his sermons and some books of spiritual guidance. A number of his letters have also survived. Feast 20 September.

Eustace the Goldsmith, died Kievan Cave monastery, twelfth or thirteenth century. Russian Church. Nothing is known of him. Feast 28 September.

Eustace White, priest and martyr, born Louth, Lincolnshire, died London, 10 December 1591. He was cut off by his family on becoming a Catholic, studied at the English Colleges in Rheims and Rome, and returned to England in 1588 to work in the West Country. He was arrested in Blandford in September 1591 and sent to London to be imprisoned, first in the Bridewell and then in Newgate. He was executed at Tyburn on the same day as **Polydore Plasden**.

Eustochia (Smargada) Calafato, bl., Poor Clare abbess, born Messina, Sicily, 25 March 1434, died there, 20 January 1468. Renowned for her beauty, Smargada Calafato came from a noble family and joined the Poor Clares *c.* 1446, taking the name Eustochia. In 1458 she was given papal permission to found a community of more rigorous discipline, under the Rule of the Franciscan Observants, which was eventually established at Monte Vergine, and of which she became abbess. During her relatively short life she gained a reputation for piety and devotion which led to her beatification in 1782.

Eustochium of Padua, bl., Benedictine, born Padua, Italy, 1444, died there, 1469. St Eustochium was born to a nun in Padua, and baptized Lucrezia Bellini. After joining the Benedictines at the age of 17, she appears to have suffered from some kind of mental disorder and was treated for demonic possession by way of imprisonment, exorcism and at times food deprivation for four years. Upon her death soon after her profession, her body was reportedly found with the name of Jesus burned on her breast. Feast 13 October.

Eustolia and Sopatra, born Constantinople (?), died there, 610 and 625 respectively. Sopatra probably was, and Eustolia may have been, a daughter of the Emperor Maurice. They founded a monastery at Constantinople. Feast 9 November.

Eustorgius, bishop, born Greece, died Milan, 518. He was bishop of Milan from 512. He ransomed those of his flock taken prisoner in the wars of the period, and was greatly admired. Feast 6 June.

Eustrathius of Armenia and Companions, martyrs, died Armenia, *c.* 303. Eustrathius was of a distinguished family. He was executed with his servant Eugenius, two of his friends named Mardarius and Auxentius, and Orestes, a soldier who was converted by Eustrathius's faith. Feast 13 December.

Eustrathius of the Kievan Cave Monastery, martyr, born Kiev (?), died Chersonesus, 1196. Russian Church. Sold into slavery after the Cave monastery had been sacked, he and 50 others became the property of a Jew who offered them the chance to convert to Judaism, which would have meant their eventual release. Eustrathius persuaded them not to apostatize, and all were then denied food and drink. After 14 days all had died except Eustrathius, who was accustomed to fasting. He was then accused of killing the others, and was crucified. When, after another 14 days, he was still alive, he was stabbed to death. His body was then thrown into the sea, but was recovered and his remains were finally returned to Kiev. Feast 28 March.

Eustrathius the Faster, see **Eustrathius of the Kievan Cave Monastery**.

Eustrathius the Wonderworker, ninth century. Feast 9 January.

Eutal, monk, born near Nineveh, died Tur Abdin. Syriac Church. A disciple of Malka, buried in the monastery of Mar Malka. Feast 9 October.

Euthalia of Lentini, died Lentini, near Catania, Sicily, 257. Said to have been executed by her brother. Feast 27 August.

Euthymius Mcedelascvili, born Zinandali, eastern Georgia, died 1804. Georgian Church. He became a monk, and by 1777 was hegumenos of his monastery of John the Baptist at Davidgaregi, a role he resigned in 1798 having earned a reputation as a theologian, preacher and friend of the poor. But in the same year his monastery was attacked by Muslim tribesmen, and he was taken into captivity, from which he was ransomed by George XII, the last king of Georgia, whose confessor he was. Feast 8 August.

Euthymius of Alexandria, martyr, died Alexandria, *c.* 305. He was a deacon. Feast 5 May.

Euthymius of Archangel, died Archangel, *c.* 1523. Russian Church. Nothing is known of him, except for the miracles surrounding his relics.

Euthymius of Carelia, the Illuminator, died 1435. Russian Church. A monk, he moved to the north of Russia in search of solitude *c.* 1400, but in 1410 founded a monastery dedicated to St Nicholas.

Euthymius of Constantinople I, patriarch, born Seleucia, Isauria, *c.* 834, died Constantinople, 5 August 917. As a youth, Euthymius joined a community of monks on Mount Olympus, Bithynia. He later served as abbot of St Theodora in Constantinople and as confessor to Emperor Leo VI the Wise (886–912), whom he convinced to protect officers in **Photius**'s party. He reigned as patriarch of Constantinople from 907 to 912. He was embroiled in the political and marital intrigues of the emperor, eventually suffering banishment. The Greek Church recognized him as a saint in 991. His *Vita* extols his virtues as a preacher, but very few of his sermons survived. He has been associated with a history of the first seven councils and the Synod of Photius's rehabilitation, but these may have been written by Euthymius (1410–16).

Euthymius of Constantinople, born Demetsana in the Peloponnese, died Constantinople, 22 March 1814. Byzantine Church. Named Eleuterius, he was educated in Constantinople, then went to Jassy where his father was a tailor, and from there to Bucharest where he decided to become a Muslim. However, after a conversion experience back to Christianity, he became a monk on Mount Athos before returning to Constantinople, where he was executed for rejecting Islam.

Euthymius of Euboea, died Euboea, eleventh or twelfth century. Byzantine Church. An ascetic, but nothing more is known of him.

Euthymius of Fuwwah, martyr, died Antinoe, Upper Egypt, 28 April c. 300. Coptic Church. Originally from Fuwwah in Lower Egypt, he is said to have died in the persecution of Diocletian.

Euthymius of Novgorod, the Wonderworker, born Novgorod, died Vjazisci, 1458. Russian Church. Named John, the son of a priest of Novgorod, at 15 he entered the monastery of St Nicholas at Vjazisci, where he took the name Euthymius. He also spent some time at the monastery of St Barlaam at Chutyn. He came to the attention of the archbishop of Novgorod, who took him into his service, and in 1429 Euthymius was chosen to succeed to the archbishopric, although he continued as far as he was able to live a monastic style of life. He returned to his original monastery shortly before his death.

Euthymius of Perejaslavl, bishop, died c. 1150. Russian Church. Thought to have come from the Kievan Cave monastery, he was bishop of Perejaslavl from 1141.

Euthymius of Sardis, bishop, died c. 829. Bishop of Sardis, he opposed the Emperor Theophilus's attempt to reintroduce iconoclasm, was exiled, and finally executed.

Euthymius of Sjanzema, monk, born Vologda, died there, 1465. Russian Church. First a monk of a monastery on lake Kubenskoe, then moved to a hermitage not far away. He then set up a monastery on the river Sjanzema, where he was joined by **Cariton**. Feast 11 April.

Euthymius of Solovki, seventeenth/eighteenth centuries. Church of the Old Believers. His life is somewhat uncertain. He seems to have been a monk in several monasteries, although eventually settling in a hermitage on an island in the White Sea, and then linking up with the Solovki monastery. When the persecution of Old Believers began in that monastery, Euthymius was taken under arrest to Moscow, then to Novgorod, and finally to Suj, where he was freed and able to return to his eremetical existence. When news came that he was nearing the end of his life, the local priest attempted to give him the last rites, but Euthymius rejected his ministrations as invalid. There was a

struggle, and the priest dropped the chalice, an incident which led to further violence, during which Euthymius was killed.

Euthymius of Suzdal, monk, born Niznij, Novgorod, 1316, died Suzdal, 1 April 1404. Russian Church. He was much influenced by Dionysius, a monk who came to live in a cave near the town, and with others began to live, with him, a life of extreme asceticism – too extreme for Dionysius, who ordered him to moderate his mortifications. A monastery was established, but when the last prince of Suzdal founded a monastery of his own in the city, Dionysius sent a protesting Euthymius to take charge of it. He was made archimandrite. He also supervised a convent of nuns – of which a niece was superior – which was founded in Suzdal a few years after his own monastery.

Euthymius of Tarnovo, patriarch, born Tarnovo, c. 1330, died Plovdiv, c. 1404. Bulgarian Church. Of a noble family, when quite young he joined the monastery of the Mother of God, also at Tarnovo – then the Bulgarian capital – but in 1350 moved to the nearby monastery founded by St **Theodosius**. A dozen years later, with Theodosius, he went to Constantinople and lived in the Studite monastery of St John. In 1365, after the death of Theodosius, he became a monk on Mount Athos, although for a time he was exiled, accused of breaking his vow of poverty. About 1371 he went back to Tarnovo and founded the monastery of the Most Holy Trinity, where was undertaken a revision of Slavic literature, a work Euthymius continued even after being elected patriarch of Tarnovo in 1375. He also wrote books of his own, doctrinal works and biographies. In 1395 Tarnovo fell to the Turks. He was condemned to death for inciting the people against the conquerors, but was eventually sent into exile. He went to the monastery of Backovo near Plovdiv, where he died.

Euthymius of the Kievan Cave Monastery, died Kiev, fourteenth century. Russian Church. Nothing is known except that he took a vow of perpetual silence. Feast 20 January.

Euthymius of Vatopedi, bl., died Mount Athos, 1275. Byzantine Church. Hegumenos of the monastery of Vatopedi on Mount Athos, he was executed for opposing the agreement reached to reunite the Latin and Greek Churches at the Council of Lyons. Feast 4 January.

Euthymius the Great, priest and monk, born Melitene, Armenia, 377, died near Jericho, 20 January 473. He was ordained in Melitene and supervised monasteries there until 405, after which he lived as a monk near Jerusalem, and then near Jericho from 411. Despite his attempts at solitary life, he attracted many converts and was ultimately consecrated a bishop by Patriarch Juvenal of Jerusalem to minister to them. One of few supporters of the Council of Chalcedon at the time (451), he influenced some to abandon their allegiance to Eutyches.

Euthymius the Younger, abbot, born Opso, near Ancyra, c. 820, died Mount Athos, 15 October 898. Baptized Nicetas, he married and had a daughter, but at 18 abandoned his family to live as a hermit on Mount Olympus in Bithynia. He went on to the monastery of Pisidion, then to Mount Athos. From Athos he went to Thessalonika and spent some time as a stylite. He then returned to Athos, where in 867 he was ordained priest. In search of the life of a hermit, he went off to an island, but was followed there by some disciples and set up a monastery, ruling as abbot for 14 years. He then went on a recruitment drive, even gathering in some of his own family in Ancyra, and as a consequence had to establish a monastery for women. He finally retired back to Mount Athos. Feast 13 May.

Eutropia of Alexandria, died Alexandria, c. 253. Feast 30 October.

Eutropius, bishop, born Marseilles, died Orange, c. 476. After a worldly early life, he became a priest when his wife died. He was bishop of Orange, north of Avignon, when the diocese had been laid waste by Visigoths. Contemporaries praised his learning and piety and exemplary conduct. Feast 27 May.

Eutropius, priest, martyred Constantinople, 406. An anti-Christian prefect falsely accused him and **Tigrius** (Tigirius), a lector, of setting fire to public buildings to avenge the exile of **John Chrysostom**.

He is said to have died under torture. Tigrius may have survived and been exiled to Mesopotamia. Feast 12 January.

Eutychian, pope, born Tuscany, reigning from 4 January 275 until his death, probably Rome, 7 December 283. Limited details of his life survive, perhaps because of the Diocletian persecution, which followed shortly after his death. He himself, however, ruled the Church at Rome at a relatively trouble-free period, and seems to have brought stability and organization to the Church, evidenced in the expansion of official Christian cemeteries at the time.

Eutychius, abbot, died 487. Feast 23 May.

Eutychius, martyr, died Ferentino, Roman Campagna, c. 300. Feast 15 May.

Eutychius, martyr, died Rome, early fourth century. According to the inscription on his tomb, he died under Diocletian by being kept in prison without food for 12 days then thrown into a well. Feast 4 February.

Eutychius, see also **Timothy**.

Eutychius of Alexandria, born Alexandria, died near Alexandria, 356. A subdeacon under St **Athanasius**, he was sent to the mines when Athanasius was deposed and died on his way there. Feast 26 March.

Eutychius of Constantinople, patriarch, born Phrygia, c. 512, died 582. First a monk then an archimandrite, he found favour with Emperor Justinian I, who ensured his succession to the patriarchate. He later fell foul of Justinian and was deposed, only to be recalled some 12 years later by Justin II, in 577. He briefly denied the doctrine of resurrection of the body, but recanted after discussion with St **Gregory the Great**, the future pope, then papal representative in Constantinople. Surviving writings include a letter to Pope Vigilius and a portion of a *Discourse on Easter*.

Eva of Liège, bl., born c. 1205, died Liège, c. 1265. A friend of **Juliana of Liège**, she became a recluse in a cell attached to St Martin's church, Liège. She succeeded in getting the feast of Corpus Christi envisioned by Juliana established after her death. Feast 14 March.

Evagrius Mgvimelli, died Schalteba, sixth century. Georgian Church. A high official of the royal court, he witnessed a dove carrying food to St **Scius**, who was living in a hermitage. He determined to join him, but Scius valued his solitude and at first tried to dissuade him, although he then accepted him as a disciple. More disciples followed, and a monastery was built at the village of Schalteba. When Scius went to live in a cave, Evagrius became hegumenos of the monastery, but after Scius's death, Evagrius himself went to live in the cave, where he died. Feast 4 January.

Evagrius of Constantinople, archbishop, died *c.* 380. Archbishop from 370 during a time of the Arian ascendancy, he was exiled and died at an unknown date and place. Feast 6 March.

Evagrius Ponticus, abbot, born Ibora, Pontus, *c.* 345, died Cellae, Egypt, 399. Byzantine Church. An acquaintance of both **Basil the Great** and **Gregory Nazianzen**, he moved to Jerusalem and was close to **Melania the Elder**. He left Jerusalem for the Egyptian desert, where he lived for the rest of his life. His writings – including a long letter to Melania laying out his spiritual doctrines – caused controversy almost immediately after his death.

Evaristus, pope, born Rome (?), died probably Rome, probably 26 October *c.* 109. The *Liber Pontificalis* states that he was of Greek ancestry, as well as giving certain unreliable data about his pontificate; but no reliable information survives. He succeeded St **Clement** *c.*100 during the reign of Trajan. His usual designation as martyr is unproven. Feast 29 October.

Eve of Liège, see **Eva of Liège**.

Eventius, martyr, died Rome, *c.*113. He is one of three Roman martyrs commemorated on this day, the others being **Alexander** and **Theodulus**. Feast 3 May.

Everard, born 1018, died 1078. He was Eberhard III, count of Nellenburg. He founded the Benedictine abbey of Schaffhausen, now in Switzerland, and became a monk there. Feast 25 March.

Everard Hanse, bl., martyr, born Northamptonshire, executed Tyburn, London, 31 July 1581. Educated at Cambridge University, he became a Protestant minister, but converted to Catholicism after falling seriously ill. He went to study in Rheims and was ordained in March 1581. He returned to England, but was arrested soon afterwards and imprisoned in Newgate. His trial began on 18 July, and on 28 July he was condemned to be hanged, drawn and quartered.

Everglislus (Ebergesilus, Ebregislus), monk, bishop of Cologne, fifth century. He is said to have died a martyr, killed by pagan thieves, in Tongres, Belgium. His martyrdom seems improbable and his whole life, presuming it to be not entirely legendary, may have been somewhat later. Feast 24 October.

Evermod, died Ratzeburg, 1178. Converted after hearing **Norbert of Xanten** preaching in Cambrai, he joined his Premonstratensian canons. He was abbot of monasteries at Gottesgnaden and Magdeburg, became first bishop of Ratzeburg, now in Germany but then Wendish territory. He is venerated as an apostle of the Wends. Feast 17 February.

Evetius, martyr, died Bithynia, 303, under Diocletian. Feast 24 February.

Evodius, Hermogenes and Callistus (or possibly Callista), martyrs, died Nicomedia (?). Feast 25 April.

Evodius of Antioch, bishop, first century. Multiple sources indicate him as the first bishop of Antioch after St Peter. He appears in various later martyrologies, but there is no surviving primary source evidence to indicate that he was martyred. He was succeeded by St **Ignatius of Antioch**. Feast 6 May.

Evroul (Evroult, Ebrulf), abbot, born possibly Bayeux, Normandy, 626, died monastery of Ouche, 706. A married nobleman, he joined the monastery of Deux Jumeaux and later became a hermit before founding the monastery where he died. His wife became a nun. Feast 29 December.

Évroul de Saint-Fuschien-au-Bois, abbot, born Beauvais, France, sixth century, died Oroër, France, 25 July c. 600. Venerated in the areas where he had been active, his remains were transferred to Beauvais in 838. Little is known for certain about his life. There are different stories about how he came to be made abbot at Saint-Fuschien-au-Bois. One version credits the bishop of Beauvais, another says that the monks petitioned to have him, and yet another that the king's influence was the determining factor. Some scholars believe that he actually lived 100 years later.

Ewald the Black, martyr, priest, born Northumbria, died Old Saxony, c. 695. After meeting St **Willibrord**, he and fellow Northumbrian priest **Ewald the Fair** set out on missionary activities c. 690. While they were guests of a Saxon overlord, his subjects murdered the two priests, fearing they would convert him and jeopardize their own religion. Feast 3 October.

Ewald the Fair, see **Ewald the Black**.

Exuperantius, see also **Sabinus and Companions**.

Exuperantius, bishop, died Ravenna, 418. From 398 he was the second bishop of Ravenna, which became the imperial capital in 403, and built the town of Argenta. Feast 30 May.

Exuperius of Toulouse, bishop, born fourth century, died after 410. Praised by St **Jerome** for his generosity to his subjects and to the monks of Palestine, Egypt and Libya. He wrote to Pope **Innocent I** for clarification regarding canonical scriptures and a reply, *Consulenti tibi*, dated February 405, contains the Canon of Scriptures as it is accepted today. It includes the deuterocanonical

books recognized by the Roman Catholic Church. St Jerome mentions him as living in 411, the latest primary source reference. Feast 1 August.

Exuplius, martyr, born Catania, Sicily (?), died there, 304. The accounts for his death suggest that he courted martyrdom by openly proclaiming his Christianity before the governor. Feast 12 August.

Eystein of Trondheim, bishop, born Norway, died Trondheim, 26 January 1198. He was archbishop of Trondheim and papal legate. During a conflict between the king and a rival, he fled to England for a while. He is credited with achieving the Church's independence from the Norwegian crown and nobility.

Ezechia, died Dabra Libanos, c. 1313. Ethiopian Church. The fourth abbot of Dabra Libanos. Feast 6 April.

Ezechiel, monk, fourth/fifth century. Coptic Church. A disciple of **Paul of Tamma**.

Ezechiel, monk, born and died Arnant, Upper Egypt, fifth century. Coptic Church. He became a hermit on a mountain near his city, but yielded to temptation and made for the city. There, however, he was bitten by a scorpion, which persuaded him to return to his hermitage, where he was refreshed by water miraculously coming from a rock. Feast 10 December.

Ezechiel Moreno Diaz, bl., bishop, born Alfaro, Spain, 9 April 1848, died Madrid, 19 August 1906. He joined the Augustinians and travelled to the Philippines, being ordained there in 1871. After working there for some time he returned to Spain as novice master, then went back to Colombia, where he became bishop of Pasto. He was renowned for his holiness of life and his readiness to help people whatever the hour of the day.

F

Fabian, pope, martyr, pontiff from 10 January 236 until his martyrdom 20 January 250. Born in Rome, he appears to have been influential politically, negotiating a previously unknown level of peace and social tolerance for the Church. A respected leader, Fabian's life was brought to an end when Emperor Decius renewed persecution against the Church upon his accession. He was buried originally at San Callistus, but his remains were discovered in 1915 at the church of San Sebastiano.

Fabiola, widow, died Rome, 399. Born of the wealthy patrician family Fabia or Fabii, she divorced her husband, reportedly for his immoral living, then married again. After her husband's death, she repented publicly for breaching the Church canons concerning divorce and spent the rest of her life in the service of the poor and the sick. She went to Bethlehem in 395, where she lived with Sts **Paula** and **Eustochium**. She was in contact with St **Jerome** and some letters between them survive. She eventually returned to Rome, where she continued to serve until her death. Fabiola, with St **Pammachius**, is known to have founded a hospital for the poor in Rome, as well as a hospice at Porto. Feast 27 December.

Fabius, martyr, died *c.* 303. He was a standard bearer in Mauretania during the Diocletian persecution. He was executed after his refusal to take part in a ceremony, which was religious in nature, exposed him as a Christian. Feast 31 July.

Fachanan, bishop, born Tulachtean, Ireland, died Ross (?), sixth century. A disciple of **Ita**, he founded the monastery of Molana, near Youghal, and also that of Ross in County Cork. He is thought to have been the first bishop of Ross. Feast 14 August.

Fahd, see **Yuhanna Abu Nagah al-Kabir and Fahd**.

Faith, martyr, died Agen, Gaul, *c.* 250 (?). Nothing is known of her, although later legends say she was of noble birth and was beheaded at the age of 12 for refusing to sacrifice to idols. Her shrine, with its famous image, is at Conques. Feast 6 October.

Falco, bl., abbot, died Cava, Campania, 1146, cult confirmed 1928. **Peter of Cava** received him as a Benedictine. He was then abbot at St Mary, the daughter house at Cirzosimo, before returning to Cava as abbot in 1141. Feast 6 May.

Falco, bl., hermit, born Calabria, died the Abruzzi, near Palena, 1440. Feast 9 August.

Famien (Famianus), monk, priest, born Cologne, *c.* 1090, died Galese, Italy, 8 August 1150. Famien went on pilgrimages to the Holy Land, to Rome and to Compostela, afterwards becoming a hermit and then, when a monastery was built nearby at Osera, a Cistercian monk. He went off once more to the Holy Land, and on his return died at Galese, where a church bears his name.

Fantinus of Syracuse, born Syracuse, Sicily, died Gioja, Calabria, 303 (?). He was converted to Christianity, and in turn converted his parents, who were martyred. He, however, fled. Feast 24 July.

Fantinus the Younger, abbot, born Calabria (?), *c.* 927, died Thessalonika, *c.* 990. After joining a monastery when only 13, he lived for 20 years as a monk before becoming a hermit. When his parents came looking for him he persuaded them, and his brothers too, to embrace the monastic life. He lived a life of strict asceticism, and wore few clothes. He is credited with correctly foreseeing the Muslim invasion of Calabria, after which he received a vision telling him to go to Greece, which he did. He became famous for miracles. Feast 30 August.

Faqada Amlak, monk, born and probably died in Tigre. Coptic Church.

Fara (Fare, Burgundofara), abbess, died near Meaux, France, 657. A noblewoman in the court of Theodebert, she defied demands by her father, Count Agneric, that she marry. St **Eustace** intervened and eventually the two made peace. She was professed in Meaux in 614, and a few years later convinced her father to build her an abbey, later known as Faremoûtiers-en-Brie, which she ruled as abbess for 37 years. The sister of Sts **Faro** and **Cagnoald**, she was responsible for the formation of Sts **Gibitrudis**, **Sethrida**, **Hildelid** and others. She has been associated with several miracles. Feast 3 April.

Faro of Meaux, monk, bishop, probably born Burgundy, died probably Meaux, *c.* 675. The son of a nobleman and brother to Sts **Fara** and **Cagnoald**, Faro was a chancellor in the court of King Dagobert I. He left his position to become a monk, and by 637 was the bishop of Meaux. **Bede** mentions him as assisting St **Adrian** of Canterbury, but otherwise little is known of his episcopate. Feast 28 October.

Fastred (Fastrade, Fastradus) de Cavamiez, bl., Cistercian abbot, born Hainault, died Paris, 1164. Fastred was received into the Cistercians at Clairvaux by St **Bernard**, and in 1148 became the first abbot of the abbey of Campron in Hainault, then the successful abbot of Clairvaux in 1157, and finally of Citeaux in 1162. Feast 21 April.

Fausta, Evilasius and Maximus, martyrs, died Cyzicus, Asia Minor, 303. Fausta was a Christian condemned to be tortured, but in the process converted the magistrate Evilasius and the praetor Maximus, who were both executed with her. Feast 20 September.

Faustina, see **Liberata**. Feast 19 January.

Faustinian, fourth century. Said to be the second bishop of Bologna, he is supposed to have reorganized the diocese after the persecution of Diocletian and been a strong opponent of Arianism. Feast 26 February.

Faustinus and Jovita, from Brescia, Lombardy, supposedly martyrs, died there second century. They were said to be brothers who preached Christianity and were beheaded under Hadrian. Their ancient cult was widespread, but suppressed in 1969. Feast 15 February.

Faustinus, see also **Simplicius and Faustinus**.

Faustus, martyr, born Greece, died there, 250. He was crucified, and used by archers as a target. Feast 16 July.

Faustus and Companions, martyrs, died Alexandria, 250. Twelve martyrs beheaded in the persecution of Decius.

Faustus, Januarius and Martial, martyrs, died Córdoba, *c.* 304. Although there is evidence of an early cult, nothing is known for sure of this group of martyrs. Feast 12 October.

Faustus of Alexandria, martyr, died fourth/early fifth century. A deacon, he was sent into exile from Alexandria with his bishop St **Dionysius**. He was executed in the persecution of Diocletian. Feast 19 November.

Faustus of Constantinople, died Constantinople, fifth century. A monk in the city. Feast 3 August.

Faustus of Riez, abbot and bishop, born Brittany, *c.* 410, died *c.* 490. Already bishop of Lérins, he became bishop of Riez, in Provence, *c.* 460, but left his see under duress for some years after opposing

Euric, the Visigoth king. A proponent of early semi-Pelagian theology, most particularly in his work *De gratia Dei*, the Second Council of Orange condemned him in 529. However, he is revered in France. Feast 28 September.

Feast of all the saints of the Kievan Cave Monastery, and of all the saints of the Ukraine, Russian Church. Feast second Sunday of Lent.

Feast of all the saints of Russia, Russian Church. Feast second Sunday of Pentecost.

Feast of all the saints of the Novgorod region, Russian Church. Feast third Sunday of Pentecost.

Feast of the Holy Fathers of the Kievan Cave Monastery who lie in the further caves, Russian Church. Feast 26 August.

Feast of the Holy Fathers of the Kievan Cave Monastery who lie in the nearer caves, Russian Church. Feast 28 September.

Feast of the saints of Belorussia, Russian Church. Feast third Sunday of Pentecost.

Feast of the saints of Carelia, Russian Church. Feast 30 October.

Feast of the saints of Kazan, Russian Church. Feast 4 October.

Feast of the saints of Kostroma, Russian Church. Feast 23 January.

Feast of the saints of Optina, Russian Church. Feast 11 October.

Feast of the saints of Pskov, Russian Church. Feast third Sunday of Pentecost.

Feast of the saints of Radonez, Russian Church. Feast 6 July.

Feast of the saints of Rjazan, Russian Church. Feast 10 June.

Feast of the saints of Rostov-Jaroslavl, Russian Church. Feast 23 May.

Feast of the saints of Siberia, Russian Church. Feast 10 June.

Feast of the saints of Smolensk, Russian Church. Feast 28 July.

Feast of the saints of Solovki, Russian Church. Feast 9 August.

Feast of the saints of Tambov, Russian Church. Feast 28 July.

Feast of the saints of Tula, Russian Church. Feast 22 September.

Feast of the saints of Tver, Russian Church. Feast 29 June.

Feast of the saints of Vladimir, Russian Church. Feast 10 October.

Feast of the saints of Volinia, Russian Church. Feast 10 October.

Feast of the saints of Vologda, Russian Church. Feast third Sunday of Pentecost.

Feast of the saints of the Caves of Pskov, Russian Church. Feast fourth Sunday of Pentecost.

Feast of the saints of the Crimea, Russian Church. Feast 15 December.

Febronia, martyr, died Hamidat, Egypt, *c.* 750. Coptic Church. According to legend, Febronia was a nun in a convent which came under attack from Muslim troops. When they were captured, Febronia claimed she had a magic ointment which would prevent any harm coming to her. Intrigued, one of the soldiers went with her. She anointed herself with sacred oil, then asked the soldier to attempt to kill her. He did so, cutting off her head. The soldiers then all fled. In this way Febronia saved her own virginity, and that of her fellow nuns. Feast 25 June.

Fechin, born Luighne, Connaught, died 665. He is said to have studied under **Nathy**, founded and been abbot of a monastery possibly at Fobhar, Westmeath, and died during a plague epidemic.

There was a cult in Scotland, notably Arbroath, although he probably never left Ireland. Feast 20 January.

Felician, born *c.* 160, died near Foligno, Umbria, *c.* 254. He had been bishop of Foligno for 56 years when, aged 94, he was arrested and tortured in the persecution of the Emperor Decius and died on his way to execution in Rome. He is patron of Foligno. Feast 24 January.

Felicissimus, and Agapitus, deacons, martyrs, died in the catacombs of Praetextatus, 6 August 258. Attendants to Pope St **Sixtus II**, they died with him at the hands of Roman soldiers ordered by the Emperor Valerian. Sixtus was beheaded, and the deacons were probably executed in the same way, along with an estimated five others. The martyrs were buried together at the cemetery of St Callistus. Their martyrdom is detailed in the Roman martyrology and in a letter by St **Cyprian**.

Felicity Pricet, bl., martyred during the French Revolution 1794, commemorated with **Monica Pichery**, **Carol Lucas** and **Victoria Gusteau**, all bl., see **Martyrs of the French Revolution**. Feast 18 January.

Felicula, Vitalis and Zeno, reputedly martyrs, died Rome, second or third century, but nothing is known. Feast 14 February.

Felim, abbot, born Sligo, Ireland, sixth century. A disciple of **Finnian of Clonard**, he apparently became abbot of Achonry. He is sometimes said to have been a bishop, although he is known as Felim the Priest, which suggests otherwise. Feast 9 August.

Felissima, see **Gracilian**.

Felix, martyr, died Dalmatia, third century. Feast 18 May.

Felix, martyr, died north Africa, date unknown. He and his fellow martyr **Gennadius** were venerated from very early times in Uzalis, a city near Utica (Bu Shatir) in proconsular Africa. Feast 16 May.

Felix, martyr, died Rome, third century. Feast 30 May.

Felix, fourth century, martyr, died Salerno. Feast 1 February.

Felix, see also **Zoëllus**.

Felix I, pope, pontiff from 3 January 269 until his death in Rome, 30 December 274. Few details survive, but he is thought to have been a Roman by birth. He is known to have ordered the deposition of renegade bishop **Paul of Samatosa**, but little else is known of his activities. Feast 30 May (suppressed 1969).

Felix III (II), pope, pontiff from 13 March 483 until his death in Rome, 1 March 492. He excommunicated Patriarch Acacius of Constantinople, thus becoming responsible for the first schism of the Eastern and Western Churches, and he also excommunicated many Catholics who had been forcibly rebaptized by Arian Vandals.

Felix IV (III), pope, pontiff from 12 July 526 until his death in Rome, 22 September 530. A 58-day gap between Felix and his predecessor, **John I**, suggests a struggle for the papacy; Felix was consecrated on the orders of Theodoric, the Ostrogoth king of Italy. He wrote 25 propositions concerning grace, which were adopted at the Council of Orange (529) and posthumously affirmed by **Boniface II**, thus ending the Pelagian controversy.

Felix and Adauctus, martyrs, died Rome, *c.* 304. Felix was a Christian priest being led out to execution during the persecution of Diocletian when an onlooker was moved to declare his own faith, and was added to (i.e., 'Adauctus') those being martyred. Feast 30 August.

Felix and Cyprian, bishops and martyrs, died north Africa, 484. These two bishops suffered under the persecution of the Vandal King Huneric, who attempted to make everyone conform to his Arianism. Felix was bishop of Abbir. Feast 12 October.

Felix and Fortunatus, martyrs, born Vicenza, died Aquileia. Two brothers. Little else is known of them. Feast 14 August.

Felix and Regula, martyrs, born north Africa (?), died Zürich, *c.* 250. Accounts of these two, said to be a brother and sister, are legendary. It is said they followed the **Theban Legion**, but escaped the massacre, only to die in Zürich. Feast 11 September.

Felix of Bourges, died Bourges, *c.* 580. Consecrated bishop by **Germanus of Paris**, he attended the Council of Paris in 573. People were said to be cured from drinking water mixed with stone dust from his first tomb slab after it was replaced by something more valuable. Feast 1 January.

Felix of Cantalice, Capuchin lay brother, born Cantalice, in the Abruzzi, died Rome, 18 May 1587. A shepherd and labourer, Felix was devoted to austerity and prayer, and was received into the Capuchins in 1543. He became a questor (i.e., a beggar for alms) in Rome for the order, and preached to and challenged powerful and poor alike, often with St **Philip Neri**. He had a special interest in the spiritual formation of children, but was also consulted by learned adults on this issue, despite his lack of education. He is buried in the church of the Immaculate Conception in Rome.

Felix of Dunwich, died Dunwich, England, 648. Sigebert, Christian king in East Anglia from 631, persuaded **Honorius of Canterbury** to send Felix, a bishop in Gaul, to be 'apostle of the East Anglians'. Although Dunwich has vanished into the sea, Felixstowe records his presence in the area. Feast 8 March.

Felix of Nantes, bishop, born Aquitaine, *c.* 513, died 6 or 8 January 582. He was appointed bishop of Nantes in 549 or 550, and sent missionaries to evangelize the area. He was involved in politics, and helped to stop the Breton invasions in 579. King Clotaire I put him in charge of the fortification of the city, and he rerouted part of the Loire river to form a natural defence. Feast 7 July.

Felix of Nicosia, bl., Capuchin lay brother, born Nicosia, Sicily, 5 November 1715, died there, 30 May 1787. A cobbler's apprentice, Felix made several attempts to join a religious order before becoming a Capuchin lay brother in 1743. He wandered as a beggar for the monastery – a common practice among poor and uneducated monks – and was known for his ministry of preaching, converting and tending to the sick. He was beatified in 1888.

Felix of Nola, confessor, priest, died probably Nola, 260. Felix, in the company of his bishop **Maximus**, was tortured but not killed for professing his faith. His apostolate afterwards, based at his church in Nola, was characterized by reports of miracles. Feast 14 January.

Felix of Rhuis, from Quimper, Britanny, died 1038. He was a hermit on Ouessant Island, then a Benedictine at Fleury at Saint-Benoît-sur-Loire. He was sent as its abbot to restore Rhuys abbey in Brittany, founded by **Gildas** and destroyed by the Normans. Feast 12 February.

Felix of Seville, martyr, died probably Seville, fourth century. He was a deacon and is greatly venerated in Seville. Feast 2 May.

Felix of Thibiuca, bishop and martyr, died Carthage, 15 July 303. He was bishop of Thibiuca, near Carthage, during the persecution of Christians under the Emperor Diocletian. He refused to hand over sacred scriptures and liturgical books to the authorities to be destroyed, and was sent to Carthage to be tried and executed.

Felix of Valois, monastic founder of the Order of the Holy Trinity for the Redemption of Captives, born Valois 1127, died Cerfroi, 4 November 1212. Perhaps of royal Valois blood, perhaps simply from the Valois province, Felix left all at an early age to live in contemplation in a wood (now Cerfroi monastery). Joined by **John of Matha**, who suggested to him the founding of an order, Felix journeyed to Rome where he and John presented the idea to Pope Innocent III. The two were kindly received and confirmed to the task of beginning their order, which grew in 40 years to 600 monasteries around the world. Feast 20 November.

Feqerta Krestos, monk. Ethiopian Church. Nothing is known of him.

Fequra Wald, monk. Ethiopian Church. Nothing is known of him.

Ferdinand, bl., prince, born Santarem, Portugal, 29 September 1402, died Fez, Morocco, 5 June 1443. Although not a cleric, he was offered appointment as a cardinal, which he refused. In 1437 he led a force against the Moors which took control of strategic Ceuta, eventually offering himself as hostage in exchange for the safe passage of his men. As a prisoner of Salà ben Salà, he was subjected to torture, solitary confinement and slavery until his death, despite rescue efforts. His secretary, João Alvarez, once freed, wrote his biography and returned his body to his birthplace.

Ferdinand of Castile III, king, born near Salamanca, c. 1201, died Seville, 30 May 1252. He was the son of Alfonso IX of Leon and was brought up there. In 1217 he was crowned king of Castile, succeeding his cousin Henry. On Alfonso's death in 1230 Ferdinand was accepted as king of Leon, so the kingdoms were reunited. Ferdinand conquered Andalucia, securing it from the Moors, and he accepted the submission of the king of Murcia. He also captured Seville, and the remaining Muslim kingdoms of Niebla and Granada came under Castile's sway. He re-established the university of Salamanca. At his death he was popularly acclaimed a saint. He was buried in Seville cathedral dressed not as a king, but as a Franciscan. He is the patron of prisoners, the poor and local rulers. In 1671 he was canonized for his services to the Crusades. His emblem is a greyhound.

Fere Mikael, monk, fifteenth century. Ethiopian Church. The son of a priest, he was educated in a monastery and become a monk. After some years he went to live in a cave, where he practised fasting and allowed himself only one hour's sleep a day. After living in this way for nine years he was elected abbot. The king appointed him governor of the province of Warab, after which he returned to his life of fasting and prayer.

Fergus, bishop, born Ireland, died Glamis, Scotland, eighth century. Little is known about him, except that he wandered over Scotland and built a number of churches dedicated to St **Patrick**. Feast 27 November.

Ferreolus, martyr, born Vienne, died there, third century. A Roman official, and a secret Christian, he was arrested for failing to apprehend **Julian of Brioude**, who had lived in his house. He refused to deny his faith, and was imprisoned. He managed to escape, but was caught, it is claimed, after swimming the Rhone and was beheaded on the spot. Feast 18 September.

Ferreolus and Ferrutio, martyrs, born France (or possibly Asia Minor), died Besançon, 212 (?). They are said to have been converted by **Polycarp** of Smyrna, and to have come, or more likely returned, to Lyons, where they were ordained by St **Irenaeus**, the first as a priest, the second as a deacon. They then evangelized the area around Besançon until they were beheaded in a persecution c. 212. Feast 16 June.

Ferreolus (Fergéol) of Grenoble, bishop, died c. 659. He is said to have been a bishop of Grenoble who was martyred by the sword. Feast 12 January.

Ferreolus of Uzès, bishop, from Narbonne, died 581. As bishop of Uzès, he focused on converting Jews in his diocese and may have been exiled by the king, Childebert, for this. He founded a monastery and wrote its Rule. Feast 4 January.

Fi... For names beginning with this combination of letters, see also **Phi...**

Fiacre, born Ireland (?), died at what is now Saint-Fiacre, France, c. 670. He is said to have come to France looking for solitude, and St **Faro**, bishop of Meaux, gave him land at Breuil, where he built a chapel in honour of the Virgin Mary and a hospice for travellers.

Fidelis of Como, martyr, died 303 (?). Either a Roman soldier who was trying to escape persecution, or a guard who released Christian prisoners during the persecution of Diocletian. Feast 28 October.

Fidelis of Sigmaringen, martyr, born Sigmaringen, Hohenzollern, 1578, died near Seewis, Switzerland, 24 April 1622, canonized 1746. A priest who joined the Capuchins, he was a successful preacher in Protestant communities and an able superior. He led a mission to convert Protestants in Grisons Canton and was murdered during a disturbance.

Fidolus (Phal), abbot, born Auvergne, died possibly Aumont, near Troyes, *c.* 540. He was the son of a Roman official taken prisoner by the Gauls and sold into slavery. Aventinus, abbot of Aumont, redeemed him. Fidolus was later abbot of Aumont abbey, afterwards called Saint-Phal. Feast 16 May.

Fillan (Phelen), abbot, born Ireland, died Glendochart, Perthshire, Scotland, eighth century. He was a nephew of St **Comgan**, and possibly became a monk in Wexford before travelling to Scotland, where he became a hermit at Pittenweem in Fife. He was elected monk of a neighbouring monastery, but resigned after some years to become a hermit again, this time at Glendochart. He died there on 9 January, but the year is unknown. Feast 26 August.

Finan of Lindisfarne, abbot, bishop, born Ireland, died Lindisfarne (?), 9 February 661. The Irish monk succeeded St **Aidan** to the see of Lindisfarne in 651 and, according to St **Bede**, engaged in missionary activity in Northumbria. His baptism of Paeda, a prince of Mercia, and Sigbert or Sigebert, ruler of the East Saxons, led to a strong Christian presence in those kingdoms. He favoured Celtic customs and the Irish method of calculating Easter over traditions emerging from Rome.

Finnbarr, born Lisnacaheragh, County Cork (?), died Cork, *c.* 610. He is said to have preached throughout southern Ireland, settling eventually as a hermit on Lough Eiroe. A number of disciples gathered around him, and he founded a monastery at Etargabail. He later founded another monastery on the south bank of the River Lee, where the city of Cork now stands, and he is said to have been consecrated the first bishop of Cork. Feast 25 September.

Finnian (Finian, Finden) of Clonard, monk, born possibly County Carlow, Ireland, *c.* 470, died probably 12 December *c.* 549–52. A great biblical scholar, Finnian founded a number of monasteries in Ireland, including Clonard, in County Meath, which was known for its strength of biblical training. He is often referred to as a bishop, but this seems unlikely. Among his students were Ss **Columba, Kieran of Clonmacnois, and Brendan the Voyager**. It seems likely that he wrote *The Penitential of Finnian*, although **Finnian of Moville** has also been suggested as its author.

Finnian of Moville, abbot, born Ireland, *c.* 495, died 579. After studying with Sts **Colman of Dromore** and Mochaw of Noendrum, he founded a monastery at Bromin, in Louth, and another at Moville, in County Down, where his students included St **Columba**. He may have written *The Penitential of Finnian*, although **Finnian of Clonard** seems the more likely author. Feast 10 September.

Fintan of Clonenagh, abbot, born Leinster, *c.* 524, died there, 17 February probably 603, although 594 has also been suggested. Taught by St **Columba** of Terryglass, he founded a monastery in Clonenagh, where students of his austere discipline included St **Comgall** of Bangor. When soldiers came to his monastery bearing the heads of their enemies, he is reported to have had them buried in the monks' cemetery in order that the monks might pray for them.

Fintan of Dún Blésce, sixth/seventh centuries, patron of Doon, Eire, supposedly died 3 January (year unknown). Variously said to be from Munster or Ulster, and to have studied under **Comgall**, he settled in Doon where, according to undocumented tradition, he founded a monastery – a holy well still exists.

Fintan (Findan) of Rheinau, hermit, born Leinster, died Schlaffhausen, 879. After being abducted as a slave by Viking raiders, the young Fintan escaped by swimming from the Orkneys to Scotland, where he was sheltered by a bishop. After making a pilgrimage to Rome, he went to the Benedictine abbey in Sabina, then travelled to an island on the Rhine, near Schlaffhausen. There he joined a group of Irish hermits and remained there until his death.

A missal, believed to have belonged to him, is preserved at Saint Gall library. Feast 15 November.

Fintan (Finian, Finton) of Taghmon (Munnu, Mundus), abbot, died Taghmon, 635. A monk for 18 years, he travelled to join the Iona Community, but was told that St **Columba** had left word before his death instructing him to found an abbey of his own instead. He did so in Taghmon, or Teach Munnu, County Wexford. At the Synod of Magh Lene in 630, he sought to retain Celtic liturgical rituals, but the decision to adopt the Roman liturgy prevailed. Feast 21 October.

Firmanus, abbot, died Macerata, 992. He was abbot of Macerata, near Ascoli Piceno, in the Italian Tronto Valley. Feast 11 March.

Firmilianus, bishop of Caesarea from *c.* 230, died Tarsus, 268. He was educated at the feet of Origen in both Cappadocia and Palestine. He supported St **Cyprian** against Pope **Stephen I** in his contention that those who had lapsed had to be rebaptized on their return to the Church; a letter by him on this theme survives in Cyprian's correspondence. In 264 he was in charge of the first of the synods of Antioch held to investigate the views of Paul of Samosata; he died en route to the second. Feast 28 October.

Firmin of Amiens I, bishop and martyr, born Pamplona, died Amiens, *c.* 303. Very little is known of his life, except that he was possibly a native of Pamplona, who was converted and became a missionary bishop, traditionally the first bishop of Amiens – he was martyred there during the Great Persecution. A later bishop, also called **Firmin** (with whom he is often confused), built the church of St Acheul over his tomb. His relics were translated to Pamplona in 1186. Feast 18 August.

Firmin of Amiens II, bishop, fourth century. Said to have been the son of a convert of **Firmin of Amiens I**, but there is some doubt as to his existence. Feast 1 September.

Firmin of Gabales, bishop, fifth century. He was the third bishop of Gabales (Gévaudan), Mende, France. Feast 14 January.

Fis, monk, fourth/fifth century, died Gabal al-Milh. Coptic Church. He became a monk on the east bank of the Nile, then, after the death of his spiritual guide **Hor**, he moved back to the west side as a hermit. After a vision, however, he founded a monastery of which he became abbot. He resigned his office towards the end of his life, and retired to Gabal al-Milh.

Five Children of Lesbos, martyrs, died Lesbos. Byzantine Church. Put to the sword for their faith at an unknown date.

Flannan of Killaloe, monk, seventh century. Practically nothing is known of him. His father was a king, the ancestor of the Irish O'Brien kings who fostered the cult of Flannan in the twelfth century. He may have worked in Scotland as well as in Ireland. Feast 18 December.

Flavia Domitilla, imperial Roman matron, regarded since the fourth century as a martyr and saint, died *c.* 100. Said to have been the daughter of the Emperor Vespasian, she was married to Domitian's cousin, Titus Flavius Clemens. Domitian banished her to the island of Pandateria when he executed Clemens in 95. According to the Roman historian Cassius Dio, she (like her husband) was accused of atheism, which may or may not imply Christian belief. Eusebius of Caesarea says she suffered as a Christian; similar claims for her husband were not made until the early ninth century. From the fourth century, Flavia Domitilla was regarded as a martyr. The cemetery of Domitilla on the via Ardeatina outside Rome was used as a Christian burial ground. Feast 12 May (suppressed 1969).

Flavia Domitilla, martyred Pontia, *c.* 90. This Flavia is the niece of **Flavia Domitilla** above, and was martyred in the same persecution. Domitian banished her to the island of Pontia, now Ponza, in the Gulf of Gaeta, where she may have been burned. Feast 7 May (suppressed).

Flavian of Antioch II, bishop, died 518. Byzantine Church. Appointed bishop of Antioch by the emperor *c.* 498, in 512 he was replaced by a monophysite.

Flavian of Antioch II, patriarch, died Petra, in present-day Jordan, *c.* 520. He was a Syrian monk, and served as delegate of the patriarch of Antioch at the imperial court in Constantinople. In 498 he himself was appointed patriarch of Antioch by the emperor, Anastasius. He tried to reach a compromise between the monophysites and the teachings of the Council of Chalcedon. Anastasius was eventually won over to the monophysite position, and Flavian was deposed by the Synod of Laodicea and went into exile in 512 to Petra, where he died from wounds incurred during the riots of 511 between the Chalcedonians and monophysites. Feast 20 July.

Flavian of Constantinople, patriarch, died Hypaepa, Lydia, 449. Patriarch of Constantinople 446–9, in 448 he excommunicated the archimandrite Eutyches for heresy concerning the person of Christ. In August 449, under imperial pressure, the decision was reversed, and Flavian and other bishops were deposed at a council in Ephesus. The Roman legates to the meeting, who had brought a Tome from Pope Leo in support of Flavian, were physically attacked – Leo described the gathering as a Robber Synod (*Latrocinium*). Flavian died not long after the council, probably from similar maltreatment. His remains were brought to Constantinople by the Empress **Pulcheria**, and he was vindicated and declared a martyr at the Council of Chalcedon in 451. Three of his letters are preserved among the works of Leo. Feast 18 February.

Flavius and Companions, martyrs, died Bithynia, *c.* 300. Flavius was bishop of Nicomedia and was executed with his brothers **Augustus** and **Augustine**. Feast 7 May.

Flavius Marcellinus, born Rome, died Carthage, north Africa, *c.* 413. A Roman tribune and notary, during a conference between Catholics and Donatists in Carthage in 411 Flavius Marcellinus became acquainted with **Augustine** of Hippo when he upheld the Catholic cause. The Donatists accused him and his brother of implication in a revolt at Heraclian, and both were condemned and executed. While he was in prison, Augustine visited Marcellinus, praised him in several of his letters, and dedicated to him his most famous work, *De civitate Dei*. Marcellinus was subsequently exonerated by the Emperor Honorius, and his name was added to the Roman martyrology by Cardinal Baronius in the sixteenth century. Feast 6 April.

Flora of Beaulieu, born 1300, died Beaulieu, 1347. She entered the priory of the Sisters of the Order of St John of Jerusalem at Beaulieu, which served as a hospice for pilgrims on the road to the shrine of Rocamadour. She had a great devotion to Mary, and had many mystical experiences. Feast 5 October.

Florentina, fl. around Seville *c.* 600. The sister of **Fulgentius of Ecija** and of **Leander** and **Isidore of Seville**, she seems to have been given a convent by Leander, who wrote for her community a work celebrating consecrated virginity and setting out a Rule of 31 chapters for virgins. Isidore dedicated his work *On the catholic faith against the Jews* to her. Her relics were discovered along with those of Fulgentius near Guadalupe, *c.* 1320, and were shared between the Escorial and the Murcia in 1593. The cult of Florentina, patroness of Plasencia, dates from the fifteenth century. Feast 20 June.

Florentius, born Ireland, died Strasbourg, seventh century. Said to have been an Irish monk who settled in Alsace, founded the monastery of Haslach, and was eventually elected bishop of Strasbourg. Feast 7 November.

Florentius of Thessalonika, martyr, born and died Thessalonika, third century. Byzantine Church. Generous to the poor, he was martyred in the persecution of Decius (?).

Florentius of Vienne, bishop, died *c.* 377. One source says that he was a fourth-century bishop who attended the Council of Valence. Another says that he lived in the third century and was martyred under Gallienus *c.* 275. Feast 3 January.

Florian, martyr, died Lauriacum (Lorch), now Austria, 304. A senior official at Noricum, he proclaimed himself Christian. The Roman governor had him scourged, flayed and thrown into the river Emms tied to a stone. He is patron of Poland, Upper Austria and Linz and is invoked against fire because he miraculously extinguished one. Feast 4 May.

Florinus, fl. Switzerland, seventh century. Florinus is the patron saint of the diocese of Chur in Switzerland. He is the subject of a number of miracle stories which are obviously legendary, and hardly any reliable details of his life have survived.

Florus, see **Titus**.

Florus, Laurus and others, martyrs, born and died Illyria, second century. Florus and Laurus were twins, both stone masons employed in building a pagan temple. During the course of this they became Christians, dedicated the temple as a church, and were then martyred by being thrown down a well. Feast 18 August.

Flosculus (Flou), bishop of Orleans, died *c*. 500. Feast 2 February.

Foilan, abbot, born Ireland, died forest of Seneffe, *c*. 655. One of three brothers of a noble family, he came to England and was given land near Yarmouth to build a monastery. When this was destroyed he crossed the Channel and settled in Nivelles. He was murdered by bandits when on a visit to other monasteries. Feast 31 October.

Folcwin, bishop of Thérouanne, France, born late 700s, died Ekelsbecke, France, 14 December 855. Folcwin became bishop of Thérouanne, Pas-de-Calais, France, *c*. 816. He belonged to an illegitimate branch of the Carolingian dynasty, which was no doubt one factor in his appointment. He attended the Synod of Paris in 846 as well as other synods, and he helped secure the relics of St Omer of Thérouanne for the abbey of Saint-Bertin. His biography was written about 100 years after his death by another Folcwin, this one the bishop of Lobbes.

Fornari-Srata, Maria Victoria, see **Victoria Fornari-Strata**.

Fortis Gabrielli, bl., born Gubbio, Umbria, died abbey of Fontevellana, 9 May 1040, cult approved 1756. He became a hermit at Camalduli, in the mountains near Scheggia, under **Ludolph**, later entering the latter's monastery at Fontevellana.

Fortunatus, see **Felix and Fortunatus**.

Forty-Four Martyrs of Palestine, died monastery of St Sabas, Palestine, 614. This group of martyrs, one of several in Palestine, were massacred at their monastery when the Persians, attacking the Byzantine Empire, invaded Palestine. The monastery founded by **Sabas** still exists, by the river Cedron near Jerusalem. Feast 16 May.

Forty Martyrs of England and Wales, between 1535 and 1680 some 357 English and Welsh Roman Catholics were put to death for their beliefs; 199 of these have been beatified and the 40 most popular of these were canonized, as representative of the whole group, on 27 October 1970. The group includes 20 religious and 13 secular priests, 4 laymen and 3 laywomen.

Forty-Two Martyrs of Syria, died 848. Feast 6 March.

Four Crowned Martyrs, martyrs, died Sirmium (Metrovica, Kosovo), 306. The four are really five: Claudius, Nicostratus, Symphorian, Castorius and Simplicius. They were Christians, the last-named being converted by observing the other four, and particularly competent stone masons, who refused to work on a statue of the pagan god Aesculapius. Because they were so skilled, the Emperor Diocletian spared them, but the townspeople were not so forgiving and they were executed by being put into boxes and thrown into the river. Their relics were brought to Rome and a basilica (Quatuor Coronati) was built to commemorate them. They were later confused with four Roman martyrs, all soldiers. Feast 8 November.

Four Hundred Martyrs of Dendera, later third, early fourth centuries. Coptic Church. They were martyred at Dendera in the persecution of Diocletian.

Foy (Faith, Foi), born Agen, France, 290, died there, by burning, 303. Her shrine at Conques, on the pilgrimage route to Santiago, notable for its bejewelled gold reliquary, was popular in the

Middle Ages and continues to flourish today. St Foy is included in the Sarum calendar and has several churches in England named after her, probably because some of her relics were taken to Glastonbury. Feast 6 October.

Franca, fl. eleventh century. She began her religious life as a solitary in Fermo, Italy, before taking vows and entering the convent, it is thought, of San Angelo in Pontano. Towards the end of her life she resumed the eremitical life in Fermo. Feast 1 October.

Franca Visalta, Cistercian, born Piacenza, Italy, 1170, died Pittoli, 1218. She joined the Benedictine convent of St Syrus when she was seven and was professed there when she was 14. Not long after this she was made abbess, but appears to have been rather severe, and was deposed. She later became abbess of the Cistercian convent at Pittoli. Feast 25 April.

Frances Anne Cirer Carbonell, bl., born Majorca, 1781, died there, 27 February 1855, beatified 1989. Already engaged in charitable work, after her parents' death she transformed the farmhouse into a community of Sisters of Charity of St Vincent de Paul and became the superior of a small community. Feast 25 February.

Frances Mézière, bl., martyr, died France, 1794. See **Martyrs of the French Revolution**. Feast 5 February.

Frances Nisch, bl., born Oberdorf-Mittelbiberach, south-east Germany, 1882, died Baden-Baden, 18 May 1913, beatified 1987. From a poor family, working as a maid, she joined the Sisters of Charity of Holy Cross in 1904, working in the kitchens. She died of tuberculosis and popular veneration grew rapidly. Feast 8 May.

Frances of Amboise, born Brittany, 1427, died Nantes, 4 November 1485. She was raised at the court in Brittany and was married, unhappily at first, to Duke Peter of Brittany. Eventually her husband joined her in charitable work among the poor and newly established religious communities. She was a friend of Bl. **John Soreth**, general of the Carmelites, and became a Carmelite herself after

her husband's death, at the convent she had helped establish in Nantes.

Frances of Rome, Frances Bussa de'Leoni, born into a rich noble family in Rome 1384, died there, 9 March 1440. Although at first reluctant to marry, she remained devoted to her husband, Lorenzo Ponziano, until his death. From early in her marriage and along with her sister-in-law she strove to live a simple, prayerful life, accompanied by work with and for the poor and sick of Rome. The two younger of her three children died in childhood. She survived the plundering of the family homes in Rome and Campagna, and the exile of her husband and son. The family was reunited in 1414 and much of their property restored. Frances nursed Lorenzo until his death in 1417, when she retired to live with the religious community of the Oblates of Mary which she had founded at Tor de'Specchi.

Frances Schervier, bl., founder, born Aachen, 3 January 1819, died there, 14 December 1876. Her father was a wealthy businessman, and she had the emperor of Austria as a godfather. Her mother died in 1832 and her elder sisters the following year, so she had to take charge of the household. She also became very active in the Catholic organizations working to relieve the poverty attendant on the Ruhr's rapid industrialization. After the death of her father, and already, from 1844, a Franciscan tertiary, she started a small religious community which eventually became the Sisters of the Poor of St Francis. In 1858 some of the nuns left for the USA, where they ministered to both sides in the Civil War – Frances herself was in the USA at the time.

Frances Tréhet, bl., martyr, born Saint-Mars-sur-la-Futaie, France, 8 April 1756, died Ernée, 13 March 1794. A nun, member of the Congregation of the Sisters of Chapelle-au-Riboul, she taught girls and cared for the sick, and was guillotined for concealing non-conforming priests a week before **Jeanne Véron** – see also **Martyrs of the French Revolution**.

Frances Xavier Cabrini, founder of the Missionary Sisters of Sacred Heart and first US citizen to be canonized, born near Lodi, Italy, 15 July 1850, died Chicago, USA, 22 December 1917. The youngest of

13 children, she had hoped to become a missionary to China, but her parents sent her to be educated as a teacher. She taught for several years following her parents' deaths, took religious vows and established one of the earliest congregations of Missionary Sisters. Her intention to go to China was thwarted when Leo XIII encouraged her to go to the USA. For the rest of her life she travelled throughout Europe and the Americas establishing congregations, schools, hospitals, orphanages and clinics.

Francis Borgia, Jesuit, great-grandson, on his father's side, of Pope Alexander VI and, on his mother's side, of King Ferdinand of Aragon, born near Valencia, 28 October 1510, died Rome, 30 September 1572. Married Eleanor de Castro in 1528 and enjoyed a privileged position at the court of the Emperor Charles V, becoming viceroy of Catalonia in 1539. On his father's death he succeeded him as duke of Gandia and retired with his wife and eight children to the family estates there. Eleanor died suddenly in 1546 and soon after Francis asked to join the Society of Jesus. On the advice of **Ignatius of Loyola** he waited a further three years until his children were settled, and meanwhile studied theology at the university he had founded at Gandia. Francis was ordained in 1551, became commissary general of the Jesuits in Spain in 1554 and father general of the order in 1565. Under his influence the Society was greatly strengthened and enjoyed both reform and expansion in Europe, the Far East and the Americas. Francis was widely recognized as a good and holy man, as well as an efficient administrator, and up to his death remained sensitive to the welfare of his family and the needs of the poor and sick. Feast 10 October.

Francis Caracciolo (Ascanio), co-founder of the Clerks Regular Minor, born into a distinguished religious family at Villa Santa Maria, Abruzzi, Italy, 13 October 1563, died Agnone, Italy, 4 June 1608. He was ordained in Naples in 1587 and later joined Fabricius Caracciolo Marsicovetere and John Augustine Adorno and helped draw up the Rule for the Clerks Regular Minor. Their intention was to engage in charitable works, to be engaged in perpetual adoration of the Blessed Sacrament, and in addition to poverty, chastity and obedience they took a fourth vow, not to aspire to any ecclesiastical office. Adorno became the first superior and Francis Caracciolo followed him in 1591 and remained in office until 1598. During this time the order spread to Rome and Francis himself established houses in Madrid, Valladolid and Alcala in Spain. He retired to a life of contemplation in 1607, but the following year went to negotiate the transfer of a house from the Oratorians in Agnone and died there after a brief illness.

Francis Chartier, martyr, born Marigné, Maine-et-Loire, France, 6 June 1762, died Angers, 22 March 1794. A secular priest, he refused to take the oath of allegiance to the revolutionary authorities and protested at the treatment of priests who would not conform. He was guillotined – see also **Martyrs of the French Revolution**.

Francis de Capillas, bl., Spanish Dominican missionary and martyr, born Baquerin de Campos, Spain, 18 August 1607, died by beheading at Fukien, China, 15 January 1648. He joined the Dominicans and went to Manila in 1631. He was ordained and from 1633 to 1641 worked in Cagayan and Babuyanes. He was sent to China, via Formosa, in 1642 and returned with Francisco Diaz to Fukien during the Tartar invasions. In 1647 Christianity was outlawed and almost immediately Francis was arrested and tortured, and later beheaded.

Francis de Posadas, bl., born Córdoba, 5 November 1644, died there, 20 September 1713. The son of a grocer, he entered the Dominicans in November 1662 in Córdoba, and was eventually ordained. He was a man of deep prayer – including mystical experiences – but he made his name as a preacher, travelling around Spain. He avoided all preferment, including the office of bishop.

Francis de Sales, bishop, joint founder of the Visitandines, born Thorens, France, 21 August 1567, died Lyons, France, 28 December 1622. Born into an aristocratic family, Francis gave up a promising career in public service in favour of the priesthood. He was ordained in 1593 and appointed provost of Geneva. Here he strove to reconvert the Calvinists of the Chablais region, and his winsome preaching drew back thousands into the Catholic fold.

Appointed bishop of Geneva in 1602, he became the spiritual director for **Jane Frances Fremiot de Chantal**, with whom he formed the Visitandine Order in 1610. His spiritual instructions were published as the *Introduction to the Devout Life* (1608) and *Treatise on the Love of God* (1616), and both became deeply influential. He was canonized in 1665. Feast 24 January.

Francis Dickenson, bl., martyr, born Otley, West Riding, Yorkshire, 1565, died Rochester, Kent, 19 or 30 April 1590, beatified 1929. Ordained at Rheims in 1589, he and **Miles Gerard** were shipwrecked at Dover and arrested. Francis was tortured and a forced confession was extracted. Francis and Miles are commemorated together. Feast 30 April.

Francis Faà di Bruno, bl., born Allessandria, Piedmont, 29 March 1825, died Turin, 27 March 1888, beatified 1988. First an army officer, he studied in Paris and was a professor at Turin University from 1859. He founded congregations to support working girls, single mothers and prostitutes. He was ordained in Rome in 1876.

Francis Fogolla, martyr, born Montereggio di Mulazzo, Massa, Italy, 4 October 1839, died Taiyuan, Shanxi, China, 9 July 1900, beatified 1946, canonized 2000. A Franciscan priest, in China since 1866, he spoke Chinese fluently. **Gregory Grassi**'s coadjutor, he was killed with his group during the Boxer Rebellion. Feast 8 July. See **Franciscan Martyrs of China** and **Martyrs of Shanxi**.

Francis Galvez, bl., born Utiel, 1578, died Yedo (Tokyo), 4 December 1623. He entered the Franciscans at Valencia in 1591 and volunteered for missionary work in the Far East. He first spent eight years in Mexico, then a few years in the Philippines learning Japanese. He arrived in Japan in 1612, only to be expelled two years later. He managed to return, and carried on his missionary work until he was captured and executed by being burned at the stake.

Francis Gárate, born Azpeitia, Spain, 3 February 1857, died Bilbao, 9 September 1929. From a poor family, he went to work at the Jesuit college at

Oduña when he was 14, and when he was 17 he himself joined the Society as a lay brother. He worked for a few years looking after sick Jesuits near Vigo, but because his own health deteriorated, he was sent to work in the Jesuit University of Deusto, in Bilboa, where for 41 years he acted as doorkeeper.

Francis-Isidore Gagelin, martyr, born Montperreux, Doubs, France, 10 May 1799, died Bāi Dâu, Saigon, Vietnam, 17 October 1833, beatified 1900, canonized 1988. A priest of the Paris Foreign Missions Society, previously cartographer at the imperial court, his body was ordered by the emperor to be dug up after three days to make sure he had not been resurrected. See **Martyrs of Vietnam**.

Francis Jaccard, martyr, born Onion, Haute-Savoie, France, 16 September 1799, died Vietnam, 21 September 1838, beatified 1900, canonized 1988. He was a priest of the Paris Foreign Missions Society. See **Martyrs of Vietnam**.

Francis Joseph de la Rochefoucauld-Bayers, bl., bishop of Beauvais, France, born Angouleme, 28 March 1755, died Paris, 2 September 1792. As a representative of the clergy in the States General of 1789, he defended the privileges of the clergy and of the court. As a result both he and his brother Pierre Louis, bishop of Senlis, were shortly afterwards declared 'enemies of the constitutional monarchy' and taken to the notorious prison of Carmes. They were both murdered in the general massacre of political prisoners.

Francis Joseph Rudigier, bishop, born Partheneu, 7 April 1811, died Linz, 29 November 1884. In 1845 Rudigier became court chaplain and tutor to Franz Josef and to Maximilian, later emperors of Austria and Mexico respectively. As bishop of Linz he zealously defended the Church's rights, opposing Josephinism and secular liberalism. He also promoted Catholic association, the Catholic press and Catholic social action. His cause for canonization was introduced in 1905.

Francis Maria of Camporosso, Italian Capuchin lay brother, born Camporosso (Imperia), 27 December 1804, died Genoa, 17 September 1866. He joined the Capuchin order in 1821, pronouncing his solemn vows four years later. He was alms gatherer for the friary in Genoa for 40 years, gaining a wide recognition for the spiritual advice and catechetical instruction he gave whilst on his begging rounds. He died of cholera, having caught the disease from those whom he was nursing, during the epidemic of 1866.

Francis of Assisi (Giovanni de Bernadone), founder of the Franciscans, born Assisi, Italy, *c.* 1181, died there, 3 October 1226. Francis came from a prosperous family and as a youth led a carefree and reckless life. He repented following a serious illness, dedicating himself to a life of prayer and service to the poor and the sick. Subsequently he renounced his wealth, embraced poverty and began itinerant preaching. He soon attracted a number of disciples, for whom he drew up a Rule characterized by simplicity of life. This was given papal approval in 1212, thereby establishing the Franciscan order. Known as 'friars minor', Francis's followers travelled extensively in their preaching journeys, Francis himself visiting Spain, eastern Europe and Egypt. In 1221 he founded an order of Tertiaries, who sought to live out Franciscan ideals while still remaining in the world. Francis's ideals, simple piety and lifestyle all combine to make him probably the supreme model of Christian sanctity. The alleged manifestation in his body of the stigmata in 1224 is often regarded as symbolic of this. He was canonized in 1228. Feast 4 October.

Francis of Cremona, bl., died 1272. Feast 18 January.

Francis of Fabriano, bl., born Fabriano, Marche region, Italy, 2 September 1251, died 22 April *c.*1322, cult approved 1775. He joined the Franciscans aged 16 and became an effective preacher, perceived as holy and wise. He was guardian (superior) of the house in Fabriano for a time and founded the first Franciscan library with his inheritance.

Francis of Fermo, see **Monaldus of Ancona**.

Francis of Geronimo (di Girolamo), Jesuit, born near Taranto, south-east Italy, 17 December 1642,

died Naples, 11 May 1716. Went to study at the Gesu Vecchio in Naples and, four years after his ordination there, entered the Society of Jesus in 1670. Despite his desire to go as a missionary to the East, he obeyed his superiors and spent the next 40 years in apostolic work in and around Naples. He enlisted the support of ordinary workers in his ministry, in what became known as the 'Oratorio della Missione'. He went to the people: in the streets and squares, in the prisons and hospitals, and even in the ships. He was an imaginative and dramatic speaker who drew vast crowds to his short sermons, his longer missions and to the confessional.

Francis of Lucera, born Lucera, Italy, 1681, died there, 29 November 1742. Baptized Donato Antonio Giovanni Fasani, he was sent by his stepfather to be educated by the Friars Minor Conventuals, and on completion of his schooling he joined the order. After his studies he was ordained in Assisi in 1705, and in 1707 returned to Lucera, where he taught and preached. He also wrote handbooks for preachers. He had a great concern for the poor, and particularly for those in prison.

Francis of Paola, founder of the Order of Minims, born Paola, Italy, 27 March 1416, died Plessis-les-Tours, France, 2 April 1507. As a youth his parents placed him in a friary, awakening in him a vocation to the ascetic life. Aged 20, he retired to a cave by the sea, where others joined him and a religious brotherhood developed. Officially established in 1474 as the Order of Minims, it was characterized by charitable works and an austere lifestyle. Francis became renowned for his sanctity, and numerous miracles were attributed to him. He spent the last 25 years of his life in France, having been summoned by the dying Louis IX for spiritual consolation, subsequently becoming the spiritual director of Louis's son, Charles VIII. He was also involved in important diplomatic missions.

Francis of Pesaro, bl., born Pesaro, *c.* 1270, died there, 1330. He joined the Franciscan Third Order *c.* 1300 and eventually went to live in a hermitage on Mount San Bartolo. He attracted disciples and established a house for them near Pesaro. He also assisted in the foundation of the Confraternity of the Annunciation to look after the sick and dying and to bury the dead. Feast 1 October.

Francis of Quebec, bl., bishop, born Montigny-sur-Aure, France, 1623, died Quebec, 1708, beatified 1980. Destined for high ecclesiastical office, he was ordained in 1647. Vicar apostolic for New France (Canada) from 1658, he founded parishes and a seminary and defended the indigenous Indians from exploitation, becoming first bishop of Quebec in 1674. Feast 6 May.

Francis of St Mary and Companions, bl., martyrs, died Nagasaki, Japan, 1627. Feast 17 August.

Francis Page, martyr, bl., born Antwerp, died Tyburn, London, 20 April 1602, beatified 1929. He was a clerk in London when the woman with whom he was in love introduced him to the Jesuit Father John Gerard – he was, indeed, arrested in the first instance because he paid so many visits to Gerard in the Tower. He purchased his release and went to study for the priesthood at Douai. He was ordained at Arras in April 1600 and returned to England in May that year. He was arrested saying mass in **Anne Line**'s house. He is commemorated with **Robert Wilkinson**, possibly his relative, with whom he was hanged, drawn and quartered.

Francis Palau y Quer, bl., born Aytona, Lérida, Spain, died Tarragona, 20 March 1872, beatified 1988. First a Discalced Carmelite, he was ordained priest in 1836 after his friary was closed. Imprisoned and exiled on several occasions when anti-Church political factions held sway, he founded two congregations of Missionary Carmelites.

Francis Patrizi, bl., born Siena, died there, 1328, cult approved 1743. Converted on hearing a sermon by the noted preacher **Ambrose Sansedoni**, he was received as a Servite friar by **Philip Benizi**. He had the gift of being able to reconcile enemies. Feast 26 May.

Francis (François) Pelletier, bl., martyred during the French Revolution, 1794, commemorated with **Jacob Ledoyen** and **Peter Tessier** – see **Martyrs of the French Revolution**. Feast 5 January.

Francis-Régis Clet, martyr, born Grenoble, France, 19 August 1748, died Wuchang Distict, Wuhan, Hubei, China, 17 February 1820, beatified 1900, canonized 2000. A Lazarist, he worked in Annecy and Paris as novice master before travelling to Macao in 1791. Much loved by his converts, who protected him during a period of persecution, he was betrayed, tortured and slowly strangled. Feast 18 February. See **Martyrs of China**.

Francis Serrano, see **Peter Sanz**.

Francis Solano, Franciscan, born Cortilla, Spain, 10 March 1549, died Lima, Peru, 14 July 1610. Joined the Franciscans in Montilla in 1569 and, after a period as master of novices, was sent to Peru in 1589. He spent the next 20 years there, successfully engaged in missionary work. He learned many of the local languages and dialects and won the affection of many throughout Peru.

Francis Xavier, pioneer Jesuit missionary to Asia, born Castle Xavier, Navarre, Spain, 7 April 1506, died Shangchuan Dao Island, China, 3 December 1552. He studied at the University of Paris (MA, 1530) along with **Ignatius Loyola**. A founding member of the Society of Jesus, he was ordained priest in 1537. He was assigned to missions in the East and arrived in Goa in May 1541. He worked with children and the poor and baptized thousands from October 1542 to December 1544. He then visited Sri Lanka (1544–5), Melaka and the Moluccas. In Japan in August 1549 he worked with state and religious leaders. In 1552 he returned to Goa and then Melaka, preparing to go to China, but died in sight of his goal. Many of his letters survive, and his catechisms. He was canonized in 1622 and proclaimed Patron of Missions, 14 December 1927.

Franciscan Martyrs of China, died 1900. It is estimated that over 100,000 Christians were put to death in the Boxer Rising which took place under the Dowager Empress Tz'u-hsi. In 1946, 29 of these, mostly Franciscan priests, brothers, sisters and tertiaries, were beatified to represent the wider group. They were: Theodore Balat, Andrew Bauer, Mary Adolphine Dierk, Elias Facchini, Bishop Antoninus Fantosanti, Bishop Francis Fogolla, Mathias Fun-Te, Joseph Mary Gambaro, Caesidius

Giacomantonio, Bishop Gregory Grassi, Mary Emiliana Grivot, Mary of Peace Guiliani, James Ien-Kutun, Mary Amandina Jeuris, Mary of Ste. Nathalie Kerguin, Mary of St Justus Moreau, Mary Clare Nanette, Thomas Sen, Peter Tchang-Pau-Nien, John Tciang, another John Tciang, Philip Tciang, Francis Tciang-Iun, James Tciao-Tcieum-Sin, Simon Tcing, Patrick Tun, Peter U-Ngan-Pau, John Van, Peter Van-al-man.

Francisco Gil de Federich de Sans, martyr, born Tortosa, Spain, 14 December 1702, died Hanoi, Vietnam, 22 January 1745, with **Alonzo Lenziana**, beatified 1906, canonized 1988. Both Dominican priests, they are the two earliest European martyrs in Vietnam for whom there are records. See **Martyrs of Vietnam**.

Franco Lippi, bl., Carmelite lay brother, born near Siena, Italy, 1211, died there, 11 April 1291. He led a life of crime until he became blind at about the age of 50. He repented and went on pilgrimage to Santiago de Compostela and regained his sight. He journeyed to Rome and then returned to Siena, where he lived as a hermit. He continued this life after he became a Carmelite lay brother, living in a small cell near to the chapel of Our Lady. In about 1340 his body was exhumed and some of his relics removed to Cremona. He first appears in Carmelite liturgy in 1672. Feast 11 December.

Françoise, see **Frances**.

Frederick, bl., abbot, from Swabia, died Ebersberg, Bavaria, c. 1071. A Benedictine at Einsiedeln in Switzerland, in 1066 he was sent with other monks to reform Hirschau abbey, Würtemberg. Falsely accused by monks there who opposed change, he was deposed in 1069 and had to retire. Feast 7 May.

Frederick, bl., abbot, born Hallum, Frisia, died there, 1175. He was the founder and first abbot of the Premonstratensian abbey of Mariengart. Feast 3 March.

Frederick Jansoone, bl., missionary, born Ghyvelde, near Lille, 19 November 1838, died Montreal, 4 August 1916. In 1864 he entered the Franciscans at Amiens, and was ordained in 1870.

He worked in Paris before being sent to the Holy Land in 1876. After his return in 1881 he was sent to Canada, where he was involved in raising funds for the Holy Places and promoting pilgrimages to them. He also excelled as a missioner and retreat giver.

Frederick of Regensburg, bl., born Regensburg, died there, 30 November 1329. Of poor parents, he eventually joined the Augustinians as a lay brother and was chiefly employed as a carpenter.

Frederick of Utrecht, bishop and martyr, died Walcheren, Netherlands, 18 July 838. He became bishop of Utrecht in 825 and sent missionaries to the northern parts of the country to evangelize the pagans. He became involved in the quarrels between the emperor, Louis the Pious, his wife Judith, and his sons. According to tradition, Louis's sons accused their stepmother of adultery, and when Frederick publicly rebuked her, she had him murdered. However, it is more likely that he was murdered by pagans in the Walcheren area who objected to his evangelizing.

Friardus and Secundellus, hermits, died c. 570. They lived near Nantes, on an island in the Loire, and were evangelists to the surrounding area. Feast 1 August.

Frideswide, born between 650 and 680, died Oxford, traditionally 735, but oldest source suggests 727. Little is known of her life, but traditionally she was a consecrated virgin, the first abbess of a convent founded in Oxford by her father, a local Anglo-Saxon ruler. After refusing an offer of marriage from the 'king of Leicester', she was by a miracle transported from Oxford and into hiding, and her suitor was struck blind (or dead – the accounts vary) for persisting in his attempts to marry her. Her monastery was recorded as having been sacked by Danish armies in the early eleventh century, but was refounded by Augustinians in 1122. From the twelfth century until the dissolution of the remaining monasteries in 1538, her shrine was a place of pilgrimage. Feast 19 October.

Fridian, see **Frigidia of Lucca**.

Fridolin, abbot, possibly sixth century. Possibly of Irish origin, he may have been a monk at Luxeuil and later founded the Benedictine abbey at Säckingen. He is seen as the apostle of the Upper Rhine. Feast 6 March.

Frigidia of Lucca, bishop and saint, died Lucca, c. 588 (?). Apparently of Irish origin, he settled as a hermit in Italy, where he acquired a reputation for his sanctity and was chosen as bishop of Lucca. After his death, his cult spread beyond Tuscany into other regions of Italy and Corsica; his relics, miraculously discovered in the eighth century, are in a church dedicated to his memory in Lucca. Most of our information about him comes from a life of which the earliest manuscripts are from the eleventh century; many scholars doubt much of its account, and in one case date Frigidia as early as the third century. Feast 18 March.

Frithebert, bishop, died Hexham, Northumbria, 766. He was consecrated bishop of Hexham, in northern England, in 735, and was for a time administrator of Lindisfarne, but otherwise little is known of him. Feast 23 December.

Frodobert, abbot, died c. 667. A monk of Luxeuil under **Waldebert**, he was founder and first abbot of Moutier-la-Celle near Troyes, where he was known for his life of prayer and great austerity. Feast 1 January.

Froilan, bishop, born Luga, Galicia region of Spain, 832, died Léon, 905. With his companion, **Attilanus**, and with the authorization of Alfonso III of Oviedo, he led the restoration of monastic observance at Moruruela in Old Castile and later throughout western Spain. He became abbot and later bishop of Léon. He was included in the Roman martyrology in 1724. Feast 3 October.

Frovinus (Frowin II), bl., abbot, died 1178. A Benedictine of St Blasien in the Black Forest, in 1143 he became abbot of Engelberg, Switzerland, where he founded a school, a library and wrote a history of the abbey. Feast 27 March.

Fructosus, bishop and martyr, died Tarragona, 259. He was bishop of Tarragona and was arrested with two of his deacons, **Augurius** and **Eulogius**

during the Valerian persecutions. Under interrogation he refused to recognize the Roman gods or sacrifice to the image of the emperor, and with his deacons was burned in the amphitheatre. Feast 21 January.

Fructuosus of Braga, Spanish monk, archbishop, died Braga, now in Portugal, c. 665. He lived alone in a mountain area of Galicia and was eventually joined by numerous pupils, and so was established the monastery of Complutum, the first of many monasteries founded by Fructuosus. In 654 he was made bishop of Dumium, and in 656 archbishop of Braga. His remains were moved to Compostela. He is usually shown with a stag, which he allegedly saved from hunters. Feast 16 April.

Frumentius, bishop, 'Apostle to the Abyssinians', born Tyre (Sur in modern Lebanon), c. 300, died Axum, c. 380. As a young man Frumentius was captured by Abyssinians while on a trading journey. At Axum he was shown favour by their king, who made him his secretary. Following the king's death, his queen persuaded Frumentius to help govern the country until the crown prince was of age. As a Christian, Frumentius used his position as a platform for evangelism, with considerable success. When he was eventually released he reported his work to **Athanasius**, who appointed him bishop of Axum c. 340. Frumentius took the title 'Abuna' (Our Father), still used by primates of the Abyssinian Church. Feast 27 October.

Fulbert of Chartres, bishop, born probably France, c. 960, died Chartres, 10 April 1028. He was educated at Rheims and one of his teachers was Gerbert, the future Pope Sylvester II. He was chancellor of the church of Chartres and treasurer of St Hilary's in Poitiers. In 990 Fulbert opened a school at Chartres which eventually drew scholars from all over Europe. In 1007 he was made bishop of Chartres, but continued to teach. The cathedral burned down in 1020 and Fulbert began an even more splendid building in its place, financed by several European monarchs. The present cathedral is, however, a later construction. Although not a monk himself, he was friendly with many monks of his time and did a lot to reform the clergy. He left many writings, including letters, treatises, hymns and sermons, and he was renowned throughout

Europe for his extensive learning and was noted for his humility, pastoral concern and practical charity.

Fulcran of Lodeve, bishop, died Lodeve, near Montpellier, 13 February 1006. According to the biography written in the fourteenth century by one of his successors (Bernard Guidonis), Fulcran came from a respected family and dedicated himself to the Church as a youth. He was consecrated bishop of Lodeve, France, on 4 February 949, strove to uphold morality in his diocese, especially among the clergy, and rebuilt many churches and convents. Revered as a saint after his death, his preserved body was burned by Huguenots in 1572.

Fulgentius of Ecija, bishop, born probably Seville, *c*. 540–60, died probably Ecija, *c*. 619. One of four saintly siblings of a distinguished Hispano-Roman family (see **Florentina, Isidore of Seville, Leander**), he became bishop of Ecija and attended the councils of Toledo (610) and Seville (619). Around 1320 his relics were discovered near Guadalupe, which led to claims that he was bishop of Cartagena; in 1593 they were shared between the Escorial and the see of Cartagena, where he had become patron saint. His cult is immemorial in Spain. Some Spanish breviaries falsely attribute to him writings by **Fulgentius of Ruspe** and Fabius Planciades Fulgentius. Feast 16 January.

Fulgentius of Ruspe, bishop, born Carthage, *c*. 460, died Ruspe, *c*. 530 (precise dates disputed). He was a former Roman civil servant who became a monk, and was appointed bishop of Ruspe in north Africa early in the sixth century. Fulgentius was a staunch upholder of the Nicene faith, which brought him into conflict with the Arian King Thrasamund; as a result Fulgentius twice suffered banishment. His admiration for the theology of **Augustine** of Hippo is evident in his writings. Feast 1 January.

Fulk of Neuilly, bl., priest and preacher of the fourth Crusade, died 2 March 1201. Nothing is known of his early life. From 1191 he served as a priest in the church of Neuilly-sur-Marne near Paris. A brilliant preacher, according to Villehardouin, Fulk inspired Count Thibault III of Champagne to ask Pope Innocent III to organize the fourth Crusade, and later Fulk preached the Crusade across France, although he died before the Crusade began.

Fulrad, abbot, born Alsace, died 784. A monk at the abbey of Saint-Denis, near Paris, he became abbot some time before 751. In 763 he visited Rome to obtain relics of Ss **Vitus, Alexander, Hippolytus** and others. He was a member of the royal council under Pepin (died 768), **Carloman** (died 771) and **Charlemagne** (768–814), and was head of the court clergy. He was involved in politics, and worked for the unification of the Frankish kingdom, which was achieved after the death of Carloman in 771. Feast 16 July.

Fursey, Irish abbot or bishop, and missionary, born near Lough Corrib, Ireland, died Mezerolles, diocese of Amiens, France, *c*. 650. He became a monk and founded a monastery in the diocese of Tuam, before travelling to England *c*. 630. He was welcomed by King Sigebert of East Anglia, who gave him lands to found a monastery at Burgh Castle, near Yarmouth. After the defeat of Sigebert in battle, Fursey travelled to Gaul (now in France), where he founded a monastery at Lagny-sur-Marne. His remains were first translated to a shrine in 654, and he was widely venerated in the Middle Ages, partly as a result of an account of his visions of heaven and hell, written by **Bede**. Feast 16 January.

Fuscian and Victoricus, martyrs, died Amiens, *c*. 285 (?). Roman missionaries to northern Gaul. Feast 11 December.

Gabinus, martyr, died Sardinia, fourth century. Feast 30 May.

Gabra, means 'Servant of'.

Gabra Amlak, monk, fourteenth century. Ethiopian Church. One of the 'seven sons of **Eustace**'.

Gabra Endreyas, monk, born Dambege, *c.* 1340, died Dabra Qozat. Ethiopian Church. Neftali by name, he married and had five children but then, as the result of a vision, he decided to become a monk, leaving his wife and children, and entered Dabra Qozat, where he was given his new name. He became abbot of the monastery.

Gabra Iyasus, monk, born Wag, mid-fourteenth century. Ethiopian Church. He had heard of the fame of **Eustace** and became his disciple, accompanying him to Alexandria to seek the blessing of the patriarch. They both lived for 14 years in the desert of Scete, then travelled to Armenia. Eustace died there, but not before advising Gabra Iyasus to go to Enfraz. Gabra Iyasus set out, but first tried to settle in some other spot. Eustace apeared to him and told him to move on, eventually to Wayna Dega, where he constructed a church and a monastery, Dabra Dabsan. He made many conversions, and he was brought food and water by a dog.

Gabra Krestos, monk, fourteenth/fifteenth centuries. Ethiopian Church. A disciple of **Zena Marqos**, who evangelized Damot.

Gabra Madhen, monk. Ethiopian Church. Feast 8 July.

Gabra Manfus Qeddus, monk, fourteenth/fifteenth centuries. Ethiopian Church. One of the most popular of Ethiopian saints, but his life as recounted is so extraordinary that it is impossible to distinguish the historical (if any) from the legendary. He is, for instance, given a lifespan of well over 500 years, 100 of which were spent standing in a lake, in penance for the sins of the people.

Gabra Marawi, monk, fourteenth/fifteenth centuries. Ethiopian Church. A disciple of **Zena Marqos**. Feast 26 February.

Gabra Maryam of Dabra Algen, monk, fifteenth century. Ethiopian Church. Founder of Dabra Algen.

Gabra Maryam of Dabra Zalkhun, monk. Ethiopian Church. Entered Dabra Zalkhun when very young and was deeply pious, making prostrations before the altar every night when the other monks had gone to bed. He was elected superior of the monastery, and was renowned for miracles. Feast 1 November.

Gabra Masqal of Gar'Alta, monk. Ethiopian Church. Founder of the monastery of Dabra Ma'ar, near Gar'Alta in Tigre.

Gabra Masqal of Guetman, monk, fourteenth/fifteenth centuries. Ethiopian Church. A disciple of **Samuel of Dabra Halleluya**, he founded a hermitage at Lagaso, in Tigre, and was renowned for miracles.

Gabra Michael, bl., martyr, born Ethiopia, *c.* 1791, died Gondar (?), 28 August 1855. A Coptic monk, well known for learning and holiness, he befriended Catholic missionaries to Ethiopia, was received in Rome by the pope and became a Catholic in 1844. He was ordained priest in Tigre in 1851 and opened a seminary. In 1855 there was a renewed persecution of Catholics. Gabra was imprisoned and threatened with death unless he reconverted to the Coptic Church, which he refused to do. He died after much torture and being marched from place to place in the entourage of the king.

Gabra Nazrawi, monk, fourteenth/fifteenth centuries. Ethiopian Church. Born of noble parents and well educated, he was a disciple of **John of Dabra Bizan**, but founded his own monastery in Tigre. He was particularly devoted to the passion of Christ, was ordained priest, and was renowned for miracles. Feast 15 December.

Gabra Seyon, monk, thirteenth century. Ethiopian Church. Brother of **Iyasus Mo'a**, he lived the life of a hermit near the monastery of Dabra Damo, where he lived in a cave. It is said of him that he spent so long standing in prayer that his legs swelled up. He had a reputation as a miracle worker.

Gabre Her, monk, fifteenth century. Ethiopian Church. Little is known about him, except that he came from Haramat.

Gabriel, abbot of St Stephen's, Jerusalem, died *c.* 490. Feast 26 January.

Gabriel, bl., born Alini, died Constantinople, 2 February 1676. Byzantine Church. When young he became a monk, then moved to Constantinople, where he became the cantor in the patriarchal church. He was determined to become a martyr, so he went out one day into the street and insulted a passing Muslim and Islam in general. He was thrown into prison and tortured, resisting all attempts to make him convert to Islam. He was therefore beheaded.

Gabriel, martyr. Church of the Old Believers, see **Alexander Guttoeva**.

Gabriel Aleksandrovic Protopopov, martyr, born Pecenegi, 26 March 1880, died Char'kov, 23 May 1938. Ukrainian Church, Moscow Patriarchate. Before his arrest he was a priest of the church of the Three Holy Bishops in Char'kov. Feast 19 May.

Gabriel Ferretti, bl., Franciscan, born Ancona, Italy, 1385, into the family of the counts of Ferretti, died convent of St Francesco ad Alto, 9 November 1456. He became a member of the Friars Minor Observant in Ancona against the wishes of his family. He became guardian of the convent of St Maria ad Alto in 1425 and was elected provincial *c.* 1434. The minister general sent him to preach in Bosnia in 1438, but his brethren solicited Eugenius IV to release him from this post as they had need of his talents. He was named guardian of St Francesco ad Alto in 1449. Feast 12 November.

Gabriel Kikodze, bishop, born Bachvi, western Georgia, 15 November 1825, died Imerethi, 25 January 1896. Baptized Gerasimos, his father was a priest, and he studied at the seminary, first in Tbilisi, then in Russia at Pskov, and finally in St Petersburg. In addition to philosophy and theology he studied psychology, and taught maths and physics as well as ecclesiastical discipline. After the death of his wife and children in 1857, possibly from a cholera epidemic, he became a monk, taking the name Gabriel. The following year he went as archimandrite to the monastery of Davidgaregi, being ordained bishop of Gori, in eastern Georgia, at the end of that year. Two years later he went to Imerethi, western Georgia. He was particularly renowned as a preacher, and his volumes of sermons have been translated into several languages. He was a consistent defender of the Georgian people, and a critic of the Tsarist regime; one of his secretaries was assassinated. He was formally canonized by the Georgian Church in 1995.

Gabriel Lalemant, martyr, born Paris, 10 October 1610, died St Ignatius Mission, 17 March 1649. He joined the Society of Jesus in Paris in 1630, arriving in Canada 16 years later. He was assigned as an assistant to **John de Brébeuf** and was martyred with him, being tortured to death the day after his companion had died. Feast, with John de Brébeuf, 19 October – see also **Martyrs of North America**.

Gabriel Mzire, monk, died monastery of Davidgaregi, 1802. Georgian Church. He became a monk at Davidgaregi, and from 1780 onwards produced a number of spiritual works, as well as translations in Georgian of some of the more important Greek Fathers of the Church. He was killed during an attack on the monastery by Muslims. Feast 17 March.

Gabriel of Alexandria I, patriarch, born Ilmay, died monastery of St Macarius, 15 February 920. Coptic Church. Born in the Delta, he entered the monastery of St Macarius as a young man and was elected patriarch in 909. Faced with the expenses of running the Church and the taxes imposed by the Muslim authorities, he had no alternative but, like his predecessor, to have recourse to simony to pay his way. Partly because he loved solitude, and partly because of the danger of living in Alexandria, he remained in the monastery throughout his period as patriarch.

Gabriel of Alexandria II, patriarch, born Old Cairo, c. 1084, died Alexandria, 5 April 1145. Coptic Church. Abu al-Ala came from a well-to-do family and had a position in the civil administration, as well as being deacon in one of Cairo's churches. He was well read and had a large library. In 1131 he was elected patriarch. He later added the office of bishop of Old Cairo. He was known as a reformer, battling against simony and banning burials within churches – even the interment of patriarchs. He was imprisoned for a time by the Muslim authorities, and successfully opposed the wish of the Ethiopian Church to have its own metropolitan.

Gabriel of Alexandria VII, patriarch, born Munsiyyat AbuA'isah, c. 1476, died Dayr al-Maymun, 26 October 1568. Coptic Church. Ibn Muhanna was the son of a priest of Old Cairo. He became a monk at the monastery of al-Suryan, where he was given the name Raphael, which was that of his father. He took the name Gabriel on being elected patriarch in 1525. During his patriarchate he restored several monasteries, including two on the Red Sea which had been destroyed by Bedouin. He

renewed links with the Church in Ethiopia, and engaged in an exchange of letters with two successive popes. Towards the end of his life he had to retire to the monastery of St Anthony at Dayr al-Maymun because of the financial demands of the sultan.

Gabriel of Bet Qustan, bishop, born Bet Qustan, died Qartmin, 648. Syrian Church. He became a monk and lived for seven years in the monastery of Ss Sergius and Bacchus, north of Hah, but then he moved to the monastery of Qartmin where he became superior, and in 634 was ordained bishop. He was renowned for miracles.

Gabriel of Constantinople II, patriarch, died 3 December 1659. Byzantine Church. Previously bishop of Ganosand Chora, he was elected ecumenical patriarch on 24 March 1657, but was promptly deposed, having been in office only a dozen days. He was then made metropolitan of Prussa, but was accused both by Jews and Muslims of proselytism, and was condemned to death.

Gabriel of Edessa, bishop. Syrian Church. Nothing is known of him.

Gabriel of Egypt, and Kirmidolis, born Egypt, died there, 1522. Byzantine Church. They were unjustly accused of fouling a mosque, and accepted martyrdom rather than abandon their faith. Their relics were sold by one of their executioners to Patriarch Joachim, who took them to the church of St Nicholas in Cairo. Feast 18 October.

Gabriel of Galata, born Tefrike, died Galata (a quarter of Constantinople), 1662. Byzantine Church. He became a Muslim and entered the Muslim army, seeing service in Cyprus. He later repented and fled to Europe, where in penance he went on pilgrimage to several shrines, after which he returned to Constantinople, proclaimed he was once more a Christian, and was executed.

Gabriel of Iviron, bl., monk, born Georgia, died Mount Athos. Byzantine Church. He lived in a cave near the monastery of Iviron on Mount Athos. It is recounted that, in 1004, he walked on the waves to rescue an icon of the Mother of God from the sea where, according to one version of the story, it had been thrown by a pious widow living near Nicaea to save it from the iconoclasts. He carried it to the monastery, but the icon mysteriously moved itself to his cave, where it remained until there was built a church for it near the gate to the monastery – from which the icon takes its name, *Portaitissa*. Gabriel's cave afterwards became a church. Feast 13 May.

Gabriel of Kaskar, monk, born Bet Aramaye, died monastery of Mahoze, 739. Syrian Church. He founded three monasteries, Mahoze (Arewan) being the first.

Gabriel of Lesnovo, hermit, born Ossoce, Macedonia, died Lesnovo, eleventh/twelfth centuries. Bulgarian Church. Born of fairly well-to-do parents, they wanted him to marry but, wishing to preserve his virginity, he prayed and the woman whom he was to marry died, leaving him free to enter a monastery. He founded a monastery not far from Kratovo, which became known as the monastery of Lesnovo. Gabriel, however, withdrew to a mountainside, where he lived as a hermit, practising hesychasm. He returned to his foundation at the end of his life. He died on 15 January, which is now his feast day, although the year is unknown.

Gabriel of Mount Athos, born near Kiev, 8 January 1849, died Novonikolaevsk, 19 October 1901. Ukrainian Church, Moscow Patriarchate. Orphaned at the age of 11, he decided to become a monk and entered the monastery of the Holy Theophany at Kiev. In 1867 he went on a visit to the Holy Land and on his journey home called at Mount Athos, where he remained, joining the hermitage of St Elias attached to the monastery of St Panteleimon and changing his name from his baptismal one of George. In 1876 he was ordained priest and held various offices, eventually becoming archimandrite of the St Elias hermitage in Istanbul. He built another such hermitage in Odessa, and was visiting one in Russia when he died. Feast 9 July.

Gabriel of Sedmiozer, monk, born Perm, 14 March 1844, died Kazan, 24 September 1915. Russian Church. Gabriel Fedorovic Zyrjanov came from a

very devout family. In 1864 he entered the monastery at Optina, but ten years later transferred to the monastery of Vysoko-Petrov at Moscow, where he was ordained deacon and given the religious name Tikon. But the urban setting did not satisfy him spiritually, and despite moving once more within the city to the monastery of the Theophany, in 1882 he moved to the monastery of the Mother of God at Kazan, where the following year he was ordained priest and became hegumenos. The same year, however, he left this monastery also, settling at the monastery of the Mother of God of Sedmiozernaja-Pustyn, still within the diocese of Kazan. In 1892 he was given the name Gabriel as his name in religion. He became archimandrite in 1902, and took charge of the spiritual direction of the students of the theological academy at Kazan. Problems within his monastery led him to move again, in 1902, to the monastery of Spaso-Eleazarov in Pskov, and although by this time he was ill, many came to see him for spiritual direction. In his final months he moved back to Kazan, to live with some friends.

Gabriel of Serbia, patriarch, died Proussa, 13 December 1659. Byzantine Church. While away in Moscow soliciting financial help for his diocese, his place was taken by one Maximus. On his return he went to complain to the Turkish vizier, who said that although Maximus had laid charges against him, he, the vizier, did not believe them. On the other hand, he was going to punish him for his activities in Moscow contrary to the Turkish authorities, unless he became a Muslim. Gabriel refused and was hanged.

Gabriel of the Upper Monastery, and Abraham, monks, seventh century. Assyrian Church. Co-founders of this monastery, possibly near Mossul.

Gabriel of Vasilevo, and Anastasia, sixteenth/seventeenth centuries. Russian Church. Two brothers, but nothing is known of them.

Gabriel Taurin Dufresse, bl., martyr, born Lezoux, near Clermont-Ferrand, 8 December 1750, died Chengtu, China, 14 September 1815. He studied at Saint-Sulpice in Paris before joining the Society for Foreign Missions and being sent to China, where from 1775 he worked in the district of Szechwan.

He was arrested during persecutions which broke out in 1784, but escaped, and then, because his presence in a house was dangerous to the inhabitants, he surrendered to the authorities. He was allowed to go free after some months in prison, provided he lived in Beijing or Macao. He chose Macao, whence in 1789 he returned to his missionary activity, this time in Chongking. In 1800 he became an assistant bishop. When persecution broke out again in 1805, he moved constantly from place to place, but in May 1815 he was captured, taken to Chengtu, and beheaded.

Gabriel the Child, born Zverka, 1684 (?), died there, 1690. Russian Church. At the age of six he was abducted by some brigands, tortured and killed. His body was thrown into a field near a Jewish village, and one of the villagers was accused, without proof, of the crime. Feast 20 April.

Gabriele Possenti, born Assisi, 1 March 1838, son of a papal lawyer, died Isola di Gran Sasso, Italy, 27 February 1862, beatified 1908, canonized 1920. Joining the Passionists in 1856, he died of tuberculosis. He is said to have remained cheerful throughout his illness. He is the patron saint of students, especially seminarians.

Gabrona of Qarta, monk, born Hordepne, near Nisibis, c. 600, died Djezireh, northern Syria. Syriac Church. Lived first in a monastery on Mount Singar, then moved to Dailak Dagh on Mount Paredon, where he died.

Gaetano Catanoso, bl., born Chorio di San Lorenzo, Reggio Calabria, 17 February 1879, died Reggio Calabria, 4 April 1963, beatified 1998. Ordained in 1902, he was a parish priest and a canon from 1930. He created the Veronican Sisters of the Holy Face in 1919 to promote this devotion and evangelize poor rural areas.

Gaius, see also **Hermes**.

Gaius, pope, elected 17 December 283, died Rome, 22 April 296. The *Liber Pontificalis* describes him as a Dalmatian, and a relative of Diocletian, but this is doubtful. He is said to have insisted on a strict observance of the clerical orders, and assigned deacons to the seven ecclesiastical districts of Rome. He was perhaps imprisoned along with the future popes **Sixtus** and **Dionysius** in 257; other accounts associate him with later persecution. The details are decidedly confused. Buried in the cemetery of Callixtus, his body was transferred in 1631 by Pope Urban VIII to the church of St Gains, though this no longer exists.

Gaius and Alexander, martyrs, died Apamea, Phrygia (modern Dinar, Turkey), c. 172. They opposed the Montanists. Feast 10 March.

Galam, priest, born Subra al-Haymah, north of Cairo. Coptic Church.

Galawdewos, monk, fifteenth century. Ethiopian Church. A disciple of **Bassalota Mikael** who undertook missionary work in the neighbourhood of Dabra San.

Galawdewos Asnaf Sagad, king and martyr, born c. 1522, died 23 March 1559. Ethiopian Church. He succeeded his father to the throne of Ethiopia when he was 18 years old. The country had been devastated by a Muslim invasion, but with the aid of the Portuguese he defeated the Muslim army and killed its emir in a battle beside lake Tana, on 23 February 1543. The country was soon afterwards subjected to a new Muslim invasion, and Galawdewos's army was defeated on 23 March 1559, in mid-Lent, while they were weakened by their vigorous fasting. The king himself was also slain.

Galdinus, cardinal archbishop, born Milan, Italy, c. 1100, died there, 18 April 1176. Born of a noble Milanese family, Galdinus served as chancellor in Milan and cardinal priest in Rome before being made archbishop of Milan and papal legate for Lombardy in 1166. As such, he worked to repair the damage done by the Victorine schism and the heretical Cathari, as well as rebuilding his city after it was destroyed by Frederick I Barbarossa. He died while preaching and was soon canonized by the then reigning pope, Alexander III.

Galgano, hermit, born Galgano Guidotti at Chiusdino, Siena, c. 1140, died Monte Siepi, 3

December 1181. He had lived a dissolute life, but was converted by a vision of the archangel Michael and became a hermit on Monte Siepi. Rather to his distress, a group of disciples gathered around him. In 1180, in order to provide a cross for the altar in his hermitage, he stuck his sword into a rock – his only known miracle. Feast 5 December.

Gall, monk and missionary, born Ireland, *c.* 550, died Swabia (modern Switzerland), *c.* 640. The younger brother of St **Deicola**, Gall became a monk at Bangor, later travelling to Gaul among a group of missionaries led by **Columbanus**. Subsequently their journey took them to Swabia, where Gall stayed for the rest of his life as a hermit and evangelistic preacher. After his death the reputed site of one of his hermitages grew into an important monastic centre (with a famous library), which was named St Gallen after him. Feast 16 October.

Gall of Clermont, bishop, born Clermont, 486, died there, 551. Of an eminent family, **Gregory of Tours** was his nephew. He became a monk at Cournon, a deacon at Clermont, then a cantor at the chapel of Theodoric. He served as bishop of Clermont from 526 until his death. He participated in various synods, convening one at Clermont in 535, and was noted for his charitable acts and for his humility. Feast 14 May.

Galla, died Rome, *c.* 550. Of patrician birth, her husband died after they had been married for only a year, and she thereafter lived in a community near St Peter's. Feast 5 October.

Gallation of Beloozero, monk, died 12 January 1506. Russian Church. A monk of the monastery of St Ferapontus, who was gifted with prophecy and became something of a 'fool for Christ'.

Gallation of Beloozero, monk, born Moscow, died Vologda, 24 September 1612. Russian Church. Born Gabriel Belski, of a noble family, but when the family fell into disgrace he was secretly hidden away in a village. When he had reached adulthood he travelled to Vologda, where he earned a living as a shoemaker. He married, but when his wife died

giving birth to a daughter, he decided to become a hermit, choosing a spot on the river Sodima, where he built himself a cell. He continued to earn a living as a shoemaker, giving his earnings to the poor, apart from what he needed for food. He lived only on bread and water, spent many hours in prayer, and bound himself in chains. He was gifted with prophecy, and foresaw the destruction of Vologda by a Polish army. He was himself killed by the invaders.

Gamalbert, bl., priest and monastic founder, died *c.* 800. Feast 17 January.

Gandolf of Binasco, bl., Franciscan hermit, born Binasco, Italy, late 1100s, died Polizzi Generosa, Sicily, *c.* 1260. Gandolf was a model Franciscan, joining the order while **Francis of Assisi** was still living. He abstained from fine foods, dressed only in coarse clothes and spent long nights in prayer. His quest for holiness and solitude took him to a hermitage near Polizzi Generosa in Sicily, where he acquired a great reputation among the townspeople for holiness and eloquence. He was especially noted for his devotion to Mary and to the passion. He was beatified by Pope Gregory XV in 1621. Feast 3 April.

Gangolf, martyr of uncertain identity, died possibly 670. This figure has been variously identified as (a) an attorney associated with the abbey of Beza in France, (b) a friend of St **Ceolfrid** and of **Bede**, or (c) a noble Burgundian warrior. He was apparently murdered at the behest of an unfaithful wife, as a result of which he has been traditionally revered as a martyr to marital fidelity. Feast 11 May.

Ganni of Hira, born Bet Aramaye, died Mount Isla, near Kaskar, sixth century. Syriac Church. A rich man, he gave all his money to the poor and became a monk in the monastery founded by **John of Kaskar**. Feast 1 October.

Gapito, see **Basil**, **Eugene**, et al.

Garima, monk, fifth/sixth century. Ethiopian Church. Baptized Yeshaq, his father was the Byzantine prefect in Egypt and Yeshaq followed his father's career, but after seven years as governor, he fled to Ethiopia where he joined St **Panteleimon**.

He was joined by others, but after a dozen years they separated and Yeshaq went to Madara, where he was renowned for his miracle-working.

Gaspar Bertoni, founder, born Verona, 9 October 1777, died 12 June 1853. He studied at the diocesan seminary and was ordained in 1800. He then served through the Napoleonic occupation of his part of Italy as a parish priest. In 1816 he founded a religious congregation in a house attached to the church of the Stigmata of St Francis. As a result the congregation came to be known as the Stigmatines: the Congregation of the Sacred Stigmata of Christ did not receive official approval until long after his death. It carried on his apostolate of fostering vocations to the priesthood and providing free education. He ran his congregation for many years effectively from his sickbed.

Gaspar del Bufalo, founder, born Rome, 6 January 1786, died there, 28 December 1837. He was educated at the Roman College and ordained in 1808. He gained a reputation for visiting the sick, caring for the homeless and teaching the catechism, and he helped his spiritual director, Canon Francesco Albertini, to establish a Pious Union of the Precious Blood in the church of San Nicola in Carvcere. He was later exiled for four years, and for some of the time imprisoned, for refusing to swear allegiance to Napoleon I. After his return to Rome in 1814, with papal support he established the Society of the Precious Blood on 15 August 1815, and opened its first house in Umbria. He also helped Bl. **Maria de Matthias** to found the Precious Blood Sisters.

Gaucherius, Augustinian abbot, born Meulan-sur-Seine, France, c. 1060, died near Limoges, France, 9 April 1140. After obtaining a good liberal education, Gaucherius moved to a hermitage near Limoges to live a contemplative life when he was 18. As other groups of contemplatives soon gathered around him, he founded an Augustinian priory there, which was called Saint-Jean of Aureil. He later also founded an Augustinian convent for women. His disciples included St **Stephen of Muret** and St Faucherius, and he was canonized by Pope Celestine III in 1194.

Gaudentius, confessor in Rhetia, now Romania, fourth/sixth century. Feast 6 May.

Gaudentius, bishop, died c. 418. He was a priest in Ivrera, near Turin, and became bishop of Novara, Piedmont, after his friend **Laurence of Novara**. He was also befriended by **Eusebius of Vercelli**. Feast 22 January.

Gaudentius of Gniezno, first metropolitan of Gniezno, born 960–70, died probably Gniezno, Poland, 1006–10. Gaudentius became a Benedictine in Rome in 988 and was ordained there. Around 996 he went on a missionary journey to Prussia with his brother, St **Adalbert**, who was martyred there. He returned to Rome in 999 to help with the canonization of his brother. While there, he was consecrated as a bishop and in March of 1000 was made archbishop in Gniezno. Little is known for surc of his activity as bishop, but in 1036 his relics were brought to Prague (Czech Republic). He has long been venerated as a saint, with his feast celebrated on 25 August, but his canonization has never been officially ratified.

Gaudiosus, bishop, fifth century. He was bishop of Brescia. Feast 7 March.

Gaufridus of Le Mans, bishop. Feast 3 August.

Gaugericus, bishop, born Yvoi, Ardennes, died Cambrai, c. 625. Ordained by St **Magnericus**, he became bishop of Cambrai where he founded a monastery. He was bishop for just under 40 years. Feast 11 August.

Gausbert, bishop, died Cahors, France, c. 906. Bishop of Cahors.

Gausbert, priest and hermit in Auvergne, died 1079. He founded the abbey of Montsalvy as a hospice for pilgrims in what had been a wild and dangerous region. Feast 27 May.

Gauzelin of Toul, bishop, date and place of birth unknown, died 7 September 962. A member of a noble Frankish family, Gauzelin became bishop of Toul in France in 922. He overcame the turbulent political climate of the times to introduce a number of ecclesiastical reforms during his episcopate, and founded or encouraged the development of a number of religious houses.

Gebhard of Constance II, bishop, born probably Bregnez (Austria), 949, died Constance, Germany, 27 August 995. The son of the count of Bregnez, Gebhard was educated in Constance under Bishop Conrad of Constance and was made his second successor by Holy Roman Emperor Otto II. As bishop, his major concern was monastic reform. To this end he founded an abbey, which was consecrated with the relics of Pope **Gregory the Great** and named for him, but eventually came to be called Petershausen because of its resemblance to St Peter's in Rome. Despite Gebhard's best efforts, the abbey never became the major centre he had hoped for. He is buried under the abbey church, and his cult is only officially followed in the former diocese of Constance.

Gebhard of Salzburg, bl., archbishop, died Salzburg, Austria, 15 June 1088. Gebhard was chaplain to Holy Roman Emperors Henry III and Henry IV and ambassador to Greece before being made archbishop of Salzburg in 1060. As such, he expanded his archdiocese, promoted monasticism and successfully supported Pope **Gregory VII** over antipope Guibert of Ravenna. He also wrote a description of the investiture controversy that occurred during his tenure. Henry IV drove him from his see, allowing him to return only two years before his death. The process for his canonization began in 1629.

Gebizo, monk, died near Venafro, Italy, 21 October 1078 or 1087. The first records of Gebizo find him making a pilgrimage in 1060 from Cologne, Germany, to Monte Cassino, Italy, where he became a Benedictine. He was known for his austere eating practices and his love of prayer and silence. Even near his death, as he was suffering greatly from a painful abscess on his chest, he continued to ask God for additional sufferings. Although called a saint by all his earliest chroniclers, there is no tradition of his veneration.

Gelasius (or Gioua-Mac-Liag), died 1174. Abbot of Derry, he became bishop of Armagh in 1138, supposedly the first Irish bishop to receive the pallium. In 1162 he ordained **Laurence O'Toole**

archbishop of Dublin. In 1170 he called a synod at Armagh in an unsuccessful attempt to prevent the Irish Church being dominated by Norman usages. Feast 27 March.

Gelasius I, pope, born Rome, although of African ancestry, died there, 21 November 496. Succeeding Felix III on 1 March 392, he strongly affirmed his position against the Caesaro-papist tendencies of the emperors. Within the Church, Gelasius affirmed the *primatus iurisdictionis* of the bishop of Rome and his supreme authority, even over against decisions of episcopal synods. Further he argued for the divine origin of the sacerdotal and the political power, claiming their mutual autonomy as well as the greater value of the bishops' sacred authority. In Rome he dealt with Manichaeism and Pelagianism while also suppressing the last outbursts of paganism.

Gelasius, martyr, died Heliopolis, Phoenicia, 297. Described as a comedian who converted during a staged mock baptism and was stoned to death by the mob, he is probably identical with **Genesius the Comedian**. Feast 26 February.

Gelasius of Rameti, bishop, fourteenth century. Romanian Church. Little is known of his life beyond his reputation for asceticism and hesychastic prayer, and that he was successful as a teacher of priests training for life as pastors in Transylvania, where the monastery of Rameti is situated. Feast 30 June.

Gemellus, martyr, born Ancyra, died there, 362. Crucified – the last martyr to be so put to death – for criticizing the pagan Emperor Julian. Feast 10 December.

Geminian of Modena, bishop, died *c.* 396. Deacon to the bishop of Modena, he succeeded him. He is remembered for sheltering bishop **Athanasius** travelling from Alexandria to exile in Gaul and for opposing Jovinianism. Feast 31 January.

Gemma Galgani, Italian mystic and stigmatic, born Borgo Nuovo di Camigliano, near Lucca, Italy, 12 March 1878, died Lucca, 11 April 1903. Born of poor but devout parents, her initial wish to become a Passionist nun was thwarted by serious illness. On several occasions between 1899 and 1901 she displayed the stigmata and other marks of Christ's passion, and experienced several ecstasies and visions of Christ, the Virgin Mary and her guardian angel. Also known for her patience, obedience and poverty in the face of her physical afflictions, she was beatified in 1933 and canonized in 1940. The publication of her correspondence with her spiritual director (1941) was important in spreading the popularity of her cult. The letters display common sense and good humour as well as piety.

Gemma of Solmona, bl., born Goriano Sicoli, Abruzzi, died there, 1439, cult approved 1890. A shepherdess who supposedly successfully resisted the sexual advances of the local count, she became a recluse for over 40 years in a walled-up cell in the church of St John the Baptist. Feast 13 May.

Gemma, see also **Hemma**.

Genesius of Arles, martyr. He was a catechumen and during his military service, while he was stationed in Arles, fulfilled the function of chancellor. During a persecution (Diocletian's or possibly Decius's) he deserted and took flight. According to his *Passio*, he did so because he had refused to register the edict of persecution. He tried to escape his persecutors by swimming to the other side of the Rhone, but was taken and decapitated. His cult was soon held in high esteem. Feast 25 August.

Genesius of Clermont, bishop of Clermont, Auvergne, died 662. He became bishop of Clermont on popular demand and, despite journeying to Rome to seek permission to lead a solitary life, continued to hold the position. He built a hospice, a monastery and St Symphorian church (where he is buried and which was later renamed St Genesius). Feast 3 June.

Genesius of Lyon, bishop, died Lyon, 11 November 678. He became bishop of Lyon in 658 and served as chaplain to Queen Bathildis.

Genesius the Comedian, martyr, patron of actors, died Rome, 303. His enacted 'baptism' performed as part of an anti-Christian satire before the Emperor Diocletian led him to publicly confess the faith – whereupon the emperor had him tortured and beheaded. Feast 25 August. See also **Gelasius**.

Genevieve, patron of Paris, born Nanterre, France, 422, died Paris, 500. Aged seven, she was inspired by a sermon to consecrate her life to God. She took the veil aged 15 and, when her parents died, moved to Paris. When Childeric the Frank besieged Paris, she made sorties to get provisions for the city. When Attila the Hun threatened to invade, she persuaded the Parisians to pray instead of abandoning the city. Attila changed his route and was defeated at Orleans. She is reputed to have saved Paris since her death, notably from an epidemic in 1129. Feast 3 January.

Gengulphus (Gangulphus, Gengulf), born Burgundy, died Avallon castle, near Vezelay, 760. A knight serving the Merovingian King Pepin the Short, a disastrous marriage led him to retire to a life of penance and almsgiving. The lover of his notoriously unfaithful wife assassinated him. Feast 11 May.

Gennadius, bl., died Constantinople, 6 April 1818. Byzantine Church. He and two companions from their monastery on Mount Athos came to Constantinople seeking martyrdom. Under torture, his companions renounced their faith, and blamed Gennadius for bringing them to the city. He was executed.

Gennadius of Astorga, bishop, patron of Astorga, died Bierzo, Spain, 936. He restored the monastery of San Pedro de Montes in 895 and became bishop of Astorga in 899. He fostered Benedictine monasticism and built an oratory for hermits in 920 and three hermitages. He resigned his see to become a solitary. Feast 25 May.

Gennadius of Cernigov, monk, born Duben, died Cernigov, *c.* 1700. Russian Church. The painter of a miraculous icon of Cernigov, and a monk of the monastery of the Most Holy Trinity and St Elias in that city.

Gennadius of Constantinople, patriarch, died Constantinople, 471. Little is known of his life before he was elected patriarch in 458. He was a biblical scholar and a staunch defender of the Chalcedonian faith.

Gennadius of Kostroma, monk, born Mogilev, died Ljubimograd, 1565. Russian Church. Baptized Gregory, he came from a noble family from which he fled so that he could enter a monastery. He went first to Moscow, then to the north of Russia. He first joined the community at Kostroma, then established a hermitage in the woods, then, when he had gathered disciples, founded the monastery of the Saviour at Ljubimograd, where he was hegumenos. He was distinguished by his gift of foresight, by his meekness, and by the fact that he taught catechism to the peasants in the surrounding region. Feast 23 January.

Gennadius of Novgorod, archbishop, born Moscow, died there, 4 December 1505. Russian Church. Born into a boyar family in Moscow, aged 20 he joined the monastery of Valaam. In 1447 he was made archimandrite of the Cudov monastery in Moscow, and in 1484 archbishop of Novgorod. At the time there was no complete Slavic version of the Bible. Gennadius set out to provide one, translating from the Latin Vulgate: it was published in 1499. He was an important liturgical reformer, and also worked on a new calendar, which was adopted by the whole Russian Church. He was an innovator in the training of the clergy, establishing for the first time in Russia special schools for their instruction. A year before his death he was deposed by the Tsar on the grounds of false accusations against his character. He retired back to the Cudov monastery.

Gentila Giusti of Ravenna, bl., died 1530. Feast 28 January.

Gentilis, bl., martyr, born Matelica, *c.* 1290, died Trebizond. He came from a noble family called Finiguerra. He became a Franciscan and was sent first to Egypt, but there encountered the Venetian ambassador to the Persian court and accompanied him to Persia, via the monastery of St Catherine on Mount Sinai. He continued on to Trebizond (Tabriz), preaching the gospel, but nothing more is known of him. He is thought to have died a martyr's death and his cult was approved in 1795, but has since been suppressed. Feast 5 September.

Genuinus (Ingenuinus), died *c.* 605. He was bishop of Sabion (a town no longer exisiting), near Brixen in the Tyrol, is said to have died in exile and is commemorated with **Albinus**, a later bishop of Brixen. Feast 5 February.

Geoffrey of Bayeux, bl., second abbot of Savigny, died 1138. After the death of Vitalis of Savigny in 1122, the founder and first abbot of Savigny, Geoffrey, a former Cluniac monk, was elected as his successor. In many ways the creator of the Congregation of Savigny, Geoffrey created the organizational framework for Savigniac expansion, and by the time of his death in 1138 the Congregation, which later merged with the Cistercians, had grown to include some 29 monasteries.

George, see also **Emmanuel**.

George, monk and hermit, died *c.* 614. Feast 8 January.

George, martyr, patron of England, soldiers, knights, archers and armourers, born Lydda, Palestine, died there, 303. He was probably a soldier martyred in the persecutions of Diocletian and Maximian. The legend of St George and the dragon appears in Irish mythology and the martyrology of Bede. He appeared in a vision at the siege of Antioch during the first Crusade. Richard I's army fought under George's patronage and Edward III founded the Order of the Garter under it. In the later Middle Ages he became patron of Venice, Genoa, Portugal and Catalonia. His popularity declined with the introduction of guns. Feast 23 April.

George, monk, seventh century. Coptic Church. A shepherd by calling, he decided suddenly to leave his herd, cross the Nile and go into the desert. For ten years he lived in the monastery of Orione, living only on raw herbs, but then, once again seeking solitude, he went off to the desert, but again found himself in a monastery, thought to be Dabra al-Baramus. He spent his final years, however, in the monastery of St Macarius. Feast 13 May.

George, martyr, died 1015. Russian Church. See **Ephraim of Novotorsk**.

George (Girgis) al-Gawhari, civil servant, born Qalyub, died Cairo, 27 September 1810. He served successive administrations of Egypt, including that of Napoleon, to whom he was close, from the 1790s until 1805, when he had to flee the capital and take refuge in Upper Egypt. He returned about a year before his death. Despite his high office, he found time for the needy and for the wants of the Church. He was the younger brother of **Ibrahim al-Gawhari**.

George (Girgis) al-Muzahim, martyr, born Damirah al-Qibliyyah in the Egyptian Delta, died 959. Coptic Church. The son of a Muslim Bedouin married to a Christian. Although at first brought up a Muslim, he always wanted to become a Christian, and did so after marrying the daughter of a priest. The news of his conversion spread and he had to flee, hiding for three years, but eventually he returned to his home town, where he was martyred. Feast 13 June.

George and Chosroes, martyrs, died 21 April 853. Armenian Church. Two Armenian princes executed for refusing to deny their Christianity. Their constancy converted one of their Muslim executioners, who was martyred with them. Feast 2 May.

George Beesley, bl., martyr, born Goosnargh, Lancashire, 1562, died London, 1 July 1591. He studied at the English College in Rheims and was ordained in 1587. He returned to England the following year and worked under the alias Passelaw. In 1590 he was imprisoned in the Tower of London and tortured. In 1591 he was moved to Newgate prison, and on 1 July was hanged, drawn and quartered in Fleet Street, along with **Montford Scott**.

George Douglas, martyr, born Edinburgh, died York, 9 September 1587. He was educated in Paris and was ordained there c. 1560. It is possible that he was a Franciscan. One of the **Eighty-Five Martyrs**.

George Errington, bl., martyr, born Hirst Castle, Ashington, Northumberland, 1554, died York, 29 November 1596. He was for a time at Trinity College, Oxford, and was frequently imprisoned for his Catholicism, on one occasion, in 1591, escaping from York castle. He was in prison again in 1593, with **John Boste**, and later with **William Knight** and **William Gibson**. They might have escaped martyrdom had it not been for a non-Catholic clergyman who pretended he wished to convert, and whom they put in touch with a Catholic priest.

George Gervase, bl., martyr, born Bosham, Sussex, 1569, died Tyburn, London, 11 April 1608. He served with Francis Drake in the West Indies, then with the Spanish army in Flanders. Ordained at Cambrai in 1603, he later became a Benedictine, was arrested in 1607 after two months in London, and hanged, drawn and quartered.

George Haydock, bl., martyr, born Cottam Hall, Preston, Lancashire, died Tyburn, 12 February 1584, beatified 1987. Ordained in France in 1581, he was arrested in London in 1582 and spent two years in prison. He was hung, drawn and quartered with **Thomas Hemerford**, **James Fenn**, **John Munden** and **John Nutter**.

George Lazarevskie and Theodosia, sixteenth/seventeenth centuries. Russian Church. The husband and daughter of **Juliana Lazarevskaja**. Feast 2 January.

George Limniotes, hermit and martyr, born c. 630, died c. 730. A hermit on Mount Olympus, he opposed iconoclasm and was martyred despite his great age after having had his hands and nose cut off. Feast 24 August.

Gregory Makar, bishop, born Armenia, died Pithiviers, France, c. 1000. He is said to have been a monk who became bishop of Nicopolis in Armenia (modern Afyonkarahisar). He fled to France and became a hermit at Pithiviers, near Orleans. Feast 16 March.

George Mazquereli, bishop, died Azquri, Georgia, ninth century. Georgian Church. Feast 2 April.

George Mtasmindeli, see **George of the Black Mountain**.

George Napper (Napier), martyr, born Oxford, 1550, died there, 9 November 1610. A student at Corpus Christi College in Oxford, he was expelled for his Catholicism, then later imprisoned for nine years. On his release he went to the English seminary in Douai, where he was ordained priest in 1596. In 1603 he returned to England and ministered in Oxfordshire until his arrest and imprisonment in July 1610. He might have escaped execution had he not, while in prison, reconciled a condemned criminal to Catholicism.

George of Aleos, bl. Byzantine Church. Little is known of him, except that to escape marriage he fled to Mount Athos. Feast 4 April.

George of Alikianos, born Alikianos, Crete, died there, 7 February 1867. Byzantine Church. The son of a priest, he refused to deny his faith and was decapitated.

George of Amastris, bishop, born Kromna, near Amastris, died there, c. 825. Born beside the Black Sea, he became a hermit in the Mount Sirik desert, then a monk at Bonyssa, and was made by popular acclaim bishop of Amastris, which city he defended against an assault by Muslim troops. Feast 21 February.

George of Antioch, bishop, died 814. A monk who became bishop of Antioch in Pisidia, he opposed the iconoclast Emperor Leo V and was exiled. Feast 19 April.

George of Attalia, martyr, born Attalia, died Krini, 25 June 1823. Byzantine Church. As a young man he became the servant of a Turk, converted to Islam and married his master's daughter. He came to regret his conversion and, pretending that he was doing on pilgrimage to Mecca, instead fled to a monastery, where he was reconciled to Christianity. He then moved to Krini, where he married a Christian, but one day his former master recognized him. He refused this time to deny his faith and was executed.

George of Bulgaria, martyr, born Sofia, died Adrianopolis, 26 1437. Byzantine Church. While in business in Adrianopolis he had an argument about Christianity with a Turk, which led to him being burned to death when he refused to deny his faith.

George of Cernica, archimandrite, born Saliste, Transylvania, 1730, died Cernica, 1806. Romanian Church. A young recruit to the monastic life, he went to Mount Athos c. 1750, but after some years returned to Moldavia and lived in various monasteries before deciding to return to Athos. At that point, in 1781, the metropolitan asked him to undertake the reform of the monastery of Cernica, near Bucharest. He much improved the life of the monastery, introducing the Rule of life lived on Athos, and much improving the celebration of the liturgy. He was made an archimandrite and given charge of other monasteries, although he finally returned to Cernica to die.

George of Chachuli ('the Writer') and Saba, monks, tenth/eleventh centuries. Georgian Church. Authors and translators of religious texts, and spiritual directors of **George of the Black Mountain**. Feast 19 December.

George of Chios, martyr, born Chios, 1785, died there, 26 November 1807. Byzantine Church. As a young man he worked as an engraver, in which profession he travelled quite widely. When in Kavala he became a Muslim, but soon regretted his action and returned home and confessed his sin. He later went to Aivali, where he became engaged to be married, but was denounced to the Turks by the brother of his bride and, this time refusing to deny his faith, was decapitated.

George of Choziba, monk, born Cyprus, died Choziba, 620. He left Cyrpus to join his brother in the Holy Land, in a monastery near Jericho, but was rejected because he was too young. Instead he was accepted by the monastery of Choziba in Wadi Qilt, where he remained for the rest of his life, surviving a Persian attack in 614 during which he was taken prisoner. He was renowned for the hospitality which, under his direction, the monastery showed to pilgrims. Feast 8 January.

George of Cyprus, afterwards Gregory, bishop in Cyprus, eighth century. Feast 5 March.

George of Gomatios, bl., died 1822.

George of Haran, bishop, died Haran, *c.* 850. Syriac Church. He became bishop in 816, but little is known of his life – indeed, he may be confused with an earlier bishop of the same name. Feast 22 February.

George of Ioannina, martyr, born Tsurchli, 1810, died Ioannina, 17 January 1838. Byzantine Church. Born in western Macedonia, he was orphaned when young and went to Ioannina in search of work. He found it with a Muslim court official who gave him a Turkish name. When George wanted to marry a Christian girl, he was cited before the court as acting against Islamic law, but his master told the court that George had always been a devout Christian and the marriage took place. Five days after the birth of his son in January 1838, George was again arrested. He was brought before the same judge who had released him two years earlier. This time, however, he was condemned to death and publicly executed. The village where he was born was renamed St George in his honour.

George of Izla, monk, died 14 January 615. Syriac Church. A monk of the monastery on Mount Izla and a convert from Zoroastrianism, he was denounced as a convert to the king, Chosroes, by a fellow Christian whom he had reprimanded, was imprisoned and put to death by crucifixion.

George of Jerusalem, patriarch, eighth century (?).

George of Limniotes, born 621, died 718. A hermit on Mount Olympus, he was martyred for his opposition to iconoclasm. Feast 24 August.

George of Lodève, bl., born near Rodez, died Lodève, *c.* 877. A Benedictine at Sainte-Foi-de-Conques in Rouergue, after the monastery's destruction by Norsemen in 862 he went to Vabres in the diocese of Rodez. He may have been bishop of Lodève in old age. Feast 19 February.

George of Magnesia, martyr, born Magnesia, died there, 24 April 1796. Byzantine Church. He was executed for wearing Turkish dress and then refusing to deny his faith when arrested.

George of Mogilev, archbishop, born Nezin, 20 November 1717, died Mogilev, 13 February 1795. Church of Belorussia, Patriarchate of Moscow. Gregory Iosifovic Konisskij came from a noble Cossack family and entered the ecclesiastical academy in Kiev. After a year in the Kievan Cave monastery he returned to the academy to teach, and was appointed archimandrite of a monastery in Kiev. In 1755 he became bishop of Belorussia, with his see at Mogilev. It was at that time part of Poland, and George had to battle to defend Orthodoxy against pressure from the Latin – on one occasion he went to Warsaw with an armed Russian escort to argue (in Latin) in favour of Orthodoxy. Although the Orthodox were eventually conceded the same rights as the Latins, George had to flee to Smolensk for four years, and only returned in 1772 when Belorussia was annexed to Russia. He then entered on a campaign to reform Orthodoxy in the whole of Belorussia, and his efforts were rewarded by the conversion to Orthodoxy of tens of thousands of Greek-rite Catholics. He wrote a number of works in defence of Orthodoxy.

George of Mytilene, archbishop, died Mytilene, 4 April 787. A strong defender of the veneration of images during the iconoclast controversy, he was also revered for his ability to prophesy and his care for the poor of the island of Lesbos, of which Mytilene is the main city. Feast 7 April.

George of Mytilene, martyr, born Georgia, died Mytilene, 2 January 1770. Byzantine Church. The slave of a Muslim, he became a Muslim himself, but in old age went before a judge to confess his reconversion to Christianity, and was executed.

George of Neapolis, bl., born Neapolis (?), died Cobia Dere, 1797. Byzantine Church. A priest of Neapolis, he was on his way to visit some Christians when he was waylaid and killed. His body was found and buried at the place of his death, but some time later a devout woman had a dream about the whereabouts of his body. It was recovered and moved to Neapolis. His relics are now to be found in Athens. Feast 3 November.

George of New Ephesus, martyr, born New Ephesus, 1756, died there, 5 April 1801. Byzantine

Church. A dissolute young man, he embraced Islam when drunk. When he repented he fled his village and went to Samos, but later returned home and confessed his faith, for which he was executed.

George of Novgorod. Russian Church. A 'fool for Christ', but nothing else is known of him. Feast 23 April.

George of Philadelphia, martyr, born Philadelphia, Asia Minor, died Caratzu, 2 October 1794. Byzantine Church. A tailor by trade, he became a Muslim in order to avoid paying money he owed to a Christian. When he afterwards repented, he spent some time on Mount Athos before going to Caratzu, giving all his money to the poor, and then proclaiming his reconversion to Christianity, for which he was decapitated.

George of Plagia (or 'the Paisanou'), died Constantinople, 14 February 1693. Byzantine Church. Although born in Mytilene, he worked as a tailor in Constantinople and was executed for refusing to deny his faith. Feast 14 February.

George of Rapsani, martyr, died 5 March 1818. Byzantine Church. Of a distinguished family, he was a teacher before being beheaded for refusing to deny his faith.

George of Retimno, see **Angeles of Retimno**.

George of Sagla, monk, born Sagla, Amara, c. 1365, died Dabra Dimo, c. 1425. Ethiopian Church. Born into a noble family, he went for his education to the monastery of St Stephen at Hayq, where he distinguished himself by his learning. He was then called back to court where he became royal preacher, but when it was suggested he marry, he said he wanted to be a monk and a priest – he was already ordained deacon – and he was eventually made superior of Dabra Dimo. He became a prolific writer and preacher, although for a time he was imprisoned after a dispute with a relative of the king.

George of Samothrace, born Samothrace, died Makri, 6 April 1835. Byzantine Church. Shot for refusing to deny his Christianity.

George of Senkursk, 'fool for Christ', fifteenth century. Russian Church. Feast 23 April.

George of Serbia, born Cratovia, Serbia, died Sofia, 11 February 1515. Byzantine Church. Born of devout parents, he fled to Sofia when his extreme good looks attracted the attention of the Turks of his native city. In Sofia he studied to be a goldsmith, but he also studied Scripture and became very learned, as a result of which he was summoned to dispute with Islamic scholars. His ability in defending Christianity led him to be dragged before a judge by a hostile crowd, and he was condemned to death by being burned alive.

George of the Arabs, bishop, died Kufa (?), 724. Syriac Church. He became bishop of the nomad Arab tribes of Mesopotamia in 686, was a translator of Aristotle, exchanged letters with the monks of Aleppo, and wrote sundry liturgical works and commentaries.

George of the Black Mountain, abbot, born 1014, died near Constantinople, 29 June 1044. He was educated at the monastery of Habuli, Georgia, and became a monk there. He went on pilgrimage to Jerusalem, then became a disciple of **George the Recluse**, who lived on the Black Mountain, near Antioch. From there he went to Mount Athos, where he was ordained and became abbot of the monastery of Iviron. He there began his life's work of translating Greek texts into Georgian, including the Scriptures and the Fathers of the Church. He refused to become a bishop, and after the Turkish invasion of Georgia took 24 orphans to Mount Athos, but he died on the way. Feast 27 June.

George of Thessalonika, archbishop, died Thessalonika, c. 1030. Byzantine Church.

George of Tsurchli, see **George of Ioannina**.

George Swallowell, bl., martyr, born Durham, England, died Darlington, 26 July 1594. He was brought up a Protestant and taught at Houghton-le-Spring, where he was a minister. He converted to Catholicism and was later arrested. He was imprisoned for a year in Durham before being tried alongside **John Ingram**. He was condemned for having converted to Catholicism and was hanged, drawn and quartered.

George the Blind, hermit, born near lake Van, died Ani, twelfth century. Armenian Church. He made a pilgrimage to Jerusalem seven times, and went once to Rome, guided by a monk called Gregory. On the latter occasion, when Gregory was killed by brigands, George's prayers brought him back to life. He spent his last years at the cathedral of Ani, where he worked many miracles. Feast 4 May.

George the Builder, the Great, monk, eleventh century. Georgian Church. He was hegumenos of the Georgian monastery of Iviron on Mount Athos from 1019, but, according to one tradition, he recruited many Greek monks, which led to tension within the monastery. He was exiled by the imperial authorities after, it was alleged, he had supported a pretender to the throne. Feast 8 December.

George the Gentle ('the Honey'), monk, born Analiwr, 1044, died Drazark, 1115. Armenian Church. He acquired his title from the gentleness of his character. For 50 years he lived in the monastery of Sevan, but then went on to reform several other monasteries, including that of Drazark where he died. He introduced the practice of praying standing for the whole night of the vigil before Sunday. Feast 30 July.

George the Recluse, born Montenegro (?), died there, 1068. Georgian Church. A monk of the monastery of St Simeon the Wonderworker, called 'the Recluse' because he lived in a cave. Feast 3 July.

George the Younger, tenth century. Pilgrim of Constantinople. Feast 11 March.

George Vsevolodovic, prince, born Vladimir, 27 November 1189, died Vladimir, 4 March 1238. Russian Church. Younger son of the grand prince of Vladimir and Suzdal, his father entrusted both cities to him, after falling out with his elder brother Constantine. This led to a four-year struggle between the two, in which Constantine emerged

victorious, but George succeeded to the title after the death of his brother in 1219. His reign brought peace to the region and he built many churches, monasteries and cathedrals in both Suzdal and Niznij Novgorod – he founded the latter city. In 1237 George attempted to establish peace with the Mongols, but the following year they invaded, besieging and eventually destroying Vladimir and other cities, including Moscow. George lost all his family in a fire which devastated Vladimir. George had himself fled, but was captured and beheaded. His reputation was that of a devout prince and a martyr. Feast 4 February.

Georgia, died *c*. 500. Said to be a young woman who became a recluse near Clermont in the Auvergne. Feast 15 February.

Gerald of Aurillac, nobleman, born Aurillac, France, 855, died there, 13 October 909. Despite inheriting the family titles, he chose to enter the religious life. He established the abbey of Aurillac following several pilgrimages to Rome. He was renowned for his justice, devotions and gift of healing.

Gerald of Braga, Benedictine and bishop, died Braga, 5 December 1108. Having entered the Benedictine order, he was invited by the primate of Spain, a fellow Benedictine, to join him in reestablishing Christianity in Spain following the defeat of the Moors. He was consecrated bishop of Braga in 1096, and his see was restored to metropolitan status in 1100.

Gerald of Mayo, abbot, born Northumbria, England, died Mayo, Ireland, 732. He was among the English and Irish monks who left Lindisfarne with St **Colman** when the Synod of Whitby disallowed the Celtic date of Easter in Northumbria. The group founded a monastery off the Mayo coast and later a house on the mainland for the English monks. He succeeded St Colman as abbot of the latter. Feast 13 March.

Gerard, bishop, died Burgundy, *c*. 940. He was a monk at Brou abbey, now Bourg-en-Bresse, a hermit, and bishop of Macon for 40 years before retiring to Brou. Feast 29 May.

Gerard Majella, born Muro Lucano, near Naples, 1726, died Caposele, 16 October 1755. A pious child, he followed his father's trade as a tailor, then entered the employ of a bishop who mistreated him. In 1745 he returned home to work as a tailor. He had tried to join the Capuchins, but had been refused. He now tried to join the Redemptorists, who again at first refused him, but then accepted Gerard as a lay brother. He was professed in 1752, and worked for the Redemptorists as a tailor, in the infirmary, and as a companion to missioners. He was renowned for great holiness of life, and for the ability to read people's souls. His constant ill-health, however, developed into tuberculosis: he died after foreseeing the date of his death.

Gerard of Brogne, abbot and monastic reformer, born Stave, Belgium, 880, died Brogne Abbey, Belgium, 3 October 959. He rebuilt an oratory in Brogne to house the relics of St **Eugene**, replaced its clerics with monks, and became its abbot in 923. He was commissioned to restore regular observation of the Benedictine Rule at the abbey of Saint-Ghislain in Hainault, and reformed the monasteries of Saint-Bavon, Saint-Pierre (where he became abbot), Saint-Bertin and Saint-Amand in Ghent, and the monastery of Saint-Remi in Rheims. His work paved the way for the Gregorian reform.

Gerard of Clairvaux, bl., died Clairvaux, 13 June 1138. He entered the Cistercian Order, despite initial reluctance, after being impressed by the fulfilment of his brother **Bernard**'s prophecy that he would be wounded, captured and freed following a battle. He accompanied Bernard to the foundation of Clairvaux and became its cellarer until his death, which is lamented by Bernard in his *Sermones in Cantica*.

Gerard of Csanad, martyr, bishop and abbot, born Sagrado, Italy, 980, died Buda, Hungary, 24 September 1046. He studied in Bologna and became abbot of the Benedictine abbey of San Gioggio. Following some time as a hermit in Bel, he tutored the son of King **Stephen I** of Hungary, who appointed him bishop of Csanad where he worked to Christianize the south-east Hungarian tribes by means of founding mission parishes with monks of various nationalities trained in Csanad. He was martyred in Buda by the deceased King Stephen's opponents. His only extant writing is the *Deliberatio Gerardi Moresanae Episcopi Supra Hymnum Trium Puerorum*.

Gerard of Sauve-Majeure, Benedictine abbot, born Corbie, France, 1025, died 5 April 1095. He was a child oblate of Corbie abbey where he later served as a cellarer. He accompanied the abbot on pilgrimage to Rome where he was ordained, and cured through the intercession of St **Adalard**. He was unsuccessful in re-establishing regular observance when abbot of Saint-Vincent, but consequently constructed a new abbey on land given to him at Sauve-Majeure, and later built a priory at Semoy and an abbey at Broqueroie – all of which prospered.

Gerard of Toul, bishop, born Cologne, Germany, 935, died Toul, France, 23 April 994. He served as a canon in Cologne before being designated bishop of Toul in 963. Here he completed the foundation of the Saint-Mansuy abbey, erected a convent for women in honour of St Gengoult, founded the Maison-Dieu, and rebuilt the cathedral.

Gerard of Villamagna, bl., Franciscan hermit, born Villamagna, Italy, 1174, died there, 13 May 1245. He went on crusade while serving as page to a Florentine knight, was captured by the Saracens and, on being released, travelled as a pilgrim to Jerusalem. On returning to Italy, he joined the Third Order of St Francis and lived as a hermit.

Gerasimus, anchorite, born Lycia, died Palestine, 5 March 475. He founded a monastery near the Jordan river following a pilgrimage to the Holy Land *c.* 451. During Lent he took no nourishment apart from the Eucharist. Tradition has it that he removed a thorn from the paw of a lion which thereafter became the monastery's pet.

Gerasimus, bl., born Leontari, in the Peloponnese, eighteenth century. Byzantine Church. He went to the Holy Land, and on his return joined the monastery of the Most Holy Trinity in Macrinitsa, of which he is considered the second founder. He was renowned for miracles, and for the manner in which he instructed the local people in their faith. Feast 15 September.

Gerasimus and Thaddeus, monks, sixteenth century. Russian Church. Disciples of **Tikon of Luchov**.

Gerasimus of Astrakhan, bishop, born Belskoe, 26 October 1809, died Astrakhan, 12 June 1880. Russian Church. Born George Ivanovic Dobroserdov into a pious family, his grandfather claimed a vision, before the child was conceived, that he would become a bishop. He early came to the attention of the bishop of Irkutsk, and he studied for the priesthood. He developed, however, a strong desire to live an eremitical life and to be a 'fool for Christ' – which was regarded at first as a sign of mental instability. He therefore gave up this idea, and continued his studies, proving himself the best student of his year. He then taught in Irkutsk, and in 1836 married and was ordained. After the death of his wife in 1841 he went to the ecclesiastical college in St Petersburg, becoming a monk, and then going to teach in Tver. In 1849 he was made an archimandrite, and was successively rector of several seminaries, and in charge of a monastery. In 1863 he became bishop of Staraja Russa, in 1864 bishop of Revel, then of Samara, and finally of Astrakhan. He was rigorous in fulfilling his office as bishop, but also maintained in his private life a monastic discipline of prayer and fasting.

Gerasimus of Boldino, monk, born Perejaslav-Zalesk, *c.* 1490, died Boldino, 1 May 1554. Russian Church. Baptized Gregory, he had an attraction to monasticism from an early age, and was accepted when only 13 into the monastery of Gorickij, where he worked as a shoemaker. He later went to the monastery of the Most Holy Trinity in his home city, where he formally became a monk, taking the name Gerasimus. In 1528 he left there, however, and in a forest near Smolensk established a hermitage. After spending some time there he was encouraged by a visit to set up a new hermitage on Mount Boldino, despite the hostility of the local inhabitants. He built some huts, and a community began to gather around him. He also

founded three other monasteries, for which he drew up a common Rule of life, stressing the role of the hegumenos – one at Vjazma, one near Kaluga, and the other near Dorogobuz. Two of those he founded still survive.

Gerasimus of Euboea, bl., fourteenth century. Byzantine Church. He travelled around Greece as a preacher, and founded a monastery.

Gerasimus of Karpenisi, bl., born Megalo Chorio, 1787, died Constantinople, 3 July 1812. Byzantine Church. Baptized George, when he was 11 he went to Constantinople where he worked in a shop. Because of an accident he found himself in great debt, and had to become a slave, in the process becoming a Muslim. After a time he repented of this, fled back to his family, and then to Mount Athos, where he became a monk at the monastery of St Panteleimon. He wanted to become a martyr as a penance for his denial of Christianity, and although at first his spiritual father tried to dissuade him, eventually he returned to Constantinople, went to see the slave-owner from whom he had fled, and was finally decapitated.

Gerasimus of Perm and Ust-Vym, bishop, died near Jaransk, 24 January 1441. Russian Church. Bishop of Perm from *c.* 1416, he was a very active missionary in what was still quite pagan territory, building churches for his converts in the diocese. It was, however, a period of considerable turmoil in the region. The people of Perm were driven from their city by incursions of local tribesmen and forced to take refuge in the forests, where Gerasimus continued to visit and encourage them. He was assassinated by one of his servants while on one of these dangerous journeys. Feast 29 January.

Gerasimus of Solovki, monk, fifteenth century. Russian Church. A hermit, disciple of **Zosimus**.

Gerasimus of the Kievan Cave Monastery, monk. Russian Church. Nothing is known of him.

Gerasimus of Vologda, monk, born Kiev, died Kajsarov, 4 March 1178. Russian Church. Originally a monk of a monastery near Kiev, in 1147 he moved to Vologda, either to engage in evangelism, or to escape the troubles around his city. He settled in a forest near Vologda and founded a monastery dedicated to the Most Holy Trinity at a place called Kajsarov – although the story is very doubtful, because this would pre-date the earliest known monastery of the region by more than a century.

Gerasimus the Younger, born near Corinth, 1509, died Zante, 15 August 1579. Byzantine Church. Of a devout and well-to-do family, he travelled around Greece, spent time on Mount Athos, and spent 12 years in the Holy Land, travelled through north Africa and went to Crete. For five years he lived in a cave on the island of Zante (Zakynthos). According to one version of the story, his solitude was so often disturbed that he fled to Cephalonia. According to another, he moved into the interior of the island where he was given a monastery, which he converted to a convent of nuns and named it the New Jerusalem. He was its hegumenos until his death. Feast 16 August.

Gerbasius, died 1830. Byzantine Church. Nothing is known of him.

Gerebernus, see **Dympna**.

Geremarus, abbot, born Vardes, France, died Saint-Germer-de-Flay, *c.* 658. He was a court official of King Dagobert I, and was married with children. In 649 he decided to become a monk, giving all his possessions to his wife. He entered the monastery at Pentale, near Brionne, and was elected abbot. However, some monks were discontented with his strict imposition of the Rule, and rather than confront them he left the abbey to become a hermit beside the river Risle. He lived there for five years, but on the death of his son the property he had left him reverted to Geremarus, so with it he founded a monastery at Flay, where he remained as abbot until his death. Feast 30 December.

Gereon and Companions, martyrs, died Cologne, *c.* 305. Said to have been members of the **Theban Legion**. Feast 10 October.

Gerius (Gerard), hermit and pilgrim, died 1326. Feast 25 May.

Gerlach, anchorite, born Houthem, Netherlands, 1100, died there, 1177. On the accidental death of his wife, he abandoned his estates and knightly life and went on pilgrimage to Rome, where Pope Eugene III agreed to his spending seven years in the Holy Land caring for the poor and the sick. When he returned to Rome, Pope Adrian IV agreed to his continuing this work in his native town. Here he lived in a huge hollow tree, which was felled with episcopal approval after critics said they suspected him of hiding gold in it. Feast 5 January.

Gerland of Girgenti, born Besançon, Burgundy, he became bishop of Girgenti, Sicily and died there, 1100. Brought to Sicily by the ruling counts, his Norman relatives, he engaged in dialogue with Jews and Muslims and is said to have converted many through peaceful persuasion. Feast 25 February.

Germaine of Pibrac, born Pibrac, France, 1579, died there, 1 June 1601. She was forced by her unloving stepmother to live with the sheep from the age of eight, and was continually neglected by the family thereafter. Working as a shepherdess in her small community, she acquired a reputation for patience and kindness. Tradition has it that sheep gathered around her staff were kept safe from wolves while she attended mass. When her grave was opened to take another corpse in 1644, her body was found to be intact. Feast 15 June.

Germanicus of Smyrna, martyr, died Smyrna, 156. Martyred with St **Polycarp**.

German (Jermyn) Gardiner, bl., martyr, died London, 7 March 1544, with **John Larke**, beatified 1929. He was a layman, secretary to Stephen Gardiner, and, like Larke, was apparently inspired by the example of **Thomas More**.

Germanus of Alaska, born Serpuchov, 1756, died island of Kadiak, December 1837. Russian Church. Born into a merchant family, in 1772 he entered the monastery of St Sergius near St Petersburg, and six years later moved to the monastery of Valaam. In 1793 the monastery sent a missionary team to Alaska, where there was a Russian settlement. The monks' voyage lasted six months. When they arrived they settled on the island of Kadiak in the Aleutians. Although they had initial success, the people of the islands turned against them. Some monks were murdered, some returned home. Germanus remained alone. He grew his own food, fished, dressed in furs, and lived an ascetical life which gradually won him great fame among the Aleutians, especially after he had cared for them during an epidemic. The local Russian community was also at first hostile to the monk, but after a time they, too, were largely won over and their leader himself became a monk after his wife's death, and his daughter became a nun. He was renowned for his miracles – once calming a storm – and also for his gift of prophecy. Feast 13 December.

Germanus of Auxerre, bishop, born Auxerre, France, 378, died Ravenna, Italy, 31 July 448. Having studied in Rome and entered the imperial civil service, he was dispatched to Gaul as military governor. Elected as bishop of Auxerre, he distributed his fortune by endowing churches and monasteries, worked to found coenobite monasticism, visited Britain to combat Pelagianism, led British forces in a bloodless battle against Picts and Saxons, promoted clerical education, and sought the alleviation of taxes in his diocese. He died in Ravenna working to prevent reprisals for a revolt in Britanny.

Germanus of Beloozero, monk, died 1508 (?). Russian Church. A disciple of St **Cyril of Beloozero**.

Germanus of Capua, bishop, died *c.* 540. Of a wealthy family, he sold all his property and gave the proceeds to the poor. He was chosen as bishop of Capua *c.* 520. A few years before this, he had been sent by the pope to Constantinople to heal the schism which had developed. (The connection between the Germanus who was a papal representative, and the one who was bishop of Capua is not certain.) Feast 30 October.

Germanus of Constantinople, patriarch, born Constantinople, *c.* 634, died there, *c.* 732. Of a patrician family, he was castrated and forced to enter the cathedral clergy when his father was condemned to death by the emperor. He became

metropolitan of Cyzicus (Kapidagi, Turkey) in 705, and a decade later patriarch of Constantinople. He was a fervent opponent of the iconoclasts, for which he was sent into exile *c.* 729. He retired to his family estates, where he died. Feast 12 May.

Germanus of Dobrugia, monk, born Casimcea, *c.* 358, died *c.* 410. Romanian Church. As a young man he was a friend of **John Cassian**, with whom he travelled to Palestine, Syria and Egypt to meet monks and learn of the spiritual life. They went to Constantinople *c.* 400, where **John Chrysostom** was bishop, and Germanus was ordained priest. In 403 he took part in the Synod of the Oak, and in 405 went to Rome to defend Chrysostom. Cassian then parted from Germanus, and nothing more is heard of him. Feast 28 February.

Germanus of Grandval, martyred 21 February 667 (?). Brought up by Modoard of Trier, he entered Romberg monastery (later Remiremont) in the Vosges, with his younger brother. He became abbot of Grandval monastery, also in the Vosges. He was killed, together with his prior **Randoald**, by soldiers of the local lord.

Germanus of Kazan and of Svjazsk, archbishop, born Starica, 1504, died Moscow, 6 November 1568. Russian Church. Baptized Gregory Fedorovic Sadyrev-Polev, and of a boyar family, aged 25 he entered the monastery of St Joseph of Volokolamsk, where he took the name Germanus. His reputation for asceticism and holiness of life was such that he was invited by the people of his native city to become hegumenos of the monastery they had built. He stayed there less than three years, but left one of his disciples as superior, before returning to Volokolamsk. In 1554 he was asked by its archbishop to help in the diocese of Kazan, which he did, also founding a monastery at Svjazsk, from which missionary activity might be carried out. In 1564 he succeeded to the archdiocese. He had only two years of intense apostolic activity in his diocese before he was asked to come to Moscow by Ivan the Terrible to take over that see. He refused to do so, but was obliged nonetheless to live in the archiepiscopal residence, where he became a critic of the deeds of the Tsar, which led to a break with the Tsar – but he was never allowed to return to Kazan. He died of the Black Death. Feast 6 November.

Germanus of Munster-Granfelden, abbot, born Trier, Germany, 610, died Munster-Granfelden, 21 February 675. After his father's death he was brought up by the bishop of Trier and later became a disciple of St **Arnulf of Metz**. He moved to the monastery of Luxeuil where the abbot, St **Walbert**, recommended him as abbot for a new monastery at Munster-Granfelden. Here he opposed peasant oppression and was consequently murdered by its perpetrator Boniface, the brother and successor of Duke Gondo who had sought his appointment as abbot.

Germanus of Novgorod, bishop, died Kiev, 1096. Russian Church. Very little is known of him. He was a monk of the Kievan Cave monastery, to which he returned shortly before his death, after serving as bishop for 18 years. Feast 10 February.

Germanus of Paris, bishop, born Autun, Burgundy, 496, died Paris, 28 May 576. He was ordained in 530 and appointed administrator and later abbot of St Symphoran. He was elected bishop of Paris where he continued to live an austere life, presided over the third and fourth Councils of Paris, attended the second Council of Tours, miraculously restored King Childebert's health, founded an abbey (later known as St Germain des Prés), and worked to bring peace to the Merovingian kingdom.

Germanus of Solovki, monk, born Totma, died Novgorod, 1479. Russian Church. He became a hermit on the edge of the White Sea, where he was joined by one Sabatius. They then moved to the Solovki islands, where they lived for six years before returning to the mainland. Germanus, however, went back to Solovki with another young disciple, Zosimus. He died in the monastery of St Anthony in Novgorod, to which he had been invited, when he was over 100 years old. Feast 30 July.

Germanus of Stolobna, monk, died Stolobna, 1614. Russian Church. Germanus came from the monastery of St Nicholas of Rostov to live on Stolobna, an island on lake Seliger, where was

buried St **Nilus**. He and another monk built a tomb for Nilus, but in 1563, after three years there, Germanus left to go on pilgrimage and returned only in 1590. He then built a church and a monastery and for the rest of his life fostered devotion to Nilus. He shares the same feast, 22 February.

Germanus, Theophilus and Cyril, martyrs, died Caesarea in Cappadocia, 250. Feast 3 November.

Germerius, bishop, died Toulouse, sixth/seventh century. He was bishop of Toulouse for 50 years and has been venerated since his own times. Feast 16 May.

Germerius, abbot and statesman, born Vardes, France, 610, died Saint-Germer-de-Flay, 660. As a nobleman, he served at the court of Dagobert I and Clovis II. He founded the monastery of Isle (now Saint-Pierre-aux-Bois), and left his wife and secular career to enter the monastery of Pentale (now Saint-Samson-sur-Risle), where he became abbot, but which he left after a quarrel to become a hermit for five years. He later founded the abbey of Flay (now Saint-Germer-de-Flay), where he was made abbot. Possibly to be identified with Geremarus.

Gero of Cologne, archbishop, died 28 June 976. He was sent to Constantinople to request the hand of Romanus II's daughter Anna's hand in marriage to Emperor Otto I's son, but received instead that of Theophano the niece of the Eastern Emperor John I Tzimisces. He also returned with the relics of St **Pantaleon**. He founded a Benedictine monastery in Thankmarsfeld (which later transfered to Nienburg) and the abbey of Gladbach. He is associated with the 'Gero-codex' of the Gospels given to Cologne cathedral.

Gerold, hermit, born 920, died Friesen, now in Austria, 10 April 978. Tradition has it that at the age of 38 he gave his lands to the Benedictine abbey of Einsiedeln, where his two sons were monks, and built himself a hermitage on a site presented to him by a friend. On his death his sons lived in his cell guarding his tomb – on which spot the abbots of Einsiedeln later built a church. Rebuilt after being destroyed in the Reformation, this now houses his relics. He is depicted in pictures with two haloed sons, or freeing a bear trapped by hounds. Feast 19 April.

Gerontius, bishop and martyr, died Italica, near Seville, *c*. 100. Said to have been bishop of Italica, and to have died by poisoning. Feast 25 August.

Gerontius, bishop and martyr, died Cagli, near Ancona, 501. He was bishop of Cervia, near Ravenna. Although murdered while returning from a synod in Rome, it is not clear that he is a martyr. A Benedictine abbey was built where he died. Feast 9 May.

Gerontius of Moscow, bishop, born Novgorod (?), died Moscow, 28 May 1489. Russian Church. Little is known of his early life. He was archimandrite of the Simonov monastery in Moscow, and in 1453 was consecrated bishop of Kolomna. In 1479 he was named metropolitan of Moscow by Tsar Ivan III, with whom, for much of the succeeding years, he was in bitter conflict, and in 1482 Ivan permitted the metropolitan of Kiev to call himself 'metropolitan of all Russia'. At this, Gerontius went back to the Simonov monastery, and would not return until the Tsar had promised not to interfere in ecclesiastical affairs. He again fell out with Ivan the following year, and went to his monastery, but this time it was he who submitted, after being asked by Ivan to resign to make way for a new metropolitan.

Gerontius of Mount Athos, died Mount Athos, fourteenth century. Byzantine Church. Little is known of him, except that he was hegumenos of a monastery close to the shore of Mount Athos, which left it open to piratical attacks, and was therefore abandoned. He built a hermitage in a safer spot on Mount Athos, dedicated to St Panteleimon. Feast 26 July.

Gerontius of the Kievan Cave Monastery, monk, died Kiev, fourteenth century. Nothing is known of his life, except that he was in charge of the choir. Feast 28 August.

Gertrude Comensoli, bl., born near Brescia, Italy, 1847, christened Caterina, died Bergamo, 18 February 1903, beatified 1989. She left the Society of St Angela Merici in 1882 to found the Adorers of the Blessed Sacrament, or 'Sacramentines', dedicated to venerating the sacrament and providing girls with a Christian education.

Gertrude of Altenburg, bl., born Wartburg, near Eisenach, September 1227, died Altenburg, 1297. The daughter of **Elizabeth of Hungary**, her father, **Louis of Thuringia**, died while on his way to the Crusade and she was placed for her education in the Premonstratensian convent at Altenburg at the age of two. She became a nun there, and at the age of 22, abbess of the convent, where she was known for her piety and her generosity. Feast 13 August.

Gertrude of Nivelles, abbess. She was born in 626 and died in 659. She is venerated in Holland and Belgium and known as a patroness of travellers. Bl. **Ida**, her mother, founded a convent on the death of Gertrude's father. Gertrude became its first abbess when Ida died. She lived such a life of asceticism that in *c*. 656 she stepped down from the abbacy and gave her last three years completely to devotional prayer. Feast 17 March.

Gertrude the Great, mystic, born Eisleben, Germany, 6 January 1256, died Helfta, 17 November 1302. From the age of five she lived at the convent of Helfta in Thuringia. Following a conversion experience at the age of 25, she led a contemplative life. She is known as one of the first to practise devotion to the Sacred Heart. Her main written works are the *Exercitia Spiritualia* and the *Legatus Divinae Pietatis*. The former is a series of meditations, the latter includes an account of her mystical experiences which centred on the person of Christ, and had an effect upon the development of the spirituality of the Cistercian Order, to which Gertrude's monastery was loosely affiliated. Feast 16 November.

Gerulf, martyr, born Meerendra, Belgium, 732, died Ghent, Belgium, 750. Legend has it that, while riding home from his confirmation at the monastery of Saint-Bavon at Ghent, his godfather was possessed by the devil and threatened to kill him despite Gerulf's warning that he would go to hell if he did. His mother realized what had happened when his horse returned riderless and had him buried at a church in Meerendra. After several miracles it was moved to the monastery at Dronghem. Feast 21 September.

Geruntius, bishop, died *c.* 472. He was bishop of Milan from *c.* 465, succeeding **Eusebius**. Feast 5 May.

Gervase and Protase, Milanese martyrs unknown until **Ambrose** discovered their bodies in 386. On 19 June he had them transferred to a recently built basilica, where they were put under the altar. This was important in two respects: firstly, the placing of relics under the altar became part of the dedication ceremony of churches and, secondly, the finding (*inventio*) of the relics by Ambrose caused many other similar findings and translations in north Italy. About Gervase and Protase themselves we know nothing since their *Passio* has no historical value. Feast 19 June.

Gervinus, abbot, born near Rheims, died 1075. A Benedictine monk and abbot of Saint Riquier in Picardy, he was known for his life of austerity and prayer. He travelled widely, visiting England in the last years of **Edward the Confessor**. He died as a consequence of contracting leprosy. Feast 3 March.

Gervinus of Oudenburg, abbot, born Flanders, died Forest of Cosfort, Flanders, 17 April 1117. He became a Benedictine monk and priest at Bergues-Saint-Winoc following a journey to Rome and two pilgrimages to Jerusalem. He left the monastery to be a hermit, but, while near Oudenburg in 1095, was elected abbot of the monastery there. He resigned in 1105 to live in the forest near the abbey.

Gery of Cambrai, bishop and patron of Cambrai, born Carignan, France, died Cambrai, 11 August 625. Mageric, bishop of Trier, conferred the tonsure on him and promised to ordain him when he had learned the Psalter by heart. He was chosen by the people of Cambrai to replace Mageric as bishop, and was consecrated by the archbishop of Rheims in 584. As bishop, he opposed paganism,

built a church to St Medard, attended a Council in Paris in 614, and went on pilgrimage to Tours.

Gezzelinus, bl., hermit, died Luxembourg, 6 August 1138. He lived as a hermit in the forests around Grunenwald near Luxembourg for some 14 years without any clothes or shelter, foraging for his food. The Cistercians claim that he was a member of their order because a monk, Achard of Clairvaux, gave him the habit of **Bernard of Clairvaux**. He was buried in the Benedictine abbey church of Maria-Munster in Luxembourg.

Gherardesca, bl., anchoress in Pisa, died *c.* 1269. Feast 29 May.

Gianna Beretta Molla, bl., born Milan, 4 October 1922, died there, 28 April 1962, beatified 1994. A married pediatric doctor, diagnosed with a uterine growth while pregnant with her fourth child, she chose from the start only to have treatment that would not harm it. She survived the birth, but died of peritonitis.

Gibrian, born Ireland, died France, *c.* 515. A priest, he was the oldest of a family of seven brothers and three sisters who all followed a popular Christian calling of the time, becoming pilgrims, *peregrini*. They settled in separate hermitages in the forest near the Marne, reasonably close together. Feast 8 May.

Gideon, see also **Barlamio of Sepuchov**.

Gideon of Capurna, martyr, born Capurna, 1766, died Tirnavo, 30 December 1818. Byzantine Church. Named Nicholas at baptism, he and his family moved to Giermi, near Velestino, and he was sent to work in his uncle's grocer's shop. He attracted the attention of a Muslim, who wanted the boy as an attendant in his harem, and when the uncle refused, he took him by force and persuaded him to become a Muslim. He quickly repented of his apostasy and fled back first to his parents' house, then set off, arriving eventually at Mount Athos where he became a monk, taking the name Gideon. He stayed there for 35 years, but decided to seek martyrdom. He returned to Velestino, proclaimed his Christian faith, was arrested, thrown in prison, and finally executed.

Gilbert, born Ham, died Meaux, 1009. He studied at St Quentin and was bishop of Meaux. Feast 13 February.

Gilbert, bl., Cistercian abbot, born England, died Toulouse, France, perhaps 17 October 1167, or possibly 1168. He was abbot of Ourscamp, near Compiègne, from 1143, and was elected abbot of Cîteaux, with responsibility for all Cistercian houses, in 1163. In that capacity he won from Pope Alexander III exemption for his order from all episcopal jurisdiction, but he failed to settle, as he attempted to do, the conflict between Alexander and the Emperor Frederick Barbarossa. When **Thomas Becket** took refuge from Henry II in the Cistercian abbey of Pontigny, Gilbert pressed him to find some other sanctuary, fearful of reprisals against the Cistercians by the English king. He is sometimes called 'the Great' or 'the Theologian', probably through a confusion with other Gilberts – no treatises can be assigned to him with certainty. He was, however, included by the Cistercians among the 'blesseds' of their order.

Gilbert of Caithness, bishop, born Scotland, died Caithness, 1 April 1245. He was archdeacon of Moray from c. 1203, then bishop of Caithness from 1223. He built Dornoch cathedral, established its clergy's constitution, founded hospices for the poor and defended the Scottish Church's independence against the archbishop of York.

Gilbert of Neuffontaines, Premonstratensian (Norbertine) abbot, born Auvergne, France, 1110, died abbey of Neuffontaines, France, 6 June 1152. After the second Crusade, he gave half his possessions to the poor and half to rebuild a convent at Aubeterre and a monastery at Neuffontaines. He joined the Premonstratensian order on completion of the monastery and became its first abbot. Many cures are attributed to him, and his intercession is believed to benefit children.

Gilbert of Sempringham, monastic reformer and founder of the Order of Sempringham, the only medieval English monastic order, born Sempringham, Lincolnshire, between c. 1083 and 1089, died Sempringham, 4 February 1189. The son of a Norman knight, Jocelin, and an Englishwoman, he was educated first in Lincolnshire and then (probably) in Paris; he returned to Lincolnshire and established a school, almost certainly at Sempringham. Before 1123 he became a clerk in the household of the bishop of Lincoln, and was ordained by Alexander the Magnificent in 1123. By 1131 he had returned to Sempringham, where he established a small religious community of seven women, which by 1147 had grown so large that he went to Cîteaux in an attempt to incorporate his monasteries into the Cistercian congregation. Reluctant to take on the administration of a small and isolated monastic order, the Cistercians declined his request. Pope Eugenius III gave his approval to the order – made up of both double monasteries and communities for men – in 1148, and by the time of Gilbert's death, the order had grown to nine double monasteries and four houses of canons. He was canonized by Pope Innocent III in 1202.

Gildas (the Wise), historian, born probably Dumbarton, Scotland, c. 516, died Houat, Brittany, 570. He was educated in Wales by Iltut and knew St Samson and Peter of Leon. He was married but then widowed, after which he became a monk and went to Ireland and ministered and preached both there and in northern Britain. He made a pilgrimage to Rome and on the way back retired to live a solitary life on the island of Houat. He established a monastery at Rhuys in Brittany and has been honoured in that region ever since. His major work is *De excidio Brittanniae liber querulus*, which outlines the history of Britain from the time of the Roman invasion down to his own period. He also berates several of the British kings and rebukes the clergy. Feast 29 January.

Gilduin, born 1052, died 1077. As a very young canon of Dol, Brittany, he was elected bishop but refused the position. Pope Gregory VII accepted his decision, but Gilduin died on his way home from Rome. Feast 27 January.

Giles, abbot and hermit, patron of cripples, beggars and blacksmiths, possibly born Athens, Greece, died c. 720. According to some sources he came from Greece to Marseilles, where he lived as a hermit near the mouth of the Rhone, and where he influenced Flavius Wamba, king of the Goths, to build the monastery for him which became the

Abbey of Saint-Giles – but it is possible that this story was concocted by the monks of Saint-Giles to free themselves from the authority of the bishop of Nimes. He later became confessor to King Charles of France. His tomb became a place of pilgrimage. Feast 1 September.

Giles Mary, bl., born Apulia, 1729, died Naples, 7 February 1812, beatified 1888. A Discalced Franciscan, working all his life as a porter, he miraculously always seemed to have enough alms for the poor. His charity was well known and he also had a reputation for healing people miraculously.

Giles of Assisi, bl., Franciscan, companion of St **Francis**, born 1190, died Perugia, Italy, 22 April 1262. He joined Francis as his third companion in 1208 and accompanied him to Rome where the approval of Pope Innocent III was obtained for the new order and he received the tonsure. He went to Jerusalem and preached in Tunis before returning to Italy to live in a series of remote hermitages, becoming famous for his mystical raptures. He settled finally in Monteripido where he was visited by Gregory IX and St **Bonaventure**. His *Dicta* denounces relaxation and intellectual pride. He was the only one of Francis's companions to be beatified. Feast 23 April.

Giles of Lorenzana, bl., born Lorenzana, Kingdom of Naples, c.1443, died there, 1518. A farmhand, he became a Franciscan lay brother and lived as a hermit in the friary garden. He was known for his love of animals. Feast 10 January.

Giles of Santarem, bl., Dominican preacher, born Vaozela, Portugal, 1184, died Santarem, (then Spain), 14 May 1265. He was endowed with five ecclesiastical benefices when young and squandered their proceeds studying medicine in Paris and going on to practise necromancy. His religious conversion prompted him to return to Spain, where he entered the Dominican order at Palencia. As a travelling preacher and teacher, he became acquainted with many prominent people. He was twice elected provincial of the Spanish province.

Gisela, bl., queen of Hungary, born c. 973, died c. 1060. Following the death of her husband **Stephen I**, she involved herself in affairs of state. Many

virtues are ascribed to her, but it is postulated that these were to contrast her with her husband's successor Peter I. She probably died in exile or in a convent – her reported death and tombstone at Passau are not considered reliable. She is not normally honoured as a saint, although she is still under consideration by the Holy See. Feast 7 May.

Gislenus, abbot, hermit near Hainault in France, born c. 650, died 9 October 681. He founded and governed the monastery of Ss Peter and Paul. Legend has it that a bear he saved from a hunt showed him the site of the future monastery. Supposedly born in Attica, he became a monk, and bishop of Athens. He is said to have resigned his see, travelled to Rome and then Hainault, met St **Amandus**, and settled on the river Haire.

Gizur of Iceland, bishop, died 1117. Grandson of one of the first people baptized in Iceland, son of the first bishop of Skalholt, Gizur succeeded him c.1080. Greatly admired for his leadership, he introduced tithes and taxation, provided for the poor and divided Iceland into two dioceses. Feast 28 May.

Glaphira of Amasea Pontica, died Amasea, 324. When the Emperor Licinius tried to violate her, she fled to the bishop of Amasea Pontica. Both were arrested and sentenced to death, but Glaphira died on the way to execution. Feast 13 January.

Gleb of Grodno, prince, died 1166. Russian Church. Little is known of him. Feast 6 July.

Gleb of Rostov, prince, died Rostov, c. 1280. Russian Church. The son of **Vasiliko of Rostov**, he was caught in a storm while travelling on lake Kubenskoe. He promised to build a sanctuary were he to be saved, which he was. He therefore built a church dedicated to the Transfiguration. He also built a monastery in thanksgiving for the cure of his child's blindness. Feast 24 July.

Gleb of Vladimir, prince, died Vladimir, 1174. Russian Church. The son of **Andrew of Bogolyubovo**, he died very young. Feast 20 June.

Gleb Vsevolodovic, prince, died river Vorksel, 1399. Russian Church. He was taken prisoner by the Lithuanians and sent to Lithuania as a hostage. In 1392 he was made grand prince of Smolensk, against the wishes of the inhabitants of that city, possibly because he had become friendly with the Lithuanians. He died fighting against the Tartars alongside the Lithuanians.

Gliceria, martyr, died Heraclea, 177. When forced to sacrifice to Zeus, instead she smashed the statue and was executed. Feast 13 May.

Gliceria of Novgorod, died fourteenth/fifteenth century. Russian Church. Her body was found incorrupt in 1572, she having died some 50 years before. Feast 13 May.

Glicerius, martyred by being drowned, c. 303. Feast 14 January.

Glicerius of Nicomedia, martyr, died Nicomedia, 303. A priest burned to death for the faith during the persecution of Diocletian. Feast 21 December.

Glodesindis, abbess, born Metz, France, 570, died 600. Glodesindis's father tried to give her in marriage against her wishes, and she fled to the cathedral of Metz. She was taken to Trier by her aunt, and instructed in the monastic life. On her return to Metz she founded a monastery of about 100 nuns. Feast 25 July.

Goar of Trier, hermit, died 570. Goar is held to have come from Aquitaine, in the days of Childebert I, king of the Franks. He built a chapel and hermitage near Oberweld. Goar was renowned for his hospitality. There are conflicting accounts of his life which have given rise to different opinions as to his dates. As well as the sixth century, he could be placed in the eighth century. Feast 6 July.

Godeleva, born near Boulogne, France, 1050, died 6 July 1070 (some accounts give date of death as 30 July). She married Bertulf of Ghistelles, a Flemish lord, at the age of 18. He left her soon afterwards, but the local bishop, at the request of Godeleva's parents, persuaded him to return. He lived with her for a time, but then had her murdered by his servants, who strangled her and dumped her body in a well. Several miracles are said to have occurred at the site of her death, and Bertulf's daughter by

his second wife is reputed to have been cured of blindness there.

Godfrey of Amiens, bishop, ecclesiastical reformer and saint, died Soissons, 8 November 1115. Little is known about his early life. He was appointed bishop of Amiens in 1104 and attempted to reform the Church by enforcing clerical celibacy, removing simony and organizing religious communes. Facing stern opposition, he withdrew to the monastery of the Grande-Chartreuse.

Godfrey of Kappenburg, bl., born Kappenburg Castle, Westphalia, 1097, died Ilbenstadt, 13 January 1127. Lord of a great estate in Westphalia, he was converted by **Norbert**, previously also a rich nobleman. Like Norbert, he gave up his possessions and took minor orders. His wife, brother and sisters also joined religious orders.

Godo, abbot, died Oyes, 26 May 690. Godo was the nephew of St **Wandville**, the founder of a monastery at Fontenellle. He was a member of the monastery until 661, when he left to found his own community at Oyes.

Godo of Troyes, abbot, seventh century. Feast 26 May.

Godric of Finchale, born Walpole, Suffolk, England, 1069, died Finchale, County Durham, 21 May 1170. He was a peddler, sailor, ship's captain and pilgrim until aged about 40. He then lived for 60 years as a hermit at Finchale, by the river Wear. Some of his hymns survive. Feast 21 May.

Goericus of Metz, bishop, died Metz, 647. Of a distinguished family of Aquitaine, he served in the royal palace, but had to leave his post when he went blind. He decided to visit his uncle **Arnulf** in Metz, where he was bishop, being guided there by his daughters. When there he regained his sight, and was inspired to become a priest. He became bishop of Metz in 625. He built churches and founded a nunnery, of which one of his daughters became the first abbess. Feast 19 September.

Gohard and Companions, martyrs, died Nantes, France, 843. Gohard, the bishop of Nantes, monks and lay people of the city, were killed when Viking raiders attacked Nantes. Gohard was saying mass at the time of the raid. Feast 25 June.

Goharinos of Sebaste and his brothers, martyrs, born Sebaste, died there, 30 July 1155. The four were arrested for their Christianity, but the first time escaped because another brother, who had converted to Islam, persuaded the authorities that they should be freed. They were rearrested and beheaded some time later – by which time one of the brothers, Ratios, had become a monk.

Golinduch, martyr, died Nixion, near Hierapolis, 591. Syriac Church. The wife of a Persian noble, she seems to have been converted to Christianity by some Greek prisoners, and took the name Mary. For converting, she was imprisoned for 18 years, and earned the title of 'the living martyr'. When finally freed, she went on a pilgrimage to Jerusalem. One version of the story suggests that she was beheaded by an angel, thus allowing her to become a martyr as a reward for the years she had spent in prison. Feast 13 July.

Gomidas Keunurgian, bl., martyr, born Constantinople, c. 1656, died there, 5 November 1707. He was an Armenian priest, married with several children. He was working in a parish in Constantinople when he decided to become a (Roman) Catholic, along with his family. Others followed his example, but because of hostility to him he went off to an Armenian monastery in Jerusalem, although there again he met hostility. This continued after he returned to Constantinople, and he went to Cyprus, where the French ambassador had him kidnapped and taken to France. This made him even more suspect, not only to the Armenians, but also to the Turkish authorities. The Armenians pressured the Turks to arrest him once he was back in Constantinople. He was beheaded.

Gonçalvo Garcia, martyred Nagasaki, 5 February 1597, canonized 1862. A Franciscan brother from India, he died with **Paul Mikki** and is venerated as the first Indian martyr. See **Martyrs of Japan.**

Gonzaga Gonza, martyr, died Uganda, 1886, canonized 1964. Converted by the Missionaries of Africa, he was imprisoned for a long period before being executed by King Mwanga of Uganda. He is commemorated with **Athanasius Bazzekuketta**. See **Martyrs of Uganda**. Feast 27 May.

Gorasdo, bishop, born Hruba Vrbka, Moravia, 26 May 1879, died Prague, 4 September 1942. Czech Church. Baptized Matthew Pavlik, he came from a pious, farming family. He was a Catholic, but with a great interest in Orthodoxy, going as a student to Kiev. He was ordained priest in Olomuc and worked in various parishes. He founded a journal called *The Observer*, and later, when he had become involved in the struggle for national independence, a monthly entitled *The Right of the People*. The independence he and others sought included a form of national Church. They first requested a 'Czechoslovakian patriarchate', but when Rome refused this, they created a national Church. Pavlik was not happy with this arrangement, however, and he and a number of others then joined the Orthodox Church, being ordained bishop in the process by the Serbian patriarch, having first become a monk and taken the name Gorasdo. He spent the next years fostering Orthodoxy in Czechoslovakia, training clergy, producing books, and keeping contact with other Churches, especially with the Church of England and the American Episcopal Church. During the German occupation in World War II he openly encouraged people to struggle for national independence. When a group of patriots assassinated the German commander in Czechoslovakia, they fled for refuge to the crypt of the Orthodox cathedral in Prague. When the Germans finally discovered the hiding place, they arrested Gorasdo and executed him. Feast 22 August.

Gordian, martyr, died Rome, c. 362. He may have been a young soldier or official in the imperial household, apparently converted when visiting a prisoner and executed by the sword. He is commemorated with **Epimachus**, in whose tomb in Rome he was buried. Feast 10 May.

Gordius, martyred c. 304. A soldier in Caesarea, Cappadocia, possibly a centurion, he was dismissed for being a Christian and retired to the desert. At the time of the persecution under Diocletian he came forward as a Christian and was beheaded. Feast 3 January.

Gorgonia, born Nazianzen (in Cappadocia, today part of Turkey), *c.* 329, died Iconium, *c.* 370. She was the eldest daughter of the bishop of Nazianzen, **Gregory the Elder**, and the sister of **Gregory of Nazianzen**. The latter composed a funeral oration to her. Born in a Christian family, she married young, was baptized just before marriage and had her husband and children also baptized. During her fairly short life she exhibited truly Christian virtues. Feast 9 December.

Gorgonius and Dorotheus, martyrs, died Nicomedia, perhaps 303. Feast 9 September.

Gorgonius and Firmus, martyrs, died Antioch (?), third century. Feast 11 March.

Gosbert, died *c.* 859. A monk, a disciple of **Ansgar**, he was the fourth bishop of Osnabruck and missionary to the Suevi in difficult times. Feast 13 February.

Goswin, Benedictine abbot and scholar, born Douai, died Anchin, near Douai, 9 October 1165 or 10 October 1166. After studying in Paris – where he was a fierce opponent of Peter Abelard – Goswin taught as a canon of Douai and, *c.* 1112, entered the nearby monastery of Anchin. A monastic reformer, he was responsible for the reform of three monasteries, and, as prior of St Médard of Soissons, gave shelter to his old adversary Peter Abelard after his condemnation by the Council of Soissons in 1121. In 1131 he became abbot of Anchin, where he encouraged the production of illuminated manuscripts.

Gothard (Godehard) of Hildesheim, bishop, born Reichersdorf, Bavaria, *c.* 960, died Hildesheim, 1038, canonized 1131. First a priest, then a Benedictine, he was a reforming abbot at the German monasteries of Tegernsee, Hersfeld and Kremsmünster. He became bishop of Hildesheim in 1022 and the alpine pass is named after him. Feast 5 May.

Gottschalk, king and martyr, born northern Germany, date unknown, died Lenzen on the Elbe, Germany, 7 June 1066. Gottschalk was a prince being educated at the monastery in Lüneburg when he left around 1030 in order to avenge the murder of King Uto, his father, by the Saxons. His rebellion was quashed, and he found himself in exile in Denmark, where he served King Canute, and then in England, where he served King Sweyn and married his daughter. He returned to his native land to rule in 1043 and worked to Christianize his realm with the aid of **Adalbert** of Bremen. He was killed in an anti-Christian uprising against Adalbert.

Gracilian, martyred Faleria, Umbria, *c.* 304. His unreliable legend is that, while in prison awaiting execution, he restored a blind girl's sight and converted her. He and **Felissima** were beheaded and are commemorated on the same day. Feast 26 May.

Gratian, bishop, born Rome (?), died Tours, *c.* 307 (?). Said to have been the missionary from Rome who established the bishopric of Tours. Feast 18 December.

Gregory, hesychast, fourteenth century. Byzantine Church. Founded the monastery of Ss Nicholas and Gregory. Feast 7 December.

Gregory, died *c.* 1005. He was a monk in Armenia. Feast 27 February.

Gregory I ('the Great'), pope, born Rome, *c.* 540 from a patrician family, consecrated pope 3 September 590, died Rome, 12 March 604. He had a legal education and in 572/3 he became *praefectus urbis*, a position which allowed him to develop his organizational skills. In 575, however, after the death of his father, he abandoned his secular career and founded a monastery in the family palace on the Celian Hill. In 578 he was ordained deacon and was sent the following year as papal nuntius to Constantinople. He returned to Rome and his monastery in 585, and in 590 he became pope. He tried, but failed, to avoid the appointment by writing to the emperor. He came into office as the city was under a plague, and did a great deal to relieve suffering and provide food. To do this efficiently he reorganized the Curia and the revenues from the land the Church owned, as well as trying to establish peace in the peninsula. He established good relations with Visigothic Spain, and sent **Augustine**, a monk, to evangelize the English. Throughout his pontificate he encouraged the growth of monasticism. He was a vigorous upholder of the prerogatives of the bishop of Rome, which meant that the relationship with Constantinople was tense. In 591 he wrote *Pastoral Care*, a reflection on the role of the bishop, which was formative for medieval bishops. His many other theological writings, his homilies and letters and his reform of the liturgy assured him a prominent place in the history of theology and Christian worship. Feast 3 September.

Gregory II, pope, born Rome, 669, elected to the papacy 19 May 715, died Rome, 11 February 731. From a wealthy family, he had acted as treasurer in the Lateran while he was a subdeacon, and as deacon had been part of a diplomatic mission to Constantinople 710–11. He possessed considerable political skills, and in 729 persuaded an alliance of Lombards and Byzantines not to lay siege to Rome. He repaired the city walls and restored churches, as well as the abbey of Monte Cassino which the Lombards had devastated. He gave active support to **Boniface** in the evangelization of Germany. He rejected Leo III the Isaurian's demand that he approve of his iconoclastic campaign, and rejected iconoclasm as heretical, adding that theology was the business of priests and not of princes. Feast 29 January.

Gregory III, pope, of Syrian origin, he was chosen by acclaim and consecrated 18 March 731, died Rome, 28 November 741. One of his first acts was to hold a synod in Rome to condemn iconoclasm, which annoyed the emperor, but Gregory also aided the emperor in the struggle against the king of the Lombards in Italy, which restored relations with Constantinople. Gregory strengthened the walls of the city and twice sent embassies to Charles Martel to ask for help from the Franks. Although none came, it established a pattern for the future. Gregory gave his backing to **Boniface**'s evangelization of Germany, and improved links between Rome and England. Feast 10 December.

Gregory V (Angelopoulos), patriarch of Constantinople, martyr, born Arcadia, Peloponnesus, 1745, died (martyred) Constantinople, 10 April 1821. He was elected ecumenical patriarch in 1797, was twice deposed by the Turkish authorities and twice reinstated, becoming patriarch finally in 1819. He concerned himself always for his flock – the entire Orthodox population of the Turkish empire. The declaration of revolution by the southern Greeks on 25 March 1821 enraged the sultan and many massacres of Christians followed. On Easter morning the patriarch was hung on his own gate, having refused the ritual offer of freedom in return for conversion to Islam. His body was taken to Odessa and eventually Athens. He was canonized in 1921. Feast 10 April.

Gregory VII, pope, born Hildebrand Rovaco, Tuscany, *c.* 1020, elected 22 April 1073, died Salerno, 25 May 1085. Hildebrand appears to have been a monk, possibly in Rome, and certainly spent some time at Cluny. He was chaplain to Gregory VI and accompanied him into exile, and having identified himself clearly with the reform party, returned to Rome in 1049 with the newly appointed Leo IX. He became a deacon, papal treasurer and prior of the monastery of St Paul Without the Walls, and an important figure in papal politics in the reigns of successive popes. He was elected by popular acclaim. He was determined to make the Roman see the effective law-making and law-enforcing authority in Western Christendom, and began by a series of synods aimed to improve the moral status of the clergy, particularly opposing simony and clerical marriage, imposing an oath of obedience on bishops and threatening to remove them if they did not impose the papal demands upon their clergy. He also wanted them to make regular visits to Rome to report on their success in carrying out papal policies. He was also deeply opposed to the system of lay investiture, according to which monarchs conferred benefices on the senior clergy, thus effectively controlling them. This was incompatible with Gregory's policies. At the Diet of Worms, summoned by the German King Henry IV early in 1076, the bishops attending declared Gregory deposed: Gregory responded by declaring Henry suspended from his royal power – rather as recalcitrant bishops were suspended from the exercise of their office. At Canossa in 1077 Henry asked pardon, which was granted. However, when a rival was chosen as king of Germany, Rudolp of Swabia, Gregory backed him, after the failure of his efforts to mediate between the two. This proved a costly mistake. In 1080 Henry had an antipope elected. In 1084 Gregory had to take refuge in Castel Sant'Angelo, and Robert Guiscard's efforts to free him, although successful, so alienated the people of Rome that the pope had to flee with Robert to Salerno.

Gregory X, bl., pope, born Teobaldo Visconti at Piacenza, 1210, elected 1 September 1271, died Arezzo, 10 January 1276. Elected at Viterbo after a vacancy of three years, Gregory had studied in Paris, had been a canon of Lyons and archdeacon of Liège before becoming a chaplain to the future King Edward I of England, and accompanying him to the Holy Land – where indeed he was when he learned of his election to the papacy, although he was not yet a priest. He returned to Rome, was ordained and consecrated. His pontificate was dominated by his desire for a new Crusade, for which he needed, and worked very successfully for, peace in Europe, and for a reunion of the Churches of East and West. The crusade was launched at the second Council of Lyons (1274), which was attended by representatives of the Byzantine Emperor Michael VIII Palaeologus. At the council was promulgated the constitution *Ubi Periculum*, which was intended so to regulate conclaves that future papal elections would not drag out as long as the one which elected Gregory himself.

Gregory bar Hebraeus, born Ibra on the Euphrates, 1226, died Maraga, 1286. Syriac Church. The son of a doctor, in 1234 he moved with his family to Antioch. In 1244 he became a monk, and two years later bishop of Gubos, then bishop of Laqabin, and in 1264 he was given charge of the territory of the patriarchate which fell within the former Persian empire. The rest of his life he spent encouraging the faithful, especially around Mosul. He wrote on a great variety of topics, including science.

Gregory Barbarigo, cardinal, born Venice, 16 September 1623, died Padua, 18 June 1697. In 1648 he was part of the Venetian embassy that went to Münster for the Treaty of Westphalia. In 1655 he was ordained, having taken a degree in law, and the next year he was helping to organize the Trestevere quarter in Rome which had been struck by the plague. In 1657 he became bishop of Bergamo and advocated the reforms of the Council of Trent. In 1660 he was made cardinal, then bishop of Padua in 1667. He gave much support to Christians who were under Muslim rule. He wrote *Regulae Studiorum* (1690) and played an important role as a candidate at three papal conclaves, especially that of 1691.

Gregory Dekapolites, Byzantine monk, born Eirenopolis, Isaurian Decapolis, c. 780, died Constantinople, 20 November 842. After completing his early education, he spent 14 years in a monastery in Isauria whose archimandrite was his maternal uncle, Symeon. He then wandered extensively in Asia Minor, Greece and Sicily, settling for periods in Syracuse and Thessalonika, from where he visited Mount Olympus and Constantinople. He survived unscathed through the second wave of persecution in the iconoclastic controversy. A life, written in the 840s, has been attributed to Ignatius the deacon, but the ascription is disputed.

Gregory, Demetrius, Artemius and Euphrosina, born Kitovo. Russian Church. Known only as miracle workers.

Gregory Grassi, bl., bishop and martyr, born Alessandria, Italy, 13 December 1833, died Taiyüanfu, Shanxi, China, 9 July 1900. Grassi joined the Order of Friars Minor in 1848, was ordained in 1856 and left for mission work in China in 1861. During his missionary work, he was made titular bishop of Ortosia and vicar apostolic for the Shanxi province of north China. He was martyred – along with a fellow bishop, seven nuns, five seminarians, and the household servants – in his episcopal residence during the Boxer Rebellion in 1900. See **Franciscan Martyrs of China** and **Martyrs of Shanxi**. Feast 4 July.

Gregory Manacihr (or 'the Persian'), martyr, died Peroz Sabur, 18 April 542. Armenian Church. Appointed governor of Georgia and Albania by the king of Persia, he caused scandal by becoming a Christian. He was imprisoned for three years, but later released and reinstated. He was, however, opposed by Zoroastrian priests, and this time condemned to death, and was beheaded.

Gregory Narek, Armenian mystical poet and theologian, born *c.* 951, son of Xosrov, bishop of Anjewac'ik', died *c.* 1001. Educated by his uncle, a philosopher, he lived in Narek monastery, and refers to himself as a priest. He seems to have acquitted himself of heresy charges by performing various miracles. He appears to have spent his later life as a cave-dwelling anchorite on the shores of lake Van. He composed 95 mystical meditations on the book of Lamentations (copies of his text were prized as talismans), a number of hymns and panegyrics, a commentary on the Song of Songs, and a letter on heresy. Feast 27 February.

Gregory of Agrigentum, bishop, born near Agrigentum, Sicily, 559, died probably 604 (though some estimates suggest later, even 638). He studied in Byzantine monasteries in Palestine and was ordained deacon in Jerusalem. After visits to Antioch, north Africa and Constantinople, he went to Rome and was appointed bishop of Girgenti. A plot was laid to besmirch his reputation by the discovery of a prostitute at his home, but he was cleared of the charge. He wrote a major Greek commentary on Ecclesiastes, in ten books. Feast 23 November.

Gregory of Assos, bl., bishop, born Akorni, near Mitylene, died Mount Priantos, 4 March (?) *c.* 1150 (?). Byzantine Church. He studied in Constantinople, visited the Holy Land, then became a monk. He was later elected bishop of Assos, but was forced to resign because of hostility, returned home and founded a monastery on Mount Priantos. Feast 4 March.

Gregory of Avnega, died Avnega, 1392. Russian Church. He was a disciple of **Stephen of Machrisca**, and went with him to found the monastery of Avnega on the river Suchoma *c.* 1370. Stephen moved on in 1386, and Gregory became superior. He was martyred during an attack by Tartars.

Gregory of Byzantium, bl., born Byzantium, died Mount Athos, thirteenth/fourteenth centuries. A

monk of the Grand Laura on Mount Athos, and teacher of **Gregory Palamas**. Feast 2 April.

Gregory of Cerchiara, abbot, born Cassano al l'Ionio, Calabria, Italy, *c.* 930, died abbey of Burtscheid, Germany, 1002. Gregory began his career as a Basilian monk and abbot at Cerchiara. He fled to Rome after the Saracen invasion and there, with the help of Empress Theophano, founded the San Salvatore around 990. The empress then sent him to Germany, where he founded and became abbot of a monastery (St Apollinaris and Nicholas) that became the centre for much dispersion of Byzantine culture and Christianity in Germany. His cult is only found among the Basilians at Burtscheid. Feast 4 November.

Gregory of Chrisi Petra, bl. Byzantine Church. Said to have been born in Asia Minor, and a monk of Chrisi Petra, but otherwise nothing is known. Feast 24 November.

Gregory of Decapolis, monk, born Irenopolis in the Decapolis, died Constantinople, 832. Byzantine Church. His parents wanted him to marry, but he fled from his home and joined a monastery where his brother was already a monk. He fell out with the hegumenos over iconoclasm and left the monastery, travelling widely and performing miracles. He suffered greatly because of his opposition to iconoclasm. Feast 20 November.

Gregory of Einsiedeln, bl., abbot, born probably in England, early 900s, died Einsiedeln, Germany, 996. Of noble English descent, Gregory was married early but left his virgin wife, with her consent, to become a monk in Rome. He came to Einsiedeln in 949 and became abbot in 964. He knew the English monastic reforms of **Dunstan** of Canterbury and regulated Einsiedeln according to the English *Regularis concordia*. He was favoured by the German Emperors Otto I (to whom he was related by marriage), Otto II and Otto III, who all enriched the abbey and helped establish its reputation. That reputation led **Gebhard II of Constance** to request monks from Gregory when the former founded Peterhausen. Miracles were said to occur at Gregory's tomb after his death. Feast 8 November.

Gregory of Elvira, bishop, died in old age after 392, possibly even after 403. He became bishop of Elvira (Spain) c. 359. A fervent anti-Arian, he did not subscribe to the formula of Rimini (359). He also fought against Priscillianism. Among his works we find a defence of the *homoousios* (*De fide*) preserved in two recensions, and several exegetical writings, among which is the earliest Western typological exegesis of the Song of Songs. His exegesis is allegorical throughout and shows familiarity with Jewish explanations of the Old Testament. Feast 24 April.

Gregory of Golutvin, monk, fourteenth/fifteenth centuries. Russian Church. A disciple of **Sergius of Radonez** who became the first hegumenos of the monastery of the Epiphany at Golutvin, which Sergius had brought into being.

Gregory of Langres, died Langres, 359. Father of **Tetricus**, great-grandfather of **Gregory of Tours**, he governed Autun, Burgundy, for 40 years. Being widowed, he was ordained and elected bishop of Langres. **Benignus of Dijon** apparently ordered him in a dream to restore his shrine and cult. Feast 4 January.

Gregory of Nazianzen, bishop, born c. 330 of a Christian family (his father **Gregory the Elder** was also bishop of Nazianzen), he died in 390. He was a close friend of **Basil of Caesarea** and **Gregory of Nyssa** (together the 'Three Cappadocians') and received a brilliant literary education in Caesarea, Alexandria and Athens. He was baptized in 358 and turned to the monastic life. Around Christmas 361 his father ordained him a priest. Because of his own ecclesiastical policy, Basil wanted him to become bishop of Sasima, a very small place in the middle of nowhere. Gregory refused this appointment and remained in Nazianzen. Later he went to Constantinople, where he became the leader of the small orthodox Neo-Nicene community in a largely Arian city. There he also preached his Five Theological Orations that gained him his surname 'the theologian'. He presided over the Council of Constantinople in 381. Soon after he went back to Nazianzen and, in 383, retreated to his estate where he died. Gregory was a fierce defender of the Nicene orthodoxy and of the divinity and consubstantiality of the Spirit. He strongly influenced later theological developments. Feast 2 January.

Gregory of Nicomedia, bl., born Nicomedia, thirteenth century. Byzantine Church. A son of devout parents, he entered a monastery, but was accused of stealing sacred vessels and had to flee to another monastery. He became an anchorite, and had a reputation as a worker of miracles. Feast 2 April.

Gregory of Novgorod, bishop, died Novgorod, 24 May 1195. Russian Church. His brother was bishop of Novgorod, and designated Gabriel (Gregory's name before his monastic profession) as his successor. Gregory became bishop in 1187.

Gregory of Nyssa, bishop and theologian, brother of **Macrina the Younger** and **Basil of Caesarea**, one of the greatest speculative theologians of the early Church and instrumental in the development of what was to become the 'orthodox' doctrine of the Trinity. Born into a wealthy Cappadocian family between 335 and 340, he died after 394. He was probably married to a Theosebeia and became bishop of Nyssa in 372, on the instigation of Basil. As a consequence of ecclesiastical politics, he was accused in 374 (?) of maladministration and removed from his see. In 378 he was able to return and after Basil's death took over his leadership of the Neo-Nicene party. At the Council of Constantinople (381) he played a prominent role and delivered the funeral oration for the local bishop Meletius. Another testimony to his rise were the funerary orations of the emperor's wife and daughter he was asked to deliver. Among his writings, the most influential is undoubtedly his *Life of Moses*, an allegorical reading of Exodus describing the journey of the soul towards God. There are many exegetical commentaries (on Ecclesiastes, the Song of Songs and the Beatitudes), a biography of Macrina, an encomium on Basil and many theological treatises, such as the *Contra Eunomium*. Feast 9 March.

Gregory of Ostia, bishop and papal legate, died Logroño, Navarre, Spain, 9 May 1044. Gregory was a Benedictine monk in Rome and abbot of the monastery of Ss Cosmas and Damian from 998 to 1004. Known for his piety and learning and favoured of Pope Benedict IX, he was elected bishop of Ostia 1033/4 and made librarian or chancellor in the Roman Church as well. He was sent by the pope as his legate to Navarre in 1039, where he reportedly freed the kingdom from locusts by making the sign of the cross. In 1754, his veneration was officially approved for Navarre. Feast 9 May.

Gregory of Pel'sma, monk, born Galic, died Pel'sma, 30 September 1441 or 1442. Russian Church. The son of an aristocratic family called Lopotov, he showed great devotion as a child and resisted the attempts of his parents to form a suitable marriage. Instead he became a monk at a monastery near his birthplace, and was ordained priest there. Because of his aristocratic connections he became spiritual adviser to the local prince, and then to the grand prince. He was disturbed by this fame, however, and left for a monastery in Rostov, where he became superior. Again his reputation grew, so he moved again, this time to an isolated hermitage beside the river Pel'sma. His hermitage in time became a new monastery as he attracted disiples. He had an especial love for the poor, and he defended them against the cruelty of princes, even on one occasion going to Moscow to remonstrate.

Gregory of Sinai, hesychast monk and writer, born near Clazomenae, 1275, died Paroria, probably 27 November 1346. Captured by the Turks in his youth, on his release he fled to Cyprus, where he became a monk. He spent some time on Mount Sinai, before moving to Mount Athos via Jerusalem and Crete. In Crete he studied with Arsenios and learned the pioneering meditative Jesus prayer ('Lord Jesus Christ, Son of God, have mercy on me', repeated over and over again), which he introduced to Athos. Turkish raids led him to flee to Paroria in Thrace, where in *c.* 1325 he established a monastery on Mount Katakekryomene, which attracted Greek and Slavic devotees and earned aid from the Bulgarian Tsar, Ivan Alexander. His main writing was the *Most Beautiful Chapters*, a series of 137 short essays on

the contemplative life; he also wrote on hesychastic prayer and on the transfiguration. One of his disciples, the future patriarch Kallistos I, composed his biography. Feast 6 April.

Gregory of Stronghili, bl., born Mistra, died island of Stronghili, thirteenth century. Byzantine Church. Against the wishes of his parents, at the age of 16 he became a monk. After some years he joined a group of monks making their way to the Holy Land, but after a series of misadventures he found himself in Rome. He later went back to the Middle East, settling eventually in Oreos in the Euboea. There he lived in an abandoned church and preached to the people. As his fame grew, he withdrew from the city to the island of Stronghili in the Gulf of Euboea. People still came to visit him, and he gathered around him a small group of disciples to follow his austere way of life.

Gregory of Suzdal, bishop, fifteenth century. Russian Church. Nothing is known of him.

Gregory of Tatew, monk, born Vayoc Jor, eastern Armenia, died Tatew, 25 December 1410. He was the spiritual heir of **John of Orotn**, whose work of teaching and fostering Armenian culture he continued. Like John, he was deeply opposed to those who were working for a reunion of the Armenian Church with the Church of Rome. He left many writings, including studies of ancient philosophers, as well as works on the Scriptures. Feast 27 April.

Gregory of the Kievan Cave Monastery, monk, fourteenth century. Russian Church. A man of great asceticism with a gift for wonder-working, he enjoyed a popular cult after his death. Feast 28 August.

Gregory of Tours, bishop, historian, born Clermont-Ferrand, probably November 538, died Tours, 17 November 594. Of an eminent Gallo-Roman family, he became bishop of Tours in 573. An opponent of King Chilperic, he won royal favour for his support for King Guntram's campaign against the aristocracy. Around 576 he began his monumental *History of the Franks*, a well-informed, if somewhat disorganized and ambitious, work which became an indispensable resource for early French history. He also produced a series of eight works on miracles, which reflect a decidedly credulous attitude, and other writings on the Fathers, the Psalms, and the Church offices.

Gregory of Utrecht, associate of St **Boniface**, born Trier, 707, died Utrecht, 25 August 776. From a leading Merovingian family, he was so impressed by an exposition of St Boniface at the convent of Pfalzel, where his grandmother was abbess, that he became a devoted disciple of the saint, who in 754 appointed him abbot of St Martin's, Utrecht. It became a great missionary and scholarly centre. On the martyrdom of St **Eoban** in 755, he assumed the administration of the see of Utrecht, although he was never formally consecrated bishop in the ensuing 20-year period.

Gregory of Verucchio, bl., born perhaps 1225, died Rieti, near Rome, 1343, cult confirmed 1769. He joined the Hermits of St Augustine aged 15, but was unjustly expelled after ten years. The Franciscans of Monte Carnerio, near Rieti, welcomed him when he was destitute and he lived apparently until the age of 118. Feast 4 May.

Gregory of Xlat, martyr, born Xlat, on lake Van, 1350, died May 1426. Armenian Church. He was brought up in the monastery of Cipnavank, although during the invasion of Tamburlaine he took refuge in the monastery of Suxaravank. After his return he wrote an account of the invasion, along with other works. He also revised the synaxarion of his Church. He died when a Turkoman band attacked the monastery.

Gregory Pahlwuni III, catholicos, born province of Tluk, c. 1093, died c. 1165. Armenian Church. He entered the monastery at Kesun and was educated there and by **Gregory the Lover of Martyrs**. He was ordained bishop at a very young age, which led to a centuries-long schism in the Armenian Church, and eventually became catholicos. He was much concerned with relations between the Churches of the Middle East, but also with Rome – the pope sent him the pallium. He wrote hymns, and composed lives of the saints.

Gregory Palamas, Greek Orthodox mystic, born Constantinople, 1296 or 1297, of a noble family with connections to the imperial court, died Thessalonika, 14 November 1359. After studies at the university in Constantinople he entered a monastery on Mount Athos at the age of 22. In 1325, however, he and several companions fled to Thessalonika to escape Turkish raids. He was ordained priest there, but established a hermitage near Beroea and lived there largely in silence until 1331, when he returned to Athos, but continued to live his eremitical life. He was attacked by the monk Barlaam from Calabria for his 'hesychastic' (silence or rest) spirituality. His defence of hesychasm was expressed in nine books, written between 1338 and 1341. In 1345 he became archbishop of Thessalonika, and ten years later, in 1354/55, he was held for ransom by the Turks. He was canonized in 1368, and he is celebrated on both 14 November and the second Sunday of the Great Lent, the latter commemorating his victory over Barlaam. Feast 14 November.

Gregory Parumula, bishop, born Mulamthuruthy, Kerala, 15 June 1848, died Kerala, 2 November 1902. Syro-Malankar Church. His family name was Geevarghese. He was ordained in 1866 and served as bishop's secretary, although eventually settling in the monastery of Vettical Dayara. In 1876 he became a bishop, with charge of three dioceses. He lived a very ascetical life, and had a great influence on all who came to know him.

Gregory Peradze, martyr, born Sakascethi, Georgia, 1899, died Auschwitz, Poland, 1944. Georgian Church. He entered the seminary in Tbilisi in 1918, then went on to study philosphy both there and in Bonn. After the annexation of Georgia by Soviet Russia, he was unable to return home and went on to do research in several countries of Europe, becoming professor of patrology in the Orthodox faculty of theology at the University of Warsaw. After the German occupation of Poland he was arrested and sent to Auschwitz, where he voluntarily entered a gas chamber in place of a Jewish father of a large family.

Gregory the Elder, bishop, born Arianzos, c. 276, died there, 374. For the first part of his life he was a civil servant and a pagan, and was converted to

Christianity in 325 by **Nonna**, his wife. They had three children, **Gregory (of Nazianzen)**, **Caesarius** and **Gorgonia**. He became bishop of Nazianzus, but then became a heretic until converted back to orthodox belief by his son Gregory. Gregory (the younger) became assistant bishop to his father in 372. Feast 1 January.

Gregory the Farmer, martyr, born Goskaja Volost, died Olonec, seventeenth century. Church of the Old Believers. Was arrested for his adherence to the old rites, then released, but later rearrested and tortured to make him abjure. Feast 10 March.

Gregory the Icon Painter, monk, died Kievan Cave monastery, twelfth century. Feast 8 August.

Gregory the Illuminator (or The Enlightener), born Armenia, died Mount Manyea, Armenia, c. 326. He was possibly of royal descent, and was brought up in Cappadocia. He returned as an apostle to Armenia and, despite opposition, converted King Tiridiates in 314. Although married, he became a bishop, setting up a diocese at Ashtishat (modern Etchmiadzin), and is the patron saint of Armenia. He eventually retired to a hermitage on Mount Manyea. Feast 30 September.

Gregory the Lover of Martyrs, monk, born 1025, died 1105. Armenian Church. He came from the noble Pahlawuni family, and was governor of Taron, of Mesopotamia and surrounding regions from 1059, in succession to his father, but eventually abandoned these duties, and his wife, for the monastic life. He was widely read in Greek and Syriac as well as his own language. In 1065 he was elected catholicos of the Armenian Church, changing his name to Gregory of Vahram. He held the office for only a few years, giving it up to research the lives of the saints, going from monastery to monastery in search of information – hence his name. Feast 8 August.

Gregory the Wise, archbishop, died Rostov, 3 May 1416. Russian Church. From being hegumenos of a monastery on lake Kubenskoe, he was elected archbishop of Rostov in 1396. In that office he fostered the growth of monastic life, especially of a strict, coenobitic kind, in his diocese, and built churches, including a new cathedral at Rostov to replace one which had burned down. He was a patron of **Andrew Rublev**. He was also deeply involved in the politics of the period, attempting to bring peace among the warring princes.

Gregory the Wonderworker, bishop, born of a pagan family in Neocaesarea (Pontus, today part of Turkey), c. 213, died c. 270–75. After his conversion to Christianity at 14, he studied rhetoric and law. In Palestinian Caesarea he met Origen and studied philosophy and exegesis for five years with him, while also receiving a training in spirituality. When leaving Caesarea, Gregory delivered a long farewell speech thanking his master. Back home he became bishop of Neocaesarea, where he performed many miracles. We also have a (probably genuine) trinitarian creed from his hand, showing the influence of Origen. Feast 17 November.

Gregory Tlay IV, catholicos, born c. 1133, died 1193. Armenian Church. He succeeded his uncle as catholicos in 1173. He opened negotiations for reunion with the see of Constantinople, but this came to nothing. He then re-established relations with Rome, and the pope sent him the pallium and other insignia.

Grimbald, scholar, born Thèronanne, Flanders, perhaps c. 825, died Winchester, England, 8 July 901. He became a monk of the abbey of Saint-Bertin, rising to become its prior. He was invited to England by King **Alfred** c. 887. According to legend, he declined the offer of the archbishopric of Canterbury on the death of Ethelred. He was appointed prior of the planned New Minster at Winchester, but died before its completion. None of his writings survive, but he exercised an important role in bringing manuscripts to England and in promoting scholarly activity. He was commemorated by the community of the New Minster. The fourteenth-century *Breviary of Hyde Abbey* is influenced by a lost medieval Life.

Guala of Bergamo, bl., Dominican bishop, born Bergamo, Lombardy, c. 1180, died Astino, 3 September 1244. When **Dominic** preached at Bergamo in 1217, Gual (Walter) Roni (Romanoni) received from him the habit of the Order of Preachers. In 1221 he became prior of the Dominican convent at

Brescia. At this time he had a vision of the glory of St Dominic, whose death, unknown to Guala, had just occurred. He established the convent at Bergamo (1222) and was associated with the founding of the nuns' convent of St Agnes at Bologna (1225), and soon after became prior of St Nicolas there. Both Honorius III and Gregory IX recognized his prudence and diplomatic skill by sending him to handle difficult missions. In 1229–30 he was elected as the bishop of Brescia, where he continued his diplomatic activities. Exiled from his see in 1239, Guala spent his last years in penitential retirement with the Benedictines at Astino.

Guarinus of Palestrina, cardinal bishop, born Bologna, Italy, c. 1080, died Palestrina, Italy, 6 February 1159. Around 1104, Guarinus, who was already a priest, joined the Augustinian order in Mortara, Italy. Twenty-five years later, upon the death of the bishop of Pavia, he was elected bishop by popular acclaim, no doubt due to his reputation for virtue, love for the poor and exemplary monastic life. He refused the honour and was imprisoned. He escaped, only to be forced by Pope Lucius II to accept a cardinal's hat and the see of Palestrina, a suburb of Rome. Pope Alexander III canonized him immediately after his death.

Guarinus (Guérin) of Sion, Benedictine and Cistercian abbot, bishop of Sion (Switzerland), born Pont-à-Mousson, Lorriane, c. 1065, died Aulps, Savoy, 27 August 1150. Guarinus entered the monastery of Molesme around 1085; in 1094, he and several others left that monastery in order to lead a more retired life at Aulps, of which he became the second abbot in 1110. After a visit from **Bernard of Clairvaux**, Guarinus arranged for Aulps to become part of the Order of Citeaux in 1136; two years later, he became bishop of Sion. He died whilst visiting Aulps and was buried there.

Guba, monk, fifth/sixth century. Ethiopian Church. An early missionary in Ethiopia. Feast 5 June.

Gudenitius of Brescia, bishop, born Brescia, died there, c. 410. He was elected bishop c. 390, and was consecrated by St **Ambrose** despite his own

unwillingness – he had left on a pilgrimage to Jerusalem in an attempt to avoid this happening. In 406 he was sent by the pope on an unsuccessful visit to Constantinople to defend **John Chrysostom**. He produced a number of homilies which survive, and built a church in Brescia. Feast 25 October.

Gudula, virgin, and patroness of Brussels, born Brabant, died c. 712. Apparently born into a noble family of Brabant, she was educated at the abbey of Nivelles and devoted her life to prayer and works of charity, living at Ham, near Alast. After her death, her remains were moved to Brussels, being placed in the church of St Michael in 1047, where her cult developed soon afterwards. She is typically depicted with a lantern, according to the legend that when a demon blew out her taper it was miraculously rekindled. Feast 8 January.

Gudwal (also Gurval or Goal), missionary and saint, died c. 640. Very little is known of his life. Probably Welsh or a Briton (perhaps from Cornwall), he was an early missionary to Brittany. He established the monastery of Plec near Locoal and several others elsewhere, and perhaps became a regional bishop. The chapel of St Stephen at Guer was probably his hermitage. His relics were moved to Picardy, then to Ghent. He now tends to be equated with Gurval, the successor of St Malo at Aleth, possibly a variant of **Tudwal**. Feast 6 June.

Guerric of Igny, bl., Cistercian abbot and theologian, born Tournai, c. 1070–80, died Igny, France, 19 August 1157. Before becoming a Cistercian monk at Clairvaux c. 1125, he was a cathedral canon and *magister scholarum* at Tournai. Elected abbot of Igny in 1138, he is best known for his sermons.

Guethenoc (or Guithern), see **Jacut**.

Guibertus (Wibert), hermit, died Gorzes, Lorraine, 962. A nobleman, he was first a soldier before retiring as a hermit on his own estates at Gembloux in Brabant. He later made Gembloux into a monastery before joining the Benedictine abbey of Gorzes. Feast 23 March.

Guido Marramaldi, bl., Dominican preacher and inquisitor, born Naples, Italy, mid-fourteenth century, died Naples, c. 1391. He was born to a noble Neopolitan family. Guido entered the Dominican order and studied philosophy and theology there. He gained a reputation as a public orator. Owing to his successful preaching, the inhabitants of Raguza erected a Dominican convent. He later became an inquisitor. He was buried in the chapel of the Rosary in San Domenico. His burial place quite soon became the centre of a cult and he received the name of Blessed Guido, but his cult has never received official approbation.

Guido of Anderlecht (known in Flemish as St Wye), died Anderlecht, 12 September 1012. Apparently the son of Brabant parents, he became a sexton in the church of Our Lady in Laeken near Brussels. After a period as a merchant, he sought to atone by undertaking a seven-year pilgrimage to Rome and Jerusalem. Thereafter he spent the brief remainder of his life in Anderlecht. Miracles attested near his tomb awakened veneration of him. Our only information comes from a dubiously reliable twelfth-century Life.

Guido of Cortona, bl., Franciscan priest, born Cortona, c. 1187, died Cortona, 12 June 1247. As a wealthy young man, he showed such impressive hospitality to St **Francis of Assisi** that he was invited to join the new Franciscan order. He founded the hermitage of Le Celle near Cortona, and lived as an ascetical priest. He was renowned for a number of miracles. His cult was approved in 1583. Feast 16 June.

Guido of Gherardesca, bl., a hermit in Campo, Italy, died 1099. Feast 20 May.

Guido of Pomposa, abbot, born Casamari, near Ravenna, c. 1010, died Borgo San Domnino, near Parma, 31 March 1046. After living for a period as a hermit, he went to the abbey of Pomposa, where he soon became abbot, and turned it into one of the chief monasteries of northern Italy. **Peter Damian** was invited to lecture there c. 1039–41. Invited to accompany Henry III to the Synod of Sutri in 1046, he took sick and died en route.

Temporarily buried at Parma, in 1047 his remains were taken to Speyer in Germany.

Guido the Lombard, bl., born probably Milan, late eleventh century, died c. 1150. Two conflicting accounts exist of his life. He is associated with the establishment of the Humiliati, a guild of men and women who worked in the wool trade in Lombard cities and dedicated themselves to the evangelical life. Some legends picture him receiving the order's Rule from **Bernard of Clairvaux**. The male branch of the order was suppressed in 1571; a few female communities persist in Italy. Guido is revered by them and by the church of Milan. Feast 6 December.

Guimera, died c. 931. He was bishop of Carcassonne. Feast 13 February.

Gulwal, before eleventh century. Said to have been female, but otherwise nothing is known. Quite possibly a variant of **Gudwal**.

Gumbert (Gundebert, Gondelbert), died c. 675. A monk, he was a Frankish bishop of Sens who retired to the Vosges, where he founded the abbey of Senones c. 660. Feast 21 February.

Gumbert of Ansbach, abbot and bishop, died perhaps c. 790. Details of his life are obscure; later legend describes him as a great lord who renounced the world and bestowed his wealth on the Church. Before 748, on family lands at Ansbach, he founded St Mary's abbey; in 786, on the guarantees of immunity and free election of abbots, he handed it over to **Charlemagne**, who gave it to Bernwelf of Würzburg c. 800. Known as St Gumbert abbey by the early tenth century, it moved to St Stefan in Würzburg. The community was suppressed in 1563. Gumbert's cult is still active in Vilchband. Feast 15 July.

Gumesindus, priest, martyred Córdoba, 852. He was killed with **Servusdei**, a monk, under Abderrahman II – see **Martyrs of Córdoba**. Feast 13 January.

Gummar, hermit, born Embleheim, died Nivesdonck, c. 775. From a distinguished Brabant household, he became a courtier of Pepin III. On the king's recommendation, he married Guini-maria; the marriage was not a success, and after eight years he obtained a separation from her. Thereafter he lived as a recluse, and along with St Rumold founded the abbey of Lierre in Flanders, whose patron saint he became. He was one of the most celebrated miracle workers of the Low Countries. Feast 11 October.

Gundecar, bl., bishop, born probably near Eich-stätt, Germany, 10 August 1019, died Eichstätt, Germany, 2 August 1075. Educated at the Eichstätt cathedral school, Gundecar was a canon there and then chaplain to Empress Agnes (*c.* 1045) before Holy Roman Emperor Henry IV named him bishop of Eichstätt in 1057. He was completely devoted to his diocese, building a cathedral, dedicating more than 100 churches and preparing the so-called *Gundecarianum*, a ritual and liturgical manual used in the education of his priests. His cult spread due to reported miracles at his grave and translation of his relics in 1309.

Gundisalvus of Braga, bl., born Vizella, Braga, Portugal, 1187, died Portugal, 1259. After ordination he was a hermit at Amaranthe before becoming a Dominican. Feast 10 January.

Gundleus (or Gwynllyw), born and died Wales, sixth century. He is commemorated with his wife Gwladys, whom he is supposed to have abducted. Cadoc, their eldest child, converted them to Christianity and persuaded them to live an austere life and then to separate and live in solitude until their deaths. Feast 29 March.

Günther of Niederaltaich, monk, born probably 955, died Hartmanice, Bohemia, 9 October 1045. Of a noble Thuringian family, Günther led a rather dissolute youth until the spiritual direction of Godard of Hildesheim helped him reform his life. He became a Benedictine in Rome and later moved to Niederaltaich, Germany. He turned down the offer to become an abbot in order to found a hermitage in the Bavarian forest. His hermitage helped open the trade route between Bohemia and Passau and was the goal of many pilgrims. He was the spiritual adviser to emperors, founder of monasteries and political mediator. He is also the patron of the abbey of Brevnov (Czech Republic),

where his tomb was located until its destruction in 1420.

Gunthildis, it is possible that three saints bore the same name:
(1) an Anglo-Saxon nun from Wimborne, England, who became an abbess in Thuringia;
(2) an abbess, whom Gundecar II, bishop of Eichstätt lists in his Pontifical. He transferred her remains from Suffersheim to his cathedral, where she was honoured among the 12 founders of Eichstätt;
(3) a maidservant, venerated at the abbey of Plankstetten in the diocese of Eichstätt, although buried at Suffersheim. If one could prove, as Bauerreiss hints, that the servant girl story was a fiction, both the abbess and servant girl might prove to be one and the same, who in turn might prove to be a follower of **Lioba**.

Gunthramus (Gontram), king, died Chalons, 592. He was a king in Burgundy who divorced his wife and executed his physician and then spent the rest of his life repenting his sins. He was proclaimed a saint on his death. Feast 28 March.

Gurias and Samonas, martyrs, born Edessa, died there, *c.* 303. Executed during the persecution of Diocletian for refusing to sacrifice to idols. Feast 15 November.

Gurius of Kazan, bishop, born Radonez, died Kazan, 2 December 1563. Russian Church. His family name was Gregory Grigoroevic Rugotin. Although noble, his family was not wealthy, and he entered the service of Prince Ivan Penkov, whom he served faithfully, but was accused by others of having had an afair with the prince's wife. He was imprisoned for two years, but then was miraculously released, and joined the monastery founded by **Joseph of Volokolamsk**. About the year 1542 he became hegumenos, an office he resigned after nine years. He was then asked by the Tsar to become hegumenos of the monastery at Selizarovo, although after only a short time in that office he was elected as the first bishop of Kazan, a diocese created in newly captured territory. He arrived there in July 1555. His first major activity was converting the inhabitants of the region to Orthodoxy, in which he had some success. He also established a monastery to carry on the work of evangelization and education. Feast 5 December.

Gurius of Saloski, monk, seventeenth century. Russian Church. Hegumenos of the monastery of the Nativity, near Novgorod.

Gurius of Solovki, see **John of Solovki I**.

Gurloes, founder, died Quimperlé, Brittany, 1057. Originally a monk of Redon, near St Lazaire, he became the first abbot of the monastery of Ste Croix at Quimperlé. Feast 25 August.

Guthlac, hermit, born England, *c.* 674, died 11 April 714. Related to the royal house of Mercia, he became a monk at Repton, then in *c.* 699 moved to an island in the Fens near the site of the subsequent Crowland abbey, which was founded in his honour by King Ethelbald in 716. He lived a life of extreme asceticism. His life is depicted on the late twelfth-century Guthlac Roll, now in the British Library, Oxford. His cult was particularly strong in the English Midlands in the Middle Ages.

Guy (Guido) of Pomposa, abbot, born near Ravenna, died near Parma, 1046. He first lived on a small island on the river Po, under the guidance of Martin, a hermit. Martin sent him to a monastery, and he eventually became abbot of Pomposa, near Ferrara. Feast 31 March.

Gwladys, see **Gundleus**.

H

Habakuk and Paisio, monks and martyrs, died Belgrade, 17 December 1814. Serbian Church. Put to death by Turks.

Habakuk, monk (?) and martyr, died Thessalonika, 6 August 1628. Byzantine Church.

Habib, Syriac Church. Recorded as the son of Gamaliel, otherwise nothing is known of him. Feast 2 August.

Habib, deacon, born Egypt, sixth century. Syriac Church. A disciple of **James of Sarug**. Feast 4 July.

Habib of Scete, monk, fourth century. Syriac Church. One of the disciples of **Awgen**. Feast 20 September.

Habta Maryam, monk, died Dabra Libanos, 22 November 1497. Ethiopian Church. According to his biographer, his life had been foretold to his mother. When he grew up, his parents wanted him to marry, but instead he became a monk, wandering from monastery to monastery, working miracles and, on one occasion, liberating souls from Sheol, as had been prophesied to his mother.

Habta Maryam, monk, born Tacazze, Tigre. Ethiopian Church.

Hadalinus, born Aquitaine, died Celles, c. 690. Along with his teacher, St **Remaclus**, he spent a time as a recluse in the wilderness of Cougnon, and later lived in Remaclus's abbey at Stavenot. He founded the monastery of Celles, near Dinant-sur-Meuse, whose eleventh-century Romanesque church survives. In 1338 the monastery moved to Visé, where Hadalinus was patron; it was suppressed in 1797. He is invoked against children's ailments. Feast 3 February.

Hadeloga, died Kitzingen, Upper Bavaria, c. 750. According to a twelfth-century Life, she was the daughter of Charles Martel. To escape an arranged marriage, she fled and established a double monastery at Kitzingen, Franconia, allegedly under inspiration from St **Boniface**, c. 745. She was subsequently reconciled with her father, who bestowed generous endowments on the monastery. She was esteemed for her care for the poor. The monastery was secularized in 1544. Feast 2 February.

Hadewych (Hadewig, Hedwig), bl., born c. 1150, died 14 April c. 1200. She was the daughter of **Hildegunde of Meer**. Together they founded the convent of Meer in 1165. This was a Premonstratensian convent near Brüderich in Prussia. She became prioress after her mother in 1183. She, her mother and brother, the prior of the monastery at Kappenberg, are all counted among the 'blessed'.

Hadid, born Singar, Nile Delta, died Matjubus al-Rumman, 27 February 1387. Coptic Church. He was first a fisherman, helping his father. He was accustomed to give away his earnings, and this gave him a reputation for sanctity. He left his village for another where he was not known, and worked as a peasant. He thought, however, that he would become a monk. He set out for a monastery, but a vision of the Virgin instead encouraged him to stay in the village of Matjubus al-Rumman, where he built a church and was ordained as its priest.

Hadoindus, bishop, died 20 August *c.* 653. Evidently of a noble family, he became bishop of Le Mans *c.* 623. He established the abbey at Evron, aided in the founding of the monastery of St Lonegisilus, and attended the councils of Clichy, *c.* 627, and Rheims, 627–30. He inherited wealth from a rich patron named Alan and bequeathed it to the church of Le Mans in 643. Buried in the church of Saint-Victor, his cult was already evident by the ninth century, when his relics were exhumed and placed in the cathedral church of Le Mans. Feast 20 January.

Hadra of Aswan, bishop, fourth/fifth century. Coptic Church. Aged 18, he married a relative, but the evening after the marriage he pleaded ill-health and the following morning entered a monastery, despite the entreaties of his family. He lived in the monastery for eight years, but then became a hermit. His reputation for sanctity and as a miracle worker grew, and he was chosen by the people to succeed to the bishopric of Aswan.

Hadra of Benhadab, monk. Coptic Church. Said to be the first to establish a hermitage on Mount Banhadab. He was also a miracle worker.

Hadulph, bishop, died *c.* 728. He was at the same time abbot of Saint-Vaast and bishop of Arras-Cambrai, both now in northern France. Feast 19 May.

Haggai, see **Hermes**.

Hainmar of Auxerre, bishop and martyr. Little is known of his life, but he served as bishop of Auxerre *c.* 717–31, apparently without ever being formally consecrated. Perhaps more active as a military commander than as a churchman, he led two of Charles Martel's expeditions against Aquitaine. He subsequently quarrelled with the king and was imprisoned in Bastogne, Luxembourg; he escaped, but was captured near Toul and executed. Feast 28 October.

Hallvard Vebjörnsson, patron saint of Oslo, died near Drammen, Norway, 1043. The only information about Hallvard's life comes from legends. According to these, he was a relative of Olaf II and died while defending a lady who had been wrongly accused of stealing. His cult is mainly confined to Norway, Iceland and parts of Sweden, and he is usually pictured in Swedish and Norwegian iconography with a millstone. Feast 14 May.

Hamai of Kahyor, monk and martyr, fourth/fifth century, died Alexandria. Coptic Church.

Hananya of Daayr al-Zafaran, bishop, died 826. Syriac Church. He founded a monastery towards the end of the eighth century before becoming bishop. Feast 21 November.

Hannibal Mary de Francia, bl., founder, born Messina, Sicily, 5 July 1851, died there, 1 June 1927. He was ordained in 1878 and went to work in one of the poorest parts of the city. He founded orphanages and two religious orders: the Daughters of Holy Zeal and, just two months later, the Rogationist Fathers. He also started movements to pray for vocations to the priesthood.

Harbay, king, twelfth century. Ethiopian Church. It is unclear for how long, or exactly when, he was king in Ethiopia, but he was deposed by his brother **Lalibala**, whom he had earlier tried to poison.

Harmina, monk, born al-Bahnasa, died Qaw. Coptic Church. Originally a shepherd, his Life recounts that he was conducted to a monastery by the apostles John and Peter, and that, after a time, he left the monastery accompanied once more by John, visiting various places and eventually settling at Qaw, where he lived in a cave and ate only dates from a heavenly palm and drank only heavenly water. Angels brought him communion.

Hartmann of Brixen, bl., abbot and bishop, born Polling, Germany, *c.* 1090, died Brixen, Italy, 23 December 1164. Hartmann became an Augustinian at Sankt Nikola in Passau, Germany, and in 1122 was moved to Salzburg to take charge of the new Augustinian chapter there. From there he was called to lead communities in Herren Chiemsee

(1128) and Klosterneuburg (1133). He was made bishop of Brixen in 1140/41 and soon founded an Augustinian priory near there in Neustift. His saintly life allowed him to rise above politics, earning him the respect of both Pope Alexander III and Frederick I Barbarossa. His veneration has been allowed in Brixen since 1784. Feast 23 December.

Hartwich of Salzburg, bl., archbishop, born *c*. 955, died Salzburg (Austria), 5 December 1023. Hartwich was the last scion of the noble Aribo-Sponheim family and served as archbishop of Salzburg from 991 until his death. His noted charity earned him grants and privileges from Holy Roman Emperors Otto II and Henry II. He is most known for his renovation of the Salzburg cathedral school and the many monasteries around the city. His veneration dates back to the 1200s. Feast 14 June.

Harwag, martyr. Coptic Church. Feast 12 December.

Hasina, martyr. Coptic Church. Feast 4 October.

Hathumarus, bishop of Paderborn. Feast 9 August.

Hedda, bishop, died 9 July 705. A monk and abbot, probably of Whitby, in 676 he was made bishop of the divided Wessex diocese, first at Dorchester, then at Winchester. He served as an adviser to King Ine on the drawing up of the king's legal code. He was a chief benefactor of Malmesbury. Many miracles were attested at his tomb. Feast 7 July.

Hedwig, born Andechs, *c*. 1174, died Trebnitz, 12 or 15 October 1243. She was of noble birth, monastery educated and said to have married Henry I of Silesia at the age of 12. The marriage brought relations with Silesia closer and Hedwig was prominent in affairs of state. She had a reputation for fortitude and piety, enabling the foundation of new monasteries and support of existing ones. She encouraged her husband to found the first house of religious women in Silesia. Piety, gentleness and austerity gave her the reputation of

a saint while still alive. She is the patron saint of Silesia. Feast 16 October.

Hedwig of Poland, born 1374, died 17 July 1399. She was the daughter of Louis Angevin, king of Hungary and Poland. When she was a year old she was betrothed to Wilhelm, of the house of Habsburg, heir to the grand duchy of Austria. After her father died, she was crowned queen of Poland in 1384. Her advisers decided that for political reasons she should marry Jagiello, the grand duke of Lithuania and Ruthenia. He was not a Christian, but promised to be baptized if they were married. Hedwig accepted the decision of her advisers, Jagiello was baptized and they were married in February 1386. This angered the Habsburgs, who spread rumours claiming that Hedwig was a bigamist, that she and Wilhelm had consummated their marriage and that Wilhelm had been crowned king. However, the Church approved of the marriage to Jagiello, and Pope Boniface IX agreed to be godfather to their child. Jagiello took on the task of Christianizing Lithuania, and Hedwig worked to unite Latin and Orthodox Christians in her lands. She gave birth to a daughter, prematurely, in 1399, but the child died after only three weeks, and Hedwig herself died four days later.

Hegesippus, born Palestine (?), died Jerusalem (?), a Greek-speaking Jewish Christian. In the years 160–80 he was in Rome, where he finished his composition of five books of *Hypomnemata* (memories). This work, used and quoted by Eusebius of Caesarea, intended to narrate, without error, the tradition of the apostolic preaching. It is a fierce polemic against Gnosticism. Feast 7 April.

Heimerad, wandering priest and hermit, born Messkirch, Baden, of serf parents, died Mount Hasungen, near Cassel, 28 June 1019. He was ordained, and served for a time in Baden, then as a chaplain to the lady of his parents' estate. After a pilgrimage to Rome and Jerusalem, he wandered Germany, settling for a while at Hersfeld abbey, then in an abandoned church given to him in Westphalia. An eccentric, he made himself very unpopular in a number of places, being publicly flogged at Paderborn; elsewhere he was revered as a saint. Ultimately he settled in a forest near Cassel, where he built a hermitage. A popular cult grew up around his tomb, where many miracles were attested; it has never been officially approved. Feast 28 June.

Helan of Cornwall, born Ireland, died Bisseuil. He spent some time in Cornwall with a group of other missionaries, before moving on to Brittany, then to Rheims, and finally to Bisseuil. Feast 7 October.

Heldrad, abbot, born Provence, died Novalese monastery, at the foot of the Italian Alps, *c.* 842. He used his inheritance on charitable projects, eventually giving everything away to look for a strict monastery. Abbot at Novalese for 30 years, he was always venerated locally. Feast 13 March.

Helen, empress, born Drepanum (Bythinia), *c.* 255, died *c.* 330. Of humble origins, she became the concubine of Constantinus Chlorus, who later rejected her. Their son, **Constantine** I, recalled her to court in 306 and made her Augusta. She performed works of charity and erected many church buildings. She made a pilgrimage to Jerusalem and believed she had found on Golgotha the true cross, a fragment of which she placed in Rome in the St Croce. Her cult, often associated with that of her son, quickly developed in East and West. Feast 8 August.

Helen Duglioli, see **Helen of Bologna**.

Helen of Arcella, bl., born Arcella, near Padua, *c.* 1208, died there, 4 November 1242. Elena Enselmini received the habit of a Poor Clare from **Francis of Assisi** himself when she was only 12 years old. She suffered from an illness throughout her life, and it was said that her only food was the sacrament. Feast 7 February.

Helen of Bologna, born Bologna, 1472, died there, 23 September 1520. Elena Duglioli wished to become a nun, but at her parents' urging married Benedetto dall'Oglio, who was more than 20 years older than she was. In fact the marriage, which lasted for 30 years, was a very happy one, and was known as such in the city. After her husband's death she gave herself entirely to good works. A

cult sprang up around her immediately after her death.

Helen of Moscow, nun, died 18 November 1547/8. Russian Church. Hegumena of the monastery founded in Moscow in 1525 to mark the reconquest of Smolensk. She had formerly been a nun in a monastery in Suzdal.

Helen of Sinope, martyr, born and died Sinope, eighteenth century. Byzantine Church. The beauty of Helena Bekiari attracted the attention of the local pasha, who raped her and imprisoned her in his house. She managed to escape, but the pasha threatened a massacre of Christians were she not returned to him. A community meeting was held, and it was agreed she had better return, but whenever the pasha came to collect her, he was held back by an invisible force. Finally he decreed that the girl should be beheaded and her body thrown into the sea. This was done, but a sailor found the sack containing both her head and her body. He took the body to Russia, but Helen's head was returned to Sinope. Feast 1 November.

Helen of Skovde (Sköfde), martyr, twelfth century. Information about her life comes from the twelfth-century St Brynolph, bishop of Skana in Sweden. Of noble birth, she remained a widow following the death of her husband and spent the rest of her life in charitable and pious works. She built the church at Skovde. She was falsely accused by her daughter's relatives of instigating the murder of her son-in-law by his own servants. She went on pilgrimage to the Holy Land, but was killed by the same relatives on her return *c.* 1160. She is buried at Skovde and many cures of the sick and disabled were reported at her intercession. She was long venerated, and the subject of many pilgrimages. Feast 31 July.

Helen of Udine, bl., Augustinian tertiary, born Udine, *c.* 1396, died there, 23 April 1458. In deep grief after the death of her husband Antonio dei Cavalcanti, she entered the Augustinian Third Order at the age of 40. She lived a life of penance, prayer and good works. Miracles are credited to her in life and after death.

Helena, see **Helen**.

Helentrudis, hermit, died Neuenheerse, Westphalia, Germany, *c.* 950. Also known as Helmtrud or Hiltrud, Helentrudis is named by Bishop Imad of Paderborn in his martyrology of 1052. According to the *Passio of St Ursula* (*c.* 975), she reportedly had a vision of St Cordula, one of the virgins supposedly killed by the Huns in Cologne, in which Cordula described her martyrdom. The *Regnante Domino*, another source of legends about St Ursula, describes pilgrimages to her grave and miracles that occurred there. Feast 31 May.

Heliconides (Heliconis), martyr, born Thessalonika, died Corinth, *c.* 250. This woman was beheaded during the persecution of Decius. Feast 28 May.

Helier, martyr, born Tongres, Belgium, died Jersey (Channel Islands), sixth century. He stayed in the monastery at Nanteuil in Normandy, where St **Marculf** was abbot, and later moved to Jersey to achieve a more solitary life. He lived in a cave and worked to convert the local people, until he was murdered by robbers or pirates to whom he had preached. Feast 16 July.

Heliodorus of Attino, bishop, born Dalmatia, 332, died Attino, Italy, 390. He became friends with St **Jerome** in Aquileia and went with him to Palestine. However, he declined to follow Jerome in becoming a hermit. He returned to Italy and was made bishop of Attino. He later gave financial assistance to Jerome for his translation of the Vulgate Bible. Feast 3 July.

Heliphotus of Achera, born Germany (?), died Cyprus. Church of Cyprus. He was the leader of five saints who had originally travelled to the Holy Land with 300 Germans (possibly crusaders), had then visited the Holy Places, but had, on their return, been blown on to the island of Cyprus, where they remained. One of them took up the role of shepherd.

Helladius, see also **Theophilus**.

Helladius, bishop, died Auxerre, France, 387. He was bishop of Auxerre for 30 years and converted his successor, **Amator**, to a life of holiness. Feast 8 May.

Helladius, died Toledo, Spain, 633. An official at the Visigothic court, he joined Agalai monastery, near the river Tagus, becoming abbot in 605 and bishop of Toledo from 615. His generosity to the poor was well known. His story is told by **Ildephonsus** of Toledo. Feast 18 February.

Hemiterius (Emeterius) and Cheledonius, martyrs, died Calahorra, Old Castille, *c.* 304. They are believed to have been soldiers. Feast 3 March.

Hemma (1), bl., Carolingian queen, born *c.* 808, died Regensburg, 31 January 876. She married Louis the German and had seven children. She became patroness and abbess of the Benedictine convent at Obermünster. Her tombstone is at Sankt Emmeram and she is reputed to be buried there, although the convent at Obermünster lays claim to her body.

Hemma (2), died Gurk, Austria (?), 1045. Brought up by **Cunegunde**, the wife of **Henry II**, she married William of Sangrau and they had two sons. Her husband died *c.* 1015, possibly while returning from a pilgrimage to Rome. One of her sons had died before her husband, but when the other son died she gave much of her money to the poor and founded monasteries, including one at Gurk, which held 20 monks and 70 nuns. It is possible that she herself entered this monastery, because she is buried in the church. Feast 29 June.

Hemming of Abo, bishop, born Balinge, near Uppsala, Sweden, 1290, died Abo, now in Finland, 22 May 1366. After studies in Uppsala and Paris, he became canon of Abo cathedral, then bishop there in 1338. He travelled with **Bridget of Sweden** on her mission to France in 1347.

Henry II, German king, Roman emperor, born Hildesheim (?), 6 May 972, died Grona, near Göttingen, 13 July 1024. Son of Henry, duke of Bavaria, he succeeded his cousin Otto III as king in 1002. He devoted his energies to consolidating

German power, spending much of his early reign in campaigns in the east and in Lombardy. In 1007 he established and generously endowed the see of Bamberg. He was crowned emperor at Rome by Benedict VIII on 14 February 1014. He intervened controversially, although with Rome's support, in ecclesiastical affairs, and supported the nascent monastic reform movement. His piety became legendary; he was canonized in 1146 (as was his wife, **Cunegund** [died 998], in 1200).

Henry de Ossó y Cervelló, bl., born Vinebre, Tarragona, Spain, 15 October 1840, died Valencia, 27 January 1896, beatified 1979. A friend and relative of **Emmanuel Domingo y Sol**, ordained 1867, he insisted that women were key to the faith. He admired **Teresa of Avila**, wrote devotional books for women and children, and created the *Compañía de Santa Teresa*.

Henry Heath, martyr, bl., born Peterborough, 1599, died Tyburn, 17 April 1643, beatified 1987. A convert, he became a Franciscan priest in Douai, staying for 19 years, teaching theology at university. At his request, apparently because he desired martyrdom, he was sent to England in 1643. He was hanged, drawn and quartered.

Henry Morse, martyr, born Brome, Suffolk, England, 1595, died Tyburn, England, 1 February 1645. Morse was converted to Roman Catholicism while studying law in London and left to study theology in Douai, France. After serving four years in an English prison for his faith, he completed his studies and was ordained in Rome. He returned to England in 1624, was again imprisoned, and completed his Jesuit novitiate while in prison in York. Morse spent the rest of his career working for the Roman Catholic Church and alternately in prison or exile for that work. He was finally executed for subverting the proper loyalties of English subjects in 1645. Feast 1 February.

Henry of Bolzano, blessed, ascetic, born Bolzano, Italy, c. 1250, died Treviso, 10 June 1315. After the death of his wife and son, he began to live in extreme poverty, devoting himself to humble trades, prayer and penance. Famed for his holiness at the time of his death, large crowds attended his funeral and his tomb in the cathedral of Treviso

became a goal for pilgrimages. Paduan Peter of Baone, later bishop of Treviso, wrote a biography of Henry in 1381. Benedict XIV confirmed the cult for the diocese of Treviso and Pius VII extended it to Trent.

Henry of Bonn, bl., Rhineland nobleman, born c. 1100, died Lisbon 1147. Henry set out from Cologne on 27 April 1147 for the second Crusade. He was among the first who responded to the plea of Alfonso I of Portugal to help free Lisbon from the Saracens. Henry fell during the siege of Lisbon. After his burial at St Vincent's church, miracles were reported at his grave and this led to his veneration as a martyr.

Henry of Clairvaux, bl., Cistercian abbot, cardinal, born at the Burgundian castle of Marcy, died 1 January 1198. He became a Cistercian in 1155 and abbot of Clairvaux in 1176. He served the popes by a mission to Archbishop Henry of Rheims in 1162 and by reconciling King Henry II of England with the Church of Canterbury in 1178. He had been active in reconciling the Albigensians and in 1181, as cardinal archbishop of Albano, assumed leadership of that mission. Before his death he persuaded Frederick Barbarossa to join the Crusade, arranged for treaties between France and England, and enrolled Philip Augustus and Henry II in what was the third Crusade.

Henry of Coquet, born Denmark, died Coquet, 1127, buried Tynemouth abbey. Escaping an unwelcome marriage, he became a hermit on this tiny island off Northumberland. Many came to consult him, attracted by his holiness and his ability to mind-read and know the future. Feast 16 January.

Henry of Heisterbach, bl., Cistercian abbot, born c. 1180, died c. 1244. Born of a noble family and educated in Paris, Henry became a canon of the church of St Cassius in Bonn. About 1200 he entered the Cistercian abbey of Heisterbach, where he was elected abbot in 1208. His reign marked a high point in the history of Heisterbach and he was effective in founding the daughter house at Marienstatt. He encouraged the important literary activity of **Caesarius of Heisterbach**, and served the Church and secular governments as a counsellor, ambassador and preacher of a Crusade.

Henry of Treviso, bl., born Bolzano, died Treviso, 1315. He left his home and moved to Treviso, where it is possible that he married and had a child. If he did so, his wife and child soon died, and he spent the rest of his life as a labourer – he was illiterate – and fulfilling with great devotion his religious duties. When too old to work he lived on alms, but anything he collected he shared with the poor he encountered. He was a very popular figure in the city, and miracles were attributed to him from soon after his death. Feast 10 June.

Henry of Uppsala, bishop and martyr, died Köylio, Finland, c. 1156. He is a somewhat enigmatic figure, an Englishman who was probably already in Rome when cardinal Nicholas Breakspear, the later Pope Adrian IV, was sent in 1151 as papal legate to Scandinavia. Henry went with him and was ordained bishop of Uppsala by the legate in 1152. The new bishop impressed St **Eric**, the king of Sweden. The bishop accompanied King Eric on a campaign against pagan marauders in Finland and converted many Finns to Christianity. One convert named Lalli refused to do the penance required of him for murder and killed the bishop. From an early date Henry has been venerated as the patron saint of Finland. By 1296 the cathedral at Abo was already dedicated to him. In 1300 his remains were translated to the cathedral at Abo (Turku).

Henry of Vitskól, bl., Cistercian abbot, died presumably Vitskól, Denmark, 11 February late 1100s. Henry joined the Cistercians at Clairvaux, where he was noticed by then abbot **Bernard of Clairvaux**. In 1143 he was sent to the abbey of Alvastra, Sweden, and became the founding abbot of the abbey at Varnhem seven years later. Forced by external conflict to leave Sweden, he became first abbot of Danish King Waldemar I's new monastery at Vitskól in 1158. In 1166 he worked to found a new monastery at either Oem or Clara-Insula. His feast, 11 February, is found in the Cistercian calender, but he has no official cult.

Henry of Zwiefalten, bl., Benedictine monk, born c. 1200, died Ochsenhausen, Germany, 4 November 1262. Henry was a respected knight in his youth before becoming prior of the Ochsenhausen priory in 1238. Although few details are known of his life, as prior he seemed to have been most concerned with the expansion of the priory library. However, he also helped obtain endowments that funded the decoration of the priory church. During his life he was renowned for great sanctity and also for healing powers. His cult seems to have been late in getting established, which may be why he is normally referred to as 'blessed' rather than 'saint'.

Henry Suso, bl., Dominican spiritual writer, born probably Constance, 21 March 1295, died Ulm, 25 January 1366. He initially entered the Dominican house there, but at 18 went through a conversion experience; he went to study at Cologne, where he was deeply influenced by Eckhart. Around 1326 he published *The Little Book of Truth*, a speculative exposition of Eckhart's teaching. Deprived of his position in 1330, he adopted an itinerant preaching ministry in Switzerland and the Upper Rhine. He served as prior of Constance 1344–6, but his community, the Friends of God, was then exiled and dispersed. He moved to Ulm in 1348, where he spent the rest of his life. He left two collections of letters and *The Little Book of Eternal Wisdom or Clock of Wisdom*, produced in German and Latin, a meditative study much read in the fourteenth and fifteenth centuries. A cult grew up shortly after his death, approved in 1831. Feast 23 January.

Henry Walpole, martyr, born Docking, Norfolk, 1558, died York, 7 April 1595. He was converted to the faith by the execution of **Edmund Campion**, in whose honour he wrote a long narrative poem, secretly printed, and offensive to the government. He went to Rheims in 1582, by way of Rouen and Paris, was admitted to the English College, Rome, and became a Jesuit priest at Paris in 1588. A chaplain to the Spanish forces in Holland, he was imprisoned by the English at Flushing in 1589 and 'sent to the Mission' in 1593. He was arrested two days after landing in Yorkshire and imprisoned, then sent to the Tower in London, where he was repeatedly tortured, before being returned to Yorkshire for trial and execution, under the Act that made it high treason for a native Englishman ordained abroad to minister as a priest in England. He was executed with **Alexander Rawlins**.

Henry Webley, bl., martyr, died Mile End Green, London, 28 August 1588. He was a layman, a friend of **William Dean**, who was executed with him.

Henry Zdik, bl., bishop, born Moravia, died Olomouc, 1150. He was related to the royal house of Bohemia, and was made bishop of Olomouc in the Czech Republic in 1126. He went on a pilgrimage to the Holy Land, where he became a member of the Premonstratensian Order (the Norbertines), and when he returned home he founded several houses of the order in his diocese, including that of Stahov, where he was buried. He was a zealous reformer in his diocese, which seems to have led to an attempt on his life. Feast 25 June.

Hensa Haymanot, monk, fifteenth century. Ethiopian Church. A disciple of **Samuel of Waldeba**.

Heraclas, hermit. Syriac Church. He had lived as a monk at the monastery of Kafar Sama.

Heraclides, martyr, died Alexandria, c. 303. Coptic Church.

Heraclius, monk and martyr, died Sazanovka (modern Anan'evo), 10 June 1937. Russian Church. Baptized Sergius Matjach, he was orphaned as a baby and brought up in a monastery, where he eventually became a monk. He was sent to Kazakhstan around the beginning of the twentieth century, and witnessed the sacking of his monastery and the massacre of its monks – he escaped by climbing the bell tower. He then went to Vernyj, where he helped **Seraphim** build his hermitage on Mount Kyzyl-zar. After the martyrdom of Seraphim he went to live in the village of Talgar, living with the family of the sacristan. When in 1928 the sacristan was arrested, he then wandered around the countryside until he was taken ill. He was looked after by the people of the village of Sazanovka, where he remained until his death.

Heraclius, Paul and Companions, martyrs, died Porto Romano, Italy, c. 305. Feast 2 March.

Herai, martyr, died Antinöe, Egypt, third/fourth century. Coptic Church. She was brought before the prefect because of her Christianity, but because of her beauty he tried to spare her. She, however, remained true to her faith.

Herculanus, bishop and martyr, died Perugia, 547. Killed by Ostrogoths when they captured the city of Perugia, of which he was the bishop. Feast 7 November.

Herculanus of Piegaro, born Piegaro, died Castelnuovo, 1451. He became a Franciscan Observant at Sarteano. He travelled to the Holy Land, but then became one of the best-known preachers in Italy, often reducing his hearers to tears. He founded a number of convents with the alms which had been given him. Feast 28 May.

Heredina, see **Justa**.

Herluin of Bec, bl., founder and first abbot of Bec, born Brionne, Normandy, c. 995, died Bec, Normandy, 26 August 1078. A knight in the service of the count of Brionne until the age of 38, he became a hermit and founded a monastic community for his followers on his land near Bonneville. In 1035 Bishop Heribert of Lisieux ordained him and named him first abbot of Bec. His zeal attracted two Italians, **Lanfranc** and **Anselm**, both of whom served long terms as prior of Bec and as archbishop of Canterbury. Lanfranc introduced the usages of Bec to England and consecrated the abbey church at Bec in 1077, just a few months before Herluin's death.

Herluka of Bernried, bl., nun, born Swabia, Germany, mid-1100s, died convent of Bernried, Augsburg, Germany, 1127. Not much is certain about Herluka's life. She began her cloistered life at Epfach, where she carried on an extensive correspondance with a nun named Deimoth, which apparently evinced great familiarity with the events of her day. She was expelled from Epfach for her pro-papal activities and retired to the convent at Bernried, where she died. Her correspondence has been lost, but from what is known, she appears to have been well educated and at least moderately influential in her day. Feast 18 April.

Herman Joseph, born Cologne, *c.* 1150, died Hoven, 1241, cult approved 1958. An ordained Premonstratensian monk at Steinfeld, he was known for his intense religious fervour, being often in ecstasy, and for his kindness and mechanical skills. He wrote prayers, hymns and mystical treatises, all lost, and promoted devotion to **Ursula**. Feast 7 April.

Herman of Alaska, Orthodox monk and missionary, born Serpukhov, Russia, *c.*1760, died Spruce Island, Alaska, 15 November 1836. He was sent to Alaska, with 12 other monks, from the famous monastery of Valaam, to evangelize the Aleuts. By 1823 he was the sole survivor. His ascetic life, gentleness with Indians and settler alike, and love of children made him a highly successful missionary, although he was never ordained priest. His last years were spent in seclusion, but his memory was always treasured by the local population. He was canonized on 9 August 1970. Feast 12 December. Regarded as the Orthodox patron saint of North America.

Herman of Heidelberg, hermit, born Heidelberg (?), died Rinchnach, near Passau, *c.* 1326. He became a monk at the monastery of Niederaltiach in Bavaria, but then became a hermit at Rinchnach. Feast 24 August.

Herman the German, Dominican missionary, flourished early 1200s. Virtually nothing is known about the life of Herman, except that he was brought into the Dominican order by St **Dominic** himself, that he co-founded a Dominican house at Friesach in 1219 (the first such house in Germany), and that he later served in Silesia (Poland). He is often grouped together with Bl. **Ceslaus of Silesia** and St **Hyacinth**, who were also among Dominic's first followers.

Hermannus Contractus, monk and scholar, born Saulgau, Württemberg-Hohenzollern, Germany, 18 July 1013, died abbey of Reichenau, Germany, 24 September 1054. Also known as Herman the Lame or Herman of Reichenau, this son of the count of Altshausen overcame great physical impairment to become a scholar in many areas of thought. He spent his entire life in the abbey of Reichenau on lake Constance, placed there by his father at the age of seven and taking monastic vows in 1043. He wrote many works, including the *Chronicon*, a list of important events from Christ's birth, and the *De sancta cruce* and *Rex regum Dei agne*, which were part of many sung Latin masses. A local cult surrounding him was confirmed in 1863. Feast 25 September.

Hermas of Rome, born Rome, died there (?), first century. Mentioned by St Paul. Feast 9 May.

Hermas, Serapion and Polienus, martyrs, died Rome. Hardly anything is known of them, except that they were said to have been dragged across rough earth until they died of their injuries. Feast 18 August.

Hermeland (Hermenland, Herbland, in French: Erblon), abbot from around Noyon, France, died Aindre, *c.* 720. As a young man he served at court before entering Fontenelle abbey, Normandy. Ordained, he founded and was first abbot of Aindre, on the island of that name in the Loire estuary. Feast 25 March.

Hermenegild, beheaded Tarragona, kingdom of the Visigoths, Spain, 13 April 585. He was son of King Leovigold, king of the Visigoths in Spain, and was brought up in the Arian faith. Hermenegild married Ingund, a devout orthodox Catholic, and was converted to Catholicism, partly through her influence and partly through that of the bishop **Leander of Seville**. Hermenegild rebelled against his father, but was defeated. He knew of his forthcoming death and was fully prepared for it when his father's soldiers appeared. Feast 13 April.

Hermes, see also **Philip of Heraclea**.

Hermes, martyred fourth century. Commemorated with **Haggai** and **Gaius**, it is said they were killed at Bologna, but this could be a town of Mesia, Asia Minor. Or they may have died at Bononia on the Danube. Feast 4 January.

Hermes, martyr, died Rome, second century. There was a basilica built over his tomb on the via Salaria. Feast 28 August.

Hermes and Companions, martyrs, died Nisibis. Syriac Church. They were, apparently, of Roman origin.

Hermias, soldier and martyr, died Comana, Cappadocia, 170. Feast 31 May.

Hermione, died Ephesus, 117 (?). A daughter of the apostle Philip. Feast 31 May.

Hermogenes, Donatus and Companions, martyrs. They were put to death by being driven into a marsh and left there. Feast 12 December.

Hermogenes of Moscow, patriarch, died 17 February 1612. Russian Church. Baptized Ermolaj, he married, and became a priest, but when he was widowed he entered the Cudov monastery at Moscow. He became archimandrite of the monastery of the Transfiguration at Kazan, and in 1589 was made bishop of Kazan. He built churches and monasteries, and was deeply committed to the 'Russification' of the region. He travelled to Moscow to take part in councils of state, and in 1606 he replaced Patriarch Ignatius, who had been put in place by the recently assassinated 'false' Tsar Demetrius. He was a capable administrator, and was succesful in rallying the people of Moscow when their city was under siege. In particular, after Moscow had been seized by the Polish King Sigismund, he roused the people against the invaders and in March 1611 was arrested and imprisoned in the Cudov monastery in the Kremlin. Even from there he continued to exhort the people by letters smuggled out of his cell, but he was slowly starved to death by his captors: six months later the Russian army drove the Polish troops from Moscow.

Hermolaus, Hermippus and Hermocrates, martyrs, died Nicomedia, 305 (?). Hermolaus was a priest who converted the doctor to the emperor, **Pantaleon**, and was martyred with him, alongside the two brothers Hermippus and Hermocrates. Feast 27 July.

Hermylus, martyred, early fourth century. An unreliable Life says he was a deacon of Singidunum (now Belgrade) who was killed under Licinius by being drowned in the Danube with his servant **Stratonicus**. Feast 13 January.

Herodion, Asincritus and Phlegon, martyrs, first century. All mentioned by St Paul, who says he was related to Herodion. Feast 8 April.

Heron, Arsenius, Isidore and Dioscorus, martyrs, died Alexandria, c. 250. Dioscorus was not in fact executed; the others were burned to death. Feast 14 December.

Herpaeses and Julian, martyrs, fourth century. Coptic Church.

Hervé, abbot, born Brittany, died Lanhourneau, sixth century. He was the son of a British minstrel at the court of the king of the Franks. The minstrel moved to Britanny and married a local girl, but their son, Hervé, was born blind. After the death of his father he was put in charge of an uncle who ran a monastic school. Although blind, he inherited the school, and decided to move it, settling at Lanhourneau, where he founded an abbey. Feast 17 June.

Hesan Mo'a, monk, fifteenth century. Coptic Church. A disciple of **Zar'a Abreham**, he founded the monastery of Dabra Bagge. Feast 31 July.

Hesperus (Exuperius), martyred Attalia, Pamphylia, c. 127. He and his family were slaves who refused their pagan owner's order to offer sacrifices to the gods. He was killed with his wife **Zoë**, and their sons **Cyriacus** and **Theodulus**. Feast 2 May.

Hesychius, monk, born Palestine, died there, fourth century. He was a disciple of **Hilarion**, whom he followed to Sicily from their monastery in Gaza, then to Dalamatia and Cyprus. Hilarion died in Cyprus, and Hesychius took his body back to Palestine, interring it in the monastery at Majuma. Feast 3 October.

Hesychius, died c. 490, bishop of Vienne. Feast 15 March.

Hesychius of Antioch, martyr, died Antioch, *c.* 305. An officer of the imperial court at Antioch, he proclaimed his Christianity when the emperor ordered a persecution, and was drowned. Feast 4 March.

Hesychius of Jerusalem, monk, church historian and theologian, active in the fifth century. In 412 he seems to have been a presbyter in Jerusalem. His *Church History*, now lost, was cited at the Council of Constantinople in 553 and reveals him as a supporter of **Cyril of Alexandria** in his stand against Nestorianism, and opposed to the Christology of **Theodore of Mopsuestia**. He played an active role in support of the Alexandrians leading up to the Council of Chalcedon. His writings, which survive only in part, included commentaries on most of the Bible and sermons. Feast (Greek Church) 28 March.

Hesychius of the Kievan Cave Monastery, monk. Russian Church. Nothing is known of him. Feast 11 December.

Hesychius the Wonderworker, born Andrapa, died Mount Maion, 781. He lived an eremetical life, but while living on Mount Maion he won fame for his miracles. Feast 10 May.

Hewald the White and Hewald the Black, martyrs, born Northumbria, died near Dortmund, *c.* 695. Brothers, distinguished by the colour of their hair. They went to Westphalia to preach the gospel, and were martyred there. Their bodies were later taken to Cologne. Feast 3 October.

Hidulf, founder, born probably Regensburg, Germany, died abbey of Moyenmoutier or Bonmoutier, France, 11 July 707. St Hidulf was first a monk in Trier, Germany, at Saint-Maximin's. He later served as a sort of auxiliary bishop for the diocese of Trier before retiring to a hermitage in the Vosges mountains. Other hermits gathered to him, and together they founded the abbey of Moyenmoutier. Feast 11 July.

Hidulf of Lobbes, monk, died Lobbes (Belgium), 23 June 707. St Hildulf was a Frankish noble and a

good friend of Pepin of Heristal. In the later part of the seventh century, he aided St **Landelin** and St **Ursmar** in their work to found an abbey in Lobbes. After the death of his wife, **Aya**, Hildulf joined the abbey and lived as a monk until his death.

Hierotheus, Eudoxia and Natalia, martyrs, born Olonec, died there, seventeenth century. Church of the Old Believers. Hierotheus was a merchant, Eudoxia was his wife and Natalia their servant. Hierotheus was held in high regard in the city, and the authorities were hesitant about punishing him for his adherence to the old rites. All three were, however, put to death on the order of Moscow. Feast 6 March.

Hierotheus of Iviron, bl., born Kalamai in the Peloponnese, 1686, died island of Giura, 13 September 1745. Byzantine Church. Intellectually brilliant as a youth, he was obliged by his parents to marry, but soon after their deaths he abandoned his family and went to Mount Athos. He later studied in Constantinople and in Venice, but then returned to Athos where he was ordained priest. At the request of the inhabitants of the island of Skopelos, he spent eight years there teaching and preaching. After his return to Athos he spent much time translating lives of the saints and combating quietism in the Orthodox Church, which brought him into conflict with the patriarch of Constantinople. Towards the end of his life, and seeking a quieter life, he retired to the island of Giura with a few of his disciples.

Hilaria, daughter of the Emperor Zeno.

Hilarion, abbot of Mount Olympus, Bithynia, eighth century. Feast 28 March.

Hilarion, monk, seventeenth century. Russian Church. Founder of the monastery, probably early in the seventeenth century, of the Dormition of the Mother of God, on the river Moca.

Hilarion, bl., martyr, born Kastro, Crete (Heracleon), died Constantinople, 20 September 1804. Byzantine Church. Baptized John, he was sent to Constantinople by his parents to learn the trade of a doctor from his uncle. Instead, however, he entered the employment of a merchant who accused him of taking money. John went to the palace to seek help, and was advised that were he to convert to Islam the sultan would indeed come to his aid. He did so, but after a few days was filled with remorse. He fled Constantinople first for the Crimea, then for Mount Athos, where he became a monk. He then returned to Constantinople, confessed that he had returned to Christianity, and was beheaded.

Hilarion Nikolaevic Zukov, martyr, born Cabanovka, died Char'kov, 16 January 1938. Ukrainian Church, Moscow Patriarchate. He worked in the village of Osinovka until his arrest in December 1937. Feast 19 May.

Hilarion of Gaza ('the Great'), monk, born Tabatha, Palestine, 291 died Cyprus, 371. His Life by **Jerome** is our only source about this Palestinian monk. A student in Alexandria, he was converted and frequented the desert cell of St **Anthony**, whose ascetic way of life he was soon to imitate at Majuma in the Egyptian desert. Disciples joined him from 329 onwards. Near the end of his life he travelled widely, seeking solitude in Egypt and elsewhere, finally dying in Cyprus. His disciple **Hesychius** took his body back to Majuma. Feast 21 October.

Hilarion of Kiev, metropolitan, born Kiev, died there, c. 1067. Russian Church. He was of a noble family with connections to the ruling family of Kiev – he was a close friend, and later confessor, of Prince **Jaroslav**. Before his election he was a priest at Berestovo, the summer residence of the prince of Kiev. As a priest, he fashioned for himself a small cave just outside the city, where he could retire for quiet prayer. In 1051 he was elected metropolitan, the first Russian to hold that position, replacing the recently deceased Greek metropolitan. This election went against Orthodox tradition: the post should have been in the gift of the patriarch of Constantinople. It was through Jaroslav's influence that Hilarion was chosen, and after the prince's death in 1054 he resigned. He then went to live in the Kievan Cave monastery, which had been begun during his episcopate, and it was probably there that he died, although there

is little or no information about him after his resignation. He left a number of writings, including a discourse on religion and the state.

Hilarion of Moglena, bl., bishop, died 21 October 1164. Byzantine Church. His episcopate was taken up with battling local heretics.

Hilarion of Optina, monk, born Kljuci, 9 April 1805, died Optina, 18 September 1873. Russian Church. Baptized Rodion Nikitic Ponomarev, his father was a tailor, and he studied tailoring in Moscow. He gained a considerable reputation as a tailor, and in 1832 moved his business to Saratov. His family had problems with other inhabitants of the city, and eventually Rodion left, and went visiting monasteries. He settled finally in the hermitage belonging to Optina, taking as his spiritual guide **Macarius of Optina**. He was ordained priest and himself became a spiritual director, with a reputation for miracles and foretelling the future. Feast 11 October.

Hilarion of Pokrovskoe, founder, died Pokrovskoe, 1476. Russian Church. A disciple of **Euphrosyne of Pskov**, he founded the monastery at Pokrovskoe on the river Zelca. His monastery was under constant threat from the Teutonic Knights, Swedish invaders and others.

Hilarion of Suzdal, bishop, born Niznij Novgorod, 1632, died Suzdal, 14 December 1708. Russian Church. Baptized Ivan, he was the son of a priest who entered a monastery after the death of his wife. Ivan was therefore brought up within a monastic community. However, he left the monastery and married. His wife died 18 months later. In 1651 he was elected bishop of Kolomna, although not yet a priest. He was not ordained until 1655, at the request of the small monastic community he had entered at Floriev – all the monks of which died of the plague. He then founded another community, running it with great strictness and attention to poverty, but also with an outreach to pilgrims. His reputation for holiness brought the community a visit from the Tsar c. 1670, and in 1681, on the Tsar's orders, he was made archbishop of Suzdal, then metropolitan a year later. He showed great energy as bishop, visiting prisons and hospitals, caring for his clergy, preaching, and all the time maintaining his strict ascetic way of life. He was removed from office in 1705 because of his blindness, but remained at the cathedral until his death. Feast 23 June.

Hilarion of the Kievan Cave Monastery, monk, died Kiev, eleventh century. Russian Church. Little is known of him, except that he had a reputation for great sanctity, eating only once a week, and praying prostrate and in tears.

Hilarion the Georgian, founder, born Kachethi, eastern Georgia, 822, died Thessalonika, c. 875. Georgian Church. The son of a noble family, he early showed interest in becoming a monk, and his father founded a monastery for him. Wishing to escape his family's attentions, however, he left this monastery for that of Davidgaregi. His reputation for holiness grew, and to get away from people's attention he went on pilgrimage to the Holy Land, remaining there in the desert as a hermit for 17 years, before a vision of the Virgin sent him back to Georgia. There he founded a convent for his sister, and returned to Davidgaregi. He then gave away all his inheritance, and founded another monastery for men. When there was an attempt to elect him bishop he once more fled, travelling to various places, including Rome – where he spent two years – and Constantinople. He founded a Georgian monastery on Mount Olympus. Finally he arrived in Thessalonika, where he swiftly gained the reputation of a miracle worker. His remains were taken to Constantinople. Feast 19 November.

Hilarion the Recluse, born Zenkino, 1774, died Troekurovo, 5 November 1853. Russian Church. Baptized Mefodievic Fokin, he was brought up by his grandmother until 14 years of age, when he returned to his parents' home. At their urging he married, but immediately after the wedding fled and tried to enter a monastery, but could not because he was technically married. He went back to his village and lived in a cave, following a strict ascetical regime. He even determined to live on a pillar to avoid the crowds who came to see him. He then started to wander from place to place and, despite the continued opposition of his wife, eventually entered a monastery at Kursk. He settled finally in the village of Troekurovo, where he gained a great reputation for holiness. He distributed whatever was given him to the poor, and established a convent of nuns. Feast 28 July.

Hilarion Tvaloeli, monk, tenth/eleventh centuries. Georgian Church. A monk of the monastery of Chachuli in southern Georgia. He was the spiritual guide of **George the Great**. Feast 24 July.

Hilary of Arles, bishop, born c. 401, died Arles, 5 May 449. A relative of St **Honoratus**, he became a monk at Lérins, then succeeded Honoratus as metropolitan bishop of Arles c. 430. He presided over notable gatherings such as the first Council of Orange (441) and the Council of Vaisson (442). In 444, having deposed a local bishop, Chelidonius of Besanion, exceeding thereby his metropolitan authority, he was deprived of his powers by Pope **Leo I**, who obtained from the Emperor Valentinian the right to direct Roman control over the Church in Gaul. He wrote a life of Honoratus which survives; he also produced letters and poetry.

Hilary of Mende, bishop, died c. 540. A Life describes him as a hermit who lived on the banks of the Tarn and attracted a group of followers, for whom he built a monastery; this is probably unreliable. He was made bishop of Mende some time prior to 535. Nothing is known of his episcopate, except that on one occasion he offered shelter to St **Leobinus** of Chartres, and that he attended the Synod of Auvergne in 535. Feast 25 October.

Hilary of Poitiers, bishop, born start of the fourth century, died Poitiers, 367. Bishop of Poitiers (France) from c. 350, he was an anti-Arian. Exiled to Phrygia by the Synod of Béziers (356), he became acquainted with Eastern theology, especially with the work of Origen. In the trinitarian conflicts he mediated between the homoousians and the homoeousians. In 361 he returned to Gaul. His moderate theological position is reflected in his works, such as *De Trinitate*. His exegesis is allegorical, as shown in his commentaries on the Gospel of Matthew and on the Psalms. Feast 14 January.

Hilary of Toulouse, bishop of Toulouse, fourth century. Feast 20 May.

Hilary, Tatian, Felix, Largus and Denis, martyred Aquileia, in the Abruzzi, *c.* 284. Hilary was bishop of Aquilea, Tatian his deacon, the others laymen, all of them beheaded. Feast 16 March.

Hilda of Whitby (more properly Hild), abbess, born Northumbria, 614, died Whitby, 17 November 680. She was the great-niece of King Edward of Northumbria and became a Christian at the age of 13, baptized by **Paulinus** at York in 627. St **Aidan** appointed her abbess of a convent at Hartlepool in 649, the earliest nunnery in Northumbria. In Whitby she founded the first double monastery for men and women in 657, an innovation from Gaul, and, although richly endowed by the Northumbrian dynasty, Hilda ruled it with great wisdom. Many of the Anglo-Saxon nobility of Northumbria entrusted their daughters to Hilda's care. Whitby became a nursery for English bishops and it was there that **Caedmon** was encouraged to write vernacular poetry. **Bede** also tells us that it was from Whitby that we have the earliest surviving Anglo-Saxon hagiographical writing in a life of Pope **Gregory I**, *c.* 700. When the Synod of Whitby met in 664 to settle the Paschal controversy between the Roman and Celtic traditions, Hilda argued in favour of keeping Celtic religious customs, including their dating of Easter. But when the decision to follow Roman customs was made under the leadership of St **Wilfrid**, Hilda concurred while **Colman** left with a splinter party of both English and Irish monks. Feast 17 November.

Hildegard of Bingen (Hildegaard), abbess, author, musician and German mystic. Born Böckelheim, 1098, died Bingen, 17 September 1179. She was brought up by the Bl. **Jutta** and had religious experiences from an early age. These caused her embarrassment and confusion so that she was reluctant to talk about them. In later life, however, she was persuaded to write them down and obtained the approval of both the archbishop and the pope. She was skilled in healing and in musical composition. She had a wide influence in her time and has recently again become well known for the breadth of her learning and teaching. Her main work recording her visions is the *Scivias*, but she wrote many other works and letters. Miracles were reported during her life and after her death. Feast 17 September.

Hildegard of Kempten, wife of **Charlemagne**, born 758, died Thionville, France, 30 April 783. Hildegard was born into a family allied with the dukes of Swabia. The second wife of Charlemagne, she was the mother of Louis I the Pious. She contributed greatly to the rebuilding of the abbeys of Kempten and St Arnulf of Metz. Thought to be buried in the latter abbey; the sisters of Kempten obtained her relics in 872 and she has been venerated as 'blessed' since the late 900s. Feast 30 April.

Hildegunde of Meer, bl., died Germany, 6 February 1183. Of noble birth, after her husband's death she joined the Premonstratensians and founded the convent of Meer in 1165 and became the first prioress. Her son was involved in the sack of Rome with Frederick Barbarossa, and to expiate his sin she built a monument. Her daughter **Hadewych** succeeded her as prioress and both are recognized as 'venerable'. Feast 6 February.

Hildegunde of Schönau, Cistercian, birth unknown, died Schönau abbey, 20 April 1188. Her merchant father dressed her as a man and named her Joseph. He took her on a pilgrimage to Rome and died during the journey. She then entered the Cistercian abbey, but died during her novitiate and was discovered to be a woman only after her death. The story was well known and she became venerated by Cistercians. There are, however, other such stories from the earliest days of monasticism. The earliest record of 'Joseph's' life is from Berthold, who shared the novitiate with her. (Feast suppressed.)

Hildelide (Hildelithe), Anglo-Saxon Benedictine abbess, born *c.* 650, died Barking, near London, *c.* 717. Of royal birth, she entered a monastery in France (Chelles or Faremoûtiers). She was invited to Barking abbey by **Erconwald**, bishop of London, to train his sister St **Ethelburga**. Hildelide became second abbess there until her death. **Bede** and **Boniface** admired her and *De Laudibus Virginitatis* by **Aldhelm** was dedicated to her. Feast 24 March.

Hipparchus and Philotheus, martyrs, died Samosata, 311 (?). They were two magistrates, converts to Christianity, who had themselves converted others. They were crucified for refusing to take part in the (pagan) celebrations for a victory of the Emperor Maximinus. Five of their converts died with them.

Hippolytus, died Loudon, c. 770. He was an abbot and bishop of Loudun. Feast 27 February.

Hippolytus of Anthioch, martyr, died Antioch, Syria. His life is confused with that of **Hippolytus of Rome**. Otherwise nothing is known of him. Feast 30 January.

Hippolytus of Avellino, martyr, fourth century. Feast 1 May.

Hippolytus of Rome, bishop, died Sardinia, 235, and was in the West the last ecclesiastical author writing in Greek. About his career we only know that he was an antipope at the time of **Callixtus I** (217–22) and that he suffered exile in Sardinia. A prolific writer, most of his works (commentaries, especially on the books of the Old Testament, heresiological, apologetical and chronographical tractates) survive only in fragments, the authenticity of which is often difficult to ascertain. Feast 3 August.

Hirenarchus, see **Irenarchus**.

Hirut, monk, born Bankol, fourteenth century. Ethiopian Church. A disciple of **Madhanina Egzi**.

Homobonus, born Cremona, Italy, died there, 13 November 1197. A tailor by trade, and married with several children, he was extraordinarily generous to the poor, possibly even to the detriment of his wife and family. He gave up work when he was 50, and devoted himself to acts of charity. He died during mass.

Honorata of Pavia, lived and died Pavia, fifth century. She was the sister of **Epiphanius of Pavia**. A nun, she was captured by Odoacer, the king of the Heruli, but was later ransomed by her brother. Feast 11 January.

Honoratus, abbot of Subiaco, near Tivoli, sixth century. Feast 23 May.

Honoratus Kozminski, see **Honoratus of Biala Podlaska**.

Honoratus (Honorius) of Amiens, bishop, born probably Port-le-Grand, France, died Amiens, c. 600. The biography of Honoratus (late eleventh century at the earliest) is unreliable; it says that he lived at the time of Pope Pelagius II (579–90). After his death, veneration of Honoratus spread and cures were attributed to him when his relics were elevated (1060). Various churches are dedicated to him; the Faubourg and Rue Saint-Honore in Paris are named after him. He is the patron of bakers. Feast 16 May.

Honoratus of Arles, bishop, died Arles, 429. A Roman living in Gaul, he became a Christian hermit. Around 405, with **Caprasius**, he founded the monastery of Lérins on that island, now opposite Cannes, based on the Rule of **Pachomius**. Ordained, he became bishop of Arles in 426. Feast 16 January.

Honoratus of Biala Podlaska, bl., born Biala Podlaska, Poland, 16 October 1829, died Nowe Miasto, 16 December 1916. Baptized Florence Wenceslaus John Kozminski, he studied art in Warsaw, and gave up the practice of his religion. In 1846 he was imprisoned on the charge of having conspired against the Russian occupiers of Poland, and during his time there he recovered his faith. In December 1848 he became a Capuchin, taking the name Honoratus. He was ordained four years later, and he worked in Warsaw as a preacher and confessor. He helped to found the Congregation of the Sisters of St Felix. In 1863 the Capuchins had to close their Warsaw house and move to Zakroczym, where they were refused permission by the Russians to leave their residence and were constantly spied upon. This continued even after they had been forced in 1892 to move to Nowe Miasto. Meanwhile, Honoratus had set up small communities, living under a form of the Franciscan Rule, but without the outward trappings of religious life. In 1895 he became superior of all Capuchins in Poland. He was also a notable spiritual writer.

Honoratus of Bourges, died 1250. Feast 9 January.

Honoratus of Milan, died Genoa, 570. Appointed bishop of Milan in 567 at a time of Arian disputes, he was driven into exile when the Lombards invaded. Feast 8 February.

Honorina, martyred Gaul, possibly Normandy. She is one of the early martyrs of Gaul with an ancient cult in Normandy, but nothing is known. Feast 27 February.

Honorius of Canterbury, missionary, fifth archbishop of Canterbury, died 30 September 653. Honorius was sent by Pope **Gregory I** to Kent, probably with the second group of Roman monks in 601, and became archbishop c. 627. Honorius's reign of consolidation was successful, including the sending of **Felix of Dunwich** to evangelize the East Angles, and the appointment in 644 of the first English bishop, the Kentish **Ithamar** of Rochester, who later consecrated Frithona, the first English archbishop of Canterbury (655). Feast 30 September.

Honorius of Dabra Segaga, monk, born Matge, Mugar, died monastery of Segaga, 27 September 1374. Ethiopian Church. Baptized Nardos, he was of a noble family, and his father was a priest. He was ordained deacon, but when his parents wanted him to marry he fled to **Takla Haymanot** and became a monk. He was accused of fathering a child and was thrown into prison, but when the woman was suffering in childbirth she admitted that someone else was the father and he was freed, and was ordained priest. After the death of Takla Haymanot he went to Tigre, and was later sent to preach in the Warab region. He gathered many disciples in the process, and founded for them the monastery of Segaga. He was exiled again for criticizing the king for marrying his stepmother, and was allowed to return only after the king's death. He also founded another community at Enaret. He fell out with the new king, and was again exiled, spending his time in various places, and was able to return only after 17 years, which time he had spent preaching, converting pagans and building churches.

Honorius of Morat, monk, fourteenth century. Ethiopian Church. A disciple of **Zena Marqos**.

Hop of Tuh, monk. Coptic Church. A hermit, living in a cave on Mount Tuh. His death was announced to him by an angel.

Hor, monk, born Bahgurah, Upper Egypt. Coptic Church.

Hor, monk, fifth/sixth centuries. Coptic Church. He exchanged letters with **Jeremiah of Saqqarah**.

Hor of Preht, monk, born Preht, Upper Egypt, fifth/sixth centuries. Coptic Church. He was a hermit, living in the desert, when he was tempted by the devil saying that he had prepared great things for him in the city. Accepting the challenge, Hor went to Alexandria where he worked for the prisoners and the poor.

Hormisdas, pope, born Frosinone, Italy, elected 20 July 514, died Rome, 6 August 523. Possibly of Persian ancestry by his name, Hormisdas was of a wealthy family and had been married: his son became Pope **Silverius** I. As bishop of Rome, Hormisdas was deeply concerned in the separation of Eastern and Western churches following the 'Henoticon' of Emperor Zeno and the demand of Emperor Anastasius that the Council of Chalcedon be repudiated. Hormisdas fought this monophysitism by means of a formula of faith which, after the emperor's sudden death in a storm, all Eastern bishops signed.

Hormisdas, martyr, died Persia, c. 420. The son of a provincial governor in Persia, he converted to Christianity and, as a punishment, was sent to look after the king's camels, a task, it was said, he was required to carry out naked. When the king offered to allow him to dress, he burned his clothes. He refused to give up his faith, but it is unclear whether he was executed. Feast 8 August.

Hormisdas Rabban, founder, born Bet Lapat, died monastery of Bet Abe, Marga, seventh century. Assyrian Church. Well born, possibly the son of a local ruler, he became a monk at the monastery near Sanat, on the modern frontier between Iraq and Turkey. He lived for a time as a monk, then as a hermit. After many years he left with a group of monks and became a hermit near Bet Edrai, near Alqos and not far from Mosul. He lived in a cave, but a number of monks gathered around him, and he became famous not just for his holiness but for the miracles he worked. But again he retired to a hermitage to live a contemplative life. At the end of his days – he lived to be 90 – he went to the monastery of Bet Abe.

Horsiesius, died Tabennisi, *c.* 380. He was a disciple of **Pachomius**, and succeeded him as abbot. His manner was too gentle, and he was replaced by **Theodore**, but when the latter died he once again became abbot. Feast 15 June.

Hospicius (Hospitius), hermit, died *c.* 580. He was a hermit at a place now named Cap-Saint-Hospice, near Nice. Apparently invading Lombards found him in chains and mistook penance for criminality. A soldier went to kill him, but his sword arm was paralysed until Hospicius made the sign of the cross. Feast 21 May.

Hotza Amiris, martyr, died Jerusalem, 1614. A Turkish soldier in Jerusalem who was so impressed by the Easter ceremonies that he became a Christian, and was executed.

Hroznata, bl., Premonstratensian crusader and monastic founder, born Tepl, Bohemia (Czech Republic), *c.* 1170, died Alt-Kinsburg (near Eger, Hungary), 14 July 1217. Hroznata was a member of the court of Henry Bretislav, prince-bishop of Prague, until the death of his wife and young son brought about a religious transformation in his life. He founded a Premonstratensian monastery at Tepl and joined the Crusade of Emperor Henry VI. When the Crusade failed, he returned to Bohemia, founded a convent on his family estate in Choteschau, and joined the abbey at Tepl as a monk and governor of the abbey's temporal affairs. He was killed by local nobles jealous of the abbey's revenues. Feast 19 July.

Hubert, bishop, born Maastricht, Holland, *c.* 656, died Fura (Tervueren), 30 May 727. A dissolute nobleman, he missed mass in order to go hunting, but saw a stag with a crucifix between his antlers and was converted. He was married, but when soon afterwards his wife died, he handed over his wealth to his only son and became a priest. He was in the entourage of Bishop **Lambert**, and when Lambert was murdered Hubert replaced him as bishop of Maastricht, although he later moved the episcopal see to Liège. (The first part of this story is identical to that of St **Eustace**.) Feast 3 November.

Hudahwi, founder, born Ber Aramaye, southern Iraq, died Hira, seventh century. Assyrian Church. He founded the monastery known as Bet Hale.

Hugh Faringdon, bl., born Faringdon, Berkshire, died Reading, 14 November 1539. His surname was Cook, but he was apparently most commonly known as Faringdon after the place of his birth. He became abbot of Reading in 1520, and was on very good terms with King Henry VIII, accepting most of his reforms, until his monastery was suppressed by the king's commissioners and he was sent to the Tower of London. He was executed outside his own monastery. Feast 15 November.

Hugh Green, bl., martyr, born London, *c.* 1564, died Dorchester, 19 August 1642. He was the son of a Protestant goldsmith, and went to Peterhouse, Cambridge. He then travelled on the continent of Europe, and became so impressed with Catholicism that he converted. He wanted to join the Capuchins, but his health was poor and he had to leave. He was ordained for the English mission in 1612, and after he returned to England he spent most of his working life as chaplain to the Arundell family at Chideock Castle, Dorset. When King Charles I issued a proclamation ordering all priests out of the country, he tried to leave, but was late in doing so. He was arrested, taken to Dorchester, and there hanged, drawn and quartered.

Hugh More, bl., martyr, born Grantham, 1563, died Lincoln's Inn Fields, 28 August 1588. He was a Protestant by origin, but was converted to Catholicism while studying at Gray's Inn. He went to Rheims to train for the priesthood, but left before ordination. He returned to England, was arrested, and promised his freedom if he were to abjure his faith. He refused.

Hugh of Anzy, bl., born Poitiers, died Anzy-le-Duc, *c.* 930. Ordained at Saint-Savin abbey in Poitou, he was a monk in several monasteries in central France, including Cluny, helping **Berno** to organize it. He was a reforming prior at Anzy-le-Duc, reputed for miracles and working to eliminate paganism. Feast 20 April.

Hugh of Auxerre, bishop, died *c.* 1136. Feast 10 August.

Hugh of Bonnevaux, Cistercian monk and abbot of Bonnevaux, born Châteauneuf d'Isère, France, *c.* 1120, died Bonnevaux, 1194. A nephew of **Hugh of Grenoble**, he entered the Cistercian monastery of Miroir *c.* 1138. Elected abbot of Léoncel in 1162 and of Bonnevaux in 1166, he founded three daughter houses. His efforts led to Frederick Barbarossa's recognition of Pope Alexander III in 1177. Feast 1 April.

Hugh of Cluny, sixth abbot of Cluny, born Burgundy, 1024, died Cluny, 29 April 1109. Son of Count Dalmace of Semur, he was educated by Bishop **Hugh of Auxerre** and entered Cluny in 1038. Made prior in 1048 and elected abbot the following year, his 60-year reign marked the high point of the Cluniac reform and the papal confirmation of Cluny's temporal and spiritual privileges. He took part in many Church councils, was appointed by the papacy to diplomatic missions to Hungary and Germany, and was at Canossa for Emperor Henry IV's reconciliation with Pope **Gregory VII**. Canonized 1 January 1120.

Hugh of Fosse, bl., first Premonstratensian (Norbertine) abbot-general, born Fosse, near Namur, *c.* 1093, died Prémontré, 10 February 1164. An episcopal chaplain before joining **Norbert** of Xanten and the Premonstratensians, he succeeded St Norbert as abbot in 1128. He guided the order through its early rapid expansion and wrote its first constitutions, as well as the first *Vita Norberti*.

Hugh of Grenoble, bishop and reformer, born Châteauneuf d'Isère, France, 1052, died Grenoble, 1 April 1132. His father, a soldier, became a Carthusian. Before his ordination, Hugh was a

cathedral canon at Valance, and he entered the service of the papal legate, Hugh of Die. In 1080, at the age of 27 and still not yet ordained, he was elected bishop of Grenoble (he was ordained immediately after his election, and was consecrated by Pope **Gregory VII** in Rome). On his election, his see was in urgent need of reform and in the course of his 52-year episcopate he was successful in reforming Grenoble, although he thought himself a failure. A friend of **Bruno** the Carthusian, his Life was written by Guigo I, prior of La Grande Chartreuse. He was canonized by Pope Innocent II in 1134.

Hugh of Lincoln, Carthusian bishop (and the first Carthusian to be canonized), born Avalon, France, 1140, died London, 16 November 1200. Educated by Augustinian canons, he left the Augustinian house of Villarbenoit to join La Grande Chartreuse, of which he later became procurator. In 1179 he was made prior of Witham by Henry II, who had founded that charterhouse after the murder of **Thomas Becket**. He became bishop of Lincoln in 1186, rebuilt the cathedral and served as royal ambassador and papal judge-delegate; three kings and three bishops carried his coffin at his funeral. He was canonized in 1220. Feast 17 November.

Hugh Taylor, bl., priest, martyr, born Durham, died by hanging York, 25 November 1585. In 1582 he went to Rheims, was ordained, and in March 1585 was sent back to England. He was arrested later that year and was the first person to die under the new statute of Elizabeth. The following day **Marmaduke Bowes**, a layman, was also hanged for having harboured Taylor. Feast 26 November.

Hugolina of Vercelli, hermit, *c.* 1330. Feast 8 August.

Hugolino Magalotti, bl., Franciscan tertiary, born Camerino, died Fiegni, 11 December 1373. From a wealthy family, he became a Franciscan tertiary, gave away all his inheritance, and lived as a hermit first at the foot of Monte Ragnolo, then later, when he was troubled by the number of people approaching his hermitage, in a more difficult place to get to, near Fiegni.

Hugolino of Gualdo Cattaneo, bl., Augustinian prior, born Bevagna, Italy, died Gualdo Cattaneo, Italy, 1 January 1260. Little is known of Hugolino's life except that he received a Benedictine community in Gualdo into the Augustianian order, becoming its prior two years before his death. A local cult evolved which encouraged charitable penitential works, and the Augustinians have venerated him as a saint since 1482. Against this history, however, there is evidence that Hugolino of Gualdo Cattaneo was the same as the fourteenth-century monk Hugolino Michaelis of Bavagna, who founded a monastery in the area c. 1340, which eventually became Augustinian in 1437. Evidence is conclusive for neither history.

Humbert of Maroilles, abbot, born Mezieres-sur-Oise, died Maroilles, 25 March c. 680. Humbert, according to tradition, was a monk and priest at Laon. When, upon his parents' death, Humbert inherited the family estate, he retired and made two pilgrimages to Rome. In 675 he gave his land to the monastery of Maroilles by a document which is still in existence, becoming also the first abbot of that monastery. Some legends claim that he became a bishop. Feast 25 March.

Humbert of Romans, bl., born Romans, near Vienne (France), c. 1194, died Valence (France), 14 July 1277. Humbert became a Dominican in 1224 after receiving his master of arts in Paris. Two years later he was appointed a professor of theology. In 1236 he was elected to the priorship of Lyons and in 1240 became the provincial of the Roman province. After also serving as provincial of France, he was elected master general of the order in 1254, a post he held for nine years. As master general, he helped the order solidify its academic and administrative practice and complete a reform of its liturgy. In 1264 he retired to Valence in order to write works on the order and on asceticism. These works are still influential within his order.

Humbert of Savoy, bl., born 1136, died Haute Combe, 1188, cult confirmed 1838. He was Humbert III of Savoy, king at 13 and tutored by **Amadeus of Lausanne**. He became a Cistercian monk in his last years. Feast 4 March.

Humiliana de Circulis, bl., Franciscan tertiary, born Florence, Italy, December 1219, died Florence, Italy, 19 May 1246. After five difficult years of marriage, Humiliana became a widow with two young girls. Because of the children, she could not fully join an order as a nun and so became a member of the Third Order of the Franciscans, or a tertiary, devoting her life to prayer, penance, church attendance and helping the poor. She was known for her meekness and courage, and miracles were ascribed to her even during her lifetime.

Humilis of Bisignano, bl., born Bisignano, Calabria, c. 1582, died there, 26 November 1637. His baptismal name was Luca, and he was a farm labourer, joining the Observant Franciscans in 1609 as a lay brother. He earned a considerable reputation as a miracle worker, and was summoned to Rome by Pope **Gregory X**.

Humilitas of Florence, born Faenza, Romagan, 1226, died Florence, 22 May 1310, cult confirmed 1721. Obliged to marry a superficial young man. When he reformed after a near fatal illness, they entered orders. First a Poor Clare, she later founded and ruled two Vallumbrosan convents. She is patron of Faenza.

Humphrey of Thérouanne, monk, died Thérouanne, 871. A Benedictine monk at Prüm in Trèves, in 856 the Emperor Lothair II appointed him bishop of Thérouanne, in what is now the Pas-de-Calais in France. He helped to rebuild the town after its destruction in 861 by Norsemen. Feast 8 March.

Hundred Thousand Martyrs, died Tbilisi, 1225. Georgian Church. Shah Gialal Ed-Din ordered the slaughter of all those who lived in the Georgian capital if they would not renounce their faith. The number of victims was swollen by all those who had taken refuge in Tbilisi. Feast 31 August.

Hunegundis (Hunegonde), founder of the monastery of Homblieres, born Lemblais, Picardy, died Homblieres, c. 690. Hunegundis was forced to marry by her parents, but at the same time vowed virginity and promised God to become a nun. She and her husband travelled to Rome, where the pope granted her request for the veil. Back in France, she founded the monastery of Homblieres (near Saint-Quentin). Feast 25 August.

Hunfried, Benedictine bishop, died Thérouanne, France, 8 March 870. Hunfried became a monk as a young man and, as abbot of Prüm, was elected bishop of Thérouanne in 856. Thérouanne was sacked by the Normans in 861, but after initial discouragement Hunfried saw it rebuilt. Subsequently he became abbot of Saint-Bertin, and attended a number of important Church councils held in France.

Huzi of Ihmim, martyr. Coptic Church.

Hwara, hegumenos, born Tella, sixth century. Syriac Church. The son of the village chief, Hwara was dumb, but was miraculously cured by **Ahha** as he was passing through, who also bestowed on the youth the monastic habit. Ahha and his companion Michael stayed in the village and founded a monastery there. Hwara succeeded Ahha as superior at the latter's death.

Hyacinth (Iaccho), Polish Dominican missionary, born duchy of Oppeln, 1185, died Krakow, 15 August 1257. He is said to have been of noble birth and met St **Dominic** on a visit to Rome in 1220. He was professed at Santa Sabina and became superior of a small group of brothers. He carried out missionary work in Denmark, Sweden and Norway and as far as the Black Sea. There is doubt about some of the facts of his life. Feast 17 August.

Hyacinth, see also **Protus and Hyacinth**.

Hyacintha Marescotti, member of the Third Order Regular of St Francis, born Vignanello, Papal States, 1585, died Viterbo, 30 January 1640. Unwillingly she entered the convent of St Bernardino in Viterbo and, after ten unhappy and unruly years, was persuaded by her confessor to renounce her behaviour and to follow a stricter regime. Thereafter she gave her life to devotion to the passion of Christ with harsh penances, poverty and humility which led to mystical prayer, and works of charity. She founded two congregations of Oblates of Mary to care for the sick and the

orphaned and, despite illness, persevered in her reformed way of life. She was beatified by Pope Benedict XIII in 1726, and canonized by Pius VII in 1807. Her reportedly incorrupt body lay in the convent in Viterbo until the church was destroyed by aerial bombardment. Feast 30 January.

Hyacinth of Amastris, died Amastris, Paphlagonia. Martyred for having cut down a sacred tree. Feast 17 July.

Hyacinth of Caesarea, martyr, born Caesarea, died c. 120. Said to have belonged to Trajan's court, and was martyred for refusing meat that had been offered to idols.

Hyersechius, monk, fourth century. Feast 7 August.

Hyginus, pope, died Rome, 142. Eusebius records that Hyginus reigned from 138 (the year of the death of **Telesphorus**) to 142, but the *Liber pontificalis* claims that he was a philosopher of Athens who reigned for four years and is buried in the Vatican near St Peter (modern excavations do not uphold this), while the Liberian catalogue says that his reign was 12 years long. The Roman martyrology lists him as a martyr, but this is unsupported by other sources. **Irenaeus** writes that during the reign of Hyginus, the Gnostic forerunners of Marcion, Valentinus and Cerdo arrived in Rome. Feast 11 January (suppressed).

Hypatius and Andrew, martyrs, born Lydia (?), died Constantinople, 735. Hypatius is said to have been a bishop and Andrew a priest. They were burned to death because of their opposition to iconoclasm. Feast 29 August.

Hypatius of Chalcedon, abbot, born Phrygia, died Chalcedon, c. 446. He was educated by his father, but ran away from home when he was 18 and went to Thrace, where he worked as a shepherd. There he began to live the life of an ascetic, and was reconciled with his father who came looking for him. He visited Constantinople, then went on to Chalcedon with two disciples. They found a deserted monastery and took it over. He was a champion of orthodoxy, and gave refuge to opponents of Nestorius, the heretical patriarch of Constantinople. He also vigorously opposed the proposal to hold the Olympic Games in Chalcedon. Feast 17 June.

Hypatius of Gangra, bishop, died Gangra, 325. After defending the divinity of Christ at the Council of Nicaea, he was martyred by stoning by a heretical mob on his return to his diocese. Feast 17 June.

Hyperechios, monk, died Egypt. One of the Desert Fathers. Feast 7 August.

Ia and Companions, born Greece (?), died Persia, 360. A slave, Ia died accompanied, it is said, by 9,000 other Christians in the reign of Shapur II. Feast 4 August.

Iazado, see **Christina**.

Iazdbozid, martyr, born Persia, died Duin, Armenia, 9 November 553. Armenian Church. He had been present at the martyrdom of **Gregory Manacihr**, and had been impressed by the martyr's constancy. He went to Armenia, where he received instruction in Christianity and was imprisoned. He was baptized in prison, shortly before his death by crucifixion.

Ibar, bishop, Ireland, *c.* 500. He is described either as a forerunner of **Patrick**, or as one of his disciples. He is known for his connection with Beg-Eire (Becc-Eriu, now Beggery) Island, Wexford harbour, where there was a monastic settlement perhaps with a school. Feast 23 April.

Ibrahim al-Gawhari, born Qalyub in the Delta, died 1795. Coptic Church. From a poor family, the son of a weaver, he came to be the chief finance officer of the Egyptian government. He was distinguished by his care of the poor, and of the Church, giving money to build or renovate churches and monasteries.

Ida of Boulogne, bl., noblewoman, born Bouillon, Belgium, *c.* 1040, died 13 April 1113. Ida was the daughter of Duke Godfrey II (Lower Lorraine) and niece of Pope Stephen IX. She married the count of Boulogne, Eustace, around 1057 and was the mother of King Baldwin of Jerusalem and of Godfrey of Bouillon. She was also grandmother of Mathilda, queen of England. Her life was noted for the practice of virtue and for her generosity, particularly to Saint-Bertin, Affligem and the convent at Nivelles. She was also a correspondent of **Anselm of Canterbury**. Feast 13 April.

Ida of Fischingen, died Fischingen, Switzerland, 1226. The legend says she was the wife of a dissolute count, who threw her from a window of his castle. She survived the fall and fled to a cave in the mountains, where she lived the life of a hermit. Many years later she was discovered, but refused to return to her remorseful husband. Because of the crowds of pilgrims who flocked to her cave, she eventually entered the convent at Fischingen. Feast 3 November.

Ida of Herzfeld, the great-granddaughter of the Emperor **Charlemagne**, died Herzfeld, Westphalia, 4 September 825. She was brought up at the court of Charlemagne and was eventually married to an Egbert (not of Kentish fame), but was widowed early and spent the rest of her life in good works, moving from her estate at Hofstadft to Herzfeld in Westphalia where her son Warin became a monk. She built a convent there and continued her exemplary life, helping the poor until her death.

Ida of Leeuw, bl., Cistercian nun, born Leeuw, Belgium, died convent of La Ramée, Brabant, Belgium, *c.* 1260. Ida entered the convent of La Ramée some time after 1216. There she was known for her love of learning and for certain mystical graces given her. During the 1500s and 1600s her cult spread throughout Belgium. Feast 30 October.

Ida of Louvain, bl., Cistercian nun, born Louvain, Belgium, early 1200s, died abbey of Roosendael, near Mechelen, Belgium, *c.* 1300. A nun at the abbey of Roosendael, Ida was said by her biographer to have been gifted with great mystical graces and by the stigmata. Although the historicity of much of her biography is doubtful, her feast, held on 13 April, was granted to the Benedictines as well as the Cistercians by Pope Clement XI in 1719.

Ida of Nivelles, bl., Cistercian nun, born Nivelles, Belgium, *c.* 1199, died convent of La Ramée, Brabant, Belgium, 11 December 1231. Ida originally joined the Kerkhem abbey, near Louvain, Belgium, when she was 16 and then moved with her community to La Ramée in 1215. She was reputed to have been given mystical graces and was devoted to the passion of Christ and the Blessed Sacrament. She is also said to have offered her sufferings for harassed priests and religious. After long suffering due to illness, she died at the age of 32. Feast 12 December.

Idesbald, bl., abbot, born Flanders, *c.* 1090, died Dune, 1167, cult approved 1894. Possibly a widower, he was ordained and became a canon of St Walburga's, Flanders, before joining the Cistercians at Dune, where he impressed the community by his sanctity and was elected abbot. Feast 18 April.

Iduberga (Ida, Itta), founder, born *c.* 592, died Nivelles, 8 May 652. Iduberga was born as daughter of a count of Aquitaine and married to the mayor of the palace, Pepin of Landen. (Two of her daughters, **Begga** and **Gertrude**, were later, after their mother, also declared to be saints). After the death of her husband, she founded the abbey of Nivelles (Belgium), freely giving herself and all her property to the endeavour. The first nuns for the new abbey came from Ireland; Iduberga was the first abbess, succeeded by her daughter Gertrude. Feast 8 May.

Ignatius, see also **Eneco**.

Ignatius Azevedo and Companions, martyrs, missionaries, Ignatius was born Oporto, Portugal, 1527, martyred off the Canary Islands, 15 July 1570. He joined the Society of Jesus in 1548 and became rector of the college at Braga before **Francis Borgia**, the general, appointed him visitor to the Jesuit missions in Brazil. Finding the missions flourishing, but short of manpower, he returned to Europe to recruit volunteers, and inspired 69 Spanish and Portuguese to come with him to Brazil. They sailed in two groups in 1570, but a Hugenot corsair, commanded by Jacques Sourie, captured them at sea, brutally slaughtered Ignacius and 39 companions on the *Santiago*, and threw their bodies into the ocean. They were beatified by **Pius IX** in 1854.

Ignatius Brianchaninov, spiritual writer and elder, born Vologda province, 5 February 1807, died Babaevsky monastery, 30 April 1867. Russian Church. Baptized Dimitri Aleksandrovic, he gave up a successful military carrier to become a monk, against the wishes of Emperor Nicholas I. In 1857 he was consecrated bishop, but after four years he retired due to ill-health and became a recluse at a remote monastery. There he wrote a large number of spiritual works both for monks and lay people. His theology was rather anti-Western for the time – certainly more so than his near contemporary, **Theophanes the Recluse**. His classics *The Arena* and *On the Prayer on Jesus* are available in English. Feast 30 April.

Ignatius, Carlampius and Panphilius, monks, died Pskov, fifteenth/sixteenth centuries. Russian Church. Three bothers, who all entered the Three Holy Fathers of the Church at Pskov, founded by **Euphrosyne of Pskov**. Ignatius was the first to enter, and became hegumenos, to be succeeded by Carlampius when Ignatius died *c.* 1470, then Panphilius followed as hegumenos after the death of Carlampius, *c.* 1495. Another brother also entered, even though he was married – his wife took a vow of chastity – and so did their father, after his wife's death.

Ignatius Delgado and Companions, martyrs, died 1838. Clemente Ignazio Delgado y Cebrián was born in 1761 or 1762 near Zaragoza. He became a Dominican and joined the mission in Tonkin

(Vietnam) in 1790. He was made coadjutor bishop in 1794 and vicar apostolic of East Tonkin in 1799. When anti-Christian persecution began again in 1838, he went into hiding along with his coadjutor Domingo Henáres. However, they were captured and put into cages, and Ignatius died of exposure before his sentence of beheading could be carried out. Domingo and Bl. Francis Chien, who was captured with him, were beheaded on 25 June 1838. Feast 12 July.

Ignatius Falzon, bl., born Valetta, Malta, 1813, died there, 1 July 1865. The son of a judge, he and all three of his brothers studied law: two of them became priests. But although Ignatius received minor orders and studied theology – he also had a degree in canon law – he felt himself unworthy of the priesthood, and instead taught catechism, and had a particular apostolate among the soldiers and sailors stationed on, or passing through, the island of Malta.

Ignatius of Antioch, bishop, born Antioch, died Rome, 107. Bishop from c. 69, we otherwise only know something about the end of his life. As bishop of Antioch he was arrested and taken to Rome. During this journey he visited several Christian communities in Asia Minor, and met **Polycarp** at Smyrna and exchanged letters. Seven of these letters have been preserved. They contain vestiges of an early theology of martyrdom and of a triple ordo (bishop, priest and deacon) in which the bishop has the central role. He died in the amphitheatre at Rome, thrown to wild beasts. Feast 17 October.

Ignatius of Beloozero, and Dositheus, monks, sixteenth century. Russian Church. Two disciples of **Cyril of Beloozero**. Ignatius was renowned for his life of silence, while Dositheus was a staunch defender of the tradition of monasticism he had received from Cyril, for which he suffered greatly from his religious superiors.

Ignatius of Constantinople, patriarch, born Constantinople, c. 799, died there, 23 October 877. Baptized Nicetas, he was the son of Emperor Michael I, but was forced to become a monk when his father was deposed in 813, and castrated. He

was elected patriarch in 846. He was deposed in 858 but reinstated in 867. Feast 23 October.

Ignatius of Gotfejski, metropolitan, born 1715, died Mariopul, on the Sea of Azov, 1786. Ukrainian Church, Patriarchate of Moscow. He was the metropolitan serving the 25,000 Greeks in the Crimea who were moved into Russian territory in 1774. He and they eventually became Russian citizens.

Ignatius of Laconi, Capuchin friar, born Laconi, Sardinia, 10 December 1701, died Cagliari, Italy, 11 May 1781. Francis Ignatius Vincent Peis came from a poor peasant family; he never learned to read or write. Even as a child he was known for his piety, which eventually led him to join the Capuchins in Cagliari in 1721 as a lay brother. Over the course of the next 60 years he served the order through the seeking of alms and works of charity, and miracles were also attributed to him. He was canonized in 1951. Feast 12 May.

Ignatius of Lomska, monk, died Vadoza, 28 December 1591. Russian Church. He became a monk at the monastery founded by **Cyril of Beloozero**, but, seeking greater solitude, he moved to a place near the city of Lomska. In search of still greater solitude, he moved again with a few disciples to Vadoza, on the river Sarja.

Ignatius of Loyola, founder of the Society of Jesus (the Jesuits), born into a noble family, castle of Loyola, Spain, 1491, died Rome, 31 July 1556. Ignatius (more correctly, Iñigo) spent his youth in the service of the treasurer to the royal house of Castile, and then in the service of the duke of Najera. He was technically a cleric, although not a priest, and served mainly on diplomatic missions. He was, however, caught up in the battle for Pamplona and had his leg broken by a French cannon ball on 20 May 1521. During his convalescence he was converted, chiefly by reading the life of Christ by Ludolph the Carthusian, and spend a year as a hermit near Montserrat, composing what became his *Spiritual Exercises*. He went on pilgrimage to Jerusalem, then spent more than a decade studying, finally at Paris, where he gathered a group of six like-minded individuals, including **Francis Xavier**, who took vows together in a chapel on Montmartre on 15 August 1534. Two years later they gathered again at Venice, hoping to travel to Jerusalem, but as this proved impossible they put themselves at the disposition of the pope. They were ordained in 1537. The bull to create a religious order was approved by Pope Paul III in September 1540, and Ignatius was elected the first superior general of the Society the following year. He spent the rest of his life running the order from its headquarters in what is now the Gesù in Rome.

Ignatius of Melitene, bishop, died 991. Syriac Church. Known as 'the pilgrim' because he was accustomed to visit regularly the monasteries around Edessa. Feast 15 October.

Ignatius of Methymna, bishop, born Pharanx, Lesbos, c. 1492, died Methymna, Lesbos, 14 October 1566. Byzantine Church. The son of a priest, he married and had children, but his wife and children died in a plague. He then became a monk, building two monasteries, one for men, the other for women, on his property, and endowing them. He was elected bishop of Methymna in 1531.

Ignatius of Ostrov and Companions, died Ostrov, sixteenth century. Russian Church. They were disciples of **Alexander of Svir**.

Ignatius of Rostov, bishop, died Rostov, 28 May 1288. He had been archimandrite of the monastery of the Epiphany at Rostov before being elected bishop in 1262. Feast 28 May.

Ignatius of Santhia, born Santhia, near Vercelli, 5 June 1686, died Turin, 22 September 1770. Baptized Lorenzo Maurizio Belvisotti, he attended the local seminary and was ordained priest. He refused to take a parish, however, preferring instead to join the Capuchins under the name of Ignatius. He worked in his home town as a confessor and spiritual director for 25 years, then as novice master. In c. 1756 he moved to Turin, where he taught catechism and gave retreats. He also wrote a book of meditations.

Ignatius of Simonov, see **Bartholomew, John and Ignatius of Simonov**.

Ignatius of the Kievan Cave Monastery, archimandrite, died Kiev, 1453. Russian Church. Renowned for his concern for the sick and his powers of healing. Feast 28 August.

Ignatius of Zagora, martyr, born Tirnovo, died Constantinople, 8 October 1814. Byzantine Church. Baptized John, his family moved when he was young to Philippopolis in Bulgaria. He thought of becoming a monk and entered a monastery, but left after six years and returned home. At this point his father was conscripted into the Turkish army, but refused to fight, and was executed. His wife and children were forced to become Muslims, but John fled to Bucharest. With a companion, he set off from there with the intention of going to Mount Athos, but was arrested by Turkish troops and forced to promise to become a Muslim. He eventually reached Mount Athos, after a time entering the monastery of Timios Podromos. Once, during a visit to Thessalonika, he witnessed a martyrdom. Wishing also to undergo martyrdom, with permission of his spiritual director he travelled to Constantinople, where he said that the promises he had made to become a Muslim were made under duress, and were not binding. He was subsequently executed.

Igor of Cenigov, prince, born 1080, died Kiev, 19 September 1147. Russian Church. He became grand prince of Kiev in 1146, but that same year the people rose against him and he was deposed. He asked permission from the usurper to enter a monastery, finally settling at the monastery of St Theodore in Kiev. However, the anger of the population had not abated, and a mob rushed into the church of the monastery and killed him.

Ildefonsus, bishop, born Toledo, died there, 23 January 667. He studied at Seville under **Isidore**, then entered the monastery of Agli, of which he became abbot. With his inheritance he founded a convent for women religious. He participated in the eighth and ninth Councils of Toledo, the city of which he was archbishop between 657 and 667. His *De viris illustribus* is a colourless continuation of earlier homonymous works. His *De perpetua virginitate Sanctae Mariae* made him the founder of the Spanish cult of Mary. Feast 23 January.

Ildefonsus Schuster, bl., abbot and cardinal, born Rome, 18 January 1880, died Milan, 30 August 1954. He was baptized Ludovico Alfredo Luigi, taking the name Ildefonsus when he became a Benedictine in 1898. He was ordained in 1904, and four years later became novice master, a post he held until 1916. He had a particular interest in history and especially liturgy, lecturing on both in Rome at various institutes. In 1918, after holding a succession of posts in the Cassinese Congregation, he was elected abbot of St Paul Without the Walls. In 1929 he became archbishop of Milan, and a cardinal. He was an energetic diocesan bishop, visiting all the parishes of his diocese several times. He was also – or became – a severe critic of the Fascist regime in Italy, refusing to bless Italian troops when Italy entered the war. He showed himself very hostile to Nazi Germany, and gave refuge to Jews fleeing the persecution, although discouraging them from receiving baptism under duress. After the war he was accused of being sympathetic to Fascism – but then so had the vast majority of Italians, and he had been one of the first to become critical of it. After the war he struggled to restore the spiritual life of the diocese through Catholic Action, through opposition to Communism, and through charitable work.

Ilga, bl., hermit, died *c.* 1115. Ilga (or Hilga or Helga) gave her name to a spring in Schwarzenberg in the forest of Bregenz (Austria), near the site of her hermitage. The spring is said to cure diseases of the eye. Traditionally, she is also the sister of Bl. **Merbot** and Bl. **Diedo**. Nothing else is known about her. Feast 8 June.

Ilia Ciavciavadze ('the Just'), born Qvareli, eastern Georgia, 1837, died 8 November 1907. Georgian Church. He came from a princely family which had fallen on hard times, and was brought up, after the death of his parents, by an aunt. He studied at Tbilisi, then in the faculty of law at St Petersburg. It was there that he began to write poetry, protesting against the social injustice suffered especially by the people of Georgia. On his return home he kept up this literary output, founded various journals, and played a considerable part in the civic life of his country, becoming, among other things, president of the Georgian national bank. In 1906 he was elected to the Russian

parliament. He was assassinated the following year. His writings are pervaded with a strong spirituality, and he was declared a saint in 1987 by the Georgian Orthodox Church. Feast 18 June.

Ilie Iorest, bishop, born Transylvania, 1600, died 12 March 1678. Romanian Church. Although born in Transylvania, he went to study in Moldavia, and there entered the monastery of Putna, becoming its abbot *c.* 1625. In 1640 he became archbishop and metropolitan of the Orthodox Church in Transylvania, with his seat in Alba Julia. The local potentate was Calvinist, and had wanted a metropolitan more sympathetic to his Protestant views. Ilie, however, had been imbued with Orthodox Romanian culture in his monastery, and energetically promoted this in his diocese. There was, therefore, a clash between the civil and the ecclesiastical authorities, and a slanderous campaign was started against the archbishop, including accusations of immorality. His property was confiscated and he was put in prison, only being released after nine months on the payment of a large bribe to the prince, and on condition he left Transylvania. He therefore returned to the monastery of Putna for the rest of his life. Feast 24 April.

Illtyd, monk, founder of the monastic school at Llantwit Major, Glamorganshire, *c.* 450 – *c.* 525. Illtyd was a Welshman who, by one account, went to Britain, joined King Arthur's court, and was later converted by St Cladoc in Glamorgan. He was assisted by the chieftain Merchion to build a church and monastery which became a centre for scholarship. Legend has it that the school was originally on an island which Illtyd miraculously rejoined to the mainland. This legend may stem from Illtyd's teaching of practical skills as well as religion, such as improved ploughing practices and how to reclaim land from the sea. Feast 6 November.

Imelda, bl., born Bologna, *c.* 1321, died Valdipietra, 12 May 1333. Of noble birth (she was a Lambertini), she entered the Dominican cloister at Valdipietra. At the time holy communion was only given from the age of 12. Imelda, being only 11, stayed in her place while the nuns received communion. It is reported that the Host appeared above her head. The priest then gave her first communion, at which point she died in the rapture of thanksgiving. Patroness of first communicants from 1910.

Imma (Emma, Imina, Immina), Benedictine abbess, died *c.* 570. The biography of Imma (twelfth century) says that she was the daughter of the duke of Thuringia, Hetan II, who erected a church in Würzburg on the Burgberg (Marienburg). Imma began a monastery there, then moved to another location at Karlsburg-on-Main (Karlstadt). Feast 25 November.

Indes, Domna and Companions, martyrs, died Nicomedia, 303. Feast 28 December.

Indract, born Ireland, died possibly Huish Episcopi, seventh/eighth century. He was apparently the son of an Irish king, gentle and holy, murdered by brigands with several companions and buried in Glastonbury Old Church. He may have been one of the then numerous wandering pilgrims, or *pergrini*. Feast 8 May.

Indrechtach, martyr, died near Glastonbury, 854. Celtic chronicles record that Indrechtach was an abbot of Iona martyred by Saxons while travelling to Rome. **William of Malmesbury** also records the story of a certain **Indract** (see above) who was murdered near Glastonbury while returning from Rome, but opinion is divided over whether or not the two are identical. Feast 5 February.

Ine, king of the West Saxons, died Rome, 726. Established new laws and encouraged religious development by founding monasteries, notably Glastonbury, and by giving money to those already in existence. He abdicated and went with his wife, Ethelburga, on pilgrimage and to live out their days in Rome. While there, they founded a home for English pilgrims, which it has been claimed was the origin of the English College. It is thought that Ine and Ethelburga are buried in the church of San Spirito in Sassia.

Iñigo, see **Eneco**.

Innocencio Canoura Arnau, martyr, born Cecilia de la Valle de Oro, 10 March 1887, died Turon,

Asturias, 9 October 1934. Baptized Manuel, he took the name Inocencio de la Imaculada when he entered the Passionist Order. He was ordained priest in September 1920. He was a learned man, who had taught a number of different subjects, and was in Turon to hear confessions of the students of the Christian Brothers' school. He was arrested with the other **Martyrs of Asturias** by a group of rebel soldiers, and executed by firing squad.

Innocent I, pope from 21 December 401, died Rome, 12 March 417. A man of great ability and firm resolution in asserting the powers of the papal office, Innocent succeeded his father, **Anastasius I**. He insisted on a uniform discipline in the Western Church based on Roman ways and custom. He endorsed the decision on the Pelagian controversy taken at Carthage in 416, and so informed the fathers of the Numidian synod, **Augustine** being one of their number. He tried to defend his friend **John Chrysostom** against Theophilus of Alexandria, but could not save him from exile. Feast 28 July (suppressed).

Innocent V, bl., born Tarantaise, Burgundy, pope from 21 January to 22 June 1276, died Rome. Pierre de Tarantaise became a Dominican, held a chair in theology at Paris, and collaborated with **Albertus Magnus** and **Thomas Aquinas** in preparing a new Rule of studies for his order. A friend of the great Franciscan **Bonaventure**, he preached his funeral sermon. He succeeded **Gregory X**, and confirmed Charles of Anjou in his office of imperial vicar of Tuscany. He resumed Gregory's negotiations with Byzantine emperor Michael VIII Palaeologus to implement Church union, and demanded that Greek clergy take personal oaths accepting the *Filioque* and the primacy of the pope; but he died as the envoys bearing these stiff demands were boarding the ship at Ancona. Feast 22 June.

Innocent XI, bl., born Benedetto Odescalchi at Como, 19 May 1611, pope from 21 September 1676 to 12 August 1689, died Rome. Greatly loved for his piety and generosity while bishop of Novara, Louis XIV of France opposed his election to succeed Clement X, and he had to struggle continuously against the absolutism of Louis in Church affairs. For similar reasons, he disapproved of the measures taken by James II of England to restore Roman Catholicism, and especially of the Declaration of Indulgence, which allowed full liberty of worship. A process of canonization begun by Clement XI in 1714 was long delayed because Innocent had shown favour to the Jansenists.

Innocent of Alaska see **Innocent of Moscow**.

Innocent of Berzo, bl., born Giovanni Scalvinoni in Brescia, Italy, 19 March 1844, died Bergamo, 3 March 1890, beatified 1961. Ordained in 1867, he became a Capuchin monk in 1874. Profoundly humble, and happiest in the background, he was esteemed for his direct answers when consulted on problems of moral theology.

Innocent of Chersonesus, born Elec, 15 December 1800, died Odessa, 26 May 1857. Ukrainian Orthodox Church. The son of a priest, he was baptized Ivan Alekseevic Borisov. He studied theology, including in Kiev, and became a monk in 1823 and was ordained priest in the same year. He taught both at St Petersburg and Kiev. As a professor of theology he had progressive views, taking much from Protestant authors, a fact which worried the Church authorities. In 1837 he became bishop of Zigirinsk, assistant bishop in the diocese of Kiev, then Vologda, then Char'kov and finally in 1848 Chersonesus, with his seat at Odessa. He was an avid student of the ancient history of his see, and of the region, built monasteries and published several theological works. He was particularly renowned for his talent as a preacher.

Innocent (Kulchitsky) of Irkutsk, missionary and bishop, born Chernigov, 1680, died Irkutsk, 27 November 1731. Russian Church. He was consecrated bishop in 1721 for Peking, but was refused entry by the Chinese emperor. He was then sent to the new Irkutsk diocese in central Siberia where he renewed the missionary work and trained translators. His labours and the climate eventually proved fatal. He was canonized in 1804 and his relics were recently recovered and re-enshrined (1990). Often called the 'apostle of Siberia'. Feast 26 November.

Innocent of Komel, monk, died Komel, 1521. Russian Church. A disciple of **Nilus Sorski**, after the latter's death he founded a monastery at Komel. He had first taken vows in the monastery of **Cyril of Beloozero**. Feast 19 March.

Innocent of Le Mans, bishop, died *c*. 542. Probably became bishop of Le Mans in 524 and was at the Synods of Orleans in 533 and 541. He did much in his diocese to restore the cathedral, churches and convents. Feast 19 June.

Innocent of Moscow, metropolitan, born Anginskoe, Russia, 26 August 1797, died Moscow, 31 March 1879. Russian Church. Baptized John Venjaminov Popov, he was the son of a sacristan, but after his father's death, when he was only seven, he was brought up by an uncle who was a deacon. He studied in the seminary of Irkutsk, married and served a church in the city. In 1823, however, he left his family and became a missionary in the Aleutian islands. He established himself on the island of Sitka and worked from there, learning the language well – he produced a grammar – and translating and writing for the people of the islands. In 1840, just after the death of his wife, he took monastic vows and was appointed bishop with responsibility for the Aleutians, and effectively for the whole of Alaska. A decade later he was raised to the rank of archbishop. After Alaska was ceded to the USA in 1869 the see was moved to San Francisco, but from 1851 it had been at Jakuzia, another new territory for the archbishop. He was looking forward to retirement when he learned that in 1868 he had been nominated metropolitan of Moscow. Among his achievements in Moscow was the establishment of a missionary society to serve the needs of Russian Orthodox missionaries. Perhaps the greatest of all Orthodox missionaries. His primary catechism, *An Indication of the Way into the Kingdom of Heaven*, was written in the Fox Aleutian dialect and from that was later translated into Russian and English.

Innocent of the Kievan Cave Monastery, monk. Russian Church.

Innocent of Tortona, bishop, born Tortona, Italy, died there, *c*. 380. According to his legends he was imprisoned during the persecution of Diocletian and later fled to Rome, where he was made a deacon and later bishop, possibly the first, of Tortona. Feast 17 April.

Innocent, Sebastia and Companions, martyrs, died Sirmium. Thirty-two Christians put to death at Sirmium (Mitrovica in Serbia). Feast 4 July.

Ionatus of Cambrai, c. 690. Feast 1 August.

Irenaeus and Abundius, martyrs, died Rome, 258 (?). They are said to have been drowned in a sewer. Feast 23 August.

Irenaeus of Lyon, bishop, born Asia Minor (?), c. 140 (?), died Lyon, c. 202 (?). He may have lived in Rome for some time. In 177 he was presbyter of the Greek-speaking community of Lyon (France). During a persecution he was sent to Rome with the *Letter of the Martyrs of Lyon and Vienne*. After his return he became bishop of Lyon and intervened to exhort Pope **Victor** (189–98) to patience with the bishops of Asia in their disagreement about the date of Easter. His main work is the *Adversus Haereses*, a refutation of diverse Gnostic currents. He is believed to have been martyred, but there is no evidence of this. Feast 28 June.

Irenaeus of Sirmium, bishop, died Sirmium, 304. Imprisoned by the governor of Pannonia, and then executed. Feast 25 March.

Irenaeus, Pellegrinus and Irene, martyrs, died Thessalonika, c. 300. Feast 5 May.

Irenarchus, monk, born Focsani, Moldavia, 1771, died Nazareth, 26 December 1859. Romanian Church. Baptized John Roset, at the age of 18 he became a monk at the monastery of Neamt, where he worked in the printing house. For 12 years he lived as a hermit, and then received permission to visit Mount Athos. He stayed there only two years, then returned to Moldavia where he went to the metropolitan for permission to found a monastery. The metropolitan ordained him priest, and he established a new monastery at Horaita. In 1838 he left Horaita and went to the Holy Land. He spent two years in Jerusalem and five in Nazareth. Just before he entered the monastery of Neamt he had a vision of Mount Tabor, and he was determined to

rebuild the church on the mountain. He died before it was completed.

Irenarchus and Acacius, see **Acacius and Irenarchus**.

Irene, see also **Irenaeus, Pellegrinus and Irene**

Irene, empress, born Athens, c. 752, died Lesbos, 9 August 803. Byzantine Church. She married the Byzantine Emperor Leo IV in 769. On the death of her husband, she became co-emperor and guardian of their son Constantine VI. She was a devoted iconodule, and her husband is said to have refused to sleep with her after discovering two icons in her room. During her regency she weakened the empire by removing competent generals who were iconoclasts. She instigated the Council of Nicaea of 787, which restored icons. She was briefly deposed (790–92), and in 797 dethroned and blinded her son, allowing her to reign alone as empress for five years, the first woman to achieve this in Byzantium. In 802, however, she herself was deposed and exiled to the islands of Prinkipo, and then Lesbos. Feast 9 August.

Irene, empress, born Hungary, died Bithynia, 1134. Byzantine Church. The daughter of the king of Hungary, she married the Byzantine Emperor John II Commenus in 1105, and founded the monastery of the Pantocrator. She herself became a nun at the end of her life, taking the name Xeni. Feast 13 August.

Irene of Chrysobalanton, hegumena, born Cappadocia, died Constantinople, ninth century. Byzantine Church. She was brought to Constantinople as a possible wife for the emperor, but instead entered the convent of Chrysobalanton, and for the final 20 years of her life ruled it as its abbess. Feast 28 July.

Irene of Kasino, see **Basil of Kasino and Irene of Kasino**.

Irene of Murom, died Murom, c. 1129. Russian Church. Wife of Prince Constantine Jaroslavic of Murom. Feast 23 June.

Irene of Portugal, nun, seventh century. She is mentioned in the tenth-century Antiphony of Léon as Virgo in Scallabi Castro. References appear in later vitae where she is described as a beautiful nun of noble birth in Thomar. She rejected the advances of her spiritual director, who gave her a potion to make her appear pregnant. A jealous former suitor had her killed. Her body is said to have floated downriver and to have become miraculously entombed in a pool at Scallabis on the Tagus in 653. The town changed its name to Santarem (Santa Irene, Ira, Eriã). Feast 20 October.

Irene of Thermes, martyr, born Thermes, Lesbos, 1452, died there, 9 April 1463. Byzantine Church. The daughter of the mayor of her home town, she was burned alive for her faith.

Irene of Thessalonika, martyr, died Thessalonika 304. Put to death with her two sisters **Chionia** and **Agape**, although Irene was sent to a brothel for two days before her death, but, according to the story, no one would approach her. Feast 3 April.

Irenion, bishop, died Gaza, 389. Bishop of Gaza in the fourth century. Feast 16 December.

Irinarchus of Rostov ('the Recluse'), born Kondakovo, 1548, died Rostov, 1616. Russian Church. Baptized Elias, he manifested a desire for a monastic life at the age of six. After the death of his father the family moved to Rostov. There he entered the monastery of Boris and Gleb, where he had a vision calling him to the life of a recluse. He locked himself into his cell, leaving only once to go to Moscow. Feast 13 January.

Irinarchus of Solovki, hegumenos, died Solovki, 17 July 1628. Russian Church. Little or nothing is known of his early life. The Solovki monastery was in a very exposed position, open to attack by Swedes and Danes, among others. He entered into a treaty with the former, but the latter remained a problem. The Tsar sent a large body of troops, and the monastery was transformed into a fortress with the help of Irinarchus, although with deleterious effects on monastic discipline. He withdrew into solitude for the final two years of his life. His tomb became a place of many miracles. Feast 9 August.

Irineus of Scete, monk, died Gaza (?), sixth century. He fled to Gaza from Scete in 570 after the incursions of the Berbers.

Irmengard (Ermengard), abbess, born Munich, 832, died Chiemsee, 16 July 866. Of royal birth, her father Louis the German made her abbess of the Benedictine convent at Buchau and then of the royal abbey at Chiemsee. She was said to have led a life of penance and virtue, devoting her life to the women in her care. She is buried in the monastery church at Chiemsee. Feast 17 July.

Irmgardis of Cologne, countess of Aspel, died on pilgrimage to Rome, *c.* 1085. Irmgardis was an heiress who spent her fortune founding cloisters, churches and charitable institutions. Much legendary material is told of her life, and she might have resided at Süchteln (where a chapel was erected to her honour) before moving to Cologne to spend the rest of her life doing works of charity. Her personality is somewhat in dispute, often confused (perhaps correctly) with Irmentrud of Aspel. Feast 4 September.

Irmina, abbess, died Weissenberg, 24 December 710. The biography written in the 1100s is considered unreliable, but portrays Irmina as the daughter of Dagobert I. She was engaged to be married, but her fiancé died before the wedding, so Irmina became a nun. She is thought to have founded the monastery of Ohren (Trier), where she was abbess. Irmina was generous to English and Irish monks, giving land to **Willibrord** and his monks for their monastery of Echternach.

Irodion of Iloezero, founder, died lake Ilo, 28 September 1541. Russian Church. A disciple of **Cornelius of Komel**, after Cornelius's death he left the monastery of Komel and established a hermitage by lake Ilo. He served as pastor to the local inhabitants, and his tomb was reputed to be a place of miracles.

Isaac, bishop and martyr, born Persia, died there, 339. Bishop of Beth-Seleucia, he suffered martyrdom with **Shapur** and others. Feast 30 November.

Isaac Jogues, martyr, born Orleans, 1607, died Ossernenon (Upper New York State), 18 October

1646. He joined the Jesuits in 1624 and went to Canada to work among the Huron 12 years later. He was taken captive in 1642, tortured and mutilated (and **René Goupil** who was with him was killed) by the Huron, but he was eventually set free and went back to France. In 1644 he returned. He was on a peace mission to the Iroquois when he was tomahawked to death. Feast, with **John de Brébeuf**, 19 October.

Isaac of al-Asmunayn, martyr, born al-Asmunayn. Coptic Church.

Isaac of Alexandria, patriarch, died Alexandria, 5 November 689. Coptic Church. He came from a well-to-do family, and rose high in the Byzantine civil service in Egypt, but when he was about to marry he fled his family and went to Scete to become a monk at the monastery of St Macarius, although he later returned to that of Terenuti to be nearer his family again. His fame reached the ears of the patriarch who appointed him his secretary, but Isaac wanted to remain a monk and returned to the monastery. As the patriarch was dying, however, he nominated Isaac as his successor. Although the election was disputed, he was made patriarch in 686. At first he enjoyed good relations with the Muslim governor, but they fell out when Isaac tried to bring peace to feuding Christian kings in Ethiopia, a feud the governor in Egypt wished to foment. There was a plot against Isaac's life, but it was discovered in time.

Isaac of Constantinople, abbot, died Constantinople, *c.* 410. He left his hermitage to publicly oppose the Arian Emperor Valens, denouncing him many times. He was imprisoned and released after Valens's death. Then revered and attracting disciples, he founded the first monastery in Constantinople, later called the Dalmatian monastery. Feast 30 May.

Isaac of Córdoba, martyr, born Córdoba, died there, 852. He became an official under the Moorish government of Córdoba, but then retired to Tabanos monastery for a time. After a time, however, he returned to the city to preach Christianity, was arrested and executed for denouncing

Mohammed. See also **Martyrs of Córdoba**. Feast 3 June.

Isaac of Dalmaton, see **Isaac of Constantinople**.

Isaac of Egypt, martyr, died 306. Feast 1 May.

Isaac of Harran, patriarch, died Harran, *c.* 760. Syriac Church. He became first bishop of Harran and then patriarch under the patronage of the local Muslim governor. The governor, however, then turned against him, had him strangled and his body thrown into the Euphrates.

Isaac of Hurin, monk, born Hurin on the Delta. Coptic Church. He worked as a shepherd, but gave his earnings to the poor. He later became a monk, although he interrupted his monastic career to help his father. When he returned to the monastery he became an anchorite.

Isaac of Langres ('the Good'), bishop, born early ninth century, died Langres, France, 880. Following the destruction by Normans of the monastery of Saint-Bénigne, Isaac was made responsible for its reconstruction. He is known to have taken part in the Councils of Soissons and Troyes, and from 859 until his death he was bishop of Langres. Feast 18 July.

Isaac of Monte Luco, monk, died *c.* 550. Isaac was a Syrian who, to escape the monophysite persecution, came to Italy, where he embraced the life of a hermit on Monte Luco. After seeing a vision of the Virgin, he established a 'laura'-like community of trained disciples. He was known for his gifts of prophecy and miracles. Feast 11 April.

Isaac of Nineveh, bishop, born Beit Qatraye (Qatar?), died monastery of Rabban Shabbor, seventh century. Assyrian Church. He became a monk, perhaps at Bet'Abe in the Marga, but was made bishop of Nineveh. He remained in this post for only five months, possibly because of theological difficulties with his fellow bishops. He withdrew to a monastery in Huzistan, and eventually to Rabban Shabbor. He wrote a number of works, especially on mysticism, which were very influential far outside the Church of which he was a member.

Isaac of Nitria, monk, died *c.* 400. Feast 14 May.

Isaac of Obnora, see **Ephraim of Obnora, with Dionysius, Jerome and Isaac**.

Isaac of Optina I, born Kursk, 31 May 1810, died Optina, 22 August 1894. Russian Church. Baptized Ivan Ivanovic Antimonov, for a time he worked in his father's business, but, refusing to marry, he entered the hermitage attached to the monastery of Optina in 1846, becoming a priest in 1858. In 1862 he was declared superior of the community by the bishop, despite the fact that he was not the monks' choice. However, he managed by his gentleness and humility to overcome the opposition, and ruled the community for 30 years. Feast 11 October.

Isaac of Optina II, martyr, born Ostrov, died Tula, 8 January 1938. Russian Church. Baptized Ivan Nikolaevic Bobrikov, his father entered the monastery of Optina, and so did he in 1884, becoming a priest in 1898. He became superior of the hermitage of Optina in 1914, and archimandrite. As a consequence of the Revolution in Russia, the monastery was closed in 1918. He was twice arrested, the second time, in 1923, being deported to Kozel'sk. Again arrested in 1930, he was deported to Belev. He was arrested again in 1937 and accused of starting a clandestine monastery. He was shot in prison in Tula. Feast 11 October.

Isaac of Scete, monk, fourth century. Coptic Church. Noted for his love of silence and of solitude.

Isaac of Tabriz (Yusuf the Persian), born Tabriz, died Samaxi, 18 April 1417. Armenian Church. Born into a Muslim family, he was converted by a vision of Christ in glory, requested baptism, and was given the name of Isaac. He was arrested almost immediately, but was thought to be mad, and released. He spent the next 40 years preaching Christianity among Muslims, making use of his knowledge of the Koran until finally, at Samaxi, in the foothills of the Caucasus, he was rearrested and condemned to death by stoning.

Isaac the Great (Sahak), catholicos, born 345, died Ashtishat, 440. Isaac was the son of **Nerses** and a descendant of **Gregory the Illuminator**. He studied at Constantinople, where he married. After the death of his wife at a young age, he became a monk. He became the tenth catholicos of the Armenian Church *c.* 389. Isaac gained from Constantinople the recognition of the metropolitical rights of the Armenian Church, and terminated the dependence of the Church upon Caesarea. He was active in national Armenian literature. With **Mesrop** he also translated much of the Bible into Armenian. In 425 he was deposed by the Persians, but was allowed to regain his see due to popular support. Feast 13 May.

Isabelle of France, bl., born France, March 1225, died Longchamp, Paris, France, 23 February 1270. The daughter of French King Louis VIII, Isabelle refused all her suitors, including a politically expedient marriage to the son of the Holy Roman Emperor, in order to devote her life to charity and hospital work. This work was often done through the Franciscan Order, which she favoured highly, although she refused to join. She also founded a convent of Poor Clares at Longchamp, Paris, and even drafted its Rule. Feast 26 February.

Isaiah, monk, born Wollo, Ethiopia. Ethiopian Church.

Isaiah, monk, sixteenth century. Russian Church. See **Alexander, Joachim and Isaiah**.

Isaiah of Aleppo, monk. Syriac Church. Very little is known of him beyond stories of miracles and visions. He is said to have been a disciple of **Awgen**, but before that to have been married to Henna, with whom he lived chastely for three years before he became a monk. He founded a monastery, but it is not certain which. Feast 15 October.

Isaiah of Edessa, bishop, seventh century. Syriac Church. He was not at first acceptable to the faithful because he was approved by the Persians. He recovered his authority somewhat, however, when he refused communion to the Emperor Heraclius, whom he rebuked for upholding the teaching of the Council of Chalcedon. Feast 4 August.

Isaiah of Krakow (Isaiah Boner), Augustinian friar, born Krakow, Poland, *c.* 1400, died Krakow, 8 February 1471. Isaiah studied at the University of Padua, where he subsequently became a lecturer in theology. He was visitor of the province of Poland in 1438, and in 1452 vicar general of Bavaria. He also taught at the University of Krakow in the 1460s. During his lifetime he was much venerated for his sanctity and Christian character, and although never officially beatified, his name bears the prefix 'blessed' among Augustinians.

Isaiah of Rostov, bishop, born Kiev, died 1090. He entered the Kievan Cave monastery, but was later appointed hegumenos of the monastery of St Demetrius in Kiev itself. In 1078, however, he became bishop of Rostov, where he was zealous in evangelizing the surrounding region. Feast 15 May.

Isaiah of Scete, monk, died Gaza, 11 August 491. Coptic Church. He became a monk in the desert of Scete, and then moved to Gaza. But nothing else is certain about him.

Isaiah of Sija and Nicanor, monks, sixteenth/seventeenth centuries. Russian Church. It is unclear where these two monks lived, except that it was near Archangel, possibly at the mouth of the river Ruc'ej. Feast 30 May.

Isaiah of the Kievan Cave Monastery, died Kiev, 1115. Russian Church. He practised silence and hard work. Feast 15 May.

Isaiah the Egyptian, monk, born Egypt, died Gaza, 488. Syriac Church. He became a monk in the desert of Scete, but then moved to Palestine, founding a monastery near Gaza. Feast 25 November.

Isaiah the Servant, died near Moscow, seventeenth century. Church of the Old Believers. A servant of a boyar called Saltykov, he remained faithful to the traditional Russian liturgy, and persuaded his master likewise. He was burned to death for his convictions.

Isaurus, Innocent and Companions, martyrs, died Apollonia, Macedonia, *c.* 270 (?). They took refuge in a cave to escape persecution, and there continued to teach Christianity, but were discovered and beheaded. Feast 17 June.

Ischyrion, martyr, died Egypt (Alexandria?), 250. An assistant to a magistrate in Egypt, he refused to offer pagan sacrifice and was executed. Feast 22 December.

Isfried, Premonstratensian bishop, died probably 15 June *c.* 1204. Isfried was a canon and provost before becoming bishop of the new diocese of Ratzeburg, Germany, in 1180. He devoted himself to the conversion of the heathen tribes east of the Elbe and was called the 'soul' of the Premonstratensians in north Germany. He also served as confessor to Henry the Lion. He is said to have practised great self-denial and miracles were ascribed to him even while he was alive.

Isidora the Fool, died Egyptian desert, *c.* 365. A nun of the convent of Tabennesi in Egypt, she was regarded as foolish by her community, but fled to the desert when she came to be thought of as holy. Feast 1 May.

Isidore Bakanja, bl., martyr, born Ikengo in what was then the Belgian Congo, died Busira, Belgian Congo, 15 August 1909. He was a convert to Catholicism in 1906, and while living in Busira became the servant of one of the directors of a mining company operating in the region. He went with his employer to Itiki, where he was badly beaten and kept in chains by a local manager who was deeply hostile to Catholicism. Although his employer took him back to Busira, he died of his injuries.

Isidore de Loor, bl., born Vrasene, Belgium, 188, died Kortrijk, 6 October 1916. The devout son of peasant farmers, at the age of 26 he joined the Passionist Order, taking his vows as a lay brother in September 1908. He served for some years as cook, porter and gardener at Wezembeek-Oppem, but was moved to Kortrijk when he developed eye trouble, which turned out to be cancer. He bore his sufferings with great patience.

Isidore of Alexandria, martyr. Said to have died at Alexandria, but nothing is known of him. Feast 5 February.

Isidore of Antioch, bishop and martyr. Nothing is known about him. Feast 2 January.

Isidore of Chios, martyr, born Alexandria, died island of Chios, *c.* 251. Said to have been betrayed by his own father. Feast 15 May.

Isidore of Egypt, priest, born Alexandria (?), died Constantinople, 404. He ran a refuge in Alexandria for pilgrims, and was a staunch defender of St **Athanasius**, as a consequence of which he was much persecuted by Athanasius's enemies and fled to Constantinople, where he became a friend of **John Chrysostom**. Feast 15 January.

Isidore of Harran, bishop. Syriac Church. Nothing is known of him. Feast 4 Febuary.

Isidore of Jur'ev and Seventy-Two Companions, martyrs, died Derpt (formerly Jur'ev), 8 January 1472. Russian Church. He was a priest serving Russian Orthodox faithful in Derpt, which had originally been founded as a Russian city and called Jur'ev. He had been actively promoting Orthodoxy among Catholics, but was then thrown into prison and later drowned with 72 of his parishioners.

Isidore of Pelusium, Egyptian presbyter and monk, born *c.* 360, probably died *c.* 435. Presbyter in Pelusium, he was forced to leave the city and lived from 405 in a monastery. His more than 2,000 letters reveal a well-educated man, full of divine wisdom. He was also a trained exegete, rejecting excessive use of allegory. Theologically he was orthodox (anti-Arian), attacking both heretics and pagans. He was not afraid to rebuke high officials, even Emperor Theodosius II, or the patriarch **Cyril of Alexandria**, because of Ephesus 431. Feast 4 February.

Isidore of Seville, bishop, born Seville, *c.* 560, died there, 636. He was the youngest child of a Spanish Romanized family devoted to the Church: his sister **Florentina** entered a convent and his two brothers, **Leander** and **Fulgentius**, both became bishops. In 600/1 he succeeded Leander as bishop of Seville. In this function he presided over the second Synod of Seville (619) and the fourth Synod of Toledo (633). He was a prolific writer. His most important work is the *Etymologiae*, an encyclopaedia of classical and Christian culture in 20 books. He was declared a doctor of the Church in 1722. Feast 4 April.

Isidore of Takinas, martyr, third/fourth century. Coptic Church. He was a soldier who had a vision, as the result of which he confessed himself a Christian and was burned to death. His body, however, remained untouched by the flames.

Isidore the Farmer, patron of farmers and of Madrid, born Madrid, Spain, 1070, died Madrid, Spain, 15 May 1130. Isidore was reputedly married to St **Maria de la Cabeza**, thus constituting one of the rare husband/wife sainthoods, but his wife is a latecomer to the story. He was employed by Juan de Vergas for most of his life. He was said to have led an unusually devout life and was associated with miracles even when he was alive. Feast 15 May.

Isidore 'Tverdislov', born Germany (?), died Rostov, 14 May 1474. Russian Church. He was born into a wealthy, possibly noble, family – possibly one of Slav descent. As a young man he abandoned his home and wandered from place to place, eventually settling at Rostov. He lived in a cabin in the marshes, spending his nights in prayer and his days wandering around the city to the jeers of passers-by. Eventually he was accepted as a holy man, and revered – his nickname Tverdislov means one whose word can be relied upon, i.e., recognizing his gift of prophecy.

Isnard of Chiampo, bl., abbot, born Chiampo, Vicenza, died Pavia, Lombardy, 1244, cult confirmed 1919. Received into his order by **Dominic** in 1219, he founded and was the first abbot of the Dominican friary in Pavia. Feast 19 March.

Iso'sabran of Erbil, martyr, born Salah al-Din, died Bet Laspar, 620/21. Syriac Church. Originally named Mahanos di Qur, and a Zoroastrian, he took the name Iso'sabran when he was converted to Christianity, with his wife, by the village priest. He kept his conversion secret for a time, but eventually professed it openly, was arrested and imprisoned. He was, however, freed and returned to his home. Desirous of martyrdom, he left his wife and began a wandering life, moving from hermitage to hermitage. He settled in a monastery near Qur, where he displayed great concern for the well-being of children and widows. He was again arrested and imprisoned – this time for 15 years – at Erbil. He was then taken for trial to Kirkuk, but was finally crucified, with others, at the village of Bet Laspar.

Iso'yab, founder, born Ba-Nuhadra, *c.* 577, died *c.* 685. Syriac Church. He studied at Qardu, then taught at the monastery of Gassa. He became a monk, however, in the monastery of Bawai of Nisibis on Mount Izla. At Bawai's death he left Mount Izla and went back to his own territory to found a monastery, although its exact location is unclear. He died there.

Iso'yab bar Qur, founder, born and died Nineveh (Mosul), seventh century. Syriac Church. He became a monk in the mountains of Adiabene, but then, because of persecution – seemingly from monophysite monks – he returned to Nineveh, where in the 570s he built a church which became the cathedral of the metropolitan of Nineveh. Feast 3 June.

Israel of Kaskar, bishop, died 872. Assyrian Church. Became bishop of Kaskar in 872, but was attacked by supporters of the rival candidate during the liturgy and died of his injuries 40 days later.

Ita of Killeedy, nun, born in the present County of Waterford, Ireland, *c.* 475, died Killeedy, County Limerick, 15 January 570. Ita resided at Cluain Credhail in County Limerick, which has since been known as Killeedy (i.e. 'The church of St Ita'). She was known for austerities, miracles and prophecies, and inspired other Irish saints such as **Brendan the Voyager**, Pulcherius (Mochoemog) and Cummian Fada. Feast 15 January.

Ithamar, bishop, born Kent, died Rochester, *c.* 656. In 644 he became the first Anglo-Saxon to be appointed to head a diocese in England – that of Rochester, in succession to **Paulinus**. Feast 10 June.

Ivan Andreevic Kononenko, martyr, born Solochi, 7 January 1880, died Char'kov, 25 May 1938. Ukrainian Church, Moscow Patriarchate. A

married man with three children, he was director of the choir of the church of the Three Holy Bishops at Char'kov. Feast 19 May.

Ivan Fedorov, martyr, died Krasnokutsk, 1941. Ukrainian Church, Moscow Patriarchate. He was smothered to death. Feast 19 May.

Ivan Petrovic Fedorov, martyr, born Seslavino, died Char'kov, 7 September 1937. Ukrainian Church, Moscow Patriarchate. He became a priest in 1930, and worked in the village of Andreevka until his arrest in August 1937. Feast 19 May.

Ivan Vasilevic Timonov, martyr, born Cernjansk, died Char'kov, 16 December 1967. Ukrainian Church, Moscow Patriarchate. He had worked as a priest in the village of Kocetok. Feast 19 May.

Ivo, bishop, born Persia, died St Ives, Cambridgeshire, seventh century. According to legend, Ivo left Persia and became a hermit in England, near the modern St Ives in Cambridgeshire. Feast 24 April.

Ivo of Chartres, bishop and author, born Chartres, France, *c.* 1040, died there, 23 December 1115. After studying at Paris and Bec, he was a parish priest in Picardy and provost of the canons-regular at Saint-Quentin in Beauvais before becoming bishop of Chartres in 1090. A prolific writer, he contributed to the establishment of the seven Sacraments, and is perhaps best known for his moderate stance in the Investiture Crisis: for Ivo, there was no objection to the king investing a properly chosen candidate after a canonical election, as everyone would understand that the king was only conferring temporal power. Feast 23 May.

Ivo of Helory, patron of lawyers, born in the manor of Kermartin, Brittany, 17 October 1253, died Trédez, France, 19 May 1303. He studied philosophy, canon law and theology in Paris and civil law in Orleans. In the Rennes district he became a diocesan judge and later in his own diocese of Treguier, where he became known as the poor man's advocate, with a gift for reconciling litigants. He was not ordained until 1284. He was a parish priest at Tredrez and at Lovannec where he built a hospital in which he ministered to the ill and poor himself. Ivo was sought out as a mediator and advocate and was noted for the austerity and piety of his life. Feast 19 May.

Iyasu, see **Joshua**.

Iyasus Mo'a, abbot, born Dahna, 25 May 1214, died Hayq, 22 November 1294. Ethiopian Church. At the age of 30 he entered the monastery of Dabra Diammo in Tigre. He later moved to a monastery dedicated to St Stephen the First Martyr at Hayq, which he effectively refounded, and over which he ruled from 1248 to 1292. He was of immense spiritual significance in the development of monasticism in Ethiopia, but he also played an important part in affairs of state. He retired into solitude for the last two years of his life, some distance from his monastery.

Izjaslav of Kiev, prince, born 1024, died Kiev, 15 November (?) 1078. He became grand prince of Kiev in 1054, after the death of his father **Jaroslav the Wise**. His hold on the throne was insecure, partly because his brothers were vying for it, partly because the people of Kiev rose up against him in 1068, accusing him of being incapable of defending them. He had to flee to Poland, and was restored to the throne by Polish troops six months later. He fled back to Poland in 1073 because of the attacks of his brothers. This time he also sought the assistance of the German Emperor Henry IV, and of the pope, asking him to confirm him as 'King of Russia'. After the death at Kiev of one of his brothers in 1076, he returned once again backed by Polish troops, but died not long after, in battle with the Cumans. He had a troubled relationship with the Kievan Cave monastery, although he had at first sought the blessing of its abbot, but he built churches, fostered (at least a little) ecclesiastical scholarship and abolished the death penalty. Feast 13 November.

Izjaslav of Vladimir, prince, died Vladimir (?), 12 April 1165. Russian Church. He was probably prince of Rostov when he is first mentioned in 1159. He was a devout man, and a successful military commander.

J

Jacinto Castañeda Puchasons, missionary, born Játiva, Valencia, Spain, 13 November 1743, martyred Ha Tay, Vietnam, 7 November 1773, beatified 1906, canonized 1988. A Dominican priest, he had worked previously in the Philippines and China. See **Martyrs of Vietnam**.

Jacob, priest, born Ethiopia. Ethiopian Church. Nothing is known of him.

Jacob, see also **James**.

Jacob Gapp, bl., martyr, born Watten, Tyrol, 26 July 1897, died Berlin-Plötzensee, 13 August 1943. He served in the Austrian forces during World War I, and was captured by the Italians just before the end of the war. He joined the Marianists in 1920, studied in Fribourg, Switzerland, and elsewhere, and was ordained in 1930. He held various posts, and from 1934 to 1938 worked at the Marianist Institute in Graz. He was strongly opposed to the Nazi party, for which he was removed from his teaching post and, eventually, felt obliged to leave Austria. He went to France, and then to Spain. But Spain he also found to be too fascist, and he went to the British consulate in Valencia, where he was teaching, in an attempt to obtain a visa to visit Britian – this was in wartime, and he was a German citizen. He was under constant surveillance by undercover Gestapo agents, who persuaded him to join them on a visit to France. There he was arrested and accused of treason. The evidence against him included the fact that he collected copies of the London-based Catholic weekly, *The Tablet*. He was beheaded.

Jacob Ledoyen, see **Francis Pelletier**.

Jacob of Alexandria, patriarch, died Tida, Nile Delta, eighth/ninth centuries. Coptic Church. A monk of the monastery of St Macarius, selected by a vision to succeed to the patriarchate in 819. For much of his patriarchate the Church suffered greatly from poverty because of the taxes imposed by the Muslim authorities, although it was saved by miracles worked by Jacob. He was, however, able to restore the monastery of St Macarius which had been destroyed by Bedouin.

Jacobinus de' Canepaci, bl., born Piedmont, 1438, died there, 1508, cult approved 1845. He was a Carmelite lay brother in the diocese of Vercelli. Feast 3 March.

Jacopone da Todi, bl., Italian poet and Franciscan, born Todi, 1228–30, died Collazone, 25 December 1306. Probably first a lawyer, he entered the Franciscan order in 1278, adhering to the branch of the Spirituals. He fought fiercely for the ideal of poverty as well as for Church reform, even subscribing to a document in which the removal of Pope Boniface VIII was demanded. He was excommunicated and in 1298 imprisoned. Five years later Benedictus XI released him. Besides numerous prose works in Latin, Jacopone also wrote 92 superb *laudi spirituali* which are often of a great beauty.

Jacut, Celtic monk, sixth century. Brother of **Winwaloe**, he is commemorated with another brother, **Guethenoc**. Both disciples of **Budoc**, they all fled from the Saxons to Britanny. The brothers were children of **Fragan** and **Gwen**. Feast 8 February.

James, died *c.* 450. He was a hermit near Cyrrhus, Syria. Feast 21 February.

James, see also **Marianus**.

James, see also **Philotheus**.

James, see also **Boris, James, Theodore I, Silvanus, Theodore II, Basil I, Demetrius, Michael, John, Basil II**.

James and John, born Menjusa, near Novgorod, died there, *c.* 1569. Russian Church. Two children, presumably killed by brigands. Feast 24 June.

James and Marian, martyrs, died Tell-dara, Persia, 347. Feast 14 March.

James and Theophilus, monks, died near Porhov, *c.* 1412. Russian Church. They joined the monastery on the island of Konevec together, and together founded a hermitage on the river Omuca, near Porhov, *c.* 1396.

James Baradeus, bishop, born Syria, died Kaison, Egypt, 30 July 578. After becoming a monk and being ordained priest *c.* 527, he was sent to the court at Constantinople where he remained until 543, when he was ordained as bishop of Edessa. He was then sent to the eastern front of the empire as a missionary to the Arabs. There he found and consecrated bishops, a large number of monophysites, thus beginning a hierarchy which survived – members of the Church are sometimes known as the Jacobites after James (Jacob).

James Bell, bl., martyr, born Warrington, Lancashire, 1525, died Lancaster, 20 April 1584, beatified 1929. Ordained a Catholic priest, he first conformed as a Protestant minister under Queen Elizabeth I. He reverted in 1581, was arrested saying mass and is commemorated with **John Finch**, with whom he was hanged, drawn and quartered.

James, martyr (?), died Constantinople, 824. He suffered for the veneration of icons. Feast 21 March.

James Bianconi, bl., born Bevagna, near Spoleto, Italy, 1220, died there, 1301. He founded the Dominican house in that town, and was its first prior. Feast 22 August.

James Bird, bl., born Winchester, *c.* 1574, martyred there, 25 March 1593, beatified 1929. Becoming a Catholic as a young boy, he studied at Douai. Back home, his activities led to his arrest. He refused to save himself by attending a Protestant church and was hanged, drawn and quartered.

James Capocci, bl., bishop, born Viterbo, died Naples, 1308, cult approved 1911. He was an Augustinian friar who became bishop of Benevento in 1302 and archbishop of Naples in 1303. Feast 14 March.

James Claxton, bl., martyr, died Isleworth (?), 28 August 1588. He went to Rheims to study for the priesthood in 1580, was ordained at Soissons in June 1582 and returned to England the following month, working mainly in York. He was captured and banished from York in 1585, returned, but was again captured and sent to London for trial and execution.

James Cusmano, bl., born Palermo, Sicily, 15 March 1834, died there of cholera, 14 March 1888, beatified 1983. A doctor and priest, he founded the Institute of Servant Sisters of the Poor and the Congregation of the Missionary Servants of the Poor to alleviate the poverty resulting from repeated famines and epidemics and to improve social conditions.

James Domai Nam and Companions, martyrs, died Vietnam, 1838. Feast 12 August.

James de Blanconibus, bl., Dominican monk, born Bevagna (Mevania), Umbria, 1220, died there, 23 August 1301 (he is also known as James Bianconi of Mevania). He joined the Dominican order at Spoleto at the age of 16, and studied theology and philosophy at Perugia, where he was also ordained. James was a noted preacher and attacked Nicolaitanism (the defence of a married clergy) so successfully that it was eliminated from Umbria.

He founded the Dominican priory of St George in Bevagna, and also directed the establishment of a convent of Benedictine nuns. A visionary – he was gifted with a vision whilst praying in front of a crucifix, and fearing the loss of his soul, in which he was comforted by being bathed in the blood from the side of Christ. On 15 August 1301 he received a further vision in which he was instructed to prepare himself for death. He died eight days later. His intact remains are at Bevagna.

James Duckett, bl., martyr from Cumbria, died Tyburn, London, 19 April 1602, beatified 1929. He became a Catholic as a young man. He married a Catholic, and used his position as a publisher and bookseller to supply Catholics with books. He was imprisoned several times and eventually hanged, drawn and quartered.

James Fenn, bl., born Somerset, *c.* 1540, martyred Tyburn, London, 12 February 1584, beatified 1929. A schoolmaster and a widower with two children, he was ordained priest in France in 1580. Captured that year in England, he ministered in the Marshalsea prison for two years. Condemned with **George Haydock**, they were hung, drawn and quartered with **Thomas Hemerford**, **John Munden** and **John Nutter**. His brothers were also priests, but escaped execution.

James Griesinger, bl., born Ulm, 1407, died Bologna, 1491. He became a soldier in Italy, but, shocked by the behaviour of the troops, he became a secretary in Capua, then returned to soldiering, but finally became a Dominican lay brother in Bologna. He was renowned for his skill at painting on glass, and also for his mystical experiences. Feast 11 October.

James Hyushei Gorobioye Tomonaga and Companions, martyrs, died Nagaski, 17 August 1633.

James Ilic Matynenko, martyr, born Korotic, 4 January 1878, died Char'kov, 16 December 1937. Ukrainian Church, Moscow Patriarchate. He had already given up his role as a priest in Malinovka when he was arrested and shot. Feast 19 May.

James Intercisus, martyr, died Persia, 421. A court official, the shah ordered his execution (he was cut up into little pieces, hence the name) after he repented his apostasy from Christianity. Feast 27 November.

James Ivanovic Redozubov, born Cuguev, died Char'kov, 19 January 1938. Ukrainian Church, Moscow Patriarchate. He spent his life as a priest in Osinovka, until arrested in December 1937. Feast 19 May.

James Désiré Laval, born Croth, Normandy, 18 September 1803, died Mauritius, 9 September 1864. He was educated first by a priestly uncle, then at the minor seminary of the diocese of Evreux. He left there, however, and went to Paris where he studied medicine. He returned to Normandy to practise, but in 1835 entered the seminary of Saint-Sulpice at Paris. After ordination he worked for a time in a parish, but then went to Mauritius as the first missionary of the newly established Congregation of the Holy Heart of Mary. He refused to live in the presbytery of the cathedral, but instead lived and worked, until ill-health drove him back to the presbytery, in a small cabin. His apostolate was to the black population: the small white population remained hostile, although an originally hostile British administration came to appreciate the work he was doing.

James Netsvetov, born Atka Island, Alaska, *c.* 1804, died Sitka, 26 July 1864. Orthodox Church in America. His father was a Russian, his mother an Aleut. The family moved in 1823 to Irkutsk, where James enrolled in the theological academy. He married in 1825, and was ordained the following year. In 1828 he set out for Alaska, arriving back on Atka Island in June 1829. His first acts were to establish a parish church and a school. In 1836 his wife died, and he thought of becoming a monk, but was dissuaded. In 1844 he moved to the Yukon, where he settled at the Inuit village Ikogmiute, travelling up and down the Yukon river and making many converts. In 1863 he was summoned by the bishop to Sitka to answer charges that had been slanderously levelled against him. He remained there, working in a parish, until his death. Feast 16 October.

James of Amidia, hermit, lived and died Diyarbakir, Turkey, *c.* 500. Feast 6 August.

James of Bitetto, bl., born Zara, Dalmatia, *c.* 1400, died Bitetto, near Bari, *c.* 1485, beatified 1700. A Franciscan lay brother in Zara, he accompanied the provincial to Italy in 1438. He was known as a holy person, highly contemplative, with the gift of prophecy and apparently experiencing levitations. Feast 27 April.

James of Borovici, died Borovici, 1540. Russian Church. A boatman, he died through being struck by lightning. He had lived as a 'fool for Christ'. Feast 23 October.

James of Bryleev, monk, fifteenth century, died near Buj. Russian Church. Of the noble Brylevcy family, he was a monk of Zeleznij Borok.

James of Cerqueto, bl., from Cerqueto, Umbria, died Perugia, 17 April 1367, cult approved 1895. He joined the Hermits of St Augustine in Perugia and devoted the remainder of his very long life to prayer. He was said to have power over wild animals and many miracles were reported at his tomb.

James of Certaldo, bl., monk and priest, born Certlado, near Florence, the son of a knight of Volterra, died Volterra, 13 (?) April 1292. He became a monk at the Camaldolese abbey of San Giusto at Volterra in 1230. After refusing the office of abbot twice, he finally accepted, only to resign the office shortly after to continue his work as parish priest of the monastery church. Here he served as a noted pastor for 40 years. Feast 17 April.

James of Edessa ('the Interpreter'), born Endeba (near Antioch), *c.* 633, died Tell Adda, 5 June. Syriac Church. Studied Scripture at the monastery of Qennesrin on the right bank of the Euphrates, then went on to Alexandria. He was appointed bishop of Edessa, but when he set about reforming the monasteries of his diocese his approach was regarded as too severe, and after four years he resigned. He then spent nine years at the monastery of Tell Adda working on the Syriac version of the Old Testament, but in 707, at the death of his successor, he returned as bishop to Edessa. He died at Tell Adda while visiting to consult the library. He wrote many works, mainly on Scripture, but also on the liturgy and other religious topics. He also wrote a grammar of Syriac.

James of Lodi, bl., born Lodi, near Milan, 1364, died there, 18 April 1404, cult approved 1933 (suppressed). He gave up his frivolous life when his daughters died. He and his wife became Franciscan tertiaries, taking vows of continence. Ordained priest in 1397, he cared for the sick and prisoners of war.

James of Mantua, bl., bishop, born Mantua, died there, 19 November 1338. He was a Dominican, and the companion of the master general of the Dominicans who in 1303 became Pope Benedict XI. He then sent James as bishop to Mantua. When his tomb was opened accidentally in 1483 his body was found intact, which gave rise to a cult. Feast 26 November.

James of Misr, bishop, died Misr (Old Cairo), 28 August 1088. Coptic Church. A monk of the monastery of St Macarius, he became bishop of Misr in 1064, although as far as possible he continued to live a monastic style of life.

James of Moscow, a 'fool for Christ', sixteenth/seventeenth centuries. Russian Church. Apart from some connection with the Novodevic monastery in Moscow, nothing is known of him.

James of Naples, bl., born Viterbo, near Rome, died Naples, 1308, cult confirmed 1911. Surnamed Capocci, and an Augustinian, he studied in Paris, eventually obtaining a doctorate in theology, and lectured there and in Italy. He was archbishop of Naples from 1302. He wrote *De regimine christiano* ('On Christian government'). Feast 13 February.

James of Nisbis, bishop, died 338. He became the first bishop of Nisbis, Mesopotamia, *c.* 308. He may have been responsible for founding the city's first theological school. He was present at the Council of Nicaea in 325, and was an opponent of Arianism. Feast 15 July.

James of Persia, martyr, died Persia, fourth century. A lawyer, he was martyred in the reign of Shapur II (310–79). Feast 22 April.

James of Psilta, bishop, born Mount Izla, died Osrhoene, sixth century. Syriac Church. In charge of the monastery of Tella d'Mauzelate. Feast 31 July.

James of Resa, born Resa, *c.* 627, died *c.* 717. Assyrian Church. At the age of 20 he became a monk at the monastery of Bet Abe in Marga, where he won disciples and gained a reputation for prophecy. For three years he was exiled from the monastery because of feelings against him, but in *c.* 685 he was summoned back as its superior. However, he preferred to remain a hermit in his cave. The bishop of Nuhadra, where the cave was situated, managed to persuade him to return, and under his direction many monks joined.

James of Rostov, bishop, born Jakovlevo, near Rostov, died near Rostov, 27 November 1392. Russian Church. In 1386, after becoming hegumenos of his monastery, he was appointed bishop of Rostov. He soon, however, ran into problems with the boyar class of the city, and had to leave it, living a hermit's life not far from the city. Such was his fame that other monks gathered around him, eventually creating the monastery of Spasso-Jaklovlev. Feast 27 November.

James of Sarug, born Qurtam, on the Euphrates, 451, died Batnan-Sarug, 29 November 521. Syriac Church. The son of a priest, he studied at Edessa, then, aged 22, became a monk. He was ecclesiastical visitor throughout Syria, and engaged in controversies with the Nestorians at Edessa. In 518 be was made bishop of Sarug. He was an important poet in Syriac (he became known as the 'harp of the Holy Spirit'), and is also credited with some liturgical and other texts. Feast 20 November.

James of Serbia, archbishop, died 1292 (?). Serbian Church. Archbishop from 1286. Said to have brought hesychasm to Serbia. Feast 3 February.

James of Solovki, hegumenos, died Kostroma, 1614. Russian Church. He was hegumenos of the monastery of Paleostrov from 1573, and was chosen as hegumenos of Solovki in 1581. The region was then regularly under attack from Swedish forces, and James built massive fortifications for the monastery. In 1597 he became archimandrite of the Ipatev monastery at Kostroma. Feast 9 August.

James of Stromyni, hegumenos, fourteenth century. Russian Church. An early hegumenos of the monastery near the village of Stromyni, on the river Dubenka. Feast 21 April.

James of Tarentaise, bishop, fifth century. He was a disciple of **Honoratus of Arles** at Lérins, the first bishop of Tarentaise, and was venerated in Chambery as the apostle of Savoy. Feast 16 January.

James of the Marches, Franciscan, born Monteprandone, Italy, 1391, died Naples, 28 November 1476. From a poor family, he was nevertheless able to take a doctorate in civil law at the University of Perugia. In 1416 he entered the Franciscans at Assisi, and after his ordination in 1420, taught and preached throughout Italy. He travelled throughout Europe and was commissary of the Friars Minor in Bosnia. He was a member of the Observant branch of the order, and was active with his confrere, **John of Capistrano**, in efforts towards reform and unity.

James of Viterbo, bl., Augustinian, bishop of Benevento and then Naples, born 1255, died 1308. Feast 13 February.

James of Voragine, bl., Dominican archbishop and writer, born Varazze, near Genoa, *c.* 1230, died Genoa, 13 July 1298. He entered the Dominicans at the age of 14 and achieved fame as a popular preacher in Lombardy. He was elected provincial of Lombardy in 1267, and was elected archbishop of Genoa in 1286, but he refused the office. He was chosen once more in 1292, and this time was obliged to undertake the office at a very disturbed time, socially and politically, in the city. His enduring fame, however, rests upon *The Golden Legend*, a compilation of the lives of popular saints, some of them legendary, and some feast days. Later dismissed as unhistorical, the work was not intended as a factual record, but as a mean to encourage devotion among ordinary Christians by describing the deeds of earlier Christians.

James of Zelezoborov, monk, born Galic, near Kostroma, died there, 11 April 1442. Russian Church. Of a boyar family, he entered the monastery of St **Sergius of Radonez**, but when he decided to become a hermit he returned to his native region, setting himself up in a forest on the left bank of the river Tebza. As he gathered disciples, he formulated a strict Rule of life for them, with great emphasis on poverty. When once in Moscow, his prayers were solicited for the health of the wife of the grand prince. She recovered, giving birth to a son, and her family – and her son when he became grand prince – were thenceforward significant donors to the monastery.

James Philip Bertoni, bl., born Faenza, Italy, 1444, died there, 1483, cult confirmed 1766. He became a Servite priest, and served all his life as procurator of the friary. Feast 25 May.

James Salès, bl., Jesuit priest, martyred Aubenas, Cévennes, France, 7 February 1593, beatified 1926 with **William Saltemouche** (or Saultemouche), Jesuit lay brother. Working when Catholics and Huguenots were in violent conflict, Salès was caught by raiders, brought before an unofficial Calvinist tribunal and killed with William, his servant, who had refused to escape.

James Salomoni, bl., born Venice, 1231, died Forli, near Ravenna, 1314. He became a Benedictine at Santa Maria Celeste in Venice and became prior at Forli, Faenza, San Severino and Ravenna. He combined prayer with reading and charity, experienced ecstasies and had the gifts of healing and prophecy. Feast 31 May.

James Strzemie, bl., archbishop, born near Krakow, 1340, died Lvov, 1 June 1409. Born into a noble family, he became a Franciscan and worked in the Ukraine as a missionary for a decade. He then became head of the Franciscan missions to western Russia, and then in 1392 archbishop of Halicz. He built churhces, hospitals and schools, and brought in more priests from Poland to help in the missionary work. He was given the title of 'Protector of the Kingdom'. Feast 21 October.

James the Almsgiver, bl., born near Chiusi, Lombardy, died there, 15 January 1304. A lawyer and priest, working with the poor in a hospital, he discovered that successive bishops of Chiusi had stolen the revenues. He won redress in the civil and ecclesiastical courts, but the bishop had him murdered.

James the Hermit, Palestine, sixth century. After either a lapse in faith or a murder, he lay hidden in a tomb as penance and became known for miracles in his lifetime. Feast 28 January.

James the Jakute, monk, died Zagorsk, fourteenth century. Russian Church. A disciple of St **Sergius of Radonez**. Feast 6 July.

James the Recluse, hermit. Syriac Church. Nothing is known about him – possibly a confusion of names.

James the Younger, bl., born Kastoria, died Adrianopolis, 1 November 1520. Byzantine Church. Originally a shepherd, he went to Constantinople where he worked as a merchant, but then entered the monastery of Timios Podromos on Mount Athos, taking the religious name of Ignatius. With a number of disciples, after a few years on Mount Athos he went to the Meteora, but was accused of raising the Greeks against the Turks. He and two of his disciples were arrested, sent before the sultan, invited to deny their faith and, when they refused, hanged.

James the Zealot, see **John of Arbela**.

James Thompson, bl., martyr, born Yorkshire, died York, 28 November 1582. He went to the English College in Rheims where he was ordained priest after less than a year, possibly because of ill-health. He returned to England to work in Yorkshire, but was arrested in August 1582, and was hanged in York.

Jane Frances Fremiot de Chantal, founder of the Order of the Visitation, born Dijon, France, 28 January 1572, died Moulin, 13 December 1641. She married Christophe, Baron de Chantal, in 1592 and they had four children. After her husband's death in 1601, Jane resolved not to remarry and took a vow of chastity. She became the spiritual daughter and friend of **Francis de Sales** and in

1610, with his help, founded the first house of the Visitation Order at Annecy. She was well liked and her order, for young girls and for widows who were not called to the austerities of the existing orders, grew rapidly. By the time of her death there were 86 Visitation houses. Feast 12 December.

Jane of Toulouse, bl., born Toulouse, died there, 1286, cult confirmed 1895. An anchoress, affiliated to the Carmelite order by **Simon Stock**, she is venerated as the founder of the Carmelite third order. She trained boys aspiring to be Carmelite friars. Feast 31 March.

Januarius (probably), bishop of Beneventum (Italy), according to the earliest liturgical tradition and his earliest *Passio*, this martyr was decapitated, together with his six companions, near Pozzuoli, 19 September 305. In 432 his relics came to Naples where, despite some temporary translations, they are still kept today. Januarius is also the city's patron saint. Since the fourteenth century a blood miracle is regularly witnessed: the saint's blood, which is preserved in two ampullae, becomes fluid again.

Januarius, see also **Faustus, Januarius and Martial**.

Januarius of Solovki, monk, fifteenth century. Russian Church. A disciple of **Zosimus**.

Jarlath, bishop, born Galway, died Tuam, sixth century. From a powerful family of Galway, he founded a monastery near modern Tuam, and opened a school there. Feast 6 June.

Jaropolk, prince, born Kiev, died between Zvenigorod and Vladimir, 1086. Russian Church. As the son of **Izjaslav**, his early years were spent in exile from Kiev, and after his father returned to Kiev he was given charge of the city of Vygorod. The feuding between claimants to Kiev continued after the death of Izjaslav, and Jaropolk found himself once more usurped and in 1085 had to flee to Poland. He returned the following year, but was assassinated by one of his soldiers in the pay of his enemies. He is recorded as being a devout Christian, a benefactor to the Kievan Cave monastery, and generous to the poor. Feast 22 November.

Jaroslav the Wise, prince, born Kiev, 978, died there, 19 February 1054. Russian Church. A son of **Vladimir**, he first ruled Rostov in the name of his father, and later Novgorod. Vladimir did not, however, bequeath the throne of Kiev to Jaroslav, and a war ensued, in which died **Boris and Gleb**, two of Jaroslav's brothers. Jaroslav eventually prevailed, but even so for a number of years had to divide his principality with yet another of Vladimir's sons. He also waged war against Constantinople and, although he was technically defeated, he concluded a marriage alliance. He attempted to break the domination of Byzantium over the Church in Kievan Rus by appointing **Hilarion**, a Russian monk, as metropolitan in Kiev in place of the customary Greek prelate. He also built the cathedral of Santa Sophia in Kiev, and although Kievan Rus was still largely pagan at his accession, despite his father's conversion, by his death Christianity was in practice the dominant faith. Feast 28 February.

Jean (in medieval names), see **John**.

Jean-Charles Cornay, martyr, born Loudun, Vienne, France, 27 February 1809, died Ha Tây, Vietnam, 20 September 1837, beatified 1900, canonized 1988. A priest of the Paris Foreign Missions Society, he was 'hewn to pieces'. See **Martyrs of Vietnam**.

Jean-Louis Bonnard, martyr, born Saint-Christo-en-Jarez, Loire, France, 1 March 1824, died Vietnam, 1 May 1852, beatified 1900, canonized 1988. A priest of the Paris Foreign Missions Society, he had arrived in Tonkin in 1850. See **Martyrs of Vietnam**.

Jeanne, see also **Joan**.

Jeanne de Lestonnac, founder, born Bordeaux, 1556, died there, 2 February 1640. From a strongly Catholic background, which included her uncle, Michel de Montaigne, Jeanne devoted herself to works of charity in Bordeaux and eventually (1607) founded the Order of Notre Dame (Company of Mary) as a counterpart to the Society of Jesus, for the education of young girls. She remained superior of the congregation until 1622 when, a victim of malicious gossip, she lost her position, but obtained redress two years later. Jeanne devoted her remaining years to her Company, and Pius XII canonized her in 1949.

Jeanne Delanoue, foundress of the Sisters of Saint Anne of Providence, born Saumur, France, 18 June 1666, died there, 17 August 1736. Following an early life dedicated to making money, she repented and experienced an ecstasy in which her vocation to help the poor was made known. She began this at once, living in incredible austerity. Her home became known as 'the house of providence' and was formally made into a religious house in 1704. She established 'houses of providence' in Brézé and Puy-Notre-Dame, feeding and housing thousands of homeless in a famine winter, by what seemed miraculous means. Feast 16 August.

Jeanne Elizabeth Bichier des Ages, co-foundress of the Daughters of the Holy Cross of St Andrew, born Le Blanc, near Poitiers, France, 5 July 1773, died Paris, 26 August 1838. After the death of her father in 1792, she conducted a successful lawsuit against the revolutionary government to save the family's property from confiscation. Jeanne settled with her mother at Bethines-Poitou, and followed a pattern of prayer and good works. She was the central figure amongst resistance to the Constitutional clergy. In 1805, along with five companions, she founded a community at La Guimetiere. The community was approved by the bishop of Poitiers in 1816. As superior, Jeanne guided the community through rapid growth, and by 1830 there were over 30 houses. Ill-health forced her to retire to Paris for the rest of her life.

Jeanne Jugan, foundress of the Little Sisters of the Poor, born Petites-Croix Brittany, 25 October 1792, died Pern, France, 29 August 1879. She spent 20 years working in the hospital at Saint Servan, and then in domestic service – in the latter occupation she used to accompany her employer visiting the sick and needy and teaching catechism. In 1837 she established a small house with a friend in Saint Servan, joined the following year by a young woman who had been entrusted to her charge. They began by chance to look after the sick and elderly. In May 1842 the small group established themselves as a religious community, with Jeanne as superior. She was re-elected the following year,

but Auguste Le Pailleur, the priest moderator of the group, dismissed her as superior: she was not even invited to the first general chapter of her order in 1847. Although the order she had founded went from strength to strength, she gained no recognition of her work in her lifetime, apart from an award of 3,000 francs from the French Academy in 1845 in recognition of her charitable work. For a time she was allowed both to beg and to assist in the foundation of new houses, but in 1852 she was sent to remain inactive for the rest of her life in the community's mother house. When she died there were 2,400 Little Sisters of the Poor caring for 20,000 aged poor in 177 houses.

Jeanne Marie de Maille, bl., Franciscan tertiary, mystic and recluse, of noble birth, Roche-Saint-Quentin, near Tours, France, 1332, died Tours, 28 March 1414. At the age of 16 she was married to Robert de Sille, but remained a virgin. When he died in 1362, she was dispossessed by his family and returned to Tours. Here she spent her days living in a simple house near to the church of St Martin in prayer and good works. Later she became a recluse, living near Clery. In 1377 she entered the third order of St Francis at Tours. She prayed unceasingly for an end to the Western schism and also sought to reform the morals of the court of Charles VI and Isabelle. Feast 6 November.

Jeanne-Marie Kerguin (Mary of Ste Nathalie), born Britanny, France, 5 May 1864, martyred Taiyuan, Shanxi, China, 9 July 1900, beatified 1946, canonized 2000. A Franciscan Missionary of Mary under **Mary Emiliana Grivot**, she had previously worked in Africa and was a member of the group killed with **Gregory Grassi**. See **Franciscan Martyrs of China** and **Martyrs of Shanxi**. Feast 8 July.

Jeanne Véron, bl., martyr, born Quelaines, France, 6 August 1766, died Ernée, 20 March 1794. In the same order as **Frances Tréhet**, with whom she worked, she was arrested with her and carried to the guillotine as she was gravely ill and possibly already dying. See also **Martyrs of the French Revolution**.

Jenaro Sanchez, bl., born Zapopán, diocese of Guadalajara, Jalisco, Mexico, 19 September 1886, died Tecolotlan, Jalisco, Mexico, 17 January 1927. He was ordained in 1911, and was walking with some parishioners in the countryside when he was arrested and hanged from a tree.

Jeremiah of Saqqarah, monk, fifth/sixth centuries. Coptic Church. According to the tradition, he built several monasteries with the assistance of John, king of Syria. One of these was that of Saqqarah, south of Cairo. Feast 29 May.

Jeremy of Valacchia, bl., born John Kostistik, Zazo, Valacchia, Romania, 29 June 1556, died Naples, 5 March 1625, beatified 1983. Having travelled to Italy, he joined the Capuchins in Naples in 1578. He spent his life nursing the sick – he died from pneumonia after walking in the rain to a sick man.

Jerome, exegete and theologian, born Strido (Dalmatia), c. 347, died Palestine, 419/20. He was one of the greatest intellects and versatile minds of antiquity. During his restless life he travelled the entire Roman Empire, took up a monastic lifestyle in various places and became secretary to Pope **Damasus**. Most of all, however, he was an erudite scholar who mastered the legacies of the Latin, Greek and biblical literature and realized the importance of reading the Bible in the original language. His most lasting contribution has been the Latin translation of almost the entire Bible (the Vulgate). There is also his *De viris illustribus*, biographies of monks, Latin translations of Greek works, homilies, letters and much more. Feast 30 September.

Jerome, died 815. He was bishop of Nevers in Burgundy. Feast 5 February.

Jerome de Angelis, bl., Jesuit and martyr, born Sicily, 1567, died Yedo (Tokyo), 4 December 1623. He had studied law in Palermo before entering the Jesuits in 1586. He was sent to Japan, but after a number of disasters, including being captured by English pirates, he found himself back in Spain and had to set out anew in 1599, arriving in Nagasaki in 1602. He worked in what is now Tokyo, and remained there secretly after the expulsion of missionaries in 1614. He was eventually captured in November 1623, and ordered to be burned at the stake. He suffered alongside **Simon Yempo**.

Jerome Emiliani, founder of the Clerks Regular of Somascha (named after the town where they founded their first house), born Venice, 1481, died Somascha, 8 February 1537, while ministering to victims of disease. As a soldier in the Venetian army he was in command of a fortress at Castelnuovo, near Treviso, which was captured and he was imprisoned. During the imprisonment he underwent a conversion and determined to devote his life and energies to plague and famine victims and especially to orphans (he was named the patron saint of abandoned children and orphans in 1928). He founded homes, hospitals and orphanages throughout northern Italy, and a house for repentant prostitutes. It is claimed that he was the first to teach catechism to children by using the question-and-answer method. His congregation was approved by the papacy in 1540. Feast 8 February.

Jerome Gherarducci, bl., died 1369. He was an Augustinian friar at Recanati, near Ascoli Piceno, in the Italian Tronto Valley. Feast 12 March.

Jerome Hermosilla Aransáez, born Santo Domingo de la Calzada, Logroño, Spain, 30 September 1800, martyred Vietnam, 1 November 1861, beatified 1906, canonized 1988. A Dominican, he succeeded **Clemente Ignacio Delgado Cebrián** as bishop and apostolic vicar of East Tonkin. He was beheaded with **Valentíne Berrio-Ochoa** and **Pedro Almató Ribera** – see **Martyrs of Vietnam**.

Jerome Lou-Tin-Mey, see **Agatha Lin-Tchao**.

Jerome of Obnora, see **Ephraim of Obnora, with Dionysius, Jerome and Isaac**.

Jerome Ranuzzi, bl., Servite priest, born Sant'Angelo in Vado, died there, 10 December 1455. He joined the Servites at the age of 20, studied in Bologna, was ordained and then taught in Servite houses in Italy. He returned to Sant'Angelo, but the duke of Urbino asked that he come to court to serve as adviser. He returned to his home town before his death.

Jerome the Recluse, monk, twelfth/thirteenth centuries. Russian Church. Nothing is known of his life. Feast 28 September.

Jesus Mendez Montoya, martyr, born 1888, died Valtierilla, 28 February 1928. He studied at Michoacan, and was ordained in 1906. He was executed in his parish. Feast 25 May.

Jieron (or Jeron, or Hieron), missionary and martyr, died Noordwijk, *c.* 856. There are differing traditions concerning his birth which place him in Egmond, Holland, England and Scotland. Little is known of him save that he was a missionary to the Friesians. He was captured and brought before a tribal assembly and was questioned, before being tortured and killed. It is said that he bore witness to his faith with great bravery. His head is at Noordwijk.

Joachim, see **Alexander, Joachim and Isaiah**.

Joachim of Opoca, monk, died 9 September 1550 (?). Russian Church. Founded the monastery at Porhov.

Joachim of Ossogovo, hermit, died 11 March 1105. Bulgarian and Serbian Churches. He established a hermitage in a cave on Mount Ossogovo, and lived a penitential life there for many years. A century later he revealed the location of his tomb to another hermit, living in the same place, and it became a place of miracles.

Joachim of St Anne Wall, see **John Wall**.

Joachim of Sartoma, monk, died Sartoma, seventeenth century. Russian Church. He lived in the monastery of Sartoma and occupied himself as a painter of icons, which he gave away to churches and monasteries.

Joachim of Siena, bl., born Siena, Italy, 1258, died there, 1305, cult approved 1609. Received as a Servite in Siena by **Philip Benizi**, he refused ordination from humility. He was seen as a saint during his life, with miracles attributed to him. Feast 16 April.

Joachim of Tarnovo I, patriarch, died Tarnovo, 18 January 1248. Bulgarian Church. Born into a noble family, he became a monk on Mount Athos. He was remarkable for the severity of the penitential discipline he imposed on himself. After a time he moved to Kressen, on the Danube, with some disciples, where they eventually established a monastery. In 1234 he was appointed to the patriarchate, which he ruled through turbulent times, both because of invasions by the Tartars and because of dynastic strife within Bulgaria, until his death.

Joachim of the Kievan Cave Monastery, monk. Russian Church. Nothing is known of him.

Joachim Royo, see **Peter Sanz**.

Joachima de Mas, founder, born Barcelona, 16 April 1783, died 28 August 1854. Joaquima de Mas y de Vedruna came from a large and wealthy family. In 1799 she married Teodoro de Mas, a pious man who had considered becoming a Franciscan. Teodoro died after 17 years of married life, and for another seven years Joaquima continued to look after her children, although she dressed as a Franciscan and led an austere life. In 1826 she founded a new order, the Carmelites of Charity, and the nuns opened a hospital. By the time of her death from cholera there were schools and hospitals across Catalonia.

Joan, see also **Jeanne**.

Joan Antide-Thouret, founder, born Sancey-le-Long, near Besançon, France, 7 November 1756, died Naples, 24 August 1826. After her mother died when she was 16, Joan ran the large family until she became a novice with the Sisters of Charity of St Vincent de Paul. She was in Paris at the time of the French Revolution, and had to make her way back to her home when the orders were dissolved. There she began a free school, but in 1796 left for Switzerland. In Switzerland, where again she lived with nuns, she was invited to open a school in Besançon. This she did in April 1799. A number of others joined her, and in 1800 a noviceship began for what became the Daughters of Charity. It was formally approved in 1819, but the archbishop of Besançon refused to accept the constitution as approved by the pope, which meant that the mother house of the congregation was closed to Joan, despite her efforts to resolve the schism.

Joan of Arc, visionary and martyr, born Domrémy, Lorraine, 6 January 1412, died Rouen, 30 May 1431, by being burned at the stake. As a child she experienced visions and heard voices which called her to a mission to save France. In 1429 she made her way to the French court and, following the examination of her claims by theologians, Charles VII allowed her to lead an expedition to Orléans. Dressed in white armour and carrying a banner with the symbol of the Trinity and the words 'Jesus Maria', she was successful in relieving the city. Six months later she was taken prisoner at Compiègne, sold to the English, tried before Pierre Cauchon, the bishop of Beauvais, and accused of witchcraft and heresy. She partially recanted, but on 23 May 1431 she once again put on male dress, was condemned as a relapsed heretic and burned. She was rehabilitated by the Church in 1456, but not declared a saint until 1920. She is patron of France.

Joan of Aza, bl., mother of St **Dominic**, born in the castle of Aza, Old Castille, c. 1140, died Calaruega, c. 1200. She married Felix de Guzman, warden of Calaruega, and having borne two sons she prayed at the shrine of St Dominic of Silos for a third child. Her prayer having been answered, she resolved to name the child Dominic in gratitude. Feast 2 August.

Joan of France, foundress of the Franciscan Annunciades, born Paris, 1464, died Bourges, 4 February 1504. She was the sister of Charles VII of France. Joan was despised by her father, probably due to the fact that she was deformed from birth. Aged just two months, she was betrothed to the duke of Orleans and was later sent to his chateau to be trained in court etiquette. At the age of 12 her marriage was solemnized, although she was badly treated by the duke, who later had the marriage annulled. Joan was now free to fulfil her lifelong ambition of founding a religious community. The Franciscan Annunciades were a community dedicated to acts of charity. The community Rule was approved in 1501 and a second house was founded at Bourges the following year. Joan adopted the name Sister Gabriella Marie and made her profession, although she never lived in the community itself.

Joan of Lestonnac, born Bordeaux, 1556, died there, 2 February 1640. Aged 16 she married Gaston de Montferrant and had seven children, five of whom survived into adulthood. She was widowed in 1597, and became a Cistercian. Then, encouraged by the Jesuits as part of their struggle against Calvinism, she founded an order of nuns, the Company of Mary, to teach girls, which had 26 houses in her lifetime.

Joan of Maillé (Jane), born 1331, died Tours, 1414, cult confirmed 1871. Married for 16 years to the Baron de Silly, but living as a virgin, after his death in 1362 she moved to Tours as a Franciscan tertiary. Feast 28 March.

Joan of Orvieto, Dominican tertiary and mystic, born Carnaiola, near Orvieto, 1264, died Orvieto, 23 July 1306. Having refused a proposed marriage, she entered the third order of St Dominic, where her director was **James of Bevagna**. She frequently received visions as well as the stigmata. In spite of her own protestations, she was venerated by the local townsfolk as a saint during her own lifetime. She was tireless in her care of the poor and sick. It was said that the best way to be assured of her prayers was to do her an injury.

Joan of Portugal, bl., religious, born Lisbon, 6 February 1452, died (of a fever) Aveiro, 12 May 1490. She was the eldest child and heiress to Alfonso V of Portugal. Ignoring family pressure to marry, and determined to remain chaste, she resolved to enter a convent. Her family forbade her from taking vows while she was heir to the throne, and it is possible that they effectively imprisoned her, but she took her vows in 1475 once the succession was secured, and assumed the Dominican habit at the convent of Jesus at Aveiro, although she was never solemnly professed, nor did she give up control of her property.

Joan of Reggio, bl., born Reggio Emilia, 1428, died there, 9 July 1491. Giovanni Scopelli was forbidden to become a nun by her parents, but when they died she decided to found a Carmelite convent in the town. She was given a house by a widow, and the widow and her two daughters joined Joan, living together and raising funds to build the convent. The convent of Our Lady of the People opened in 1485, and Joan was the first prioress.

Joan of Santa Lucia, bl., religious, born Fonte-chiuso, Italy, 4 September (year unknown), died there, 16 or 17 January *c.* 1105. She joined the Camaldolese convent of St Lucia at Bagno. Little else is known of her life. In 1287 her remains were transferred to the parish church at Bagno. Some time later the cessation of the plague in the town was ascribed to her intercession. She became the town's patroness in 1506. Feast 16 January.

Joan of Signa, bl., recluse, born Signa, near Florence, *c.*1245, died there, 9 November 1307. At the age of 23 she became a recluse at a cell in Signa, leading a life of austerity and prayer for over 40 years. She had the reputation of being a miracle worker. Joan is claimed by the Franciscans, the Carmelites, the Vallombrosan monks and the Augustinians as a tertiary, although there is no direct evidence to support the claims. In 1348 the cessation of an epidemic at Signa was attributed to her intercession. Feast 17 November.

Joan Soderini, bl., born Florence, 1301, died there, 1 September 1367. She belonged to a noble family. She refused to marry, and instead joined the Third Order of Servites, which had been established in Florence by **Juliana Falconieri**, whom she succeeded as prioress.

Joanna, Camaldolese nun, died 1105. Feast 16 January.

Joanna Maria Bonomo, bl., born Asiago, Lombardy, 15 August 1606, died Bassano, 1 March 1670, beatified 1783. A Benedictine in Bassano from 1620, she apparently received the stigmata in 1637. The priests and bishops responsible for her monastery, mistrustful of mystics, bullied her, but despite their opposition, she was twice elected abbess.

Joanna Maria of the Cross, ven., poet and founder of two convents of Poor Clares, born Roverto, Italy, 8 September 1603, died Roverto, 26 March 1673. In 1650 she founded the Convent of Poor Clares of St Charles in Roverto and became its abbess. In 1672 she founded the convent of Poor Clares of St Anne in Borgo Valsugana and was influential in founding a Carmelite convent nearby. She worked to establish peace during the Thirty Years War. She wrote *Evangelici Spirituali Sentimenti*, an unpublished autobiography and much poetry – becoming known as 'first poetess of the Trentino'.

Joannes (in medieval names), see **John**.

Joannicius of Devic, born Montenegro, died Devic, 2 December 1430. Serbian Church. He lived in a cave in Montenegro, but so many came to visit him that he eventually fled to the uninhabited region of Devic. A monastery was later built on the spot.

Joannicius of Serbia II, patriarch, born Prizren, Kosovo, died near Pec, 1354. Serbian Church. He was chancellor to the king, but in 1338 was raised to the office of archbishop of Pec. When the king decided to take the title of emperor (Tsar), his see was made patriarchal. This took place in 1346, although without the approval of the patriarch of Constantinople, so a schism developed between the Churches which was not resolved until after Joannicius's death. Feast 3 September.

Joannicus ('the Great'), monk, born Bithynia, *c.* 754, died there, 846. He was a swineherd until he joined the Byzantine army, then led a dissolute life for a time, but was then converted. He remained in the army for a while, then went back to Bithynia, where he entered a monastery on Mount Olympus. He gained a reputation for healing and as a spiritual guide. While in the army he had been an iconoclast, but after his conversion he was a defender of the veneration of images. Feast 4 November.

Joasaph (or Josaphat), in medieval legend the son of Abenner, an Indian king. As it had been prophesied in his infancy that he would be converted to Christianity, he was subsequently kept locked in a palace. He escaped and was converted by the hermit Barlaam. The story dates from the eighth century, and appears to have been composed in order to glorify Christian monasticism. The name 'Joasaph' would appear to be a corruption of 'Bodisatva', a title of the Buddha. Joasaph has been commemorated in the Roman martyrology on 27 November.

Joasaph Bolotov, bishop and missionary, born near Tver, 22 January 1761, died (drowned) off the Alaskan coast, 1799. Russian Church. He became a monk and later abbot at the Valaam monastery and was appointed to head the famous mission to Russian America (Alaska). After a successful beginning, he was appointed first bishop of Kodiak for Alaska. He was consecrated bishop in Siberia, but was shipwrecked before he could enter his diocese. Revered still as the first Orthodox bishop of America. Feast 22 January.

Joasaph of Belgorod, Russian Orthodox bishop, born Poltave province, 8 September 1705, died 10 December 1754. He was appointed bishop of Belgorod through the direct intervention of Empress Elizabeth and became a zealous pastor, constantly travelling around his vast and poor diocese. Miracles were attributed to him in his lifetime and even more so after his death, when his tomb became a shrine for pilgrims. He was not canonized until 1911, one of the last such ceremonies before the revolution. Feast 10 December.

Joasaph of Niznij Novgorod, recluse, sixteenth century. Russian Church. Nothing is known of his life.

Joasaph of Vologda, bishop, died 1570. Russian Church. Became bishop of Vologda some time in the 1550s. Possibly a former hegumenos, and author of saints' lives.

Joavan, bishop, born Ireland, died Brittany, *c.* 570. He came to join his uncle **Paul of Léon** at the monastery of Landevenic, and afterwards travelled with him to Britain. Paul ordained him coadjutor bishop of Léon. Feast 2 March.

Job of L'Govskie, born Volokolamsk, *c.* 1592, died Cir, 9 May 1681. Church of the Old Believers. Baptized John Timofeev Lichacev into a boyar family, at 17 he joined the monastery of St **Sergius of Radonez**, but then founded a hermitage at Mogilev and later a monastery near Tver. He was in time a candidate for the patriarchal see of Moscow, but he attempted, successfully, to avoid

this by pretending to have gone mad and hiding. He abandoned his monastery completely, however, when the new liturgy was introduced, and founded another at L'Govskie, near Rylsk, which followed the old ways. He had to leave this one, too, because of persecution, and founded yet another monastery on the river Cir, where he died.

Job of Moscow, patriarch, born Starica, died there, 9 June 1607. Russian Church. His baptismal name was John, and he came from a devout family – his mother became a nun. He joined a monastery in Starica, where he gained a reputation for both gentleness and learning, especially scriptural studies. About 1559 the monastery was visited by Ivan the Terrible, who was impressed by Job and had him made an archimandrite and hieromonk. He then became archimandrite of a monastery in Moscow. In 1581, after ten years in Moscow, he was named bishop of Koloma, then in 1586 bishop of Rostov. Finally, in December 1587, he became metropolitan of Moscow. After negotiations with the patriarch of Constantinople, in January 1589 the see of Moscow became the 'patriarchate of Moscow and all Russia', and Job succeeded to that title. As patriarch he was particularly concerned with improving the administration of his see, but also with missionary work throughout Russia, constructing monasteries and canonizing new saints. In the dynastic struggles he backed Boris Godunov, who succeeded to the throne, and Job carried out Russia's first imperial coronation. However, after the death of Godunov in 1605, he refused to accept the 'false' Demetrius, was attacked while celebrating the liturgy and exiled back to Starica. In exile he became blind, and when asked to return to the patriarchate he refused, although he returned to Moscow for a short time in 1607 a few months before his death. Feast 2 July.

Job of Niznetagil, monk, eighteenth century. Church of the Old Believers. Baptized John, he joined the Old Believers in 1725, when already a priest. He established a parish at Niznij Tagil in the Urals, which became a major place of pilgrimage for Old Believers.

Job of Pocaev, monk, born Galicin, *c.* 1550, died Pocaev, 28 October 1651. Russian Church. Baptized John Zelezo, at the age of ten he entered the monastery of the Transfiguration at Ugornickij, where he took the name Job. After his ordination he became hegumenos of the monastery of the Exaltation of the Cross at Dubenski. He stayed there for 20 years, but at the end of that time fled to the monastery at Pocaev to escape from all the attenton his sanctity was attracting. Both that monastery and his earlier one were very active in struggles over the Uniate Churches.

Job of Raifskaia Pustyn, martyr, born Odessa, 1880, died near Raifskaia Pustyn, 7 April 1930. Russian Church. Born Ivan Andreevic Protopopov, he served first in Kiev, then transferred in 1917 to the diocese of Kazan, and entered the monastery of the Dormition at Svijazsk. When that was closed after the Russian Revolution he moved to Raifskaia Pustyn, where he was ordained. After that monastery was closed he served in a nearby parish. He was arrested in January 1930 and was later shot. Feast 14 January.

Job of Solovki, monk, born Moscow, 1635, died Anzer, 6 March 1720. Russian Church. Baptized John, he became a priest in Moscow, and many were attracted to his liturgy because of his devotion to the services and his use of the chant. Although for a time the confessor of the imperial household, he was devoted to the poor and the imprisoned. He was, however, falsely accused of supporting a fanatic who was opposed to the Tsar, and was therefore sent to the Solovki monastery where he lived so ascetical a life that he was known to the other monks as 'the faster'. It was when he became a monk that he was given the name Job. The Tsar came to realize the holiness of Job, and wanted him to come back to court, but instead he retreated to an even more isolated spot on the island of Anzer where there was a hermitage. He became the superior of the hermitage, and imposed upon it a very strict Rule of life. Later, with two of his monks, he went on to found another such hermitage in an even more remote spot, aided by the support of the Tsar and Tsarina.

Job of Uscel, monk, died Uscel, 5 August 1628. Russian Church. Founder of the monastery at Uscel, although originally of the Solovki monastery, and killed by brigands.

Job of Vladimir, monk, fifteenth century? Russian Church. Archimandrite of Vladimir.

Johannes (in medieval names), see **John**.

John, see also **Anthony and John**.

John, see also **Cyrus**.

John, see also **Xenophon**.

John, bishop of Autun, died *c.* 475. Feast 8 May.

John, martyr, died 29 April 1210. Coptic Church. The story is unclear, but he may have been a monk of the monastery of St Macarius who converted to Islam, then suffered martyrdom by beheading when he converted back to Christianity.

John, prince, born Srem, northern Serbia, died there, 10 December 1502. Serbian Church. The son of Ss **Stephen** and **Angelina**, he was last ruler of Srem. He was noted for his piety.

John, martyr in Lithuania, see **Anthony, John and Eustace**.

John, see also **Boris, James, Theodore I, Silvanus, Theodore II, Basil I, Demetrius, Michael, John, Basil II**.

John I, pope, born Tuscany, consecrated 13 August 523, died Ravenna, 18 May 525. Senior deacon on his election, and already old, he was pro-Eastern in sentiment and introduced to the West the Alexandrian method of dating Easter. He went to Constantinople on the instructions of Theodoric, king of Italy, to dissuade the emperor from persecuting Arians on the Italian peninsula. John was treated with great respect by the emperor, but he refused to grant Theodoric's demand that Arians who had been forced to convert to Catholicism should be free to revert to Arianism. Theodoric was furious, but John died suddenly in Ravenna before the king could wreak vengeance.

John II, catholicos, died 1048. Georgian Church. A monk of the monastery of Kalipos, near Antioch in Syria, he was elected in 1033. Feast 3 March.

John III, Ducas Vatatzes, Eastern Orthodox saint, born Dioymotaichos, Byzantine Empire, 1193, died 3 November 1254. He was the son-in-law of Theodore I, whom he succeeded in 1222. Twice John III defeated his rivals and conquered Asia Minor. He allied himself with the Bulgarian Tsar Arsen and besieged Constantinople. On Arsen's death, John annexed territory in Bulgaria. He was involved in negotiations with the Holy Roman Empire – after his first wife died, he married the daughter of the Emperor Frederick II – and the papacy, in an attempt to win back Constantinople which was still occupied by the Latins (he was ruling from Nicaea). He improved agriculture and stockbreeding, built hospitals and poorhouses, and was revered as St John the Merciful.

John IV, patriarch of Constantinople, died 2 September 595. First a deacon at Hagia Sophia, later patriarch (582–95) under emperors Tiberius II and Maurice, John was popular at court as well as renowned for his asceticism – hence his nickname 'John the Faster'. He is known primarily for his assumption of the title 'ecumenical patriarch', the apparent arrogance of which proved controversial to Pope **Gregory I** and other primates. At his death, John left only a cloak, a blanket and a prayer stool. Feast 12 September.

John al-Rabban, monk, born Cairo, died Samannud, fourteenth century. Coptic Church. The son of a wealthy family, he entered a monastery south of Cairo, but spent some time in a number of different houses, including some in the Holy Land. He was ordained a priest. He died in the city of Samannud, in the Delta.

John Alcober, see **Peter Sanz**.

John Almond, martyr, born Allerton, near Liverpool, died Tyburn, London, 5 December 1612. He was educated in Ireland, then studied for the priesthood in Rome and was sent to the English mission in 1602. He was once captured, but was either released or escaped, before being arrested again in 1612, sent to Newgate prison, and executed at Tyburn.

John Amias, bl., born Wakefield, Yorkshire, martyred York, 16 March 1589, beatified 1929. A widower, he was ordained in France 1581, was arrested and hanged, drawn and quartered with **Robert Dalby**.

John and Paul, martyrs, died *c.* 361. John and Paul were martyred in Rome during the reign of Julian the Apostate (361–3); their legend, which is not historically reliable, claims that they were eunuchs of Constantina, daughter of **Constantine the Great**; that they were converted, then beheaded secretly by the emperor's command and buried in their house on the Caelian Hill. This house was built into a Christian basilica in the second half of the fourth century by the senator Byzantius and his son Pammachius, and is still one of the most important memorials of early Christianity in Rome. Feast 26 June.

John Andrew Houben (Charles of St Andrew), born Munstergeleen, Holland, 11 December 1821, died Mount Argus, Dublin, Ireland, 5 January 1893, beatified 1988. A Passionist priest, he came to England after his ordination in 1852. He worked in England and Ireland for the rest of his life, and people everywhere flocked to him for his blessing and advice.

John Angelo Porro, bl., born near Milan, *c.* 1451, died there, 1506. He joined the Servites and was sent to Monte Senario, where he remained for the next two decades, gaining a great reputation for holiness. He was then sent as master of novices to Florence. He was more of a contemplative by nature, although he worked to reform the houses of his order in which he lived. Feast 24 October.

John Baptist Chon Chang-un, see **Peter Ch'oe Hyong Hyeng**.

John Baptist de la Salle, founder of the Institute of the Brothers of the Christian Schools – the de la Salle Brothers, born Rheims, 30 April 1651, into a wealthy and noble family, died St Yon, Rouen, 7 April 1719. He entered the seminary of St Sulpice, Paris, in 1670, and was ordained priest in 1678. Inspired by a layman, he assisted in the establishment of schools and recruited teachers for them, accommodating the teachers in his own house. In 1683 he resigned his canonry at Rheims, distributed his wealth to the poor and devoted his energies to the improvement of teachers. With 12 of his teachers, he formed the Institute of the Christian Schools, which did not get papal approval until 1725. La Salle established teachers' colleges at Rheims in 1687, at Paris in 1699 and at St Denis in 1709, at the same time steadily increasing the number of schools for boys under his control. He wrote his revolutionary *Conduite des écoles Chrétiennes*, which replaced individual instruction with classroom teaching, then new, and in the vernacular. In 1698 he opened a college for the aristocratic Irish followers of James II who had followed him into exile in France. La Salle countered much opposition from the secular masters, from the Jansenists, and from his own Brothers of the Institute because of reported severity in the training of his novices. His fledgling Institute weathered these storms as De La Salle schools spread throughout France and Italy and, during and after the French Revolution, into the British Isles and eventually throughout the world. The founder retired in 1717 to St Yon. His other main writings are *Les devoirs du chrétienne* (1703), *Recueil de différents petit traites à la usage des Frères des Écoles Chrétiennes* (1711), and several books of meditations. Many subsequently founded religious congregations are modelled on his ideas. Pope Leo XIII canonized him in 1900 and Pope Pius XII named him patron of teachers in 1950.

John Baptist Mazzucconi, bl., born Rancio di Lecco, near Milan, 1 March 1826, died Woodlark Island, near Papua New Guinea, 1855. He came from a wealthy family. He decided to become a foreign missionary, and was ordained in 1850. In 1852 he went to Rooke Island (now Kampalap Siassu), where he contracted malaria. He was sent to Sydney for treatment. On his way back his ship was driven ashore at Woodlark Island, some 400 miles from Rooke Island, where the local people were very hostile. He and the boat's crew were all killed. The exact date is not known. Feast 7 September.

John Baptist Nam Chong-Sam, martyr, born Ch'ungju, Korea, 1812, died Seoul, 7 March 1866, beatified 1968, canonized 1984. He was a civil servant, becoming a regional governor, then a teacher. A known Catholic, he went on official business to a French bishop. Jealous officials then initiated a general persecution of Catholics – see **Martyrs of Korea**.

John Baptist of the Conception, bl., Trinitarian reformer, writer and mystic, born Almadovar del Campo, Spain, 10 July 1561, died Córdoba, 14 February 1613. He studied philosophy at Almadovar and theology at Baeza and Toledo. In 1580 he entered the Trinitarian order and was admired for his virtue, mortification and prayerfulness. He was professed in 1581 and was made official preacher at La Guardia and Seville. In 1594 he was made superior at Valdepenas. He was a prolific writer on theology and mysticism. At Valdepenas he reformed (although he said 'restored') the order by adding the use of sandals and other austerities to the Rule. He established 19 houses of the Discalced Friars. Today these Discalced Trinitarians form the surviving branch of the Trinitarian Friars as founded by **John of Matha** (1213) and **Felix of Valois** (1198).

John Baptist Righi of Fabriano, bl., born Ancona, 1469, died Massacio, 1539, cult approved 1903. He was a Franciscan who lived as a hermit. Feast 11 March.

John Baptist Rossi, born Voltaggio (Genoa), 22 February 1698, died Rome, 23 May 1764. From an impoverished family and of a sickly constitution, Jean Baptist needed a special dispensation to be ordained in 172. He became a canon of the church of Santa Maria in Cosmedin, where a cousin was already a canon. He proved himself an outstanding and popular priest, much sought after as a confessor. He was concerned for the temporal and spiritual welfare of the poor, preaching in marketplaces, hospitals, prisons and at any gathering of the poorer classes. He was particularly concerned with the homeless, and established a residence for homeless women. Leo XIII canonized him in 1881.

John Baptist Scalabrini, bl., bishop and founder, born Fino Mornasco, near Como, 8 July 1839, died Piacenza, 1 June 1905. The son of a devout family – his father was a wine merchant – he entered the seminary and was ordained on 30 May 1863. He then taught at the seminary, and eventually became its rector. His next post was as a parish priest in Como, and in 1875 he became bishop of

Piacenza. He was very active in his diocese, and became particularly concerned over the welfare of emigrants. To this end he founded the Missionaries of St Charles in 1887, and in 1895 the Missionary Sisters of St Charles, who worked with migrants in the USA.

John Baptist Spagnuolo, see **Baptist of Mantua**.

John Baptist Turpin du Cormier and Companions, martyrs, see **Martyrs of Laval**.

John bar Abdun, patriarch, born 1004, died Thracia, 1033. Syriac Church. Accused of not adhering to the Chalcedonian faith, he was arrested in the monastery of Barid and taken to Constantinople, where he was put on trial in Hagia Sophia in June 1029. He was then exiled to a monastery on Mount Ganos in Thracia.

John bar Aphtonia ('the Great'), monk, born Edessa, c. 489, died Qennesrin, 4 November 538. Syriac Church. He entered the monastery of St Thomas in Seleucia when he was still very young. In 518, however, there was a campaign against the anti-Chalcedonians. The monks of the monastery who rejected Chalcedon were supposed to leave the monastery, but appear not to have done so, instead electing John as their superior. In 531, however, the campaign was renewed, and this time John and his community established a new monastery, with him as its archimandrite, at Qennesrin on the Euphrates. It became renowned for the quality of its learning. John himself wrote a number of works. Feast 4 November.

John bar Nagore, martyr, born and died Bartelli, near Mosul. Syriac Church. Killed by his father, a carpenter, because of his Christianity.

John bar Penkaye, born Finik, c. 660, died Kamul, c. 735. Syriac Church. He became a monk at Kamul, although later lived for some time as a hermit. He had wide interests, but especially in the study of history, and left a number of writings.

John Bassano, bl., religious, reformer and diplomat, born Besançon, France, 1360, died Córdoba, 14 February 1613. In 1378 he entered the Augustinian monastery in Besançon and in 1390 the

Celestines in Paris. He was later sent to found a monastery in Amiens, where he became the director of St Collette. Between the years 1411 and 1441 he was prior in Paris, and provincial of France five times. During this period he travelled extensively. He was sent by Charles VII of France on a diplomatic mission to try to persuade the antipope Felix V to resign his claim to the papacy. This mission was unsuccessful. In 1443 he was called upon by Pope Eugene IV to reform the monastery at Collemaggio. Feast 26 August.

John Beche, bl., abbot and martyr, died Colchester, 1539. His surname may have been Marshall; his religious name was Thomas. A graduate of Oxford, he was abbot of St Werburgh's, Chester, before becoming abbot of Colchester in 1533. With his friends **Thomas More** and **John Fisher** he was an opponent of Henry VIII's Act of Supremacy, but appears to have been tried and convicted for opposing the suppression of his monastery. Feast 15 November.

John Benincasa, bl., Servite hermit, born Florence, 1376, died Monticelli, 9 May 1426. At a very young age he entered the Servite house at Montepulciano, and became a hermit on Mount Montagnata near Siena at the age of 25. He was a rigorous ascetic, and was often sought out by the locals for spiritual advice. It is said that his death was announced by the spontaneous ringing of the local church bells. Feast 11 May.

John Berchmans, Jesuit student, born Diest, Belgium, the son of a shoemaker, 13 March 1599, died Rome, 13 August 1621. Amid the religious controversy in the Netherlands, he was educated in Dienst by Premonstratensians, then at the seminary in Malines as a servant to one of the cathedral canons, and finally, in 1615, at the newly opened Jesuit college in Malines. Influenced by news of Jesuit martyrs, he became a novice at Malines, during which time his mother died and his father was ordained and became a canon of Malines. In 1618 he went (on foot) to study philosophy in Rome.

John Bodley, bl., martyr, born Wells, Somerset, England, 1549, died Andover, England, 2 November 1583. He studied at Winchester and Oxford before he converted to Catholicism. He then went to Douai to study law, returning to England to get married. He was arrested in 1580, and remained in prison for three years. Along with **John Slade**, he was found guilty of refusing to accept the supremacy in matters spiritual of Queen Elizabeth, and was hanged.

John Bosco, priest, founder of the Salesian Order, born near Turin, 1815, died there, 31 January 1888. Experienced religious visions from about the age of nine, and dedicated his life to the care, education and training of vulnerable boys and young men. Entered the seminary in 1831 and went on to further theological studies in Turin. Beginning with combined Sunday schools and recreation activities for boys, he went on to set up evening classes and eventually, with his mother as housekeeper, took some homeless boys into their home. Later he set up hostels where, in addition to receiving food, shelter, education and spiritual guidance, they could learn a trade. A positive and encouraging, rather than punitive, approach was taken in matters of discipline. In 1859 Don Bosco established the Pious Society of St Francis de Sales to continue and develop all the aspects of his work which, in 1872, was extended to girls and young women. By the time of his death there were about 750 Salesians in over 60 houses in Europe and in North and South America.

John Boste, martyr, born Dufton, Westmoreland, England, c. 1543, died Dryburn, near Durham, England, 24 July 1594. Trained at Oxford, Boste became a Roman Catholic in 1576 despite having taken the Oath of Supremacy. In 1580, he travelled to the English College at Rheims, France, to train for the priesthood and returned to England in 1581. He travelled secretly around the country, mostly in the north, in the livery of Lord Montacute, illegally promoting the Roman Catholic faith. He was betrayed and arrested in September 1593. After serving time in the Tower of London and refusing to reveal other Roman Catholics, he was sent to Durham for trial. He was accused of high treason, waived his right to a trial to spare a jury the guilt of his blood, and died forgiving his executioners and inspiring his colleagues. He was canonized as one of the **Forty Martyrs** of England and Wales.

John Bretton (Britton), bl., martyr, born West Riding, Yorkshire, died York, 1 April 1598, beatified with other English martyrs 1987. He led a difficult life, sometimes in hiding and, as a Catholic, paying fines. Accused, apparently from malice, of treason against Queen Elizabeth, he was executed when he was about 68.

John Buoni, bl., founder, born Mantua, c. 1168, died there, 1249. After the death of his father, he earned a living as an entertainer (jester) and lived a debauched life. In 1208 he nearly died, and the experience made him change his ways. He lived for a time as a hermit near Cesena, leading an extremely austere life. He attracted disciples, and formed them into a community under the Rule of St Augustine. They became known as the Buoniti, but not long after his death were amalgamated with another order. Feast 23 October.

John Buralli, bl., born Parma, 1208, died Camerino, 19 March 1289, cult approved 1777. As minister general of the Franciscans in 1248, he visited all European friaries incognito, seeking to heal divisions in the order. After stepping down, he lived at the Grecchio hermitage, leaving occasionally to undertake papal missions.

John Busnaya, monk, born near Mosul. Syriac Church. Apparently a monk of the monastery of Qaraqos. Feast 1 November.

John Calabria, founder, born Verona, 8 October 1873, died there, 4 December 1954. The son of a cobbler, he was educated at a charitable institute, but one of the priests noticed his piety and tutored him for a scholarship. Although his studies were interrupted by military service, he was eventually ordained, but in the meantime he had started giving shelter to poor children. After he became rector of a church in the city, he was able to establish a house to provide a more permanent home for the street children of Verona. Lay people came to help him, and he founded the religious institute for men that became the Poor Servants of Divine Providence. The Congregation received diocesan approval in 1932, and papal approval in 1949. He later went on to found a similar organization for women, the Poor Women Servants of Divine Providence. Before his death his two foundations had spread throughout Italy and across the world.

John Calabytes, monk, born Constantinople, c. 415, died there, c. 450. He ran away from home when still very young to become a monk. After a time he became a hermit, and lived in a hut in the grounds of his parents' house, although they did not recognize him until he revealed his identity on his deathbed. A church was later built on the spot. The story is quite possibly legendary. Feast 15 January.

John Cantius, see **John of Kanti**.

John Cassian, born Romania (?), c. 360, died Marseilles, 433. He became a monk at Bethlehem, went to Egypt to study monasticism, then to Constantinople where he was a supporter of **John Chrysostom**. He travelled to Rome to defend Chrysostom, and then settled in Marseilles, where he founded two monasteries. His writings were influential in the development of monasticism in the West, and were commended by both **Augustine** of Hippo and **Benedict**. Feast 23 July.

John Chachuleli, bishop, eleventh/twelfth centuries. Georgian Church. Presumably originally a monk of the Georgian monastery of Chachuleli, he became in 1019 a monk on Mount Athos, and then it seems bishop of Bolnisi in southern Georgia. He wrote a number of works, including homilies. Feast 10 March.

John Chanztheli, martyr, tenth century. Georgian Church. A monk of the monastery of Chanztha in southern Georgia, he went on a pilgrimage to Jerusalem, but during his return journey was taken captive in Baghdad and, when he refused to convert to Islam, was executed.

John Charles Cornay, martyr, born Poitiers, 27 February 1809, died Ban Ho, Tonkin, Vietnam, 20 September 1837. A member of the Paris Foreign Mission Society, he was arrested in 1835 and imprisoned. Because of his fine voice he was forced to sing to his captors. He was eventually beheaded, and his body hacked into little pieces.

John Chrysostom, bishop of Constantinople, born Syrian Antioch, between 344 and 354, died in exile in the small town of Comana (Pontus, today in Turkey), 14 September 407. After an outstanding education he turned his back on a worldly career and had himself baptized. He became a lector and studied exegesis with Theodore of Tarsus. Then he retired to the mountains near Antioch to live a severely ascetic life. However, his health suffered too much and after six years he returned to the city (378). In 381 he became a deacon, in 386 a presbyter. In 398 he was more or less coerced to become bishop of Constantinople. Chrysostom did not succeed in establishing good relations with the imperial court. Because of his attempts to reform the clergy of Constantinople and the enmity of Theophilus of Alexandria, he was twice exiled. He died during the second term of exile. Among his writings, his homilies particularly stand out – he was probably the greatest preacher of the early Church. Most of them are exegetical or theological, while always betraying a genuine concern for the less privileged. Feast 13 September.

John Climacus, abbot, born possibly Palestine, c. 525, died Thole, near Mount Sinai, possibly 30 March 605. He was married, but after the death of his wife became a monk and hermit. When he was 70 he was elected abbot of Mount Sinai, retiring back to his hermitage a decade later. He wrote *Ladder (Klimax) to Paradise*, a treatise of spiritual exercises which became very influential throughout the Church and gave rise to his name, and *To the Shepherd*, on spiritual fatherhood.

John Colombini, founder of the Congregation of Jesuati, born Siena, Italy, c. 1300, died en route to Aquapendente, 31 July 1367. He was a rich and influential businessman who gradually left materialism behind and sought the spiritual life and service to the poor and sick. With the eventual acquiescence of his wife, he began a life of apostolic poverty. He attracted many young men to join him, and the families of the richer and more influential amongst them cause him to be banished from Siena. He and a group of followers traversed Tuscany preaching and serving the poor, and on their return to Siena were welcomed and honoured. They were eventually approved by Pope Urban V, a week before Colombini died. Their main apostolate was the care of the sick, especially those with the plague, and the burial of the dead. They also led a life of prayer and mortification. Abuses crept into the Congregation and it was suppressed in 1668.

John Cornelius, bl., martyr, born Bodmin, Cornwall, 1557, executed Dorchester, 4 July 1594. He was educated at Exeter College, Oxford, and became a fellow of the college in 1575, but was expelled three years later for being a Catholic. He studied for the priesthood in Rheims and Rome, and was ordained in 1582. He returned to England in September 1583 and worked as a chaplain for the Arundell family. He was arrested in 1594 and taken to London, where he was tortured for the names of those who had helped him. He refused to reveal any information, and was sent to Dorchester to be tried. On 2 July he was found guilty of being a priest and sentenced to be hanged, drawn and quartered, along with three laymen who had been arrested with him. They are known collectively as the Dorchester Martyrs.

John da Lecceto Chigi, bl., born Maciareto, near Siena, 1300, died there, 28 October 1363. He became a lay brother with the Augustinians of Lecceto and led an exemplary life in Vallaspra, Siena and Pavia, and later once again in Siena.

John Damascene, theologian, born *c.* 650, in an influential family in Damascus, he died certainly before 754. After a career at the caliph's court, he retired *c.* 700, when Christians were excluded from government offices, to the monastery of St Sabas near Jerusalem. Later he received priestly ordination. In the iconoclast controversy he defended the veneration of images. His most important work is the *Source of Knowledge*, a kind of systematic theological compendium (including a catalogue of heresies). He also wrote moral, ascetic and homiletic works. Feast 4 December.

John Danilovic, prince, born Moscow, *c.* 1290, died there, 31 March 1340. Russian Church. The son of Prince **Daniel of Moscow**, he succeeded to the throne after the death of his brother Gregory in 1325. It was very largely thanks to John's efforts that Moscow came to establish itself as the chief city of Russia. He built the cathedral of the

Dormition in the Kremlin, and entered a monastery shortly before his death.

John de, see also **John of**.

John de Brébeuf, martyr, born Normandy, 1593, died Canada, 16 March 1649. De Brébeuf joined the Society of Jesus and went to Canada in 1615, arriving in Quebec to assist the Franciscans who were already there. De Brébeuf first worked among the Algonquin, then with the Huron, but did not make any converts. He returned to France, but went back again in 1632, accompanied on this occasion by **Anthony Daniel**. They were later joined by five others, including **Isaac Jogues** and **Charles Garnier**. The missions to the Huron were beginning to make progress, but de Brébeuf and **Gabriel Lalemant** were attacked in March 1649 by an Iroqois war party, the enemies of the Huron, and were killed, de Brébeuf on 16 March and Lalemant the following day. See also **Martyrs of North America**. Feast 19 October.

John de Britto, bl., Jesuit missionary, born Lisbon, Portugal, 1 March 1647, died by beheading Oreiour, India, 11 February 1693. He was brought up at court and joined the Jesuits in 1662. He was sent to Madura in southern India and was in Goa in 1673. He did the 30-day Spiritual Exercises in Ambalacarte near Crangamore, joined a noble caste and learned the languages of India before proceeding to Madras and Vellore. He was imprisoned in 1684 and then expelled, but returned to India in 1691. Two years later he was executed following his attempts to get the newly converted Teriadevan to dismiss all but one of his wives.

John de Castillo, born Spain, 1596. See **Roque González**.

John de la Lande, see **John Lalande**.

John de Ribeira (Ribera), born Seville, 1532, died Valencia, 1611. Ordained in 1557, bishop of Badajoz, archbishop of Valencia, he was among those who worked to expel the Moriscos (converted descendants of the Moors) from Valencia in 1609. Beatified 1796, canonized 1960, during periods of similar Catholic integralism. Feast 6 January.

John della Pace, bl., founder, born Pisa (?), died there, *c.* 1332. A hermit who founded the Brothers of Penance. Feast 12 November.

John Discalceatus, bl., born Saint-Voregay, Brittany, *c.* 1280, died Quimper, 15 December 1349. Becoming a Franciscan friar in 1316, he went barefoot for over 13 years and was devoted to charitable deeds, even giving away his clothes. He died of a plague. Many miracles led him to be popularly held a saint and commemorated in the Franciscan Order, but this never attained ecclesiastical approval.

John Doan Trinh Hoan, martyr, born Kim-Long, Vietnam, *c.* 1789, died near Doug Hoi, Vietnam, 1861, canonized 1988. He was an enthusiastic priest who was beheaded and is commemorated with **Matthew Nguyen Van Phuong** – see **Martyrs of Vietnam**. Feast 26 May.

John Dominici, bl., cardinal, born Florence, died Buda, Hungary, 10 June 1419. Of humble birth – and afflicted with a stammer – he entered the Dominican Order, studied in Paris, then taught in Venice. He wrote on theology and on education, and was sufficient of an artist to be able to illuminate the manuscripts himself. He became confessor to Pope Gregory XII, and was created cardinal: it was he who informed the Council of Constance that Gregory was prepared to resign to help end the Western schism. Pope Martin V, elected at Constance, made him legate to Bohemia, where his task was to suppress the Hussites, but the king refused to allow him to do so and he set off back to Rome, but died on the way.

John Duckett, bl., martyr, born Underwinder, Yorkshire, 1613, died Tyburn, London, 7 September 1644. He studied at Douai, became a priest in 1639, and went in 1643 to work in County Durham, where he was arrested on 2 July. He was sent to London with **Ralph Corby**, and the two were together hanged at Tyburn.

John Duns Scotus, bl., Franciscan, priest, philosopher, theologian and teacher, born probably at Moxton, near Roxburgh, 1265, died Cologne, 8 November 1308. He was taught by an uncle at the friary at Dumfries, and entered the order. He went to Oxford *c.* 1290 and was ordained in 1291. From 1293 to 1296 he was a student in Paris, but then returned to Oxford to lecture on the *Sentences* of Peter Lombard, 1297–1301. He studied, and then taught, at Paris again until 1307, when he was sent to teach at Cologne, where he died. He wrote commentaries on Aristotle and many other works in his short lifetime, but his most important work is the commentary on the *Sentences*, based on his notes from his Oxford lectures. His thought incorporated elements from **Augustine** within the Aristotelianism influential at the time. In particular he advocated that Love and Will were of first importance in distinction from the primacy of Knowledge and Reason of St **Thomas Aquinas**. He is also known as the first theologian of note to defend the immaculate conception and the inevitability of the incarnation irrespective of the fall. The Scotist system was particularly influential in medieval times and was accepted by the Franciscans as a basis for doctrine. In the Middle Ages he was known by the nickname of 'Doctor subtilis' – 'the subtle teacher'.

John Elisaeus, hermit, 1312. Feast 9 August.

John Eudes, missionary, born Ri, Normandy, 1601, died Caen, 19 August 1680. Having been educated by the Jesuits, he became a priest in 1625 and served in the Oratory at Paris. For several years he worked as a missionary in various regions of France. In 1641 he founded the Order of our Lady of Charity, a charity formed to care for fallen women. In 1643 he established at Caen the Congregation of Jesus and Mary (the Eudists). He is best known for promoting the devotion to the Sacred Hearts of Jesus and Mary. His written works include *Le Coeur admirable de la Mère de Dieu* (1670) and *La Vie et le royaume de Jésus* (1637).

John Felton, bl, martyr, died London, 8 August 1570. His wife Mary was servant and childhood friend to Queen Elizabeth I, and the Catholic family was allowed access to the clergy without recrimination as a consequence. In this way, Felton obtained copies of **Pius V**'s papal bull excommunicating Elizabeth. He published them in England. When confronted, he admitted his involvement, and was tortured. He sent a ring to Elizabeth by way of reconciliation, but maintained his belief in papal supremacy. He was executed at St Paul's Cathedral, his corpse desecrated as that of a rebel.

John Finch, bl., martyr, born Eccleston, Lancashire, died Lancaster, 20 April 1584, beatified 1929. A yeoman farmer who first conformed under Queen Elizabeth I, he reverted to Catholicism, being open about it and helping priests. He is commemorated with **James Bell**, with whom he was hanged, drawn and quartered after two years in prison.

John Fingley, bl., martyr, born Barneby, Yorkshire, died York, 8 August 1586. He studied at Caius College, Cambridge, before going to the English College at Rheims, where he was ordained priest in 1580 and sent on the English mission the following year, when he worked in York. He was arrested in York, and hanged, drawn and quartered.

John Fisher, cardinal, theologian, and martyr, born Beverly, Yorkshire, 1459, died London, 22 June 1535. He was educated at Cambridge, ordained priest in 1491 and gained the patronage of Lady Margaret Beaufort, whose confessor he became in 1497, encouraging her patronage of the university of Cambridge, where she founded a Chair of Divinity in 1503 and Christ's College in 1505. St John's, its sister college, was supervised by Fisher in 1511 and he persuaded Erasmus to lecture in Greek there 1511–14. He became president of Queens' College as well as chancellor of the university and, in 1504, bishop of Rochester. Although he strongly opposed the teachings of Martin Luther, he was a dedicated and scholarly humanist and not opposed to moderate reforms in the Church. He became confessor to Queen Catherine of Aragon in 1529 and opposed King Henry VIII's attempts to divorce her as well as his title of Supreme Head of the Church in England and the Supremacy Act of 1534. He was condemned for not reporting the subversive prophecies of Elizabeth Barton and for his refusal to take the Oath required by the Act of Succession, and was imprisoned in the Tower with **Thomas More**. In 1535, to the additional fury of Henry VIII, Pope

Paul III created Fisher cardinal. He was put on trial, condemned for treason and beheaded on Tower Hill. Fisher's theological work on the real presence in the Eucharist later influenced the Fathers at the Council of Trent. His complete Latin *Opera* were first published in 1597 at Würzburg. Some of his works against Luther, *Assertionis Lutheranae Confutatio* (1523) and a body of vernacular sermons, especially one on the penitential psalms (1508), were published in England.

John Forest, bl., born possibly Oxford, martyred Smithfield, London, 1538, beatified 1886. A Franciscan priest at Greenwich, he was a confessor of Catherine of Aragon. After the divorce of Henry VIII he spent four years in prison until he was burned at the stake for rejecting the Oath of Supremacy. Feast 22 May.

John-Francis Regis, missionary, born Fontcouverte, Narbonne, 31 January 1597, died Lalouvesc, Ardeche, 31 December 1640. The son of wealthy parents, he was educated by Jesuits at the college in Bezier and elsewhere, and at the age of 18 he entered the Society himself. He worked in Toulouse with victims of the plague, and taught at Pamiers, but his skill as a preacher persuaded his superiors to send him as a missionary around France. From then on Regis devoted his life to converting the Huguenots. His influence reached all classes and brought about a lasting spiritual revival throughout France. Miraculous cures were attributed to him, and thousands immediately venerated him as a saint at his death. **John-Baptist Mary Vianney** ascribed his own vocation and his accomplishments to Regis. Clement XII declared him a saint in 1737. His legacy includes the Sisters of Saint Francis Regis, known as the Religious of the Cenacle, founded in 1830.

John Gabriel Perboyre, martyr, born Le Puech, near Cahors, 6 June 1802, died Ou Tchang Fou, China, 11 September 1840. At the age of 15 he went, with his brother Louis, to the seminary of the Congregation of the Mission. Although his brother was sent on the mission, John's academic ability kept him first at the seminary of Saint Flour, and then in Paris as master of novices. When Louis died in China, John was sent in 1835 to replace him. He worked in Hunan, then in Hupeh. In 1839 there was renewed persecution of the missionaries, possibly because of the British attack on China. He was arrested and tortured, and eventually strangled.

John Grove, bl., martyr, died Tyburn, London, 24 January 1697, with **William Ireland**, beatified 1929. Grove looked after the secret Jesuit house in London. They were falsely accused with **Thomas Whitbread**, **John Fenwick** and **Thomas Pickering** of wanting to murder Charles II when Titus Oates invented the 'Popish Plot'. He was hanged, drawn and quartered.

John Gualbert, abbot and founder of the Vallombrosans, born Florence, Italy, 995, died Passignano, Italy, 12 July 1073. Soon after the murderer of one of his kinsmen asked for his forgiveness on Good Friday, John became a Benedictine monk at St Miniato in Florence. He went to Camaldoli in search of a more ascetic way of life sometime before St **Romuald of Ravenna**'s death in 1027, but around 1030 he left Camaldoli to lead an eremitic life at Vallombrosa. The monastery he founded at Vallombrosa in 1038 incorporated *conversi* to perform manual labour.

John Hogg, see **Edmund Drake**.

John Houghton, Carthusian martyr, born Essex, *c.* 1487, died Tyburn, 4 May 1535. After taking a degree in law from Christ's College, Cambridge in 1506, he studied privately for the priesthood and served as a secular priest for several years until he entered the London Charterhouse *c.* 1515. He served as prior of Beauvale (Nottinghamshire) 1530–31, and was unanimously elected prior of the London Charterhouse in 1531. Imprisoned in the Tower for refusing to swear to the Act of Succession in 1534, he was martyred at Tyburn.

John Ingram, bl., martyr, born Herefordshire, England, 1565, died Gateshead, 26 July 1594. He was brought up a Protestant, but converted and went to the English College in Douai. He went on to Rheims in 1582, but was captured by Calvinist soldiers and held to ransom, along with some of his companions. He escaped and reached Rheims and in 1584 went to the English College in Rome, where he was ordained in 1589. He left for

Scotland in 1591 and worked there for 18 months, until persecution broke out in Scotland. He went to England, but was immediately arrested. In 1594 he was taken to the Tower of London and tortured, but he refused to give any information. He was tried in Durham along with **George Swallowell** and **John Boste**, and was hanged, drawn and quartered in Gateshead.

John Ireland, bl., martyr, died London, 7 March 1544, with **John Larke**, beatified 1929. He was a secular priest.

John Jones (Buckley), Franciscan priest and martyr, born Clynog Fawr, Wales, 1559, executed Southwark, 12 July 1598. In *c.* 1590 he joined the Franciscan Order at Pontoise in France, was professed in 1591, and returned to England in 1592. In 1597 he was arrested and imprisoned on the charge that as a priest ordained abroad he had returned to minister in England. He was found guilty by his own admission and was executed on 12 July 1598 at Southwark. He was canonized by Pope Paul VI in 1970 as one of the **Forty Martyrs of England and Wales**.

John Joseph of the Cross, Franciscan, born Ischia island, southern Italy, 15 August 1654, died Afila, 5 March 1739. Born Carolo Gaetano Calosirto, he joined the Franciscans of the Alcantarine Reform in Naples in 1670 and lived a life of great austerity. In 1674 he founded a monastery in Afila, Piedmont, himself assisting in its construction. He was ordained and became the superior and in 1702 was made vicar provincial of the Alcantarine Reform in Italy.

John Kaloktenis, born Constantinople, died Tebe, *c.* 1190. Byzantine Church. His father wanted him to serve in the imperial court, but John preferred to become a monk, and soon afterwards was created metropolitan of Tebe, where he was concerned to improve both the affairs of the Church and the social conditions of his flock.

John Kama, monk, died 21 December 858. Coptic Church. John's parents arranged a marriage for their only son when he was still very young, but as he wanted to be a monk, he lived with his wife as brother and sister until both agreed that she should enter a convent and he an abbey. He joined the monastery of St Macarius, but then moved on to that of **John Kolobos**, and eventually constructed his own beside the Red Sea.

John Kama of Aged, monk, fourteenth/fifteenth centuries. Ethiopian Church.

John Kama of Dabra Libanos, monk, fourteenth/ fifteenth centuries. Ethiopian Church. Abbot of Dabra Libanos at the time when it came to the fore in Ethiopian monasticism. Feast 29 January.

John Kemble, priest and martyr, born near Hereford, 1599, of a Wiltshire family, died Hereford, 22 August 1678. He studied at the English College, Douai, was ordained priest in 1625 and returned to England, where he set up mission centres in Herefordshire and Gwent. After the Popish Plot (1678), and at the age of 80, he was arrested and tried for being a seminary priest. Sentenced to be hanged, drawn and quartered, he was first taken to London and offered release if he would give details of the nonexistent plot. He was then sent back to Hereford prison where the sentence was carried out. Kemble was canonized in 1970 by Pope Paul VI as one of the **Forty Martyrs of England and Wales**. Feast 25 October.

John Kocurov, martyr, born Bigil'dino-Surka, near Rjazan, 13 June 1871, died Carskoe Selo, 31 October 1917. The son of a priest, he studied at Rjazan and then at St Petersburg before marrying, being ordained and volunteering for the Alaskan mission. He was sent, however, to Chicago. He was raised to the rank of archpriest, and was very active in the restructuring of the Russian Orthodox Church in America. In 1907 he returned to Russia to work in St Petersburg. In 1916 he was made parish priest of the cathedral church at Carskoe Selo, and it was there that he was assassinated by revolutionaries.

John Kolobos ('the Dwarf'), monk, born Tese, Egypt, *c.* 339, died by the Red Sea, 409. Byzantine Church. He became a hermit in the desert of Scete *c.* 357, living near the monastery of St Bishoi. He went on to found his own monastery, but this was destroyed by raiders and he went to live by the Red Sea for the final two years of his life. Feast 9 November.

John Koucouzelis, bl., born Durazzo, died Mount Athos, fourteenth century. Byzantine Church. His father having died when he was very young, his mother sent him to Constantinople to study. In time he became a distinguished musician, in charge of the music at the imperial palace. He himself, however, wanted to live as a monk, and he left for Mount Athos, resisting all the emperor's entreaties to return. His surname means 'beans and peas' – a nickname given him. Feast 1 October.

John Koulikas, martyr, died 8 April 1564. Byzantine Church. Martyred for refusing to deny his faith. Feast 18 April.

John Kovarov, martyr, born 1878, died St Petersburg, 13 August 1922. See **Benjamin of Kazan**.

John Lalande, martyr, born Dieppe, died Auriesville, New York State, 19 October 1646. John Lalande was a layman who was assisting the Jesuit missionaries working among the Huron. He was accompanying **Isaac Jogues** when they were captured by Iroquois. He was beheaded. Feast, with **John de Brébeuf**, 19 October.

John Lantrua, bl., Franciscan priest and martyr, born Triona, Italy, 25 March 1760, died Changsha, China, 7 February 1816. He joined the order in 1777 and was ordained in 1784, serving in Italy until he left for China in 1798, his long journey delaying his arrival until 1800. His apostolate in the provinces of Hunan, Hupen and Kiaugsi was conducted, despite political unrest and religious persecution, from 1802 to 1815, when he was arrested, tortured and put to death by strangulation. His remains were taken to Macao in 1819 and later to Rome, where they rest in the church of St Maria in Aracoeli.

John Larke, bl., martyr, born London, died there, 7 March 1544, beatified 1929. He was rector of St Ethelburga, Bishopsgate, from 1504 and, from 1530, parish priest in Chelsea of **Thomas More**. Apparently inspired by his parishioner, he was charged with attempted treason and hanged, drawn and quartered with **John Ireland** and **German Gardiner**.

John Le Vacher, ven., missionary, consul and martyr, born Ecouen, France, 15 March 1619, died Algiers, 28 July 1683. He was ordained in 1647 in the Congregation of the Missions and in the same year was sent to Tunis by St **Vincent de Paul** as missionary to the Christian slaves. From 1648 to 1653, and again from 1657 to 1666, he acted as French consul in Tunis as well as holding apostolic appointments there and in Carthage. On his return to Algiers from France in 1668 he was appointed vicar apostolic in Algiers, Tripoli, Tunis and Morocco. When a French military force invaded Algiers in 1683 he refused to renounce his faith and was cruelly martyred.

John Lego, bl., priest, part of a group executed Angers, France, 2 January 1794. He is commemorated with his brother **René**, also a priest. See **William Repin**, and **Martyrs of the French Revolution**. Feast 1 January.

John Leonardi, founder, born near Lucca, Italy, c. 1541, died Rome, 9 October 1609. After practising for a time as a pharmacist in Lucca, he was ordained priest in 1572 and became a fervent reformer dedicated to combating Protestantism and promoting the Counter-Reformation. In 1574 he founded the Order of Clerks Regular of the Mother of God, which received episcopal sanction in 1583 and papal approval in 1595. He was prominent in charitable works and initiated the Confraternity of Christian Doctrine, which encouraged the training of laymen in the Church. Leonardi was supported by St **Philip Neri**, and he co-founded at Rome the Colegio Urbano which, under the charge of the Congregation for the Evangelization of Peoples, still trains priests for the foreign missions. The mother church of the Clerks Regular is Sta Maria Campitelli in Rome, where Leonardi's relics are kept. He was canonized in 1938. Feast 9 October.

John Liccio, bl., Dominican preacher, born Càccamo, Sicily, c. 1426, died there, 1511. Influenced by Pietro Geremia, John joined the order as an adolescent in the monastery of Santa Zita in Palermo, founded the monastery of the Holy Spirit

in Polizzi in 1469, and that of Càccamo in 1487. Throughout his life, Liccio demonstrated a spirit of profound humility and total dedication to the poor. Miracles were associated with him during his life and during the transfer of his relics, which led to his beatification by Benedict XIV in 1753. Feast 14 November.

John Lloyd, martyr, born Brecon, 1630 (?), hanged Cardiff, 22 July 1679. John Lloyd studied at Valladolid and laboured in the Welsh mission for 25 years until the outbreak of the Titus Oates persecution, when he was arrested on the charge of saying mass and imprisoned in Cardiff castle. No other charges were made against him, but his priesthood sufficed to condemn him, and a fellow priest named **Philip Evans**, in May 1679. He was canonized in 1970.

John Lobedau, bl., Franciscan, born Torun, Pomerania, c. 1231, died Chelmo, 9 October 1264. He became a Franciscan at Torun and was then sent to Chelmo. Pious, learned and devout, miracles reputedly performed through his intercession led him to be the patron of sailors and fishermen.

John Lockwood (alias Lassels, Lascelles), bl., martyr, born Yorkshire, 1555 or 1561, died York, 13 April 1642, beatified 1929. Ordained in Rome, he escaped death twice after arrests but was eventually hanged, drawn and quartered, despite local protests because of his age. He was executed with **Edmund Catherick**, whom he encouraged to the end.

John-Louis Bonnard, born Saint-Christo-en-Jarez, Loire, France, 1 March 1824, martyred Vietnam, 1 May 1852, beatified 1900, canonized 1988. A priest of the Paris Foreign Missions Society, he had arrived in Tonkin in 1850. See **Martyrs of Vietnam**.

John Macias, born Ribera del Fresno, Estremadura, 2 March 1585, died Lima, Peru, 16 September 1645. As a boy he worked as a shepherd in Estremadura. He decided to go to South America, where he worked on a cattle farm before entering the Dominican Order in Lima as a lay brother in 1622. From then on he worked mainly as the doorkeeper, but his spare time he devoted to the poor, and to prayer. Throughout his life he experienced visions. He was a friend of **Martin de Porres**.

John Mangleli, bishop, died 1751. Georgian Church. A monk of the monastery of Bertubani, he became bishop of Manglisi because of his reputation for holiness.

John Marinoni, bl., Theatine, born Venice, died Naples, 13 December 1562. Francesco Marinoni became a priest in Venice, and eventually a canon of St Mark's cathedral. In 1528, however, he joined the Theatine order, taking the name John. He became superior of the Theatine community in Naples, where he established *montes pietatis*, a form of credit union for the poor.

John-Martin Moÿe, bl., missionary, and founder of religions congregations, born Cutting, Lorraine, France, 27 January 1730, died Trier, Germany, 4 May 1793. Educated in Strasbourg and Metz, Moÿe was ordained in 1754 and spent 17 years in pastoral work in Metz, founding there the Sisters of Divine Providence in 1762 to help with the education of the poor. He spent the years from 1773 to 1784 as a missionary in China, where he founded the Institute of Christian Virgins to teach mothers and children in their homes. He then returned to pastoral work in France. After the revolution, he moved the Sisters to Trier in 1791, but it was suppressed by the advancing French army in 1792 (although later restored in 1816). Moÿe died in a typhus epidemic the following year.

John Mary Mzec, martyred Uganda, 1887. He was converted by the White Fathers, suffered a cruel death as a young man and is seen as one of **Charles Lwanga**'s companions. Feast 27 January.

John-Mary-Robert Lamennais, bl., founder, born St-Malo, 1780, died Ploërmel, Brittany, 26 December 1860. The older brother of Felicité Lamennais, he studied privately and under the Abbé Vielle, who had asylum in the family household during the revolution, and was ordained in 1804. He became vicar general to several bishops, during which time he helped establish, following the revolution, schools, colleges, seminaries and convents. He helped found the ultramontane Congregation of St Peter, and in 1817 founded the Institute of the Brothers of Christian Instruction, modelled on **John Baptist de la Salle**'s congregation, but with an apostolate to serve the poorer country districts. By the time of Lamennais's death there were some 800 members of the congregation working in France and in the French colonies. The mother house was in Ploërmel, where a statue was erected in his honour. He collaborated in a number of the early publications which appear under his brother's name.

John Mason, bl., martyr, born Kendal, died Tyburn, London, 10 December 1591. He was a manservant of a Mr Owen in Oxfordshire, but was arrested with **Edmund Gennings**, whom he had been assisting.

John Menard, bl., martyr, died Angers, 1794. See **Martyrs of the French Revolution**. Feast 16 February.

John Morosini, founder of St Giorgio, Venice. A kinsman of **Peter Orseolo**, the Venetian doge and hermit who resigned to enter the religious life, he accompanied **Romuald of Ravenna** to Cuxa in 978, and led a coenobitic life there. Unlike his companions Romuald of Ravenna, Peter Orseolo and John Grandenigo, he did not become a hermit, and eventually returned to Venice where he founded the monastery of St Giorgio.

John Munden (or Mundyn, or Mondayne), bl., born Dorset, 1543, martyred Tyburn, London, 12 February 1584, beatified 1929. A schoolmaster, he was ordained in Rome *c.* 1582 and arrested as soon as he returned to England that year. He was hung, drawn and quartered with **Thomas Hemerford**, **James Fenn**, **John Nutter** and **George Haydock**.

John Nelson, bl., martyr, born Skelton, Yorkshire, *c.* 1533, died Tyburn, London, 3 February 1578, beatified 1886. A late vocation, he was ordained in France in 1576 and sent to England where he became a Jesuit. He was hanged, drawn and quartered. His two brothers were also priests in England, but were not martyred.

John Nepomucene Neumann, bishop, born Prachitz, Bohemia, 28 March 1811, died Philadelphia,

USA (he dropped dead on the street), 5 January 1860. He studied at the diocesan seminary, then at Charles University, Prague. Inspired to be a missionary in America, he was ordained priest in New York in 1836, entered the Redemptorists in 1842, and was appointed bishop of Philadelphia in 1852. He visited the larger parishes of his diocese annually and the smaller ones every two years. He once walked 25 miles to confirm an invalid boy. He founded nearly 100 schools and 50 churches, and began the cathedral in Philadelphia. He wrote a number of books, including a much-used catechism, and contributed articles to Catholic journals. He was canonized in 1977.

John Ni Youn-Il, catechist, martyred Korea, 1867, see **Martyrs of Korea**. Feast 20 January.

John Nutter, bl., born near Burnley, martyred Tyburn, London, 12 February 1584, beatified 1929. Ordained in France in 1582, arrested in 1583, he spent time in the Marshalsea prison and the Tower of London. He was hanged, drawn and quartered with **Thomas Hemerford**, **James Fenn**, **John Munden** and **George Haydock**. His brother **Robert Nutter** was martyred in 1600.

John of, see also **John de**.

John of Alexandria I, patriarch, born Alexandria, died there, 29 April 503. Coptic Church. A monk of the monastery of St Macarius, and the first to be chosen, in 494, from that community of monks to be patriarch.

John of Alexandria II, patriarch, died Alexandria, 22 May 515. Coptic Church. A monk, although it is uncertain of which monastery, he was elected to succeed his relative **John of Alexandria I**.

John of Alexandria IV, patriarch, born Bana Abu Sir, died 799. Coptic Church. A monk at his election, possibly of the monastery of St Macarius. He was chosen by lot – his name was selected three times – in 775. He enjoyed a time of peace in Egypt for Christians, and he was able to rebuild some of the ruined churches. There was also a famine, and he dispensed aid to the poor of all types, not just Christians, from the wealth of his see. The last years of his rule saw a revival of persecution of Christians and the destruction of churches.

John of Alexandria VI, patriarch, born Old Cairo, died Alexandria, 6 January 1216. Coptic Church. Originally a wealthy, though pious, merchant called Magd Ibn Gaib Ibn Surur, he was elected patriarch while still a layman. He was a strict enforcer of the canons.

John of Arbela, bishop, with **James the Zealot**, died Bet Lapat, 344. Armenian Church. Executed by order of Sharpur.

John of Armant, bishop, born Armant, Upper Egypt, third/fifth centuries. Coptic Church. Born into a pagan family of carpenters, his brother encountered Christians and was converted; so was John on hearing his brother's story. The brother joined a monastery, but John remained at home. He was chosen as their bishop by the Christians of Armant. As bishop he was successful in converting many of the pagans, and successful, too, in defending his flock from the oppressive authorities.

John of Avila, mystic, born Almodóvar del Campo, near Toledo, 1500, died Montilla, 10 May 1569. Of Jewish descent, he studied law (1514–15) before devoting himself to a life of austerity and prayer. He later studied philosophy under Domingo Soto at Alcala. Upon the death of his parents he sold all his property, was ordained priest in 1525 and was prepared for missionary work in Mexico. He was dissuaded from this path by the archbishop of Seville, who encouraged him to revive the faith in Andalusia. John became one of the most effective preachers of his age, although he was summoned before the Inquisition for preaching of the dangers of wealth. He was subsequently acquitted. After a nine-year ministry in Andalusia, John returned to Seville. He later visited many other Spanish towns, despite being in great physical pain for the last 17 years of his life. He was a friend of St **Teresa of Avila**, and was responsible for the conversion of St **Francis Borgia** and St **John of God**.

John of Bankol, monk, fifteenth century. Ethiopian Church. A disciple of **Madhanina Egzi**.

John of Bastone, bl., Sylvestrine monk, born early thirteenth century, died Fabriano, 24 March 1290. He taught grammar at Fabriano, Italy, before becoming a priest, and was resident as a Sylvestrine Benedictine in the monastery of Monte Fano for 60 years.

John of Bergamo, bishop, died *c.* 683. He became bishop of Bergamo in about 670, and probably attended the Council of Milan in 678. He worked to eliminate Arianism in his diocese, and attended the Synod in Rome in 680 with Pope St **Agatho**, to respond to the Eastern emperor on the question of monothelitism. Feast 11 July.

John of Beverley, bishop of York, born Harpham, Humberside, died Beverley, 7 May 721. He studied at Canterbury under St **Adrian**, then became a monk at **Hilda**'s monastery in Whitby. He succeeded **Eata** as bishop of Hexham (687), where he was renowned as a man of piety who cared for the poor and the handicapped. He ordained **Bede** both deacon and priest. He succeeded Bosa as bishop of York (705). He founded the monastery of Beverley and retired there in 717. In 1307 his relics were translated – Henry V ascribed his victory at Agincourt on his translation to John's intercession.

John of Bridlington, prior of St Augustine's, Bridlington, born Thwing, near Bridlington, died 10 October 1379. He studied at Oxford, and became canon at St Augustine's and eventually prior (1362). He was greatly loved, and was regarded as a man of deep piety alongside a great ability as an administrator, exercising the duties of his office with considerable success. He was canonized by Boniface IX in 1401. Feast 21 October.

John of Capistrano, Franciscan, born Capistrano, Italy, 1385, died Villach, Hungary, 23 October 1456. He studied in Perugia and became governor there in 1412. He married, but the marriage was never consummated, and when John decided some time later to join the Franciscans, which he did in 1416, the marriage was annulled. He went with **Bernadine of Siena** on his preaching tours and undertook some preaching himself. He was ordained in 1425 and became a preacher renowned throughout Italy. He also helped in the Franciscan reforms and was sent several times as ambassador

for the Holy See to France and Austria. He travelled through Europe preaching against the Hussites. In 1454 he was at the Diet of Frankfurt and accompanied Hunyady throughout the campaign against the Turks. He wrote mainly against the heresies of his day.

John of Caramola, bl., Cistercian monk and ascetic, born Toulouse, died Chiaramonte, 26 August 1339. He was, for many years, a hermit on Mount Caramola in Italy, living a life of great austerity. He was reputedly given the gift of prophecy. Due to illness he gave up the life of a hermit and became a lay brother at the Cistercian monastery of Santa Maria of Sagittario at Chiaramonte. He continued to live an austere life, feeding upon a little bread and water. It is said that his bed was so small that it was impossible to lie down in a normal position. After his death many miracles were attributed to his intercession.

John of Cathares, abbot, died 813. The monastery was situated at Nicaea. John was a strong opponent of iconoclasm, and died in exile from his monastery. Feast 27 April.

John of Chatillon, abbot and bishop, born Chatillon, Brittany, *c.* 1098, died St Malo, 1 February 1163. A monk at Clairvaux under St **Bernard**, he himself founded other Cistercian abbeys, and went on to become bishop of Aleth. He transferred the see to the Isle of Aaron, which he renamed St Malo. He was also abbot of the St-Croix monastery of the canons regular of St Augustine at Guingamp. Whilst bishop he was involved in lengthy litigation when he tried to replace monks from Marmoutier with the canons regular in his cathedral. He is also known as John de Craticula ('of the grating') because of the iron grating around his tomb.

John of Chinon, born Brittany, died Chinon, sixth century. He settled as a hermit between Tours and Saumur, where he was renowned for the holiness of his life. Feast 27 June.

John of Choziba, metropolitan, born Upper Egypt, *c.* 450, died Choziba, *c.* 530. Byzantine Church. He entered the monastery of Choziba in Wadi Qilt *c.* 480, and in 516 was elected bishop of Caesarea.

He did not hold the office long, however, and resigned to return to his monastery. Feast 3 October.

John of C'mskacag, martyr, died 10 September 1405. Armenian Church. A priest in the city of C'mskacag in central Anatolia. Although married, he lived in chastity, and his virtue aroused the envy of other clergy, who drove him from the city. He and his parishioners built another church, but his enemies got permission from the local ruler to destroy the church and demand that John deny his faith. When he refused, he was executed. Feast 27 March.

John of Crete, martyr, born Sfakia, Crete, died Nea Ephesus, 15 September 1811. Byzantine Church. Although born in Crete, he moved to Ephesus where he worked on a farm. While celebrating a local saint's day with some friends at Nea Ephesus, a dispute broke out with some Turks, in the course of which one of the Muslims was killed – although not by John. John, however, was accused and imprisoned, but was offered his freedom were he to convert to Islam. He refused and was hanged.

John of Dabra Bizan, monk, born Ahse'a nel Bur, 1371, died Dabra Bizan, 7 October 1449. Ethiopian Church. Originally called Zar'a Haymanot, he was early attracted to the monastic life. By chance he met abbot **Philip of Dabra Bizan** and he decided to join him there. When Philip felt he was about to die, he proposed John as his successor. This aroused considerable hostility among the monks, because John had not long been in the monastery. The community was, however, afflicted by plague and after many died, opposition ceased. Under John's rule the monastery flourished: it grew in numbers and in buildings.

John of Dabra Libanos, monk, born Dablat, died Dabra Libanos, 11 March 1559. Ethiopian Church. After joining the monastery of Dabra Libanos, he became skilled in music and received the habit from **Enbaqom**. After the Islamic invasion the monastery was destroyed and the monks scattered, but John gathered some of them together again, went back to the monastery and began to rebuild it. He died in battle, supporting the king against the invaders.

John of Dabra Sege, monk. Ethiopian Church. Feast 7 October.

John of Dalyata, monk, born Ardamust (Kawasi, near Mosul), died Mount Dalyata, eighth century. Assyrian Church. He became a monk c. 700 at the monastery at Qarsu, but seven years later went to Mount Dalyata in search of solitude, where he became a mystical writer of some importance, dwelling on the symbolic significance of creation.

John of Daylam, monk, born Bet Qira (Gayyara), c. 660, died 26 January 738. Syriac Church. He entered a monastery when still very young, but because of a famine the monks had to disperse. He and a number of others went to live in the mountains of modern Iraq, but he was captured by the people of Daylam and he lived in their city for some 20 years, converting many to Christianity. He then went on pilgrimage to Jerusalem, on the journey working many miracles, even for Muslims. He went on to establish a monastery for Persian monks not far from Basra, on the river Tab, but a clash between Persian and Syriac-speaking monks led him to build a second one on the opposite bank. He died just after the building was finished.

John of Dukla, patron of Poland and Lithuania, born Dukla, near Tarnow, Poland, 1414, died Lvov, Ukraine, 29 September 1484. He became a Franciscan Conventual, and was guardian at Krosno and Lvov, and then Custos. A model of charity and virtue, he became blind in later years, although he continued to minister, preach and hear confessions. He was also active in helping to repel a Tartar incursion in 1474. His tomb is in the church of the Bernardines at Lvov, where many miracles have been reported. Feast 3 October.

John of Egypt, hermit, born Assiut, Egypt, c. 300, died Lycopolis, 394. A carpenter by profession, he joined a monastery at an early age and later became a hermit in a cave on Mount Lykos. Here he remained for the rest of his life, living a life of great austerity. He was widely sought out for spiritual advice, communicating only through a small window. Reputed to have the gift of prophecy, he was known as 'the seer'. According to tradition, he foretold the victories of the Emperor

Theodosius I over Maximus and Eugenius, as well as the death of Theodosius in 395. Feast 27 March.

John of Epirus, martyr, born Albania, *c.* 1789, died (martyred) Ithaca, 23 September 1814. Byzantine Church. Unusually for a martyr of the Turkish period, he was born a Muslim and not baptized until adulthood. After baptism he married and led an obscure life, but was discovered by the authorities. He was executed, but his body was secretly buried in a nearby monastery. Feast 23 September.

John of Gales, martyr, died Kufstein, *c.* 1785. Romanian Church. He was a priest in the village of Salistea in Transylvania at the time of the reunion of some of the Orthodox with Roman Catholicism. The civil authorities hoped to press all Orthodox priests into this union, but John resisted. Troops were sent to arrest him, but he fled. Instead they mistreated his wife, and a neighbour who came to her help was killed. He was eventually arrested and imprisoned in Sibiu. He was later secretly transferred to other prisons, finally dying in Kufstein.

John of God, founder of the Brothers Hospitallers, born Portugal, 1495, of Christian parentage, died Granada, Spain, 8 March 1559. After a pious upbringing he later renounced the practice of religion and became a soldier. At about the age of 40 he rediscovered his faith. He hoped for martyrdom in Morocco, but when this was denied him he journeyed to Spain, coming under the influence of **John of Avila** in 1538. He became somewhat excessive in his piety, devotion and penitence, but later directed his energies towards helping the poor and sick, founding the Brothers Hospitallers. In 1886 he was declared patron of hospitals and sick people by Pope Leo XIII.

John of Gorze (also known as Jean de Vandiers), abbot, born Vandiers, France, died Gorze, *c.* 975. He was the son of an affluent landowner, and studied at Metz and later at the abbey of Saint-Mihiel. After the death of his father he took care of the estate, but continued his studies at Toul. Upon returning from a pilgrimage to Rome, he came under the influence of Einold, the archdeacon of Toul. In 933 he followed Einold to the abbey of Gorze where, with their companions, they re-established monastic discipline. In 953 he travelled

to Córdoba as envoy to Otto I. Following the death of Einold, John succeeded him as abbot of Gorze, where he played a major role in the monastic reform movement of which Gorze was the centre. Feast 27 February.

John of Granada, bl., martyred Granada, Spain, 1397, commemorated with **Peter of Granada**. Feast 19 May.

John of Gunanqe, monk, born Tigre, fourteenth century. Ethiopian Church. A disciple of **Madhanina Egzi**.

John of Harran, bishop. Syriac Church. Exiled by the Emperor Justin I in 518.

John of Hira ('the Blue'), bishop, seventh/eighth centuries. Syriac Church. A monk of Bet Hale, near Hira, before becoming its bishop.

John of Jarenga and Longinus, monks, sixteenth century. Russian Church. Two pious lay brothers of the Solovki monastery who were drowned while transporting material for a new construction at the monastery. Their bodies were found on the shore still incorrupt, and they were buried in the church of St Nicholas at Jarenga, where their tomb was the site of many miracles. Feast 9 August.

John of Jerusalem II, bishop, born *c.* 356, died Jerusalem, 10 January 417. He became bishop in 387, and was an enthusiastic supporter of Origen. His friendship with St **Jerome** turned sour and John refused access to the holy places of his city to the monks of Jerome's monastery in Bethlehem. He later welcomed Pelagius to Jerusalem, and when the complaint was made that Pelagius was at odds with St **Augustine** of Hippo, John replied, 'I am Augustine here.'

John of Kamul, hermit, born Bet Garmai, died Mount Gudi, fourth century. Syriac Church. A Zoroastrian royal official, he was converted after witnessing the martyrdom of the catholicos Sahdost. He attempted to persuade Sharpur, who was his cousin, not to persecute Christians, but was himself denounced and had to flee. He was received into Christianity by **Awgen**, but then lived the life of a solitary on Mount Gudi.

John of Kanti, born Kanti, Silesia, 23 June 1390, died Krakow, 24 December 1473. He was educated at the University of Krakow, and stayed on to lecture there. For some reason, unrecorded, there was a student protest and he left Krakow to serve as a parish priest in Bohemia for a number of years. He was not a great success at that either, and returned to the university where he remained for the rest of his life. By the time he died, however, he was a much admired figure, both because of his learning and because of the austere holiness of his life. Feast 23 December.

John of Kargopol, monk, fifteenth century. Russian Church.

John of Kaskar, born Kaskar, died Gabal Hamrin, fifth century. Syriac Church. He went to the monastery on Gabal Hamrin c. 430, after a series of visions. Feast 1 October.

John of Kazan, martyr, born Niznij Novgorod, died Moscow, 1529. Russian Church. He was living in Kostroma when he was abducted by Tartars and made a slave at Kazan. He was tortured to make him embrace Islam, but he refused. He was eventually thrown out into the snow, his hands fettered, but the fetters fell off, the snows melted, and he made his way to Moscow to relate his story just before he died.

John of Kfone, monk. Syriac Church. A disciple of **Awgen**.

John of Kiev II, born Constantinople, died Kiev, 1089. Russian Church. Well educated in his youth, he became metropolitan of Kiev in 1076. During his rule he created two further episcopal sees, took part in the 1086 Synod of Constantinople, and engaged in controversy over the liturgy with an antipope. Feast 31 August.

John of Konitsa, martyr, born Konitsa, died Vrachorion, 23 September 1814. Byzantine Church. His father was a dervish, and he was called Hassan. Hassan too became a dervish, but in the course of time converted to Christianity, taking the name John. He settled at Machalas, where he married and found work on a farm. Eventually his father learned of his conversion and sent people to attempt to convert him back. When this failed he was arrested and eventually beheaded. Feast 4 January.

John (Sergeyev) of Kronstadt, Russian Orthodox priest and healer, born near Archangel, Russia, 19 October 1829, died Kronstadt, 20 December 1908. A married priest who served a poor parish at the naval base near St Petersburg. He undertook extensive charitable and educational projects and transformed his church liturgically, with daily liturgies, frequent communion and public confession (because of the numbers involved). Popular as a healer throughout Russia, he travelled widely and attended the dying Emperor Alexander III. His published works were many, but the most famous was *My Life in Christ*, a spiritual diary which was translated into English and presented to Queen Victoria. He prophesied the revolution in the clearest terms. Canonized by the Russian Church Abroad in 1964 and inside Russia after the fall of communism in 1990. Feast 20 December.

John of La Verna, bl., Franciscan priest, born Fermo, near Ancona, Italy, died La Verna, 9 August 1322. At the age of ten he joined the Augustinian canons, and three years later the Franciscans. After residing in hermitages at both Ancona and Fermo, he eventually settled in a hermit's cell at La Verna c. 1290. He is reputed to have had the gift of prophecy, along with mystical experiences. These included visions of the Virgin Mary, the Sacred Heart of Christ, St **Francis** and St **Laurence**. In the later years of his life he preached widely throughout Tuscany. Feast 13 August.

John (Pommers) of Latvia, martyr and bishop, born near Riga, 1876, died (martyred) 12 October 1934. Russian Church. Born of a Latvian family recently converted to Orthodoxy, he was consecrated bishop in Russia, but when Latvia became independent, he was elected archbishop of Riga. He worked tirelessly to reconcile the Russian and Latvian members of his flock and did much to publicize the persecution of the Church in the Soviet Union. In 1934 the Soviet Secret Police (NKVD) managed to enter the country, destroy his papers, torture him and burn him alive below the cathedral at Riga. Feast 29 September.

John of Licopolis, see **John of Egypt**.

John of Lodi, Benedictine monk, born Lodi, Italy, c.1025–30, died Gubbio, 7 September 1105. After an education in the liberal arts, he joined a group of hermits at Fonte Avelana c. 1065. He became the travelling companion of St **Peter Damian**, whose biography he wrote following the latter's death. In 1080 he became prior to the hermitage at Fonte Avelana. In 1104 he became bishop of Gubbio.

John of Mardin, bishop, born Edessa, died Mardin (?), 1165. Syriac Church. His baptismal name was Joseph. As bishop, from 1125, he was particularly active in rebuilding the monasteries and churches in his region. Feast 12 July.

John of Matera (also known as John of Pulsano), Benedictine monk, born Matera, kingdom of Naples, 1070, died Pulsano, near Monte Gargano, 20 June 1139. He spent many years moving from one monastic house to another in a bid to find one which was conducive to his severe mortifications. For many years he lived as a hermit, and founded a small monastery at Ginosa, which was later dispersed by the Normans. Whilst preaching at Bari he narrowly escaped being burned as a heretic. Around 1130 he founded a community at Pulsano which adopted a strict Benedictine Rule. He ruled over the monastery until his death.

John of Matha, founder, born Faucon, Provence, 23 June 1160, died Rome, 17 December 1213. Said to have been of Provencal nobility and educated at Aix-en-Provence. He then went for a time to live as a hermit, but afterwards went to Paris to study theology and was ordained in 1197. He is said to have been inspired while saying his first mass with the idea of founding an order whose purpose was to redeem captives. He founded the Hospitaller Order of the Most Holy Trinity for the Redemption of Captives, which received papal approval in 1209. Feast 8 February.

John of Mecklenberg, bishop and martyr, died 1066. He was one of many missionaries who preached the faith in Iceland during the eleventh century. His date of birth and details concerning much of his life are unknown. Sometime after 1055 he was made the first bishop of Mecklenberg and was sent to witness among the Slavic tribes, including the Wends in Saxony. In 1066, during an uprising, he was captured. Refusing to deny his faith, he was tortured, having both his hands and his feet amputated. Decapitated, his head was impaled on a spike and offered to the tribal god Redigast. He was erroneously called the first American martyr, because the territory Veindland (land of the Wends) is wrongly associated with Vinland, the reputed Norse settlement in North America.

John of Meda, born Meda, near Milan, died Brera, 26 September 1159. He was a nobleman who became a priest, then a hermit near lake Como. There was an existing community of penitents there, which he turned into a religious order, the Humiliati, suppressed in 1571.

John of Monemvasia, martyr, born Geraki, Monemvasia, died Larissa, 21 October 1773. Byzantine Church. His town was captured by Albanians in 1770, and his father killed. He was taken as a prisoner to Larissa and sold as a slave to a Turk. His master became fond of him and tried to persuade him to become a Muslim, but when the young man refused, the Turk stabbed him to death.

John of Monte Marano, bishop and monk, eleventh century. He is reputed to have been a Benedictine monk. He became bishop of Monte Marano in Italy in 1074. A champion of the poor, he is also reputed to have performed many miracles. There is a tradition which claims that he was a disciple of **William of Vercelli**, the founder of the abbey of Monte Vergine, although this has no historical foundation. Feast 17 August.

John of Montfort, bl., Knight Templar, born Voralburg, Austria, died Nicosia, 25 May 1177. A nobleman, he was a crusader of the twelfth or thirteenth century. He was wounded in a battle at Jerusalem against the Saracens and taken to Cyprus, where he died. There is some doubt about the exact year of his death. His body was interred at the abbey church of Beaulieu in Nicosia, where he was venerated until the Turkish conquest of 1571. Feast 24 May.

John of Montmirail, bl., Cistercian monk, born Montmirail, near Chalons-sur-Marne, 1165, died abbey of Longpont, 29 September 1217. He was a loyal knight in the service of King Philip II Augustus of France. He turned his back on a worldly life and founded a hostel near his castle, where he personally cared for the sick. In later life he left his wife and children and became a Cistercian monk at the abbey of Longpont in the diocese of Soissons. He displayed extraordinary devotion to the virtues of obedience and humility.

John of Moscow, 'fool for Christ', born Vologda, died Moscow, 3 June 1589. Russian Church. He worked as a water carrier in his home city, while practising a strict ascetical life. He then moved to Rostov as a 'fool for Christ', going about half-naked, wearing iron chains on his body and an iron hat on his head. He then moved on to Moscow where he went about in the same way, whatever the weather. He earned a reputation both for holiness of life and for healing the sick. Feast 3 July.

John of Mozaj, 'fool for Christ', died either 1492 or 1592. Russian Church.

John of Neamt-Hozevitul, hermit, born Crainiceni, 23 July 1913, died Jordan valley, 4 August 1960. Romanian Church. He was baptized Elias, and was largely brought up by his deeply devout grandmother. In 1932 he entered the monastery of Neamt, although he visited other monasteries and spent some years in military service as a medical orderly before taking vows at Neamt in 1936, receiving the name John. The same year he was given permission to visit the Holy Land, where he lived as a hermit for eight years, looking after the sick. He was ordained priest in Jerusalem, and became hegumenos of the monastery of St John the Baptist in the Jordan valley. After some years, seeking greater solitude, he and a disciple went to the monastery of St George Hozevitul, where he lived as a hermit.

John of Nepomuk, born Pomuk, Bohemia, c. 1340, martyred Prague, 20 March 1393. Born John Wolflin, he was educated in Prague and was ordained priest. As vicar-general of the archdiocese of Prague, he incensed Wenceslas IV by resisting the monarch's attempts to suppress an abbey in order to create a see for one of his favourites. There is also a tradition that he angered the king by refusing to betray the queen by breaking the seal of the confessional. As a consequence, and on the king's orders, he was drowned in the river Moldau. His recovered body became the centre of veneration. He was canonized in 1729. Feast 16 May.

John of Nicomedia, martyr, died Nicomedia, 303. He was executed for destroying copies of the decree of Diocletian about sacrificing to idols. Feast 7 September.

John of Novgorod, archbishop, born Novgorod, died there, 7 September 1186. Russian Church. The son of a priest, he joined the monastery of the Annunciation with his brother, taking the name Elias. He was appointed bishop of Novgorod and displayed both great personal holiness of life and concern for his clergy and for the poor. In 1166 he was raised to the rank of archbishop – the first of Novgorod. In 1170 he is credited with saving his city from the army of the prince of Suzdal by his prayers and by a procession carrying an icon of the Virgin. Throughout this time he was known by his monastic name, but assumed his baptismal one when he was dying.

John of Numrus, martyr, born Abu al-Numrus, near Giza, died Cairo, 22 February 1562. Coptic Church. Seized from his family when only seven, he was raised in the city of al-Mahallah, in the Delta. His father found him, however, and managed to rescue him, taking him to the monastery of St Paul on the Red Sea. Some years later John went to the governor of Cairo, saying he was a Christian, and was executed.

John of Ojun, catholicos, born Ojun, Armenia, c. 650, died 729. Armenian Church. Renowned for his learning, he was elected catholicos in 718 and made considerable efforts both to reorganize his Church and to move towards unity with the Syriac Church. He wrote a number of works, including studies on the liturgy, but he is particularly remembered for his holiness of life and his concern for canon law. Feast 17 April.

John of Orotn, born Orotn, 1315, died 1388. Armenian Church. Of a noble family, he was a monk of the monastery of Tat'ew, where he founded a school. He was himself very learned, and left a number of writings. He was a great supporter of the specific culture of the Armenian Church. Feast 6 January.

John of Pake, monk, born Minya, Upper Egypt, fifth/sixth centuries. Coptic Church.

John of Panaca, born Panaca, Armenia, sixth century. He fled from Armenia because of the persecution by the monophysites and came to Italy, where he founded a monastery at Pinna, Umbria, of which he was abbot. Feast 19 March.

John of Parallos, bishop, born *c.* 540, died 15 December *c.* 615. Coptic Church. Of a wealthy family, he first spent his money on building a hospital and caring for the sick. One of those in his charge was a monk, and he decided to join a monastery himself, although he then became a hermit. He was created bishop of the troublesome diocese of Parallos. He managed to convert many of the heretics to the Coptic faith.

John of Parma, abbot, born Parma, died there, 990. A cathedral canon, he went six times to Jerusalem, becoming a Benedictine there. As abbot of St John's, Parma, from 983, he had it adopt the Cluniac observance. He is a patron of Parma. Feast 22 May.

John of Parma, bl., Franciscan minister general, born Parma, 1209, died Greccio, 1289. He taught logic at Parma for many years, and became a Franciscan *c.* 1233. He then studied in Paris. A popular preacher and teacher, he was elected minister general of his order in 1247. He travelled widely throughout Europe, and endeavoured to restore the order to its original standards of asceticism and discipline. He worked tirelessly in an attempt to reunite the East and West, although without success. His austerity of life made him many enemies and he was accused of heresy in Rome. He resigned his office in 1257, retired into the hermitage of Greccio, and lived a solitary life for over 30 years. In 1289 he was chosen to go on a mission to Greece in a further attempt at reunification, but died. Feast 20 March.

John of Pavia, bishop, died Pavia, 813. He was bishop from 801. Feast 27 August.

John of Perugia and Peter of Sassoferrato, bl., martyrs, died Valencia, 29 August 1231. John was a priest, Peter a lay brother. Together they went to Spain to attempt the conversion of the Muslims. They settled in Valencia, but when they tried to preach they were arrested and executed.

John of Poliboton ('the Wonderworker'), bishop, died *c.* 750. Bishop of Poliboton in Phrygia, and a vigorous opponent of iconoclasm. He had a reputation for working miracles, which effectively meant that the emperor could not persecute him for his opposition. Feast 5 December.

John of Prado, bl., born Morgobejo, Leon, Spain, martyred Marrakesh, Morocco, 1631, beatified 1728. An ordained Observant Franciscan, he preached and held various posts in Spain. At his request he went to Morocco with two others to minister to Christian slaves. He was imprisoned and burned alive. Feast 24 May.

John of Prislop, hermit, born Silvasul de Suss, died there, fifteenth/sixteenth century. Romanian Church. He entered the monastery of Prislop near his birthplace, but after some years retreated to a hermitage he made for himself beside the river. It is said he was accidentally killed by a musket shot from a huntsman. Feast 13 September.

John of Pskov, recluse, died Pskov, 24 October 1616. Russian Church. He lived in a cell hollowed out of the wall of the fortress of Pskov. Feast 24 October.

John of Puttivl, martyr, thirteenth century. Russian Church. Prince of Puttivl, he was killed by Tartars.

John of Qalyub, martyr, died Cairo, 26 November 1582. Coptic Church. A monk of a monastery in Wadi al-Natrun, he was ordered to convert to Islam but refused and was hanged.

John of Qartmin, bishop (?). Syriac Church. Feast 10 November.

John of Rasca, bishop, died 1608. Romanian Church. He entered the monastery of Rasca, where as a monk he was known not only for the asceticism of his life but for his translations of the Fathers of the Church into Romanian. He became the first bishop of Husi in 1598, and then bishop of Radauti in 1605, but retired to his monastery when near death.

John of Ravenna, bishop, died *c*. 494. Bishop of Ravenna from 452, he is said to have shielded his people from the anger of Attila the Hun, and also protected them when Theodoric of the Ostrogoths captured the city. Feast 19 January.

John of Reome, monk, born Courtangy, *c*. 450, died Reome, 28 January 544. One of the pioneers of the monastic life in Burgundy. He became a monk at Lérins and later, at the instigation of his bishop, founded a monastery at Reome (now Menetreux) called Saint-Jean-de-Reome or Moutier-Saint-Jean-en-Auxois. Here he introduced the Rule of Macarius of Egypt. He had a reputation for sanctity, and many miracles were attributed to him.

John of Rieti, bl., born Castel Porziano, Umbria, died Rieti, *c*. 1350. He entered the Hermits of St Augustine at Rieti, where he spent the rest of his life in prayer and contemplation. Little otherwise is known of his life. Feast 1 August.

John of Rila, hermit, born Skrino, near Sofia, *c*. 880, died Mount Rila, 18 August 916. He left home as a young man, sold his possessions and distributed the proceeds to the poor, then entered a monastery. After a number of years, seeking greater solitude, he established a hermitage on Mount Rila, where he was visited by King Peter I of Bulgaria. Others joined John, and a monastery was eventually established. Feast 19 October.

John of Rostov ('the Merciful'), 'fool for Christ', died Rostov, 3 September *c*. 1580. Russian Church. Nothing is known of his origins, although the fact that he carried with him a Psalter in Latin suggests that he came originally from the West. Despite having no fixed place to live, he was much sought out for his spiritual advice, and after his death his tomb became renowned for miracles. Feast 12 November.

John of Sagittario, bl., born Toulouse, France, died Sagittario, near Naples, *c*. 1330. He was first a hermit on Mount Caramola, Basilicata, Italy, then became a Cistercian lay brother at the monastery of Sagittario. Feast 26 August.

John (Gonzalez) of Sahagún, born Sahagún, 1430, died Salamanca, 11 June 1479. He was educated at the Benedictine abbey near his home town, and was ordained priest in 1455. He became a canon of the cathedral of Burgos, but after ministering there for a time felt the need of further theological education and went to the university at Salamanca. He stayed in Salamanca, working in a parish, but then was taken ill and needed an operation. He promised that, if he survived the operation, he would join a religious order. He did indeed survive, and became an Augustinian, being professed in 1464 and rising to be in charge of the house in Salamanca. He was renowned as a preacher, and for denouncing the sins of society: it was rumoured that his death was brought about by poison, at the behest of an adulterous woman he had reprimanded – although this is unlikely. Feast 12 June.

John of St Dominic, bl., Dominican, martyred Japan, 1619. See **Martyrs of Japan**. Feast 19 May.

John of St Martha, bl., Franciscan, martyr, died Meako, Japan, 1618. Feast 16 August.

John of Salerno, bl., Dominican friar, born Salerno, *c*. 1190, died Florence, 9 August (or 10 September) 1242. Educated at the university of Bologna, in 1219 he received the habit from St **Dominic** himself, who sent him to introduce the order into Florence. In Florence he founded the priory of Santa Maria Novella and, later, the monastery of Dominican nuns at Ripoli. He was commissioned by Pope Gregory IX to preach against the heretical Patarines, a Manichaean sect. Feast 9 August.

John of Sanhut, martyr, died Egypt, *c*. 303. Feast 3 May.

John of Scete, monk, born Subra Mansina, c. 585, died desert of Scete, 675. Coptic Church. He entered the monastery of St Macarius in the desert of Scete when he was 18, and became a priest, and then hegumenos. He was three times taken prisoner by marauding bands, but each time returned to the monastery, of which he eventually became abbot.

John of Selalo, monk. Coptic Church.

John of Serres, martyr. Byzantine Church. Born into a wealthy family at Serres. He was accused of having said he would embrace Islam. He insisted he had never done so, but was imprisoned. After further efforts to convert him had failed, his execution was ordered.

John of Sezenovo, born Potudani, 1791, died Sezenovo, 14 December 1839. Russian Church. He was a bonded servant called John Lukic Bykov, but an extremely difficult one, although devout. He eventually fled his home and his master and started wandering around pilgrimage shrines, including the Kievan Cave monastery. In 1817 he was at the monastery at Zadonsk, where he became a 'fool for Christ'. He had a great reputation for holiness and was treated with considerable veneration wherever he went. He finally settled in the village of Sezenovo. There he lived a life of extreme asceticism, and he had a reputation for working miracles.

John of Shanghai, archbishop, born Adamovka, 4 June 1896, died Seattle, 2 July 1966. Russian Church Abroad. Michael Borisovic Maksimovic came from an important family and studied at the military school at Poltava, then in the faculty of law at Char'kov, before working as a lawyer in Char'kov. In 1921 his family moved to Belgrade, and there he enrolled in the faculty of theology and became a monk, adopting the name John. He lived a very ascetic life as a monk, but in 1934 he was sent to China as bishop of Shanghai by the Russian Orthodox Church Abroad, being raised to the rank of archbishop in 1946. He dedicated himself to the liturgical worship of his cathedral and to the care of the poor, gaining a reputation as a healer. He had to leave China in 1949, and was appointed bishop for émigré Russians in Western Europe, operating first from Paris and later from Brussels.

In 1962 he was moved to San Francisco. Throughout he continued his strict regime of fasting and other ascetical practices. Feast 19 June.

John of Simonov, see **Bartholomew, John and Ignatius of Simonov**.

John of Solovki, monk, died Solovki, 18 April 1492. Russian Church. A disciple of **Zosimus** and famed for his fasting.

John of Solovki I (also John II) **and Gurius**, monks, seventeenth century. Russian Church. Feast 9 August.

John of Solovki, monk, born Dvina, died Slovoki, 28 January 1699. He lived apart from the monks in the forests around the island monastery, dressed only in a long shirt, whatever the weather. He settled finally in the monastery, where he continued to live a life of extreme asceticism. When he lived apart he would always refuse alms. He is commemorated with **Thomas, Iriodion, Michael and Basil**, all with John 'fools for Christ'.

John of Spetse, martyr, born island of Spetse, 1800, died Chios, 3 February 1822. Byzantine Church. A merchant, he and his brother **Stamatius** were caught in a storm and driven onto the island of Chios. They got their boat repaired, but the shipbuilder reported them to the authorities as Christians. Several of the crew were killed immediately, including the captain. John and his brother were imprisoned and eventually beheaded.

John of Suceava ('**John the New**'), martyr, born Trebizond, died Cetatea Alba, 1330. Romanian Church. A merchant by trade, he travelled around the cities of the Black Sea coast. He was a devout Christian, and was not afraid to say so openly. One man, jealous of him, said to the Tartar authorities that he had undertaken to become a Muslim. He was therefore brought before the judge, but steadfastly refused to deny his faith. He was beheaded. His relics were later taken to the Moldavian city of Suceava. Feast 2 June.

John of Suzdal, bishop, died monastery of Bogoljubovo, Suzdal, 15 October 1372. Russian Church. He seems to have become bishop in 1340, after being consecrated in Constantinople. He spent his last years in the monastery of Bogoljubovo.

John of Svatogorsk, monk, born Kursk, 20 September 1795, died Svatogorsk, 11 August 1867. Ukrainian Church. John Krukov spent his early years apprenticed to a candlemaker before setting up on his own. He married, but when his wife died he became a monk at Glinsk, where he was given the name Joachim. He was, however, invited to join the newly founded monastery at Svatogorsk. Although he did so, after a very few years he became a hermit within the monastery, living an extremely ascetical life. The community was opposed to him doing this, and were hostile, but he had a great popular following in the surrounding district, and a reputation as a healer. He died in the monastery's infirmary.

John of Tella d'Mauzelat, bishop, born Callinicia (Raqqa), *c.* 484, died Antioch, 6 January 538. Syriac Church. After a rather dissolute youth, he joined the monastery of Zakka in his home town, and became bishop of Tella in 519. There was much conflict between the supporters of Chalcedon and its opponents – of whom he was one – and he was forced for some time to return to his monastery, and then to go on pilgrimage. This took him to Constantinople, but the emperor's efforts could not change his mind. He was arrested and tried in 537, and imprisoned in Antioch.

John of Thasos, martyr, born Maries, Thasos, died Constantinople, 1652. Byzantine Church. He moved to Constantinople when he was 14. He was accused of mocking Islam, and was executed.

John of the Cross (Juan de Yepes y Alvarez), Carmelite mystic and poet, joint founder of the Discalced Carmelites, born Fontiveros, Spain, 24 June 1542, died Ubeda, Spain, 14 December 1591. He became a Carmelite friar at Medina in 1563, but the laxity of the order caused disillusionment. He sought admission to the Carthusians, but **Teresa of Avila** persuaded him to remain in the Carmelites and seek reform from within, and with her he formed the order of Discalced (i.e., without shoes, but meaning in effect 'reformed') Carmelites. Meeting opposition, he was imprisoned in 1577, but escaped, subsequently holding various

positions in the Discalced Carmelites. Further opposition saw him banished to Andalusia in 1591, where he died. His poems and other writings are among the great masterpieces of Spanish literature, notably *The Spiritual Canticle, The Dark Night of the Soul, The Ascent of Mount Carmel* and *The Living Flame of Love.* He was canonized in 1726. Feast 14 December.

John of the East, monk, fourteenth century. Ethiopian Church. It is impossible to distinguish the reality from the legend: he was born in Palestine, spent many years in different monasteries and in evangelizing the countryside, and apparently died aged 500.

John of the Goths, bishop, born Crimea, died Amastris (modern Amasserah on a peninsula jutting out into the Black Sea), *c.* 800. His father had been an Armenian soldier. Bishop in the Crimea from 761, he was an opponent of iconoclasm. He attended the second Council of Nicaea in 787, which condemned iconoclasm. On his return from the council his diocese was invaded by Khazars, and he was imprisoned but managed to escape and spent the last four years of his life at Amastris. Feast 26 June.

John of Tobolsk, metropolitan, born Nezin, 1651, died Tobolsk, 10 June 1715. Russian Church. After studying, and then teaching, at the ecclesiastical academy in Kiev, he became a monk of the Kievan Cave monastery. He achieved prominence in the monastery not only for his spiritual life, but also as a preacher. He was sent, when still quite young, as representative of the monastery to the Tsar, to seek help against the Turkish threat. The Tsar gave the monks the monastery of Svensk, and John was made its superior. The archbishop of Cernigov made him archimandrite of the monastery at Eleck, and announced that he should succeed to the archbishopric; he was made bishop of Cernigov in 1697. In Cernigov he attempted to raise the educational standards of the clergy, and founded a printing press which produced several of his own works. He also supported financially the Russian monks on Mount Athos. In 1710 he was moved to the see of Tobolsk, in Siberia, where he attempted to carry on much the same pastoral regime as in Cernigov.

John of Tossignano, bl., bishop, born Tossignano, Italy, 1386, died 1446. He studied law at the university of Bologna, and joined the Jesuati, the lay organization founded by **John Colombini** specializing in nursing and works of charity. He translated parts of the Bible, several sermons and other works into Italian. He was appointed bishop of Ferrara in 1431. Between 1437 and 1439 Pope Eugene IV moved the Council of Basle to Ferrara, during which time the pope, the emperor and the patriarch of Constantinople stayed there. John was known for his spirituality and learning. Feast 25 July.

John of Triora, martyr, 1816. See **Martyrs of China**. Feast 7 February.

John of Uglic, prince, born Uglic, died Vologda, 19 May 1523. Russian Church. Because of a military coup he was thrown into prison in 1490 and died still in captivity. He had in the meantime taken monastic vows, and the monastic name of Ignatius.

John of Uglic, born Uglic, 1657 (?), died there, 25 June 1663. Russian Church. He was murdered and his body left in a ditch. It was discovered by shepherds who saw a light shining from it. The relics were later reported to have worked miracles. Feast 23 May.

John of Ustjug, 'fool for Christ', born Puchovo, near Ustjug, died 1494. Russian Church. He came from a pious family, and after his father's death his mother entered a convent in Orlov, where he, too, lived for a time. He then began to wander the streets of the city as a 'fool for Christ', praying by night and wandering by day. Feast 29 May.

John of Valence, bl., bishop, born Lyons, *c.* 1070, died Valence, 21 March 1146. He was ordained priest and later became a canon of Lyons cathedral. He wished to enter the monastic life at Citeaux, but went instead on pilgrimage to Santiago de Compostela. Encouraged by a dream, he eventually entered Citeaux in 1114. In 1118 he was sent to found the monastery of Bonnevaux. He later established four daughter houses. In 1141 he became bishop of Valence. He was noted for his care of widows and orphans, and for his commitment to social justice. Feast 21 April.

John of Vercelli, bl., Dominican master general, born Mosso Santa Maria, Italy, 1205, died Montpellier, 30 November 1283. Born as John Garbella, he studied in Paris and went on to teach civil and canon law at Paris, and later at Vercelli. Around 1230 he was received into the Dominican order and by 1245 had become prior of Vercelli. In 1255 he was appointed vicar general for Hungary and, in 1256, prior of San Nicolo at Bologna. Between the years 1257 and 1264 he was provincial of Lombardy, and from 1264 to 1283 sixth master general of the order. In this post he personally visited nearly every house of the order, with the exception of those in Spain. He presided at 20 general chapters, and sent many encyclical letters. He urged perfect obedience to the constitution of the order. He was responsible for the building of the Arca, into which the body of St **Dominic** was translated. In 1278 he declined the patriarchate of Jerusalem. Feast 1 December.

John of Verchotur'e, 'fool for Christ', seventeenth/eighteenth centuries. Russian Church. Feast 16 April.

John of Wallacia, martyr, born Wallacia, 1647, died Constantinople, 12 May 1662. Byzantine Church. Captured and taken into slavery when the Turkish army overran the country, he killed his owner, who was making sexual advances to him. His fate was left in the hands of the dead man's wife. She wished to marry him, which would have meant him denying his Christianity. He refused, was taken to Constantinople and hanged.

John of Warneton, bl., bishop, born Warneton, near Arras, now northern France, died 27 January 1130. A disciple of **Ivo of Chartres**, he was a monk at Mont-Saint-Eloi, near Arras, then a reluctant bishop of Thérouanne and an active monastic reformer. He was strict but gentle, refusing to prosecute would-be assassins.

John of Wifat, martyr, died *c.* 1443. Ethiopian Church.

John of Xlat, born Bznunik, died there, 22 February 1438. Armenian Church. A singer by profession, he aroused the envy of a woman who falsely claimed that he had promised to marry her

– which would have meant converting to Islam. Under threats of torture he agreed to deny his faith, but when he was being led in procession he repented his apostasy, proclaimed himself a Christian, and was stoned to death.

John of Zichina, bishop, born Serres, 1258, died monastery of Podromos, 12 December 1333. Byzantine Church. He was brought up and educated by an uncle on Mount Athos. In 1288 he was elected bishop of Zichina, much to his uncle's displeasure. He would only agree to his nephew accepting the office if he undertook to support the monastery of Podromos, which the uncle had founded. This was agreed, and John carried out this duty to the extent that he is considered a founder of the monastery. So successful was the monastery that John founded another in Serres.

John Ogilvie, martyr, born Drum-na-Keith, Scotland, 1580, died Glasgow, 10 March 1615. He was brought up a Calvinist, but was educated in France and was converted to Catholicism at Louvain in 1596. He studied also at Regensburg, entering the Society of Jesus in 1599. For the next decade he worked at Gratz and Vienna, but, being transferred from the Austrian province to the French, he was ordained priest at Paris in 1610. In 1613 he travelled back to Scotland disguised as a horse-dealer and soldier. He found that the Scottish Catholic nobility had conformed to Protestantism at least in appearance and, being unable to make much impression on them, he travelled to London and then to Paris, but was ordered back to Scotland by his superiors. He then ministered to congregations in Edinburgh, Renfrew and Glasgow, where he was arrested, tortured and examined. He was sent to Edinburgh, where every effort was made to induce him to conform. At his trial he declared his willingness to shed his blood in defence of the king's temporal power, but said he could not obey in matters of spiritual jurisdiction which had been unjustly seized. He wrote up an account of his arrest and treatment in prison which was smuggled out by his visitors. He was canonized in 1976. Feast 10 March.

John Paine (Payne), martyr, born Northamptonshire, England, died Chelmsford, England, 2 April 1582. Paine is thought to have come from a Protestant background, but the date and circumstances of his conversion to Catholicism are unknown. He studied at Douai and was ordained in 1576, after which he returned to England. He ministered in secret as chaplain to Lady Petre, a staunch Catholic, but was eventually betrayed and arrested. He was interrogated and tortured in the Tower of London before being tried, and was condemned for treason on the strength of his Catholic priesthood, and put to death.

John Paleolaurites, hermit, died Palestine. Feast 20 April.

John Patrizi, born Samzche, southern Georgia, died Ghelati, eleventh/twelfth centuries. Georgian Church. Born of a distinguished family, he was educated in Constantinople and then in various monasteries, finally possibly in the Georgian monastery of Petrizoni, in Bulgaria. He then moved to the academy at Ghelati. He translated many works into Georgian from Greek, and had a considerable influence on the development of the Georgian language. He was also acquainted, unusually, with the writings of some of the Neoplatonists. Feast 10 February.

John Pelingotto, bl., born Urbino, Italy, 1240, died there, 1 June 1304. Belonging to a leading local family, he joined the Third Order of St Francis in 1255 and devoted himself to prayer and the service of God. In 1300 he made a pilgrimage to Rome for the celebration of Pope Boniface VIII's jubilee year, where he was described as 'the holy man from Urbino'. After his death he was buried in the chapel of St Francis in his native city. Feast 1 June.

John (Jean-Gabriel) Perboyre, martyr, born Puech, Montgesy, France, 6 January 1802, died China, 11 September 1840, beatified 1889, canonized 1996. A Lazarist (Congregation of the Mission) priest, he held important posts in Rome before being sent to China in 1835 – at his request, to replace his brother who had died en route. He was denounced, tortured and slowly strangled. See **Martyrs of China**.

John Peter Néel, born Soleymieux, Sainte-Catherine, France, 18 October 1832, martyred Kaiyang, Guizhou, China, 18 February 1862, beatified 1909, canonized 2000. A priest of the Paris Foreign Missions Society, he was killed with Martin Wu Xuesheng, his Chinese catechist. See **Martyrs of China**.

John Pibush, bl., born Thirsk, Yorkshire, 1567, martyred Southwark, London, 18 February 1601, beatified 1929 with **William Harrington**. Ordained in Rheims in 1587, he worked in England calling himself Foster and Gravenor. Arrested in Gloucestershire, he spent six years in prison in London before his execution, developing tuberculosis during this time.

John Plessington, martyr, born Dimples Hall, Lancashire, c. 1637, died Chester, 19 July 1679. Ordained at the English College, Valladolid, in 1662, he returned to the English mission and ministered at Holywell, the shrine of St **Winefride**. He then became tutor in the Massey household at Puddington, while being in reality a missionary. He objected firmly to the marriage of a prominent Catholic heiress to a Protestant, which caused his betrayal and arrest at the time of the Titus Oates conspiracy. Although the authorities were unable to involve him in the plot, they charged him with being a priest and executed him.

John Psychaitas, imprisoned and exiled during the persecution by the iconoclasts, died c. 820. Feast 24 May.

John Raptis, martyr, born Mariais, died Constantinople, 18 April 1526. Byzantine Church. A tailor by trade, he moved to Constantinople, where he conceived of the idea of becoming a martyr. His spiritual adviser tried to dissuade him, but he was adamant, saying he had dreamed that he was being burned alive for the faith. When he was falsely accused of having undertaken to embrace Islam, then reneged on his promise, he was ordered to be burned alive, but was ransomed by the patriarch. Not long after, however, he was again ordered to be executed. A fire was made, and he was thrown on to it, but a neighbour put out the flames. Some Christians, seeing his suffering, paid someone to behead him.

John Rigby, martyr, born Harrack Hall, Wigan, Lancashire, 1570, died London, 21 June 1600. Of little formal education, Rigby had left the Church but became reconciled. While at the Old Bailey to plead the case of his master's daughter for non-appearance on a recusant charge, he admitted his own reconciliation to Catholicism, a capital offence. In Newgate prison he rejected any compromise with the queen's Church, and went to a barbaric death saying distinctly on the scaffold, 'God forgive you. Jesus receive my soul.'

John Roberts, monk and martyr, born Trawsfynedd, north Wales, 1577, died Tyburn, London, 10 December 1610. He studied at Oxford, but left to enter the Inns of Court in London. He became a Catholic after travelling on the continent in 1598, and entered the English college at Valladolid. The following year, however, he became a Benedictine monk in Valladolid, moving on to an abbey in Santiago de Compostela. In 1602 he returned as a missionary to England. He was several times expelled, but managed to return. During one period of exile in Douai he set up a house for English monks which later became the abbey of St Gregory. In 1607 he came back again to London, and was again expelled. In December 1610 he was arrested while saying mass, and executed.

John Roche, born Ireland, died Tyburn, London, 30 August 1588. He was a servant who assisted **Margaret Ward** in helping a prisoner to escape.

John Ruysbroeck, bl., born Ruysbroeck, near Brussels, 1293, died Groenendael, 1381. He left his home village at the age of 11 to live with his uncle, who was canon of the cathedral in Brussels. He became a priest in Brussels, but in 1334 left the city with his uncle to set up a hermitage at Groenendael. They attracted other clergy to the hermitage, and constituted the group as canons regular of St Augustine, taking their vows as such in 1350. His mystical writings had a very considerable influence.

John Sandys, bl., martyr, born Lancashire (?), died Gloucester, 11 August 1586. A scholar at Oriel College, Oxford, he worked as a tutor in Gloucestershire before going to the English College at Rheims in 1583. He was ordained just under a year later, and returned to England in October 1584. He was captured and sentenced to be hanged, drawn and quartered.

John Sarkander, born near Cieszyn, Silesia, now Poland, 20 March 1576, died Olmütz, now Czech Republic, following torture, 17 March 1620, canonized 1995. A parish priest in Moravia during the Thirty Years War, Protestants accused him of helping Polish Catholic enemies. He refused to divulge information learned in the confessional.

John Sciavteli, monk, twelfth/thirteenth centuries. Georgian Church. A monk of the monastery of Ghelati towards the end of his life, after serving the royal court for many years. He was a poet and writer of hymns.

John Shert, bl., born Shert Hall, near Macclesfield, Cheshire, martyred Tyburn, London, 1582, beatified 1886. He converted after studies at Brasenose College, Oxford, and was ordained at Douai in 1576. He is commemorated with **Thomas Ford** and **Robert Johnson**, executed with him. Feast 28 May.

John Slade, bl., martyr, born Milton, Hampshire, died Winchester, 30 October 1583. He studied at New College, Oxford, and became a teacher. He was arrested on the grounds that he denied the royal supremacy over the Church, and was tried at Winchester. There was a further trial four months later, after which he was executed.

John Sordi (or Cacciafronte), bl., bishop and martyr, born Cremona, northern Italy, died Vicenza, 1183. Abbot of St Lawrence (1155), a Benedictine abbey in Cremona, then a hermit when banished by the emperor. Bishop of Mantua (1174), then of Vicenza (1177), he was killed by a man he had reprimanded for stealing church funds. Feast 16 March.

John Soreth, bl., born Normandy, *c.* 1405, died Angers, 25 July 1471. He became a Carmelite at the age of 16, and after being ordained went to university in Paris. He gained his doctorate in 1438 and was elected prior provincial of the order in France two years later. In 1451 he was elected prior general of the order, and he was re-elected every five years, until his death. He worked to reform the order without causing a split, and encouraged the development of a Carmelite Rule for nuns. He was also responsible for the formal institution of a Carmelite Third Order, and drew up a Rule for the tertiaries in 1455. He died of cholera at Angers.

John Southworth, martyr, born Lancashire, *c.* 1590, died Tyburn, London, 28 June 1654. He entered the seminary at Douai in 1613 and was ordained at Cambrai just under five years later. He considered becoming a Benedictine, and served for a time as a chaplain to Benedictine nuns in Brussels. He returned to England to work in Lancashire *c.* 1626. He was arrested soon afterwards and imprisoned, although variously sentenced to be executed and to be banished, until 1637, first in Lancashire but most of the time in London. He then worked in London, where he was again arrested in 1654, and this time put to death. His body was taken to Douai, but was brought back to England and placed in a shrine in Westminster Cathedral in 1930.

John Speed (also called Spence), bl., martyred Durham, 4 February 1594, beatified 1929. A layman, he was hanged for helping priests, notably taking them to safe houses, and is counted as one of the four 'Durham martyrs of 1594' with **John Boste**, **George Swallowell** and **John Ingram**.

John Storey, bl., martyr, born northern England, *c.* 1504, died Tyburn, London, 1 June 1571. He studied, then taught, law at Oxford, and became the first regius professor of law. In 1537, after marrying and leaving Oxford, he practised law in London and became a member of parliament. He was briefly imprisoned for opposing the anti-Catholic legislation of King Edward VI, then went to Louvain. He returned in the reign of Queen Mary, and was active as a lawyer in prosecuting Protestants. He was imprisoned again when Elizabeth came to power, but escaped, and he and his family fled to Louvain. He was kidnapped by English agents and brought back to London where, despite protesting that he was no longer a subject of the queen but of the king of Spain, he was hanged, drawn and quartered.

John the Almsgiver, bishop, born Amathus (?), Cyprus, died there, 11 November 619. He came from a wealthy family, went into a secular career and married, but after his wife died childless he turned to religion – although little or nothing is known of his life before the emperor made him, possibly while still a layman, patriarch of Alexandria in 610. He was an ardent defender of Chalcedonian orthodoxy, and a great builder of churches in his region, but he was best known for his generosity towards the poor and for organizing the care of those who needed it. He was particularly concerned about the plight of refugees from the Islamic conquest. When, however, Arab forces threatened Egypt, he withdrew from Alexandria intending to make his way to Constantinople, but he visited his home town en route, and died there. Feast 23 January.

John the Cabinet Maker, martyr, born Galata (Constantinople), died Constantinople, 26 February 1575. Byzantine Church. A cabinet maker to the sultan, he had as an apprentice a young Turk who rose to great heights in the sultan's service. The apprentice asked John about Christianity, but when it was explained to him that Mohammed was not considered a prophet by Christians, he reported John to the authorities for defaming Islam. John was imprisoned, tortured, sent for some time to be a slave on the galleys, and eventually beheaded.

John the Camel-Driving Bishop, eighth century. Syriac Church. John had been bishop to Syriac Christians in Egypt when he was captured by Bedouins and, as a slave, put in charge of camels. His identity was discovered when Maran Zha, bishop of Hadita in Tigre, heard him singing Syriac chants. John refused to be ransomed, and died soon afterwards.

John the Dwarf, martyr, born Thessalonika, died Smyrna, 12 May 1802. Byzantine Church. His father was a shoemaker who moved his family to Smyrna. John was an extremely pious youth who much desired martyrdom. He therefore converted to Islam, then announced that he was abandoning Islam for Christianity. He was beheaded.

John the Faster, patriarch, see **John IV**, of Constantinople.

John the Faster and another John, monks, eleventh/twelfth centuries. Two monks of the Kievan Cave monastery of whom nothing is known.

John the Goldsmith, martyr, born Sumla, Bulgaria, died there, 14 May 1802. His shop was close to the house of a Turkish family, the daughter of whom was much attracted to John. When he refused her advances, she reported to the authorities that he had tried to violate her. He was offered his freedom if he would deny his faith, but he refused and was beheaded.

John the Great Sufferer, died Kiev, *c.* 1160. A monk of the Kievan Cave monastery, he suffered greatly from temptations of the flesh, and wrote a book recounting his battles to overcome them. In a vision he was told to live in solitude, and by that means to overcome the devil. Feast 18 July.

John the Hidden, monk, died Dabra Libanos, 14 August *c.* 1410. Ethiopian Church. Chosen as abbot because of his outstanding piety and simplicity, he received a vision of the Virgin.

John the Iberian, abbot, died Mount Athos, *c.* 1002. He was a nobleman and a successful soldier until middle age, when he left his wife and family to enter the monastery on Mount Olympus, in Bithynia. He went to Constantinople to free his son, who had been taken hostage, and they both returned to Mount Olympus. In about 970 they moved to Mount Athos and joined the laura of St **Athanasius the Athonite**. John's brother-in-law, John Thornikios, joined them on Mount Athos and together they began building a separate monastery *c.* 980. When John Thornikios died, John tried to leave for Spain. However, he was prevented from doing so by the order of the emperor and was made abbot of the new monastery, which he ruled over until his death, even while bedridden in his final years. Feast 12 July.

John the Patriarch, eighth century. Syriac Church.

John the Prior, died Zedazeni, *c.* 887. Georgian Church. Prior of the monastery of Zedazeni, he was killed during an assault on the monastery by Muslim troops. Feast 12 December.

John the Russian, born Ukraine, *c.* 1690, died Prokopion, 27 May 1730. Byzantine Church. He joined the Russian army, took part in the war against the Turks, and was captured, becoming a slave in Prokopion, Cappadocia, where he lived effectively the life of a hermit while looking after his owner's animals. At first efforts were made to try to convert him to Islam, but he refused, saying that while he was a Christian he would serve his master well. This greatly impressed the owner, and John continued to live in his cave for the rest of his life, attending a Greek Orthodox church nearby. He became renowned not just for the holiness of his life, but for his ability to work miracles, and after his death his relics were taken to the local church, eventually finding their way to Halkis, where they have become a site of pilgrimage.

John the Scholar, died *c.* 543. He was a disciple of St **Sabas**. Feast 4 January.

John the Silent, monk, born Nicopolis, Armenia, 454, died desert of Judea, 559. He was orphaned when only 18, and used his inheritance to found a monastery. Ten years later he was made bishop of Colonia. Again after some ten years he visited Constantinople, then made his way to Jerusalem, becoming a monk in the monastery of St Sabas and spending the final years of his life in silence. Feast 13 May.

John the Sinner, born Carmona, Andalusia, 1546, died Jerez de la Frontera, 3 June 1600. His name was Juan Grande, John Great (or Large), and he worked for a time in the linen trade in Seville before beginning his own business in his home town. When he was 22 he gave away all his money and became a hermit. Later he moved to Jerez and started to care for the sick and for prisoners. Benefactors started a hospital for him, which he affiliated with the Order of St **John of God**, which he himself joined. He also cared for orphans. He died of plague while nursing the sick. He is known as 'John the (great) Sinner' because of his own play on his name, introducing himself as 'Juan Grande Pecador'.

John the Solitary, monk. Syriac Church. He lived in the monastery of Zuquin for 25 years, for much of the time as a hermit within the monastery. But he was then forced to leave, with a good number of other monks, because of theological disputes in the community. For the final dozen years of his life he settled in another monastery, which is unknown.

John the Spaniard, bl., born Almza, near Leon, 1123, died near Geneva, 1160. He studied at Arles, then became a hermit, and afterwards joined a Carthusian monastery, eventually moving to La Grande Chartreuse, where he became prior. He was sent to make a new foundation off Reposoir, near Geneva. Feast 25 June.

John Theristus, born Sicily, died Calabria, eleventh century. His Calabrian mother had been enslaved by Saracens. He escaped to Calabria and became a Benedictine monk. He is called the harvester, *Theristus*, as he is said to have produced a miraculous harvest. Feast 23 February.

John Thules, bl., born Whalley, Lancashire, 1568, martyred Lancaster, 18 March 1616, beatified 1987. Ordained in Rome in 1592, he was arrested in Northumberland in 1593, twice escaped and was arrested again, and was hanged, drawn and quartered with **Roger Warren**.

John Torniche, founder, tenth century. Georgian Church. Torniche was his name as leader of Georgia's army, John the name he took when he entered the Greek monastery of St Athanasius on Mount Athos. A great man, Georgians followed him to the monastery, which was too small, but there was not enough money to found another one. Then a rebellion took place in Constantinople. The monk John agreed to lead Georgian troops against the usurper. He was successful and came back to Mount Athos with plunder enough to build the monastery of Iviron for Georgian monks. Feast 14 December.

John Vanakan, monk, born Tawus, 1185, died monastery of Xoranasat, 1251. Armenian Church. A learned man, sometimes called 'the doctor', he founded several monasteries, including that in which he died. In 1236 he was captured by the Tartars and made a slave, but a ransom was paid for his release. After that he retired to his monastery to write, including works on the Scriptures, theological studies and a history. Feast 29 January.

John-Baptist Mary Vianney, patron of parish priests, known as the Curé d'Ars, born Dardilly, near Lyon, 8 May 1786, died Ars, 4 August 1859. He had little formal education, and his youth was spent herding cattle. At 18, he began to study privately for the priesthood with Abbé Balley. He was called up for military service, but deserted and remained in hiding until a general amnesty was declared in 1810. He returned to his studies, but was dismissed because of his inability to learn Latin. Abbé Balley again resumed his private tutoring, won John-Baptist two special examinations, and he was finally ordained in 1815. Assigned to the remote village of Ars-en-Dombe, which was seriously lacking in a true sense of religion, he lived a most ascetical life, existing for years on little more than potatoes. He restored the church, visited every family and taught catechism; from the pulpit he chided his flock for drunkenness, blasphemy, profanity, obscenity, dancing and working on Sundays. In eight years he transformed the religious life of Ars, and achieved almost worldwide fame, with tens of thousands of visitors coming every year to seek his counsel. He was credited with an ability to read hearts, and many miracles and wonders were attributed to him. During his last years, he regularly spent up to 18 hours a day in the confessional. He was canonized in 1925, and declared patron of parish clergy by Pope Pius XI in 1929.

John Vicentius, bishop and hermit, died probably 12 December 1012. A bishop in the area of Ravenna, he fled the city, it is said, because of his great popularity and became a hermit on Monte Pirchiriano, Piedmont, where he assembled around him a group of hermits called Santa-Maria della Celle. There he built a chapel which by 1000 became the abbey of San Michele di Chiuse, and in 1006 he assisted in the foundation of San Salutore in Turin. Feast 21 December.

John Wall, martyr, born Chingle Hall, Lancashire, 1620, died Worcester, 22 August 1679. He was sent to Douai at the age of 13, entered the English College, Rome, was ordained in 1645 and 'sent to the Mission' in 1648. In 1651 he was professed as a Franciscan at St Bonaventure's Friary, Douai, taking the name Joachim of St Anne. He returned to England in 1656 and laboured with great zeal for

20 years in Warwickshire. During the turbulence caused by the Oates Plot in 1678, Wall was apprehended at Rushoch Court, near Bromsgrove, and confined to Worcester gaol for refusing the Oath of Supremacy, his priestly status having been declared. He was sent to London to be questioned concerning the Oates Plot and, although proved innocent of conspiracy, was condemned for his priesthood in 1679, and executed. His head, recovered after his execution, was preserved at Douai until the French Revolution, when it was lost. He was canonized in 1970.

John Woodcock, bl., martyr, born Clayton-le-Woods, Lancashire, 1603, died Lancaster, 7 August 1646. He studied under the Jesuits at St Omer and in Rome, but became a Franciscan at Douai in 1631, taking the name Martin of St Felix. He remained on the continent until, after hearing a sermon on martyrdom, he resolved to return to England. He was arrested as soon as he arrived in Lancashire, and was in prison for two years before his execution.

John Yi, bl., martyred Korea, 1867. He is commemorated with **Stephen Min** – see **Martyrs of Korea**. Feast 30 January.

John Yi and Companions, martyrs, died Seoul, Korea, 1839. There were seven martyrs in addition to John. Feast 20 August.

John Zedazzneli and Companions, born Syria, sixth century. A group of monks, led by John, came from Syria into what became Georgia, to evangelize its people. Some of the monks became bishops and travelled to other lands. Feast, of the group of 13, 4 November.

Jolenta of Hungary, bl., princess, born Hungary, c. 1235, died Gniezno, 1298. She was the daughter of King Bela IV of Hungary and her mother was the daughter of the emperor of Constantinople. She was also the grandniece of St **Hedwig**, niece of St **Elizabeth of Hungary**, and sister of **Margaret of Hungary**. At the age of five she was put in the care of her sister, **Kunigunde**, queen of Poland. She later married Duke Boleslas VI the Pious of Kalisz. With him she founded the Poor Clare convent at Gniezno. In 1279 the duke died and Jolenta, along with her youngest daughter, joined Kunigunde (also widowed) in the Poor Clare convent at Stary Sacz. Jolenta later moved to Gniezno, where she became abbess. Feast 15 June.

Jon Ogmundsson, bishop, born Breidabolsstadur, Iceland, 1052, died Iceland, 23 April 1121. He travelled extensively, perhaps even as far as Rome. He brought back with him from his travels Saemund the Learned, who founded the famous Icelandic school at Oddi. Ogmundsson was a priest in Breidabolsstadur when it was decided to divide Iceland into two dioceses. He became the first bishop of Holar. During this time he was responsible for renaming the days of the week in Iceland, to rid them of their pagan association. Feast 8 March.

Jonah, monk, born Armant, seventh/eighth centuries. Coptic Church. Born into an influential family in Upper Egypt, he joined the monastery where his uncle Victor was a monk. Victor educated him in the ways of the spirit, and he became known for his miracles, including the conversion of a Muslim. He died aged 72.

Jonah, monk, born Hagara Masqal, Eritrea, c. 1396, died 1491. Coptic Church. Baptized Habta Egzi, he took the monastic name of Job when he joined the monastery of his uncle Daniel, Dabra Sina. He later himself founded monasteries, and gained many disciples.

Jonah and Vassa of Pskov, born Moscow, died Pskov. Russian Church. Jonah was baptized John, and was a priest in charge of the Russian church in Derpt (modern Tartu, in Estonia). During a persecution of Orthodox, John fled with his wife Mary and their children to the cave which had been dwelt in by **Mark of Pskov** by the river Kamenec, which was reputed to hold a miraculous icon of the Mother of God. When Mary was taken ill, she became a nun with the name Vassa, and died in 1472. John then became a monk with the name Jonah. He began to develop the cave into what became the Pskov Cave monastery. He died in 1474. Feast 29 March.

Jonah, Gurius and Germanus, monks, died Pecenga, northern Carelia, 1590. Russian Church.

Monks of the monastery of Pecenga, they were killed with 48 other monks and 65 lay people when their monastery was attacked by Swedish troops.

Jonah Kurnosov, monk, eighteenth century. Church of the Old Believers. Superior of a small monastery near Semonovo, he was an important writer of polemical tracts.

Jonah of Jasezero, monk, born Soksi, Olonec, died Jasezero, c. 1614. Russian Church. Little is known of his early life, before he founded the hermitage beside lake Jasezero. He dedicated himself to the construction of the hermitage, and also constructed a canal between lake Jasezero and lake Sennoj.

Jonah of Kazan, and Nettarius, monks, born Zastol'ja, died Kazan, c. 1565. Russian Church. A father and son of the boyar class who came to assist Bishop Gurius of Kazan, but both became monks, changing their names from John and Nestor respectively. Feast 4 October.

Jonah of Klimency, born Novgorod, died Klimency, 6 June 1534. Russian Church. Baptized John Kliment'ev, he was the son of a wealthy merchant, and himself engaged in trade until he was caught in a storm crossing a lake and vowed to become a monk if he were saved. He landed safely on the island of Klimency on lake Onezskoe, where he built a chapel. He went back to Novgorod, became a monk, then returned to Klimency where eventually he created a monastery, although he refused to be its superior, remaining there as an ordinary member of the community. Feast 28 March.

Jonah of Manchuria, bishop, born Kaluga, 1888, died Manchuria, 7 October 1925. Russian Church Overseas. The son of a priest and baptized as Vladimir Pokrovskij, he studied at Kaluga, then at Kazan before ordination. He took the name Jonah on becoming a monk of the monastery of Optina, although he taught at Kazan. In 1918 he went to Perm, but was arrested and sent to Tobolsk. En route he was freed by the White Army, of which he became a chaplain, with the title of hegumenos. After the victory of the Soviet army he left for China, where he became bishop of Chankou, having charge of all Russian exiles in China and Manchuria. He was very much admired by his flock for his pastoral care.

Jonah of Moscow, metropolitan, born Soligalic, near Kostroma, died Moscow, 31 March 1461. Russian Church. He began his monastic life at the monastery of Chalic, then moved to the Simonov monastery in Moscow. In 1433 he was elected bishop of Murom and Rjazan, where he successfully evangelized the non-Christians in his region, but only two years later he was sent to Constantinople to be consecrated metropolitan of Kiev on the orders of the Grand Prince Basil the Blind. Instead of Jonah, however, Isidore was consecrated, although Jonah was promised the right of succession. Four years later Isidore was deposed for heresy – namely supporting the reunion of Rome and Constantinople agreed at the Council of Florence – but because of the political situation in Russia a synod to elect Jonah did not take place until 1448. Throughout Basil's political misfortunes, Jonah remained loyal to the grand prince, even taking over the leadership of Moscow when Basil was exiled. He also firmly opposed attempts by the pope, backed by the king of Poland, to replace him with a metropolitan who was in sympathy with the efforts to reunite the Churches of East and West.

Jonah of Novgorod, bishop, born Novgorod, died there, 5 November 1471. Russian Church. Baptized John, he entered a monastery in his native city, and became hegumenos. He was chosen as bishop of the city by its citizens in 1458, and was a steadfast defender of its independence against the claims of Moscow, and of the metropolitan **Jonah**.

Jonah of Odessa, born Odessa, 14 September 1855, died there, 30 May 1924. Ukrainian Church, Moscow Patriarchate. He was the son of a deacon. He married – and had nine children – and was ordained priest in 1886. After ordination he worked first in the countryside, in the village of Kardaovka, before returning to Odessa in 1897. In 1901 he became a parish priest and made the celebration of the Eucharist the centre of parish life. He himself led a life of severe asceticism, spending long hours in prayer in his church. He was also very hospitable to the poor, and especially to orphans: he had himself been orphaned when very young. When the Church in the Ukraine was beset by division over loyalty to Moscow, he remained steadfastly faithful to the patriarch of Moscow.

Jonah of Pergamo, hermit, fourth century. Church of Cyprus. Little is known about him. He appears to have lived in a cave near the church in Pergamo, and after his death was much revered locally. Feast 11 October.

Jonah of Perm and Ust-Vym (the Great), bishop, died Ust-Vym, 6 June 1470. Russian Church. He became bishop in 1455. Successor to **Pitirim of Perm**, he managed to convert many of the pagan tribes whose incursions had destroyed the peace of the region. He was able to build churches and founded a monastery dedicated to St John the Evangelist to spread the Christian message. Feast 29 January.

Jonah of Pertoma, see **Bassianus of Pertoma and Jonah of Pertoma**.

Jonas, martyred 326/7. A monk in Persia during King Shapur's persecution, he and another monk, **Barachisius**, were arrested for encouraging nine Christians prior to their martyrdom. Each was told that the other had apostatized, but neither believed this, and they were tortured and killed extremely cruelly. Feast 29 March.

Jordan Forzate, bl., monk, born Padua, c. 1158, died Venice, 1248. He studied law before becoming a Camaldolese monk. He later became prior of San Benedetto Novello in Padua, the rebuilding of which he instigated. In 1231 he was appointed examiner in the canonization process of **Anthony of Padua**. He also played a decisive role in the quarrel between Frederick II and the popes as *doctor decretalium* of the city council of Padua. In 1237 he was imprisoned by Ezzelino III of Romagna, but was freed by Frederick in 1239, and took refuge in Aquileia. He finally settled in the monastery of Della Celestia in Venice. His body was moved to the cathedral of Padua in 1810. Feast 7 August.

Jordan of Pisa, bl., born Pisa (?), died Piacenza, 1311. He entered the Dominicans at Pisa in 1280, after having studied at Paris. He worked in Florence and in Pisa, and was renowned for his eloquence – and for the fact that in preaching he used the Tuscan dialect rather than Latin. He was appointed professor of theology in Paris in 1311, but died on his way there. Feast 19 August.

Jordan of Saxony, bl., Dominican, second master general of the Order of Preachers, born diocese of Mainz, died at sea, 13 February 1237. A German noble, he studied in Paris where he received the Dominican habit from **Dominic** himself on Ash Wednesday 1220. By 1221 he had already become provincial of the Lombardy province, which at that time was the most important province in the order. Shortly after that he succeeded Dominic as master general. He visited many houses of the order, enlarging and strengthening them. A preacher of some note, he encouraged many vocations to the religious life (it is said he encouraged more than 1,000 vocations to the Dominican order). A great writer on spiritual matters, his letters of spiritual direction are still read to this day. He also wrote the first biography of St Dominic. He died in a shipwreck whilst returning from the Holy Land. Feast 14 February.

Josaphat, martyr, seventeenth century. Church of the Old Believers, A holy monk of the monastery of St Cyril, but after the liturgical reforms which he could not accept, he left the monastery and set out to become a hermit. En route, however, he had a vision telling him to proclaim his beliefs. He therefore went to Moscow, where he expressed his opposition to the reforms and was martyred. Feast 4 May.

Josaphat, monk, died Vetka, Poland, 1695. Church of the Old Believers. He was a disciple of **Job of L'Govskie**, and lived in his monastery. Job had him ordained, but when the Old Believers were persecuted from 1674 onwards, Josaphat left Job and went to Vylev, an Old Believer village in Poland. As he had not been ordained by an Old Believer bishop, he was not at first welcome. He left, but later returned, and the people of the village of Vetka asked him to serve as their priest.

Josaphat Kuncevyc, bishop and martyr, born Volodymyr, Volyns'kyj, now in the Ukraine, 1580, died Vitebsk, Belarus, 12 November 1623. Born

John Kunsevyc, he entered the monastery of the Holy Trinity in Vilnius in 1604. He was a man of deep spirituality, prayer and asceticism. In 1617 he became bishop of Polock (Polotsk) and was noted for his tireless preaching. He supported the Union of Brest, which had concluded in 1596. He was killed by some opponents of the union of the Ukrainian-Belorussian Church with Rome. Josaphat was the first Eastern saint to be formally canonized by the Roman Catholic Church.

Josaphat of Belgorod, bishop, born Ukraine, 1705, died Belgorod, December 1754. Russian Church. Of a noble family, and named Joachim Andreevic Gorlenko, he studied at Kiev and in the course of his studies he visited the Kievan Cave monastery and conceived the desire to become a monk. He secretly entered the monastery of Mezigorsk, where he was given the name Hilarion, changing it to Josaphat in 1725, shortly before being ordained priest. In 1734 he became superior of the monastery near Lubno, which flourished under his supervision. In 1748 he was made bishop of Belgorod in the Ukraine. It was in a parlous state, but he was indefatigable in visiting the parishes and encouraging the clergy. Feast 10 December.

Josaphat of Moscow, bishop, died Zagorsk, 25 July 1555. Russian Church. A monk of the monastery of St **Sergius** at Zagorsk – for a time he was its hegumenos – he was made metropolitan of Moscow in 1539 by one of the warring clans of boyars. As metropolitan he worked to bring reconciliation to the factions, which was not appreciated by his patrons, who deposed him in 1542, sending him off first to Belozersk, then five years later bringing him back to Zagorsk, where he occupied himself in his writing and his book collecting.

Josaphat of Snetogorsk, Basil of Mirozsk and Companions, martyrs, died Snetogorsk, 4/5 March 1299. Russian Church. Josaphat was hegumenos, and possibly the founder, of his monastery at Snetna, not far from Pskov. He was killed with Basil, from a monastery not far away, when Pskov was attacked by the Livonian Order. Some 30 monks and priests were killed. Feast 5 March.

Josaphat of Spasokubensk, monk, died Spasokamennoe, 10 September 1453. Russian Church. His baptismal name was Ndrew, and he was the son of the prince of Zaozero, but after his father had been killed in battle he did not succeed to his office because of dynastic struggles, and instead entered the monastery of Spasokamennoe, although the hegumenos was at first hesitant about accepting so high profile a figure. He took the name Josaphat and lived a very ascetical life, eating, it was said, only once a week. His prince uncle came to visit him, offering him money to found his own monastery, but Josaphat wished to remain at Spasokamennoe.

Josaphat of the Meteora, bl., born Trikala, *c.* 1350, died in the Meteora, *c.* 1423. Byzantine Church. Named John at baptism, his father was Simon Uresis Palaeologus, the king of Thessaly, and John succeeded to the throne when he was 20. When he was 22, however, he determined to become a monk, entering the monastery of the Transfiguration in the Meteora, and taking the name Josaphat. He remained there for the rest of his life, apart from two periods in which he lived on Mount Athos. He became hegumenos of the monastery, and was responsible for considerable building work which was paid for by his sister. Despite his royal ancestry, he was known for the simplicity of his life.

Joscio, bl., monk, died Saint Bertin, France, 30 November 1163. Virtually nothing is known of his life, save that he was a monk at Saint-Bertin. According to legend, five roses are said to have sprouted from his head after death, each bearing a letter of the name Maria. His grave was under the small choir altar at Saint-Bertin, and the miracle of the roses was depicted in the ambulatory of the choir. Feast 30 November.

José Fernández de Ventosa, missionary, Dominican priest, born Ventosa de la Cueva, Avila, Spain, 3 September 1775, martyred Vietnam, 24 July 1838, beatified 1909, canonized 1988. See **Martyrs of Vietnam**.

José Isabel Flores, martyr, born Teul, Zacatecas, Mexico, 28 November 1866, died Zapotlanejo, 21 June 1927. A student at the seminary in Guadalajara and ordained in 1896, he was marked by his devotion to Mary. He was shot for refusing to accept the laws proscribing the liberties of the Church. Feast 25 May.

José María Díaz Sanjurjo, martyr, born Santa Eulalia de Suegos, Lugo, Spain, 25 October 1818, martyred Vietnam, 20 July 1858, beatified 1951, canonized 1988. A Dominican priest and bishop, he was apostolic vicar of Central Tonkin. See **Martyrs of Vietnam**.

José Maria Robles, martyr, born Jalisco, Mexico, 3 May 1888, died Tocolotlan, 26 June 1927. Ordained in 1888, and with a deep devotion to the Sacred Heart, he was parish priest at Tocolotlan from 1920. In his previous parish he had established the Congregation of Victims of the Eucharistic Heart of Jesus, now known as Sisters of the Sacred Heart of Jesus. He was hanged from a tree. Feast 25 May.

José María Rubio Peralta, bl., born Dalias, Almeria, Spain, 1864, died Aranjuez, 2 May 1929, beatified 1966. Ordained in 1887, he was mainly a diocesan seminary teacher in Madrid until becoming a Jesuit in 1906. He worked in the poorest parts of Madrid, preaching in simple terms that touched people.

José Melchór García-Sampedro Suárez, born Cortes, Asturias, Spain, 26 April 1821, martyred Vietnam, 28 July 1858, beatified 1951, canonized 1988. A Dominican priest and bishop, he was auxiliary apostolic vicar of Central Tonkin. See **Martyrs of Vietnam**.

Josémaria Escriva de Balaguer, founder of Opus Dei, born Barbastro, Spain, 9 January 1902, died Rome, 26 June 1975. Educated by the Piarists in Barbastro, then in the State Instituto in Logroño before entering the seminary there in 1918. He subsequently studied in Zaragoza and Madrid. It was in Madrid in 1928 that he decided to found Opus Dei, although it was some time before it took its final form. During the Spanish Civil War he had to flee Spain, but then returned to Burgos, in the hands of the Nationalists, to begin his work again. He moved the headquarters of Opus to Rome in 1947, and remained there until his death, apart from many journeys to visit members of the organization.

Joseph, monk, died Dabra Tabor. Ethiopian Church. He was ordained deacon, but then became a monk in the monastery of a relative, Zachariah. With Zachariah he went to Tigre, where he lived in the desert for some years in strict asceticism. He was then ordained priest. After the death of Zachariah he increased his fasting and was much tempted by the devil, from whom he was defended by Michael the Archangel. He visited Jerusalem and Rome, and then came back to Dabra Libanos. A number of disciples had gathered around him, and he gave them a Rule of life. Feast 27 May.

Joseph, see also **José**.

Joseph, monk, fifth century. Coptic Church. He was the secretary of Senute of Atripe.

Joseph, patriarch. Syriac Church. Possibly the patriarch of Antioch, who died in 792.

Joseph Baldo, bl., born Puegno, near Brescia, 13 February 1843, died Ronco all'Adige, 24 October 1915. The son of a farmer, at 16 he entered the seminary at Verona, was ordained aged 22, served as a curate in a rural parish, and then returned to the seminary as vice rector. During this time he wrote a number of books and also served as a spiritual director, but he wanted to return to parish work, which he did in 1877, becoming the priest at Ronco all'Adige, which he served for the remainder of his life. He opened a school and started a savings bank. He founded the Little Daughters of St Joseph to do hospital work, and a number of other confraternities and pious associations.

Joseph Benedict Cottolengo, born Bra, kingdom of Sardinia (now Italy), 3 May 1786, died Chieri, 30 April 1842. He was ordained in 1811 and served as a canon in Turin from 1818 to 1827. He became aware of the great need for medical and social services and founded the hospital known as Piccola Casa della Divina Providenza (the Little House of Divine Providence). This became a massive complex, serving the mentally ill, the aged, those with physical disabilities, penitent women and orphans. It also trained the religious in nursing skills. He founded 14 religious congregations, including the Brothers and Sisters of St Vincent de Paul (Cottolenghine), the Daughters of Compassion, and the Hermits of the Holy Rosary. This network of caring institutions continued to grow and still thrives. In 1917 Cottolengo was beatified, and in 1934 he was canonized.

Joseph Benedict Dusmet, bl., bishop, born Palermo, Sicily, 1818, died 4 April 1894, beatified 1988. A Benedictine, ordained in 1842, he became abbot of San Niccoló, Catania, in 1858, archbishop of Catania in 1867, and cardinal in 1889. He reformed his diocese and helped the poor, giving them everything he had.

Joseph Busnaya, monk, born Ba-Bosa (modern Bozan), died 979. Assyrian Church. He started his monastic life at the monastery of Rabban Hormizd near his birthplace, but then moved to Bet Sayyare.

Joseph Cafasso, Italian priest, moral theologian and spiritual director, born Castelnuovo d'Asti, Piedmont, 15 January 1811, died Turin, 23 June 1860. Studied at Chieri, was ordained in 1833 and did further studies in Turin, at the Institute of St Francis, where the emphasis was on combating the Jansenist tendencies prevalent in northern Italy. He became lecturer in moral theology at the Institute and in 1848 was made rector. One of his students was **John Bosco**. Besides his teaching in the seminary, he did a lot of work with the laity: he gave lectures, preached, gave spiritual direction and was confessor. His writings include *Meditazione e instruzione al clero* (1892).

Joseph Calasanz ('Calasanctius'), in religion 'a Matre Dei', founder of the Piarists, born Barbastro, Aragon, 11 September 1556, died Rome, 25 August 1648. He studied at several Spanish universities before being ordained priest in 1583. He went to Rome in 1592, where he was patronized by the Colonna family. He became greatly involved in working with the poor and homeless and in their education. He was influential in the founding of the first free school in Rome in 1597. He founded the Piarist Order to further facilitate the work of educating the poor.

Joseph Chang Songji, bl., martyred Seoul, Korea – see **Martyrs of Korea**. Feast 26 May.

Joseph Dang Dinh Vien, martyr, died Hung-An, Vietnam, 1838. A diocesan priest. Feast 21 August.

Joseph de Anchieta, bl., missionary and linguist, born San Cristobal de la Laguna, Tenerife, 19 March 1534, died Reritiba (Anchieta), 9 June 1597. Related to the family of **Ignatius of Loyola**, he studied at Coimbra, entered the Society of Jesus in 1551, and went to the missions in Brazil two years later to work among the Puru and Guarani Indians. He learned Tupi, the language of the coast, wrote grammars and dictionaries as well as catechetical and pastoral manuals, and became provincial of Brazil (1577–87). During 44 years as a missionary, Anchieta is remembered for his apostolic work, his lofty ideals and a reputation for heroic deeds. He is reputed to have suppressed cannibalism and to have protected the chastity of Christian Indian women against the lust of pagan barbarians. No one has been so readily termed a saint and 'father of Christianity' in colonial Brazil – indeed, the bishop of Bahia gave him the name 'Apostle of Brazil' in the eulogy at his funeral.

Joseph Díaz Sanjurjo, bishop and martyr, born Lugo, Spain, 1818, died Vietnam, 20 July 1857. He studied at the university of Compostela and became a Dominican in 1842. He was ordained in 1844 and went to Vietnam as a missionary. He was rector of the seminary at Luc-Thuy until it was destroyed in 1847 in a popular uprising, sparked by the persecution of the missionaries by the emperor, Tu Duc. He became bishop of East Tonkin (now Bui Chu diocese) in 1852. In 1857 the persecution of missionaries intensified, and Joseph was denounced and arrested. The mandarin condemned him to death and his body was thrown into the river at Nam-Dinh.

Joseph Do Quang Hien, martyred Vietnam, 1840. He was a Dominican – see **Martyrs of Vietnam**. Feast 9 May.

Joseph Fernández de Ventosa, Dominican priest, born Ventosa de la Cueva, Avila, Spain, 3 September 1775, martyred Vietnam, 24 July 1838, beatified 1909, canonized 1988 – see **Martyrs of Vietnam**.

Joseph Freinademetz, bl., born Bodia, Tyrol, 15 April 1852, died of typhus, Taickianckwau, China, 28 January 1908, beatified 1975. Ordained in 1875, **Arnold Janssen** sent him to China as a Divine Word missionary in 1879. He became a wandering preacher, adopting Chinese dress and identifying with peasants, ignoring the elites.

Joseph Gerard, bl., born Bouxières-aux-Chênes, France, 1831, died southern Africa, 1914, beatified 1988. Joining the Oblates of Mary Immaculate, he worked in southern Africa, moving to northern Basutoland in 1876. He built a mission, convent and school, cared for the sick and suffering and was greatly respected. Feast 29 May.

Joseph Giandieri, catholicos, died 1770. Georgian Church. He was a monk of Dodo Garegeli, but was elected patriarch in 1755, then dispossessed of his see when a former patriarch was reinstated. He retired to live a hermit's life. Feast 17 October.

Joseph Herman, Premonstratensian mystic and writer, born Cologne, Germany, 1150, died convent of Hoven, Cologne, Germany, 7 April 1241 (?). Having had spiritual visions from an early age, Herman joined the Premonstratensians when he was 12 and was sent from Steinfeld abbey to Frisia to finish school, after which he returned. At Steinfeld he served as chaplain of the local Cistercian nuns and was noted as a clockmaker. His exemplary life led him to be called 'Joseph'. Some of what he wrote is now lost, but his surviving hymns and prayers (including possibly the *Summi regis cor aveto*, the earliest hymn about the Sacred Heart) reveal an affectionate piety that foreshadows the Devotio Moderna.

Joseph Lambton, bl., martyr, born Malton, Yorkshire, 1568, died Newcastle upon Tyne, 24 July 1592. He studied at the English College in Rheims from 1584, went to Rome in 1589 and was ordained in 1592, with a dispensation for being under age. He returned to England that year, but was arrested in Newcastle upon Tyne after only a short while. He was condemned for being a seminary priest working in England and was hanged, drawn and quartered at the age of 24.

Joseph Manyanet y Vives, bl., born Tremp, Catalonia, 7 January 1833, died Barcelona, 17 December 1901. He studied at the Piarist college in Barbastro, then at seminaries in Lerida and Urgel. He was ordained in 1859 and worked for five years in Tremp before moving to Barcelona. He founded three Congregations: one to look after the education of boys, and two for girls. He also started a newspaper called *The Sacred Heart*. He was in part responsible for Gaudi's decision to design and build the cathedral of the Sagrada Familia in Barcelona.

Joseph Marchand, martyr, born Passavant, Doubs, France, 17 August 1803, died Saigon, Vietnam, 30 November 1835, beatified 1900, canonized 1988. A priest of the Paris Foreign Missions Society, he is said to have been flayed alive. See **Martyrs of Vietnam**.

Joseph Mary Gambaro, bl., born Novara, Italy, 7 August 1869, martyred Hengzhou, China, 7 July 1900, beatified 1946. A Franciscan priest, in China since 1896, he supervised the Christian community at Yenchow. He was captured during the Boxer Rebellion while trying to reach Hengzhou by boat, and was stoned with his companion Antony Fantosati. See **Franciscan Martyrs of China**.

Joseph Moscati, born Benevento, near Naples, 25 July 1880, died Naples, 27 April 1927, canonized 1987. A doctor from 1903, he worked at the hospital of Santa Maria del Popolo, or Incurabili, becoming director in 1911. He practised medicine tirelessly, seeing it as his religious vocation. Feast 12 April.

Joseph Nascimbeni, bl., born near lake Garda, Italy, 22 November 1851, died Castelletto di Brenzone, 21 January 1922, beatified 1988. Ordained in 1874, he was curate then parish priest at Castelletto. In 1892 he founded with Mother Maria Mantovani the Congregation of Little Sisters of the Holy Family. Feast 22 January.

Joseph Nguyen Van Luu, martyred Vietnam, 1854 – see **Martyrs of Vietnam**. Feast 2 May.

Joseph of Astrakhan, metropolitan, born Astrakhan, 1597, died there, 11 May 1671. Russian Church. He became a monk, then archimandrite of the monastery of the Most Holy Trinity, before becoming archbishop of Astrakhan in 1659, and being raised to the rank of metropolitan in 1667 while he was in Moscow. He became caught up in a Cossack revolt against Moscow, and although he said he remained outside politics, a group of Cossacks attacked him in his cathedral, carried him up to a high point and threw him off.

Joseph of Bisericani, monk, born near Neamt, fifteenth/sixteenth centuries. Romanian Church. As a young man he entered the monastery of Bistrita, but then visited the Holy Land and settled in the desert, where a group of disciples gathered around him. They lived for the most part a solitary life, meeting just once a week to eat together. The group later moved back to Moldavia and settled on Mount Bisericani, where they built a monastery and kept to the same Rule they had developed in the Holy Land.

Joseph of Biswaw, monk, born Qift, Upper Egypt, died Mount Benhadad. Coptic Church. A rich man, he gave all his wealth to the poor and became a monk.

Joseph of Chaleplis, martyr, born Chaleplis, died there, 4 February 1686. Byzantine Church. Put to death for refusing to convert to Islam after – it was claimed – he had promised to do so.

Joseph of Crete, bl., monk, born Atokeramo, Crete, *c.* 1540, died Heraklion, 22 January 1611. He was educated in the monastery of St John the Theologian near Heraklion, but was early left an orphan, and very rich. He was generous to the poor, but eventually divided his wealth in three parts – one for Mount Athos, one for the Holy Land, and the third part for himself. This last part, however, he continued to distribute to the poor. He became head of the monastery.

Joseph of Cupertino, Franciscan priest, born in poverty at Cupertino, near Brindisi, Italy, 17 June 1603, died Osimo, 18 September 1663. Born Joseph Desa, he had a very unhappy childhood and was resented by his mother, who was widowed shortly after his birth. He was refused admission by the Conventual Friars Minor and was then dismissed by the Capuchins as a result of his awkwardness. He finally became a stable boy at the Franciscan convent of La Grotella near Cupertino, where he was admitted as a novice in 1625. Although very backward in his studies, he was ordained priest in 1628. His life from then on was one of extreme austerity, accompanied by a series of miracles and ecstasies which included levitation. Because of the disturbance caused by this, he was not allowed to take part in community duties for some 35 years, and was even denounced to the Inquisition. In 1639 he was removed from the curiosity of the people to Assisi and then to the convent of the Capuchins in 1653. Finally, in 1657, he was removed to the conventual house at Osimo, where he remained in strict seclusion for the rest of his life.

Joseph of Duin, martyr, born near Duin, died there, 24 October 1170. He was a Persian by birth, but was attracted to Christianity and was secretly baptized. Returning from a pilgrimage to the Holy Land, he was arrested, but refused to deny his Christianity and was executed after a long imprisonment.

Joseph of Kozlov, monk, died Kozlov, seventeenth century. Russian Church. He set himself up as a hermit *c.* 1627. When a small community gathered around him he built a monastery. The nearby city of Kozlov postdates the arrival of Joseph. Feast 28 July.

Joseph of Leonessa, Capuchin friar, born Leonessa, Italy, 8 January 1556, died Amatrice, Italy, 4 February 1612. The son of a nobleman – his family name was Desideri – his parents died when he was 15 and he was brought up and educated by his uncle, Battista, who was a professor at Viterbo. In January 1573 he joined the Capuchin Order, and was later ordained to the priesthood. A noted preacher, he arrived in Contantinople in 1587, where he ministered to galley slaves and preached in the city. This led to great hostility, and his imprisonment. On his release he attempted to enter the royal palace, but was caught and condemned to death by the sultan. Having been left hanging by hooks through his hand and foot for three days, he was released. He returned to Italy where he became widely known for his preaching and his care for the poor and sick. Feast 4 February.

Joseph of Marmures, bishop, born Marmures, Romania, died 1711. Romanian Church. Of a noble family named Stoica. He was elected bishop when a widower, and had to take monastic vows before his consecration. He was chosen as someone who might strengthen the faith of the Orthodox, just as the Greek-rite Catholics were making efforts to convert them to Rome. He was arrested and imprisoned in Hust in 1705 for his zeal in defence of Orthodoxy. He was freed in 1711 thanks to a popular outcry, but never regained his see. Feast 24 April.

Joseph of Optina, monk, born Gorodisce, 2 November 1837, died Optina, 9 May 1911. Russian Church. He was brought up as a very devout child but, having been left an orphan, had to take a number of different jobs to earn a living. In 1861 he visited the monastery of Optina, where he was offered a post as assistant to **Ambrose of Optina**, which he accepted, and three years later entered the monastery, when he changed his name to Joseph from his original Ivan Efimovic Litovkin. He became a priest in 1884. He had received a vision of the Mother of God when he was eight, and he was to receive other visions of Mary while in the monastery. He became superior of the hermitage attached to Optina in 1894, which he had to give up because of ill-health in 1905. Feast 11 October.

Joseph of Pskov, martyr, died Pskov, 4 March 1299. With the monk **Constantine of Pskov**, he was killed during an attack by the Livonian Order.

Joseph of Raifskaia Pustyn, martyr, born 1888, died near Raifskaia Pustyn, 7 April 1930. Baptized Ivan Illarionovic Gavrilov, he entered the monastery in 1907, and during World War I served as a cook. In 1923 he was ordained priest. When the monastery was closed he remained in the vicinity, serving the parishes. In January 1930 he was arrested immediately after the liturgy, along with others, including members of the congregation. He was imprisoned and later shot. Feast 14 January.

Joseph of Solovki and Companions (Joseph the Younger, Alexis, Ephraim, Sebastian, Theodoulus, Tikon, Tryphon), monks, seventeenth century. Russian Church. A group of monks who lived in the woods as hermits, but belonged originally to the monastery of Solovki. Feast 9 August.

Joseph of the Kievan Cave Monastery, fourteenth century. Russian Church. Known as 'the Great Invalid', he was very sick, and vowed that were he to be cured he would spend his life serving the monks of the Kievan Cave monastery. He was indeed cured, and lived a life of great asceticism, serving the community. Feast 28 August.

Joseph of Thessalonika, bishop and martyr, born Constantinople, *c.* 760, died there, 15 July 832. He joined the monastery of St John the Baptist in Constantinople with his brothers and father, after they had been driven out of the monastery they founded at Sakkoudion by the Emperor Constantine VI, over a quarrel concerning the emperor's adulterous marriage. Joseph became bishop of Thessalonika in 806 or 807, but when St **Nicephorus** was appointed patriarch in 809 Joseph refused to recognize him, as he had not been ordained, and Nicephorus had Joseph imprisoned. He was banished to the Princes' Island in the Sea of Marmara for two years for refusing to celebrate mass with the priest who had blessed Constantine's marriage, and spent six years in exile between 815 and 821 during the iconoclast persecution.

Joseph of Timisoara, metropolitan, born Dubrovnik, 1568. Serbian Church. His baptismal name was James: he took Joseph when he entered a monastery on Mount Athos. He lived in several, becoming the hegumenos of one. In 1650 he became the metropolitan of Timisoara, but retired to the monastery of Partos for the last period of his life. Feast 15 September.

Joseph of Tsenti, monk, born Faw. Coptic Church. He and a friend both became monks near the city of Faw, but later withdrew to live an eremitical life on Mount Tsenti, near Biswaw.

Joseph of Volokolamsk, founder, born Jazvisce-Pokrovskoe, near Volokoloamsk, *c.* 1440, died Volokolamsk, 9 September 1515. His baptismal name was John Sanin, and the family had originally come from Lithuania. They were deeply embedded in Orthodoxy: both John's parents entered religious life and so did two of his brothers, as well as other relatives. At the age of 20 John also entered religious life, first at a monastery near Tver, then at one at Borovsk, invited there by **Paphnutius of Borovsk**, who became his spiritual director. It was there that he made his monastic profession in 1460. In 1477 he became hegumenos of the monastery, but met with opposition from some members of the community and left, spending time in a number of other monasteries (including a return to Borovsk) before leaving for his native territory with seven other monks. In 1479 he settled at Volokolamsk, building first a church dedicated to the Dormition of the Mother of God, and eventually a monastery which, despite the strictness of its Rule, quickly attracted new monks, many of them from the aristocracy. For much of the remainder of his life, Joseph was engaged in controversy, both on theological issues and particularly on the right of monasteries to own property – which he strongly upheld. In addition to his Rule, of particular significance in the development of the coenobitic tradition in Russian Orthodoxy, he left a large number of writings.

Joseph of Walaqa, monk, fourteenth/fifteenth centuries. Ethiopian Church. He was sent by **Zena Marqos** to evangelize Walaqa.

Joseph of Zaonikievo, born Obuchovo, *c.* 1530, died Zaonikievo, 21 September 1612. Russian Church. Hilarion (his baptismal name) suffered with eye problems, for the healing of which he prayed constantly to Ss **Cosmas and Damian**. Eventually they appeared to him in a vision and told him to go to a certain place, where he found an icon of the Mother of God. He was healed there – as was another blind man whom the local bishop had sent to test the story – and Joseph established a monastery there, although he would not himself take the office of hegumenos, but remained a simple monk. Feast 21 September.

Joseph Oriol, born Barcelona, Spain, 23 November 1650, died there, 23 March 1702, canonized 1909. Ordained in 1676, he supported his poor mother as a tutor and, after her death in 1686, travelled to

Rome. Returning home, he lived a life of strict asceticism, curing many people in the region.

Joseph Pignatelli, Jesuit, born Saragossa, 27 December 1737, died San Pantaleone, Italy, 11 November 1811. Joseph led the Society of Jesus after its expulsion from Spain (1767), and went to Bologna when Clement XIV suppressed the entire order in 1773. He could not join the remnant in White Russia because of ill-health, but worked to establish a vice province in Parma – the general in St Petersburg named him provincial of Italy in 1803. From Rome, Joseph directed the re-establishment of the Society in Sardinia (1807), and opened colleges at Rome, Orvieto and Tivoli. He greatly facilitated the full restoration of the Society in 1814. Pius XII canonized him in 1954. Feast 28 November.

Joseph Ta, martyred Tongking, 1859, commemorated with **Dominic Kahm** and **Lucy Thin** – see **Martyrs of Vietnam**. Feast 13 January.

Joseph Tchang Ta-Pong, bl., born Kouy-tcheou Province, China, c. 1754, martyred there, 12 March 1815, beatified 1909. Always religious, baptized in 1800, after arranging for his junior wife to marry another Christian, he worked as a catechist. Denounced by a family member, he refused to abjure and was crucified.

Joseph the Painter, bl., martyr, died Constantinople, 1819. Byzantine Church. He appears to have belonged to a monastery on Mount Athos, although he was not a monk, and he was arrested while in Constantinople.

Joseph the Priest, died 1763. Georgian Church. A devout priest from southern Georgia. He is said to have climbed one of the highest peaks in the Caucasus, never ascended before, and there found the crib of the patriarch Abraham, a fragment of which he took to the king. Feast 7 October.

Joseph Tjyang Tjyon Keni, born Suwon, Korea, 1802, martyred there, 30 March 1866, beatified 1968, canonized 1984. A catechist after his conversion, his house was used as a seminary in Paeron. He was tortured and killed with others

during a time of general persecution – see also **Martyrs of Korea**.

Joseph Tomasi, cardinal, born Sicily, 1649, ordained 1673, died Rome, 1 January 1713, beatified 1803, canonized 1986. A Theatine priest, Greek and Hebrew scholar, called the 'prince of liturgists', he analysed translations of the Psalms in his *Psalterium* and edited ancient texts. People claimed cures in his lifetime from touching his clothing.

Joseph Vaz, bl., apostle of Ceylon (Sri Lanka), born Goa, 21 April 1651, died Kandy, Sri Lanka, 16 January 1711. Ordained in 1676, Vaz laboured in Goa until he was able to found a group of Oratorians in 1685 to go to Ceylon, where the Dutch denied religious freedom to Catholics. He arrived there in 1686, disguised as a beggar to avoid persecution. Notwithstanding many hardships, he had success and won the confidence of the king of Kandy, who restored religious liberty. Other Oratorians joined him, and the territory was geographically divided so as to assign responsibility among them. The faith spread rapidly and Vaz, who was revered for the holiness of his life, resisted with difficulty the conferment of ecclesiastical honours. By the time of his death, more than 70,000 persons openly professed the faith in Ceylon. Feast 16 January.

Josepha Naval Girbés, bl., born Algamesí, near Valencia, Spain, 1820, died there, 24 February 1893, beatified 1988. Unable to leave home due to chronic ill-health, she joined the St Vincent de Paul Association, taught the girls in her village and was known for her ability to reconcile those involved in quarrels.

Josepha of Benigamin, bl., born near Valencia, Spain, 1625, died Benigamin, 21 January 1696, beatified 1888, better known in Spain as Inés (Agnes), her given name. She joined the Congregation of Discalced Augustinian Hermitesses in Benigamin. Many came to consult her, including high-ranking people, drawn by her counselling abilities.

Josephine Bakhita, nun, born southern Sudan, c. 1869, died Schio, Italy, 8 February 1947.

Kidnapped and enslaved as a child, she was eventually sold in 1883 to an Italian family who took her home to care for their daughter. In Italy, with the support of the Church, she was declared free, was baptized on 9 January 1890 and joined the Daughters of Charity. She was considered holy during her life. The people of her town prayed for her protection during World War II and Schio was spared bomb damage, as she had promised. She was beatified in 1992 and declared a saint in 2000.

Joshua of Dabra Daret, monk. Ethiopian Church. Little is known of him except that, it is recorded, he remained for so long immobile in prayer that his body began to resemble that of a dead man.

Joshua of Gar Sellase, monk, born 1468, died Dabra Libanos, 13 October 1508. Ethiopian Church. As a child he was raised from the dead, so his parents set him to the study of Scripture, and he was ordained priest. On the way back from the ordination he was set upon by robbers, but saved by an angel, who told him he was to become a monk. His life was full of similar miracles, and of temptations which he overcame with the help of angels. Much of his time as a monk he spent at Dabra Libanos, but he also lived in a hermitage near to it, and founded his own monastery at Gar Sellase, north-east of Dabra Libanos. However, he returned to the latter monastery to die.

Joshua the Great, king and martyr, died lake Tana, 13 October 1706. Ethiopian Church. He became king of Gondar in 1682. He was devout, and much improved the well-being of his people through his social and economic reforms. He was also interested in opening relations with other countries, including those of Europe. He was forced to abdicate, however, and, as a devout man, retired to a monastery on lake Tana, where he was killed by his enemies.

Jovinian, martyr, died Auxerre, third century. He is supposed to have been reader to bishop **Peregrinus** and been martyred after the bishop's death. However, the story of Peregrinus being first bishop of Auxerre is not reliable. Feast 5 May.

Jovita, see **Faustinus**.

Juan de Castillo, born Spain, 1596. See **Roque González**.

Juan Diego, visionary, born Tlayacac, near Mexico City, 1474, died there, 30 May 1548. A Christian Indian, he saw a vision of Mary on three occasions, the first on 9 December 1531. She appeared on a hill at Tepeyac, near what is now Mexico City, as a young Indian girl speaking Nahuatl, his own language. She told him to instruct the bishop to build her a shrine on the hill. The Spanish bishop refused to believe that the Virgin could appear as an Indian or choose an Indian as her messenger, until her image was mysteriously imprinted on Juan's cape. The Virgin of Guadeloupe, as she is known, remains a potent symbol to all Mexicans. Feast 9 December.

Judicael of Quimper, king, born Brittany, died Gael, near Vannes, 658. The brother of St **Judoc** and the last independent king of Brittany. According to Fredegar, King Dagobert I insisted that Bretons obey his rule; Judicael responded and a peaceful solution was reached with the help of Bishop **Ouen** of Rouen and **Eligios of Noyon**. He entered the abbey of St-Jean-Baptiste, later called St-Meen-Gael, where his spiritual director, **Meen**, was a monk. It is possible that he entered the monastery twice, the first time being called back by his family. Feast 17 December.

Judith, see **Salome and Judith**.

Judoc (Josse), prince and hermit, born Brittany, died St-Josse-sur-Mer, 668. He was offered the crown when his brother abdicated to become a monk. Judoc refused, and instead went on pilgrimage to various shrines, including Rome, in the course of which he became a priest. He then became a hermit at Ponthieu: the place, St-Josse-sur-Mer, is named after him. At the beginning of the tenth century his relics were brought to Winchester, where they were placed in the new minster then being built. Feast 13 December.

Julia, born Carthage, martyred Cape Corso, north Corsica, sixth century. Her legend describes her as a woman sold by the Vandal conquerors to a pagan Syrian merchant who landed in Corsica. She defied the pagan ruler's order to participate in a sacrifice and was crucified. Feast 22 May.

Julia della Rena (Julia of Certaldo), bl., born Certaldo, 1319, died there, 9 January 1367. In domestic service in Florence, she became an Augustinian tertiary at the age of 19. She returned home and lived for 30 years in a cell alongside the local church. She once rescued a child from a burning building.

Julia Eustochium, born Rome, c. 370, died probably Bethlehem, c. 419. The daughter of St **Paula**, the two were in contact with St **Jerome**, and were ultimately forced to leave Rome when a letter concerning virginity written by Jerome to Julia in 385 (Ep. 22) caused controversy. They travelled through Syria and Egypt before building four monasteries in Bethlehem, for which Julia assumed responsibility in 404 after her mother's death. Feast 28 September.

Julian, see also **Caesarius and Julian**.

Julian, see also **Lucian**.

Julian, see also **Philotheus**.

Julian, martyred possibly Antioch, fourth century. He and his wife **Basilissa** are supposed to have agreed to a celibate marriage and made their home into a hospital for the poor. He is commemorated with other martyrs: **Anthony**, a priest; **Anastasius**, a convert; **Marcionilla** and her small son **Celsus**. Feast 6 January.

Julian, martyr, died Alexandria, 250. According to Eusebius, quoting Bishop Dionysius of Alexandria, Julian was an infirm old man when he was killed under Decius by being burned with quicklime. Several companions died in the same way, including his friend Cronion (Eunus in Latin), a soldier. Feast 27 February.

Julian, martyr, died Anazarbus, Cilicia, c. 302. Of senatorial rank, he was tortured then thrown into the sea in a sack filled with scorpions and vipers. His body was recovered and buried at Antioch, where **John Chrysostom** gave a sermon praising him. Feast 16 March.

Julian Alfredo Zapico, martyr, born Cifuentes de Rueda, 24 December 1903, died Turon, Asturias, 9 October 1934. Baptized Vifridio, he joined the de la Salle Brothers on 4 February 1926. He had arrived in Turon only a month before his martyrdom. He was arrested with the other **Martyrs of Asturia** by a group of rebel soldiers, and executed by firing squad.

Julian Casarello de Valle, bl., born Valle, Istria, died there, 1349, cult approved 1910. He was a Franciscan. Feast 1 May.

Julian, Marcian and Companions, martyrs at Constantinople, c. 729. Feast 9 August.

Julian Maunoir, bl., born near Rennes, France, 1606, died Plévin, near Quimper, 28 January 1683, beatified 1951. A Jesuit from 1625, ordained in 1637, he worked in Brittany, where Celtic pre-Christian beliefs were strong. He learned Breton and, with other priests, helped form the long-lasting Breton rural Catholic life.

Julian of Alexandria, bishop, died Alexandria, 4 March 192. Coptic Church. A learned priest of Alexandria, he was elected bishop in 180.

Julian of Antioch, patriarch, died 595. Syriac Church. A monk of Qennesre before his election in 591.

Julian of Brioude, martyr, died Brioude, in the Auvergne, third century (?). He is said to have been a soldier, who took refuge in the Auvergne when the governor of Vienne started to persecute Christians. He was found at Brioude, and beheaded. Feast 28 August.

Julian of Caesarea, martyr. Of doubtful authenticity, but said to be a Syrian priest. Feast 25 August.

Julian of Caesarea, martyr, born Cappadocia, died Caesarea, c. 308. Recorded as having offered himself for martyrdom when he saw others being martyred. He was burned alive. Feast 17 February.

Julian of Cuenca, bishop and patron saint of Cuenca, born Burgos, Castile, sometime between 1113 and 1138, died Cuenca, 28 January 1208 (?).

He had taught theology at Palencia before becoming archdeacon of Toledo in 1182. In 1196 he became the second bishop of Cuenca, a city which had been captured from the Moors in 1177. As bishop he was responsible for drawing up the constitutions of the cathedral chapter. He was renowned as a pastor who cared for the poor and the sick. A number of miracles were attributed to him, including one in which he provided grain for the city. After his death his shrine became a place of pilgrimage where cures were reputedly effected.

Julian of Le Mans, traditionally first bishop of Le Mans, France, died *c.* 400 (?). Unreliable sources claim that Julian was a Roman nobleman and evangelist in the Le Mans area, where many churches are dedicated to him. His cult was probably popularized by Henry II, born at Le Mans and baptized in the church of St Julian. Julian's legend claims that he performed miracles, calling him one of Christ's 72 disciples and Simon the Leper. He is occasionally confused with the mythical **Julian the Hospitaller**. Feast 27 January.

Julian of Saba, monk. Born Heliopolis, Syria, *c.* 300, died Orshoene, 377/8. Julian lived first in a cave in the desert of Orshoene, between Antioch and Euphrates, with a group of disciples. He built a church in Sinai on the rock where God was said to have appeared to Moses. He refuted Arian claims of allegiance between 364 and 378. Feast 17 January.

Julian of St Augustine, bl., born Medinaceli, Spain, *c.* 1550, died Spain, 1606, beatified 1825. Several times dismissed from the Franciscan novitiate as mentally unstable because of his extreme austerities and devotions, he eventually became a lay brother. He proved an eloquent preacher with the gift of prophecy. Feast 8 April.

Julian the Hospitaller, a legendary account claims that Julian, a nobleman, killed his parents when they were paying him a surprise visit: he thought the couple in the bed were his wife and another man. He and his wife then made a pilgrimage to Rome to seek absolution, and on their return established a hospice by a river for travellers and the poor. Feast 12 February.

Juliana, martyr, died possibly near Naples, *c.* 305. She is also described as a martyr who died in Nicomedia, Asia Minor, although that seems less likely as her relics are supposedly at Cumae, near Naples. She was a virgin and is depicted with a dragon. Feast 16 February.

Juliana, see also **Paul**.

Juliana Chigi, bl., possibly connected with the famous Chigi family, died Siena, 1400. After being widowed four times, she spent her remaining years as a tertiary of St Augustine.

Juliana Falconieri, founder of the Sisters of the Third Order of Servites, born Florence, 1270, died there, 12 June 1341. Julia was born into a respected Florentine merchant family. Her uncle was St **Alexis Falconeri**. Devout from youth, Julia founded the Third Order, remaining the superior until her death. The order cared for the sick and did works of mercy. On her deathbed, desiring to receive communion but being unable to because of vomiting, Julia asked for the host to be placed on her chest. The host disappeared, Julia died, and a cross such as had been on the host was said to appear on her chest. Feast 19 June.

Juliana of Bologna, died *c.* 435. She agreed to her husband becoming a priest and brought up their four children. **Ambrose of Milan** mentions her piety and charity to the poor. Feast 7 February.

Juliana of Lazarevo, born Murom, died Niznyj Novgorod, 10 January 1604. The daughter of an official at the court of Ivan the Terrible, she was left an orphan at seven, and was brought up by various relatives. At 16 she married George Osorgin, also a courtier, and moved to his property at Lazarevo. She was deeply devout, practising great mortifications – including regular prostrations – and after two of her sons were killed, for which she blamed herself, she wanted to enter a convent, but her husband dissuaded her, although he agreed that she might live in chastity. Unable to read and write, she had her children read the Scriptures to her. In the great famine in Russia at the beginning of the seventeenth century – by which time she was a widow – she fed the hungry as far as she was able, but then had to move to a property near Niznyj Novgorod, and then dismiss all her servants.

Juliana of Liège, abbess and visionary, born Retinnes, near Liège, 1192, died Fosses, near Namur, 5 April 1258. An orphan, she joined the Augustinian convent of Mont Cornillon, where in 1222 she became prioress. As the result of a vision she dedicated herself to establishing the feast of Corpus Christi, persuading her local bishop to allow its celebration: he fixed the day as the first Thursday following the octave of Trinity Sunday. The feast was extended to northern Europe in her own lifetime and, a year after her death, to the whole Church (by Pope Urban IV, who had been archdeacon of Liège). Juliana herself, however, was exiled from Mont Cornillon and spent her final years first at a monastery in Namur and then as a recluse at Fosses. **Eva of Liège** succeeded in getting Juliana's idea accepted.

Juliana of Nicomedia, martyr, died Nicomedia, *c.* 305. She was a Christian in a pagan family, and when her father proposed she marry a young pagan, she said she would not do so until he became prefect of Nicomedia – which he achieved. She then said she would not marry him unless he became a Christian, which he refused. Her angry father took her before a tribunal and denounced her as a Christian. She was executed. Feast 16 February.

Juliana of Novgorod, died 1383. Russian Church. The mother of **Nicola Kocianov**. Feast 21 December.

Juliana of Sol'vycegodsk, sixteenth/seventeenth century. She came from the village of Ulijanovsk, but otherwise nothing is known.

Juliana of Vjaz'ma, princess and martyr, died Torzok, 1406. Russian Church. She was the wife of **Simeon Mstislav**, prince of Vjaz'ma, who followed his lord, George of Smolensk, into exile in Torzok. George was infatuated with Juliana, and killed Simeon. Juliana rejected his approaches, and she too was killed and her body thrown into a river. George then fled for refuge to the Golden Horde, but later repented and entered a monastery. Feast 21 December.

Juliana Olsankaja, princess, died *c.* 1540. Russian Church. The daughter of Prince George Dubrovicki Olsanski, she died when only 16, but had demonstrated great devotion during her short life. Feast 18 October.

Juliana Puricelli, bl., Augustinian, died Novara, 1501. Feast 15 August.

Julitta, martyr, born Iconium, died Isauria, *c.* 304. The mother of **Cyriacus**, she moved from her home town to avoid persecution, but was nonetheless caught up in the persecution of Diocletian. Feast 16 June.

Julitta, martyr, died *c.* 303. Julitta lived in Caesarea during the reign of Diocletian. She was a widow and was denounced as a Christian by a man who wanted to take over her estates. She was ordered to sacrifice to Zeus, but refused, and was burned and decapitated. Feast 30 July.

Julius I, pope between 6 February 337 and 12 April 352, born Rome, died there. He was dragged into the Arian controversy when **Athanasius** and **Marcellus**, both condemned by Arians and in exile in Rome, sought his support. Julius took their part and managed to have the emperors convene a synod in Serdica (Sofia). After the departure of the Easterners, Julius's decision in favour of Athanasius and Marcellus was approved by the Westerners, who in this way accepted the right of bishops condemned by a provincial council to appeal to the Roman see. The episode shows a glimpse of the very gradual unfolding of the theory of papal primacy.

Julius Alvarez Mendoza, martyr, born Guadalajara, Mexico, 20 December 1866, died San Julian, Jalisco, 30 March 1927. Ordained in 1894, he was arrested while riding out to say mass in an outlying farm. Feast 25 May.

Julius and Aaron, martyrs, died Caerleon, Wales, 304. If historical, they were probably traders. Feast 1 July.

Julius the Veteran, martyr, died Durostorum, by the Danube (Silistria, Bulgaria), *c.* 304. He had been a soldier for 27 years, secretly a Christian, when he was questioned and admitted this. The Roman prefect tried to save him, but he refused to compromise and was killed by the sword. Feast 27 May.

Junipero Serra, bl., Franciscan missionary to Central and North America, born Petra, Majorca, 24 November 1713, died Monterey, California, 28 August 1784. He joined the Franciscans in September 1730, was educated at the university in Palma, Majorca, where he became professor of philosophy. In 1749 he was sent to the college in San Fernando, Mexico, but undertook missionary work among the indigenous population in the Sierra Gorda mission. After serving there for nine years he was recalled to Mexico, but in 1767 was appointed superior of a group of Franciscan missionaries who made their way northwards along the coast of California. He founded 21 missions in Upper California, the first being at San Diego (16 July 1769). He was a remarkable preacher, and was given the right to confirm his converts, even though he was not a bishop – then an unusual privilege. He was beatified in 1987.

Jurii Novicki, martyr, born 1882, died St Petersburg, 13 August 1922. See **Benjamin of Kazan**.

Just of the Holy Sepulchre, monks. Georgian Church. Three monks commemorated together, John, Stephen and Isaiah, belonging to the monastery of the Holy Sepulchre in Jerusalem. Feast 4 November.

Justa, possibly martyred Cagliari, Sardinia, c. 300, with **Justina** and **Heredina**. Feast 14 May.

Justa and Runa, see **Rufina and Justa**.

Justin, monk, fourteenth/fifteenth centuries. Ethiopian Church. Very little is known about him. His life recounts the fact that a group of hermits, visiting his parents' house, predicted that he would be a holy man and a great teacher, that he was sent to study Scripture, that he worked miracles, and that he was a monk for almost 100 years.

Justin de Jacobis, Vincentian missionary bishop to Ethiopia, born San Fele, Italy, 1800, died Alghedien, Eritrea, 31 July 1860. He was ordained in 1824, became prefect apostolic of a new mission to Ethiopia in 1839 and in 1847 was made vicar apostolic. He had great sympathy for the Ethiopian Church and used its liturgy. In turn, internal dissent in the country encouraged more openness towards Roman Catholicism. In 1844 he built a seminary at Gwela and a school for Ghe'ez and Catholic theology. His mission was particularly successful amongst the mountain tribes. His good relations with Ethiopian authorities declined after the appointment in 1855 of Abuna (metropolitan) Salama, who saw de Jacobis as a rival. He was arrested, but his work continued through the many priests he had ordained – some of them married – and the Roman Catholic Church continued to grow.

Justin Martyr, Christian apologist, born Samaria c. 100, died by beheading c. 165. He was trained in philosophy, particularly Stoicism and Platonism, and became a Christian c. 130. He continued to teach, but now his teaching was in the defence and explanation of Christianity to Jews and pagans alike, first in Ephesus, where he engaged in his famous dialogue with the Jew Trypho, and later in Rome, where he opened a school. His *Apologies* (c. 155 and 161) meet accusations against Christianity and endeavour to explain its beliefs and practices to pagan minds. Feast 1 June.

Justin of Chienti, may have died c. 384, or c. 540. Always venerated at Chienti, he is described as the first bishop of the city. Feast 1 January.

Justina, martyr, died Padua, second century (?). Although venerated from before the sixth century, nothing is known of her life. She is said to have been converted by a disciple of St Peter, and put to death by the sword. Feast 7 October.

Justina, see also **Justa**.

Justina Bezzoli, bl., born Francuccia, Arezzo, died there, 1319, cult confirmed 1890. She was a Benedictine in both St Mark's and All Saints convents and also a recluse at Civitella. Feast 12 March.

Justinian, hermit and martyr, died island of Ramsey, Wales, sixth century. Said to have been murdered by brigands. Feast 23 August.

Justinian I, emperor, born Tauresium, Macedonia, 482, died Constantinople, 14 November 565. Byzantine Church. Justinian's uncle Justin was head of the imperial guard in Constantinople, and succeeded to the throne in 518. Justinian was a close adviser, and succeeded his uncle in 527, two years after marrying the former actress **Theodora**. The basis of his policy was the restoration of the Roman Empire, by attempting to win back both north Africa and Italy, in which enterprise he was partly successful. Another aspect of the same policy was the restoration of the law, expressed only a few years after his accession to the throne by the publication of the Code which is named after him. The Code shows the strong influence of Christianity on the law under Justinian, and he took a very considerable role in the ecclesiastical politics of the time, the suppression of heresy playing a large part in his policies. He produced a number of significant theological writings, both in the form of letters and of treatises.

Justinian II, emperor, born Constantinople, 669, died there, 14 November 711. Byzantine Church. He became emperor in 685 on the death of his father. He was at first successful. He pursued a policy of reconciliation between Rome and Constantinople, although he insisted on – and called a council which accepted – the equality of the two sees, a position rejected by the bishop of Rome. Heavy taxation led to an uprising against him in 695, and he was exiled to the Crimea after being mutilated: his nose was cut off, and he was given the nickname 'Split Nose'. He returned to power in 705, backed by Slav and Bulgar troops. He once again worked for reconciliation with the bishop of Rome, and sent troops to Italy to defend him. He was the first Byzantine emperor to put the figure of Christ on his coinage. Feast 15 July.

Justino Orona Madrigal, martyr, born Mexico, 1877, died Cuquio, 1 July 1928. Ordained in 1904 after studies at the seminary of Guadalajara. At the time of the persecution, with his assistant priest **Atilano Cruz Alvarado** he was serving four different parishes. He and Atilano were captured while on a ranch with his brother, who was also killed with him.

Justus, monk. Ethiopian Church.

Justus, monk, seventh century. Coptic Church. A disciple of **Samuel of Kalamon**. Feast 5 January.

Justus and Pastor, martyrs, born Complutum (Alcalá de Henares, Spain), died there, 304. Two young boys, one aged 13, the other 9, who so encouraged Christians being persecuted for their faith that they, too, were beheaded. They are patrons of both Alcalá and Madrid. Feast 6 August.

Justus of Beauvais, martyr, died Beauvais, c. 305. Supposedly a young man, possibly a boy, beheaded for being a Christian. Nothing else is known about him. Feast 18 October.

Justus of Canterbury, fourth archbishop of Canterbury, died Canterbury, c. 627. Most of what is known of Justus comes from **Bede**, who tells us that Justus was one of the second wave of missionaries sent to England by **Gregory the Great** in 601. He was made bishop of Rochester by **Augustine** in 604. Following a pagan backlash he fled to Gaul, but returned and in 624 was made archbishop of Canterbury.

Justus of Lyons, bishop, born Vivarais, died Lyons, c. 390. He served as a deacon in Vienne before becoming bishop of Lyons. After attending the Council of Aquileia in 381 he decided to become a hermit, and went off to the Egyptian desert instead of returning home, but a messenger was sent to bring him back. According to one version of the story the messenger failed, and also stayed as a hermit in Egypt. According to the other, more plausible, version, Justus returned. Feast 14 October.

Justus of Urgel, bishop, died Urgel, c. 550. He is the first known bishop of Urgel, near Tarragona, Spanish Catalonia. He attended councils at Toledo (527) and Lérida (546). Three of his brothers were bishops in Spain and **Isidore** includes him in his work *Viri Illustres* (*On Famous Men*). Feast 28 May.

Jutta, bl., recluse, born c. 1090, died Disbenberg, c. 1136. She became a recluse near Mons St Disibodi and was joined in 1106 by St **Hildegard**, who was then aged eight. A group of noble women gathered around them, to whom Jutta acted as prioress. On her death she was succeeded by Hildegard. Feast 22 December.

Jutta of Heiligenthal, bl., Cistercian abbess, born Essleben, Germany, died Heiligenthal, 1250. A group of pious women living in an independent community at Essleben, wishing to live by a Rule, founded a Cistercian convent at Heiligenthal. Jutta was its first abbess (1234–50). Pilgrimages were made to her tomb before the high altar. Her relic, an arm to which a golden cup was attached, was said to cure the sick, and was held at the Julius hospital in Würzburg, but is now lost. Feast 12 May.

Jutta of Huy, bl., born near Liège, 1158, died there, 13 January 1228. Married against her will, widowed young, she worked in a leper hospital before living as an anchorite, walled up near the lepers. She had mystical experiences, gave counsel to many and was credited with the gift of foreknowledge.

Jutta of Sangerhausen, anchoress, born Sangerhausen, Germany, died Kulmsee (now Chelmza, Poland), Prussia, 12 May 1260. Although wanting to enter religious life, she married to please her parents. After her husband's death she settled as an anchoress in Prussia, nursing the sick and lepers. Her spiritual directors were **John Lobedau** and Bishop Heideinreich. Her devotion was to the Sacred Heart of Jesus.

Juvenal, martyr, born Ekaterinburg, 1761, died Alaska, 2 July 1796. Russian Orthodox Church in America. Baptized as James Govoruchin, he was a state official, but in 1791 entered the monastery of Valaam and was ordained. In 1794 he went to Alaska as a missionary, and was martyred there, after conducting many baptisms.

Juvenal Ancina, bl., bishop, born Fossano, Piedmont, Italy, 19 October 1545, died Saluzzo, 31 August 1604. He studied at Montpellier, in Sicily, then in Padua and finally at Turin, where in 1561 he became professor of medicine. A devout young man, he cared for the poor without payment. In 1575 he moved to Rome, where he came under the influence of **Philip Neri**, and with his brother joined the Congregation of the Oratory. He was

sent to live for ten years in Naples, where he took a particular interest in the welfare of those in the hospital. He was recalled to Rome, but he fled from the city when it seemed likely he would be made a bishop. He was eventually ordered to accept the bishopric of Saluzzo, where he found himself involved in a dispute with the duke of Savoy over the rights of the Church. He died in the city after being poisoned by a Franciscan whom he had rebuked for having an affair with a nun. Feast 30 August.

Juvenal of Jerusalem, patriarch, died Jerusalem, 458. He was bishop of Jerusalem from 422 and took part in the Councils of Ephesus and Chalcedon. His defence of orthodoxy brought him many enemies, and for a time he had to take refuge in Constantinople. It was he who established the patriarchate of Jerusalem (hitherto it had been a bishopric) by uniting the three Roman provinces within Palestine, and assuming the right to ordain bishops for the region. He also fixed the feast of Christ's Nativity for Jerusalem as 25 December. Feast 2 July.

Juvenal of Narni, bishop, possibly from the East, died Narni, central Italy, c. 376. He is said to have been a priest and a doctor who was consecrated bishop by Pope **Damasus I**. He apparently saved his city from Ligurian invaders by mobilizing all the townspeople to pray together. Feast 3 May.

Juvenal of Rjazan, archbishop and martyr, born Livna, 15 January 1878, died Novosibirsk, 24 October 1937. Russian Church. Eugene Aleksandrovic Masloskij came from a noble family, took vows as a monk in 1899 and the following year entered the ecclesiastical academy in Moscow. After graduating he was sent to teach at the seminary in Pskov, where he became hegumenos of the monastery of Spaso-Eleazarskij, and in 1910 archimandrite of the Jur'ev monastery in Novgorod. In 1914 he became bishop of Kaira, then in 1923 archbishop of Kursk, but the following year was deported to the Solovki monastery for anti-Soviet activities. While there he was named archbishop of Rjazan. He was released from exile, and engaged in fervent pastoral activity in his diocese, but was rearrested in 1936 and deported once more, this time to Siblag. He nonetheless kept up a correspondence with some to whom he had been giving spiritual direction, and for this he was again condemned, and shot.

Juventinus, martyr, died Antioch, Syria, with **Maximinus**, 25 January 363. Christian officers of Emperor Julian the Apostate (although Christians had been banned from the emperor's army), they were apparently overheard criticizing Julian's anti-Christian activities. Arrested, they refused to retract and were beheaded. There may have been a third martyr, Longinus.

Juventius of Pavia, died 397. According to tradition, **Hermagoras**, bishop of Aquileia, sent him with **Syrus** to evangelize Pavia, of which he became first bishop. Feast 8 February.

Kaichosro the Georgian, monk, born Georgia, died Jerusalem, 1558. Georgian Church. He was very active in refounding the Georgian monastery in Jerusalem, as well as founding the church of St Nicholas near the church of the Holy Sepulchre. Feast 16 June.

Ka'il, monk, fifteenth century. Coptic Church. A convert from Islam, when his father came to visit him he too was converted, and entered the monastery of St John in Scete.

Kakubilla (or Cacucabilla, Cacucila, or Cucacilla), a mythical saint popular in the fifteenth century. It is said that her name, which is reminiscent of Columcille, goes back to St **Columba**, who was invoked against demons and thunderstorms. In Germany the saint was invoked against rats and mice, and in the abbey church of Adelberg in Wurtemberg there is a portrait of a saint with two mice bearing the title 'Cutubilla'.

Kantara, Thirteen Martyrs of, see **Thirteen Martyrs of Kantara**.

Karag, abbot. Syriac Church. Feast 4 July.

Karolina Gerhardinger, bl., founder of the School Sisters of Notre Dame, born Stadtamhof, Bavaria, 20 June 1796, died Munich, Germany, 9 May 1879. At 18 she told her school headteacher she wanted to be a nun, but he persuaded her to found a community of itinerant teaching sisters, along the lines attempted unsuccessfully in the seventeenth century by **Peter Fourier** – a revival of the Canonesses of Our Lady – using Pestalozzi's teaching methods. She was not allowed to take her vows, assuming the religious name Mary Teresa, until her community had demonstrated its self-sufficiency. She was superior of the community from 1839 to her death.

Kateri Tekakwitha, see **Catherine (Kateri) Tekakwitha**.

Katharine Kaspar, ven., founder of the Poor Handmaids of Christ, born Dernbach, near Montabaur, Germany, 26 May 1820, died there, 2 February 1898. In 1848 in Dernbach she founded her congregation to care for the sick, which was approved by the diocese in 1851. Largely because of the Church/state antipathy in Prussia, her movement was established in the USA in 1868 and in England in 1875. Her cause for beatification was introduced in 1946.

Katherine Drexel, founder, born Philadelphia, 26 November 1858, died Cornwells Heights, Pennsylvania, 3 March 1955. She was born into an extremely wealthy banking family and inherited a massive fortune, which she wished to give to a missionary congregation for the evangelizing of the black and native American population of the USA. She asked the advice of Pope Leo XIII, who suggested that she herself become a missionary. She therefore entered the novitiate of the Sisters of Mercy at Pittsburgh in 1889, but two years later founded, in her family's summer house at Toresdale, Pennsylvania, the Blessed Sacrament Sisters for Indians and Coloured People. Her 49 foundations in the USA included Xavier University in St Louis in 1915. She was declared a saint in 2000.

Kaw, martyr, born al-Fayyum, died *c.* 305. Coptic Church. Martyred, it is claimed, in the company of some 500 other Christians.

Kea Maryam, monk, fourteenth/fifteenth centuries. Ethiopian Church. A disciple of **Zena Marqos**. Feast 26 February.

Kenan, bishop. Syriac Church. Feast 13 June.

Kendeas of Cyprus, fourth century. Church of Cyprus. Said to have been a hermit in the desert of the Holy Land who, with many others, had to flee the region and was shipwrecked with them near Paphos in Cyprus. Kendeas lived in a cabin he constructed, and became renowned for his miracles of healing. Feast 9 March.

Kenelm, died 812 or 821. Son of Kenulf (or Coenwulf), king of Mercia from 796 to 821. According to legend, Kenelm succeeded his father as king at the age of seven, but was murdered a few months later on the order of his jealous sister, who was punished by her eyes falling out. However, it is more likely that he lived to be somewhat older, and possibly died in battle. He was buried in Winchcombe. Feast 17 July.

Kenneth (Canice, Cainnech, Canicus), abbot, born Glengiven, County Derry, *c.* 525, died Aghaboe, *c.* 599. Educated by St **Finnian of Clonard**, he became a close friend of St **Columba** and founded monasteries across Ireland, most notably Aghaboe in Laois, Drumahose in Derry, and Cluian Bronig in Offaly. He frequently visited Columba at Iona, where a cemetery and a church were dedicated to him. An effective preacher, he also spent periods of his life as a hermit, especially on deserted islands. In his solitude he copied books, including a manuscript of the Four Gospels. In Scotland his principal church was Inchkenneth in Mull; other churches which bear his name include Kilchennich in Tiree, Kilchainie in South Uist, and the abbey of Cambuskenneth. Some churches in Kintyre and Fife claim to have been founded by him. His journeys to Scotland included one with St Columba to King Brude at Inverness. Feast 11 October.

Kentigern (also known as St Mungo), missionary-bishop and saint, died Glasgow, *c.* 612. According to legend, he was born in southern Scotland, the grandson of a British prince, and taught by St Serf in a monastic school at Culross. He became bishop of the Britons of Strathclyde and founded the church of Glasgow. He spent a period away from Scotland to avoid persecution, in Wales, where he established the monastery of Llanelwy (St Asaph), and in Cumbria. His reputed tomb stands in Glasgow cathedral. We are heavily dependent on a dubious twelfth-century Life for what we know of his career. Feast 13 January.

Kessog (Mackessog), bishop and martyr, born Cashel, Tipperary, said to have died Bandry, Scotland, *c.* 560. A monk who became bishop in the area around Loch Lomond, he had a sanctuary at Luss and is the patron saint of Lennox. Feast 10 March.

Ketevan, queen of Georgia, martyr, died Isfahan, 13 September 1624. She lived at a time when Georgia was divided internally and threatened by both the Turkish and Persian Muslims. In 1615 the Persian shah invaded the country and Ketevan was imprisoned for ten years in Isfahan. She always refused to accept Islam and was eventually tortured to death with hooks and red-hot coals, at a public ceremony. This was witnessed and recorded in detail by visiting Augustinian friars who stole her remains, it is claimed, and took them to Goa.

Kevin, abbot, born Leinster, died Glendalough, County Wicklow, Ireland, *c.* 618. He was educated at the monastery at Kilmanach, was ordained priest, but then became a hermit at Glendalough. He later founded a monastery near his former hermitage. He is said to have made a pilgrimage to Rome, and to have lived until he was 120. Feast 3 June.

Keyne, born Wales, died there (?), sixth century. Said to have been the daughter of a Welsh king who took a vow of virginity and travelled in Herefordshire and possibly Cornwall before returning to Wales. She is said to have founded several churches. It is possible that Keyne was a man. Feast 8 October.

Kieran of Clonmacnois, abbot, born Connaught, Ireland, c. 512, died Clonmacnois, c. 545. One of the so-called 'Twelve Apostles of Ireland', he studied first under **Finnian of Clonard**, then lived with **Enda** in the Aran Islands, and after that visited **Senan** on the Shannon river. With eight companions he founded the abbey of Clonmacnois on the west bank of the Shannon, which he ruled over for only seven months before his death. Feast 8 September.

Kilian (Chillen) of Aubigny, hermit, born Ireland, died Aubigny, France, 670. A relative of St **Fiacre**, but little else is known of him. Legend says that upon returning from a pilgrimage to Rome, he met **Faro**, bishop of Meaux, who gave him land at Aubigny (near Arras) for a hermitage. Feast 13 November.

Kilian of Würzburg, monk, possibly bishop, missionary, martyr, born Ireland, c. 640, died Würzburg, 8 July c. 689. Kilian went to pagan Würzburg as a missionary, along with Colman, a priest, and Totnan, a deacon, arriving in 686, and saw the conversions of Duke Gozbert and many of his subjects in east Franconia and Thuringia. However, the duke had married his brother's widow Geilana, and Kilian informed him that this was unlawful for a Christian. While her husband was absent, Geilana murdered the three missionaries, burying them along with their vestments, books and sacred vessels. Although their work did not continue, **Boniface** found evidence of it upon his arrival in Thuringia.

Kjeld (or Ketllus, or Exuperius), born Vennig, near Randers, Denmark, c.1105, died Viborg, 27 September 1150. He became canon regular at the cathedral of Our Lady in Viborg. He later became provost, but lost the office as a result of excessive generosity, only to be reinstated by Pope Eugene III. He preached in favour of the expedition against the Wends in 1147, and had planned to lead the Slavic missions, but died before he could do so. His cult is confined to Denmark.

Klug, martyr. Coptic Church. A priest who died on 15 January. Otherwise nothing is known.

Krestos Bezana, monk, born Tembien, Tigre, fourteenth century. Ethiopian Church. Known only through the life of **Thaddeus of Ta'amina**. He was a monk of Dabra Ta'amina.

Krestos Samra, nun, fifteenth century. Ethiopian Church. Of a wealthy family, she married the son of a royal chaplain and had many children. One day, becoming angry with a slave, she killed her. Filled with remorse, she prayed that if God brought the woman back to life, she would dedicate herself to his service. This happened, and she then put on the dress of a monk and went to Dabra Libanos, leaving her family behind her. She then moved to lake Tana, where she founded a convent on the island of Guangut. In her convent, where she practised an extreme asceticism, she had a number of remarkable visions. Feast 18 July.

Kuksa, monk and martyr, born Kiev (?), died Vjatka, twelfth century. Originally a monk of the Kievan Cave monastery, he was sent as a missionary to Slav tribes on the river Oka, and was killed by them. On the day of his death, in the monastery's church, his friend **Pimen the Faster** called out that he had been slain at dawn. Feast 27 August.

Kuksa of Odessa ('the New'), monk, born Garbuzinka, 1874, died 1964. Ukrainian Church, Moscow Patriarchate. Born Kosma Kirillovic Veliko, and of a peasant family, he entered the Russian monastery on Mount Athos in 1894, although he was illiterate – he struggled to learn to read and write. In 1912 he was expelled with other monks because of their Slav origins, and went to the Kievan Cave monastery, where he was given the name Kuksa. Like other monks, he worked during World War I as a nurse. In 1917 he was ordained priest, and after the closure of the monastery continued to work in Kiev at the only church which remained open. He was arrested in 1938 and imprisoned for five years in Siberia. He remained there after his imprisonment, but in 1948 his spiritual disciples, of whom he had gained a good number during his years in Kiev, helped him to return to that city, and to the Cave monastery, which had been reopened during the German occupation. His fame as a spiritual guide, however, irritated the Soviet authorities, and he was sent to a monastery at Pocaev. The superior at Pocaev was somewhat hostile, and he again transferred, this time to the monastery of St John the Theologian in Cernovcy. He was able to keep up his contact with his followers through letters, and their visits. When, in 1960, this monastery was closed, he went to a hermitage near the summer residence of the patriarch at Odessa, where he served as superior, but was unable to keep up his contacts, and his last years where spent in isolation. His death renewed the popular esteem in which he had been held. Feast 16 September.

Kunigunde, empress of Germany, born *c*. 980, died convent of Kaufungen, Hesse, Germany, 3 March 1033 or 1039. The daughter of a count of Lux-embourg, Kunigunde married Duke Henry IV of Barvaris *c*. 998. When her husband became Emperor Henry II, she was crowned empress in 1014. She was a strong advocate and adviser to her husband, but is better remembered for giving her dowry to found the diocese of Bramberg (1007). In 1024, after her husband died, she entered the convent of Kaufungen, which she had founded in 1017. Many miracles are told of her life, and legend says that she and her husband took vows of per-petual virginity (probably because their marriage was childless). She was canonized in 1200.

Kunigunde, bl., patroness of Poland and Lithuania, born *c*. 1224, died Stary Sacz, Poland, 1292. Daughter of King Bela IV of Hungary, in 1239 she married Prince, later King, Boleslas V (the Chaste). It was a marriage in which sexual abstinence co-existed with lifelong harmony, and saw the estab-lishment of hospitals, churches and convents and help for the work of the Franciscans. Widowed in 1279, she withdrew to the convent of Poor Clares which she had founded at Stary Sacz. When the Turks invaded Poland in 1287, the nuns took refuge in Pyenin. The castle was besieged, but after Kunigunde's prayers for its safety the Turks with-drew. Pope Clement XI named her patroness of Poland and Lithuania in 1715. Feast 24 July.

Kurbur, martyr. Syriac Church. Said to have been a Roman magistrate. Feast 26 March.

Kvabtachevi, martyrs of, see **Martyrs of Kvabtachevi**.

L

Ladislaus of Gielniow, bl., Franciscan missionary, born Gielniow, diocese of Gniezno, Poland, *c.* 1440, died 4 May 1505. Educated at Krakow, he became a Franciscan and in 1487 the provincial of the Polish Bernardine province. He founded an Observant (one where the Rule of St **Francis** was strictly carried out) convent as a training centre of missionaries for Lithuania. He wrote poems on the passion of Christ and on the Virgin Mary, in whose honour he introduced a special rosary. In 1498 he helped defeat an invading Tartar and Turkish army through a campaign of mass prayer. He was proclaimed patron of Poland and Lithuania in 1753. Feast 4 May.

Ladislaus of Hungary, king, born Poland, 1040, died Nitra, modern Slovakia, 29 July 1095. Elected king (against his will) by the Hungarian nobles in 1077, the early years of his reign were troubled by opposition from his cousin Solomon, a rival claimant to the throne, which took 12 years to subdue. Once this was achieved, Ladislaus, an ardent champion of Christianity, devoted himself to the evangelization of his pagan subjects. He built many churches, and enacted enlightened civil and religious laws. He was canonized in 1192. Feast 27 June.

La'eka Maryam, prince, sixteenth century. Ethiopian Church. The son of a king, he was captured in battle against Muslims, and castrated. He was then taken as a prisoner to the Yemen, but managed to escape and returned home. He was devout, generous to the poor, a builder of churches and, on his deathbed, freed all his slaves. Feast 28 July.

Laetus, bishop and martyr, died Leptis Minor, *c.* 484. King Huneric of the Vandals, an Arian, had decreed that all Catholic churches in Africa be closed and the possessions of their clergy turned over to Arian clergy. Laetus, bishop of Leptis Minor, was imprisoned and burned at the stake; other bishops of Byzacene (Fusculus, Germanus, Mansuetus and Praesidius) were tortured and driven into the desert, where they also lost their lives. Feast 6 September.

Lalibala, king, born Lalibala (then called Roha), died *c.* 1230. Ethiopian Church. He was persecuted by his brother Harbay, who suspected him of plotting to overthrow him. He was exiled to Tigre where he married **Masqal Kebra** – an act for which Harbay had him flogged. He went on pilgrimage via Egypt to Jerusalem, where he had a vision of Christ, who commanded him to create the ten rock churches in the town which still bears his name. On his return to Ethiopia, Lalibala seized power from his brother and became king. Feast 19 June.

Lambert, bishop, died 688. A monk at Fontenelle under **Wandregisilus**, he succeeded him as abbot, attracting many disciples, including **Erembert** and **Condelus**. He became archbishop of Lyons *c.* 679 and founded Donzère abbey in Provence. Feast 14 April.

Lambert, bishop, born Maastricht, between 633 and 638, died Liège, between 698 and 705. Following the death of Childeric II, Ebroin, mayor of the palace, exiled Lambert from his see at Maastricht to the abbey of Stavelot, where he remained for seven years. After the assassination of Ebroin, order was re-established by Pepin of Herstal and Lambert resumed his bishopric. Later, Lambert became a missionary bishop in Kempenland and Brabant. He died violently in Liège, only a village at that time. It is generally believed that he was martyred for his condemnation of the adultery of Pepin with the sister of his wife, who then became the mother of Charles Martel. The city of Liège grew up around his relics. Feast 17 September.

Lambertenghi of Como, bl., Franciscan (called 'Master of the Cloister'), born Como, Italy, 1440, died Valverde, 25 March 1513. He joined the order at the age of 20 and entered the convent of St Donato, near Como, where he succeeded to the offices of preacher, vicar and prior to various communities. His love of austerity and devotion to the passion of Christ led to an intensity of penitential practices which are alleged to have included the use of an iron chain to discipline his body, and sleeping in a coffin into which nails had been driven. Miraculous powers have been attributed to him and his body is reported to be incorrupt in Forli cathedral.

Lambros, martyr, born Samothrace, died Makri (?), 1835. Byzantine Church.

Landelin (Landelinus), abbot, born Vaux, France, died Crespin, *c.* 686. At 18 he turned to a life of violence and crime together with other young men, but reformed his life when one of his friends was killed. Becoming a hermit at Lobbes, his godliness attracted disciples, and he formed a monastery in 654. Seeking solitude, he travelled to Aulen, to Wallens, and finally to Crespin. In each place he attracted followers whom he organized into communities. He served as abbot in Crespin until his death. Feast 15 June.

Landoald, missionary to the Netherlands, died *c.* 688. Landoald is believed to have been a Lombard who became a priest in Rome, and was sent by Pope **Martin I** along with **Amand** and others as missionaries to the Netherlands. Landoald was supported by Childeric II of Austrasia, and ministered in the Maastricht area, building a church in Winterhoven. Feast 19 March.

Landry (Landericus), bishop, died Paris, *c.* 660. Landry, as bishop of Paris, was known for his concern for the poor. During one famine, he even sold church fixtures to provide food for the hungry. He was the founder of St Christopher's Hospital, which eventually became the famous Hotel-Dieu. Feast 10 June.

Landry, abbot, bishop, died *c.* 730. The son of **Vincent Madelgarius** and **Waldetrude**, Landry was the abbot at Soignies abbey (Hainault, Belgium) and Hautmont (Nord, France). Later he served as a missionary bishop in the area of Brussels (Melsbroek). His relics lie at the collegiate church of Soignies; he is venerated there and in Melsbroedied. Feast 17 April.

Landulf of Evreux, bishop, died Evreux, before 614. All that is reliably known about Landulf is that he was bishop of Evreux, and that *c.* 600 he exhumed the relics of **Taurinus** (late fourth century), who had been the first bishop of Evreux, building a church to honour him. Feast 13 August.

Lanfranc, bl., archbishop, born Pavia, Italy, *c.* 1005, died 28 May 1089. After an early life as an itinerant scholar, he came to northern France and entered the abbey of Bec in 1042, where he rapidly gained a reputation as an able monastic administrator, being appointed prior in 1045. In 1063 he was appointed abbot of St Stephen's, Caen, France, at first making an enemy of William of Normandy by opposing his marriage to a cousin. This rift was subsequently healed, and Lanfranc became William's most trusted counsellor, being made archbishop of Canterbury in 1070 following the conquest of England. He continued to employ his organizational skills in this office, overhauling the administration of the English Church. Lanfranc also wrote a number of theological treatises, the most important of which is *De Corpore et Sanguine Domini*, which anticipates the later doctrine of transubstantiation.

Lantbert of Freising, bishop, died Freising, 19 September 955 or 957. He was appointed bishop of Freising in 937 or 938, presiding during the Hungarian invasion and domestic opposition to the Emperor Otto I. He was present at the Synod of Augsburg in 952 and he has been venerated locally as a saint since the eleventh century. The few details of his life have been supplemented by legends associated with his childhood, the period of the Hungarian invasions and the ravaging of his city, and the safe deliverance of the cathedral due to Lantbert's prayers. Feast 19 September.

Lanvinus (Lanuin), bl., abbot, born Normandy, died Calabria, 11 April *c.* 1120, cult approved 1893. Entering the Grande Chartreuse under **Bruno** *c.* 1090, he accompanied him to Calabria, succeeding him as abbot of the two Italian charterhouses in 1101. He consolidated the order in Italy and was active in Church affairs.

Laserian, abbot, born Ireland, died there, 639. Possibly from the royal family of Ulster, he became a monk, then abbot, at the monastery in Leighlin, County Carlow, where there is a well associated with his cult. He promoted Roman usage in the controversy dividing the Irish Church, notably over Easter dating. Feast 18 April.

Laudatus, abbot, seventh century. Feast 15 January.

Laudomar (Launomar), hermit, abbot, died Chartres, *c.* 590. Laudomar's first short biography was written shortly after his death, most likely by a disciple. He studied with the priest Chirmirius, then was ordained and served as a pastor in Chartres. Later he became a hermit at La Perche, where his reputation for holiness and miracles grew. So many disciples gathered that he went to found the monastery of Curbio (*c.* 570) and became the first abbot. After his death his relics were translated to Blois and a monastery was built in his honour and named after him (St-Lomar, 924). Feast 19 January.

Laudus (Lo), bishop of Coutances, died *c.* 568. Not much is known about Laudus, except that he took part in councils at Orleans in 533, 538 and 541. He buried Paternus in 549. His name was given to St-Lo (Manche), and to a college and railway station at Angers. Feast 22 September.

Launomorus, abbot, died *c.* 593. Feast 19 January.

Laura Vicuña, bl., born Santiago, Chile, 5 April 1895, died Las Lajas, Argentina, 1908, beatified 1988. After her mother's lover tried to assault her, she asked to join the Salesian Sisters, but was refused because of her mother's lifestyle. She died soon after from stress and this man's beatings. Feast 22 January.

Laurence, martyr, died Rome, 10 August 258. One of the deacons of Pope **Sixtus II** (257–8), he was martyred in the persecution under Valerian. According to a tradition preserved by various early writers, when ordered to surrender the treasures of the church he presented the poor, saying, 'These are the church's treasure.' For this he is said to have been slowly roasted to death on a gridiron. The scene is much depicted in art, but many scholars believe the story unreliable. A chapel was built over his tomb in Constantine's time, at St Cyriaca on the via Tiburtina, which in turn became linked with the late sixth-century San Lorenzo fuori le Mura. His sainthood is much celebrated in the Roman tradition, in the Canon of the Mass and in the Litanies. Feast 10 August.

Laurence, second archbishop of Canterbury, died Canterbury, 2 February 619. According to **Bede**, Laurence, one of 13 monks who left Rome with Augustine in 595 and arrived in Britain in 597, shared in the work there and was consecrated bishop by Augustine in 604 as his successor. Discouragement with and fear of the paganism of King Eadbald tempted him to flee to Gaul. A vision of Peter, who flogged him for his intended desertion, left visible stripes on his back. Showing this evidence to Eadbald resulted in the king's conversion and the evangelization of Kent and neighbouring provinces. Feast 3 February.

Laurence, monk, died Vetka, Poland, 1776. Church of the Old Believers. He joined the Old Believers community at Vetka towards the end of the seventeenth century. When it was attacked he hid in nearby woods, on the river Uza. He founded a monastery for Old Believers there.

Laurence, see also **Cassian and Laurence**.

Laurence Giustiniani, see **Laurence Justinian**.

Laurence Humphrey, bl., martyr, died Winchester, 1591. He was a convert to Catholicism, and worked with the poor and helped prisoners. He fell ill with a fever and in a delirious state apparently shouted that the queen was a whore and a heretic. He was reported and brought to trial. Despite his protestations of loyalty, he was condemned to be hanged, drawn and quartered in Winchester. Feast 7 July.

Laurence Justinian, first patriarch of Venice, and spiritual writer, born Venice, Italy, 1381, died there, early January 1456. At the age of 19 he entered the Canons of San Giorgio, was appointed superior at Vicenza in 1407, and became four times general of the Congregation between 1423 and 1431. Appointed bishop of Castello in 1433, he transferred to Venice in 1451. He was noted for the simplicity of his personal life, his charity and apostolic zeal, but above all for the depth of his spiritual writings. In 15 written works and a collection of sermons, there was one dominant theme derived from the saint's own early mystical experience of a vision of the Eternal Wisdom. The essence of his teaching was the theory that all spiritual development was founded on and progressed in an understanding of the incarnate Word espoused to the Wisdom of Love. Feast 5 September.

Laurence Loricatus, bl., hermit, born Siponto, Apulia, died Subiaco, 1243. After accidentally killing someone, he went on pilgrimage to the shrine of St James at Compostela, and on his return became a monk at Subiaco and subsequently a hermit. His nickname derives from the coat of mail he wore next to his skin as a form of penance. Feast 16 August.

Laurence Ngon, martyred Vietnam, 1862, commemorated with **Michael Ho Dinh Hy** – see **Martyrs of Vietnam**. Feast 22 May.

Laurence of Brindisi, Franciscan theologian, born as Ceasare de Rossi at Brindisi, then in the kingdom of Naples, 22 July 1559, died Lisbon, 22 July 1619. He was educated by his uncle at St Mark's in Venice, and when he was 16 he joined the Capuchins at Verona, taking the name Laurence. He pursued his higher studies, particularly in the biblical languages, at the university of Padua. He became definitor general of his order in 1596 and was frequently re-elected to that position. He was

sent on missions to convert the Jews in Germany and to combat Lutheranism, in the course of which Laurence and his companions founded friaries at Prague, Vienna and Gorizia. In 1602 he was elected vicar general of the Capuchins. He was sent by the emperor to persuade Philip III of Spain to join the Catholic League and while on that diplomatic mission he founded a Capuchin house in Madrid. Laurence was chosen as peacemaker in several royal disputes, being sent as papal nuncio to the court of Maximilian of Bavaria. In 1618 he was again called out of retirement by the rulers of Naples to intercede for them with Philip III against the duke of Osuna's tyranny. After persuading the king, who was in Lisbon, to recall Osuna, he returned to his lodging and died there. Laurence's main writings are in the nine volumes of his sermons, but he also wrote a commentary on Genesis, and several treatises against Luther. He was made a doctor of the Church by Pope John XXIII in 1959. Feast 21 July.

Laurence of Cernigov, monk, born Karil'skoe, 1868, died Cernigov, 11 January 1950. Ukrainian Orthodox Church, Moscow Patriarchate. Baptized Lukja Evseevic Proskura, he came from a peasant family in Karil'skoe, near Cernigov. He entered the monastery of Richla, not far from his home village, where he immediately took charge of the music – he had been a very young choirmaster in the village church. He later moved to the monastery of the Trinity at Cernigov. He was ordained, and became a well-known preacher. He travelled to the Holy Land, and to Mount Athos, before becoming hegumenos. After the Communist Revolution he ran a clandestine monastery – literally underground – but also served the local church whenever possible. When the church was closed, he performed the liturgy in secret. During the German occupation he reopened the Trinity monastery, and it became the main focus of spiritual life for the region, remaining open even after the German army had been driven out and Communist power restored.

Laurence of Kaluga, 'fool for Christ', died Kaluga, 10 August 1515. Russian Church. He lived on a hill not far outside Kaluga and went about with bare feet, whatever the weather. He sometimes lived in the palace of the prince, and is said to have saved the prince's life in a battle with the Tartars in 1512.

Laurence of Megara, bl., born Megara, Attica, died Salamis, 9 March 1707. Byzantine Church. Baptized Lambros Kanellos, he came from a pious family, married, and had two sons. One day while working in the fields he had a vision of Mary, who told him to go to Salamis to restore a church in her honour. After Mary had appeared to him on several occasions, he did as he had been commanded, moving to Salamis and becoming a monk – his wife became a nun. Such was his reputation for holiness and for miracles that other monks gathered about him. He died in the monastery of Phaneromeni.

Laurence of Ripafratta, bl., Dominican friar, reformer and preacher, born Ripafratta, near Pisa, Italy, 23 March 1373 or 1374, died Pistoia, 28 September 1456. He joined the Dominican Reformed Congregation in Italy and was a leading figure in the reforms inaugurated by **Raymond of Capua**. Laurence was appointed professor of philosophy and theology at the priories of Fabriano and Pistoia, and also as prior. He was noted for his austerity and his charitable works, and was counsellor to **Antoninus** when the latter was bishop of Florence. Feast 27 September.

Laurence of Siponto, died *c.* 546. He was bishop of Siponto, Apulia, from 492 until his death and is supposed to have built the sanctuary of St Michael on Mount Gargano. Feast 7 February.

Laurence of Turov, monk and bishop, born Kiev, died Turov, 1194. Russian Church. Laurence fell out with the monks of the Kievan Cave monastery – to which he belonged – because they would not permit him to become a hermit. So he moved to the monastery of St Demetrius, also in Kiev, and there gained fame as a healer and caster-out of demons. He was reconciled with the Cave monastery community after he had sent there a man possessed by demons who had been cured as he reached the entrance to the monastery. In 1182 he became bishop of Turov. Feast 29 January.

Laurence of Villamagna, bl., Franciscan friar and preacher, born Villamagna, Abruzzi, Italy, 15 May 1476, died Ortona, 6 June 1535. The son of a noble family, he overcame family objections and entered the order at the Friary of Our Lady of Grace at Ortona. During the course of his studies he showed exceptional ability and, after his ordination, specialized in preaching, in which he was markedly successful. His eloquence was generally acknowledged and he preached in almost every city in Italy.

Laurence Ouang-Pin, bl., see **Agatha Lin-Tchao**.

Laurence O'Toole (Lorcan ua Tuathail), archbishop of Dublin, born probably near Castledermot, County Kildare, 1128, died Eu, Normandy, 14 November 1180. He was taken as a hostage when aged ten, and released to the bishop of Glendalough two years later. He was educated there and became abbot in 1148. In 1161 he was elected the second archbishop of Dublin. He was a reformer, removing the secular canons from Christ Church, Dublin and bringing in the canons regular of Arrouaise, becoming one of them himself. In 1162 he was appointed archbishop of Dublin and took a leading part in opposing the Anglo-Norman invasion of Ireland. He was at the reforming Synod of Cashel to which Pope Alexander III had sent letters urging acceptance of the English King Henry II as overlord. In 1175 he was at the Council of Windsor representing Rory O'Connor, high king of Ireland. In 1179 he travelled through England to Rome to attend the Third Lateran Council. In 1180 he acted as a peacemaker between the English and Irish kings, but Henry II had the ports closed to prevent Laurence's return. He was following Henry II to the continent when he took ill and died in the house of the Aroasian canons at Eu, in which cathedral he is buried. He was the first Irishman formally to be canonized (in 1225). Feast 14 November.

Laurence Richardson, bl., born Great Grosby, Lancashire, martyred Tyburn, London, 30 May 1582, beatified 1886. He studied at Brasenose College, Oxford, and was ordained at Douai in 1581. He is commemorated with **Luke Kirby**, **William Filby** and **Thomas Cottam**, with whom he was executed.

Laurence Ruiz and Companions, martyrs, died Japan, various dates. Laurence Ruiz had Christian parents, a Chinese father and a Filipina mother, and was born at Binondo, Manila, c. 1600. He worked with the Dominicans as a sacristan, was married and had children. In July 1636 he was falsely accused of murder, and fled the country with three Dominicans and a number of others who were going to Japan, despite the persecution of Christians at that time. The group was arrested in Okinawa shortly after their arrival, taken to Nagasaki, and there slowly burned to death. Laurence died 28 September 1637. With him are also commemorated 15 others, French, Spanish and Japanese Dominicans, a Japanese Augustinian and a Japanese layman. Feast 28 September.

Laurence the Illuminator, born Syria, died near Rome, 576. A Syrian Catholic, he came to Italy escaping persecution, was ordained and founded a monastery near Spoleto. Bishop of Spoleto for 20 years, he resigned and founded Farfa abbey near Rome. His title refers to his gift for healing blindness. Feast 4 February.

Laurence the Recluse, died Kievan Cave monastery, thirteenth/fourteenth century. Russian Church. Nothing is known, except that he lived as a recluse in a dark cave. Feast 20 January.

Lawrence, see **Laurence**.

Lazarus, prince, born Prilip, Macedonia, 1329, died Kossovo ('the Field of Blackbirds'), 15 June 1389. He was at the court of the Tsar Stephen Dusan, then at that of **Stephen Uros**, before taking charge of Serbia in 1371 after the disastrous battle of Cirmen, near Adrianople. He strengthened his hold over the Balkans by a series of dynastic marriages. By building churches and supporting monasteries he also won the backing of the Serbian Church, and he mediated a reconciliation between the Serbian patriarch and the patriarch of Constantinople. His purpose was to build a strong Christian alliance against the Muslims. He lost his life, however, in the battle of the Field of Blackbirds, which effectively left the Balkans open to the Turks.

Lazarus, priest and martyr, born Romanov-Borisoglebsk, died Pustozersk, 14 April 1682. Church of the Old Believers. A priest of his native city, he was one of a group who were promoting spiritual renewal in the Russian Orthodox Church before the advent of the liturgical reforms of Nikon, to which he was completely hostile. For his opposition he was arrested and sent to Siberia for ten years, before being allowed to return to Moscow in 1665. For his continued hostility he was reduced to the lay state and excommunicated, had his tongue cut out, and was imprisoned at Pustozersk. He continued his campaign by letter, and as a consequence had his right hand cut off. Finally he, and other prisoners, were put to death.

Lazarus of Harsinas, Syriac Church. Feast 4 May.

Lazarus of Milan, bishop, died c. 450. As bishop of Milan during the invasion of the Ostrogoths, he was active in the defence of his people. Feast 14 March.

Lazarus of Murmansk, born Constantinople, died Murmansk, fourteenth/fifteenth centuries. Russian Church. Lazarus was sent on a mission to **Basil of Novgorod**, but decided to stay in the city. At the death of Basil, however, he asked permission to settle on the remote island of Murmansk, on lake Onega. This was among tribes who had not yet been converted to Christianity, and they were hostile – on one occasion he had to take refuge in a cave where he heard a voice telling him to build a church there in honour of the Dormition. The voice also promised that the pagans would be converted. His holiness and his gift of healing did indeed convert the local people, and a group of monks gathered around him. Feast 8 March.

Lazarus of the Caves of Pskov, monk, born Opoca, 1733, died Pskov, 27 May 1824. Russian Church. He was the well-loved parish priest of Opaca, but on the death of his wife he entered the cave monastery of the Dormition at Pskov, taking vows in 1785. He was severely ascetic, wearing chains on his body. He became the monastery's treasurer, and was generous to the poor and to visitors. His tomb immediately became the site of pilgrimage.

Lazarus of Tur Abdin, bishop, died 763 (?). Syriac Church. Possibly a monk of Qartmin before becoming bishop. Feast 3 January.

Lazarus of Zagug, Syriac Church. Feast 3 January.

Lazarus the Bulgarian, born Kambrova, Bulgaria, died Pergamon, 23 April 1802. He was a shepherd near Pergamon, and on one occasion, while he was asleep, his dog attacked a Muslim woman. She, however, told her husband that it was Lazarus who had attacked her. He was arraigned before a judge and, although he had no difficulty proving his innocence, he was condemned to death unless he converted to Islam, which he refused to do.

Lazarus the Confessor, martyr, fourth century. Syriac Church. Possibly a monk of the monastery of Qartmin, executed for verbally attacking a Persian general. Feast 3 August.

Lazarus the Confessor, stylite and founder, born near Magnesia, 968, died Mount Galesius, 8 November 1054. He began his religious life as a solitary and then entered the monastery of St Sabas, near Jerusalem, where he was ordained. Lazarus founded three monasteries near Ephesus, one in honour of the Saviour, the second of the Resurrection, and the third of the Mother of God at Mount Galesius. From a stylite pillar near the monastery church he directed the monastic life, drawing up a Rule for the spiritual guidance of the monks, and in relation to their temporal tasks emphasizing the need to care for the poor.

Lazarus the Iconographer, born Armenia, died Cyprus, 867. He became a monk in Constantinople and an icon painter, dedicated to the task of restoring icons defaced during the iconoclast period. He was sent as ambassador to Rome, but died on his way there. Feast 23 February.

Lea, died Rome, c. 383. On becoming a widow she joined **Marcella**'s community and spent the rest of her life serving the nuns. Feast 22 March.

Leander of Seville, bishop, born Cartagena, Spain, c. 540, died Seville, 600. After the untimely death of his father he took care of the education of his younger brother, later to be known as **Isidore of Seville**. Afterwards he embraced the religious life and did his best to spread Catholicism among the Arian Visigoths. He was exiled to Constantinople, where he met the future Pope **Gregory the Great**.

After his return he was entrusted with the tutelage of Prince Reccared and with his initiation in the Catholic faith. As archbishop of Seville (from 584), he convened some local synods. Leander wrote, among other works, *De institutione virginum*. Feast 27 February.

Lebdeyos, monk, seventeenth century. Ethiopian Church. He founded a monastery at May Gundi as a defence against the Chalcedonian faith, which had been introduced into Ethiopia after the conversion of its king to Catholicism.

Lebdna Dengel, king, born c. 1495, died 2 September 1540. Ethiopian Church. He came to the throne at the age of 12 in 1508. He defended Ethiopia against the Muslims, but was defeated. Feast 12 September.

Lebuinas (Lebwin), monk, patron of Deventer, Holland, born into an Anglo-Saxon family in England, died Deventer, c. 780. He had a monastic education, was ordained priest and went to Utrecht, whence he was sent as missionary to Overyssel. He built a chapel at Wulpe, by the river Yssel, and then a larger church and residence at Deventer which was later sacked by Saxons trying to stop the spread of Christianity. Lebuinas escaped and determined to take up the matter with the Saxon Assembly. He proclaimed to the gathered Saxon leaders the Christian message and foretold their own downfall if they persisted in their idolatry. He was only spared death by the intervention of one of their own noblemen, Buto, who told of the miraculous cure of one of his servants and convinced the gathering to practise tolerance and respect towards the Christians. Lebuinas returned to rebuild his church, but it was destroyed again by Saxons soon after his death. Feast 12 November.

Leger, see **Leodegar**.

Lelia, born and died Ireland, sixth century. Probably related to Limerick, but nothing else is known about her. Feast 12 August.

Leo, abbot, seventh century. Feast 25 May.

Leo, fourth century. He was a disciple of **Hilary of Poitiers**. Feast 3 February.

Leo, born 703, died 787. He was a priest in Ravenna who became bishop of Catania in Sicily. He had a reputation for great learning and in Sicily is called *il Maraviglioso*, the wonderworker. Feast 20 February.

Leo, see also **Emmanuel**.

Leo I ('the Great'), pope, born Rome, elected pope 29 September 440, but before that he had already been an influential deacon at the papal court, as his political mission to Gallia on the request of the Empress Galla Placidia shows, died Rome, 10 November 461. As bishop of Rome he applied himself to establish unity within the community by reacting against, for example, both the Priscillianists and the Manichaeans. This concern for the purity of the faith also guided his actions on the international scene, foremost in the Nestorian controversy. Meanwhile he asserted the primacy of the Roman bishop, against the claims of the political capital, Constantinople. On the political level he tried to defend his fellow citizens against the invasions of the Vandals and the Huns – he apparently persuaded Attila not to attack Rome. Of his writings, 97 sermons and 143 letters have been preserved.

Leo II, pope from 17 August 682 to 3 July 683, born Sicily, died Rome. Leo succeeded **Agatho** I, and seems to have been elected in June 681, but had to wait some 18 months before receiving the imperial mandate from Constantine necessary for his consecration. The only fact of historical interest with regard to Leo is that he approved of the decision at the Council of Constantinople (681) to condemn Pope Honorius I as a supporter of heresy in the monothelite controversy. During Leo's pontificate the dependence of the see of Ravenna upon that of Rome was finally settled by imperial edict.

Leo III, pope from 27 December 795 to 12 June 816, born Rome, died there. Leo succeeded Hadrian I, and his pontificate covered the last 18 years of the reign of **Charlemagne**. Although unanimously elected, he aroused the hostility of Hadrian's relatives, and after a violent physical assault (799) he fled to Charlemagne's court at Paderborn. Escorted back to Rome, he was fully rehabilitated. Shortly afterwards, on Christmas Day 800, Leo crowned Charlemagne in St Peter's, and the assembled crowd acclaimed him as emperor of the Romans. Leo accepted the dogmatic correctness of the *Filioque*, but judged inopportune the emperor's request to include it in the Nicene Creed (810). Assisted by the emperor's rich gifts, Leo did much to adorn the churches of Rome and other cities of Italy.

Leo IV, pope from 10 April 847 to 17 July 855, born Rome, died there. Leo succeeded Sergius II, and his pontificate was chiefly distinguished by his efforts to repair the damage done by the Saracens, who sacked Rome in 844. He built and fortified with a 40-foot wall a suburb on the right bank of the Tiber still known as the 'Civitas Leonina'. In 853 he is said to have 'hallowed' the young Alfred as future king of England. He sought to bring under his authority Anastasius Bibliothecarius (Anastasius the Librarian, later an antipope) and Hincmar of Rheims, but the history of this struggle belongs rather to the reign of **Nicholas I**.

Leo IX, pope from 12 February 1049 to 19 April 1054, born Bruno, son of Count Hugh of Egisheim, Alsace, 21 June 1002, died St Peter's, Rome. Leo succeeded Damasus II, and his reign marks the beginning of papal reform from its decadence of the previous century and a half. He did much to foster a new ideal of the papacy: at the Easter Synod (1049) celibacy was enforced on all clergy, and shortly afterwards councils promulgated decrees against simony and clerical unchastity. Leo travelled extensively, pressing home the need for renewal, assisted by Hildebrand (**Gregory VII**), **Humbert** and St **Peter Damian**. He condemned Berengar of Tours for his eucharistic doctrine that no material change in the elements is needed to explain the eucharistic Presence. His later years were marred by military defeat by the Normans at Civitate (1053), as well as a breach with Michael Cerularius and the Eastern Church.

Leo, Donatus and others, martyrs, died Africa (or possibly Rome). A group of 13 martyrs. Feast 1 March.

Leo Ignatius Mangin, Anne Wang and Companions, bl., martyred China, 1900, beatified 1955. This was a group of four French Jesuits and over 50 Chinese men, women and children killed during the Boxer Rebellion. See also **Martyrs of China**.

Leo Luke, abbot, born Corleone, Sicily, *c.* 885, died Monteleone, Calabria, *c.* 980. Became a monk at a young age at the abbey of St Philip in Argira. Arab raids led him and many of his fellow monks to Calabria, *c.* 940, where he became a disciple of St **Christopher** of Collesano. He succeeded Christopher as abbot at the monastery he founded near Monteleone, serving for more than 20 years until his own death. Feast 1 March.

Leo of Cava, bl., Benedictine abbot, born 1239, died La Cava, near Naples, 19 August 1295. Elected abbot of La Cava in 1268, he encouraged the development of the abbey's scriptorium and built the monastery's cloister and chapel of San Germano. The abbey suffered greatly during his reign due to the Sicilian Vespers and the subsequent loss of their Sicilian holdings.

Leo of Montefeltro, hermit. Feast 1 August.

Leo of Optina, monk, born Karacarov, 1768, died Optina, 11 October 1841. Baptized Lev Danilov Nagolkin, he was born into a family of merchants, and for a time pursued the career of a merchant, travelling all over Russia. In 1797, however, he entered the hermitage of Optina, two years later moving to that of Belobereg, where he took the name Leonid and was ordained priest. For a time he served as superior at Belobereg, but gave it up and moved to a smaller hermitage in 1808, and shortly afterwards was given the name Leo. In 1811 he moved to Valaam, but his popularity as a spiritual director aroused the hostility of other monks, and he moved again, finally returning to Optina in 1829. Once again his popularity gave rise to hostility, but he had powerful friends who defended him. Some nuns under his influence, however, ran into difficulties, and he was accused of heresy, being for a time exiled to the islands of Solovki.

Leo of Rouen, bishop and martyr, born Carentan, Normandy, *c.* 856, died near Bayonne, 900. He is said to have resigned as bishop of Rouen to preach in the Basque country and in Navarre, then laid waste by Saracens, and to have been beheaded by pirates. Feast 1 March.

Leo Thaumaturgus, bishop, miracle worker, died *c.* 785. Leo was bishop of Catania, Sicily. He was a well respected figure, especially by Emperor Leo IV, who invited him to court in Constantinople, and by Emperor Constantine IV, who requested his intercession. The name Thaumaturgus means 'wonderworker'. Feast 20 February.

Leobard, recluse, died *c.* 593. Leobard's parents wished him to marry, but after their death he became a recluse in Tours, under the direction of **Gregory of Tours**, and he remained there for 22 years. Leobard also founded and became the first abbot of the abbey of Mormoutier. Feast 24 January.

Leobard (Liuberat), abbot, died *c.* 665. Leobard was a disciple of **Waldebert** and founded the abbey of Maursmunster (*c.* 660). Feast 8 August.

Leobinus (Lubin), bishop, born near Poitiers, died *c.* 556. First a hermit, then a priest, abbot of Brou and finally a distinguished bishop of Chartres. Feast 14 March.

Leocadia, martyr, born Toledo, died there, *c.* 304. She died in prison in the persecution of Diocletian. She is patron of Toledo. Feast 9 December.

Leodegar (Leger), bishop of Autun, born *c.* 616, died near Sarcing, the Somme, 679. He was brought up in the Frankish court, and then by his uncle who was bishop of Poitiers. As abbot of St Maxentius at Poitiers he introduced the Rule of St **Benedict**. In 653 he was made bishop of Autun and imposed the same Rule on all religious houses in his charge. He became involved in the dispute over the claim to the throne and was eventually banished, blinded, tortured and beheaded. He was soon revered as a saint and a following emerged throughout France. Feast 2 October.

Leonard, bl., abbot, died 1255. Abbot of La Cava, near Salerno, from 1232. Feast 18 August.

Leonard Murialdo, founder of the Pious Congregation of St Joseph, born Turin, Italy, 26 October 1828, died Turin, Italy, 30 March 1900. Murialdo studied and was ordained in Turin (1851), and dedicated himself to educating poor boys in the city. In 1857 he became director of the oratory of San Luigi and in 1866 rector of the Collegio Artigianelli, which aimed to give youths a Christian education and some trade skills. In 1873 he founded the Pious Congregation of St Joseph, serving as its first superior general. He was a tireless worker for the Catholic worker movement in Italy, serving on many committees and national societies and initiating at least two publications. He was beatified in 1963 by Pope Paul VI and canonized by him in 1970.

Leonard of Noblac, hermit, died *c.* 559. Virtually unknown until the eleventh century, he is alleged to have been the son of a Frankish nobleman and was converted by St **Remigius**, apostle of the Franks. After his conversion he lived in a cell at Noblac, near Limoges, where he founded an abbey. His cult spread rapidly in the twelfth century, possibly stemming from a legend of the returning crusader who had offered thanksgiving for his release at Leonard's shrine. Although his historical existence is unproven, in England alone 177 churches are dedicated to him, and two towns, one in Sussex and one in Roxburgh. He is the patron of prisoners, peasants and horses. Feast 6 November.

Leonard of Port Maurice, Franciscan friar, born Porto Maurizio, Liguria, Italy, 20 December 1676, died Rome, 26 November 1751. He was educated at the Jesuit college in Rome and professed as a Franciscan in 1697. From 1709 he was based in Florence, where he initiated a 40-year apostolate of missions, combining preaching, Lenten courses, retreats and the promotion of devotions, in particular the Way of the Cross. From 1730 he conducted similar missions in Rome, Umbria, Genoa and the Marches. He was employed – unsuccessfully – by Pope Benedict IV as an emissary in a political dispute between the feuding Corsicans and their overlord in Genoa. Leonard is buried in St Bonaventura al Palatino in Rome, and was canonized in 1867. He was declared patron of popular missions in 1923. Feast 26 November.

Leonidas of Alexandria, martyr, died Alexandria, 202. The father of Origen. Feast 22 April.

Leonidas of Posechon'e, monk, died Posechon'e, 1549. Russian Church. A disciple of **Adrian of Posechon'e**, he was originally a monk of the monastery of **Cornelius of Komel**, which Adrian and he left in 1540 to live as solitaries. They lived for three years at Posechon'e beside the river Votcha, then went to Moscow to get the approval of the metropolitan for the establishment of a monastery. They then returned to Posechon'e. Feast 5 March.

Leonidas of Ust'neduna, founder, born Posechon'e, 1551, died Ust'neduna, 17 July 1654. Russian Church. He came from a pious, farming family, and worked the land until about the age of 50, when he had a vision of the Virgin which caused him to become a monk in the monastery of Kozeozersk, near Archangel. While there he once again had the vision, and it was repeated when he went to the Solovki monastery. He then went to the monastery of St Nicholas at Morzev, as he had been instructed to do in his vision. The vision had told him to take an icon of the Virgin from St Nicholas's monastery to Mount Turin, which he did, although he met with hostility from the local people when he built a cabin next to the river. He was, however, eventually helped by a local inhabitant to build a church, and, with the permission of the metropolitan of Rostov, he eventually founded a monastery. He was ordained, and became the superior of the community. While building the monastery he had to construct a canal to drain the land. In the course of doing this he was bitten by a snake, but simply ignored the bite: the name of the canal, Neduna, which gave its name to the monastery, reflects this event. During his last years he gave up the office of superior and lived in his cell, only coming out for the liturgy.

Leonius, bl., Benedictine abbot and reformer, died 26 October 1163. Educated by Benedictines, he became a monk at the age of 22 and embraced the ideals of the Cluniac reform. He served as prior of Hesdin until he was made abbot of Lobbes in 1131. He served in that office until he was elected abbot of Saint-Bertin in 1137, where he established a school. A friend of St **Bernard of Clairvaux**, he took part in the second Crusade.

Leontie of Radauti, see **Leontius of Radauti**.

Leontius, Attus and Companions, martyrs. Feast 1 August.

Leontius of Caesarea, bishop, died Caesarea, 337. He was an opponent of Arianism. Feast 13 January.

Leontius of Karichov, founder, died Karichov, 1492. Founder of the monastery of Karichov. Feast 18 July.

Leontius of Monemvasia, born Monemvasia (Peloponnese), 1377, died Mount Athos, 1452. Byzantine Church. From a wealthy family, he went to work in Constantinople, but returned to Monemvasia after his father's death. When his mother entered a convent, he left his wife and children and entered a monastery on Mount Athos. Feast 11 December.

Leontius of Moscow, born Kaluga, died Belivo, near Moscow, c. 1750. Church of the Old Believers. He came from a family of merchants, and worked for a time as a priest in Moscow, and travelled widely, visiting Constantinople, the Holy Land and Egypt. His travels convinced him that both the Russian and the Greek Orthodox Churches had strayed from the truth. When he returned from his travels he settled in Vetka, where he served the Old Believer community, but when Catherine the Great allowed Old Believers to return to Russia he settled at Belivo.

Leontius of Pamphylia and Companions, martyrs, died Perga, c. 300. Leontius and two other citizens, Attius and Alexander, plus six farm labourers (Cindeus, Mnesitheus, Cyriacus, Menaeus, Catunus and Eucleus), were executed for destroying the temple of Artemis. Feast 1 August.

Leontius of Radauti, monk, born Radauti, died there, 1432. Romanian Church. As a child he was attracted to life as a hermit, when he encountered hermits in the nearby forests. As soon as he could, he entered the monastery of Bogdano, where he was given the name Lawrence. After a time,

however, disturbed by the number of visitors who came to see him, he retired to the forests as a hermit. Yet such was his fame that a group of disciples gathered around him, and he founded a monastery with a very strict Rule. When Radauti became a diocese, he was named its first bishop and worked in his diocese for many years, retreating back into the forest monastery before his death: it was at this point that he was given the new monastic name of Leontius. Feast 1 July.

Leontius of Rostov, bishop and martyr, born Constantinople (?), died Rostov, north of Moscow, 1077. He may have come from Constantinople, or more likely from Kiev: he was the first monk of the Kievan Cave monastery to become a bishop, probably in 1051. He was the third bishop of the still largely pagan Rostov, and a highly successful evangelist, in part because of the gentleness of his character, but nonetheless he died of ill-treatment at the hands of the pagans. Feast 23 May.

Leontius of the Kievan Cave Monastery, monk, fourteenth century. Russian Church. He joined the monastery when still very young, and had remarkable musical abilities. He died quite young. Feast 20 August.

Leontius of Tripoli and Companions, martyrs, died Phoenicia, c. 75. Leontius himself was born in Greece, but served in Tripoli, north Africa, as an officer in the Roman army. He was particularly generous to the poor, and the governor of Phoenicia sent two soldiers to arrest him, Hypatius and Theodulus. They, however, were so impressed that they converted and were martyred with him. Feast 18 June.

Leontius of Ustug, 'fool for Christ', died Ustug, 18 July 1492 (?).

Leontius the Elder, bishop, died Bordeaux, 541. He preceded **Leontius the Younger** as bishop of Bordeaux. Feast 21 August.

Leontius the Mirovlita, bl., monk, died Mount Athos, 1600. Byzantine Church. A monk of the Athonite monastery of St Dionysius, where he lived in strict asceticism for 60 years, he was called *mirovlita* because of the perfume which arose from his body after death.

Leontius the Younger, bishop, died Bordeaux, 565. He had been a soldier, but settled at Bordeaux, and married. He was, however, elected bishop of the city. Feast 11 July.

Leopold Mandic, born Castelnuovo, Dalmatia, 12 May 1866, died Padua, Italy, 30 July 1942. Bogdan Mandic went to the Capuchin seminary at Udine in the Veneto region at the age of 16, and two years later entered the novitiate at Bassano and took the name Leopold. He was ordained priest in 1890, and became a confessor at the Capuchin monastery in Venice. In 1897 he returned to Dalmatia and was put in charge of the monastery at Zara, and finally in 1909 he moved to Padua, where he spent the rest of his life hearing confessions for between 10 and 15 hours a day.

Leopold Mandic, born Castelnuovo, southern Dalmatia, 1866, died Padua, 30 July 1942, canonized 1983. He was small and frail, but was accepted by the Capuchins at Udine, near Venice, aged 16, being ordained priest in 1890. He worked in Italy and Dalmatia, living in Padua from 1906. Feast 14 May.

Leopold of Austria, margrave, born Gars, *c.* 1075, died 15 November 1136. He was educated by St **Altmann of Passau**. Initially loyal to Pope Innocent II in the investiture contest, he changed his allegiance to support the Emperor Henry V, and he married Agnes, the emperor's widowed daughter. Of his six sons, two were distinguished: the historian Otto of Freising, and Archbishop Conrad of Salzburg. Leopold refounded the Canons Regular at Klosterneuberg in 1108, later founding the Cistercian abbey at Heiligenkreuz and the Benedictine monastery at Kleinmariazell. He renounced his claim to the German throne in 1125, and is buried at Klosterneuberg. Canonized in 1485, he was declared national patron of Austria in 1663. Feast 15 November.

Leopold of Gaiche, bl., born Gaiche, near Perugia, 1733, died Spoleto, 2 April 1815. He became a Franciscan in 1751, was ordained in 1757 and taught philosophy and theology. In 1768 he began

47 years of missionary activity in Umbria and the Papal States. When Napoleon seized the Papal States and suppressed religious houses, Leopold withdrew to a hut. He was imprisoned briefly for his refusal to take an oath to the new regime. After Napoleon's fall in 1814, Leopold withdrew to Monteluco and spent his last months in prayer. He wrote *Diario delle S. Missioni*.

Leovigild and Christopher, martyrs, died Córdoba, 852. Two monks of a monastery near Córdoba, beheaded by the Muslim authorities. Feast 20 August.

Lesbos, Five Children of, see **Five Children of Lesbos**.

Leucius, see also **Thyrsus**.

Leucius of Brindisi, bishop. There are two saints of this name commemorated on the same day. One was the first bishop of Brindisi, apparently a missionary from Alexandria, who died *c.* 180. The other was bishop there late fourth/early fifth century. Feast 11 January.

Leucius of Volokolamsk, died Volokolamsk, *c.* 1492. Russian Church. He started his monastic career in the monastery of Borovsk, where he gained fame as a spiritual guide. He eventually retired to the region of Volokolamsk, where he founded a hermitage by the river Ruza.

Leutred (Leufred, Leufridus, Leufroy), abbot, born near Evreux, France, died 738. Leutred was educated locally, and at Condat and Chartres. For a time he taught boys, then became a hermit and later a monk under the Irish **Sidonius** of Rouen. Eventually he returned home and built the monastery La-Saint-Croix-Saint-Ouen, later called La-Saint-Croix-Saint-Leufroy, where he served until his death. Feast 21 June.

Libanus, monk, died Tarqa, fifth/sixth century. Ethiopian Church. Married to the daughter of a Byzantine emperor, he was commanded by the archangel Gabriel to leave his wife and children and become a monk, then an apostle in Ethiopia. He was eventually summoned to Axum by the metropolitan, but incurred his – and the king's –

anger by denouncing corruption. He lived in various places, finally preaching to the pagans of Tarqa. Feast 11 January.

Liberata, from Como, died 580. With her sister **Faustina**, who also died in 580, she founded the nunnery of Santa Margarita in Como. Feast 19 January.

Liberatus, martyred Africa, 484, with his wife and sons. Feast 23 March.

Liberatus of Loro, born Loro Piceno, south of Macerata, died Soffiano, *c.* 1260. Very little is known of him. He is said to have been related to noble families of Loro, and to have been very strict in his observance of the Rule. Feast 6 September.

Liberatus Weiss, bl., martyr, born Konnersreuth, Bavaria, 4 January 1675, died Ethiopia, 3 March 1716, with **Samuel Marzorati** and **Michael Fasoli da Zerbo**, all Franciscans, beatified 1988. Liberatus led a team to Ethiopia, where some monophysite Christians wished to reunite with Rome. Victims of political upheavals, they were stoned to death after a trial in which they insisted on the two natures of Christ.

Liberd, see **Leobard**.

Liberius (Oliver), hermit of Ancona, in the Marches, east central Italy, ninth/tenth century. Feast 27 May.

Liberius Wagner, priest and martyr, born Mülhausen, Germany, 1593, died Altenmünster, 9 December 1631. Brought up a Lutheran, he converted to Catholicism, studied in Strasbourg, and was ordained priest in 1625. He was sent to the parish of Altenmünster, but was assassinated because of his Catholicism, during the invasion of the town by Swedish troops.

Libertius of Hamburg, bishop, died 1013. Feast 4 January.

Licerius, bishop, born Lerida, Tarragona (?), died Pyrenees, *c.* 548.

Licinius (Lesin), bishop, born *c.* 540, died *c.* 616. As a cousin of King Clotaire I of France, Licinius became a courtier at the age of 20, and was created count of Anjou by King Chilperic. However, when his fiancée contracted leprosy, he decided to become a monk. In 586 he was elected bishop of Anjou and spent the remainder of his life in the ministry to his diocese. Licinius is known for his compassion for the poor and is credited with miracles. Feast 13 February.

Lidanus, Benedictine abbot and monastic founder, born Antina, Sicily, *c.* 1026, died Monte Cassino, Italy, 1118. Lidanus probably began his monastic career at Monte Cassino in Italy, which he is said to have entered at an early age. He later founded the monastery of St Cecilia at Sezze, where he is remembered for his help in draining the Pontine marshes and where his relics are still venerated. As an old man he retired as abbot of Sezze, and returned to Monte Cassino. Feast 2 July.

Lietbert of Cambrai-Arras, bishop, born Brabant (Belgium), died probably Cambrai, France, 23 June 1076. Lietbert followed his uncle as bishop of Cambrai in 1051 and spent much time defending his flock from the machinations of the local civil authorities. He was briefly exiled from his see by those authorities, but returned to lead a pilgrimage to the Holy Land around 1054. He was unable to complete the pilgrimage because of the growing Saracen threat. Feast 23 June.

Limnaeus, Syria, fifth century. A hermit, he was first **Thalassius**'s disciple, with whom he is commemorated. He then trained with Maro before walling himself up in a stone enclosure. Limnaeus also ministered to the blind at two houses for them near his hut. Feast 22 February.

Linus, bishop, regarded as the first bishop of Rome after the apostles Peter and Paul and conventionally given the dates *c.* 68 – *c.* 78 for his pontificate. Nothing is really known with certainty about Linus. An early Christian by this name sent greetings, possibly from Rome, in 2 Timothy 4.21. **Irenaeus** and Eusebius of Caesarea both mention him as bishop. Feast 23 September (suppressed 1969).

Lioba (Leoba, Liobgytha), abbess, born Wessex, England, *c.* 700, died near Mainz, 780. A nun and relative of **Boniface**, Lioba corresponded with the missionary bishop. When Boniface wrote in 748 to ask for nuns to help him in Germany, 30 were sent, including Lioba, whom he made abbess at Bischofsheim in Mainz. 'The Life', written by Rudolf of Fulda 50 years after Lioba's death on the testimony of four of her companions, paints a charming picture of the abbess's wisdom, zeal and holiness, and of her nuns, required to learn Latin and industrious in the scriptorium, the kitchen, the bakery, the brewery, the garden and in prayer. See also **Gunthildis**. Feast 28 September.

Liphardus and Urbicius, abbots, died Meung-sur-Loire, sixth century. Liphardus was a lawyer who became a monk at Micy, but he and Urbicius left the abbey to become hermits near Meung-sur-Loire. They attracted disciples and founded an abbey, of which Liphardus was the first abbot, and Urbicius the second. Feast 3 June.

Liqanos, monk, born Constantinople, fifth/sixth centuries. Ethiopian Church. One of the 'Nine Saints' who were missionaries in Ethiopia. Liqanos settled in a hermitage near Axum. Feast 7 December.

Liutbirg, anchoress, died Wendhousen, *c.* 880. Little is known of Liutbirg's early life, but she was enclosed *c.* 824 by Bishop Thiatgrim of Halberstadt in a hermitage near the church at Wendhausen. She there instructed young girls in church music and handicrafts, and offered her prayers and counsel to those who sought them, among whom were Bishop Haimo of Halberstadt, and Bishop **Ansgar** of Bremen. Feast 28 February.

Livarius of Metz, martyr, died Marsal, south of Metz, 451. A twelfth-century legend has it that Livarius (Livier) was martyred by the Huns in 451, but if there is any historical basis to the legend he is more likely to have been a martyr in the Hungarian incursions of the ninth or tenth centuries. His relics were removed in the tenth century to the abbey of St-Vincent in Metz, and thence to the church of St-Polyeucte in Metz, now the church of St Livarius. Feast 17 July.

Lollia, martyr, born Lystra, died Ancyra, *c.* 303 (?). She was converted to Christianity by Eustochius of Caesarea, and put to death by the governor of Ancyra. Feast 23 June.

Loman of Trim, bishop (?), born Britain, died Trim, Ireland, *c.* 450. He is said to have been the son of the sister of **Patrick**, and to have accompanied Patrick on his missionary journey to Ireland. He was sent to the area around Trim, where, according to some versions of his life, he became bishop. Feast 11 October.

London Martyrs: Edmund Gennings, Polydore Plasden, Swithin Wells, John Mason, Sydney Hodgson, Eustace White and **Brian Lacey**. Feast 10 December.

Longinus, abbot, born Cilicia, died Egypt, fifth century. Coptic Church. After deciding to become a monk, he travelled to Syria and finally settled in the monastery of Enaton in Egypt. He rejected the Chalcedonian creed, despite a direct request by the Emperor Marcion to accept it. Feast 28 January.

Longinus, see also **Vindemialis**.

Longinus of Jarenga, see **John of Jarenga and Longinus**.

Longinus of Korjazem, monk, died Korjazem, 1540. Russian Church. He began his monastic life in the monastery of St Paul in Obnora, but in 1515, with a disciple called Simon, he moved to a hermitage on the river Korjazem, near the monastery of St **Cornelius of Komel**. Simon moved on to found another monastery, but Longinus remained. His hermitage eventually became a monastery itself, rather against Longinus's wishes. Feast 10 February.

Longinus of Murom, died Murom, 1653. Church of the Old Believers. An archpriest, he opposed the reforms of the patriarch Nikon. Nikon excommunicated him, whereupon he attacked the patriarch. He was stripped of his vestments and imprisoned naked – but was then dressed by angels. He was exiled to Murom, where he died.

Longinus of the Kievan Cave Monastery, monk, thirteenth/fourteenth centuries. Russian Church. He was the gatekeeper of the monastery, but was gifted with the ability to read people's hearts, which led to many conversions. Feast 16 October.

López y Vicuña, Vincenta, see **Vincenta López y Vicuña**.

Louis IX, king of France, born Poissy, 25 April 1214, died of fever near Tunis during a Crusade in north Africa, 25 August 1270. He inherited the throne when only 12, but took over the government of his country only in 1235. His way of life, even as a child, was characterized by great religious devotion, and as king by a concern for justice and the building of churches and hospitals. He was also a very considerable politician and exercised control over his barons, repressing several rebellions. He led France into two Crusades, one from 1248 to 1254, part of which time he spent in captivity, and the other in 1270 against Tunis, although he fell sick and died almost immediately on his arrival. Robert de Sorbon was a friend and occasional confessor of the king, who encouraged and financially assisted him in the foundation of what eventually became the Sorbonne.

Louis Batiz Sainz, bl., martyr, born San Miguel del Mezquital, Mexico, 13 September 1870, died Chalchihuites, Zacatecas, Mexico, 14 August 1926. He was ordained in 1894, and worked in the seminary at Duyrango, then as parish priest at Chalchihuites. He was arrested and shot simply for being a priest. Feast 25 May.

Louis Bertrán, friar, born Valencia, 1526, died there, 9 October 1581. He became a Dominican priest, and was for many years the novice master. He became famous because of his work among the poor in Valencia during a plague. He was approached for guidance by **Teresa of Avila**. In 1562 he went to what is now Colombia, before working in some of the Caribbean islands. He returned to Spain after six years on this mission and tried to persuade the government to take action against the abuses suffered by the local inhabitants from the Spanish conquerors, although without success. He trained missionaries for the Americas until his death.

Louis d'Aleman, bl., cardinal archbishop, born Arbent-en-Bugey,France, *c*. 1390, died Salonne, near Arles, 17 September 1450. A canon lawyer, Louis took a lead at the Council of Basel (1439), and nominated Amadeus VIII of Savoy as antipope Felix V, for which Eugene IV excommunicated him. However, he recanted when Felix abdicated, and Nicholas V restored him to his previous position. He died with a reputation for sanctity. Clement VII proclaimed him 'blessed' in 1521. Feast 16 September.

Louis-Gabriel Taurin Dufresse, born Lezoux, Puy-de-Dôme, France, 8 December 1750, martyred Chengdu, Sichuan, China, 14 September 1815, beatified 1900, canonized 2000. A bishop, from the Paris Society of Foreign Missions, he was beheaded and his head stuck on a pole to intimidate local Christians – with apparently the opposite effect. See **Martyrs of China**.

Louis Guanella, bl., founder, born Franciscio di Campodocino (Sondrio), Italy, 19 December 1843, died Como, Italy, 24 October 1915. Guanella came from a poor family, entered the diocesan seminary (1854) and was ordained (1866). During his pastoral works in the village of Savogno he had so great a concern for the spiritual and temporal needs of his parishioners that they built a monument in his honour shortly after his death. While pastor in Pianello Lario, he opened a hospice for orphaned and abandoned children (1878). He started similar institutions in several Italian cities. To perpetuate his work, Guanella founded the Daughters of St Mary of Providence and also a religious congregation for men, the Servants of Charity, originally (1904) known as the Sons of the Sacred Heart. Both institutes have spread to other countries, especially to Switzerland. Visits to these regions stimulated Guanella to aid Italian immigrants. Through his friendship with Davide Albertario and Giuseppe Toniolo he also became a pioneer leader in the social question. Guanella promoted the apostolate of the press and wrote about 50 popular devotional, historical and pedagogical works.

Louis-Marie Grignion de Montfort, founder, born Montfort-sur-Meu, France, 31 January 1673, died St Laurent-sur-Sèvre, 28 April 1716. He was ordained a priest in Paris, and worked at Nantes, then Poitiers. Here he founded a religious congregation, the Daughters of Wisdom (the La Sagesse nuns), then he founded the Montfort Fathers for missionary and retreat work, and to spread devotion to the Blessed Virgin Mary. Pope Clement XI named him missionary for France, and Grignion preached in parishes in western France. He was unpopular because he insisted on working with and evangelizing the poorest, especially in hospitals. Only posthumously in 1842 was his work *True Devotion to the Blessed Virgin* discovered. He was beatified in 1888 and canonized in 1947.

Louis Moreau, bl., bishop, born Betancour, French Canada, 1824, died Canada, 24 May 1901, beatified 1987. Ordained in 1846, and bishop of Saint-Hyacinthe, east of Montreal, from 1876, he was an active leader, persuasive speaker and clear thinker. He founded parishes, formed priests, developed schools and organized the care of the sick.

Louis of Arnstein, ven., Premonstratensian count and lay brother, born Arnstein, Germany, 1109, died Gummersheim, Germany, 25 October 1185. Louis and his wife entered the Premonstratensian Order in 1139, mutually agreeing to do so. He converted his ancestral home into a Premonstratensian abbey, gave away his material goods to the order and to relatives, and helped to found five religious houses. Although he lacks an official beatification, he does have a feast – 25 October.

Louis of Casoria, ven., Franciscan religious founder, born Casoria, Naples, 11 March 1814, died Posillipo, 30 March 1885. Baptized Arcangelo Palmentieri, he established a society for Catholic intellectuals and the periodical *Carità*, and undertook charitable enterprises throughout Italy, including hospitals and refuges, and homes for the handicapped and the elderly. He founded the Brothers of Charity at Naples in 1859, and the Grey Sisters of St Elizabeth in 1862, both congregations for the education of poor children.

Louis of Thuringia, bl., born Hesse, 28 October 1200, died Otranto, 1227. He was married, when a child, for political reasons, to the daughter of the

king of Hungary, **Elizabeth of Hungary**. The marriage was a very happy one, and he encouraged his wife's devotions. He was himself a just and generous ruler. He died of malaria at the outset of the sixth Crusade. Feast 11 September.

Louis of Toulouse, bishop, born Brignioles, Provence, 1274, died there, 19 August 1297. Born into a noble family, he spent much of his youth as a hostage of the king of Aragon at Barcelona. He was deeply devout and was particularly attracted to the Franciscan Order, which he vowed to enter after recovering from a dangerous illness. When he was freed in 1295 he was required to marry the sister of the king of Aragon, but he refused. Pope Boniface VIII appointed him bishop of Toulouse before he was ordained priest, and he succeeded in making his profession as a Franciscan only a few days before being ordained bishop. As bishop of Toulouse he continued to live the life of a poor religious, but concluded that he was unsuited to the post and tried to resign. He was not allowed to do so, but died on his way back to Toulouse from visiting his sister in Barcelona.

Louisa, see **Louise**.

Louise Albertoni, bl., born in or near Rome, 1473, died there, 31 January 1533, cult confirmed 1671. Happily married but widowed young, she joined the Third Order of St **Francis**, gave up her wealth and lived in prayer and poverty. She is said to have had visions and to have levitated.

Louise de Marillac, founder, born Ferrières-en-Brie, near Meaux, 12 August 1591, died Paris, 15 March 1660. After the death in 1625 of her husband, Antony Le Gras (they had married in 1613), she supported the work of St **Vincent de Paul**. She established a house in Paris in 1633 for women who might care for the poor – the origins of the Daughters of Charity for whom she drew up a Rule of life. Her congregation grew rapidly and at the time of her death there were over 40 houses of the Sisters in France. She was canonized in 1934, and is the patron saint of social workers.

Louise de Monataigne, bl., born Le Havre, France, 14 May 1820, died Moulins, 27 June 1885. She came from a wealthy and devout family, and was sent to a boarding school run by the Faithful Companions of Jesus at Chateauroux. She there developed a devotion to the Sacred Heart, but also to St **Teresa of Avila**. She first thought of becoming a Carmelite like St Teresa, but, aged 23, made a vow to devote herself to propagating devotion to the Sacred Heart. In 1848 she founded the Guild of the Tabernacle at Montluçon, and in 1874 the Pious Union of the Oblates of the Sacred Heart, of which she became mother general in 1880. The congregation was to be both active and contemplative – with veneration of the Eucharist in the tabernacle and devotion to the Sacred Heart, but also running orphanages and schools.

Louise of France, ven., Carmelite nun, born Versailles, 15 July 1737, died St Denis, 23 December 1787. The daughter of King Louis XV, Louise entered the Carmelite convent at St Denis in 1770, taking the name Thérèse de St Augustin. There she exercised considerable spiritual influence as novice mistress and prioress. She dedicated herself to penances for the conversion of her father, to the Rule and to the Church; she wrote a series of meditations on the Eucharist, and a spiritual testament. Her cause was introduced in 1873.

Louise of Savoy, bl., widow and Poor Clare, born Savoy, 28 December 1462, died Orbe, Switzerland, 24 July 1503. The daughter of Bl. **Amadeus of Savoy** and Yolanda of France, granddaughter of Charles VII and niece of Louis XI, Louise married Hugh of Orléans. When he died in 1490, she dispersed her fortune and entered the Poor Clare monastery at Orbe. She became an exemplary religious and an inspiring abbess, noted for her hospitality to the Franciscan friars. Pope Gregory XVI confirmed her cult in 1839.

Luarsab, king and martyr, born 1587, died Shiraz, Persia, 20 March 1622. Georgian Church. King of Karthli (eastern Georgia) from 1606, he allied himself with the king of Kacheti against Persian domination. The two kings led a disastrous expedition against the Persians, after which Kacheti was destroyed. To save Karthli, Luarsab appealed to the shah, who demanded that he convert to Islam. Lursab refused and was imprisoned, then eventually strangled. Feast 22 June.

Lubin, see **Leobinus**.

Luchesius of Poggibonsi, bl., Franciscan tertiary, born Gaggiano, near Florence, Italy, c. 1181, died Poggibonsi, Italy, 28 April 1260. Luchesius was a merchant with a reputation for greed when he underwent a religious conversion. Afterwards, upon meeting **Francis of Assisi** (c. 1213), he and his wife sold their possessions (excepting only a small field that he farmed) and devoted their lives to charity. They were the first to be admitted by Francis into his Third Order in 1221. Luchesius is said to have been gifted with ecstatic prayer and the miracle of levitation.

Lucia Khambang, martyr, born Viengkuk, 1917, died Sonkong, 26 December 1940. She had entered the Order of the Lovers of the Cross in 1931, and was working at the Sonkong mission. She and several others (see **Martyrs of Thailand**) were marched to the cemetery and shot. Feast 16 December.

Lucian, martyred Beauvais, c. 290. He is commemorated with **Maximian** and **Julian**, and all are supposed to have been missionaries from Rome. Feast 8 January.

Lucian, Marcian, Florus, Heraclius, Titus and Florus, martyrs, died Nicomedia, c. 250. Feast 26 October.

Lucian, Metrobius, Paul, Zenobius, Theotimus and Drusus, martyrs, died Tripoli. Feast 24 December.

Lucian of Antioch, martyr, born possibly Samosata or Edessa, c. 240, died Nicomedia 7 January 312. It seems that he was a priest living an ascetic life. During the persecutions under Maximinus Daia he was brought before the emperor in Nicomedia, where he was questioned, leading to his suffering a martyr's death. Feast 7 January.

Lucian of Perejaslav, born Kostroma, died Perejaslav, 1655. Russian Church. For a time he lived in strict silence near a church which had an icon of the Nativity of the Mother of God. When a community grew around him, he founded the hermitage of the Nativity of the Mother of God. In c. 1650 he also founded a monastery of nuns. He was said to have both eloquence and a gift for prophecy. Feast 8 September.

Lucian of the Kievan Cave Monastery, martyr, died 1243. Russian Church. Feast 15 October.

Lucian Petrovic Fedorov, martyr, born Izjum, 13 October 1895, died there, 10 January 1938. Ukrainian Church, Moscow Patriarchate. He was ordained in 1920 and spent his priestly life serving the church attached to the cemetery. Feast 19 May.

Lucillian, Claudius, Hypatius, Paul and Dionysius, martyrs, died 273. They are said to have been martyred in Byzantium (i.e. the future Constantinople), but that is unlikely, although their relics were brought there. Feast 3 June.

Lucillian and Companions, martyrs, died Nicomedia, 273. Lucillian is said to have been a pagan priest of Nicomedia (modern Izmit, Turkey) who converted to Christianity late in life, and was imprisoned. In prison he met four young Christians, Claudius, Hypatius, Paul and Dionysius, whose faith he strengthened. They were all executed, along with Paula, a woman who brought them food. There are various versions of this story. Feast 3 June.

Lucius, king, Britain, second century. Mentioned by **Bede** and other sources as the first Christian king of Britain, he remains otherwise unknown. Feast 3 December.

Lucius I, pope, born Rome, elected 25 June 253, died Rome, 5 March 254. He was exiled by the emperor on his election, but returned almost immediately when the new emperor, Valerian, seemed ready to tolerate Christians. Little or nothing is known of his pontificate, and it is not clear that he died a martyr's death as was later reported. He showed himself sympathetic to those who had abandoned the faith during persecution. Feast 4 March (suppressed 1969).

Lucius, Absolon and Lorgus, martyrs, died Caesarea, Cappadocia. Feast 2 March.

Lucius of Adrianople, martyr, bishop, died 350. As an opponent of Arianism he was exiled from his see, restored, then imprisoned again. Some of his followers were killed in the riots, and are also honoured as saints. Feast 11 February.

Lucius of Cyprus, probably to be identified with **Lucius of Cyrene**. Feast 20 August.

Lucius of Cyrene, first century. Said to have been the first bishop of Cyrene. Feast 6 May.

Lucretia, martyred Córdoba, Spain, 15 March 859. See **Eulogius of Córdoba** and **Martyrs of Córdoba**.

Lucy, martyred, born Syracuse, Sicily, died there, 303. Tradition claims that St Lucy practised her faith through the distribution of goods to the poor during the persecution of Diocletian. For doing do she was given over to the political authorities by the man to whom she was engaged. She was much venerated by the early Church, as is demonstrated by the Canon of both the Roman and the Ambrosian Mass. Feast 13 December.

Lucy Brocadelli, bl., born Narnia, Umbria, 13 December 1476, died Ferrara, 15 November 1544. One of 11 children, she wished to become a nun, but her guardian – her father had died – betrothed her to a young man with whom she refused to have any physical relationship, and they parted after three years. She then joined the Dominicans, living first in Rome and then in Viterbo, where she began to experience the stigmata. When he heard of this, the duke of Ferrara built a convent for her in his city, to which she went, having to be smuggled out of Viterbo in a basket. After the death of the duke in 1505, Lucy was replaced as prioress of the convent, and she lived the rest of her life in obscurity.

Lucy Filippini, born Tarquinia, Italy, 13 January 1672, died Montefiascone, Italy, 25 March 1732. An orphaned, highly gifted child, Lucy was found as a young girl by Cardinal Barbarigo, explaining the faith to crowds in the marketplace in Corneto. He took her to be raised and instructed by the Poor Clares in Montefiascone. As an adult, she founded places of Christian education for girls and women across Italy, including one in Rome at the request of Pope Clement XI. She is buried at the cathedral in Montefiascone.

Lucy Kim, see **Barbara Kim**. See also **Martyrs of Korea**.

Lucy of Caltagirone, bl., born Caltagirone, Sicily, died Salerno, thirteenth century. A member of the Franciscan tertiaries, she spent almost all her life in the Franciscan convent at Salerno, where she won renown for the holiness of her life, and miracles were attributed to her. Little is otherwise known about her. Feast 26 September.

Lucy Thin, martyred Tongking, 1859, commemorated with **Dominic Kahm** and **Joseph Ta** – see **Martyrs of Vietnam**. Feast 13 January.

Ludan (Luden, Loudain), died Alsace, c. 1202. He is supposed to have been a Scottish or Irish pilgrim returning from Jerusalem who died at Scherkirchen, where he is venerated. Feast 12 February.

Ludfred of Pavia, bishop, died c. 875. Feast 30 January.

Ludger of Münster, bishop, and missionary to the Saxons, born near Utrecht of wealthy parents, 744, died Münster, 26 March 809. He was impressed by the missionary work of St **Boniface** and, after studies in Utrecht, went to York to study under **Alcuin**: there he was ordained deacon. He was ordained priest at Cologne in 777. In 775 he continued the missionary work of **Lebuinas** at Deventer. Later he evangelized the Frieslanders whilst living in Dockum. In 785 he visited Rome, then entered the monastery of Monte Cassino. But in 787 **Charlemagne** called at the monastery, and sent him to evangelize the Saxons of Westphalia. He built an abbey at what came to be called Münster (after *monasterium*) and in 803 he was appointed bishop of the region. He died whilst continuing his evangelistic work and was buried in the Benedictine monastery in Werden. Feast 26 March.

Ludmilla, martyr, patron of Bohemia, born near Melnik, Bohemia, c. 860, died Tetin Castle, near Poderrady, 15 September 921. She married Borivoj, the first Czech prince to adopt Christianity, and helped him to establish Christianity in their region. They built Bohemia's first Christian church near Prague. She was responsible for bringing up her grandson **Wenceslas**, who became king c. 921. It was an attempt to prevent her influencing Wenceslas that led to her assassination, by strangling. She was immediately hailed by Christians as a martyr. Feast 16 September.

Ludolf of Corvey, abbot, died abbey of Corvey, Germany, 13 August 983. Ludolf became abbot of Corvey in 965 and was known for his deep spirituality, his promotion of the monastic school (which gained a good reputation under his leadership), and for having the gift of extrasensory perception. He was also known as a dutiful follower of Rome, where he once went on pilgrimage, and for surrounding his abbey with a high protective wall.

Ludolf of Ratzeburg, bishop, died Wismar, Germany, 29 March 1250. Little is known of Ludolf before he became bishop, except that he was a member of the Premonstratensians (Norbertines). Upon becoming bishop of Ratzeburg in 1236, Ludolf imposed his strict Premonstratensian Rule on his cathedral chapter. He was known for his spiritual discipline and for his conflicts with the local civil authorities. His struggles with Duke Albert of Sachsen-Lauenburg, including being imprisoned and ill-treated, eventually led to his death.

Lüfthildis (Leuchteldis, Liuthild, Lufthold, Luchtel), tradition has it that Lüfthildis flourished in Germany in the ninth century, and that she retired to a hermitage, having been persecuted by her stepmother for her generosity to the poor. Miracles having occurred after her death, her grave became the centre of a cult for the cure of head and ear maladies, first reported by Caesarius of Heisterbach in 1222. Her bones were translated in 1623 and enclosed in a marble sarcophagus in 1902. Feast 23 January.

Luke, founder, born Constantinople (?), died Tesfamba, Skete, fourteenth century. Ethiopian Church. Said to have founded the monastery in which he died.

Luke, abbot of St Saviour's, Sicily, died 1149. Feast 27 February.

Luke Belludi, bl., Franciscan, born near Padua, *c.* 1200, died there after 9 June 1285. From a rich family, Belludi received the habit of the Friars Minor from St **Francis** himself, became a close companion of St **Anthony of Padua**, and attended him at his death at Aracoeli in 1231. As provincial minister he continued building the great basilica in which are enshrined Anthony's remains and Luke's own. Pope Pius XI confirmed his cult in 1927. Feast 17 February.

Luke Hwang Sok-tu, martyr, born Yonp'ung, Korea, 1811, died there, 30 March 1866, beatified 1968, canonized 1984. He resisted family pressure to give up his new faith, became assistant to **Antony Daveluy** and was tortured and killed with him and others during a time of general persecution – see also **Martyrs of Korea**.

Luke Kirby, priest and martyr, born Bedales, north Yorkshire, *c.* 1548, died Tyburn, London, 30 May 1582. He received a university education in England before attending the English College at Douai. He was ordained priest in 1577, and returned to England in 1580. He was immediately arrested at Dover, imprisoned in London, and tortured. In November 1581 he was tried for an alleged and fictitious plot against the queen, along with **Edmund Campion**, **Ralph Sherwin** and **Alexander Briant**, and was sentenced to be hanged, drawn and quartered. The execution itself was delayed until May the following year. He was canonized by Pope Paul VI in 1970 as one of the **Forty Martyrs of England and Wales**. He is commemorated with **William Filby**, **Laurence Richardson** and **Thomas Cottam**, with whom he was executed.

Luke Kiyemon, bl., martyr, born Japan, died Nagasaki, 1627. He was a Franciscan tertiary, and was beheaded. Feast 27 August.

Luke of Armento, monastic founder, born Sicily, early 900s, died Armento, Italy, 19 October 993. Luke began his monastic career at a Greek monastery in Agira. From there he moved to a hermitage in Reggio di Calabria. He left there *c.* 959 seeking to escape the Saracen raids. He spent seven years in Noa, then moved to San Giuliano and finally to Armento *c.* 969. Everywhere he went, he restored churches, engaged in charitable work and founded religious communities. Feast 13 October.

Luke of Belgorod, bishop, born Kiev (?), died Belgorod, *c.* 1090. Russian Church. A monk of the Kievan Cave monastery, he became bishop of Belgorod at an unknown date.

Luke of Jerusalem, monk and martyr, died Jerusalem, 27 June 1273. Georgian Church. He went to Jerusalem to prepare the way for his mother, who had become a nun after the death of her husband. He stayed, however, as a monk of the Holy Cross monastery. The monastery was closed by the Ottoman authorities to be turned into a mosque, and Luke at first plotted to assassinate the governor of the city, but then thought better of it. He challenged the governor, however, who offered him preferment were he to convert to Islam. He refused, and was beheaded.

Luke of Rostov, bishop, died Vladimir, 10 November 1189. Russian Church. He was hegumenos of a monastery in Berestovo before being chosen by the grand prince as bishop of Rostov. He remained close to the prince as a counsellor.

Luke of Simferopol, bishop, born Ker, 14 April 1877, died Simferopol, Crimea, 11 June 1961. Ukrainian Orthodox Church, Moscow Patriarchate. Baptized Valentin Feliksovic Vojno-Jaseneckij and of a noble family, he studied at Kiev and became a doctor, working first in the Far East, where he married a nurse in the military hospital – they had four children. After holding various positions, in 1917 he moved to the new university at Tashkent, where he became professor of surgery. His wife died about this time, and he took vows and was ordained priest. He served in the cathedral, while continuing his work at the university medical school. In 1923 he came bishop of Tashkent, changing his name to Luke. Soon after his consecration he was arrested and sent to Siberia by the Soviet authorities. He returned in 1926, but was arrested again in 1930. This time he was sent to Archangel, where he continued his medical work. He returned in 1933, but was arrested for a third time in 1937 and this time was exiled to Krasnojarsk. When his exile was over, however, he did not return to Tashkent, but remained in Krasnojarsk, where he was named bishop, while he was still working in the local hospital for those wounded in the war. The hospital was moved to Tambov in 1944, and Luke was made bishop of that city. In 1946 he won the Stalin Prize for medical work, and gave much of the prize money to children who had suffered from the war. His importance was a problem for the Soviet authorities, who decided in 1946 to send him to Simferopol in the Crimea. There again he became bishop, and did much to reform the diocese, while still working as a doctor. He remained bishop until the end of his life, although he became blind in 1956. Feast 29 May.

Luke of Triglia, born Lyaconia, died Triglia. Byzantine Church. Hegumenos of the monastery at Vatheos Ryakos, near Triglia. Feast 7 Sepember.

Luke the Stylite, born Anatolia, died Chalcedon, ninth/tenth centuries. Byzantine Church. He was at first a soldier, then a monk and priest. He lived for three years on a column before going to Mount Olympus, where he put a stone in his mouth to prevent hmself from speaking. He later moved to Chalcedon, where he again lived on a column for 45 years. Feast 11 December.

Luke the Treasurer, monk, born (?) and died Kiev, thirteenth century. Russian Church. A monk of the Kievan Cave monastery.

Luke the Younger, died near Corinth, 955. Originally from the island of Aegina, he became a hermit on Mount Joannitsa near Corinth. Called Thaumaturgus, the Wonderworker, during his life because of his miracles, after his death his cell became an oratory called Soterion, the Place of Healing. Feast 7 February.

Luke the Younger, bl., martyr, born Adrianopolis, died Mytilene, 23 March 1802. Byzantine Church. He moved to Constantinople, where he became a Muslim. Swiftly regretting this action, he fled to the skete of St Anna on Mount Athos. In order to atone for his sin, he went to Mytilene, where he said he had abandoned Islam, and was hanged.

Luke Zidjata, bishop, died Kopys, 15 October 1058. Russian Church. He became bishop of Novgorod in 1035, chosen by the grand prince **Jaroslav the Wise** to mark a break with the domination of Constantinople over the Russian Church. During his episcopate he built churches and monasteries. He died on his return journey to Novgorod from Kiev, where he had been for three years. Feast 10 February.

Lull, missionary bishop, successor of **Boniface** of Fulda, a monk of Malmesbury abbey, England, died Hersfeld, 787. A cousin of Boniface, Lull went out to help in the missionary work in Germany, eventually succeeding Boniface as bishop in Mainz. Lull's correspondence reveals an appreciation for books and a desire to build a library of books from England, as well as pastoral concerns and zeal for the observance of the canons. He founded a monastery at Bleidenstadt in Nassau, and refounded the abbey of Hersfeld in Hesse, where he retired in his old age. Feast 16 October.

Lupicinus, abbot, died Jura, c. 480. He was brother to **Romanus of Contat**, with whom he founded the monasteries at Contat and Leuconne in the Jura and whom he succeeded as abbot at Contat. Feast 21 March.

Lupicinus and Felix, fifth century. They were both bishop of Lyons. Feast 3 February.

Lupus of Châlon, bishop, died c. 601. He was bishop of Châlon-sur-Saône, reputed for his charity to the suffering. Feast 27 January.

Lupus of Limoges, bishop, died Limoges, 638. Feast 22 May.

Lupus of Novae, died near Svishtov, Bulgaria. Although said to have been a martyr in Thessalonika, it is more likely that he died at Novae, near Svishtov, where there was a memorial basilica. Feast 23 August.

Lupus of Sens (St Loup), bishop, born Orléanais, c. 573, died Brienon, near Sens, c. 1 September 623. Educated and ordained by his maternal uncles, the bishops of Orléans and Auxerre, in 609 he was appointed bishop of Sens, with popular support.

He spent a time in exile in Picardy for his support for Sigebert of Austrasia, where he is said to have made many converts. He was restored in 614, and attended the Council of Paris in that year. Buried in the monastery of Sainte-Columbe-les-Sens, which he had founded, his relics were translated to a new church in 853. Many churches in France are dedicated to him. He is invoked by epileptics. Feast 1 September.

Lupus of Troyes, bishop, born Toul, Gaul, *c.* 393, died Troyes, 479. He was married for several years, but when the marriage ended by mutual consent, his wife became a nun and he entered the monastery at Lérins. He was made bishop of Troyes *c.* 426. When Attila and the Huns invaded, Lupus agreed to become a hostage in exchange for sparing the province. However, when he eventually returned to Troyes he was accused of helping the enemy and was forced into exile. He spent two years as a hermit before returning to Troyes. Feast 29 July.

Lutgardis, mystic, born Tongeren (Belgium), 1182, died Aywières (Belgium), 16 June 1246. At the age of 12, Lutgardis was sent to a convent, presumably because her father had lost her dowry in a business venture. She became a nun at the age of 20 because of a vision of Christ. For the next 12 years, she had numerous mystical visions and experiences. Around 1216, she left the Benedictines for the stricter Rule of the Cistercians, living at their abbey in Aywières. Known for her spiritual wisdom as well as for her visions and prophecies, Lutgardis is considered one of the leading mystics of the 1200s.

Luxorius, martyr, died Forum Trajananum (modern Fordingiano, Sardinia), *c.* 303. A soldier, he is said to have more or less converted himself by reading the Christian Scriptures, and was one of the first to be executed in the persecution of Diocletian. Feast 21 August.

Lydwina, bl., born Schiedam, near Rotterdam, 1380, died there, 14 April 1433, cult approved 1890. An invalid after an ice-skating accident aged 15, she suffered progressively worse disability and pain. Reported as experiencing visions and having miraculous powers, an investigation into possible diabolical possession cleared her of this accusation.

Lyon, Martyrs of, see **Pothinus**.

Mabe'a Maryam, monk. Ethiopian Church. Commemorated in the district of Tegulet.

Mabe'a Sellase, monk. Ethiopian Church. Commemorated in Tigre.

Mabe'a Seyon, monk, fifteenth century. Ethiopian Church. From a wealthy family, at the age of 18 he entered the monastery of St John and was ordained deacon. His parents wanted him to marry, but he increased his penitential practices and was eventually, after 46 years as a deacon, ordained priest, after which he lived for another nine years. He was blessed with many visions – of Christ sitting on his arm, of the Virgin and, in the Eucharist, of a white lamb.

Macanisius, bishop, born Ireland, died there, *c.* 514. A disciple of **Patrick**, and said to have been made a bishop by him. He went on a pilgrimage to the Holy Land and Rome, and on his return founded the diocese of Connor, becoming its first bishop. Feast 3 September.

Macarius, martyr. Coptic Church. Nothing is known about him except that he was, apparently, drowned. Feast 30 May.

Macarius, martyr, born Egypt, died Satanuf, Egypt, 16 July *c.* 302. Coptic Church. The son of a minister in the government of Diocletian, he became a Christian, and was tortured and exiled, first to Nikiu, then to Satanuf, where he was beheaded. Feast 8 September.

Macarius, see also **Amphilochius, Macarius, Tarasius and Theodosius**.

Macarius Chachuli, hegumenos, eleventh century. Georgian Church. Known as 'the great faster', he joined the monastery of Chachuli in southern Georgia in the early part of the eleventh century, and rose to become its hegumenos. Feast 21 December.

Macarius Glucharev, archimandrite, born 1792, died 1847. Russian Church. He studied in St Petersburg, and taught in Ekaterinoslav. He became head of a seminary in Kostroma, but then entered first the Kievan Cave monastery, then that of Glinsk. From his time as a student he had been interested in mysticism, and he dreamed of opening a centre in Moscow where Orthodox, Catholics and Lutherans could meet. Instead, however, he went off to Tomsk, where he started the Spiritual Mission of the Altaj, a region of southern Siberia, as a result of which many in the region were baptized and churches and schools were opened. While there he began a translation of the Bible into modern Russian from the Hebrew. He continued this even after he was appointed superior of the monastery of the Most Holy Trinity at Optina. He wished to continue this work in the Holy Land, and in 1847 received permission to make a pilgrimage there, but he died just before setting out. Feast 18 May.

Macarius Makris, bl., born Thessalonika, died Constantinople, 7 January 1431. Byzantine Church. Of Jewish birth, he became a monk on Mount Athos and later hegumenos of the monastery of the Pantocrator in Constantinople and chaplain to the emperor. He died in a plague. Feast 8 January.

Macarius of Alexandria, martyr, died Alexandria, 250. There is some confusion over this Macarius. He was possibly a potter, put to death with three others in the same trade, Rufinus, Justus and Theophilus, at Alexandria. Other versions list Rome as the place of execution. The feast day of Macarius himself is 8 December, but of the group is either 28 February or 30 October.

Macarius of Alexandria I, patriarch, born Subra, near Alexandria, died Alexandria, 20 March 952. Coptic Church. As a young man he became a monk at the monastery of St Macarius, and was elected patriarch in 932. He visited his mother, who reprimanded him for being proud of his office, and from then on he lived an edifying life.

Macarius of Alexandria II, patriarch, died Alexandria, 1 September 1128. Coptic Church. A monk of the monastery of St Macarius, he was elected patriarch in 1102. There were conflicts between himself and the monks of St Macarius, with the clergy, and with leading Christian figures in Alexandria, but little or nothing is known of his pastoral activity.

Macarius of Antioch, bishop, born Antioch, died Ghent, 1012. Said to have been a bishop in Antioch before travelling to the West as a pilgrim, and dying of the plague in Belgium. The story is highly unlikely. Feast 10 April.

Macarius (Notaras) of Corinth, bishop and spiritual writer, born Corinth, 1731, died Chios, 17 April 1805. Byzantine Church. Both as bishop and writer he helped to sustain and revive the Greek Church under Turkish rule. He is most famous as the co-compiler (with **Nicodemus of the Holy Mountain**) of the *Philokalia*; indeed, he was probably the more important figure in the publication of this collection.

Macarius of Jerusalem, bishop, died Jerusalem, c. 333. Elected c. 312, he has been thought to be the Macarius who was labelled an 'uneducated heretic' by Arius in his letter to Eusebius of Nicomedia. He

attended the Council of Nicaea (325) and there is a tradition that he actively participated in the debate against the Arians. Macarius was of the opinion that Jerusalem ought to have precedence over Caesarea. Constantine drafted a letter assigning construction of the Church of the Holy Sepulchre to Macarius. Feast 10 March.

Macarius of Kanev, see **Macarius of Ordez**.

Macarius of Kios, martyr, born Kios, Bithynia, died Prusa, 6 October 1590. Byzantine Church. Baptized Manuel, he trained as a tailor. His father converted to Islam, but the rest of his family did not. On one occasion he went to Prusa to buy materials for his trade, and met his father who had him forcibly circumcized. The young man then went to Mount Athos and became a monk, where he lived for 12 years, receiving the monastic name of Macarius. He then went to Constantinople, where he obtained a document testifying that he had been forcibly converted to Islam. He then entered the monastery of Chalki in Constantinople. Some time later he returned to Prusa, where he proclaimed his Christian faith. At first the document he had obtained in Constantinople saved him from execution, but he was eventually imprisoned, tortured, stoned, and finally beheaded.

Macarius of Koljazinsk, monk, born 1402, died 1483. Russian Church. Of a noble family, and born Matthew Koza. He married, but his wife died three years later, and he entered the monastery of St Nicholas at Klobukovo. After a time he entered a hermitage with nine companions, and eventually built a monastery dedicated to the Most Holy Trinity which, because of its position on the Volga river, came to play an important part in the political history and economic development of Russia. Feast 17 March.

Macarius of Krasnagora, founder, died Krasnagora, 10 January 1636. Russian Church. At one time the parish priest of Jurol, Miron, as he was then called, was chosen in a vision to the hegumenos **Barlamio**, bishop of Suzdal, to have charge of a miraculous icon of the Virgin, which he placed at an isolated spot near Cernogora (now Krasnagora). Miron's wife had died, so he became a monk with the name of Macarius and received permission to start a monastery at Cernogora, the building of which began in 1607. The monastery to survive until it received gifts of two other icons of the Virgin. Feast 22 August.

Macarius of Menjuga, hegumenos, died Menjuga, seventeenth century. Russian Church. Nothing is known of him except that his tomb was venerated as that of a saint.

Macarius of Moscow, metropolitan, born c. 1482, died Moscow, 31 December 1563. Russian Church. He was baptized Michael, of a noble family, and entered the monastery of Paphnutius at Borovsk, taking the name Macarius. He was ordained priest at 24, and shortly afterwards became archimandrite of the monastery at Luzevsk. Aged 50, he became archbishop of Novgorod. He introduced the coenobitic life into the monasteries and convents of his diocese, after the Rule of Luzevsk, built or remodelled churches, provided liturgical books, and generally improved the religious life of the diocese. He wrote the lives of the saints according to the liturgical year, an immense work which took him 12 years. In 1542 he was elected metropolitan of Moscow. As metropolitan he crowned Tsar Ivan the Terrible, and after Ivan's victory over the Tartars in 1552 he built the cathedral of the Protection of the Mother of God – later called St Basil's Cathedral – in what is now Red Square. In the great fire of 1547, in which 1,700 people died, he lost the sight of one eye. He greatly encouraged the people to rebuild the city. Feast 30 December.

Macarius of Novgorod (the Roman), monk, born Rome, died Novgorod, c. 1550. Russian Church. Originally of a wealthy Roman family, but was attracted to the Orthodox Church and came as a pilgrim to the monastery of **Alexander of Svir** at Novgorod. He lived as a hermit some distance from the monastery on the river Lenza, and followed a penitential life, wearing heavy chains about his person. Against his wishes a community built up around him, and a monastery was established of which he became hegumenos. Shortly before his death he handed over charge of the monastery to a disciple, and went to live again as a hermit on an island. Feast 15 August.

Macarius (Makary Ivanov) of Optina, monk, born Kaluga, 20 November 1788, died Optina hermitage, 7 September 1860. Russian Church. Baptized Nichael Nikolaevic Ivanov, he gave up a brilliant career to become a monk and was appointed confessor at Optina in 1836. Thereafter he received visitors from all over Russia. His letters of spiritual advice form five published volumes. He was influential in spreading the practice of the Jesus Prayer and helped translate patristic texts into modern Russian. His Russian *Letters of Spiritual Direction* are also available in English.

Macarius of Ordez, monk, died 1532. Russian Church. Founder of a monastery of the Dormition at Ordez. Feast 9 August.

Macarius of Ovruc, martyr, died Kanev, 7 September 1678. Russian Church. Son of a devout family, he entered the local monastery, of which he became hegumenos. After the monastery was destroyed by Polish troops he moved, still as hegumenos, to a monastery at Kanev, which was also destroyed and Macarius martyred.

Macarius of Pelecete, monk, born Constantinople, c. 750, died 'Aphrysia' (unknown island), 829. Macarius entered the monastery of Pelecete in Bythnia, succeeded St **Hilarion** as abbot, and received ordination from Tarasius, patriarch of Constantinople. Renowned for his holiness and miracles, Macarius opposed the iconoclast Emperor Leo V, the Armenian, and suffered imprisonment and torture. Freed by Michael II, he continued to refuse to accept the heretical teaching, and was exiled, as a septuagenarian, to the island where he died. Feast 1 April.

Macarius of Pis'ma, monk, born near Kostroma, fourteenth/fifteenth centuries. Russian Church. He entered the monastery of **Sergius of Radonez**, but, seeking greater solitude, he returned to his own region and settled by the river Pis'ma, where a community gathered and a monastery was eventually founded. Feast 10 January.

Macarius of Solovki, monk, fifteenth century. Russian Church. A disciple of **Zosimus**.

Macarius of the Kievan Cave Monastery, died Kiev. Russian Church. He is said to have been miraculously cured as a baby, and became a monk when very young. Feast 19 January.

Macarius of Tkow, bishop, died Alexandria, *c.* 452. Coptic Church. He accompanied the patriarch **Dioscorus** to the Council of Chalcedon in 451. On the journey Dioscorus had two visions, and Macarius performed two miracles. Macarius did not know Greek, and when he was in the presence of the emperor he upbraided him in Coptic for his support for the position of Pope **Leo**. For their opposition to the definition about the nature of Christ reached at Chalcedon, Dioscorus was exiled, while Macarius was martyred on his return to Alexandria by being kicked in the stomach.

Macarius of Vysokoezero, founder, died Vysokoezero, 1683. Russian Church. He died a violent death, attacked by brigands, after founding the hermitage at Vysokoezero.

Macarius of Zabyn, monk, died Zabyn, 1623. Russian Church. He died at the age of 84 with a reputation for working miracles. Feast 22 January.

Macarius of Zeltovoda, monk, born Niznij Novgorod, 1349, died Zeltovoda, 25 July 1444. Russian Church. Born into a wealthy family, at a very young age he entered a cave monastery at Niznij Novgorod, unbeknown to his parents. After three years they discovered him, and tried to persuade him to leave, but he refused. However, in order to escape the reputation for holiness that was building around him, he left the monastery and settled on the river Luch. Again his presence attracted attention, and he moved to a cave that he dug out on the left bank of the Volga, which again became a monastery. From there he preached to the people around, converting many. In 1439 the Tartars attacked Niznij Novgorod, and also the monastery, killing the monks and taking Macarius prisoner. Although he was later released, he was ordered to leave the region by the khan, and went to Galic. He finally settled near lake Zeltovod, where he died.

Macarius the Agorite, bl., martyr, died 1527. Byzantine Church. A disciple on Mount Athos of the former patriarch **Niphon II**, he got Niphon's approval to seek martyrdom. He went to Thessalonika, where he publicly preached Christianity, was thrown into prison and, when he refused to deny his faith, was executed. Feast 14 September.

Macarius the Alexandrian, hermit, born Alexandria, *c.* 300, died desert of Nitria, 390. He converted to Christianity *c.* 340, after working as a maker of sweets in Alexandria. He was a great ascetic – too ascetic for the monks of Pachomius's monastery, who drove him out. A number of hermits gathered around him in the Nitrian desert, and he became their abbot. Feast 2 January.

Macarius the Faster, monk, born Kiev (?), died there, twelfth century. Russian Church. A monk of the Kievan Cave monastery. Feast 19 January.

Macarius the Great, abbot, born Upper Egypt, *c.* 300, died monastery of Scete (Wadi Natrun), 390. A cattle herder or camel driver by trade, he became a hermit in Scete, where a community gathered around him, and a monastery was established which still bears his name. He was influenced by – and may have known – **Anthony of Egypt**. He was ordained priest in 340, and in 374 was exiled for a time with **Macarius the Alexandrian** to an island in the Nile because of his support of **Athanasius**. Stories about him, and some of his sayings, are included among the *Sayings of the Desert Fathers*, although the *Spiritual Homilies* once attributed to him are now thought to have been composed in Syria. Feast 15 January.

Macarius the Roman (1), born Rome, died monastery of the Dormition on the river Lezna, 1550 (?). Russian Church. Feast 19 January.
(2) born Rome, died Mesopotamia. Byzantine Church. He lived naked, covered only by his beard, which reached to his feet. Feast 23 October.
(3) see **Macarius of Novgorod**.

Macarius the Scot, bl., Benedictine abbot, born Ireland or Scotland, *c.* 1100, died probably monastery of Sankt Jakob, Würzburg, Germany, 1153. He was a Benedictine at the abbey of Regensburg, Germany, when, in 1139, he was made abbot of the monastery of Sankt Jakob. He made a journey to Rome to obtain relics for his community. His body was moved to the abbey church in 1615, and after this many miracles were attributed to his intercession. Feast 19 December.

Macarius and Julian, martyrs, died Syria. Feast 12 August.

Macartan (Marcatin, Maccarthen, in Irish: Aedh mac Cairthinn), bishop, born Ireland, died Clogher, Ireland, c. 505. He was an early disciple of **Patrick**, who is supposed to have ordained him bishop of Clogher. Feast 24 March.

Macedonius Kritophagus ('the barley eater'), hermit, died Syria, c. 430. A wandering hermit, who slept under a roof only for the last few years of his life. Feast 24 January.

Macedonius of Constantinople II, died Gangra, c. 517. Effectively appointed patriarch in 495 by the emperor, in place of Euphemius who was exiled, Macedonius insisted, like his predecessor, on maintaining the faith as defined at Chalcedon. The emperor tried to have him assassinated, and in 511 exiled him to Ancyra, although he later moved to Gangra for his own safety. Feast 25 April.

Macedonius, Patricia and Modesta, martyrs, died Nicomedia, 304. Said to have been a married couple and their daughter. Feast 13 March.

Macedonius, Theodulos and Tatian, martyrs, died Meros, Phrygia, 362. The were executed after breaking the idols in a newly reopened temple. Feast 12 September.

Machan, abbot, died c. 653. Feast 24 January.

Machar, bishop, born Ireland, died in the region of modern Aberdeen, Scotland, c. 540. Baptized by **Colman**, he came to Scotland with **Columba**, and preached in the Aberdeen area. Feast 12 November.

Mackessog, see **Kessog**.

Maclovius (Malo, Machutus, Maclou), missionary to Brittany, born probably Wales, died near Saintes (Archingeay), between 618 and 640. Maclovius worked in the area around Aleth (Saint-Servan) and the estuary of the Rance, and in the area now

bearing his name, St Malo. He was consecrated the first bishop of Aleth, but throughout his life also spent periods as a hermit. Biographies from the ninth century paint a picture of a rugged pioneer missionary on horseback, singing and preaching loudly, making both friends and enemies as he travelled. Feast 15 November.

Macrina the Elder, born Neocaesarea, Pontus (today part of Turkey), died there, c. 340. She was probably converted to Christianity by **Gregory Thaumaturgus**. During the persecution of Maximinus Daia she survived by hiding with her family for some years in the mountains. She was the grandmother on the paternal side of **Basil the Great**, **Gregory of Nyssa** and **Macrina the Younger**, and was a decisive factor in their religious education. Feast 14 January.

Macrina the Younger, born Cappadocian Caesarea, c. 327, died Pontus, 19 July 379 (or 380). She was the elder sister of **Basil the Great** and **Gregory of Nyssa**. After the death of her fiancé she founded a monastery on a family estate, together with her mother **Emmelia** and former slaves. Gregory of Nyssa wrote her biography. By attributing to her the role of imaginary teacher in his *On the Soul and Resurrection*, he showed high esteem for her spiritual influence and learning. With her mother she founded a convent on the river Iris, where they spent the last years of their lives. Feast 19 July.

Macrobius, bishop and martyr, died Egypt, fourth century. Feast 26 February.

Macrobius, monk, sixth century. Coptic Church. Son of the governor of Tkow, he travelled with **Severus of Antioch** on a visit to the monasteries of the region, and decided himself to join the monastery of **Moses of Abidos**, where he was joined by his three brothers. He then became a founder of monasteries, and was summoned to Alexandria to be ordained priest.

Macrobius and Julian, martyrs, died 321 (?). Macrobius was born in Cappadocia, and martyred at Tomi in what is now Romania; Julian died in Galatia. Feast 13 September.

Madhanina Egzi, monk, thirteenth/fourteenth centuries. Ethiopian Church. A disciple of **Takla Haymanot**, he founded the convent of Dabra Bankol, near Axum.

Ma'eqaba Egzi, monk. Ethiopian Church. Monk of Dabra Bakur, in Tigre.

Madeleine, see **Magdalen**.

Maedoc (Aidan) of Ferns, born Connaught, Ireland, died there (?), c. 626. It is said he was educated at **David**'s school in Wales, founded three monasteries in Ireland and was first bishop of Ferns, County Wexford. His staff, bell and reliquary with satchel are still kept in Ireland. Feast 31 January.

Maelrubha (Malrubius), abbot, born Ireland, c. 642, died Applecross, Wester Ross, 722. A monk at Bangor, County Down, he went to Scotland aged 29, probably first to Iona. He established a monastery at Applecross and, based there, he evangelized a large area, including the Isle of Skye. Feast 21 April.

Mafalda of Portugal, born Portugal, 1206, died there, 1257, cult confirmed 1793. Daughter of King Sancho I, she became a Cistercian nun at Arouca after her marriage was annulled for consanguinity, living an austere life. She founded a pilgrims' hostel and a hospital for widows, and rebuilt Oporto cathedral. Feast 1 May.

Magdalen, martyr, sixteenth century. Ethiopian Church. Of royal birth, she was crucified by Muslims. Feast 7 June.

Magdalen Albrici, bl., Augustinian abbess, born Como, Italy, 1400, died Brumate (near Como), 13 or 15 May 1465. Orphaned when young, Magdalen entered St Andrew's convent at Brumate, where her many virtues soon commended her to the office of abbess. Said to have been a visionary, she promoted holiness among her nuns and reputedly worked miracles. In 1455 she founded a convent in Como. Feast 15 May.

Magdalen Fontaine, and three other Sisters of Charity of St Vincent de Paul, bl., martyrs, died Paris, 27 June 1794, during the French Revolution, beatified 1920. All guillotined as a result of planted evidence of anti-state activity, the others were Frances Fanton, Joan Gérard and Frances Lanel (superior) – see also **Martyrs of the French Revolution** and **Martyrs of Cambrai**.

Magdalen Gabriella Canossa, religious founder, born Verona, Italy, 2 March 1774, died there, 10 April 1835. She was educated privately by her uncle and from 1799 devoted herself to the care of poor girls, rather in opposition to her father. In 1802 she gave housing to some of these girls and three years later opened a school for them. She was joined by others and in 1808 founded the Daughters of Charity of Canossa (Canossian Sisters), whose apostolate was to education and nursing.

Magdalen Panattieri, bl., born Trino-Vercellese, Italy, c. 1444, died there, 13 October 1503. A devout woman, she became a Dominican tertiary and worked among the poor and with children. Her example of prayer persuaded the Dominicans in the town to adopt a stricter observance of their Rule.

Magdalen Son, see **Augustine Pak**.

Magdalen Sophie Barat, founder of the Sacred Heart Society, born Yonne, France, 12 December 1779, died Paris, 25 May 1865. In 1800 her teacher/ brother (who was a priest) took her to Paris so she could study. There she was persuaded to join a religious order. She followed this group to Amiens and in 1802 became their superior general and head of the school for girls. In 1804, in Grenoble, she founded the second house of the Sacred Heart Society. She spent the rest of her life attempting (with reasonable success) to extend her institute and to keep its constitution safe from the attitudes of the post-revolutionary society from which her pupils came. Even the chaplain of the Amiens house was involved in attempting to reshape the constitution, but she resisted him and such change for the whole of her life. She travelled widely to spread her order around the world.

Magenulf, born Westphalia, died Bodeken, c. 857. Of noble birth, he was the godson of the Emperor **Charlemagne**. He was educated at Paderborn, and became a priest. He established a monastery for women on his estate, and spent his life preaching around Westphalia. Feast 5 October.

Maginus, martyr, born Tarragona, Spain, died there, *c*. 304. A missionary in the area around Tarragona, martyred under Diocletian. Feast 19 August.

Maglorius (Maelor), abbot, born Glamorgan, Wales, died between 575 and 586. Of Irish origin (son of Umbrafel), Maglorius was educated by **Illtyd** at Llaniltyd Lawr. A disciple of **Samson**, Maglorius travelled with him as a missionary to Brittany, and there founded monasteries under the protection of King Childebert. Eventually, he succeeded Samson as bishop of Dol. In his old age, Maglorius retired to the island of Sark, where he founded a monastery and lived as a hermit. Miracles were attributed to him – the healing of a skin disease of a chieftain in Sark, who gratefully gave him land, and the driving out of a dragon in Jersey. Feast 24 October.

Magnabod (Maimbeuf) of Angers, bishop, born Angers region, *c*. 574, died Angers, after 635. As his biographer writes, Magnabod came from a respected family, and was both spiritual and studious. Bishop **Licinius** ordained Magnabod and later gave him charge of the Challones-sur-Loire monastery. Magnabod became bishop of Angers (*c*. 610), attended synods (Paris 614, Clichy 627), wrote a biography of St Maurilius of Angers, and built a church dedicated to St Saturninus. Feast 16 October.

Magnericus, bishop, born Trier (?), died there, 25 July 596. Magnericus was raised in Gaul, in the household of Bishop Nicetius of Trier, who later ordained him. Bishop Nicetius was exiled by King Clotaire I (the bishop had excommunicated the king due to his corruption and licentiousness). Magnericus accompanied him into exile, returning the following year. He was named first Frankish bishop of Trier six years later. In 585 Magnericus gave shelter to another exiled bishop, Theodore of Marseilles, when banished by Gunthamnus of Burgundy, even pleading with King Childebert II on his behalf.

Magnus (Magnoaldus, Maginaldus, Mang), monk, missionary to the Algau, died Füssen, Bavaria, *c*. 750. Little is reliably known about the life of Magnus. Supposedly he crossed the river Lech at St Manstritt ('footstep of St Magnus') and built a cell, where afterwards the monastery of Fussen was founded, and there he died. In 851, when the relics of Magnus were moved to the new church of Füssen, a manuscript was said to have been found which was the story of the saint's life written by his companion Theodore, but due in part to historical inaccuracies this is now believed to date from the time of the removal of the relics, with even later additions, and to be unreliable. Feast 6 September.

Magnus of Fabrateria, martyr, died third century. This is thought to be a mistaken identification, and no such person existed. Feast 19 August.

Magnus of Orkney, born *c*. 1075, died Egilsay, 1116. Son of a Viking earl of Orkney, after becoming a Christian he began a life of prayer. His cousin had him murdered over their inheritance. Traditionally regarded as a martyr, he is said to have appeared to Robert the Bruce before Bannockburn. Feast 16 April.

Maharshapur, Narses and Sebokt, martyrs, died Persia, 421. Maharshapur was a Persian nobleman who, with Narses and Sebokt, was accused of destroying a Mazdean temple. All were offered their freedom were they to convert, but all refused to do so. Narses and Sebokt were executed immediately (418), but Maharshapur was kept in prison for three years before being thrown into a pit to starve to death. Feast 10 October.

Maimbod, martyr, born Ireland, died near Kaltenbrunn, Alsace, *c*. 880. He appears to have been one of the *peregrini*, Irish monks who wandered Western Europe over a period of 200 years. It is said that pagans killed him while he was preaching or praying. A local cult developed around his remains. Feast 23 January.

Mainard, bishop of Urbino, died 1088. Feast 9 May.

Maiulus, martyred Byzema, Libya, *c*. 200. Feast 11 May.

Majolus (Maieul) of Cluny, monastic reformer and fourth abbot of Cluny, born Avignon, 906, died Souvigny, 11 May 994. Also known as Mayeul, he studied at Lyon, became archdeacon of Mâçon, and became a Cluniac monk after refusing the bishopric of Besançon. Appointed coadjutor in 954, he became abbot of Cluny in 965. The Cluniac reform spread widely during his reign, and he reformed abbeys in Burgundy, France and Italy. In 974 Emperor Otto II offered him the papacy, which he refused. Hugh Capet asked him to reform Saint-Denis, and he died on his way to Paris at the abbey of Souvigny.

Majorus, martyr, died Gaza, fourth century. Feast 15 February.

Makbeba Dengel, monk, fifteenth/sixteenth century. Ethiopian Church. A disciple of **Theodore**, the founder of the monastery of Adyabo in Tigre.

Makhlouf, see **Charbel Makhlouf**.

Malachias, martyr, born Rhodes, died Jerusalem, *c.* 1500. He went to Jerusalem to live a hermit's life there when still a young man. For some reason he fell foul of the Turkish authorities, and was executed for refusing to deny his faith.

Malachy, archbishop of Armagh, born Armagh, 1094, died Clairvaux, whilst travelling to Rome, 2 November 1148. He was ordained in 1119 and elected abbot of Bangor four years later. He became bishop of Connor the following year (1124) and was chosen for Armagh in 1132, although he was only able to take possession of his see two years later. He was very enthusiastic about the monastic system in Gaul and on his journey to Rome in 1139 visited **Bernard of Clairvaux**. On his way back he persuaded five Cistercians to return with him to Ireland, and they established a Cistercian abbey at Mellifont, County Louth, in 1142. He was making a second visit to Rome, again calling at Clairvaux, when he died. Feast 3 November.

Malard of Chartres, bishop, died *c.* 650. He participated in the Council of Châlon-sur-Saône in 650. Feast 15 January.

Malati, martyr, born Egypt, died there, 19 May 1803. Executed by the Muslims for collaborating with Napoleon during the latter's occupation of Egypt.

Malo, see **Maclovius**.

Mamas (Mammas, Mamans), martyr, born Gangra, died Caesarea, 275 (?). A shepherd, executed in the reign of Aurelian for his faith. Feast 17 August.

Mamas of Gudgude, monk, born Tigre, died there. Ethiopian Church. He evangelized part of Tigre.

Mamelchtha, martyr, born Bethgarme, Persia, died there, *c.* 344. Said to have been a Zoroastrian priestess (or alternatively a priestess of Artemis) who became a Christian, and was recognized as such by her baptismal robe. She was then stoned to death. Feast 5 October.

Mamerto Esquiú, Franciscan bishop and theologian, born San José, Argentina, 1826, died Córdoba, Argentina, 1883. As bishop of Córdoba, Esquiú became well known in Argentina during the nineteenth century because of his involvement and interventions in public affairs, which did much to bring stability to the country. Through numerous writings he also made significant contributions to Catholic theology in such areas as moral theology, Christology and metaphysics. Esquiú was widely revered and respected for his piety and Christian charity, and among Argentinians is considered a saint.

Mamertus, bishop, born near Lyons, died Vienne, near Lyons, *c.* 475. He was bishop of Vienne by 463. He earned a rebuke from Pope Hilary in 464 for consecrating a bishop of Die and for interfering in an attempted settlement between the sees of Arles and Vienne. He is famous for introducing the processional litanies on the days prior to Ascension Day as an appeal against natural disasters such as volcanic eruptions and earthquakes; these were the forerunner of the later Rogation Days. Feast 11 May.

Manasse, monk, born Alexandria, sixth century. Coptic Church. A relative of **Abraham of Farsut**, he became a monk in a Pachomian monastery, and went on to found a monastery of his own. Feast 19 January.

Mancio Shibata, see **Martyrs of Omura**.

Mancius, martyr, died Evora, Portugal, fifth/sixth century. Described as of Roman origin, he was apparently bought as a slave by Jewish traders, who took him to Portugal, where they killed him. Feast 21 May.

Manfred Settala, bl., died 1217. He was a priest and hermit. Feast 27 January.

Mansuetus, Severus, Appianus, Donatus, Honorius and Five Companions, martyrs, died Alexandria, 483 (?). They were martyred for their support for the Chalcedonian formula. Feast 30 December.

Manuel II Palaeologus, emperor, born 1350, died 21 July 1425. Byzantine Church. He was son of John V. At Constantinople he was besieged by the Turks, but he diplomatically established peaceful relations with the Ottoman Turks, whose advance and conquest of the Byzantine Empire he held back for 50 years. Manuel also pursued religious and literary affairs, and finally retired to a monastery.

Manuel Morales, martyr, born Mesillas, Mexico, 8 February 1898, died Chalchihuites, near Zacatecas, Mexico, 14 August 1926. He had been in the seminary at Durango, but had to leave to support his family. After leaving the seminary he married and had three children. He was president of the League for the Defence of Religious Freedom. He tried to obtain the release of **Louis Batiz Sainz**, but was arrested, and shot with him. Feast 25 May.

Manuel of Crete, martyr, born Sphakia, Crete, died Chios, 15 March 1792. Byzantine Church. He had been forced to become a Muslim in 1770, while imprisoned. On his release he went to Mykonos, where he married and had six children. When he discovered that his wife had been unfaithful, he removed the children and went to live in another house. His wife's parents, however, informed the Turks that he had once been a Muslim, and he was beheaded.

Manuel of Rethymnon, martyr, born Rethymnon, Crete, died there, 28 October 1824. Byzantine Church.

Manuel of Samothrace, born Samothrace, died Makri, 6 April 1835. Byzantine Church.

Manuel, Sabel and Ismael, martyrs, born Persia, died Chalcedon, 362. Three brothers, sent by the Persian ruler to negotiate with the Emperor Julian who, finding they were Christians, had them executed. This event was a contributory cause of the war between Rome and Persia. Feast 17 June.

Mappalicus and Companions, died Carthage, c. 250. Under the persecution of Decius, Christians who would not abjure were imprisoned and tortured to change their mind. Mappalicus died under torture, followed by about 17 others, many of whom died of starvation in prison. Feast 19 April.

Marana and Cyra, hermits, born Beroea, Syria, died there (?), fifth century. Two brothers who became hermits. Feast 3 August.

Mar'awi Krestos, monk, born Axum, died Scete (Tigre), thirteenth century. Ethiopian Church. A priest of Axum, he wanted to live a more ascetical life and retired to the desert of Scete. He worked many miracles, including, in a time of famine, multiplying loaves.

Marcel Callo, bl., martyr, born Rennes, Brittany, 6 December 1921, died Mauthausen concentration camp, 19 March 1945, beatified 1987. A printer and member of Jeunesse Ouvrière Chrétienne (Young Christian Workers), he continued his Catholic activities when a conscripted labourer in Germany, and was arrested for these. He died of starvation and tuberculosis.

Marcella, born into Roman aristocratic circles, c. 325, she died after torture during Alaric's sack of Rome, 410. She married when she was still very young, but was widowed after only six months, and then rejected a new offer of marriage from the consul, despite the pleas of her mother. Having heard about the flowering ascetic movements in Egypt, she started a community with her mother and many other aristocratic women in her palace on the Aventine. **Jerome** acted as their spiritual guide and master in the Scriptures (382–5). Marcella's monastic settlement was for many decades a centre of intense monastic living. Feast 31 January.

Marcellianus, bishop of Auxerre, died 337. Feast 13 May.

Marcellin Joseph Benoit Champagnat, founder, born Marlhes, 20 May 1789, died La Valla, 6 June 1840. He came from a devout family, and entered the minor seminary at Verrieres and then the major seminary at Lyon, joining the seminary in Lyon at the same time as **John-Baptist Mary Vianney**, the future curé d'Ars. A group of friends in the seminary determined to devote themselves to establishing a religious institute devoted to Mary, and it fell to Champagnat to create the order of brothers. After ordination he was appointed to the parish of La Valla. In 1817 he brought together the first two members of what was to become the Little Brothers of Mary, the Marist Brothers. In 1836 the Marist Brothers were entrusted with the mission to Oceania. He himself became a member of the Society of Mary (for priests) in 1836. He believed that the priests, brothers, nuns and laity should be integrated into one society, but this did not happen, and the enterprise of creating the Marist group of congregations was fraught with problems, which perhaps contributed to Champagnat's relatively early death.

Marcellina, born Trier, c. 330, died Rome, c. 400. She was the elder sister of St **Ambrose**, and often advised him on spiritual matters. She gave herself to the service of God in 353, and lived a life of fasting and penance in a private house in Rome. Feast 17 July.

Marcellinus, see also **Argeus**.

Marcellinus, pope, born Rome (?), elected 30 June 296, died Rome, 25 October 304. Nothing is known of him before his election, but during the persecution of Diocletian he apparently complied with orders to hand over sacred texts and to offer incense to pagan gods, as did some of his presbyters who all later became popes. This apostasy was cited by the Donatists as evidence of his moral

failure, and was clearly an embarrassment to later churchmen. According to some traditions, he was filled with remorse for his failing, and days later sought execution at the hands of the authorities. He was buried in the cemetery of Priscilla on the via Salaria. There is in fact no evidence that he was martyred, although he came to be venerated as a saint. His death left the Church of Rome without a leader for more than three years. Feast 26 April.

Marcellinus Akimetes, see **Marcellus Akimetes**.

Marcellinus and Peter, Roman martyrs, died 304. Marcellinus was a priest, Peter an exorcist. Evidence of their cult is early and strong: feasts in sacramentaries and calendars, survival of tombs, verses by **Damasus**. They were buried in the catacomb of Tiburtius, via Lavicana, over which a church was later built. They are also mentioned in the Roman Canon. In 827 Pope Gregory IV sent their relics to Einhard, former secretary and biographer of **Charlemagne**, to enrich his monastery at Seligenstadt. Records of miracles are extant. Feast 2 June.

Marcellinus Flavius, fifth-century Roman tribune, notary, and a friend of St **Augustine** of Hippo, died Carthage, north Africa, c. 413. In 411 during a conference between Catholics and Donatists in Carthage he became acquainted with St Augustine when Marcellinus upheld the Catholic cause. The Donatists accused him and his brother of implication in a revolt at Heraclian, and both were condemned and executed. Whilst in prison Augustine visited Marcellinus, praised him in several of his letters, and dedicated to him his most famous work, *De civitate Dei*. Marcellinus was subsequently exonerated by the Emperor Honorius, and his name was added to the Roman Martyrology by Cardinal Baronius in the sixteenth century. Feast 13 September.

Marcellinus of Ancona, bishop, born Ancona, died c. 566. He became bishop of his native city. Feast 9 January.

Marcellinus of Embrun, bishop, from Africa, died France, 13 April 374. A priest, he evangelized in what is now the Dauphiné with Vincent and Domninus (also venerated), working from

Embrun in the Hautes Alpes. Bishop of Vercelli, he had to hide in the mountains from Arian persecution. Feast 20 April.

Marcellus, see also **Sabinus and Companions**.

Marcellus I, pope, born Rome, elected bishop of Rome, March 308, only after a difficult succession procedure, died in exile, January 309. While he was pope he reorganized the city's parishes. With regard to the readmission of the *lapsi* (those who disavowed their faith during Diocletian's persecution), he took a firm stance that ultimately led to his removal and exile, probably on the orders of the Emperor Maxentius. Feast 16 January.

Marcellus and Maura, martyrs, born Moscow, died Kola peninsula, eighteenth century. Church of the Old Believers. Marcellus was a soldier, and gaoler of **Theodosia** Morozova, who was an Old Believer. So impressed was he by Theodosia that Marcellus became one too, and was imprisoned, then exiled to the Kola peninsula. He embraced the eremitical life and retired to live alone, eventually dying in exile. Maura, however, was burned to death. Feast 16 October.

Marcellus Akimetes, abbot, known as Marcellus the Righteous, born Apamea, Syria, died near Constantinople, *c.* 485. He became abbot of a monastery near Constantinople. The community were known as *Akoimentoi*, 'sleepless' monks, hence the name. In daily shifts they sang God's praises continuously. Marcellus attended the Council of Chalcedon in 451. Feast 29 December.

Marcellus and Companions, martyrs, died Tomi, on the Black Sea, fourth century. Marcellus (or Marcellinus) is said to have been a tribune, and his companions included Mannea, his wife, two of their children, John and Bybla, Serapion the Christian priest, and Peter, a soldier. An alternative version, giving somewhat similar names, has them as executed at Oxyrynchus in Egypt. Feast 27 August.

Marcellus of Apamea, bishop, born Cyprus, died Apamea, Syria, 389. He was governor in Cyprus, but after the death of his wife was appointed bishop of Apamea, where he was killed by pagans while trying to destroy idols in a temple. Feast 14 August.

Marcellus of Chalon-sur-Saône, legendary figure who is supposed to have been martyred in 175 during the reign of the Emperor Marcus Aurelius (121–80). A cult and a church in his honour are mentioned by St **Gregory of Tours**. Feast 4 September.

Marcellus of Die, bishop, born Avignon, died Bareuil, Provence, 474. He was consecrated bishop of Die by Maurertus, bishop of Vienne, who was in conflict with the metropolitan city of Arles. Marcellus was temporarily imprisoned and exiled by the Arian king of the Burgundians, but eventually returned to his see where he became distinguished by his piety and zeal as a pastor. His cult at Die was confirmed for the diocese of Valence by Pope Pius IX. Feast 9 April.

Marcellus of Nicomedia, martyr, died Nicomedia, 349. A priest of the city, he was killed by Arians, being thrown over a cliff. Feast 26 November.

Marcellus Spinola y Maestre, bl., archbishop, born Isle of San Fernando, Cadiz, Spain, 14 January 1835, died Seville, 19 January 1906, beatified 1987. He focused on social welfare, creating orphanages and workers' organizations, visiting hospitals and prisons and opening his residence to the poor. Archbishop of Seville from 1896, in 1902 he founded the Congregation of the Handmaids of Mary Immaculate and the Sacred Heart.

Marcellus the Centurion, martyr, born Rome. His *Acts* place his death in Leon, Spain, and, more convincingly, in Tangier, 298. During the celebrations of the birthday of the emperors Diocletian and Maximian, Marcellus publicly declared himself a Christian. A centurion, first class, he renounced his military oath, judging it to be incompatible with the practice of the Christian religion. He was arrested and condemned to death by the sword. Feast 30 October.

Marchelm, born England, died Oldenzaal, *c.* 760. He was a missionary to the Frisians, working with St **Willibrord**. He worked in Friesland and

Guelderland for about 15 years, and was then sent to Overyssel with St **Lebuinas**. Feast 14 July.

Marcian, martyr, said to have died Tortona, Piedmont, *c.* 120. He is supposed to have been a disciple of **Barnabas** and to have been bishop of Tortona for 45 years. Feast 6 March.

Marcian, emperor, born Thrace (?), 396, died Constantinople, 26 January 457. Byzantine Church. He married **Pulcheria**, sister of the emperor, and succeeded as emperor in 450, being the first to be crowned by the patriarch. Financial reforms made his reign one of considerable prosperity. Theologically, his reign is marked by his successful repression of monophysitism, Marcian himself attending the sixth session of the Council of Chalcedon (451). But he had to resort to arms to enforce its theological decrees. He enjoyed good relations with Pope **Leo**, correspondence with whom survives. Feast 16 February.

Marcian and Martyrius, priests (?), died Constantinople, *c.* 338. Imprisoned, and eventually put to death, by the Emperor Constantius for opposing Arianism. Feast 25 October.

Marcian José Lopez y Lopez, born El Pedregal, Guadalajara, 15 November 1900, died Turon, Asturias, 9 October 1934. Baptized Filomeno, he joined the de la Salle Brothers on 20 September 1916. He was hard of hearing and had other health problems, and did not teach in the school. He was arrested with the other **Martyrs of Asturias** by a group of rebel soldiers, and executed by firing squad.

Marcian, Nicander, Apollonius and Companions, martyrs, died Egypt, *c.* 304.

Marcian of Constantinople, priest, born Rome, died Constantinople, 471 (?). Born of a noble family, he was ordained *c.* 455 and became treasurer of the church of Hagia Sophia. He gave away much of his inheritance. Because of his ascetical way of life he was suspected of heresy, and for a time was persecuted. Feast 10 January.

Marcian of Cyrrhus, monk and ascetic, born Cyrrhus, Syria, *c.* 300, died desert of Chalcis, north

Syria, *c.* 381–91. Son of a patrician family, he chose instead the lifestyle of a hermit in fasting and prayer. Two of his disciples, Eusebias and Agapetus, encouraged others to follow the ascetic way of life, but Marcian, out of humility, refused either to become their abbot or to be ordained as a priest. He ordered that on his death his body be concealed, and his burial place was only discovered 50 years later. Feast 2 November.

Marcian of Iconium, martyr, died Iconium, Asia Minor, 241. Feast 11 July.

Marciana, empress. Byzantine Church. Not identifiable, but her feast occurs 27 January.

Marcionilla, killed with her small son **Celsus**, see **Julian**.

Marcolinus of Forli (Marcolino Ammani), bl., monk, born Forli, 1317, died 2 January 1397, cult confirmed 1750. A Dominican from an early age, always an exemplar of religious life, after his death he was considered a saint by his fellow monks.

Marculf, abbot, born Bayeux, died on one of the Channel Islands, *c.* 610. Ordained aged 30, he evangelized the countryside, then built a monastery for his followers by the sea at Nanteuil, now St-Marcouf. Entreated for skin diseases, he is associated with the healing of the 'King's Evil' claimed by French kings. Feast 1 May.

Mardarius the Recluse, monk, died Kiev, thirteenth century. Russian Church. A monk of the Kievan Cave monastery, although apparently living apart from the other monks. Feast 13 December.

Mardonius, Musonius, Eugenius and Metellus, martyrs, died Neocaesarea. Burned to death. Feast 24 January.

Mareas, bishop and martyr, died Persia, 342. Bishop of Bayt-Lapat, he was put to death with a large number of priests, bishops and lay people by Shah Shapur II. They were being sympathetic to the Roman Empire. Feast 22 August.

Margaret Clitherow, martyr, born York, 1556, died there, 25 March 1586. She was the daughter of a sheriff of York who converted to Roman Catholicism in 1574. She was charged at York Assizes in 1586 with sheltering Roman Catholic priests, but refused to answer charges in order to protect her children from having to testify against her. She died by being crushed to death. Her canonization took place in 1970 and she was included as one of the **Forty Martyrs** canonized by Paul VI.

Margaret Colonna, bl., born Rome, died Palestrina, 20 September 1284. The daughter of Prince Odo Colonna, she was expected to marry into the Roman aristocracy. Instead she left Rome for Palestrina, and there established a convent of Poor Clares. She wished to become one of them herself, but ill-health prevented it. She nonetheless led a holy life, and became famous for miracles. Feast 7 November.

Margaret d'Youville, founder, born Varennes, Quebec, 15 October 1701, died Quebec, 23 December 1771. Her full name was Marguérite Dufrost Lajemmerais. In 1721 she married François You de la Découverte, or François Youville, a fur trader, although engaged also in illicit trade with the native Americans. He died after they had been married eight years, leaving her with considerable debts, which she paid off by opening a store, and with two small sons, both of whom eventually became priests. In 1737 she established a community in a poor area of Montreal to care for the poor – something which was not at first welcomed by the people of the neighbourhood. Members of the community wore grey dresses, and became known as 'the grey nuns'. In 1747 they took over the running of the hospital in Quebec, and found themselves nursing both French and English soldiers wounded in the struggle to control Canada. See also **Mary Marguerite d'Youville**.

Margaret Faventina, bl., abbess, died Florence, c. 1330. The abbess of the Vallombrosan monastery in Florence. Feast 26 August.

Margaret Mary Alacoque, Visitandine nun, born Lauthecourt, France, 22 July 1647, died Paray le Monial, 17 October 1690. She had an unhappy childhood marked by ill-health. In 1671 she entered a convent at Paray le Monial. Between 1673 and 1675 she received a number of visions telling her to spread devotion to the Sacred Heart, and to establish a feast in its honour. These were treated as delusions by her superiors, but opposition declined with the support of her confessor **Claude de la Colombière** SJ. She was beatified in 1864 and canonized in 1920. Feast 16 October.

Margaret Mary Hallahan, ven., foundress of the English congregation of St Catherine of Siena of the Third order of St Dominic, born London, 23 January 1803, died Stone, Staffordshire, 11 May 1868. She came from a very poor Irish family and had only two years of elementary education at an orphanage at Somers Town in London. She then began 30 years of service as a maid and nurse. She lived in Bruges, Belgium, and became a Dominican tertiary in 1837. In 1842 she returned to England, and in 1844 founded a small community of Third Order Dominicans in Coventry. Bishop Ullathorne, then vicar apostolic but afterwards bishop of Birmingham, gave encouragement. Other foundations were made, but in 1853 the whole community there was transferred to St Dominic's at Stone, which became the mother house of the congregation. Mother Hallahan's devoted Christian life and indefatigable energy as well as excellent administrative skills led her to set up five convents, several schools and orphanages, four churches and a hospital for incurables. Her cause for beatification was introduced in 1936.

Margaret of Antioch (Marina), martyr, born Antioch, Pisidia, died there, c. 303. Patron saint of women in labour. She has been honoured in the Eastern Church since the seventh century, but not as a devotion in the West until the twelfth century. She is often depicted with a dragon (symbolic of evil). Feast 20 July (suppressed 1969).

Margaret of Cortona, penitent, born Laviano, Tuscany, 1247, died Cortona, 22 February 1297. After the murder of her seducer by whom she had a son, Margaret underwent a conversion, went to Cortona to put herself under the guidance of Franciscans there, and led a life of public penance for 29 years, becoming a Franciscan tertiary. To support herself and her son she nursed elderly women in Cortona, but she gave that up to look after the sick poor in her own house, and later in the community she founded in Cortona, with the approval of the bishop. She early became the recipient of mystical experiences, and appeared to have had the gift of healing. Her holiness was recognized long before her death, and she was proclaimed a saint by the people as soon as she had died. Her incorrupt body remains in Cortona.

Margaret of Hungary, born 1242, died 18 January 1271. The daughter of Bela I of Hungary, she entered the Dominican convent in Veszprém when only four years old, in fulfilment of a vow made by her parents. Her parents later founded a convent on Hasen Insel, near Buda, where she went in 1252, and where she spent the rest of her life, taking her solemn vows when 18 and fighting off her father's wish to marry her to the king of Bohemia. The fame of her holiness and her penitential practices was widespread even during her lifetime. There were frequent attempts to have her canonized, and Pius VII permitted her to be venerated as a saint.

Margaret of Lorraine, bl., born Vaudemont, Lorraine, France, 1463, died Argentan, 2 November 1521. In 1488 she married René, duke of Alençon, but was widowed with three young children by 1492. During her son's minority she ruled the duchy and, coming under the influence of **Francis of Padua**, she adopted an ascetic lifestyle and, when finally free from family responsibilities, joined the Third Order of St Francis of Assisi and withdrew from the court. In 1513 she founded a convent at Argentan where the Rule of St Clare was observed. Later she refused the office of abbess for herself. She was buried at Argentan, where her reportedly incorrupt body was venerated until it was profaned by the Jacobins in 1793.

Margaret of Metola, bl., born Metola, Italy, 1287, died Città di Castello, 13 April 1320. She was of noble birth but suffered from severe disabilities of blindness, dwarfism and a hunchback, and she was kept hidden by her parents from the age of 6 to 16, when they abandoned her. She became a Dominican tertiary and, despite her multiple handicaps, devoted herself to the sick, the dying, and to prisoners in the city's jail. Many miracles were attributed to her after her death, and she was beatified in 1609.

Margaret of Ravenna, bl., born Russi, near Ravenna, 1442, died there, 1505. She presented as blind, but was probably partially sighted as she was accused of hypocrisy. Helped by a priest, she formed a religious association for lay people, which did not survive her. Feast 23 January.

Margaret of Roskilde, born Denmark, died Ølse, near Køgc, Denmark, 25 October 1176. A relative of the archbishop of Lund, Margaret was strangled by her husband, who then attempted to make her death look like a suicide. When they tried to buried her on unhallowed ground, a mysterious light was said to have shone around, causing people to believe in her sanctity. After an investigation, her husband confessed to his crime, and she became the object of local veneration.

Margaret of Savoy, founder, born Pinerolo, Italy, 1382, died Alba, Liguria, 23 November 1464. Her father was Count Amadeus of Savoy, her mother the sister of (the antipope) Clement VII. She married the marquis of Montferrat, but after his death refused other suitors, became a Dominican tertiary and established a community at Alba which, according to some accounts, she ruled with excessive strictness. She was even accused of being a heretic. She had a reputation for performing miracles, and for receiving visions.

Margaret of Scotland, queen of Scotland, born Hungary, c. 1045, died Edinburgh Castle, 16 November 1093. Her father was the son of Edmund Ironside, her mother a Hungarian princess, and she grew up in the fervently Christian Hungarian court until summoned to England in 1057 by **Edward the Confessor**. After his death and the Norman Conquest the family took refuge in Dunfermline, Scotland, with King Malcolm III, whom she married c. 1069. She corresponded with Archbishop Lanfranc of Canterbury, and is said to have summoned a council for the reform of the practices of the Church in Scotland, the decisions being known as the Five Articles of Margaret. Her support of the Church included the provision of the Queen's Ferry for pilgrims to St Andrews, and monastic endowments. Her children maintained her strong Christian commitment. She was canonized in 1249.

Margaret of the Blessed Sacrament (Margarite Parigot), ven., Discalced Carmelite nun, and promoter of devotion to the Divine Infancy, born Beaune, France, 1619, died there, 26 May 1648. She is reported to have received her first holy communion at the age of 11, entered the Discalced Carmelite convent in 1631, and was professed with the name of Margaret of the Blessed Sacrament in 1634. Her spiritual progress was directed by the Oratorians Fathers Parisot (1637–43) and Blaise Chaduc (1643–8). She was the principal apostle of devotion to the Infancy of Jesus, a cult which spread throughout France. The cause for her beatification was introduced in 1905. Although she put nothing in writing, her spiritual experience and confidences were gathered by her prioress and published, and were the sources of biographies and translations into the principal European languages.

Margaret Pole, bl., born Farleigh Castle, Somerset, England, 14 August 1473, executed Tower of London, 28 May 1541. From the Plantaganet royal family, she married Richard Pole in 1491 and had five children – one of whom, Reginald, became a cardinal. Richard died in 1505. Henry VIII admired her and appointed her in 1513 as countess of Salisbury in her own right, and later governess of Princess Mary. When Margaret opposed Henry's divorce, he imprisoned her and had her beheaded without a trial – also thereby eliminating a possible centre of resistance and contender for the throne.

Margaret Ward, martyr, born Congleton, Cheshire, died Tyburn, London, 30 August 1588. She was in service with the Whittles, a London Catholic family, when she was arrested for helping a secular priest, William Watson, to escape from Bridewell prison. She smuggled a rope into his cell which, left dangling from a cornice of the roof after his escape, was traced to Margaret. **Robert Southwell** described her torture to the Jesuit general Claudius Acquaviva: 'she was flogged and hung up by the wrists, the tips of her toes just touching the ground so that she was crippled and paralysed'. She refused to reveal Watson's whereabouts, nor would she accept freedom if she attended a Protestant service. She was canonized in 1970.

Margarito Flores, martyr, born Mexico, 1899, died Tuliman, 12 November 1927. He studied at the seminary of Chilapa, then taught there. He moved to Mexico City and taught in a school during the persecution of the Church, but was arrested. On his release he returned to the seminary, and then to a parish. He was arrested on his way to take up his post, and shot. Feast 25 May.

Marha Iyasus, monk, born Goggiam. Ethiopian Church.

Marha Krestos, abbot, born Enaraqan, 6 August 1408, died 19 January 1497. Ethiopian Church. He was ordained while still very young, and then joined the monastery of Dabra Libanos. He became abbot in 1463, after his predecessor had been exiled, unjustly accused of plotting against the king. In the council of 1477 he opposed the plan, backed by the majority of Ethiopian bishops, to seek a metropolitan from among themselves rather than leaving it to the patriarch of Alexandria. It was his view which eventually won the day.

Mari, bishop, died Seleucia-Ctesiphon, c. 150 (?). Said to have been a disciple of **Addai**, and sent by him to Nisibis (Nusaybin, south-eastern Turkey), whence he travelled in Mesopotamia converting thousands. Both Chaldeans and Nestorians regard him as the founding apostle of their Church. Feast 5 August.

Maris, hermit, Syria, fifth century. Feast 19 February.

Maria, see also **Mary**.

Maria Clorinda Andreoni (Vittoria in religion), born San Casciano in Val di Pesa, Florence, Italy, 13 June 1836, martyred Tianjin, Hebei, China, 20 June 1870. A Daughter of Charity of St Vincent de Paul – see **Martyrs of China**.

Maria Cristina of Savoy, ven., queen, born Caligari, Sardinia, 14 November 1812, died Naples, 31 January 1836. She was the youngest child of King Victor Emmanuel 1 (1759–1824), king of Sardinia. Her desire to enter religious life was not granted and she was married to Ferdinand I, king of Naples. Fulfilling her state obligations, nevertheless she maintained her charitable and pious practice and exercised an exemplary influence on the court and on those around her. Stories about her ill-treatment by her husband may be unfounded, but she died giving birth to her only child, who became Francis II, the last Bourbon king of Naples. Her cause was introduced in 1889, and her heroic virtues approved in 1937.

Maria Crocissa Di Rosa, foundress of the Handmaids of Charity, born Brescia, Italy, 6 November 1813, died there, 15 December 1855. After her mother's death in 1824, Paolina Francesca Maria (her name at baptism) was entrusted for her education to the Visitandines (1824–30). Then she took charge of her father's household and developed a talent for organization and supervision. During a devastating cholera epidemic (1836) Paola and her companion Bagriella Bornati won wide admiration by caring for the sick. The foundation in 1840 of her religious congregation was popularly called at first the Hospitable Adorers. Maria Crocifissa went to Rome in 1850 and obtained approval of her institute's Rule. Basic to her spirituality was the imitation of Christ's sorrowful life; this led her to infused contemplation and inspired her with the idea of aiding the sick and the poor, the sorrowful members of Christ's Church. The chapel in the mother house at Brescia is her burial place. She was beatified on 26 May 1940, and canonized on 12 June 1954.

Maria de la Cabeza, born Madrid, died there (?), twelfth century. Said to have been the wife (he was known to have one) of **Isidore the Farmer**, but nothing is known of her. The name refers to the fact that the claimed relic is of a skull. Feast 9 September.

Maria de Matthias, bl., Italian foundress, born Vallecorsa, Frosinone, 4 February 1805, died Rome, 20 August 1866. Inspired at an early age to dedicate her life to prayer and good works, Maria founded the Congregation of Sisters Adorers of the Most Precious Blood, dedicated to the education of youth, and opened a school at the request of the bishop of Anagni (1834). She established some 60 houses in Italy. Feast 1 October.

Maria Domenica Mazzarello, foundress, born Marnese, Piedmont, 9 May 1837, died Nizza

Monferrato, 14 May 1881. A dressmaker and a member of a local sodality, Maria taught her trade to local girls, and so impressed **John Bosco** during a visit to the village in 1865 that he placed her in charge of a school for girls established by herself. She founded, with ten companions, the Daughters of Our Lady Help of Christians (Salesian Sisters) for the education of poor girls, under a Rule written by John Bosco. The Congregation gradually spread to France and Argentina, and had 250 members at her death.

Maria Francesca Gallo (of the Five Wounds), Franciscan religious and mystic, born Naples, Italy, 25 March 1715, died Naples, 8 October 1791. Baptized as Anna Maria Rosa Nicoletta, Gallo was deeply pious from childhood and became a Franciscan tertiary in 1731, devoting herself to works of charity. She is said to have had the gift of prophecy, and among numerous mystical experiences is reputed to have manifested the stigmata. During her lifetime she suffered much misunderstanding, as well as poor health and intense spiritual conflicts. She was canonized in 1867.

Maria Gabriella Sagheddu, bl., born Dorgali, Sardinia, 17 March 1914, died near Rome, 23 April 1939, beatified 1983. In 1935 she became a Trappist nun at Grottaferrata abbey near Rome. She believed her special mission was to pray for Christian unity, this at a time when ecumenism had little support.

María Miguela of the Blessed Sacrament Desmaisières, foundress of the Handmaids of the Blessed Sacrament and of Charity, Sisters Adorers, born Madrid, 1 January 1865. María de la Soledad Miguela Desmaisières Lopez de Dicastillo, viscountess of Jorbalén, early displayed zeal for the ascetical life and for charitable works. During a cholera epidemic in Madrid in 1834 she attended the plague-stricken and set up home assistance boards to aid them. In 1845 she established a home for 'fallen' or endangered young women. To perpetuate this work she founded her religious congregation in 1859, and acted as superior general until her death. Papal approval came in 1866. Men who had preyed on these women caused the foundress to be slandered, but by 1865 the institute numbered seven houses. The order has since grown in Europe, Latin America and Japan. María died after contracting cholera while attending to her own religious during an epidemic. She was beatified on 7 June 1925, and canonized on 4 March 1934, by Pope Pius XI. Feast 25 August.

Maria of Radonez, see **Cyril and Maria of Radonez**.

Maria Phon, martyr, born Sonkong, 1926, died there, 26 December 1940. She was a helper on the mission station. She and several others (see **Martyrs of Thailand**) were marched to the cemetery and shot. Feast 16 December.

Maria Silesia Chappuis, ven., Visitation nun, born Souhières, France (now Switzerland), 16 June 1793, died Troyes, 7 October 1875. She entered the Visitation Order in 1814, became superior and novice mistress at Troyes in 1826–37 and at Paris 1838–44, and collaborated with Louis Bresson in founding the Oblate Sisters of St Francis de Sales in 1866 and the Oblates of St Francis de Sales c. 1871. Her cause for beatification was introduced in 1897.

Maria Teresa Goretti, martyr, born Corinaldo, Italy, 16 October 1890, died 6 July 1902. A peasant girl, responsible for the care of her family, following the death of her father. On 5 July 1902 she was mortally wounded by Alessandro Serenelli, a young man who stabbed her with a stiletto while attempting to rape her. She died the next day after forgiving him. Canonized in the presence of her killer in 1950.

Maria Theresia Haze, ven., founder of the Daughters of the Holy Cross of Liège, born Liège, Belgium, 27 February 1782, died there, 7 January 1876. As a child, she went through difficult times, her parents' property being confiscated and the family persecuted during the French Revolution. With Canon Jean Habets (died 1876) she founded her religious order in 1833. The Sisters' work covered a wide area of social, as well as spiritual, activities – teaching in schools, nursing the sick, taking care of needy women, especially of women in jail. Her congregation spread to England, Germany and India during her lifetime. Her cause for beatification was introduced in 1910.

Mariam, queen, eleventh century. Georgian Church. She married George I of Georgia, but he died in 1019 soon after the birth of their child, and Mariam was regent during her son's infancy. She was a notable benefactor of the Georgian monastery of Iviron on Mount Athos, and of the church of the Holy Cross at Jerusalem.

Mariana Giuliani (Mary of Peace), born L'Aquila, Italy, 12 December 1875, martyred Taiyuan, Shanxi, China, 9 July 1900, beatified 1946, canonized 2000. She was assistant to **Mary Emiliana Grivot** and a member of the group killed with **Gregory Grassi** – see **Franciscan Martyrs of China** and **Martyrs of Shanxi**. Feast 8 July.

Marianus (Marian), martyr, died Lambesa, Numidia (now Tazoult, Algeria), 6 May 259. Marian, a reader, and **James**, a deacon, both from Numidia, were tortured on the rack and put in prison, where they experienced visions. They were killed with swords, and their bodies thrown into the river Rummel. Feast 6 May.

Marianus Scotus, bl. (Muiredach Mac Robhartaigh, or Murdoch McRoberts), died c. 1080. One of many Irish wandering monks or *peregrini*, he and his companions reached southern Germany on their way to Rome. They settled in Regensburg, where he worked at copying sacred texts and composed works of his own. Feast 9 February.

Marie, see **Mary**.

Marina, see **Margaret of Antioch**.

Marinus and Asterius, martyrs, died Caesarea, Palestine, 262. Marinus was a centurion who became a Christian, was denounced and executed. Asterius was the Christian who buried his body, but it is not clear that he, too, was a martyr. Feast 3 March.

Marinus and Leo, details of the lives of both are based largely on legends which grew up centuries later. According to the legends, Marinus and Leo were Dalmatian Christians who were condemned to work on repairing the walls of Rimini during the persecution of the Emperor Diocletian, c. 304. During this time they showed concern for their fellow prisoners and converted some to Christianity. Separately they retired as hermits, Marinus to Mount Titano, and Leo to Montefeltro. Marinus was made a deacon, and Leo may have been ordained as priest in 359 by Bishop Gauentius. The site of Marinus's hermitage is reputed to have become a foundation of a monastery and the tiny republic of San Marino.

Marinus of Anazarbus, according to his (legendary) *Passio*, he was an old man living in Anazarbus (Cilicia). During Diocletian's persecution, probably in 285, he was accused of being a Christian. Brought to Tarsus before the governor of the province, he refused, even after torture, to renounce his faith. He was decapitated and his body thrown for the dogs and other wild beasts. Two of the Christians who were in the neighbourhood took advantage of a thunderstorm and succeeded in seizing the relics, which they hid in a cavern and later returned to Anazarbus. Feast 8 August.

Marinus of Dalmatia, born Albe, Dalmatia, died in what is now San Marino, fifth century. Said to have been a stonemason brought from Dalmatia to work on Monte Titano (modern San Marino), where he was a great evangelist. When falsely accused of being someone's husband, he retired to a hermitage. Feast 4 September.

Marinus of Jur'ev, bishop, eleventh century. Russian Church.

Marinus of Rome, martyr, born Rome, died there, 283. Said to have been the son of a senator of the city. Feast 26 December.

Marinus of Tersoos, martyr, *c.* 303. Feast 8 August.

Maris, an alternative form of Marius: see **Marius, Martha, Audifax and Abachum**.

Marius, Martha, Audifax and Abachum, martyrs, born Persia, died Rome, 270. They came from Persia to bury the Roman martyrs, but were themselves martyred by beheading or, in the case of Martha, by drowning. The story is very unlikely. Feast 19 June (suppressed 1969).

Marius of Avenches, chronicler and bishop, born Autun, 530 or 531, died Lausanne, 31 December 594. As Bishop of Avenches from 574 until his death, he transferred his episcopal see from Avenches to Lausanne. He compiled a *Chronicle* of the years 455–581, continuing the work of Prosper of Aquitaine, recording contemporary events in Italy and the Orient as well as matters in Burgundy. Marius is described as thoroughly Roman in culture and convinced himself of the permanent survival of the Roman Empire, despite surrounding barbarism. He was buried in Lausanne, and his cult was approved in 1605.

Mark, monk, born Walqayt. Ethiopian Church.

Mark, martyr. Church of the Old Believers. See **Alexander Guttoeva**.

Mark I, pope, born Rome, elected 18 January 336, died 7 October 336. Little or nothing is known of Mark, beyond the fact that he was the son of Priscus, and a Roman. It may have been Mark who laid down that the bishop of Rome should always be consecrated by the bishop of Ostia.

Mark and Mucian, martyrs. Died by beheading, date and place unknown. Onlookers, inspired by their example, declared themselves Christians and were executed with them, one being a small boy. Feast 4 October.

Mark and Stephen, martyrs, died Antioch, Pisidia, 305 (?). Feast 22 November.

Mark Barkworth, bl. (also called Lambert), born near Searby, Lincolnshire, 1572, martyred London, February 1601, beatified 1929. Ordained in Spain in 1599, he was hanged, drawn and quartered with **Roger Filcock**. He had become a Benedictine in Spain and is venerated as the first English Benedictine martyr. Feast 27 February.

Mark Chong Lu-bai, martyr, born Korea, 1794, died there, 11 March 1866, beatified 1968, canonized 1984. He was a teacher, then, becoming a Catholic fairly late in life, he was a catechist. He was tortured and beheaded with **Alexius Ou Syei-Yeng** during a time of persecution – see also **Martyrs of Korea**.

Mark Criado, bl., born Andújar, southern Spain, 25 April 1522, died near La Peza, in the Alpujarras, 25 September 1568. He joined the Trinitarian Order when only 14 years old, and after his studies was sent to preach in various places around Granada where the influence of Islam was still strong. He was killed by stoning during a Muslim uprising.

Mark dei Marconi, died Mantua, 1510. He was a Hieronymite friar. Feast 24 February.

Mark Fantuzzi, bl., born Bologna, Italy, 1405, died Piacenza, 1479, cult approved 1868. He became a priest in the strict Observant Franciscans, was a successful preacher in all Italy and travelled throughout Europe and Palestine as vicar general. He successfully opposed the pope's plan to merge all Franciscan branches. Feast 10 April.

Mark, John and Theophilus, monks, died Kiev, twelfth/thirteenth centuries. Russian Church. Mark's task in the monastery was to excavate graves for the deceased monks. Among the monks were the close friends John and Theophilus who wished to be buried in the same grave. Feast 29 December.

Mark Körösi, born Crisium, Croatia, 1589, died Kosice, 7 September 1619. Of a noble family, he was educated by the Jesuits, but became a diocesan priest. He studied in Rome, and on his return was appointed to the diocese of Esztergom in 1615. By 1619 he was working in Kosice, in what is now Slovakia. When a Protestant prince marched on Kosice, he was arrested along with the Jesuits **Stephen Pongracz** and **Melchior Grodecz**, and was executed.

Mark, Marcian and Companions, martyrs, died Egypt, 304 (?). Mark and Marcian are said to have been brothers. Feast 4 October.

Mark of Alexandria II, patriarch, died Nabaruwah, 17 April 819. Coptic Church. He was ordained deacon by the patriarch John Vi, who took him into his service, although for a time he became a monk and fled to the desert, but was called back. He was afraid he would be chosen as patriarch at the death of John, and again fled, only to be brought back and consecrated bishop in 799. As patriarch he was a great upholder of the monophysite faith, and he also had a reputation as a miracle worker. In conflicts over the succession in Baghdad, Egypt collapsed into anarchy, and Mark had to flee to a city in the Delta, where he died.

Mark of Alexandria III, patriarch, born Syria, died Alexandria, 1 January 1189. Coptic Church. A layman called Abu al-Faragi Ibn Abui As'ad when elected in 1167, and living in Old Cairo, he had a troubled patriarchate. Under Saladin there were discriminatory laws against Christians, and some churches and monasteries were destroyed. There was also a breakaway group in the Church, led by a blind monk, who joined the Melchites.

Mark of Athens, born Athens, died Mount Tarmaq, Egyptian desert, fourth century. Byzantine Church. He went to live (for, it is recorded, 90 years) as a hermit on Mount Tarmaq, and was famous for the strictness of his asceticism and his knowledge of the Scriptures. Feast 5 March.

Mark of Arethusa, bishop and confessor, born between 250 and 270, died Arethusa, Mount Lebanon, 28 March 389. He is thought to have been active in the dispute over Arianism and may have joined the semi-Arians, attending their synods, but he died in the Orthodox faith. He was responsible for the destruction of pagan temples, building churches on their sites. Unhappily, the reign of the Emperor Julian the Apostate left Mark to the mercy of his fellow townsmen, who exacted their revenge with the most vicious tortures. He survived, even winning the admiration of his tormentors, and eventually was pardoned by the emperor. His cult was approved by Pope Clement VIII in 1598. Feast 29 March.

Mark of Belavin, founder, seventeenth century. Russian Church. Originally a monk of the monastery of St Elias, he moved to a spot near lake Belavin c. 1630, and established a monastery there. Feast 8 November.

Mark of Chios, martyr, born Thessalonika, died Chios, 5 June 1801. Byzantine Church. His mother was from Smyrna, which is where he lived, and where he married in 1788. A few years later he travelled to New Ephesus, where he was arrested for adultery, but escaped with his life only after converting to Islam. He immediately repented, and fled. He then travelled to Venice, but could not find peace, and decided to seek martyrdom. He therefore returned to New Ephesus, but his spiritual director told him that his desire for martyrdom would only bring trouble to the local Christian community. He travelled to Chios, went before a judge to confess his faith in Christ and, after attempts to persuade him to deny Christianity had failed, was beheaded.

Mark of Crete, martyr, born Crete, died Smyrna, 14 May 1643. Byzantine Church. Although born in Crete, he lived in Smyrna. He was captured by pirates when quite young, and forced to become a Muslim. Later in life he travelled to Constantinople, and there he returned to Christianity. He returned to Smyrna, declared his faith in Christ, and was beheaded.

Mark (Eugenikos) of Ephesus, metropolitan, born Constantinople, 1391, died there, 23 June 1444. Of noble birth, and baptized Manuel, he took the name Mark when he became a monk in 1418. He became well known as a theologian, and was approached by the Emperor John VIII Paleologus who was seeking reunion with Rome. He was subsequently elected metropolitan of Ephesus in 1437, and was appointed a member of the commission to discuss the theological issues which were to be debated at the forthcoming Council of Ferrara-Florence. He attended the council, but was an adversary of union, and, alone among the Eastern bishops, refused to sign the accord between the two Churches. The emperor returned with Mark to Constantinople, where the metropolitan was enthusiastically welcomed by the people for his stand against union with Rome on the terms agreed. To persuade him to change his mind, the emperor then offered him the patriarchal see of Constantinople, but he refused it, and returned to Ephesus. Such was the pressure on him there, however, that he decided to go to Mount Athos. The ship taking him there put into Limnos, where on the orders of the emperor he was arrested. He was in prison for two years, but from the island where he was held wrote his 'Encyclical to all the Orthodox' which put the anti-union case. When he was freed he went to Constantinople,

where he led the anti-union movement. He wrote a number of theological works, some of which treat specifically with matters where Orthodoxy is in disagreement with Western Christianity. Feast 19 January.

Mark of Jerusalem, bishop, died 156. First non-Jewish bishop of Jerusalem. He served for 20 years before being martyred. Feast 22 October.

Mark of Modena, bl., born Mocogno, near Modena, died Pesaro, 21 September 1498. A member of the Scalabrini family, he joined the Dominican Order. He served as prior of the Dominican house in Pesar for many years, and was renowned for miracles.

Mark of Montegallo, bl., born Montegallo, 1425, died Vicenza, 19 March 1496. A doctor, he and his wife decided together in 1452 to become Franciscans. He was an eloquent preacher and developed pawnshops for the poor, making loans at minimal rates, raising the start-up capital through his preaching.

Mark of Pskov, monk, born Kiev (?), died Pskov, fourteenth century. Russian Church. He is presumed to have been a monk of the Kievan Cave monastery, who came to Pskov and established himself in a forest nearby, where the cave monastery was later established by **Jonah and Vassa**. Feast 29 March.

Mark of Sarov, monk, born Kursk, 1733, died Sarov, 4 November 1817. Russian Church. He had as a child a vision of the Last Judgement, which encouraged him to embrace the religious life. However, at first he lived in a wood as a 'fool for Christ', only later entering a monastery at Sarov, taking first, in 1778, the name Methodius, then in 1811 the name Mark. Even as a monk he lived outside the monastery, in a hermitage, where he was joined by a small group of monks. He maintained complete silence for much of his life. After he became ill he was transferred back to the monastery, where he died.

Mark the Anthonian, born al-Mansat al-Kubra, died St Anthony's monastery on the Red Sea, 2 June 1386. Coptic Church. A pious child of poor parents, he entered a monastery near his home village when he was 23, but because the monks lacked fervour he returned home. He then went to the monastery of St Anthony on the Red Sea, and also spent some time at the monastery of St Paul, but he lived according to a very strict regime, dwelling in a cave he had excavated himself.

Mark the Fool, monk, born near Alexandria, died there, sixth century. Coptic Church. He became a monk in the Egyptian desert, but was much tempted to fornication, so travelled to Alexandria where he pretended to be mad, so that people would despise him. His holiness of life was recognized by **Daniel of Scete**, who arranged for his burial as a holy man.

Mark the Hermit, died Egyptian desert, c. 400, aged about 100. He is called Mark the Wonderworker in the *Menaion*, writings used in the Byzantine rite, but the only miracle reported is the curing of a hyena's blind whelp. Feast 5 March.

Marmaduke Bowes, bl., martyr, born Appleton, Cleveland, died York, 26 November 1585. Although Bowes was a Catholic, he conformed to the Church of England until he encountered **Hugh Taylor**. When he heard that the priest had been arrested he went to York to try to obtain his freedom, but was himself thrown into jail, and with Hugh was hanged, drawn and quartered.

Maro of Ayn Ward, hegumenos. Syriac Church. Said to have baptized 2,000 people of Nisibis.

Maro of Cyrrhus, hermit, died near Emesa, on the Orontes. He lived near Cyrrhus in Syria as a hermit with many disciples. St **John Chrysostom** was a friend. Maro was buried between Apamea and Einesa and a monastery grew up near his grave. In Lebanon the Maronites take their name from this saint. Feast 14 February.

Martha Kim, see **Barbara Kim**, see also **Martyrs of Korea**.

Martha Le Bouteiller, bl., born Percy, France, 2 December 1816, died Normandy, 18 March 1883, beatified 1990. Professed in the community of **Mary Magdalen Postel** in 1842, she eventually

looked after all the convent's practical matters. Close to the superior, **Placide Viel**, she also suffered from the opposition to her superior.

Martha of Pskov, princess, died Pskov, c. 1300. Russian Church. Her baptismal name was Mary, she was the daughter of the prince of Vladimir, and was married to the prince of Pskov. She bore him several children. After his death she entered a convent. Feast 8 November.

Martha of Tambov, nun, born Saransk, died Tambov, 1 September 1800. Russian Church. Born Martha Petrovna Aparina into a noble family, after the death of her father they moved to Kirsanov. Even as a child she displayed great piety, looking after the poor and going on pilgrimages. A small community grew up around her and her sister, although she refused to serve as its superior. The community lived together in a house in Tambov, owned by her brother. Her tomb became a centre of pilgrimage. Feast 28 July.

Martha the Egyptian, nun. Coptic Church. A public sinner in her youth, she repented, gave away all her wealth, and entered a convent, which she never left in the remaining 25 years of her life.

Martial, see also **Faustus, Januarius and Martial**.

Martial of Limoges, bishop, died Limoges, c. 250. A completely fabricated account claims that he was converted by Christ in Palestine, and came to France as an evangelist. But nothing is known about him, except that it is unlikely he was a martyr. Feast 30 June.

Martin, hermit, died Mondragone, Italy, c. 580. Known to Pope **Gregory I**, he lived in a cave, having chained himself to a rock so that he could not leave on a mere whim. Feast 3 August.

Martin, abbot in Aquitaine, sixth century. Feast 8 May.

Martin I, pope, born Todi, elected 5 July 649, deposed 17 June 653, died in the Crimea, 16 September 655. Before his election Martin had served as apocrisarius, or papal ambassador, in Constantinople. He accepted election without awaiting imperial approval, and immediately held a synod at the Lateran which condemned monothelitism (the belief that there was only one will in Christ), contrary to the emperor's wishes. The emperor had Martin arrested and, although very ill, transferred to Constantinople, where he was tried and condemned to death. The sentence was commuted to banishment to Chersonesus, in the Crimea, where he soon died, although not before the Romans had elected Eugenius I to succeed him. He is the last pope to be venerated as a martyr. He is mentioned by name in the Canon of the Mass in the Bobbio Missal. Feast 13 April.

Martin de Porres, Dominican lay brother, healer, born Lima, Peru, 9 December 1579, died there, 3 November 1639. He was of mixed African and Spanish parentage and was apprenticed to a barber-surgeon before becoming a Dominican lay helper at the age of 15, and eventually a lay brother. His skills and powers of healing both physical and spiritual suffering became renowned both within and beyond the monastery. He engaged in extreme ascetical practices, but was a fount of love and hope for all who encountered him.

Martin Luc Huin, born Guyonville, France, 28 October 1836, died Korea, 30 March 1866, beatified 1968, canonized 1984. Joining the Paris Foreign Missions Society in 1863, he went to Korea in 1865. He was tortured and killed with others during a time of general persecution – see also **Martyrs of Korea**.

Martin Lumbreras, bl., Augustinian and martyr, born Zaragoza, 1598, died Nagasaki, 11 December 1632. After joining the Augustinians in 1619, he was sent to the Philippines, where he served in Manila as novice master. In August 1632, however, he and **Melchior Sánchez** sailed for Japan. They were soon arrested and executed.

Martin Manuel, born Auranca, near Coimbra, Portugal, martyred Córdoba, 1147. He was archpriest of Soure, near Coimbra, and was captured by the Saracens, dying in prison as a result of ill-treatment. Feast 31 January.

Martin of Braga, bishop, born Hungary, 520, died Braga, Portugal, 580. He went as a monk to the Holy Land, then returned to the Iberian peninsula, where he became bishop of Braga. He seems to have introduced monasticism into the region. Feast 20 March.

Martin of Léon, born Léon, Old Castille, died 1203. He was an Augustinian canon regular at San Marcelo and St Isidore in Leon, and a Scripture scholar, writing many works. Feast 12 January.

Martin of Tours, monk and bishop, born Sabaria, now Szombathkely, Hungary, where his father was in the Roman garrison, c. 316–17, died monastery of Candes, France, which he had founded, 8 November 397. Martin's parents, who were pagan, sent him to Pavia to be educated and there he decided to become a Christian, although only after he had served some three years in the army. He was baptized in 339, but remained in the army until 356, by which time he probably already knew Bishop **Hilary of Poitiers**. He made himself Hilary's disciple and set out on a spiritual pilgrimage, including a return to his family home, where he converted his mother. He was back in Poitiers by 360, and established a hermitage at Ligugé, near the city but in the countryside, where he was joined by many disciples, creating the first monastery in France. He was elected bishop of Tours in July 370, or possibly 371. He continued, however, to live like a monk, and continued to found monasteries, of which the first was at Marmoutier: he saw such foundations as a means of evangelizing the countryside, which he viewed as his major task as bishop. In the controversy over Priscillian, 384–6, he defended the Spanish bishop, even though he did not approve of his doctrine, because he did not wish an ecclesiastical matter to be decided by the secular powers. His missionary activity spread far outside his own diocese, and he became one of the most popular saints of the Middle Ages, especially in France. The church which Augustine of Canterbury took over on his arrival in England, for instance, was dedicated to Martin. A basilica, with a monastery attached, was built at his tomb, which quickly became an important place of pilgrimage.

Martin of Turov, monk, died Turov, c. 1150. Russian Church. He was a servant in the employ of successive bishops of Turov who became a monk, and a solitary, living in the bishop's house. Feast 27 June.

Martinian of Beloozero, monk, born Berezniki, 1397, died monastery of St Terapons, 12 January 1483. Russian Church. His baptismal name was Michael. He entered the monastery of Beloozero when he was 13, and was an exemplary monk in his prayer and fasting. He eventually sought permission to live as a hermit beside a lake at some distance from the monastery. After a while he was invited to join the monastery of St Terapons, which prospered under his spiritual guidance. He was then called to be hegumenos of the monastery of St **Sergius of Radonez**, but he was unhappy with this role in a large monastery so close to Moscow, so he returned to St Terapons, where he again took up the role of spiritual guide.

Martinian of Palestine, died Caesarea, c. 400. A hermit, he was tempted by a local woman, but persuaded her to become a nun. Feast 11 February.

Martyrius, see also **Sergius**.

Martyrius of Novgorod, archbishop, died near lake Seregeri, 24 August 1199. Russian Church. He was hegumenos of the monastery of the Most Holy Saviour, and was elected bishop of Novgorod in 1193. He was a great builder of churches. He died while on a journey to Vladimir. Feast 16 February.

Martyrius of Zeleneck, monk, born Velike-Luki, died Zeleneck, 1 March 1603. He was left an orphan when very young, and was brought up by a guardian, a priest, who founded the monastery of the Mother of God at Velike – which Mina, as Martyrius was called before he became a monk, entered. He later decided to become a hermit not far from his home town, but subjected as he was to temptations, he decided to return to monastic life in the monastery of the Mother of God at Tichvin. He himself then founded a monastery on an island nearby.

Martyrius the Deacon and Martyrius the Recluse, lived and died Kiev (?), thirteenth/fourteenth centuries. Russian Church. Monks of the Kievan Cave monastery. Feast 25 October.

Martyrs of Alexandria, Egypt, died 257. These are the Christians tortured and killed during the persecution of Valerian. Feast 10 August.

Martyrs of Alexandria, Egypt, died 260. These are priests and deacons commemorated as martyrs because they are said to have died as a direct result of deciding to nurse the sick during an epidemic under Valerian. Feast 28 February.

Martyrs of Alexandria, Egypt, died 342. They were reportedly killed on Good Friday when Arians and pagans invaded all the churches. Feast 21 March.

Martyrs of Alexandria, Egypt, died 356. Catholics worshipping in church were ordered to be killed by an Arian officer. Bishop **Athanasius** was there, but escaped. Feast 28 January.

Martyrs of Alexandria, Egypt, died 372. A great many Catholics were massacred by Arians when their bishop **Athanasius** was exiled for the fifth time. Feast 13 May.

Martyrs of Alexandria, Egypt, died 390. A mob of worshippers of Sarapis massacred many Christians who had refused to sacrifice to his statue. Theodosius, emperor at the time, had the temple razed and replaced by a Christian church. Feast 17 March.

Martyrs of Alexandria. Coptic Church. A large number of Christians, mainly but not only Copts, who died for their faith in the unrest in Egypt at the end of the fourteenth century.

Martyrs of Armenia, the Seven, hermits, died Taron, 28 October 604. These seven men, four of whom were said to have been Greek, the remainder technically Persians, Armenia being then under Persian rule, were hermits attracted to the monastery of Glak, near lake Van in Armenia, because of the fame of its abbot. As hermits, however, they lived in the surrounding forest, and came from time to time to the monastery. When the monastery was attacked the monks were accustomed to take their precious objects and flee to a nearby fortress. When in 604 they were again caught up in the war between Byzantium and Persia, the monks fled, but the hermits came to the monastery to look after it, and were martyred. Feast 30 September.

Martyrs of Asturias, died Turon, 9 October 1934. These are eight de la Salle Christian Brothers, and a Passionist priest who was celebrating mass for them when they were arrested on 5 October by troops opposed to the government in Madrid. They were put in prison for four days, then taken to the cemetery and shot, together with two officers loyal to the government. There were **Cyril Bertrand Tejecdor, Marcian José Lopez, Julian Alfredo Zapico, Victoriano Pio Cano, Benjamin Julian Andres, Augusto Andres Fernández, Benito de Jesús Sáez, Aniceto Adolfo Gutierrez, Innocencio Canoura Arnau**. The uprising lasted only 15 days. Feast 9 October.

Martyrs of Cambrai, bl., died Cambrai, France, 27 June 1794. Nuns of the daughters of Charity of St Vincent de Paul, they ran a small school for girls at Arras, and nursed the sick. After the French Revolution they were allowed to continue nursing, only in lay dress. They were, however, arrested in February 1794, taken to Cambrai, tried and sentenced to death. They were Madeleine Fontaine, the superior, Françoise Lanel, Thérèse Fantou and Jeanne Gérard. They went to the guillotine singing a hymn.

Martyrs of China, bishops, priests and lay people, Chinese and European, martyred over three centuries. After a century during which European missionaries – notably the Jesuits – were respected by the emperors, Pope Clement XI in 1704 forbade inculturation, leading to some early executions. Sustained persecution began in the nineteenth century, at a time when the European powers were enforcing concessions on the Chinese administrations, culminating in the Boxer Rebellion of 1900 when many thousand Christians – Catholic and Protestant – were martyred. See also **Franciscan Martyrs of China**. Feast 17 February.

Martyrs of Compiègne, died 17 July 1794. A group of Carmelite nuns from Compiègne left their convent but carried on their Carmelite way of life, as far as possible, while living in private houses and wearing secular dress, to try to avoid capture. However, they were arrested in June 1794 on the charge of plotting against the republic, and a layman named Mulot de la Ménardière, who had been helping them, was also arrested. They were taken to Paris, condemned to death and guillotined on 17 July. The 16 nuns who were executed were Marie Madeleine-Claudine Lidoine, in religion Sr Thérèse de Saint Augustin; Marie-Anne Françoise Brideau, Sr Saint-Louis; Marie-Anne Piedcourt, Sr de Jésus-Crucifié; Anne-Marie Madeleine Thouret, Sr Charlotte de la Résurrection; Marie-Claude Brard, Sr Euphrasie de l'Immaculée Conception; Marie-François de Croissy, Mère Henriette de Jésus; Marie-Anne Hanisset, Sr Thérèse du Coeur de Marie; Marie-Gabrielle Trézel, Sr de Saint-Ignace; Rose Chrétien de Neuville, Sr Julie-Louise de Jésus; Marie Annette Pelras, Sr Marie-Henriette de la Providence; Angélique Roussel, Sr Marie du Saint-Espirit; Marie Dufour, Sr Sainte-Marthe; Elisabeth Julietter Vérolot, Sr Saint-François-Xavier; Marie-Geneviève Meunier, Sr Constance; and Catherine and Thérèse Soiron.

Martyrs of Córdoba, martyred there, 822–59. Most died in the 850s when, inspired by **Eulogius**, 30–50 Christians chose martyrdom by publicly declaring their faith in the divinity of Christ, an insult to Mohammed for the Muslim rulers of Spain. The authorities destroyed churches and punished Christians, fuelling more martyrs until the movement ended with Eulogius's execution. Feast 11 March.

Martyrs of Garegi, died desert of Garegi, seventeenth century. Georgian Church. Said to be 600 monks from the several monasteries in the Garegi desert who were killed by Persian looters at Easter, when they were all gathered to celebrate the feast. The Persians offered to spare their lives were they to embrace Islam, but all the monks refused, and, after a time of prayer, were slaughtered.

Martyrs of Garegi, died Garegi, 1851. Georgian Church. Six monks killed by Muslim invaders of the monastery of Davidgaregi when they tried to prevent the looting. Feast 12 August.

Martyrs of Gorkum, see **Nicholas Pieck and Companions**.

Martyrs of Japan, bishops, priests and lay people, mainly Japanese and European, martyred between 1597 and 1640; a group of 205 were beatified in 1867. Thousands converted in the 50 years after **Francis Xavier**'s arrival, but persecution began with the first group execution, of **Paul Mikki** and 25 others. Several thousands were martyred, usually by slow burning, in small groups or in mass executions. Many of those who apparently renounced their faith by trampling on images stayed Christian in secret and communities of their descendants remain, mainly around Nagasaki. Feast 6 February.

Martyrs of Korea, died Korea, between 1839 and 1867. Sometimes listed as **Andrew Kim, Paul Chong** and Companions, they include French missionaries as well as Korean Catholics among the 103 who have been canonized. Feast 20 September.

Martyrs of Kvabtachevi, died monastery of Kvabtachevi, 1393. Georgian Church. A large number of monks and lay people took refuge in the monastery of Kvabtachevi after Tamburlaine's troops had sacked the former capital of Georgia, Mzcheta. The troops surrounded the monastery, and demanded that the refugees abandon Christianity for Islam. When they refused, the soldiers burned down the building, killing all those inside. Feast 10 April.

Martyrs of Laval, bl., died in and around Laval, 1794. There was a particularly savage persecution of the Church in the Laval region of France in 1794, during which hundreds died, 19 of whom were beatified. On 21 January, 14 priests were executed, including **John Baptist Turpin du Cormier**, who was parish priest of Laval and rural dean, under whose name the others are commonly remembered. Those guillotined in addition were: John Mary Gallot, Joseph Mary Pellé, René Ludwig Amboise, Julian Francis Morvin de la Gérardière, Francis Duchesne, James André, Andrew Duliou, Ludwig Gastineau, Francis Migoret Lambarière, Julian Moulé, Augustine Emmanuel Philippot, Peter Thomas, John Baptist Triquerie OFM. See also **Martyrs of the French Revolution**. Feast 19 June.

Martyrs of Lyon, see **Pothinus**.

Martyrs of Mar Saba, martyred there, 797. Arab raiders attacked this still existing community in Palestine demanding money and valuables. The monks had no money and refused to say where the church vessels were hidden. Twenty were killed, some by being trapped in a fire. Feast 19 March.

Martyrs of Mount Sinai, fourth century, a group of monks, their exact number unknown, who were killed in different episodes by desert Bedouins and are commemorated together. See also **Martyrs of Sinai and Raithu**. Feast 14 January.

Martyrs of Nagasaki, bl., died 1622. Fifteen died on this date, either burned alive, or beheaded. Feast 19 August.

Martyrs of Nicomedia, died Nicomedia (modern Izmit, Turkey), 300–303. Four groups of martyrs are listed in the Roman martyrology as having been executed in Nicomedia under Diocletian, sometimes in very large numbers – numbers which are now discounted by historians of the persecutions. Their feasts are celebrated on 18 March, 23 June, 23 December and 25 December.

Martyrs of Omura, died Omura, Japan, 12 September 1622. Six Japanese martyrs are commemorated as being burned to death on this day – all converts to Christianity: Mancio Shibata, Dominic Mogoshichi, and four companions.

Martyrs of Orange, died Orange, July 1794. These martyrs were nuns who lived in the two convents in the town of Bollène during the French Revolution. One was an Ursuline convent, and the other was the Perpetual Adorers of the Blessed Sacrament, or the Sacramentines. The nuns were arrested when they refused to take the republican oath on the grounds that it was anti-religious. They were imprisoned in the town of Orange, and during the month of July, 32 were executed. Feast 9 July.

Martyrs of Persia, died Seleucia-Ctesiphon, Persia, 344. This is a group of mainly priests and monks, with some lay men and women, beheaded during the persecutions of King Shapor II. Their story tells how a woman from Arbela, Yazdandocta, supported them in prison and buried them secretly. Feast 17 April.

Martyrs of Raithu, see **Martyrs of Sinai and Raithu**.

Martyrs of Rome, died Rome, 64–8. Executed under the Emperor Nero for allegedly setting fire to the city. Ss Peter and Paul were among the victims of this persecution. Feast 30 June.

Martyrs of Russia, Russian Church. Many hundreds of bishops, priests, monks and others who were killed, or imprisoned, between the 1917 Revolution and the outbreak of World War II. (In fact the list includes a number who died from 1905 onwards.) Feast 25 January.

Martyrs of Samaria, 1,480 martyrs, died Samaria, 615.

Martyrs of Samosata, died Samosata (modern Turkish city of Samsat; the ruins have been flooded by the building of a dam), 297. They were crucified for refusing to perform a pagan rite in celebration of the victory of Maximian over the Persians: Abibus, Hipparchus, James, Lollian, Paragnus, Philotheus and Romanus. Feast 9 December.

Martyrs of Samothrace, died Makri, Thracia, 6 April 1835. Five martyrs, of whom Manuel, Gideon, George and George the Younger were from Samothrace, and Michael was from Cyprus. They are now honoured as protectors of the island.

Martyrs of September, bl., died Paris, 1 and 2 September 1792. One hundred and ninety-one people died in four Parisian prisons on these two days and are venerated together. Most of them are priests. The total number who died is some 1,400. Feast 2 September.

Martyrs of Scete, monks, died Scete, 444. The 49 monks slaughtered by barbarian invaders. However, associated with the story is a messenger from the emperor, who had enquired of **Isidore** of Scete whether he would have a son and heir. When the imperial messenger arrived, with his son John, Isidore had just died, but returned to life to tell the emperor that as long as he was infected by heresy –

as a supporter of the Chalcedonian definition – he would never have an heir. The imperial messenger and his son both also died in the massacre. Feast 21 January.

Martyrs of Scillium, died Scillium, north Africa, 180. Speratus, Narzales, Cythinus, Veturius, Felix, Acyllinus, Laetantius, Januaria, Generosa, Vestina, Donata and Secunda, died at Scillium, near Carthage (now in Tunisia), in the reign of Septimius Severus. A seemingly authentic account of their trial survives. Feast 17 July.

Martyrs of Sebaste, died Sebaste, Armenia (Sivas in Turkey), 320. According to the story, 40 Christian soldiers were immersed in a freezing lake for their faith. One apostatized, but his place was taken by another soldier who was converted by the sight of their constancy. According to some versions of the story, only one survived, St Mellitus, but he died almost immediately afterwards; other versions have it that those who survived the night in the lake were beheaded. Feast 10 March (suppressed in the Roman calendar).

Martyrs of Shanxi, martyred Taiyuan, Shanxi, China, 9 July 1900, beatified 1946, canonized 2000. This was the largest group of Catholics executed together during the Boxer Rebellion, 26 people, all Franciscans. Led by **Gregory Grassi**, the Europeans were: Theodore Balat, Andrew Bauer, Elias Facchini, Francis Fogolla, Mary Emiliana Grivot, Anna Catharina Dierks, Mariana Giuliani, Pauline Jeuris, Jeanne-Marie Kerguin, Mary Clare Manetti, Anne-Françoise Moreau – see also **Franciscan Martyrs of China**. Feast 8 July.

Martyrs of Sinai and Raithu, died c. 312 and c. 510 respectively. Monks of the caves on Mount Sinai, and of monasteries in the wilderness along the Red Sea coast, they were killed in the first instance in the persecution of Licinius, in the second by barbarian tribes. There died in these martyrdoms 38 monks in the first, and 43 in the second. The martyrdom of the monks on Mount Sinai was witnessed by an Egyptian monk who escaped the slaughter, of those of the wilderness of Raithu by Nilus the Faster. Feast 14 January.

Martyrs of Sirmium (Metrovica in Serbia), died 303. (1) Seventy-two Christians died as a group. Feast 23 February. (2) Seven women died as a group. Feast 9 April.

Martyrs of Syria (1) died 517. Three hundred and fifty monks, adherents of the teaching of the Council of Chalcedon, put to death by opponents of the council. Feast 31 July.
(2) died Emesa (Homs), 773. A large group of women said to have been put to death by Muslim invaders. Feast 14 November.

Martyrs of Thailand, died Songkong, 1940. **Philip Siphong, Agnes Phila, Lucia Khambang, Agatha Phutta, Bibian Khamphai, Maria Phon** and **Cecilia Butsi**. Feast 16 December.

Martyrs of the Crimea, died Crimea, 1937/8. Ukrainian Orthodox Church, Moscow Patriarchate. Seven priests and monks, and one bishop, Porphyrius of Simferopolis, shot on 2 December 1937.

Martyrs of the French Revolution, bl., died 1792–4. From 1790, the revolutionary authorities required bishops, priests and religious to swear an oath of loyalty – many refused. On 10 August 1792, 300 clergy, imprisoned in Paris for refusing, were killed. In 1793 the death penalty was decreed for this refusal, and many died until public opinion stopped the executions. Over 100 people guillotined during 1794 were beatified in groups at different times during the twentieth century. Feast 2 January.

Martyrs of the Oates Plot, bl., five Jesuits were executed at Tyburn, London, and are commemorated, 20 June 1678: Thomas Whitebread, the Jesuit provincial, James Fenwick, William Harcourt, John Gavan and Anthony Turner. In all some 45 Catholics were executed, among them **William Ireland, John Grove, Thomas Pickering, Richard Langhorne, Oliver Plunket, John Plessington, Thomas Thwing, John Kemble, Edward Coleman** and **William Howard**.

Martyrs of the Solovki Monastery, died seventeenth century. Church of the Old Believers. Died in the mid-seventeenth century during the eight-year-long siege of the Solovki monastery for refusing to accept the new rites. The first to die was the monk John, the monastery's chronicler, who lived slightly apart from the monastery proper in a hermitage. He was held in prison for a year, then beheaded. A number were killed during the final assault on the monastery in January 1676. The archimandrite, Nicanor, was among those killed. Feast 29 January.

Martyrs of the Spanish Civil War, during the Spanish Civil War, between July 1936 and April 1939, 6,832 priests and religious were killed, apparently because of their profession of their faith. Many more lay Catholics were executed, but as the Nationalists adopted a Catholic banner it is usually difficult to say whether they died for their faith or for their political or military allegiance. Over 230 victims have been beatified as martyrs, and over 1,000 more have causes for beatification. Feast 22 July.

Martyrs of the Theban Legion, see Theban Legion, martyrs.

Martyrs of Uganda, see **Charles Lwanga**.

Martyrs of Utica, died Utica, north Africa, third/fourth century. Utica was near Carthage, now in Tunisia. There were said to have been 300 martyrs. Feast 18 August.

Martyrs of Valenciennes, bl., died Valenciennes, 17 and 22 October 1794. A group of Ursuline nuns executed on the grounds that they had returned to France without permission (during earlier troubles they had fled to what is now Belgium) and because they were running religious schools. Five were tried and executed on 17 October, and the remaining five a few days later, including the superior, Marie Clotilde Paillot, and a lay sister who had been overlooked, Cordule Barré, who jumped of her own accord on to the wagon taking them to the guillotine. The names of the other religious were Marie Augustine Dejardin, Marie Vanot, Laurentine Prin, Ursula Bourla, Louise Ducrez and Scholastique Leroux; Anne Josephine Lerroux, the sister of Scholastique, had been a Poor Clare, and Livina Lacroix and Anne Marie Erraux had been Bridgettines, but their orders had been suppressed. Feast 17 October.

Martyrs of Vietnam, bishops, priests and lay people, Vietnamese and European, mainly martyred between 1745 and 1862 (when the emperor signed a treaty with France), beatified in groups between 1900 and 1951, 117 of them canonized together in 1988. Christians were tortured and killed in successive waves of persecution. From 1832, the emperor banned foreign missionaries, executing those found in the country, and ordered Vietnamese Christians to renounce their faith by trampling on a cross – those who refused were branded. Feast 2 February.

Marutha of Maiferkat, bishop, died Maiferkat, Persia, *c.* 415. A friend of **John Chrysostom**, he reorganized the Church in Syria after the persecution under Shah Shapor II. He also collected the relics of the martyrs of the persecution, and wrote hymns in their memory. Feast 4 December.

Marutha of Tikrit, metropolitan, born Surzaq (in the north of modern Iraq), died Tikrit, 2 May 649. Syriac Church. He became a monk at the monastery of Nardos, then moved to the monastery of Zakka, near Edessa. He was elected metropolitan in 629 of a diocese then under Byzantine control, although the region was conquered by Arabs in 657. He was a great builder of churches, and of at least two monasteries.

Maruthas, died Syria, *c.* 415. Bishop of Maiferkhat in Syria, he persuaded Yesdigerd I, king of Persia, to stop persecuting his Christian subjects, although persecution was renewed after Maruthas died. He left many writings, and because of these is regarded as the chief of the Syrian Doctors. Feast 16 February.

Mary, see also **Xenophon**.

Mary, martyr, fourth century (?). Said to have been a Christian slave in a pagan household. During the persecution of Christians her master, Tertullus, hid her for her safety, but was discovered and had to hand her over. She was tortured when she refused to renounce her faith, but, although sentenced to death, she was allowed to escape by a sympathetic

soldier. She is nonetheless regarded as a martyr because of her sufferings. Feast 1 November.

Mary-Aimée Tillet (Aurélie in religion), born Aulnay-la-Rivière, Loiret, France, 16 July 1836, martyred Tianjin, Hebei, China, 20 June 1870, she was a Daughter of Charity of St Vincent de Paul. See **Martyrs of China**.

Mary Angela Astorch, bl., abbess, born Barcelona, 1 September 1592, died Murcia, 2 December 1663. The last of five children, her mother died shortly after she was born, and at the age of 11 she entered a Capuchin convent, although she did not enter the noviceship itself until several years afterwards, when she was given the name Maria Angela. She was selected to make a new foundation in Zaragossa in 1614, where she served first as mistress of novices, then as abbess. Again in 1645 she left the convent to make a new foundation, this time in Murcia, where again she was abbess and where she died.

Mary-Angélique Lenu (Thérèse in religion), born Paris, France, 5 January 1832, martyred Tianjin, Hebei, China, 20 June 1870, she was a Daughter of Charity of St Vincent de Paul. See **Martyrs of China**.

Mary Anna Sala, bl., born Brivio, near Lecco, Italy, 21 April 1829, died Milan, 24 November 1891. She came from a devout family, and was sent to a school run by the Sisters of St Marcellina. There she decided to enter the order, but could not do so immediately because of family problems. She eventually entered in 1848, and after her profession taught in the order's schools until, dying of throat cancer, she had to retire to the infirmary.

Mary Ann of Quito, born Quito, Ecuador, 1618, died there, 26 May 1645, canonized 1950. She was a penitential and austere solitary in her sister's house, under Jesuit direction. She publicly offered her life to save Quito, experiencing an earthquake and epidemic. Both ceased and she died shortly after. Feast 26 May.

Mary-Anne Pavillon (Eugénie in religion), born La Tourlandry, Maine-et-Loire, France, 11 February 1823, martyred Tianjin, Hebei, China, 20 June

1870, she was a Daughter of Charity of St Vincent de Paul. See **Martyrs of China**.

Mary-Anne Vaillot and Forty-Six Companions, bl., martyrs, died Angers, 2 January 1794, beatified 1984, see **William Repin and Companions**. Feast 1 February.

Mary Bartholomaea Bagnesi, bl., born Florence, 1514, died there, 28 May 1577, cult approved 1804. Wishing to be a nun, she apparently had a nervous breakdown when told to marry, and remained bedridden. People came to her as she became known for healing the sick, reconciling opponents and converting many.

Mary Bertilla Boscardin, nurse, born Brendola, Italy, 6 Octobeer 1888, died Treviso, Italy, 20 October 1922. Baptized Anna Francesca, she became part of the Dorothean community at Vicenza in 1907, taking the name Mary Bertilla. She continued to nurse in the Treviso hospital with children stricken with diphtheria as her special charge. She was known for her display of courage and faith to wounded soldiers during the latter part of World War I.

Mary Catherine de Longpré, bl., born Saint-Sauveur-le-Vicomte (Manche), France, 1632, died Quebec, 9 May 1688, beatified 1989. A nun, a Hospitaller of Mercy of the Order of St Augustine, she became known for her nursing and counselling skills. She continued with this work in Quebec. Feast 8 May.

Mary-Catherine of Cairo, bl., born Giulano, Rome, 1813, died Cairo, 6 May 1887, beatified 1985. A Franciscan nun at Ferentino, she left for Cairo in 1859 as a missionary. Lack of support from Ferentino led her to found the Franciscan Missionary Sisters of Egypt, becoming the first superior. Feast 6 May.

Mary Clare Manetti (Mary Chiara), born 9 January 1872, near Rovero, Italy, martyred Taiyuan, Shanxi, China, 9 July 1900, beatified 1946, canonized 2000. A Franciscan Missionary of Mary under **Mary Emiliana Grivot**, she was a member of the group killed with **Gregory Grassi** – see

Franciscan Martyrs of China and **Martyrs of Shanxi**. Feast 8 July.

Mary Crescentia Hoss, see **Crescentia Hoss**.

Mary de Cervelló, Mercedarian religious, born Barcelona, Spain, 1 December 1230, died there, 19 September 1290. A member of a noble family, Mary was educated privately by **Bernardo de Corbera**, the founder of the Mercedarians. Mary took religious vows at 18, and became a Mercedarian herself, establishing a second order with a ministry to the sick and poor. She is reputed to have had spiritual gifts of prophecy and discernment – notably in regard to ships in distress, which she is said to have saved through her intercessions.

Mary de la Dive, bl., martyred France, 1794 – see **Martyrs of the French Revolution**. Feast 26 January.

Mary Deluil-Martiny, bl., born Marseilles, 1841, martyred there, 27 February 1884, beatified 1989. She developed the Daughters of the Heart of Jesus from an existing group of nuns, creating three houses in France and Belgium. Her convent's gardener, Louis Chave, fanatically anti-religious, attacked her and she died of her injuries.

Mary di Rosa, founder, born Brescia, 6 November 1813, died there, 15 December 1855. The daughter of an industrialist, and baptized Paula, she had to look after her father after the death of her mother. She found time, however, to care for the poor of the city, and was especially active during an outbreak of cholera. After the epidemic had run its course she opened a house for abandoned young women, and gathered helpers to work with her in the house, and also with nursing in the city's hospital. During the troubles in mid-nineteenth-century Italy she set up a military hospital. The women working with her formed themselves into the Congregation of the Handmaids of Charity, and the first members took their vows in 1852. When she took vows, Paula changed her name to Mary of the Crucified.

Mary Emiliana Grivot (Mary Hermina of Jesus), born Burgundy, France, 28 April 1866, martyred Taiyuan, Shanxi, China, 9 July 1900, beatified

1946, canonized 2000. She was the superior of the orphanage run by the Franciscan Missionaries of Mary and a member of the group killed with **Gregory Grassi** – see **Franciscan Martyrs of China** and **Martyrs of Shanxi**. Feast 9 July.

Mary Enrica Dominici, bl., born near Turin, 1829, christened Caterina, died Turin, 1894, beatified 1978. Joining the Institute of Sisters of St Anne and Providence in 1850, she was superior general from 1861. She developed the Institute during difficult times, always emphasizing the importance of humility. Feast 21 February.

Mary-Eugénie Milleret, born Anne-Eugénie in Metz, France, 26 August 1817, died Antevil, 10 March 1898, beatified 1975. She came from an unbelieving family, but was converted after hearing the sermons of the Dominican preacher Lacordaire in Notre Dame cathedral, Paris. She entered the novitiate of the Visitation nuns, but did not take vows, feeling herself called to start a congregation dedicated both to teaching and to the observance of the monastic rule. She started the Sisters of the Assumption in 1839, combining a contemplative life with educating women. Superior for life from 1858, she saw the order expand rapidly worldwide.

Mary Euphrasia Pelletier, born Noirmoutier Island, Brittany, 1796, died Angers (from cancer), 1868, canonized 1940. In Tours in 1814 she joined the Institute founded by **John Eudes** to rescue and protect young women from prostitution. She expanded and reorganized the Order, refounding it as the Good Shepherd Sisters. Feast 24 April.

Mary Fortunata Viti, bl., born Veroli, Italy, 10 February 1827, died there, 20 November 1922. Her baptismal name was Anna Felice, and she was born into a fairly prosperous family. After her mother died, and her father's business collapsed, she had to become a servant to earn money for the family to live on. In 1851, however, she entered the Benedictines at Veroli, and served the community as a lay sister in a number of different posts.

Mary Frances of Naples, born Naples, 1715, died there, 6 October 1791. Baptized Anna Maria Rosa Gallo, she was very devout, and refused to marry – for which her father beat her. He eventually allowed her to become a Franciscan tertiary, when she took the name of Mary Frances of the Five Wounds. She continued to live at home, and suffered ill-treatment from her father. For nearly the last 40 years of her life she worked as a housekeeper for a priest. She lived an austere life, and is said to have experienced the stigmata. She served as a spiritual guide to many lay people.

Mary-Joseph Adam (Joséphine in religion), born Arbrefontaine, Namur, Belgium, 2 April 1836, martyred Tianjin, Hebei, China, 20 June 1870, she was a Daughter of Charity of St Vincent de Paul. See **Martyrs of China**.

Mary-Joseph Cassant, ven., Trappist-Cistercian, born Casseneuil-sur-Lot, France, 6 March 1879, died abbey of Notre Dame du Désert, 17 June 1903. He wanted to be a priest, but was not thought to be physically or intellectually strong enough for the priesthood. In 1894 he became a choir religious in the Trappist-Cistercian abbey of Notre Dame du Désert, where he was professed on 24 May 1900. With the help of his spiritual father André Malet, later the abbot, who recognized his spiritual perception, he was ordained priest on 12 October 1902. His cause for beatification was introduced at Rome on 19 February 1956.

Mary Joseph Rosella, founder, born Albisola Marina, Italy, 27 May 1811, died Savona, 7 December 1880. Baptized Benedetta, she was the daughter of a potter, and unable to find the dowry then necessary to enter a religious order. When she was 19, therefore, she became a maid with a family in Savona, but then offered to help the bishop of the city with the pastoral care of young women. She and two cousins settled in a house in Savona, calling themselves the Daughters of Our Lady of Mercy. When the Congregation was formally established Benedetta took the name Mary Joseph. Her foundation spread around Italy, and to the Americas, in her lifetime.

Mary Kasper, bl., born Dernbach, Germany, 1820, died there, 2 February 1888, beatified 1978. After a vision, she founded the Poor Handmaids of Jesus Christ in 1851, living mainly in small communities. In her lifetime, she opened houses in

Holland, the USA and England and the order is now widely spread.

Mary McKillop, founder, born Melbourne, Australia, 15 January 1842, died Sydney, 8 August 1909. With Father Julian Woods, Mary McKillop established the Sisters of St Joseph of the Sacred Heart in Adelaide, and pronounced her vows in 1866 as Mother Mary of the Cross. She tried to adapt the new community to a colonial environment, but was opposed to a degree that the local bishops suppressed the community and excommunicated Mother Mary; however **Pius IX** reinstated the congregation. She founded 160 Josephite houses and 117 schools. At her death the Sisters numbered about 1,000, and had spread to New Zealand and Ireland by 1964. The Order ran refuges and orphanages without proselytizing and she is seen today as a pioneer in feminism, and care for aboriginal Australians and for the environment.

Mary Magdalen de' Piazzi, born Caterina di Geri de' Pazzi, Florence, 1566, died Florence, 25 May 1607, canonized 1669. She became a Carmelite, professed in 1584. She had mystical experiences all her life from the age of 12, and suffered greatly physically and mentally, all of which was witnessed, dated and recorded.

Mary Magdalen Martinego, abbess, born Brescia, Italy, 1687, died 1737. She joined the Capuchin abbey of Our Lady of the Snows at Brescia when she was 18, and took her vows in 1706. She served as a novice mistress, and was twice elected abbess, in 1732 and 1736. Feast 27 July.

Mary Magdalen Postel, foundress, born La Bretonne, Normandy, 28 November 1756, died Saint-Sauveur-le-Vicomte, 16 July 1846. Postel opened a school for poor children and maintained their religious instruction during the French Revolution. In 1807 she and three others took vows of religion in a new community, the Sisters of the Christian Schools of Mercy, for the education of girls, with a Rule from John Baptist de la Salle for the Brothers of the Christian Schools. An imaginative educator, the congregation flourished under her leadership.

Mary Mancini, bl., Dominican prioress, died 1431. Feast 22 January.

Mary Margaret Caiani, founder, born Poggio, near Florence, 2 November 1863, died Florence, 8 August 1921. Baptized Maria Anna Rosa, she was early on determined to be a nun, but had a clear idea of what she wanted her life to be. She entered one religious order, but found it did not suit and left. With two friends, she then opened a school. Her group became a religious community in 1902, with the name of the Institute of Franciscan Minims of the Sacred Heart: Anna took the name Mary Margaret.

Mary Marguerite d' Youville, foundress of the Grey Nuns, born Varennes, Canada, 15 October 1701, died Montreal, 23 December 1771. She was the niece of Pierre de la Verendrye, pioneer explorer of the Canadian Northwest, and great-granddaughter of Pierre Boucher, 'the father of Canada'. She married at 20, and although operating a family business, devoted much time to charity. She was widowed in 1730, after eight years of unhappy marriage to a man despised in Canada and in France for defrauding Indians and merchants by illegal trade. She was left with four sons, who all became priests. In 1737, she and three companions formed a small community and began caring in their home for the destitute. Despite misunderstanding, open hostility and even violence from the people of Montreal, they persevered in their good work, and the authorities asked Marguerite in 1749 to administer the general hospital, then in ruins. This led, with the sanction of Louis XV, to the founding of the Grey Nuns in 1753, for whom she organized a religious life, inaugurated closed retreats for women, began the first home for foundlings in North America, and opened hospital wards for soldiers. See also **Margaret d'Youville**. Feast 1 April.

Mary of Alexandria, nun, born Alexandria, died there, seventh century. Coptic Church. A member of a rich family, she rejected all attempts to arrange a marriage, and after the death of her parents she gave away her fortune and entered a convent near Alexandria. After 15 years as a nun she became a recluse, observing strict ascetical discipline.

Mary of Crete, martyr, born Crete, died there, May 1826. Byzantine Church. She was shot dead by a Turkish soldier, when she rejected his advances.

Mary of Egypt, born Alexandria, died desert of Jordan, fifth century. According to what is almost certainly a legend, Mary was a prostitute who converted after a visit to the Holy Sepulchre in Jerusalem, thereafter living as a hermit in the desert wearing only her long hair, and doing penance for her sins. Feast 2 April.

Mary of Jesus, bl., born Tartanedo, Spain, 18 August 1560, died Toledo, 13 September 1640. Baptized Maria Lopez de Rivas, she was sent as a child to Aragón where she was put under the spiritual direction of a Jesuit. He recommended she join the Carmelites as reformed by **Teresa of Avila**. This she did in Toledo. In Teresa she had a staunch supporter, and very early was put in charge of novices, a post she held several times, as well as that of prioress. She gained a reputation for being a saint during her own lifetime.

Mary of Jesus Crucified, bl., born Zabulon, not far from Nazareth, 5 January 1846, died Bethlehem, 26 August 1876. Baptized Mariam Baouardy to an Arab family of the Melkite Rite. Her parents died when she was two years old, and she was brought up by an uncle who in 1846 took her to Alexandria. An attempt was made to convert her to Islam, but she refused, and was punished – which included being wounded by a scimitar. She became a servant in different Christian families, working in Alexandria, Jerusalem, Beirut and Marseilles. In France she managed, after several attempts, to join the Carmelites: one of the problems for the orders she approached were the visions, and even the stigmata, which she experienced. Her stigmata became more visible when she went with a group of Carmelites from Paul to work as missionaries in India in 1870, and as a consequence she had to return to France. She persuaded her superiors to allow her to open a Carmelite convent in Bethlehem. The building opened in November 1876, and she was planning a further convent in Nazareth when she died, as a result of a fall.

Mary of Mattias, bl., born Vallecorsa, near Frosenone, Italy (then in the Papal States), 4 February 1805, died Rome, 20 August 1866. At the age of 17 she was inspired by a sermon of **Gaspar del Bufalo** to dedicate herself to teaching poor children. She opened her first school in Acuto in 1834, then a second one in her family home. She gained her first recruit in 1835, and eventually established the Congregation of the Adorers of the Precious Blood. She moved to Rome to take charge, at the request of **Pius IX**, of a hospice there. By the time she died there were 70 schools.

Mary of Oignies, bl., Belgian mystic and Beguine, born Nivelles, Brabant, 1177, died Oignies, 23 June 1213. She married at 14 and encouraged her husband to lead a life of poverty and abstinence, nursing lepers in their own home. Her mysticism and miracles attracted attention and she moved to Oignies where she could live under the spiritual direction of James de Vitry. With other Beguines she anticipated the changes in Catholic devotion to the Passion of Christ and the Holy Eucharist. Feast 23 June.

Mary of Providence, bl., born Eugénie Smet Lille, 1825, died Paris, 7 February 1871, beatified 1957. After several false starts, she founded the Helpers of the Holy Souls, dedicated to prayer, to deliver souls in purgatory, and to practical help for those in need – those suffering a purgatory on earth.

Mary of St Joseph, bl., founder, born Choroni, Venezuela, 25 April 1875, died Maracay, 2 April 1967. Baptized Laura Evangelista Alvarado Cardozo, she moved with her parents to Maracay. There Laura worked in a small hospital started by a local priest and with him she founded the Sisters Hospitallers of St Augustine, although the name was later changed to Augustinian Recollects of the Heart of Jesus. She took the name Mary Joseph as a member of this Congregation. She established houses for the sick, the disabled, and for orphans. She retired from the position of superior in 1967.

Mary of the Angels, bl., born near Turin, c. 1660, died there, 16 December 1717. Before she entered the Carmelite convent in Turin her name had been Marianna Fontanella, and she was the ninth of 11 children. She lived most of her life in the Turin Carmel, although she would have preferred to stay at Moncaglieri, a small foundation which she herself had made in 1702. She was renowned as a mystic during her lifetime.

Mary of the Apostles, bl., founder, born Mullendoch Castle, Gladbach, Germany, 1833, died Rome, 25 December 1907. Marie Thérèse von Wüllenweber came from an aristocratic family, but early felt the call to religious life. First she attempted to set up a house of Franciscan tertiaries, but this was unsuccessful. Then, inspired by John Jordan, the founder of the Salvatorians, she established the Congregation of the Sisters of the Divine Saviour.

Mary of the Incarnation (1. Mde Acarie), bl., married woman and Carmelite nun, born Barbara Avrillot at Paris, 1 February 1566, married, at 17, Peter Acaric, a French treasury official and minor noble, died Pontoise, 18 (?) April 1618. She was educated in a convent at Longchamps, and was early noted for her piety. After her marriage she became famous for charitable works, chief among which was bringing the Carmelites of the Teresian reform to Paris in 1604. Although not at this time a nun, she was almost an unofficial novice mistress, guided by her friends **Pierre de Berulle** and **Francis de Sales**. Her husband died in 1613, and she entered the Carmelites at Amiens the following year. All three of her daughters were Carmelites, and one of her three sons a priest. She later moved to Pontoise. She was beatified in 1791. Feast 18 April.

Mary of the Incarnation (2. Marie Guyard), bl., born Tours, 28 October 1599, died Quebec, 30 April 1672. She married, although reluctantly, at 17, a silk manufacturer called Martin and had a son who became a Benedictine, but her husband died only two years later. Raising her son prevented her from entering the recently established Ursuline convent in Tours until he was 12 years old. Two years later she was appointed mistress of novices. She developed a desire to go on the missions, and was permitted to leave for Quebec in 1639, accompanied by a number of other nuns. Two years later the foundation stone of the first Ursuline convent in North America was laid. She worked among the Iroquois – having set about learning their language as soon as she arrived –

until her death. She left a number of spiritual writings.

Mary of the Incarnation of the Sacred Heart, bl., born Quetzaltenango, Guatemala, 26 October 1820, died Tulcan, Ecuador, 24 August 1886. Baptized Maria Vicenta Rosal Vasquez, she joined the Sisters of Bethelehem in her home town, but found them less observant than the Rule required. She moved to another convent, but that was no better, so she moved back, eventually becoming prioress. Her reforms were, however, not welcomed, and she went on to found another convent which could keep more strictly to the Rule. During an anti-clerical period in Guatemala, she had to move to Costa Rica. She set up a number of new convents of her reform in South America. She died after a fall from her horse near Tulcan in Ecuador, while visiting one of her foundations.

Mary of Vladimir, princess, born Bohemia, died Vladimir, 1206. Russian Church. By birth a Catholic, she married Grand Prince Vsevolod II, and founded a convent of the Dormition in Vladimir, which she entered, taking the name Martha, after the death of her husband, and where she died. Feast 23 June.

Mary Paradis, bl., born L'Acadie, Quebec, 1840, died Sherbrooke, Canada, 3 May 1912, beatified 1984. A Marianite Sister of the Holy Cross from the age of 17, she taught in Canada, then at St Vincent's orphanage, New York. She founded the Little Sisters of the Holy Family, approved in 1880, becoming superior for life.

Mary-Pauline Viollet (Louise in religion), born Communauté, Saône-et-Loire, France, 11 October 1852, martyred Tianjin, Hebei, China, 20 June 1870. She was a Daughter of Charity of St Vincent de Paul. See **Martyrs of China**.

Mary Repetto, bl., born Voltaggio, northern Italy, 1 November 1807, died Genoa, 5 January 1890, beatified 1991. She was infirmarian of the Conservatorio del Refugio, a community of lay women in Genoa. The sick and poor whom she treated and nursed during cholera epidemics called her the 'holy nun'.

Mary Rivier, bl., born Auvergne, France, 1768, died there, 3 February 1838, beatified 1982. In poor health all her life, and marked by the experience of the Revolution, she founded the Sisters of the Presentation to care for orphaned and abandoned children and to help underprivileged mothers look after their children.

Mary Rose Durocher, foundress of a religious congregation, born St Antoine, Canada, 6 October 1811, died Longueuil, Canada, 6 October 1849. She worked in Beloeil parish, where she established the first Canadian parish sodality with help from the Oblates of Mary Immaculate. In 1843, at the request of the bishop of Montreal, she co-founded the Congregation of the Sisters of the Holy Name of Jesus and Mary at Longueuil, which was canonically established in 1844. She worked to promote the religious and general education of poor young women and set up schools for 400 students. She was beatified on 23 May 1982.

Mary Rose Molas y Vallvë, founder, born Reus, north-east Spain, 1815, died Tortosa, 11 June 1876. The daughter of shopkeepers in Reus, and baptized Rosa, she wanted to join a religious order, but her father, a widower, forbade it. When she was 26 she left home and joined some nuns working in a hospital at Reus. She was then sent as superior to a house in Tortosa. She and 12 other members of the order she had joined decided to found another order devoted to caring especially for children in need – the Sisters of Our Lady of Consolation.

Mary Schinina, bl., founder, born Ragusa, Sicily, 10 April 1844, died there, 11 June 1910. She was born into a noble Sicilian family. She was very distressed by the vast differences between the rich and poor, and she began to work with young people under the direction of a Carmelite. After the death of her mother in 1884 she wanted to join an enclosed religious order, but the archbishop persuaded her to continue her work with the poor, and in 1889 she and a handful of other women founded the Sisters of the Sacred Heart, putting into their new foundation their own money and property.

Mary-Séraphie Clavelin (Marie in religion), born Névy-sur-Seille, Jura, France, 30 November 1822, martyred Tianjin, Hebei, China, 20 June 1870. She was a Daughter of Charity of St Vincent de Paul. See **Martyrs of China**.

Mary Siedliska, bl., founder, born Roszkowa Wola, Poland, 12 November 1842, died Rome, 21 November 1902. Baptized Franciszka, she was brought up in a wealthy family and was well educated. The family was not particularly devout, and Franciszka's desire to become a nun was opposed by her parents. They went on a long tour of Europe, and in Cannes her father finally agreed. Franciszka determined from the start to found a new order, one dedicated to the hidden life of the Holy Family. The Congregation of the Holy Family was founded in Rome in 1875. It spread quickly, to Poland, the USA, France and England, working particularly with Polish émigrés.

Mary Soledad Acosta, founder, born Madrid, 26 December 1826, died there, 11 October 1887. The second of five children, she was baptized Manuela. She considered becoming a Dominican nun, but was persuaded instead to start a community to look after the sick. They eventually became a congregation called the Handmaids of Mary Serving the Sick, with Mary Soledad, as she became, at their head until her death.

Mary Teresa de Soubiran La Louvière, born Castelnaudary, May 1835, died Paris, June 1889. From a noble family, she wanted to become a religious, but she was persuaded instead to become a Béguine, as an uncle wanted to found a community of Béguines at Castelnaudary. She went to Ghent to study their life, and returned home to found the community in the mid-1850s. It was then that she took the name Mary Teresa in place of her baptismal name Sophie. Under her guidance, the Béguines began to develop into something like a religious community, but this Mary Teresa found unsatisfactory, and she decided to found a new order, which she did in September 1864 with some of the Castelnaudary community, in nearby Toulouse. They called themselves the Society of Mary the Helper (Marie Auxiliatrice). They taught small children and ran a hostel for working women, which became their chief apostolate. In 1871, however, there was elected as assistant mother general a Mother Mary Frances, who intrigued to get Mary Teresa expelled from the order. This happened in 1874, and Mary Teresa went to live with the Sisters of Charity, an order which she finally joined in 1877 and remained in until she died of tuberculosis. Shortly afterwards Mother Mary Frances was removed from office, and left the order. It transpired that she had deserted her husband, but was still legally married, and could not validly have become a nun. Feast 20 October.

Mary-Teresa-Eugénie-Josèphe Marquet (Elisabeth in religion), born Montenaeken, Limburg, Belgium, 18 November 1842, martyred Tianjin, Hebei, China, 20 June 1870. She was a Daughter of Charity of St Vincent de Paul. See **Martyrs of China**.

Mary Teresa Ledóchowska, bl., foundress, born Loosdorf, Austria, 29 April 1863, died Rome, 6 July 1922. She studied at the college of the 'English Dames' in Sankt Pölten. She became a lady-in-waiting in the court of the grand duchess of Tuscany in Salzburg and later became a close companion of the duchess. In 1886 she met some Franciscan Missionaries of Mary and became interested in the foreign missions. Three years later, a meeting with Cardinal Lavigerie convinced her of the need for missionaries to Africa. She had great literary ability and edited several journals, including *The Echo of Africa*, which she founded in 1889. In 1893 she founded a missionary association, the Sodality of St Peter Claver. The sodality was formally approved in 1899, and was dedicated to work for the African missions. Mary Teresa initiated the production of Bibles and catechisms in various African languages, and worked on literacy programmes in Africa. In 1900 she organized an international anti-slavery conference in Vienna.

Mary the Armenian, martyr, born Armenia, died Cairo (?), thirteenth century. Coptic Church. She was the slave of a Muslim soldier. When she rejected his advances he told the sultan that she was a Muslim and was going to deny her faith. The sultan ordered her to be burned alive.

Mary the Consolatrix of Verona, c. 770. Feast 1 August.

Mary Theresa of the Sacred Heart, bl., born Liège, 27 February 1782, died there, 7 January 1876. Baptized Johanna Haze, her father was secretary to the bishop, but had to flee because of the French Revolution, and died shortly afterwards. Johanna wanted to join a religious order, but the conditions of the day made it impossible. Instead she worked at her embroidery, and in a school run by one of her sisters. In 1830 the situation improved, and she founded the Daughters of the Holy Cross of Liège to work with the sick and to teach catechism.

Mary Victoire Thérèse Couderc, bl., foundress of the Religious of the Cenacle, born Sablieres (Ardeche), France, 1 February 1805, died Lyon, 26 September 1885. In 1826, taking the name Thérèse, she joined a teaching congregation at Aps. A hostel she started for female pilgrims to the tomb of St **John-Francis Regis** soon evolved into the Congregation of the Cenacle, with Thérèse appointed superior in 1828. Here women made retreats following the spiritual exercises of St **Ignatius of Loyola**. The Jesuits, who oversaw the institution, strongly shaped the nature of the growing congregation. In 1837 she made her perpetual vows and renounced her own authority. The congregation then went through a period of chaos and mismanagement. Thérèse herself was slighted and humiliated, but bore all this stoically. From 1855 until her death, she again served in positions of responsibility. In 1951 she was beatified.

Maryam Kebra, queen, born Ethiopia, died there, sixteenth century. Ethiopian Church.

Masabki, Francesco, Mooti and Raphael, martyrs, died Damascus, nineteenth century (?).

Masqal Bezana, monk, died Tigre, thirteenth/fourteenth centuries. Ethiopian Church. Founder of the monastery of Dabra Ta'amina.

Masqal Kebra, queen, thirteenth century. Ethiopian Church. Wife of King **Lalibala**, whom she married before he succeeded to the throne. She played an active part in the political life of the country, and after her husband's death helped her son to succeed to the throne. Feast 4 August.

Mastoc, catholicos, born Elivard, 833, died Garni, 898. Armenian Church. The son of a priest, he entered the monastery of Mak'enoc, and after ordination went to the island of Sevan where he rebuilt the church and monastery. He was elected catholicos in 897. Feast 13 October.

Maternus, bishop, born Cologne (?), died Trier, *c.* 340. Very little is known of him, although he is thought possibly to have been the first bishop of Cologne. He attended the Roman Council of 313. Feast 14 September.

Matilda of Germany, born Westphalia, *c.* 895, died Quedlinburg, 14 March 968. She was married to Henry I (The Fowler) of Germany and had a reputation for humility, piety and generosity. On the death of her husband, there was disunity over which son should succeed him, with Matilda supporting the loser. Both sons later rejected their mother, accusing her of impoverishing the crown with her generous almsgiving. She then renounced all her possessions and retired to Westphalia. She was eventually reconciled to her sons, but spent her life in church building and the building and support of many monasteries.

Matrona of Thessalonika, martyr, died Thessalonika, 350 (?). Said to have been the servant of a rich Jewish woman who, on discovering she was a Christian, had her put in prison, where she died. Feast 15 March.

Matta, founder, born Abgarsat, fourth century. Assyrian Church. He became a monk near his home, but was forced by persecution to flee to Gabal Maqlub, a mountain north-east of Mosul. Later, with other monks, he moved to the mountain of Alpap, where the monastery they founded became one of the most important in the Eastern Church. Feast 25 July.

Matthew (Matthias), bishop, died *c.* 120. Of Jewish descent, he was bishop of Jerusalem during a period when his people were scattered. Feast 30 January.

Matthew Correa, born Tepechitln, Zacatecas, 23 July 1866, died Durango, Mexico, 6 February 1927. He was parish priest at Valparaiso when he was arrested and taken to the prison at Durango. He heard the confessions of several of his fellow inmates, and was shot for refusing to reveal what they had said.

Matthew (Major) Flathers, bl., martyr, born Weston, Yorkshire, *c.* 1560, died Yorkshire, 21 March 1608, beatified 1987. Educated at University College, Oxford, and ordained at Arras in 1606, he was arrested, banished, caught again and hanged, drawn and quartered.

Matthew Le Van Gam, martyr, died Vietnam, 11 November 1847. He was a Vietnamese sea captain, martyred for smuggling foreign priests into the country. See **Martyrs of Vietnam**. Feast 11 May.

Matthew Nguyen Van Phuong, martyr, born Ke-Lay, Vietnam, *c.* 1801, died near Dong-Hoi, 1861, canonized 1988. He was a catechist who was beheaded because of his occupation. He is commemorated with **John Doan Trinh Hoan** – see **Martyrs of Vietnam**. Feast 26 May.

Matthew of Agrigento, bl., bishop, born Agrigento, Sicily, died Palermo, 1450. He originally joined the Conventual Franciscans, but then entered the Observant Friars. He became a friend of **Bernardine of Siena**, with whom he travelled around Italy, preaching. He returned to Sicily to reform the Church there, and became provincial superior of his order. He founded more houses both there and in Spain. He became friendly with the king and queen of Aragon, and in 1442 King Alfonso V appointed him bishop of Agrigento. He did not want to accept the post, and did so only on the instructions of the pope. He resigned it as soon as he could, and tried to return to his order, but the Observants were reluctant to have him back, not least because they could not afford his medical expenses. He died in a Conventual house in Palermo. Feast 21 October.

Matthew of Alexandria I, patriarch, born Banu Ruh, 1337, died Old Cairo, 3 December 1409. Coptic Church. After working as a shepherd during his childhood, he entered a monastery in Upper Egypt at the age of 14 and was ordained four years later, after which he went to the monastery of St Anthony on the Red Sea. He then went on pilgrimage to Jerusalem, where he worked as a labourer. On his return to the monastery he was arrested and taken to Cairo, along with **Mark the Anthonian**. He was freed in Cairo, however, and went to the monastery of al-Muharraq. This was a somewhat lax house, but Matthew's example brought the community to a stricter observance of the Rule. In 1378 he was elected patriarch, much against his will. He turned his residence in Old Cairo effectively into a monastery, and continued his monastic style of life. He had developed great wisdom, and he was consulted not only by Christians but also by the government of Egypt – he became a good friend of the sultan. The attitude of the government towards Christians changed towards the end of his life, and he advised Christians to flee the cities. He was himself accused of treason because he had exchanged letters with the king of Ethiopia, who had also sought his advice, but he died before he could be formally charged.

Matthew of Alexandria II, patriarch, died Cairo, 10 September 1465. Coptic Church. Born Sylayman al-Sa-idi, he took the name Matthew when he entered the monastery of al-Muharraq. He became patriarch in 1452. He was buried beside **Matthew of Alexandria I** in the monastery of al-Handaq.

Matthew of Cerneevo-Sackij, monk, sixteenth century. Russian Church. A Cossack by birth, he founded the monastery of Cerneevo-Sackij at the orders of the Tsar on newly annexed territory. Matthew used the new monastery as a base for evangelizing the local people. Feast 28 July.

Matthew of Girgenti, bl., bishop, died 1451. He was a Franciscan. Feast 7 January.

Matthew of Jaransk, monk, born Vjatlka, died Jaransk, 27 May 1927. Russian Church. Baptized Mitrofan Kuz'mic Svecov, his father was a shoemaker. He joined the monastery in his home town, but in 1899 moved to the monastery of Prorocick, not far distant. When the monastery was shut down in 1921, he remained in the area as a spiritual guide to many. His tomb became a centre of pilgrimage.

Matthew Talbot, ven., Irish reformed alcoholic, born Dublin, 2 May 1856, died there, 7 June 1925. He first worked as a messenger with a wine merchant and then with the Port and Docks Board. He later became a builder's labourer, spending all his money on drink until, in 1884, he 'took the pledge' and became a total abstainer from alcohol. He became increasingly devout, attending mass daily, which, with the demands of his job, meant rising at 4.00 a.m. He adopted other ascetic practices, including sleeping on a wooden bed and fasting. He gave most of his earnings to charity. His final job was in a timber yard, where he worked until the day before he died. He died on his way to mass: it was then found that he had bound his body with chains as a form of mortification.

Matthew the Potter, monk, born Asfant, eighth century. A priest, he earned his living by fishing, but then entered a monastery. He won considerable fame as a healer.

Matthia of Metalica, bl., abbess, died Metalica, near Ancona, Italy, 28 December c. 1300. The daughter of Count Guarniero Nazzarei, she was determined to become a Poor Clare, even though at first the convent would not accept her. She eventually became the abbess, and after her death miracles were reported.

Matthias Kalemba, martyred Uganda, 1886, canonized 1964. He was among those converted by the Missionaries of Africa and put to death by King Mwanga of Uganda – see **Martyrs of Uganda**. Feast 30 May.

Matthias of Addeqe, monk, died Addeque, fifteenth century. Ethiopian Church. Born Terita Egzi, he followed his elder brother into the monastery of Dabra Maryam, but finally settled at Addeqe, south of Asmara.

Matthias of Gogiam, monk, fourteenth/fifteenth centuries. Ethiopian Church. Founder of the monastery of Dabra Dima at Goggiam.

Matthias of Jerusalem, see **Matthew**.

Maturinus, priest, born Larchant, northen France, died Rome, fourth century. The son of pagan parents, he was attracted to Christianity, was baptized when only 12, and then converted his family. He became a priest, much trusted by his bishop, was a missionary, and had a remarkable gift as an exorcist. It was as such that he was sent to Rome, where he died. Feast 1 November.

Maughold of Man, bishop, Ireland, died Isle of Man, *c.* 498. A cruel pirate or oppressor, he was converted by **Patrick**, who banished him as a penance. Landing by chance on the Isle of Man, he lived as a hermit until elected bishop, when he started evangelizing. Feast 27 April.

Maura, see also **Timothy of Antinoë**.

Maura, possibly fourth century. **Gregory of Tours** relates that the relics of two virgins, Maura and **Britta**, were found while **Euphronius** was bishop of Tours before him. Nothing is known about them. Feast 27 January.

Maura, born Troyes, France, 827, died there, 21 September 850. A precociously spiritual child, through her prayers she brought about the conversion of her dissolute father, and after his death remained at home with her mother, praying especially for her brother, who became bishop of Troyes.

Maura, nun, born Bistrita, Moldava, seventeenth century. Romanian Church. Her baptismal name was Mary. She joined a community of hermits, originally all men but later joined by women. Although she lived strictly under obedience, she felt that her life was not satisfactory because she had to think of looking after the other women. With permission, she therefore went to Mount Panaghia where she lived in great simplicity and poverty, although she was visited by many people seeking her spiritual guidance.

Maura of Constantinople, martyr, died Constantinople. Feast 30 November.

Maurice and Seventy Companions, see **Theban Legion**, martyrs.

Maurice of Carnoët, abbot, born Croixanvec, Brittany, *c.* 1114, died Carnoët, Brittany, 9 October 1191. Maurice became a monk at the Cistercian abbey of Langonnet in 1143 and was made abbot

in 1147. In 1171 the duke of Brittany asked him to found a monastery in Carnoët, where he was made abbot in 1176. He was known for his miracles, and the abbey was renamed St Maurice after his death. His cult was eventually approved in 1869. Feast 13 October.

Maurontius, abbot, born northern France, 634, died Marchiennes, near Douai, France, 702. The son of **Adalbald** and **Rictrude**, he became a monk and founder and first abbot of Breuil-sur-Lys monastery, near Douai. He was for a time chancellor to Theodoric I and is patron of Douai. Feast 5 May.

Maurus, see also **Papias**.

Maurus, see also **Titus**.

Maurus, monk, died Glanfeuil, later St Maur-sur-Loire, 15 January 584. Put into St **Benedict**'s care by his parents when aged 12, he is said to have founded an abbey at Glanfeuil in France and, after giving up the abbacy, spent the remainder of his life in solitude. But nothing certain is known about Maurus beyond these doubtful details in a biography ascribed to Odo of Glanfeuil. Feast 15 January.

Maurus of Bodon (Marius, May), abbot, died *c.* 550. He founded Bodon, in Sisteron diocese, France. Feast 27 January.

Mawes, bishop, sixth century. It is unclear where he was from. Some accounts associate him with Wales and Cornwall, others with Brittany, yet others with Ireland. Feast 18 November.

Maxellenids, martyr, born Caudry, near Cambrai, died there, *c.* 670. She had told her parents that she wanted to become a nun, but they insisted on her marrying a certain Harduin of Solesme. She then fled and hid, but Harduin found her, and when she tried to escape he hit her with his sword and killed her. He was immediately struck blind. Her tomb was the site of many miracles, and her body was therefore moved to a larger church at Caudry. During the procession with her body, Harduin confessed his crime, and was cured. Feast 13 November.

Maxentius, abbot, born Agde, north of Perpignan, *c.* 445, died St-Maixent-l'Ercole, 515. Baptized Adjutor, he entered a monastery at Agde, but became famous for his sanctity, and decided to leave Agde for a place where he was unknown. He entered a community near Poitou, changing his name to conceal his identity. But again he became renowned for his sanctity, and was elected abbot. He resigned shortly before his death, and lived nearby as a hermit. Feast 26 June.

Maxima, see **Montanus**.

Maximian, see also **Lucian**.

Maximian of Constantinople II, bishop, born Rome, died Constantinople, 434. He was a vigorous opponent of the Nestorian heresy. Feast 21 April.

Maximian of Ravenna, born Pola, 498, died Ravenna, 22 February 556. The Emperor Justinian made him bishop of Ravenna in 546. The first in the West to call himself 'archbishop', he was effectively primate of Italy for long periods. He built or completed several basilicas and produced many books.

Maximilian, martyr, died Theveste (Tebessa, Algeria), *c.* 295. He is said to have been executed in Numidia because he refused military service in the Roman army. Feast 12 March.

Maximilian, bishop, died Cilli, Styria, *c.* 284. Born of a wealthy family, he is said to have given away his wealth and devoted himself to the spiritual life. At Rome, he was sent by Pope Sixtus II to Noricum, between Styria and Bavaria, where he became first bishop of Lorch, near Passau. He served for 20 years, and was martyred during Numerian's persecution. Feast 12 October.

Maximilian Maria Kolbe, Franciscan priest, born Zdunska Wola, Poland, 8 January 1894, died (executed) Auschwitz, Poland, 14 August 1941. Kolbe joined the Franciscans in 1910 and was ordained in 1919. He taught at a Polish seminary and founded a religious community which published Christian journals and newspapers. Following the Nazi occupation of Poland, these publications assumed a patriotic, anti-Nazi stance, leading inevitably to Kolbe's arrest and imprisonment in the Auschwitz concentration camp. There he exercised a solicitous priestly ministry to other prisoners, which culminated in him offering himself for execution in the place of a younger man with a wife and family. Kolbe was canonized by fellow Pole John Paul II in 1982, and in the presence of the man he had saved.

Maximilian of Lorch, bishop and martyr, born Cilje, died there, *c.* 281. The apostle of Pannonia, he became bishop of Lorch, which is not far from Linz in Austria. He is patron of the diocese of Passau. Feast 12 October.

Maximinus, see also **Juventinus**.

Maximinus of Aix, bishop, fifth century (?). Nothing is known about him. One legend has it that he arrived with Lazarus in the first century. Feast 8 June.

Maximus, martyr, died Asia, third century. Feast 14 May.

Maximus, see also **Cassius and Companions**.

Maximus, see also **Tiburtius**.

Maximus and Olympiades, died Persia, 251. Noblemen who were executed in the persecution of Decius. Feast 15 April.

Maximus of Alexandria, bishop, died Alexandria, 282. He was a priest of the city of Alexandria who took over running the bishopric during the exile of **Dionysius**, and was elected bishop the year he died. Feast 27 December.

Maximus of Apamea, martyr, died Cuma, Italy, 304. Feast 30 October.

Maximus of Chinon, founder, died Chinon, near Tours, *c.* 470. He was a disciple of St **Martin of Tours** who became a hermit, and then the founder of a monastery at Chinon. Feast 20 August.

Maximus of Ephesus, martyr, died Ephesus, 251 (?). A merchant, he proclaimed his faith and was executed. Feast 30 April.

Maximus of Jerusalem, bishop, born Jerusalem, died there, *c.* 350. Having suffered mutilation during the persecution under Diocletian, he became bishop in 333, but then went over to the Arians. However, he later returned to Orthodoxy. Feast 5 May.

Maximus of Moscow, 'fool for Christ', died Moscow, 1433/4. Russian Church. He went about the streets of the city calling upon the people of Moscow to repent of their sins.

Maximus of Pavia, bishop, died *c.* 514. He attended councils in Rome under Pope Symmachus. Feast 8 January.

Maximus of Riez, bishop, born near Digne, Provence, died Riez, *c.* 460. He entered the monastery at Lérins and became abbot there after the founder, **Honoratus**, became bishop of Arles. He managed, by hiding, to avoid being elected bishop of Fréjus, but was prevailed upon to become bishop of Riez, although he continued to live as far as possible according to the monastic Rule. Feast 27 November.

Maximus of Tot'ma, 'fool for Christ', born Tot'ma (?) 1565, died there, 1650. Russian Church. He was a priest in the city of Tot'ma, but became a 'fool for Christ', praying, fasting and going about naked. He had a reputation as a wonderworker.

Maximus of Turin, bishop, born *c.* 350 (?), was certainly bishop of Turin in 398, died Turin, between 408 and 423. This is all that is known for sure about him. His works, mainly some 90 sermons, some of dubious authenticity, reveal him as a pastor genuinely concerned about his flock, rather than as a speculative theologian. His sermons show a marked influence of Ambrosius. In them he reacts against idolatry, hypocrisy, laxity, corrupt clerics, Arianism and despondency because of the German incursions. Feast 25 June.

Maximus of Trier, bishop, born Silly, near Poitiers, died Trier, *c.* 357. He moved to Trier, succeeding his teacher **Agricius** as bishop in 333. A renowned opponent of Arianism, notably at the Milan, Sardica and Cologne Councils, he gave practical help to its victims, welcoming **Athanasius** and **Paul of Constantinople**. Feast 29 May.

Maximus, Quintilian and Dadas, martyrs, born Durostorum, died Ozobia, 303. Three brothers, from what is now Bulgaria, beheaded during the persecution of Diocletian.

Maximus Sandovich, martyr, born Zhdenia, Austrian Galicia, 30 September 1886, died (shot) Gorlice, 6 September 1914. He was born a Greek Catholic (uniate), but studied in Russia and was ordained priest. Thereafter he was an Orthodox missionary in his home region, then part of the Austrian Empire, and converted several villages. He was arrested, and when World War I began he was executed, without trial, for treason, as the Orthodox were considered pro-Russian. Canonized by the Orthodox Church of Poland in 1994 at Gorlice. Feast 6 September.

Maximus the Confessor, a prolific writer and Greek theologian, born into Byzantine aristocracy, *c.* 580, died Skhemaris, on the Black Sea, *c.* 662. Brought up in Constantinople, he became secretary to the Emperor Heraclius, but resigned, possibly because of the emperor's doubtful orthodoxy, and became a monk at Chrysopolis (Scutari), where he was eventually elected abbot. He was an active opponent of the monothelitism embraced by the Emperor Constans II. He was imprisoned for six years, then, when he was about 82 years old, put on trial in Constantinople, had his tongue cut out and his right hand cut off, and was sentenced to life imprisonment. He died shortly after his arrival at Skhemaris. He is called 'the Confessor' because of the sufferings he endured for his faith. Feast 13 August.

Maximus the Greek, monk, born Arta, Greece, *c.* 1470, died December 1556. Baptized Michael Trivolis, he came from a noble family. He travelled to Italy and entered the Dominican Order in Florence in 1502, but had left by 1504. He then went to Mount Athos and entered the monastery of Vatopedi, where he took the name Maximus. In 1516, however, he was sent to Moscow to organize a Greek-language library. He learned the Russian language on the way, and arrived in Moscow only in 1518. After he had finished his work in the library – in the course of which he also translated the Psalter into Russian – he was asked to stay on to translate a commentary on the Acts of the Apostles, and to advise on revision of liturgical books. He was, however, put on trial in 1525 and imprisoned in a cell in the monastery of Voloko-lamsk by a hostile metropolitan of Moscow, Daniel, who accused him of criticizing the practices of the Russian Church and particularly of Russian monasticism, although a more immediate cause for his downfall may have been a letter criticizing the Tsar for entering a second marriage because his first wife had not given birth to an heir. He was eventually transferred in 1551 to another monastery where he enjoyed greater freedom. In 1554 he was invited to attend a synod of the Russian Church, but refused to go. He was buried in the monastery of St **Sergius**, and his tomb became a place of pilgrimage long before his holiness was formally recognized by the Russian Church. His letters, autobiography and a great many other writings survive as an important witness to the religious culture of sixteenth-century Russia.

Maximus the New, prince and archbishop, died Srem, 1546. Serbian Church. Son of the prince of Serbia **Stephen the Blind**, he was baptized George. He took the name Maximus when he entered the monastery of Kupinovo in 1496. He was invited with his mother to Wallacia, c. 1505, where he was asked to help reorganize the Church. He was appointed archbishop of Wallacia, and in 1509 of Srem, where he built a monastery. Feast 18 January.

Maximus, Theodore and Ascepiodotus, martyrs, born Marcianopolis (in what is now Bulgaria), died Adrianopolis, c. 310. Feast 15 September.

Mazmura Dengel, monk, fifteenth century. Ethiopian Church. He wrote a hymn in honour of Mary.

Mazmura Krestos, monk, born Adua, Tigre. Ethiopian Church.

Mazre'eta Krestos, monk, fourteenth century. Ethiopian Church. Founder of the monastery of Dabra Hamalmal in Tigre.

Mechtild of Hackeborn (Mechtilde, Matilda von Hackeborn-Wippra), born Eisleben, Saxony, 1240 or 1241, died Helfta, 19 November 1298. Of a noble Thuringian family and sister of Gertrude of Hackeborn. She was born very weak and baptized immediately. The celebrant prophesied that she would lead a saintly and long life. At the age of seven she begged to be allowed to enter the monastery of Rodardsdorf. As a young nun she became known for her humility, fervour and friendliness. Subject to divine revelations, she was sought out by many for advice. At the age of 50, two nuns to whom she had confided the revelations wrote a book about them, *The Book of Special Grace*. Feast 19 November.

Mechtild of Magdeburg, mystic, writer and Béguine, born into a noble family in Saxony, c. 1210, died c. 1280. She became a Béguine at Magdeburg, where she led a contemplative and penitential life. She was subject to visions, which she was instructed to write down by her confessor. She later moved to the Cistercian convent at Helfta (1270). Her book *Das Fliessende Licht der Gottheit* had great influence in medieval Germany.

Medard, bishop of Noyon, born Salency (Picardy), c. 456 or 470, died Noyon, 8 June c. 545–560. Medard, born of a noble Frankish father and a Gallo-Roman mother, was pious and studious from childhood, leading to his ordination and (despite his objections) consecration as bishop of Vermand. Because of barbarian turmoil, Medard moved his see to Noyon, a more secure location. Upon the death of the bishop of Tournai, Medard was asked by King Clotaire to rule that diocese also. Medard is also known for consecrating **Radegund** as a deaconess after King Clotaire had murdered her brother.

Medericus, abbot, born Autun, France, died Paris, c. 700. He entered a monastery at Autun when very young and eventually became abbot. As he was much sought after for spiritual advice, he decided to leave the monastery and become a hermit, which he did for a time, but then he had to return because of ill-health. Towards the end of his life he went to the shrine of St **Germanus** at Paris, and remained in that city, living in a simple cell, until his death. Feast 29 August.

Méen (Mewan), abbot, born Gwent, Wales, died Wales (?), sixth century. Nothing is certain about Méen, but he appears to have moved from Wales to Cornwall, then on to Britanny, and founded there two abbeys, that at Brocéliande, and the one named after him, St-Méen. He is reported to have been a relative of **Samson** of Dol, and to have returned to Wales before his death. Feast 21 June.

Meinhard, bishop, born Holstein, *c.* 1135, died Ilskile (?), near Riga, 14 August 1196. He was an Augustinian Canon Regular of the abbey of Sege-berg in Holstein. He began his mission to the peoples of the Eastern littoral of the Baltic in the 1170s or early 1180s, establishing himself at Ilksile where he built a small fort.

Meinrad of Einsiedeln, died Einsiedeln, 21 January 861. In *c.* 836 Meinrad, a monk of Reichenau, came to live in solitude near lake Zurich in Swit-zerland, having had to abandon an earlier hermi-tage beside the lake because of the number of his visitors. He was murdered by robbers. Later his demesne was occupied by hermits – *Einsiedeln* means 'hermitage' – and a Benedictine monastery was founded here, named after him.

Meinwerk of Paderborn, bl., bishop, died Pader-born, Germany, 5 June 1036. A noble and friend from youth of Emperor Henry II, Meinwerk was made bishop of Paderborn by the emperor in 1009, reputedly so that he could restore it with his own personal wealth. Meinwerk did make his diocese richer, obtained donations for the emperor him-self, and was known as a meticulous, even pater-nally petty, administrator. He spent much of his time in building and decorating, both for the cathedral and the town.

Mel (Melchno), born Britain, died Ireland, *c.* 490. He was reputedly one of four nephews of **Patrick**, sons of his sister, who went with him to Ireland. He became first abbot-bishop of Ardagh. Feast 6 February.

Mel, died Bardsey Island (Ynis Enlli), Wales, sixth century. He and **Sulian**, who are commemorated together, were monks and disciples of **Cadfan**. Feast 13 May.

Meladius, monk, thirteenth century. Russian Church.

Melaine, bishop, born Placet, Brittany, died there, *c.* 530. He was elected bishop of Rennes after working in Brittany as a monk and priest. He was active in Church affairs outside his diocese, and died in a monastery he had built at Placet, although his remains were taken to the cathedral at Rennes. Feast 6 November.

Melangell, abbess, died Pennant Melangell, Wales, possibly seventh century. She is supposed to be an Irish or Welsh princess who took refuge in Powys to escape marriage. She became a recluse and later an abbess. There is still a restored twelfth-century shrine to her at Pennant Melangell, near Llangy-nog. Feast 27 May.

Melania the Elder, born into an aristocratic family, Rome, 342, died Jerusalem, *c.* 410. When she was 21 she lost her husband and two of her three children. She turned to an ascetic lifestyle, left her eight-year-old son with his inheritance in Rome and travelled with other ascetic women and slaves to Alexandria. Then she lived for a while in the Egyptian desert, from where she travelled to Jer-usalem. There she founded a double convent over which she presided for many years. She came in contact with many famous men, including her spiritual master Rufinus of Aquileia, **Jerome** and **Augustine**. Feast 8 June.

Melania the Younger, born Rome, *c.* 385, grand-daughter of **Melania the Elder**, died 31 December 439. After the early death of both their children, she and her husband **Pinianus** adopted an ascetic lifestyle, against the will of their families. With their money they started and kept alive many spiritual communities and charitable institutions. They founded convents in Sicily and Africa and travelled to Egypt and Palestine. On the Mount of Olives they built a convent, where Melania spent the last years of her life after her husband's death.

Melanippus, see **Cosconius**.

Melas, bishop, died *c.* 385. He was a monk who was appointed bishop of Rhinocolura, east of Port Said. He was an opponent of Arianism, and was exiled. Feast 16 January.

Melasippus, Carina and Anthony, martyrs, died Ancyra, 360. They were a husband and wife with their son – or daughter (Antonia) – who died in the persecution of Julian. The son/daughter was beheaded; the parents were tortured to death. Feast 7 November.

Melchior García Sampedro, bishop and martyr, born Cortes, Asturias, Spain, 26 April 1821, died Vietnam, 28 July 1858. In 1845 he became a Dominican at Ocaña. He was posted as a missionary in Tonkin (Vietnam), which was particularly dangerous due to the anti-Christian policies of the emperor. He was made coadjutor to the vicar apostolic of the region, **Joseph Díaz Sanjuro**, whom he succeeded as bishop. In 1858, bishop Garcia was ambushed and taken prisoner, tortured, and eventually killed.

Melchior Grodecz, martyr, born Cieszyn, Silesia, 1584, died Kosice, Slovakia, 7 September 1619. He studied at the Jesuit college in Vienna, joined the Society of Jesus in 1603 and met **Stephen Pongracz** at the noviceship in Brno. He taught in Prague. By 1619 he was working in Kosice with Stephen and **Mark Körösi** when the three were executed by Protestant troops.

Melchior Sánchez, bl., Augustinian and martyr, born Granada, 1599, died Nagasaki, 11 December 1632. He entered the Augustinians when he was 19, and was sent to the Philippines, where he worked as a missionary in Mindanao, learning the local languages. In 1632, however, he volunteered to go with **Martin Lumbreras** to Japan, where he was promptly arrested and executed.

Melchisedech, monk, died Mida, sixteenth century. Ethiopian Church.

Melchisedech and Karapet, martyrs, died Van, fourteenth/fifteenth century. Armenian Church. Two young men accused of defacing a Muslim

tomb. They were given the opportunity to convert to Islam, but refused and were executed.

Melchisedech of Dagina, monk, born Dagina, near Axum. Ethiopian Church.

Meletius, bl., monk, thirteenth century. Byzantine Church. A monk of the monastery of Galisou in Asia Minor, he had his tongue cut out in 1275 for his defence of Orthodoxy against those – including the emperor – who were fostering better relations with the Latin Church.

Meletius and Isacius, bishops and martyrs, died Cyprus (?). Feast 21 September.

Meletius of Antioch, bishop, born Melitene, Armenia, died Constantinople, 381. He was elected bishop of Sebaste in 358, and patriarch of Antioch in 360. He was exiled for his opposition to Arianism, but was allowed back in 378. He died at the Council of Constantinople. Feast 12 February.

Meletius of Char'kov, bishop, born Poltava, 6 November 1784, died Char'kov, 29 February 1840. Russian Church. Of a noble family, Michael Ivanovic Leontovic, as he was called, was brought up in poverty after the death of his family. He studied at Ekaterinoslavl and at St Petersburg, being for some time a teacher of ancient Greek in St Petersburg. He went on to hold other academic posts, but in 1820 became a monk and from 1821 to 1823 was archimandrite of the monastery of Kuteensk Orsansk, and then held similar positions elsewhere, before being elected bishop of Cigirinsk in 1826. Two years later he was moved to Perm, and three years after that became archbishop of Irkutsk. Finally, in 1835, he moved to Char'kov. In all of these bishoprics he undertook the same tasks, improving the educational standards of the clergy and preaching to the non-Christians in the region.

Meletius of Sebastopol, bishop, died 295 (?). Mentioned by Eusebius, who came to know him when he took refuge in the Holy Land during the persecution of Decius. Feast 4 December.

Meletius, Serapion and Philaret, monks, died Kiev, thirteenth century. Monks of the Kievan Cave monastery.

Meletius the Younger, bl., born Mutalaski, Cappadocia, *c.* 1035, died Mount Cytheron, 1 September 1105. Byzantine Church. His parents wished him to marry, but he wanted to become a monk. He ran away from home to Constantinople where he entered a monastery. After some years he decided to go on pilgrimage to Jerusalem and Rome, but on the way he lived for nearly 30 years in the monastery of St George at Tebe before continuing the journey, first to Jerusalem, where he stayed for three years, and then to Rome, continuing on to Spain. He returned to Tebe, where he was received with great honour, but did not stay, moving to Mount Cytheron in Boeotia, to the monastery of the Paraclete, where he became hegumenos. Under his direction the monastery grew considerably, and became an important cultural centre for that part of Greece.

Melitina, martyr, died Marcianopolis (now in Bulgaria), *c.* 150. Feast 15 September.

Melito of St Sabas, abbot, sixth century. Feast 3 January.

Melito of Sardis, bishop, died Sardis, near Smyrna, *c.* 180. Nothing is known of his life, but his several writings were held in high esteem. He is best known now for his Easter homily. But he is known to have sent an apology for – a defence of – Christianity to the emperor. Feast 1 April.

Mellitus, third archbishop of Canterbury, died Canterbury, 24 April 624. He was possibly a monk at St Andrew's monastery in Rome and part of the second cohort of missionaries sent in 601 to help **Augustine** in Britain. He was consecrated bishop of the East Saxons in 604 with his see in London – St Paul's was built as his cathedral. After a brief banishment to France, he returned to Britain and became archbishop of Canterbury in 619.

Memmius, bishop, third/fourth century. First bishop of Châlons-sur-Marne. Feast 5 August.

Menas, martyr. Coptic Church.

Menas, monk. Coptic Church. A monk of the Thebaid.

Menas of al-Asmunayn, monk and martyr, born Ihmim, died al-Asmunayn, seventh century. Coptic Church. He died at about the time of the Arab capture of Egypt. He upheld the divinity of Christ in debate with the head of Muslim troops, who ordered his execution.

Menas of Bawit, monk. Coptic Church. Possibly the abbot of the monastery of Bawit.

Menas of Constantinople, patriarch, participant in the Three Chapters controversy, born Alexandria, *c.* 500, died Constantinople, 552. He was ordained to the priesthood in Constantinople. When Anthimus was removed from the patriarchate of that city by Pope Agapitus because of the former's monophysite leanings, Menas was consecrated as the new patriarch by the pope. Menas opposed the teachings of Origen and signed Emperor Justinian's condemnation of the Three Chapters, which were Nestorian documents. This caused Pope Vigilius, whose opinion on this issue mirrored his fluctuating relationship with Emperor Justinian, to excommunicate Menas on two separate occasions, only to be reconciled with him later. Menas did not live long enough to witness the pope's eventual condemnation of the Three Chapters. Feast 25 August.

Menas of Egypt, martyr, died Alexandria, *c.* 300. An Egyptian officer in the Roman army. Feast 11 November.

Menas of Nikiu, bishop, seventh century. Coptic Church. A monk of the monastery of St Macarius who was elected bishop of Nikiu.

Menas of Tmuis, bishop, born Sammanud, died Tmuis, 3 November 768. Coptic Church. He was obliged by his parents to marry, but lived in chastity with his wife, both of them winding chains about their body in mortification. However, he eventually entered the monastery of St Anthony, and then moved to that of St Macarius. He was chosen as bishop of Tmuis, an office which he held for many years – he is said to have lived to the age of 95.

Meneus and Capito, martyrs. Feast 24 July.

Menignus, martyr, died Parium, Hellespont, *c.* 250. A dyer, he tore down the imperial edict against Christians, for which he had his fingers chopped off and was later beheaded. Feast 15 March.

Menodora, Metrodora and Nymphodora, martyrs, died Bithynia. Three sisters. Feast 10 September.

Meradioc, born Wales, died Britanny, sixth century (?). Nothing at all is known of him for sure, although his name indicates Wales as his place of birth, and there are parishes in Britanny dedicated to him, which suggests he went there, probably from Cornwall, where he is credited with founding the church at Cambourne. Feast 7 June.

Merbot, bl., martyr, died Alberschwende, near Bregenz, Austria, 23 March 1120. According to legend, Merbot was the brother of Bl. **Diedo of Andelsbuch** and Bl. **Ilga**. A Benedictine monk at Mehrerau, he was made pastor of the church in Alberschwende when it was acquired by the abbey. Settlers killed him, but later, over his grave, a chapel was built that became a pilgrimage site. Feast 19 March.

Mercurius, monk, born Manbarta, 23 August 1290, died Dabra Demah, 12 December 1420. Ethiopian Church. He was ordained priest and began to preach, founding five churches. At Dabra Semana he received the habit of a monk. He continued his travels after a while, settling for a time, when he was 50, at Dabra Agd in Goggiam, where he eventually became superior of the monastery. He then lived for a while in Axum, but retreated to Gadama Gorasa because the fame of his holiness brought crowds to his door. There he formed his disciples, both men and women, into a religious community, but a few years later was again on his travels, to the Holy Land and to Alexandria. He also visited Armenia. When he returned to Ethiopia he founded two communities, one male, one female, at Dabra Demah. He made one more journey to Armenia, and on his return founded yet another monastery at Barbar Zagi. When he was just over 100 years old, he returned to Dabra Demah, where he continued an active life until he was 130.

Mercurius, martyr, died Cappadocia, *c.* 251. According to legend, he was a soldier who distinguished himself in the defence of Rome. When, however, he was required to offer sacrifice to the gods, he refused. He was taken to Caesarea in Cappadocia to be beheaded. Feast 25 November.

Mercurius of Smolensk, bishop. Russian Church. Probably an eleventh-century bishop. His remains are at the Kievan Cave monastery. Feast 7 August.

Mercurius of Smolensk, soldier and martyr, born Smolensk, died there, 1239. Russian Church. A story of a soldier who, almost single-handedly, turned back the Mongol army of Batu from the city of Smolensk (which was indeed the only major city not to fall to the Mongols at the time). He took on this task because of a vision of the Virgin, but the vision also said that he would be slain immediately afterwards – as indeed happened.

Mercurius the Faster, monk, died Kiev, fourteenth century. Russian Church. A monk of the Kievan Cave monastery. Feast 28 August.

Merewenna, abbess, died Romsey, Hampshire, tenth century. Feast 29 October.

Mesrop, an important figure in Armenian culture, born Hassik, province of Taron, *c.* 361, died Valarsabad, 441, a year after becoming patriarch. The correct version of his name is probably Mashtotz, and his life is told in a biography by his pupil Korium in the middle of the fifth century. Mashtotz was skilled in languages, being knowledgeable in Greek, Persian and Syriac, and was secretary to King Chosroes II. In 390 he abandoned this life, first to be a monk, then a missionary, which led to his commissioning a translation of the Bible into Armenian for the use of his converts. There being no Armenian alphabet at the time, he devised one (406), from which developed an independent Armenian literature and culture. He created schools across the country to teach the new alphabet, and adapted it for other neighbouring regions he evangelized. He succeeded Sahak III as patriarch in 440. Feast 25 November.

Methodia of Kimolos, recluse, and healer, born island of Kimolos, 10 November 1865, died there,

5 October 1908. She was widowed early and took monastic vows, but lived entirely alone in a little mountain cell, only leaving it to receive communion on Sundays. She received large numbers of (only) female visitors and is an example of a 'spiritual mother'. She was never formally canonized, but her body was enshrined in a new church, a service composed in her honour, and she was entered into the Greek Church calendar of saints. Feast 5 October.

Methodius, archbishop, born Thessalonika, *c.* 815, died Velehrad (Czech Republic), 6 April 885. He and his brother **Cyril** were born into a senatorial family and both became priests. They were sent, *c.* 863, to Moravia as missionaries at the request of the local ruler, who wanted the liturgy and the Bible in the vernacular. In Moravia they encountered German missionaries who distrusted them, and they decided to return to Constantinople. They were, however, invited to Rome by Pope Nicholas I, but were received there by his successor, Hadrian II, who consecrated both of them bishops and created the archdiocese of Sirmium for Methodius. The Germans continued to oppose him, however, and for a time he was imprisoned and only released on the instruction of Pope John VIII. Some claimed that the use of Slavonic in the liturgy was contrary to orthodoxy, but Pope John supported Methodius and confirmed him as archbishop. He and his brother were declared patron saints of Europe – with St **Benedict** – by John Paul II. Feast 14 February.

Methodius of Constantinople ('the Confessor'), patriarch, born Syracuse, died Constantinople, 847. He went to Constantinople looking for preferment, but instead felt the call to religious life. He founded a monastery on the island of Chios, but was then called back by the patriarch to help run the diocese. He was an opponent of iconoclasm, and was sent to Rome by fellow opponents to inform the pope of what was going on. On his return he was imprisoned (in 821), and stayed there for seven years. He was briefly in prison again some year later, was badly beaten and his jaw broken, but in 842 was appointed patriarch by the Empress Theodora. He called a council which asserted the lawfulness of venerating images. He was also a hymn writer. Feast 14 June.

Methodius of Crete, martyr, born Vizari, Crete, died Lampi (?), 9 July 1793. Byzantine Church. He became hegumenos of the monastery of the Assumption, and was elected bishop of Lampi. He was imprisoned, and then executed, by the Turks.

Methodius of Olympus, bishop (?). His life is clouded with uncertainty. He lived at the turn of the third and fourth centuries. He may have been bishop of Olympus (Lycia), but Tyrus, Patara and Philippi are also associated with his name. He may also have died a martyr's death. We know for sure that he is the author of *Symposion*, a dialogue in which ten young women praise the virtue of virginity. Several other writings are preserved only in fragments, or in a Palaeoslavonic translation. Feast 20 September.

Methodius of Penosk, hegumenos, died Penosk, 1392. Russian Church. A disciple of **Sergius of Radonez**, whose permission he asked to establish a hermitage on the river Pesnosa. He soon attracted disciples to his cell, and began a new monastery. Feast 4 June.

Methodius of Pocaev, monk, died 1353. Russian Church. A monk of the Kievan Cave monastery who took refuge in the mountains of Pocaev during the Tartar invasion, and stayed there to develop a new monastery. Feast 10 October.

Metranus, martyred Alexandria, *c.* 249. He was an Egyptian. His bishop and contemporary **Dionysius of Alexandra** described how he was crushed with stones. Feast 31 January.

Metras, martyr, born Alexandria, died there, *c.* 250. Feast 31 January.

Metrius the Farmer, born Paphlagonia, died Constantinople (?), eighth/ninth centuries. He found a great deal of money, but instead of keeping it, he returned it to its rightful owner. That night an angel appeared to him and promised him a much longed-for son, who eventually became valet to the Emperor Leo VI. Feast 1 June.

Metro, hermit in Verona, eighth century. Feast 8 May.

Metrophanes of Byzantium, bishop, died Byzantium, 325. He became bishop of Byzantium, the future Constantinople, in 313. He was too ill to attend the Council of Nicaea in 325, but sent a representative. Sometimes regarded, anachronistically, as the first patriarch of Constantinople. Feast 10 September.

Metrophanes of Vladimir, archbishop and martyr, died Vladimir, 7 February 1238. Russian Church. He had been hegumenos of the monastery of the Nativity of the Mother of God in Vladimir before becoming bishop in 1226. He died, with many others, when the Mongols attacked his cathedral during a liturgy, and set it on fire. Feast 4 February.

Metrophanes of Voronez, bishop, born Antilochnovo, 1623, died Voronez, 23 November 1703. Russian Church. Baptized Michael, he became priest of his local village, but when he was widowed at the age of 40, he became a monk at the monastery of the Dormition at Zolotnikovo, near Suzdal. Although simple and illiterate, he became through his spiritual wisdom hegumenos of two monasteries, and was then made bishop of Voronez when the diocese was created in 1682. He became a close friend and supporter of Tsar Peter the Great, personally contributing money to the development of Peter's fleet. He built churches and preached widely in his diocese, suppressed the Old Believers, and was opposed to the introduction to Voronez of foreign workers for the shipyards, not least because they were not Orthodox Christians.

Mewan, see **Méen**.

Mexico, Martyrs of, see **Christopher Magallanes**.

Michael al-Buhayri, monk, born Asnin al-Nasara, 1847, died monastery of al-Muharraq, 10 February 1923. Coptic Church. He entered the monastery of al-Muharraq at the age of 20, and was ordained priest in 1874. He was close to the hegumenos Bulus, who was desposed in 1869, and his successor was ill-disposed to Michael. He worked as a bookbinder and copier of manuscripts, but also as the spiritual director of the monks. He continued to attend the offices in the church, despite going blind in 1908 and being hard of hearing. He was known as a healer and worker of miracles.

Michael al-Dimyati, martyr, born Damietta, died Cairo, c. 1175 (?). Coptic Church. He entered the monastery of St John in Scete, but then abandoned the monastery, travelled to Cairo, converted to Islam and married. A week after the marriage he repented, giving up his faith, declared himself a Christian once again, and was condemned to death.

Michael al-Tuhi, martyr, born Tuh al-Nasara in the Delta, died Cairo, 23 December 1523. Coptic Church. He learned to read and write, and at the age of eight was ordained deacon. He married, and became the village priest before he was 15. When he was 15 he had reason to go to Cairo, travelling by boat. On the return journey he was accused by some of his fellow passengers of having spoken against Islam, and was taken in chains back to Cairo. He was condemned to be burned alive, but when the flames failed to touch him, he was beheaded.

Michael and Arsenius, monks, ninth century. Georgian Church. They were co-founders of the monastery on Mount Olympus in Bithynia. Feast 3 May.

Michael and Siris, martyrs, died Mardin. Assyrian Church. Brother and sister.

Michael ('the Black') and Theodore, martyrs, died 20 September 1245 (?). Russian Church. Michael was the son of the prince of Cernigov, and was born c. 1185. He ruled successively a number of principalities, although he was always most attached to Cernigov. In 1240, while he was on the throne of Kiev, representatives of the Golden Horde came to discuss peace terms, but were killed by the people of the city. Realizing this would lead to further warfare, Michael went to Hungary and Poland, looking without success for support against the Golden Horde. He therefore returned to Cernigov and went to visit the Khan, accompanied by a boyar named Theodore. He was expected, before meeting the Khan, to perform certain pagan rites, which he refused to do, and was executed. Theodore was then offered the throne of Cernigov if he would perform the rites, but he too refused and was executed. See also

Boris, James, Theodore I, Silvanus, Theodore II, Basil I, Demetrius, Michael, John, Basil II.

Michael Carvalho, Peter Vasquez, Louis Sotelo, Louis Sasanda and Louis Bana, bl., martyrs, died Simabara, Japan, 1624. They were roasted to death. Feast 25 August.

Michael Cernorizec, monk, born Edessa, died Jerusalem, *c.* 860. After the death of his parents he distributed all his wealth to the poor and became a monk at the monastery of St Saba in Palestine. He was given the task of carrying the produce of the monastery to Jerusalem for sale. On one occasion, when he rejected the advances of the queen, he was accused of speaking against Islam and was condemned to death by poison. The poison, however, left him untouched, and he was pierced with a sword.

Michael de la Mora, martyr, born Tecalitlán, Jalisco, Mexico, 19 June 1874, died Cardona, Colima, 7 August 1927. Ordained in 1906 and parish priest in Colima, he was constantly harried by government troops and decided to flee to his brother's ranch. On the way there he was asked by a woman to perform the marriage service for her daughter. The conversation was overheard, he was arrested and shot in a stable. Feast 25 May.

Michael de Santis, mystic, born Vich, Catalonia, 1591, died Valladolid, 10 April 1625. Michael made a vow of chastity at the age of eight, joined the Order of Trinitarians at Barcelona in 1603 – although he later moved to a stricter, reformed branch of the order where he was professed in 1609 – and became a priest in Portugal. He displayed extraordinary mystical gifts, such as levitation when rapt in ecstasy: while preaching in Salamanca, he is reported to have been raised into the air in sight of all his audience. A famous preacher, his favourite topic was the ransom of Christian captives of the Moors.

Michael Fasoli da Zerbo, bl., Franciscan, born Zerbo, near Pavia, Italy, 3 May 1676, martyred Ethiopia, 3 March 1716, with **Liberatus Weiss**, beatified 1988.

Michael Febres Cordero, born Ecuador, 1854, died Spain, 9 February 1910, beatified 1977, canonized 1984. Born with a physical disability affecting his legs, always deeply spiritual, he joined the de la Salle Brothers in 1868. He became a distinguished teacher of Spanish, writing several textbooks. His body is in Ecuador.

Michael Garicoïts, founder of the Bétharram Fathers, born Ibarre, Basses-Pyrénées, France, 15 April 1797, died Bétharram, 14 May 1863. Born of a poor peasant family, he was ordained in 1823. After a period of parish work, he became professor at the seminary of Bétharram (1826). While he was serving as its superior (1831–3), the seminary was moved to Bayonne, but Garicoïts stayed to found the Bétharram Fathers (1832), a congregation devoted to mission and teaching work. He also founded numerous schools and colleges. A leading figure in efforts to re-Christianize the Basses-Pyrénées and re-establish a Church presence in that region, he was beatified in 1923 and canonized in 1947.

Michael Georgievic, prince, died Vladimir, 20 June 1177. Russian Church. He replaced his brother as prince of Vladimir, restoring the wealth of the Church, which had been confiscated, and restoring to power local people rather than foreign nobility. In his brief reign he brought order to the city: so much so that the cities of Rostov and Suzdal chose to put themselves under his leadership.

Michael Ghebre, bl., martyr and theologian, born Mertoule-Miriam, Ethiopia, 1790, died Cerecia-Ghebaba, Ethiopia, 28 August 1855. As a monophysite monk he was renowned for his holiness and theology. Following a visit to Rome, he recast his theology to take account of Catholic Christology, but was suspected of Arianism by his metropolitan. He subsequently became a Roman Catholic, establishing a seminary at Gaula and translating the catechism and Catholic theological works into Ethiopian languages. He was later ordained and became a member of the Vincentian congregation. In 1855 he was imprisoned at the instigation of the metropolitan and died in chains. Feast 1 September.

Michael Giedroyc, bl., born Giedroyc castle, near Vilnius, Lithuania, died Krakow, 1485. He was severely physically disabled, being a dwarf and lame. Soon after becoming an Augustinian canon at our Lady of Metro in Krakow, he moved to a cell by the church, living as a hermit. Feast 4 May.

Michael Giurgea, born Slatina, died there, eighteenth century. Romanian Church. Slatina was a village in which Catholics and Orthodox had lived in harmony. However, after the 1716 uprising of the Austrians against the Turks, there was increasing pressure by the Catholics on the Orthodox to convert. In 1745, when the campaign of proselytism was at its height, Michael was chief among those who refused to convert, even when threatened with being burned alive. His courage served as an inspiration to the other Orthodox of the village.

Michael Gobroni, martyr, died fortress of Qveli, 914. Georgian Church. Michael was captain of a small force defending the fortress of Qveli in southern Georgia against Muslim attacks. When the fortress was taken, the defenders were offered their liberty if they converted to Islam. They refused, and were decapitated in front of Michael to persuade him to deny his faith. He still refused, and was martyred. Feast 17 November.

Michael (Michel) Ho Dinh Hy, martyr, born Nhulam, Vietnam, c. 1808, died An-Hoa, near Hué, Vietnam, 1857, canonized 1988. He was superintendent of the royal silk mills. Of Christian parents, he long ignored his faith, but eventually became a leader of the Christian community. He is commemorated with **Laurence Ngon** – see **Martyrs of Vietnam**. Feast 22 May.

Michael Kozal, bl., martyr, born Nowy Folwark, Poland, 25 September 1893, died Dachau, Germany, 26 January 1943, beatified 1987. Ordained 1918, he was parish priest, seminary teacher and bishop from 1939. Sent to Dachau in 1941, he gave spiritual guidance and celebrated mass whenever he could. He was killed by lethal injection.

Michael Nakaxima, bl., martyr, born Maciai, Japan, died Mount Unzen-Dake, Shimabara, 1628. He had hidden Jesuit missionaries in his house, and then himself joined the Society of Jesus. He was executed by having scalding water from the hot springs of a volcano poured over him. Feast 25 December.

Michael of Adrianople, martyr, born Adrianople, died there, c. 1490. Byzantine Church. Born into a well-to-do family, he married and had children, but his wife died when he was still young. He was a significant figure in the city and in the service of the sultan, a position which he used to help his fellow Christians. His success in representing Christians, and his wealth, aroused the envy of some of the Muslims, who took him before a judge, saying that he had contravened the law. The judge offered him his freedom were he to deny his faith, but he steadfastly refused to do so, despite being imprisoned and tortured. The judge eventually asked the sultan for advice, and he ordered him to be executed. Feast 17 February.

Michael of Agrapha, martyr, born Granitsa of Agrapha, Eurytania, died Thessalonika, 1344. Byzantine Church. He was brought up by pious parents, and married, then moved to Thessalonika where he worked as a baker. While there, however, he declared that he wanted to become a monk, but his relatives dissuaded him, saying that he could not do so without the consent of his wife. One day in the bakery he had a theological debate with a young Muslim, who reported him to a judge, and he was put in prison. That night he had a vision of Christ encouraging him, and the following day, having again refused to deny his faith, he was burned alive. Feast 10 March.

Michael of Alexandria I, patriarch, died Alexandria, 12 March 767. Coptic Church. A monk of the monastery of St Macarius before his election in 744. He was patriarch during a time of great conflict, in part with the Melkite Christians, but also with the Muslim government of Egypt. He was imprisoned several times, and thousands of Christians apostatized. When the oppression by the government led to a rebellion, Michael was held as hostage and was released only when the Muslim ruler was assassinated – not by Christians, but by another party among the Muslims. The persecution did not cease under the new rulers of Egypt, and continued until Michael's death.

Michael of Alexandria II, born Alexandria (?), died monastery of St Macarius, 17 April 851. Coptic Church. After being a monk in the desert of Scete, he was elected patriarch in 849. He was a weak character, but a holy man.

Michael of Alexandria III, patriarch, died 15 February 907. Coptic Church. Elected in 880, he spent a year in prison after a dissident bishop, whom he had deposed, reported to the Egyptian authorities that he was a very rich man. He protested that he did not have any money, but was forced to pay a large amount, effectively a tax on the Church, before he was released.

Michael of Alexandria IV, patriarch, died Old Cairo, 25 May 1102. Coptic Church. A monk of the monastery of St Macarius, he had retired to a hermitage in the desert before he was chosen in 1092. He chose to live in Old Cairo and his patriarchate was marked by conflict between himself and the bishop of Old Cairo, which might have led to his being deposed, had he not died. He was also known for his generosity to the poor.

Michael of Alexandria V, patriarch, died 29 March 1146. Coptic Church. He was a monk of the monastery of St Macarius, as was the favoured candidate, but the latter was opposed by a group of powerful figures within the Coptic Church, and it was decided to choose the new patriarch by lot. Michael was thus selected, despite the fact that he was neither literate nor in priestly orders. He was consecrated in July 1145. He was a forceful personality, and very strict, imposing his will during his relatively short patriarchate by sending people to prison when necessary. Before his death he went back to the monastery of St Macarius.

Michael of Chernigov, prince and martyr, born Novgorod, died Saraj, 20 September 1246. Son of the duke of Novgorod, he was in Hungary attempting to get the assistance of the king against the Tartars after they had sacked Kiev in 1240. When he returned he established himself in Chernigov, but this city, too, was destroyed by the Tartars in 1241. In 1245 he was summoned to the Tartar camp at Saraj on the Volga. He was told he had to abjure his faith, which he refused to do, and

he was beheaded, along with one of his boyars, Theodore. Feast 21 September.

Michael of Klopov, 'fool for Christ', born Moscow, died 1456. Russian Church. Son of the prince of Moscow, he suddenly arrived anonymously at the monastery at Klopov in 1412, and continued to live a strict ascetic life there, until he was recognized by a visiting prince. He remained there until his death, with a reputation for sanctity, working miracles and prophecy. Feast 11 January.

Michael of Naqadah, bishop. Coptic Church.

Michael of Nuhadra, founder, born Nuhadra (?), died Alqos, 1 November 429. Assyrian Church. He was baptized by **Awgen**, and was with him as a monk on Mount Izla, but had to flee during the persecution of Julian the Apostate, when he went to the Holy Land. He later returned to Alqos, north of Mosul, where he lived for the rest of his life, and founded a monastery.

Michael of Qamulah, monk. Coptic Church. A monk of the Thebaid.

Michael of Smolensk, bishop, died Zagorsk, fourteenth/fifteenth centuries. Russian Church. After serving as hegumenos in the monastery of Smonov, he was appointed bishop of Smolensk. In 1336 or 1388 he went to Moscow, and then travelled to Constantinople with Pimen, metropolitan of Moscow. He arrived in Constantinople at the end of June 1389, although Pimen died on the way. The patriarch in Constantinople then sent Cyprian to be metropolitan in Moscow, and Michael travelled back with him. It is unclear whether he ever returned to the see of Smolensk. He spent the final few years of his life in the monastery of the Most Holy Trinity.

Michael of Smolensk, prince, died 1290. Russian Church. Son of **Theodore of Smolensk**. When Theodore was visiting the Golden Horde, the boyars elected Michael in place of his father and would not let Theodore return to the city. Nothing is known of Michael's life.

Michael of Synnada, bishop, born Constantinople (?), died Galatia, *c.* 820. He was appointed bishop of Synnada in Phrygia (in the modern province of Broussa, Turkey) by **Tarasius**, patriarch of Constantinople, in 787. A firm opponent of iconoclasm, he was exiled to Galatia by the Emperor Leo IV. Feast 23 May.

Michael of Taril, founder. Syriac Church. A follower of **Sabriso**, he eventually founded his own monastery in the village of Kilisa, south-west of Erbil.

Michael of Tver, prince, born Pskov, 1333, died Tver, 26 August 1399. Russian Church. His father was the deposed prince of Tver, who fled for safety to Pskov. After his death in 1339 Michael was brought up in Novgorod. In 1364, after the death of his older brothers in a plague, Michael became prince of Tver, although the nominal ruler was his uncle Basil, prince of Kasin. He entered an alliance with Lithuania, and with a Lithuanian army attacked his uncle Basil and forced him to sign a peace treaty. Basil died the following year (1368), leaving Michael as undisputed prince. He had, however, made an enemy of Prince Demetrius of Moscow, who attacked several times, forcing Michael to turn once again to Lithuania, and to the Tartars – who granted him the title of grand prince – for support. The closing years of his rule were peaceful. He showed great care for his subjects, ruling them with justice, and for the future defence of his city. He built churches, and covered with gold the cupola of the cathedral of Tver. Less than a week before his death he entered the monastery next to the cathedral in Tver, and became a monk.

Michael of Vjaznikov, hermit, died Vjaznikov, 1422. Russian Church. A layman who belonged to the monastery of the Dormition at Vjaznikov and practised great austerities, including wearing chains about himself. He had a reputation as a miracle worker. Feast 9 November.

Michael Paknanas, martyr, born Athens, died there, 9 July 1771. Byzantine Church. He was a gardener in Athens who used to sell food to people on the periphery of the city. On one occasion, as he was returning, he was arrested by Turkish soldiers and accused of carrying supplies to the Greek rebels. He was offered his freedom if he converted

to Islam, but he refused to do so, and was put to death by the sword. Feast 9 July.

Michael Parecheli, born Norghialisi, southern Georgia, died Parechi, ninth century. Georgian Church. Originally a monk of the monastery of Miznazori, he moved to that of Chanztha, but later became a hermit at Parechi, living in a cave he had himself dug, and where he was buried.

Michael Pro, bl., martyr, born Guadalupe, Zacatecas, Mexico, 13 January 1891, died Mexico City, 23 November 1927. The son of a mining engineer, Michael was sent to the Jesuit college in Mexico City, but had to leave because of ill-health. He then went to a state school, but was withdrawn because of its anti-Catholic bias. He was then educated privately. At 15 he became his father's secretary, but in 1911 he joined the Jesuits. When rebels attacked the noviceship, Michael fled to the USA, and was later sent to Spain, Nicaragua and Belgium to complete his studies. He was ordained at Enghien, Belgium, in 1925, returning the following year to Mexico. By this time the Church in Mexico was being persecuted: Michael lived with his family, now in Mexico City, and operated secretly. After an attempt on the life of the president-elect, he was arrested, charged with the bomb plot (even though the perpetrator had confessed) and summarily executed by firing squad.

Michael Rua, bl., born Turin, 1837, died there, 6 April 1910, beatified 1972. He worked with **John Bosco** from the start of the Salesians. He took vows in 1855, was ordained in 1860, and succeeded him as head of the order. He greatly expanded the order, developing its missionary aspect.

Michael the Monk, born Susan, died Mosul (?), fourth century. Assyrian Church. He is called 'the companion of angels' because his birth was announced by the archangel Gabriel. At 30 he became a monk, and a few years afterwards went to live as a solitary. He became a disciple of **Awgen**, whose life he wrote. He later returned to the district of Mosul to evangelize the people, and the foundation of a monastery north-west of Mosul is attributed to him. Feast 13 October.

Michael the Soldier, born Potuka, died Bulgaria, c. 880. The legendary story of a soldier who, like St **George**, battled with a dragon. Feast 22 November.

Midius. Coptic Church.

Miguel, see **Michael**.

Milburga, died Wenlock, England, c. 715. A granddaughter of Penda, king of Mercia, daughter of Mereweld and **Ermenburga** of Mercia, sister to **Mildred** of Thanet and Mildgyth, she founded Wenlock, Shropshire (now Much Wenlock), and was second abbess. She was said to have power over birds and her tomb was the focus of a cult until the dissolution of the monasteries. Feast 23 February.

Mildred, abbess, died c. 700. She was the daughter of King Mereweld of Mercia. She was educated in Paris, but returned to England and became a nun at the abbey founded by her mother at Minster-in-Thanet. She became abbess after her mother's death, and died herself after a long illness around the end of the seventh century. Feast 13 July.

Milica, princess, died monastery of Ljubustinija, fourteenth century. Serbian Church. She married Prince **Lazarus** in 1353, and after his death served as regent for her son **Stephen Lazarevic**. In 1398 she founded the monastery of Ljubustinija, becoming a nun there in 1393, taking the name Eugenia. Feast 19 July.

Millán (Emilian), hermit, born 473, died near the monastery of La Cogolla, 574. A shepherd in his youth, he became a hermit at the age of 20 in the mountains not far from Burgos, near the village of Berceo in the Rioja region of Spain. He became a priest, and the local bishop insisted he look after a parish, at which he was not a success. He therefore returned to the solitary life, although by this time with a group of disciples. His hermitage is thought to have been near the present monastery of La Cogolla. He is one of the patrons of Spain. Feast 12 November.

Milles, bishop and martyr, born Persia, died there, c. 360. He was bishop of Susa, and was martyred by being hacked into pieces. Feast 22 August.

Milo, born Auvergne, died Benevento, Campania, 1076. He was a canon of Paris and dean of the chapter, who became bishop of Benevento in 1074. Feast 23 February.

Miltiades, pope from c. 311, born Rome, died there, 10 January 314. Elected bishop of Rome shortly after the Edict of Toleration, Miltiades's role in the legalization of Christianity is not known. He did, however, play a role in the Donatist controversy. At the initiative of Emperor **Constantine**, he convened a synod in Rome to consider both the election of Caecilian as bishop of Carthage and what the response of the Church should be to those who, like Caecilian, had allegedly apostatized under persecution. At the synod, Miltiades did not endorse the strict stand of the north African bishops and confirmed the election of Caecilian, excommunicating his rival Donatus. Feast 10 December.

Miles Gerard, bl., martyr, born Wigan, Lancashire, 1549, died Rochester, Kent, 19 or 30 April 1590, beatified 1929. Ordained at Rheims in 1583, he and **Francis Dickenson** were shipwrecked at Dover and arrested. Francis and Miles are commemorated together. Feast 30 April.

Milutin, king, died Banjska, 29 October 1321. Serbian Church. A very successful king of Serbia from 1282, expanding its territory by strategic alliances – including with the pope – and through his five marriages. He was a great founder of churches and monasteries. Feast 30 October.

Mina of Polock, bishop, died Polock, 20 June 1116. Russian Church. A monk of the Kievan Cave monastery, he became the first bishop of Polock in December 1105.

Mirak of Tabriz, martyr, born Tabriz, died 24 March 1486. Armenian Church. Of noble birth, he entered the service of the shah despite being a Christian, and served as Armenian ambassador to Venice, the Papal States and Naples. He used his position to win better treatment for Christian prisoners, and built churches. But his success earned him the emnity of some at the court. There was a conspiracy against him, and he was ordered to convert to Islam, which he refused to do. He was executed.

Mirdat, king and martyr, died Baghdad, fifth century. Georgian Church. He was ruler of eastern Georgia from *c*. 408–10, and was captured in battle against the Persians. Taken to Baghdad, he was offered his freedom if he converted to Islam, but he refused and, after a long imprisonment, was executed. Feast 18 July.

Mirian, or Meribanes, first Christian king of Iberia (east Georgia), born Iberia, *c*. 282, died Iberia, 361. Mirian was a scion of the house of Mihran, one of the monarchial houses of Iran, and was made king of Iberia by the Iranians to counterbalance the Roman presence in Armenia. He was converted in 334 through the ministry of St **Nino** and was baptized along with his subjects by priests sent by Constantine in 337. Feast 1 October.

Mirin, born Ireland, died Paisley, Scotland (?), seventh century. Possibly a disciple of **Comgall**, he may have been abbot of Bangor before working as a missionary in Scotland, possibly in the Paisley area. Feast 15 September.

Miro, bishop on Crete, fourth century. Feast 9 August.

Misael, monk, died Fayyum, seventh/eighth centuries. Coptic Church. An orphan at seven, and in the care of the local bishop, he entered the monastery of Dayr al-Qalamun, in Fayyum, at the age of 12. He progressed quickly in the spiritual life, and was granted the gift of prophecy. He asked his abbot, Isaac, for permission to become a hermit, which was granted. Before he left the monastery, however, Misael prophesied that there would be a famine and that he would return to defend the monastery. Isaac therefore laid in supples of food, but when the famine came the local governor attempted to confiscate these. The monastery was defended by a troop of soldiers, who turned out to be hermits under the leadership of Misael.

Misael, Nicetas and Theophanes, monks, seventeenth century. Russian Church. Monks of the Solovki monastery.

Misael of Abalack, monk, born Lipojarskoe, near Tambov, 29 June 1797, died Abalack, 19 August 1852. Russian Church. He was baptized Pavel Ivanovic Fokin, the son of a deacon. He studied in the seminary at Tobolsk. Although attracted to the ascetical life, his parents insisted that he marry, which he did in 1819, and he was ordained the following year. He ministered in his home village, and had three children. In 1839 his wife died, and he became a monk at the monastery of the Mother of God in the town of Abalack, to which he had been moved a few years earlier, taking the name Misael. He went on to become hieromonk at the cathedral of Tobolsk, confessor to the bishop, and spiritual guide to many of the clergy. Feast 10 June.

Mochta, abbot, born England, died Louth, Ireland, fifth century. Said to have been a disciple of **Patrick**. He was born of Christian parents who brought him to Ireland when he was a child. Feast 19 August.

Mochua, abbot, born Achonry, district of Connacht, Ireland, died Derinish, County Cavan, 657. A warrior before he became a monk, he founded the monastery at Derenish, where he died, but also that of Timahoe and possibly others, including in Scotland. Feast 24 December.

Mocius, martyr, died Byzantium (Constantinople), *c*. 300. A priest in Amphipolis (modern Amfipoli), Thrace, he is said to have destroyed a pagan altar while the consul was offering sacrifice. He was arrested and sent to Byzantium, where he was beheaded. Feast 10 May.

Modan, died possibly Rosneath monastery, Dumbarton, Scotland, *c*. 550 (or perhaps eighth century). He is supposed to have been a monk who preached around Stirling and Falkirk, was made abbot against his will and meditated alone in the mountains. He is titular saint of the high church in Stirling. Feast 4 February.

Modestus, died Carinthia, *c*. 722. He was a Benedictine monk under **Virgilius of Salzburg** and a missionary bishop in Carinthia. Feast 5 February.

Modestus, see also **Vitus**.

Modestus and Ammonius, martyrs, died Alexandria. Feast 12 February.

Modoaldus (Modoald, Modowald, Romoald), bishop, born Aquitaine, died Trier, Rhineland, 640. He served the Merovingian king Dagobert I, who appointed him bishop of Trier in 622. He participated in the Council of Rheims in 625 and eventually persuaded the king to repent of his immoral behaviour. Feast 12 May.

Moling, bishop, born Kinsellagh, County Wexford, Ireland, died monastery of Tech Moling (modern St Mullins, Carlow), 697. Said to have been related to the kings of Leinster, he entered the monastery at Glendalough, then founded his own abbey at what is now St Mullins. He became bishop of Ferns, and settled a quarrel with the kings of Leinster over the tribute to be paid by the Church. He resigned his see and retired to his monastery some years before his death. Feast 17 June.

Molua, abbot, born Ossory, Ireland, died 608. Said to have been a herdsman who went to Bangor in Wales to study, became a priest, and then established several monasteries, including Clonfert-mulloe, near Offaly. Feast 4 August.

Moluag, bishop, born Ireland, *c.* 520, died Rossmarkie, Scotland, 592. He became a monk at Bangor, then travelled to Scotland, founding the monastery at Lismore *c.* 562. He evangelized the region of Ross, and went as far as the Outer Hebrides. Feast 25 June.

Mommolinus of Noyon, bishop, born Coutances, Nomandy, died *c.* 686. He became a monk at the abbey of Luxeuil, and then with two companions became a missionary in the region around St Omer in northern France. He started a monastery at what is now St-Mommélin, then another at Sithiu. He became bishop of Noyon in 660, and established yet another monastery at St Quentin. Feast 16 October.

Mona, bishop, fourth century. He was bishop of Milan. Feast 25 March.

Monaldus of Ancona, Francis of Fermo and Antony of Milan, bl., martyrs, died at Arzenga, Armenia, 1286. They were Franciscan friars sent as missionaries to Armenia. Feast 15 March.

Monegundis, born Chartres, France, sixth century, died Tours, France, *c.* 570. After her two daughters died in childhood she became an anchoress. She built a cell and lived there in solitude until she gained a reputation for her healing powers. To avoid this fame she moved to Tours, where she built a hermitage near the shrine of St **Martin**. Here she was joined by many women wishing to dedicate themselves to solitude and prayer, and they founded the convent of St-Pierre-le-Puellier. Feast 2 July.

Mon(n)ica, mother of St **Augustine of Hippo**, born Tagaste (Numidia), 331, died Ostia, Italy, autumn 387. Married to the pagan Patricius, who later converted to Christianity under her influence, she had three children: Navigius, Augustine and a daughter. Monica followed Augustine's spiritual growth closely, including his struggles to free himself from Manichaeism. After a futile attempt to arrange a marriage for him, she attended his baptism by St **Ambrose** at Easter 387. She died on her way home to Africa. Feast 27 August.

Monica Pichery, see **Felicity Pricet**.

Montanus and Companions, martyrs, born Carthage, died there, 259. He is one of eight Christians, most of them priests and all disciples of **Cyprian**, who were arrested, tortured and executed. They left their own account of their imprisonment, and their deaths were described by eyewitnesses. Feast 23 May.

Montanus and Maxima, martyrs, died Sirmium (Srem Metrovica), 304. A husband – said to have been a priest – and wife, drowned in the river Save for their faith. Feast 26 March.

Montford Scott, bl., martyr, born Hawstead, Suffolk, died London, 1 July 1591. He studied at Cambridge, but went to Douai in 1574. He was captured in England in 1576, but he had returned to Douai by 1577 and was ordained in Brussels in June that year. He was sent to England, but was soon arrested in Cambridge and was sent to London. However, in the 1580s he was again working as a priest in East Anglia, until he was captured in Hawstead in December 1590. He was sent to prison in London, and was hanged, drawn and quartered the following year in Fleet Street, along with **George Beesley**.

Morandus, Benedictine prior, born near Worms, Germany, c. 1115, died Altkirch, Alsace, France. Morandus was trained and ordained in Worms and became a monk at the abbey of Cluny upon returning from a pilgrimage to Santiago de Compostela. His exemplary life led him to be named prior, first of the monastery of Auvergne and then of Altkirch in Alsace. He was buried in Altkirch, and his tomb soon became a place of pilgrimage. He is said to have fasted during Lent eating only grapes, for which he has become a patron of wine growers, and his emblems in art are a bunch of grapes and a pruning knife. Feast 3 June.

Moses, bishop, died c. 389. An Arab by birth, he was a hermit before becoming a wandering bishop among the then animist Arab nomads in the Middle East. Apparently a warrior queen called Mavis had fought the Romans and agreed to peace, provided Moses became their bishop. Feast 7 February.

Moses and Ammonius, martyrs, died Astas, Bithynia, c. 250. Two soldiers, first condemned to the mines for their faith, then burned alive. Feast 18 January.

Moses bar Kipha, bishop, born Kuhayl, died 903. Syriac Church. He became a monk c. 823 in the monastery of St Sergius on Mount Arido, and was elected bishop of Bet Raman-Bat Waziq, on the Tigris, north of Tikrit.

Moses Khorenatzi, bishop (?), fifth century. Armenian Church. All that is known of him is contained in his *History of Armenia*, which is an important source of information about early Armenia. He claims to have been a disciple of **Isaac the Great** and of **Mesrop**. The details of his life contained in this work are, however, not reliable. It has been suggested that he was a bishop, and that he was possibly martyred.

Moses Macinic, born Sibiel, Transylvania, died Kufstein, Austria, eighteenth century. Romanian Church. He was ordained priest in Bucharest c. 1745. As a disciple of **Bessarion of Romania**, he opposed those who were working for reunion between the Orthodox and Catholic Churches, which was imperial policy. He was imprisoned for 17 months in Sibiu. In 1750 he signed a declaration about the sufferings of the Orthodox in Transylvania, and some years later took a petition to Vienna on their behalf. This resulted in his imprisonment in Kufstein. In July 1784 his wife petitioned the imperial government for his release, but received the reply that they had heard nothing of him for 30 years – which can only imply that he had died in prison. Feast 21 October.

Moses of Abidos, monk, sixth century. Coptic Church. One of several children, he became a monk and, filled with zeal for the gospel – which he had committed to memory – he pulled down pagan temples in his region. He founded the monastery of Abidos, and also other monasteries both for men and for women.

Moses of Africa, martyr, died north Africa, c. 250. Feast 18 December.

Moses of Awsim, bishop, eighth century. Coptic Church. He was a monk in the desert of Scete for 18 years before being elected bishop of Awsim (an area south of Cairo). He played an important role, despite ill-health, in the election of the patriarch **Michael of Alexandria I**, using force to constrain opponents of his election. He was bishop for 20 years.

Moses of Beloozero ('the Prophet'), monk, died c. 1492. Russian Church. Said to have prophesied that his monastery at Beloozero would be relocated three times – which came to pass. Feast 23 February.

Moses of Novgorod, archbishop, born Novgorod, died there, 25 January 1362. Russian Church. Baptized Metrophanes, he came from a wealthy family and, when quite young, entered a monastery at Tver. He became hegumenos at the monastery of St George in Novgorod, and in 1324 bishop of the city. It was a difficult time because of the Tartar invasions. He built and fortified churches and monasteries, he had liturgical books copied, and he looked after the material as well as the spiritual needs of the people. In 1330 he retired to a monastery, but 20 years later returned to the city, retiring again to a monastery in 1357.

Moses of Optina, monk, born Borisogglebsk, 15 January 1782, died Optina, 16 June 1862. Russian Church. Baptized Timothy Ivanovic Puilov, he was the brother of **Andrew of Optina**. He worked with his father in Moscow, but had always been attracted to the ascetical life and for a year lived in a hermitage. In 1808 he entered the monastery of Bejan Sven. In 1811, however, he went to live as a hermit in the forest of Roslavl. At the request of the patriarch **Philaret**, he moved in 1821 to the hermitage of Optina. The following year he was ordained priest and in 1826 became superior of the community. In 1853 he became an archimandrite. Feast 11 October.

Moses of Rome, martyr, died Rome, 251. He was a priest of Rome, and a leader of a group of priests opposed to the antipope Novatian. After an imprisonment of almost a year, he was among the first to die in the persecution of the Emperor Decius. Feast 24 November.

Moses of the Kievan Cave Monastery, monk, thirteenth/fourteenth centuries. Russian Church. He punished his body by wearing chains about it. He particularly delighted in singing the psalms. Feast 28 August.

Moses Rabban, monk, died monastery of Bet Sayyare, 947. Syriac Church. Feast 15 November.

Moses the Arab, bishop, died Sinai peninsula, c. 372. A hermit, he became a missionary among the Bedouin. Feast 7 February.

Moses the Black, monk, born Egypt, c. 330, died desert of Scete, 405. Moses began his life as a servant of an Egyptian official, was dismissed for immoral behaviour, and soon took up the life of an outlaw. The details of his conversion are not recorded, but he next appears at the monastery of Petra in the desert of Scete. There, through the help of St **Isidore**, he was able to overcome his

violent nature and was ordained a priest by **Theophilus of Alexandria**. He remained at his monastery when it was threatened by the Berbers and perished there with five of his fellow monks. Feast 28 August.

Moseus, martyred 250. He was a soldier, arrested with **Ammonius**, also a soldier, for supporting Christians during the persecutions of Decius. Both were condemned to forced labour in the mines of Bithynia before being burned at the stake. Feast 18 January.

Moseus, see also **Antoninus**.

Mount Sinai, Martyrs of, see **Martyrs of Mount Sinai**.

Mstislav II, prince, born Kiev, died 1172. Russian Church. He was given the throne of Perejaslavl by his father, who was prince of Kiev. Because of feuding in his family, he had to abandon that city and take refuge at Sluck, but eventually recovered Kiev in 1167. Less than two years later, however, **Andrew of Bogoljubovo** succeeded in driving him from Kiev, giving the throne to his younger son Gleb. Mstislav in turn drove Gleb out in 1170, and was welcomed back by grateful citizens, but was not able to hold the city and went to Volynia, returning again with an army in 1172, but dying before he could attempt to retake it. Feast 23 June.

Mstislav of Novgorod, prince, born Novgorod, died there, 14 June 1180. Russian Church. He was elected prince in 1179, and was renowned for his piety as well as for his courage on the battlefield. As he lay dying he asked to be taken into church, where he received communion.

Mstislav of Novgorod ('the Bold'), born Novgorod, died Torcesk, 1228. His father had been a much loved prince of Novgorod, but Mstislav was passed over for the succession at his death, the throne passing to Vsevolod. In 1209, however, the people of Novgorod proclaimed him prince, and he set about reorganizing the administration – which entailed exiling the bishop and bringing in another. He did not stay continuously in Novgorod, but also occupied Galic, leaving Novgorod to be run by others. When the Mongols first invaded in 1223, he organized the princes to oppose them, but they lost the battle of the river Kalka in May that year. Although Mstislav returned safely to Galic, he found that the city had been sacked by Poles and Hungarians. He then established an alliance with the Hungarians by marrying a daughter to a Hungarian prince. He retired from the governance of Galic and went to live at Podolok, but regretted having done so and started to create an army to win back the city. He died en route to Kiev, having pronounced vows as a monk. Feast 4 October.

Mstislav of Vladimir, prince, born Vladimir, died there, 18 or 28 1173. Russian Church. He was a highly successful military leader on behalf of his father, the prince of Vladimir, leading expeditions against several Russian cities – including Novgorod – and against the Bulgars. He was recorded as pious. Feast 28 March.

Mstislav-Theodore of Kiev, prince, born Vladimir, died 1132. Russian Church. He became prince of Kiev in 1125, and was known for his mercifulness and his gift of prayer. Two of his sons, **Vsevolod of Pskov** and **Rostislav of Smolensk**, are also venerated as saints. Feast 15 April.

Mucianus (Mutien) Wiaux, born Louis Joseph in Mellet, Belgium, 20 March 1841, died Malonne, 30 January 1917, beatified 1977, canonized 1989. A Christian Brother, he taught for 60 years. In poor health, he was not a good classroom teacher, but excelled at one-to-one work, bringing out the best in pupils.

Mucius, martyr, born Byzantium, died there, 304. Supposedly of a Roman family living in Byzantium, he became a priest in Macedonia, but was martyred at Byzantium for overturning pagan altars. Feast 13 May.

Mui, martyr, died Alexandria, fourth century. Coptic Church. Held a prisoner in Alexandria, he worked many miracles.

Mummolus, abbot, died abbey of Fleury, 678. He was the second abbot of the monastery of Fleury. Feast 8 August.

Munchin of Limerick (Mainchin, Manchén – 'little monk'), late seventh century. Patron of Limerick and considered its first bishop (although there is no evidence that he was a bishop), he is called 'the Wise' in early texts. Prince Feardomnach is said to have given him Sitband island. Feast 2 January (3 January in Limerick).

Mungo, see **Kentigern**.

Mylor, martyr. The legend is of a boy, the heir to a dukedom, who was first banished to a monastery and then beheaded to prevent him succeeding to his estate. Again according to the legend, this took place in Brittany, although some versions transfer it to Cornwall or Devon. Feast 1 October.

Myron, martyr, born Heraclea, Crete, died there, 20 March 1793. Byzantine Church. A handsome boy of devout parents, he worked as a tailor. He was accused of seducing a Turkish boy and, being taken before the judge and despite proving his innocence, he was forced either to abjure his faith or to be executed. He refused to deny his faith, and was hanged.

Myron of Crete ('the Wonderworker'), bishop, born Knossos, Crete, c. 250, died there, c. 350. Feast 8 August.

Myron of Cyzicus, martyr, died Cyzicus, c. 250. A priest of Cyzicus on the Sea of Marmara, he attempted to prevent the destruction of his church during the persecution of Decius, and was killed. Feast 17 August.

Myrope of Chios, martyr, born island of Chios, died there, c. 251. She was whipped, and subsequently died in prison of her injuries, for burying those who had died during the persecution of Decius. Feast 13 July.

Na'Akweto La'Ab, king, born *c*. 1204, died 1250. Ethiopian Church. The son of King **Harbay**, and brought up at the court of **Lalibala**, he founded a church, and led an army against the pagan kingdom of Goggiam. He seems to have overthrown Lalibala, but was then overthrown himself, and spent the rest of his life living in a church dressed as a penitent.

Nabis, bishop, born Qift, died Aydab, fourth/fifth century. Coptic Church. He worked in his parents' wine press before becoming a monk. At the age of 40 he became bishop of Aydab, a diocese on the Red Sea. However, rather than settle in Aydab itself, he took up residence in a small church in his home village, going to Aydab only for major feast days.

Nabraha, died fourth century. Coptic Church. He was exiled in the reign of Diocletian, but came back under Constantine and lived as an ascetic for the rest of his life.

Nahyud of Dabra Sihat, monk, fourteenth century. Ethiopian Church. Dabra Sihat was a large monastery in Eritrea, with some 350 monks. Nabyud was remembered for his visions. Feast 27 January.

Naharwah, martyr, born al-Fayyuum, died Antioch, third/fourth century. Coptic Church. He decided to offer himself for martyrdom during the persecution of Diocletian, and set off for Alexandria in order to do so. A vision informed him that, rather than Alexandria, he ought to go to Antioch. As there was no boat available, he was transported there by St Michael the archangel.

Nahum of Ochrida, one of the companions of **Clement the Bulgarian**.

Nana, queen, fourth century. Georgian Church. She was converted to Christianity by St **Nino**. Nino had come to live in the cottage of the gardener to the royal palace at Mzcheta. When Nana was taken ill she summoned Nino, who had a reputation as a healer, but Nino instead demanded that the queen come to her. She did so, was healed, and began her instruction in Christianity. Feast 1 October.

Na'Od, king, died 31 July 1508. Ethiopian Church. He came to the throne in 1495. He was magnanimous to his enemies, a great friend of the monks **Habta Maryam** and **Iyasu di Gar Sellase**, whom he held in high esteem and consulted on difficult issues.

Narcisa de Jesús Martillo Morán, born Nobul, Ecuador, 1837, died Lima, Peru, 8 December 1869. The child of farm labourers, after their deaths she moved to Guayaquil, where she worked for 15 years before moving on to Lima. She was deeply devout, and subjected her body to extraordinary ascetical practices – she would, for instance, hang upon a cross wearing a crown of thorns.

Narcissus, see also **Argeus**.

Narcissus of Jerusalem, bishop, died Jerusalem, *c*. 215. After accusations against him, he disappeared. When he was found, he resumed the administration of his diocese only with reluctance, and St **Alexander** was moved from his own diocese to assist him. Feast 29 October.

Narsetes, see **Nerses**.

Natalia, see also **Aurelius and Natalia**.

Natalia of Nicomedia, born Nicomedia, died Constantinople, c. 311. The wife of the martyr **Adrian of Nicomedia**, she helped persecuted Christians, but survived the persecution herself. Feast 1 December.

Nathalan of Aberdeen, died c. 678, cult confirmed 1898. Apparently he was a pious nobleman who locked his right hand to his leg and went thus to Rome as penance for 'murmuring against God'. Having miraculously found the key, he was made bishop by the pope. Feast 8 January.

Nathanael of Nitria, monk, died Nitria, c. 375. He spent all his life in the one cell. Feast 27 November.

Nathy, bishop, born and died Ireland, sixth century. Said to have been the son of the four-times-married Dediva, and first bishop of Kilmore. Feast 9 August.

Naucratius, hegumenos, died Constantinople, 848. He was a disciple of **Theodore the Studite**. After being driven from Constantinople for his defence of the veneration of images, he returned to be made hegumenos of the Studium monastery. Feast 8 June.

Nazarius, metropolitan, born 1870, died Rodinouli, 25 August 1924. Georgian Church. Baptized Nestor Lezhava, he studied at the seminary in Tbilisi and was ordained in 1892. He became parish priest of Choni, a small village, before going on to further studies in Kiev. He returned to Georgia in 1909 and held various posts before being elected metropolitan of Kutaisi and Ghelathi in 1918. He strongly opposed the atheism of the Soviet Union after its takeover of Georgia, and was arrested and shot during the consecration of a church at Rodinouli.

Nazarius of Lérins, fourteenth abbot of the monastery of Lérins, probably some time during the reign of the Merovingian Clotaire II (i.e. 584–629, although some put his death c. 450). He opposed the heathens in France, destroyed a sanctuary of Venus near Cannes and founded on its site a convent for women, which the Saracens destroyed in the eighth century. Feast 18 November.

Nazarius of Murmansk, see **Eleazar of Murmansk, with Nazarius and Eumenius**.

Nazarius of Sarov, monk, born Anosovo, 1730 (?), died 1809. Russian Church. Baptized Nicholas, in 1752 he entered the hermitage of the Dormition at Sarov. In 1776 he was ordained priest. He had a reputation for great asceticism, and the metropolitan of Novgorod asked him to come to his diocese to help restore the monastery of Valaam, which he did, also constructing a new hermitage. He sent ten of his followers to the Alaskan mission. In 1801 he resigned the office of superior and three years later returned to Sarov. Feast 25 July.

Neagoe Basaarab, prince, born Wallacia, 1481, died there, 1521. He was educated by the monks of the monastery of Bistrita, and retained all his life a deep interest in spiritual and theological matters. He had a clear idea of the duties towards society of a Christian prince, which he recorded in a book dedicated to his son Theodosius.

Nectan, born Wales, died Hartland, Devon (?), sixth century (?). He founded churches in Devon and Cornwall, and is said to have been killed by brigands. Feast 17 June.

Nectarius (Nektarios Kephalas) of Aegina, bishop, born Thrace, 10 October 1846, died Athens, 8 November 1920. Byzantine Church. He was consecrated metropolitan of Pentapolis in the Alexandrian patriarchate, but was expelled by other bishops jealous of his rapid promotion. He arrived penniless in Greece, where he directed a small seminary and later (1908) became chaplain to a convent on the island of Aegina. He wrote many theological works, but it was as confessor and spiritual adviser that he became revered. After his death huge numbers of miracles were attributed to his intercession and his shrine is one of the most popular in the Orthodox world. Canonized 1961. Feast 9 November.

Nectarius of Constantinople, bishop, born Tarsus, Cilicia, died Constantinople, 27 September 397. He was appointed bishop by the emperor in 381, although it seems likely that he was not yet a Christian, and was married. However, his appointment was confirmed by the Council of Constantinople then in session. He presided over the council from then on. During his episcopacy he faced difficulties with the Arians. Feast 11 October.

Nemesius, martyr, born Egypt, died Alexandria, 250. Feast 19 December.

Nemesius and Companions, martyrs, died Alexandria, 257. Nine bishops, who received a letter of encouragement from **Cyprian** of Carthage. There may be some confusion with the previous **Nemesius**. Feast 10 September.

Neophytus, bl., born Constantinople, died Mount Athos, eleventh century. The son of a duke, and secretary to the emperor in Constantinople, he eventually decided to become a monk on Mount Athos, where he entered the monastery of Dochiariou. He became hegumenos, and built a new church, as well as fortifying the monastery against Saracen pirates. He finally became the chief of all the monks on Mount Athos.

Neophytus and Meletius, monks, seventeenth century. Romanian Church. Two monks of the monastery of Cozia, they came to Mount Salbaticul, dug out caves for themselves, and lived rigidly ascetical lives there for some 30 years in the case of Neophytus, and 40 for Meletius.

Neophytus of Nicaea, martyr, born Nicaea, 296, died there, 310. Feast 20 January.

Neophytus of Vatopedi, bl. Byzantine Church. He once heard an icon of the Mother of God speak to him. Feast 21 January.

Neomartyrs, see **Martyrs**.

Neot, died 877 (?). According to tradition he was a Saxon monk of Glastonbury, who was ordained priest by Bishop Aelfheah, visited Rome seven times and preached frequently near Bodmin. He was a kinsman of Aelfred, king of the West Saxons, whom he is said to have reproved for his harsh rule. He became a hermit in Cornwall and was buried at the place now called St Neot. His relics were brought to Crowland c. 1003. Feast 31 July.

Nereus, martyred Terracina Island, c. 100. He and **Achilleus** were Praetorian soldiers who apparently experienced a sudden conversion. Their unreliable story says they were exiled first to Pontia Island with **Flavia Domitilla**, before being beheaded on Terracina. Feast 12 May.

Nerses ('the Great'), born Armenia, c. 333, died c. 373. Educated in Cappadocia and married to a Mamikonian princess, he was the father of St **Isaac the Great**. After his wife's death, he became an ecclesiastic and c. 363 was consecrated patriarch of Armenia by force. He set out to reform the Church, which aroused the hostility of King Arshak III, who exiled him. He was recalled in 369 by the dissolute King Pap and poisoned by him at a meal. Feast 19 November.

Nerses of Lambron, born Cilicia, 1153, died Tarsus, 1198. A nobleman, and a nephew of Nerses Klayetski – by whom he was ordained – he became bishop of Tarsus in 1175. He was actively concerned to bring about the reunion of the Armenians with the Roman Church, which came about in 1198. He was a translator of works by the Fathers of the Church into Armenian. Feast 17 July.

Nerses of Sahgerd, bishop, martyr, died Sahgerd, fourth century. Executed under the Persian king Shapur II, although the king himself had begged the old man – he was over 80 – to conform to the Persian religion. A young man, Joseph, and several others were beheaded at the same time. Feast 19 November.

Nerses Šnorhali ('the Gracious'), catholicos of the Armenians, born near the modern Elazig (Turkey), 1102, died Hromkla, the Armenian patriarchal see, 15 August 1173. He was archbishop, or catholicos, of the Armenians from 1166 in succession to his brother Gregory III. He opened discussions with the patriarch of Constantinople about reunion of the two Churches, accepting the Byzantine calendar and, more controversially, the doctrine of the Council of Chalcedon on the two natures of Christ.

Although unsuccessful in this, his efforts to achieve reunion with the Church of Rome were brought to completion by his nephew **Nerses Lambron**. As well as being a significant theologian of the Armenian tradition, he was an outstanding poet of the nation. Feast 13 August.

Nestor, see also **Basil, Eugene**, et al.

Nestor, martyr, died Perga, 251. Bishop of Magydus in Pamphylia when the Emperor Decius renewed persecutions, he sent people into hiding but refused to leave himself. He was tortured before being crucified. Apparently highly respected, it was said the pagans also prayed for him as he died. Feast 25 February.

Nestor and Tribimaeus, martyrs at Perge in Pamphylia (a city once some eight miles east of modern Antalya, Turkey), third century. Feast 1 March.

Nestor, Ephrem and Euthymius, hermits, fourteenth century. Serbian Church. Three hermits who lived in the Decani. Feast 11 November.

Nestor of Thessalonika, martyr, died Thessalonika, 303. Said to have been challenged to a duel by a pagan, which he won, but the emperor ordered his death anyway. Feast 8 October.

Nestor the Illiterate, monk, died Kiev, fourteenth century. Russian Church. A monk of the Kievan Cave monastery, during the liturgy he would think of God. Feast 28 October.

Nettarius and Theophanes, bl., born Ioannina in the Epirus, died in the Meteora, 7 April 1550 and 17 May 1544 respectively. Byzantine Church. Brothers of the noble Apsarades family, they entered a local monastery, then moved to Mount Athos, and then, at the request of the patriarch, returned to Ioannina where they established a monastery on an island on the lake. After some years, however, they moved to the Meteora, where they built another monastery with the help of monks from a neighbouring institution. From the start this was a coenobitic monastery, where the monks received a good formation.

Nettarius of Aegina, bishop, born Silivria, Thrace, 1 October 1846, died Aegina, 8 November 1920. Byzantine Church. Baptized Anastasias Kefalas, he left his home town and went to live in Constantinople, then found a job as a teacher on the island of Chios. There he entered a monastery, taking the name Lazarus. When he was ordained deacon in 1877 he took the name Nettarius. He moved to Athens for further studies, and was ordained priest there in 1886. He served in the patriarchate, and in 1889 was appointed metropolitan of the Pentapolis. He continued to serve in a number of offices before being made rector of the school at Risarios in 1894, where he stayed for 15 years. He was responsible for the establishment of a convent at Aegina, and when he retired on grounds of ill-health in 1908 he went to the convent, where he died. He published a number of books, especially of his sermons, and articles. Feast 9 November.

Nettarius of Bezeck, hegumenos, died Bezeck, 1492. Russian Church. He began his monastic career in the monastery of **Sergius of Radonez**, then became a hermit at Bezeck. He was famed for his holiness of life and his rigid asceticism, and drew a number of disciples. He built a monastery at Bezeck, and was chosen as hegumenos. He gained a reputation as a miracle worker. Feast 13 April.

Nettarius of Karyes, bl., born Empitolion (modern Monastiri), c. 1430, died Karyes, 5 December 1500. After his father became a monk at an advanced age, Nettarius himself did likewise on Mount Athos. He then helped to establish a small monastery at Karyes, where he died of old age at about 70, famed for his sanctity.

Nettarius of Optina, monk, born Elec, 1853, died Cholmisci, 12 May 1928. Russian Church. Baptized Nikolai Vasil'evic Tichonov and from a very poor family, he went to work as a clerk for a rich merchant. When the head clerk wanted to arrange a marriage with his daughter, Nikolai went for advice to **Ambrose of Optina** and became a monk, taking the name Nettarius. Although rigidly ascetic in his style of life, he nonetheless gave himself to the study of secular literature, learned foreign languages and immersed himself in world culture.

He developed a spirituality which incorporated Christian devotion with humane learning. He became a priest in 1898 and from 1912 was the confessor at Optina. After the 1917 Revolution he prepared his disciples for life under an atheistic regime. In 1923, when the hermitage of Optina was being torn down, he was arrested and condemned to death, but was reprieved, being sent into exile, first to Plochino and finally to Cholmisci.

Nettarius of Tobolsk, bishop, born Ostaskov, 1586, died monastery of St Nilus, Tver, 15 January 1667. Russian Church. Baptized Nikolai Pavlovic Teljasin into a peasant family, he entered the monastery of St Nilus the Stylite in 1599 and was ordained in 1613. He became superior in 1614 and ran the monastery well, in particular building up a great library. In 1636 he became archbishop of Tobolsk and Siberia. As archbishop he ran the diocese effectively, but asked permission to resign the office in 1636, which was refused, and again in 1639, when his request was accepted. He returned to his monastery – which he had taken a vow never to leave – and once again became superior in 1647. Feast 10 June.

Nettarius of Tver, hegumenos, fifteenth/sixteenth centuries. Russian Church. Hegumenos of the monastery of the Intercession of the Mother of God at Tver. Feast 7 April.

Nettarius the Obedient, monk, died Kiev, twelfth century. Russian Cchurch. A monk of the Kievan Cave monastery. Feast 29 November.

Newaya Iyasu, monk, born Abnat. Ethiopian Church.

Nicander and Hermas, martyrs, died Myra, second century. Said to have been, respectively, a bishop and a priest. Feast 4 November.

Nicander of Egypt, martyr, died Egypt, c. 304. Said to have been a doctor who ministered to Christians, and was beheaded. Feast 15 March.

Nicander of Gorodno, monk, sixteenth/seventeenth centuries. Russian Church. Founded a monastery on lake Gorodno. Feast 15 March.

Nicander of Pskov, monk, born Videleb, near Pskov, 1507, died Porchov, 1 October 1581/2. Russian Church. Baptized Nikon. He wanted to enter a monastery at the age of 17, but was unable to do so, possibly because of his poverty. Instead he went to work for a merchant in Pskov, and learned to read and write. He then went from place to place visiting monasteries, but settled for 12–15 years as a solitary near Novgorod. He then went to the monastery of Krypeck where he was accepted, thanks to the generosity of the merchant for whom he had worked. Again he returned to his life as a hermit, but because of temptations and other dangers, he went back again to Krypeck, although he lived as a solitary near the monastery after spending some time within its walls filling various offices. As a solitary, however, he was visited by many for spiritual guidance, which rather upset the monastic community. He therefore returned to his first hermitage, where he remained for the rest of his life, although each Lent he would go to the monastery of Demjan to receive communion. Feast 24 September.

Nicanor, bl., born Thessalonika, 1491, died Mount Kallistratos, Macedonia, 7 August 1549. Byzantine Church. Baptized Nicholas, he came from a wealthy family. After the death of his parents he gave his money away and became a monk. After some years he went to Mount Kallistratos, preaching to the people as he went. On the mountain he lived in a cave, and built a small church dedicated to St George. He went on to build a monastery, dedicated to the Transfiguration, on the summit of Mount Kallistratos. His sanctity attracted many to the monastery, and it became a major institution in western Macedonia, reviving Orthodoxy in the aftermath of the Turkish occupation.

Nicanor and Isaiah, see **Isaiah of Sija and Nicanor**.

Nicarete, born Nicomedia, died Constantinople (?), c. 410. A wealthy woman who moved to Constantinople and lived a holy life there, apparently being skilled in healing. She was a supporter of **John Chrysostom**, and may have been driven into exile with him. Feast 27 December.

Nicasius, bishop and martyr, died Rheims, 451 (?). He was bishop of Rheims during the barbarian invasions, and was killed at the door of his church while trying to protect his flock. Feast 14 December.

Nicephorus, abbot in Bithynia, Asia Minor, now Turkey, died 813. Feast 4 May.

Nicephorus, founder. Byzantine Church. Founder of the important monastery in Charsianon in Cappadocia. Feast 23 October.

Nicephorus and Gennadius, monks, died lake Vaze. Russian Church. Both disciples of **Alexander of Svir**, Gennadius settled in a hermitage on the bank of lake Vaze, not too far from Svir. Nicephorus developed this hermitage into a monastery after Gennadius's death. Feast 9 February.

Nicephorus and Niphon, monks. Monks of the Kievan Cave monastery.

Nicephorus Irbachi, monk, born Kachethi, eastern Georgia, 1585, died 1658. Georgian Church. Baptized Nicholas Cioloqashvili-Irubakidze. He became a monk while in Rome, studying at the Greek College. He returned to Georgia in 1608, and when the Persians conquered Georgia in 1614 he moved to Jerusalem. In 1625 he was sent on a diplomatic mission to Rome, and then returned to Georgia, to serve in the church at Metechi. In 1632 he became a counsellor to the grand duke of Samegrelo, but in 1643 returned once again to Jerusalem, as hegumenos of the Georgian monastery of the Holy Cross. He was extremely successful, and shortly after he returned to the court of the grand duke he was appointed patriarch of the Georgian Church. When the grand duke died, however, his successor accused him to being too close to Catholicism, and put him in prison where, after a year, he died.

Nicephorus of Antioch, martyr, died Antioch, Syria, 260. Feast 9 February.

Nicephorus of Borovsk, monk, fourteenth century. Russian Church. A disciple of **Sergius of Radonez**. Feast 6 July.

Nicephorus of Chios, bl., born Cardamila, island of Chios, 1750, died Chora, 1821. Byzantine Church.

Baptized George, he entered the monastery of Nea Monì, moved to Chora, and was brought back to Nea Monì as hegumenos. There was considerable unrest in the monastery, and he did not stay, moving to the monastery of St George at Resta, although he was taken ill, and died, while visiting Chora. Feast 1 May.

Nicephorus of Constantinople, born Constantinople, 758, died there, 2 June 828. As imperial secretary to the court at Constantinople, he zealously opposed the iconoclasts and attended the second Council of Nicaea. Although he was a layman, he was made patriarch of the city in 806, but in 813 Leo the Armenian, who was himself an iconoclast, became emperor and banished him to the monastery of St Theodorus on the Bosphorus, which he had founded, and he spent the last years of his life there. In 846 the Empress Theodora had his body brought to Constantinople on 13 March, which became his feast day.

Nicephorus of Kaluga, monk, fifteenth century. Russian Church.

Nicephorus of Mendikion, see **Nicetas of Mendikion**.

Nicephorus of Mount Athos, born southern Italy, died Mount Athos, c. 1300. He was opposed to the reunion of Rome and Constantinople, and was exiled, although he was probably able to return to Athos in 1282. He wrote a number of spiritual works.

Nicephorus of Solovki, monk, born Novgorod, died Solovki, 1617. Russian Church. Eager to become a monk, he went to the monastery of Solovki, but was rejected because he was too young. He stayed working there, however, following the monastic life as far as possible. He decided that he wanted to become a hermit, left the monastery and went into the forest, where he lived for 12 years. Feast 9 August.

Nicephorus of the Crimea, martyr, died Theodosia, Crimea, 12 March 1730. Russian Church. A priest, he was brought before the Muslim ruler of the Crimea and offered his freedom if he were to deny his faith. He refused and was executed.

Nicephorus Phocas, emperor, born Constantinople, 910, died there, 10 December 969. Byzantine Church. He came from a distinguished family, one member of which had been emperor in the early seventh century. He held a number of senior posts in the imperial army, eventually becoming commander-in-chief. In 963, after the death of the Emperor Romanus II, he was proclaimed emperor, marrying Romanus's widow although he was 30 years older than she was. He conducted a number of military campaigns, more successfully in the East than in the West, but the cost of running the army led to a devaluation of the currency and higher prices. There was a conspiracy against him, and he was assassinated. He was a profoundly religious man, and he had wanted to have it proclaimed that those who died in battle were martyrs, something which the patriarch refused to do on the grounds that killing was an offence. He also promoted monasticism.

Niceta and Aquilina, martyrs, died Lycia. In fact originally two soldier saints, their names were turned into those of prostitutes converted by the (legendary) St **Christopher**. Feast 24 July.

Nicetas, martyr, died Nyssa, thirteenth century. Baptized Theodore, he adopted the name Nicetas out of devotion for the saint in whose church he served as a lector. With his uncle and two other young men he found himself in Nyssa during Ramadan. Not knowing Muslim customs, they were accused of offending Mohammed. Brought before the judge, they were offered their lives if they converted. Only Nicetas refused to deny his faith, and was burned to death.

Nicetas Dobrynin, martyr, born Suzdal (?), died Moscow, 11 July 1682. Church of the Old Believers. He was a priest of the cathedral of the Nativity of the Mother of God at Suzdal. He composed a petition against the innovations in the liturgy introduced by the Patriarch Tikon. He was arrested and taken to Moscow. His petition was condemned, he was reduced to the status of a layman, and imprisoned. He went on to abjure his Old Believer beliefs in order to gain his freedom, but immediately afterwards repented of having done so. In July 1682 there was a debate on the issue of the reforms in the Kremlin in Moscow. Nicetas

continued to defend the old ways. He was again arrested, and was put to death in Red Square.

Nicetas, John and Joseph, founders, born Chios, twelfth century. Byzantine Church. The three were originally hermits, but with the aid of the Byzantine emperor, who was exiled on Chios, they founded Nea Monì. They were themselves later accused of heresy and exiled for a time, but they were eventually exonerated, and returned to their monastery.

Nicetas, Nicephorus, Clement, Cyril and Isaac, founders, born Novgorod, died there (?), eleventh/twelfth centuries. Russian Church. Five brothers, surname Alfanovy, founders of the monastery of Sokol'niki. Feast 4 May.

Nicetas of Apollonia, bishop, died c. 735. Bishop of Apollonia in Bithynia, but banished from his diocese because of his opposition to iconoclasm. He died in exile. Feast 20 March.

Nicetas of Borovsk, monk, fifteenth century. Russian Church. He was a disciple of **Sergius of Radonez**, and a monk of the monastery at Borovsk, but otherwise nothing is known for certain about him. Feast 1 May (?).

Nicetas of Constantinople, monk, born Paphlagonia, c. 763, died there, c. 838. He was a courtier at the Byzantine court, and a relative of the Empress Irene. He was an opponent of iconoclasm, but when the iconoclasts appeared to triumph under Leo V he entered a monastery and was eventually exiled to Paphlagonia.

Nicetas of Mendikion, abbot, died Constantinople, 824. Abbot of the monastery of Mendikion, on Mount Olympus in Bithynia, he opposed iconoclasm, and as a consequence was imprisoned on an island in the Sea of Marmara. When released, he returned to Constantinople and lived as a hermit. Feast 3 April.

Nicetas of Mount Athos ('the Slave'), martyr, born Albania, died Serra, 4 April 1808. Russian Church. Originally a slave, he entered the Russian monastery of St Panteleimon on Mount Athos, then, wishing to live in total silence, he entered a hermitage. He eventually developed the desire to suffer martyrdom. He went to Serra, where he started to preach and to criticize Islam, and was executed.

Nicetas of Nisyros, martyr, born Mandraki, island of Nisyros, 1716, died Chios, 21 June 1732. Byzantine Church. He was the son of a wealthy family, which had become Muslim to preserve its status. The family moved to Rhodes. Nicetas was a fervent Muslim, but when he was 14, and his mother told him about their conversion to Islam, he abandoned his family and fled to Chios, where he went to the monastery of Nea Monì and told his story. He became a monk there, and spent some time as a hermit. He conceived the idea of becoming a martyr, something his monastic superiors would not permit, but one day he was arrested by a Turkish official for not having paid the tax owed by Christians. While under arrest, he was recognized by a passing clergyman, who called out to him using the Muslim name his parents had bestowed on him after their conversion. He was brought before a judge for having abjured Islam, and after imprisonment and torture, was executed.

Nicetas of Novgorod, bishop, born Kiev, died Novgorod, 13 January 1109. Russian Church. He became a monk of the Kievan Cave monastery, but was tempted by the devil with the sin of spiritual pride, and was possessed by the devil. The other monks drove out the devil, he did penance, and then lived a life of great humility and obedience. In 1096 he was elected bishop of Novgorod.

Nicetas of Paphlagonia, monk, born Paphlagonia, died Katisia, near Constantinople, 838 (?). A nobleman, he moved to Constantinople when he was 17 and entered the service of the Empress Irene. He became a general in the imperial army, but at the age of 50 entered a monastery in Constantinople. He was sent into exile for opposing iconoclasm. Feast 6 October.

Nicetas of Perejaslavl ('the Stylite'), monk, died Perejaslavl, 1196. Russian Church. He had been a tax collector and oppressed the poor, but, having converted, he became a monk and not only lived a life of extreme asceticism, but undertook personally a number of public building works, including

two wells. He became famous for his healing powers, but was killed by a group of bandits who came to him on the pretext of seeking a blessing, but in reality hoping to steal gold which they believed he had. Having killed him, they bound his body in chains and threw it into a river.

Nicetas of Remesiana, bishop and ecclesiastical author, born *c.* 350, died after 414. He was bishop of Remesiana in Dacia – today Bela Palanka in Serbia. We know only that he was a friend of **Paulinus of Nola**, whom he visited twice (in 398 and 402). From his works (preserved only in fragments), *Instruction for Baptismal Candidates* and several other writings (including hymns and liturgical sermons) are important. The authenticity of several other works is insecure. Feast 22 June.

Nicetas the Goth, martyr, born Ukraine, died Moldova, 378. From a noble Ostrogoth family, he was converted by Ulfilas and was ordained priest. He was executed for his faith by the king of the Ostrogoths. Feast 15 September.

Nicetas the Goth, martyr, born in what is now Romania, died there *c.* 375. Possibly ordained by Ulfilas, he was put to death in the persecution of Christians by the pagan Visigoth chieftain Athanaric. Nicetas's relics were taken to Mopsuestia. Feast 15 September.

Nicetas the Younger, bl., martyr, born *c.* 1765, died Serres, 4 April 1808. Byzantine Church. It is unclear where Nicetas came from: he appears to have given different responses at different times. His parents were secretly Christian, but pretended to be Muslims. Nicetas himself decided to become a monk and went to Mount Athos, where he became a monk of the monastery of St Panteleimon. He was concerned, however, with the status of his parents, and decided to offer himself as a martyr, despite the opposition of his monastic superiors. He left Athos, and went to Serres in eastern Macedonia. He spent the night in a monastery, then secretly slipped away and went to a mosque, where he began a dispute with a Muslim teacher. He was imprisoned and eventually hanged.

Nicetius of Besançon, died Besançon, before 610, cult confirmed 1900. There is confusion regarding his dates, but he was a Merovingian bishop, originally bishop of Noyon, who is said to have restored both the buildings and the community of the church in Besançon after the city had been devastated by the Huns. Feast 8 February.

Nicetius of Trier, died Trier, c. 566. After entering a monastery at Limoges and becoming its abbot, he was made by King Theodoric the twenty-fifth and last of the Gallo-Roman bishops of Trier. The barbarous Franks in his diocese were little more than nominal Christians, cruel and violent in behaviour. He excommunicated persistent offenders, including the kings Theudebert I and Clotaire, who exiled him for a time. Personally ascetic and charitable, he restored discipline and orthodoxy among the clergy, founded a school of clerical studies and rebuilt the cathedral. Feast 5 December.

Nicetus, bishop, died c. 449. He was a bishop of Vienne, near Lyons. Feast 5 May.

Nicholas, patriarch, born Georgia, died there, 1591. The son of King Levan of Katcheti, and the brother of his successor, Alexander II, he was patriarch – catholicos – of the Georgian Church from 1584. Feast 18 February.

Nicholas I, pope, born Rome, 820, died there, 13 November 867. Made subdeacon by Pope Sergius II and deacon by Leo IV, he was elected pope on 24 April 858. In the difficulties after the collapse of **Charlemagne**'s empire, he upheld Christian morality and authority against worldly bishops and ambitious princes, and built and endowed several churches in Rome. He encouraged the Church's missionary activity and secured the position of the papacy in Western Europe. He was one of the greatest medieval popes.

Nicholas II (Alexandrovich), emperor of Russia, born Gatchina, 6 May 1868, died (shot) Ekaterinburg, 17 July 1918. His life inevitably belongs to the political history of Russia, but he has been continually revered as saint and martyr by Russian Orthodox believers from the moment of his death. He was patron and active helper of numerous charities, Orthodox missionary endeavours and other Christian causes (including world peace). Due to his efforts, St **Seraphim of Sarov** was canonized. His complete lack of resistance to exile, imprisonment and certain death made him a modern example of the ancient Russian 'Passion-Bearers' who were martyrs for justice in the face of violence and aggression. Canonized, together with all the 'New Martyrs', by the Russian Orthodox Church Abroad on 1 November 1982. The 'New Martyrs' included the members of his family, his wife Alexandra, his daughters Olga, Tatiana, Maria and Anastasia, and his son Alexis. There also died three of his servants, and his doctor. Feast 4 July.

Nicholas III, patriarch, died 1280. Georgian Church. He was catholicos of the Church in eastern Georgia from 1240. He was a firm upholder of the rights of the Church, both against the feudal nobility of Georgia, who were tempted to side with the Mongol invaders, and against the invaders themselves. Feeling himself a failure in his struggle to purify the Church, he resigned in the year of his death.

Nicholas Albergati, bl., cardinal and bishop of Bologna, born Bologna, 1375, died Siena, 10 May 1443. He entered the Carthusian Order in 1394, having begun to study for the law. He became superior of several houses and, in 1417, the clergy and citizens of Bologna chose him for their bishop, which only the express command of his superiors could induce him to accept. He continued to follow the Rule of his order, was zealous for the reform of regular and secular clergy, and a great patron of learned men, among whom was Aeneas Sylvius, afterwards Pius II. Martin V and his successors charged him with important diplomatic missions, thrice to France and thrice to Lombardy, between 1422 and 1435. He was made a cardinal in 1426, attended the Council of Basle in 1432, 1434 and 1436 as legate of Eugenius IV, and also opened the Council of Ferrara, where (and at Florence) he had much to do with the reconciliation of the Greeks. The pope held him in the highest esteem, consulted him in most things, made him grand plenipotentiary, and visited him when he was ill.

Nicholas Appleine, bl., canon of Nevers, died 1466. Feast 11 August.

Nicholas Cabasilas, bl., mystic, born Thessalonika, 1322, died there, 1392. Cabasilas was a family name taken from his mother, whose brother Nilus was the metropolitan of Thessalonika. He went to Constantinople to study, but returned in 1342 because of the civil war. At the end of it, however, he was invited back to Constantinople to serve the new emperor, which he did for some seven years. This was a time of conflict, not only over hesychasm, but also about reunion of the Churches of East and West, which he strongly opposed. From 1354 he seems to have given up all interest in political questions to concentrate on religious ones, and in 1362 he returned to Thessalonika on the death of his father. His mother became a nun, and he eventually entered the monastery of Manganon, where he lived for the rest of his life. It is not certain that he ever became a priest. His major work is *Concerning Life in Christ* and in it he outlines how spiritual union with Christ can be achieved through the sacraments of baptism, confirmation and the Eucharist. He was sympathetic towards **Gregory Palamas** in the hesychast controversy, and in a short pamphlet defends Palamism against Nicephoras Gregorias. Feast 20 June.

Nicholas Dvali, martyr, born Georgia, died Damascus, 19 October 1314. Georgian Church. He first entered a monastery in Georgia, but then went to live in the Holy Cross monastery in Jerusalem. He decided to seek martyrdom by publicly attacking Islam. He was arrested and tortured, but was freed by his fellow monks and sent to Cyprus. From Cyprus he went to Mount Athos, but the desire for martyrdom remained. He returned to Jerusalem, but was sent on to Damascus. He was arrested three times for attacking Islam, and twice the Christians in Damascus obtained his freedom. He was on his way back to Jerusalem when he was arrested again, and beheaded.

Nicholas Factor, Franciscan, born Valencia, 1520, died there, 1582. The son of a tailor, at 17 he joined the Franciscans with the hope of going on the foreign missions. Instead he was sent to preach around Spain, which he did with great ardour and to great effect. He was a friend of several future saints and generally much admired, despite his possibly overzealous austerities. Feast 23 December.

Nicholas Garlick, bl., martyr, born Derbyshire, *c.* 1554, died Derby, 24 July 1588. He entered the English College in Rheims in 1581, was ordained in 1582, and returned to England early the next year. He was arrested after being betrayed by a Catholic prisoner and was banished in 1585. He returned immediately to England, and was arrested in 1588 along with **Robert Ludlam**. Both were tried in Derby, were condemned for being seminary priests working in England, and were hanged, drawn and quartered.

Nicholas (Nils) Hermansson, born Skeninge, Sweden, 1331, died Linköping, Sweden, 24 July 1391. Educated at Paris and Orleans, he was ordained priest and appointed tutor to the sons of St **Brigid of Sweden**. Eventually he became bishop of Linköping. He was a tireless preacher, and greatly dedicated to pastoral work in his diocese. He is greatly honoured in Sweden as a liturgist and poet.

Nicholas Horner, bl., martyr, died London, 4 March 1590. A tailor, hanged for providing **Christopher Bales** with a jerkin, on the same day, beatified 1987.

Nicholas Karamonos, martyr, died Smyrna, 19 March 1657. Byzantine Church. Nothing is known of his earlier life, but for some reason, in March 1657, he was heard to declare that he would convert to Islam, and then to deny it. He was imprisoned, deprived of food, and died. Feast 6 December.

Nicholas Lancicius (Laczycki), ven., Jesuit ascetical writer, born Nesvizh (Nieswiesz), Lithuania, 10 December 1574, died Kannas (Kovo), 16 March 1652. Through his studies he abandoned Calvinism in 1590 and two years later entered the Society of Jesus at Krakow, moving on to Rome where he was ordained in 1601. In 1608 he transferred to the Academy of Wilna in Poland where he taught Hebrew, Scripture and theology, becoming rector at Kalisz and Krakow, and provincial of the Lithuanian province from 1631 to 1635. His many books on the spirit and organization of the Society of Jesus include *De Meditationibus rerum divi-narum*, and *De praestantia instituti S.J.* In 1650 Bollandus published Lancicius's collected works in two voloumes (Antwerp), subsequently translated into several languages.

Nicholas Light of the Georgians, hymn writer, fourteenth century. Georgian Church. Son of King **Demetrius II**, but little is known of him, and hardly any of the prayers and hymns he wrote have survived.

Nicholas Michailovic Zagorovski, martyr, born Achtyrka, 1872, died near Char'kov, 1944. Ukrainian Church, Moscow Patriarchate. A priest in Char'kov in the Ukraine, he was very popular among the people, so much so that he was arrested in 1923 and deported. In 1941 he was able to minister in Obojan, but with the German occupation of Char'kov he returned there, and retreated with the German forces. He died on the way to Persmysl. Feast 19 May.

Nicholas of Aarhus, bl., born Jutland, *c.* 1150, died Aarhus, Denmark, 1180. An illegitimate son of King Canute Magnusson, he spent some time at the Danish court and then went to his estates near Aarhus, where he lived a simple, holy life. He was popularly regarded as a saint, but never recognized by any formal process.

Nicholas of Cernigov, prince, died Kiev, 14 October 1143. Russian Church. When driven from Cernigov by the Tartars, in February 1106 he entered the Kievan Cave monastery, the first Russian prince to become a monk, taking the name Nicholas in place of Svjatosa. He lived the ordinary life of a monk, cultivating a garden and building a church out of his own funds.

Nicholas of Chios, martyr, born Caries, island of Chios, died there, 31 October 1754. When he was 20 he was in Magnesia working as a bricklayer. He was persuaded to convert to Islam. After he returned home he was arrested, made to dress in Islamic clothes, and given the name Mohammed. He was, however, persuaded by a monk to return to Christianity, was arrested and decapitated.

Nicholas of Constantinople, martyr, born Constantinople, died there, 1732. Byzantine Church. Feast 12 November.

Nicholas of Constantinople I, patriarch, born Constantinople, 852, died there, 15 May 925. Born of an Italian slave on an estate of the Patriarch Photius, he was a government official, but on Photius's fall in 886 became a monk. Soon after being made patriarch of Constantinople in 901, he was deposed during the dispute over the Emperor Leo VI's fourth marriage. When recalled in 912, he persuaded Pope John X to end the schism by allowing the emperor a dispensation for reasons of state. The Greek Church canonized him. Feast 15 May.

Nicholas of Constantinople II, patriarch, born Constantinople (?), died there, 996. Known as 'Chrysoberges', he was patriarch from 983. It was during his patriarchate that Russia was converted to Christianity. Feast 16 December.

Nicholas of Corinth, martyr, born Psari, near Corinth, 1520, died Constantinople, 14 February 1554. Byzantine Church. He moved to Silivri, a place near Constantinople, to work as a servant. He was accused of having offended Islam by his manner of life, and was offered the chance to abjure Christianity. He refused to do so, and was beheaded. Feast 14 February.

Nicholas of Flüe, born near Sachseln, Canton Oberwalden, Switzerland, 21 March 1417, died there, 21 March 1487. The son of wealthy peasants, he was a soldier, judge and cantonal councillor. In 1467, after a quarter-century of married life, his wife and ten children agreed to him departing to live for 19 years as a hermit at Ranft, reputedly with no food besides holy communion. He was esteemed as 'Bruder Klaus' in Switzerland, and his influence with the confederates in 1481 averted a civil war. Feast 21 March, but in Switzerland, as its patron saint, 25 September.

Nicholas of Forca Palena, bl., founder, born Forca Palena, *c.* 1349, died 1449. He was ordained a priest in his home town, then went to Rome to join a community of hermits at the church of the Holy Saviour. He became superior of the group, and parish priest. He then went to Naples and later Florence, starting communities there before returning to Rome. He put the hermits under the patronage of St **Jerome**. There was already a congregation of hermits with Jerome as their patron founded by **Peter of Pisa**, and the two combined to form the Hieronymites. Feast 1 October.

Nicholas (Kasatkin) of Japan, bishop and missionary, born Berjozvskij, near Smolensk, 1 August 1836, died Tokyo, 3 February 1912. Russian Church. Baptized Ivan Dimitrrevic Kasatkin, in July 1860 he became a missionary in Japan and succeeded in founding a fully indigenous local church entirely staffed by Japanese priests. By 1904 there were 260 congregations, and he was made archbishop of Tokyo in 1906. He also supervised a complete translation of the Orthodox liturgical books and other basic texts. Feast 3 February.

Nicholas of Karpenesi, born Karpenesi, died Constantinople, 23 September 1672. Byzantine Church. When he was 15 he accompanied his father, a grocer, to Constantinople to study. He first needed to learn Turkish, and so was apprenticed to a Turkish barber. The barber wanted him to convert to Islam, and gave him an Islamic text to read, claiming, after he had done so, that the reading of the text signified the young man's conversion. He denied it, was taken before a judge, and condemned to death by beheading. Feast 23 September.

Nicholas of Kiev, metropolitan, died Kiev, *c.* 1106. Russian Church. He may originally have been Greek. He criticized the princes for their feuding, saying that it left the territory of Russia open to pagans.

Nicholas of Magnesia, martyr, born Giagia Kioi, died Magnesia, 1776 or 1796. Byzantine Church. Aged 22, he went with permission to Magnesia. While there he was arrested because he was dressed as a Turk, and it was alleged that he wished to convert to Islam. When he refused to do so, he was imprisoned, and finally executed.

Nicholas of Metsovon, martyr, born Metsovon, Epirus, died Trikkala, 17 May 1617. Byzantine Church. He went to Trikkala to work as a baker.

He converted to Islam, but immediately regretted his action and returned to Metsovon. Some time later he had to return to Trikkala, where he was recognized by a Muslim who tried to blackmail him. Nicholas decided to embrace martyrdom, and on another visit to Trikkala he was arrested, beaten, and then burned alive.

Nicholas of Mitylene, martyr, born Mitylene, died there, 16 January 1771 or 1777.

Nicholas of Myra, born Pararia, Lycia, Asia Minor, died Myra, 6 December 345 or 352. A popular saint in both the Greek and Latin Churches, but little is known about him. He is said to have made a pilgrimage to Egypt and Palestine during his youth. Appointed bishop of Myra, he was imprisoned during the persecution of Diocletian, but released by Constantine. He was said to have been present at the Council of Nicaea, although his name is not among the names of the bishops attending the Council. In 1087 Italian merchants stole his body from Myra and took it to Bari, Italy. Because of the story that he secretly provided poor young women with money for their dowries, he is often depicted carrying bags of gold, and he is the origin of 'Santa Claus'.

Nicholas of Ochrid and Zhicha (Nikolai Velimirovich), bishop and writer, born Valjevo, Serbia, 23 December 1880, died St Tikhon's monastery, Pennsylvania, 18 March 1956. Serbian Church. He studied in Switzerland, Germany, England and Russia. He obtained British support for Serbia during World War I and his whole life was devoted to both his Church and his people. In 1941 he was arrested by the Germans, together with Patriarch Gabriel, and sent to Dachau concentration camp where he spent two years. Instead of returning to Yugoslavia after the war, he went to America, where he continued to lecture and write. His most famous work is *The Prologue of Ochrid* – lives and meditations on the saints. He was canonized in 1987. Feast 5 March.

Nicholas of Novgorod, born Novgorod, died there, 1392. Russian Church. He came from a wealthy family, but lived his life as a 'fool for Christ', wandering the streets of the city – he lived near the cathedral of Santa Sophia – and maintaining a hostile rivalry with his fellow 'fool for Christ', **Theodore**, who lived on the opposite bank of the river. Feast 27 July.

Nicholas of Prussia, bl., born Prussia, c. 1379, died Genoa, 1456. He was one of the original members of the reformed abbey of St Justina at Padua under the Ven. Ludovico Barbo, founder of the Benedictine Cassinese congregation. He resided successively at Padua, Venice, Padolirone, and finally at the abbey of San Niccolò del Boschetto, near Genoa, where he was novice master and prior. Feast 23 February.

Nicholas of Pskov, born Pskov, died there, 28 February 1576. Russian Church. A 'fool for Christ', he became so famous as he went about the street proclaiming the gospel that, when Ivan the Terrible came to the city, he asked to see him. Nicholas put before the Tsar a plate of meat which the Tsar refused, saying that he was a Christian and, as it was Lent, did not eat meat. Nicholas replied that although he was a Christian, he was killing Christians. Ivan, abashed, saved the city from the destruction he had intended.

Nicholas of Rethymnon, martyr, died Rethymnon, Crete, 28 October 1824. One of four Cretan martyrs (**George, Manuel** and **Angelo of Rethymnon**). Feast 1 September.

Nicholas of Sibenik, born Sibenik, Dalmatia, died Jerusalem, 1391. Nicholas Tavelic joined the Franciscans in Italy, and was sent to the Holy Land. With **Peter of Narbonne**, **Deodatus of Rodez** and **Stephen of Cuneo** they determined to preach Christ to the Muslims, and proclaimed their intention before the judge. They were put to death. Feast 14 November.

Nicholas of Sicily, bl., born Sicily, died Skotini, Greece. Byzantine Church. He became a monk in Sicily, but then moved to the Euboea, possibly as a consequence of the Saracen invasions of Sicily, which might place him in the ninth century. He first settled at the monastery of Charadra, then moved to Neotakos (the modern Skotini) where, with the help of monks from Charadra, he constructed a new monastery and became its hegumenos.

Nicholas of Spetses, martyr, born Spetses, died Chios, 1822. Feast 3 February.

Nicholas of Thessalonika, martyr, born Constantinople, died Caries Thermis, Mitylene, 9 April 1463. Byzantine Church. A monk in Constantinople, he went to Caries Thermis after the fall of the city, and was there killed by Islamic troops when they attacked the monastery, along with **Raphael**.

Nicholas of Tmutorakan, bishop, eleventh century. Russian Church. A monk of the Kievan Cave monastery, he was chosen as the first bishop of Tmutorokan, which lay between the Black Sea and the Sea of Azov.

Nicholas of Tolentino, born Sant' Angelo, March of Ancona, Italy, c. 1245, died Tolentino, Italy, 10 September 1306. He made his profession as an Augustinian friar in 1253 and was ordained priest. He devoted himself to pastoral work among the poor and destitute, preaching almost every day. He is recorded as having achieved remarkable conversions and frequent miracles. He spent his last 30 years at Tolentino, where he was interred, and fragments of his body are said to foretell calamities by bleeding, as in 1452 before the fall of Constantinople and in 1510 before the Reformation. Feast 10 September.

Nicholas of Vrulla, bl., martyr. Byzantine Church. Feast 11 July.

Nicholas of Vunena, bl., martyr, died Mount Vunena, c. 902. Byzantine Church. A soldier sent by the Emperor Leo the Wise to take charge of the defence of Larissa in Thessaly. When it fell to the Arabs, Nicholas fled with some other soldiers to Mount Ternavo, where he became an ascetic. He was captured and tortured, but managed to escape, and this time went to Mount Vunena, where he continued his ascetic life. Again, however, he was attacked, and this time run through with a lance. Feast 9 May.

Nicholas Owen, martyr, born Oxfordshire, died Tower of London, 2 February 1606. He was a carpenter by trade, and possibly a servant to **Edmund Campion**. He was imprisoned several times, but released. He was employed to build hiding places – 'priest's holes' as they came to be known – in houses frequented by priests, and he was finally captured while in one of these at Hinlip Hall in Herefordshire, after hiding for a fortnight without being discovered. He had become a Jesuit lay brother in 1577. He died under torture.

Nicholas Paglia, bl., administrator and preacher, born Giovinezzo, near Baria, Italy, 1197, died Perugia, 11 February 1255. When studying law at Bologna, he heard St **Dominic** preach in 1218 and joined his order, founding priories at Trani, Perugia and perhaps Todi, and becoming provincial of the Roman province 1230–35 and 1255. Pope Gregory IX got him to reform the Benedictine monks of St Antonio. He was a good preacher and a charitable administrator. Feast 14 February.

Nicholas Pieck and Companions, martyrs of Gorkum, died 1572. During the struggle for Dutch independence from Spain, the Calvinist, anti-Spanish Les Gueux ('Sea Beggars') captured Gorkum and took all the Catholic clergy prisoner. They were offered freedom if they would denounce the doctrine of the blessed sacrament, but they refused. They were then offered freedom if they would deny the primacy of the pope, and when they refused they were taken to a deserted monastery at Ruggen and hanged. Feast 9 July.

Nicholas Planas ('of Athens'), born Naxos, Greece, 1851, died Athens, 2 March 1932. Byzantine Church. He spent all his adult life ministering in different parish churches in Athens. He is a recent example of 'foolishness for Christ's sake' and was treated with contempt by most of his fellow clergy. His absolute simplicity and gentleness attracted a devoted group of followers, who later wrote down their recollections. Miracles have been continuously claimed at his tomb, and he was eventually canonized under popular pressure. Feast 18 February.

Nicholas Politi, bl., born Aderno, near Patti, Sicily, 1117, died Mount Etna, 1167. He married, but abandoned his wife on their wedding night, and became a hermit on Mount Etna. Feast 17 August.

Nicholas Postgate, bl., martyr, born Whitby, Yorkshire, died York 7, August 1679. He studied at Douai in 1621, and was ordained seven years later. Two years after that he returned to England and worked for the rest of his life in Yorkshire until his arrest in his eightieth year.

Nicholas Saggio, bl., born Longobardi, Calabria, died there, 1709, beatified by Pius VI in the eighteenth century. He was a lay brother in the order of Minims of St Francis of Paola. Feast 2 February.

Nicholas Sergeevic Emov, martyr, born Verchnij Saltov, 3 February 1908, died Char'kov, 16 January 1938. Ukrainian Church, Moscow Patriarchate. He was ordained in 1923, and spent his priestly life in the village of Ternovaja. He was arrested in December 1937, and shot the following January. Feast 19 May.

Nicholas Stenson, bishop, born Copenhagen, 1 January 1638, died Hamburg, 25 January 1686. The son of a goldsmith, he studied in Copenhagen, Amsterdam and Leyden, and became a doctor of medicine. His scientific interests were, however, extremely wide, including geology as well as anatomy and physiology. He became a Catholic in Florence in 1667, and a priest in 1675. For a time he served as a tutor at the Florentine court, but was then appointed vicar apostolic for Scandinavia. Three years later he went on to be an assistant bishop of Münster, in which capacity he was assiduous in visiting the parishes of the diocese. He left that city, however, after a dispute about the election of a new bishop, and was invited to Hanover, where the duke was a recent convert to Catholicism. He spent the final years of his life in various cities of northern Germany, always retaining an interest in his home country. He was greatly admired for his scientific acumen, but even more for the saintliness of his life. After his death his body was taken to Florence for burial.

Nicholas Tavelic, martyr, born Sibenik, Dalmatia, died Jerusalem, 14 November 1391. Nicholas Tavelic joined the Franciscans in Italy, and was sent to the Holy Land. With **Peter of Narbonne**, **Deodatus of Rodez** and **Stephen of Cuneo** they determined to preach Christ to the Muslims, and proclaimed their intention before the judge. They were put to death.

Nicholas the Mystic (Nicholas I), patriarch, died Constantinople, 925. Originally a monk of the monastery of St Tryphon in Chalcedon, he was patriarch of Constantinople from 895 until 906, when the Emperor Leo the Wise deposed and exiled him when he would not approve the emperor's fourth marriage. He became patriarch again, from 911, after the emperor's death. The appellation 'Mystic' comes from his membership of the mystic, or secret, council at the Byzantine court. Feast 15 May.

Nicholas the Pilgrim, born Greece, died Trani, Italy, 1094. Apparently simple-minded, he was a shepherd until his mother persuaded a monastery to take him in. The monks, however, irritated by his constant chanting of *Kyrie eleison*, ejected him after a while and he travelled to Italy, where he likewise went about chanting. He lived off alms, and frequently had a large crowd of children around him. Many miracles were attributed to him after his death, and he was canonized in 1098. Feast 2 June.

Nicholas the Studite, born Crete, 793, died Constantinople, 4 February 868. A student at the monastery of the Studion at Constantinople, he went into exile with the abbot during the iconoclastic persecution and, when able to return, himself became the abbot. Under the Emperor Michael he would not recognize the usurper Photius and was deposed. When the rightful patriarch, **Ignatius**, was restored by the Emperor Basil, Nicholas considered himself too old to become abbot again and remained a simple monk. He was famous as a scribe.

Nicholas Timofeevic Migulin, martyr, born Malaja Volca, 4 December 1872, died Char'kov, Ukraine, 13 November 1937. Ukrainian Church, Moscow Patriarchate. He worked all his life in the diocese of Char'kov, and he was shot there. Feast 19 May.

Nicholas Woodfen, bl., martyr, born Leominster, Herefordshire, *c.* 1550, died as Devereux, an alias, with **Edward Stransham** at Tyburn, London, 21 January 1586, beatified 1987. After ordination in

Rheims, France, in 1581, he returned with Stransham to England and worked among lawyers at the London Inns of Court. He was hanged, drawn and quartered.

Nicodemus, archbishop, died 1323. Serbian Church. He was a monk, and then from 1312 hegumenos of the Serbian monastery on Mount Athos. In 1317 he became archbishop of Serbia and contributed to the reforms of the Serbian Church, particularly with regard to the liturgy. He was buried in the monastery of Pec, and his tomb was the site of many miracles.

Nicodemus of Beria, bl., monk, born Beria, Macedonia, died Thessalonika, thirteenth century. Byzantine Church. After becoming a monk he lived in extreme asceticism as a hermit for many years, but later he went to Thessalonika, where he entered the Philocalli monastery. His behaviour, however, caused consternation, because he frequented prostitutes. The hegumenos sent him away, and from then on he lived in perfect chastity and again rigid asceticism. He gave away what little money he had, and preached to prostitutes to change their ways. The protectors of the prostitutes therefore killed him. As he was dying, he asked to be taken to the monastery, but the hegumenos would not let him enter. He was buried near the monastery, and his tomb began to give out a sweet smell. When the tomb was opened his body was found to be incorrupt. Many miracles are attributed to him.

Nicodemus of Elbasan, bl., martyr, born Elbasan, Epirus, died 11 July 1722. Byzantine Church. Baptized Nicholas Dedes, he was a tailor in Elbasan who became a Muslim, and circumcized all his sons except one, who fled to Mount Athos. He went to try to bring him back, but instead was persuaded to return to Christianity and himself became a monk, taking the name Nicodemus. After some time as a monk, he decided to offer himself for martyrdom. He returned to Elbasan, was recognized as having abjured Islam, and was beheaded.

Nicodemus of Kostroma, archbishop, born Progresino, 29 November 1868, died 21 August 1938. Baptized Nikolai Vasil'evic Krotkov, he studied in the local seminary, then taught in a parish school before going for further studies to Kiev, where he became a monk. In 1905 he was made rector of the seminary in Pskov, and became an archimandrite. In 1907 he became bishop of Akkerman, then in 1911 of Cigirinsk. In 1921 he was transferred to Tavria and Simferopol. He was imprisoned from 1929 to 1932, and on his release was sent to Kostroma, which he administered until 1936, when he was again arrested on the charge of opposing the confiscation of Church property. He was imprisoned at Jaroslavl, and died still in gaol. Feast 23 January.

Nicodemus of Kozeer, monk, born Ivankovo, near Rostov, died Kozeer, 3 July 1640. Russian Church. Baptized Nikita, and of a peasant family, he worked as a blacksmith in Jaroslavl and Moscow. Believing himself called to the monastic life, he went to the Cudovo monastery, where he was accepted. He wanted to live as a solitary, and after some time went to the north, lived for six months in the monastery of Kozeer, but then established a hermitage for himself not far away, in a forest, where he lived for 37 years. The local people came to him for spiritual guidance.

Nicodemus of Mammola, born Ciræ, *c.* 900, died Mammola, Greece, 25 March 990. When young he became a Basilian monk under St Fatino's spiritual guidance and later went to Mount Cellerano, where his strict form of life drew many followers to his hermitage. In *c.* 975 he established a monastery in the woods near Mammola in Greece which was dedicated to him after his death. Feast 12 March.

Nicodemus of the Holy Mountain (the Hagiorite), monk and spiritual writer, born Naxos, Greece, 1749, died Mount Athos, 14 July 1809. Byzantine Church. Baptized Nicholas Kallivurtsi, he came from a devout family, and his mother became a nun. He spent some time studying in Smyrna before becoming a monk of Athos in 1755. There he collaborated with **Macarius of Corinth** in producing anthologies of patristic and spiritual writings which had long been neglected, most famously the *Philokalia* (which was soon translated into Slavonic and Romanian). From this five-volume collection, published in Venice in 1782, can be dated the beginning of the great spiritual and monastic revival of nineteenth-century Orthodoxy. Nicodemus was a strong supporter of frequent communion. He was proclaimed a saint in the Eastern Church in 1955. Feast 14 July.

Nicodemus of the Meteora, martyr, died 1551. Very little is known of him. A monk of the Meteora, he was forced to become a Muslim. When he refused he was executed. Feast 16 August.

Nicodemus of Tismana, born Prilep, *c.* 1320, died Tismana, 23 November 1406. Romanian Church. His father was a Greek, his mother Serbian, and the family was of noble origins. While still quite young he went to Mount Athos, where he became a monk and a priest. He set up a community near the modern Romanian city of Drobeta-Turnu, south of the Danube, but then moved north to Vodita, where he built a church. In 1375 he was sent on a diplomatic mission to Constantinople by his relative Lazar, prince of Serbia, in an attempt to reconcile the Serbian and Byzantine Churches. But that same year there was a Hungarian invasion, and Nicodemus retreated to the mountains, where he founded a new monastery of Tismana, which specialized in copying books. Feast 26 December.

Nicodemus of Vatapedi, bl., died Mount Athos, fourteenth century. Byzantine Church. Originally a monk at a monastery near Chalcedon, he was forced to flee, probably because of the Turkish invasion, and settled at the Vatopedi monastery on Mount Athos, where he became the teacher of **Gregory Palamas**.

Nicomedes, martyr, died Rome. Buried on the via Nomentana, but no dates are known. Feast 15 September.

Nicostratus, Antiochus and Companions, martyrs, died Caesarea, Palestine, 303. Nicostratus was head of a troop of Roman soldiers, all of whom suffered martyrdom. The story is doubtful. Feast 21 May.

Nikon, martyr, died *c.* 1114. A monk of the Kievan Cave monastery, he was a disciple of **Kuksa** and accompanied him on his missionary journey to preach to the Vjatici, when they were martyred. Feast 22 September.

Nikon and Companions, martyrs, died Taormina, Sicily, *c.* 250. Nikon was solider in the imperial army who became a Christian, and then a monk in Palestine. With his disciples (199 of them) he fled to Sicily during the persecution of Decius, but they were put to death at Taormina. Feast 23 March.

Nikon and Tikon of Sokolovo, monks, died near Zvenigorod, sixteenth century. Russian Church. Monks of the hermitage of Sokolovo, and brothers. They died at Sokolovo, and were buried in the woods. A chapel was later erected over their tomb. Feast 16 June.

Nikon of Novgorod, and Denis, monks. Nothing reliable is known about them.

Nikon of Optina, monk, born Moscow, 26 September 1888, died Pinega, 1931. Russian Church. Baptized Nikolai Mtrofanovic Beljaev, he entered the hermitage of Optina in 1907. He was ordained priest in 1917. He was imprisoned in 1919, but after his release remained in the monastery even though most monks were deported. In 1924 he was obliged to leave Optina and went to Kozelsk, where he worked in the cathedral. He was again arrested in 1927, and from 1928 to 1930 was in a concentration camp in Kem, being sent into exile in Archangel at his release. He settled at Pinega, but shortly afterwards died of tuberculosis, from which he had suffered since his youth. Feast 11 October.

Nikon of the Kievan Cave Monastery, hegumenos, died Kiev, 23 March 1088. Russian Church. One of the first monks of the Kievan Cave monastery, he angered the prince by admitting as a monk the prince's treasurer, without the prince's permission. He was exiled to Tmutorokan, where he built a monastery, and where he became an important figure in the life of the city: the people sent him as envoy to request Prince Gleb as their ruler. He then returned to Kiev, but was again exiled to Tmutorokan, where he was cordially received by Prince Gleb. He stayed there for ten years, until 1078, when Gleb was assassinated, and then returned to Kiev, where he became hegumenos and was responsible for the decoration of the monastic church.

Nikon the Penitent (Metanoiete), born Pontus, died in the Peloponnese, 998. The son of a wealthy landowner, he was born in what is now Turkey. He entered a monastery as a young man and lived there for a dozen years, but so successful was his preaching that he was sent as a missionary, first to Crete, then to Sparta, and afterwards to other places in Greece. His name recalls the constant theme of his preaching, repentance. He died in a monastery. Feast 26 November.

Nikon the Thirsty, monk, died Kiev, twelfth century. Russian Church. From a rich family, he became a monk of the Kievan Cave monastery, but was taken prisoner with many fellow monks during an invasion by the Cumans. Because he came from a wealthy background, the leader of the Cumans expected a large ransom for him, but when he refused to be ransomed he was kept prisoner without food or water, or any warmth. He was, however, mysteriously transported out of prison by angels, and taken back to Kiev. Feast 11 December.

Nilammon, anchorite, fifth century. A monk who was chosen bishop against his will, and barricaded himself in his cell to avoid the ordination service. Feast 6 June.

Nilus Erichiotis, monk, born Constantinople, *c.* 1230, died Thesprotia, 1336. He belonged to the Lascaris family. He left Constantinople for the Akimiton monastery on the Bosphorus. When the Byzantine emperor recaptured Constantinople in 1261 he returned there, but only after a visit to the Holy Land. He was opposed to those who favoured the reunion of Constantinople with Rome, for which he was exiled to Mount Athos. He returned later, but again went into exile, living in various places before establishing a monastery on Mount Thesprotia in Epirus. Feast 16 August.

Nilus of Ancyra ('the Wise'), born Ancyra, died there, *c.* 430. Believed to have been an imperial official at Constantinople, he became a hermit with his son on Mount Sinai. He was a friend of St **John Chrysostom**, was ordained by the bishop of Eleusa in Palestine and became the founder and superior of a monastery near Ancyra. He is now best remembered as an ascetical theological and biblical writer. Feast 12 November.

Nilus of Rossano, born Rossano, Calabria, died Grottoferrata, *c.* 1005. A Greek of Italy, he joined the Basilian monks of St Adrian's abbey, Calabria, and became abbot there. In 981 the Saracens drove the monks to Vellucio, where they settled on land given them by the abbey of Monte Cassino. In obedience to his decree shortly before his death at Frascati, near Rome, his disciple **Bartholomew of Rossano** founded there the abbey of Grottaferrata under St Basil's Rule and in the Greek rite. Feast 26 September.

Nilus of Stolobnoe, monk, born Zabenskoe, died island of Stolobnoe, 7 December 1554. Russian Church. When still young he entered the monastery at Krypetskoe, but *c.* 1515 he became a hermit beside the river Ceremcha. When his fame drew large crowds, he retreated in 1528 to the island of Stolobnoe on lake Saliger, although once again the crowds followed him there.

Nilus Sorski, monk, born Moscow, 1433, died hermitage of Sora, 7 May 1508. Russian Church. Of aristocratic origins, he entered the monastery of **Cyril of Beloozero**. He spent some time in the East, visiting Constantinople and Mount Athos before returning, settling in a hermitage beside the river Sora, not far from Cyril's monastery. A small community gathered there under his guidance. In 1490 he attended a Church synod in Moscow where he spoke out against the persecution of heretics, although he was ready firmly to condemn their teachings. In 1503 another synod in Moscow was held to discuss Church property, where he spoke out firmly against the assimilation of the Church to political power. In neither position was he able ultimately to carry the day, and he retired back to his hermitage. Well versed in the Church Fathers and in the Bible, he himself produced a number of important theological and, especially, spiritual works.

Nilus the Mirovlite, born Aghios Petros, in the Peloponnese, 1601, died Mount Athos, 13 November 1651. Byzantine Church. Baptized Nicholas Terzakis, he became a priest in the local monastery where his uncle Macarius was also a monk, but the two decided to go to Mount Athos, where they dwelt in a cave. After Macarius's death Nilus sought even greater solitude until his own death. His corpse gave off a sweet smell, hence the name 'the Mirovlite'.

Nine Brothers Chercheulidze, born Marabda, eastern Georgia, died there, 3 March 1625. Georgian Church. The nine brothers vowed not to leave the field of battle and to defend their country and their faith against Persian invaders. They all perished in the battle, as did their mother and their sister, who were caring for the wounded.

Ninian, born Cumbria, *c.* 360, died Whithorn, *c.* 432. The son of a converted Cumbrian British chieftain, he was said by **Bede** to have been educated at Rome, where he was consecrated bishop in 394 and sent to evangelize Scotland. Travelling through Tours on the way, he met St **Martin**, to whom he later dedicated the church (commonly called Candida Casa) which he built at Whithorn in Wigtownshire. From here he and his monks evangelized the Britons and Picts; it was long a centre of learning for the Welsh and Irish missionaries and his tomb there was a shrine for medieval pilgrims. Feast 16 September.

Nino of Georgia, born Cappadocia (?), died Bodbe, Katcheti, Georgia, fourth century. Nino is regarded as the apostle of Georgia. She is said to have been taken there as a captive, and because of her holiness and her gift of miracles was able to bring the king to embrace Christianity, and to seek clergy from the Emperor Constantine. She retired to a hermitage at the end of her life. Feast 14 January.

Niphon, bl., born Lukovo, Epirus, 1315, died Mount Athos, 14 June 1411. The son of a priest, he first became a monk on Mount Giromeron, then went to Mount Athos where he was ordained. For some time he lived in a monastery, but then became a hermit. He was renowned for his miracles, during his life as well as after his death.

Niphon II, patriarch, born Constantinople, died Mount Athos, 11 August 1508. Byzantine Church. He was a scholar in his youth, and became a monk on Mount Athos. He was appointed bishop of Thessalonika because of his learning, and was elected patriarch of Constantinople in 1486, but was deposed in 1489 because of slanders about him. He went into a monastery in Constantinople, but was reappointed patriarch in 1497. On this occasion he visited Wallachia. In 1498, however, he was exiled to Adrianopolis, but was once again recalled in 1502. He was offered another bishopric, but refused it, spending the last years of his life on Mount Athos.

Niphon of Kozeozero, monk, died Moscow (?), *c*. 1565. Russian Church. A solitary beside lake Koza, near Archangel, he was joined by a Christian Tartar who had taken the name **Serapion**. Others joined them, and they decided to found a monastery. Niphon went to Moscow to seek permission for this, but died either there, or on the journey.

Niphon of Novgorod, bishop, died Kiev, 1156. Russian Church. Originally a monk of the Kievan Cave monastery, he became bishop of Novgorod in 1130. He was deposed for refusing to recognize the metropolitan of Kiev, Clement, who had been elected uncanonically, but was freed from his exile in Kiev by the grand prince and returned to Novgorod. He died at the monastery in Kiev when he returned to the city to greet the new, canonically elected, metropolitan.

Niphon of Telegovo, monk, sixteenth century. Russian Church. Founder of the monastery at Telgovo, but nothing else is known of him.

Nivard, bl., born *c*. 1100, died *c*. 1150. The youngest brother of St **Bernard**, whom he joined at Clairvaux, later becoming novice master at Vaucelles. Little is known for certain about his subsequent life, and his cult is not confirmed. Feast 7 February.

Noe Mawaggali, martyr, died Uganda, 1886, canonized 1964. He was a potter, among those converted by the Missionaries of Africa, who was put to death by King Mwanga of Uganda – see **Martyrs of Uganda**. Feast 30 May.

Noel Chabanel, martyr, born Saugues, France, 2 February 1613, died St Jean, Canada, 8 December 1649. He joined the Society of Jesus in Toulouse in 1630, and worked in Toulouse and Rodez before leaving for the mission to the Hurons in 1643, two years after his ordination. He found living among the Hurons and learning their language very difficult indeed, but took a vow that, despite his problems, he would stay there for the rest of his life. He escaped death when a group of Christian Hurons were attacked by the Iroquois, although his companion **Charles Garnier** did not survive. But the day after Charles Garnier's death, Noel Chabanel was shot and killed by a Christian Huron who blamed him for all the evils that had fallen on his family. Feast, with **John de Brébeuf**, 19 October.

Noël Pinot, bl., martyr, died 1794. He was parish priest of Louroux-Béconnais. See **Martyrs of the French Revolution**. Feast 21 February.

Nolawi, monk, born Goggiam. Ethiopian Church.

Nolawina Her, monk, thirteenth/fourteenth centuries. Ethiopian Church. A disciple of **Takla Haymanot**.

Non (Nonna, Nonnita), died Britanny, *c*. 540. Mother of **David of Wales**, she may have been married to Sant, a local chieftain, and David is variously described as her only, or her eldest, child. She is patron saint of Dirinon, Brittany, where her supposed tomb is in the church. Feast 3 March.

Nonna, died Nazianzen, 374. The wife of **Gregory of Nazianzen**, whom she converted to Christianity. Their three children were **Gorgonia, Gregory** and **Caesarius**. Feast 5 August.

Nonnosus, monk, died Mount Soracte, sixth century. Prior of the abbey of Mount Soracte, northeast of Rome. His miracles are recorded by Pope **Gregory the Great**. Feast 2 September.

Nonnus, bishop, died *c*. 458. He had been a monk in Egypt before being made bishop of Edessa. Feast 2 December.

Norbert of Xanten, born Xanten, Cleves, *c*. 1080, died Magdeburg, 6 June 1134. Born of a princely family, he obtained ordination to support his worldly life at the imperial court, but in 1115 an escape from death during a thunderstorm led to his conversion. After failing to reform the canons at Xanten, he gained papal permission to become an itinerant preacher. In 1120 at Prémontré near Laon he founded an order of canons, since called Norbertines or Premonstratensians; and in 1126 he was made archbishop of Magdeburg. Feast 6 June.

Nostrianus, died *c.* 450. He was bishop of Naples and combated Arianism and Pelagianism. Feast 14 February.

Notburga, born *c.* 1265, died Rattenburg in the Tyrol, 1313 (an alternative account puts her in the ninth or tenth centuries). She was employed as a maidservant, first in a noble household and then in a peasant family. Although poor herself, she became beloved for the attention she gave to people less fortunate than herself. Her shrine was established at Eben in the Tyrolese Alps. Feast 14 September.

Nothelm of Canterbury, archbishop, born London (?), died Canterbury, *c.* 740. He assisted **Bede** in his *Ecclesiastical History* by supplying information about Kent, and by researching in the papal archives in Rome. Otherwise very little is known of him. Feast 17 October.

Notker, bl., born Switzerland, *c.* 840, died there, 912, cult approved 1512. A monk at St-Gall abbey, he taught music, wrote *Liber Hymnorum* (Book of Hymns, 884), and became master of the monastic school. He developed the use of sequences, hymns sung before the Gospel, composing about 40, possibly with **Tutilo**. Feast 6 April.

Notker of Liège, bl., born 940, died Liège, 10 April 1008. Of a noble Swabian family, he was made prince-bishop of Liège by his uncle, the Emperor Otto I, in 969. As its 'second founder' he improved the moral and intellectual standard of its clergy and built schools and churches. The cathedral school of St-Lambert was remarkable in Europe. He also rebuilt the cathedral-like church at Aachen, but it was burned down in 1185. His relics at Liège are not genuine. Feast 9 or 10 April.

Nun' Alvares de Pereira (Nonnius), bl., born Sernache de Bomjardin, near Lisbon, 24 June 1360, died Lisbon, 1 November 1431. He was of a very distinguished family, married at 17, and had three children. He was placed in charge of the Portuguese army, and proved a highly successful commander. In 1422 he became a Carmelite lay brother at the house he had himself founded – his wife had died in 1387 – and remained there to the end of his life.

Nunilo and Alodia, martyrs, born Huesca, Spain, died there, 851. Two sisters, with a Christian mother and a Muslim father. Under pressure to marry, they decided to go to live with a Christian aunt. It was then decreed that children of Muslim fathers had to follow the religion of the father. Efforts were made to persuade them to convert, but they refused to do so, and were beheaded. Feast 22 October.

Nuntius Sulprizio, bl., born Pescosansonesco (Pescara), Abruzzi, 1817, died Naples, 5 May 1836, beatified 1963. Orphaned young, he started working with a blacksmith at the age of nine. Suffering from painful illnesses from the age of 14 until his early death, he was declared a patron of young working men for his patience and chastity.

Nup, monk, born Bilad, Upper Egypt, third/fourth centuries. Coptic Church. He became a monk early in life, and during the persecution of Diocletian was arrested and, after refusing to burn incense before the idols, was exiled for seven years in the Pentapolis. After the accession of **Constantine** he went to a monastery on the Basla mountains, but was summoned to Constantinople by the emperor. Before he set off he was consecrated bishop against his will, and in Constantinople was laden with gifts, although he would accept only those intended for the Church. He returned to his monastery, and died there.

O

Octavian of Savona, bishop, born Burgundy, *c.* 1060, died Savona, Italy, 1132. A nobleman, he entered the monastery of St Peter at Pavia, and later was appointed bishop of Savona. Feast 6 August.

Oda of Canterbury, see **Odo of Canterbury**.

Oddino of Fossano, bl., born Fossano, Piedmont, 1334, died there, 7 or 21 July 1400. He was parish priest of the church of St John the Baptist in Fossano, and was reputed for his care of the poor. He was appointed provost of the collegiate chapter of Fossano in 1374. He later resigned and became a Franciscan tertiary, and made his house into a shelter for the poor. In 1381 he went on a pilgrimage to the Holy Land, and was held prisoner by the Turks for a time. When he returned he was made governor of the Guild of the Cross, an association caring for pilgrims and for the sick. He built a hospital and hospice, and a new church, and was again elected provost in 1389 or 1396. The plague came to Fossano in 1400 and he cared for the victims, eventually succumbing to the disease himself. Feast 7 July.

Odilia, patroness of Alsace, born Oberheim, *c.* 660, died Niedermunster, *c.* 720. She is thought to have been the daughter of a Frankish lord, Adalricus, to have been born blind and later to have recovered her sight miraculously. She founded a nunnery in a castle granted to her by her father at a place which became known as Odilienberg in the Vosges mountains, and became abbess. This abbey was a famous centre for pilgrims, and was visited by **Charlemagne**, Pope **Leo IX** and possibly Richard I of England. The water of the well is said to cure eye disease. She later founded another nunnery at Niedermunster. Feast 13 December.

Odilo of Cluny, fifth abbot of Cluny, born probably in the Auvergne, *c.* 962, died abbey of Souvigny, 31 December 1048. He became a cleric in St Julien in Brioude, but then entered Cluny in 991, was made within the year assistant to the abbot, and succeeded as abbot in 994 – which is when he was also ordained. He was a person of great virtue, often hard on himself but gentle with others. He expanded the work of the Cluniac houses, increasing their number from 37 to 65 during his administration. Odilo was a competent administrator, centralizing many of the houses around Cluny itself, and was highly respected by popes and emperors. He was responsible for introducing the 'Truce of God' as well as All Souls' Day (2 November), eventually extended from Cluny to the whole Church. He was canonized in 1063. Feast 11 May.

Odo of Cambrai, bl., also known as Odo of Tournai, bishop and theologian, born Orléans, France, died Anchin abbey, near Arras, 19 June 1113. He taught at Toul and Tournai, introduced Cluniac reform to his monastery, St-Martin of Tournai, and was elected bishop of Cambrai in 1095. Several of his theological works survive.

Odo of Canterbury ('the Good'), a Dane, but probably born in East Anglia, died Canterbury, 2 June 958. He was rejected by his family when he converted to Christianity, and was adopted by a nobleman in the entourage of King Alfred. He took orders, and was appointed to the see of Ramsbury in 927. He at first declined the see of Canterbury offered to him by King Edmund, on the grounds of not being a monk. Nevertheless, the king persisted and he received the Benedictine habit from Fleury and accepted the offer of the see. He was active in renovating buildings and restoring the morals of the clergy. Feast 4 July.

Odo of Cluny, abbot of Cluny and son of a Frankish knight, Abbo, born Tours, 879, died Cluny, 18 November 942. After studying in Paris and returning to the abbey of St Martin at Tours, he was sent to the abbey school at Beaume, becoming its abbot in 924, and eventually succeeding St **Berno** − who had also been his predecessor at Beaume − as abbot of Cluny in 927. He was largely instrumental in establishing the dominance of this monastery, through the reforms he carried out of other monasteries in France and Italy: he established the monastery of Our Lady on Rome's Aventine Hill. During his abbacy the monastic church of St Peter and St Paul was completed. His writings include three books of moral essays, a work (the *Occupatio*) on redemption, and some sermons. Feast 11 May.

Odo of Novara, bl., born Novara, *c.* 1105, died Tagliacozzo, Italy, 1200, cult confirmed 1859. A Carthusian, made prior of Geyrach monastery, Slavonia, he left to escape the bishop's persecution. He became chaplain to a convent at Tagliacozzo. He seems to have had the gift of healing. Feast 14 January.

Odulf, born Brabant, died Stavoren, 855. He was a member of the nobility and a canon of the cathedral of Utrecht, whence he was sent, by **Frederick of Utrecht**, to work among the Frisians. He founded a church and monastery at Stavoren. Feast 12 June.

Oengus the Culdee, monk, born Ulster, died Dysartenos, *c.* 824. A monk at Clonenagh monastery, a hermit at Dysartenos, he then hid as a servant at Tallaght monastery near Dublin until abbot **Maelruain** recognized him. Together they wrote the *Martyrology of Tallaght*. Oengus also wrote the *Festilogium* (*Félire* in Irish) and *Pedigrees*

of Irish Saints and became abbot-bishop of Clonenagh. Feast 11 March.

Oidilwald, see **Ethelwald**.

Olaf II, Olaf Haraldson, king, patron saint of Norway, helped to establish Christianity in his native country, born 995, died Stiklestad, Norway, 1030. Having spent several years raiding the French and English coasts, he was converted to Christianity in Rouen, Normandy, in 1013. He returned to Norway in 1015, claiming the throne. He completed the conversion of Norway begun by Olaf I, building many churches throughout Norway and introducing clergy into the country. Due mainly to his severity in eradicating heathenism, Norway was invaded in 1028 by Canute II, king of England and Denmark, and Olaf went into exile at Novgorod. Returning to Norway in 1030, he was killed at the battle of Stiklestad. Canonized in 1164. Feast 29 July.

Olbianus, bishop and martyr, died Anaea, Asia Minor, *c.* 300. Feast 29 May.

Oldegar, political counsellor and crusader, born Barcelona, Spain, 1060, died there, 1 March 1137. Oldegar held a number of minor ecclesial posts in Barcelona before becoming prior of St-Adrian in Provence in 1099 and then abbot of St-Ruf in Avignon in 1113. He was elected bishop of Barcelona in 1116, and in 1118 was appointed by the pope and the count of Barcelona-Provence to re-establish the metropolitanate of Tarragona. He attended a number of councils, including the first Lateran Council in 1123, and helped pave the way politically for the union of Aragon and Catalonia. Feast 6 March.

Oleg of Brjansk, prince, died Brjansk, *c.* 1285. Russian Church. In 1274 he took part with his father in an attack on Lithuania, then he went to see his sister, but when he returned to Brjansk he abdicated and became a monk, taking the name Basil. He built the monastery of the Theophany at Brjansk, and lived a strictly ascetical life. Feast 20 September.

Oleg the Handsome, prince and martyr, died Rjazan, 1237 (?). Prince of Rjazan, and a convert to

Christianity, he was captured when his city was taken by the Mongols. Attracted by his good looks, the khan offered him his freedom were he to abjure his faith, but he refused to do so, and was executed.

Olga (Helga), born Pskov, *c.* 890, died Kiev, 11 July 969. Of royal birth, she avenged herself for her husband's death and this event is described with approval by Nestor in the *Primary Chronicle*. He also paints a picture of a highly competent ruler. At some later date she was baptized and attempted to gain autonomy for the Russian Church, negotiating both with Rome and with Byzantium, visiting Constantine Porphyrogenitus at Constantinople. She also wrote to the Emperor Otto I asking for missionaries, because her own conversion had not been followed by her people at that time. She was given a Christian burial and recognized as a saint. Feast 11 July.

Oliver Plunkett, martyr, archbishop of Armagh and the first Irishman to be canonized since **Laurence O'Toole** in the twelfth century, born Loughcrew, County Meath, 1 November 1629, into an old English family, executed Tyburn, London, 11 July 1681, the last of the Irish bishops to die a martyr's death. After early education in Dublin he was sent to the Irish College in Rome under the care of the papal legate. He was ordained for the Irish mission in 1654, but because of the penal laws his return to Ireland was much delayed; he stayed in Rome from 1645 to 1669 and was professor in the college of the Propaganda Fidei, where he also acted as agent for the Irish clergy. He also served much among the poor and infirm in the hospital of Santo Spirito. He was appointed archbishop of Armagh in 1669 and duly consecrated at Ghent in November of that year. During his ten-year episcopate he was unceasing in his efforts to build up the Church in Ireland, holding synods, confirming, ordaining, and travelling incessantly throughout the country. Catholicism was given only occasional tolerance in this period, so that in effect he administered much in secret or in remote forests and hillsides. Plunkett was also a thoroughly conscientious archbishop in rooting out clerical abuses. He established the Jesuits at Drogheda, where they opened a school and a seminary. He was forced into hiding in 1673 and from then until his arrest in 1679 his life was one of danger and physical hardship. He was charged with implication in the Titus Oates Plot, conspiring to bring about an armed rebellion. On the evidence of an apostate priest he was first imprisoned in Dublin castle, then removed to Newgate in London. In a travesty of a trial, Plunkett was found guilty of high treason. He was hanged, drawn and quartered at Tyburn, the last Catholic to be martyred there, and was canonized on 12 October 1975.

Ollegarius (Oldegar), archbishop, born Barcelona, died Tarragona, 1137. Dedicated to the Church as a child, he chose the celibate life, was an abbot, bishop of Barcelona, then archbishop of Tarragona. He rebuilt churches destroyed by the Moors and supported those fighting them. Feast 6 March.

Olvianus, see **Olbianus**.

Olybia, Leone and Eutropia, martyrs, died Palmyra, Syria, 303. The two sisters Olybia and Leone were burned alive for their faith, and the 12-year-old Eutropia was used for target practice by archers. Feast 15 June.

Olympias, born between 361 and 368 into a rich, influential family in Constantinople, died Nicomedia, between 408 and 410. After the early death of her husband, a high imperial official, she refused a second marriage. Because of her ascetic lifestyle and her many donations to the Church, she became at the age of 30 a deaconess in the Church of Constantinople. She started an ascetic community which shared her life of service and soon counted 250 adherents. Very close to several bishops, especially **John Chrysostom**, she fell into disgrace together with him and was exiled. Seventeen letters from this period, written by Chrysostom to her, have been preserved. Feast 25 July.

Olympias, bl., martyr, born in the Peloponnese, died Lesbos, May 1235. She became prioress of the nunnery of Carie Thermis, on Lesbos, and was martyred when the house was attacked by pirates.

Olympius of Aïnoi, bishop (of what is now Enez, Turkey), died *c.* 340. A strong supporter of

Athanasius against the Arians, he was sent into exile, and died there. Feast 12 June.

Omer of Thérouanne, bishop of Thérouanne, died *c.* 670. Upon the death of his mother, Omer and his father entered the monastery of Luxeuil (*c.* 615). There, under Eustachius, Omer became proficient in the study of the Scriptures. In 637, when King Dagobert sought a bishop for Thérouanne, the capital of the Morini in Belgic Gaul, Omer was consecrated. At one time the city had been Christianized, but had later relapsed into paganism. Omer succeeded in restoring true faith and practice. Along with monks of Luxeuil (Bertin, Mommolin and Ebertan) he founded Sithin abbey, which became an important spiritual centre, and also the church of Our Lady of Sithin with a small monastery. Feast 9 September.

Onesima, hermit, born Antioch (?), died Egypt. Syriac Church. Said to be the daughter of a king, she spent 40 years as a hermit in the Egyptian desert before going to the monastery of Tebnesi, where she lived for another 40 years, pretending to be mad, so that her holiness would not be observed. When her holiness was finally revealed she fled from the monastery.

Onesimus of Kiev, monk, twelfth/thirteenth centuries. Russian Church. A monk of the Kievan Cave monastery. His remains were discovered in 1675 after an earthquake. Feast 12 July.

Onesiphorus, monk, died Kiev, 1148. Russian Church. A priest-monk of the Kievan Cave monastery, one of his priestly pentients died unrepentant of his sin. Onesiphorus permitted him to be buried nonetheless, but the impenitent monk appeared to him and reproved him for allowing the burial. Feast 9 November.

Onuphrius, martyr, born Cabrova, 1786, died Chios, 4 January 1818. Baptized Matthew, at the age of eight, he declared that he wanted to become a Muslim, to annoy his devout parents, and was only just rescued from the hands of the Turks. Later in life he became a monk on Mount Athos, taking the name Manasses. He changed it to Onuphrius, however, before setting out for Chios in search of martyrdom. Dressed as a Turk, he

presented himself before a judge and declared himself to have become a Christian. He was beheaded.

Onuphrius Garegeli, monk, born Guria, western Georgia, died 1733. Georgian Church. He was baptized Othar Maciutadze, and *c.* 1680 he moved to eastern Georgia because his brother had become confessor to the queen of Karthli. Othar became a monk at the monastery of Davidgaregi, then became hegumenos *c.* 1690. He set about reviving religious life in the monastery, building churches and enriching the monastic library, and conducted a campaign against the feudal lords selling their slaves, and especially against them selling slaves to Muslims. Feast 29 September.

Onuphrius of Katroma, monk, sixteenth century. Russian Church. Founder of the monastery of Katroma, but nothing else is known. Feast 12 June.

Onuphrius of Kursk, bishop and martyr, born Posad-Opole, 2 April 1889, died Blagovescensk (?), 1 June 1938. Ukrainian Church, Moscow Patriarchate. Baptized Anthony Maksimovic Gagaljuk, his father was murdered when he was only four years old, and the family home set on fire, so he was brought up in an orphanage in Lublin. He studied in Cholm and St Petersburg. He twice believed himself cured of pneumonia by the intercession of St **Onuphrius**, which is the name he took when becoming a monk in St Petersburg in 1913. He became a professor at the monastery of Grigorievo-Bizjukovy, but when this was sacked after the revolution he went to Borislavl, then on to Krivoj Rog, in both palces working in the cathedral. He was made bishop for Odessa and Cherson in 1922, and the following year archbishop of Elizabetgrad. He was arrested, and eventually sent to Char'kov, but when freed returned to Odessa. He was arrested again in 1926, and imprisoned, but continued to write articles. He was unexpectedly freed in 1929 when in prison in Tobolsk, and he was sent as bishop to Staryj Oskol. He was allowed by the authorities only to celebrate in one church, and was forbidden to leave the city. He was again arrested and freed, and appointed to the diocese of Kursk with the rank of archbishop. In June 1935 he was re-arrested and sent to a concentration camp, where he was shot:

the day is known, but the exact location is uncertain. Feast 19 May.

Onuphrius of Preveza, bl., died monastery of the Nativity of the Mother of God, on the island of Koronisia, near Preveza, Greece. Feast 12 June.

Onuphrius of Pskov, monk, died Malye, near Izborsk, 12 June 1592. Russian Church. Founded a monastery of the Nativity of the Mother of God at Malye, near Izborsk, which in turn is near Pskov.

Onuphrius of Romanov, died Romanov-Borisoglebsk. Russian Church. A 'fool for Christ', but nothing else is known of him.

Onuphrius of Solovki, monk, fifteenth century. Russian Church. A disciple of **Zosimus**.

Onuphrius of Vologda, see **Ausentius of Vologda**.

Onuphrius the Egyptian, hermit, died Upper Egypt, c. 400. He lived for 70 years on water and vegetables in the Egyptian desert, near Hermopolis. It is also said that he wore nothing, but covered himself with his long hair. Feast 12 June.

Oprea Miklaus, died Kufstein, in the Tyrol, eighteenth century. Serbian Church. A devout shepherd, he was imprisoned for his resistance to Catholics. Feast 21 October.

Optatus, bishop of Milevis, north Africa, died c. 370. Little is known for sure about him except his writings against Donatists, produced between 367 and 375. Book I argues against the foundations of Donatism, books II–VI argue that there is no catholicity amongst them, and book VII claims that repentant Donatists can be readmitted to the Church. **Augustine**'s refutation of Donatism was influenced by Optatus's work. Feast 4 June.

Optatus and Companions, died Saragossa, Spain, 304. A hymn by the fourth-century poet Prudentius says that 18 Christians died, but not how. It describes in detail the tortures of Encratis (Engrazia), a virgin called a 'living martyr', implying she survived. A popular local saint, she became associated with this group. Feast 16 April.

Optina Elders, Russian Church. This group of monks is generally reckoned to number 14 – the earliest, Moses, born 15 January 1782 and the last, Isaachius, martyred in 1937. They all belonged to the Optina hermitage in the Kaluga district, which was a centre of spiritual direction and renewal inspired by the hesychast tradition, brought to Russia by disciples of **Paisius Velichkovsky**. Most of the elders made themselves available to visitors who came from all over the Russian empire. Several counselled also by correspondence. Optina was closed by the Soviet authorities in the 1920s and the last elders all suffered varying degrees of persecution. See separate entries for **Macarius** and **Ambrose of Optina**. Canonized in 1990. Feast day 11 October.

Orentius, Heros, Pharnacius, Firminus, Firmus, Cyriacus and Longinus, martyrs, died 304 (?). Said to be seven brothers, all soldiers, sent into exile for their faith and martyred in various places. Feast 24 June.

Orestes, martyr, born Tyana, Cappadocia, died 304. Feast 9 November.

Orientius, bishop, died probably Auch, southern France, early fifth century. A hermit in the Lavendan valley near Tarbes, the people of Auch insisted he became their bishop, which he was for over 40 years. Feast 1 May.

Orlando de Medici, hermit, probably born Milan, died Borgone monastery, Salsmaggiore, near Parma, Italy, 15 September 1386. He lived as a solitary in Borgone for about 26 years. His bones were taken to St Bartolomeo's church in Busseto, Cremona, and since the end of the fourteenth century many miracles have been attributed to him and his cult has flourished. Feast 15 September.

Orosia, martyr, died Bayonne, eighth century (?). Everything is doubtful about Orosia, except the fact of a cult. She is said to have been of a noble family in the region of Bayonne, refused to marry a Muslim chief, fled to the mountains, but was captured and executed. Feast 25 June.

Orsiesius, see **Horsiesius**.

Ortolana (Hortulana), mother of Ss **Clare** and **Agnes** of Assisi, died near Florence, before 1238. Always very devout, she travelled as a pilgrim to the Holy Land *c.* 1192 before marrying Count Favarone di Offreduccio of Assisi. She had four children. After the death of her husband, she joined her third daughter, Beatrice, at the convent of the Poor Clares at San Damiano near Florence. She was buried near her daughters in the church of St Clare in Assisi. Feast 2 January.

Os, monk, born Caesarea, fifth/sixth century. Ethiopian Church. A Greek monk, he was one of the 'Nine Saints' who came to Ethiopia after the Council of Chalcedon in 451. He belonged to the monastery of Quezara. Feast 13 December.

Osanna, bl., born Montenegro, 1493, died 27 April 1565, cult approved 1928. An Orthodox Christian, she became a Catholic, an anchorite and a Dominican tertiary, living in two successive cells attached to churches. She chose her name to honour **Osanna of Mantua**, attracted disciples and is venerated by Orthodox and Catholics.

Osanna of Mantua, bl., mystic, born Mantua, 17 January 1449, died there, 20 June 1505. She had a visionary experience when she was a small child and became a Dominican tertiary. She lived at home and followed a life of prayer, helped the poor and the sick and interceded on behalf of victims of injustice. Her own model was the Dominican friar Savonarola of Florence, and like him she was critical of Pope Alexander VI. Feast 18 June.

Osburga, abbess, died Coventry, England, *c.* 1018. Nothing is known of her, except that she was abbess of the convent in Coventry from the time that it was founded by **Cnut** before he was king. Miracles were attributed to her shrine. Feast 30 March.

Osmund, bishop, born Seez, Normandy, died Salisbury, 4 December 1099. He was a Norman and followed William I to England, possibly as a chaplain, and as William's chancellor assisted with the compilation of the Domesday Book. He became bishop of Salisbury in 1078 and built a cathedral at Sarum (not the present one, which dates from 1225), which he consecrated in April 1092. He also

organized the cathedral chapter, which was a model for others. Feast 4 December.

Oswald, king and martyr, born Northumbria, *c.* 605, killed in battle, possibly at Oswestry ('Oswald's Tree'?), 5 August 642. When his father Ethelfrith died, Edwin seized the throne, forcing Oswald into exile on Iona. Here he was converted to the Christian faith. Returning to Northumbria after Edwin's death, he set about spreading the Christian faith through the help of **Aidan**, sent from Iona for this purpose to the see of Lindisfarne. Oswald was killed by Penda of Mercia in the seventh year of his reign. Feast 5 August.

Oswald of Worcester, archbishop, born probably Denmark, exact date unknown, *c.* 925, died Worcester, England, 29 February 992. Oswald was educated by the archbishop of Canterbury and ordained at the monastery of Fleury, which he had entered. He served as bishop of Worcester (961) and archbishop of York (972) – although he continued as bishop of Worcester. During his episcopal tenure, he worked to found and reform religious houses and was one of the primary promoters of the Anglo-Saxon monastic revival of the 900s. His methods were peaceful and by example. Along with **Dunstan**, another monastic reformer, he crowned kings Edgar, **Edward** (the martyr) and Ethelred II. Feast 28 February.

Oswin, king and martyr, born Deira (modern Yorkshire), died Gilling, Yorkshire, 20 August 651. At the death of his father, Oswin was taken to Wessex for safety, where he became a Christian. Oswin returned to claim the kingdom of Deira in 644. In 651 he was attacked by his brother Oswiu, but rather than face a battle with subsequent loss of life, he dismissed his troops and retired to a property at Gilling, where he was murdered on the orders of his brother.

Osyth, martyr, born Mercia, died Crich, Essex, *c.* 675. Of noble birth, she was educated in a convent and wished to become a nun, but her parents insisted on her marrying Sighere, king of the East Saxons. When the king was about to consummate the marriage, a white stag emerged, which he went off to hunt, and by the time he had returned Osyth had become a nun. Sighere then established a convent for her at Crich, near Colchester in Essex, where she lived until she was beheaded by pirates for refusing to adore their pagan gods. She picked up her head, carried it to a church and placed it on the altar there. Feast 7 October.

Othmar (Otmar, Audemar, Audomar), abbot, born *c.* 689, died Werd, near Stein-am-Rhein, Switzerland, 16 November 759. Educated for the priesthood at the imperial court, in 719 he was invited to direct a colony of monks who had settled near the grave of St **Gall**. He built them a monastery and gave them a Rule. For defending the autonomy of the house, he was imprisoned and exiled, and established the first house for lepers in Switzerland. In 769 his remains were returned to the abbey of Sankt Gallen, and in 867 they were buried in a church named for him. Feast 16 November.

Otto, died *c.* 1120. He was a hermit at Ariano, Sannio. Feast 23 March.

Otto Neururer, bl., martyr, born Piller, Landeck, 25 March 1882 , died Buchenwald concentration camp, Germany, 3 (?) June 1940. He entered the junior seminary at Brixen in 1895 and was ordained in 1907. He worked in a number of parishes before being appointed to Götzens in 1932. He was arrested in 1939 for his hostility to the changes brought by the Nazis, and in March was sent to Dachau, then, in September, to Buchenwald. There in June 1940 he was hanged by his feet until he died, for engaging in the conversion of one of the inmates. His death was admitted on 3 June. Feast (with **Jacob Gapp**) 13 August.

Otto of Bamberg, bishop and missionary, born Swabia, 1060, died Bamberg, 30 June 1139. Having worked as a teacher and priest in Poland, he was appointed chancellor for Henry IV, Holy Roman emperor, in 1101. He became bishop of Bamberg in 1106. In this office he carried out a reform of his diocese, creating over 20 monasteries and completing the cathedral. Otto did much to heal the breach between pope and emperor in the celebrated Investiture Contest in Henry V's time, and to bring about the Concordat at Worms in 1122. In 1124 he undertook the first of two missionary journeys to Pomerania (Poland), successfully converting many of the inhabitants. Canonized in 1189.

Ouen, statesman, biographer, archbishop of Rouen, born Sancy, near Soissons, *c.* 609, died Clichy-la-Garenne, near Paris, 24 August 683 or 684. Ouen was educated at St Medard abbey and served in the courts of Clothaire II and Dagobert I (as chancellor to the latter). He founded the abbey of Rabais in 634 or 636, was ordained and then consecrated archbishop of Rouen in 640 or 641. Ouen fought pockets of paganism in his diocese, wrote the biography of his friend St **Eloi**, which is an important historical/ecclesiological source, and continued as a statesman, upholding Ebroin, the mayor of the palace, against the aristocracy, and negotiating peace between Neustria and Austrasia in Cologne at the invitation of Thierry I. His fatal illness struck as he returned from Cologne.

Pachomius, bl., Byzantine Church. Shares a feast with **Mamanta** and **Hilarion**. Feast 6 May.

Pachomius, monk and martyr, born General'scino, c. 1890, died Kazakhstan, 1936. Russian Church. Baptized Procorus Petrovic Rusin, he joined the monastery of St Peter and Paul, Cernigov, but in 1910 moved to what is now Kazakhstan as a missionary. He was ordained priest there, probably in 1914. In 1916 he left the monastery and went to live at Vernyj, and then went to live with **Seraphim** on Mount Kyzyl-zar. After the death of Seraphim he went to a remote region and then in 1928 he moved to Tashkent. In 1930 he was living in the mountains of Dzagal-Abad. He was arrested in 1935 on the charge of having established a secret religious community, and the following year was sentenced to three years in a prison camp, but was then unexpectedly shot.

Pachomius of Keno, founder, fifteenth/sixteenth centuries. Russian Church. Nothing is known of him, except that he was founder of the monastery of the Transfiguration on lake Keno, towards the end of the fifteenth century. Feast 15 May.

Pachomius of Nerechta, anchorite, born Vladimir, died Nerechta, 23 March 1384. The son of a priest, he was very devout as a child, and when aged 21 he entered the monastery of the Nativity at Vladimir. He eventually – and reluctantly – became a priest, and was appointed hegumenos of the monastery of Ss Constantine and Helena, founded by the bishop of Vladimir. After a time, however, he handed over his responsibilities to a fellow monk and went to live as a hermit in Nerechta, beside the river Gridevka. There he established a monastery, for which he provided a Rule laying down that every monk had to work to maintain himself and own nothing.

Pachomius of Russia, bl., martyr, born Russia, died Usaki, Turkey, 21 May 1730. Byzantine Church. Captured by Tartars as a young man, he was sold to a Turk as a slave, and lived in Usak. His owner tried, but failed, to convert him to Islam. He succeeded in escaping, and went to live on Mount Athos. While there he began to think of martyrdom, and with the support of his spiritual director he returned to Usak, was arrested, and beheaded. Feast 7 May.

Pachomius of Spaso-Kamennyj, monk, fifteenth century. Russian Church. Originally a monk of Spaso-Kamennyj, he and **Dionysius of Glusic**, seeking a more ascetic way of life, left the monastery in the 1390s and settled beside lake Kuben, where they found an abandoned monastery. After a time, however, Dionysius moved on, seeking an even more ascetical life, leaving Pachomius alone. His date of death is not known, and the new monastery eventually became a dependency of their original one.

Pachomius the Great, abbot, founder of coenobitic monasticism, born Esneh, c. 290, died Tabennisi, north of Thebes, 346. One of the great monastic fathers, after serving in the army, he became a hermit at Schenesit under **Palaemon**. Dissatisfied with eremitic life, he settled in Tabennisi and developed the first *coenobium*, a monastery based on the full communal life. His second foundation at Pbou became the mother house in a federation of nine monasteries and three convents over which he presided. The Rules of Pachomius were composed in Coptic and translated into Latin (by **Jerome** in 404), Greek and Ethiopian. They influenced in some degree all subsequent monastic Rules, such as that of St **Benedict**, and thus the form of monasticism that prevails today. Feast 9 May.

Pachomius the Romanian, born Gledin, Transylvania, 1674, died Lvov, Poland, 1724. Baptized Petru Pencu, the son of a priest, in 1694 he entered the monastery of Neamtu in Moldavia, taking the name Pachomius. In 1702 he became hegumenos, but resigned the office two years later and spent a further two years travelling in Russia. On his return to the monastery, and with the approval of the monks, he retired with a group of disciples to a deserted spot about an hour's distance, to live a more hermit-like existence in the forests on the slopes of Mount Chiriacu. In 1707 he was elected bishop of Radauti, but in 1714 he returned to Mount Chiriacu. Two years later, however, war between Austria and the Tartars drove him into exile, at first in Transylvania, then in Poland, where he died.

Pacian of Barcelona, bishop, born Spain, *c.* 310, died Barcelona, before 392. The main source of information about Pacian is **Jerome**'s *De viris illustribus*, a book dedicated to his son, Dexter, the praetorian prefect, in which Pacian is praised for his learning, sanctity and pastoral zeal. His extant writings are *De Baptismo*, a sermon on baptism and original sin; *Contra Novatianos*, three letters to Sympronian on the Novatian heresy; *Paraenesis sive exhortatensis libellus*, on the forgiveness of sins. The first letter to Sympronian contains the famous line: 'My name is Christian, my surname, Catholic.' Feast 9 March.

Pacificus of Cerano, bl., born Novara, Italy, 1424, died Sardinia, 14 June 1482. He was educated by the Benedictines, but entered the Observant Franciscans. He preached throughout Italy, and was sent by the pope to Sardinia. After returning to Novara he wrote a book of moral thelogy, then went off again on a preaching tour, but in 1480 he was sent again to Sardinia, both as visitor to the Observant houses and to inspire a crusade against the Muslims. He died in Sardinia, although at his request his body was brought back to Cerano, where he had been preaching before he set out. Feast 9 June.

Pacificus of San Severino, born San Severino, March of Ancona, 1 March 1653, died there, 24 September 1721. Baptized Carlo Antonio Divini, he was very strictly brought up by a priest uncle, and at 17 joined the Friars Minor of the Observance, taking the name Pacificus. He was ordained in 1678. He then taught philosophy, as well as travelling around giving missions, but became ill and went nearly blind. He continued to hold office in his order, in both San Severino and Forano, although he finally settled in the former in 1705. He had many mystical experiences, and could foresee the future.

Paisius, see also **Habakuk and Paisio**.

Paisius Grigorevic Moskot, martyr, born Peski Radkovskie, 8 December 1869, died Char'kov, 15 December 1937. Ukrainian Church, Moscow Patriarchate. He became a monk of the monastery of the Dormition at Svatoogosrsk, and was ordained priest in 1911. At the closure of his monastery he moved to the diocese of Tver and until 1936 worked in a village in Siberia. In 1936, however, he returned to his native village and exercised a ministry from his house until he was arrested and shot. Feast 19 May.

Paisius of Chlendar, monk, born *c.* 1725, died 1773. Bulgarian Church. At the age of 20 he entered the Bulgarian monastery of Chlendar on Mount Athos. This is the first thing that is known of him, apart from the fact that he came from the diocese of Samokov, south-west Bulgaria. As a consequence of arguments between Greek and Serbian monks about the merits of their respective countries, he began a history of the Bulgarian people, which he completed in 1762 at the Bulgarian monastery of Zographou. He appears later to have gone on a pilgrimage to Jerusalem, but the place of his death is not known, nor even with certainty the year. Although much copied, the vast manuscript which he wrote, despite continued ill-health, was not printed until 1844, but it then appeared at a time of Bulgarian national resurgence and made Paisius, whose name had been almost forgotten, a major figure in Bulgarian nationalism. Feast 19 June.

Paisius of Galic, archimandrite, died Galic, 23 May 1460 (or 1463). Russian Church. He carried a copy of an icon of the Dormition to Moscow, where he was welcomed by the grand prince, the ringing of bells, and great crowds of people. His monastery, on the banks of lake Galic, was taken under the grand prince's protection.

Paisius of the Kievan Cave Monastery, monk, died Kiev, fourteenth century. Russian Church. A close friend of the monk **Mercurius**. Feast 19 July.

Paisius of the Kievan Cave Monastery, monk, born Lubna, 8 July 1821, died Kiev, 17 April 1893. Ukrainian Church, Moscow Patriarchate. Baptized Procopius Grigorevic Jarockij, he grew up a very devout child – so devout that he gave all his attention to religious things, including friendship with the monks of the Kievan Cave monastery, and failed his school examinations and had to leave. He secretly fled from his home and went to the monastery, where he became an assistant cantor. He eventually joined the monastery, taking the name Paisius, but because of his eccentricities he was sent to the hermitage of Goloseevo where he adopted the role of a 'fool for Christ'. Although in 1855 he returned to the monastery proper, in 1856, during the liturgy, he left the church and began to wander around the streets of Kiev with an iron staff in his hand and wearing dirty, torn clothes. His behaviour attracted many followers, and earned him a reputation for miracle working.

Paisius of Uglic, founder, born Bogorodskij, near Kasin, died Uglic, 6 June 1504. Russian Church. Baptized Paul, he was orphaned at the age of ten and was sent to his uncle **Macarius**'s monastery at Kaljazin for his education. He entered the monastery a year later, when he was only 11, taking the name Paisius. He was employed in the transcription of manuscripts. In the mid-1470s Paisius decided he would prefer to live a more solitary life and in 1476, with the support of the prince of Uglic who had known his parents, he founded a small hermitage with a group of monks who joined

him. He was ordained priest and, again with the support of the princely family, developed a monastery of some 50 monks. He was believed to have great powers of healing and miracle working: when a fire swept through areas of Uglic he went in procession with his monks, carrying an icon, and the flames stopped immediately.

Paisius of Vaga, monk. Russian Church. Nothing is known of him.

Paisius the Great, monk, born Egypt, died there, fourth century. A disciple of **Pambo**, he was remarkable for his fasting. Feast 19 June.

Paisius Velichkovsky, abbot, born Poltava, Ukraine, 21 December 1722, died Niamets monastery, Romania, 15 November 1794. Baptized Peter, he rejected the Latinized theology of the Kiev Academy and travelled to Mount Athos to become a monk. He founded several monasteries on hesychast principles in Moldavia, as the Russia of Catherine II was anti-monastic. The houses used both Slavonic and Romanian and from there the Slavonic *Philokalia,* which he translated, was disseminated. Paisius thus began the monastic revival of nineteenth-century Russia.

Palaemon, abbot, died Tabenna (Tabennisi), near Thebes, 325. He was an early Egyptian hermit, persecuted under Diocletian, who trained **Pachomius** in the monastic life. When Pachomius wrote the first known coenobitical rule, they worked together to organize hermits. Feast 25 January.

Paldo, see **Tasso**.

Palladius, bishop, born Ireland, died Brittany, after 432. According to the *Chronicon* of Prosper of Aquitaine, **Celestine I** sent Palladius, a Roman deacon, to the Irish Christians as their first bishop to combat Pelagianism. He is recorded as being an associate of **Germanus**, bishop of Auxerre, a delegate to the British Church. Early lives of St **Patrick** portray Palladius as an unsuccessful missionary who abandoned his task, or died, leaving the way open for Patrick, then in Gaul, who is supposed to have received permission from Germanus to continue Palladius's work in Ireland, which was based mainly in County Wicklow, near to the spot where he arrived. Feast 6 July.

Palladius of Antioch, hermit, died Antioch, Syria, c. 390. A friend of **Simeon the Elder**, he is said to have raised someone to life to prove his innocence, after being himself accused of murder. Feast 28 January.

Pambo, monk, born Egypt, died there, c. 390. An early disciple of **Anthony**, he learned to read so that he could read the Bible and be ordained priest. He joined **Ammon** in Nitria, Lower Egypt, and was one of the founders of the monasteries of the desert of Nitria. His reputation for wisdom spread far beyond Egypt, bringing many to talk to him, including **Athanasius**. **Melania the Elder** also came, and was with him when he died. Feast 18 July.

Pambo the Recluse, monk, died Kiev, 1241. Russian Church. A monk of the Kievan Cave monastery, he was taken prisoner during one of the invasions of Kiev, and kept a captive after refusing to deny his faith. He was eventually freed – it is said miraculously – and was able to return to the monastery. Feast 18 July.

Pamin, monk, born Minyat Hasib, died al-Asmunayn, Egypt, third/fourth centuries. Coptic Church. The son of a priest, and originally a servant in a noble family, he became a monk but then, attracted by the idea of martyrdom, he went to Antinoë, where he publicly professed his faith and was imprisoned during the persecution of Diocletian. He was freed on the death of the emperor, and settled at al-Asmunayn, where he had a reputation as a miracle worker, including healing the wife of the Roman governor. He died on 5 December, but the year is unknown.

Pammachius, born Rome, c. 340, died there, 410. A senator of the Furian family and a friend of **Jerome**, who dedicated several works to Pammachius, including commentaries on the Minor Prophets and on Daniel. After the death of his wife Paulina, daughter of St **Paula**, he took the monastic habit and used his wealth for charitable causes, among them the famous hospital for pilgrims at Portus and the church of Ss Giovanni e Paolo, in Rome. A

peaceful man, he disapproved of Jerome's lack of moderation in the controversy between him and Rufinus on the subject of Origen. St **Augustine** addressed his Epistola 58 to Pammachius. Feast 30 August.

Pamphilus, born Berytus (Beirut), c. 240, died Caesarea, Palestine, 16 February 310. A pupil of **Pierius** at Alexandria, he had a deep veneration for the teaching of Origen and wrote an *Apology for Origen* with the help of **Eusebius of Caesarea**, who in turn held Pamphilus in great esteem. **Jerome** testifies to Pamphilus's authorship of the first five books, but when he became an anti-Origenist, Jerome discredited the work and attributed it all to Eusebius, who added a sixth book after Pamphilus's martyrdom, and called himself Eusebius Pamphilus. Feast 1 June.

Pamphilus and Companions, martyrs. dcb Those who died with Pamphilus are thought to have been Valens, a deacon, Paul of Jamnia, who was a notable evangelist, Pophyrius, who was Pamphilus's pupil, Theodoulus, who had been a servant to the governor of Caesarea, Seleucus, and others. Feast 1 June.

Panacea de Muzzi, bl., born Quorona, 1378, died Ghemme Novara, Piedmont, 1383. Her father remarried after the death of her mother, and her stepmother was extremely hostile. She worked as a shepherdess, but was very pious and was often to be found at prayer. Her stepmother murdered her with a spindle while she prayed. Feast 27 March.

Panaghiotis of Caesarea, martyr, born Caesarea, died Constantinople, 24 June 1767 (?). Byzantine Church. As a young man he became a Muslim, possibly under pressure, but later abjured Islam and returned to Christianity, for which he was martyred.

Panaghiotis of Jerusalem, martyr, nineteenth century. Byzantine Church. He was in the service of the Turkish governor of Jerusalem and accompanied him on a visit to a mosque. This was regarded by some Turks as an insult to their religion. He was taken prisoner and sent to Damascus, where he was tried and beheaded when he refused to abjure Christianity. The date of this is uncertain, but it occurred a few years before 1839, when an English missionary wrote down this account.

Panaghis, bl., born Luxuri, Cephalonia, 1801, died there, 7 June 1888. He studied in Cephalonia and earned a living by teaching there, but eventually entered the monastery of Blacherna on the island of Dias, near Cephalonia. His mother's entreaties persuaded him to return to his native island, where he was ordained priest. He looked after the people of the island, even after entering the monastery of St Spyridion, just outside Luxuri, after the death of his mother. He became its hegumenos, and was hailed as a saint by the people of his island immediately after his death.

Panarius of Nicomedia, martyr, died Nicomedia, 303. Secretary to the Emperor Maximian. He at first concealed his Christianity during the persecution, but then proclaimed it, and was beheaded. Feast 19 March.

Pancras, boy martyr, born Rome, died there, 304 (?). There are no reliable historical data about him, but it seems certain that a martyr of this name existed in the early fourth century. Pope **Symmachus** built a church over his tomb in the via Aurelia where he suffered decapitation a month after his conversion, when not yet 14. The first church built at Canterbury bore his name and contained a portion of his relics; the railway station in London is so called from its location in the parish which held the old cemetery of St Pancras. Feast 12 May.

Pancras of the Kievan Cave Monastery, monk, died Kiev, thirteenth century. A hieromonk, he was reputed to have the gift of miracles. Feast 9 February.

Pansirion, see **Paul**.

Pansous, martyr, died Alexandria, 250. The son of wealthy parents, he gave all his money to the poor and went to live as a monk in the desert, but he was executed during the persecution of Decius. Feast 15 January.

Pantaenus, born Sicily, died *c.* 200. He was a Stoic philosopher and a convert to Christianity. He taught at the catechetical school in Alexandria, and became head of the school in about 180. He was famous for his learning and effective teaching skills, and one of his pupils was the theologian Clement of Alexandria. Feast 7 July.

Pantaleon, martyr, died Nicomedia, *c.* 305. Nothing is known for certain about him, but legend would have Pantaleon a physician in the court of Emperor Galerius at Nicomedia, who, although brought up a Christian, fell into apostasy because of the evil example of the palace. A Christian called **Hermolaus** led him back to the faith. He suffered martyrdom when Diocletian gave orders to purge the court of Christians. He is honoured as one of the patron saints of physicians, second only to St Luke. Feast 27 July.

Pantaleon, monk, born Constantinople (?), died near Axum, Ethiopia, late fifth/early sixth century. Ethiopian Church. He came from a distinguished Byzantine family and had become a monk early in life, but came to Ethiopia after the Council of Chalcedon as one of the 'Nine Saints' who evangelized Ethiopia. Then, according to the account written long after the event, he became a hermit near Axum. He never sat, or slept, or ate. Feast 17 October.

Pantaleon of Cernigov, bishop, died Cernigov, 1142. Russian Church. Feast 27 July.

Panteleimon, alternative spelling of **Pantaleon**.

Papas, martyr, died Laranda, Lycaonia, Asia Minor (modern Caraman, Turkey), fourth century. Feast 16 March.

Papas, martyr, died Sicily (?), *c.* 303. Feast 28 June.

Paphnutius, a disciple of St **Anthony** and bishop of Upper Thebaid, died *c.* 360. In the persecution under Maximin Daia he suffered such great hardship and cruelty, losing one eye, that the assembled bishops at the Council of Nicaea, which he attended, were amazed at his fortitude. It used to be thought that he dissuaded the council from ordering all clergy to put away their wives. Feast 11 September.

Paphnutius, an anchorite who suffered martyrdom in 305 under Diocletian, according to the Roman martyrology. Feast 24 September.

Paphnutius, bishop, tenth/eleventh centuries. Coptic Church. A monk of the monastery of St Macarius, he lived only on raw herbs, a practice he continued even when, after 35 years in the monastery, he was ordained bishop. He served as bishop for 32 years. He died on 6 May, but it is unknown which year – just as it is unclear of which diocese he was in charge.

Paphnutius, father of **Euphrosyne**, born Alexandria (?), died Egyptian desert, *c.* 480. The not very likely story of Euphrosyne names him as her father. According to the story, he became a monk in the Egyptian desert. Feast 25 September.

Paphnutius of Balachna, founder, sixteenth/seventeenth centuries. Russian Church. The founder of a monastery at Balachna.

Paphnutius of Borovsk, born Kudinov, near Borovsk, died there, 1477. Russian Church. Aged 20, he entered the monastery of the Mother of God at Vysok, not far from Borovsk, of which he eventually became hegumenos, a post which he held for 13 years before falling seriously ill and resigning the post. When he recovered his health he left the monastery and, with a few disciples, established a hermitage on the left bank of the river Isterva, where he built a church dedicated to the Nativity of the Mother of God. Basil Jaroslavic, the prince of Borovsk, was at first hostile to him, but when he, along with other Russian princes, was captured by the khan of Kazan in 1445, he undertook to become reconciled with Paphnutius when he was free, and when liberated he sought the monk's forgiveness. From then on Paphnutius became an adviser to Basil and his family. Paphnutius was remarkable for the rigour of his fasting – going without eating for a week before receiving communion, and doing so in silence, and for his chastity – he would allow no one to touch him. There were many stories of his ability to heal the sick and to read hearts. He predicted his own death a week before it occurred. Feast 1 May.

Paphnutius of Dendara and his 546 Companions, martyrs, died Dendara, near Thebes, 303 (?). Feast 24 September.

Paphnutius of Jerusalem, martyr, died Jerusalem. He is recorded as having been a priest, but nothing else is known about him. Feast 19 April.

Paphnutius of Keno, monk, died Keno, 15 May 1515. Russian Church. A monk of the monastery of the Most Holy Saviour at Keno.

Paphnutius of Pbow, monk, died Pbow, 346. Coptic Church. The younger brother of **Theodore of Tabennisi**, who joined the monastery of Tabennisi after his brother, and was appointed by **Pachomius** to be treasurer of his major foundation of Pbow. He died in an epidemic.

Paphnutius the Archimandrite, monk, fifth century. Coptic Church. Abbot of the monastery at Tabennisi. He visited the patriarch **Dioscorus of Alexandria** in exile on the island of Gangra. He died on 31 May, but it is not known in which year.

Paphnutius the Buffalo, anchorite and priest of the desert of Scete. Date of death unknown, but when **John Cassian** visited him in 395, he is reported to have been 90 years old. In 397 he held a public reading of the letter of the Patriarch Theophilus of Alexandria condemning anthropomorphism as contrary to the Christian doctrine that God is strictly incomparable and incomprehensible. Feast 20 July.

Paphnutius the Recluse, monk, died Kiev, thirteenth century. Russian Church. It is recorded of him that, from the time he became a monk until his death, he did not cease to weep. Feast 15 February.

Papias, martyred Rome, *c.* 303. He and another Roman soldier, **Maurus**, died under Maximian. Feast 29 January.

Papias, Diodorus, Conon and Claudian, martyrs, born Pamphylia, Asia Minor, died there, *c.* 250. Four shepherds. Feast 26 February.

Papias of Corinth, martyr, born Corinth, died there, *c.* 250. Imprisoned for being a Christian, then drowned in the sea. Feast 31 January.

Papias of Hierapolis, bishop, died Hierapolis, Asia Minor (near the modern Pammukale, Turkey), *c.* 130. Nothing is known of his life, although he is said to have heard St John the Evangelist and to have known **Polycarp**. He wrote *Explanation of the Sayings of the Lord*, no longer extant, but which is referred to by **Irenaeus** and **Eusebius of Caesarea**, from which comes some information about the origins of the Gospels. Feast 22 February.

Papylus, martyr, born Pergamon, died Thyatira (modern Akhisar, Turkey), *c.* 250. A doctor, and also a deacon. Feast 13 October.

Papylus, see also **Carpus**.

Paramarubyananda, Swami, see **Jules Monchanin**.

Paramonus of Balsatia and his 370 Companions, martyrs, died Balsatia (in Mesopotamia), *c.* 250. After the governor had ordered the arrest of the 370 Christians, Paramonus was converted by their constancy and suffered martyrdom with them. Feast 29 November.

Parasceve, born Rome, died there, *c.* 180. Said to have been the daughter of wealthy Christian parents and born on a Friday (hence the name). She gave away all her wealth and preached Christianity, for which she was martyred. Feast 26 July.

Parasceve of Kevrolsk, died Kevrolsk, near Archangel, sixteenth century. Russian Church. Nothing is known of her, although she is sometimes said to be the sister of **Artemis of Verkola**. However, her tomb in Kevrolsk, found in 1610, is claimed as the source of many miracles. Feast 30 June.

Parasceve of Rzev, Russian Church. Nothing is known of her, although an icon said to represent her was brought to Moscow and a church dedicated to her there.

Parasceve of Trebizond, martyr, died Trebizond, 1659. Byzantine Church. A distinguished citizen of Trebizond who was hanged for the faith.

Parasceve the Younger, born Epivates, Thracia, died Constantinople, tenth century. Of wealthy parents, she gave away all her money and exchanged clothes with a poor girl before going off to Constantinople, Heraclion and Jerusalem, where she lived for five years in a convent. She eventually returned to Constantinople, where she died. Feast 14 October.

Paregorius, see **Philotheus**.

Parmenius and Companions, martyrs, died near Babylon, Persia, *c.* 250. Parmenius, Helimenas and Chrysotelus were priests, Luke and Mucious were deacons. All were beheaded during the persecution of the Emperor Decius. Feast 22 April.

Paronloys, martyr, born Theodosia, Crimea, *c.* 1550, died there, 1567 or 1568. At the age of about 18 he was falsely accused of having converted to Islam, then reverted to Christianity. He was taken before a judge, but released. He was, however, again arrested and put in prison, where he was comforted by visions of Armenian saints, especially of **Gregory the Illuminator**. He was finally executed. Feast 15 May.

Parsnuus, monk and martyr, *c.* seventh century. Coptic Church. He was accused of insulting Islam, and was beheaded. The day of his martyrdom was 9 December, but the year is unknown.

Parthena of Edessa, born Edessa, died there, 9 January 1376 (?). Byzantine Church. When in 1375 Edessa was besieged by the Turks, Parthena's father let them in after an eight-month siege, and then converted to Islam. He attempted to give his daughter to the pasha as a mistress, but she steadfastly rejected his advances and was martyred by being buried alive on a hill just outside the city.

Parthenius, see **Calocerus**.

Parthenius of Constantinople III, patriarch, martyr, born Mytilene, died Constantinople, 24 March 1657. Byzantine Church. He became bishop of Chios, then almost immediately, in 1656, was elected patriarch. He was, however, accused of conspiring against the Turkish regime, arrested, and told to abjure his faith, which he refused to do, and was put to death.

Parthenius of Kiev, monk, born Simovo, 24 August 1790, died Kiev, 25 March 1855. Ukrainian Church, Moscow Patriarchate. Baptized Peter Ivanovic Krasnopevcev, his father was a sacristan and he studied at a religious school, then in the seminary at Tula. Although his parents wanted him to marry, he decided in 1819 to enter the Kievan Cave monastery, taking the name Paphnutius. In 1830 he became a priest. In 1838 he took the name Parthenius when he was raised in monastic rank. A man of intense spirituality, he was blessed with visions.

Parthenius of Lampsakos, bishop, born Melitopolis, died Lampsakos (Lapseki, Greece), c. 340. The son of a deacon, he worked as a fisherman. He overcame his illiteracy to study the Scriptures, was ordained and eventually became bishop of Lampsakos. Feast 7 February.

Parthenius of Radovisi, bishop and martyr, born Vatsounia, Thessaly, died Radovisi, 1777. Byzantine Church. He had a reputation for miracles, especially curing diseases in sheep. Feast 21 July.

Paschal I, pope, born Rome, elected 24 January 817, died Rome, 11 February 824. He studied in the school attached to the Lateran, joined the papal civil service and, when elected, was abbot of the monastery of St Stephen. Relations between pope and emperor (Louis the Pious) were good, until Louis's son Lothair came to Rome to be crowned co-emperor (for the second time) in 823. Lothair appeared to usurp some papal authority while in the city, something welcomed by Paschal's enemies. Two of them were executed, much to the anger of Louis, although Paschal disclaimed responsibility. Paschal protested against the revival of iconoclasm in the East, and provided refuge for Greek monks driven out by the iconoclasts. He also built several splendidly decorated churches. He was, however, unpopular in Rome itself for his dictatorial manner, and an unruly crowd interrupted his funeral. His claims to sainthood were not recognized before the sixteenth century, and his feast, 14 March, is no longer celebrated.

Paschal Baylon, Franciscan lay brother, born Torre-Hermosa, Aragon, 24 May 1540, died Villareal, Castellon, 15 May 1592. A shepherd until the age of 24, Paschal lived a life of austerity and prayer, and entered the convent of Franciscans of the Alcantarine reform where he practised extreme mortification. He continued throughout his life to be particularly devoted to the cult of the Blessed Sacrament. On a mission to France he defended the doctrine of the Real Presence, at risk to his life by the Calvinists. Canonized in 1690, Pope Leo XIII designated him patron of all eucharistic congresses and societies. Feast 17 May.

Paschasius Radbertus, Carolingian theologian, born Soisson, c. 785, died Corbie, near Amiens, 26 April 865. Paschasius entered the Benedictine abbey of Corbie under Adalard the Elder, a cousin of **Charlemagne**, whom he accompanied into Saxony in 822. Elected abbot, he attended the Council of Paris in 847, but resigned in 849 and devoted himself to study. He wrote a biography of Adalard, a *Commentary on the Book of Lamentations*, a *Commentary on St Matthew*, and his most famous work, *De Corpore et Sanguine Domini*, composed for the monks in Corvey in Saxony, and the first doctrinal monograph on the Eucharist. He was possibly the most important theologian of his generation.

Pasicrates and Companions, martyred Silistria, now in Bulgaria, c. 304. This group of four Roman soldiers was formerly remembered as being martyred with **Julius the Veteran**. Feast 25 May (suppressed).

Pasicrates, Valentinus and Companions, martyrs, died Silistra, Bulgaria, c. 302. Four soldier-martyrs. Feast 25 March.

Passarion, founder and bishop, fourth/fifth centuries. He founded a monastery in Jerusalem and became assistant bishop of the city. Feast 11 August.

Pastor, Vitorinus and Companions, martyrs, died Nicomedia, c. 311. A group of seven martyrs. Feast 29 March.

Patapius, hermit, born Egypt, died Constantinople. Feast 8 December.

Patasius, monk, born Faw, Egypt, died there, fourth/fifth century. Coptic Church. He became a monk in a monastery near Faw, but later became a hermit with a great reputation for sanctity and for healing. He died on 18 January, but the year is unknown.

Patermuthius, monk, born al-Bahnasa, fifth/sixth century. Coptic Church. He became a monk at some unknown monastery, where he attracted many disciples. He was venerated in the White Monastery of **Senute of Atripe**. He died on 3 December, but the year is unknown.

Patermuthius, Copres and Alexander, martyrs, died Alexandria, c. 363. Copres was a hermit, who converted Patermuthius, who was a brigand. They were said to have been executed together with Alexander, a soldier, under the Emperor Julian. Feast 9 July.

Paternus of Avranches, bishop, from Poitiers, France, died 564. A monk at Ansion, Poitou, he left with the monk Scubilio (venerated locally) for a solitary life at Scissy, near Granville, Normandy. Attracting disciples, they established the monastery later called St-Pair. He was bishop of Avranches from c. 547. Feast 15 April.

Paternus of Vannes, bishop, Britanny, fifth century, cult confirmed 1964. He was apparently the first bishop of Vannes, Britanny, consecrated by **Perpetuus of Tours** in 467. He founded a monastery in Vannes and may have died in exile. Feast 21 May.

Paternus of Wales, abbot, probably from southeast Wales, fifth or sixth century. He founded and was abbot of Llanbadarn Fawr monastery near Aberystwyth, and was bishop there. He was later portrayed as a missionary famous for his charity and mortifications. A legend has him visiting Jerusalem with **David** and **Teilo**. Feast 15 April.

Patiens of Lyon, bishop, born Lyon, died there, c. 480. Born into a wealthy family, he became bishop of the city c. 450. He built churches, combated the Arian heresy, and took care of the poor. He also wrote a number of books, including a collection of sermons, which survive. Feast 11 September.

Patricia, born Constantinople, died Naples, c. 665 (?). Said to have belonged to the imperial family, she went on pilgrimage from Constantinople to Jerusalem, but then settled as a nun in Naples. Feast 25 August.

Patrick, 'Apostle of the Irish'. The chronology is not certain, but Patrick appears to have been born in Britain near the village of Bannavem Taburniae (the exact location is unknown, but somewhere along the north-west coast), c. 386, and died in Ireland, c. 460. Brought up a Christian, the son of a Roman official who was also a deacon (Patrick's grandfather was a priest), captured by pirates and taken to Ireland at the age of 16, Patrick made his way back to Britain and trained for the ministry. At some point he went as 'Bishop in Ireland' (his own phrase, *Epistola*, para. 1), and there spent his life evangelizing, ordaining clergy and instituting monks and nuns. In addition to the *Epistola* to Coroticus (a chieftain in Britain), his other work to have survived, the *Confession*, is a moving personal account of his spiritual pilgrimage. The dispute over the chronology of Patrick's life centres on the reference in the chronicle of Prosper of Aquitaine to the sending of **Palladius** by **Celestine I** to be 'the first bishop of the Irish', and that Patrick, then in Gaul, received permission from St **Germanus**, delegate to the British Church, to continue the work of Palladius in Ireland. There is no certain connection between the two men, but Patrick's birth is inferred from the likely date of his mission to Ireland (431), and his death is therefore not likely to have occurred later than c. 460. The *Irish Annals*, compiled two centuries later, admit also that Patrick may have lived a generation later and died c. 490. Feast 17 March.

Patrick, Acacius, Menander and Polyaenus, martyrs, died Bursa, c. 360. Patrick was the bishop of the city, near the Sea of Marmara, during the reign of Julian the Apostate. Feast 19 May.

Patrick of Vladimir, born Greece, died Vladimir, 3 July 1411. Russian Church. Although a Greek priest, he became treasurer of the church of the Dormition at Vladimir. When the Tartars attacked the city in 1411 Patrick hid the church's treasures under the floor. He resisted all attempts through torture to make him reveal their whereabouts.

Paul, martyr, died Gaza, *c.* 308. See **Thea, Valentina and Paul**.

Paul, martyred fourth century, commemorated with his brothers **Pansirion** and **Theodotion**. Feast 24 January.

Paul, martyr, died Ptolemais (Acre), Palestine, *c.* 270. The brother of **Juliana**. Feast 17 August.

Paul, martyr, died Nicaea. Nothing else is known. Feast 19 December.

Paul, martyr, died Lebanon. Nothing else is known. Feast 24 December.

Paul, martyr, born Rome, died there, *c.* 361. He was the servant of Constantia, daughter of **Constantine**, but refused to serve in the household of the Emperor Julian the Apostate, and was beheaded. Feast 26 June.

Paul, see also **Peter**.

Paul I, pope, born Rome, pope from 29 May 757, died Rome, 28 June 767. Paul succeeded his brother Stephen II, and his pontificate is chiefly remembered for his close alliance with Pepin III of the Franks. He reorganized the temporal power of the papacy, and tried unsuccessfully to effect a reconciliation with the iconoclastic emperor of the East, Constantine Copronymus. He has been considered a firm, even harsh, ruler, but the times were disorderly and his biographer rather shifts the blame for his behaviour on to tyrannical subordinates.

Paul and Companions, martyrs, died Numidia, second century. Feast 18 January.

Paul and Cyriac, martyrs, died Tomi, Romania. Feast 29 June.

Paul and Juliana, martyrs, died Ptolemais (modern Ptolemaida, western Macedonia), third century. Feast 4 March.

Paul and Salfana, martyrs, born Arus. Coptic Church. They died on 20 December, but the year is not recorded.

Paul Aurelian, born Wales, died St-Pol-de-Léon, Brittany, *c.* 575. He was a disciple of **Illtyd**, and educated at Llanwit Manor, before going, possibly, to Caldey Island and then to Cornwall. With 12 companions he then crossed to Brittany, founding a monastery on the island of Ushant of which he was abbot, before becoming bishop of what is now St-Pol-de-Léon. He is said to have lived to over 100 years old. Feast 12 March.

Paul Chong, martyr, born 1795, died Seoul, 22 September 1839. A Korean nobleman, whose father and elder brother had died in an earlier persecution – and whose mother and sister were to be martyred shortly after he was – he was active in reviving the Church in Korea after the previous suppression, and wrote a book explaining to the government why Christians were no threat to the stability of the country. He travelled to Beijing at least nine times to try to encourage priests to return, and wrote to the pope. When they did come back he regularly went to the frontier to meet them, escort them across the country, and give them hospitality in his own house. Feast of the **Martyrs of Korea** 20 September.

Paul Constamonitis, bl., martyr, born Giannina, died Thessalonika, 1821. Baptized Peter, he came into contact with a monk from the monastery of Constamonitis on Mount Athos, travelled there and became a monk, taking the name Paul. In 1821, however, he was arrested, taken to Thessalonika, and executed. Feast 12 June.

Paul, Cyril, Eugene and Companions, martyrs, died Antioch, Syria. There were seven in all. Feast 20 March.

Paul Evergetinos, bl., founder, born Constantinople, died near there, at the monastery of Evergetinos, 11 April 1054. In *c.* 1049 he left the home of his parents to live in an isolated house belonging to his family, where he lived an ascetic life. A group gathered around him, creating a monastery, of which he was the hegumenos. To him is attributed the *Ascetical Anthology*, much read by monks and laity alike.

Paul Hanh, martyr, died near Saigon, Vietnam, 1859, canonized 1988. He gave up his Christian faith and joined a band of outlaws. When arrested as a criminal, he declared himself a Christian, and as a consequence was horribly tortured and beheaded. See **Martyrs of Vietnam**. Feast 28 May.

Paul, Heraclius and Companions, see **Heraclius, Paul and Companions**.

Paul Hong, John Yi, Peter Maubert and Barbara Tchoi, martyrs, died Korea, 1840. See **Martyrs of Korea**. Feast 1 February.

Paul KeyeT'ing Chou, bl., martyr, died 1900. Feast 8 August.

Paul Le-Van-Loc, died Korea, 1859. See **Martyrs of Vietnam**. Feast 13 February.

Paul Lieu (Lieou), also called Ouen Yen, martyr, died China, 1818. He encouraged his sons in prison and died strangled. He was executed in the wave of persecution in China. See **Martyrs of China**. Feast 17 May.

Paul, Longinus and Zena, martyrs. Coptic Church. All that is known is the day of their death, 21 October.

Paul Michailovic Krasnokutski, martyr, born Pokrovskoe. Ukrainian Church, Moscow Patriarchate. After his ordination he worked in the village of Zaroznoe, but in 1930 was interned and was never heard of again. Feast 19 May.

Paul Mikki, and 25 others, martyrs, including children, martyred Nagasaki, 5 February 1597, all canonized 1862. The first martyrs in Japan, the group included Franciscans, Jesuits and lay people. Paul was a Japanese Jesuit. The Franciscan brother **Gonçalvo Garcia** is venerated as the first Indian martyr. The others were: Peter Baptist Blásquez, Martin de Aguirre, Francis Blanco, Franciscan priests; Francis de la Parilla, Philip de las Casas, Franciscan brothers; James Kisai, John Soan, Jesuit brothers; and Japanese lay people, the adults Franciscan tertiaries and the children altar servers: Michael Cosaqui, his son Thomas, Thomas Danki, Francis Danto, Antony Doynan, (aged 12), Leo Ibaraki, his brother Louis and nephew Paul, Gabriel Ize, Leo Karesuma, John Quizia, Cosmas Raquiza, Peter Sukejino, Paul Susuki, Bonaventure of Mikayo, Matthias of Mikayo, Francis Kichi of Mikayo (from Korea). See **Martyrs of Japan**. Feast 6 February.

Paul My, martyr, Vietnam, died 1839. Feast 18 December.

Paul of Benhadab, monk, born Danfiq, Qina. Coptic Church. He worked as a carpenter before becoming a monk on Mount Benhadab, where eventually he became abbot. He lived for a time in a cave once occupied by **Peter the Great**. He was renowned for his visions and raptures, and died on 13 November, but it is unclear in what year or century this was.

Paul of Constantinople, bishop and martyr, born Thessalonika, died Cucusus, Armenia, *c.* 350. Paul succeeded Alexander as patriarch of Constantinople in 337, only to be displaced in 341 by the Arian Eusebius of Nicomedia, upon whose death the Orthodox Christians recalled him, but the Arians elected Macedonius, who had the support of the Emperor Constantius, and Paul again went into exile in the West. Under pressure from Constans I, Paul regained his see in 346. On Constans's death in 351, the Arians again drove Paul into exile, where they strangled him. A close friend of **Athanasius** and Pope **Julius I**, he zealously upheld Orthodoxy. Feast 7 June.

Paul of Constantinople III, patriarch, born Constantinople, died there, 693. He had been secretary to Emperor Justinian II before becoming patriarch in 686. Feast 2 September.

Paul of Constantinople IV, eighth century.

Paul of Corinth, bishop, tenth century. He was bishop of Corinth in Achaia. Feast 27 March.

Paul of Cyprus, martyr, born Cyprus, died there, 775. He refused to trample on a crucifix during the iconoclast persecution, and was roasted to death. Feast 17 March.

Paul of Dabra Libanos, born *c*. 1510, died Ayd, 1580. Ethiopian Church. He became a monk at Dabra Libanos *c*. 1530, but later visited other monasteries, settling eventually, only a couple of years before his death, at Ayd.

Paul of Edessa, bishop, died Egypt, *c*. 619. Syriac Church. He was bishop of Edessa from the mid-590s, but in 609, because of the Persian invasions, he left for Cyprus and in 616 went with other exiles to Egypt. Feast 23 August.

Paul of Glusica, hermit, fifteenth century. Russian Church. Nothing is known for certain about this figure, except that he apparently chose to live as a solitary near the hermitage of Glusica, which caused some concern to its superior, who feared the development of another monastery nearby.

Paul of Jamnia, martyr, died Caesarea, Palestine, fourth century (?).

Paul of Kolomna, bishop and martyr, born Kolycevo, near Niznij Novgorod, died Novgorod, 3 April 1656. Church of the Old Believers. He became bishop of Kolomna in October 1652, and in 1654 he was the only bishop openly to reject the liturgical reforms – for which he was reduced to the rank of layman and exiled to the north, where he continued to preach. He was then moved to the monastery of Chutynskij at Novgorod, where it seems he was either burned alive, or suffocated. He was immediately hailed as a martyr by the Old Believers.

Paul of Latros ('Paul the Younger'), born Constantinople, died Latros, 15 December 956. His father had been an officer in the imperial army, and his brother Basil became a monk first in Bithynia then on Mount Latros. Paul wished to follow Basil, but his elder brother forbade him to do so, putting him in the charge of the abbot of Kratia. Paul was able a few years later to become a solitary on Mount Latros, but so many disciples

gathered around him that he went off to an even more remote spot on the mountain, and even eventually withdrew to a cave on Samos. But again disciples flocked to him, and he re-established three monasteries which had been destroyed by Muslim invaders. Towards the end of his life he returned to the monks on Latros.

Paul of Narbonne, bishop, born Rome (?), died Narbonne, *c*. 290. According to **Gregory of Tours**, he was one of several missionaries, many commemorated as saints, who were sent to Gaul from Rome. He became a bishop. Feast 22 March.

Paul of Nisibis, metropolitan, born Prat Maysan, died Nisibis, 573. Syriac Church. He became metropolitan of Nisibis *c*. 544, and was used as an emissary by Chosroes to the Emperor Justinian. In 572, when the Byzantines were besieging Nisibis, he sent a message to the emperor telling him he ought to speed up his attack because the Persians were reinforcing the defences, but Justinian ignored the advice, and failed to capture the city. When Chosroes discovered Paul's treachery, he demanded that the catholicos depose Paul, but the catholicos, who largely owed his position to the metropolitan, hesitated, and Paul died before he could act.

Paul of Obnora, founder, born Moscow, 1317, died Obnora, 10 January 1429. Russian Church. He became a monk when about 20 years old, entering the monastery of the Nativity at Priluki, not far from Uglic. It had been founded by **Sergius of Radonez**, and after a few years Paul moved to Sergius's monastery of the Most Holy Trinity. He undertook various offices, but after a time went to live in nearby woods as a hermit. He lived in this way for 15 years before seeking even further solitude, travelling to the north of Russia and visiting various monasteries before finally settling, *c*. 1389, at the confluence of the rivers Nurma and Obnora. There was another hermit living close by, **Sergius of Nurom**, who was also a disciple of Sergius of Radonez, and the two struck up a deep friendship. A small community grew up at Obnora and Paul received permission to establish a monastery, but he himself continued to live apart from it. He is said to have lived to the age of 112.

Paul of Plousias, bishop, died 850. Bishop of Plousias/Prusa (modern Bursa, Turkey) and an opponent of iconoclasm, for which he was exiled. He died in exile. Feast 8 March.

Paul of Prusa, bishop, died Egypt, 840. Bishop of Prusa, Bithynia, he was exiled to Egypt as a result of his opposition to the iconoclasts. Feast 7 March

Paul of Tamben, monk, born Tigre. Ethiopian Church.

Paul of Tamma, monk, born Tamma, near Tkow, fourth century. Coptic Church. He lived with his disciple Ezechiel on Mount al-Asmunayn, and his life recounts his various journeys and encounters with different holy men. The more curious part of this account, however, tells of his seven attempts at suicide for love of Christ, after each of which Christ returned his life to him. He eventually died on 4 October, but it is not known in which year.

Paul of the Cross, founder, born Ovada, Italy, 3 January 1694, died Rome, 18 October 1775. Paul Danei led a life of prayer and great austerity until, in 1720, mystical experiences inspired him to found a congregation of men totally dedicated to the passion of Christ. Ordained in 1727, he drew up a Rule and retired to Monte Argentario, where the first Passionist 'Retreat' opened in 1737. Pope Benedict XIV approved the Rule in 1741. He also founded a contemplative community of women Passionists. One of the most celebrated preachers of his age, especially on the passion, he became famous as a miracle worker and spiritual director. Feast 19 October.

Paul of the Peloponnese, bl., martyr, born Kalavryta, died Tripoli, 22 May 1818. Byzantine Church. Baptized Panaghiotis, he worked as a shoemaker, and as a result of a squabble over payment, was thrown into prison where he declared he would rather become a Muslim than pay the sum due. He was, however, released, and went to Tripoli, where he declared that he had indeed converted. He almost immediately repented of his action, and went to Mount Athos. After some years there he decided to seek martyrdom. He returned to Tripoli, where he proclaimed his Christianity, was arrested and beheaded.

Paul of Thebes (Paul the Hermit), traditionally the first Christian hermit, born in the Thebaid, date unknown, died in the Egyptian desert, c. 340. According to **Jerome**'s *Vita Pauli*, the only authority, Paul suffered in the Decian persecution (249–51) and fled to the desert, where he lived for some 100 years a life of prayer and penitence in a cave. St **Anthony** is said to have visited him when he was 113 years old and later to have buried him, wrapped in a mantle which he had himself received from St **Athanasius**. In later art, Paul is commonly shown with a palm tree or two lions. Feast 10 January.

Paul of Tobolsk, metropolitan, born Galicia, western Russia, 1705, died Kiev, 1770. Russian Church. Baptized Peter Konjuskevic. He studied in Kiev, then remained in the academy teaching, becoming a monk in 1773. He moved to Moscow to teach, then went as archimandrite to the monastery of St George at Novgorod. He became metropolitan of Tobolsk in 1758. His Siberian territory was sparsely populated and he had few priests, but he reorganized the seminary and established parishes. When in 1764 he protested at the secularization of Church property, he was stripped of his office and sent back to the Kievan Cave monastery, where he spent the rest of his life in a regime of rigorous asceticism. Feast 4 November.

Paul of Trois-Châteaux, bishop, born Rheims, died Dauphiné, c. 405. He escaped barbarian invasions and settled as a hermit near Arles. He became bishop of Trois-Châteaux (*Augusta Tricastrinorum*), a now extinct diocese. Feast 1 February.

Paul of Verdun, died c. 649. First a courtier, he became a hermit near Trier and later a monk, and was appointed by the Merovingian king Dagobert I as bishop of Verdun. He restored the Church community there and took part in the contemporary evangelization eastwards. Feast 8 February.

Paul of Vilnius, martyr, died Vilnius, seventeenth century. Russian Church. Possibly of a noble family, he died during the Polish persecution of the Orthodox. Feast 3 May.

Paul of Xeropotamus, founder, third century (?). Founder of the monastery of Xeropotamus on Mount Athos, and said to be the begetter of the rule that no female animal at all should exist on the Holy Mountain. Feast 28 July.

Paul, Pausirion and Theodotion, born Egypt, died there, c. 305. All brothers. The first two were Christians, and were martyred for their faith. Seeing this, Theodotion converted and also died. Feast 24 January.

Paul, Tatta and their Four Sons, martyrs, born Damascus, died there. The sons were Sabinian, Maximus, Rufus and Eugene. Feast 25 September.

Paul the Interpreter, monk, sixth/seventh century. Syriac Church. It is unclear who this is, possibly identical with **Paul of Edessa**. Certainly he had lived in Egypt, took part in the reconciliation of the Syriac Church with Alexandria, and attended the Synod of 616. Feast 15 February.

Paul the Obedient, monk, died Kiev, thirteenth century. A monk of the Kievan Cave monastery, simply described as 'wonderful in his obedience'. Feast 10 September.

Paul the Russian, martyr, born Russia, died Constantinople, 3 April 1683. Byzantine Church. He was captured by Tartars, and only freed from prison after some Christians paid a ransom. He married a Russian who had also been released from captivity, and the two moved to Constantinople. There he developed what seems to have been epilepsy. His wife wanted to take him to a church for healing, but he refused, and called upon some Turks to help him as he was being forcibly taken there. He said he wanted to become a Muslim, but, when he suddenly recovered his senses, he refused to convert, and was beheaded.

Paul the Simple, monk, born Egypt, died there, 340. Said to have become a disciple of St **Anthony** after his wife was unfaithful to him. Feast 7 March.

Paul, Valentina, Thea and Companions, martyrs, died Caesarea, Palestine, fourth century.

Paula, foundress, born Rome, 5 May 347, died Bethlehem, 26 January 404. Of noble birth and a widow at 31 with five children (among whom was St **Eustochium**), Paula became a disciple of St **Jerome** and, with Eustochium, followed him to Palestine in 385, and then to Bethlehem, where she used her wealth to found a monastery for monks, a convent for nuns and a guesthouse for pilgrims. She studied the Scriptures under St Jerome, who wrote her eulogy in *Epistola 108*. Her granddaughter cared for Jerome in his old age.

Paula Cerioli, bl., foundress, born Soncino, Italy, 28 January 1816, died Comonte di Seriate, 24 December 1865. In 1835 she married a wealthy widower, had three children who died, and was widowed in 1854. Thereafter she devoted her money and energy to the care of orphan girls through her foundation in 1857 of the Sisters of the Holy Family at Bergamo, and was helped by Giovanni Caponi of the Brothers of the Holy Family to look after orphan boys. She was beatified in 1950.

Paula Frassinetti, founder of the Dorothean religious congregation, born Genoa, Italy, 3 March 1809, died Rome, 11 June 1882. Sister of **Giuseppe Frassinetti**. Owing to ill-health, she was prevented from fulfilling her early wish to join a religious community, and so in 1834 she founded her own institute for the education of girls from all levels of society. The Dorotheans were granted papal approval in 1863. New houses were founded across Italy and in Portugal and Brazil, with Paula serving as superior general until she died.

Paula Gambara Costa, bl., born Brescia, 1473, died 1515. Married young to an unsympathetic and unfaithful husband, she persisted in her penances and charities, was a member of the Third Order of St Francis, and eventually converted him to a peaceful and celibate life together. Feast 24 January.

Paula of Montaldo, bl., born Montaldo, near Mantua, 1443, died Mantua, 1514. She became a Poor Clare at Mantua, serving three times as abbess. She was a renowned mystic. Feast 18 August.

Paulina, princess, died Münsterschwarzach, 1107. A German princess, after her husband's death she founded the double monastery of Paulinzelle at Zelle. Feast 14 March.

Pauline Jeuris (Mary Amandina), born Limburg, Belgium, 28 December 1872, martyred Taiyuan, Shanxi, China, 9 July 1900, beatified 1946, canonized 2000. A Franciscan Missionary of Mary under **Mary Emiliana Grivot**, she was in charge of the dispensary in their orphanage and was a member of the group killed with **Gregory Grassi** – see **Franciscan Martyrs of China** and **Martyrs of Shanxi**. Feast 8 July.

Pauline of the Suffering Heart of Jesus, bl., foundress, born Vigolo Vattaro, Italy, 16 December 1865, died Sao Paulo, Brazil, 9 July 1942. Amabile Wisenteiner emigrated with her family to Brazil in 1875 and settled in Santa Catarina. In 1890 she and a friend founded the Little Sisters of the Immaculate Conception, dedicated to caring for the sick and elderly. In 1895 Amabile moved to Nova Trento and received episcopal approval for the congregation. She made her religious vows, taking the name Pauline of the Suffering Heart of Jesus. She moved to Sao Paulo in 1903, and opened several houses for the congregation. In 1909 a misunderstanding by the archbishop meant that she had to step down from her role as superior, and from then until her death she lived as a sister. Her congregation received papal approval in 1933.

Paulinus, patriarch of Aquileia, born Ciovidale, Friuli, *c.* 750, died Aquileia, 11 January 802. A noted grammarian and scholar, in 787 **Charlemagne** appointed him a master in the palace school and patriarch of Aquileia. One of his main concerns was to suppress adoptionism, taught by Epilandus of Toledo and Felix of Urgel. This he did at the Councils of Regensburg, Frankfurt and Cividale. His writings include two anti-adoptionist works, *Libellus Sacrosyllabus contra Epilandum* and *Libri iii contra Fillicem*. Feast 28 January.

Paulinus of Nola, bishop, born Bordeaux, *c.* 353, died Nola, 431. From a prominent family and well educated, Paulinus qualified for the senate and served as governor of Campania. He married Therasia and went to live in Spain, where, after the death of their only child, they returned to Campania to lead a monastic life near the tomb of St **Felix** at Nola. He became bishop of Nola *c.* 409. Acquainted with many notable Christians of his time, he corresponded with **Sulpicius**, **Augustine** and **Martin of Tours**, among others. Some 50 of his letters to Sulpicius Severus, Augustine, **Jerome** and others are extant. Feast 22 June.

Paulinus of Trier, bishop, died Phrygia, 358. A disciple of St **Maximin**, he succeeded him in the see of Trier and, a strong opponent of Arianism, was banished to Phrygia after the Synod of Arles (353). His relics were brought back to Trier in 396. Feast 31 August.

Paulinus of York, first bishop of the Northumbrians and archbishop of York, born Rome (?), died Rochester, 10 October 644. **Gregory I** sent Paulinus to England in 601 to assist **Augustine** of Canterbury in his mission. He was ordained bishop in 625. He escorted Æthelberg, a Christian, to be the bride of Edwin, king of Northumbria, whom he converted to the faith two years later. Edwin assigned York to Paulinus as his see. Honorius I sent the pallium to Paulinus, as a sign of his status as a metropolitan at York, but he never wore it in his cathedral because after Edwin was slain at Hatfield Chase in 633, Paulinus retired to Kent, where he became bishop of Rochester.

Pausiacus, bishop, died Synnada, Phrygia, 606. He was a monk who, because of his virtuous life, was chosen bishop of Synnada where he was vigorously opposed to heretics. He was brought to Constantinople to tend the Emperor Maurice, whom he cured of sickness, and who ordered that the bishop be given annually 16 ounces of gold. Feast 13 May.

Pedro, see **Peter**.

Pelagia, martyr, born Antioch, Syria, died *c.* 311. Pelagia's name occurs in the Canon of the Ambrosian Mass of Milan, and her fate is known from praise of her by Ss **Ambrose** and **John Chrysostom**. Only 15 years of age when Roman soldiers surrounded her house during a persecution by Diocletian, she threw herself from a window into the sea to preserve her chastity. Feast 9 June.

Pelagia of Tarsus, born Tarsus, died there, *c.* 302. She is said to have become a Christian after refusing to marry the son of Diocletian. The emperor then wanted her to be his mistress, but she refused and he ordered her to be burned to death. Feast 8 October.

Pelagia the Penitent, died *c.* 457. A celebrated dancer and courtesan who, converted by St **Nonnus**, bishop of Edessa, went to Jerusalem disguised as a man and lived a life of penance on the Mount of Olives. Feast 8 October.

Pelagius, martyr, died Córdoba, 925. As a boy of ten he had been left as a hostage in Córdoba. After three years, when the ransom had still not been paid, he was offered his freedom provided he renounced Christianity. He refused to do so, and was executed. Feast 28 August.

Pelagius of Laodicea, bishop, died Laodicea (?), *c.* 381. He was exiled for opposing the Arianizing policies of the Empeor Valens, but returned to his see after Valens's death. Feast 25 March.

Pelayo, see **Pelagius**.

Peleus and Companions, martyrs, died Phunion, near Petra, 310. Peleus and Nilus were bishops, Elias was a priest and Paterninus was a layman, all from Egypt. They were burned to death after being removed from the quarries in Palestine to which they had been sent, during the persecution of Galerius. Feast 19 September.

Peleusius, martyr, died Alexandria. Nothing is known of him, beyond the fact that he was a priest. Feast 7 April.

Pellegrine, see also **Irenaeus, Pellegrinus and Irene**.

Pellegrine, Astius and Companions, martyrs, died Dyrrachium (Durres, Albania), *c.* 117. Astius was the bishop of Dyrrachium, and was crucified. Apart from Pellegrine, the others were Lucian, Pompeius, Hesychius, Papias, Saturninus and

Germanus, all of them refugees from Rome who sympathized with Astius. They were arrested and thrown overboard, bound in chains. Feast 7 July.

Pentecost Martyrs of Alexandria, died there, 357–8. Feast 21 May.

Peregrine, bl., died 1232. He was a priest of San Severino, Piceno. Feast 27 March.

Peregrine Laziosi, born Forli, Romagna, 1265, died there, 1345, canonized 1726. Repenting of assaulting **Philip Benizi** during a political meeting, he became a Servite priest, founding a house in Forli in 1322. He was a zealous preacher and spiritual director. His leg – he suffered badly from varicose veins – was miraculously healed the day before its planned amputation. Feast 1 May.

Peregrine of Falerone, bl., born Falerone, Italy, died San Severino, 1240. Son of the lord of Falerone, he went to the university of Bologna and there heard **Francis of Assisi** preach. He immediately decided to join the Franciscans, although he did so not as a priest but as a lay brother. Feast 6 September.

Pergentius and Laurentius, martyrs, born Arezzo, Italy, died there, 251. Said to have been two students of wealthy families who converted to Christianity and died in the persecution of Decius. They were selected for execution because of their zeal in spreading the faith. The story is, however, thought to be fictional. Feast 3 June.

Pergius, monk, died Kiev, thirteenth century. Russian Church. A monk of the Kievan Cave monastery. Nothing is known of him.

Pergrinus, bishop and martyr, possibly born Rome, died Bouhy, east of Alençon, 304. He is traditionally, but erroneously, venerated as the first bishop of Auxerre, sent there in the third century by Pope **Sixtus II**. He is now believed to have been a victim of the persecution of Diocletian. Feast 16 May.

Peroz, martyr, died Bet Lapat, 5 September 421. Syriac Church. When first arraigned for his

Christianity he returned to pagan worship, but soon repented, and was executed.

Perpetua and Felicity, martyrs, born Carthage, died there, 203. *The Acts of Perpetua and Felicity* tells how Perpetua and her slave, with other cate-chumens in Carthage, were imprisoned and after their baptism condemned to execution in the arena. The document, perhaps written by Perpetua herself in Latin, later translated into Greek and possibly edited by Tertullian, also tells of the interesting visions of Perpetua and the priest Saturus, also martyred, who had instructed the women in the faith. Beautifully written, the text is a precious record because it is contemporary with the events – or so it used to be thought, although there are now some doubts. Perpetua and Felicity are mentioned in the Roman calendar of 354; the basilica dedicated to them was among the most important in Carthage. Feast 7 March.

Peter, died 380. He was the second bishop of Alexandria. Feast 14 February.

Peter, see also **Ananias**.

Peter, see also **Emmanuel**.

Peter, monk. Coptic Church. A disciple of **Isaiah of Scete**. He died on 13 October, but nothing else is known.

Peter, hermit, eleventh century. Coptic Church. He lived at Singar, and performed numerous miracles.

Peter, martyr, died Troas, 251. He was a young man from the Hellespont who died with **Andrew**, **Paul** and **Dionysia**. Feast 15 May.

Peter, priest. Coptic Church. He was ordained priest against his wishes, but from then on cele-brated the Eucharist daily. Famous for his prayer and fasting, he was also renowned for miracle working. He died on 1 March, but the year is unknown.

Peter Almató Ribera, born San Feliú Saserra, Barcelona, Spain, 1 November 1830, martyred Vietnam, 1 November 1861, beatified 1906,

canonized 1988. A Dominican priest, he was beheaded with **Jerome Hermosilla Aransáez** and **Valentine Berrio-Ochoa** – see **Martyrs of Vietnam**.

Peter and Companions, martyrs, died Nicomedia, 303. All members of the household of the Emperor Diocletian, they were tortured and put to death when they refused to sacrifice to the gods. Peter was the emperor's major-domo. Feast 12 March.

Peter and Febronia, princes, born Murom, died there, 1228. Peter was the son of the prince of Murom. He married Febronia, a commoner, apparently after having been healed by her of a skin complaint. When he succeeded to the throne the boyars demanded that he either divorce Feb-ronia or abdicate and, believing in the sanctity of marriage, he chose the latter. This was, however, followed by considerable unrest, so he was asked to return, and the two ruled piously and justly until shortly before their deaths, when they both took vows as religious. They died on the same day. Feast 25 June.

Peter and Hermogenes, martyrs, died Antioch, Syria. Peter seems to have been a deacon, Her-mogenes his servant. Feast 17 April.

Peter Apselamus (or Balsamus), martyred by crucifixion at Aulona, near Hebron, fourth cen-tury. There is a reference to a Peter Absalon (Abselame), burned at Caesarea at the same per-iod, who may or may not be the same man. Feast 11 January.

Peter Arbués, martyr, born Epila, Zaragoza, c. 1440, died Zaragoza, 16 September 1485. He became a canon regular at Zaragoza, and studied in Bologna. On his return he was appointed inquisitor for Aragón, a task which he approached with such zeal that there was a conspiracy to murder him. He was killed while praying in the cathedral at Zaragoza, despite the armour he was wearing beneath his clothes. Feast 17 September.

Peter Aumaître, martyr, born Angoulême, France, died Korea, 30 March 1866, beatified 1968, cano-nized 1984. Joining the Paris Foreign Missions Society in 1857, he went to Korea in 1863. He was tortured and killed with others during a time of general persecution – see also **Martyrs of Korea**.

Peter Bartolomeevic Dorosenko, martyr, born Cuguev, died Char'kov, 17 January 1938. Ukrainian Church, Moscow Patriarchate. He was ordained priest in 1906, and served until his arrest in the village of Preobrazenka. Feast 19 May.

Peter Canisius, Jesuit theologian, born Nijmegen, Netherlands, 8 May 1521, died Fribourg, Switzerland, 21 December 1597. Canisius studied theology at Cologne and Mainz, after which he became a Jesuit and founded a house of the order in Cologne. He was a staunch defender of Roman Catholic beliefs in opposition to Protestantism, and was the author of the *Summa Doctrinae Christianae* (or *Catechismus Major*), which was published in 1555 and has subsequently appeared in over 130 editions. In 1556 he was appointed provincial of Upper Germany, and founded several Jesuit colleges. Protestantism's ultimate failure to establish itself in southern German territories was largely due to the vigour with which Canisius revived and consolidated Roman Catholicism in those areas. He was canonized in 1925 and simultaneously made a doctor of the Church.

Peter Casani, ven., Piarist, born Lucca, Italy, 8 September 1570, died Rome, 17 October 1647. He was a companion of the founder of Pious schools, for which he wrote a Latin grammar. He became secretary-general and rector of St Panteleon, Rome, and was the author of works on theology and exorcism. In Germany he was effective in preaching and in raising money for charity. Ladislas IV invited him to Poland to inspect proposed sites for Piarist schools. The process of his beatification, introduced in 1922, was held up by the loss of the relevant documents.

Peter Chanel, first martyr of the South Seas, born Cuet, diocese of Belley, France, 1803, died island of Fortuna, New Hebrides, 28 April 1841. After being ordained in 1827 for the diocese and serving for four years in the parishes of Ambérieux as a curate and then as parish priest at Crozet, he became one of the earliest members of the Missionary Society of Mary (the Marists). In 1836 he went as a missionary to the New Hebrides. He was murdered by the inhabitants of the island of Futuma on 28 April, after the ruler's son had become a Christian. Canonized in 1954.

Peter Ch'oe Hyong Hyeng and John Baptist Chon Chang-un, martyrs, died Korea, 1866, beatified 1968, canonized 1984 – see **Martyrs of Korea**. Feast 10 March.

Peter Chrysologus, bishop and doctor, born Imola, Italy, *c.* 380, died there, December 450. He was a deacon at Imola, and was made archbishop of Ravenna by the Emperor Valentinian III some time between 425 and 430. He was given the title 'Chrysologus', which means 'golden worded', due to his reputation for being a great preacher. Feast 30 July.

Peter Claver, missionary, born Verdu, Catalonia, *c.* 1580, died Cartagena, Colombia, 8 September 1654, known as 'Apostle of the Negroes'. He studied at the university of Barcelona and joined the Society of Jesus when he was 20. He was sent to the Jesuit college in Majorca, returned to Barcelona to study theology, and in April 1610 was sent at his own request to Cartagena. He at once began ministering to the slaves who arrived from Africa in terrible conditions. Following ordination in 1615, he declared himself 'the slave of the negroes for ever', and championed their cause against the slave owners. He devoted himself to their temporal and spiritual welfare, and is said to have baptized some 300,000 people. Leo XIII canonized him in 1888. Feast 9 September.

Peter Cubicularius, martyr, died 303. Feast 24 February.

Peter Damian, reformer, born Ravenna, 1007, died Faenza, 23 February 1072. An uncompromising prelate against the evils of the day, Peter upheld clerical celibacy and struggled against simoniacal practices of the clergy. Made cardinal bishop of Ostia (1057), he enjoyed great authority in the Church for his learning, zeal and integrity. His *Liber Gratissimus* defended the validity of orders conferred by simonists, against the rigorist views of Cardinal Humbert; his *Liber Gomorrhianes* attacked the moral decadence of the clergy. Never formally canonized, his cult began after his death, and in 1828 Leo XIII proclaimed him a doctor of the Church. Feast 21 February.

Peter de Betancur, bl., born Tenerife, Canary Islands, 1619, died Guatemala, 25 April 1667, beatified 1980. In 1649 he travelled to Havana, then Guatemala. A Franciscan tertiary from 1652, he worked with poor children, slaves and indigenous people. He founded two secular institutes to work with women and men, the Sisters and Brothers of Bethlehem.

Peter de Jesus Maldonado, martyr, born Sacramento, Mexico, 1892, died Chihuahua, 11 February 1937. Because of the persecution of the Church in Mexico, he studied part of the time in El Paso, Texas, and was ordained there in 1918. He returned to work in Santa Isabel, Chihuahua, and survived the worst of the persecution in the 1920s. It broke out again in the early 1930s, and he was arrested several times, once being exiled to El Paso. He was, however, blamed for a fire in a local school, was seized by a drunken mob, and beaten. He was taken to hospital in Chihuahua, and died there. Feast 25 May.

Peter, Dionysius and Companions, martyrs, born Alexandria (?), died there, 257 (?). A group of martyrs who were banished to Libya in 250, but allowed to return, only to be executed later. Dionysius may have been the patriarch of Alexandria. Feast 3 October.

Peter Doan Van Van, martyr, born Vietnam, c. 1780, died Son-Tay, Vietnam, 1865, canonized 1988. He was a local catechist who was beheaded – see **Martyrs of Vietnam**. Feast 25 May.

Peter Donders, bl., born Tilburg, Holland, 27 October 1809, died Batavia, Surinam, 14 January 1887, beatified 1982. Ordained in 1841, he went to Surinam, a Dutch colony, and worked in the leper colony. He also sought to evangelize indigenous peoples and runaway slaves. He became a Redemptorist in 1867.

Peter Dorie, see **Simeon**.

Peter Duong, martyr, born Tonkin, Vietnam, died Annan. A catechist. Feast 18 December.

Peter Esqueda Ramirez, martyr, born San Juan de los Lagos, 1899, died Tecaltitlan, 22 November 1927. He was a seminarian when the seminary was closed. He had already been ordained a deacon, and worked as such in his home parish. He was ordained two years later, in 1916. After the persecution broke out in 1926 he continued to work secretly, but was discovered and shot. Feast 25 May.

Peter Faber, bl., born Villaret, Savoy, 13 April 1506, died Rome, 1 August 1546. In 1525 he went to Paris to study and shared lodging with **Francis Xavier**. He also met **Ignatius of Loyola** and became one of his earliest associates. He was ordained in 1534 and took vows with the incipient Society of Jesus in the same year. In 1537 he led a small group to Venice to meet up again with Ignatius and from there he travelled to Rome. He was sent as the pope's representative to the Diet of Worms in 1540 and to Regensburg the following year. He was shocked both by the problems wrought by the Reformers and by the decadent Church against which they were protesting. He set about reforming the clergy rather than arguing with the Reformers. At the end of the year he was called back to Spain by Ignatius, but within six months was back in Germany, where he laboured in Speyer, Mainz and Cologne for another 19 months. In 1544 he went back to Spain, where he taught and preached in all the main cities, but his health was weakening and after journeying to Rome in 1546, to meet up again with Ignatius, he developed a fever and died.

Peter Fourier, co-founder (with **Alix le Clerq**) of the Canonesses Regular of Our Lady, born Mirecourt, Lorraine, France, 1565, died Gray, Haute Saone, 9 December 1640. He joined the Canons Regular of St Augustine in 1585. After his ordination in 1589 he pursued his doctoral studies before taking charge of the abbey parish at Chaumousey, and later the parish at Mattaincourt. When his efforts to reform practices and to provide free education for boys had failed, he enlisted the support of Alix le Clerq and three other women, the nucleus of the new religious order, to set about providing for the education of girls. His later reforming efforts met with greater success, and in 1632 Peter became superior general of the reformed Congregation of Our Saviour. The congregation successfully established the provision of boys' education.

Peter Francis Jamet, bl., born Fresne, France, 1762, ordained 1787, died Caen, 12 January 1845, beatified 1987. He refused to take the Revolutionary oath, but survived. He ministered to those with physical and mental disabilities. He was rector of Caen University 1822–30 and is remembered for a French sign dictionary for deaf-mutes.

Peter-Francis Néron, born Bornay, Jura, France, 21 September 1818, martyred Ha Tây, Vietnam, 3 November 1860, beatified 1909, canonized 1988. He was a priest of the Paris Foreign Missions Society – see **Martyrs of Vietnam**.

Peter Frassati, bl., born Turin, 6 April 1901, died 4 July 1925. Son of Alfredo Frassati, founder of the newspaper *La Stampa* and Italian ambassador in Berlin, and the painter Adelaide Ametis. He studied industrial engineering in Turin, and as a student became involved in a number of political movements, such as the Italian Catholic University Federation and the anti-fascist Partito Populare Italiano. He was also an active member of several religious organizations, and in 1922 became a Dominican tertiary, taking the name Jerome. He often visited the sick, and it may have been through this ministry that he contracted poliomyelitis, the disease that killed him.

Peter Fremond and Five Companions, martyrs, died Angers, 1794. The others were his sister Katherine, Mary Louise du Verdier de la Sorinière, Louise Margaret Bessay de la Voute, Mary Anne Hacher du Bois and Louise Poirier. See **Martyrs of the French Revolution**. Feast 10 February.

Peter Friedhofen, bl., founder, born Weitersburg bei Vallendar, 25 February 1819, died Koblenz, 21 December 1860. He was a chimney sweep, whose work brought him into contact with many poor people. He conceived the idea of founding an order of laymen to help the poor, and was encouraged to do so by the local bishop, although he had at first suggested that Peter join an already existing order. He founded the Congregation of the Brothers of Mercy, with episcopal approval in

1850, which expanded in his lifetime to several places in Germany. He moved the headquarters of his congregation to Koblenz in 1850 after the Princess von Wittgenstein had promised her support.

Peter Gambacorta (Peter the Hermit), hermit and religious founder, born Pisa, Italy, 16 February 1355, died Venice, Italy, 17 June 1435. Although a member of Pisa's ruling family, Gambacorta opted for a life of seclusion and went to live in the wilderness near Urbino. He was joined there by other hermits, as a result of which he formed the Poor Hermits of St Jerome, which was given papal recognition in 1421. Other foundations of the order were established in Venice, Pesaro and Treviso. Gambacorta's asceticism was severe, and on one occasion brought him before the Inquisition. He was beatified in 1693, but his order ceased to exist in 1933, when it was suppressed because it had become too small.

Peter George Frassati, see **Peter Frassati**.

Peter Geremia, bl., born Palermo, Sicily, 1399, died Sicily, 1452. Becoming a Dominican in Bologna, he was sent to Sicily in 1427, to Oxford in 1430, attended the Council of Florence and, refusing all offers from the pope, returned to Sicily, where he was a renowned preacher and reformer of religious life. Feast 3 March.

Peter Gonzalez, Dominican preacher and missionary amongst the Spanish fisher-folk, born Astorga, 1190, died Santiago de Compostela, Easter Sunday, 14 April 1246. Of noble birth, he was confessor to the king of Castile, and later worked among the sailors of Galicia, which led to him being adopted as the patron saint of sailors, confused with St **Elmo**.

Peter Hong, see **Augustine Pak**.

Peter Igneus ('of the fire'), bl., died Vallombrosa, 8 February 1089. As the monk Peter Aldobrandini, he took the ordeal by fire for the people of Florence who had challenged their bishop. He was successful and the bishop was deposed. Peter was later bishop of Albano and cardinal, and a much travelled papal legate.

Peter Julien Eymard, founder, born La Mure d'Isère, France, 4 February 1811, died there, 1 August 1868. He founded the Society of the Blessed Sacrament for men and the Servants of the Blessed Sacrament for women. Dedicated to eucharistic devotion, he wrote, among other works, *La Sainte Communion* and *L'Eucharistie et la Perfection Chrétienne*. He was also responsible for the founding of the Archconfraternity of the Blessed Sacrament and the Priests' Eucharistic League. Feast 2 August.

Peter Martyr, inquisitor, born Verona, *c.* 1205, died near Milan, 6 April 1252. Although born into a predominantly Catharist (Albigensian) family, Peter grew up a Catholic. He attended the university of Bologna and, after deciding to enter the Dominicans, received the habit from **Dominic** himself and became a renowned preacher and dedicated controversialist against the Cathari. Innocent IV appointed him inquisitor (1251) in Milan and Como, and he and his companion were assassinated by the Cathari near Milan. Peter prayed for his murderer as he died. **Fra Angelico** depicted him in a famous fresco in the convent of San Marco, Florence, with a wounded head, his fingers to his lips.

Peter Mogila, bishop and theologian, born Moldavia, 21 December 1596, died Kiev, 22 December 1646. Ukrainian Church, Moscow Patriarchate. He studied theology in the west and became metropolitan of Kiev in 1632. His theological works and liturgical revisions show strong Latin influences, although he remained firmly Orthodox. His *Orthodox Confession* (1640) and *Brief Catechism* influenced the decrees of the Council of Bethlehem (see **Dositheus of Jerusalem**). He was canonized in Ukraine in 1996.

Peter Nicholas Factor, see **Nicholas Factor**.

Peter Nolasco, founder of the Order of Our Lady of Ransom (Mercedarians), born Barcelona, *c.* 1182, died there, 25 December *c.* 1256. Little is known of Peter's early life, but by the mid-1220s he was engaged in his life's work of ransoming the Christian slaves of Muslim masters in Catalonia. When others associated themselves with his activities, the Mercedarian Order began to take shape,

and Gregory IX approved it in 1235. Urban VIII canonized Peter in 1628.

Peter of Alcántara, Franciscan mystic and reformer, born Garavita, Alcántara, 1499, died Arenas, 18 October 1562. Peter entered the Franciscans in 1515 after studies at Salamanca, joining the stricter branch (the Observants) in 1517. He was ordained in 1524. Peter fostered the discalced reform, a controversial movement within the Friars Minor, the adherents being known as Alcantarines, who continued to exist as one of the four branches of the Observants until all were united in 1897. A man of the greatest austerity and mortification, a renowned mission preacher and spiritual director, he advised **Teresa of Avila** in her reform of the Carmelites. Canonized in 1669, the Sacred Congregation of Rites made him patron saint of Brazil in 1826. Feast 19 October.

Peter of Alexandria, bishop and martyr, died Alexandria, 25 November 311. Eusebius describes him as 'a model bishop, remarkable alike for his virtuous life and for his keen study of the scriptures'. Bishop from *c.* 300, he survived the persecution of Diocletian, and followed a policy of leniency towards those who had apostatized through fear of torture. While himself in hiding, another bishop, Melitius of Lycopolis, who favoured a more stringent policy towards the lapsed, usurped Peter's authority at Alexandria. Peter returned to his see in 311, but was beheaded by Maximin Daia shortly afterwards. A little of his work survives in fragments, from which it appears that he opposed Origenism. Feast 26 November.

Peter of Alexandria III (Peter Mongus – The Stammerer), patriarch, born Alexandria, died there, 29 October 490. Coptic Church. An ardent opponent of the Council of Chalcedon, he became patriarch of Alexandria in 477 and established an accord with Acacius, patriarch of Constantinople, which led to what became known as the Acacian Schism between Rome and Constantinople. Peter was excommunicated by Pope Felix III in 484.

Peter of Alexandria IV, patriarch of Alexandria, died Alexandria, 19 June 569. Coptic Church. A monk of Daayr al-Zugag, he was elected patriarch only two years before his death. No theologian, he chose **Damian** as his secretary and adviser, and was succeeded by him.

Peter of Anagni, bishop, born Salerno, died Anagni, 1105. He became a monk at Salerno, then bishop of Anagni from 1062. He took part in the first Crusade. Feast 3 August.

Peter of Antioch, patriarch, died monastery of Gubba Baraya, between Aleppo and Manbig, 22 April 590/91. Syriac Church. He strengthened ties with the patriarchate of Alexandria.

Peter of Argos (The Wonderworker), born Constantinople, *c.* 855, died Argos, ninth century. He and his brother Paul became monks together in Constantinople. He refused a request to be bishop of Corinth, Paul being appointed in his stead, but eventually accepted the bishopric of Argos, winning the great respect and love of the people of the city. Feast 3 May.

Peter of Atroa, born near Ephesus, 773, died St Zachary, near Atroa, Asia Minor, 1 January 837. Joining **Paul the Hesychast**, he succeeded him as abbot of St Zachary. Persecuted during the iconoclast conflicts, he moved around western Asia Minor and the eastern Mediterranean, repeatedly dispersing his monks for safety and recreating communities.

Peter of Bulgaria, king, died 969. Feast 30 January.

Peter of Canterbury, drowned near Boulogne, *c.* 607, cult confirmed 1915. A companion of **Augustine** on the mission to the Anglo-Saxons in 597, he became first abbot of Canterbury monastery. Probably the monk sent back to brief the pope, he died on a mission to Gaul. Feast 6 January.

Peter of Capitolias, bishop and martyr, born Capitolias, Palestine, died Busra, Hauran, 715. Originally a hermit in Transjordan, he became bishop of Busra in Arabia, and was stoned to death for attacking Islam. Feast 4 October.

Peter of Castelnau, bl., martyr, born near Montpellier, died St-Gilles, on the Rhône, 15 January 1208. A Cistercian monk, he campaigned as papal legate against the Cathars in the French Midi. He was assassinated on the orders of Count Raymond of Toulouse, and this incident sparked off the bloody crusade against the Cathars.

Peter of Cava, abbot, born Peter Pappacarbone at Salerno, Italy, died Cava monastery, 1123. A monk at Cava, he went to Cluny, then returned to Cava, where he eventually became abbot. He overcame opposition and reformed the monastery along Cluniac lines, leading to an increase in vocations and donations. Feast 4 March.

Peter of Cava II, bl., abbot, died 1208, cult confirmed 1928. He was ninth abbot of Cava, Campania, from 1195 to his death, and was described as 'an enemy of all litigation'. Feast 13 March.

Peter of Cerekovo, martyr, sixteenth/seventeenth centuries. Russian Church. Priest of the village church in Cerekovo, he was killed during a Polish invasion. His tomb, discovered in 1615, was the site of many miracles. Feast 9 July.

Peter of Cetigne, metropolitan, born Njegos, Montenegro, 1 April 1749, died Cetigne, 18 October 1830. Serbian Church. He became a monk when only 12, and later metropolitan of Cetigne, where he devoted himself to bringing peace to warring families in the area. Although he was a bishop, he continued to live in a cell as a simple monk.

Peter of Chavanon, born Langeac, the Auvergne, *c.* 1005, died Pébrac, 8 September *c.*1080. After his studies he returned as a priest to Langeac, but in *c.* 1060 he decided to found a community of canons at Pébrac.

Peter of Constantinople, born Constantinople (?), 829, died there, 867. Of a wealthy family, he served in the imperial army. He was taken prisoner, but escaped, with divine assistance, as a result of which he became a monk, first on Mount Olympus, then for the last eight years of his life at the monastery of St Phocas in Constantinople. Feast 9 October.

Peter of Galatia, hermit, born Galatia, died Antioch, *c.* 429. Byzantine Church. He is said to have left home at the age of seven to become a hermit.

He travelled to Jerusalem, and then to Antioch, where he walled himself up in a tomb for the rest of his life. He was a worker of many miracles. Feast 1 February.

Peter of Galatia, monk, died Antioch, ninth century. Byzantine Church. He had a very similar life to his namesake above. Feast 25 November.

Peter of Granada, see **John of Granada**.

Peter of Kazan, martyr, sixteenth century. Russian Church. A Tartar who embraced Christianity and had allied himself with the Russians. When the army of which he was a part was captured by Tartars, he was condemned as a traitor. Feast 24 March.

Peter of Kiev, metropolitan, born Volynia, Galicia, c. 1260, died Moscow, 21 December 1326. The son of a boyar, at 12 he entered a monastery and dedicated himself to the spiritual life. After a number of years he became a hermit beside the river Rata, where he developed his talent as a painter of icons, and where he founded a monastery, dedicated to the Transfiguration, of which he was the hegumenos. He was visited there by Maximus, metropolitan of all Russia, to whom he gave an icon still revered in the cathedral of the Dormition in Moscow. At the death of Maximus, Peter went to Constantinople on an embassy from the prince of Galicia, as a result of which Peter was consecrated in 1308 as metropolitan of Kiev and of all Russia – which was not what the prince had intended. At this time Kiev had been left in ruins by the Tartars, and Peter established himself instead at Vladimir. He was active not only in attempting to establish peace among warring Russian princes, but went to negotiate with some success concerning tolerance for Christians from the Golden Horde. He was a frequent visitor to Moscow, then a small city, and the governor of the city, John Kalita, persuaded him to transfer his residence to Moscow, building a new cathedral, of the Dormition, in the Kremlin. Peter chose the site of his tomb within the cathedral, still unfinished at his death. He was canonized at a synod in Vladimir a year after his death. He is considered as the protector of the city of Moscow, and much venerated.

Peter of Korisa, hermit, born Ujmir, south-west of Pec, died Korisa, Kosovo, thirteenth century. A poor farmer, after the death of his parents both he and his sister became hermits, Peter eventually moving to Korisa. Feast 5 June.

Peter of Krutitsa, martyr and bishop, born Storozevoe, Voronezh province, Russia, 28 June 1862, died (shot) Verkhne, Ural prison, Chelyabinsk, 10 October 1937. Russian Church. Baptized Peter Fedorovic Polyansky, he studied at Voronezh and Moscow, then taught in Moscow and St Petersburg. He became a monk in 1920, and bishop of Podolsk. He was almost immediately arrested and deported, but was allowed back in 1923 when he was raised to the rank of archbishop and, the following year, to the rank of metropolitan of Krutitsa. After the death of Patriarch Tikhon in 1925 he was one of the three successors nominated in the patriarch's will. As the other two bishops were in exile, he administered the Church amid the persecution and confusion caused by the Soviet government. His refusal to capitulate completely to the Communists led to his confinement and eventually exile to Tobolsk. Thereafter his sentences were constantly renewed and increased to keep him from contact with other bishops, but he was commemorated as head of the Russian Church everywhere until his death was confirmed, the Soviet authorities saying that he had died in prison.

Peter of Luxembourg, bl., bishop and cardinal, born Lorraine, France, 1369, died Carthusian monastery, Villeneuve, France, 2 July 1387. The son of Guy of Luxembourg, count of Ligny, Peter was orphaned at the age of four. He was educated in Paris and was made a canon of Notre Dame in 1378, archdeacon of Dreux and Brussels in 1381, and canon of Cambrai in 1382. He was appointed bishop of Metz in 1384 by the antipope Clement VII, and was made a cardinal two months later. Peter used armed troops to take control of Metz, as it was occupied by supporters of Pope Urban VI. However, he was driven out by political opponents in 1385, and in 1386 joined Clement VII in Avignon.

Peter of Mogliano, bl., born Marche, Italy, 1442, died 25 July 1490. He studied law at the university of Perugia, became an Observant Franciscan in 1467, and was later ordained as a priest. He was vicar provincial of the Marche for three terms, and in 1472 was a commissary to Crete. He was very much loved by the local people, and towards the end of his life was known simply as 'the holy father'.

Peter of Mount Athos, hermit, born Constantinople, died Mount Athos, ninth century. Byzantine Church. After serving in the imperial army, being captured and imprisoned in Samara, he was released by the intervention of St **Nicholas**. He then travelled to Rome and from there to Mount Athos. Feast 12 June.

Peter of Narbonne, see **Nicholas of Sibenik**.

Peter of Nicomedia, martyr, died Nicomedia, 303. An official in the palace of Diocletian at Nicomedia, he was tortured for his faith before being roasted alive. Feast 12 March.

Peter of Osma, bishop, born Berry, France, died Osma, Spain, 1109. He became a monk of Cluny, and was later sent to Spain where he became archdeacon of Toledo and then bishop of Osma. Feast 2 August.

Peter of Pavia, bishop, died c. 743. He was bishop for a short time in Pavia in Lombardy. Feast 7 May.

Peter of Pisa, bl., founder, born Pisa, 1355, died there, 1435. The father of **Peter Gambacorta** was the ruler of Pisa, but when he was 26 he fled the court and took up residence near Pisa on Monte Bello. There he founded an order called the Hermits of St Jerome, which was approved in 1421. He is the brother of the Bl. **Clare Gambacorta**. Feast 17 June.

Peter of Poitiers, bishop, died Chauvigny, 1115. Bishop of Poitiers from 1087, he helped **Robert of Arbrissel** found Fontrevault monastery. He convened the 1110 Council of Poitiers that excommunicated the French king for repudiating his wife. Threatened by the illegally remarried count of Poitou, he excommunicated him. He died in exile. Feast 4 April.

Peter of Raifskaia Pustyn, martyr, born Elanbuj, 1906, died near Raifskaia Pustyn, 7 April 1930. Russian Church. Peter Tupicyn had entered the monastery of Raifskaia Pustyn as a novice just before it was closed. He then wandered around the diocese, earning a living wherever he could, but eventually settling in Belo-Bezovodnaja, where **Sergius of Raifskaia Pustyn** served as the parish priest. He was arrested with Sergius and others in January 1930, and shot. Feast 14 January.

Peter of Rufa, bl., martyr, born Piedmont, 1320, died Susa, 2 February 1365, cult approved 1865. A Dominican and a talented scholar, he became inquisitor general in Piedmont in 1351 as part of the struggle against the Waldensians, two of whom murdered him.

Peter of St Joseph Betancur, bl., born Tenerife, Canary Isles, 1626, died Guatemala City, 25 April 1667. His family were poor, and his first occupation was as a shepherd. He left for Guatemala in 1650, finally arriving on 18 February 1651. He was so poor that he was forced to join the daily bread queue at the Franciscan friary. Here he befriended the missionary Fray Fernando Espino, who found him work in a local textile factory. In 1653 he entered the local Jesuit college, hoping to become a priest, but his lack of intellectual ability forced him to give this up. In 1655 he joined the Third Order of St Francis. He founded a hospital for the poor, an oratory, a school, and a hostel for the homeless, and dedicated his life to alleviating the suffering of the poor. He had small chapels erected in the poorer districts of Guatemala City. Every 18 August he would gather the children to sing the Seven Joys of the Franciscan Rosary in honour of the Virgin Mary. This custom is still practised in Guatemala today. Known as the 'St Francis of the Americas', he died in the hospital which he had founded.

Peter of Sassoferrato, see **John of Perugia and Peter of Sassoferrato**.

Peter of Scete, monk. Coptic Church. Called 'the devout', nothing else is known of him apart from the day of his death, 20 January.

Peter of Sebaste I, born Caesarea, Cappadocia, died Sebaste, Armenia, 391 (?). The younger brother of **Basil** and **Gregory of Nyssa** and brought up, after his parents' death, by **Macrina**, his eldest sister. In 362 he became abbot of Basil's monastery, was ordained in 370 and then bishop of Sebaste in 380, attending the Council of Constantinople a year later. Feast 9 January.

Peter of Siena, bl., born Siena, died there, 1289. Peter Tecelamo was a maker of combs, and married, but after the death of his wife he entered the Franciscan Third Order, using the money he earned by his trade to support the Franciscans. He lived in a cell attached to the Franciscan house. Feast 4 December.

Peter of Spaso-Kamennyj, monk, fifteenth century. Russian Church. A monk of the monastery of Spaso-Kamennyj towards the middle of the fifteenth century, but previously he may have been a hermit on the river Kubin.

Peter of Tarentaise, archbishop, born near Vienne, 1102, died Bellevau, 14 September 1174. Peter joined the Cistercians at Bonnevaux, and became first abbot of Taruivé in Savoy and archbishop of Tarentaise. With great difficulty he reformed his diocese, founding many hospitals. He supported Pope Alexander III against Emperor Frederick I Barbarossa, and undertook a mission from him to reconcile Henry II and Louis VII of France. Venerated as a saint even in his lifetime, Celestine III canonized him in 1191.

Peter of Tomsk, born near Kuzneck, Siberia, 1800, died there, 1820. Of a noble family, he entered the army, but managed as a soldier to live the life of an ascetic, and became a hermit in the woods near his home village. His rigorous life weakened him, and one day when chopping wood he inflicted a wound on his leg which brought an early death. Feast 10 June.

Peter of the Peloponnese, martyr, born Tripoli, died Temisi, Asia Minor, 1 January 1776. Byzantine Church.

Peter of Trebizond, martyr, died Trebizond. Nothing is known of him, except that he appears to have been fairly young at his death, which occurred possibly in the second half of the fifteenth century.

Peter of Treja, bl., died Sirolo, Piceno, 1304. He was a Franciscan friar who preached throughout Italy with **Conrad of Offida**. Feast 19 February.

Peter of Trevi, born Carsoli, in the Abruzzi, died Trevi, near Subiaco, c. 1050. A diocesan priest, he preached in the region around Subiaco. Feast 30 August.

Peter of Xizan, see **Stephen of Xizan and Peter of Xizan**.

Peter Ortiz de Zárate, ven., priest and martyr, born Jujuy, Argentina, 1622, died in the Chaco, 27 October 1683. He was a rich and devout landowner who, after the death of his wife in 1653, studied with the Jesuits and was ordained in 1659. He organized and funded a missionary expedition, leaving Jujuy with two Jesuits on 18 October 1682. They founded two settlements in the forests of the Chaco, among apparently friendly Indian people. But he was killed the following year, together with one of his companions, the Jesuit Father Salinas.

Peter Pascual (Paschasius), bl., bishop and martyr, born Valencia, 1227, died Granada, 1300. He studied in Paris, taught in Barcelona, became tutor to the son of the king of Aragon, and then was appointed to the see of Granada, although this was still in the hands of Muslims. In 1296 he was made bishop of Jaén. This city, too, was still under Muslim domination, but Peter exercised a pastoral ministry there. He was, however, taken captive and sent to Granada, where he died in prison. Feast 6 December.

Peter Poveda, bl., founder and martyr, born Jaén, Spain, 3 December 1874, died Madrid, 27 or 28 July 1936. He was offered a scholarship by the bishop of Guadix to the seminary there, and was ordained in April 1897. He was made canon of the basilica at La Santina, the shrine of the Virgin Mary in Covadonga, and in 1911 he opened a student residence in Oviedo, called the St Teresa of Avila Academy. This was the starting point of the Teresian Association, devoted to the spiritual and pastoral formation of teachers. The first members were women involved in teaching at all levels, and most notably in higher education for women. Peter was made canon of Jaén cathedral in 1913, and in 1914 opened an *academia* for women graduates of the university of Madrid. He was appointed chaplain of the royal palace in 1921 and moved to Madrid, still devoting much of his time to the Teresian Association. The Association received papal approval in 1924. As a prominent Catholic educator, Peter was an obvious target for revolutionary elements when the Spanish civil war broke out. He was abducted from the Teresian house in Madrid by revolutionary militia on 27 July 1936, and his body was found the next day. Feast 28 July.

Peter Prokop'ev, monk, born Povenec, 1673, died Vyg, 1719. Church of the Old Believers. He was related to **Andrew** and **Simeon Denisov**, and came from the same village. He had a particular interest in liturgical ceremonial, and drew up the Rule for the monastery on the river Vyg which Andrew Denisov had founded. He also wrote lives of the Old Believer saints. Feast 16 January.

Peter Regalado, born Valladolid, Spain, 1390, died La Aguilera monastery, 30 March 1456, canonized 1746. A Franciscan friar, he followed the founder's primitive Rule and worked with other friars to restore it. He was renowned in life for his generosity to the poor and miracles were reported after his death.

Peter Rene Rogue, bl., martyr, born Vannes, France, 11 June 1758, died there, 1 March 1796. Rogue joined the Vincentians, and refused to subscribe to the Civil Constitution of the Clergy during the revolution. Forbidden to exercise his priestly functions, he continued to do so in secret until apprehended in 1795. He ministered to his fellow prisoners until he was guillotined. Pius XI beatified him in 1934.

Peter-Rose-Ursule-Dumoulin Borie, born Beynat, Corrèze, France, 20 February 1808, martyred Vietnam, 24 November 1838, canonized 1988. A priest of the Paris Foreign Missions Society, he was a bishop and apostolic vicar of West Tonkin – see **Martyrs of Vietnam**.

Peter Ryou Tjeng Rioul, martyr, died Korea, 31 December 1866. He was only 13 when he was strangled. See **Martyrs of Korea**. Feast 17 February.

Peter Sanz and Companions, martyred Fuchow, China, 1748. Peter and four others – **Francis Serrano**, **Joachim Royo**, **John Alcober** and Francis Diaz – all Spanish Dominicans, were among the first to be executed in the wave of persecution in China that began in the nineteenth century – see **Martyrs of China**. Feast 26 May.

Peter, Severus and Leucius, martyrs, died Alexandria. It is possible that only Severus was a martyr. Feast 11 January.

Peter Snow, bl., martyr, born Ripon, Yorkshire, died York, 15 June 1598. He studied for the priesthood at Rheims, was ordained at Soissons in March 1591, and returned to England – under the name of Sharp – shortly afterwards. He was arrested in May 1598 in the company of **Ralph Grimston**, described as a gentleman of Nidd, also in Yorkshire, who tried to prevent the arrest, and was executed with him.

Peter Tessier, bl., see **Francis Pelletier**.

Peter the Aleut, martyr, born Aleutian Islands, died San Francisco, 8 September 1815. Russian Orthodox Church in America. He was a young Alaskan (Aleutian) Indian of the Orthodox faith who, on a trading expedition down the Pacific coast, was captured by Spaniards in California. He was tortured to make him change his faith, but he refused. He died after his hands and feet were cut off. Never officially canonized, but venerated as a martyr by all the American Orthodox. Feast 12 December.

Peter the Egyptian, hermit. A disciple of Abba Lot, and one of the Desert Fathers. Feast 27 January.

Peter the Great, monk. Coptic Church. His cave is mentioned in the life of several saints, but nothing is said of him.

Peter the Iberian, bishop, born Georgia, 411, died Gaza, 491. Georgian Church. The son of a king of

Iberia (i.e. Georgia), and named Murvanos, from the age of 12 he was sent to the imperial court in Constantinople as a hostage. He then became a monk, taking the name Peter, and was ordained priest in 445. He travelled widely in Syria and Egypt, founding monastic houses and hospices for pilgrims, eventually settling in a monastery near Gaza, where he was made bishop. Feast 2 December.

Peter the Spaniard, born Spain, died Veroli, before the eleventh century. He was a Spanish pilgrim to Rome who became a hermit at Babuco, near Veroli, south-east of Rome. As mortification he wore chainmail next to his skin. Feast 11 March.

Peter the Venerable, bl., abbot of Cluny, born Montboissier, Auvergne, c. 1092, died Cluny, 25 December 1156. Peter made his profession at Cluny under St **Hugh**, and became abbot in 1122, ruling 200–300 monks at Cluny and many dependent houses throughout Western Europe. An able administrator, he held that monastic life should include humane studies, and in 1143 promoted the first translation of the Koran into Latin. He supported polemics against his great friend St **Bernard**, gave shelter to Abelard at Cluny, wrote against the Muslims, against Peter de Bruys and against the Jews (1144–7); his writings show little acquaintance with the Fathers, but profound knowledge of the Scriptures. Feast 11 May.

Peter the Wonderworker, see **Peter of Argos**.

Peter Thi, priest and martyr, born Vietnam, 1763, died Hanoi, 21 December 1839.

Peter Thomas of Famagusta, bishop, born Périgord, 1305, died Cyprus, 1366, from wounds received in action at Alexandria. A Carmelite at 21, he held posts as papal legate, became archbishop of Crete in 1363 and Latin patriarch of Constantinople in 1364, and worked for Church unity. Feast 6 January.

Peter ToRot, bl., martyr, born Rakunai, Papua New Guinea, 1912, died there, 17 July 1945. His father, the village chief, and his mother had been among the first converts to Catholicism in the area, and Peter joined a mission school in 1930, to become a lay catechist. He married Paula IaVarpit in 1936. In 1942 all missionaries were imprisoned by the Japanese, but Peter was allowed to continue his work until the military police imposed a more rigorous regime, forbidding Christian worship and reintroducing the practice of polygamy. In early 1945, Peter was arrested because of his opposition to polygamy, and was given a lethal injection on 17 July.

Peter Truat, martyr, born Tonkin, died Annan, Vietnam, 1839. Feast 18 December.

Peter Wright, bl., born Slipton, Northamptonshire, 1603, died Tyburn, London, 19 May 1651. He became a Jesuit in Flanders in 1629, and later was a chaplain in the Royalist army. He was arrested and executed as a priest by Parliamentarians under the Commonwealth.

Peter Zarevic, prince, died Rostov, 1290. Russian Church. He was the son and heir (*zarevic*) of the Khan Berka. He became a Christian, taking the name Peter, and lived at Rostov. He founded a monastery dedicated to Ss Peter and Paul. Feast 29 June.

Pethion, catholicos, died 740. Syriac Church. Catholicos from 731 until his death. This was a time of peace for the Church, under a tolerant caliph.

Pethion of Dasen, monk. Syriac Church. Possibly the founder of a monastery.

Petrock, born Wales (?), died Padstow, Cornwall, sixth century. Probably the son of a chieftain and, as recounted in the ancient Latin life of St Cadoo, from the royal family of Gwent. After studies in Ireland (where he perhaps instructed St **Kevin**), he made his way to Cornwall and founded monasteries at Padstow (i.e., Petrockstowe) and Bodmin. In the late twelfth century a Breton canon regular stole his body from Bodmin and took it to St Méen in Brittany, where he is venerated as St Perreux, and whence originated the Latin *Vita Petroci*. Feast 4 June.

Petronilla, martyr, born Rome (?), died there, c. 251. The only thing that is known for certain is that she is represented as a martyr in a fourth-century fresco. The previous story, now discounted, was that she lived in the first century and ministered to the apostle Peter, even being described as his daughter. Feast 31 May.

Petronilla of Moncel, bl., from Troyes, died Burgundy, 1355. She was first abbess of the Poor Clare convent at Moncel, Burgundy, founded by King Philip the Fair. Feast 1 May.

Petronius, monk, born Gog, near Qina, fourth century. Coptic Church. The successor of **Pachomius**, he came from a wealthy family, but retired to one of his family's estates to live an eremitical life. A group grew around him, but he then came to know Pachomius, and Pachomius put him at the head of his community at Tsmine. He died soon afterwards, on 19 July, although the year is uncertain.

Petronius, born Gaul (?), died Bologna, *c.* 450. Petronius's *Vita* describes him as the son of the praetorium of Gaul, and he himself may have held civil office before becoming bishop of Bologna. He erected a church and monastery dedicated to St Stephen, modelled on the Church of the Holy Sepulchre in Jerusalem, which he had visited. His relics were discovered in Bologna in 1141, and the *Vita* is highly controversial. In any case he is now commemorated in the church of San Petronio, a vast gothic structure in Bologna. Feast 4 October.

Petronius of Die, bishop, died *c.* 465. He was the son of a senator in Avignon who became a monk at Lérins and was bishop of Die from *c.* 456. Feast 10 January.

Phambaldus, monk, died near Le Mans, sixth century. Feast 16 August.

Pharaïldis (Varelde, Verylde, Veerle), died Flanders, *c.* 745. According to legend, she was married against her will and treated brutally by her husband, and after his death she dedicated herself to God. A spring she made flow was credited with healing powers, and she is a patroness of Ghent. Feast 4 January.

Phi..., see also **Fi...**

Philaret Dozdov, metropolitan, born Kolomna, 26 December 1782, died Moscow, 19 November 1867. Russian Church. Baptized Basil Michajlovic, his father was a priest in Kolomna. In 1799 he entered the seminary of the Most Holy Trinity of St **Sergius of Radonez**, where he proved himself a brilliant student, staying on after completing his studies to teach Hebrew. In 1806 he became a monk, taking his name from St **Philaret the Almsgiver**. He was sent to teach in St Petersburg, and in 1811 was raised to the rank of archimandrite, becoming rector of the ecclesiastical academy a year later. There he began what was almost a life's work, translating the Gospel of John into Russian. In 1817 he became bishop of Revelsk, then two years later archbishop of Tver. In 1821 he became metropolitan of Moscow. He was particularly active in overseeing the religious schools, for which he produced the basic text on Russian Orthodoxy. He also showed great concern for the monastic life in his diocese, again producing a basic guide to the religious life. He was renowned as a preacher, and published a book of his homilies. He helped to draft the decree of Alexander II emancipating the serfs.

Philaret the Almsgiver, born Amneia, Paphlagonia, died Constantinople, 789. Byzantine Church. A wealthy man, born into a noble family, he distributed all his wealth to the poor, reducing himself and his family to poverty. His granddaughter married the Emperor Constantine. Feast 1 December.

Philaster, bishop and anti-heretical writer, born Spain, died Brescia, Italy, *c.* 397. Philaster became bishop of Brescia and took part in the Council of Aquileia (381). In *c.* 385 he wrote a treatise refuting 12 Jewish and 128 Christian heresies. The material, largely drawn from **Irenaeus** and **Epiphanius**, includes the notable heretic Simon Magus, as well as persons who believed only that the stars occupied a fixed place in the heavens, rather than being set in place each evening by God. Despite this lack of perspective, however, the book filled a need and St **Augustine** made use of it. Feast 18 July.

Phileas of Thumis, martyr, died Alexandria, 4 February 306. Of noble birth and great wealth,

Phileas became bishop of Thumis in the Nile Delta. He and three other bishops protested to Meletius, bishop of Lycopolis, that his adherents had invaded their dioceses, thus beginning the Meletian Schism. Imprisoned during the Diocletian persecution and tried by Culcianus, governor of Egypt, Phileas was beheaded along with Philoromus, a Roman official. A letter to his people in Thumis from his dungeon is preserved by Eusebius in his *Ecclesiastical History*; the *Acta* of his martyrdom are considered authentic.

Philemon, monk, fourteenth century. Ethiopian Church. Son of the governor of Sebta, he was ordained deacon and then decided, against his family's wishes, to become a monk. The first time he tried to enter a monastery he was brought back home, but he soon escaped and became a monk at Dabra Maryam. He then moved to the monastery of Ta'amina, where his uncle was abbot. When his uncle was killed by brigands, he took his place as abbot. He was renowned for the strictness of his life, and for his constant prayer. He went to visit Jerusalem, but on his return was advised to go into the desert, which he did with some disciples, creating a new community.

Philemon and Apollonius, born Antinoe, Egypt (?), died Alexandria, 305 (?). Apollonius was the deacon who converted Philemon, an actor. They were executed in Alexandria. Feast 8 March.

Philemon and Appia, died Colossae, Asia Minor, 70 (?). St Paul wrote to Philemon about his runaway slave. Appia is thought to have been Philemon's wife. Both are said to have been stoned to death. Feast 22 March.

Philemon and Domninus, born Rome (?). Missionaries in Italy. Feast 21 March.

Philibert of Rebais, abbot, born Eauze, *c.* 618, died abbey of Noirmoutier, 20 August 684. Of a noble family in Gascony, in 636 Philibert took the monastic habit at Rebais under St **Ouen**; he later founded the monastery of Jumièges and a convent for women at Pavilly, on land given him by Clovis II. For denouncing the injustice of Ebroin, mayor of the palace, in 674, he lost his post and retired to

the island of Her, where he established the monastery of Noirmoutier.

Philip Benizi, born Florence, 15 August 1233, died Todi, 22 August 1285. He came from a noble family, and studied medicine at Paris and Padua before practising in Florence. Always a devout young man, he studied the Scriptures in his spare time. In 1254, as a result of a vision, he decided to join the newly founded Servite Order, which was located at Mante Senario not far from Florence. He joined as a lay brother, and undertook menial tasks until his scholarship was revealed by a chance encounter, and he was ordained. He held a number of posts in the order, eventually becoming general of the order in 1267. When it was rumoured that he was a candidate for the papacy in 1268, he went and hid in the hills until the danger was passed. He created the Order of Servite Nuns, and sent out the first Servite missionaries. When he felt that he was dying he went to the poorest house of the order to spend his last days.

Philip de Jesus Casas Martinez, proto-martyr of Japan, born Mexico City, 1 May 1572, died Nagasaki, Japan, 5 February 1597. Of Spanish parentage, at 17 he joined the Franciscans in Puebla, then left to become a merchant and went to Manila. Here he rediscovered his vocation, took the habit and was ordained in 1593. On 18 October 1596 the ship in which he was travelling back to Mexico was wrecked on the coast of Japan. He was taken into the Franciscan convent of Miyaco, Kyoto, but shortly afterwards the Japanese authorities ordered the execution of the missionaries, with whom he requested to be included, and they were all crucified. He was beatified on 14 September 1627 and canonized on 8 June 1862.

Philip Evans, martyr, born Monmouth, England, 1645, died Cardiff, 22 July 1679. Evans became a Jesuit in 1665 and after his ordination in Liège (1675), he worked in south Wales. In 1678 he became a target as part of Titus Oates's plot to persecute Catholics. Later that year, a price was placed on his head by John Arnold of Abergavenny, a justice of the peace and hunter of priests. Following his arrest on 2 December, Evans refused to take the oath of allegiance and was subsequently imprisoned for three weeks of solitary confinement. In May 1679 he was brought to trial and convicted of being a priest.

Philip Howard, born Arundel House, London, 28 June 1557, died Tower of London, 19 October 1595. He was the son of Thomas Howard, fourth duke of Norfolk. He succeeded his grandfather as earl of Arundel, his father having been executed. After a rather dissolute youth he turned to religion when his chances of preferment at Elizabeth's court had diminished. Under the inspiration of his wife, who had become a Roman Catholic, and of his friend **Edmund Campion**, he converted to Catholicism, being received into the Church in September 1584. He was arrested as he tried to leave England the following year, and was imprisoned in the Tower of London. He was found guilty of treason, but the death sentence was not carried out. It has been alleged that he was poisoned: as he lay dying he asked to see his wife and children, and this was refused unless he conformed, which he would not do. In 1970 he was canonized as one of the **Forty Martyrs of England and Wales**. His body is in Arundel, at the cathedral, dedicated to him and to Our Lady.

Philip Michailovi Ordinec, martyr, born Miropol, 1 June 1888, died Char'kov, 25 May 1938. Ukrainian Church, Moscow Patriarchate. He was married with four children, and served as choirmaster of the church of St Nicholas in Char'kov until his arrest.

Philip Neri, founder of the Oratorians, born Florence, 1515, died Rome, 26 May 1595. Educated by the Dominicans of San Marco, and attracted to the memory of Savonarola, Philip went to Rome in 1533 and co-founded the Confraternity of the Most Holy Trinity, for the care of pilgrims, who in the Jubilee year 1575 numbered 145,000. Following his ordination, the confessional and spiritual conferences at San Girolamo became his apostolate. The growing community became the Congregation of the Oratory, approved by Gregory XIII in 1575. Revered as a saint during his lifetime, Philip's gentleness, gaiety and warm personal devotion to Christ made him known as the 'Apostle of Rome'. Gregory XV canonized him in 1622.

Philip of Agirone, born Sicily, died there, fifth century. He is said to have been a priest who was the first missionary sent to Sicily, but the story as told is improbable. He was supposed to have the gift of exorcism and is venerated in the hill town of Agirone. Feast 12 May.

Philip of Dabra Bizan, monk, born October 1322, died Dabra Bizan, 29 July 1406. Ethiopian Church. After living as a monk and then a hermit, he and some disciples founded a monastery, particularly to look after orphans. Because his monastery was close to the sea, he came into contact with Muslim merchants, with whom he established very good relations. From there he evangelized, and founded 25 churches. He proposed a reform of Sabbath observance which led to a clash with his metropolitan and his exile to the island of Havq, where he remained until c. 1403, after which he spent four years preaching in Amara, before returning to his monastery at the end of his life.

Philip of Dabra Libanos, monk, born Lat, 1274, died Gergesa, 22 July 1348. Ethiopian Church. He became a monk, despite his parents' wish that he should marry. He went to Asbo, where he was welcomed by **Takla Haymanot**, and where, after Takla Haymanot's death, he built up a large community. He and 12 companions were sent on missionary journeys by the metropolitan, but, because he reproved the king for having married the wife of his father, he was exiled. A new king allowed him to return. Then the metropolitan was himself exiled because he opposed the king when he took three wives. Philip was summoned to court, but exiled once more for his opposition to the king. The king's soldiers killed several of Philip's companions, as well as some who lived nearby and supported the monks, but Philip himself escaped. Some time later, feeling that his end was near, he went to Gergesa where, after a few days, he died.

Philip of Gortina, bishop, died Gortina, Crete, c. 180. The author of a treatise against Gnostic heretics.

Philip of Heraclea and Companions, martyrs, died Adrianople, 303. Philip was bishop of Heraclea, **Hermes**, a former senator, was a deacon, and

Severus was a priest. During the persecution under Diocletian, Severus went into hiding, but Philip and Hermes remained conducting services. They refused to sacrifice to the gods, and were imprisoned and tortured. Severus then handed himself over, and all three were transferred to Adrianople, where they were again tortured, and finally burned to death. Feast 22 October.

Philip of Moscow I, bishop, died Moscow, 5 April 1473. Russian Church. By 1455 he was bishop of Suzdal, and was elected metropolitan of Moscow in 1464. He collaborated actively with Prince Ivan III in the establishment of Moscow's dominance over Russian territory. He clashed with the patriarch of Constantinople over the union between the Roman and Orthodox Churches proposed at the Council of Florence, and later fell out with Ivan over his Westernizing policies. He refused to preside at the marriage of Ivan to a Byzantine princess who had been educated at Rome. He began the cathedral of the Dormition in the Moscow Kremlin.

Philip of Moscow II, metropolitan, born 1507, died Tver, 23 December 1569. Russian Church. Baptized Theodore Stepanovic Kolycev, he came from a boyar family. Although destined like his father for a career at court, he decided to become a monk, a decision perhaps encouraged by the persecution of his family, who had backed the losing side in a power struggle. He fled to the village of Chizach, where for a time he worked as a shepherd, then went to the Solovki monastery, where he was elected abbot in 1548. As superior he was highly successful, and the monastery grew in numbers, wealth and influence. Tsar Ivan IV initiated a campaign against the influence of the boyars, and also tried to force the Church to do his wishes. He chose Philip as metropolitan of Moscow in 1566. Philip, however, was hostile to the Tsar's anti-boyar policy, and in the cathedral of the Dormition in 1568 openly refused the Tsar his blessing. The Tsar then accused Philip of immoral behaviour, put him on trial, and had him condemned. He was imprisoned first in Moscow, then in a monastery in Tver, where, on the instructions of the Tsar, he was assassinated. Feast 15 October.

Philip of Zell (Celles), died Zell, c. 770. He was a hermit near Worms, on the Rhine, who was a friend of the Merovingian king Pepin. He founded a monastery, calling it after his own cell, or *Zell* in German. There is now a town of that name. Feast 11 May.

Philip Rinaldi, bl., born Lu, Monferrato, 28 May 1856, died Turin, 5 December 1931. He was educated in the Salesian college in Mirabello, and there encountered **John Bosco**, the founder of the Salesians. He decided to join the order, and was ordained priest in December 1882, by which time he was already master of novices. He served for a time in Spain, but was brought back to Turin after the death of John Bosco, and became the superior general in 1922.

Philip Siphong, martyr, born Nonseng, died Songkong, 16 December 1940. He was a married man with five children, and was a teacher in the village. He took over leadership of the community when the parish priest was expelled. He was summoned to the police station, and was tortured and killed. Feast 16 December.

Philip Suzanni, bl., born Piacenza, died there, 1306, cult approved 1756. He was an Augustinian friar in Piacenza who was known for his life of prayer. Feast 24 May.

Philip the Cantor, seventeenth century. Church of the Old Believers. He was cantor to the Tsar, but rejected the reforms of Nikon, and joined the Old Believers. He was put to death after torture. Feast 29 November.

Philip the Deacon, first century. One of the first deacons, he worked in Samaria. Feast 6 June.

Philip, Zeno, Narses and ten children, martyrs, died Alexandria. Feast 15 July.

Philippa Mareri, bl., born in the Abruzzi, near Rome, died (quite young) near Rieti, possibly 16 February 1236, cult confirmed 1806. She apparently defied her rich parents to follow **Francis of Assisi**'s teaching. They eventually provided a building on their land where, under the direction of **Roger of Todi**, she became the first abbess of a Poor Clares' convent.

Philo of Cyprus, bishop, died *c.* 394. Feast 24 January.

Philogonius of Antioch, bishop, died Antioch, 324. A lawyer, as bishop he was a protector of the poor, and of the faith against the Arian heresy. Feast 20 December.

Philologus, born Rome, died there (?), first century. Mentioned by the apostle Paul.

Philomenus of Ancyra, bishop, died Ancyra, 275 (?). Died in the persecution of Aurelian. Feast 29 November.

Philonidis, bishop and martyr, died Cyprus, *c.* 303. He is reputed to have committed suicide in prison, rather than be subjected to further torture. Feast 29 August.

Philossenus of Mabbug, bishop, born Tahal, died Gangra, Paphlagonia, 10 December 523. Assyrian Church. His family came from Tur Abdin. He was well educated, and wrote a number of Gospel commentaries and other spiritual works. He was accused of being a monophysite, but his explanation of his faith to the Emperor Zeno led to his appointment as bishop in 485. When the Emperor Justinian succeeded to the throne, however, he fell from favour and was exiled to Gangra, where he was suffocated accidentally by smoke from the kitchen. Feast 18 February.

Philothea, hermit, born Molivot, Pamphilia, died there. Russian Church. She had practised fasting and prayer from a young age, and when she was given in marriage she persuaded her husband Constantine to live virginally. After his death she retired to an island on a nearby lake and lived a hermit's existence. Feast 7 December.

Philothea of Arges, born Tarnovo, *c.* 1206, died there, 1218. Romanian Church. A child of deep religious faith, her mother died when she was very young, and her father punished her for her religious practices. She commonly gave to the poor the greater part of the food she was taking out to her father in the fields, and when he discovered this he struck her such a blow that she died. Feast 7 December.

Philothea of Athens, born Athens, 1522, died there, 19 February 1589. Byzantine Church. Born into a noble family and baptized Regula, she was married at 14, but her husband died three years later and, although her parents wanted her to marry again, she gave herself up to an ascetic life. After the death of her parents she founded a convent. She also founded, among other things, a hospital and a school, and cared for orphan children. Her convent was, however, attacked by Turks in August 1588: she was wounded and left for dead. She survived this ordeal by just a few months. She was declared a saint only a few years after her death.

Philotheus, see also **Hipparchus and Philotheus**.

Philotheus I Kokkinos, patriarch, born Thessalonika, 1300, died 1379. Byzantine Church. After living for a time on Mount Sinai as a monk, he moved to the Grand Laura on Mount Athos, where he encountered **Gregory Palamas** and learned the doctrine of hesychasm. He eventually became hegumenos of the Grand Laura before being elected metropolitan of Heraclea in 1347, and he began to play a major role in the life of the Church. He became patriarch of Constantinople at the emperor's wish in 1353, but resigned the following year when the emperor resigned. He returned to Mount Athos, but was again elected to Constantinople in 1364, using his second period of office, until 1376, actively to promote hesychasm. He was also active in efforts to reunite the Churches of East and West, and to assert the authority of Constantinople over Moscow, something he achieved when one of his close supporters became metropolitan there. He wrote many works promoting hesychasm, but also lives of saints and exegetical works, among others. Feast 11 October.

Philotheus of Tobolsk, metropolitan, born 1650, died Tjumen, 31 May 1727. Russian Church. Born of a noble family in the Ukraine and named Lescinski. He studied in Kiev, married and became a priest, but after the death of his wife he became a monk in the Kievan Cave monastery, then was sent as superior to a monastery in Sveno. He became metropolitan of the vast Siberian diocese of Tobolsk in 1702. He organized, and himself made, many missionary journeys, converting the pagans, so that the number of parishes more than doubled. He used the monks of Kiev as missionaries. He resigned his see in 1711 and gave himself even more to his missionary activity, but he was re-elected in 1715 on the death of his successor. He resigned again on the grounds of ill-health. He entered the monastery of Tjumen, which he had earlier restored, and again occupied himself with missionary work. Feast 10 June.

Phocas, martyr, died Antioch, *c.* 320. He is said to have been suffocated in his bath. Feast 5 March.

Phocas the Gardener, martyr, died Sinope, on the Black Sea, fourth century (?). Said to have kept a garden at Sinope, where he lived just outside the city gate. During a persecution (it is not clear which), the soldiers sent to execute him arrived at the city when the gate was shut. They lodged with Phocas, telling him the purpose of their journey. He said he knew the man they were looking for and would direct them to him in the morning. When they learned that their host was the one for whom they were searching, they did not know what to do, but beheaded him only after he had insisted that martyrdom was the greatest honour that could be bestowed on a Christian. Feast 22 September.

Photius, see also **Archelaus**.

Photius of Constantinople, patriarch, born Constantinople, *c.* 820, died there, 6 February 891. Byzantine Church. He was a layman at the imperial court when he was made patriarch in 858, but his predecessor, Ignatius, refused to abdicate. The bishop of Rome was asked to intervene and reinstated Ignatius, an action which was deeply resented in Constantinople. He remained patriarch until 867, when Ignatius returned, continuing in office until 878, when Photius again came back. He was important in the Orthodox Church for his rejection of Western attempts to add the *Filioque* to the creed. Feast 6 February.

Photius of Moscow, metropolitan, born Malvasia, in the Peloponnese, died Moscow, 11 July 1431. Russian Church. While in Constantinople on a mission for his own metropolitan of Malvasia, he was chosen because of the holiness of his life to be the metropolitan of Moscow, where he arrived at Easter 1410. Shortly afterwards the Tartars attacked Moscow and destroyed the cathedral of the Dormition, while Photius himself was, by chance, in a monastery outside the walls of the city. In the absence of any civil government in the aftermath, the cathedral's property was stolen, and one of Photius's first tasks was to attempt to recover it. He then incurred the displeasure of Prince Vitovt, who accused him of showing no interest in the bishops of Lithuania who were under his charge. He then went on to accuse Photius of simony. Eventually, however, Photius was able to reassert his authority over Lithuania and over Galizia. He was also able to act as mediator in arranging the marriage between the daughter of the prince of Moscow and the son of the Byzantine emperor.

Pierina Morososi, bl., martyr, born Fiobbio, near Bergamo, northern Italy, 7 January 1931, died there, 6 April 1957. A factory worker from the age of 15, she was a pious and active parishioner, impressed by the example of **Maria Teresa Goretti**. She died of head injuries after a brutal attempted sexual assault.

Pierius, born Alexandria (?), died Rome, *c.* 310. The priest head of the catechetical school in Alexandria. Feast 4 November.

Pigimi, hermit, born Egypt, died there. Feast 7 November (?).

Pihur, Pisurah and Abnirah, martyrs, died Egypt, thirteenth century (?).

Pimen, monk, born Egypt, *c.* 350, died Scete, *c.* 450. He and two of his brothers, Anubias and Paisius, were monks in Scete, but had to take refuge in a former pagan temple on the Nile at Tereneuthis when they were forced out of their monastery by barbarians. Pimen was famous for his asceticism, and it is said he travelled from place to place to avoid crowds coming to see him. Many of his sayings are recorded in the *Sayings of the Desert Fathers*. Feast 27 August.

Pimen of Kiev, metropolitan, died Chalcedon, 11 September 1389. Russian Church. Nothing is known of him before 1379, when he was archimandrite of the Gorickij monastery at Perejaslavl-Zalesk. He was travelling to Constantinople with Michael, who was seeking to be recognized as metropolitan of Kiev when he died in a storm at sea. Pimen was chosen in his stead, but when the news reached Moscow in February 1381, Grand Prince Demetrius refused to recognize the legitimacy of the choice and had Pimen arrested and sent to Tver. In 1382 Moscow was sacked by the khan, and both Demetrius and his preferred candidate for metropolitan, **Cyprian**, fled. Cyprian went to Tver, which was then in the hands of one of Demetrius's rivals, and the grand prince was furious. He sent Cyprian off to Lithuania and installed Pimen as metropolitan. There were further intrigues between the two claimants, involving journeys to Constantinople to receive the blessing of the Byzantine patriarch, and it was on one such that Pimen suddenly died, leaving Cyprian as the only claimant. He was buried at Chalcedon, and although his name was included among the saints in the seventeenth century, the appropriateness of this has been questioned.

Pimen of Novgorod, archbishop, died Tula, 25 September 1571. Russian Church. A monk probably of the monastery of St Cornelius Belozerskij, he became archbishop of Novgorod in November 1553. It was he who discovered the remains of **Nicetas of Nogorod**, the source of many miracles. In 1570 Ivan the Terrible removed him from his post and exiled him to a monastery, where he died of starvation.

Pimen of Rostov, hermit, died Rostov, sixteenth century. Russian Church. A recluse who lived in a hermitage dependent on the monastery of the Epiphany at Rostov. He lived on an island, and wore chains around his body. Feast 23 May.

Pimen of Vernyj, bishop and martyr, born Vailevskoe, near Novgorod, 5 November 1879, died Vernyj (modern Almaty), 16 September 1918. Baptized Peter Zacharovic Belikov and the son of a priest, he studied in Novgorod and Kiev, becoming a monk with the name Pimen in 1903, and a priest the following year. He was sent as a missionary to Urmija in Persia, where he worked with great success until 1911, when he was brought back to

Russia, made archimandrite and assigned to the seminary of Archdonsk. He went back to Urmija the following year, but in 1914 was made rector of the seminary at Perm. As such he was one of the leaders of a nationalist movement which saw the renewal of the Russian people through the Church. In 1916 he was consecrated bishop to oversee the mission in Urmija, but the following year he went to Vernyj. After the Russian Revolution he vigorously opposed socialism and the decrees of the Soviet government in general, as a consequence of which he was arrested and summarily executed. His place of burial is unknown; a pilgrimage developed, however, to the place of his execution.

Pimen of Zographou, born Sofia, died monastery of Cerepis, near Sofia, 3 November 1618. Bulgarian Church. Baptized Paul, at the age of 16 he entered the Bulgarian monastery of Zographou on Mount Athos, where he attained fame for his sanctity, as well as for his talents as a copyist and an icon painter – talents which gave rise to jealousy among his fellow monks. He was ordained priest, but lived for 15 years in a small house on the monastery's property. He decided, because of a vision, to return to his native land, where he is said to have helped decorate some 300 churches as he travelled around.

Pimen Salos, monk, thirteenth century. Georgian Church. He was a monk at the Davidgaregi monastery, and then became a missionary among the people of the northern Caucasus, where he lived in a cave hollowed out of rock. Feast 16 March.

Pimen the Faster, monk, born Kiev (?), died there, twelfth century. Although it happened many miles away, he announced the death of his friend **Kuksa**. Feast 27 August.

Pimen the Ill, monk, born Kiev, died there, 1110. Russian Church. A monk of the Kievan Cave monastery, the community hesitated to receive him because of his illness, which lasted until shortly before his death. Feast 7 August.

Pinhas, martyr, died Awsar, near Cizre, fourth/fifth centuries. Syriac Church. He is said to have lived for 30 years as a hermit on the White Mountain (al-Gabal al-Abiad) before being martyred. He died on 28 April, but the year is unknown.

Pinianus, see **Melania the Younger**.

Pinitus, bishop, died Knossos, Crete, *c.* 180. Bishop of Knossos. Feast 10 October.

Pio, Padre, see **Pius Forgione of Pietrelcina**.

Pionius, martyr. Died Smyrna, *c.* 250, during the Decian persecution, having been arrested while celebrating the anniversary of the martyrdom of St **Polycarp**. Pionius's death is described in *Acta Pionii*, allegedly recorded by eyewitnesses and known to Eusebius as a reliable document. Although not to be identified as the author of the legendary *Life of St Polycarp* (400), he may well be the Pionius mentioned at the end of the *Martyrdom of St Polycarp*. Feast 1 February.

Pior, monk, born Egypt, died Scete, *c.* 395. A disciple of **Anthony**, he became a priest in Nitria. Feast 17 January.

Pior the Hermit, monk, died Kiev, thirteenth or fourteenth century. Nothing is known of him, except that he lived as a recluse. Feast 28 August.

Pirminius, abbot, died Hornbach (?), *c.* 753. A Visigoth refugee from Aquitaine or Spain during the Moorish invasions, according to a ninth-century *vita*, Pirminius founded Reichenau (*c.* 724) and other monasteries among the Alemanni in Baden and Alsace, which became important centres of religious and cultural development. He is regarded as the author of *Dicta Pirminii*, or *Scarapsus*, a brief account of salvation history which circulated widely in Carolingian times; it contains the earliest commentary on the present form of the Apostles' Creed. Feast 3 November.

Pisentius of Armant, monk, born Armant, Qina province, fourth/fifth centuries. Coptic Church. A carpenter by trade, he converted to Christianity and became a monk. He gathered around him 35 disciples, among whom was **Patasius**. His brother was the bishop **John of Armant**. He died on 13 July, but the year is unknown.

Pisentius of Armant, bishop, born Armant, died Isna, *c.* 630 (?). Coptic Church. He was sent to be educated by his uncle, who was abbot of the monastery of Tud. He joined the monastery, and some years later was elected bishop of Armant. Later still he was also given charge of the diocese of Isna, vacant because of the Persian occupation of Egypt, and it was there that he died on 16 December, although the year is uncertain.

Pisentius of Coptos (Qift), bishop, born Sabra, near Armant, *c.* 569, died Coptos, 7 July 632. Coptic Church. He came from a fairly well-off family, and as a young man looked after the family's herds. He then became a monk at the monastery of Febamone, before becoming a hermit, with three followers. In 598 he became bishop of Coptos. He was particularly concerned to improve the standard of the clergy. He was renowned for miracles.

Pitirim of Perm and Ust-Vym, bishop, born Jaroslavl, died Ust-Vym, 19 August 1455. Russian Church. The successor of **Gerasimus of Perm**, he lived for a time in Moscow, where he baptized the future Ivan III, and was archimandrite of the monastery of St Michael the Archangel. As bishop he suffered, as had Gerasimus, from incursions of brigands and pagan tribes – on one occasion his residence and the cathedral were sacked and the sacred vessels stolen. The situation was made worse by the troubles brought by warring factions among the Russian princes. He was, however, successful at converting at least some of the pagans in the region, and hostility gradually declined. Nevertheless, he was martyred on the orders of one of the tribal leaders just after celebrating a *Te Deum* in a field to mark the end of a drought. Feast 29 January.

Pitirim of Tambov, bishop, born 1644, died Tambov, 28 July 1698. Russian Church. Baptized Procopius, he was archimandrite of the monastery of St John at Vjazma, near Smolensk, from 1677 until he was appointed to the bishopric of Tambov in 1685. This was still something of a frontier diocese, dwelt in by pagans and deported criminals as well as Old Believers. He built churches, convents and monasteries, and engaged in missionary activity among the non-Christians. He also used to retire to a cell in the Treguljavy monastery.

Pitirun, monk, died Thebaid, *c.* 410. A disciple of **Anthony**, he later became head of a monastic community. Feast 29 November.

Pius I, pope from *c.* 140, born Aquileia, died Rome, 155 (?). Both Eusebius and **Jerome** place his accession in the fifth year of Antonius Pius (142), and his reign at 15 years. According to the *Muratorian Fragment*, he was a brother of Hermas, author of the *Shepherd*, an account of a series of revelations made to Hermas by different heavenly visitors. There is no evidence for the tradition that Pius died a martyr. Feast 11 July (suppressed 1969).

Pius V, pope from 1566, born Bosco Marengo, Lombardy, 17 January 1504, died Rome, 1 May 1572. Baptized Antonio Ghislieri and ordained a Dominican in 1528, taking the new name Michele, he made a career in the Inquisition, which led to him becoming a cardinal and Inquisitor General of Christendom (1558). **Charles Borromeo** assisted him to be elected as Pius IV's successor. He worked zealously for the reform of the Church and compelled bishops and clergy to accept the recommendations of the Council of Trent. He struggled against the spread of the Reformation, encouraged the Spanish invasion of England, and famously excommunicated Queen Elizabeth I (1570) when she imprisoned Mary Stuart. He succeeded in forming the alliance of Spain and Venice which defeated the Ottoman Turks at Lepanto in 1571. Feast 30 April.

Pius IX, bl., pope from 1848, born Senigallia, Italy, 13 May 1792, died Rome, 7 February 1878. Baptized Giovanni Maria Mastai Ferretti and of a noble family, he studied in Volterra and in Rome and was ordained in 1819. He remained in Rome, working in the papal administration, until he was appointed archbishop of Spoleto in 1827 and of Imola in 1832. He was made a cardinal in 1839. His election to the papacy in 1846 was widely welcomed because he was believed to be a modernizer, but attitudes to him changed after the uprisings in Rome in 1848, and he had to flee to Gaeta. In 1854 he proclaimed the dogma of the immaculate conception. In 1869–70 he held the First Vatican Council as Rome, the last bastion of the Papal States, fell to the Italian army. Feast 7 February.

Pius X, pope from 1903, born Riese, near Treviso, 1835, died Rome, 20 August 1914. Born Giuseppe Melchior Sarto, he succeeded Leo XIII and signified that his rule should be pastoral rather than political, as stated in his first encyclical, *E supremi Apostolatus*. However, political considerations forced themselves upon him, and he condemned the French proposal that, in separating Church and state (1905), the latter should control Church property. He thus secured independence from state interference. In the field of social policy, Pius laid down the principles of Catholic Action in *Il fermo proposito*, with the aim of restoring Christ to his rightful place within the home, the schools and society in general; social action and the labour question were integral to the total programme. He gave a lasting stimulus to the spiritual life of the faithful, and laid the foundations of the modern Liturgical Movement in his reform of the Breviary, and in his *motu proprio*, which restored Gregorian chant to its traditional place in the liturgy. Venerated as a saint in his lifetime, Pius XII canonized him in 1954. Feast 21 August.

Pius Brunone Lanteri, ven., founder, born Cuneo, Italy, 12 May 1759, died Pinerolo, Turin, 5 August 1830. Ill-health forced Lanteri to leave the Carthusians and he studied for the secular priesthood, receiving a laureate in theology at the university of Turin in 1782. He declined all preferments and devoted himself to apostolic and charitable work amongst students, seminarians, soldiers and workers. He was active in the Amicizia Christiana, an association founded by Nikolaus von Diessbach SJ, which utilized the press and secret meetings similar to Freemasonary. In 1815 Lanteri was co-founder of the Congregation of the Oblates of the Virgin Mary, approved by the Holy See in 1826 and numbering 200 centres by 1963. The cause for his beatification was introduced in Rome in 1952.

Pius Campidelli, bl., Passionist, born Trebbio, near Florence, 29 April 1868, died San Vito di Romagna, 2 November 1889. Baptized Luigi, he joined the Passionists aged 14. While still in his studies, he was taken ill with tuberculosis and died. He was beatified in 1985.

Pius Forgione of Pietrelcina, friar, born the son of a shepherd of Pietrelcina, Italy, 25 May 1887, died San Giovanni Rotondo, 23 September 1968. Having nurtured since the age of five the desire to consecrate himself to God for ever, Francesco Forgione entered the Capuchin Order at Morcone in 1903 and was ordained in 1910. He lived an uneventful life until he was assigned to the friary at San Giovanni Rotondo, where in 1918 he received the visible signs of the stigmata. Known as 'Padre Pio', he had to cope with suspicion, embarrassment and disciplinary action as a consequence of the phenomenon. The Vatican, cautious in its deliberations, forbade him to say mass publicly and restricted his activities for 13 years, until Pope Pius XI lifted the ban in 1933. He remained at San Giovanni for 50 years, attracting people from all over the world who came seeking spiritual favour, intercession and direction. His one monument is the hospital he founded, Casa Sollivo della Sofferenza. Pope John Paul II visited his tomb in 1987, and canonized him in 2002.

Placide Viel, bl., born Victoire Eulalie Jacqueline in Normandy, 1815, died there, 4 March 1877, beatified 1951. Joining the community started by **Mary Magdalen Postel** in 1833, she succeeded her as abbess in 1846. She accepted humiliation from opponents to avoid a damaging split before leading a great expansion of the order in France and abroad.

Placidus and Sigisbert, early eighth century. Sigisbert was a monk at the abbey of Luxeuil, in what is now northern France, worked as a missionary around the upper Rhine, and founded a hermitage at Disentis, in modern Switzerland. Placidus was an influential man, possibly a lawyer, and was a friend and supporter of Sigisbert. The ruler of Chur was unhappy about the Frankish influence of Sigisbert. He prevented the hermitage from becoming a monastery, and had Placidus murdered, c. 720. Sigisbert, who became abbot of the monastery, died some time after that. Feast 11 July.

Placidus Riccardi, bl., born Tomasso at Spoleto, Umbria, 24 June 1844, died Rome, 15 March 1915, beatified 1954. He joined the Benedictines in 1865, becoming a priest in 1871. He was the priest at Farfa monastery in the Sabine Hills for 20 years,

ministering to local people, nearby religious houses and pilgrims.

Placilla, empress, died Constantinople, 14 (?) September 385/6. Byzantine Church. The devout wife of the Emperor Theodosius and a generous distributor of alms to the poor.

Plato of Ancyra, martyr, died Ancyra (Ankara, Turkey), 306. Feast 22 July.

Plato of Constantinople, hegumenos, born Constantinople, 732, died there, 4 April 813. From a wealthy family, he became a monk in the Symboleon monastery on Mount Olympus in Bithynia, before moving to the Sukkodion monastery near Constantinople, of which he became hegumenos. He was a vigorous opponent of iconoclasm and was several times exiled, but was allowed to return. He retired from direction of the monastery in 794, appointing as his successor **Theodore the Studite**.

Platonides, deaconess, died Nisibis, 308 (?). She founded a women's monastery at Nisibis. Feast 6 April.

Plutarch and Companions, martyrs, born Alexandria, died there, 202. They were members of the catechetical school in Alexandria. Feast 28 June.

Podius, bishop, died 1002. Son of the margrave of Tuscany, he joined the Augustinians and was bishop of Florence 990–1002. Feast 28 May.

Podlasie, Martyrs of, see **Vincent Lewoniuk and Companions**.

Poemen, see **Pimen**.

Polius, see **Timothy**.

Pollion, martyr, born Cybalae (Vinkovci, Croatia), died there, 304 (?). Died by being burned alive. Feast 28 April.

Polycarp, martyr, born c. 70, died Smyrna, 23 February c. 155. One of the Apostolic Fathers, Polycarp links together the apostolic age and that of nascent Catholicism. St **Irenaeus** says in a letter to Florinus that Polycarp 'had intercourse with

John (the Apostle or Elder), and with the rest of those who had seen the Lord'. John later made him bishop of Smyrna. Other sources for his life are the *Epistle of Polycarp to the Church at Philippi*, wherein he describes his visit to the bishop **Anicetus** at Rome and their discussions with regard to Quartodeciman celebration of the festival of Easter; the *Epistle of Ignatius the Martyr to Polycarp*; and the *Epistle of the Church at Smyrna to the Church at Philomelium*, one of the most precious texts of the second century, which gives an account of the martyrdom of Polycarp on a burning pyre. Feast 23 February.

Polycarp and Theodore, martyrs, died Antioch, Syria. Feast 7 December.

Polycarp of Brjansk, monk, died Brjansk, 1620/21. Russian Church. Baptized Peter Ivanovic Borjatinskij, he came of a princely family, and had a career in politics, diplomacy and the army before falling from favour in 1591 and being sent to Tjumen. In 1599, however, he moved to Brjansk and became a monk. He founded in that city the monastery of the Transfiguration, where he died. Feast 23 February.

Polychronius of Babylon, martyr, died 250 (?). Said to have been bishop of Babylon, in Persia. Feast 17 February.

Polychronius of Ganphanetus, martyr, died Ganphanetus, c. 350. He was a lector who showed such zeal against Arian heretics that he was ordained priest, but was later attacked and killed by the heretics. Feast 7 October.

Polydore Plasden, martyr, born London, 1563, executed there, 10 December 1591. Ordained at the English College, Rheims, in 1586, Plasden returned to the English mission and laboured in Sussex. He went to London and, with **Edmund Gennings**, was arrested while saying mass in the house of **Swithin Wells**. Condemned for high treason, he protested his loyalty to Queen Elizabeth, while remaining faithful to his religious convictions. Sir Walter Raleigh, who supervised the execution, ordered leniency, directing that Polydore be hanged until dead before dismemberment began.

Polyeuctus, patriarch, born Constantinople, died there, 970. He was bishop of Constantinople from 956. Feast 5 February.

Polyeuctus, Candidianus and Philoromos, martyrs, died Alexandria, third century (?).

Polyeuctus of Melitene, martyr, born Melitene, Armenia, died there, third century. From a Greek family, he was a soldier in the Roman army and a convert to Christianity. His friends and relatives attempted to persuade him to give up the faith, but he remained steadfast, and was tortured and beheaded with his friend Nearchus. He became the subject of Corneille's tragedy *Polyeucte*. Feast 7 January.

Polyeuctus the Younger, patriarch, born Constantinople, died there, 970. Byzantine Church. He was a monk in Constantinople before becoming patriarch in 956. It was he who baptized **Olga**, princess of Kiev, who visited Constantinople during his patriarchate, and thus opened the way for the conversion of Russia. Feast 5 February.

Polyeuctus, Victorinus and Donatus, martyrs, died Caesarea, Cappadocia. Feast 21 May.

Pompeius and Companions, martyrs, died Carthage, 250. A group of some 50 martyrs who died by decapitation. Feast 10 April.

Pompilio Pirrotti, born Montecalvo Irpino, Campania, Italy, 1710, died Campi Salentina, near Lecce, 15 July 1756. Domenico Pirrotti joined the Clerks Regular of the Religious Schools, also known as 'Piarists' or Scolpini. He took the name Pompilio Maria when he was professed in 1728, and he was ordained priest in 1732. He moved around Italy, preaching and hearing confessions, but in Naples the local clergy took objection to his success and persuaded the king that, because of his popularity, he was politically dangerous. He was exiled, but public outcry forced the king to recall him. Pompilio worked to spread devotion to the Sacred Heart, and founded a confraternity in Montecalvo in its honour. He was sent to the Congregation's house in Campi Salentina in 1765, and died the following year.

Pomposa, see **Columba and Pomposa**.

Pontian, pope, elected 21 July 230, born Rome, died Sardinia, 28 September 235. The *Liber pontificalis* refers to him as a Roman, son of Calpurnius; Eusebius says he reigned for six years. Little else is known of his origins or activities, except that he must have presided over the Roman synod which approved the condemnation of Origen by Demetrius, bishop of Alexandria, in 230. Exiled to the mines of Sardinia by Maximilian Thrax in 235, along with the antipope **Hippolytus**, he died the same year of harsh treatment on the 'island of death'. The bodies of both were returned to Rome and buried by Pope Fabian in the Catacombs of St **Callixtus**. Feast 11 August.

Pontian, martyred Spoleto, Italy, *c.*169. He was put to death by the sword under Marcus Aurelius. Feast 19 January.

Pontius, biographer of St **Cyprian**, born north Africa, died Carthage, *c.* 260. Cyprian's deacon at Carthage, Pontius followed him into exile at Curubis. According to St **Jerome**, Pontius wrote *Vita et Passio Cypriani*, the latter's earliest biography. Feast 8 March.

Pontius, died Avignon, 1087. He was abbot of St Andrew's. Feast 26 March.

Pontius of Faucigny, abbot, born in the Savoy, died Sixt, 26 November 1178. Of a noble family of the Savoy, he became a canon regular at Chablais, then founded another monastery at Sixt, which formally became an abbey in 1155.

Poppo of Stavelot, abbot, born Deinze, 978, died Marchienne-au-Pont, 25 January 1048. After a career in the army and pilgrimages to the Holy Land, Poppo became a monk at the monastery of St Thierry, near Rheims. He was invited to join the abbey of St-Vanne and to undertake reform of several abbeys in Flanders and Lorraine. He succeeded to the abbatial see of Stavelot-Malmédy in 1020. He was admired by the Emperor Henry II, and served him as a political adviser. Feast 23 January.

Porcarius and Companions, martyrs, died monastery of Lérins, *c.* 732. Porcarius was the abbot of the monastery. When Saracen pirates were sighted he evacuated the youngest monks and students from the island – which is opposite Cannes in Provence – but he and 500 or so monks were massacred. Feast 12 August.

Porphyry of Caesarea, martyr, died Caesarea, Palestine, 309. He was martyred after protesting that the bodies of some other Christian martyrs should not be left without burial. His courage gave rise to the martyrdom of St **Seleucus**. Feast 16 February.

Porphyry of Gaza, ascetic and bishop, born Thessalonika, *c.* 347, died Gaza, 26 February 420. Porphyry had been a monk in Egypt for ten years, according to Mark the Deacon, and in Palestine before being ordained in 392 and named bishop of Gaza, a hotbed of paganism. He tirelessly instructed his people, won many converts and succeeded, with help from Empress Eudoxia, in repressing the persecutions in his diocese. Feast 26 February.

Porphyry the Mime, martyr, born Ephesus, died Alexandria (?), fourth century. A 'jester' in the service of the governor of Alexandria. He became a Christian and, when it was demanded that he abjure the faith, he refused and was beheaded. Feast 4 November.

Possidius, bishop, born north Africa, *c.* 370, died Mirandola, near Mantua (?), *c.* 440. One of **Augustine**'s first disciples at Hippo, Possidius became bishop of Calama in Numidia (*c.* 400), and helped Augustine in his struggle against Donatism and Pelagianism. They were lifelong friends. Possidius attended Augustine when he died at Hippo in 430, and wrote a short but valuable sketch of the great bishop. The Vandal invasion drove him first from Calama to Hippo, and then to Italy. Feast 16 May.

Potamine, martyr, died Alexandria, 304 (?). A slave girl. Feast 7 June.

Potamius and Nemesius, martyrs, died Cyprus or Alexandria. Feast 20 February.

Potamon (Potamion), bishop and martyr, died Egypt, c. 340. Bishop of Herakles, Upper Egypt, sent to the mines for his faith in 310, he was freed under Constantine, lame and blind in one eye. He attended the Councils of Nicaea and Tyre. A supporter of **Athanasius**, he died after Arians attacked him. Feast 18 May.

Pothinus, bishop and martyr, born Asia Minor, c. 87, died Lyon, 177. The first bishop of Lyon, Pothinus is said to have been a disciple of St **Polycarp**, who sent him to Gaul in the mid-second century. Taken in the persecution under Marcus Aurelius, he died in prison aged 90, after being maltreated and stoned. Feast 2 June.

Praecordius, hermit, sixth century. Lived in what is now Belgium. Feast 1 February.

Praejectus, martyred Volvic, central France, 676. Educated by **Genesius**, and an active bishop of Auvergne from 666, he may have reported a bad local ruler to the king, who executed the man. Friends of this man murdered Praejectus while he was travelling back from the king's court. Feast 25 January.

Prandota, bl., bishop of Krakow, born Bealaczóv, Poland, early thirteenth century, died Krakow, 21 September 1266. Little is known of his early life, except that he seems to have studied abroad and on his return became a canon of Sandomierz. As bishop of Krakow from 1242, he did much to secure the canonization of St **Stanislaus** in 1255, an event which bolstered national unity and put an end to in-fighting among the princes. He was also eager to encourage missionary activity, although in this he had, for political reasons, less success. He also encouraged the growth of religious orders in his vast diocese, and was renowned for his generosity to the needy. His tomb in the cathedral at Krakow quickly became, and long remained, a centre of pilgrimage.

Praxedes (Prassede), martyr, born Rome, died there, second century. Her spurious *Acta* has it that Praxedes sheltered Christians during the persecution of Marcus Aurelius, and that she and St Prudentiana were sisters, since she is buried next to her in the Catacomb of Priscilla. It is a recorded

fact that her remains were transferred to the church of St Praxeda built by Pope Paschal I (817–24). Feast 21 July.

Primus, see also **Cyrinus**.

Primus and Felician, martyrs, born Rome, died there, c. 297. They were two brothers of the Roman nobility who had devoted themselves to the care of Christians, especially those in prison. They were executed just outside Rome by beheading. Feast 9 June.

Primus, Cyril and Secundarius, martyrs, died Antioch, Syria. Feast 2 October.

Priscus and Companions, born Africa, died Italy. Priscus died Capua (?), c. 450. He is said to have been an African bishop, possibly of Castra, who was set adrift with his priests in a boat without a rudder by the Vandals. The priests are named as Tammarus, Rosius, Heraclius, Secundinus, Adjutor, Mark, Augustus, Elpidius, Canion and Vindonius. The story is that they reached Italy, where he became bishop of Capua. Feast 11 February.

Priscus, Malchus and Alexander, martyrs, died Caesarea, Palestine, 260. They were thrown to wild beasts during public games. Feast 28 March.

Privatus, bishop and martyr, died Gévaudan, France, 260. He was beaten to death by barbarians. Feast 21 August.

Probus of Rieti (central Italy), bishop, died c. 570. **Gregory the Great** describes him seeing two saints, **Juvenal** and **Eleutherius**, in a vision as he was dying. Feast 15 January.

Proclus and Hilarion, martyrs, died Ancyra (Ankara, Turkey), 115. Feast 12 July.

Proclus of Constantinople, patriarch, born Constantinople, died there, 24 July 447. Consecrated bishop of Cyzicus in 426, Proclus could not occupy his see and remained in Constantinople as a popular preacher; he delivered a famous sermon on the *Theotokos* (the one who gave birth to God), which Nestorius said did not accord with the full humanity of Christ, and himself proposed

Christotokos in its place. Elected patriarch in 434, Proclus gained popular support by his moderate view of Orthodoxy, although he attacked the beliefs and morals of the Jews in classical fashion. He is said to have introduced the Trisagion – 'Holy God, Holy and strong, Holy and immortal, have mercy on us' – as a feature of Orthodox worship. Feast 24 October.

Procopius, see also **Basil**.

Procopius, martyr, born Varna, Bulgaria, died Smyrna, 25 June 1810. Byzantine Church. At the age of 20 he became a monk on Mount Athos, but did not stay. He eventually found himself in Smyrna, where he became a Muslim. He almost immediately regretted his decision, confessed his failing, and returned to Christianity, as a consequence of which he was executed.

Procopius of Caesarea ('the Great'), martyr, born Scythopolis, Palestine (Beth Shean), died Caesarea, 303. A reader in the church at Scythopolis, and an interpreter of Syriac. He was beheaded under Diocletian, the first martyr of that persecution in Palestine. Feast 8 July.

Procopius of Sazava, abbot, born Bohemia, died Sazava, near Prague, 1053. He was educated in Prague, married, became a priest of the Byzantine rite, and eventually canon of the cathedral in Prague. He later became a hermit, and later still founded a Basilian monastery at Sazava. Feast 4 July.

Procopius of Ustjansk, bl., seventeenth century. Russian Church. Nothing is known of him, but his relics, at Ustjansk, were the source of many miracles. Feast 8 July.

Procopius of Ustjug, miracle worker, born Lubeck, died Ustjug, 8 July 1303. Russian Church. He was originally a merchant whose affairs took him to Novgorod. He was very attracted by the rites of the Russian Church, and was received into it, giving away all his wealth and becoming a monk at the monastery of Chutyn. Such was the fame of this conversion that crowds of people came to see him in Novgorod. He therefore left the city for Ustjug, where he became friendly with **Cyprian of Ustjug**.

During the day he would wander around the streets in bare feet, and at night he would pray outside the churches. He was a worker of miracles, and had the gift of prophecy.

Procopius of Vjatka, bl., born near Vjatka, 1578, died 1627. Russian Church. He left home at the age of 20 and lived in Vjatka as a 'fool for Christ'. Feast 21 December.

Procorus and Bassianus, monks, sixteenth century. Russian Church. They were founders of the hermitage of the Saviour by the river Jastreba, near Vladimir. Procorus died on 8 July 1592, and was followed by Bassianus. Feast 23 June.

Procorus and Companions, martyrs, died Vjazniki, seventeenth century. Church of the Old Believers. A group of monks fled to the forests of Vjazniki, near Vladimir, to escape the persecution of those who resisted the liturgical reforms of the Patriarch Nikon. In 1665 an expedition was launched to deal with this group. Procorus, the leader, died just as they arrived at his cell. Babila, who was a convert to Orthodoxy from Western European Protestantism, was one of the firmest opponents of the reform. He was captured, imprisoned, and finally burned to death. Feast 3 January.

Procorus of Jurev Gora, monk, seventeenth century. Russian Church. Known only through the life of **Diodorus**, he apparently lived with Diodorus when he sought solitude at Jurev Gora.

Procorus of Kiev, died Kiev, 1107. Russian Church. He was renowned for eating only bitter bread, but during time of scarcity – because of invasions – he distributed his bread to the needy, and it tasted sweet, for which he was regarded as a miracle worker. Feast 10 February.

Procorus of Pcinja, hermit, born near the present Stip, in Macedonia, eleventh century. Rather than marry, he left home and became a hermit in a cave by the river Pcinja, in northern Macedonia, where he lived for 32 years. Then, because his fame was growing, he retired even further into a remote forest. Feast 15 January.

Procorus of Rostov, bishop, died Jaroslavl, 7 September 1328. Russian Church. In 1314 he founded a monastery near Jaroslavl where an icon had been found, dedicated to the Transfiguration, of which he became hegumenos. In 1322 he was instrumental in saving the city of Rostov from invasion by Tartars. He was close to **Peter**, who was metropolitan of Russia and a strong supporter of Moscow becoming the effective centre of the nation. Procorus promoted his canonization, not least by writing a life of the metropolitan. After Peter's death he was effectively governing the Church in Russia until a new metropolitan could be appointed, and in that capacity consecrated the cathedral of the Dormition in Moscow. Feast 7 September.

Procorus the Georgian, monk, died near Jerusalem, 12 February 1066. Georgian Church. As a young man he joined the monastery of Zqarostavi in southern Georgia. After some years he went on pilgrimage to the Holy Land, where he stayed in the monastery of St Sabas, and began himself to build a monastery in Jerusalem, which he named the Holy Cross. He began building c. 1025, and it was completed in 1058. He was joined by some 80 Georgian monks, and became the hegumenos, but in 1061 he resigned and went to live as a hermit in the desert of Arnon. Feast 17 January.

Proculus, Ephebus and Apollonius, martyrs, died Terni, Umbria, 273. Proculus may be identical with a fourth-century martyr of that name, said to have been bishop of Terni. Feast 14 February.

Proculus of Bologna, bishop and martyr, born Bologna, died there, c. 542. He was martyred by Arian Goths, two years after being elected bishop. Feast 1 June.

Proculus of Terni, martyr, died early fourth century, under Maxentius. He was supposed to have been bishop of Terni, but there is no authority for this – he may be the third-century martyr of that name, commemorated on 14 February. Feast 14 April.

Proculus the Soldier, martyr, died Bologna (?), c. 304. A soldier in the army of Diocletian. Feast 1 June.

Prosper of Aquitaine, theologian, born Aquitaine, c. 390, died Rome, after 463. At Marseilles, Prosper defended **Augustine** against the Pelagians, and the opposition to his teachings on grace and predestination current among the disciples of **John Cassian**. In reply Augustine wrote *De praedestinatione sanctorum*, and *De dono perseverantiae*. After Augustine's death (430), he sought **Celestine I**'s support for Augustinian doctrines, in defence of which he published a number of works, as well as against **Vincent of Lérins** and Cassian. After the latter's death (c. 435) he modified his strict Augustinianism, rejected predestination to damnation, and affirmed the will of God to save all men, although he believed in fact that a great number could not attain salvation. Feast 25 June.

Prosper of Reggio, bishop, died Reggio nell'Emilia, Italy, 25 June 466. He was bishop for 22 years, and is reputed to have given away all his possessions to the poor, but little else is known of him.

Protadius (Prothadius), bishop, died Besançon, c. 624. He was bishop of Besançon. Feast 10 February.

Protasius Chong, martyred Korea, 1839 – see **Martyrs of Korea**. Feast 20 May.

Proterius, patriarch, martyr, born Alexandria (?), died there, 28 February 458. He was imposed as patriarch after Dioscorus was removed from office because of his opposition to the Council of Chalcedon. Proterius inherited a divided city, and when imperial protection faltered, he was stabbed to death.

Protogenes, bishop, born Carrhae, Syria (Altinbasak, Turkey), died there, fourth century. He was a priest who was sent into exile because of his opposition to Arianism, but was recalled towards the end of the fourth century, and became the city's bishop. Feast 6 May.

Protonice, queen, first century. Syriac Church. She is venerated in the Syriac Church as the wife of the Emperor Claudius. Before her marriage she became a Christian and travelled to Jerusalem, when James was still bishop, and there discovered the true cross.

Protus, see also **Cantius**.

Protus and Hyacinth, martyrs, died Rome. There is no date for their deaths, except that, according to the inscription on his tomb, Hyacinth was buried on 11 September. The charred remains of Protus have been found, which suggests that he may have been burned to death. Feast 11 September.

Provinus, bishop, born Gaul, died Como, Italy, *c.* 420. A disciple of **Ambrose of Milan**, he succeeded **Felix** as bishop of Como in 391. Feast 8 March.

Prudentius, bishop, born Spain, died Troyes, 6 April 861. Prudentius became chaplain at the court of Louis the Pious, and bishop of Troyes *c.* 843. In the controversy on predestination, he defended the monk **Gottschalk of Orbais** against **Hincmar**, with *Epistola ad Hincmarum*; he taught the 'Augustinian' doctrine of double predestination, and wrote a treatise entitled *Praedestinatione contra Joannem Scotium (Erigena)*, whom Hincmar had called to his aid. He also wrote a continuation of the *Annales Bertiniani* for the years 835–61, valuable for the history of the Frankish Empire. Feast suppressed.

Psoi, monk, born Absunah, died Mount Atripe, fifth century. Coptic Church. He was a shepherd living a rather dissolute life, but when taken gravely ill he promised to reform were he to be cured – as he was. He then became a monk on the mountain of Atripe. His spiritual guide was Pgol, the uncle of **Senuti of Atripe**, and he, Senuti and Pgol formed a small community. He died on 30 January, but the year is unknown.

Psoi of Scete, monk, born Sansah, died Antinoë (Ansina), 2 June 417. Coptic Church. He became a monk when aged 20 or so in the desert of Scete, eventually settling in a cave beside what became the monastery of al-Suryan. In 407 he had to flee from Scete because of barbarian invasions, and went to Antinoë, where he lived with **Paul of Tamma** until his death.

Psoi of Tud, monk, died mountain of Tud. Coptic Church. He became a monk as a young man, and died on the mountain of Tud, south of Thebes,

where he was buried. Many miracles were associated with his tomb.

Ptolemy, Coptic martyr, see also **Apaiule and Ptolemy**.

Ptolemy, bishop, died Minuf al-Ulya, Egypt, seventh/eighth century. Coptic Church. He was a fellow monk with the future patriarch **Simon I**, who, after his election, made him bishop of Minuf al-Ulya. Feast 16 July.

Publia, died Antioch, 362. She established a small community in her house. It happened that she and her community were singing as the Emperor Julian the Apostate passed, and he thought the words of the psalm were deriding him. Julian said he would have them executed on his return, but he was killed in battle with the Persians before he could do so. Feast 9 October.

Publius, bishop, martyred *c.* 212. Traditionally, he was the man described in Acts who befriended Paul after his shipwreck on Malta and was killed under Trajan. He may have been the first bishop of Malta, or possibly bishop of Athens. Feast 21 January.

Publius, Julian and Companions, martyrs, died Africa. Feast 19 February.

Publius of Athens, bishop, second century. An opponent of the Montanists. Otherwise nothing is known of him. Feast 12 November.

Publius of Zeugma, abbot, born Zeugma (Belkis, Turkey), died there, 380. The son of a senator, he gave away all his possessions and became a hermit. A community grew up around him, which he divided into two – one being Greek, the other Syriac-speaking – and for whom he developed a strict Rule of life. Feast 25 January.

Pudentiana, martyr, born Rome, died there, second century. According to the Roman martyrology, a Roman virgin of the early Church, a daughter of St Pudens and the sister of St **Praxedes**. The cult seems to rest on a mistaken interpretation of Pudentiana as a noun rather than an adjective, denoting the founder of *ecclesia*

Pudentiana in Rome as St Pudens. The *Acta* of Ss Pudentiana and Praxedes, printed by the Bollandists, are not earlier than the eighth century. Feast 19 May.

Pulcheria, Byzantine empress, born Constantinople, 19 January 399, died there, July 453. The daughter of Emperor Arcadius, elder sister of **Theodosius the Younger** and a woman of uncommon ability and deep piety, Pulcheria had made a vow of virginity, and led a secluded life away from the court. A strong defender of Orthodoxy, she induced her brother, Theodosius, to condemn Nestorianism (two separate persons in the incarnate Christ), and received a letter of gratitude from **Cyril of Alexandria**. On the death of her brother (450) she became empress, took the aged senator **Marcian** as her consort, and forthwith organized a General Council to meet at Chalcedon in 451; she attended the sixth session in person. She has been venerated as a saint since the Middle Ages. Feast 10 September.

Qasis of Hah, monk, sixth century. Syriac Church. Feast 15 September.

Qawestos, monk, thirteenth/fourteenth centuries. Coptic Church. A cousin of **Takla Haymanot**, he was one of the 12 selected to evangelize parts of Ethiopia – he was sent to the Mahgel.

Qawma, born Mayperqat, died near Tikrit (?), sixth/seventh century. Syriac Church. He was baptized Simeon, became a monk, but then went to live in a tree, which he did until he was 90.

Qayyuma of Baz, monk, fourth/fifth centuries. Syriac Church. He evangelized the region of Baz, in the Hakkari, where his shrine remains at Swa'uta.

Quadratus, second century. Very little is known of him, except that he wrote an apology, or defence, of Christianity addressed to the Emperor Hadrian. Feast 26 May.

Quadratus of Corinth and Companions, martyrs, died Corinth, 258. Feast 10 March. Feast 26 March.

Quadratus of Magnesia, first century. Said to have been a contemporary with the apostles. Feast 21 September.

Quadratus of Utica, bishop, third century. Bishop of Utica in north Africa, and praised by St **Augustine**, but otherwise nothing is known of him. Feast 21 August.

Quadratus, Theodosius, Emmanuel and Companions, martyrs, died Asia Minor, 304. Quadratus was a bishop, who died with 42 companions.

Quartus, martyr, born Capua, died Rome, fourth century. He was executed with **Quintus**, also from Capua and commemorated today. Feast 10 May.

Quentin, martyr, died St Quentin, northern France. Possibly the son of a Roman senator, and a missionary to the region around Amiens. Feast 31 October.

Quinidius, bishop, died Vaison, Provence, *c.* 579. He was a hermit at Aix before becoming bishop of Vaison. Feast 15 February.

Quinta, martyr, born Alexandria (?), died there, 249. She is said to have been martyred by being dragged behind a horse. Feast 8 February.

Quintianus, bishop, died Seleucia, fourth century (?).

Quintianus and Irenaeus, martyrs, died Armenia. Feast 1 April.

Quintilius, bishop and martyr, died Nicomedia. Feast 8 March.

Quintius, died Lipari, *c.* 284. Feast 2 March.

Quintus, see **Quartus**.

Quiriacus, priest of Trier, fourth century. Feast 6 March.

Quiricus and Julitta, martyrs, born Iconium (Konya, Turkey), died Tarsus, 304. Julitta is said to have been a widowed noblewoman, and Quiricus her small son. He was beaten to death because he had scratched the face of the magistrate. She was executed immediately afterwards for her faith. Feast 16 June.

Quirinus, martyr, died Rome, *c.* 269. All that is known is that he was killed under Claudius II and buried by the Persians **Marius, Martha and companions**, who were themselves killed for this. Feast 25 March.

Quirinus of Siscia, bishop and martyr, born Siscia (Siseck, Croatia) (?), died Sabaria (Szombathely, Hungary), 308. He is said to have fled his city to escape persecution, but was captured and taken to Sabaria, where, having refused to abjure Christianity, he was drowned. Feast 4 June.

Quiteria, martyr, died Aire, fifth century. Her unreliable story says that she fled from her father, a prince of Galicia, who wanted her to marry and renounce Christianity. He had her pursued and beheaded. She is greatly venerated in the ancient province of Navarre, now south-west France and northern Spain. Feast 22 May.

Quna of Edessa, bishop, born Edessa, died there (?), *c.* 313. He was bishop from 303 to his death, and was responsible for the city's cathedral.

Quodvultdeus, bishop, born Carthage (?), died Naples, *c.* 450. Bishop of Carthage, he was exiled by the Arian king Genseric in 439. Feast 19 February.

Rabanus Maurus, monk and theologian, born Mainz, *c.* 780, died Winkel (Rhine), 4 February 856. Rabanus went to Tours *c.* 802, to study with **Alcuin** and St **Martin**. His literary output began in 810 with the poem *De laudibus sanctae crucis*; there followed *De institutione clericorum*, a manual for the use of priests, relying heavily on St **Augustine**, St **Gregory the Great** and **Isidore**; *De computo*, on the division of time and the date of Easter. He also wrote extensive commentaries on the Bible (Pentateuch, Ruth, Proverbs, Jeremias, Ezekiel, Wisdom, Matthew, the Pauline Epistles). Rabanus compiled his writings, as did Alcuin, with the help of pupils, and they are important for their role in the Carolingian Renaissance.

Rabbula, bishop, born Kenneshnu, near Aleppo, *c.* 350, died Edessa, 435. Syriac Church. Rabbula converted to Christianity and threw himself into Christian ascetic practices, sold his possessions and separated from his wife and kinsfolk. He lived for a time in a monastery, then as a hermit. Chosen to succeed Diogenes as bishop of Edessa on the latter's death in 411, he readily accepted without any of the customary show of reluctance. He ruled his diocese with extraordinary energy, insisted on discipline among the clergy and monks under his authority, and combated all heresies with fierce determination. A friend of **Cyril of Alexandria**, he translated his treatise *De recta fide* into Syriac. He died after 24 years of episcopal life, immensely lamented by his people. Feast 19 February.

Rabbulas, abbot, born Samosata (Samsat, Turkey), 476, died Constantinople, 530. He was well educated as a young man, but retreated into the mountains as a hermit before going to Phoenicia, where he founded a monastery. He eventually came to Constantinople, where he also founded a monastery. Feast 19 February.

Rachel, nun, born Dorogobuz, near Smolensk, 1833, died Borodino, 27 September 1928. Russian Church. Baptized Mary, she came from a wealthy, devout family. She determined to enter religious life, despite efforts by her parents to persuade her to marry. In 1851 she secretly left home and entered a convent at Smolensk. After seven years there she left the convent and went on pilgrimage around Russia, settling in 1872 at the convent of the Saviour at Borodino where, in 1915, she took the name Rachel. She was by this time the oldest member of the community, and much venerated for her prayer life, her visions and her skill as a spiritual director.

Radbod of Utrecht, monk and bishop, born Namur, *c.* 850, died Deventer in what is now Holland, 29 November 917. Educated at the court of Charles the Bald, Radbod became a monk, taught the famous Abbot Hugo and, in 900, became bishop of Utrecht. The Normans drove him out the following year and he went to nearby Deventer, from where he carried on his diocesan duties. He furthered the Utrecht tradition for learning, wrote poetry, history and a work on St **Martin**, and the Catholic university of Nijmegen bore his name until 1923. Renowned for charity and pastoral rule, Radbod tried to eradicate the traces of the Frisian pagans, of whom his great-grandfather had been the last king.

Radegund, queen of the Franks, 518–87, born Erfurt, died Poitiers, 13 August 587. Born a Thuringian princess, Radegund fell as booty, aged 12, to Theodoric, king of Austrasia, and Clothar I, king of Neustria, whom she married after six years of prayer in retirement. Clothar led a dissolute life, so Radegund left him in 555 and, with his help, founded a convent at Poitiers, where she had gathered some 200 high-born converts by 587. Radegund collected relics, notably one of the true cross, which gave the name Holy Cross to the convent. Having installed an abbess, she lived as a simple nun in her own community. She is said to have cured a blind man who attended her funeral, and her cult began immediately afterwards, bringing about her popular canonization.

Radegund, died Chelles, France, 680. Goddaughter to **Bathilde**, queen of France, they lived in Chelles monastery. Dying, Bathilde prayed that Radegund might die first so as not to be left alone in the world. The girl apparently fell ill and died the day before Bathilde. Feast 28 January.

Rainald of Bar, bl., abbot of Citeaux, died Provence, 1150. From the family of the counts of Bar-sur-Seine, Rainald joined the Cistercians at Clairvaux, and St **Bernard** nominated him abbot of Citeaux in 1133. Rainald helped to repair the rift that had developed between Bernard and Abelard. His only extant work is part of the *Instituta generalis capituli*, a collection of statutes published by his successor, Goswin, *c.* 1150. Feast 16 December.

Rainand of Ravenna, bl., archbishop, born Milan, *c.* 1250, died Ravenna, 18 August 1321. Boniface VIII entrusted Rainand with several important missions: bishop of Vicenza, legate on a peace mission to England and France in 1299, director of spiritual affairs in the Romagna, and archbishop of Ravenna in 1302. He was also papal commissioner for the investigation of the Knights Templar in central and northern Italy. **Pius IX** beatified him in 1852.

Rainerius, bishop and martyr, born Italy, died Split, modern Croatia, 1180. He was originally a Camaldolese monk, but was then appointed bishop of Cagli in 1156, and of Split in Dalmatia in 1175, where he was murdered while attempting to restore the property of the Church. Feast 4 August.

Rainerius of Arezzo, bl., Franciscan, born Arezzo, died Borgo San Sepolcro, 1 November 1304. Feast 12 November.

Ralph Ashley, see **Edward Oldcorne**.

Ralph Corby, bl., martyr, born Maynooth, near Dublin, died Tyburn, London, 7 September 1644. His family was English, and they returned to England when he was five years old. His father, mother and two sisters all entered religious orders, his father becoming a Jesuit, as did Ralph himself and his two brothers. He went on to the mission in England in 1632, and worked in County Durham until he was arrested while saying mass near Newcastle. He was sent to London with **John Duckett**, a diocesan priest arrested at about the same time. Both were held in Newgate, and hanged together at Tyburn.

Ralph Grimston, see **Peter Snow**.

Ralph Milner, see **Roger Dickenson and Ralph Milner**.

Ralph of Bourges, bishop, born Cahors (?), died Bourges, 21 June 866. He was the son of the count of Cahors, and entered the monastery of Solignac, near Limoges. He served as abbot to a number of different monasteries, including that of St-Medard at Soissons. He was appointed bishop of Bourges in 849, and made a number of monastic foundations of his own, including that of Sarrazc in Quercy. He was a learned man, and produced a book of instructions for the clergy of his diocese. He is also known to have written letters on points of Church law to the pope of the day.

Ralph of Fusteia, bl., founder, died near Rennes, 1289. Founder of the monastery of St Sulpice, near Rennes. Feast 16 August.

Ralph Sherwin, martyr, born Rodsley, Derbyshire, 1549, died London, 1 December 1581. After graduating from Oxford he went to Douai to become a priest, in 1577, and then moved on to Rome. He was in the party of **Edmund Campion**

which, in 1580, set out for England. He was arrested in London in November, was severely tortured, and then condemned to death alongside Campion.

Raphael Chylinsky, Franciscan, born Poznan, Poland, 1694, died Krakow, 2 December 1741. Baptized Melchior, when he was 21 he entered the Franciscans in Krakow and, although studying in Warsaw and elsewhere, he returned to Krakow to minister to the poor, the sick and the dying during one of the most difficult periods of Polish history, when the country was fought over by Germans, Russians and Swedes.

Raphael Guizar y Valencia, bl., bishop, born Cotija, Mexico, 26 April 1878, died Mexico City, 6 June 1938. As a pastor he worked in various regions of Mexico, but also in Cuba, Guatemala, Colombia and the Southern states of the USA. He became bishop of Veracruz in 1919.

Raphael Kalinowski, friar, born Vilnius, Lithuania (then Vilna, and in Russia), 1 September 1835, died Wadowice, Poland, 15 November 1907. The son of a professor of mathematics, and baptized Joseph, he studied agronomy for a while, but then went to the academy of military engineering in St Petersburg. As a lieutenant in the army he worked on the construction of a railway, and then was promoted to captain and sent to Brest-Litovsk. In the Polish rising of 1863 he joined the insurgents, was arrested and sent to Siberia for nine years. It was there that he finally decided to become a priest. He first worked in Paris as a tutor, then went to Graz in Austria where he became a Carmelite, taking the name Raphael. He was ordained in 1882. He held a number of offices in the order, including being prior in Wadowice, where he spent the last years of his life. He was well known for the holiness of his life, but also for his role in the uprising. He was canonized in 1991 by John Paul II, who had himself been born in Wadowice, and who had a particular affinity to the spirituality of the Carmelites.

Raphael of Agapia, monk, born Bursucani, province of Barlad (now Galati), c. 1560, died monastery of Agapia, c. 1640. Romanian Church.

Nothing is known of him, although he has been much venerated.

Raphael of Baanato, monk, sixteenth/seventeenth centuries. Serbian Church. He was originally a monk of the Chlendar monastery on Mount Athos, then moved to the monastery of Baanato (modern Zrenjanin), where his tomb was renowned for miracles. Feast 16 August.

Raphael of Thermi, bl., martyr, born Ithaca, c. 1405, died Thermi, 9 April 1463. Byzantine Church. Baptized George. He went to Athens, where he became a monk. After the fall of Constantinople he fled to Mytilini on Lesbos, where he entered the monastery at Thermi. He was put to death during a Turkish invasion of the island.

Raphaela Porras y Ayllón, foundress, born Pecho Abad, Córdoba, 1 March 1850, died Rome, 6 January 1925. The youngest of 13 children, Raphaela and her sister Dolores were the first novices of the Society of Mary Reparatrix (1875). They remained in Córdoba when the Society moved to Seville and founded the Handmaids of the Sacred Heart of Jesus, dedicated to perpetual adoration, teaching and catechetics. Rome approved the Society in 1886, and Raphaela became first superior general. By 1961 the Handmaids had 61 houses and more than 2,700 members. She was canonized in 1977.

Raphaela Ybarra de Villalonga, bl., born Bilbao, Spain, 1843, died there, 1900, beatified 1984. Married, she brought up her children and those of her dead sister. She opened centres for working girls, an orphanage, a shelter for unmarried mothers, and founded a congregation for this work. Feast 23 February.

Randoald, see **Germanus of Grandval**.

Raymond (Ramon) Lull, early missionary to Muslims, born Palma, Majorca, c. 1235, stoned to death, Bougie, Algiers, 29 June 1315. He spent his youth in the court of Aragon, and was converted in 1257, becoming a hermit and then a Franciscan tertiary. His goal became to preach, write books to convince unbelievers, and set up colleges to train missionaries to Islam. He engaged Muslim and

Jewish scholars in debate and travelled widely, including to Paris where he taught for a time, to find support for his plans to evangelize the Islamic peoples, but had little success other than the foundation of the college of Miramar in 1276 for the study of Arabic. He attempted to build a system whereby one could fathom all religious truth by way of logical argument. In one of his works, *Ars Magna*, he tried to show that all possible knowledge could be deduced from first principles. This resulted in his condemnation by Gregory XI in 1376. Lull was stoned to death by Muslims in Bougie, north Africa.

Raymond Nonnatus, friar, born Portello, *c.* 1204, died Cardona, 31 August 1240. Raymond's surname derives from his reputed birth by caesarean section after his mother's death. He joined the Mercedarian Order *c.* 1224, and is credited with noteworthy activity in ransoming captives in Moorish north Africa and in Spain. The details of Raymond's life are not well authenticated, the earliest *vita* written long after his death. He is the patron of midwives and mothers in labour, and of the innocent charged with crime. A painting of him preaching, by Carlo Saraceni (1585–1625), is in St Adrian's church, Rome.

Raymond of Capua, bl., friar, born Capua, Italy, *c.* 1330, died Nuremberg, Germany, 5 October 1399. Raymond became a Dominican and spiritual director of St **Catherine of Siena**, with whom he tried to reconcile Florence and the Tuscan League with the papacy. He also worked with Catherine at Avignon in 1376 to return Gregory XI to Rome and end the schism. His *Legenda* (1477) is important on Catherine's life and spirituality. He also wrote a biography of St **Agnes of Montepulciano**, whom he knew in 1363, and a treatise on the Magnificat. Leo XIII confirmed his cult in 1899.

Raymond of Fitero, abbot, born Tarazona, Spain, died Toledo, 1163. Known in Spain as Raimondo Serra, he entered the order in France, but soon participated in the foundation at Fitero, Navarre (1140), where he became abbot. King Sancho III of Castile accepted Raymond's offer to defend Calatrava against the Moors in 1158, and granted the fortress to him. Raymond made it into a

monastery, whence he transferred his monks, welcoming warriors who offered their help or who wished to take the habit. Thus was created the Order of Calatrava, which received papal approval in 1164. Never formally canonized, his remains are in the cathedral of Toledo. Feast 15 March.

Raymond of Peñafort, canonist lawyer, born Vilefranca de Penades, *c.* 1175, died Barcelona, 6 January 1275. Raymond joined the Dominicans in 1221, and wrote his most influential work, *Summa de casibus*, a systematic treatment of doctrinal and canonical questions for confessors. Gregory IX then called him to Rome as his confessor. Elected third master general of the Dominicans in 1238, he resigned in 1240 to return to Spain and an apostolate to the Jews and Moors, writing, preaching and working against heresy and Islam. Feast 7 January.

Raymond of Roda-Barbastro, monk, born Durban, south of Toulouse, died Huesca, 21 June 1126. Prior of the Augustinian monastery of St Saturninus in Toulouse, Raymond became bishop of Roda, and then of Barbastro, in northern Aragon. Famed as a zealous bishop of outstanding personal virtue, he was driven from his see in the political turmoil of the time, despite the intervention of Paschal II. Raymond accompanied Alfonso I of Castile on his Cutanda campaign and his expedition to Malaga. On the return journey he fell ill and died. Alfonso later restored Barbastro to the jurisdiction of Roda.

Raymond of Toulouse, patron of Toulouse, born Toulouse, died there, 3 July 1118. Dedicated by his parents to St **Saturninus**, Raymond abandoned the religious life, married, and after the death of his spouse, devoted himself to charitable works. He was generous to the poor, built and endowed a hospital for poor clerics and rebuilt the church of St Saturninus. His cult dates from 1652, following the ending of an epidemic attributed to his intercession.

Raymund Palmerius, born Piacenza, 1140, died there, 27 July 1200. At the age of 15, Raimondo Zanfogoni went with his mother on a pilgrimage to Jerusalem. She died on the journey home and Raymund returned alone carrying a pilgrim's palm branch, earning him the nickname 'Palmerius'. In about 1178 he had a vision of Christ telling him to take care of the poor in Piacenza. He spent the rest of his life carrying this out. He founded a hostel for the poor and sick, and several other institutions to help those in need. He looked after orphans and pilgrims, prisoners and repentant prostitutes. After his death he was buried in a chapel near the church of the Twelve Apostles, and miracles have been reported at his tomb.

Raynald of Nocera, born Nocera, Umbria, died 1225. Born of German parents, he became a Benedictine at Fontavellana. He was bishop of Nocera from 1222 and is the city's patron. Feast 9 February.

Raynald of Ravenna, bishop, died Ravenna, 1514. Bishop of Ravenna. Feast 18 August.

Raynerius, see **Rainerius**.

Razhden the Martyr, born Persia, died Zromi, eastern Georgia, *c.* 457. Georgian Church. He held an important post at the court of the shah, and was converted to Christianity when he accompanied a Persian princess to the court of **Vachtang Gorgasali**, the king of Georgia, when she was given in marriage to the king. However, relations between Georgia and Persia deteriorated, and Razhden became one of the commanders in the Georgian army in their battles with the Persians. He was taken prisoner, and attempts were made to persuade him to abjure his Christianity. He was eventually shot dead with arrows while tied to a cross, thus becoming the first martyr of the Georgian Church. Feast 3 August.

Rebecca Ar-Rayyes, nun, born Himlaya, Lebanon, 29 June 1832, died Grabta, Lebanon, 23 March 1914. Baptized Boutrossieh, her mother Rafqa (Rebecca) died when she was six, and she did not get along with her stepmother. She worked as a maid, but felt called to the religious life. Her father stopped her, but at 21 she joined an order at Bikfaya, taking the name Agnes. This order was merged with the Order of the Sacred Heart of Jesus in 1871, but Agnes decided to join the Order of St Anthony of the Maronites, taking the name Rafqa. From 1885 her health, and particularly her sight,

deteriorated, but she continued to work until by 1907 she was completely blind. She prayed that she would be granted one more hour of sight so she might see one of the nuns who had been particularly kind to her, and this happened. Miracles were reported from almost immediately after her death. She was canonized in 2001.

Redemptus of the Cross, bl., martyr, born Portugal, died Sumatra, 29 November 1635. Baptized Tomas Rodriguez da Cunha, he was originally a soldier but later joined the Discalced Carmelites and was sent to Goa. There he was sent with **Dionysius of the Nativity** on an ambassadorial expedition to Sumatra, where several of the party were put to death for their faith, including the two Carmelites.

Regina, martyr, born Alise, France (?), died Autun. She is said to have been of pagan parents, but brought up by a Christian nurse, and became a Christian, which led to estrangement from her parents. When she refused to marry the local prefect, she was tortured and beheaded. Feast 7 September.

Reginald of Orleans, bl., preacher, born Orleans, 1183, died Paris, 1 February 1220. Reginald studied at Paris and became dean of the canons of St-Aignan, Orleans. St **Dominic** received him into his order in 1218, following a near-fatal illness during which, in a vision, Our Lady is said to have shown Reginald the Dominican habit. He went to Paris in 1219 to help the young Dominican foundation at the university, where he died. Acclaimed for his preaching and holy life, **Pius IX** beatified him in 1875.

Regulus (Rieul), died Senlis, France, *c.* 260. Said to be of Greek origin, he is revered as the first bishop of Senlis. Feast 30 March.

Reineldis, martyr, born Kontish, near Antwerp, died Saintes, Belgium, *c.* 680. Daughter of St **Amalburga** and sister of St **Gudula**. She went on a seven-year pilgrimage to the Holy Land, returning with a large number of relics. She went to live at Saintes, south-west of Brussels, and remained there until she was murdered by barbarian raiders, along with a servant and a subdeacon named Grimoald. Feast 16 July.

Remaclus, bishop, born Aquitaine, died Stavelot, in the Ardennes, 3 September *c.* 675. He studied under **Sulpicius** in Bourges, then became abbot of a newly founded monastery at Solignac. He moved to the abbey of Cugnot (now in Luxembourg), and then became adviser to King Sigebert III of Austrasia. He encouraged the king to found a monastery at Stavelot, from which he and his monks evangelized the countryside.

Rembert of Bremen-Hamburg, archbishop, died Bremen, 11 June 888. Rembert became a monk at Turnholt near Bruges, where he met St **Ansgar**, whom he succeeded as archbishop of Hamburg, and whose biography he wrote. He is reported to have evangelized parts of Scandinavia, but that is doubtful. He is buried near the cathedral church in Bremen.

Remigius of Lyon, archbishop, died Lyon, 28 October 875. Chaplain of Lothair I and Charles II, Remigius succeeded Amulo in the see of Lyon, in the midst of the predestination controversy. Although disapproving of Gottschalk's views, he was no partisan of his adversary archbishop Hincmar of Rheims, as he considered neither to have done justice to the thought of St **Augustine** on the subject. He took part in the councils of Langres (859) and Toucy (860), and attempted to regain confiscated Church property.

Remigius of Rheims, bishop, 'Apostle of the Franks', born Laon, *c.* 437, died Rheims, 13 January *c.* 533. Scion of an influential family: his father Aemitius, count of Laon, his mother St Cilinia, his younger brother St Principius, Remigius became bishop at the age of 22. A great friend of Clovis, he converted the king to Christianity and baptized him, along with 3.000 Franks (according to **Gregory of Tours**), on Christmas Day 496, following Clovis's defeat of the Alamanni at the battle of Tolbiac. Clovis became known as the eldest son of the Church, whose influence in the subsequent history of Christianity in the West has been inestimable. Remigius's relics have lain in the abbey of St-Remi since 1049. Feast 1 October.

Remigius of Rouen, archbishop, died Rouen, *c.* 772. An illegitimate son of Charles Martel and brother of Pepin III, he succeeded Rainfroi as archbishop of Rouen in 755. While on a mission to Paul I (760) and Desiderius, king of the Lombards, Remigius was impressed by the chant of the monks, and brought some back to introduce Gregorian chant and Roman liturgical practice in the Frankish kingdom. His name has figured in the Rouen Breviary since 1627. Feast 19 January.

René Goupil, martyr, born Anjou, 1606, died Canada, 1642. As a young man he joined the Jesuits, but his health was judged unsatisfactory, and he left to study medicine. He then offered to accompany Jesuit priests to Canada. He worked for a time in a hospital in Quebec before accompanying **Isaac Jogues** on a missionary expedition. They were both captured by Iroquois, and tortured. René Goupil was tomahawked to death after being seen giving a child a blessing. Isaac Jogues had received him into the Society of Jesus as a lay brother sometime before. Feast, with **John de Brébeuf**, 19 October.

René Lego, see **John Lego**.

Renée-Marie Feillatreau, bl., martyr, born Angers, 8 February 1751, died there, 28 March 1794, beatified 1984. Accused of anti-revolutionary activities for hiding vestments and vessels and supporting the royalist 'Vendéens', she was really condemned to the guillotine for attending masses said by nonconforming priests – see also **Martyrs of the French Revolution**.

Renilda of Eyck, eighth century. She was an abbess in the diocese of Lyon, and was said by her biographer to have been highly accomplished, having been sent to the nunnery at Valenciennes to be educated. It is uncertain, however, whether that nunnery existed in her time. Feast 6 February.

Reparata, martyr, died Caesarea, 250. Feast 8 October.

Restituta, martyr, died Carthage, 304. She was a young African woman. Her relics are thought to be in Naples. Feast 17 May.

Restituta Kafka, bl., martyr, born Helene, Brno, now Czech Republic, 1 May 1894, died Austria, 30 March 1943, beatified 1998. A nun and a skilled operating theatre sister, she was denounced by her surgeon at Mödling hospital for continuing her religious activity, banned by the Nazis, and was beheaded in prison.

Restitutus, martyr, died Rome, *c*. 299. The account of his martyrdom is unreliable. Feast 29 May.

Restitutus, Donatus, Valerianus, Fruttuosa and Companions, martyrs, died Antioch, Syria, 305 (?). A group of 16 in total, said to have been Syrians. Feast 23 August.

Rheginus, bishop and martyr, born Chalcedon, died Phasula, near Limassol, Cyprus. Byzantine Church. Feast 20 August.

Rheginus, martyr, died 355. He was bishop of Thessaly. Feast 25 February.

Rheticus, bishop, born Burgundy, died Autun, fourth century. He was bishop of Autun from 310, attended the Lateran Synod in 313 and is supposed to have taught the elements of the Christian faith to the Emperor Constantine. Feast 15 May.

Ricerius, bl., died 1236, cult confirmed 1838. While studying in Bologna in 1222, he heard **Francis of Assisi** preaching and immediately joined him. He was ordained, became provincial minister of the Marches and apparently died young. Feast 7 February.

Richard, born Wessex, England, died Lucca, Tuscany, *c*. 720. He was the father of **Willibald, Winnibald** and **Walburga**, venerated as evangelizers of Germany. A cult developed around their father's burial place, with miracles reported. A story developed that he was 'Richard, king of the English', but his real name is not known. Feast 7 February.

Richard Bere, bl., martyr, born Glastonbury, died Marshalsea prison, London, 1537. A monk of the London Charterhouse, he was starved to death for refusing to acknowledge the royal supremacy. Feast 9 August.

Richard Fetherston, bl., martyr, died Smithfield, London, 30 July 1540. He was educated at Cambridge and became a doctor of divinity, and in 1523 was made archdeacon of Brecon, south Wales. He taught Latin to Princess Mary until 1533, and in 1529 spoke before Convocation for the validity of the marriage of King Henry VIII and Catherine of Aragon. In July 1540 he was convicted of high treason, for denying Henry's supremacy over the Church, and was hanged, drawn and quartered along with **Edward Powell** and **Thomas Abel**.

Richard Gwyn, martyr, born Llanidloes, Montgomeryshire, Wales, 1537, died Wrexham, 17 October 1584. He was educated at St John's College, Cambridge, and became a schoolmaster at Overton in Flintshire (Clwyd). He married, and had six children, three of whom survived. He was eight times arraigned for recusancy, several times fined, tortured or placed in the stocks. The eighth time he was condemned to death.

Richard Hill, see **Edmund Drake**.

Richard Holiday, see **Edmund Drake**.

Richard Hurst, bl., martyr, born Broughton (?), near Preston, Lancashire, died there, 29 August 1628. He was a fairly wealthy farmer and well known as a Catholic. In the scuffle that followed an attempt to arrest Richard, a man fell and died of his injuries. Richard was indicted on the charge of murder. He was offered his life if he agreed to take the oath of allegiance, but he refused.

Richard Kirkman, bl., martyr, born Addingham, West Riding, Yorkshire, died York, 22 August 1582. He went to Rheims to study for the priesthood in 1577, and was ordained there in 1579, returning to England just over three months later. He worked as a chaplain, then ministered in Yorkshire and Northumberland before being arrested in August 1582. He shared a cell in York castle and was executed with **William Lacey**.

Richard Langhorne, bl., martyr, died Tyburn, London, 14 July 1679. He was a prominent Catholic and a barrister, and was accused of complicity in the so-called Popish Plot of 1678. He was held in Newgate prison for eight months and tried at the Old Bailey in June 1679, charged with plotting to kill the king. Despite obvious inconsistencies in the evidence against him, he was condemned to death and was hanged, drawn and quartered.

Richard Langley, bl., martyr, born Grimthorpe, Yorkshire, died York, 1 December 1586. Married with five children, he was a wealthy man who gave priests refuge on his estates during the persecutions in England. He was arrested for doing so in October 1586, and hanged.

Richard Leigh, bl., martyr, born London, 1561, died Tyburn, London, 30 August 1588. Educated at Douai, Rheims and the English College in Rome, he was ordained priest in 1586. He was arrested on 4 July 1588 and imprisoned in the Tower of London before being executed.

Richard Lloyd, born Wales, died Tyburn, London, 30 August 1588. He was executed for giving assistance to a priest, **Robert Morton**.

Richard Martin, bl., martyr, born Shropshire, died Tyburn, London, 30 August 1588. He was executed for giving assistance to a priest.

Richard Newport (alias Smith), bl., martyr, born Harringworth, Northamptonshire, 1572, died Tyburn, London, 30 May 1612, beatified 1929. A convert to Catholicism, he was ordained in Rome in 1597 and worked in London. Repeatedly arrested and banished, he is commemorated with **William Scott**, with whom he was hanged, drawn and quartered.

Richard of Chichester, bishop, born Wyche (Droitwich), c. 1198, died Dover, 3 April 1253. Richard became chancellor of Canterbury under St **Edmund of Abingdon**, whom he accompanied in his exile, and was there at his death. Elected bishop of Chichester (where he instituted the offering for the cathedral at Chichester, later known as 'St Richard's pence'). In 1244, Henry III at first refused Richard, and only gave way under threat of excommunication by Innocent IV. A man of deep spirituality and an excellent administrator, he preached the Crusades and showed much eagerness to reform the manners and morals of the clergy, and to introduce greater reverence into the services of the Church. Miracles were reportedly wrought at his tomb in Chichester. Canonized by Urban IV in 1262, his shrine in Chichester cathedral was destroyed by order of Henry VIII in 1538.

Richard Pampuri, born Trivolzio, near Pavia, 2 August 1897, died Milan, 1 May 1930, beatified 1981. Baptized Erminio, he trained as a doctor when it was decided that his health was not strong enough for him to be a missionary priest as he wished. He practised as a doctor in Morimondo, a poor region near Milan, and founded the Band of **Pius V** as organized good Samaritans to help the poor in Milan. In 1927 he joined the Order of St John of God, changing his name to Richard (Riccardo) and becoming responsible for dental care for the poor in Brescia. He died of pleurisy.

Richard Reynolds, martyr, born Devon, c. 1487, died Tyburn, London, 4 May 1535. Richard became a Benedictine monk at Syon abbey, Isleworth, where he achieved prominence as a preacher and spiritual adviser. Henry VIII sought the backing of Syon in his divorce proceedings, but failed. Reynolds was arrested and sent to the Tower, where he stoutly disputed to Cromwell Henry's claim to lead the English Church. Condemned for treason, Richard was executed at Tyburn. He was canonized in 1970.

Richard Rolle of Hampole, bl., hermit, born Thornton, Yorkshire, c. 1290, died Hampole, 29 September 1349. Richard early felt a call to the solitary, but not enclosed, life and settled at Hampole, near Doncaster, where he died of the plague. The most widely read English mystical writer of his time, his poetry and prose have survived in some 400 manuscripts, of which the more important are *De Incendio Amoris*, in defence of the contemplative and ecstatic life, and how he reached the highest point of divine rapture; and, despite his anti-feminist leanings, his writings for Margaret Kirkby and other holy women at Yedingham: *Ego Dormio*, *On the Love of God*, *The Form of Perfect Living*, and their attainment through contemplation.

Richard Sergeant, bl., martyr, born Gloucestershire, died Tyburn, London, 20 April 1586, beatified 1987. He studied at Rheims, was ordained in Laon in 1583 and returned to England, calling himself Lee or Long. He is commemorated with **William Thompson**, with whom he was hanged, drawn and quartered.

Richard Thirkeld, bl., martyr, born Coniscliffe, County Durham, died York, 29 May 1583, beatified 1886. He was at Queen's College, Oxford, and was already quite old when he studied at Douai and Rheims, being ordained in April 1579, returning to England the following month. He worked in Yorkshire, was captured in York itself, and was hanged, drawn and quartered. Feast 29 May.

Richard Whiting, bl., last abbot of Glastonbury, martyr, died Tor Hill, Glastonbury, 15 November 1539. Educated at the abbey under **Richard Bere**, he was ordained in Wells Cathedral in 1501. He was nominated by Cardinal Wolsey to succeed Bere on his death in 1525, a selection formally witnessed by **Thomas More**. As a member of the House of Lords, he was immediately involved in Henry VIII's divorce, but prudently took no stand on the matter, although privately unsympathetic. In 1534, he and his 51 monks took the Oath of Royal Supremacy. Glastonbury was the greatest of the great monasteries, a target for suppression and destruction and a source of great wealth for the king. Cromwell's visitor, Robert Layton, found such good order in 1535, however, that the monastery was left unmolested. Cromwell continued to assure Whiting that there would be no suppression, but in 1539 Layton and the royal commission arrived without warning, interrogated the weak and sickly old abbot, perceived his 'cankered and traitorous heart', and took him to the Tower for examination by Cromwell himself. They searched the monastery and found valuable articles hidden away, which enabled them to change treason to robbery as a basis for arresting Whiting. He remained adamant in the faith, and was secretly and without trial condemned to death. He was taken back to Glastonbury, laid on a trundle and dragged through the town to be hanged, drawn and quartered. Feast 1 December.

Richardis, born Alsace, c. 840, died Andlau, 18 September 895. The daughter of the duke of Alsace, she married, aged 22, Charles the Fat, who was crowned Holy Roman emperor in 881. She was a devout woman, who founded several monasteries, including that at Andlau, to which she retired after being accused of adultery with the highly respected bishop Liutward of Vercelli, and where she died.

Richarius (Riquier), born Celles, near Amiens, northern France, died near Crécy, 26 April c. 645. A pagan, he became a Christian priest, preaching in northern France and England. He became known, founded a church at Celles and eventually retired to the forest of Crécy, where he created a monastic community.

Rictrude, born Gascony, 612, died Marchiennes, near Douai, France, 678. Influenced by **Amandus**, then living in the family house, she married **Adalbald**. After her husband's murder, Amandus persuaded the king, Dagobert, to let her enter Marchiennes monastery. Their four children, including **Maurontius**, are also venerated. Feast 12 May.

Rigobert of Rheims, bishop, died c. 743. A monk and abbot of Orbais, Champagne, he became archbishop of Rheims in 721. Banished by Charles Martel, he returned to Orbais and eventually became a hermit. Feast 4 January.

Rigomerus of Meaux, bishop, sixth century. Feast 4 January.

Ripsima and Companions, martyrs, died Armenia, 303 (?). A group of 78 martyrs. According to the story, Diocletian, in Rome, wanted Ripsima as his wife. She fled with her companions to Armenia, where the king tried to violate her. She, however, grappled with him, and his guards came to defend him, killing Ripsima and her companions. Feast 30 September.

Rita of Cascia, nun, born Roccaporena, Umbria, 1377, died Cascia, 22 May 1457. After the murder of her tyrannical husband her two sons vowed to kill the assassins, but she prayed that they would not be able to do so – and both died. Despite her lack of means and education, she joined the Augustinians in 1413 after several attempts, owing, it is related, to supernatural intervention after they had first refused her. She lived a life of heroic penance that won the admiration of all her contemporaries. Through her own austerity and sufferings, including a painful wound on her forehead, she became known as the 'Saint of Desperate Cases'. Her symbol is roses, which are blessed in commemoration on 22 May, in Augustinian churches.

Robert Anderton, martyr, born Isle of Man, 1560, died Newport, Isle of Wight, 25 April 1586, beatified 1929. Ordained at Rheims in 1584, he was tried in Winchester and London. He is commemorated with his friend **William Marsden**, with whom he was hanged, drawn and quartered, the only priests condemned by royal proclamation.

Robert Bellarmine, cardinal, born Montepulciano, 4 October 1542, died Rome, 17 September 1621. He came from a distinguished family (his mother was a sister of Pope Marcellus II), and was well educated in the arts and humanities. He entered the Society of Jesus in 1560, taught classics, and then was sent in 1569 to Louvain, where the following year he became the university's first Jesuit professor, lecturing on the *Summa* of **Thomas Aquinas**. While there he also produced a Hebrew grammar. In 1576 he was appointed to the Roman college of the Jesuits to teach 'controversial theology', i.e., to discuss the views of the Reformers. His *Disputationes de controversiis Christianae Fidei adversus huius temporis hereticos* were published between 1586 and 1593. His views on the indirect papal power in secular affairs nearly resulted in the first volume of this being put on the *Index of Forbidden Books* in 1590. In 1592 he became rector of the Roman college, and two years later provincial superior in Naples. In 1597 he was made papal theologian by Clement VIII, and a cardinal two years later. From 1602 he was archbishop of Capua, but resigned his see on becoming prefect of the Vatican library in 1605, and from then on served in the papal Curia. Apart from his disputes with Protestant theologians, he was also involved in the controversy over grace – one of the major disputants, Leonard Lessius, had been a student of his – and in the Galileo affair, in which he was somewhat sympathetic to Galileo. Also a person of great generosity towards the poor, and of

personal austerity, he spent the last years of his life writing spiritual works. The process for his canonization began soon after his death, but was not concluded, for political reasons, until 1930. The following year he was declared a doctor of the Church.

Robert Bickerdike, bl., martyr, born Knaresborough, Yorkshire, died York, 8 August 1586. He lived in York, and was arrested there for being reconciled to Roman Catholicism, and for holding what were deemed treasonable opinions. He was hanged, drawn and quartered.

Robert Dalby, bl., martyr, born Hemingborough, Yorkshire, died York, 16 March 1589, beatified 1929. Previously a Protestant minister, he was arrested on landing at Scarborough in 1588 and hanged, drawn and quartered with **John Amias**.

Robert Drury (or Drewrie), bl., born Buckinghamshire, *c.* 1567, martyred Tyburn, London, 26 February 1607, beatified 1987. Ordained in Spain, he returned to England in 1605, was arrested in 1607 after the Gunpowder Plot and hanged, drawn and quartered under the alias of Hampden.

Robert Hardesty, bl., martyr, died York, 24 September 1589. A layman, he was arrested for sheltering **William Spencer**, and was executed with him. One of the **Eighty-Five Martyrs of England, Scotland and Wales**.

Robert Johnson, bl., from Shropshire, martyred Tyburn, London, 28 May 1582, beatified 1886. Originally a manservant, he was ordained at Douai in 1576 and then worked in London from September 1580. He is commemorated with **Thomas Ford** and **John Shert**, executed with him.

Robert Lawrence, Carthusian monk and martyr, born Dorset (?), England, died Tyburn, London, 4 May 1535. He gained his degree in law at Cambridge in 1508 and, after his profession at the London Charterhouse, became prior at Beauvale in 1531. In 1535, following King Henry VIII's Act of Supremacy, Lawrence with two fellow priors sought to negotiate with Thomas Cromwell. But he proved obdurate and all three were imprisoned in the Tower, tried in Westminster Hall, and condemned to be hanged, drawn and quartered. Lawrence is one of the **Forty Martyrs of England and Wales** canonized by Pope Paul VI in 1970. Feast 25 October.

Robert Ludlam, bl., martyr, born Radbourne, Derbyshire, *c.* 1551, died Derby, 24 July 1588. He went to the English College in Rheims in 1580, was ordained the next year, and returned to England in 1582. In 1588 he was arrested in Padley along with **Nicholas Garlick**. Both were condemned for being seminary priests working in England, and were hanged, drawn and quartered.

Robert Morton, bl., martyr, born Bawtry, Yorkshire, died Lincoln's Inn Fields, 28 August 1588. He first left England in 1568 to travel in Europe, staying for three years with a priest uncle in Rome. In 1573 he began to study at Douai, but returned home and married. In 1578 he and his wife decided to leave England, but were arrested. He was eventually released, but his wife died, so he returned to Rome to study for the priesthood in 1586. He returned to England the following year, but was arrested in London almost immediately.

Robert Nutter, bl., martyr, born Clitheroe, Lancashire, *c.* 1556, died Lancaster, 26 July 1600. He went to Rheims in 1579 and was ordained at Soissons in 1581. He returned to England and worked under the alias Askew until his arrest in 1584. He was imprisoned in the Tower of London and tortured, and was banished from England in 1585. He set out to return later that year, but was arrested after the ship he was on was intercepted. He argued that he had not been attempting to return to England, but had been brought back by force, and escaped immediate execution. He was imprisoned in the Marshalsea, and moved to Wisbech in 1588. He remained there until 1600, when he tried to escape. He was soon captured, however, and was tried along with **Edward Thwing**. Both were hanged, drawn and quartered.

Robert of Arbrissel, bl., hermit, wandering preacher, and founder of the Order of Fontevrault, born Arbrissel, Brittany, *c.* 1055, died Orsan, France, 25 February 1116 or 1117. After studying at Paris, he was archpriest at Rennes from 1085 to 1090, taught briefly at Angers, and then lived as a hermit in the forest of Craon, where he established a house of canons at La Roë to house his followers. Given a papal licence to preach by Pope Urban II, he resigned the abbacy of La Roë and began a career as a wandering preacher. He converted many to the religious life, and to house his many followers he was forced to build a double monastery at Fontevrault *c.* 1100. He placed the order under the control of an abbess, **Petronilla**, shortly before his death. He was buried at Fontevrault. The several attempts to canonize him all failed.

Robert of Bruges, bl., abbot, born Bruges, died Clairvaux, 29 April 1157. Persuaded by **Bernard of Clairvaux** to accept the monastic vocation in 1131, Robert became first Cistercian abbot in 1139 at Our Lady of Dunes abbey in Flanders. He succeeded Bernard as second abbot of Clairvaux in 1153. He is mentioned in the Cistercian martyrology of 1491, as well as in the Missal of 1526.

Robert of Chaise-Dieu, abbot, born Auvergne, central France, *c.* 1000, died 1067, canonized 1070. A priest who became a solitary, he attracted disciples, so he founded Chaise-Dieu abbey (House of God). To ensure a simple life of prayer and manual labour, he established small daughter houses, with perhaps five monks in each. Feast 17 April.

Robert of Knaresborough, bl., born York, *c.* 1160, died Knaresborough, Yorkshire, 24 September 1218. A devout youth, he trained for the priesthood, but instead of continuing entered the Cistercian abbey at Morpeth. It was not long before he decided this form of life did not suit him, and instead went to live as a hermit at Knaresborough, beside the river Nidd. He lived in a cave, which he had for some years to share with a knight who was hiding from King Richard I. He was later offered a chapel at Rudfarlington, but was driven out of there and took refuge in the priory at Hedley before returning to Rudfarlington. There, however, he fell foul of the constable of Knaresborough castle, who had the buildings in which he lived pulled down, forcing Robert to return to his original cave. His brother, who was mayor of York, built a chapel beside the cave. After his death the hermitage passed to Yves, one of Robert's disciples.

Robert of Molesme, founder of the monastery at Citeaux. Born Troyes, *c.* 1027, died Molesme, 1110. He first became a monk at Moutier-la-Celle, then was appointed abbot of Tonnerre. He next became a hermit, but with a group of hermits he founded the monastery of Molesme in 1075. While prior at Molesme, he became dissatisfied with the Rule of life and Robert and others were permitted to leave and to organize a new monastery at Citeaux based on the original interpretation of the Benedictine Rule. Some 18 months later he was ordered to return as abbot to his former monastery at Molesme. The Cistercian movement introduced a wave of reform and Citeaux continued to prosper under **Alberic**, **Stephen Harding** and St **Bernard**. Feast 29 April.

Robert of Newminster, abbot, born Yorkshire, died Newminster, 7 June 1159. Educated in Paris, and a parish priest in Yorkshire, Robert joined the Cistercians, helped to found Fountains abbey, and then founded the abbey of Newminster, near Morpeth in Northumberland, in 1139. The abbey grew rapidly, establishing three daughter houses in less than ten years. Robert's tomb at Newminster became the scene of numerous miracles and of popular pilgrimage until the Reformation.

Robert of Soleto (Robert of Sala, Salle), bl., monk, born Sala, 1273, died Morrone, 18 July 1341. Received into what became the Celestine Order by Peter of Morrone (later Celestine V) in 1289, Robert founded monasteries and hospices for the sick and orphans. Contemporaries revered him for his spirit of penance and devotion to the Sacred Passion.

Robert Southwell, poet and martyr, born Horsham St Faith, England, 1561, died Tyburn, London, 21 February 1595. A member of a predominantly Catholic family, Southwell was educated by Jesuits in Douai and Paris, becoming a Jesuit himself in 1578 in Rome. He was ordained in 1584 and taught at the English College before returning to England in 1587 to work clandestinely for the cause of English Catholicism. During the course of this, his secret presses published several works of experimental poetry, which influenced Shakespeare and are today highly regarded by literary scholars. Southwell was eventually betrayed, and

was captured and imprisoned in 1592. Following prolonged torture, Southwell's priesthood finally condemned him, and he was put to death at Tyburn in 1595. He was beatified by Pope Pius XI in 1929 and canonized as one of the **Forty Martyrs of England and Wales**.

Robert Sutton, bl., martyr, born Burton-on-Trent, Staffordshire, 1544, died Stafford, 27 July 1588. Educated at Christ Church, Oxford. He went to the English College in Douai in 1577, and the following year was ordained and sent back to England. He was banished in 1584, but returned to England and worked as a priest in Staffordshire. He was captured in July 1588 and tried in Staffordshire. He was condemned for being a priest ordained abroad and working in England, and was hanged, drawn and quartered.

Robert Thorpe, bl., born Yorkshire, martyred York, 31 May 1591, beatified 1987. He was ordained at Rheims in April 1585, and returned to England the following month to work in Yorkshire. He was captured at the house of **Thomas Watkinson**, an older widower. They were executed – and beatified – together.

Robert Wilkinson (alias John Wilson), bl., martyr, born Hemingborough, Yorkshire, *c.* 1579, died Tyburn, London, 20 April 1602, beatified 1929. He studied at Douai and Rome, being ordained in 1602. Ill, he went to London for treatment and was immediately arrested. He is commemorated with **Francis Page**, with whom he was hanged, drawn and quartered.

Roch (Roque, Rocco), healer of the plague-stricken, born Montpellier, France, *c.* 1350, died Angera, Italy, *c.* 1378. Little is known of Roch's life, and the *vita* by Francis Dindo, although chronologically impossible and of doubtful value, credits him with curing many victims of the plague in the town of Aquapendente, and in other cities. His cult first appeared in Montpellier in 1410, and he was invoked against the plague in an outbreak in 1414 during the Council of Constance. His relics are venerated in Venice. Feast 16 August.

Roderigo, martyr, died Córdoba, Spain, 13 March 857, with **Solomon**. Roderigo was a priest denounced to the Muslim authorities by his Muslim brother. Solomon, who had repented of renouncing his Christian faith, became a friend in prison – see **Martyrs of Córdoba**.

Rodrigo Aguilar Aleman, martyr, born Mexico, 1875, died Ejutla, 28 October 1927. Ordained in 1905, at the time of his death he was parish priest in Union de Tula. Having been denounced to the authorities, he decided to hide, but was found and shot in the main square of Ejutla. Feast 25 May.

Roger Cadwallador, bl., martyr, born Streeton, Herefordshire, died Leominster, 27 August 1610. He studied at the English College in Rheims, and then at Valladolid, where he was ordained priest in February 1592. Eighteen months later he returned to England, to work in Herefordshire. He was involved in controversy over the status of Catholics in England, protesting along with others that he was prepared to recognize Elizabeth as the lawful sovereign, while retaining allegiance to Rome in religious matters – a position the English government was not prepared to accept. He was arrrested on Easter Sunday 1610, and imprisoned in Hereford, where he refused to accept the new oath of allegiance to the crown – drawn up in 1606 and condemned by the pope. He was condemned to be hanged, drawn and quartered.

Roger Dickenson and Ralph Milner, bl., martyrs, died Winchester, 7 July 1591. Roger Dickenson went to the English College at Rheims in 1582 and was ordained the next year at Laon. He returned to England in May 1583 and worked as a priest before being arrested at the end of the year. He may have been exiled in 1585, but is next heard of in Winchester, where he met **Ralph Milner** (or Miller). Ralph Milner became a Catholic as an adult and was imprisoned several times because of his Catholicism. He helped Fr Roger and gave him shelter. Both were arrested in January 1591 and taken to London, where they were imprisoned in the Clink. They were sent back to Winchester for trial and were condemned to death, Fr Roger for being a seminary priest working in England, and Ralph for assisting him.

Roger Filcock (also called Arthur Nayler), bl., born Kent, martyred London, February 1601, beatified

1987. Ordained in Spain, he returned to England in 1597 and joined the Jesuits two years later, but before starting his novitiate was hanged, drawn and quartered with **Mark Barkworth** and immediately after **Anne Line**. Feast 27 February.

Roger le Fort, bl., bishop, born Ternes, Limousin, France, died Bourges, 1 March 1367/8. Professor at Orleans, Roger became bishop there in 1321, and of Limoges in 1343. Dedicated to the apostolate, austere in his personal life, and noted for his charity, he founded the Celestine priory at Ternes. Venerated during his lifetime, his tomb became a place of pilgrimage.

Roger of Ellent, bl., monk, born England, died Ellent, France, 4 January, after 1162. Roger joined the Cistercians at Lorroy-en-Berry, Bourges, and in 1143 became first abbot of Ellent, in the Champagne. His *vita*, considered unreliable, records that Archbishop Henry of Rheims, brother of King Louis VII, did not like the bread offered to him by the monks, and granted to the monastery as much land in Attigny as could be ploughed by five yoke of oxen in a year, to provide better grain.

Roger of Todi, bl., friar, born Todi, Umbria, died there, 5 January 1237. Received into the Franciscans by St **Francis** himself, who referred to Roger as an exemplar of charity in his *Speculum perfectionis* and appointed him spiritual director at the convent of Poor Clares in Rieti. His friend Gregory IX called him a saint and approved his cult for the city of Todi, where he is buried. Thomas of Pavia, in his dialogues, credited him with 16 miracles, and Benedict IV approved his feast.

Roger Warren, bl., martyr, died Lancaster, 18 March 1616, beatified 1987. A Catholic weaver, he escaped from prison with **John Thules**, but was rearrested and hanged, drawn and quartered with him.

Roland de Medici, see **Orlando de Medici**.

Rolendis, princess, born France, died Villers-Poterie, Belgium, seventh/eighth centuries. A thirteenth-century *vita* describes Rolendis as the daughter of a king in Gaul, probably the Lombard Desiderius. To avoid marriage she fled to the convent of St Ursula in Cologne, but died en route in Villers-Poterie. Her cult developed early around the relics contained in her eighth-century sarcophagus. Feast 13 May.

Roman Adame Rosales, martyr, born Teocaltiche, Jalisco, Mexico, 7 February 1859, died Yahualican, Jalisco, 2 April 1927. A student at the seminary of Guadalajara, and a priest from 1890, he was forced into hiding but carried out his ministry secretly. When captured and shot, one of the firing squad refused to fire, and was himself executed. Feast 25 May.

Romanov Family, martyrs, see **Nicholas II**.

Romanus, martyr, died Rome, 258. Said to have been a soldier converted to Christianity by St **Laurence**, martyr, and was consequently martyred the day before Laurence. However, an alternative version says that he was a doorkeeper at one of the churches in Rome. Feast 9 August.

Romanus, monk, martyred Syria, 780. Feast 1 May.

Romanus, bl., martyr, born Carpenissi, died 1684. Byzantine Church. He went as a young man to the Holy Land, entering the monastery of St Sabas. He was much taken by stories of martyrdom, and desired to suffer in that way. He went to Thessalonika, where he professed his faith and was condemned to death. However, the death penalty was commuted to work as a galley slave, from which some Christians ransomed him, and he went to Mount Athos. After a time, and unhappy at not becoming a martyr, he went to Constantinople where, having again insulted Muslims, he had his tongue torn out, and was executed.

Romanus ('the wonderworker'), hermit, died Antioch, fifth century. He was a hermit who lived on a mountain near Antioch. Feast 9 February.

Romanus and Barulas, martyrs, died Antioch, 304. Nothing is known of Barulas, although he was said to have been a boy; Romanus was a deacon. Feast 18 November.

Romanus Melodus, religious poet, born Emesa, Syria, c. 490, died Constantinople, c. 555–65.

Perhaps of Jewish extraction, Romanus came to Constantinople during the reign of Anastasius I. His Akathistos Hymn, *Kontakia* (on the Nativity), 24 alphabetically arranged stanzas in praise of the Virgin Mary, composed after she appeared to him in a vision on Christmas Eve, is still one of the most widely known and best-loved liturgical texts of the Byzantine Church, and is rated as a masterpiece of world literature. He is believed to have written a great many hymns, only a few of which have survived. Feast 1 October.

Romanus of Antioch, martyr, born Palestine, died Antioch, 304. A deacon in Caesarea. He publicly warned Christians not to sacrifice to idols, was arrested and ordered to be burned. A rain storm put out the pyre, however, and his tongue was then pulled out. Nonetheless, he continued speaking, and was finally put to death by strangulation. Feast 18 November.

Romanus of Contat, died there, c. 460. A hermit in the Jura mountains, others joined him, including his brother **Lupicinus** and his sister. He founded a monastery at Contat – becoming abbot – then one at Leuconne, followed by a convent at La Beaume. Feast 28 February.

Romanus of Kirzac, hegumenos, died Kirzac, 29 July 1392. Russian Church. Romanus was the monk chosen by **Sergius of Radonez** to govern the monastery he had founded at Kirzac, near Vladimir, when he left the monastery of the Most Holy Trinity because of the hostility of the monks to the severity of its Rule. He later returned to the Trinity monastery, but sent Romanus to be ordained by the metropolitan.

Romanus of Perekom, monk, died Perekom, c. 1554 (?). Russian Church. The biographer of **Ephraim of Perekom**, and probably his successor at the monastery which he had founded.

Romanus of Rjazan, prince and martyr, died 1270. Russian Church. Executed by the Khan Meng Timur after being accused of insulting the khan by a collector of taxes, then imprisoned, and put to death for refusing to abjure Christianity. Feast 19 July.

Romanus of Tarnovo, monk, died *c.* 1370. Bulgarian Church. A disciple of Theodosius of Tarnovo, whom he accompanied to Mount Athos, and was with him when he founded the monastery at Tarnovo. He took charge of the monastery when Theodosius travelled to Constantinople. Feast 17 February.

Romanus of Uglic, prince, born 1235, died Uglic, 1285. Russian Church. His father died in exile at Vladimir, and he took over the city of Uglic after the death of his elder brother in 1261. He was a pious man, founding monasteries, building churches, and undertaking acts of penance. Feast 3 February.

Romanus the Bulgarian, born Bdyn (now Vidin), Bulgaria, *c.* 1325, died Ravanitza monastery, Serbia, 16 January *c.* 1375. A monk, he moved around to follow a master or escape unrest. Called *Kaloromano*, 'good Romanus', he spent several years in Zagora, Bulgaria, and on Mount Athos, where he taught monks of many nationalities.

Romaric, abbot, died Remiremont, 653. A widowed nobleman at the Merovingian court, he entered the abbey of Luxeuil, but *c.* 620 he founded a monastery on his former estate. As he had daughters from his marriage, he also founded beside it a convent for women. He founded them with the assistance of his friend **Arnulf of Metz**, who was the first abbot, but after Arnulf retired to a hermitage the task fell on Romaric. Feast 8 December.

Romedius, bl., hermit, fourth century. Feast 15 January.

Romeo, bl., died Lucca, 1308. He was a Carmelite lay brother, travelling with **Avertanus** to the Holy Land when they died on the way, possibly of the plague. Feast 4 March.

Romuald of Ravenna, founder of the Camaldolese Order, born Ravenna, Italy, *c.* 952, died Val di Castro, near Fabriano, Italy, 19 June 1027. His father having killed a kinsman, Romuald entered the monastery of Sant' Apollinare-in-Classe to do penance on his behalf. After three years as a monk, he received permission to join the cluster of hermits gathered around the ascetic **Marinus** in the Veneto. Together, Romuald and Marinus spent some four years leading an ascetic life as wandering hermits in central and northern Italy. In 978, at the invitation of Abbot Guarinus of Cuxa, they left Italy for a hermitage in the Pyrenees. Romuald returned to Italy some ten years later in order to strengthen his father's monastic vocation. Emperor Otto III greatly admired Romuald, and appointed him abbot of his old monastery of Sant' Apollinare-in-Classe. His abbacy was not a success, and after about a year he resigned in order to return to the eremitic life. His most important eremitical foundations were Camaldoli and Vallombrosa.

Romulus, martyr, died Melitene, Armenia, 112 (?). Said to have been an official of the Emperor Trajan who was executed for having criticized him for permitting the persecution of Christians. Feast 5 September.

Ronan, missionary bishop, seventh century. Ronan is venerated in Brittany and may have been Irish, although several saints of that name are venerated in Ireland, such as Ss Ronan of Lough Derg, of Lismore, of Down, of Meath; the most famous is Ronan Find, son of Berach of Louth, who died *c.* 664 and whose cult spread abroad, perhaps as far as Brittany. Feast 1 June.

Roque González, Jesuit missionary and martyr, born Asunción, Paraguay, 1576, died Rio Grande do Sul, Brazil, 15 November 1628. After his ordination in 1599, González felt his work to be the evangelization of the indigenous South Americans. After serving as priest and vicar general of his own diocese, he entered the Society of Jesus in 1609. In 1615 he left his diocese to found the settlement of the Reduction of Itapúa among the natives of Rio Grande do Sul in Brazil. He founded several other settlements before being killed by the natives he served in the Reduction of Todos los Santos. He was beatified in 1934 together with his fellow Jesuits, both Spaniards, **Alonso Rodriguez** and **John (Juan) de Castillo**, the first martyrs of South America to be so recognized. They were canonized in 1988.

Rosalia, recluse, died Montepellegrino, near Palermo, 1160. A Basilian, or possibly a

Benedictine nun, information concerning Rosalia's life before the seventeenth century is unreliable. She is the patroness of Palermo, where, during a plague that raged there in 1624, a vision granted to one of the stricken led to a search for her remains, which were found in a grotto on Monte Pellegrino. The plague abated when they were brought to Palermo. A supposedly autographic inscription on the wall of the cave identified her, and confirmed her having chosen to live there for the love of Jesus Christ. Urban VIII added her name to the Roman martyrology in 1630. Feast 4 September.

Rosalie du Verdier de la Sorinière, bl., martyred Angers, 2 January 1794. She was a nun of Calvary, guillotined with a group led by **William Repin** – see **Martyrs of the French Revolution**. Feast 27 January.

Rose of Lima, first saint of the New World, born Lima, 20 April 1586, died there, 24 August 1617. Baptized Isabel de Flores, Rose became a Dominican tertiary, and took St **Catherine of Siena** as her model, living a life of remarkable austerity and penance in a cell she had built in the garden of the family home. In a room of the house she set up an infirmary, where she cared for destitute children and infirm elderly people. The Inquisition pronounced her great mystical gifts and social activities as directed by impulses of grace. Clement X canonized her in 1671, and proclaimed her patron of Peru, the Americas, the Indies and the Philippines. Feast 23 August.

Rose of Viterbo, third order Franciscan, born Viterbo, 1235, died there, 6 March 1252. Having reputedly received an apparition from Our Lady that cured her, Rose joined the Third Order Secular of St Francis, and championed the cause of Callistus III against Emperor Frederich II. At 15 she tried to enter the convent of St Mary, but was refused admission and retired to a cell in her father's house. She died at 17 and her body remains incorrupt after seven centuries. Callistus canonized her in 1457. Feast 4 September.

Rose Phillipine du Chesne, missionary, born Grenoble, 29 August 1769, in a merchant family, died St Charles, Missouri, USA, 18 October 1852. Educated in early life by the Visitation nuns, she

was prevented from joining the community by her father and therefore devoted herself to good works. She bought the convent buildings in 1802 and after failing to revive the religious life there she joined the Society of the Sacred Heart at the invitation of its foundress. Professed in 1804, she eventually realized her calling to be a missionary in America. Here she and other sisters established schools, first at St Charles, then in New Orleans, St Louis and elsewhere. In old age she attempted to set up a school for native Americans at Sugar Creek (Kansas). Age, health and language difficulties frustrated this attempt and she died ten years later in conditions of extreme personal poverty. She was canonized in 1988. Feast 17 November.

Rose Venerini, born Viterbo, 9 February 1656, died Rome, 7 May 1728, beatified 1952, canonized 15 October 2006. Recognized as an excellent teacher after opening a free girls' school in Viterbo in 1685, she then organized schools and teacher training colleges throughout Italy, the last in Rome in 1713. She did not herself found a religious order, but one was created out of the group of women whom she gathered to help her with her work. Today Venerini Sisters work among Italian immigrants.

Rose Wang-Hoei, bl., martyr, died China, 1900. Died in the Boxer Rebellion. Feast 16 August.

Roseline, nun, born Chateau d'Arcs, Fréjus, France, 1263, died Celle-Roubaud (Provence), 17 January 1329. Roseline entered the Carthusians at the age of 15, practised severe penances and worked miracles, becoming prioress at Celle-Roubaud *c.* 1300. She is venerated throughout France and is pictured as a Carthusian nun with maniple and stole, i.e., with the symbols of priesthood.

Rostislav of Kiev, prince, died 1167. Russian Church. The third son of **Mstislav II (the Great)**, prince of Kiev, he was troubled by the internecine strife which had affected the Russian states, and when he became prince he attempted to bring peace. He wanted to become a monk, and surrounded himself with monks as advisers, among them Polycarp of Kiev, who urged him to remain in charge of his city. He was stricken with plague when visiting Smolensk, and attempted – but failed

– to return to Kiev before his death so that he could take monastic vows at the Kievan Cave monastery. Feast 14 March.

Ruadhan, abbot, born Leinster or Munster, Ireland, died Lorrha (Lothra), now County Tipperary, *c.* 584. A disciple of **Finnian of Clonard**, he founded Lorrha monastery, which became one of the most important in Munster. He is one of the 12 apostles of Ireland. Feast 15 April (suppressed).

Ruben, monk. Syriac Church. Possibly a stylite. Feast 4 August.

Rudesind, abbot, born Galicia, 907, died Celanova, 977, canonized 1195. Bishop of Dumium (Mondoñedo) at 18, then administrator of Compostela, he founded the Benedictine monastery of Celanova, becoming abbot there. Feast 1 March.

Rudolf Aquaviva and Companions, martyrs, died Cuncolim, India, July 1583. Rudolf (or Rodolfo) Aquaviva was the son of the duke of Atri, in Naples. He was born in 1550, became a Jesuit in 1568, and after being ordained in Lisbon was sent to work in Goa, India. When the Great Mogul asked for missionaries to be sent to his court to discuss religion, Fr Rudolf was chosen to lead the group, and set off for Agra in 1579. He was later sent to take charge of the mission in Salcete. Sometime shortly before 1583, two Jesuit priests, Alphonsus (Alfonso) Pacheco and Peter (Pietro) Berno, were involved in an expedition to Cuncolim, a centre of Hindu religion. They took part in the destruction of temples and sacred buildings, in line with the royal decree of 1546 ordering the destruction of Hindu images and the suppression of Hindu festivals in Portuguese territories. In July 1583, Fr Rudolf, Fr Alphonsus and Fr Peter decided to launch another missionary campaign to Cuncolim, along with another Jesuit priest, Anthony (Antonio) Francisco, and Francis (Francesco) Aranha, a temporal coadjutor. The village leaders met them with force, but Fr Pacheco stopped the Catholic laymen from firing on the Indians and the five Jesuits were killed, along with a number of lay Christians who were with them. Feast 25 July.

Rufina and Justa, martyrs, died Seville, 287. They died for refusing to sell as vessels for pagan worship the earthenware they had made. Feast 19 July.

Rufina and Secunda, martyrs, recorded as having been martyred in the Valerian persecution (*c.* 257), and buried on the via Cornelia at the ninth milestone. Feast 10 July.

Rufinus of Assisi, bishop and martyr. Said to have been the first bishop of Assisi. Nothing is known of him. Feast 11 August.

Rufinus of Capua, bishop, died Capua, fifth century. Feast 27 August.

Rufinus, Silvanus and Vitalicus, martyrs, died Ancyra (Ankara, Turkey). Said to have been three child martyrs. Nothing more is known.

Rufus and Rufinian, martyrs, died Apollonias, Bithynia (?), third century. Said to have been brothers. Feast 9 September.

Rufus and Zosimus, martyrs, born either Antioch or Philippi (?), died Rome, *c.* 107. Companions in martyrdom of **Ignatius of Antioch**, and mentioned as such by **Polycarp**. Feast 18 December.

Rufus of Capua, see **Rufinus of Capua**.

Rufus the Recluse, born Kiev, died there, fourteenth century. He lived as a hermit in a cave at some distance from the Kievan Cave monastery, of which he was a monk. Feast 8 April.

Rumilus and Conindrius, bishops, *c.* 450. Nothing is known of them, although they may have come from Ireland to the Isle of Man, of which they were the first bishops. Feast 28 December.

Rumwold, born King's Sutton, Northamptonshire, died there, seventh century. Said to have been a member of the Mercian royal family. He was baptized only three days after his birth, but nonetheless made a profession of faith, and preached, before dying. After his death his remains were taken to Buckingham, where there was a shrine to the infant prodigy. Feast 3 November.

Rupert Mayer, bl., German Jesuit, born Stuttgart, 23 January 1876, died Munich, 1 November 1945. Mayer became a preacher of parish missions in Germany, Switzerland and the Netherlands, and co-founded the Sisters of the Holy Family, a mission to the very poor. In 1925 he inaugurated the Banhofsmission, a ministry to travellers. One of the first to recognize the incompatibility of Nazism and Christianity, he became an object of police attention when the Nazis came to power in 1933. Mayer regarded Hitler as 'hysterical' and, forbidden to preach, he was arrested in 1939 and sent to Sachsenhausen concentration camp, although he actually spent the war in Ettal abbey. He returned to Munich in 1945 and resumed preaching, but died six months later. His tomb soon became a place of pilgrimage and John Paul II beatified him in 1987. Feast 3 May.

Rupert of Bingen, born Bingen, near Mainz, died there, fourth century. He and his mother Bertha consecrated themselves to God after a pilgrimage to Rome. He built several churches before they became hermits on a hill near Bingen, now called Rupertsberg. He is said to have died aged 20. Feast 15 May.

Rupert of Ottobeuren, bl., abbot, died Ottobeuren, 1145. He was prior of a monastery in the Black Forest before becoming abbot of Ottobeuren in 1102. Rupert introduced the Cluniac reforms as elaborated in the constitutions of Abbot William of Hirsau, whose monastery had contributed to the cause of ecclesiastical reform in Germany. Feast 15 August.

Rupert of Salzburg, founder and first bishop of Salzburg, born France (?), died Salzburg, 27 March 718. A descendant of the Frankish Merovingian royal line, he became bishop of Worms, then moved into what is now Austria. Rupert founded the oldest monastery in Austria, Sankt Peter (*c.* 700), on the ruins of ancient Juvavum with a community of Irish-Celtic monks, and also the convent of Nonnberg, entrusted to his niece Erentrude as first superior; both these communities later became Benedictine. With his companions, Rupert evangelized the country around Salzburg, built churches, civilized the people,

developed the local economy by opening the salt mines, and gave Juvavum its modern name of Salzburg.

Rusinos, monk, born province of Mokk. Armenian Church. He was the treasurer of the monastery of P'as, and of great holiness, although this was unknown to his fellow monks until one had a dream in which he saw Rusinos in heaven. He then became famous, but wishing to escape such attention, he tried to leave the monastery. The other monks barred the way, but he opened the door with the sign of the cross, and left. Nothing more was heard of him. Feast 5 April.

Rusticola, abbess, died Aix-en-Provence, 632. Feast 11 August.

Rusticus of Cahors, bishop and martyr, born Albi, died Cahors, 629. He served as archdeacon at Rodez before becoming bishop at Cahors in 622. He was killed by brigands, and his body thrown into the river. Feast 18 August.

Rusticus of Narbonne, bishop, died Narbonne, *c.* 461. He was the son of a bishop, and after studies in Rome – where he seems to have known St **Jerome** – decided to become a monk. He was elected bishop of Narbonne *c.* 427. It proved a difficult diocese to govern, not least because of the barbarian invasions, and he asked Pope **Leo** for permission to resign, which was refused. Feast 26 October.

Rutolius, martyr, died Africa, in what is now Algeria, *c.* 250. He paid a fee to be exempted from offering sacrifice to the pagan gods, but was nevertheless arrested and executed. Feast 2 August.

Ruways, born Yamin, in the Delta, *c.* 1334, died Dayr al-Handaq, 18 October 1404. Coptic Church. He was the son of poor parents, and a camel driver. When his father converted to Islam, during a persecution against the Christians of Egypt, he fled his home for Cairo and then Upper Egypt, changing his name from Furayg to Ruways (which had been a nickname). He then travelled around Egypt, eating little, sleeping where he could, and living a life of prayer and asceticism, although never becoming a monk. He was once flogged and imprisoned, but took the opportunity to preach to his fellow prisoners. For the last decade or so of his life he was very ill, but did not ask God for renewed health, although many others were cured by his prayers. The headquarters of the Coptic patriarch are situated near the church in which he was buried, and the complex bears his name.

S

Sa'ad of Edessa, bishop, died Edessa, 324. Syriac Church. He was bishop of Edessa from 313, and continued the building of the cathedral begun under his predecessor. Feast 20 April.

Saba, see **Sabas**.

Sabaia, nun, died Tazrisi, Samzache, southern Georgia, eleventh century. Georgian Church. She was superior of the convent of Tazrisi when the sister of **George the Great** was placed there. Feast 30 December.

Sabas, see **Barsonuphius of Tver II, and Saba**.

Sabas of Chachuli, see **George of Chachuli ('the Writer') and Saba**.

Sabas, ninth century, disciple of Ss **Cyril** and **Methodius** and a companion of **Clement the Bulgarian**. Feast (with Clement) 17 July.

Sabas, monk, born Mutalaska, Cappadocia, 439, died near Jerusalem, 532. After several years of life as a solitary, he founded, to the south of Jerusalem, the Mar Sabas Lavra, which still exists. Unusually for a monk of that period, and with some reluctance, he was ordained to the priesthood in 490, and soon after was created superior of all the hermits in Palestine by the patriarch of Jerusalem. Strongly orthodox in his theology, he played a leading role in the struggle against the monophysites and the Origenists. A typicon of the Eastern Church bears his name. Feast 5 December.

Sabas, priest in Bulgaria, ninth century. Feast 9 August.

Sabas Gusniaazad, monk, born Beth Glal, near Diyala, in what is now Iraq, died 488. Syriac Church. He came from an important family, and was a convert from Zoroastrianism through the good offices of a Christian nurse. He became a monk, and worked as an evangelist among the Kurds, founding many churches and religious houses. For the last three years of his life he retired to a monastic cell. Feast 20 August.

Sabas Ioannitis, monk, born in the Epirus, died Limni, fifteenth century. Byzantine Church. A monk at the monastery of Timios Podromos at Limni, renowned for the austerity of his life. Feast 3 February.

Sabas of Kalimnos, bl., born 1862, died island of Kalimnos, 1948. He became a monk at the hermitage of St Anna on Mount Athos, before going to Jerusalem and living for 17 years at the monastery of Ss Johan and George, and at the monastery of St Sabas. He went back to Greece, to the island of Aegina, and later to Patmos. He died on the island of Kalimnos.

Sabas of Krypec, monk, born Lithuania (?), died Krypec, 28 August 1495. Russian Church. He possibly became a monk at Pskov in the 1450s, at the monastery of **Euphrosynus of Pskov**. With Euphrosynus's blessing, after a time he went off to a solitary spot to become a hermit, there building a church dedicated to John the Theologian. Disciples gathered, forming a new monastic community, but like Euphrosynus he refused to become hegumenos. He lived an extremely austere life, having in his cell only an icon, a mat and his monastic habit. He was consulted for spiritual advice by many, but women were strictly forbidden to enter the monastery.

Sabas of Moscow, hegumenos, died Moscow, 1378. He was the successor of **Andronicus** at the monastery of the Holy Face at Moscow. Feast 16 June.

Sabas of Mosok, died Mosok, near Vladimir, sixteenth century. Russian Church. He was the parish priest of Mosok, and revered as a miracle worker. Nothing else is known of him. Feast 23 June.

Sabas of Nigdi, martyr, born Nigdi, Asia Minor, died Constantinople, 12 November 1762. Byzantine Church. He was beheaded for his faith, although nothing else is recorded about him.

Sabas of Serbia I, first archbishop of the Serbian Orthodox Church, born Ras (Serbia), between 1170 and 1175, died Turnovo, Bulgaria, 12 or 14 January 1236. Son of the Serbian ruler **Simeon Stephen Nemanja**, at 17 he ran away to become a monk on Mount Athos, where he and his father founded Hilandar monastery. Later, as abbot of Studenica in Serbia, he preached, taught and interceded in political crises. In 1219 Sabas went to Nicaea, to Patriarch Manuel I Sarantenos and Emperor Theodore I Lascaris, in exile from Constantinople and the Crusaders' Latin kingdom, to present Serbia's request for its own archbishop. Sabas himself was consecrated (Easter 1219 or 1220), which enabled the Serbian Church to be autocephalous and self-perpetuating. Due to Sabas's work, Serbia, on the border between Rome and Constantinople, lies in the Orthodox world.

Sabas of Serbia II, archbishop, died Pec, 1271. Serbian Church. He was a nephew of **Sabas of Serbia I**, and was baptized Predislav. He took the name Sabas when he entered the monastery of Chlendar on Mount Athos. For a while he was bishop of the Zahum region, with his see at Ston, near Dubrovnik, but in 1266 he took charge of the Serbian Church. Feast 8 February.

Sabas of Serbia III, archbishop, died Pec 26, July 1316. Serbian Church. He was hegumenos of the monastery of Chlendar on Mount Athos before becoming a bishop in Kosovo, and then from 1309 archbishop of Serbia.

Sabas of Solovki and Nestor of Solovki, monks, seventeenth century. Russian Church. Sabas was a layman who worked for the Solovki monastery on the White Sea, but seeking greater solitude, he went into the woods and lived as a hermit for 11 years. Nestor was another solitary who lived nearby. Although the dates of their deaths are uncertain, they probably both occurred *c.* 1635. Feast 9 August.

Sabas of Storoza, monk, died Storoza, 3 December 1406. Russian Church. He came to the monastery of the Most Holy Trinity at the time of St **Sergius of Radonez**. When Prince Demetrius Donskoj defeated the khan in 1380 he decided to found a monastery to commemorate the event, asking Sergius to find the place. Sergius did so, on the river Dubenka, where he began the building of a church dedicated to the Dormition of the Mother of God. Sergius apponted Sabas to take charge of it. After Sergius's death, his disciple **Nikon** took over, but when Nikon became a hermit for six years, Sabas was called to be hegumenos of the Trinity monastery. While Sabas was in charge, Sergius's godson, Prince George Dmitrevic, came to visit, and he requested that Sabas return with him to bless his house. Sabas agreed, intending to return to the monastery, but Prince George asked him to found yet another monastery, this time at Storoza, on the Moscow river, not far from Zvenigorod. Overcome by the beauty of the place, Sabas built a church dedicated to the Nativity of the Mother of God, and a cell for himself. However, a group of disciples came to join him, forming a community, on which Sabas imposed the same Rule as that of the Trinity monastery. It was richly endowed by the prince.

Sabas of Suroz, archbishop. Russian Church. Nothing is known of him, although at Suroz, the modern Sudak in the Crimea, there are the remains of a church which is probably where he was buried, before the twelfth century. Feast 2 April.

Sabas of the Kievan Cave Monastery, bl., died Kiev, twelfth/thirteenth century. Russian Church. He was known as a miracle worker. Feast 24 April.

Sabas of Visera, monk, born Kasin, 1381, died Visera, 1 October 1460 or 1461. Russian Church. He came from the noble Borozdin family. He was a pious young man and became a monk, and, although it is unknown which monastery he entered first, it seems that c. 1397 he was co-founder, if not founder, of a monastery at Tver, where he remained until 1412 before going to Mount Athos. He returned from Athos, not to his monastery, but to the life of a mendicant, wandering around the monasteries in the region of Novgorod, until he settled at Visera, not far from Novgorod, where he lived as a hermit. The archbishop of Novgorod rebuked him for establishing himself in this spot without his permission, but Sabas won him over and was able to build a church there, and eventually cells for the other monks who came to form a community around him.

Sabas of Zeleznoborvsk and Benjamin of Zeleznoborvsk, martyrs, fifteenth century. Russian Church. Presumably two monks who were killed by a Tartar attack on their monastery, but nothing else is known of them.

Sabas Reyes Salazar, martyr, born Mexico, 5 December 1879, died Tototlan, Jalisco, Mexico,13 April 1927. A student at the seminary in Guadalajara, he was ordained in 1911, and became parish priest at Tototlan. The village was attacked by government troops – he hid, but was discovered and shot. Feast 25 May.

Sabas Stagiron, bl., martyr, died 1821. Byzantine Church. Nothing more is known of him.

Sabas the Goth, martyr, died Rome, 270. A soldier with Gothic ancestry, he died with some 70 colleagues. Feast 24 April.

Sabas the Goth, martyr, died Tirgovisti, Romania, 372. A reader in church, and a Visigoth, he refused to eat food which had been sacrificed to the gods, and was drowned in the river Mussovo, along with several others. Feast 12 April.

Sabas the Younger, abbot, died Calabria, 995. Abbot of a monastery in Calabria. Feast 5 February.

Sabasius of Tver, monk, died Tver, fifteenth century. Russian Church. Founder of a monastery near Tver, which was remarkable for the austerity of its Rule. Feast 2 March.

Sabbatius, hermit. Syriac Church. Feast 3 May.

Sabina, martyr, Italy, early second century. Her *acta*, written much later, say she was a widow from Umbria who was converted by her servant, Serapia – who came from Antioch in Syria. The *acta* states that in the persecution under Hadrian both were arrested, but while Serapia was killed, Sabina was initially released, only to be rearrested and put to death the following year. The church of St Sabina on the Aventine Hill is believed to contain her relics. Feast 29 August.

Sabina, martyr, born Samos, died Troyes (?), 275. She is venerated at Troyes together with her brother **Sabinian**. Feast 29 August.

Sabinian of Troyes, martyr, born Samos, died Troyes, possibly 275. According to local tradition, he came to Gaul from Samos with his sister **Sabina**, who is also said to have been martyred there in 275. Feast 24 January.

Sabinus and Companions, martyr, died Damascus. These were were 16 Syrian martyrs. Those named are Julian, Maximus, Macrobius, Cassia and Paula, in addition to Sabinus. Feast 20 July.

Sabinus and Companions, martyrs, died Spoleto, c. 303. Sabinus is said to have been a bishop who was arrested during Diocletian's persecution for breaking a statue of Jupiter. His deacons **Marcellus** and **Exuperantius** were killed before he was, and are buried in Assisi, but Sabinus himself was sent back to prison, where he worked miracles and converted the Roman governor – who was then put to death, as was Sabinus. Feast 7 December.

Sabinus of Canosa, born Canosa di Puglia, southern Italy, c. 515, died Puglia, 566. He was bishop of Canosa and an emissary of Pope Agapitus I to

Constantinople for the council presided over by Patriarch Mennas. Feast 9 February.

Sabinus of Hermopolis, martyr, died Antinoë, 287. An Egyptian nobleman, he was drowned in the Nile. Feast 13 March.

Sabinus of Piacenza, bishop, born Rome (?), died Piacenza, Italy, 420. He was sent by the pope to help resolve the Meletian schism at Antioch, and was then appointed bishop of Piacenza. Feast 11 December.

Sabinus of Poitiers, martyr, died Poitiers, fifth century. Said to have been a disciple of St **Germanus of Auxerre**. Feast 11 July.

Sabriso, hegumenos, born Nineveh (Mosul, Iraq), died Bet Nuhadra, *c.* 612. Assyrian Church. He was a disciple of **Abraham of Kaskar**, and entered his monastery on Mount Izla. He later left, believing that the regime had become too lax under Abraham's successor, and settled in the mountainous region on the Iraq-Turkey border, at Bet Nuhadra, where he founded a monastery with other monks who had left at the same time. Feast 1 October.

Sabriso, catholicos, born Peroz-Abad, in the east of modern Iraq, *c.* 520, died 604. Syriac Church. He was a shepherd, but then studied for the priesthood at Nisibis (Nusaybin in Turkey). He then became a hermit on Mount Qardu. Reluctantly he accepted the bishopric of Lasom, and in 596 became catholicos, thanks to the direct intervention of Chosroes II, who much admired him and in whose company he was when he died. He was able to free Christian captives and found churches. Feast 18 September.

Sabriso of Awana, monk, born Awana, Tikrit, died *c.* 650. Syriac Church. He was attracted to the monastic life, and *c.* 630 founded a monastery 'of the Martyrs'. He was offered, but refused, the bishopric of Adiabene (Arbil, Iraq).

Sabriso of Bet Garmai, metropolitan, sixth/seventh century. Syriac Church. Only remembered because he instituted 'the Fast of Nineveh' at a time of plague.

Sacerdos, bishop in Aquitaine, died 720. Feast 5 May.

Sadalaberga, born Laon, died there, 22 September *c.* 665. The sister of **Bodo**, she married twice. Her first husband died soon after the marriage, and she believed this was a sign from God that she should enter a nunnery, which she did. At her father's insistence, however, she agreed to marry a nobleman called Blandinus, and they had five children. The marriage was successful, but late in life Blandinus became a hermit, and Sadalberga joined a monastery she herself had founded at Poulangey. She later returned to Laon, however, and founded a new monastery, which evolved into a double monastery which Blandinus joined as well. Sadalberga ruled as abbess, and after her death her place was taken by her daughter **Anstrudis**. There are many variants of this story.

Sadhost of Seleucia and Companions, martyrs, died Bei-Lapat, Persia, 345. Deacon to Simeon Barsabae, he succeeded him as bishop after his execution, thus becoming the metropolitan of Seleucia-Ctesiphon in Persia. He was put to death with 128 of his flock. He himself was kept in prison for five months before execution; the others were beheaded immediately after their arrest. Feast 20 February.

Sadoc of Sandomierz and Companions, bl., martyrs, died Sandomir, Poland, 1260. A disciple of St **Dominic**, he founded a Dominican priory in Sandomir, where he and the other 48 members of his community were massacred during a Mongol raid. Feast 2 June.

Sadqan ('The Just'), martyrs, born Syria, died Ethiopia, fifth/sixth centuries. A group of Syrian monks who evangelized Ethiopia and were martyred in the course of their mission. Feast 28 October.

Sagar, bishop and martyr, died Laodicea, Phrygia, *c.* 275. The bishop of Laodicea in Phrygia. Feast 6 October.

Sahma, monk, born Antioch, Syria, died Sadenya, Ethiopia, fifth/sixth century. Ethiopian Church.

One of those with **Zamik'ael Aragawi** who came to evangelize Ethiopia. Feast 24 January.

Salama, metropolitan, born Egypt, died Ethiopia, 13 August 1388. Ethiopian Church. Possibly a monk of the monastery of St Macarius at Wadi Natrun, he became metropolitan in 1348, and was responsible for the translation of numerous texts from Arabic.

Salamanes the Silent, born Kapersana on the Euphrates, died 390. He lived as a hermit in a cave near the bank of the river, and is remembered as the first hermit to take upon himself the vow of silence. Efforts were made to persuade him to be ordained, but he refused. Feast 23 January.

Salib, martyr, born Hur (Ibsadah), near al-Asmunayn, died Cairo, 29 November 1512. Coptic Church. His parents forced him against his will to marry, but he and his wife agreed to live in chastity. This they did for a time, then Salib left his home and started visiting monasteries. He was forced back, but he was eventually allowed his freedom to choose. By then, however, he had decided on martyrdom. He began preaching Christianity wherever he was, was arrested, taken to Cairo and executed there.

Sallita, born Egypt, died either Bet Zabdai, on Mount Saba, near Penek, or Balad, north-west of Mosul. Syriac Church. Nothing is known of him, or of his reasons for coming to Syria, but two places claim to be the locality of his death. Feast 19 September.

Sallita, martyr, died Egypt, 362. Possibly an (Arian) governor of Egypt more properly named Artemius, who was executed under the Emperor Julian the Apostate for rising up against him. He was transformed into a saint in the ninth century.

Salome, born Warab, died monastery of Dabra Libanos, 1 May, mid-fifteenth century. Ethiopian Church. She was a pious child, and was determined to dedicate herself to God. When her parents tried to force her into marriage, her suitor was prevented from approaching her, and she fled. She spent some time visiting the monasteries of Ethiopia, eventually settling as a nun at Dabra Libanos.

Salome, martyr, born Georgia (?), died Jerusalem, thirteenth century. Georgian Church. She was a nun in a convent in Jerusalem who converted to Islam, but quickly repented of her act and reverted to Christianity, for which she was tortured and beheaded. Feast 20 July.

Salome, bl., abbess, born Krakow, died Sandomierz, 17 November 1268. She was the daughter of the prince of Krakow, and was married, when only three, to the six-year-old son of the king of Hungary. They were taken prisoners for a time, after which the marriage was solemnized, and Salome's husband ruled Dalmatia and Slavonia until his death in battle in 1241. The following year Salome returned to Poland and founded a convent of Poor Clares at Sandomierz, which she eventually entered herself, and became abbess.

Salome and Judith, anchorites, died Altaich, Bavaria, ninth century (?). They are reputed to have been two English princesses: Salome went on a pilgrimage to the Holy Land, but on her return settled at Altaich as an anchorite, where Judith found her when she was sent to look for her – but she settled at Altaich herself, also as an anchorite. The English 'princesses' cannot be identified. Nor can the abbot of Altaich who is supposed to have given them a home. Feast 29 June.

Salome and Perozhavr, fourth century. Georgian Church. Both women were nobly born: Salome was the daughter of the Armenian King Tiridates, while Perozhavr was the mother of one of the grand dukes of Karthli. Both were witnesses of the death in Kuchethi of St **Nina**. Feast 15 January.

Salvador Lara Puente, born 13 August 1905, died near Chalchihuites, Mexico, 14 August 1926. He was president of Catholic Action in Chalchihuites, and had attempted to obtain the release of **Louis Batiz Sainz**, and as a consequence died with him. Feast 25 May.

Salvator Lilli, bl., martyr, born Cappadocia, east of Avezzano, Italy, 19 June 1853, died Marasc, Armenia, 22 November 1895. He became a

Franciscan in 1870, and when the religious orders were suppressed in Italy he went to Palestine, living first in Bethlehem, then in Jerusalem, where he was ordained in 1878. Two years later he was sent to Marasc in Armenia, where he ministered with great success for 15 years. He was then sent to Mujuk-deresi. During the Turkish persecution of the Armenians, he was repeatedly advised to leave the country, but refused. He was arrested, taken to Marasc, and there bayoneted to death with several members of his parish, who were all beatified with him in 1982. Feast 19 November.

Salvator of Orta, born Santa Coloma, near Gerona, Spain, 1520, died Cagliari, Sardinia, 1567, canonized 1938. A Franciscan brother from 1540, he became known for curing people while out begging. Annoyed by the resulting crowds, his superiors moved him repeatedly, but people always found him. Feast 18 March.

Salvius, martyr, born and died proconsular Africa, second century. Feast 11 January.

Salvius, bishop, born Albi, died there, 10 September 584. He was a lawyer who abandoned his profession after some years and entered a monastery near Albi, where he eventually became abbot, although he preferred to live as a recluse. In 574 he was made bishop of Albi, and was a defender of **Gregory of Tours** against a charge of calumny against the queen. He died of plague, after ministering to the people of his city who were suffering from the disease.

Samonas, see **Gurias and Samonas**.

Samosata, Martyrs of, see **Martyrs of Samosata**.

Sampson, see **Samson**.

Samra Ab of Dabaka Balasa, fourteenth century. Ethiopian Church. A disciple of **Zena Marqos** in the evangelization of the Muslims of Adal.

Samra Krestos, monk, born Adua, Tigre, fourteenth century. Ethiopian Church. A monk of Dabra Wifat, renowned for his miracles, but little else is known of him.

Samson, bishop, born south Wales, *c.* 486, died probably at Dol, Brittany, sometime after 557. He was ordained by St Dubric and became a monk, and later abbot, of the monastic community on Caldey Island. He is thought to have visited Ireland and to have lived for a while in a cave near the river Severn. He was made a bishop and, following a vision, went to Cornwall and then on to Brittany, where he founded the monastery at Dol which was to be at the hub of much missionary activity. He was also bishop there, although no diocese existed as such for some time afterwards. He was present at the Councils of Paris in 553 and 557. Feast 28 July.

Samson the Hospitable (or Xenodochius), born Constantinople (?), died there, *c.* 530. He came from a wealthy family which claimed to be descended from the Emperor **Constantine**. He studied medicine in order to devote himself to the care of the poor and sick. He gave away much of his wealth, and founded a hospital. He was ordained priest because of his piety. Feast 27 June.

Samthann, abbess, died Ireland, 739. She is said to have been offered in marriage but refused and became a nun, either in Donegal or County Cavan. She was apparently a good administrator, for **Funech** summoned her to Clonbroney abbey in County Longford to take over from her. Feast 18 December.

Samuel, see also **Elias, Jeremias, Isaias, Samuel and Daniel**.

Samuel Marzorati, bl., martyr, Franciscan, born Biumo, Italy, 10 September 1670, martyred Ethiopia, 3 March 1716, with **Liberatus Weiss**, beatified 1988.

Samuel of Benhadar, monk, died 17 December, year unknown. Coptic Church. He was ordained priest by the bishop of Qift, and placed at the head of a monastic community on Mount Benhadar. He is recorded as living off bread flavoured with salt.

Samuel of Dabra Halleluya, monk, died Dabra Halleluya, 26 July 1347. He was the son of a priest, and was baptized Na'akweto La'ab, changing his name to Samuel when he became a monk. He studied under his maternal uncle **Abiya Egzi** before becoming a disciple of **Anthony** of Da'ero. He eventually went to live as a hermit in the desert with **Gabra Masqal**, and the two of them founded the monastery Dabra Halleluya between Mareb and Adua in Tigre.

Samuel of Edessa, born Edessa (Urfa, Turkey), died Constantinople, c. 490. A priest at Edessa, and a controversialist against the Nestorians and monophysites. Feast 9 August.

Samuel of Kalamon ('the Confessor'), monk, born Tkello, near the city of Pelhip, c. 597, died al-Qalamun, province of Fayyum, 4 December 695. Coptic Church. The son of a priest, he was ordained a subdeacon at the age of 12, by which time he was already showing signs of wanting to be a monk. His parents wished him to marry, but he refused to do so. He was ordained deacon at 18. Four years later his father died, after which he left his village for the desert of Scete, coming eventually to the monastery of St Macarius, where he became a monk and was ordained. He rejected all the efforts of the emperor to make him accept the Chalcedonian formula, for which he was tortured almost to death (hence the title 'the Confessor') and lost one eye. He then left the monastery and went to the district of al-Fayyum with four companions, where he became abbot of a large monastery and gained a reputation as a miracle worker. The persecution did not cease, however, and he had to flee again, this time settling at a spot called Takinas, where he found a ruined church buried under the desert sand and restored it, again creating a monastery. One day a passing group of barbarians took him prisoner, then sold him as a slave. He worked as a camel herdsman for three years, his master trying to marry him to another slave – even going so far as to chain the two together – but he remained chaste and was eventually liberated, being taken to the monastery of Kalamon (al-Qalamun) in Fayyum, where he remained for 57 years. He gathered many disciples, so many that he had to extend the monastic church, and was visited by many notables, partly at least because of his reputation as a miracle worker.

Samuel of Qartmin, monk, born Estin, north of Mardin, died 4 May c. 410. Syriac Church. He

founded a monastery near to his village, but then for three years became a hermit on a mountain north-east of Nisibis. A number of disciples gathered around him, and he founded a monastery for them, where he lived for seven years, being ordained priest by the bishop of Sawur.

Samuel of Qoyasa, monk, born Macalle, fourteenth/fifteenth century. Ethiopian Church. A disciple of **Madhanina Egzi**, he became a hermit, then founded the monastery at Qoyasa.

Samuel of Saqurt, monk, fourteenth century. Ethiopian Church. A disciple of **Madhanina Egzi**, he was a monk in Tigre.

Samuel of Tarita, monk, born Tigre, died Dabra Tarita, Tigre, fourteenth century. A disciple of **Madhanina Egzi**.

Samuel of Wagag, monk, born Zem (Bulga, Ethiopia), died Yazarzar, 27 October, year unknown, fifteenth century. Ethiopian Church. He is said to have been born while his mother was on her way back from church, holding the Eucharist in his right hand. At the age of seven he was handed over for his education to **Takla Haymanot**, who had foretold his birth. After he had become a monk and was ordained priest, he set out for Wagag, where he founded a monastery and evangelized the surrounding region. He became widely known for his miracle-working, for his battle against demons and magicians, and his preaching. He also founded many churches.

Samuel of Waldeba, monk, born Axum, fourteenth/fifteenth century. Ethiopian Church. Of pious parents, he was orained deacon, and then betrothed to a rich young woman. However, he went off to Bankol, to the monastery of **Madhanina Egzi**, where he became a monk. After two years he met his father, by this time a widower, who also decided to become a monk. They went to the monastery of Wayna, where his father died. Samuel then went into the desert. He had a reputation for miracle-working, and for visions. On one occasion he was taken captive by brigands, who refused to release him, when they discovered who he was, until he had performed a miracle: a cloud came down and took him back to his hermitage. He was also renowned for his familiarity with wild animals, on one occasion assisting a lion to give birth. He died aged 100.

Sana, martyr, died Pelusium, 19 April, third/fourth century. Coptic Church. A soldier, and a companion of **Isidore of Takinas**, they were condemned to death by the governor of Pelusium (near Damietta in the Nile Delta), although Sana was first sent to Alexandria.

Sanctinus, bishop, died Verdun, 584. There is also a bishop of Meaux with the same name, reputed to have died c. 300. The two may be identical. There is a shrine of Sanctinus at Verdun. Feast 7 January.

Sanctus of Urbino, bl., Franciscan, died Ancona, 1390. Feast 14 August.

Sandratus, abbot, born Trier (?), died Gladbach, 986. A monk of Trier, in 972 he was sent by the Emperor Otto I to reform the monastery at St Gall. He went on to become abbot of Gladbach, and from 981, apparently simultaneously, of Weissenburg. Feast 24 August.

Sanducht, martyr, died Armenia, early second century. She is said to have been the daughter of the king of Armenia, and one of the very first converts to Christianity, put to death by her father.

Sansno, Coptic Church. Nothing is known of this saint, except that two churches are dedicated to him.

Sanusios I, patriarch, born Batanun in the Nile Delta, died al-Mahallah al-Kubra, 19 April 880. Coptic Church. He became a monk at the monastery of St Macarius, and eventually hegumenos there. While in Cairo on business for his community, he was elected patriarch, the electors having failed to agree on anyone else. He was taken to Alexandria and consecrated as patriarch in January 858. He combated simony in the Church, which was widespread because of the heavy taxes churchmen had to pay to the state, and was a firm opponent of heresy. He also improved the supply of water to Alexandria. In 861 a new governor was sent to Egypt who vastly increased the taxes on the patriarch. Sanusios protested, then went into

hiding for six months, but ultimately had to find the money through increased charges on bishops and wealthy Christians, which led in turn to many abjuring the faith. The regime in Egypt was unstable, with governors following one after another in quick succession. The consequence was increased difficulty for Christians, with churches and monasteries being attacked. Sanusios himself assisted with building new fortifications for the monasteries. In the end he had to leave Alexandria and take refuge in al-Mahallah al-Kubra, although even there he was imprisoned for a month, and only released after a rich Christian had paid a ransom, because of accusations made against him by a monk. He died soon after he was released.

Saqaw'a Dengel, monk, died Dabra Zalkhun. Ethiopian Church. The son of a priest, when he was 30 his father entered the monastery of Dabra Zalkhun and became its abbot. Saqaw'a Dengel then entered the same monastery, and succeeded his father as abbot. He is reported to have healed a paralysed man. Feast 8 November.

Sarah, born Egypt, died Saintes-Maries-de-la-Mer, France, first century. Also known as Sarah the Black, she is said to have been the servant of the two Marys, who, according to the legend, came to France after the crucifixion. She is the patron saint of gypsies. Feast 19 August.

Sarapamones, martyr, born Asmun, Upper Egypt, died al-Qusiyyah, north of Asyut, fourth century. Killed with his wife and son by an Arian governor on 3 February, although the year is not known.

Sarapamones Abu Tarhah (Sarapamones the veiled one), bishop, born al-Sarqiyyah in the Nile Delta, died 1853. Coptic Church. In his youth he sold oil on the streets of Cairo, where he was once accused of killing someone. To prove his innocence he raised the person from the dead, who then protested that Salib (his original name) was not guilty, so the young man was released. He then entered the monastery of St Anthony, and was consecrated bishop of al-Minufiyah, taking the name Sarapamones. He had a gift for miracles, and a great love for the poor. When distributing alms to the poor he always covered his face – hence his name. As bishop he had responsibility for marriage cases in the patriarchate.

Sarapamones of Scete, monk, born Upper Egypt. Coptic Church. He was a monk of the monastery of St John in Scete. After being there for 30 years he was named hegumenos, and he held this post for another 20 years, after which for 15 years he lived as a recluse. He ate only on Saturdays and Sundays. He died on 1 March, but the year is unknown.

Saraqa Berhan, monk, fifteenth century. Ethiopian Church. First a hermit, he later founded a monastery at Alaughien, which was miraculously defended from attack when suddenly the land around it became swampy, and the enemy was attacked by a swarm of bees.

Sarbel (Sarbil, Sarvel) and Bebaia, martyrs, born Edessa, died there, second century. Sarbel was a pagan priest who converted to Christianity, Bebaia his sister. Both died for their faith. Feast 29 January.

Sarmatas, martyr, died Egypt, 357. A disciple of St **Anthony**, he was killed when his monastery was attacked by barbarians. Feast 11 October.

Sarmeanes, catholicos, eighth century. Georgian Church. Nothing is known of him except that he was head of the Church in Georgia. Feast 21 August.

Sarra of the Nile, nun, died Egypt, fourth/fifth century. Feast 13 July.

Sarsa Petros, monk, born Enabse, Goggiam, Ethiopia, fifteenth century. He founded the monastery of Dabra Warq in Goggiam.

Saturninus, born Carthage, died Rome, c. 308. A priest who was beheaded on the Salarian Way, together with a deacon called Sisinnius. Feast 29 November.

Saturninus, martyred Carthage, 304. A priest, he led his congregation in professing their faith, together with **Dativus**, a senator, when all were arrested under Diocletian. The men and women,

including Saturninus's children, were all tortured and seem to have died in prison as a result. Feast 12 February.

Saturninus and Lupus, martyrs, died Caesarea, Cappadocia. Feast 14 October.

Saturninus of Toulouse, bishop and martyr, born Africa (?), died Toulouse, third century (?). Apparently a missionary bishop who evangelized Toulouse and the region around it. He is said to have had a small church in his house, next door to a temple. When the temple idols stopped prophesying, the presence of a Christian bishop was blamed, and he was put to death. He was much venerated in south-west France and northern Spain under the variant name of St **Sermin**. Feast 29 November.

Saturninus, Theophilus and Revocata, martyrs. Feast 6 February.

Saturninus, Thyrsus and Victor, martyrs, died Alexandria, c. 250. Feast 22 March.

Satyrus, martyr, died Achaia, Greece. Said to have been put to death for insulting the gods. Feast 12 January.

Satyrus, see also **Titus**.

Satyrus, born Trier (then in Gaul), c. 330, died Milan, c. 379. What is known of Satyrus comes from the recollections of his brother, **Ambrose of Milan**. He was born at Trier, but the family moved back to Rome after the death of their father. He became a lawyer, then a civil administrator, but when Ambrose was elected bishop he moved to Milan to assist him in running the diocese, although still only a catechumen. A brush with death at sea made him request baptism. He died suddenly in the arms of Ambrose. Feast 17 September.

Sava, see **Sabas**.

Savin, born Barcelona (?), died Tarbes (?), fifth century (?). Said to have been the apostle of the region of France around Lourdes before becoming a hermit. Feast 9 October.

Savina Petrilli, bl., founder, born Siena, 1851, died there, 18 April 1923. She began by teaching religion to her brothers and sisters, and this inspired her to think that her first mission was to teach catechism to street children. She founded the Sisters of the Poor of St Catherine of Siena, with a broad remit to help the poor, the sick and the elderly.

Sawl, born and died Wales, sixth century. The father of St **Asaph**. Feast 15 January.

Sayat-Nova, martyr, born Tbilisi, *c.* 1712, died 1795. Armenian Church. He came from an Armenian family, and in his younger days was a weaver. He married and had four children. He became acquainted with the poetical and musical traditions of Persia, and became well known as a singer. In 1740 he was appointed by the king of Georgia as a court musician and composer, bringing Persian styles into Georgian music – he composed in Russian and Turkish, as well as Armenian and Georgian. After a time he felt a growing distaste for the intrigues of the court, and his music and poetry expressed an increasing desire to turn to spiritual things. In 1760 he abandoned both the court and his family and entered a monastery. He was ordained priest, but his success as a poet and composer pursued him, and he returned to Tbilisi. When Persia invaded Georgia in 1795, he felt he had to leave his monastery to look after two of his children, their mother having died. He sent them safely into Russia, but he himself was killed when the Persian troops attacked the monastery in Tbilisi where he was staying.

Sayfa Mikael, monk, born Eggala, Eritrea, *c.* 1644, died Sa'ad Embla, 27 October 1740. He became a monk at Beta Qerqos in Tigre, but then with a number of disciples he founded his own monastery, dedicated to the Trinity, in Eritrea at Sa'ad Embla ('the White Mountain'), south of the city of Karan. He chose the spot because it was on the borders of Muslim-held territory, and he wanted his monastery to be a beacon of Christianity. It was richly endowed by successive emperors, one of them even building a retreat near it, intending to retire there before his death – although he died while on his way there. Sayfa Mikael played a considerable part in the theological disputes of the period between the monks of the different monasteries, and was also actively hostile to Catholic missionaries who were attempting to make headway in Ethiopia. He had himself a strong missionary impulse, preaching the faith in surrounding regions, as well as teaching in many of the monasteries of the country.

Schecelinus, bl., hermit, died Luxembourg, *c.* 1138. Feast 6 August.

Scholastica, died near Monte Cassino, Italy, 547. Sister of **Benedict**, she founded a nunnery close to his monastery. It is said they met annually and that she obtained a thunderstorm from God to keep Benedict longer with her on their last encounter before her death. Their joint tomb survives at Monte Cassino. Feast 10 February.

Scialva, see **Bidzina, Scialva and Elisbar**.

Scio Garegeli, monk, martyr, born Vedzisi, near Tbilisi, died monastery of Davidgaregi, 1 June 1700. Georgian Church. He was married as a young man, but widowed shortly afterwards, so decided to become a monk at the monastery of Davidgaregi, where he quickly gained a reputation for the holiness of his life and his dedication to prayer and fasting. When the monastery was sacked by Muslim tribesmen from the Caucasus, Scio and three other monks attempted to prevent them carrying away icons and other sacred and valuable objects, and were killed.

Sciota Rustveli, born Rustavi, province of Mescheti, southern Georgia, died Jerusalem (?), thirteenth century. Georgian Church. He was a distinguished member of the aristocracy, and treasurer to Queen Tamara. He gave a large donation to the monastery of the Holy Cross in Jerusalem, which he is believed to have entered as a monk towards the end of his life. He is the author of a famous Georgian poem. Feast 25 May.

Sciuscianik, grand duchess, died Zurtavi, 17 October 475. Georgian Church. She came from an aristocratic family, and married Varsken, the grand duke of Karthli who, in 467, converted to Zoroastrianism to gain favour with the king of Persia.

When he returned to Zurtavi he announced his change of religion, but told the clergy that he had no intention of persecuting Christians. Sciuscianik, however, was extremely angry at her husband's action, and made clear her feelings in public. In April 469 she was sent to prison in chains – which she refused to allow anyone to remove. Her actions won her great respect from the Georgian people which survives down to the present day, not least because the account of her sufferings, written not long after her death in prison, is one of the earliest and best examples of Georgian literature.

Scubillion Rousseau, bl., born Annay-la-Cité, near Dijon, 22 March 1797, died St Leu, Réunion, 13 April 1867. His baptismal name was Jean-Baptiste: he took the name Scubillion when he joined the de la Salle Brothers and worked in various parts of France before being sent to the island of Réunion in the Indian Ocean. Apart from teaching in the school, he spent his evenings teaching catechism to the slaves, and he came to represent them before the government.

Sebald, hermit, born Italy (?), died in the Reichswald, Germany, eighth century. Before travelling to Germany as a missionary with **Willibald**, he had been a hermit at Vicenza. He lived as a hermit in Germany, but evangelized the countryside around his hermitage. Feast 19 August.

Sebastia, see **Innocent, Sebastia and Companions**.

Sebastian, martyr, died Rome, 288 (?). An army officer under the Emperor Diocletian. When the fact that he was a Christian became known, he was tied to a tree and used for target practice, although the arrows did not kill him, and he was beaten to death. Feast 20 January.

Sebastian Kimura, bl., born Hirado, Japan, 1565, died Nagasaki, 10 September 1622. The grandson of one of the converts of **Francis Xavier**, he joined the Jesuits, served as a catechist in Miyako, and was sent to Macao to study theology. He was ordained in Nagasaki in 1601, the first Japanese to become a priest. When persecution broke out two decades later, he was told to leave Nagasaki, where he was working, but was arrested before he could do so. He was imprisoned in Suzuta with **Charles**

Spinola and others, but then burned to death by being slowly roasted over a fire just outside Nagasaki.

Sebastian Maggi, bl., Dominican, born Brescia, died Genoa, 16 December 1496. He came from a distinguished Genovese family, and joined the Dominican order when he was 15. He was a successful preacher, and held many offices in his order. He was, for a time, the superior of Savonarola.

Sebastian Newdigate, bl., martyr, born Harefield, Middlesex, died Tyburn, London, 19 June 1535. From a pious family (a sister became a Dominican nun), he studied at Cambridge university, married and had a daughter. After the death of his wife in 1524, he entered the Carthusians in London. He first accepted the supremacy of the king over the Church in England, although adding 'in so far as the law of God allows'. He was eventually arrested for disloyalty to the crown, was imprisoned in the Marshalsea, then the Tower of London, and eventually condemned to be hanged, drawn and quartered.

Sebastian of Aparicio, bl., born La Gudiña, Orense, Spain, 20 January 1502, died Puebla, Mexico, 25 February 1600. His parents were peasants, and he worked as a shepherd and as a hired hand before becoming a valet in Salamanca. When he was 31 he emigrated to Mexico, settling in Puebla, where again he worked on the land, but also in many other jobs, including road building. He became quite wealthy, although he gave away much of his money to the poor. He married twice, but outlived both his wives. When he was 72 he entered the Franciscans as a lay brother, and spent the rest of his life begging for alms for his community. Even during his life he had a reputation as a miracle worker.

Sebastian of Esztergom, bishop, died Esztergom, 1036. He was consecrated in 1002, the second bishop of Esztergom, and was an ally of King **Stephen I** of Hungary in evangelizing the Magyars. Feast 30 December.

Sebastian of Karaganda, monk, born Orel, 1884, died Karaganda, 19 April 1966. Russian Church.

Baptized Stephen Vasilevic Formin, he became a monk at the monastery of Optina Pustyn in 1906. He was ordained a priest in 1927, and from the following year until 1933 he served as a parish priest at Kozlov. In 1933 he was arrested and sent to a prison camp at Karaganda in Kazakhstan. When he was released in 1943 he remained in Karaganda, where he gathered a small group of monks – it rapidly became bigger – and eventually founded a church. He remained as priest – the only one – in Karaganda until his death. In 1957 he became an archimandrite, and he was able to train others for the priesthood. Immediately after his death pilgrimages began to his tomb.

Sebastian of Posechone, monk, died Posechone, 1492 (possibly 1542). He occupied a hermitage not far from the city of Posechone. When a group of disciples gathered around him, he decided to found a monastery not far from Romanovo, on the river Sochot. Feast 26 February.

Sebastian Rostok, ven., bishop, born Grottkau, Silesia, 24 August 1607, died Breslau (now Wroclau), 9 June 1671. A member of the cathedral chapter of Breslau during the Thirty Years War, Rostok was engaged principally in providing spiritually and materially for some 600 parishes of the diocese restored to Catholicism at the command of Ferdinand III. It fell to Rostok to renew religious practices in these churches and to staff them with clergy. He became bishop of the diocese in 1665.

Sebastian Valfré, bl., born Verduno, near Alba, Italy, 1651, died Turin, 30 January 1710. He became a priest of the Oratory in Turin and was appointed superior in 1661. He is remembered for his missions in Piedmont and Switzerland and for his work with young people. He was seen as a caring confessor and as a saint in his lifetime.

Sebastiana, martyr, born Marcianopolis, died Heraclea, c. 90. Said to have been a disciple of Paul the Apostle, she was arrested in Marcianopolis, but when all attempts to execute her failed, she was sent to Heraclea, where she was beheaded. Feast 16 September.

Sebbe, king, died London, c. 694. King of the East Saxons (Essex), he reconverted his people to Christianity after they had fallen back into paganism. A devout man, shortly before his death he resigned the crown and took the monastic habit. He is said to have founded the first monastery at Westminster. Feast 29 August.

Secunda and Runa, see **Rufina and Secunda**.

Secundinus, martyr. Feast 1 August.

Secundinus, see also **Agapius**.

Secundinus, bishop, died Apulia, Italy, fifth/sixth century. He was a bishop in Apulia. Feast 11 February.

Secundinus, bishop, born France, died Ireland, 447. Sent from Gaul to assist **Patrick** in the conversion of Ireland, he was possibly a bishop before he arrived. He was left in charge when Patrick went to Rome, according to one version of Patrick's life. Feast 27 November.

Secundinus of Córdoba, martyr, died Córdoba, 306 (?). Feast 21 May.

Secundus, martyr, died Asti, Piedmont, possibly 119. According to the account of his life, after becoming a Christian he was beheaded for ministering to **Marcianus**, an imprisoned Christian, and burying his body after he had been beheaded. He is the patron saint of Asti. Feast 31 March.

Secundus, Carpophorus and Companions, martyrs, died Como, 295 (?). A group of soldiers, in addition to those named there were Exanthus, Cassius, Severinus and Licinius. Feast 7 August.

Secundus, Darius, Paul and Zosimus, martyrs, died Nicaea. Feast 19 December.

Secundus of Alexandria and Companions, martyrs, died Alexandria, 357. Secundus was a priest, put to death with some of his laity by the Arian patriarch George. Feast 21 May.

Sege Dengel, monk, fifteenth century. Ethiopian Church. Nothing is known of him beyond the fact that he was the composer of a hymn in honour of Mary.

Sege Sellase, monk. Ethiopian Church. Feast 29 March.

Seleucus, martyr, died Casearea, Palestine, 309. Died after praising the constancy of St **Porphyry of Caesarea**. Feast 16 February.

Seleucus, martyr, born Syria. Feast 24 March.

Seleucus, Hieronides, Leontius, Serapion, Valerius and Straton, martyrs, died Alexandria, 300 (?). Leontius and Serapion were brothers, Hieronides was a deacon. All were drowned at sea. Feast 12 September.

Senan of Scattery Island (Inis Cathaigh), born Corca Bhaisin, County Clare, Ireland, died Inis Cathaig, 8 March 544. A monk, and born into a Christian family, he founded the monasteries of Iniscarra near Cork, Inis Mor on Canon Island, Mutton Island in County Clare and Scattery Island in the Shannon river estuary, near his birthplace.

Senator, bishop, born Milan, died there, *c.* 480. He was a young priest when he attended the Council of Chalcedon as the legate of Pope **Leo I**. Later he became archbishop of Milan. Feast 29 May.

Sennen, see **Abdon and Sennen**.

Senoch, abbot, born Poitou, died St-Senou, Touraine, 576. A convert to Christianity, he became a hermit at what is now St-Senou. Three years before his death he left his hermitage for a time to greet the new bishop of Tours, **Gregory**, and the two became firm friends. He is said to have helped repair bridges, and is patron of bridge builders. Feast 24 October.

Senophons, monk, died Robejka, 26 June 1262. Originally a monk of the monastery at Chutyn, near Novgorod, he became a solitary and eventually founded a monastery on the river Robejka, not far from Chutyn.

Senufe, martyr, born Egypt, died there, *c.* 300. Coptic Church.

Senufe, monk, martyr, died Cairo, 11 May 1164. Coptic Church. A monk of the monastery of St Macarius, he was caught up in a civil war while visiting Cairo, and ordered to become a Muslim or be executed. He refused to deny his faith, was killed and his body burned.

Sequanus, abbot, born Mesmont (?), Burgundy, died St-Seine-l'Abbaye, *c.* 580. Founder of the abbey in which he died, possibly after living for a while as a hermit. Feast 19 November.

Serana (Fina), born San Geminiano, Tuscany, died there, 1253. Never a nun, she appears to have followed the Benedictine Rule at home. This may have been because she suffered all her life from painful diseases that others found repulsive and led to her being neglected. Feast 12 March.

Seraphim, bl., born Zeli, 1527, died Dombu, 6 May 1602. Byzantine Church. He entered when still quite young the monastery of the Prophet Elias on Mount Karkara, about an hour from his home. There he lived in a cave, and built himself a small church. He was still visited by his parents, and after a time he asked them to place him in another nearby monastery, although he stayed there only six months before moving to Mount Sagmatio, at the summit of which was the monastery of the Transfiguration. There he stayed for ten years, during which time he was ordained priest, but then he decided to become a solitary at Dombu. In response to a vision he determined to build a monastery there, which he began with the approval of the patriarch. But his strong personality made enemies, he was reported to the Turkish authorities as a swindler, and was arrested and taken to Livadia. His captors let him go free, however – thanks, it is said, to two miracles he performed on their behalf – and he returned to his monastery.

Seraphim, born Montegranaro, 1540, died Ascoli Piceno, 12 October 1604. Baptized Felice a Rapagnano and a shepherd in his youth, at the age of 18 he joined the Capuchins as a lay brother. He was unpopular, and was sent from house to house, until he settled at Ascoli Piceno where he worked as the doorkeeper. He had a particular apostolate to the poor of the town. Feast 17 October.

Seraphim, martyr, born Gluchov, *c.* 1870, died Mount Kyzyl-zar, Kazakhstan, 11 August 1921. Russian Church. Baptized Alexander Efimovic Bogoslov, while still very young he joined the monastery of Glinskaja Pustyn near Kursk. He then moved to a missionary monastery in what is now Kazakhstan. He was a painter of icons and a singer, and in 1909 was ordained priest. He later created a hermitage with **Anatolius of Odessa** on Mount Mochnataja, where many came looking for advice and spiritual direction. The two monks then moved to Mount Kyzyl-zar, where again Seraphim became a director to many. The two were killed by Red Army soldiers who had spent the night in their hermitage.

Seraphim Cicagov, bishop, martyr, born 1856, died Butovo, 11 December 1937. Russian Church. He was born into a military family, and baptized Leonid Michailovic Cicagov. He was commissioned into the artillery of the imperial guard, and in the Russo-Turkish war of 1877–8 he was decorated for bravery. From 1878 he took **John of Kronstadt** as his spiritual director. He married the following year, and after a few years left the army and was ordained priest in 1893, working in Moscow. In 1895 his wife died, and he decided to become a monk, entering the monastery of St **Sergius of Radonez**. In 1905 he became bishop of Suchumi, then in quick succession of Orel, Kilinev and, in 1912, archbishop of Tver. In 1918 he was named metropolitan of Warsaw, but could not go there. In 1921 he was exiled to a remote part of Russia, but in 1928 he became metropolitan of what was by then Leningrad. He retired in 1933 and went to live in Moscow. He was arrested in November 1937, despite the fact that he was extremely ill, and was shot.

Seraphim of Karditsa, archbishop and martyr, born Bezula, Agrapha, died Constantinople, 4 December 1611. Byzantine Church. He became a monk at an early age, then archbishop of Phanar and Neochorion. When the archbishop of Larissa, Denis the Philosopher, raised a rebellion against the Turks, Seraphim was accused of being involved. He was offered his life were he to abjure Christianity, but he refused to do so, and was executed.

Seraphim of Sarov, monk, born Kursk, 19 July 1759, died Sarov monastery, 2 January 1833. Russian Church. Baptized Procoro Mosnin, he worked for a time in his brother's business, but at the age of 18 he decided to become a monk. He made a pilgrimage to the Kievan Cave monastery and, with the blessing of **Dosithea of the Kiev Caves**, he became a monk at Sarov in 1780. In 1794 he entered total seclusion in the nearby forest for 16 years, followed by another 15 years in silent prayer in the monastery. In 1825 he opened his room to all visitors, and his fame as a healer, a miracle worker and a spiritual adviser spread throughout Russia. In the final years of his life he gave a great deal of time to founding, and then caring for, a convent of nuns for which he formulated a Rule of life, including the rule of perpetual silence. He left no writings, but his famous *Conversation with Motovilov* on the acquisition of the Holy Spirit has been constantly reprinted. He was canonized at the insistence of the imperial family in 1903. Feast 2 January.

Seraphina of Sezenovo, nun, born Nizne-Lomov, 14 September 1806, died Sezenovo, 13 February 1877. Russian Church. Baptized Eutimia Efimova Morgaceva, she came from a large peasant family. She refused to marry, saying she wanted to dedicate herself to God in prayer and Bible reading, and working in the fields. In 1823 she began living in a small cell near the parish church, earning her living by working at various tasks. In 1838 **John of Sezenovo**, whom she had taken as her spiritual director, put her in charge of collecting money for a new church he was building. For two years she went about collecting alms, and then in 1840 she settled in the small community which John had begun in Sezenovo. She continued to collect money for the new foundation, and from 1844 to 1852 lived in St Petersburg. After the creation of a nunnery had been formally approved, she was in charge of acquiring icons and other items for the foundation, dedicated to St **John of Kazan**. In 1853 she became the superior of the community, taking the name Seraphina. Feast 28 July.

Seraphina Sforza, bl., born Urbino, 1434, died Pesaro, 8 September 1478. Baptized Sueva, she was early left an orphan, and was brought up in Rome by her uncle Cardinal Colonna. In January 1448 she married Alessandro Sforza, lord of Pesaro. Although the marriage started happily enough, it began to degenerate and Alessandro accused her of trying to poison him. He threw her out of their home, and she was taken in by a convent of Poor Clares. Although Alessandro eventually came to ask her forgiveness, she remained in the convent to the end of her life, eventually becoming its abbess.

Serapion, martyr, died Alexandria, first century. Feast 21 March.

Serapion, bl., martyr, born England (?), died Algiers, 1240. Said to have been born in England, but had served in the army of Alfonso IX of Leon before meeting the founder of the Mercedarians, **Peter Nolasco**, and joining the order. He went to Algeria to ransom Christian captives, but on his third trip he was held in prison while the balance of the ransom was being found. In prison he converted a Muslim to Christianity, for which he was crucified. Feast 14 November.

Serapion and Companions, martyrs, died Alexandria. Their names, in addition to Serapion, were Cerulus, Pupulus and Gaius. Feast 28 February.

Serapion Garegeli, hegumenos, born Imereti, western Georgia, died Garegeli, 1742. Georgian Church. He became a monk at Davidgaregi, and in 1719, on the recommendation of the king of Kacheti, he was made superior of the monastery, a post he held almost to the end of his life. He had a wide reputation as a miracle worker. In his last days he retired to a hermitage. Feast 24 August.

Serapion of Alexandria, martyr, born Alexandria, died there, 252. Thrown from the roof of his house by an anti-Christian mob. Feast 14 November.

Serapion of Antioch, bishop, died Antioch, *c*. 211. Very little is known of him, apart from his work against heretics, and his rejection, after studying it, of the 'Gospel of Peter'. Feast 30 October.

Serapion of Ceremsan, archimandrite, born Saratov, 1823, died Ceremsan, 10 January 1898. Church of the Old Believers. Baptized Simeon Ignatevic Abcin into a family of Old Believers, when he was 18 he travelled around centres of his

faith and eventually settled at the Slavskij monastery in Romania, where he became a priest. He returned to Russia in 1863 and settled at Ceremsan, where he and some other Old Believers founded a small monastery, of which he became hegumenos. There was some persecution – he was put in prison for a time – but the monastery developed into a large community, and in 1893 he became archimandrite. He was well known for the sanctity of his life and the depth of his devotion to the liturgy, which he celebrated daily. There was an attempt to make him a bishop, but he refused. His tomb quickly became a place of pilgrimage.

Serapion of Izborsk, founder, sixteenth century. Russian Church. Founder of the monastery of the Mother of God at Lamech, in the Izborsk region. Feast 12 June.

Serapion of Kozeozero, monk, born Kazan, died monastery of Kozeozero, 27 June 1611. He was a Tartar by birth, named Turtas Changavirovic. He was taken prisoner by Ivan IV in 1552 and taken to Moscow, where he became a Christian, assuming the name Sergius. After living for a time in Moscow he decided to become an ascetic, and spent some time beside lake Koza near Archangel as a solitary. There he met **Niphon of Kozeozero**, and put himself under Niphon's direction. They lived together for 18 years before Niphon died, and Serapion took charge of the community which had gathered around the two men.

Serapion of Pskov, monk, died 1481. Russian Church. A monk of the monastery of the Saviour at Pskov, he was a companion of the founder **Euphrosyn** when both retired to live as hermits. They were also active in evangelizing the surrounding region. Feast 8 September.

Serapion of Thmuis, bishop, born Egypt, died there (?), *c*. 370. A monk, he became bishop of Thmuis, a city in Lower Egypt, and a vigorous opponent of Arianism. He was a friend both of **Anthony** and **Athanasius**. He was bishop from *c*. 339, but was exiled in 359. Feast 21 March.

Serapion of Vladimir, bishop, died Vladimir, 1275. Russian Church. A monk of the Kievan Cave monastery, he became bishop of Vladimir in 1275.

He saw the Tartar invasions as divine punishment for the sins of the people of Russia. Five of his sermons survive. Feast 12 July.

Serapion the Sindonite, monk, born Egypt, died there, c. 356. One of the Desert Fathers, he was renowned for having no possessions except the sheet (*sindon*) in which he wrapped himself. Feast 21 May.

Serapion Zarsmeil, hegumenos, born Klargethi, southern Georgia, ninth century. Georgian Church. He became a monk while still quite young, was ordained priest and, with his brother John and the help of the local duke, founded the monastery of Zarma. Feast 29 October.

Serenicus, hermit, born Spoleto (?), died Le Mans, 669. He travelled to Rome and France following angelic guidance. A monk and deacon, maybe at St Paul Outside the Walls, he became a hermit near the river Sarthe, perhaps founding a monastery. He may have had a brother, Serenus, with a similar life. Feast 7 May.

Serenus of Sirmium, martyr, born Greece, died Sirmium (modern Mitrovica, Serbia), c. 303. He fled from Greece because of Diocletian's persecution, and became a gardener at Sirmium where his faith was unknown. In a dispute with a pagan, however, he confessed his Christianity, and was martyred. Feast 23 February.

Serenus the Gardener, martyred c. 307. He lived an ascetic life, working his garden in Syrmium, in Croatia. Falsely accused by a woman whose advances he had rejected, he was acquitted of insulting her. Then charged with being a Christian, he assented and was beheaded. Feast 23 February.

Sergius and Bacchus, martyrs, died Arabissus, 303. Two Christian Roman army offcers who refused to worship the gods and were paraded through the streets of Arabissus in Cappadocia dressed as women before being executed. Feast 7 October (suppressed 1969).

Sergius and Barbara, born Mandera (?), near Novgorod, fifteenth/sixteenth century. They were husband and wife, named Stephen and Vassa before becoming religious, and the parents of **Alexander of Svir**. After the birth of their son, whom they named Amos, they decided to live in chastity. Everything that is known about them comes from the life of their son.

Sergius and Germanus, monks, fifteenth/sixteenth century. Russian Church. They are venerated as the founders of the monastery of Valaam, on an island on lake Ladoga, in the north-west of Russia, near the Russian-Swedish border, now Valamo in Finland. Traditionally they are thought to have been Greek, and to have established the monastery in the tenth century. In fact the monastery was set up towards the end of the fifteenth century. The work was begun by one Ephrem, accompanied by Sergius. Ephrem, however, went elsewhere, so that Sergius was the effective founder of the monastery. He withdrew from his foundation when some of the monks rebelled against him, and went to live at a monastery in Novgorod. He was succeeded by Germanus as hegumenos. Feast 28 June.

Sergius and Martyrius, martyrs, died Persia, fourth century. Martyrius was the son of Sergius.

Sergius I, pope, born Palermo, of a Syrian family, consecrated 15 December 687, died 9 September 701. He studied in Rome, and became priest in charge of the church of St Susanna. He was elected on **Conon**'s death after two other candidates disputed the election between them. Sergius was the popular choice and had the backing of the imperial representative. He nonetheless soon clashed with the Emperor Justinian II, who called a council in 692 without inviting any Western bishops. It was concerned chiefly with disciplinary matters, but its decisions cut across Western practice. Justinian persuaded the papal representative in Constantinople to sign the acts of the council, but Sergius himself refused to do so. When an imperial representative was sent either to extract a signature or to arrest the pope, the imperial order supported Sergius and turned on the imperial official, who had to seek refuge from Sergius. He showed considerable interest in the Church in England, and in the missionary work of **Willibrord**, making him archbishop of the Frisians. Sergius also concerned himself with the liturgy, improving the churches of Rome, adding the *Agnus Dei* to the liturgy, introducing processions for certain feasts, and beginning the celebration of the feast of the Exultation of the Cross. Feast 8 September.

Sergius, Maurus and Panteleimon, martyrs, died Bisceglie, near Bari, Italy, 117 (?). Nothing is known of them. Feast 27 July.

Sergius of Caesarea, martyr, died Caesarea, 304. A priest, and possibly a hermit before he was put to death under Diocletian. Feast 24 February.

Sergius of Constantinople, born Constantinople, died 820. He was exiled – with his wife Irene – because of his defence of the veneration of icons, and died in exile. Feast 13 May.

Sergius of Constantinople, patriarch, born Constantinople (?), died there, July 1019. Byzantine Church. A relation of the Patriarch **Photius**, and well educated, he was abbot of a monastery in Constantinople before being appointed patriarch in July 1001. It was he who claimed the title 'ecumenical patriarch'. Feast 12 April.

Sergius of Huzri, deacon. Syriac Church. Nothing is known of him. Feast 24 February.

Sergius of Kiev II, monk. Russian Church. Said to have been outstanding for his obedience, but otherwise nothing is known of him.

Sergius of Malopinega, monk, born Novgorod, died Maloinezskij, 16 November 1585. Baptized Semen Markianovic Nekljud, he was the son of a nobleman who was in the service of the archbishop of Novgorod. Sergius was ordained priest and for 62 years served in the village of Maloinezskij, on the river Pinega. He became a monk shortly before his death, taking the name Sergius.

Sergius of Melitopol, bishop and martyr, born Petropavlovsk, 1872, died Karaganda, 20 November 1937. Russian Church. Baptized Sergej Michailovic Zverev, his father was a priest. He studied at St Petersburg, and became director of music at the imperial court. He then went to the theological academy at Moscow and was ordained priest. He worked in the Crimea, and was given the title of archpriest, but then became a monk and

was advanced to the rank of archimandrite. In 1922 he became bishop of Sebastapol. He then became bishop of Melitopol. In 1926 he was imprisoned for two years, at the end of which time he was made an archbishop. From 1929 until his death he was archbishop of Elec, and in charge of the diocese of Veronez. He was sent to a prison camp at Karaganda in 1935, and was shot there.

Sergius of Nurom, monk, died Komel, 7 October 1413. Russian Church. He received his training as a monk on Mount Athos, but then came to Moscow and entered the monastery of St **Sergius of Radonez**. He stayed there a good many years, but then went north to Komel to live as a solitary. There he was joined by many other monks. His monastery was suppressed in 1764, and the saint's remains were moved to the parish church at Nurom.

Sergius of Perejaslavl, monk, died Perejaslavl, 9 December 1685. Russian Church. He was the founder of the Fedorovskij nunnery at Perejaslavl. Feast 23 May.

Sergius of Radonez, founder, born Rostov, 3 May 1314, died monastery of Zagorsk, near Moscow, 25 September 1392. Baptized Bartholomew, Sergius was born into a noble and pious family at Rostov, but when the principality was annexed to Moscow, the family moved there. Bartholomew's mother and father decided to enter religious life, and after their deaths in 1334 Bartholomew determined to do likewise, and formally became a monk in 1337, taking the name Sergius. At the beginning he lived alone, in a hermitage in the forest at Radonez, but a community grew around him, all living as hermits until an emissary of the patriarch of Constantinople suggested they form a community. They did so, after consulting the metropolitan of Moscow, and elected Sergius as abbot. They called it the monastery of the Holy Trinity. Further foundations followed, and Sergius is regarded as the founder of Russian monasticism. He was canonized in 1448.

Sergius of Raifskaia Pustyn, martyr, born Mansurovo, 1875, died 10 August 1930. Baptized Pavel Ivanovic Guskov, he entered the monastery of Raifskaia Pustyn in 1898, and was ordained in

1910. He was, at the revolution, superior of the monastery, but when it was closed he became parish priest nearby. He was arrested, but freed, in 1929, but was arrested again in January 1930 and tortured to reveal the supposed whereabouts of the monastery's treasure. Feast 14 January.

Sergius of Suchtoma, monk, born Kazan, died Suchtoma, 1609. Russian Church. He travelled to Palestine, and then spent three years at Constantinople before going to Novgorod, then entering the Solovki monastery. He only formally became a monk, however, after he joined the monastery of the Resurrection at Cerepovec, near Suchtoma. He is said to have had the gift of working miracles. Feast 19 May.

Sergius of Tella, bishop, born Tella, died c. 590. Syriac Church. He accompanied **James Baradeus** to Constantinople, then succeeded him as bishop. Feast 2 July.

Sergius of Zuqnin, monk. Syriac Church. Monk of the monastery at Zuqnin, near Amed, and possibly to be identified with the Sergius who was superior of the monastery of Qennesrin. Feast 30 December.

Sergius Pavlovic Zipulin, martyr, born Belsk, 21 December 1872. Ukrainian Church, Moscow Patriarchate. He worked in several churches in Char'kov until his arrest in October 1937. He was sent to a concentration camp, and afterwards deported, and was never heard of again. Feast 19 May.

Sergius Sein, archimandrite and martyr, born 1870, died St Petersburg, 13 August 1922. See **Benjamin of Kazan**.

Sergius, Stephen and Companions, martyrs, died Palestine, 796. Monks of the monastery of St Sabas, Palestine, who died in an attack by Bedouin. Twenty were killed, some escaped, and one of the last, Stephen the Poet, wrote an account of the event. Feast 20 March.

Sergius the Confessor, born Constantinople, ninth century. With his wife Irene he was a strong defender of the cult of images, for which he was exiled under the reign of Emperor Theophilus

(828–42). He and Irene both died in exile. Feast 13 May.

Sergius the Obedient, monk, died Kiev, thirteenth century. Russian Church. Nothing is known of him, apart from what is indicated by his title. Feast 7 October.

Sergius, Theodore, Mary and Companions, martyrs, died Egypt, fourth century (?).

Serlo, bl., born Cherisy, near Chartres, died monastery of Savigny, Normandy, 1158. In 1140 he became abbot of Savigny, and managed the union of the reformed Benedictines, which Savigny represented, with the Cistercians. Feast 10 September.

Sermin, see **Saturninus of Toulouse**.

Servatius (Servais), bishop, born Armenia (?), died Tongres, 384. He was bishop of Tongres, now Belgium, and attended the Councils of Sardica in 343 and Rimini in 359. **Athanasius** stayed with him during his exile. Feast 13 May.

Servilius, see **Zoëllus**.

Servulus, born Rome, died there, c. 590. A paralysed beggar who was left by his family at the door of San Clemente in Rome, and despite his illness was constantly praising God. The story is told in the *Dialogues* of St **Gregory**. Feast 23 December.

Servusdei, see **Gumesindus**.

Set, monk. Ethiopian Church. An evangelist in Adua.

Seth, archimandrite, eighth century. Coptic Church. He became superior of **Shenoudah of Atripe**'s White Monastery. He died 24 January, but the year is not recorded.

Seven Holy Sleepers, born Ephesus, died there. According to the legend, they were walled up in a cave in 250, during the persecution of Decius, went to sleep, and were found still alive in 362. Feast 27 July (suppressed).

Seven Martyrs of Armenia, see **Martyrs of Armenia**.

Seven Martyrs of Samosata, see **Martyrs of Samosata**.

Severian, see also **Severinus**.

Severianus, martyr, born Chalcedon, died there, 298. Feast 22 August.

Severianus, born Sebaste, Armenia, died there, 320. He was a senator of Sebaste (near modern Mersin, Turkey) who openly professed Christianity. Feast 9 September.

Severianus of Scythopolis, bishop and martyr, died Scythopolis, Palestine (modern Beth Shean), 452 (?). He was a supporter of the Chalcedonian definition, and was martyred by the definition's opponents on his return to Palestine after the council. Feast 21 February.

Severianus, Victor, Zoticus, Eusebius and Companions, martyrs, died Nicomedia (Izmit, Turkey), 303 (?). They and others were said to have witnessed the martyrdom of St **George**, but then were later themselves beheaded. Feast 20 April.

Severinus (Severian), martyr, died Julia Caesarea, Mauritania, third century. He was burned to death with **Aquila**, his wife. Feast 23 January.

Severinus, abbot, born Burgundy, died Switzerland, sixth century. He is said to have been abbot of Agaunum in Switzerland and to have healed Clovis, the first Christian king of the Franks. Feast 11 February.

Severinus Boethius, see **Boethius**.

Severinus of Bordeaux, bishop, died Bordeaux, c. 420. It is said that he came from Cologne, where he had been bishop, and replaced **Armand**. Feast 23 October.

Severinus of Noricum, monk, apostle of Noricum (Austria), died there, 8 January c. 480. His life was written some 30 years after his death by a disciple. He seems to have been from Italy, possibly Rome

itself, but spent his early years in the desert in the East. Some time in the middle of the fifth century he moved to Noricum, where he founded a number of monasteries, although he himself lived in a hermitage.

Severus, see also **Philip of Heraclea**.

Severus, bishop, born Ravenna, died there, c. 348. He was bishop of Ravenna from 283 and accompanied the papal legate to the Synod of Sardica in 344. Feast 1 February.

Severus, died St Sever de Rustan, c. 500. A nobleman who became a priest and worked near Tarbes in France. A village is named after him. Feast 1 August.

Severus, died Interocrea, in the Abruzzi, c. 530. He was parish priest of Interocrea (Androcca) in the Abruzzi, whence his relics were taken to Münster-Maifeld in the tenth century. **Gregory the Great** writes that he brought a man back to life long enough for him to receive the last rites. Feast 15 February.

Severus bar Maqa, patriarch, died 681. Syriac Church. He was elected patriarch in 668 (as Severus II), but his term of office saw a major dispute within the Church, which was not resolved until after his death. He had, however, written to his fellow bishops suggesting how it might be settled.

Severus, Mennon and Companions, martyrs, died Bizya, Thrace, c. 300. Severus was a priest, Mennon a centurion. They were beheaded, and 37 soldiers originally from Plovdiv in modern Bulgaria were burned to death. Feast 20 August.

Severus of Agde, abbot, fifth century. Feast 25 August.

Severus of Antioch, patriarch, born Sozopolis, Psidia, c. 459, died Noïs, Egypt, 8 February 538. Syriac Church. Not a Christian at birth, he was baptized in Tripoli in 488 after studying in Alexandria and Beirut. He became a monk in Gaza, then a priest, and founded his own monastery. He went to Constantinople in 508, protesting at the treatment of Christians who did not accept the Chalcedonian definition, and remained there until 511. He was elected patriarch of Antioch in November 512, but then exiled to Egypt because of his opposition to Chalcedon, and remained there for 20 years. He was sent into exile once again in 536.

Severus of Kafar'Ze, born Kafar'Ze, near Midyat, now in Turkey. Syriac Church. He was superior of the monastery of Qartmin, now in eastern Turkey. Feast 29 February.

Severus of Samosata, bishop, died Kaysum, *c.* 640. Syriac Church. The brother of **Athanasius the Camel Driver**, he was bishop of Samosata (Samsat, Turkey) from 595. He went with his brother to negotiate reunion with the patriarch of Alexandria, and was later one of the 12 bishops who escorted Athanasius to meet the Emperor Heraclius after the recapture of the Holy Cross. He was accustomed to spend half the year as a monk, and half visiting his diocese. When he felt death approaching, he went to the monastery of Kaysum where he conducted his own funeral service, dying immediately afterwards. Feast 18 November.

Severus the Mathematician, monk, born Nisibis, died Qennesre, 667. Syriac Church. He became a monk at the monastery of Qennesre, and *c.* 638 became bishop of Qennesre. He produced many works, now lost, scientific writings as well as theological. A number of translations from Greek into Syriac of scientific works, including works on astronomy, are attributed to him.

Sexburga, abbess, died 6 July *c.* 699. Daughter of the king of the East Angles and sister of **Ethelreda** and **Withburga**. She married King Erconbert of Kent and had two sons and two daughters, **Ercongota** and **Ermengild**. She founded a convent at Minster-in-Sheppey and became abbess there after her husband died in 664. She moved to the abbey of Ely and succeeded her sister Ethelreda as abbess there in 679.

Shapur, bishop and martyr, born Persia, died there, 339. He was bishop of Beth Nictor, and as such made many converts. He was then accused, with **Isaac, Mahanes, Abraham** and **Simeon**, of

both interfering with Mazdeism and collaborating with Rome. Shapur II had them executed. Feast 30 November.

Sharbel Makhlouf, see **Charbel Makhlouf**.

Shenoudah, martyr, died seventh century. Coptic Church. Nothing is known of him, apart from the day of his death, 7 July.

Shenoudah, monk, died Nusa, in the Delta, eleventh century. Coptic Church. Nothing is known of him, except that his prayers freed his brother from prison.

Shenoudah of al-Bahnasa, martyr, died Oxyrhynchus (modern al-Bahnasa), *c.* 300. Coptic Church. He was imprisoned for his faith under Diocletian, but was miraculously released which led to him being accused of magic. He was then killed, and his body thrown to dogs – although they would not touch it. He died on 10 March, but the exact year is not recorded.

Shenoudah of Atripe, archimandrite, born Senalot, died 1 July 451 or 452. He began life as a shepherd, looking after his father's flock. Because of his health, his father took him to see his maternal uncle, a monk at the White Monastery, and Shenoudah remained with him, becoming abbot of the monastery after his uncle's death *c.* 385. As abbot of the White Monastery he had charge not only of a community of 2,200 monks, but of a convent of 1,800 nuns. Shenoudah imposed the Rule of St **Pachomius**, although with modifications to make it much stricter. Two of the modifications were particularly important: he introduced a written profession, to be signed by each person on becoming a monk or nun, and he allowed a monk, after a certain length of time in the community, to become a hermit. In 431 he attended the Council of Ephesus, and is said to have been ordained archimandrite during the council by **Cyril of Alexandria**. He is said to have died at the age of 119.

Sidhum Bisay, martyr, born Damietta, Egypt, died there, 13 March 1844. Coptic Church. While going to church he was set upon by a mob and accused of insulting Islam, was badly beaten, and died at home of his injuries. As a result of protests, the governor of Damietta and the judge before whom he had been tried were removed from their posts.

Sidonius Apollinaris, bishop, born Lyon, *c.* 430, died Clermont Ferrand, 480. He studied at Arles, married the daughter of Avitus, who became Roman emperor in 456, and had three daughters. When Avitus was deposed he joined the insurrection to try to place him back on the throne. The insurrection failed, but Sidonius managed to ingratiate himself with the new emperor, Majorian, and gained a post at Rome. This he had to abandon when Majorian was killed in 461. Sidonius went back to Gaul, but returned to Rome in 467 and was made, for the following year, prefect of the city. He went home again in 469 and, rather against his wishes, was made bishop of the Auvergne, with the centre of his see at what is now Clermont Ferrand. He was, however, an effective bishop, or seems to have been, defending his people as far as he was able from the vicissitudes of the time – which included the surrender of the Auvergne to the Arian Goths in 475. He was briefly exiled for his opposition to the new regime, but came back to his bishopric where he spent his last years editing his letters. He also wrote poetry, some of which survives. Feast 21 August.

Sigebert, Merovingian king, born 632, died 656. Inheriting Austrasia, the eastern part of the kingdom of his father, Dagobert I, he ruled peacefully with his brother Clovis, who reigned in the western half. He endowed hospitals, churches and monasteries, including Stavelot and Malmédy. Feast 1 February.

Sigebert, king and martyr, born East Anglia, died there, 27 September 637. Possibly the stepson of Redwald, king of East Anglia, he left England for France, where he became a Christian. On his return as king in 631 he attempted to convert the people of East Anglia with the help of **Felix** and **Fursey**. Sigebert resigned his throne to his brother and entered a monastery at what is now Bury St Edmunds, but when in 637 the kingdom was invaded by the pagan King Penda, he was urged to lead the East Anglians into battle – which he agreed reluctantly to do, on condition that he was not required to carry a weapon. He died in the battle.

Sigfrid, abbot, died Wearmouth (in what is now Sunderland), 688. A deacon, he was elected acting abbot of Wearmouth in 686 while **Benedict Biscop** was away in Rome. Feast 22 August.

Sigfrid, born England, died Scandinavia, *c.* 1045, possibly canonized 1158, cult established in Scandinavia by the thirteenth century. A monk, King Ethelbert apparently sent him as missionary to Norway in 995, when Scandinavia was largely pagan. He worked for many years there and in Sweden and Denmark. Feast 15 February.

Sigiramnus, also known as **Cyran**, abbot, born Berri, died Lonrey, *c.* 655. From a noble family, he served in the Frankish court, but rejected his father's wish that he marry and instead became a cleric at Tours. He inherited his father's fortune, but gave it away. The king, however, gave him an estate in the forest of Brenne, where he built an abbey. He also built an abbey at Lonrey, where he became abbot. Feast 4 December.

Sigisbert, see **Placidus and Sigisbert**.

Sigismund, king, died Orleans, 523. A Vandal, he was converted to Catholicism from Arianism in 515, the year before he became king of Burgundy. He founded the monastery of St Maurice in the Valais, to which he retired to live a life of penance after ordering the murder of his son at the instigation of his second wife. He came out of seclusion to lead his army against the Franks, but was defeated and fled, disguising himself as a monk. He was, however, caught and executed. Feast 1 May.

Sigo, bishop, died Clairmont, *c.* 873. He was bishop of Clairmont in Aquitaine. Feast 10 February.

Silouan the Athonite, see **Silvanus of Mount Athos**.

Silvanus, see also **Boris, James, Theodore I, Silvanus, Theodore II, Basil I, Demetrius, Michael, John, Basil II.**

Silvanus, monk, died Kiev. Russian Church. Two monks of the Kievan Cave monastery of this name are celebrated as saints, although little is known of either. One is called 'the Faster'.

Silvanus, monk, born Palestine, fifth century. Coptic Church. A disciple of **Macarius**, 12 of the *Sayings of the Desert Fathers* are attributed to him. He lived at Scete, Sinai and Gaza, and died on 27 March, but the year is unknown.

Silvanus, see also **Zoëllus**.

Silvanus of Emesa, bishop and martyr, died Emesa (Homs), third century. He was arrested along with his deacon, Luke, and a reader, Makius, and after being imprisoned they were thrown to the wild beasts in the amphitheatre. Feast 29 January.

Silvanus of Gaza and Companions, martyrs, died Gaza, *c.* 303. Silvanus served in the Roman army before becoming a priest in Gaza, and later bishop. He preached Christianity throughout Palestine, and was sent to the mines after preaching in Caesarea. He was eventually released and returned to Gaza, where in the persecution of Diocletian he and 39 others were beheaded for their faith. Feast 14 October.

Silvanus of Kiev, monk, died Kiev, thirteenth/fourteenth centuries. A monk of the Kievan Cave monastery, he had the gift of healing and of prophecy. Feast 10 July.

Silvanus of Mount Athos, monk, born Sovksoe, near Tambov, 1866, died Mount Athos, 24 September 1938. He was in the Russian army, serving in St Petersburg, before becoming a monk in the Russian monastery of St Panteleimon on Mount Athos in 1892. He served in a number of posts within the monastery, but he also gained a great reputation as a spiritual guide. It was the publication of his spiritual diary, however, which brought him (posthumous) fame, displaying a spirituality not far removed from that of St **Teresa of Lisieux**.

Silvanus of Troas, bishop, born Constantinople (?), died Troas, in the Dardanelles, *c.* 450. He was a rhetorician (i.e., more or less the equivalent of a lawyer) at Constantinople before becoming a monk in the city. He was then made bishop of Philippopolis (Plovdiv, Bulgaria), but then transferred to Troas because he could not stand the cold. A former lawyer himself, he forbade his clergy from working in the courts. Feast 2 December.

Silverius, pope, born Frosinone, the son of Pope **Hormisdas**, consecrated 8 June 536, deposed 11 November 537, died 2 December 537. He was forced upon a reluctant Rome by the last Ostrogoth king of Italy, and had strong Ostrogoth sympathies. He was stripped of his office in March 537 by the Byzantine general Belisarius – who accused him of plotting with the Goths – so that the way would be open for the appointment of Vigilius, the Empress Theodora's candidate. He was deported, but the emperor ordered him to be taken back to Rome to stand trial. Vigilius, now in office, had him deported again, this time getting from him a statement of his abdication. He died shortly afterwards, and is venerated for his sufferings for the orthodox faith – Theodora being a monophysite.

Silvester, see **Sylvester**.

Silvin, died possibly near Arras, *c.* 720. He may have been an Irishman at the court of the Frankish king, then left for Rome where he was ordained. He became a bishop, with no fixed see, living very simply and evangelizing in pagan north-eastern France. Feast 17 February.

Silvius, bishop of Toulouse, died *c.* 400. Feast 31 May.

Simbert, bishop, died Augsburg, *c.* 809. He was educated at the monastery of Murbach in Alsace, entered the monastery, and eventually became abbot. In 778 he was appointed bishop of Augsburg, while retaining his office as abbot of Murbach. He improved the learning and discipline of the clergy. Feast 11 October.

Simeon, see also **Simon**.

Simeon and Companions, martyrs, died near Irgen, *c.* 1660. A number of Cossacks, tortured and then killed by their commanding officer, Athanasius Paskov, during a military campaign. Their martyrdom was reported by the archpriest **Avvakum**. The number of martyrs is unclear. In addition to Simeon, Cyprian, Joseph and Basil are mentioned.

Simeon bar Sabba and Companions, martyrs, died Ctesiphon, Persia, 341. Simeon was the bishop of Seleucia-Ctesiphon and was executed for his faith in the reign of Shapur II, together with very many other priests, bishops and lay people. Feast 21 April.

Simeon Denisov, born Povenec, *c.* 1681, died Vyg, 25 September 1740. Church of the Old Believers. With his father Dionysius, he left the village of Povenec and settled at the monastery on the river Vyg which had been founded by his brother **Andrew**. On a visit to Novgorod he was arrested for teaching heretical doctrine, and spent four years in prison before managing to escape back to his monastery, where he still for some time remained hidden in the cell of his brother. He collected much material for the lives of saints, and became one of the major defenders of Old Believer doctrine. After the death of Andrew in 1730 he was unwillingly elected head of the community. In 1739 he was again arrested and spent six months in prison, after which his health declined. Feast 24 May.

Simeon Inauridze, archimandrite, died Davidgaregi (?), eighteenth century. He was the superior of at least two monasteries in the desert of Davidgaregi, and a man of considerable practical resourcefulness, as well as a miracle worker with the gift of prophecy. Feast 4 September.

Simeon Kirillovic Oskin, martyr, born Pescanoe, 24 May 1880, died 5 September 1937. Ukrainian Church, Moscow Patriarchate. He was ordained after the revolution, and worked in the village of Pecegnei before his arrest in June 1937.

Simeon Mcedlidze, martyr, died Kutaisi, 25 August 1924. Georgian Church. After studying at the ecclesiastical academy in St Petersburg he returned home to teach. He married, and then became priest as his father had been. From 1913 he began to publish religious journals, promoting in particular the culture and spirituality of the Georgian Church. Under the Soviet regime he was accused of spreading anti-Communist propaganda, was arrested and executed.

Simeon Metaphrastes, born and died Constantinople (?), tenth century. Probably a civil servant who, at the request of the Byzantine emperor, collected together lives and legends of the saints (*Metaphrastes* = 'the Recorder'). Nothing is known of his life. Feast 9 November.

Simeon Mstislav, prince and martyr, died 1406. Russian Church. He was at the court of the prince of Smolensk when that city fell to the Lithuanians, and he fled to Novgorod and then on to Moscow. He was made governor, with George of Smolensk. George was attracted to Simeon's beautiful wife **Juliana of Vjaz'ma**. She held off his advances and called for help. Simeon came to his wife's assistance, but was killed by George. His wife was tied hand and foot and thrown into a freezing river, where she likewise died. George repented his act, and died in a monastery. Feast of Simeon and Juliana 21 December.

Simeon of Dara, bishop, eighth century. Syriac Church. Feast 25 February.

Simeon of Edessa, bishop, died Edessa (?), 665. Feast 23 December.

Simeon of Emesa, monk, born Emesa (Homs, Syria), died there, *c.* 585. He lived for nearly 30 years at the monastery of St Gerasimus on the river Jordan, and then returned to Emesa, where he lived as a 'holy fool'. Feast 1 July.

Simeon of Fafo, monk. Syriac Church. He was superior of the monastery of Qartmin. Feast 11 January.

Simeon of Jerusalem, bishop and martyr, died Pella, *c.* 107, apparently aged 120. He became bishop of Jerusalem probably *c.* 62 after the martyrdom of St James the Younger. When Jerusalem fell in 70, the Christian community moved across the Jordan, to Pella. Eusebius wrote that Simeon knew Jesus. Feast 27 April.

Simeon of Harran, bishop, born Tur Abdin, *c.* 655, died Harran, 734. Syriac Church. He went to school at the monastery of Qartmin, then became a monk there *c.* 670. Shortly afterwards he and a few other monks founded another monastery at Sirwan. He then went on to establish other monasteries and churches. In *c.* 700 he became bishop of Harran.

Simeon of Kafar Abdin, monk, born Edessa, died Kafar Abdin, near Samosata (Samsat). Syriac Church. He became a monk in Edessa, but refused to become superior of the monastery. He left with a disciple and went to the foot of a mountain at Kafar Abdin, where they established themselves in a cave. He is reputed to have worked many miracles.

Simeon of Pangarati, monk, born Piatra Neamt, died Gurghiu, Transylvania, *c.* 1476. Romanian Church. Aged about 20, he entered the monastery of Bistrita. After some years he went with a number of disciples to the region of Pangarati, where they built cells. Towards the end of 1461 he was ordained priest and appointed hegumenos of the hermitage he had begun: at that time it contained about 12 disciples. When the Turks invaded in 1476 he and his monks moved to Transylvania, where they joined the monastery of the Dormition at Casiva, near Gurghiu.

Simeon of Polirone, born Armenia (?), died Polirone, near Padua, Italy, 1016. A hermit from Armenia, he went on pilgrimage to Jerusalem, Rome and Santiago de Compostela in Spain, settling finally in the Cluniac monastery of Polirone. Feast 26 July.

Simeon of Oigona, monk. Syriac Church. Nothing is known of him.

Simeon of Qarqafta, monk, eighth century (?). Syriac Church. He may have been the founder of the monastery of Qarqafta, but it is not clear where this monastery was. Feast 1 October.

Simeon of Qartmin, born Qartmin, died there, 13 January 433. He is said to have been healed by a monk called Samuel who was living near his village, and then himself became a monk – at the age of four and a half. The two then founded a monastery nearby, *c.* 396. Just over a decade later, after the death of Samuel, Simeon became head of the monastery. By the time of his death the monastery is said to have had over 700 monks. Feast 2 October.

Simeon of Radonez, bl., fourteenth/fifteenth century. Russian Church. He was a disciple of St **Sergius of Radonez** and was named 'the Silent', because he took upon himself no monastic offices or external obligations, but dedicated himself entirely to the life of asceticism. He is reported to have had a vision of a divine light descending upon Sergius and the chalice during the liturgy.

Simeon of Smolensk, metropolitan, born Tobolsk, died Smolensk, 4 January 1699. Russian Church. Baptized Sergius Moljubov, he entered the monastery of Ss Boris and Gleb at Rostov, and in 1672 was appointed superior of the Cave monastery at Niznij Novgorod. In 1676 he became bishop of Smolensk, being consecrated at the cathedral of the Dormition in Moscow. As bishop he set about constructing a new cathedral in Smolensk, and many churches in his diocese. He was granted the title of metropolitan in 1681, but the growing importance of Simeon in the Russian Church irritated the patriarch, and he was removed from his see to spend two years in the monastery of St **Sergius**. After his return he governed his diocese for two more years before his death. Feast 28 June.

Simeon of Syracuse, hermit, born Syracuse, died 1035. He was educated in Constantinople, then became a hermit in Palestine before joining a monastery near Mount Sinai, then became a hermit on the mountain. He was sent back to Europe by the monastery to collect money for its upkeep, but his ship was captured by pirates and only Simeon escaped, finding his way to Antioch. He then set out again, travelling much of the way with a monk he met called Cosmas. The two finally arrived in France, where Cosmas died, and where Simeon discovered that the duke of Normandy, from whom he had expected to collect money for the monastery, had died. He travelled on to Trier, where he met the archbishop, who wanted to go on a pilgrimage to the Holy Land, and Simeon agreed to act as a guide. The two reached the Holy Land,

and both then returned to Trier where Simeon became an anchorite. He is thought to have been only the second person to be formally canonized by the pope (in 1042). Feast 1 June.

Simeon of Thessalonika, bishop, born Constantinople, c. 1370, died Thessalonika, September 1429. Byzantine Church. He was an outstanding student, and then a teacher, possibly a university teacher, at Constantinople, where at some point he became a monk. In 1416 he was appointed archbishop of Thessalonika. It was a difficult period for the city, its population being divided between those, led by the governor, who wanted to hand its defence over to the Venetians, and those who preferred to hand it over to the Turks. The governor, Andronicos Palaeologos, decided to hand it over to the Venetians in 1423, and then became a monk on Mount Athos. Simeon gained from the Venetians an undertaking not to install a Latin hierarchy, but in the event the city fell to the Turks shortly after Simeon's death. He was the author of numerous books on theology and the liturgy, as well as poems. Feast 15 September.

Simeon of Todi, bl., born Todi, Umbria, died Bologna, 1322. A Hermit of St Augustine from 1280, he was a famous preacher, prior of several houses and provincial of Umbria. When unjustly accused of misdeeds, he remained silent rather than damage the order by defending himself. Feast 20 April.

Simeon of Trebizond (Trabzon, Turkey), martyr, born Trebizond, died Constantinople, 1653. Byzantine Church. He was accused of killing a Jew in a brawl, but was offered his freedom were he to convert to Islam. He refused, and was martyred. Feast 14 August.

Simeon of Trier, hermit, born Syracuse, Sicily, died Trier, 1035. Having studied at Constantinople he went to the Holy Land, where he was a hermit and then a monk. He went to St Catherine's monastery on Mount Sinai, but again became a hermit – on top of Mount Sinai. He was sent by the abbot of St Catherine's to Europe to collect alms for the monastery, but never returned, staying instead as a hermit in Trier. Feast 1 June.

Simeon of Tver, bishop, died Tver, 1289. Russian Church. Driven from his original see of Polock by Lithuanian soldiers, he became the first bishop of Tver and built a cathedral there, completed just after his death.

Simeon Salos, born Syria, sixth century. On a pilgrimage to the Holy Places he met John, also a Syrian, and they decided to become monks. Simeon's approach to spirituality was through humility, believing that we should not only willingly accept the humiliations of everyday life, but also actively seek to be humiliated. He was a well-educated man, but deliberately copied the behaviour of those who were mentally disturbed, and was given the Greek nickname *salos* (mad). Feast 1 July.

Simeon, Simon de Bretennières, Peter Dorie and Bernard Beaulieu (last three arrived in Korea, 1865), martyrs, died Korea, 1866, beatified 1968, canonized 1984 – see **Martyrs of Korea**. Feast 8 March.

Simeon Stephen Nemanja, king and monk, born Podgorica, now in Montenegro, c. 1113, died Mount Athos, 1200. He was of noble birth, although his family links are unclear, one of four brothers who gradually expanded what became the Serbian state. There were battles between the brothers, but after the death of one of them, the others collaborated, with Stephen as their leader. Having first clashed with the Byzantine emperor, in 1172 he surrendered to him and emerged as ruler of Serbia (then called Raska) with the backing of the emperor. In 1180 he took advantage of the troubles in Constantinople to acquire more territory, including Kosovo and Nis, which then served as the capital of his kingdom. A new treaty was agreed with Byzantium in 1190, guaranteeing Stephen's hold over the territories he had gained. In 1196 he abdicated in favour of his son, and became a monk on Mount Athos, taking the name Simeon. His youngest son, **Sabas**, was already there, and together they created the Serbian monastery of Chilandar. Stephen founded several other monasteries (most importantly that of Studenica) and churches. He was almost immediately revered as a saint, and his relics were said to have miraculous powers: he became known as Simon the Myrrh-Flowing. Feast 26 February.

Simeon Stylites (the Elder), born Sisan, near Aleppo, Syria, c. 388, died Telanisson, near Antioch, 2 September 459. The first and most famous of the 'pillar saints', he worked as a shepherd before joining a monastery. The excesses of his penances and fasting were such that he was soon forced to remove himself from the community into a hut, where he continued his life of prayer and austerity. Three years later he moved on to a rock in the desert, but his fame had spread and he was besieged by pilgrims seeking his wisdom and blessings. He had a small pillar erected with a platform at the top on which he lived. It was replaced with increasingly higher pillars over the years. He wrote letters, including one to the Emperor Leo in support of the Council of Chalcedon, from his pillar, addressed those assembled below and, by means of a ladder, pilgrims and others were able to speak to him personally. The remains of the pillar, on which Simeon spent 36 years in all, and of the four basilicas built in his honour, survive at Qal'at Sim'an. Feast 5 January.

Simeon Stylites (the Younger), born Antioch, Syria, 521, died there, 24 May 597. Orphaned as a small boy, he was looked after by a hermit called John who was the spiritual guide to a small community. Simeon himself says that he was living on a pillar before he had lost his first teeth, and he continued to do so for almost 70 years. He stayed close by John's pillar until the hermit died, John keeping Simeon's austerities under control, but after John's death he gave full rein to his ascetical practices. He moved several times to different pillars, and while on the ground he was ordained priest. He finally settled near Antioch at the 'Mountain of Miracles'. A basilica was built around him, the ruins of which still survive. He is thought to have been the author of several spiritual treatises and hymns. Feast 3 September.

Simeon Stylites, died Hegca, Cicilia, fifth century. Nothing is known of him, except that he seems to have been struck by lightning while on his pillar.

Simeon Stylites of Lesbos, bl., born Mytelene, Lesbos, c. 765, died September 844. Byzantine Church. He became a monk on Mount Idi, near Troy, where his brother was already a monk, and was ordained priest at the age of 22. He later returned to Mytelene, and joined a monastery there. He built a pillar and sat upon it, giving himself up to prayer and fasting. He was, however, forced into exile by an iconoclast bishop of the city, then travelled around the Aegean giving support to others suffering the consequences of iconoclasm. In 843 he went to Constantinople to take part in a council to bring an end to iconoclasm. While in Constantinople his brother was made archbishop of Mytelene, and the two returned to Lesbos together, Simeon dying shortly afterwards. Feast (with his two brothers David and George) 1 February.

Simeon the Elder, died Mount Sinai (?), 390. A hermit near Antioch in Syria, he later founded two monasteries on Mount Sinai. Feast 28 January.

Simeon the Greek, monk. Syriac Church. Nothing is known about him except that he had a large number of disciples. Feast 18 November.

Simeon the Just, missionary, died Merkusino, 1642. Russian Church. Although born into a noble family, he left his home and went wandering through the countryside, helping peasants in their work for no pay. He eventually found himself in the region of Perm, in an area where there were still many non-believers. He began from then on to preach the gospel. He died when he was only about 35 years old. Feast 12 September.

Simeon the New Theologian, born Galatea, Paphlagonia, 949, died Constantinople, 1022. He was of noble birth, and served at the imperial court in Constantinople before entering the Studion monastery at the age of 27. He had wanted to enter at 14, but his spiritual director would not allow him to do so. Once he had become a monk he intensified his prayer and fasting. He had already received visions before becoming a monk, and afterwards his mysticism increased. This seems to have alienated the other monks of the Studion monastery, which may possibly account for his move to the monastery of St Mamas, still in Constantinople, of which he became abbot in 981. Even there the strict discipline he imposed angered some of the monks, and there was an attempt on his life. In 1005 he resigned as abbot, to live nearby. He wrote important works on Byzantine mysticism, but these were also not always well received, and he was banished from Constantinople. He settled across the Bosphorus at the monastery of St Makrina. Feast 12 March.

Simeon the Seafarer, monk. Syriac Church. Nothing is known of him. Feast 21 May.

Simetrius and Companions, martyrs, died Rome, *c*. 159. This was a group of 23 people, arrested while praying in the church of St Praxides and beheaded without trial. Feast 26 May.

Simon, see also **Simeon**.

Simon, bl., born Kavala. Byzantine Church. He was a monk of an unnamed monastery, who was sent by his abbot in search of three fellow monks who had been captured and sold into slavery in Africa. He eventually found one of them, and when the slave master tried to beat him off, he found himself paralysed. Simon was then regarded as a magician and taken before the judge, but he proceeded to heal the paralysis. The judge was so impressed that he let him go free, with his fellow monks, and any other Christians he wished to take. On their way home, the group ran out of water while at sea, and Simon miraculously made the sea water drinkable. Feast 19 November.

Simon, monk. Ethiopian Church. He was a monk of Dabra Daga, but little else is known about him. Feast 8 August.

Simon Bocusai Kiota and Magdalen, martyrs, died Cocura, Japan, 1620. Magdalen was Simon's wife. They died by being crucified upside down. Feast 16 August.

Simon Hoa, martyr, born Vietnam, died there, 12 December 1840. The doctor and mayor of his local community, he became a Catholic and was beheaded for his faith.

Simon of Alexandria, patriarch, born Syria, died Alexandria (?), 701. Coptic Church. He was committed to **Agaton**, patriarch of Alexandria, by his parents, and educated by him. He was then sent to the Enaton monastery, where he became a priest. The abbot of Enaton, John, was elected patriarch and went to seek the approval of the Muslim ruler, but while he was there, a bishop who had voted in favour of John suddenly withdrew his support, and indicated that Simon should be patriarch. The other bishops agreed and Simon was duly consecrated, although in practice John acted as patriarch, while Simon continued to live the life of a monk. Simon does not seem to have enjoyed as good relations with his clergy as he did with the Muslim ruler, and there is a story that some priests tried to poison him.

Simon of Alexandria II, patriarch, died Alexandria, 30 September 830. Coptic Church. He was a monk of the monastery of St Macarius, and accompanied his abbot to Alexandria when the abbot was elected patriarch. He was chosen to follow him, but died after less than six months in office.

Simon of Cascia, bl., friar, born Umbria, *c*. 1295, died possibly Florence, 2 February 1348. An Augustinian preacher, he had a devoted following of penitents. He is regarded as the (disputed) author of theological works, controversial at the time but popular until *c*. 1540, which may have influenced Luther.

Simon of Créspy, count, born Créspy, near Senlis, 1048, died Rome, 1082. He was count of Créspy, and related to the wife of William of Normandy. He succeeded his father in 1072, and supported William against Philip I of France. He wanted to become a monk, but William wanted him to marry his daughter Adela. Simon set off for Rome, possibly to discuss the legality of the marriage as he and Adela were already related, but on the way stopped at the monastery of St Claud at Condat, where he became a monk. He continued as an adviser to William, but also to Pope **Gregory VII** and others. He was buried in St Peter's basilica, although his remains were eventually moved back to his abbey. Feast 30 September.

Simon of Jurevec, born Brtaskij, near Kostroma, died Jurevec-Povolzskij, 4 November 1584. Russian Church. He left home as a young man, and lived in woods as a 'fool for Christ' near the village of Elnati. He fasted, went about barefoot, and wore only a simple gown whatever the season of the year. He became so wild looking that the priest of Elnati took him in out of pity. He lived in the village for 15 years, living off alms and helping the people of the village. He then went to Jurevec-Povolzskij, where he lived in the doorways of churches, especially that of the monastery of the Ephiphany. He died after receiving a beating and being thrown into the cellar of a house where he had been accepting hospitality. His relics occasioned many miracles.

Simon of Lipnicza, born Lipnicza Murowana, Poland, *c.* 1440, died Krakow, 18 July 1482. He studied at Krakow university, and after graduating became a Franciscan and was ordained priest before 1465. He was the official preacher at Wawel cathedral, and in 1478 was made definitor of the order in Krakow. He cared for the sick during the outbreak of plague in Krakow in 1482, and later that year succumbed to the disease himself.

Simon of Minuf, born Nile Delta, died there, seventh century (?). Nothing is recorded of him. Feast 10 December.

Simon of Moscow, bishop, died Moscow, 30 April 1511. From 1490 to 1495 he was superior of the monastery of the Most Holy Trinity, founded by St **Sergius**, after which he was consecrated as metropolitan of Moscow. He tried to reform the lives of monks and priests, and although he at first supported the seizure of Church property by Ivan III, he later went on to oppose it. When **Joseph of Volokolamsk** clashed with the prince of Volokolamsk and the bishop of Novgorod, Simon was an energetic supporter of Joseph.

Simon of Novgorod, archbishop, died Novgorod, 15 June 1421. Russian Church. Baptized Sampson, he was a monk of the monastery of Chutyn before being elected archbishop of Novgorod in 1415. He built a number of churches, some with his own money, quashed a revolt by blessing the people, and saved Novgorod from a flood. Feast 14 February.

Simon of Perejaslavl, bishop and martyr, died Perejaslavl, 1239. Russian Church. He was

probably a monk of the Kievan Cave monastery before becoming bishop. He was killed by Tartars when they attacked the city.

Simon of Rimini, bl., Dominican, born Rimini, died there, 1319. Simone Ballachi joined the Dominican house in Rimini as a lay brother when he was 27. He looked after the garden and taught catechism to children. He went blind aged 57, and was later bedridden, all of which sufferings he bore cheerfully, giving him a reputation for sanctity even in his lifetime. Feast 3 November.

Simon of Sojga, hermit, born Solvycegodsk, died Sojga, 24 November 1562. Russian Church. Baptized Simon Tentjukov, he became a monk in the monastery of **Cornelius of Komel**, and then at the monastery of Ss Boris and Gleb at Solvycegodsk. With his friend Longinus he established himself eventually in a hermitage on the river Sojga, where in 1541 he established a monastery dedicated to the Transfiguration.

Simon of Suzdal, bishop, twelfth century. Russian Church. Nothing is known of this bishop of Suzdal. Feast 10 May.

Simon of Vladimir, bishop, died Vladimir, May 1226. Russian Church. Originally a monk of the Kievan Cave monastery, he then became hegumenos of the monastery of the Nativity at Vladimir, then first bishop of the city *c.* 1215. He was close to the princely family of Vladimir, and when they were driven out in 1217 Simon followed them, becoming bishop of Suzdal instead, and building a cathedral there which was consecrated a year before his death. He was, however, able to return to Vladimir on the death of the usurper. He produced several works, the most important of them being a long letter to his friend Polycarp, still a monk of the Kievan Cave monastery, about the joys of monastic life compared to that of a bishop. Feast 120 May.

Simon of Volom, priest and martyr, born Volokolamsk, died Volom, 12 July 1644. Baptized Simeon Michajlovic, he became a tailor in Ustug. After travelling around various Russian monasteries, aged 24 he became a monk at the monastery of St Macarius on the river Pinega, but then in 1613 he became a hermit in the forest of Volom, where he cultivated his own food and begged alms from local villagers. A community grew up around him, and he received permission and a grant of land to build a monastery. He was ordained priest, and in 1620 became superior of the community. The villagers, however, resented the loss of their land. They destroyed the church, and there were several threats on his life. On one occasion he was found alone in the monastery because the other monks had gone off to the liturgy in a nearby church, and he was beaten to death.

Simon Stylites, see **Simeon Stylites**.

Simon Stock, born *c.* 1165, died Bordeaux, France, 16 May 1265. It is thought that Simon Stock was originally so named because of a legend that as a young man he lived as a hermit inside a tree trunk, although the story has no historical basis. Evidence suggests he was an Englishman who visited the Holy Land and there encountered early Carmelites, whom he joined. When it became impossible for them to remain in the Holy Land, Simon returned to Aylesford in England, and in 1254 was elected general superior of the order at a council held in London. He founded many houses in England and elsewhere, especially in university towns. He is principally remembered for his 'vision of the scapular', in which the Virgin Mary appeared to him holding a Carmelite scapular and declaring that whoever died in it would be saved. This gave rise to the belief that whoever lived and died as a Carmelite could not be eternally damned. Although he died in Bordeaux, his relics were returned to Aylesford. Feast 16 May.

Simon Yempo, bl., Jesuit, born Nozu, Japan, died Yedo (Tokyo), 4 December 1623. He had become a Buddhist monk as a young man, but was converted to Christianity and became a Jesuit lay brother. He was expelled with other missionaries in 1614, but returned to assist **Jerome de Angelis** as a catechist, and was martyred alongside him.

Simplicianus, bishop, died Milan, 401. As a priest, he was consulted by **Augustine** of Hippo about Neo-Platonism. He succeeded **Ambrose** to the see of Milan. Feast 15 August.

Simplicius, pope, born Tivoli, consecrated 3 March 468, died Rome, 10 March 483. His pontificate was largely concerned with an attempt to keep the Eastern empire loyal to the decisions of the Council of Chalcedon of 451, under Pope **Leo**, about the nature of Christ. Emperor Zeno and his patriarch Acacius were attempting, without technically breaching Chalcedon, to reunite the monophysite (i.e., 'one nature') protagonists with the Chalcedonians. In Rome itself Simplicius converted a public building for use as a church, the first known example of this.

Simplicius, martyred Sardinia, 304. He was buried alive. Feast 15 May.

Simplicius, bishop, died *c.* 477. He was a married man with children when he became bishop of Bourges, Aquitaine. He fought against the Arian Visigoths. Feast 1 March.

Simplicius and Faustinus, martyrs, early fourth century. According to legend, Simplicius and Faustinus were Roman brothers, and were either beheaded or drowned for refusing to sacrifice to the gods. Their bodies were saved by their sister, Beatrice, who buried them in the cemetery of Generosa. Their relics were moved to the church of Santa Bibiana in the seventh century, and were later transferred to Santa Maria Maggiore. Feast 29 July.

Sinisius, martyr, died Antinoë, third century. Feast 10 May (?).

Sinoda, monk, born Waj, died lake Tana, *c.* 1433. Ethiopian Church. He became a monk at a monastery on an island on lake Zuai, then moved to Goggiam, where he founded the monastery of Dabra Semmona. He was exiled for political reasons to the island of Daq, on lake Tana, in 1434, the king ordering his hands and feet to be cut off. He died of his wounds.

Siricius, pope, born Rome, consecrated December 384, died Rome, 26 November 399. A deacon under Pope **Damasus I**, he was a popular choice as bishop of Rome, both among the people and with the emperor. He was firm and direct in government, issuing his decrees in the manner of an imperial official, to be binding in local churches in the West. Although he was a vigorous defender of orthodox doctrine, he criticized bishops who had condemned the heretic Priscillian to death. He created a vicariate of the papacy at Thessalonika, thus challenging the authority of the patriarch of Constantinople.

Sirin, martyr, born Kirkuk, *c.* 538, died Seleucia-Ctesiphon, 28 February 559. Assyrian Church. Possibly of royal blood and brought up as a Mazdean, but at the age of 18 she became a Christian and left court circles, although without disclosing her conversion for a year. She was then thrown into prison, but was eventually sent to the king at Seleucia-Ctesiphon, where she was strangled.

Sirin and her Children, martyrs, born Bet Zadoq, died 24 August 445. Assyrian Church. She moved to what is now Kirkuk, and worked as a baker. When she learned of the martyrdom of many Christians in the city, she took her two children and presented herself before the persecutor, the governor **Tahmazgerd**, and confessed that they too were Christians. They were executed, despite attempts to persuade her elder child to renounce his faith. Feast 26 August.

Sirmium, Martyrs of, see **Martyrs of Sirmium**.

Sirun, martyr, born Hizan, died there, 14 January 1476. A young Armenian, his mother converted to Islam. When he refused to do likewise, he was tortured and died of his wounds.

Sisebutus, abbot, died San Pedro de Cardeña, near Burgos, Spain, 1086. Abbot of the important monastery of San Pedro from 1056, he appears to have been the friend of the legendary 'El Cid', to whom the latter entrusted his family when he was exiled. Feast 9 February.

Sisinnius, Diocletius and Florentinus, martyrs, died Ancona, Italy, 303. Feast 11 May.

Sisinnius, Martyrius and Alexander, martyrs, born Cappadocia, died Tyrol, 397. They came as missionaries to Italy, and were sent by the bishop of Trent (Triento) to evangelize the Tyrol. There,

however, they were set upon by a pagan mob and killed. Feast 29 May.

Sisinnius of Constantinople, born Constantinople, died there, 427. He was a devout priest of the city, renowned both for his piety and for his learning. He was elected patriarch in 425, but lived only a couple of years afterwards. Feast 11 October.

Sisinnius of Cyzicus, bishop, died Cyzicus, *c.* 325. He was bishop of the see of Cyzicus, which was on what is now the Kapu-Dagh peninsula in Turkey. During the persecution of Diocletian he was tied behind a horse which was then set free to gallop – but survived. Feast 23 November.

Sisoes, monk, died Egypt, 429. He went to the desert of Scete for some years, but felt that it was too crowded and crossed the Nile to St Anthony's Mountain, where he remained for some 70 years. Some time before his death he moved closer to the Red Sea, but thought better of it and returned to the mountain. He gathered a number of followers around him. He is sometimes known as Sisoes the Great. Feast 4 July.

Sisoes and Theophilus, monks, died Kiev, thirteenth century. Mentioned in the lists of saints of the Kievan Cave monastery to which they belonged, in fact little or nothing is known of them. Feast 28 September.

Sisoj, monk, died Kiev, thirteenth century. Russian Church. A monk of the Kievan Cave monastery, he was renowned for his asceticism, and for the fact that he foresaw his death. Nothing more is known of him. Feast 28 August.

Sithney, monk, born Britain, died Sithney, Cornwall (?), *c.* 529. He went to Guic-Sezni in Brittany and founded a monastery there, but presumably returned to Cornwall before he died: his tomb was said to have been in Sithney, although his relics are in Sezni (also named after him). A legend of St Sithney says that God offered him the choice of being the patron saint of young women or of male dogs, and he chose the latter as less troublesome. Feast 4 August.

Siviard, abbot, born France, died monastery of St-Calais, near Le Mans, 729 (?). His father was abbot of the monastery of St-Calais before him. He wrote a life of the founder, **Carileffus** (Calais). Feast 1 March.

Sixtus I, pope, consecrated *c.* 116, died 125. Nothing is known about him. It is unclear whether he died as a martyr, as tradition suggests he did. Feast 3 April.

Sixtus II, pope and martyr, consecrated August 257, died Rome, 6 August 258. He was probably of Greek origin, and little is known of his pontificate except that he restored good relations with the Church in Africa, damaged by Pope **Stephen I**. He did this without sacrificing his principles, for a letter has survived from Sixtus to **Dionysius of Alexandria** defending the validity of baptism administered by heretics. On the day of his death he was dragged from the chair where he was sitting teaching, in the cemetery of Praetextatus, and beheaded on the spot, together with some of his attendant deacons.

Sixtus III, pope, born Rome, consecrated 31 July 432, died Rome, 19 August 440. Sixtus's chief concern, in the aftermath of the Council of Ephesus (431), was to reconcile warring factions without betraying the decrees of the council. In this he was largely successful, as he was in maintaining for the most part good relations with the patriarch of Constantinople, without giving up papal claims, for example, to have jurisdiction over the disputed area of Illyricum (roughly the Balkans). He built Rome's first recorded monastery, and rebuilt the Liberian basilica as Santa Maria Maggiore, to celebrate the Council of Ephesus and, in its iconography, to proclaim papal authority.

Slebhene, abbot, born Ireland, died Iona, 767. He was elected abbot of Iona in 752. Feast 2 March.

Slemun the Weeper, bishop, died monastery of Ahrun, near Balad (?), eighth century. Syriac Church. He became bishop of Hadita, on the Tigris, in the middle of the eighth century. Although punished by the governor of the city for having converted some Muslims to Christianity (he was beaten and forced to shave his beard), he

later established good relations with the governor. He was vehemently opposed to the special taxes placed on Christians, which had led to many apostasies, and was exiled to a monastery for his pains. He was allowed back after three years, but then took part in a rebel synod opposed to the new patriarch. This was a miscalculation, and he was sent off to the monastery of Ahrun, where he wept for seven years. Feast 31 July.

Smaragdus, priest, born Rome (?), died there, 303. He ministered to the Christian slaves working on the building of the baths of Diocletian, but was martyred, apparently alongside Ss **Cyriac, Largus** and others. Feast 8 August.

Smbat the Confessor, born Armenia, died Samarra, *c.* 855. Armenian Church. He was a military leader who was taken hostage when Armenia was invaded by Bula, and taken to Samarra. Most of the other hostages, when offered their freedom in return for renouncing their faith, apostatized, but Smbat refused to do so, and died in prison. Feast 13 June.

Smbat the Martyr, king, born Armenia, died Siwnik, 914. Armenian Church. His reign, which began in 890, was one of continual warfare, both because of family rivalry and because of external attacks. After being defeated at the siege of Kapoyt Berd, he was taken to the siege of Ernjak, but steadfastly refused to call upon the defenders of that fortress to surrender. He was then given the opportunity to deny his faith, but refused to do so, and was beheaded. Feast 8 May.

Snorhawor, martyr, born Scrutari, Armenia, died there, 1494. She was a childless widow who lived with her brother. Her brother killed a Kurd, and then fled immediately. Snorhawor was blamed, but was offered her freedom were she to abjure Christianity. She refused, and was condemned to death. Feast 31 October.

Socrates and Dionysius, martyrs, died Perga, Pamphylia (modern Perge, Turkey), 275. They were soldiers in the imperial army who became Christians and were martyred. Feast 19 April.

Sola, see **Sualo**.

Solangia, martyr, born Villemont, near Bourges, died there, *c.* 880. From a modest rural family, she worked guarding her father's sheep. A son of the count of Poitiers, the local lord, killed her when she resisted his attempt to sexually assault her. She is widely venerated in the region. Feast 10 May.

Solochon, Pamphamer and Panphilion, martyrs, born Egypt, died Chalcedon, 305. Three soldiers who were clubbed to death for their Christianity. Feast 17 March.

Solomon, martyr, died Córdoba, Spain, 13 March 857, with **Roderigo** – see also **Martyrs of Córdoba**.

Solomon, bishop, died Ephesus. Bishop of Ephesus. Feast 2 December.

Solomon of Brittany, king, born Cornwall, died Brittany, fifth century. Said to have been assassinated by rebels. Feast 25 June.

Solomon of Brittany, king and martyr, born Brittany, died there, 874. He fought the Franks, and did penance for the sins of his youth. He was assassinated, and is regarded as a martyr. Feast 25 June.

Sophia, born Cappadocia, died Bethlehem, *c.* 500. She was the mother of St **Sabas**, and followed him to the Holy Land, where she lived out her life in the convent of St **Paula**.

Sophia and Irene, martyrs, died Egypt, *c.* 200. Feast 18 September.

Sophia of Aenus, born Aenus, Rhodope (modern Rodopi), died there, tenth century. Byzantine Church. After the death of her six children she dedicated herself to the care of the poor, then later became a nun. Feast 4 June.

Sophia of Fermo, martyr, died Fermo, Italy, *c.* 250. Feast 30 April.

Sophia of Minden, martyr, died Minden, Germany (?), *c.* 303. Feast 3 September.

Sophia of Rome, died Rome, *c.* 115. Said to have been the mother of three daughters, Faith, Hope and Charity, who were martyred. She herself died peacefully when visiting their tomb. Feast 30 September.

Sophia of Suzdal, princess, died Suzdal, 16 December 1542. Russian Church. Baptized Soilomonia Jurjevna Saburova, in 1505 she married the grand prince of Moscow and all Russia, but was found to be barren and was separated from her husband. In 1525 she was accused of sorcery, which provided her husband with grounds for divorce. She was then sent to the convent of the Protection of the Mother of God at Suzdal, where she died. Feast 23 June.

Sophianus of Drynoupolis, bl., bishop, born Politsani Pogoniu (?), died there, 1711. Byzantine Church. He was hegumenos of the monastery of St Athanasius at Politsani, where he established a school to preserve the national culture. That was in 1672. Some years later he was elected bishop of Drynoupolis in the Epirus. After a few years, however, he resigned his see, possibly because of conflict with the Turkish authorities, and retired back to the monastery, spending the rest of his life preaching and teaching in the region. Feast 26 November.

Sophronius, bl., monk, born Epirus, died Mount Athos, 1770. His parents wished him to marry, but on the night of the wedding he fled to Mount Athos, where he eventually settled for 50 years in the hermitage of Santa Anna and was renowned for his holiness of life. Feast 18 August.

Sophronius of Bulgaria, Orthodox bishop, born Kotelin, Bulgaria, 1739, died Bucharest, 22 September 1813. Consecrated bishop of Vratsa, he laboured to protect his flock from arbitrary mistreatment by the Turkish authorities and also translated spiritual literature into colloquial Bulgarian. He was forced out of Bulgaria and went to Bucharest, where he continued to write for his people. There he also wrote his own *Life and Sufferings*. Canonized by the Bulgarian Church in 1964. Feast 22 September.

Sophronius of Cioara, martyr, born Cioara (Alba Julian), Romania, died Curtea de Arges, eighteenth century. Romanian Church. The son of a priest, he become a monk at a monastery in Wallachia, and then became a hermit. He founded a small monastery which in 1757 was destroyed by (Catholic) Hungarian troops. There had been an attempt by the authorities in Vienna to unite the Romanian Orthodox Church with Rome: Sophronius was active in opposing this policy, and was created a bishop for the Orthodox because of this. He was for a time imprisoned at Boblina, but then released because of pressure from his fellow Orthodox. He fled to Carpathia, where he went about encouraging the Orthodox. In 1761 there was a synod in Transylvania which reached an agreement that the two faiths should live in harmony. That same year, however, there was renewed persecution of the Orthodox by Vienna, some 150 monasteries being destroyed. Sophronius fled back to Wallachia, and retired to a monastery at Curtea de Arges. Feast 21 October.

Sophronius of Cyprus, archbishop, died Constantia, Cyprus, sixth century. He was renowned as a scholar of the Scriptures. Feast 8 December.

Sophronius of Irkutsk, bishop, born Cernigov, 25 December 1703, died Irkutsk, 30 March 1771. Russian Church. The son of a priest, and baptized Stephen Kristalevskij, he grew up in Berezan near Perejaslavl, then studied in Kiev and entered the monastery of the Transfiguration at Krasnogorsk, where his brother was in charge, taking the name Sophronius. He became treasurer of a monastery, then of the bishop of Perejaslavl, where he worked for eight years. While in St Petersburg on business, he was asked to become a member of the community of the monastery of Alexander Nevski in that city, and in 1743 became treasurer there. He served in this office for three years before being appointed vicar of the monastery, with responsibility for running it. He improved the monks' course of study and created a library, as well as building a church for the monastery. In 1753 he was appointed bishop of Irkutsk, although he did not arrive there until nearly a year later, spending much of the intervening time learning about his new diocese. He immediately set about reforming the structures of the diocese and the monasteries and convents of the region. He was also determined to improve the schooling available, he went on visits to the parishes of his diocese, and built new churches – six of them in Irkutsk alone. He was particularly concerned to encourage missionary activity among the pagans still in his region, using the monasteries for this purpose. In all this he maintained very much the life of a monk, in prayer and fasting.

Sophronius of Jerusalem, patriarch, usually identified as 'the Sophist', born Damascus *c.* 560, died Alexandria 638. He accompanied John Moschus on his travels, recorded in *The Spiritual Meadow*, and then lived as a monk in Egypt from about 580, before moving near to the Jordan and in 616 to Bethlehem. He became patriarch of Jerusalem in 634, and died in 638, shortly after negotiating the surrender of Jerusalem to the Arabs. He then left for Alexandria. He was the chief opponent of monothelitism in his later years. His writings include Lives of the Alexandrians Cyrus and John, sermons and poems. Feast 11 March.

Sophronius of Vraca, bishop, born Kotel, Balkans, 1739, died Bucharest, September 1813. Bulgarian Church. Born Stojko Vladislavov, he came from a well-to-do family, although he was orphaned fairly early in life. He became a priest in 1762. He worked first in his native city, but because of the Russian-Turkish war he had to leave it in 1774 and went to Mesembria, where he worked in rural parishes. After 20 years he retired to live with some relatives in Arbanisi, near Veliko Tarnovo. The metropolitan of that city suggested that he might become bishop of Vraca in a wild part of the Balkan mountains, constantly menaced by warring bands. He once had to hide, disguised as a woman, in a harem, and from 1800 to 1803 he was held prisoner at Vidin. He used the time to study and write, and when he was freed he went to live in Bucharest where he continued to do likewise. He produced a large number of books, mainly on religious themes, including an autobiography, *The Life and Sufferings of Sophronius the Sinner*. Feast 11 March.

Sophronius the Recluse, monk, died Kiev, thirteenth century. Russian Church. He read the entire Psalter every day, and wore iron chains around his body. Feast 11 March.

Sorus, hermit, died Gaul (France), sixth century. Feast 1 February.

Sosthenes and Victor, martyrs, died Chalcedon, fourth century. Said to have been executioners, who were converted by the sufferings of St **Euphemia**. Feast 10 September.

Sostratus and Companions, martyrs, died Sirmium (Mitrovica, Serbia), fourth century. Feast 8 July.

Sosus and Companions, martyrs, died near Rome, *c.* 303. Sosus was a deacon. His companions were named Januarius, Proclus and Faustus. Feast 21 April.

Soter, pope, born in the Campania, consecrated *c.* 166, died Rome, *c.* 174. We know he sent a gift to the Church at Corinth, because a letter of thanks has survived. It was during his pontificate that Easter became an annual feast of the Church. It is common to celebrate Soter as a martyr, but there is no evidence that he was one. Commemorated with **Gaius**. Feast 22 April (suppressed 1969).

Soteris, martyred 304. Claimed with pride by **Ambrose** as a close relative, he describes her as a wealthy and beautiful young woman, who had consecrated herself to God and was tortured and beheaded for her faith. Feast 11 February.

Sozomen, seventh century. Church of Cyprus. One of the saints – said to be 300 in number – who fled from the Muslim invasions to Cyprus, and settled in a cave at Potamia. It is possible that there were two saints of the same name, one of whom had settled at Carpasia and became a bishop. They are commemorated on successive days, of Carpasia on 20 November, and of Potamia on 21 November.

Sozon, martyr, born Lycaonia, died Cilicia, *c.* 303. Originally named Tarasius and a shepherd, he converted to Christianity taking the name Sozon. He then went about preaching. He broke the hand off a golden idol, and sold the gold to feed the poor. For this he was burned alive. Feast 7 September.

Speratus and Companions, martyrs, died 180. Also known as the Scillitan martyrs, they were arrested in the first year of the reign of the Emperor Commodus, taken to Carthage and questioned. They were offered a pardon if they would worship Roman gods and acknowledge the divinity of the emperor. They refused, and were executed. Their names are Speratus, Aquilinus, Cittinus, Donata, Felix, Generosa, Januaria, Laetantius, Nartzalus, Secunda, Vestia and Veturius. Feast 17 July.

Speusippus, Eleusippus, Meleusippus and Leonilla, martys, died Cappadocia, *c.* 175. The first three were triplets, Leonilla was their grandmother. Feast 17 January.

Spiridon, bishop, born Cyprus, died there, *c.* 348. He was bishop of Tremithus in Cyprus and was probably one of the bishops at the Council of Nicaea (325) and definitely at the Council of Sardica (343). He had been a shepherd, and continued to look after sheep even as a bishop. Feast 14 December.

Spiridion and Nicodemus, monks, died Kiev, *c.* 1150. Russian Church. Spiridion came from a peasant family, and had no education. He taught himself the whole of the Psalter by heart, and was accustomed to recite it as he worked in the kitchen. Nicodemus was his closest friend among the monks. Both were renowned for their virtue. Feast 31 October.

Spiridion Makarovi Evtusenko, martyr, born Solonicevka, 31 October 1883, died Char'kov, 25 May 1938. Ukrainian Church, Moscow Patriarchate. He worked as a deacon in Char'kov, attached to the church of the Three Holy Bishops. Feast 19 May.

Spiridion Potemkin, archimandrite, born Smolensk, died 1665. Church of the Old Believers. He was from a well-to-do family, and had been educated in Poland. He had relatives in Moscow, and he became archimandrite of the monastery of the Protection of the Mother of God at Moscow. He was then proposed as bishop of Novgord, but refused the appointment because of his hostility to the new rites. He wrote in defence of the old ways, and became the first significant theologian of the Church of the Old Believers.

Stamatius of Spetse, martyr, born island of Spetse, 1804, died Chios, 3 February 1822. Byzantine Church. He travelled to Turkey with his brother **John of Spetse**, was arrested, and eventually beheaded on Chios.

Stamatius of Volos, martyr, born Volos, Thessalia, died Constantinople, 1680. Byzantine Church. He came to Constantinople with a delegation from his village to protest at the taxes being levied by the local authority. As spokesman for the group he raised the anger of the Turks, who claimed that he had undertaken to become a Muslim and had reneged on this promise. He was condemned to death.

Stanislaus, bishop and martyr, born Szczepa-nowski, near Krakow, Poland, 26 July 1030, died Krakow, 8 May 1079. He was born into a noble family and was educated at Gniezo and – possibly – Paris before becoming a priest at Krakow. He held various offices in the diocese, and was made bishop of the city in 1072, much against his will. He was an outspoken critic of King Boleslaus II for his evil life, and particularly for seizing the lands of the Church. Boleslaus ordered his assassination, and he was stabbed to death in the chapel of St Michael, just outside Krakow, although his body was interred in the cathedral of the city. The king fled to Hungary, and died in exile.

Stanislaus Kostka, patron of Poland, born Rost-kovo, Poland, 28 October 1550, died Rome, 15 August 1568. Born into the Polish nobility, he studied at the Jesuit college in Vienna. Against family opposition, he managed to enter the Jesuit novitiate of St Andrew in Rome in 1567, where he lived for a few months in faith and spiritual fervour. He was canonized in 1736.

Stephana Quinzani, bl., born near Brescia, 1457, died Soncino, 2 January 1530. A member of the Third Order of St **Dominic** from the age of 15, she worked with the poor and sick, founded a convent at Soncino near Cremona, had ecstatic seizures, showed the stigmata in her hands and feet, and left letters.

Stephen, died 815. He was abbot at Triglia, Bithynia, and a firm defender of the veneration of icons, for which he was exiled. Feast 26 March.

Stephen, hegumenos. Syriac Church. Possibly a disciple of **Samuel**, superior of the monastery of Qartmin, whom Samuel converted from paganism. Feast 19 March.

Stephen, Coptic Church. Died 15 September. Nothing else is known about him, not even the century of his death.

Stephen I, pope, born Rome, died there, 2 August 257. He became pope on 12 May 254 and was immediately called upon by the bishop of Lyon, Faustinus, to take action against Marcion, the bishop of Arles who had become a follower of the schismatic Novatus. He took no action and help was sought from **Cyprian** of Carthage, who in turn appealed to the pope, and it seems he complied. Stephen was also called on to intervene in another dispute arising from the Decian persecution, this time in Spain where he declared two of those apparently guilty of apostasy to be restored to the Church. In a later dispute with Cyprian he maintained, against Cyprian, that those baptized in schismatic sects need not be rebaptized when they joined the 'true Church'. The *Liber Pontificalis* cites Stephen as suggesting that clergy should wear special clothes when engaged in liturgical celebrations.

Stephen I, king of Hungary, born Gran, 975, died 15 August 1038. He became a Christian, with his father Geza, and was baptized by **Adalbert of Prague** in 985. As king from 997 he set out to Christianize his country. He was a supporter of the papacy and asked the pope if he could establish episcopal sees throughout Hungary. This was granted and he received a royal crown from the pope with which he was crowned in 1001. He founded a monastery in Jerusalem and pilgrims' refuges in Rome, Ravenna and Constantinople. He was distraught when his son **Emeric** was killed and there would be no devout Christian to succeed him. He was canonized in 1083 together with Emeric. Feast 16 August. (In Hungary it is kept on 20 August, the day of the translation of his relics to Buda.)

Stephen Aleksandrovic Andronov, martyr, born Zolocev, 15 September 1867, died Char'kov, 13 November 1937. Ukrainian Church, Moscow

Patriarchate. He became a priest in 1923, and worked in Prisib before his arrest and execution. Feast 19 May.

Stephen and Timothy of Kuben, monks, fifteenth century. Russian Church. They appear to have been monks living beside lake Kuben, although it is possible that Timothy was a hermit in the region, but nothing is known for certain about them.

Stephen Bandelli, bl., born Castelnuovo, near Piacenza, Italy, died Saluzzo, near Turin, 1450. He became a Dominican at Piacenza, was a student of canon law, and held a professorship at Pavia. He was well known as a preacher, and much sought after as a confessor. Feast 12 June.

Stephen Corumani, bl., hermit, died *c.* 1165. Feast 5 January.

Stephen Harding, abbot, born Sherborne, Dorset, England, *c.* 1050, died abbey of Clairvaux, 28 March 1134. He was educated at the monastery of Sherborne and later studied in Paris and Rome. On his way back from Rome he passed through Burgundy, stopped at the abbey of Molesme, and in 1098, under the guidance of the abbot, **Robert**, decided to join the community. He went with Robert and others to Citeaux, to establish a reformed foundation there, and became prior under the second abbot, **Alberic**, and then abbot in 1100. The abbey had become impoverished and few people had come to join them, until in 1112 **Bernard**, along with 30 of his confreres, joined the community and from then on it began to flourish. Stephen was an excellent organizer and 13 new foundations had been established from Citeaux before his death, with an administrative and pastoral system to match, the 'Charter of Charity'. This was approved by Callistus II in 1119.

Stephen Min, bl., martyr, died Korea, 1840. He is commemorated with **John Yi** – see **Martyrs of Korea**. Feast 30 January.

Stephen of Antioch, patriarch and martyr, died Antioch, 481. He became patriarch in 478, after Peter the Fuller had been exiled for rejecting the Council of Chalcedon. Stephen was, however, assassinated by Peter's followers. Feast 25 April.

Stephen of Châtillon, bishop, born Châtillon-les-Dombes, *c.* 1150, died Die, 7 September *c.* 1208. When he was about 25 he became a Carthusian at Portes-en-Bugey, but *c.* 1208, at the insistence of Innocent III and against his own wishes, he became bishop of Die.

Stephen of Chenolakkos, abbot, died Moudania, Asia Minor (Mudanya, Turkey), eighth century. He became a monk at monasteries in Palestine, including that of St Sabas, before going to Constantinople, where he successfully sought the help of the patriarch in founding the monastery of Chenolakkos, at Moudania. Feast 14 January.

Stephen of Cuneo, see **Nicholas of Sibenik**.

Stephen of Decani, king and martyr, born *c.* 1275, died Zvecan, 11 November 1331. Serbian Church. His parents divorced when he was about six, so that his father could marry a Byzantine princess, and he was exiled to what is now Montenegro. Some time later, however, his father had him blinded and sent to Constantinople as a hostage. He spent much of his time in Constantinople in the Pantocrator monastery, where he impressed everyone by his piety and wisdom, and where he had visions. His sight was restored by St **Nicholas of Myra**, who came to him in one such vision. In 1331, when his father died, he returned to the Serbian court to demand his inheritance. His brother refused the proposal to share power, and there was a struggle in which Stephen emerged victorious, largely through the support he enjoyed from the Orthodox Church. He was crowned in 1322, together with his son Dusan, who was called 'the young king'. Under Stephen, Serbia became a major power, but a conflict broke out between Dusan and himself, which he lost. Dusan imprisoned his father in the city of Zvecan, in Kosovo, where he died, possibly suffocated on the orders of his son, which is why he is called a martyr.

Stephen of Gusin, monk. Russian Church. Nothing is known of him, apart from the fact that he was the founder of the monastery of Gusin – although it is unclear where the monastery was located. Feast 13 January.

Stephen of Kiev, bishop, died Kiev, 27 April 1094. He was hegumenos of the Kievan Cave monastery. He left the monastery and founded another nearby with the same Rule. In *c.* 1080 he became bishop of Vladimir-Volynskij. After his death he was buried in the monastery he had founded.

Stephen of Kostroma, hegumenos, seventeenth century. Russian Church. Nothing is known of him, except that he was the hegumenos of the monastery of the Saviour at Kostroma – although there were two monasteries of the Saviour at Kostroma, and it is not clear to which he belonged. Feast 14 July.

Stephen of Lenaios, martyr, born Lenaios, Egypt, died there, *c.* 305. Coptic Church. He was priest of his native village, a second-generation Christian, and was put to death there some time between 305 and 311 for refusing to sacrifice to the pagan gods. Lenaios was in Middle Egypt, north of the modern Mallawi.

Stephen of Lyon, bishop, died Lyon, *c.* 515. As bishop of Lyon, he was active in converting the Arians in Burgundy to Catholicism. Feast 13 February.

Stephen of Machrisca, founder, born Kiev, died Machrisca, 14 July 1406. Russian Church. He became a monk at a monastery in Kiev, but in *c.* 1355 he left for Moscow, then became a hermit at a place called Machrisca, not far from the monastery of **Sergius of Radonez**. A small community grew up around him, and *c.* 1358 a monastery was founded to which Sergius himself came when problems within his own monastery forced him to leave. Stephen had to leave his foundation for a time because of hostility from one of the neighbouring families, who feared they might lose their land to the monastery. He settled as a hermit, with his disciple **Gregory of Avnega**, at Vologda, but later returned and spent the final years of a long life in his foundation.

Stephen of Mar Saba, born Damascus, *c.* 725, died Sabas monastery, Palestine, 794. Educated at the monastery by his uncle, **John Damascene**, he eventually lived partly in silent prayer – his real wish – and partly using the gifts of prophecy and counsel received after a 'transfiguration' experience. Feast 31 March.

Stephen of Muret, born Auvergne, *c.* 1047, died near Limoges, 1124, canonized 1189. He founded an extremely strict eremitical community, refusing any written Rule except 'Christ's Gospel'. After his monks moved to Grandmont in Normandy, it became the Grandmontine Order. There were three foundations in England. Feast 8 February.

Stephen of Obazine, bl., monastic reformer, founder and first abbot of Obazine, born Vierjo, near Limoges, *c.* 1085, died Bonaigue, 8 March 1159. A diocesan priest, he became a hermit under the influence of one of **Robert of Arbrissel**'s disciples. His eremitical community became an abbey in 1142, and with its daughter houses merged with the Order of Citeaux in 1147. Although never officially canonized, his cult was approved by Pope Clement XI in 1701.

Stephen of Omsk, born Tomsk, 1806, died Omsk, 2 April 1877. Russian Church. His full name was Stephen Jakovlevic Znamenskij and his father was a priest. He married in 1824, was ordained in the same year and worked in various cities before being appointed in 1854 as rector of the cathedral in Omsk. He was a humble man, ate little, was a vegetarian, dressed poorly. He was much sought after as a spiritual guide. Feast 10 June.

Stephen of Perm, bishop, born Ustug, 1340, died Moscow, 26 April 1396. The son of a priest, he entered a monastery in Rostov and was ordained there. An excellent linguist, he decided to become a missionary to the Ziryans, a people of Perm on the western edge of the Ural Mountains. He learned their language, and invented a script for it so he could translate the Scriptures into it. Although the pagan population was at first hostile, he gradually won them over and in 1383 was consecrated as the first bishop of Perm. This led to a clash with the bishopric of Novgorod, which claimed jurisdiction over this region, but Stephen managed to establish good relations with the city. He built churches and monasteries, and established colleges for training clergy for his new diocese. He died in Moscow, while on a visit there.

Stephen of Perm, monk, seventeenth/eighteenth centuries. Russian Church. Baptized Avraam, he was a servant to a noble house in Rostov, then becoming a monk in the city, where he gained a reputation for holiness of life. Feast 9 December.

Stephen of Rieti, abbot, died Rieti, c. 560. He was abbot at Rieti near Rome, and was known to be devoted to prayer, being described by **Gregory the Great** as 'rude of speech but of cultured life'. Feast 13 February.

Stephen of St Sabas (Sabaita), monk, ninth century. A monk of the monastery of St Sabas in Palestine, he was renowned as a poet, and particularly for a long poem on the passion of Christ. Feast 28 October (?).

Stephen of Sebaste, bishop and martyr, died Sebaste, 23 June 1387. Armenian Church. He was summoned before the emir and accused of conspiring against him. When it became evident that the charge was false, the emir threatened to execute him if he did not convert to Islam. Stephen refused, and was executed by being cut in half. Two priests who had accompanied him to the emir, Sylvester and Theodore, were beheaded.

Stephen of Serbia ('the First Crowned'), king, died Serbia, 24 September 1224. Serbian Church. Stephen succeeded his father in 1196 when the latter became a monk at the monastery of Studenica, which he had founded under the name of **Simeon**. Supported by his brother **Sabas**, he showed himself sympathetic to Catholicism, and sought the crown of Serbia. He approached Pope Innocent III, who agreed to his request, but then countermanded it because of opposition from Hungary. He renewed his request under Innocent's successor, Honorius III, this time successfully: he became 'the first crowned' king of Serbia in September 1217. He was also anointed as king by Sabas in his cathedral church at Zica in 1220.

Stephen of Solovki, monk, fifteenth/sixteenth centuries. Russian Church. Nothing is known of him. Feast 9 August.

Stephen of Sorb, see **Stephen of Xizan and Peter of Xizan**.

Stephen of Sweden, bishop and martyr, born Germany, died Uppsala or Norada, Helsingland, 1075 (?). A monk of the abbey of Corbie in Saxony, he went to Sweden as a missionary and was put to death. Feast 2 June.

Stephen of Tigre, monk, born Agame, Tigre, c. 1394, died Gewatr, c. 1445. Ethiopian Church. He was the son of a district chief who died before his birth. He was entrusted to an uncle, and when still very young entered the monastery of Qoyasa. He was a somewhat retiring individual, and tended to disassociate himself from his fellow monks. Nonetheless, he was entrusted with teaching some of the junior monks, and developed ideas which were at odds with those traditionally held. He therefore established his own monastic community with a group of disciples in 1428. Chief among his ideas was to break with the political power in Ethiopia, thus depriving his monastery of public funds. He attracted many followers, and thus weakened the other monasteries in his region. They complained, and he was summoned before the king, but found innocent. This was c. 1430. But in 1434 there was a new king, who was irritated at Stephen's independence and his refusal to prostrate himself before him. He was condemned to go into exile at Gewatr, largely Muslim territory, and he died there. Feast 27 December.

Stephen of Xizan and Peter of Xizan, martyrs, died Xizan, 2 June 1424. Armenian Church. They were two priests of Xizan who, along with many others, had abjured their faith. Repenting of their apostasy, they decided to confront martyrdom, and they went about the city proclaiming their faith. They were martyred, and their bodies burned. Their execution encouraged another apostate, **Stephen of Sorb**, to return to his faith, and he was martyred nine days later.

Stephen Pongracz, martyr, born Alvinc, Transylvania, 1583 (?), died Kosice, Slovakia, 8 September 1619. He entered the Society of Jesus at Brno, where he met his fellow martyr **Melchior Grodecz**. After studies in various places he went to the Jesuit College at Hummenné. By 1619 he was working in Kosice, with Melchior and **Mark Körösi**, a diocesan priest who had studied with the Jesuits and knew both Stephen and Melchior. When a

Protestant army invaded, the three were put to death. Feast 7 September.

Stephen Stiljanovic, prince, died Serbia, *c.* 1540. The exact place and date of his death are not known, but he was buried in the monastery of Sisatovic, near Fruska Gora, although his remains were moved to Belgrade during World War II. He was renowned for his generosity to the poor, and for his defence of Serbia against both the Ottomans and the Christian West. Feast 4 October.

Stephen the Blind, prince, died Italy, 1477. Serbian Church. He was a hostage of the Sultan Murat II when, together with his brother, he was blinded, then for a short period he became prince of Serbia, ruling Srem, with its capital at Smederevo, which was all that was left of an independent Serbia. When that fell in 1459 he fled to Albania, where he married **Angelina**, a Byzantine princess, after which he moved with his family to Italy.

Stephen the Faster, Theodosius and Timothy, monks, died Kiev. Russian Church. Nothing is known about them.

Stephen the Great and Holy, prince, born Borzesti, died Putna, 2 July 1504. Romanian Church. He owed his fame to the fact that, in the second half of the fifteenth century, his defence of Moldova was a bulwark against the invasion of Europe by the Ottomans: he called for a common front against the Muslims from all Christian leaders of Europe, regardless of their particular creed. His personal life was unhappy – he married four times, and was three times left a widower. He built monasteries and churches, and was a patron of Moldavian culture. His tomb became a place of pilgrimage almost immediately after his death.

Stephen the Tall, prince, died 19 July 1427. Serbian Church. He succeeded to the throne of Serbia after the death of his father **Lazarus** at the battle of Kosovo. Exploiting a momentary weakness on the part of the Ottomans, he was able to reunite Serbia from the Danube to the Adriatic. He was a great protagonist of the veneration of his father, and he founded several monasteries.

Stephen the Younger, martyr, born Constantinople, died there, 764. As a young man he spent some time in a monastery, but after the death of his father he returned home, sold his estate, and with his mother and sister went to Bithynia where they each entered a monastery. He became the abbot of St Auxentius's monastery in Constantinople in 744, but then resigned to live as a hermit. During the iconoclast controversy the emperor attempted to win him over, but Stephen remained firmly in favour of the veneration of images. He was therefore banished to an island in the Sea of Marmara for two years before being brought back and put on trial before the emperor. When he still remained firm he was scourged, dragged through the streets, and eventually clubbed to death. Some 300 others are said to have suffered at the same time. Feast 28 November.

Stephen-Théodore Cuénot, born Le Bélieu, Doubs, France, 8 February 1802, died Vietnam, as a prisoner, 14 November 1861, beatified 1909, canonized 1988. A priest of the Paris Foreign Missions Society, in the country since 1829, he became a bishop and apostolic vicar of Cochinchina. He worked in hiding during a time of persecution – see **Martyrs of Vietnam**.

Stephen Uros V, emperor, died 2 December 1371. Serbian Church. A meek and gentle individual, he was the last Serbian monarch to be titled 'Tsar': under him the nation divided up into principalities. He was buried at Fruska Gora, in the monastery of Jazak, although his remains were moved to Belgrade during World War II.

Stephen Vinh, martyr, died Vietnam, 1839. A Dominican tertiary. Feast 19 December.

Stilla, bl., born near Nuremberg, Germany, died *c.* 1140. Her family were the counts of Abenberg. She lived at home as a nun, and may have helped to endow the convent at Heilbronn. She built a chapel dedicated to St Peter in 1136. She may have made a vow of virginity in this chapel before St Otto, bishop of Bamberg. She also wanted to build a monastery, but died before it could be started. Feast 19 July.

Strato, martyr, died Nicomedia, *c.* 301. Said to have been martyred by having his legs tied to two trees bent towards each other, then released. Feast 9 September.

Strato, Philip and Eutychianus, martyrs, died Nicomedia, 301 (?). Said to have been executed by fire. Feast 15 August.

Stratonicus, see **Hermylus**.

Sturmi, abbot, born Lorch, Austria, *c.* 705, died Fulda, 17 December 779. He was entrusted by his parents to St **Boniface**, was educated at the abbey of Fritzlar, and for some years after his ordination to the priesthood he became a hermit. In 744, with Boniface, he founded the abbey at Fulda, and Sturmi became its first abbot. He travelled to Italy to visit Monte Cassino to study the Benedictine Rule. Pope **Zacharias** gave Fulda the privilege of being immediately accountable to the papacy rather than to the local bishop, which the bishop of Mainz, **Lull**, was unwilling to accept and Sturmi was banished from the monastery for a time, although the monks refused to accept any other superior. He and his monks were active evangelists of the Saxons.

Sualo, hermit, born Britain, died Heidenheim, 3 December 794. He followed St **Boniface** to Germany, and was ordained priest by him. After his master's death he lived the life of a solitary: the village of Solnhofen recalls his hermitage.

Sudislav of Pskov, prince and monk, died Kiev, 1063. Russian Church. The youngest son of **Vladimir of Kiev**, 'the Baptizer', he was blind from birth, but was given the principality of Pskov when his father divided out his territories. In 1035 his brother Jaroslav imprisoned him in Pskov, so as not to have to share power with him, and he was not freed until Jaroslav's death in 1058. He was set at liberty by Jaroslav's sons, on condition that he stayed out of political life. He retired to the monastery of St George in Kiev for the rest of his life.

Sulian, see **Mel**.

Sulpicius of Bourges I, archbishop, died Bourges, 591. He became archbishop of Bourges in 584. Feast 29 January.

Sulpicius of Bourges II, archbishop, died Bourges, 647. A noble from Béziers, he decided in early life to live as a celibate, and became archbishop of Bourges in 624. He is said to have converted everyone in his diocese not already a Christian. He resigned his see towards the end of his days to devote himself to the care of the poor. He is the Sulpicius of the church and seminary of St Sulpice in Paris. Feast 17 January.

Sunniva, princess, born Ireland, died island of Selje, Norway, tenth century (?). With her brother Alban and a large number of women she fled Ireland and, via Scotland, found herself on the island of Selje. There they were attacked by the local inhabitants and, fearing for their viriginity, the women prayed that they be spared. A rock fall then blocked the entrance to the cave where they were sheltering, and Sunniva's body was later found incorrupt behind the fall. Their remains were later buried at Bergen. Feast 8 July.

Suranus, abbot, died Sora, Umbria, Italy, *c.* 580. He distributed all the goods of his monastery to refugees from the Lombards. When the Lombards arrived at his monastery and found nothing left, they killed him. Feast 24 January.

Susanna, martyr, born Rome, died there, *c.* 295. There is an elaborate story of Susanna refusing suitors of the imperial court, and Diocletian ordering her to be beheaded as a consequence, a narrative probably concocted some two centuries after the events it purports to describe. Feast 10 August.

Susanna Chobyoye, bl., martyr, died Nagasaki, 1628. She was hanged naked on a tree for eight hours to shame her into denying her faith. When this failed she was again imprisoned, then beheaded with her husband **Peter** as one of the **Martyrs of Japan**. Feast 12 July.

Susanna, Marciana, Palladia and their Children, martyrs, died Galatia, second century. They were said to have been the wives and children of

Christian soldiers. It was claimed that their constancy converted their executioners. Feast 24 May.

Susanna of Eleutheroplis, martyr, died Eleutheroplis, Palestine, 362. She was converted to Christianity, and became a deaconess at Eleutheroplis, which lay between Gaza and Jerusalem.

Susanna, see also **Archelais**.

Svjatoslav, prince, born 1027, died Kiev, 27 December 1076. Russian Church. He was the son of **Jaroslav the Wise**, and in 1054 he became prince of Cernigov and, from 1073, grand prince of Kiev, a title for which he had to battle with his brother **Izjaslav**, who was backed by a Polish army, having been driven out of the city by a popular uprising. He was a generous donor to the Kievan Cave monastery, then just beginning, and a great supporter of ecclesiastical culture.

Svatoslav of Jurev, born Vladimir, 27 March 1196, died Jurev Polskij, 3 February 1253. Russian Church. He was the son of Vsevolod III, and when his father's dominions were divided out at his death, he received Smolensk. He later became prince of Perejaslavl and in 1220 prince of Jurev Polskij. In 1238 he also became prince of Suzdal, although that was seized by **Alexander Nevski** for his own brother. In 1247 he became grand prince of Vladimir, but that title, too, was taken from him the following year. He was buried in the cathedral of the city, which he himself had ordered to be built. His place at Jurev Polskij was taken by his son **Demetrius**, who became a monk shortly before his death. He died at Jurev Polskij in 1269, and was buried beside his father. Feast (of them both) 3 February.

Swithbert the Elder, bishop, born Northumbria, died Kaiserwerth, 713. A monk, he went to Friesland with **Willibrord** in 690, but in 693 returned to England to be consecrated bishop by **Wilfrid**. On his return he evangelized in what is now Westphalia, but was driven out by Saxon invaders, and settled on the island of Kaiserwerth on the Rhine, where he founded a monastery. Feast 1 March.

Swithbert the Younger, bishop, born England, died Werden, Westphalia, 807. He became bishop of Werden. Feast 30 April.

Swithin, born Wessex, died Winchester, 2 July 862. He was educated in Winchester and became chaplain to the king of Wessex and tutor to his son. When the son became king, he made Swithin bishop of Winchester in 852. He was originally buried outside the walls of the minster, but in 971 his body was moved to a shrine inside the newly rebuilt cathedral. His relics disappeared when his shrine was destroyed in 1538, in the Reformation. It is unclear why the belief arose in England that the weather on his feast day, 15 July, would be the weather of the following 40 days. One theory is that a similar belief is associated with Ss Processus and Martinian, on whose feast day St Swithin died.

Swithin Wells, schoolmaster and martyr, born Brambridge, Hampshire, c. 1563, died London, 10 December 1591. He had originally conformed to the established Church, and ran a school in Wiltshire. He had openly converted to Catholicism by 1585, when he came to London and took a house in Grays Inn Lane. It was while saying mass there that **Edmund Gennings** was captured. Wells and his wife, who was later released, were also taken, and Gennings and Wells were executed together in Grays Inn.

Syagrius of Autun, bishop, born France, died Autun, 600. He was bishop of Autun from c. 560 and was highly respected by Pope **Gregory I**, who sent **Augustine of Canterbury** to him on his way to England. Feast 2 August.

Syagrius of Nice, bishop, died Nice, 787. A monk at Lérins, he was a relative of **Charlemagne**. He himself founded a monastery, dedicated to St Pons, at Cimiez, and became abbot there before being made bishop of Nice in 777. Feast 23 May.

Sybillina Biscossi, bl., born Pavia, 1287, died there, 1367, cult approved 1853. An orphan, blind at 12, she was looked after by Dominican tertiaries. In 1302 she became a recluse near the Dominican friary and was known for her penance and miracles. Feast 19 March.

Sydney Hodgson, bl., martyr, died Tyburn, London, 10 December 1591. Arrested with **Edmund Gennings**.

Sylvester I, pope, born Rome, consecrated 31 January 314, died Rome, 31 December 335. Legend asserts that he baptized the Emperor **Constantine** and that he was the recipient of the *Donation of Constantine*, an eighth century document purporting to be a record of the emperor's conversion and profession of faith, and which allegedly granted wide temporal rights to Sylvester and his successors. Little is known of his life, but recognition of the primacy of the see of Rome increased during his period of office. He did not attend the Council of Nicaea in 325, but was represented by two legates.

Sylvester Gozzolini, bl., abbot, born Osimo, near Ancona, *c.* 1177, died near Fabriano, 1267. He was sent to study law, but switched to theology. When he came back to Osimo his zeal for reform annoyed the local bishop. He had received a valuable benefice which, in 1227, he resigned and for a time lived as a hermit. In 1231 he decided to found a monastery, which he did on the ruins of a pagan temple on Monte Fano, near Fabriano. His interpretation of the Rule of St **Benedict** was extremely strict, but there were nonetheless 11 monasteries in what came to be known as the Silvestrian Congregation by his death. Feast 26 November.

Sylvester of Assisi, friar, born Assisi, died there, 1240. A nobleman, he sold **Francis of Assisi** stone to rebuild a church, and when he saw Francis distributing alms, complained that he had not been paid enough. Francis gave him more money, but this weighed heavily upon Sylvester's conscience, and he eventually joined Francis and became one of his closest advisers, travelling around with him. Feast 6 March.

Sylvester of Kiev (1), monk, died Kiev. Russian Church. A monk of the Kievan Cave monastery, recorded simply as obedient, and a miracle worker. Feast 2 January.

Sylvester of Kiev (2), hegumenos, died Kiev, twelfth century. Russian Church. He continued the chronicle of **Nestor**, and was hegumenos of the Vydubickij monastery in Kiev. Feast 2 January.

Sylvester of Kiev (3), monk, died Kiev, twelfth century. Russian Church. He may be identical with (1) above.

Sylvester of Nicosia, abbot, twelfth century. He was of the Order of St Basil. Feast 2 January.

Sylvester of the River Obnora, hegumenos, died 25 April 1479. Russian Church. A follower of **Sergius of Radonez**, he became a hermit in the woods beside the river Obnora, not far from Jaroslavl. For a year he lived without anyone knowing where he was, living off the herbs of the forest. This food was inadequate, and he nearly died, until he was fed by an angel. The peasant who found him then brought him bread. After this many people came to live with him, and with the permission of the metropolitan of Moscow he founded a monastery, of which he became the hegumenos.

Sylvester of Valdiseve, bl., born Florence, 1288, died there, 1348. Baptized Ventura, he worked in the wool trade until he was 40, when he became a lay brother at the Camaldolese monastery in Florence, where he worked in the kitchen. He remained illiterate, but gave very good spiritual advice. Feast 9 June.

Sylvester Ventura, monk, born Florence, died there 1348. He worked in the cloth trade before becoming a Camaldolese lay brother at Florence. He worked as a cook in the monastery kitchen, and it was said angels did the cooking for him. He was much given to ecstasies and visions, and was greatly sought after as a spiritual director. Feast 9 June.

Sylvia, born Rome, died there, 572 (?). The mother of Pope **Gregory I**. Feast 3 November.

Symeon, see **Simeon**.

Symmachus, pope, born Sardinia, pope from 22 November 498, died Rome, 19 July 514. A convert from paganism who strictly upheld Roman doctrine and papal claims. He was the successful papal candidate – supported by the clergy and the majority of the laity in opposition to the archpriest Laurence, who was favoured by the aristocratic laity – following the death of Pope Anastasius II. After a bloody struggle between the factions in Rome, the candidacy of Symmachus was endorsed by the Arian King Theodoric. Later in his reign he opposed the Henoticon, supported by the Emperor Zeno, as being contrary to the Catholic faith and expelled the Manichaeans from Rome. He sent the pallium to Bishop **Caesarius** in Arles (the first bishopric outside Italy to receive the honour) and confirmed its primacy over the Gallican and Spanish Churches. He introduced the singing of the *Gloria* (by bishops only) on Sundays and feast days, helped the poor, including those persecuted by the Arians, and embellished St Peter's and other churches in Rome.

Symphorian, martyr, died Autun, France, third century. He was beheaded, it was said, for showing disrespect to the pagan deities of Autun. Feast 22 August.

Syncletica, recluse, born Alexandria, died there, fourth century. A wealthy woman, she lived as a recluse in an abandoned tomb until she was 83. She suffered greatly physically and mentally. Feast 4 January.

Synesius and Theopemptus, see **Theopemptus and Theonas**.

Synesius of Rome, martyr, died Rome, 257. A reader in a Roman church. Feast 12 December.

Synesius of Siberia, monk, born Priluka, 1698, died Irkutsk, 10 May 1787. Russian Church. In 1746 he was made superior of the hermitage of the Most Holy Trinity at St Petersburg, then in 1754 he became superior of the monastery of the Ascension at Irkutsk. He was an advisor to bishop **Sophronius of Irkutsk**. He helped to create the monastery of the Ascension, and was a model of monastic living. Miracles were attributed to his relics soon after his death. Feast 10 June.

Syra of Troyes, born Ireland, died Troyes, France, seventh century. The sister of St **Fiacre**, she became a hermit near Troyes. Feast 8 June.

Syra of Châlons-sur-Marne, abbess, died Châlons-sur-Marne, *c.* 660. She was a nun at Farmoutier, then became abbess at Châlons-sur-Marne. Feast 23 October.

Syrus of Genoa, bishop, died Genoa, *c.* 380. Bishop of the city from *c.* 324. Feast 29 June.

Syrus of Pavia, bishop. Said to have been the first bishop of Pavia. It is unclear when he lived. Feast 9 December.

T

Taamna Egzi, monk, born Tigre, fifteenth century. A disciple of **Andrew of Saffea**.

Tahmazgerd, martyr, died 25 September 445. Assyrian Church. He was governor of Nisibis (modern Nusaybin, south-west Turkey) and travelled to Karkha d'Beth Slob (modern Kirkuk) to take part in the persecution of Christians there. He was so impressed by the patience with which the Christians underwent their suffering that he put an end to the persecution, saw to the honourable burial of the martyrs, and became a Christian himself. When the king heard of this he ordered that Tahmazgerd reconvert, or that he too be martyred. He refused all efforts to persuade him to abjure Christianity, and was put to death.

Takasta Berhan, monk, fourteenth century. Ethiopian Church. He was founder of the monastery of Dabra Dimah in Goggiam.

Takla Adonay, monk. Ethiopian Church. A monk of Dabra Libanos, commemorated with **Tawalda Madhen**. Feast 18 July.

Takla Alfa, abbot, born Wasan Amba, fourteenth century. Ethiopian Church. His parents wanted him to marry, but three days before the wedding he fled to Dabra Dimah. There he became a monk and a priest. He was renowned for the rigour of his asceticism, and when he was 35 the monks, under pressure from the king, forced him to become abbot. He continued his life of asceticism, and intensified his giving of alms: when he had nothing left for the poor he distributed the church furnishings. He died at the age of 75, shortly after returning from an expedition preaching to the people of the region.

Takla Hawaryat, monk, fifteenth century. Ethiopian Church. He was selected for an ecclesiastical career by his parents, and he was ordained deacon. His parents then wished him to marry, but instead he left home and became a monk at Dabra Libanos. The abbot wanted him to be ordained, which he was, although against his will. He left the monastery and eventually settled in a large cave. He then decided to make a pilgrimage to Jerusalem in order to seek martyrdom, and went on a round of the monasteries to get the monks' blessing. One of them, however, foretold that he would never go to Jerusalem. He continued to wander in Ethiopia, preaching and converting both pagans and Jews to Christianity, and calling Christians to repentance. He eventually returned to his cave on Mount Gabarmna in Mugar, where he and his disciples destroyed the idols and set fire to the homes of the idol-worshippers. He died at Mugar on 6 December, but the year is not recorded.

Takla Haymanot, abbot, born Zorare, Selales (modern Etisa), died 30 August 1313 (?). Ethiopian Church. He was ordained deacon while still quite young, possibly *c*. 1270. He then married, but was soon a widower. He began preaching in his own region, which was still partly pagan, but then entered the monastery of Dabra Hayq. He stayed there for ten years before moving to Dabra Dimo in Tigre, possibly because he was thinking of making a pilgrimage to Jerusalem, but three years later returned to his home territory where he founded Dabra Asbo in Gerarya, later to be called

Dabra Libanos, as a centre for evangelization. A number of other monasteries in Ethiopia also owe their origin to Takla Haymanot. He played a significant part in the coming to power of Yekuno Amlak in 1270, which was achieved with the support of the clergy of the country. Takla Haymanot spent the last years of his life as a recluse.

Takla Iyasu, martyr. Ethiopian Church. Killed by pagans, but little else is known about him. Feast 12 August.

Takla Mikael, monk. Ethiopian Church. Feast 11 August.

Takla Samaet, Ethiopian Church. Feast 12 October.

Takla Seyon, monk, fifteenth century. Ethiopian Church. Nothing else is known.

Talawe Krestos, monk, thirteenth/fourteenth century. Ethiopian Church. He was commander of the royal army before becoming a monk and a follower of **Takla Haymanot**.

Tamar Gohar, martyr, died Ostan, 1398. Armenian Church. A woman of especial beauty, because of a Kurdish invasion she and her family were forced to flee to an island on lake Van. Five years later she was recognized in the city of Ostan and accused of having abjured Islam. She was stoned to death.

Tamara the Queen, died 1213. Georgian Church. She became queen of Georgia in 1184, after the death of her father who had named her as his heir. The nobility tried to limit her powers, because she was a woman, but she gradually won them back. Her reputation, and that of her country, was greatly enhanced by two important victories over the Turks. She was a great patron of the Church, establishing churches and monasteries, particularly the rock monastery of Varzia. Feast 1 May.

Tanco, bishop and martyr, born Ireland, died Saxony, 808. He was abbot of the Benedictine abbey of Neustadt and then bishop of Werden. He was a missionary to the Saxons and was killed by a pagan mob. Feast 16 February.

Tarasia of Portugal, see **Teresa of Portugal**.

Tarasius, original name of **Sozon**.

Tarasius, see also **Amphilochius, Macarius, Tarasius and Theodosius**.

Tarasius, patriarch, born Constantinople (?), died there, 25 February 806. His father was the prefect of Constantinople and he entered state service, becoming secretary to the Empress Irene II. Although not in orders, he became patriarch of Constantinople by popular acclaim in 784, but only with the agreement of the empress to the suggestion that he would try to restore Church unity. Pope Hadrian I gave reluctant approval and agreed to participate in the second Council of Nicaea in 787, which rejected iconoclasm and restored unity between Rome and Constantinople. Tarasius was involved in several controversies after this, but eventually became venerated as a saint.

Tarsicia of Rodez, died Rodez, c. 600. She is supposed to be a granddaughter of the Frankish king Clotaire II and a sister of **Ferreolus of Uzès**, who became a recluse near Rodez. Feast 15 January.

Tarsicius, martyr, born Rome (?), died there, third century. Killed while carrying the Eucharist either to sick Christians, or to imprisoned ones. Feast 26 August.

Tarsicius, Zoticus, Cyriac and Companions, martyrs, died Alexandria. Feast 31 January.

Tarsilla, see **Tharsilla**.

Tarsius and John, martyrs. They were beheaded. Byzantine Church. Feast 20 June.

Tasfa Iyasus, monk. Ethiopian Church. He was named 'the Just'. Feast 29 January.

Tassach, bishop, died Raholp, County Down, Ireland. He was an early disciple of **Patrick**, and was renowned as a craftsman. He became the first bishop of Raholp.

Tassilo, duke, born Bavaria, died Lorsch, near Frankfurt, c. 790. He was duke of Bavaria, and as such a founder of many abbeys and churches. He became himself a monk, at Jumiège in France, but later moved to Lorsch. Feast 13 December.

Tasso, abbot, born Benevento, died abbey of San Vincenzo, on the Voltorno river, *c.* 729. A monk of the abbey of Farfa, with his brothers **Paldo** and **Tato** he founded the monastery of San Vincenzo, and became its second abbot. Feast 11 January.

Tataq, martyr, born Adiabene, died Seleucia-Ctesiphon, *c.* 420. He was steward to the Persian King Yazdegerd I, but provoked his anger by suddenly leaving his post and becoming a monk. He refused to return to his duties, and was consequently beheaded.

Tathai, born Ireland, died Caerwent, Wales, sixth century. With a group of disciples he came to Caerwent, or Gwent, and established a school, as well as the monastery of Landathan. Feast 26 December.

Tation, martyr, died Claudiopolis (Mut, near Adana, in what is now Turkey), 304 (?). He was beheaded. Feast 24 August.

Tato, see **Tasso**.

Tatulus, Varus and Thomas, hermits, died Armenia, fifth century. Feast 21 February.

Tatwin, archbishop, died Canterbury, 30 July 734. He was a monk of the monastery of Bredon in Mercia and became archbishop of Canterbury in 731. He wrote a book of riddles, and a grammar, which survive.

Taurinus of Evreux, bishop, died Evreux, 412. Nothing is known of him. Feast 11 August.

Tawalda Madhen (1), monk, fifteenth century. Ethiopian Church.

Tawalda Madhen (2), monk. Ethiopian Church. Commemorated with **Takla Adonay**. Feast 18 July.

Teilo, bishop, born near Penally, Wales, died Llandeilo Fawr, Powys, sixth century. He spent some time in Brittany with **Samson** of Dol, and died as abbot of Llandeilo Fawr, the monastery he

had founded. When three places in Wales disputed his body, it was apparently miraculously multiplied into three. Feast 9 February.

Telemachus, martyr, died Rome, *c.* 400. Apparently originally a hermit from the eastern part of the empire, he was stoned by the crowd when he tried to stop a gladiator fight, protesting that the games represented 'the superstition of idols' and 'polluted sacrifices'. When the Emperor Honorius learned this, he put an end to such displays. Feast 1 January.

Telesphorus, pope, elected *c.* 125, died Rome, *c.* 136. The name suggests that he was Greek, possibly from Calabria, but little else is known about him, although it is probable that he died a martyr. Feast 5 January (suppressed 1969).

Ten Martyrs of Crete, died Gortyna, Crete, 250. They suffered in the persecution of Decius, and a village near Gortyna is still called 'The Ten Holy Ones'. Their names were Theodulus, Saturninus, Eporus, Gelasius, Eunician, Zoticus, Cleomenes, Agathoopus, Basilides and Evaristus. Feast 23 December.

Terence, bishop and martyr, born Hungary, died Foglia, Italy, *c.* 251. He had fled the persecution in Hungary, but was put to death near Pesaro, of which he has become the patron saint. Feast 24 September.

Terence Albert O'Brien, bl., martyr, born Limerick, 1601, died there, 30 October 1651. He became a Dominican in 1622, then provincial in charge of Dominicans in Ireland, then bishop of Emly. He was captured and put to death after the siege of Limerick.

Terence and Companions, martyrs, died Carthage, 250. Fifty martyrs in all, who had been thrown into a snake pit, but emerged unharmed, and then were beheaded. Feast 10 April.

Terence and Fidentius, martyrs, born Chalcedon, died Todi, Umbria, Italy, *c.* 305. They came to Rome from Syria seeking martyrdom during the persecution of Diocletian. Attempts to execute them in Rome failed, but then an angel appeared to the executioners with a message telling them to take their captives to Todi, where they were successfully beheaded. Feast 27 September.

Terence, Neonilla and their Children, martyrs, died 250. Feast 28 October.

Terence of Imola, born Imola, Italy, died Faenza, twelfth century (?). He was born near the cathedral in Imola, and was ordained deacon. He was remarkable for his care for the poor and needy, and for healing, so much so that he fled the area and went to Faenza. There the same thing happened, and he retreated into the countryside as a hermit. Feast 30 July.

Terence of Luni, bishop and martyr, died Sarzana, Italy, ninth century. Bishop of Sarzana, near La Spezia, he was reported to have been killed by robbers. Feast 15 July.

Teresa Benedicta of the Cross, see **Edith Stein**.

Teresa Bracco, bl., martyr, born Santa Giulia, Savona, Italy, 24 February 1924, died there, 28 August 1944. A very devout child, and a mystic, she was shot by a German soldier after resisting his attempts to rape her.

Teresa Couderc, see **Mary Victoire Thérèse Couderc**.

Teresa Eustochio Verzeri, bl., born Bergamo, Italy, 1801, died Brescia, 3 March 1852. Baptized Ignazia, she came from a noble family. She tried three times to become a Benedictine nun at Bergamo, but failed each time, and began to teach girls at her own home. In 1831 she founded the Institute of the Daughters of the Sacred Heart of Jesus, dedicated to teaching, but also to running orphanages, homes for the elderly and other charitable undertakings. Approval came from Rome in 1841, and she spent the rest of her life guiding her order and drawing up a constitution, as well as keeping in touch, through letters, with her communities around the world.

Teresa Grillo Michel, bl., born Alexandria, 25 September 1855, died there, 25 January 1944. Baptized Maddalena Parvopassau, her father was senior doctor at a hospital in Alexandria. She was educated in Italy, but returned to Alexandria where in 1877 she married Captain Giovanni Michael, but he died of sunstroke after a military parade in 1891, and she sank into a depression. She only recovered from this when she started to care for the poor, selling her own house to buy a much larger building to house the needy. In January 1899 she and eight of her helpers in Alexandria founded the Congregation of the Little Sisters of Divine Providence, which she spent the rest of her life guiding.

Teresa Jornet e Ibars, also known as Teresa of Jesus, born Aytona, Spain, 9 January 1843, died Valencia, 26 August 1897. Her parents were pious peasants. She joined the Poor Clares, but was forced to return home due to ill-health. She later founded her own religious community to provide care for the elderly. Later, along with ten companions, she took the habit at Barbastro, but soon transferred the mother house to Valencia, where it remains to this day. She continued to be superior general until her death. By this time the institute had 103 houses.

Teresa Kim, see **Agatha Yi**.

Teresa Margaret Redi, born Arezzo, Italy, 15 July 1747, died Florence, 7 March 1777. Baptized Anna Maria, she was educated at a convent in Florence. Always very devout, at the age of 17 she decided to become a Carmelite, and entered a Carmel in Florence. She worked mainly in the infirmary, and was reputed to have the gift of healing.

Teresa Mary of the Cross, bl., born Campo Bisenzio, near Florence, 2 March 1846, died (of cancer) 23 April 1910, beatified 1986. She opened a free school, establishing a group of Carmelite tertiaries to teach poor children. This became the Sisters of the Third Order of St Teresa of Jesus in 1904.

Teresa of Avila (Teresa of Jesus), mystic and reformer, born Avila, 28 March 1515, died Alba de Tormes, 4 October 1582. Initially educated at home, she spent just over a year in her mid-teens at the Augustinian school in Avila, but had to leave because of ill-health, which she suffered throughout her life. In 1535 she left her family and joined the Carmelites in Avila. Although disapproving this move, her father eventually gave his blessing. Teresa, intent on pursuing a life of religious perfection, entered more and more deeply into prayer and began to experience a series of visions and ecstasies. So that she and others could lead a life of greater mortification, she determined to open a house where the primitive Rule of the Carmelites would be observed. The convent of St Joseph was opened, against much opposition, in 1562 and this was followed, against similar opposition, by several more Discalced houses both for women and, with the aid of **John of the Cross**, for men. On the instructions of her spiritual advisers she wrote her *Life*, and also began a book for the sisters, *The Way of Perfection*. These and her other writings, including *Foundations* and *The Interior Castle*, are all regarded as classics of the spiritual life. Teresa was declared a doctor of the Church in 1970.

Teresa of Calcutta (Mother Teresa), bl., founder, born Skopje, Macedonia, 26 August 1910, died Calcutta, 5 September 1997. Baptized Agnes Gonxha Bojaxhiu into an Albanian family, she joined the Sisters of Loreto at Rathfarnham, Ireland, in 1928. Having expressed what she understood as her call to work in India, she was sent as a novice to study and work in Darjeeling, and in 1929 went to work in the Loreto school in Calcutta. In 1946 she became convinced that God wanted more from her, and felt increasingly called to serve the very poor. In 1948, with her superior's permission, she left the Loreto convent, took the name Teresa and, dressed in a simple blue and white sari, went to live in a Calcutta slum area where she cared for the destitute and the dying and taught the children of the very poorest. She was soon joined by others, among them those she had taught, and in 1950 the Missionaries of Charity was approved as a new religious order. In 1963 the Missionary Brothers of Charity was established and in 1969 the International Co-Workers of Mother Teresa. Mother Teresa established the work of the order worldwide, including in the cities of the supposedly privileged West, where many of the destitute, desperate and dying have benefited from the acceptance and care of the sisters. In 1979 she was awarded the Nobel Peace Prize.

Teresa of Lisieux, nun, born Alencon, 2 January 1873, died Lisieux, 30 September 1897. Drawn to religious perfection early in life, she entered the Carmelite convent at Lisieux at 15, and professed in 1890. In 1895, on the feast of the Trinity, she conceived the wish to offer herself as a victim to the merciful love of the Lord. A few days later, as she was praying the Way of the Cross, a shaft of fire penetrated her: God had ratified her request. In April 1896, Teresa haemorrhaged for the first time and she was happy to be going soon to heaven. However, her faith in another world was severely tested in the following weeks, made the more burdensome by her growing desire 'to pass her heaven doing good in the world'. Fortified by Our Lord's promise, 'Where I am, there you will be also,' she reacted to this temptation by multiplying her acts of faith and offering her sufferings for the unbelieving. A year after her death appeared *Histoire d'une âme*, her autobiography, to which the superior, Agnes, her older sister, had appended fragments of letters, poems, prayers and souvenirs. She was canonized in 1925 by Pope Pius XI, who declared her 'the star of his pontificate'. In 1927 he named her patron of the missions, the equal of **Francis Xavier** and, in 1944, she joined **Joan of Arc** as patroness of France.

Teresa of Portugal, queen, died Lorvao, 1250. She was the daughter of King Sanco I of Portugal, and married King Alfonso IX of Leon. There were children, but the marriage was annulled because she and Alfonso were cousins. She then returned to Portugal, and went to live in a Cistercian convent at Lorvao near Coimbra. She did not at first take vows, and at one point left the convent to settle a dispute among her children over their inheritance, but then returned, took vows, and spent the rest of her life as a nun. Feast 17 June.

Teresa of the Andes, born Santiago, Chile, 13 July 1900, died Los Andes, 12 April 1920, canonized 1993. She joined the Carmelites aged 19, after which her strong spirituality deepened further, as her letters and spiritual journal make clear. She died of typhus, making her final vows on her deathbed.

Teresa Verzeri, bl., born Bergamo, Lombardy, 31 July 1801, died Brescia, 3 March 1852, of cholera, beatified 1946. Unsettled in the Benedictine monastery she first joined, she was encouraged to leave and in 1841 founded the Daughters of the Sacred Heart of Jesus, who combine a contemplative life with working with young girls and women.

Teresa Yi, see **Barbara Kim**, and **Martyrs of Korea**.

Ternan, bishop, born Scotland, died Abernethy, Scotland, fifth/sixth centuries. He was a missionary to the Picts – Abernethy being the capital of the Pictish kings – but little else is known about him. Feast 12 June.

Tetricus, bishop, died Burgundy, 572. Son of **Gregory of Langres** and uncle of **Gregory of Tours**, he succeeded his father as bishop of Langres c. 540. Feast 18 March.

Tetricus, bishop and martyr, died Auxerre, c. 707. He became bishop of St Germanus (Germain) at Auxerre by popular acclamation, and was killed by his archdeacon as he slept. Feast 18 March.

Thaddeus MacCarthy, bishop, born Munster, Ireland, c. 1455, died Ivrea, in the Alps, 24 October 1497. He came from a noble family, and studied with the Franciscans at Kilcrea before going to Rome. There the pope appointed him as bishop of Ross in 1482. The assistant bishop there believed he had a right to the bishopric, and complained to Rome. Thaddeus was suspended by the pope, and had to leave the diocese. He went back to Rome. This time the pope made him bishop of Cork and Cloyne. However, his opponents had already seized his cathedral there, and he went back to Rome to plead his cause. He was reinstated by the pope and set off back to Ireland, but died at Ivrea, in a hospice of the Canon Regulars of St Bernard. Feast 25 October.

Thaddeus of Dabra Bartarwa, martyr, born Sebta, province of Hamasen, fourteenth century. Ethiopian Church. After the death of his mother, Thaddeus, his sister and his father all entered the monastery of Quahayn, where Thaddeus was ordained deacon. They were, however, forced to leave the monastery because of opposition to them and they went to Tembien, where his sister died

after falling from a tree while collecting fruit. Their father died shortly afterwards, and Thaddeus joined the monastery of Dabra Bankol, where he became a monk and was ordained priest. He had gathered a number of disciples, and together they founded a new monastery on Mount Bartarwa. With two of his disciples, Thaddeus was killed when bandits set fire to the church in which they were seeking refuge.

Thaddeus of Dabra Maryam, monk, born Zoare, died lake Tana, c. 1345. Ethiopian Church. He was brought up by a priest relative from the age of five to 30. He was related to **Takla Haymanot**, and probably became a monk at his monastery, Dabra Libanos, from which he founded Dabra Maryam. He was a successful evangelist, making converts not only among the pagans of the region, but also converting the Muslim governor. He was renowned for his care for the poor of the area. Feast 6 February.

Thaddeus of Ta'amina, monk, died Qola, fourteenth century. Ethiopian Church. He founded the monastery of Ta'amina at Qola in Tigre.

Thaddeus of Tver, bishop and martyr, born Vasildursk, 12 November 1872, died Tver, 31 December 1937. Russian Church. Baptized Ivan Vasilevic Uspenskij, the son of a priest, he studied theology in Moscow and was ordained in 1897. He taught in the seminary in Smolensk, then held a number of other offices in the Church before being consecrated bishop of Vladimir Voylynskij in 1908. Even as a bishop he lived a life of strict asceticism, giving away to the poor all that he possessed. In 1921 he was appointed archbishop of Astrakhan, was arrested soon afterwards and spent 1922–3 in prison. He was imprisoned again while visiting Moscow in 1926, and on his release was appointed to the see of Tver. In 1936 the state authorities ordered that he be transferred to Kostroma, but he refused to abandon his diocese, was arrested and shot.

Thaddeus the Studite, martyr, died Constantinople, 816. He was a monk of the Studion monastery in Constantinople. During the iconoclast controversy he was imprisoned and tortured for his defence of the veneration of images, and was eventually put to death. Feast 29 December.

Thais, penitent, died Egypt, fourth century. She was a prostitute, converted by one of the Fathers of the Desert, possibly **Paphnutius**. She then sold all her possessions and remained in a convent for the rest of her life, never leaving her cell. Feast 8 October.

Thalassius and Limnaeus, monks, died Cyrrhus, Syria, fifth century. Thalassius founded a monastery at Cyrrhus, which was joined by Limnaeus. Limnaeus was famed for his miracles. Feast 22 February.

Thalelaus and Companions, martyrs, died Aegae, c. 284. Thalelaus, born in the Lebanon, was a doctor at Anarbus (modern Anavarsa, Turkey) who was put to death for the faith at nearby Aegae. His constancy converted two of his executioners, Asterius and Alexander. Feast 20 May.

Thalelaeus the Weeper ('Epiclautos'), hermit, died Gabala, near Laodicea (modern Latakia, Syria), c. 450. He lived next to a pagan temple, for a time in a barrel, and won many converts.

Thalia, martyr, Syriac Church. The small son of a king who was murdered and his body hidden. While a priest was saying mass the child appeared, saying that he forgave his assassin because he had greater joy in heaven than before, and he showed the people where his body was hidden.

Thalia, monk. Syriac Church. A monk of Qartmin. Feast 1 February.

Thalia of Cyrrhus, martyr, died Gbayl. Syriac Church. When he was born his parents received a revelation saying that, by the age of two, he would have slain the king and destroyed idols. When the governor in Jubeil (Gbayl) came to hear of this, he threw the parents in prison and had the boy brought before him. At that moment 60 idols in the temple fell to the ground and smashed. The boy was then thrown into a furnace, but rain came and put out the flames, so he was sent off to prison again. This time the prison doors opened and he walked free, into the bedroom of the governor,

who now had him cut into three parts and the remains thrown out of the city. They were found by two fishermen – except that the boy was whole again, and alive. The fishermen were converted. They were beheaded, and the boy was again tortured, this time to death. His remains were gathered together and a church was built over his grave.

Thalus, see **Trophimus and Thalus**.

Thamel and Companions, martyrs, died Persia, c. 125. He was a converted pagan priest, and was put to death with a number of other converts, including his sister. Feast 4 September.

Tharachus, Probus and Andronicus, martyrs, died Tarsus, 304. Tharachus himself was said to have been a retired officer, the other two civilians. They were beheaded. Feast 11 October.

Tharsilla, born Rome, died there, 24 December c. 550 (?). The eldest sister of **Gregory the Great**'s father, and brought up in her father's house almost as if a nun.

Thea, Valentina and Paul, martyrs, died Gaza, c. 308. The three lived in Palestine during the persecution begun by Emperor Diocletian, under the rule of the governor Firmilian. Thea was arrested in Gaza, and Firmilian had her tortured for her outspokenness after she refused to give up her Christianity. Valentina witnessed the trial and called out in Thea's defence, and so was also arrested. Both were burned to death. Paul was beheaded at Gaza on 25 July 308, and before his death prayed aloud for Christianity, and for the judge, emperor and executioner. Feast 25 July.

Theban Legion, martyrs, born Upper Egypt, died St-Maurice-en-Valais, Switzerland, 287 (?). This legion, recruited in Upper Egypt, was sent against the Gauls. They were required to sacrifice to idols, but all refused to do so on the grounds that they were Christians. Led by Maurice, they then withdrew from the rest of the army, and were all slaughtered at a place then called Agaunum. According to this account, the number of martyrs was nearly 7,000, or according to another version, one in ten of the legion were put to death. Feast 22 September.

Thecla, see also **Archelais**.

Thecla and Companions, martyrs, died Persia, fourth century. Thecla, Martha, Mary, Ennatha and Mariamne were arrested together with a priest called Paul. The women refused to renounce their faith, but Paul did so, at which he was ordered to execute the women. Feast 31 May.

Thecla of Gaza, martyr, born Bizya, died Gaza, Palestine, 304. She was put to death by being thrown to wild beasts with **Agapius**. Feast 19 August.

Thecla of Kitzingen, abbess, born England, died Kitzingen, Germany, c. 790. A nun of a convent in Wimborne in Wessex, she went c. 749 to assist **Boniface**. She was a nun at Bischofheim before becoming abbess of Ochsenfurt and finally of Kitzingen. Feast 15 October.

Thecla of Perejaslavl, nun, born Mcensk (?), died Perejaslavl, fifteenth/sixteenth centuries. Russian Church. She was the mother of **Daniel of Perejaslavl**, and moved to that city because of her husband's work. After his death she became a nun in a convent in the city. Feast 25 May.

Themistocles and Dioscorus, martyrs, died Myra, Asia Minor, 253. Themistocles was a shepherd who was put to death for refusing to reveal the whereabaouts of Dioscorus. Feast 21 December.

Theobald of Alba, born Vico, near Mondovi, died Alba, 1150. Born into a noble family, he was converted to living a simple life by reading the Scriptures. He became a cobbler, but when the master cobbler wanted him to marry his daughter, he went on a pilgrimage to Compostela. When he returned he worked as a porter, gave away his wages and cared for the sick. Feast 1 June.

Theobald of Provins, born Provins, France, 1017, died 1066. He was the son of the count of Champagne, but decided to become a hermit in the manner of the Desert Fathers. He and a companion, Walter, settled in the forest of Pettingen in Luxembourg, where they gained a reputation for sanctity which attracted people to come to see them. They then decided to go on pilgrimage, to Compostela in Spain, and to shrines, including those of Rome, in Italy. They then settled at Salaniga, near Vicenza, where Walter died. Theobald's reputation for holiness was such that his parents heard of it, and came to visit him. His mother decided to stay at Salaniga as an anchorite. Shortly before he died, Theobald became a Camaldolese monk. Feast 30 June.

Theobald (Thibaud) of Vienne, bishop, born Toluon, Isère, died Vienne, 21 May 1001. Orphaned early in life, he became a priest and was consecrated bishop in 957. He was a reformer, associated with **Odilo of Cluny**.

Theocharis and Apostolos Duias, bl., born Arta, north-west Greece, died there. Byzantine Church. Two brothers, sons of a priest of Arta, Theocharis being born c. 1765, dying in 1829, and Apostolos, who was slightly the younger, dying in 1846. Theocharis became a teacher in the town, but their father wanted them to marry, then become priests. Both refused to do so, choosing instead to establish a small monastery for themselves near the church of Santa Sophia.

Theocleta the Wonderworker, born Asia Minor, died Constantinople, c. 840. Byzantine Church. After her marriage, she persuaded her husband to allow her to live as his sister, and passed all her time in spiritual deeds. Feast 21 August.

Theocletus, bishop, died Sparta, c. 898. Byzantine Church. He was bishop of Sparta. Feast 2 December.

Theoctista, hermit, born Lesbos, died Paros, tenth century (?). She fled from Lesbos because of Muslim raids on the island. Feast 10 November.

Theoctistus, monk, born Palestine (?), died there, 451. He was a friend of St **Euthymius the Great**, and was originally a monk of the monastery of Pharan, before founding his own monastery in the wilderness of Judea with Euthymius. He was its first abbot. Feast 3 September.

Theoctistus of Cernigov, bishop, died Cernigov, 1123. Russian Church. He was a monk of the Kievan Cave monastery, and became hegumenos. In 1108 he was elected bishop of Cernigov.

Theoctistus of Novgorod, bishop, died Novgorod, 23 December 1310. Russian Church. He was hegumenos of the monastery of the Annunciation, near Novgorod, when he was elected bishop of that city in 1299. He built a number of churches in the city, but retired from office in 1308 to return to his monastery. Feast 23 January.

Theodard of Maastricht, born Maastricht, died near Speyer, *c.* 670. A disciple of **Remaclus**, he probably entered the monastery of Stavelot before becoming bishop. He was killed by robbers as he passed through the forest of Bienwald, on his way to see King Childeric II of Austrasia. Feast 10 September.

Théodard of Narbonne, bishop, born Montauriol, now in Montauban, died there, 893. After studying law, he was ordained and became archdeacon to, then successor of, Archbishop Sigebold of Narbonne. He freed Saracen captives and sold church treasures to feed the hungry during a long famine. Feast 1 May.

Theodomar, bl., bishop and martyr, born Bavaria, died Ascalon, Palestine, 1102. He was a nobleman who became a monk at the monastery of Niederaltaich. He was made abbot of a monastery in Salzburg, and then bishop of that city in 1090. He was a supporter of the reforms initiated by Pope **Gregory VII**, for which he was put in prison. He was released on the undertaking that he would go on the first Crusade, during which he was captured by the Turks, imprisoned, then executed for refusing to become a Muslim. Feast 28 September.

Theodora, martyr, died Thessalonika, fourth century. Byzantine Church. She was the daughter of the pagan Emperor Maximian, and was converted after accidentally coming across a group of Christians worshipping. She hid her new faith from those about her, and had a room in her house turned into a chapel. One day, however, her mother asked her to join in pagan worship for the safety of her father in battle. When she refused, her faith was revealed, and she was executed.

Theodora and Didymus, martyrs, died Alexandria, 304. Theodora was born in Alexandria, but sold as a slave to a brothel when she refused to marry and have children. From the brothel she was rescued by Didymus, a Christian soldier, who changed clothes with her in the brothel. Both were brought before the judge and executed together. There are a number of variants on this story. Feast 28 April.

Theodora I, empress, born Constantinople, *c.* 495, died there, 548. Byzantine Church. She was the wife of Justinian I, who married her in 523, having had amended the law that forbade the marriage of a patrician to a woman of servile origin shortly before his accession, at which he made her an independent and equal co-ruler, inserting her name with his own in the oath of allegiance. In the religious strife which distracted the empire, Theodora took part with the monophysites, while Justinian was a warm upholder of the decrees of Chalcedon, and she was influential in having Justinian adopt his reactionary policy which, especially in the dispute over the 'Three Chapters', sought to reconcile the monophysites and the Chalcedonians, even at the expense of the decrees of Chalcedon. Although she had, according to Precopius, lived a dissolute early life, she was a woman of outstanding intellect and learning and, as empress, was shrewd, courageous in the Nika riots (532), when she rallied the emperor and court, a moral reformer and an example of true Christian piety, observing the feasts and fasts punctiliously. She did not suffer any affront, and had a reputation for severity. Although condemned by Baronius as *civis inferni*, Paul Silentiarius called her 'St Theodora' two years after her death. Feast 14 November.

Theodora Guerin, see **Theodore Guerin**.

Theodora of Arta, queen, bl., born Thessalonika, died Arta, thirteenth century. She became the wife of Michael Ducas, king of Arta, and had a son. The king left her for another woman for two years, but was eventually persuaded to return to her, not least because of her qualities as an administrator. They founded a number of churches in Arta, and after the death of Michael she became a nun, living a life of great austerity, at a convent she had herself founded. Feast 11 March.

Theodora of Caesarea, born Caesarea, Cappadocia, died there, eighth century. Byzantine Church. She was the daughter of a noble family who, while she was still a child, entrusted her to the care of the convent of Santa Anna. Emperor Leo the Isaurian, an iconoclast, wanted to marry her to one of his courtiers. She was brought from her convent to Constantinople, but on the evening of the wedding the city was attacked, and her new husband died in its defence. Theodora used the resulting confusion to escape from the city and return to Caesarea. When the imperial emissary came to bring her back, he discovered she had already become a nun. She lived the remainder of her life in the convent, renowned for her asceticism. Feast 30 December.

Theodora of Niznij Novgorod, princess, born Tver, died Galic, 1347. Russian Church. Of a noble family, she was married, aged 12, to Prince Andrew of Suzdal. After his death, and being childless, she entered the convent of the Conception of the Mother of God at Galic, which she had herself founded, and lived there a life of great asceticism. Feast 16 April.

Theodora of Sihla, hermit, born Vanatori, *c.* 1650, died Sihla, *c.* 1720 (?). Romanian Church. She married at her parents' instructions, despite her strong desire to become a nun. After the death of her parents, and being childless, she and her husband parted, and she entered the convent of Varzaresti on Mount Buzau. Her husband became a monk, receiving the name Elephteriu. During the Turkish attack on Vienna, some of the invaders found their way to the region in which Theodora was, and she and some of the other nuns fled to a more remote spot, where they established a small monastery, of which she became the superior. She served in this office for a decade, but then became a hermit in the forest of Sihla for the rest of her life. By chance Elephteriu was present for the funeral of Theodora, and recognized his wife. Feast 7 August.

Theodora of Thessalonika, bl., born Aegina, 812, died Thessalonika, 29 August 892. Byzantine Church. Baptized Agapi, she was the daughter of a priest who, after the death of his wife in childbirth, became a monk. At the age of seven she was married to a rich man, and at about the same time, or possibly before her marriage, she and her (future) husband were forced to flee, with many others, to Thessalonika because of Saracen attacks on their island. Two of her three children died in childhood, the other, **Theopista**, survived. After the death of her husband she became a nun at the convent of St Stephen, where she spent the remaining 55 years of her life, with a reputation for great sanctity. Feast 3 August.

Theodora the Empress, died Constantinople, 867. Wife of iconoclast emperor Theophilus and mother of Michael the Drunkard, she tried to restore the veneration of images before retiring to a convent. Feast 11 February.

Theodora the Penitent, hermit, born Alexandria, died there, 491. A sinner, presumably a prostitute, who repented and became a hermit for the rest of her life. In some versions of her story she entered a monastery as a monk, and hid her gender until her death. Feast 11 September.

Theodore, see also **Maximus, Theodore and Ascepiodotus**.

Theodore, king, died 1413. Coptic Church. King from 1412, he died while on a military expedition. He is recorded as being particularly devoted to the Church. Feast 23 June.

Theodore, martyr, died Kvelethi, 1609. Georgian Church. He was priest in the village of Kvetheli, and saved the life of King **Luarsab** when the Turks took the priest prisoner and demanded to know the king's location. Theodore decided to attempt to fool the Turks by taking them the wrong way, for which he was executed after much torture. The king escaped, and Theodore became a Georgian folk-hero.

Theodore, martyr. See also **Michael Chernigov**.

Theodore, monk, born Kerak, Palestine, died Apamea, Bithynia, 841. With his brother **Theophanes**, Theodore became a monk in the monastery of Sabas, where both gained a reputation for learning. He was ordained priest, and with his brother went to Constantinople at the behest of the patriarch of Jerusalem to protest at the emperor's iconoclast policy. They were exiled by the emperor, and returned to Constantinople only at his death. They were again banished in 829, and brought back two years later, still opposed to iconoclasm. As a punishment they were apparently tattooed with a verse proclaiming the reason for their punishment, and then banished once again, this time to Apamea in Bithynia, where Theodore died. Feast 27 December.

Theodore, patriarch, died 657. Syriac Church. It is unclear who this is. Possibly it is an Egyptian monk who became patriarch in 649, and died in 657. It may also be a misreading of a manuscript and may refer to **Theodosius of Alexandria** (536–67). Feast 1 November.

Theodore I, pope, born Jerusalem, died Rome, 14 May 642. Byzantine Church. He was the son of a bishop, and was possibly a refugee from the Arab invasions of Palestine and, as a Greek, was well versed in the theological controversies of the time. The chief issue was the number of wills in Christ – not an arcane argument because the belief that there was only one ('monothelitism') would imply that Christ was not fully human. The deposed patriarch of Constantinople, Pyrrhus, travelled to Rome to recant his belief in monothelitism, and Theodore promptly recognized him as the lawful patriarch. But when he found that his recantation did not regain him his see, he withdrew it, and went off to the imperial court at Ravenna. Theodore excommunicated him. When the emperor tried to bring peace among the warring parties by producing a document which simply insisted on the definitions of the first five councils, and forbidding any further discussion, the papal representative at Constantinople refused to sign, was exiled, and the office of the papal ambassador was closed. Theodore himself died before being presented with this document (the 'Typos'). Because of his opposition to monothelitism, Theodore is regarded as a saint in the East. Feast 18 May.

Theodore I and Theodore II, see also **Boris, James, Theodore I, Silvanus, Theodore II, Basil I, Demetrius, Michael, John, Basil II**.

Theodore and Basil, martyrs, died Kiev, eleventh century. Russian Church. Theodore had been very rich before he became a monk, and was constantly tempted by wealth, against which he was warned by his friend Basil. One day the devil revealed to him the whereabouts of much riches, hidden by brigands in the monastery. Thanks to Basil, Theodore was not tempted, but news of the treasure reached Prince Mstislav, who came to the monastery demanding to know where it was. Theodore said he knew, but had forgotten. He was tortured to make him reveal its location, and then so was Basil. Both died, but Basil was able to prophesy that the prince would die from an arrow wound, which came to pass. Feast 11 August.

Theodore and John, martyrs, died Kiev, tenth century. Russian Church. Theodore, whose pagan name had been Tur, had served in the army of Byzantium and became a Christian, as did his son John. The pagan priests in Kiev selected John as an offering to the gods, but Theodore refused. The mob then sacked his house, and both were carried away and thrown down a ravine. They were the proto-martyrs of Russia. Feast 12 July.

Theodore and Luke, martyrs, died Mezen, 1670. Church of the Old Believers. Theodore was born at Mezen, but travelled through various cities as a 'fool for Christ'. At Ustug he came to encounter **Avvakum**, who persuaded him of the errors of the new Russian liturgy, and then sent him to Moscow, where he handed to the Tsar Avvakum's letters. He then lived with Avvakum's family by the river Mezen where, in 1670, he was interrogated, found guilty for his Old Believer convictions, and was put to death. With him there died Luke, orginally from Moscow where he had worked as a cobbler. Feast 18 June.

Theodore and Pausilippus, martyrs, died Byzantium (the future Constantinople), *c.* 130. Feast 9 April.

Theodore Balat, martyr, born near Albi, France, 23 October 1858, died Taiyuan, Shanxi, China, 7 July

1900. A Franciscan priest, he spoke good Chinese and was chaplain to the sisters who were killed with him and **Gregory Grassi** during the Boxer Rebellion. See **Franciscan Martyrs of China** and **Martyrs of Shanxi**.

Theodore Gabras, martyr, born Trebizond (?), died Theodosiopolis (Erzurum, eastern Anatolia), 10989. Byzantine Church. He was a successful military commander at Trebizond, but he was eventually captured by the Turks who took him to Theodosiopolis, where he was martyred.

Theodore Guerin (Mother Guerin), born Etables-sur-Mer, Brittany, France, 2 October 1798, died St Mary-of-the-Woods, Indiana, 14 May 1856. Her parents, Laurent and Isabelle Guerin, christened her Anne Thérèse. After early education at a private school, she undertook the care of her invalid mother until 1823, when she entered the recently founded Congregation of the Sisters of Providence. After taking her vows on 8 September 1825, she was appointed superior of the school in the industrial town of Rennes, where she remained for eight years. When transferred to Soulaines, she was noted for the excellence of her methods in teaching mathematics. In 1840, answering an appeal from Bishop Celestine de la Hailandriere Vincennes, Sister Theodore and five companions left to establish a mother house in Indiana. Upon arriving, she opened an academy for girls, chartered in 1846, the first in Indiana. She also established the mother house and Institute of St Mary's and ten schools during her 16 years of labour.

Theodore Ioannovic, Tsar, born Moscow, 1557, died there, 7 January 1598. Russian Church. Elected Tsar in 1584, in spite of his obvious unsuitability, the country was run by a council of regency, dominated by Boris Godunov, his brother-in-law. Theodore diverted himself by entertainments, but also by prayer, the liturgy and weekly pilgrimages to churches and monasterics, of which he was a great builder and decorator. It was during his reign, although thanks to Godunov, that the Moscow patriarchate was established.

Theodore Ivanov, martyr, died Pustozersk, 14 April 1682. Church of the Old Believers. A learned man, a deacon at the cathedral of the Annunciation in Moscow, and one of the most significant early opponents of the new Russian liturgy, arguing that the changes proposed were not on the basis of the ancient models of the Greek Church but were influenced by Western practices. He was arrested in 1665, and excommunicated the following year. He was imprisoned, but then conformed in order to gain his liberty. He soon repented of his action, and started his opposition again. This time his tongue was cut out, and he was again imprisoned. He was then deported. His tongue recovered, so it was again mutilated, and his right hand was cut off. He was put to death with **Avvakum** after 15 years' imprisonment.

Theodore, Oceanus, Ammianus and Julian, martyrs, died *c.* 310. They were burned at the stake. Feast 4 September.

Theodore of Adyabo, monk, fifteenth century. Ethiopian Church. His monastery was in Tigre.

Theodore of Alexandria (1), bishop and martyr, died Alexandria, 609. He was bishop from 607, and was tortured and put to death by heretics. Feast 3 December.

Theodore of Alexandria (2), martyr, died Alexandria, *c.* 303 (?) He was imprisoned because of his faith, then thrown into the sea. When he survived this ordeal he was beheaded. Feast 12 September.

Theodore of Alexandria (3), monk, sixth century. Coptic Church. One of the monks forced to leave the desert of Scete because of Berber incursions.

Theodore of Alexandria (4), monk, martyred in Alexandria. Feast 31 May.

Theodore of Alexandria II, patriarch, died Alexandria, 1 February 743. Coptic Church. A monk of Timnuwah monastery, he was elected in 731. He was gentle and peaceable, and was able to build and restore churches.

Theodore of Amasea, see **Theodore Tiro**.

Theodore of Antioch, died Antioch (?), fourth century. During the reign of Julian the Apostate (361–5), and when he was only 15 years old,

Theodore transported the relics of St **Babylas** from Daphne to Antioch. For this he was arrested and tortured, but survived into old age. Feast 24 November.

Theodore of Byzantium, martyr, born Constantinople, 1774, died Mitylene, 17 (27?) February 1795. Byzantine Church. He was a painter, working in the sultan's palace. He became a Muslim, but almost immediately regretted his act and fled to Chios. He confessed his sin and went to Mitylene, where he admitted he had abjured Islam, and was executed.

Theodore of Caesarea, martyr, died there, 1204. Armenian Church. He fell into debt to a Muslim, and was taken before a judge when he was unable to pay. To save himself, he undertook to convert to Islam, but almost immediately repented and fled to Xirsehir. He was recognized there, and brought back in chains to Caesarea, where he was executed.

Theodore of Canterbury, archbishop, born Tarsus, Cilicia, *c.* 602, died Canterbury, 19 September 690. The candidate, Wighard, whom Kings Oswy and Egbert had set to be consecrated to the see of Canterbury after the death of **Deusdedit** in 664, died on his way to Rome. Pope Vitalian chose Hadrian, abbot of a monastery near Naples, but he was reluctant to take the post and suggested the 66-year-old Theodore, a holy and learned monk. Vitalian accepted the nomination, but insisted that Hadrian, as well as **Benedict Biscop**, go with Theodore to ensure his orthodoxy. Theodore was consecrated in Rome in 668. His journey to Canterbury took a year, during which time he learned English and familiarized himself with the situation of the Church in England. He took possession of his see on 27 May 669. He did much to unify the Church in England: he visited all the churches, endorsed the good teaching and morals he found, reformed abuses, introduced the Roman chant in the Divine Office, and reformed the governance of the Church by reorganizing dioceses and confirming new bishops. He resolved two disputes at York in favour of **Wilfrid**. He held two important synods of the whole Church, one at Hertford in 627 and another at Hatfield in 679. Theodore and Hadrian attracted many pupils eager to learn Latin and Greek, astronomy and mathematics, as well as

theology, and this learning spread throughout the country. He produced a number of written works, including a famous penitential.

Theodore of Crowland and Companions, martyrs, died Crowland, 5 April 870. Abbot of Crowland in Lincolnshire, Theodore died with a number of his community when his abbey was sacked by Vikings.

Theodore of Cyreme, bishop and martyr, died Cyreme (in modern Libya), *c.* 310. He was put to death for refusing to hand over manuscripts of the Bible which he had himself copied. Feast 4 July.

Theodore of Dabra Libanos, abbot, died Dabra Libanos, fourteenth/fifteenth century. Ethiopian Church. It is known he was exiled for a time, so it seems he was involved in the political and religious struggles of his time. Feast 14 May.

Theodore of Edessa, bishop, born Palestine (?), died Edessa, eighth century. Byzantine Church. He became a monk at the monastery of St Sabas in Palestine, but was then made bishop of Edessa. He was a theologian and controversialist. Feast 19 July.

Theodore of Egypt, monk, died Egypt, fourth century. A disciple of St **Ammon**. Feast 7 January.

Theodore of Kama, martyr, born Jerusalem, died Kama, 21 April 1323. Russian Church. He was executed by the Bulgar people on the Volga river for preaching Christianity. Nothing else is known of him.

Theodore of Kamen, monk, thirteenth century. Russian Church. His name is associated – but erroneously – with the foundation of the monastery of Spaso-Kamenskij on lake Kuben. He is said to have been placed in charge of the monastery by Prince Gleb Vasilkovic.

Theodore of Kaskar, monk, seventh century. Syriac Church. He founded a school and monastery at Kaskar, and in old age retired to a hermitage, where he lived off wild plants and stood all the time, to the detriment of his legs. On one occasion, in a period of drought, his prayers brought rain.

Theodore of Kythera, hermit, born Koronis in the Peloponnese, died island of Kythera, tenth century. Byzantine Church. He was a married priest, with two children, but he left his family and travelled to Rome and elsewhere, before settling on the (then) deserted island of Kythera. Feast 12 May.

Theodore of Maqarat, monk, born Adua, Tigre. Coptic Church. Nothing is known of him.

Theodore of Marseilles, bishop, died 514. Feast 2 January.

Theodore of Mytilene, born Mytilene, died there, 30 January 1784. Byzantine Church. As a young man he was forced to become a Muslim, but much later repented and went to Mount Athos. He then returned to Mytilene, and was executed, his body being thrown into the sea, although it was afterwards recovered.

Theodore of Novgorod, prince, born Perejaslav-Zalesk, 1219, died Novgorod, 1233. Russian Church. The brother of **Alexander Nevski**, he was sent by his father in 1228 to rule Novgorod, but he died there on the eve of his wedding. He was renowned for his generosity to the needy. Feast 5 June.

Theodore of Novgorod, bl., born Novgorod Velikij, died there, 19 January 1392. Russian Church. From his youth he practised a strict asceticism, attended all the liturgies, embraced complete poverty, and eventually walked the streets of the city, talking nonsense and earning beatings for the offence he gave. He was in verbal combat with another 'fool for Christ', **Nicholas of Novgorod**, who lived on the other side of the river. He was thought to have the gift of foretelling the future.

Theodore of Ostrog, prince, died 1483. Russian Church. He was a notable defender of his people against the Poles and against the Tartars. By 1440 he was one of the most powerful of the Russian princes, but in 1441 he became a monk at the Kievan Cave monastery, taking the name Theodosius, and he remained there until his death. As prince he was a great builder of churches. Feast 11 August.

Theodore of Pavia, bishop, died Pavia, 778. He was bishop from 743, and a vigorous critic of the Arianism of the Lombard kings, which led to his frequent exile. Feast 20 May.

Theodore of Perge, martyr, died Perge, c. 150. Theodore was conscripted into the Roman army at Perge (near modern Antalya, Turkey), but refused to worship idols. The judge called his mother, Philippa, to persuade him, but instead she encouraged him in his constancy. His commitment also converted a pagan priest, Dioscorus, and other soldiers, **Socrates and Dionysius**. All were imprisoned, and eventually put to death. Feast 19 April.

Theodore of Rjazan, prince and martyr, died 1237. Russian Church. After George Ingarevic, prince of Rjazan, was defeated in battle by the Khan Batyj, the Mongol leader demanded a tenth of all that the prince possessed. The tribute was taken to the khan by George's son Theodore. The khan then demanded to see Theodore's wife, whom he had heard was very beautiful. Theodore refused, saying it was not right to show a Christian wife to an infidel – after which he was tortured and killed. When she heard of the death of her husband, Theodore's wife Euphrasia, who was probably from Constantinople, threw herself from a precipice together with her one-year-old son John. Theodore, Euphrasia and John are all regarded as martyrs, and were much venerated.

Theodore of Rostov, monk, born Novgorod, died Rostov, 22 October 1409. Russian Church. Theodore founded the monastery at Ustja, not far from Rostov. He was joined three years after his own arrival by Paul. Theodore became hegumenos of the nascent monastery. When the monastery was finished, Theodore entrusted it to Paul, and went off to the Vologda region, where he founded another monastery with some monks from Rostov on the White Lake, at the mouth of the river Kovza. When he knew he was dying, Theodore returned to the monastery at Rostov, dedicated to Ss Boris and Gleb. After his death, Paul ruled both monasteries.

Theodore of Rostov and Suzdal, bishop, born Greece (?), died Suzdal, 1023. Russian Church. He became bishop of Rostov c. 990, but was driven out by the largely pagan inhabitants, and then established a church at Suzdal, at that time still a small village. In 1010 Boris (of **Boris and Gleb**) came to govern Rostov, and Theodore re-entered the city with him, but when Boris was recalled he was once again forced to flee to Suzdal, where he died. Feast 8 June.

Theodore of Salahunik, martyr, third century. Armenian Church. He was the son of the governor of Salahunik in Armenia. He was healed of a long illness by **Gregory the Illuminator**, and became a Christian. Knowing that his father would force him to return to the worship of idols, he fled, but was found, and was put to death for his faith. Feast 11 May.

Theodore of Samothrace, martyr, died Makri, 6 April 1835. Byzantine Church. During the Greek uprising against the Turks he was sold as a slave, and became a Muslim. When he was able to return, he regained his Christianity, and was put to death along with **George, George the Younger and Michael**.

Theodore of Sebaste, martyr, died Sebaste, 1156. A monk of the monastery of the Holy Cross at Sebaste, he was accused of defaming the emir who had put to death his father and uncles. Although offered his freedom were he to convert, he remained faithful, and was executed. Feast 1 June.

Theodore of Smolensk, prince, born Smolensk, c. 1237, died Jaroslavl, 18 September 1297. Russian Church. From his father, Theodore inherited the city of Mozajsk, where he spent his childhood, and after his marriage in 1260 became also prince of Jaroslavl. The khan of the Golden Horde, having conquered Russia, made an alliance with the Russian princes and Theodore was particularly favoured. While he was away at war, the throne of Jaroslavl had been usurped by his first son, and he was not able to return there, so he lived at Saraj, the capital of the Horde, and married – he was a widower – a daughter of the khan, who was baptized Anna. Theodore was able to build churches across the territory of the Horde, and converted many to Christianity. He returned to Jaroslavl in 1290, and began to reorganize the city, again building churches. About 1297 he was able to

reassert his hereditary right over Smolensk. That year he became a monk, interrupting the liturgical process to ask forgiveness of the people of the city. His elder son David by his marriage to Anna succeeded him at Jaroslavl. Both David and Theodore's younger son Constantine were regarded with Theodore as saints. Feast 19 September.

Theodore of Starodub, prince, died Starodub (?), 23 June 1330. Russian Church. He was named Jaroslav at birth: Theodore was bestowed on him as a Christian. Prince of the small city of Starodub, he was chosen, among others, to represent Moscow in negotiations with Tver in 1319. He was put to death for political reasons by Khan Uzbek of the Golden Horde.

Theodore of Sykeon (Sikion), bishop, born Sykeon, Asia Minor, died there, 613. He was a convert, his father running a stage on the imperial messenger service. Already reputed for his exorcisms, he became a hermit in his teens, was ordained, and became a monk in Jerusalem. Returning home, he established a monastery and church, and was bishop of Anastasiopolis (not far from the modern Ankara) for ten years before retiring to his monastery. Feast 22 April.

Theodore of Tabennisi, see **Theodore the Sanctified**.

Theodore of the Dardanelles, martyr, born Hellespont, died Dardanelles, 2 August 1690. As a young man he moved to the Dardanelles, where he grew olives. He was approached by a Turk who wanted him to marry his daughter, but for that Theodore would have to convert. He refused to do so. Sometime later he was ill, and was healed by the Turk, who claimed that in return for the healing Theodore had undertaken to convert. Theodore still refused. He was imprisoned, tortured and beheaded in front of the French consulate.

Theodore of Tomsk, died Tomsk, 20 January 1864. Russian Church. Baptized Fedor Kuzmic Kuzmin, he first appeared in the city of Krasnoufimsk, near Perm, where his behaviour brought him to the attention of the police. He was deported to the region of Tomsk, where he lived in several different places. His life was modest and prayerful, he ate little, and spoke quietly, although he was a good speaker. He taught children to read and write, and taught Christians their faith and respect for authority. He was thought to have the ability to foretell the future. He became acquainted with a rich merchant of Tomsk, and towards the end of his life lived in his house. Miracles were attributed to him. He was also believed by many to have been the Tsar Alexander I, thought to have died in the Crimea.

Theodore of Tver ('the Good'), bishop, born Kasin, near Tver, died Tver, 1367. Russian Church. He was elected bishop in 1342, and became involved in the political conflicts for control of the city, attempting to bring reconciliation among the various parties. In 1353, when the patriarch of Constantinople nominated two metropolitans of all Russia, Theodore refused to accept Romanus, the one eventually appointed, a situation which became all the more difficult when Romanus came to live at Tver, where he was treated with great honour by the prince. Theodore built, or improved, many churches in his diocese, particularly the cathedral. In 1361, because of the continuing conflicts, both political and religious, he resigned his see and retired to a monastery. During his episcopate he was also engaged in theological controversy with the bishop of Novgorod over the nature of the earthly paradise.

Theodore of Valais, bishop, fourth century. The first bishop of Valais. Feast 16 August.

Theodore of Vladimir, bishop, died Vladimir, 1286 or 1287. Russian Church. He was hegumenos of a monastery in Kiev before he became bishop of Vladimir in 1276. Feast 23 June.

Theodore of Vologda, prince. Russian Church. He is recorded among the saints of Vologda, but is otherwise unknown, and is probably a case of mistaken identity.

Theodore Scribon, patriarch, martyr, died Alexandria, 609. Patriarch from 607, he was a supporter of the Chalcedonian definition.

Theodore the Branded, martyr, born Kerak, in what is now Jordan, 775, died Apamea, Bithynia,

c. 841. The brother of St **Theophanes**, he grew up in Jerusalem and entered the monastery of St Sabas. He became known as a writer of hymns, and was a strong defender of the cult of images, for which both he and his brother were banished to an island in the Black Sea. They were allowed back to the monastery in 820, but then in 829 were summoned to Constantinople, where they were tortured: Theodore had lines of verse engraved into his forehead. They were then banished, and Theodore died in prison. Feast 27 December.

Theodore the Sanctified, abbot, born Upper Thebaid, Egypt, c. 314, died 368. While still young he wished to enter the monastery of **Pachomius**, despite the protests of his family, and Pachomius managed to reconcile them. He remained close to Pachomius, and was thought by the monks to be the obvious person to take charge of the abbey of Tabennisi after Pachomius had retired to the monastery of Pabau. Pachomius, however, would not approve, and accused Theodore of ambition. In 346 there was an outbreak of plague, in which Pachomius died. Even while dying he refused to name Theodore, and eventually **Horsiesius** became abbot, although he placed Theodore in charge. Theodore was abbot for more than 20 years, ruling over all Pachomius's monasteries. Feast 27 April.

Theodore the Silent, monk, died Kiev, thirteenth century. Russian Church. His particular form of asceticism was to keep silent. Nothing else is known. Feast 28 August.

Theodore the Studite, born Constantinople, 759, died Akritas, 11 November 826. Ordained priest in 787, he became abbot of the monastery of Symboleum on Mount Olympus in Bithynia in 794. He was banished to Thessalonika for opposing the (second) marriage of the emperor, but was released following the seizure of power by the Empress Irene. He returned to his monastery, but moved it to the Studion monastery in Constantinople after it became vulnerable to Arab raiders. He was a leading figure in the opposition to iconoclasm, which again led to his exile, first to Mysia and then to Anatolia. In the meantime he had again clashed with an emperor over the appointment of a layman as patriarch and the reinstatement of a priest who had blessed the emperor's adulterous marriage. On this occasion he was exiled to Princes' Island on the Sea of Marmara. The iconoclast controversy was dragging on, and Theodore was again forced to leave Constantinople. He established himself, with other exiled monks, on the Akritas peninsula, which is where he died. Not only was he a vigorous opponent of iconoclasm, he was also eager to see better relations between Constantinople and the see of Rome, and he reformed monasticism in a manner which spread from the Studion monastery throughout the world of Eastern Christendom.

Theodore the Younger, martyr, born Adrianopolis, died Melagina, *c.* 1360. Byzantine Church. He was captured by Turks when still a child, and taken to Melagina in Asia Minor where he was obliged to become a Muslim. After some years – possibly quite a long time – he met a priest and told him that he wanted to return to Christianity. The priest sent him first to the patriarch at Constantinople, then he returned to Melagina, where he openly proclaimed his faith. He was arrested and executed.

Theodore Tiro, martyr, died Euchaita (near modern Amasya, Turkey), 17 February 306. He is said to have set fire to a statue of a pagan god. He was possibly a soldier, but not a general as the later legend has it (*tiro* means 'recruit', although it may also mean that he was originally from Tyre, or even that he belonged to a cohort that had been stationed at Tyre, and named after that city). He was burned following torture for his Christian faith. He is venerated in the East with George and Demetrius as one of three 'warrior saints'. He was the patron of Venice before St Mark.

Theodore Tokmacev, martyr, born Posechone, died Moscow, seventeenth century. Church of the Old Believers. A well-educated nobleman, he was arrested for his faith as an Old Believer, and was burned alive. Feast 1 December.

Theodore Trichinas, hermit, born Constantinople (?), died there, fourth century. His name means 'the hairy', from the hair shirt which was his only garment. Feast 20 April.

Theodoret of Kola, bl., monk, born Rostov, *c.* 1490, died Kola, 17 August 1571. Russian Church. At the age of 15 he joined the Solovki monastery of the Transfiguration, where he lived for ten years, before making a pilgrimage around other Russian monasteries, and from 1521 to 1525 living as a hermit near the monastery founded by **Sergius of Radonez** – an enforced solitude, imposed by the Grand Prince Basil IV, for Theodore's defence of one of his imprisoned opponents. He then went to the north of Russia, settling at Kola, where he lived for 20 years before seeking ordination at Novgorod. While there he sought funds to found a monastery at Kola. For reasons which are unclear, he was forced to leave Kola. He served from 1547 to 1594 as hegumenos of a small monastery near Novgorod, then was sent by the Tsar to Suzdal as archimandrite of a monastery in that city. There was further trouble in this new monastery, with the monks who thought he was imposing too strict a Rule, and with the bishop, whom he rebuked for his manner of life. He was accused of being sympathetic to heretics and was driven out. Again he spent some time going from one monastery to another, eventually ending his life in his own foundation at Kola. His fame rests particularly upon his earlier period at Kola, where he was a successful missionary among the Lapp people of the region, perhaps drawing upon his knowledge of their language gained at Solovki.

Theodoric (Thierry), abbot, born Aumenancourt-le-Grand, near Rheims, died 1 July 533. Forced by his relatives to marry, he persuaded his wife to give up her marital rights so that he could become a priest. He was reputedly a pupil of **Remigius**, and founded a monastery at Mont d'Or, near Rheims. He was a healer, and miraculously cured King Theodoric I of a serious eye disease.

Theodoric II of Orleans, bishop, died Tonnerre, 1022. A monk of St-Pierre-le-Vif at Sens, he was called to court as a counsellor and later became bishop of Orleans. He died while travelling to Rome. Feast 27 January.

Theodosia and Companions, martyrs, died Borovsk, 1 November 1675. Church of the Old Believers. Theodosia was born in Moscow on 21 May 1632. When she was 17 she married a courtier, Gleb Morozov. After his death in 1662 she inherited great wealth, but she was more interested in things of the spirit, the Old Believer **Avvakum** being her spiritual guide. When Avvakum was exiled she declared her allegiance to the old beliefs openly, and was deprived of her fortune. She was imprisoned at Borovsk, together with her sister the Princess Eudoxia, and a companion named Maria Danilova. They were deprived of food, and Eudoxia died on 11 September 1675, while Maria survived until the beginning of December. Feast 11 September.

Theodosia Lazarevskaja, sixteenth/seventeenth centuries. Russian Church. The daughter of **Juliana Lazarevskaja**. Feast 2 January.

Theodosia of Caesarea and Companions, martyrs, died Caesarea, Palestine, 303 (?). She is reported to have been the mother of St **Procopius**, and hid with 12 other women during the persecution of Diocletian. Feast 29 May.

Theodosia of Constantinople, martyr, born Constantinople, died there, 745. She was orphaned as a child and brought up in the convent of St Anastasia in Constantinople. During the iconoclast controversy troops came to the monastery to destroy the icon of Christ. She and other nuns resisted. They were beaten and dragged through the streets, and Theodosia was killed by a soldier. Feast 29 May.

Theodosia of Tyre, martyr, died Caesarea, Palestine, 2 April 308. Arrested for comforting prisoners, probably Christians, she was tortured and executed. She is commemorated with **Apphian**.

Theodosia of Vladimir, princess, died Novgorod, 4 May 1244. Russian Church. She was originally named Rostislava, but received the name Theodosia at her baptism. She married **Jaroslav Vsevolodovic** of Novgorod, and she was the mother of **Alexander Nevski** and **Theodore of Vladimir**. Towards the end of her life she became a nun, taking the name Euphrosyne.

Theodosius, bishop and martyr. Syriac Church. He died in a lime kiln. Feast 26 November.

Theodosius, bishop, died Trapezus (Trabzon, north-east Turkey), 1392. Byzantine Church. He was hegumenos of the Philotheou monastery on Mount Athos before being appointed bishop of Trapezus in 1375. He persuaded the emperor to build a new monastery on Mount Athos, the Dionysiou. Feast 11 January.

Theodosius, monk, died Vetka, Poland, *c.* 1710. Church of the Old Believers He was ordained at Rylsk, where he was a monk of the monastery of St Nicholas. When persecution of Old Believers began he decided he could not in conscience accept the new rites, and became a hermit. He was arrested, and imprisoned for seven years in the monastery of St Cyril at Beloozero. On his release he fled to the forest of Kerzensk, where he organized a community of Old Believers, but was again obliged to flee, eventually leaving Russia and settling in the village of Vetka in Poland, among a community of Old Believers.

Theodosius, see also **Amphilochius, Macarius, Tarasius and Theodosius**.

Theodosius I ('the Great'), emperor born Cauca, north-west Spain, *c.* 345, died Milan, 395. Byzantine Church. He became emperor at Sirmium in 379, and shortly after his baptism the following year he ordered all Christians to profess the faith of the bishops of Rome and Alexandria, that is to say the Nicene Creed. Totally unsympathetic to Arianism, he deposed Demophilus of Constantinople, the Arian bishop, and installed **Gregory of Nazianzen**. Arianism and other heresies became legal offences, sacrifice was forbidden, paganism outlawed, and all church buildings returned to Catholics. The Council of Constantinople abolished Arian claims and its acts were ratified by Theodosius, who published a decree establishing Catholicism as the religion of the empire. Theodosius showed a willingness, in his relations with St **Ambrose of Milan**, to recognize the limitations of the state in regulating ecclesiastical affairs and in 390, after the massacre at Thessalonika, accepted Ambrose's dictum that, even in political matters, the emperor was subject to the Church's moral judgements. Feast 17 January.

Theodosius and Timothy, see **Stephen the Faster, Theodosius and Timothy**.

Theodosius of Alexandria I, patriarch, died Constantinople (?), 22 June 567. Coptic Church. He was a deacon in Alexandria, and served as secretary to **Timothy of Alexandria III**, and was elected on his death. However, he was driven out of the city by supporters of a rival patriarch, and did not return for some years. When he was at last back in Alexandria, the emperor demanded that he accept the Council of Chalcedon, which he refused to do. He was removed from his see, and brought to Constantinople in 537.

Theodosius of Antioch, abbot, born Antioch, died there, *c*. 412. He founded a monastery near Rhosus (Alexandretta) in Cilicia. Feast 5 February.

Theodosius of Argos, born Athens, 862, died Argos. Byzantine Church. A wealthy man, he gave away all his possessions and went to live in the Peloponnese at Argos, where, because of his powers of healing, he was regarded as a magician. He was, however, defended by the bishop of Argos. Feast 7 August.

Theodosius of Auxerre, bishop, died Auxerre, 516. He was bishop of Auxerre from *c*. 507. Feast 17 July.

Theodosius of Cerepovec, see **Athanasius of Cerepovec**.

Theodosius of the Caucasus, monk, born Perm, 3 May 1841, died Mineralnye Vody, 8 August 1948. He was baptized Theodore Fedorovic Kasin. He was ordained deacon and then priest on Mount Athos in 1897. In 1901 he became superior of his monastery, but resigned the post in 1905. He then wandered around many places in Russia, from 1912 in Kuban in the south of the country. In 1915 he joined the ultranationalist Union of the Russian People, and was for a time its president. In 1925 he was deported to the north of Russia, but on his release settled in Mineralnye Vody in the north Caucasus, where he was able to conduct a secret ministry, particularly one of healing – with herbs and holy water. He acquired a reputation for miracles. He died of malaria.

Theodosius of Cernigov, archbishop, born Uglic, died 1696. Russian Church. His father was a priest, and he studied to be a priest at Kiev, becoming a monk of the Kievan Cave monastery. He became hegumenos of a monastery in Kiev, then of one at Cernigov. He spent some time in Moscow on diplomatic affairs, for which he was awarded the title of archbishop. Many miracles were attributed to him both before and after his death. Feast 5 February.

Theodosius of Kiev, abbot of Kiev, died 1074. Feast 3 May.

Theodosius of Moscow, bishop, died Zagorsk, October 1475. Russian Church. He was archimandrite of the Cudov monastery in Moscow, and in 1455 was named as archbishop of Rostov. Two years later, however, for various misdemeanours, he was reduced to the lay state, but shortly afterwards was pardoned. In 1461 the metropolitan Jonah, who had disciplined Theodosius, died, having named Theodosius as his successor. His appointment occurred without reference to Constantinople. That had been true also of Jonah, but the appointment of Jonah had divided the Russian Church, which Theodosius managed to reunite. He also attempted to improve relations with the other Orthodox Churches. His efforts to improve the morals of the clergy met with such resistance in Moscow that in September 1464 he was forced to resign his see under the pretext of ill-health. He first went to the Eudov monastery in Mosow, and then to that of St **Sergius of Radonez**, where he died.

Theodosius of Novgorod, bishop, born 1491, died Volokolamsk, 26 February 1563. He became a monk at the monastery of St **Joseph of Volokolamsk** in 1523, and in 1531 was appointed head of a monastery in Novgorod. In 1542 he became bishop of Novgorod. Because he opposed the secularization of Church goods, he was deposed by Tsar Ivan IV and returned to his original monastery, where he died.

Theodosius of Pecersk, monk, born Vasilev, near Kiev, 1029, died Kiev, 3 May 1074. Russian Church. He was a disciple of **Anthony of Pecersk**, whom he met at Kiev after a failed attempt to make a pilgrimage to the Holy Land, thus becoming one of his first disciples and a member of the community which became the Kievan Cave monastery. He formally became a monk *c.* 1055, and after Anthony retired into solitude he was governed by Anthony's successor, Barlaam, before himself becoming hegumenos in 1062. Under him the monastery flourished, and a Rule was imposed which he acquired from the Studite monastery at Constantinople.

Theodosius of Sij, monk, died Sij, 19 October 1688. Russian Church. Head of the monastery at Sij.

Theodosius of Totma, monk, born Vologda, died Totma, 1568. After the death of his parents he entered the monastery of the Saviour at Priluki. After some years he was put in charge of the salt pans owned by his monastery at Totma. He established good relations with the local population, and when he decided to stay there and establish a new monastery, they helped him. He was also approached by the bishop of Rostov to look after another group of monks who had been abandoned by the founder of their monastery. For many years he conducted both monasteries, although never in priest's orders, and while imposing upon himself the greatest austerities.

Theodosius of Turnovo, monk, died Constantinople, 27 November 1363. Bulgarian Church. He became a monk at Vidin, in north-west Bulgaria (modern Arcarad), but then left there for the monastery at Turnovo. Still not satisfied with the form of religious life observed there, he visited several monasteries and encountered **Gregory of Sinai** and joined his monastery on Mount Paroria on the Black Sea, becoming one of Greogry's most faithful followers. When the monastery came under attack by Turks, he was sent to the Bulgarian king to seek help and protection. After the death of Gregory he refused to replace him as abbot, and with a disciple went to Mount Athos and elsewhere, returning to Paroria and then going on to Turnovo, where he established his own monastery at Kefalarevo. This grew quickly and became a centre of Bulgarian culture. He died while on a visit to the patriarch of Constantinople.

Theodosius the Coenobiarch, abbot, born Cappadocia, 423, died Palestine, 529. He went to the Holy Land to become a monk, and eventually built a monastic city near Bethlehem, organized into language groups (Greek, Armenian and Arab) with three infirmaries and four churches. As abbot general of monastic communities – *coenobia* – in Palestine, he worked with **Sabas**, superior of the hermit monks, against the monophysite heresy. Feast 11 January.

Theodosius the Younger, emperor, born Constantinople, 11 April 401, died there, 28 July 450. Byzantine Church. He was appointed his father's successor when only two, and came to the throne in 408. The affairs of state he tended to leave to his sister **Pulcheria**, and to his wife Eudoxia, whom he married in 421. For most of the time they managed to keep the empire at peace, and many threats, if not all, were coped with through diplomacy. He was more interested in the arts than in politics, and in 425 founded the first proper university. He called the ecumenical Council of Ephesus in 431. He died from a fall from his horse when hunting. Feast 29 July.

Theodota, martyr, died Nicaea, 304 (?). Supposedly a mother who died in the persecution of Diocletian with her three sons, **Evodius, Hermogenes and Callistus**. They died by being thrown into a furnace. Feast 2 August.

Theodota the Penitent, died Philippolis (Plovdiv, Bulgaria), *c.* 318. She was a repentant prostitute. Feast 29 September.

Theodotion, see **Paul**.

Theodotus and Companions, died Ancyra (Ankara, Turkey), fourth century. The fictional story is of an innkeeper who acquired the relics of **Valens**. He recovered the bodies of seven young women – the Companions – drowned for their faith, was betrayed and decapitated, and his own body recovered and buried. Feast 18 May (suppressed).

Theodotus and Theodota, martyrs, died Caesarea, Cappadocia (Kayseri, Turkey), *c.* 120. They died at the same time as St **Hyacinth**, and share his feast. Feast 3 July.

Theodotus of Amid, bishop, born Not, died Aglosh, 698. Syriac Church. He was brought up in the monastery of Qennesre on the Euphrates, becoming a monk there, and remaining until *c.* 666, when he went for five years on pilgrimage to Sinai and Jerusalem, and finally to Egypt. He returned to Syria, and again visited several monasteries, dying at Aglosh. For a time he served as a bishop of Amid, but he resigned the post *c.* 693 to return to the monastic life. Feast 15 August.

Theodotus of Caesarea and Companions, martyrs, died Caesarea, Cappadocia (Kayseri, Turkey), 270 (?). The companions of Theodotus's martyrdom were his mother, foster-mother and father. Feast 31 August.

Theodotus of Cyrene, bishop, fourth century. Feast 19 January.

Theodotus of Cyrenia, bishop, died Cyrenia, Cyprus, *c.* 321. He was imprisoned for the faith, but survived. Feast 6 May.

Theodotus of Laodicea, bishop, died Laodicea (Latakia, Turkey), 334. An Arian, included among the Western saints by mistake. Feast 2 November.

Theodula (Dula), martyred Nicomedia, Asia Minor, fourth century. She was the slave of a Roman soldier, who killed her when she would not give herself to him. Feast 24 January.

Theodula and Companions, martyrs, died Anazarbus (modern Anazarva, Turkey), *c.* 303. Her constancy under torture converted a number of bystanders, who all died with her, being thrown into a furnace. Feast 5 February.

Theodulph, abbot near Rheims, sixth century. Feast 1 May.

Theodulus, see also **Eventius**.

Theodulus, see also **Hesperus**.

Theodulus and Companions, martyrs, died Crete, 250. There were in all ten martyrs. Feast 23 December.

Theodulus of Caesarea, martyr, died Caesarea, Palestine, 309. He was a servant in the household of the governor, who ordered him to be executed for his faith. Feast 17 February.

Theodulus of Sinai, monk, born Ancyra (Ankara), died Mount Sinai, fifth century. He was the son of **Nilus of Ancyra**, and lived with him on Mount Sinai. He was captured and sold into slavery, but was then redeemed and returned to his monastery. Feast 14

Theodulus the Stylite, born Constantinople, died Edessa, fifth century. A wealthy man of Constantinople, after the death of his wife he sold all he had and became a pilgrim, finally settling on a column near Edessa, where he lived for 30 years. Feast 3 December.

Theogenes, see also **Cyrinus**.

Theogenes, martyr, died *c.* 257. Feast 26 January.

Theognius, bishop, died Bethlehem, 527. He was bishop of Bethlehem. Feast 8 February.

Theognostes, monk and martyr, died Mount Kyzyl-zar, Kazakhstan, 11 August 1921. Originally a monk of the monastery of Glinskaja Pustyn, he moved to what is now Kazakhstan as a missionary *c.* 1900. He left there in 1916 and went to Vernyj (modern Aalma Ata), where he assisted **Seraphim** in building his hermitage on Mount Kyzyl-zar. Together with Seraphim, he was shot by troops of the Red Army who had spent the night at the hermitage.

Theognostes of Kiev, metropolitan, born Greece, died Moscow, 11 March 1353. Russian Church. He was a monk in Constantinople before being consecrated metropolitan of Kiev and all Russia by the patriarch of Constantinople in 1327. He strongly supported the claims of Moscow to dominate the other Russian principalities, and in 1328 excommunicated the rebellious prince of Tver. He travelled widely around Russia and Lithuania, and went twice to visit the Golden Horde – once to seek, and obtain, a tax exemption for the clergy. He built churches in Moscow, and oversaw the decoration of the cathedral of the Dormition in the

Kremlin. It was he who consecrated the wooden church which was the start of the monastery of the Most Holy Trinity, founded by **Sergius of Radonez**. He died of the plague, and was buried in the cathedral of the Dormition.

Theognostes of Peremsyl, monk, died Peremsyl, 1545. Russian Church. He founded the monastery of the Dormition at Peremsyl, on the river Zidra. Otherwise nothing is known of him.

Theonas, see **Theopemptus**.

Theonas of Alexandria, patriarch, died Alexandria, 300. He was elected patriarch in 281. Feast 23 August.

Theonas of Thessalonika, archbishop, born Mitylene, died 1542. He became a monk on Mount Athos, then with his spiritual director went to the Meteora and elsewhere. But his director and two other disciples were executed by the Turks in 1519. He took their relics back to Mount Athos and stayed there for two years. He then moved to Alatista, where he renovated a ruined monastery, creating with it a school and a hospital. In 1535 he was elected metropolitan of Thessalonika, where he founded the monastery of St Anastasia, and remained until his death. Feast 4 April.

Theopemptus and Theonas, martyrs, died Nicomedia, 284. Theopemptus was a bishop, whose martyrdom converted Theonas, who was a magician. The story is also attributed to **Synesius and Theopemptus**. Feast 3 January.

Theophana, princess, born Wallachia, c. 1330, died Vidin, Bulgaria. She was the daughter of Prince Bararab I of Wallachia, and at baptism was called Theodora. She was given in marriage to the Bulgarian tsar, Ivan Alexander, and had three children, but in 1355 she was rejected by her husband and sent to the convent at Vidin, where she became Theophana, and where she remained to the end of her life. She lived a life of humility and penance, and was regarded as a saint almost immediately after her death.

Theophanes, born Kerak, Palestine, died Nicaea, 845. His story is as his brother **Theodore**'s, except

that he did not die in exile, but returned to Constantinople and was honoured as a confessor for the faith and made bishop of Nicaea. He also wrote hymns. Feast 27 December.

Theophanes, founder, born Lesbos, died there, eleventh century (?). Byzantine Church. He founded a monastery on Mount Ordimnos on Lesbos, although he also lived as a hermit in a cave nearby.

Theophanes, martyr, born Constantinople (?), died there, 8 June 1559. He embraced Islam as a boy, but then repented and became a monk. After a time he went back to Constantinople and confessed his change of heart, for which he was executed.

Theophanes, bl., wonderworker, born Ioannina, Epirus. Byzantine Church. Nothing else is known of him.

Theophanes and Companions, martyrs, died Constantinople, 818. They were four officials at the imperial court – Papias, Strategus and Jacob in addition to Theophanes – who were persecuted for their opposition to iconoclasm. Theophanes was put to death, but the others survived to become monks. Feast 4 December.

Theophanes of Ioannina, born Ioannina, died sixteenth century. Byzantine Church. He went to Mount Athos and rose to become hegumenos of the Dochiariou monastery. When the Turks took as slaves the young men of Dochiariou, Theophanes went to Constantinople to free his nephew. The two returned to Mount Athos, then went on to the hermitage of St John the Baptist at Verria. Theophanes later founded another monastery at Naousa, Paros, and he and his nephew looked after both monasteries. Theophanes died at Verria, but his remains were brought back to Naousa. Feast 19 August.

Theophanes of Sigriane, founder, born Constantinople, 759, died Thasos, Macedonia, 818.

Theophanes of Soli, born Nicosia, Cyprus, died Cyprus, 1550. Byzantine Church. He became a monk at Nicosia, and then, reluctantly, bishop of

Soli, a post from which he resigned to spend his last years in a monastery.

Theophanes of the Meteora, founder, born Constantinople, died in the Meteora, 1544. He and his brother Nectarius were born into a well-known family, and both became monks on the island on lake Ioannina. They then went to Mount Athos, but eventually moved to the Meteora where they re-established monastic life and built a church. Feast 17 May.

Theophanes the Ascetic, monk, died Kiev. Russian Church. A monk of the Kievan Cave monastery, he was renowned for his fasting. Feast 11 October.

Theophanes the Confessor, historian, born Constantinople, *c.* 760, died Samothrace, 12 March 817. He was a court official, and married, but he and his wife both entered monasteries – more correctly, Theophanes founded one himself on Mount Sigriane, but was exiled to Samothrace because he rejected iconoclasm. In his *Chronographia*, which follows a strict chronological narrative, he has hardly a good word to say for any emperor after **Constantine I**.

Theophanes (Feofan Govorov) the Recluse, bishop and spiritual writer, born Orel district, 10 January 1815, died Vyshi monastery, 6 January 1894. Russian Church. Baptized George Govorov and the son of a priest, he entered a monastery in February 1841 and rose to become bishop of Tambov in 1859, but in 1866 retired to become a recluse at a small monastery. There he wrote many letters of spiritual direction, produced Russian versions of the *Philokalia* and composed his own spiritual works on the Jesus Prayer and other topics. His *Path to Salvation* is available in English (1996). Feast 10 January.

Théophanes Vénard, martyr, born near Poitiers, 21 November 1829, died Hanoi, 2 February 1861. From a pious family – one brother became a bishop – he studied locally, then in Paris. He was ordained in 1852, and two years later went to Vietnam after 15 months spent in Hong Kong. There was already a persecution of Christians in progress when he arrived, and he had to operate secretly. He was arrested in November 1860 and

was kept in a wooden cage and beheaded after refusing to trample on the cross. He translated the New Testament into Vietnamese and became an inspiration for **Teresa of Lisieux**. See **Martyrs of Vietnam**.

Theophano, empress, born Constantinople, died there, 892. Byzantine Church. She was the first wife of Emperor Leo VI ('the Philosopher'), and was known for her charitable work for the poor. Feast 16 December.

Theophilatus of Stavropol, bishop, born Makovec, 1818, died Stavropol, 11 May 1872. Baptized Feodor Gubin and the son of a deacon, he became a monk in 1842. In 1850 he became an archimandrite, and rector of the seminary at Kaluga, then in 1857 rector of the seminary of Volynia. He was made an assistant bishop of Novgorod in 1862, and was appointed to Kavkaz the following year, the seat of the bishop being at Stavropol. He was a particularly diligent bishop, and a man of great personal holiness.

Theophilus, see also **Sisoes and Theophilus**.

Theophilus, see also **Theophylact**.

Theophilus, friar, born Corte, Corsica, 1676, died 1740, canonized 1930. Becoming a Franciscan in Naples in 1693, he was ordained and taught theology at Civitella, Roman Campagna. He later preached in Italy and Corsica and worked for the revival of Franciscan observance. Feast 19 May.

Theophilus, martyr, died Alexandria. Feast 8 September.

Theophilus, monk, born Zichni, Macedonia, *c.* 1460, died Mount Athos, 8 July 1548. Byzantine Church. While still young he became a monk, and made close study of the Scriptures. After his ordination he went about Greece trying to reinvigorate Orthodox life under the Turkish regime. For this work he was summoned, with his friend Acacius, by the archbishop of Thessalonika, to meet the patriarch at Constantinople. They were then sent to Alexandria, as representatives of the patriarch of Constantinople. After this mission, Theophilus and Acacius went on to Mount Sinai, then to Damascus, where they were handed letters by the patriarch of Antioch to give to the patriarch of Constantinople, and then back to Jerusalem, where Acacius died. Theophilus returned to Constantinople, and the patriarch kept him there. In 1510 he moved to Mount Athos, living on the Holy Mountain for the remainder of his life, apart from a visit to Thessalonika – where there was a plan, which he foiled, to make him archbishop.

Theophilus and Helladius, martyrs, died Libya. Theophilus was a deacon, and Helladius a layman. They were burned to death. Feast 8 January.

Theophilus and James, monks, died monastery of Omuc, 21 October 1412. Russian Church. They lived for a time on the island of Konovec before founding a monastery on the river Omuc, not far from Porchov. They appear to have died on the same date.

Theophilus of Alexandria, patriarch, born Memphis, died Alexandria, 15 October 412. Coptic Church. Left an orphan – with his sister – while still very young, he was taken into slavery by a pagan, but both childen managed to escape, apparently during an earthquake. By chance they encountered St **Athanasius**, who took them into his care. Theophilus's sister married, while Theophilus himself became a priest and Athanasius's secretary. He was elected patriarch himself in 385. He was a vigorous campaigner against paganism, tearing down temples and other buildings associated with the gods, and building churches. In his campaign he employed Egyptian monks. He fell out with some of them, however, when they accused him of accepting the (heretical) teachings of Origen, and they took their charge to Constantinople, where they received the backing of **John Chrysostom**. Theophilus turned this to his own advantage, and at a synod in 403 managed to get Chrysostom deposed. This act brought him into conflict with Pope **Innocent I**, who excommunicated him. Miracles were attributed to Theophilus both during his life and after his death.

Theophilus of Antioch ('the Apologist'), bishop, died Antioch, 181. A pagan, he was converted by reading the Scriptures, and in 169 became bishop of Antioch. He wrote a three-volume *Apology* for Christianity. Feast 13 October.

Theophilus of Bulgaria, born Bulgaria, died *c.* 750. He became a monk at the monastery on Mount Seleution, but was exiled for opposing the iconoclastic Emperor Leo IV. Feast 2 October.

Theophilus of Caesarea (1), see **Dorothy**.

Theophilus of Caesarea (2), bishop, died Caesarca, Palestine, *c.* 195. He was opposed to those – the Quartodecimans – who wanted to celebrate the feast of Easter on the Jewish Passover, rather than on a Sunday. Feast 5 March.

Theophilus of Corte, born Corte, island of Corsica, 1676, died Fucecchio, 1740. Baptized Biagio Arrighi, he became a Franciscan in 1693 and was ordained in Naples. After teaching theology for a time, he became a missioner in Italy, and then in Corsica. He also worked for the reform of his order. Feast 19 May.

Theophilus (Feol) of Kiev, monk and 'fool for Christ's sake', born near Kiev, October 1788, died 28 October 1853. Ukrainian Church, Moscow Patriarchate. He became a monk, but soon began to act in a strange manner, dressing and talking in a way which shocked many. Others began to visit him for help and advice, although he often threw wealthy people out. He was said to have predicted the disasters of the Crimean War to Emperor Nicholas I. Long venerated locally, he was canonized in Ukraine in 1994.

Theophilus of Novgorod, archbishop, died 6 October (?) *c.* 1480. Russian Church. A monk of the monastery of Oren, he served as treasurer of the diocese of Novgorod during the 1460s, and was elected archbishop of the city in 1471. Novgorod had established links with Poland-Lithuania in an attempt to preserve its independence of Moscow, but this was interpreted by the metropolitan of Moscow as a move to Latinize the Church of Novgorod. Ivan III sent an army against Novgorod, and the city was forced to surrender. In December 1471 Theophilus was consecrated bishop at Moscow. Novgorod made an attempt to re-establish links with Poland-Lithuania in 1478, and Ivan again sent an army, this time occupying the city and sending Theophilus to the Cudov monastery in Moscow, where he remained until his death.

Theophilus of Zante, martyr, born Zante, died Chios, 24 July 1635. Byzantine Church. He was a sailor by trade, and was offered a place on a Turkish ship. He refused, and the Turkish owner, taking offence, accused him of pretending to be a Muslim. He denied it, but was taken before a judge and ordered to be forcibly circumcized. He managed to escape immediately afterwards, and went to Samos, then returned to Chios, where he was recognized by a Turk and again taken before a judge and accused of having abjured Islam. He was burned alive.

Theophilus the Penitent, died Adana, Cilicia (now in Turkey), c. 538. He is said to have been archdeacon of Adana, and was deposed from his post by a calumnious charge against him. The devil appeared to him and offered him a pact in which, in return for his soul, he would be reinstated. He agreed, but then repented, and the Virgin Mary appeared to him, returning the contract. This, as developed in *The Golden Legend* of **James of Voragine**, is the origin of the Faust legend. Feast 4 February.

Theophilus the Younger, martyr, born Constantinople, died Cyprus, 30 January 792. He was in command of the Byzantine forces on Cyprus which were defeated by the fleet of Harun al-Rashid. He was offered his freedom in return for apostasy, but refused. He was then imprisoned for four years before being executed. Feast 22 July.

Theophylact of Nicomedia, bishop, born Asia Minor, died Caria (Kariye, Turkey), Macedonia, 845. He moved from somewhere in the East to Constantinople in 780, and became an important figure at the court of the emperor. After some years, however, he became a monk, and in 816 was named bishop of Nicomedia. He was strongly opposed to iconoclasm, and was exiled to Caria. Feast 7 March.

Theopista, lived and died Egypt, fourth century (?). Coptic Church. She was a married woman, with a son. When her husband died she went to the bishop and asked to become a monk. He told her to wait for a year, and then if she still wanted to do so, he would make her a monk. She then lived for the year as a recluse in her house, looked after by her 12-year-old son. At the end of the year she died. Feast 1 January.

Theopista, born Aegina, ninth century. She was the daughter of **Theodora of Thessalonika**, and with her she entered the monastery of St Stephen. In 868, when her mother refused to be elected hegumena, Theopista herself took on the role. Feast 3 August.

Theopista, see also **Eustace**, martyr.

Theosebius, born Arsinoe, Cyprus, died Cyprus. Byzantine Church. He was a wealthy married man, who abandoned his family and became a hermit. Feast 12 October.

Theotecnus, martyr, died Antioch, c. 310. He was a military commander at Antioch. During the persecution of Maximian he was stripped of his rank for refusing to worship pagan gods, was dressed in women's clothes and put among the female slaves, in the hope that this would break his spirit. It did not, and after various tortures he was put to death. Feast 10 October.

Theotonius, born Gorfeo, Spain, 1086, died Coimbra, Portugal, 1166. He studied at the university of Coimbra before becoming archpriest in Viseu. His preaching drew many people. He travelled twice to Palestine before joining the Canons Regular of St Augustine at Coimbra, becoming abbot. He was a counsellor to the royal family, and the king believed his prayers ensured victory over the Moors. Feast 18 February.

Therapon of Borovenka, monk, fourteenth/fifteenth centuries. Russian Church. Founder of the monastery of the Dormition on the river Borovenka, not far from Kaluga.

Therapon of Constantia, bishop and martyr, born Germany, died Cyprus, 632 (?). Byzantine Church. According to tradition, he was born of a wealthy family in Germany. He gave up his wealth to study, and became a bishop, but was driven from his diocese and came to Cyprus. When the island was taken by Muslim invaders, he was martyred while celebrating the liturgy. Feast 14 May.

Therese of Lisieux, see **Teresa of Lisieux**.

Thesesius, martyr, died Cappadocia, *c.* 230. Feast 1 June.

Thetmar, born Bremen, died Neumünster, 1152. A missionary among Slavs with St **Vicelin**. He may have been a Premonstratensian canon (a Norbertine). Feast 17 May.

Theuderius, abbot, born Arcisse, near Vienne, died Vienne, *c.* 575. He became a monk at Lérins, then returned to Vienne, but after building a church and a monastery he returned to Arcisse, where he also established a monastery. Towards the end of his life he was again called back to Vienne. Feast 29 October.

Theusetas and Companions, martyrs, died Nicaea. Martyred with Theusetas were his son Horres, together with Theodora, Nymphadora, Marka and Arabia. Feast 13 March.

Thialtild, abbess, ninth century. Feast 30 January.

Thirteen Martyrs of Kantara, monks, died Nicosia, Cyprus, April–May 1231. The 13 monks of the Kantara monastery were persecuted for their orthodox faith during the Latin domination of the island. They were required to defend their beliefs before the Latin-rite bishop in Nicosia, and were kept in prison in the meantime. When they would not recant they were handed over to a certain Andrew, who had been questioning them in the first place and whose imprisonment was even harsher than that of the bishop. One of the monks, Theodoret, died of mistreatment on 5 April 1231, the others were executed on 19 May of the same year.

Thirty Fathers of the Kievan Cave Monastery. Russian Church.

Thirty-Three Martyrs of Palestine, martyrs. An unknown group. Feast 16 August.

Thomais of Alexandria, martyr, died Alexandria, 476. The wife of a fisherman, she rejected the advances of her father-in-law, and was murdered by him. Feast 14 April.

Thomais of Lesbos, bl., born Lesbos, *c.* 910, died Constantinople, 1 January 948 (or 951). She and her husband Stephen moved from Lesbos to Constantinople, where she was killed by her violent husband. She was buried in the monastery at Constantinople where her mother was prioress. Feast 3 January.

Thomas, monk, born Sinsif, died there, 20 (?) May *c.* 451. Coptic Church. He lived his life as a monk and hermit near his village, where he was visited by **Shenoudah of Atripe**, who later returned to bury him, when he learned of his death by a vision.

Thomas, patriarch, died Constantinople, 610. He was bishop of Constantinople from 607. Feast 20 March.

Thomas, see also **Tatulus**.

Thomas Abel, bl., martyr, born *c.* 1497, died Smithfield, London, 30 July 1540. He studied at Oxford and became a doctor of divinity. He was chaplain to Queen Catherine, as well as her tutor in music and languages. In *c.* 1532 he wrote *Invicta Veritas*, a book supporting the validity of the marriage of Catherine and Henry VIII, for which he was imprisoned in the Tower of London. He was released, but rearrested, and was eventually convicted of high treason in July 1540 and sentenced to be hanged, drawn and quartered, along with **Edward Powell** and **Richard Fetherston**.

Thomas Alfield, bl., martyr, born Gloucester, 1552, died Tyburn, London, 6 July 1585. He was brought up a Protestant and studied at King's College, Cambridge. He was a fellow there from 1571 to 1575, when he converted to Catholicism. In 1580 he went to Douai to study for the priesthood, and was ordained at Châlons in 1581. He returned to England, but was arrested in April 1582, taken to the Tower of London and tortured. He renounced his Catholicism and was released, but repented shortly afterwards and was arrested again in June 1585. He was charged with distributing copies of

Cardinal Allen's book *A True, Sincere and Modest Defence of English Catholics*. He admitted to this, but claimed that the book was loyal to the queen. He refused to admit that the queen was head of the Church in England, and was sentenced to be hanged, drawn and quartered.

Thomas Aquinas, philosopher and theologian, born Roccasecca, near Monte Cassino, *c* 1225, died Fossanuova, near Maenza, 7 March 1274. Eminent in the history of European thought, he is its most important and influential scholastic theologian and philosopher, of whom Pope Pius XI said that the Church had made him 'her very own'. He joined the Dominicans in 1244, after which he was kidnapped by his shocked and disapproving family and shut up for a year, but he would not change his mind. On his release he went to study at Cologne, where **Albert the Great** soon recognized his genius, and the two were in profound intellectual sympathy. He became master in theology in 1256. The rest of Thomas's life was spent between Paris and Italy, studying, lecturing, preaching and, above all, writing incessantly. During his first teaching appointment at Paris he wrote a defence of the mendicant orders against William of St Amour, a commentary on the *Sentences* of Peter Lombard, *De Ente et Essentia*, and works on Isaiah and Matthew. In 1259 he began *Summa contra Gentiles*, a treatise on God and his creation argued partly by the use of pure reason, without faith, against Islam, Jewry, heretics and pagans. Islam had produced famous Aristotelian thinkers, and Thomas's aim was to answer them from Aristotle himself. In 1266 he started his *Summa Theologiae*, a great theological synthesis of theology and a comprehensive statement of his mature thought on all the Christian mysteries; it proceeds through objections and authoritative replies in each article to a concise summary of his views on the matter under discussion, after which the various objections are answered. The work is organized in three parts which treat respectively of God and creation, the human person as a free moral agent, and Christ as the way of man to God. He treated sacred doctrine as a single discipline embracing the whole life of the Church, including worship, morals and spiritual practice. Various of his teachings were attacked during his life and after his death, but from 1278 general chapters insisted

that his writings be respected and defended within the order. He was canonized in 1323 by John XXII. Thomism was revived in the sixteenth century, and by the time of the Council of Trent the Church had accepted the substance of his teaching as an authentic expression of doctrine. In 1567 **Pius V** declared him doctor of the Church; in 1879 Leo XIII's bull *Aeterni Patris* enjoined the study of Aquinas on all theological students as a clear, systematic philosophy capable of defending Christian tradition from contemporary attack. In 1880 Thomas was declared patron of all Catholic universities and, in 1923, Pius XI reiterated his authority as a teacher. In 1974 Pope Paul VI proposed Thomas as a model for theologians, not only for his doctrinal positions, but also for his openness to the world of his day. Since Vatican II there has been another revival of Thomistic studies and renewed interest in his teaching, not limited within confessional boundaries, notably on the value of his thought on moral development. Feast 28 January.

Thomas Atkinson, martyr, born East Riding, Yorkshire (or possibly Leeds), *c.* 1546, died York, 11 March 1616. He was ordained at Laon in 1588, and returned to England to work in and around York. He was arrested in 1616 at Willitoft, in the home of a Mr Vavasour, and was executed.

Thomas Becket, archbishop and martyr, born London, 21 December 1118, murdered Canterbury cathedral, England, 29 December 1170. He was educated at Merton priory and in Paris. He worked as a merchant in London before joining the household of the archbishop of Canterbury, who made him archdeacon and recommended him to King Henry II, whom he subsequently served well as chancellor from 1154. The king appointed him archbishop of Canterbury in 1162, seeing this as a way of imposing royal authority over the Church. But Becket opposed the king's attempts and, after several years of conflict and efforts at reconciliation, the king declared he wanted rid of him. Four knights murdered the archbishop as he prepared for vespers. The people acclaimed him as a saint and the king had to acknowledge his crime by fasting, walking barefoot to Canterbury and submitting to scourging. Becket was canonized in 1173.

Thomas Bellaci, born Florence, 1370, died Rieti, 31 October 1447. A dissolute young man, he was accused of a crime he did not commit, but no one would believe him except a priest he met by chance. The shock changed his life. He joined the Observant Franciscans at Fiesole as a lay brother. Even though he was only a lay brother he was appointed master of novices, and promoted reform in the order. He then went to preach throughout Italy and Corsica, and when aged over 70 was sent to Syria to promote better relations with the Eastern Church. He was arrested for preaching Christianity, and expected (and hoped) to be martyred, but was rescued by the pope. He was on his way to Rome to ask to be allowed to return to Syria when he died.

Thomas Belson, bl., martyr, born Ixhill Lodge, near Oakley, Buckinghamshire, c. 1565, died Oxford, 7 July 1589. He studied at Oxford, then went to Rheims, and was arrested on his return and put in the Tower. He was released, but banished. He did not, however, leave the country, and was arrested at the Catherine Wheel Inn in Oxford. He was sent to London, but then returned to Oxford, where he was condemned to death by hanging.

Thomas Bosgrave, bl., martyr, born Dorset, died Dorchester, 4 July 1594. A Dorset landowner, he was executed for helping **John Cornelius**.

Thomas Corisin, bl., born Orvieto, died there, 1343. He joined the Servite Order as a lay brother, and spent his life in Orvieto collecting alms for the friary. Feast 23 June.

Thomas Cottam, bl., martyr, born Lancashire, 1549, died Tyburn, London, May 1582. He completed his degree at Oxford in 1568. While teaching in London he converted to Catholicism under the influence of Thomas Pound. In 1577 he went to Douai, later attracting other English converts there. He was ordained in 1580, but poor health stopped him being accepted by the Society of Jesus. After spending time in Rome, Lyon, and again in Douai, he returned to England. He was arrested at Dover on the basis of information from an English priest-catcher named Sledd. He escaped, but rather than endanger the man who had helped him, Cottam gave himself up. After imprisonment and

torture, he was tried and condemned in 1581. He was received into the Society of Jesus before his execution.

Thomas de Cantalupe, see **Thomas of Hereford**.

Thomas Felton, bl., martyr, born 1568, died Isleworth, near London, 28 August 1588. He was a Franciscan – a Minim – and had only returned to England for his health, meaning to go back to his monastery, but was captured, imprisoned, twice released, but rearrested.

Thomas Ford, bl., born Devon, martyred Tyburn, 1582. He converted at Trinity College, Oxford, and was ordained at Douai in 1573. He worked in Oxfordshire and Berkshire and was captured with **Edmund Campion**. He is commemorated with **John Shert** and **Robert Johnson**, executed with him. Feast 28 May.

Thomas Garnett, martyr, born London, 1575, died London, 23 June 1608. He studied at St Omers and at the English College, Valladolid. He was the nephew of Henry Garnett, the Jesuit superior in England, and came to England with the Benedictine **Mark Barkworth**. He was admitted to the Society of Jesus in 1604. He was seized at the port on his way to the Jesuit novitiate in Flanders and sent to the Tower of London. In 1606 he was among the 46 priests banished from the country. Later he was betrayed to the civil authorities by the apostate priest Rouse, and was executed at Tyburn.

Thomas Ghengoro, wife and son, bl., martyrs, died Japan, 1620. They died by being crucified upside down. Feast 16 August.

Thomas Helye, bl., born Biville, Normandy, c. 1187, died Vauville, La Manche, 19 October 1257. He was well educated and became a teacher, first in Biville, then in Cherbourg. He then studied in Paris and was ordained, returning to Biville to work. Although appointed a parish priest, he employed a curate and went about the region preaching and hearing confessions. His tomb soon earned a reputation for miracle working.

Thomas Hemerford, bl., martyr, born Dorset, 1554, died Tyburn, London, 12 February 1584. He studied at Oxford, but then left for the continent. He was ordained in Rome in 1583, and left almost immediately for England, where he was captured that year. He was held in the Marshalsea and the Tower of London before being hanged, drawn and quartered, with **James Fenn, John Munden, John Nutter** and **George Haydock**.

Thomas Holford, bl., martyr, born Aston, Cheshire, 1541, died Clerkenwell, London, 28 August 1588. The son of a Protestant minister, he converted to Catholicism and in August 1582 went to study at Rheims. He was ordained at Laon less than a year later, then returned to England almost immediately to work in Cheshire and London. He was captured in Nantwich in May 1585, but managed to escape while being taken to London. He was recaptured, again in Nantwich at the house of **Swithin Wells**, in 1588, and again taken to London for trial and execution.

Thomas Holland, bl., Jesuit and martyr, born Sutton Hall, near Prescott, Lancashire, 1600, died Tyburn, London, 12 December 1642. The son of Thomas Holland, he went to school at the Jesuit college at St Omer, became a Jesuit and was ordained in 1624. For some years he served in different posts in Jesuit houses on the continent, but c. 1635 he returned to England. He was arrested in October 1642, and executed on account of his priesthood.

Thomas, Iriodion, Michael, John and Basil, 'fools for Christ'. See **John of Solovki** – however, only Thomas is still venerated. Feast 3 June.

Thomas Johnson, bl., martyr, died Marshalsea prison, London, 20 September 1534. A member of the London Charterhouse, he and ten other Carthusians refused to take the Oath of Supremacy, were imprisoned in the Marshalsea, and left to starve to death.

Thomas Kuong, martyred China, 1860 – see **Martyrs of China**. Feast 30 January.

Thomas Mary Fusco, bl., born Pagani, near Salerno, Italy, 1 December 1831, died there, 24 February 1891. The son of a pharmacist, his father died when he was still young, and his education

was left in the hands of an uncle who was a priest. He himself was ordained priest in 1855, and then opened a school in his own house. He was a missioner in southern Italy, and founded a number of organizations to help the poor, including the Daughters of Charity of the Precious Blood, to run orphanages.

Thomas Maxeld, bl., martyr, born Enville, Staffordshire, c. 1585, died Tyburn, London, 1 July 1616. He was born in prison at Maer Hall, where his mother was under arrest for harbouring a priest. He went to Douai when he was about 18, but was sent home in 1610, as he was considered unsuitable for the priesthood. However, he returned in 1612 and was ordained in 1614. He was sent to England, but was arrested after only three months. He was kept in Gatehouse prison for eight months before trying to escape. The attempt was thwarted and he was moved to Newgate to be tried. Despite the intervention of the Spanish ambassador, the duke of Gonmar, Thomas was sentenced to be hanged, drawn and quartered.

Thomas More, statesman, martyr, born London, England, 7 February 1477, died there by beheading, 6 July 1535. More attended school in London and at the age of 12 entered the service of Cardinal John Morton, who remain an important influence on his life. He went to Oxford and finished his legal training at Lincoln's Inn. He was called to the bar in 1501, and entered parliament in 1504. He married in 1505 (and married again, when he was widowed, in 1510), although he had considered entering the Carthusian Order and had spent some time living in the London Charterhouse. More was noted both for his statecraft, serving Henry VIII in many roles including speaker of the House of Commons and, after the disgrace of Cardinal Wolsey, lord chancellor (1529–32), and for his humanism, best represented by his friendship with Erasmus and by his work *Utopia* (1516). He actively opposed Protestantism both as a controversialist (he wrote a book against William Tyndale) and as a judge. He was imprisoned in the Tower of London in April 1534, and 15 months later executed for high treason by Henry VIII for refusing to submit to the Oath of Supremacy, which acknowledged the king as head of the newly created Church of England. In the Tower he wrote his *Dialogue of Comfort against Tribulation*, the finest of his spiritual writings. He was canonized in 1935 alongside **John Fisher**. Feast 22 June.

Thomas Netter, bl., Carmelite theologian, born Saffron Walden, Essex, *c.* 1370, died Rouen, France, 1430. His order having sent him to study at Oxford, he attended the Council of Pisa in 1409 and in England was prominent in persecuting the Wycliffites. He was appointed Henry V's confessor and a representative at Constance in 1415. In 1419 he went to Poland to support the papal army against the Hussites. As spiritual adviser to Henry VI, he accompanied him to France in 1430. He wrote to confute the Lollards and Hussites. Feast 2 November.

Thomas of Biville, see **Thomas Helye**.

Thomas of Constantinople I, patriarch, born Constantinople (?), died there, 610. Byzantine Church. He was sacristan in Hagia Sophia, and was elected patriarch in 607. Because of a strange occurrence durng a procession, when the processional crosses began to shake, he foresaw the troubles – the Persian wars – which were to befall the Byzantine Empire. Feast 21 March.

Thomas of Cori, bl., monk and priest, born Cori, in the Latium, 1655, died 1729. A shepherd who became an Observant Franciscan in 1675, he was ordained and worked among the people in the mountains around Subiaco, in the Latium. Feast 11 January.

Thomas of Dima, monk, fourteenth/fifteenth centuries. Ethiopian Church. A disciple of **Takasta Berhan**.

Thomas of Farfa, hermit, born Maurienne, died Farfa, *c.* 720. He went to the Holy Land on pilgrimage, and on his return settled as a hermit near Farfa, where he restored the abbey.

Thomas of Florence, see **Thomas Bellaci**.

Thomas of Germanicia, bishop, died Samosata, 542. Syriac Church. He was exiled from his diocese in 519, and died in exile. Feast 25 June.

Thomas of Hales, monk, died Dover, 2 August 1295. An aged monk who died when his priory at Dover, a dependency on the monastery of Christ Church, Canterbury, was attacked by French raiders. All the monks fled except Thomas, who was asleep and was unaware of the incursion. When the raiders demanded to know the whereabouts of the monks' treasure, he refused to tell them and was killed. He was never formally canonized, despite efforts to do so, but there was a popular cult of Thomas.

Thomas of Harran, bishop, died Harran, 738. He was a monk of Qartmin and a disciple of **Simeon of Harran**, whom he succeeded as bishop in 734. Feast 5 July.

Thomas of Hereford, bishop, born Hambledon, Buckinghamshire, *c.* 1218, died Montefiascone, 25 August 1282. He came from a noble family – his father was baron de Cantalupe – and studied in Oxford, Paris and Orleans. He returned to Oxford in the mid-1250s and became chancellor of the university in 1261. He was appointed chancellor of the realm in 1265 by barons who had rebelled against King Henry III. When they were defeated he went to Paris, but later returned as chancellor of the university. In 1275 he became bishop of Hereford. He was a conscientious prelate, and also served in high offices of state. In 1282, however, he fell out with the archbishop of Canterbury, and was excommunicated. He went to Rome to put his case to the pope, but died while in Italy. His body was brought back to Hereford, and miracles were soon reported at his tomb. He was canonized in 1320. Feast 25 August, but 3 October in England and Wales.

Thomas of Mount Maleon, hermit, died Mount Maleon, tenth century. He had been a soldier, but gave up his position and his wealth and retired to Mount Maleon, a remote part of Mount Athos, although his reputation as a spiritual guide soon spread. Feast 7 July.

Thomas of Qorera, monk, fourteenth century. Ethiopian Church. He was a disciple of **Eustace of Sarabi**.

Thomas of Rimini, feast 1 August.

Thomas Tolentino, bl., born *c.* 1260, martyred Tana, near Bombay, 1321, cult approved 1894. A Franciscan missionary, he worked in Armenia, Persia, India and possibly China. He was being sheltered with three other Franciscans by Nestorian Christians in Tana, when the Muslim rulers tortured and beheaded them for attacking Islam. Feast 9 April.

Thomas of Villanova, bishop, born Fuenllana, Spain, 1486, died Valencia, 8 September 1555. He was called 'of Villanova' (Villanueva) from the home of his parents, although they had moved to Fuenllana before his birth. He studied in Alcalá de Henares, and joined the faculty to teach philosophy. In 1516 he joined the Augustinians in Salamanca. He was ordained priest two years later, and held various senior offices in his order. He succeeded in avoiding being made archbishop of Granada, but in 1544 he was consecrated, in Valladolid, to the see of Valencia. In his new office he continued to wear his religious habit for as long as possible. He was a very active bishop, visiting the parishes of his diocese, preaching and taking especial care of the poor.

Thomas Percy, bl., earl of Northumberland and martyr, born 1528, died York, 22 August 1572. His father and uncle had taken part in the Pilgrimage of Grace, an uprising against King Henry VIII, and his father was executed. The family was restored to favour under Queen Mary, Thomas becoming the seventh earl. He continued for a while to prosper under Queen Elizabeth I, but in 1569 he and the earl of Westmoreland led a rising in the north against the new religion. The uprising collapsed, and for a time Thomas was on the run in Scotland, but he was finally captured there and sold to the English crown. He was offered his life were he to abjure his Catholicism, but refused.

Thomas Pickering, bl. martyr, born Skelmergh, near Kendal, Cumbria, 1620, martyred Tyburn, London, 9 May 1679. Becoming a Benedictine lay brother in Douai in 1660, he worked at the Queen's Chapel. He was one of those whom Titus Oates falsely accused of plotting to kill King Charles II, and went serenely to his death.

Thomas Pilchard, bl., martyr, born Battle, Sussex, *c.* 1557, died Dorchester, 21 March 1587, beatified 1987. Educated at Balliol College, Oxford, ordained at Laon in 1583, he was arrested and banished in 1585, then returned and was arrested again – he was apparently recognized because of a squint. He was hanged, drawn and quartered.

Thomas Plumtree, bl., martyr, born Lincolnshre, died Durham, England, 4 January 1570, beatified 1886. He studied at Corpus Christi College, Oxford, and became rector of Stubton in Queen Mary's reign and a recusant Catholic under Elizabeth I. Chaplain to **Thomas Percy**, earl of Northumberland, he took an active part in the 1569 rising in the north, becoming known as the 'Preacher of the Rebels'. He was executed in the marketplace at Durham.

Thomas Pormont, bl., born Lincolnshire, martyred St Paul's Churchyard, London, 20 February 1592, beatified 1987. Ordained in Rome in 1587, he worked in London – under the names of Whitgift, Meres and Price. He was befriended by **Robert Southwell**, was arrested, escaped, rearrested and executed.

Thomas Reynolds (real surname Green), born Oxford, c. 1560, martyred Tyburn, London, 21 January 1642. He studied in France and Spain before being ordained in 1592. He then worked for nearly 50 years in England, the last 14 in prison. He was executed with **Alban-Bartholomew Roe**.

Thomas Sherwood, bl., born 1551, martyred Tyburn, London, 7 February 1578. Assistant to a draper, and from a devout Catholic family, he was planning to become a priest. He was held in the Tower of London, tortured for information and hanged. His mother also later died in prison.

Thomas Somers, bl., priest and martyr, born Westmoreland, died Tyburn, London, 10 December 1610. Also known as Wilson, Somers had been a teacher before entering the English College at Douai in February 1605. He was quickly ordained and returned to England in 1606. He was expelled in mid-1610, but again returned to England in October, only to be arrested and executed in London.

Thomas the Dephourkinus, hegumenos, ninth/tenth century. He could work miracles, and had the gift of prophecy. Feast 10 December.

Thomas Tsuji, martyr, born Sonogi, near Omura, Japan, *c.* 1571, died Nagasaki, 7 September 1627. He was educated by the Jesuits, and joined the Society in 1589. When Jesuits were banished from Japan he went to Macao, but returned to work secretly four years later. As a Japanese, he was able to mix with the people more easily than the European Jesuits, and he saw them being rounded up and executed. He suffered a bout of depression, and asked to be released from his vows. By the time permission arrived he had changed his mind, but his superiors would not allow him back for six years. Once reinstated in 1626, he was arrested almost immediately while saying mass at the house of Louis and John Maki. All three were imprisoned. Thomas resisted attempts by his family to persuade him to abjure his faith, and he was burned alive, with Louis and John.

Thomas Tunstal, bl., martyr, born Whinfell, near Kendal, died 1616. He went to the English College in Douai in 1606, was ordained, and was sent back to England in 1610. He was arrested soon after returning and spent several years in various prisons. When he was brought to trial, the judge offered him the Oath of Supremacy, but he refused to take it, and was condemned to be hanged, drawn and quartered. Feast 13 July.

Thomas Watkinson, see **Robert Thorpe**.

Thomas Welbourn, bl., martyr, born Hutton Bushel, Yorkshire, died York, 1 August 1605. He was a (lay) schoolmaster who was arrested and condemned for preaching Catholicism.

Thomas Whitaker, bl., martyr, born Burnley, Lancashire, September 1611, died Lancaster, 7 August 1646. He was at school in Burnley, then at St Omer. He studied in Valladolid and came back to England in 1639. He was captured, but escaped, then was captured again and imprisoned at Lancaster, where he was executed.

Thomas Woodhouse, bl., martyr, born Lincolnshire, died Tyburn, London, 19 June 1572. He was ordained towards the end of the reign of Queen Mary, and served in Lincolnshire. With the accession of Queen Elizabeth he lost his living, and served as a schoolmaster in Wales. He was arrested in 1561 while saying mass and was confined in the Fleet prison in London. In 1572 he wrote a letter to Lord Burghley urging him to persuade the queen to submit to the pope, a letter which Burghley took as evidence of high treason, and he was tried and executed. He became a member of the Society of Jesus before his death.

Thomasius of Costacciaro, bl., born Costacciaro, died Monte Cupo, 1337. From a peasant family, he joined the Camaldolese at Sitria, then became a hermit at Monte Cupo, Umbria. Feast 25 March.

Thomian, archbishop, died Armagh, *c.* 660. He was archbishop of Armagh from 623. Feast 10 January.

Thraseas, bishop and martyr, died Smyrna, *c.* 170. Bishop of Eumenia (Ishekli, near Brusa, Turkey). He was possibly a Quartodeciman, i.e., he held that Easter should be celebrated on the day of the Jewish Passover, rather than on a Sunday. Feast 5 October.

Thyrsus, martyred Apolonia, Phrygia, 251, with **Leucius** and **Callinicus**. Their supposed relics reached Constantinople, then Spain and France. Thyrsus is celebrated in the Mozarabic liturgy and is the patron of Sisteron cathedral in the Basses Alpes, France. Feast 28 January.

Thyrsus and Projectus, feast 24 January.

Tiburtius, martyr, died Rome. Together with **Valerius** and **Maximus**, he has been venerated from an early date, but nothing reliable is known. They may have been executed and buried together, or separately. Their remains were translated together to the cemetery of St Callixtus. Feast 14 April.

Tigides and Remedius, bishops, died Gap, France, fourth/fifth century. They were successive bishops of Gap in the French Alps. Feast 3 February.

Tigrius (Tigirius), see **Eutropius**.

Tikhon of Amanthus, bishop, born Amanthus (modern Limassol), Cyprus, died there, 425. His father was the owner of a bakery, and Tikhon used to give away free bread to the poor, among many other acts of charity. He became a lector, then deacon, and was chosen as bishop of his city. He was a vigorous opponent of the remnants of paganism on his island. Feast 16 June.

Tikhon of Karacev, monk, sixteenth century. Russian Church. Founder of the monastery of the Resurrection at Karacev – although there is some confusion about which monastery, and its precise location. Feast 16 June.

Tikhon of Krestogora, monk, died Krestogora, *c.* 1690. Russian Church. He founded a hermitage by the river Vochma, the church of which became the parish church of Tichonovo.

Tikhon of Lukh, born Lithuania, died Lukh, 16 June 1503. Russian Church. Baptized Timothy, and a soldier, he left Lithuania, where he had originally become a monk, because he did not approve of reunion with Rome. He settled on the banks of a river near Lukh, where he built a cell and, when others joined him, a monastery. His tomb was renowned for miracles.

Tikhon of Medyn, monk, born Moscow (?), died Medyn, 1492. Russian Church. He became a monk in Moscow, then moved to a deserted spot near Medyn, where he lived in the hollow of an oak tree.

Tikhon (Bellavin) of Moscow, patriarch of Moscow, born Pskov province, Russia, 19 January 1865, died Moscow, 7 April 1925. Russian Church. Baptized Basil, he studied at Pskov, then at St Petersburg, becoming a monk when he was 26. When he was 34 he was appointed a bishop, and was sent as vicar to the diocese of Cholmsk, but was then appointed bishop for North America in 1898. He greatly extended the Russian diocese there, accepting dozens of former uniate parishes and encouraging the liturgical use of English. In 1917 he was elected the first Russian patriarch since the seventeenth century. He led the Church against the Bolshevik persecution and protested against the laws from the beginning. For this he was imprisoned, abused, threatened and finally probably poisoned. He was buried in his beloved Donskoy monastery. Feast 26 September.

Tikhon of Zadonsk, bishop and spiritual writer, born Korock, near Novgorod, 1724, died Zadonsk monastery, 13 August 1783. Baptized Timothy Savelevic Sokplov, where his father was sacristan. His father died when he was very young, leaving the family in utter poverty. Nonetheless, he managed to study in Novgorod and then at the theological academy in Kiev, paying his fees by working as an agricultural labourer. In 1754, when he had completed his studies, he was appointed to teach Greek. Four years later he became a monk and a priest. He taught for a few years at Tver, then in 1761 was consecrated bishop of Kerksgolm and Ladoga. In 1763 he was appointed to the important Voronezh diocese, where he set about reforming the life of the clergy – but, possibly because of the hostility his reforms had aroused, he resigned in 1767 and the following year moved to a small monastery not far from Voronezh, and then from 1769 until his death lived in seclusion at Zadonsk. His spiritual writings have always been popular in Russia and include *Journey to Heaven* and *Instructions to the Clergy*. Feast 13 August.

Tillo (Tilloine, Theau), born Saxony, died Solignac, France, *c.* 702, ancient cult in Belgium and France. Captured in the Low Countries, he was ransomed and baptized by **Eligius**, who sent him to evangelize around Courtrai. After Eligius's death, Tillo lived as a recluse near Solignac abbey in Limousin. Feast 7 January.

Timolaus and Companions, martyrs, died Caesarea, Palestine, 303. Timolaus and seven companions were beheaded in the persecution of Diocletian. Feast 24 March.

Timothy, hermit, died Mount Olympus, seventh century. Feast 21 February.

Timothy, bishop, seventh century. Feast 1 August.

Timothy, martyr, died Mauretania, second/third century. He, **Polius** and **Eutychius**, all commemorated on the same day, were deacons in this African province of the Roman empire, killed probably under Diocletian. Feast 21 May.

Timothy and Diogenes, martyrs, died Philippi, Macedonia, 345 (?). They were possibly put to death by Arians. Feast 6 April.

Timothy and Faustus, martyrs, died Antioch, Syria. Feast 8 April.

Timothy and Theodore, monks, seventeenth century. Russian Church. Timothy was born in the village of Aleksino, near Tula, and became a hermit near the Solovki monastery. Of Theodore nothing is known, and he may be the same person. Feast 9 August.

Timothy and Theodosius, see **Stephen the Faster, Theodosius and Timothy**.

Timothy of Alexandria I, bishop, died 385. He was patriarch from *c.* 380.

Timothy of Alexandria II ('Ailouros'), bishop, died Alexandria, 31 July 477. Coptic Church. His nickname means 'the cat', or 'the weasel'. As a priest, he opposed the Council of Chalcedon and organized monophysite resistance to it in Egypt. In 458 he was exiled by Emperor Leo I, acting under pressure from Pope **Leo I**, when he had become bishop of Alexandria after the assassination of his orthodox rival **Proterius**. He regained the bishopric briefly, after being recalled from exile in 475.

Timothy of Alexandria III, bishop, died Alexandria, 7 February 535. Coptic Church. He was elected patriarch in 517, and despite his anti-Chalcedonian views, was left largely untroubled because he enjoyed the protection of the Empress **Theodora**, who took him as her spiritual guide.

Timothy of Antinoë, martyr, died Upper Egypt, *c.* 286. He was a church reader at Penapeis, near Antinoë, who refused to hand his sacred books to the Roman authorities. He and his wife of two days, **Maura**, who also defied this order, were executed by being nailed to a wall. Feast 3 May.

Timothy of Edessa, bishop, died Edessa, *c.* 761. Syriac Church. He became bishop in 754.

Timothy of Esphigenou, martyr, born Paraora, Thracia, died Adrianopolis, 29 October 1820.

Byzantine Church. Baptized Triandafillos, he married, but his wife fell in love with a Muslim and she abandoned both her husband and her faith. Timothy managed to persuade her to return to him, but only if he became a Muslim also, which he did. For a time they lived in their home village as Muslim, but secretly Christian. They eventually left the region, the wife entered a convent and the husband became a monk on Mount Athos, at the monastery of Esphigenou, taking the name Timothy. After some years there he conceived the idea of martyrdom. With two others who had a similar desire he went to Kassani, where the three attempted to reconvert lapsed Christians. They were arrrested, but only Timothy was beheaded.

Timothy of Eurippos, bl., bishop, born Kalamos, Greece, 1510, died island of Kea, 1590. Byzantine Church. The son of a priest, he was sent to Athens to study, then returned to Eurippos, where he was ordained and eventually became the bishop. His episcopate coincided with a persecution of Christians, and he had to flee into the mountains, settling on Mount Pentelicos, where there were many other ascetics, and he founded a monastery, of which he was hegumenos. He wanted, however, to live as a hermit, so he left his monastery and, after visiting various places, settled on the island of Kea, where he again founded a monastery. Feast 16 August.

Timothy of Gaza, bishop and martyr, died Gaza, 304. He was bishop of Gaza, and was burned alive for the faith. Feast 19 August.

Timothy of Kuben, see **Stephen and Timothy of Kuben**.

Timothy of Montecchio, born Montecchio, near Aquila, Italy, 1414, died Fossa, 1504. He was a Franciscan Observant. Feast 22 August.

Timothy of Opoca, born Voronici, died Novgorod, 1569. He was a shepherd, and extremely devout. Twice in 1563 he had visions, while on the hillsides with his sheep, of the icon in the village church, the Tenderness of the Mother of God. In 1569 he organized a procession from his village carrying the icon to the top of Mount Sinica – subsequently named the Holy Mountain, during which miracles occurred. He went to Novgorod and started preaching about the miracles which had occurred, but the bishop put him in prison as a trouble-maker, and he died there.

Timothy of Prusa, bishop and martyr, died Prusa (Cius, on the Sea of Marmara), *c.* 362. He was bishop of Prusa, and highly successful at converting pagans in his region. Emperor Julian the Apostate ordered his imprisonment, but he still continued to preach even from prison, and was then beheaded. Feast 10 June.

Timothy of Pskov, see **Dovmont of Pskov**.

Timothy of Rome, martyr, born Rome, died there, 306 (?). Feast 22 August.

Timothy of St Nicholas, monk, died lake Kuben, 1492. A monk of the monastery of St Nicholas on lake Kuben, not far from Vologda. He was renowned as a wonderworker.

Timothy of Symboli, born Italy, died Asia Minor, 795. Byzantine Church. A monk of the Symboli monastery near Mount Olympus in Bithynia, he became a hermit in later life. Feast 21 February.

Timothy, Polius and Eutychius, martyrs, died Mauritania (modern Morocco), c. 303. They were three deacons. Feast 21 May.

Tiridates, king, fourth century. Armenian Church. He was a contemporary of Diocletian, and like him was a persecutor of Christians, but went mad. He was healed by St **Greogry the Illuminator** and was converted, with his wife Askhen and his sister Khosrovidukht. Feast 12 December.

Titian, bishop, died 476. He was bishop in Liguria. Feast 1 May.

Titian of Brescia, bishop, born Germany (?), died Brescia, 536 (?). Bishop of Brescia. Feast 3 March.

Titian of Oderzo, bishop, died near Venice, 650. Bishop of Oderzo, near Venice. Feast 16 January.

Titus, martyred possibly third century, comme-morated with the martyrs **Florus**, **Satyrus** and **Maurus**. Feast 25 January.

Titus Brandsma, bl., born Boslward, Holland, 23 February 1881, died Dachau concentration camp, 26 July 1942. He came from a pious family – one of his brothers beame a Franciscan priest, and four of his five sisters were nuns – and he attended a Franciscan Minor seminary, but could not enter the order because of ill-health. He then joined the Carmelites, taking vows in 1899. He was a talented student, and after his ordination in 1905 taught philosophy in Nijmegen, becoming rector for the university in 1923. He also worked as a journalist, editing the local paper. He became an outspoken opponent of Nazism from 1935 onwards, for which he was arrested in 1942 and deported to Dachau, where he was executed by a lethal injection.

Titus of Jurevec, hermit. Russian Church. A hermit at Jurevec, by the Volga river. But nothing else is known.

Titus of Kiev, monk, died Kiev, 1190. Russian Church. All that is known is a story told in a letter from Bishop **Simon of Vladimir**. Titus had a great friend among the monks of the Kievan Cave monastery, Evagrius, but the two fell out bitterly. The antipathy went on for several years, until Titus was dying, and wished to be reconciled. Evagrius had to be brought forcibly to Titus, and when the latter asked forgiveness, Evagrius said he would never forgive him in this world or the next, at which he fell dead, and Titus recovered.

Titus Pescernik, died Kiev, fourteenth century. Russian Church. A soldier, he became a monk at the Kievan Cave monastery, and for the remainder of his life wept bitterly for his sins. Feast 28 August.

Titus the Wonderworker, hegumenos, died Con-stantinople, ninth century. Byzantine Church. He was a monk of the Studion monastery, and an opponent of iconoclasm. Because of his rigorous asceticism he was rewarded with the gift of per-forming miracles. Feast 2 April.

Torello, bl., born Poppi, Tuscany, 1201, died there, 1281, cult confirmed by Benedict XIV. Repenting his bad life, he became a hermit near his old home and lived for 50 years walled up in his cell. He was a Vallombrosan oblate. Feast 16 March.

Toribio Alfonso de Mogrovejo, archbishop, born Mayorga de Campos, Leon, November 1538, died Saña, Peru, 23 May 1606. After university studies in Salamanca and Coimbra, Mogrovejo was named inquisitor of Grenada, an important ecclesiastical post, in 1574. In this work he gained a reputation for fairness and moderation. Despite the fact that he was not ordained, he was appointed archbishop of Lima in 1579. Through the next year, he received the necessary minor orders, was ordained, and finally consecrated bishop in 1580. In Lima he instituted a programme of needed reform that was eventually adopted by most of the Roman Catholic missions in the Western hemisphere. He died from an illness contracted during a pastoral visitation. In 1727 he was canonized by Pope Benedict XIII. Feast 23 March.

Toribio of Astorga, bishop, died Astorga, *c.* 460. He was bishop of Astorga, Spain. Feast 16 April.

Toribio Romo Gonzalez, martyr, born Mexico, 1900, died Tequila, 25 February 1927. He studied at the seminary in Guadalajara, and was ordained in 1922. He was a very effective preacher, and during the persecution he moved from place to place in a vain attempt to avoid detection, saying mass in a disused factory. Feast 25 May.

Torquatus and Companions, martyrs, died Spain, third century. Seven bishops are commemorated as saints in the Mozarabic liturgy for evangelizing Spain. Torquatus was active at Guadix, near Grenada. The others were: Ctesiphon at Verga, Secundus at Avila, Indaletius at Urci near Almeira, Caecilius at Granada, Hesychus at Gibraltar and Euphrasius at Andujar. Feast 15 May.

Tranquilino Ubiarco, martyr, born Mexico, 1899, died Tepatitlan, 5 October 1928. His studies were constantly interrupted by the persecution of the Church in Mexico, but he was eventually ordained in 1923 and sent to Tepatitlan. He was arrested there and permitted to hear the confessions of his fellow prisoners before he was shot. Feast 25 May.

Triandaphillus of Zagora, martyr, born Zagora, Thessaly, died Constantinople, 8 August 1680. Byzantine Church. He became a sailor, but was arrested by the Turks who demanded that he abjure Christianity. He refused and was executed.

Tribimaeus, see **Nestor and Tribimaeus**.

Triverius, monk, born Neustria, died *c.* 550. He lived as a hermit near Thérouanne monastery, then went to Dombes. Feast 16 January.

Troadius, martyr, died Neocaesarea, 250.

Trojan (Troyen), bishop, died Saintes, *c.* 550. Supposedly the son of a Jewish father and Saracen mother, he became a priest under **Vivian**, whom he succeeded as bishop of Saintes (Aquitaine). Feast 10 February.

Trond, see **Trudo**.

Trophimus, bishop, third century. Bishop of Arles. Feast 29 December.

Trophimus and Eucarpius, martyrs, died Nicomedia, 304 (?) As soldiers they were sent to capture Christians, but were themselves converted, and were burned alive. Feast 18 March.

Trophimus and Thalus, martyrs, born Stratonicea, Lydia, died Laodicea (Latakia, Syria), *c.* 300. They were crucified. Feast 11 March.

Trophimus and Theophilus, martyrs, died Rome, 302 (?). They were beheaded. Feast 23 July.

Trophimus, Dorymedion and Sabbatius, martyrs, died Antioch, Syria (?), 277. Feast 19 September.

Trophimus of Suzdal, died Suzdal. Russian Church. A 'fool for Christ', but otherwise nothing is known of him. Feast 19 September.

Trudo (Trond), born Hasbaye, Brabant, *c.* 630, died there, *c.* 692. He studied at Metz, then became a missionary in his native region. He founded a monastery on his own lands, at what is now known as St Trond, near Louvain, and a convent near Bruges. Feast 23 November.

Trumwin, bishop, died Whitby, England, c. 704. Originally a monk of Whitby, he became bishop in Scotland in 631, and had a monastery at Abercorn. When political events turned against him, he was forced to return to Whitby. Feast 10 February.

Tryphenes of Cyzicus, martyr, born Cyzicus (on the Kapu-Dagh peninsula in the Sea of Marmara), died there. She was tortured for her faith, then thrown to the wild beasts. Feast 31 January.

Tryphyllius, bishop, died Nicosia, c. 370. A lawyer and a disciple of St **Spiridion**, he became bishop of Nicosia, and was a staunch supporter of **Athanasius**. Feast 13 June.

Tryphon of Campsada, martyr, died Nicaea, 251 (?). Feast 1 February.

Tryphon of Constantinople, patriarch, died Constantinople, 933. He became a monk in Constantinople when still quite young. In 928, when the patriarch Stephen died, the Emperor Romanus wanted his son Theophylact to become patriarch, but he was too young. Romanus then suggested to Tryphon that he become patriarch until his son was old enough. Three years later he asked Tryphon to resign, but Tryphon refused, believing that Theophylact, who was only 20, was not a proper person to serve in that office. Eventually the emperor removed Tryphon by a mixture of trickery and force, and he returned to his monastery. He lived in his monastery for another year before his death, when he was buried with the other patriarchs. Feast 19 April.

Tryphon of Pecenga, monk, born Novgorod, 1495, died 15 December 1583. Russian Church. Baptized Metrophanes, and the son of a priest, he one day heard a voice which called him, saying, 'You will serve me in a solitary place.' He took this to mean he was to spread the gospel to the pagans on the peninsula of Kola on the Arctic Sea. The local people were at first hostile, but became more receptive as he learned their language. As he was not a priest, he could not baptize his converts, so

he went to Novgorod where he became a monk, received ordination, and was given permission to start a monastery on the river Pecenga, along the banks of which he had been living. He himself helped to build the church, and he lived there for the rest of his life, in an extremely inhospitable region where life was particularly harsh. After his death many miracles were reported.

Tryphon of Rostov, bishop, died Jaroslavl, 30 December 1468. He was hegumenos of the monastery of St Cyril at Beloozero. In the struggle between the Grand Prince Basil of Moscow and Demetrius Semjaka of Galic, he backed the former, who triumphed and did not forget the support he had received. Tryphon came as an archimandrite to Moscow, and was a counsellor to the prince, as well as his confessor. In June 1462, after the death of Basil, he was named bishop of Rostov, a position he resigned in August 1467 to spend his last days in the monastery of the Saviour at Jaroslavl. Feast 1 February.

Tudwal, bishop, sixth century, born Wales (?), died Tréguier. After living in a hermitage off the Welsh coast, he is said to have settled in Brittany with members of his family and some monks. He became bishop of Tréguier. Feast 1 December.

Tutilo, monk, born Germany, c. 850, died Switzerland, 27 April c. 915. A monk at St-Gall abbey who became master of the monastic school, he was famous for his various artistic skills, with paintings and carved ivory bindings surviving. Contemporary with **Notker**, he probably worked with him on musical compositions.

Twenty-Six Saints of Mount Athos, martyrs, thirteenth century. Byzantine Church. Monks of the monastery of Zographou. Their monastery was burned down, and they died within it, for refusing to accept the possibility of reunion between the Orthodox and Latin Churches. Feast 22 September.

Typasius, martyred, possibly third century. He was beheaded. Feast 11 January.

Tyrannius and Companions, martyrs. Tyrannius and Zenobius were martyred at Antioch in 310,

Silvanus died at Emesa, and two Egyptian bishops, Peleus and Nilus, died in the mines in Palestine. All, however, are commemorated as one group, on the same day. Feast 20 February.

Tysilio, abbot, born Powys, died there, *c.* 642. He was born into the royal house of Powys in north Wales, and despite his father's disapproval decided to enter a monastery at Meifod, although he later founded his own monastery in Anglesey. Seven years later he returned to Anglesey as abbot. The rest of his life is possibly a confusion with that of another saint. It is said he went to Britanny and founded churches there, but it is slightly more likely that he died in Powys. Feast 8 November.

Ubald, bishop, born Gubbio, Italy, died there, 1160. When he was dean of the cathedral chapter he induced the canons to live a common life. He himself wanted to be a hermit, but was dissuaded, and in 1128 he became bishop of Gubbio. Feast 16 May.

Ubald, bl., born Florence, *c.* 1245, died San Senario monastery, 9 April 1315, cult approved 1821. A wealthy, turbulent young man, he became a Servite priest after hearing **Philip Benizi** preach. He was seen as gentle and holy, with miracles attributed to him during his life, and became Philip's confessor.

Ubaldesca of Pisa, born Calcinaia, near Pisa, 1136, died Pisa, 28 May 1206. At the age of 16 she became a member of the Hospitaller Order of St John of Jerusalem and for the rest of her life worked in the hospital attached to her monastery in Pisa, caring for the sick. After her death her body was taken back to her home town.

Ugandan Martyrs, see **Charles Lwanga**.

Ulpian, martyr, born Syria, died Tyre, Lebanon, *c.* 304. Said to have been put to death by being tied in a sack with a dog and a snake, and then thrown into the sea. Feast 3 April.

Ulrich of Augsburg, bishop, born Zurich, 890, died Augsburg, Germany, 4 July 973. He was born into the family of the counts of Dillingen, and after completing his education at the monastery of St-Gall in Switzerland, returned and stayed with the bishop of Augsburg, his uncle, St **Adalbero**. Ulrich himself became bishop in 923. After the Magyar

invasion in 926, Ulrich played a large part in organizing the city's defences, and Augsburg held out until Emperor Otto defeated the Magyars in 955. Ulrich retired from his see in 972 and appointed his nephew Adalbero in his place. He was criticized for nepotism and was called before the Synod of Ingelheim, but Adalbero died before taking up the post. Ulrich was canonized in 993 by Pope John XV, the first recorded papal canonization.

Ultan of Ardbraccan, bishop, died Ardbraccan, County Meath, Ireland, 657. Not a great deal is known about him. He was renowned for his learning, and seemingly for his skills as an illuminator. He may have taught in the monastic school at Ardbraccan, where he was bishop. Feast 4 September.

Unno, bishop, born *c.* 880, died Birka, September 936. A monk at Korvey in Westphalia, he served as chaplain to the provost of the cathedral of Bremen, and in October 916 became archbishop of Hamburg-Bremen. Under the protection of King Harald Bluetooth of Denmark he evangelized that country, then crossed to Sweden, first calling at Birka (Bjorko, an island on lake Malar) and then travelling as far north as Uppsala. He was taken ill and set out to return, but died on the way. Feast 17 September.

Urban I, pope from 222, born Rome, died there, 230. Little is known of his pontificate. He is sometimes said to have been a martyr, but there was no persecution in Rome during his time in office. Feast 19 May (suppressed 1969).

Urban II, bl., born Chatillon-sur-Marne, *c.* 1042, pope from 12 March 1088, died Rome, 29 July 1099. Odon de Chatillon studied at Rheims under St **Bruno**, who afterwards became his most trusted adviser, and in 1070 entered the monastery of Cluny. He was called to Rome where **Gregory VII** made him cardinal bishop of Ostia in 1080. He was elected to the papacy in 1088, adhered to the Gregorian reform, and sought ways to restore relations with the Byzantine Church. He presided at the Council of Melfi (1089), which renewed the prohibitions against simony, lay investiture and the marriage of priests. At Piacenza (1095) he declared the ordinations of Clement III, the anti-pope, and his adherents, void and, in response to an appeal from the Byzantine emperor Alexis I Commenus, called on Christian warriors to defend the Eastern Church. At Clermont, in the same year, Urban preached the first Crusade, the most memorable achievement of his pontificate. However, if his success in preaching the Crusade illustrated the remarkable recovery of the papacy, his vision of 'rapprochement' with Byzantium and Church unity was doomed to failure. The division was only reinforced with a stronger, more centralized government in the emergence of the Roman Curia and a growth in the influence of the college of cardinals. Urban died before the news of the capture of Jerusalem by the Crusaders could reach him.

Urban V, bl., born Guillaume de Grimoard at Grisac, France, 1310, pope from 28 September 1362, died Avignon, 19 December 1370. He studied at Montpellier, became a Benedictine in Marseilles and then returned to Montpellier to teach canon law, before becoming abbot of St Germain at Auxerre in 1352 and of St Victor at Marseilles in 1361. He was elected pope as a compromise candidate in a much disputed election, the first choice having turned down the office, and as a moderate reformer lived a monastic lifestyle in the papal palace. In 1367 he returned the papal Curia to Rome, taking up residence in the Vatican, the papal palace of the Lateran being uninhabitable. He was eager to forward the reunion of the Churches of East and West, and was visited in Rome by the Byzantine emperor, although nothing further was achieved. He made efforts to rebuild Rome, including the Lateran, but

unrest in Italy and renewal of the war between England and France in 1370 forced his return to Avignon, where he died a couple of months after his arrival.

Urban of Langres, bishop, fifth century. Feast 23 January.

Urban, Theodore, Menedemus and Companions, martyrs, died Nicomedia, 370. Eighty priests of Constantinople were put to death by the Arian emperor Valens after they had petitioned him to end the persecution of Catholics. Feast 5 September.

Urbitius, died *c.* 450. He was bishop of Metz. Feast 20 March.

Urosica, prince, died *c.* 1312. Serbian Church. Son of the king of Serbia, Stephen Dragutin, he is reported to have led a blameless life and to have become a monk, taking the name Stephen, on his deathbed. He was buried in the monastery of Prapac. Feast 11 November.

Urpasian, martyr, died Nicomedia, 295. A servant in the household of the emperor. He was burned to death. Feast 13 March.

Ursicius, martyr, born Illyria, died Nicomedia, 304. A military tribune. He was beheaded. Feast 14 August.

Ursmar, bishop, possibly born Floyon, northern France, *c.* 640, died Lobbes, now Belgium, 18 April 713. Perhaps a monk at Lobbes, he was elected abbot there *c.* 689, and probably made bishop at that time. He extended the abbey, built a church and founded other monasteries to evangelize Flanders.

Ursula and Companions, martyrs, born Britain, died Cologne, fourth century. This completely legendary story recounts that Ursula was crossing the English Channel with 11,000 virgins on the way to her wedding when they were driven ashore. She and her companions then went to Rome, and returned by way of Cologne, where they were martyred by Huns. Feast 21 October (suppressed).

Ursula Ledochowska, bl., born Loosdorf, Austria, 17 April 1865, died Rome, 29 May 1939, canonized 2003. Baptized Julian, and born into a noble family, with an Austrian father and Polish mother, she was brought up – after the death of her father and the subsequent financial difficulties for her mother – under the protection of her uncle, a cardinal. She joined the Ursulines at Krakow, Poland, taking the name Ursula. At the request of Pope **Pius X** she moved to and worked secretly in St Petersburg, founding the Ursulines of the Sacred Heart (Grey Ursulines) there, approved after World War I. In 1914 she moved to Scandinavia, even publishing a catechism in Finnish, before returning to Poland in 1920. Pope Benedict XV asked her to come to Rome. In addition to her language and administrative skills, she was a distinguished public speaker. In 1989 her body was taken back to the Grey Ursuline mother house in Pniewy, Poland.

Ussik, catholicos, born Armenia, 305, died Thordan, near Daranalis, Armenia, 345. Armenian Church. The son of the catholicos (and nephew of **Gregory the Illuminator**), he was brought up at the royal court, and married. His wife bore twins, but after that he abandoned his family and went to live as an ascetic. After the death of his father he was in turn elected catholicos. He was not afraid to upbraid the king for his immoral behaviour. In 345, when the king tried to enter the church where he was presiding at the liturgy, Ussik barred his way. The king, furiously angry, struck him with a staff. His clergy came to assist him, and carried him to the village of Thordan, but despite their ministrations he died there. Feast 1 December.

Vaast, see **Vedast**.

Vachtang Gorgasali, king, died 502. Georgian Church. He was king of eastern Georgia during the final years of the fifth century and battled constantly, and successfully, with Persia to achieve independence for his kingdom. He restructured the Georgian Church and united all his bishops behind the struggle for independence, and repaired relations with Constantinople for the same purpose. He is remembered for founding the city of Tbilisi, although it was his son who moved the capital there from Mzcheta. Feast 30 November.

Vahan Goltnaci, martyred Rusafah, Syria, 737. Feast 18 March.

Valentina, see **Thea, Valentina and Paul**.

Valentine, martyr, died Rome, second half of the third century. Two Valentines are mentioned in early martyrologies as having feast days on 14 February. One was a Roman priest and the other bishop of Interamna, modern-day Terni, and both appear to have been buried on the Flaminian Way. The current Porto del Popolo, previously the Flaminian Gate, was also known as the Gate of St Valentine. It is not clear whether there really were two people, or whether there was just one who became the protagonist of two different legends. The association of Valentine with lovers appears to be due to the belief that his feast day was the day on which the birds began to pair. Feast 14 February.

Valentíne Berrio-Ochoa de Aristi, martyr, born Ellorio, Vitoria, Spain, 14 February 1827, died Vietnam, 1 November 1861. Originally a missionary in the Philippines, he was apostolic vicar of Central Tonkin, and in 1857 became a bishop. He was beheaded with **Jerome Hermosilla Aransáez** and **Pedro Almató Ribera**. See **Martyrs of Vietnam**.

Valentine of Chur, bishop, died 548. Feast 7 January.

Valentine of Rhaetia, bishop, died Mais, Tyrol, *c.* 400. He was an abbot who became missionary bishop of Rhaetia. His body was eventually translated to Passau. Feast 7 January.

Valerian, see also **Eugenius**.

Valerian, martyr, died Lyons, 178. Feast 15 September.

Valerian, bishop and martyr, died north Africa, 457. Died in the persecution of the Arian King Genseric, having been driven from his house and forced to live on the street when he was over 80 years old. Feast 15 December.

Valerian, bishop of Cemele, southern Gaul, died *c.* 460. Not much is known about him, but he was present at the Councils of Riez (439) and Viason (442). He defended the jurisdictional rights of Arles against Pope Leo the Great and was reputed to be semi-Pelagian in his theological outlook. His writings include *Epistola ad Monachos de Virtutibus et Ordine Doctrinae Apostolicae* and 20 homilies found in the seventeenth century, their subject matter being largely moral and ascetic. Feast 23 July.

Valerian, Macrobius, Gordian, Elias, Zoticus and Lucianus, martyrs, died Tomi, Scythia, fourth century. They died at Tomi, a city on the Black Sea, during the persecution of Licinius. Feast 13 September.

Valerius, see also **Tiburtius**.

Valerius, died *c.* 320. He is said to have been the second bishop of Trier and supposedly a disciple of the apostle Peter. But he was probably bishop there in the early fourth century. Feast 29 January.

Valerius of Limoges, hermit, sixth century. Feast 10 January.

Valerius of Saragossa, died there, 315. Bishop of Saragossa, he and his deacon **Vincent** were arrested under Diocletian. Valerius survived and was exiled, returning eventually to his see, and is commemorated with Vincent. Feast 22 January.

Valéry, see **Walaricus**.

Vardan and Companions, martyrs, died Avarayr, 26 May 451. Armenian Church. Prince Vardan led an uprising of the Armenian nobility against the attempt by the Persians to convert Armenia to Zoroastrianism. The uprising was unsuccessful, and Vardan and his companions fell in the battle of Avarayr, but the Persian king nevertheless decided to abandon his proselytizing. Feast 5 August.

Vardan of Datvan, martyr, born Datvan, a town not far from lake Van, died there, 1421. Armenian Church. He tried to dissuade the local emir from persecuting Christians, and was imprisoned then executed. Feast 4 January.

Varmundus, bl., bishop of Ivrea, *c.* 1010. Feast 1 August.

Varus, see also **Tatulus**.

Varus and Companions, martyrs, died Upper Egypt, 307. Varus was a Roman solider who was guard of a prison holding six monks who had been condemned to death for their faith. When one of them died in prison, Varus himself took his place, and was hanged from a tree. Feast 19 October.

Vedast, bishop, born France, *c.* 455, died Arras, *c.* 539. A priest in Merovingian Gaul, he is said to have persuaded the king, Clovis, to be baptized by **Remigius** by curing a blind beggar. Later bishop of Arras, he worked to restore church and city, both devastated by Vandals. His cult developed in England. Feast 6 February.

Venantius Fortunatus, bishop and poet, born Treviso, near Venice, *c.* 530, died Poitiers, *c.* 610. He travelled widely in Europe, and for a time was spiritual director to the former Queen **Radegund** and her abbess **Agnes of Poitiers** at the Holy Cross monastery in Poitiers, where he served as steward and then chaplain. He was encouraged to publish his poetry (which wove classical forms with a more medieval mysticism and symbolism) by his friend **Gregory of Tours**, with whom he corresponded. His *Vexilla Regis* and *Pange Lingua Gloriosi* came to form part of the Office of Holy Week in the Western Church. He was a popular figure in Poitiers, and *c.* 599 was chosen to be the city's bishop. Feast 14 December.

Venerius, bishop, died 409. He was a bishop of Milan who had been ordained deacon by **Ambrose**. He faithfully supported **John Chrysostom**. Feast 6 May.

Verda, see **Daniel and Verda**.

Veremund, born Navarre, died there, 1092. Joining the Benedictine abbey of Hyrache as a boy, he became abbot *c.* 1050. Renowned for his love of the poor, he is credited with several miracles, mainly of healing. He won approval for the use of the Mozarabic rite. Feast 8 March.

Verena, born Egypt (?), died Zurzach, Switzerland (?), fourth century. Little or nothing is known of her except legends which recount that after her conversion she became a hermit, then travelled to what is now Germany, and finally to Switzerland.

She also has connections with the **Theban Legion**. Feast 1 September.

Veronica, first century. When Jesus fell as he was carrying the cross on the way to Calvary, a woman in the crowd took pity on him and wiped his face with a towel, and an exact image of Jesus' face was left on the cloth. The woman has been named Veronica, and nothing else is known about her, although attempts have been made to identify her with other women mentioned in the New Testament. Feast 12 July.

Veronica Giuliani, abbess, born Mercatello, Urbino, 1660, died Umbria, 9 July 1727. She became a Capuchin at the convent of Città di Castello in Umbria after seeing a vision of Our Lady. She had a particular devotion to the passion, and had several visions of Jesus's suffering. In 1681 an imprint of the crown of thorns appeared on her head, and on Good Friday 1697 she developed the five marks of the stigmata, which stayed with her until her death. She undertook numerous tests and examinations, and was constantly watched by a lay sister, but the marks remained. In 1688 she became novice mistress, and she held this post for 30 years, even after becoming abbess. She was first elected abbess in 1717, and was re-elected every three years until she died of apoplexy in 1727.

Veronica of Binasco, bl., born Binasco, near Milan, 1445, died Milan, 13 January 1497. A poor peasant, she taught herself to read and write in order to become a nun, and joined St Martha's (Augustinian) convent in Milan as a lay sister, where she had the responsibility of collecting alms for the convent. She constantly meditated on Christ's suffering and had numerous visions.

Vertanes, catholicos, born Armenia, died there, 341. Armenian Church. A son of **Gregory the Illuminator**, and himself the father of two sons, he succeeded his brother as catholicos in 333. He spread Christianity to the still-pagan areas of Armenia, and is credited with proposing the notion of a national Church.

Viator, hermit, died at what is now St Viâtre, near Blois, sixth century. Said to have been a monk at a monastery near Blois, and the worker of many miracles, he became a hermit near the village which now bears his name. Feast 5 August.

Vicelin, bishop, born Hamelin, Germany, *c.* 1086, died Neumünster, 12 December 1154. He studied at Paderborn, then became a canon of Bremen cathedral. In 1126 he began to evangelize the peoples of northern Europe, first from a base at Lübeck, then at Wippenthorp near Bremen. To produce clergy for the mission, he founded three Augustinian monasteries. His missionary activity was often disrupted by incursions of raiders, and one of his foundations was destroyed. He was made bishop of what is now Oldenburg, but became crippled, possibly before he was able to take up his bishopric, and retired to the first of his foundations to die.

Vicinius, bishop, died Sarsina, near Ravenna, fourth/fifth century. The first bishop of Sarsina. Feast 28 August.

Victor, martyr, died Cereso, near Burgos, *c.* 950. He is said to have been a priest martyred for converting Muslims. Feast 26 August.

Victor, martyr, born Novgorod, died (?) 1936. Russian Church. Baptized Victor Matveevic Matveev, he had been seriously ill as a child, and was cured by **John of Kronstadt**. He then embarked on the life of a pilgrim, wandering from place to place across Russia. When the revolution broke out he was in Vernyj (modern Alma Ata), where he lived as if a monk on Mount Gorel'nik. Some time after that he adopted the life of a 'fool for Christ'. He was arrested in 1935, accused of establishing a secret religious community, and condemned to five years in a prison camp at Karaganda. He was, however, thrown out of the plane while being transported there.

Victor, martyr, died Rome, fourth century. Feast 17 May.

Victor, monk, born Sara'e, Eritrea, thirteenth/fourteenth century. Ethiopian Church. Nothing else is known of him.

Victor, see also **Adrio**.

Victor I, born Africa, pope from 189, died Rome, 198. The principal event of his pontificate, and an important step in the history of the papal supremacy, was the 'Quartodeciman' controversy, for the settlement of which he ordered synods to be held throughout Christendom. He himself assembled a Council at Rome, where he insisted that Polycrates of Ephesus, and other Eastern bishops, conform to the Roman practice of keeping Easter only on Sunday, rather than on 14 Nisan, whatever the day of the week. Although he threatened them with excommunication otherwise, it seems that he was dissuaded from such severity by St **Irenaeus** and other bishops. Among other incidents of his pontificate, Victor deposed the presbyter Florinus for defending Valentinian doctrines, and excommunicated Theodotus, the founder of dynamic monarchianism. According to St **Jerome**, Victor was the first ecclesiastical authority to write in Latin, but it seems he wrote nothing but his encyclicals, which would have been published in both Latin and Greek, so this claim is doubtful. He was venerated as a martyr, but there is no evidence that he died of violence, nor is there any to confirm the *Liber Pontificalis* report that he was buried near St Peter in the Vatican. Feast 28 July (suppressed 1969).

Victor III, bl., pope, born Daufer, *c.* 1027, elected 24 May 1086, died Monte Cassino, 16 September 1087. He was related to the Lombard dukes of Benevento and was a pious man. He had been a hermit, and was a monk at Benevento (taking the name Desiderius) at Monte Cassino, where he became abbot, rebuilt the monastery, expanded its library and generally encouraged scholarship, and then in 1059 he became a cardinal with responsibility for the monasteries in southern Italy. In his position as cardinal he undertook several diplomatic missions on behalf of the papacy, and was with **Gregory VII** on his deathbed. He did not accept the papacy when elected, but retired to Monte Cassino and was only persuaded to take up the office a year later. Although consecrated in Rome, he was never able to establish full control over the city. He held an important council at Benevento, which reiterated the main themes of the reforms of Gregory VII.

Victor and Companions, martyrs, died Nicomedia, 303 (?). Those who died, in addition to Victor, were Zoticus, Zenon, Acindinus, Caesareus, Severianus, Christopher, Theonas and Antoninus. Feast 20 April.

Victor and Corona, martyrs, died Syria, 176. A husband and wife. Feast 14 May.

Victor Nikolaevic Javerski, martyr, born Korocino, 2 April 1873, died Char'kov, 13 January 1938. He worked before his arrest in various churches in Char'kov. Feast 19 May.

Victor of Marseilles, martyr, late third century. Very little is known for certain about his life. He may have been a Christian officer in the Roman army, and he encouraged local Christians not to give in to persecution, particularly when the Emperor Maximian visited Marseilles. Victor was denounced before the emperor, and was tortured and killed. Feast 21 July.

Victor of Su, martyr, born Qasr Su, near Abnub, died Musa, 1 December, third/fourth century. Coptic Church. He joined the army when still very young, and apparently rose to a significant post under Diocletian, but when the edict was issued that all had to sacrifice to idols he refused, and after many sufferings he was burned to death.

Victor of Tabennisi, monk, fifth century. Coptic Church. The archimandrite of the monastery at Tabennisi, he accompanied **Cyril of Alexandria** and **Shenoudah of Atripe** to see the emperor at Constantinople. Before he left, however, the abbess of a monastery told him that she was his mother, and that the Emperor Theodosius II was his father. When he learned he had a son, Theodosius wanted to make him a prince, but Victor refused and returned to Egypt, and at Pbow built a church in honour of St **Pachomius**.

Victor the Hermit, born Troyes, France, died Saturniac (St Vittre), *c.* 610. He came from a noble family, and was well educated. He became a priest, and then a hermit and miracle worker. Feast 29 August.

Victor the Moor, martyr, born Mauritania, died Milan, 303. Probably a black man, a Christian from an early age, he was a soldier in the Praetorian guard. Miracles were claimed at his tomb and in 1576 **Charles Borromeo** translated his relics to Milan. He is a patron of Milan. Feast 8 May.

Victor, Victorinus, Claudian and Bassa, martyrs, died Nicomedia, Bithynia, possibly third century. Bassa was the wife of Claudian. They are said to have died in prison. Feast 6 March.

Victoria, martyr, see **Acisclus**.

Victoria and Anatolia, martyrs. They were sisters who lived in or around the Sabine hills, to the north-east of Rome. Anatolia is described in a fourth-century document as a worker of miracles, and she and Victoria are mentioned together in the *Hieronymian Martyrology*, which dates from the fifth century. Nothing is known of the circumstances in which they were martyred. Feast 10 July.

Victoria Díez, bl., martyr, born Seville, 11 November 1903, died Rincón, near Hornachuelos, 12 August 1936. She was a teacher, but wanted to become a missionary. She joined the Teresian Association, founded by **Peter Poveda**, in order to combine her spirituality with teaching. She was sent to Hornachuelos, west of Córdoba, and dedicated the rest of her life to teaching there. When a law was passed in 1933 forbidding religion to be taught in state schools, she organized catechetical classes for the mothers of her pupils, so that they could teach their children. She believed that women would become a powerful force in the Church. After the outbreak of the civil war, the local committee for the defence of the republic began arresting those who might be in favour of the uprising, and this included Catholic teachers. She was arrested on 11 August 1936 and force-marched, along with 17 others, to an abandoned mine, where they were shot dead the next morning. Feast 28 July.

Victoria Fornari-Strata, bl., founder of the contemplative Order of the Annunciation, referred to as the 'Celestial Annunciades' or 'Blue Nuns', born Genoa, Italy, 1562, died there, 15 December 1617. After the death of her husband she took a vow of chastity and lived a holy life, bringing up her six children – five of whom joined religious orders. When they were all settled she set about establishing her new contemplative order. Maria Victoria and ten companions took solemn vows in 1605. Communities were established early on in Burgundy, France and Germany. The order, which makes altar linens and vestments, is regarded by some as being rather rigid. Feast 12 September.

Victoria Gusteau, see **Felicity Pricet**.

Victoria Rasoamanarivo, bl., born Tananarive, Madagascar, 1848, died there, 21 August 1894. She was born into a powerful family, studied in the missionary school run by the nuns of St Joseph of Cluny, and became a Catholic, converting from her traditional religion, in 1863. The following year she married: it was a difficult marriage, but she remained with her husband until his death, persuading him to convert to Catholicism. In 1883 there began a three-year persecution of Catholicism on Madagascar, but Victoria used her status to defend, and also to care for, other Catholics.

Victoriano Pio Cano, martyr, born San Millan de Lora, 7 July 1905, died Turon, Asturias, 9 October 1034. Baptized Claudio Bernabè, he entered the de la Salle Brothers on 30 August 1921. A gifted musician, he had arrived in Turon less than a month before his martyrdom. He was arrested with the other **Martyrs of Asturias** by a group of rebel soldiers, and executed by firing squad.

Victorianus, Frumentius and Companions, martyrs, died Carthage, 484, for refusing to become Arians. Victorianus had been proconsul in Africa. Feast 23 March.

Victorianus of Asan, born Italy (?), died Spain, *c.* 558. He travelled to France, then settled in what is now Aragon. Abbot of Asan, he had a reputation as a teacher of orthodox monastic observance at a time of division between Christian sects. Feast 12 January.

Victoricus, see **Fuscian and Victoricus**.

Victorinus, see also **Cassius**.

Victorinus, bishop and martyr, died Pruj, Slovenia, 303. Very little is known about him except that he was a learned man, who had produced commentaries on Scripture, quoted by several Fathers of the Church. Feast 2 November.

Victorinus and Companions, martyrs, born Corinth, died Diospolis in the Thebaid, Egypt, 284 (?). They were exiled from Corinth to Egypt because of their faith, and were martyred there. Victorinus's companions are listed as Victor, Nicephorus, Claudian, Dioscorus, Serapion and Papias. Feast 25 February.

Victorius, see **Polyeuctus**.

Victricius, bishop, died Rouen, c. 407. He was a convert to Christianity as a soldier, which led him to ask to be allowed to leave the army. For this he was flogged and condemned to death, but was surprisingly released. He became bishop of Rouen in 386, where he established a monastery and several churches, as well as converting many in the surrounding countryside. He was widely respected among bishops, and his advice was frequently asked. Towards the end of his life he was accused of heresy, but cleared. Feast 7 August.

Vietnam, Martyrs of, see **Martyrs of Vietnam**.

Vigilius, bishop and martyr, born Trento, Italy, died Rendena, 405. He studied in Athens, and became bishop of Trento soon after his return. He was stoned to death in the valley of Rendena, where he was preaching, after he had thrown his cloak over a statue of a pagan god. Feast 26 June.

Vigor, bishop, born in the Artois, northern France, died Bayeux, c. 537. Educated in Arras, he decided to become a priest, but had to flee from his home in order to do so, hiding out near Bayeux. He was eventually ordained priest there, and was highly successful as an evangelist. He was elected bishop of the town in 513. Feast 1 November.

Villana of Florence, bl., born Florence, 1322, died there, 29 January 1361. She was born into the wealthy Botti family. Although she tried to run away from home at the age of 13 to become a nun (she was rejected), after she married she led a worldly life, before joining the Third Order of St **Dominic**. She then begged for the poor, was said to have visions and was venerated as a saint during her lifetime.

Vilmos Apor, bl., bishop, martyr, born Segesvar, Transylvania, 1892, died Györ, Hungary, 2 April 1945, beatified 1997. Ordained in 1915, he was parish priest in Gyula, Hungary, and bishop of Györ from 1940, committed to the poor and to ecumenism. A Russian soldier shot him on 30 March as he protected a girl. Feast 1 April.

Vincent, martyr, died Léon, Spain, 630. Feast 11 March.

Vincent de Paul, apostle of charity, born Pouy (Landes), April 1581, died Paris, 27 September 1660. Son of a peasant family, he became a priest in 1606 and, according to his own account, was captured by pirates and made a slave in Tunisia before returning to Avignon with his former master, whom he converted. In 1608 he went to Paris, where he met Pierre Berulle, who profoundly influenced his life, and engaged him as tutor to the family of P-E De Gondi, general of the galleys, and this gave Vincent the opportunity of compassionate work among the unfortunate galley slaves and convicts. His gradual conversion to God's work had begun, and he was to embrace a life of heroic charity. St **Francis de Sales** gave him charge of the convents of the Visitation Order in Paris and, with St **Jane Frances Fremiot de Chantal**, he founded the Visitandines, whose superior he was from 1622. In 1625 he founded the Congregation of the Missions (Lazarists, or Vincentians) to give missions to country people and to train priests. With **Louise de Marillac**, he founded the Sisters of Charity, who are entirely devoted to the care of the sick and the poor. In 1638 he created the first viable home for foundlings. Vincent sent his missionaries abroad to north Africa for the relief of Christian slaves, and into heretic countries to win them to Catholicism. In France he founded a hospice for men, another, La Salpetriere, for the indigent poor, and yet another for foundling children. Vincent de Paul was not a profound or original thinker, but his success was a result of natural talents and a tremendous amount of work, sincere dedication over many years and, above all, a profound spiritual life. The piety that he practised and taught was simple, non-mystical, Christocentric and oriented towards action, and few have accomplished as much. He was canonized in 1885. In 1883 the Society of St Vincent de Paul (a lay association for personal service to the poor) was founded by Frederic Ozanam.

Vincent Ferrer, born Valencia, *c.* 1350, the son of an Englishman who had settled in Spain, died Vannes, France, 5 April 1419. He received the Dominican habit in Valencia in 1367, taught philosophy at Lerida, and was sent as a deacon to preach in Barcelona. He was sent to Toulouse for a year after being accused of prophesying, but later returned to Spain where he converted the rabbi Paul of Burgos, who became bishop of Cartagena. In the Great Schism he sided with Clement VII and his successor, Pedro de Luna, who took the name Benedict XIII: Vincent went to Avignon and attempted to persuade Benedict to reach an agreement with his Roman rival. When he failed in this, Vincent set off on preaching tours of southern France, Switzerland and northern Italy. In 1405 he went to Flanders, returning to Spain in 1407 where he preached even in the Islamic areas of the region. In 1414 he went to Perpignan to try once again to persuade Benedict to resign, but again failed. He told King Ferdinand of Castile and Aragon that he would be justified in withdrawing support from Benedict, thereby assisting in the ending of the schism. His final years were spent preaching in northern France. He was canonized in 1455.

Vincent Grossi, bl., founder, born Pizzighettone, near Cremona, Italy, died Vicobellignano, 7 November 1917. He studied for the priesthood at the diocesan seminary and was ordained in 1864. After several postings, he was sent in 1883 to Vicobellignano. There he organized a group of young women to look after the spiritual well-being of the girls of the parish, and this group became the nucleus of the Institute of the Daughters of the Oratory. This received papal approval, but only after the founder's death, with a reputation for great holiness of life.

Vincent Kadlubek, bl., bishop, born in the Palatinate, died Poland, 1223, cult approved 1764. He studied in France and Italy, became bishop of Krakow in 1208, resigned in 1218, and became a Cistercian at Jedrzejo. Feast 8 March.

Vincent Lewoniuk and Companions, martyrs, died Podlasie, Poland, 24 January 1874. The 13 men were killed while attempting to defend their Greek-rite parish church from being taken over as an Orthodox parish, as Tsar Alexander II had instructed.

Vincent Madelgarius, born Strépy, modern Belgium, died 14 July *c.* 677. He married St **Waldetrude** and had four children. Madelgarius and Waldetrude later decided to separate and lead religious lives. Madelgarius founded a monastery in Hautmont, and took the name Vincent when he became a monk there. In 653 he moved to Soignies and established another monastery there, which he handed over to his son **Landry**, bishop of Metz, shortly before his death.

Vincent of Aquila, bl., Franciscan lay brother, died 1504. Feast 7 August.

Vincent of Lérins, theologian, born Toul, into an aristocratic family, died monastery of Lérins (now called St-Honorat, on an island near Cannes), *c.* 450. Little is known of his life, although a contemporary says he had been a soldier before being attracted – with his brother Loup – to the monastic life, entering Lérins *c.* 425. His fame rests particularly on his *Commonitorium*, and also on a collection of excerpts he made from the writings of St **Augustine**. Both books were written under the pseudonym of 'Pilgrim'. The *Commonitorium* enunciates the principle that to distinguish orthodoxy from heresy it is necessary to accept '*quod ubique, quod semper, quod ab omnibus*', 'what is everywhere, always and by all' believed. The greater part of the book is an historical study demonstrating this principle. This 'Vincentian canon' deeply influenced John Henry Newman. Feast 24 May.

Vincent of Novye Krupcy, monk, died Novye Krupcy, 1773. Church of the Old Believers. Already a monk, he moved to the Old Believers' community at Vetka in Poland towards the end of the seventeenth century. He settled in the monastery established by **Lawrence** near the village, but five years later moved on to become a hermit near Krupcy, another Old Believer community. Because of his evident holiness many were attracted to him, and he not only established a new monastery (to which the monastery of St Lawrence later moved) but also a new village – Novye Krupcy. He was aged about 100 when he died.

Vincent of Saragossa, martyr, born Huesca, Spain, died Valencia, 304. Deacon to bishop **Valerius**, he was tortured under Diocletian and died of his wounds. He was widely venerated and his story, with gory details, is in the *Peristephanon* by Prudentius. He is patron of vinedressers. Feast 22 January.

Vincent of Vologda, monk, died Vologda, seventeenth century. Nothing is known of him. Feast 19 March.

Vincent Pallotti, founder, born Rome, 21 April 1795, died there, 22 January 1850. The son of a grocer, he was ordained in 1818 and for a time became a teacher of theology. He then took up pastoral work, starting numerous guilds and credit unions to help the working class. In 1835 he founded the Pious Union of the Catholic Apostolate to mobilize priests and lay people. He was also interested in mission work, especially with Muslims, in the reunion of the Eastern and Western Churches, and the return of England to the Catholic faith. He also founded the Pious Society of the Missions (the Pallotine Fathers) to work in urban areas. Radical for the time, he was opposed by Church authorities, but supported by successive popes.

Vincent Strambi, bishop, born Civitavecchia, 1 January 1745, died Rome, 1 January 1824. At the age of 15 he entered the seminary at Montefiascone, but after meeting **Paul of the Cross**, in 1768 he became a member of the Passionist Congregation. He taught and held various offices in the Congregation before, in 1801, being made bishop of Macerata and Tolentino. He worked with considerable success to renew the spiritual life of the diocese and to help the poor, but was expelled in 1808 when he refused to take the oath of allegiance to Napoleon. He was only able to return after the

defeat of Napoleon. He resigned his see in 1823 and went to Rome as adviser to Pope Leo XII.

Vincent the Presbyter, fifth/sixth centuries. Feast 13 January.

Vincent Vilar David, bl., martyr, born Manises, near Valencia, 28 July 1889, died there, 22 February 1937. He was the youngest of eight children, and with his brothers ran the ceramics factory they had inherited. However, David's commitment to Catholic social doctrine on the treatment of workers made it difficult for him to be a partner, and he eventually started his own factory. In 1922 he married Isabel Rodes Reig. After the declaration of the republic and the anti-religious propaganda which followed, he started evening classes to teach Catholic doctrine. He also sheltered priests in his house. In 1937 he was arrested for his Catholic activities, and although defended by some trade unionists who knew him as a very good employer, he was shot – possibly unintentionally.

Vincenta López y Vicuña, founder, born Cascante, Navarre, 22 March 1847, died Madrid, 26 December 1890. From a middle-class family, Vincenta studied in Madrid, and became interested in the life of young working girls. She lived a common life there with a small group for five years. In 1876 she founded the Daughters of Mary Immaculate for Domestic Services, and pronounced vows two years later. The Congregation received papal approval in 1888 and soon spread to Europe and Latin America. The Daughters numbered some 2,000 in 81 houses by 1961. Vincenta was canonized in 1975.

Vincentian, hermit, died *c.* 730. He was a disciple of **Meneleus** and became a hermit in the Auvergne. Feast 2 January.

Vincenza Gerosa, co-founder of the Sisters of Charity of Lovere, born Lovere, Lombardy, 29 October 1784, died there, 28 June 1847. Her family were wealthy but quarrelsome – which led to her mother dying in poverty and Gerosa having to be carefully advised on retaining her patrimonial rights. On inheriting the family fortune, she converted one of her houses into a hospital. She later became co-founder of a religious institute with

Bartolomea Capitanio, after whose death she ran it herself. When it gained ecclesiastical approval, she was elected superior.

Vindemialis and Companions, martyrs, died Africa, *c.* 485. He and his companions, **Eugenius** and **Longinus**, were bishops who had vigorously opposed Arianism in the Council of Carthage. They were viciously tortured before being beheaded on the orders of the Arian Vandal king, Hunneric. Feast 2 May.

Vindicianus, bishop, died *c.* 712. A disciple of **Eligius**, he was a bishop of Arras-Cambrai who opposed the excesses of the Merovingian rulers. He spent his final years mainly in St Vaast abbey in Normandy. Feast 11 March.

Virgilius of Arles, died *c.* 618. He was a monk at Lérins, then abbot of St Symphorian at Autun. Afterwards he became bishop of Arles, and as such probably ordained **Augustine** as bishop of Canterbury. He was rebuked by Pope **Gregory I** for forcibly converting Jews. Feast 5 March.

Virgilius of Salzburg, bishop, born Ireland, died Salzburg, 27 November 784. After a monastic education in Ireland he set off, possibly for the Holy Land, but in France was befriended by Pepin the Short, who sent him on a diplomatic mission to Duke Odilo of Bavaria. Odilo made him abbot of the monastery of St Peter in Salzburg, and wanted to appoint him bishop. **Boniface**, however, objected, alleging heretical views. Virgil appealed to Rome, and his appeal was upheld. He built Salzburg's first cathedral, and not only sent missionaries to Carinthia, but for a time went himself.

Virginia Centurione-Bracelli, bl., born Genoa, 2 April 1587, died there, 15 December 1651. Of a noble family of Genoa, she was obliged to marry the dissolute Caspar Bracelli when she was 15, bearing him two daughters. After the death of Caspar five years later, Virginia took a vow of chastity and devoted herself to the care of the poor of the city, and especially of orphans. She established the Order of Our Lady of Mount Calvary to carry on her work. It took its name from the empty convent of Monte Calvario, to which in 1631 she transferred her activities from what had been the house of her mother-in-law – although shortly afterwards, finding Monte Calvario too expensive, she moved to other accommodation.

Viridiana (Veridiana), hermit, born Castel Fiorentino, died there, 1236 or 1242. After a pilgrimage to Compostela, she became a walled-up recluse. She lived thus for 34 years attached to a Vallombrosan abbey. Feast 1 February.

Vitalis, see also **Felicula**.

Vitalis, martyr, born Bologna, died there. His body, along with that of his slave **Agricola**, was discovered in the Jewish cemetery in 392. Agricola had been made to suffer first, in the hope that his martyrdom would make Vitalis deny his faith, but it had the opposite effect. Vitalis was put to death by crucifixion. Feast 4 November.

Vitalis, abbot, died 990. He was a hermit who founded monasteries in Calabria and was abbot of Rapolla in Basilicata. Feast 9 March.

Vitalis, died Umbria, 1370. He was a monk of Monte Subasio, near Assisi, who moved to Santa Maria delle Viole, also near Assisi, where for 20 years he was a hermit under the guidance of the abbot of Monte Subasio. Feast 31 May.

Vitalis Grandin, ven., Oblate missionary and bishop, born St Pierre-la-Cour, France, 8 February 1829, died St Albert, Canada, 3 June 1902. In 1851 Grandin joined the Oblates of Mary Immaculate, was ordained in 1854 and sent as a missionary to Canada, where he began work in Île-à-la-Crosse, Saskatchewan. In 1857 he became auxiliary bishop of St Boniface but did not learn of it until 1859. In 1871 he moved from Île-à-la-Crosse to St Albert upon becoming bishop there. He interceded during the Métis revolt (1855) and as bishop strongly defended the rights of both Indians and Catholics. His cause for canonization was introduced in 1937.

Vitalis of Gaza, monk, died *c.* 625. When already old, he scandalized people by the way in which he tried to save fallen women, but he was vindicated after his death. Feast 11 January.

Vitalis of Savigny, bl., hermit, wandering preacher and founder of the Congregation of Savigny, born Tierceville, near Bayeux, France, 1060–65, died Savigny, 16 September 1122. A chaplain to Count Robert of Mortain, he left *c.* 1095 in order to become a wandering preacher and hermit in the forests of Craon. The abbey of Savigny was established *c.* 1115. The Congregation of Savigny greatly influenced English and Norman monasticism, but was torn apart by dissent among her English houses and merged with the Order of Citeaux in 1147. Feasts 16 September and 7 January.

Vitalis, Revocatus and Fortunatus, martyrs, died Smyrna. A bishop and two deacons. Feast 9 January.

Vitesindus of Córdoba, martyr, born Córdoba, died there, 855. Living under Muslim rule in Spain, he officially conformed to Islam while remaining a Christian in secret. He was an old man when he declared his faith in public, possibly inspired by **Eulogius of Córdoba**, and was executed. See **Martyrs of Córdoba**. Feast 15 May.

Vitonus, bishop, died Verdun, *c.* 525. Effectively appointed bishop of Verdun by Clovis, king of the Franks, although as second choice. He was a successful evangelist of the countryside around his city. Feast 9 November.

Vitus, martyr, born Syracuse, died Rome (?), *c.* 300. He was said to be the son of the Roman governor of Sicily, who converted to Christianity under the influence of **Modestus**, his tutor, and **Crescentia**, his nurse. When his father found out he tried to have them imprisoned, but they escaped to Rome, where, however, they were captured and put to death. Crescentia and Modestus are believed to be legendary. Vitus himself is the saint after whom 'St Vitus's Dance' is named. Feast 15 June.

Vivaldus, bl., died Etruria, 1320. He was a Franciscan hermit. Feast 1 May.

Vivian, bishop, died Sanctes, France, *c.* 460. Feast 28 August.

Vladimir, founder, died Serpuchov, 1522. He founded a monastery dedicated to the Most Holy Trinity near Serpuchov in 1498, and ruled it until his death.

Vladimir and Agripina, prince and princess, died Rzev, thirteenth century. Russian Church. Little or nothing is known about them, but they were venerated as miracle workers after their deaths, and Vladimir was said to have returned to defend his city from attack from time to time. Although never officially canonized, they enjoyed a considerable cult at Rzev. Feast 15 July.

Vladimir and Companions, martyrs, died Vladimir, 2 and 6 February 1238. Russian Church. This group of martyrs died during the Mongol attack on Vladimir in February 1238. The first to die was the young prince Vladimir, who had been captured by the Mongols at Moscow. He was killed outside the walls of Vladimir in an effort to intimidate the inhabitants of the city. On 6 February, when it seemed that the Mongol attack was imminent, a number of nobles and the two princes Vsevolod and Mstislav, with their wives and their mother, took monastic vows. Many died, either directly at the hands of the Mongols, or in the cathedral when the invaders set it on fire. The two princes, however, died fighting outside the walls of the city. Feast 23 June.

Vladimir John the Baptist, prince, born Zeta (in modern Montenegro), died Prespa (in modern Macedonia), 22 May 1016. His principality of Zeta was attacked by Samuel, king of Macedonia, and Vladimir was taken prisoner. While held by Samuel, he fell in love with Samuel's daughter, and the two were married. On the death of the Macedonian king – and the death of his legitimate heir – it seemed possible that Vladimir would succeed to the throne, but he was killed by Samuel's nephew to secure the throne for himself. He was remembered as a devout man – he had attended a church service immediately before his assassination – and a founder of monasteries, in one of which, Elbasan in central Albania, his remains were eventually buried.

Vladimir (Wlodzimierz) Laskowski, bl., martyr, born Rogozno, Poland, 31 January 1896, died Gusen, Austria, 8 August 1940. A priest of the archdiocese of Poznan, he died in a Nazi concentration camp and was beatified by Pope John Paul II on 13 June 1999, along with 107 other victims of the same persecution.

Vladimir Nikolaevic Vasilevski, martyr, born Tashkent, 6 January 1892, died Char'kov, 11 January 1938. Ukrainian Church, Moscow Patriarchate. He became a priest in 1924, and worked until his arrest in December 1937 in the village of Vedenskoe. Feast 19 May.

Vladimir (Bogoyavlensky) of Kiev, bishop and martyr, born Malye Moroski, Tambov province, Russia, 1 January 1848, died Kiev, 25 January 1918. Russian Church. Baptized Basil Nikiforovic, he was, uniquely, metropolitan successively of Moscow, St Petersburg and Kiev. As senior bishop he presided over the Church Council of Moscow (1917–18). He began his ecclesiastical career teaching in the seminary at Tambov, and after his ordination in 1882 he worked in the cathedral of Kozlov, eventually becoming its parish priest. Four years after his ordination his wife died, and he became a monk, changing his name to Vladimir. He held various monastic positions, including that of superior of the Antoniev monastery at Novgorod. His first appointment as a bishop was as vicar of the diocese of Novgorod, then he became archbishop of Samara in January 1891, just as that city was suffering from a plague of cholera. He spent five years as exarch of Georgia, before embarking on the distinguished career outlined above, being appointed to Moscow in February 1898, in November 1912 to St Petersburg, and just three years later to Kiev. He was tortured and murdered by Bolshevik irregulars at the Kievan Caves monastery – the first of very many bishops of the Russian Church to be martyred. Feast 25 January.

Vladimir of Kiev ('the Baptizer'), prince, born Kiev, c. 956, died there, 15 July 1015. A Viking by origin, he became prince of Kiev in 970, although he had to flee only two years later because his brothers rose against him. He fought his way back to power, establishing himself with the aid of the Byzantine emperor, whose daughter he married. He became a Christian, and a zealous one. Although his efforts to impose Christianity by force were not wholly successful, he began the process which converted first Kiev and then the rest of Russia to Christianity. His Christianity was moreover not simply skin-deep: he changed his own private life and became gentler in his treatment of those who had offended him, and of prisoners. He was generous to the poor. After the death of his first wife Anna, he married a niece of the German Emperor Otto I. He died during an expedition against one of his sons. **Boris** and **Gleb** were also his sons, and suffered from the internecine strife that afflicted his family.

Vladimir of Novgorod, prince, born Novgorod, 1021, died there, 1052. Russian Church. He was entrusted by his father, Grand Prince Jaroslav, with the governorship of Novgorod from the age of 14. He took part in the disastrous attack on Constantinople in 1043, but managed to make his way back to Novgorod. He was a devout Christian, making careful study of the Scriptures and building the cathedral of the Divine Wisdom in his city, where he was buried. He and his mother were proclaimed saints in 1439.

Vodoaldus (Voel, Vodalus, Vodalis), hermit, died near Soissons, c. 720. He was an Irish or Scottish monk who went as a missionary to Gaul, where he became a recluse. Feast 5 February.

Volusian, bishop, born Tours, died Toulouse, 496. He became bishop of Tours in 491, but, repeatedly harassed by the Goths, he was driven into exile. Other accounts say that he was beheaded by the Goths, and this led to him being venerated as a martyr. Accounts of his life mention his unhappy marriage. Feast 18 January.

Vsevolod of Pskov, prince, born Novgorod, died Pskov, 11 February 1138. Russian Church. His father was Prince **Mstislav-Theodore of Kiev**, and Vsevolod was brought up in that city, becoming its ruler in 1117. The first years of his rule were marked by the setting up of schools and monasteries and the building of churches. He was also a warrior, attacking Finns and Estonians, and was also involved, unsuccessfully, in an attempt to win the throne of Perejaslavl. He entered the city, but had to flee again almost immediately. He was not, however, welcomed back by the people of Novgorod, who were angered by his apparent breaking of a promise to remain in that city until death. His effort to win them over by an attack on Suzdal ended disastrously, and the people of Novgorod looked for another prince to defend them. Vsevolod was, however, welcomed by the people of Pskov as their prince, where once again, as he had at first in Novgorod, he took care of the poor and the sick, and built churches, all the time preparing for death by prayer and fasting.

Vulagius, bishop, born Rue, near Abbeville, northern France, died Regnière Ecluse, 645. When the priest of Rue died, the villagers asked Vulflagius to serve them. The bishop agreed, although he was married with three daughters, provided he and his wife agreed to live celibate lives. They promised to do so, but failed to keep their promise. He was full of remorse, and went on a pilgrimage to the Holy Land in expiation. On his return he became a recluse at Regnière Ecluse, where he died. Many people came to consult him. His three daughters all became nuns. Feast 7 June.

Vulmar (Wulmer), abbot, born Boulogne, France, c. 620, died 700. He entered the abbey of Hautmont in Hainault as a servant. He was eventually ordained and went to live in a hermitage near Mount Cassel. He founded a monastery near Calais, known as the abbey of Samer, and founded a convent at Wierre-aux-Bois. Many miracles were attributed to him during his life, and these continued at his tomb after his death.

Walaricus (Valéry), abbot, born Auvergne, France, died near the Somme estuary on the North Sea, *c.* 620. A monk at Auxerre and Luxeuil, then a missionary in north-west France, evangelizing most of the coastal area, he founded a monastic settlement that became the Columban abbey of Leuconay. Feast 1 April.

Walatta Maryam, nun. Ethiopian Church. She was a nun of Dabra Warq in Goggiam, but nothing else is known of her.

Walatta Petros, nun, born Dawaro, 1594, died Quarasa (?), 1644. Ethiopian Church. She came from a noble family and was married young to one of the king's advisers. She had three children, all of whom died young. Although the marriage was at first happy, when the king converted to Catholicism and her husband supported him, Walatta Petros fled to a convent. She was arrested and brought back. Her husband asked pardon for her, and she was sent to live with his brother. She continued to campaign against Catholicism, however, and won many adherents, for whom she founded a number of communities. When the royal infatuation with Catholicism waned, Walatta was received back into favour.

Walatta Seyon, nun. Ethiopian Church. She was the founder of Dabra Quesquam and Jamma in Wallo.

Walburga of Heidenheim, abbess, born Wessex, England, *c.* 710, died Heidenheim, 25 February 779. She was raised and educated at Wimborne in Dorset, went as a missionary to Germany at the request of St Boniface, entered the double monastery of Heidenheim, founded by her brothers according to Anglo-Saxon models, and succeeded her brother **Winnibald** as superior. She was one of the most popular medieval saints; she especially favoured the education of German women and, unlike the cult of other women saints of the time, she was venerated as a patroness against hunger and disease in an area exceeding by far the radius of her activities. Each year from October to February, oil ('Walburga's oil') flows from a stone slab near her relics at Eichstatt, and is collected in small bottles for use with prayers of healing for the sick.

Wald, bishop, seventh century. He was bishop of Evreux. Feast 31 January.

Waldebert, abbot, died Luxeuil, in the Vosges, France, *c.* 665. A nobleman, he became a monk at Luxeuil (Haute Savoie), then a hermit close by. Abbot at Luxeuil for 40 years, he replaced the Rule of **Columbanus** by that of **Benedict**. He founded other monasteries and with **Salaberga** founded St John the Baptist nunnery at Laon. Feast 2 May.

Waldetrude (Waltrude), died Mons, now Belgium, *c.* 688, cult approved 1679. Daughter of **Waldebert** and **Bertilla**, sister of **Aldegund**, she married **Vincent Madelgarius**. Their children, **Aldetrude**, **Dentelin**, **Landry** (**Landericus**) and **Madelberta**, are saints. She founded a convent at Chateaulieu, in Mons, where she is patron. Feast 9 April.

Walfrid (Galfrido della Gherardesca), born Pisa, died Palazuolo, *c.* 756. Married with adult children and eminent in Pisa, he and his wife Thesia chose the religious life. Walfrid founded two monasteries for them both near Pisa, where others joined them, including some of their children. Feast 15 February.

Walstan of Bawburgh, born Bawburgh, Norfolk, died Norfolk, 1016. He was an agricultural labourer in Taverham, near Bawburgh, who gave what little he had to the poor and healed people and animals. Farm people venerated at his shrine until its destruction during the Reformation. Feast 30 May.

Walter, bl., died Guimaraes, now in Portugal, c. 1258. An early follower of **Francis of Assisi**, he was sent to Portugal to establish the order there. Feast 2 August.

Walter of L'Esterp, abbot, born Conflans castle, near river Vienne, died L'Esterp, Limousin, 11 May 1070. He joined the Augustinian Canons at Dorat, eventually becoming abbot for 38 years. He is recalled as gentle to his community, charitable to the poor and with a special gift for reconciling sinners.

Walter (Gautier) of Pontoise, abbot, born Andainville, Picardy, northern France, c. 1030, died Pontoise, 8 April 1095. He was first abbot of the new monastery at Pontoise. Craving solitude to pray, he left several times, but eventually accepted Pope **Gregory VII**'s order to accept his office and was an outspoken reformer.

Wandregisilus, abbot, born Verdun, France, c. 600, died July 668. He was married, but in c. 628 he and his wife decided to separate and he became a monk at Mountfacon. He soon moved to St-Ursanne in the Jura Mountains in order to live a solitary life. He later moved to the abbey of Romain-Moûtier, on the Isère, and stayed there for about ten years. He was also ordained there by St **Ouen**. He founded an abbey at Fontenelle in Normandy, which subsequently became one of the leading monasteries in France. Its church was consecrated in 657. Feast 22 July.

Warada Qala Egzi, monk, born Tigre. Ethiopian Church.

Wenceslas, martyr, duke of Bohemia, born Prague, c. 907, died Alt-Bunzlau, 28 September 929. His grandmother, **Ludmilla**, raised him as a Christian until she was killed by his pagan mother, who ruled as regent until Wenceslas came of age. He put his duchy under the protection of King Henry the Fowler of Germany, and invited German Christian missionaries into Bohemia. He is the 'good king' of the Christmas carol. He was murdered at the door of a church by his pagan brother Boleslav.

Werburga (Werburgh, Werbyrgh or Werburth), born 650, died Threckingham, England, c. 700. Daughter of Wulfhere, king of Mercia, and **Ermengild**, granddaughter of **Sexburga** and great-niece of **Etheldreda**, she entered Ely abbey and was later in charge of several Midlands nunneries. There was a popular cult in Chester, where her body was taken in 1095, until her shrine and relics were destroyed under Henry VIII. Feast 3 February.

Werenfried, missionary, born England, died Arnhem, in what is now the Netherlands, c. 760. He was a colleague of **Willibrord**. Feast 14 August.

Wibert, see **Guibertus**.

Wiborada (Guiborat), martyr, born Klingnau, Switzerland, died near St-Gall, 926, canonized 1047. Always living alongside her brother Hatto, after he joined the Benedictines at St-Gall she became a walled-up recluse nearby in 915. She is considered a martyr because she refused to flee invading barbarians, and she died at their hands. Feast 2 May.

Wigbert, abbot, born England, died Fritzlar, near Kassel, Germany, c. 745. Invited by **Boniface** to help evangelize Germany, he became abbot of the monastery at Fritzlar, then of Ohrdurf, but returned to Fritzlar to prepare for death. Feast 13 August.

Wilfrid, bishop, born possibly Ripon, Yorkshire, c. 634, died near Oundle, Northamptonshire, 709. He was educated at Lindisfarne, Rome and Lyon, and on his return to England became abbot of Ripon. He was a major protagonist of Roman, rather than Celtic, practices, a view which triumphed at the Synod of Whitby. He was chosen to be bishop of York, but when he returned in 666 from France, where he had gone to be consecrated, he discovered that **Chad** had been installed in his place. He was, however, granted the see by Archbishop **Theodore of Canterbury** three years later. When, a decade later, Theodore divided his enormous diocese without consulting him, Wilfrid appealed to Rome. Rome granted his appeal, but the king of Northumbria would not accept the decision, and imprisoned and then exiled Wilfrid, who went to what is now Sussex to preach Christianity and to found a monastery at Selsey. He was reinstated in 686, but with limited jurisdiction. In 703 a synod deprived him yet again of the see of York, and of his monasteries. Again he appealed to Rome, and was vindicated, but in 705 a compromise was reached by which he was left with the diocese of Hexham and his monasteries, but not the see of York. Feast 24 April.

Wilfrid the Younger (Wilfrid II), bishop, died Ripon, c. 744. He studied at Whitby when **Hilda** was abbess, and was coadjutor to Bishop **John of Beverley**, succeeding him as bishop of York in 721. **Bede** describes his outstanding holiness, and he appears to have been especially interested in education. He retired to a monastery in 732. Feast 29 April.

Wilfrida, see **Wulfhilda**.

Willehad, bishop, born Northumbria, England, died Blexen, Lower Saxony, 8 November 789. He appears to have known **Alcuin**, so it may be that he too was educated in York. He emerges into history in the late 760s when he was sent by the king of Northumbria to evangelize the Frisians. In 780 **Charlemagne** sent him to the Saxons, but he had to flee in 782. He then went on pilgrimage to Rome, and afterwards settled in the abbey of Echternach. He returned to his mission to the Saxons in 785, and two years later was made the first bishop of the new diocese of Bremen, being consecrated at Worms. He built the first cathedral at Bremen, dedicated to St Peter.

William, thirteenth century. A priest in Piedmont. Feast 7 February.

William Andleby, bl., martyr, born c. 1552, executed York, 4 July 1597. The son of John Anlaby of Etton, William was brought up a Protestant. He was educated at St John's College, Cambridge, and graduated in 1572. At the age of 25 he went to join the Dutch Protestants in fighting the Spanish, and on the way visited the English College in Douai. He met with William Allen, founder of the college, and as a result of these meetings eventually converted to Catholicism and decided to become a priest. He was ordained in 1577 at Cateau-Cambrésis. He returned to England the following year and worked for nearly 20 years before being arrested. In 1597 he was tried and convicted of ministering as a priest and was sentenced to be hanged, drawn and quartered.

William Brown, bl., martyr, died Ripon, 5 September 1605. A layman arrested with **Thomas Welbourn**, but little is known of him.

William Davies, bl., martyr, born probably Crois, Yris, north Wales, died Beaumaris, Wales, 27 July 1593. He studied at Rheims, was ordained priest in 1585 and returned to minister in Wales. In 1591 he was arrested at Holyhead and imprisoned in Beaumaris castle. He was, it seems, able to celebrate mass and receive visitors who wanted to consult or convert him. He was a popular figure and was moved from prison to prison in an attempt to stem the flow of his popularity and in renewed attempts to get him to convert. He was eventually returned to Beaumaris where, despite opposition by the populace, he was hanged, drawn and quartered.

William Dean, bl., martyr, born Linton, Yorkshire, died Mile End Green, London, 28 August 1588. A converted minister, he went to Rheims in 1581, was ordained at Soissons, then returned to England in 1582. He ministered for two years before he was arrested and banished in January 1585, but returned the following November. He was imprisoned in March 1588.

William Filby, bl., born Oxfordshire, c. 1555, martyred Tyburn, London, 30 May 1582, beatified 1886. He studied at Lincoln College, Oxford, was ordained at Rheims in 1581, and arrested at Lyford Grange with **Edmund Campion**. He is commemorated with **Luke Kirby**, **Laurence Richardson** and **Thomas Cottam**, with whom he was executed.

William Freeman, bl., martyr, born Yorkshire, died Warwick, 13 August 1595. He was at Magdalen College, Oxford, before going to Rheims to study for the priesthood. He was ordained in September 1587 and returned early the following year to England, to work in Warwickshire and Worcestershire. He was arrested in Worcestershire in January 1595, imprisoned at Warwick, and there was hanged, drawn and quartered.

William Gibson, bl., martyr, born Ripon, Yorkshire, died York, 29 November 1593. He spent many years in prison for his faith, and was martyred with **George Errington** and **William Knight**.

William Harrington, bl., martyr, born Felixkirk, Yorkshire, 1566, died Tyburn, London, 18 February 1594. He went to school in Douai and afterwards joined the Jesuits, but had to leave because of ill-health. He was arrested on his return to England, but was released, and returned to Felixkirk for seven years, before returning to the continent to study for the priesthood. Ordained in Rheims in 1592, he was captured in 1593 at the house of Henry Donne (brother of the poet, who died – apparently of the plague – in prison as a direct consequence) and was hanged, drawn and quartered.

William Hart, bl., born Wells, Somerset, 1558, martyred York, 15 March 1583, beatified 1886. Having recovered from surgery for the stone, he studied at Douai, was ordained in Rome and returned to England in 1581, working in and around York. Arrested in December 1582, he was hanged, drawn and quartered.

William Horn, bl., martyr, died Tyburn, London, 4 August 1540. A lay brother of the London Charterhouse, in 1537 he was kept in prison in the Marshalsea with nine of his brethren, all of whom died of ill-treatment and starvation. William survived, and was sent to the Tower of London for three years before being tried, found guilty for denying the royal supremacy, and hanged, drawn and quartered.

William Howard, bl., martyr, born 30 November 1612, died London, 29 December 1680. He was brought up as a member of the Church of England, although in a family which had strong Catholic connections. After his marriage in 1637 – the service was conducted by a Catholic priest in deference to his bride's family – he became Viscount Stafford, and started to practise as a Catholic. This meant that he and his family had to leave the country for long periods, his estate was sequestered, and he was only restored after the restoration of the monarchy in 1660. He then made efforts to gain more toleration for Catholics, but was implicated by Titus Oates in the 'Popish Plot', was imprisoned and executed on Tower Hill.

William Gunter, bl., martyr, born Raglan, Wales, died Shoreditch, London, 28 August 1588. He went to Rheims in 1583, was arrested in June 1588, and condemned to death on 20 August that year.

William Ireland, bl., born Lincolnshire, England, 1636, martyred Tyburn, 24 January 1697. He studied with the Jesuits at St Omer, then joined the Society. He was professed in France in 1673, and later he worked in London, returning in 1677. He was falsely accused with **Thomas Whitbread**, **John Fenwick** and **Thomas Pickering** of wanting to murder Charles II when Titus Oates invented the 'Popish Plot'. He was hanged, drawn and quartered with **John Grove**.

William Knight, bl., martyr, born South Duffield, Yorkshire, 1573, died York, 29 November 1596. He was reported as a Catholic to the authorities by a relative who wanted to obtain his land – William's father having died. He was imprisoned first in what is now King's Manor, York, before being moved to York castle, where he met **George Errington** and **William Gibson**, with whom he suffered martyrdom.

William Lacey, bl., martyr, born Horton, West Riding, Yorkshire, c. 1531, died Knavesmire, near York, 22 August 1582. A lawyer, he was married to a widow, the mother of a Jesuit, and he too was suspected of being a Catholic. From 1565, when he was dismissed from his post, he was hunted as a Catholic and eventually left his wife and family, went to France and then to Rome. He was ordained priest in Rome (with a special dispensation, as he was married), and returned to York. He was arrested on leaving York castle, where he had been ministering to Catholic prisoners. With **Richard Kirkman**, he was hanged, drawn and quartered.

William Marsden, bl., born Goosnargh, Lancashire, martyred Newport, Isle of Wight, 25 April 1586, beatified 1929. Educated at Brasenose College, Oxford, he was received into the Church at Douai, then ordained at Rheims in 1585. He returned to England in February 1586, was seized almost immediately, and was tried in Winchester and London. He is commemorated with his friend **Robert Anderton**, with whom he was hanged, drawn and quartered, the only priests condemned by royal proclamation.

William of Aebelholt, abbot, born Paris, *c.* 1127, died Aebelholt, Denmark, 6 April 1203. Son of a noble family, William became a Canon Regular of Sainte-Geneviève-de-Paris. Absalon of Lund, bishop of Roskilde, called him to Denmark to reform the house of canons on Eskilsø. As first abbot of Aebelholt (1175), he exerted great influence as a writer and teacher and acted as an intermediary in Franco-Scandinavian controversies; he worked for peace, and for freedom of the Church. His cult began with numerous miracles shortly after his death, and he was canonized in 1224.

William of Aquitaine, founder, born *c.* 755, died Gellone abbey, Languedoc, 28 May 812. A cousin of **Charlemagne**, who appointed him count of Toulouse and protector of his son Louis the Pious, king of Aquitaine. William recaptured Barcelona from the Moors (803), and founded a monastery at Gellone, near Aniane, where he was professed as a lay brother in 806, with **Benedict of Aniane** as his spiritual director. He also founded nearby a monastery for women. He appears in several *Chansons de geste* as William *au court-nez*; his biographical material is contained in the eleventh-century *Ardonis vita Benedicti abbatis Anianensis*.

William of Arnaud, bl., martyr, died Avignoult, 1242. Little is known of William's life until 1234, when **Gregory IX** appointed him inquisitor for

four dioceses in Provence; his zeal in rooting out heresy was such as to have him banished from Toulouse, although he is said to have converted many by his 'sweetness and charity'. Lured to a castle at Avignoult by the bailiff of Count Raymond VII of Toulouse, William and his 11 companions were murdered, giving rise to reports of miracles and cures, and confirmation of a cult by **Pius IX** in 1866. Feast 29 May.

William of Bourges, archbishop of Bourges, born Arthel, 1150, died Bourges, 10 January 1209. William became abbot of the Cistercian monastery at Fontaine St-Jean (1184), then of Châlis (1187). Named archbishop of Bourges in 1200, he lived a life of strict observance, and died while preparing a crusade against the Albigenses. He is buried in his cathedral. Pope Honorius III canonized him in 1218.

William of Gellone, see **William of Aquitaine**.

William of Eskhill, see **William of Aebelholt**.

William of Firmatus, hermit, perhaps bishop, born Tours, died Mantilly, 24 April *c.* 1095. Educated at Tours, a canon of St Venantius, William became a soldier and physician. He retired to the wilderness with his mother, and lived as a hermit after her death. Renowned for his sanctity, miracles were credited to him, including the freeing from prison of Count Baldwin of Boulogne, later king of Jerusalem. Stephen of Fougères, bishop of Rennes, wrote his life.

William of Hirsau, bl., second abbot of Hirsau, born 1026, died at the abbey of Hirsau, 4 July 1091. He entered the monastery of St Emmeran in Regensburg as a child oblate, and in 1069 was named abbot of Hirsau. He was a supporter of the reforms of **Gregory VII**, and eventually adopted a form of the Cluniac observance for his monastery, and for those founded from Hirsau. He wrote treatises on music and on astronomy.

William of Malavalla ('bad valley'), born France (?), died near Siena, 10 February 1157. He abandoned his military career, made several pilgrimages as penance and eventually became a hermit after two attempts to establish a monastic community.

After his death, a community of Guliemites, Hermits of St William, formed on the spot. It was later absorbed into other orders.

William of Norwich, alleged child-martyr, born near Norwich, 1132, died there, 22 March 1144. A tanner's apprentice aged 12, William is said to have been enticed from his home on Tuesday of Holy Week into the house of a Jew in Norwich. His mutilated body was found in Mousehold Wood on Holy Saturday. According to Thomas of Monmouth, a monk and the only authority for the legend, William had been crucified by the Jews during Passover. This earliest known example of blood accusation against the Jews was investigated in 1759 by Cardinal Lorenzo Ganganelli (Clement XIV), who refuted the legend absolutely. The cult of William dates from 1151, when many visions and miracles were reported at his tomb.

William of Notre Dame de l'Olive, hermit, born Brabant, died Mariemont, 10 February 1240. A baker early in life, William became a Canon of St Norbert (Premonstratensian) at Aisne, but soon left to live as a hermit at Mariemont in Belgium. He founded Notre Dame de l'Olive, an abbey for women that became affiliated with Citeaux; the first nuns came from Fontenelle and from Moustier-sur-Sambre.

William of Rochester, born Perth, Scotland, died near Rochester, England, 1201. A fisherman, he adopted a foundling, David. They left for the Holy Land, but David murdered him. When the woman who found him was cured of her mental illness through contact with his body, a popular cult began. Feast 23 May.

William of Roskilde, bishop, born England, died Roskilde, Denmark, 1074. Said to have been a chaplain to King Canute, and returned with him to Denmark, where he set about evangelizing the people and was eventually created bishop of Roskilde, which was then the seat of the Danish kings. Feast 2 September.

William of St-Brieuc, bishop, born St-Brieuc, Brittany, date unknown, died there, 1234. He was ordained in St-Brieuc, was a canon in Tours, and became bishop of St-Brieuc *c.* 1220. He argued

with the duke of Brittany, Peter Mauclerc, about the rights of his see, and was expelled for two years. He went to Poitiers, but had returned to St-Brieuc by 1230. After his death he was buried in the cathedral, and when his body was exhumed in 1248, the year after his canonization, it was found to be incorrupt. Feast 29 July.

William of Toulouse, bl., theologian and mystic, born Toulouse, 1297, died Paris, 18 May 1369. William entered the Augustinian Order at 19, and lectured at Paris. He had a special devotion to the souls in purgatory, read the lives of the saints often, and sought to model his life on theirs; he overcame many temptations in his struggle for perfection. Miracles accumulated after his death, his cult was approved 50 days later, and confirmed in 1893.

William of Vercelli, abbot, born Vercelli, Piedmont, 1085, died monastery of San Salvatore, Goleto, near Nusca, 25 June 1142. As a youth William became a hermit and built a monastery at Monte Vergine, near Avellino, and a celebrated shrine there to Our Lady (1124). When disagreements arose with other monks, William moved to Serra Cognata and founded other monasteries, including the one near Nusca where he died. He also founded (in 1119) the now extinct congregation of Benedictine monks called Williamites.

William of Volpiano, abbot, born in the castle on Isola S. Giulio, on lake Orta, Italy, 962, died abbey of Fécamp, 1 January 1031. He was the son of the count of Volpiano, and entered as a child oblate the monastery of San Genuario, near Vercelli. In 987 he met Abbot Majolus of Cluny, and returned with him to Cluny. Majolus entrusted him with the reform of a number of monasteries, one of which, St Bénigne at Dijon, elected him abbot in 990, at which point he was ordained priest. A large number of monasteries followed the reforms he instituted, and by the time of his death he ruled some 40 houses. A small number of his letters and sermons, and a single treatise, survive.

William of York (Fitzherbert, also known as William of Thwayt), archbishop, died, possibly of poisoning, York, 8 June 1154. About the year 1139 he was canon and treasurer of York Minster. On the death of the previous archbishop in 1140 he was proposed for the vacant see. He was supported by the king and in Rome by Henry of Blois, but stood in opposition to Henry Murdac, a Cistercian monk who enjoyed wide ecclesiastical support, including that of Theobald, the archbishop of Canterbury, and, again in Rome, by **Bernard of Clairvaux**. William was suspected of simony, and it was alleged there was undue royal pressure in his nomination. He was, however, able to clear his name, and in 1143 he was consecrated archbishop by the papal legate. He reformed the diocese and won the affection of the people. When Eugenius III, a Cistercian, came to the papal throne he took up the cause of Murdac and William was deposed. He travelled to Rome and later took refuge with Henry of Blois in Winchester. Both Eugenius and Murdac died in 1153, and the incoming pope, Anastasius IV, restored William to the see of York and gave him the pallium, which he had never before collected, although it had been bestowed by Pope Lucius II. He returned to York to popular acclaim, and when everyone escaped unharmed when a bridge over the river Ouse collapsed, the supposed miracle was attributed to him. He died suddenly within a month of his return.

William Pattenson, bl., born Durham, martyred Tyburn, 22 January 1592. Ordained in Rheims in September 1587, he returned to England just over a year later. He then worked in the West Country. Arrested in Clerkenwell, London, it is said that he converted six fellow prisoners, and was therefore hanged, drawn and quartered as painfully as possible.

William Repin and Companions, bl., martyrs. There were in all 98 other priests, religious and lay people who died during the French Revolution, all beatified in 1984. William Repin himself died at Angers, 2 January 1794. Those guillotined included the priest brothers **John** and **René Lego** and **Rosalie du Verdier de la Sorinière**, nun of Calvary. See also **Martyrs of the French Revolution**.

William Richardson (also called Anderson), bl., martyr, born near Sheffield, 1572, died London, 27 February 1603. After looking after imprisoned priests at Wisbech, he studied in Spain from 1592, returning to England in 1600. He was arrested in

London, and was the last priest martyred under Elizabeth I, executed a few days before the queen died.

William Saltemouche, see **James Salès**.

William (Maurus) Scott, bl., from Chigwell, Essex, martyred Tyburn, London, 30 May 1612, beatified 1929. He converted while studying at Trinity Hall, Cambridge, and in 1604 became a Benedictine at St Facundus, Satagún, Spain. Repeatedly arrested and banished, he is commemorated with **Richard Newport**, with whom he was hanged, drawn and quartered.

William Spencer, bl., martyr, born Gisburn, Yorkshire, c. 1555, died York, 24 September 1589. He studied at Oxford, then at the English College at Rheims. He was ordained priest in September 1583, and returned to England just under a year later. Little is known of his missionary activity. He is one of the **Eighty-Five Martyrs of England, Scotland and Wales**.

William Tempier, bl., died Poitiers, 1197. A Canon Regular at St-Hilaire-de-la-Celle, Poitiers, he became bishop of the city and defended Church freedoms. Feast 29 March.

William Thompson (alias Blackburn), bl., born Blackburn, Lancashire, martyred Tyburn, London, 20 April 1586, beatified 1987. He studied at Rheims, was ordained in 1584 and in England was chaplain to **Anne Line**. He was captured at Harrow-on-the-Hill and is commemorated with **Richard Sergeant**, with whom he was hanged, drawn and quartered, aged about 26.

William Ward, bl., martyr, born England, c. 1565, died Tyburn, London, 26 July 1641. Records of his early life and background are confused, and he may have been born William Webster. This is the name he is given in the records of the English College at Douai, where he studied from 1604. He was ordained in 1608 and travelled to Scotland, where he was arrested and imprisoned for three years. He went to England and was arrested again and held in Newgate prison until he was banished in 1613. Over the next 30 years he worked in London, between spells in various prisons. In 1641 the persecution of Catholics was intensified, and when William was arrested in July that year he was tried and condemned to death by being hanged, drawn and quartered.

William Way, bl., martyr, born Exeter, August 1562, died Kingston on Thames, near London, 9 September 1588. He studied for the priesthood at the English College, then at Rheims, and was ordained in September 1586. Later that year he travelled to England. He was arrested in London some six months later, imprisoned in the Clink, and after refusing to recognize the jurisdiction of the bishop of London, was condemned to be hanged, drawn and quartered. He is one of the **Eighty-Five Martyrs of England, Scotland and Wales**. Feast 23 September.

Willibald, born Wessex, England, 21 October 700, died Eichstätt, Germany, 7 July 786. A nephew of St **Boniface**, he was educated at Waltham in Hampshire. In 720 he set out on pilgrimage with his father **Richard** and his brother **Winnibald**. Richard died at Lucca in Italy. The brothers carried on and toured the Middle East, including the holy places of Palestine: Willibald later dictated an account of their travels to a nun. On the way home they visited Constantinople, and were back in Italy in 730. For ten years he stayed at the monastery of Monte Cassino, but then went to assist Boniface. He became a priest, and in 742 bishop of Eichstätt. He founded a monastery at Heidenheim, where Winnibald and his sister **Walburga** came to live.

Willibrord, missionary archbishop, born Northumbria, 658, died Echternach, Luxembourg, 7 November 739. He studied under **Wilfrid** at Ripon, became a monk and at the age of 20 joined a community in Ireland, where he was ordained. In 690 he went with a group of confreres on a mission to Frisia, and was welcomed at the court of Pepin of Herstal. He quickly secured papal support for his mission, and in Rome in 695 Pope Sergius I consecrated him archbishop of the Frisians. He established a cathedral in Utrecht and in 698 established the monastery of Echternach, from which he made missionary journeys as far as Denmark, Heligoland and Thuringia. He encountered opposition from the pagan Duke Ragbod, but after the duke's death he was able to return to

Frisia, where he enjoyed the support of **Boniface** in repairing the damage wrought by the duke. He was buried in the abbey at Echternach, where his shrine became a centre of pilgrimage. He is the patron saint of the Netherlands and Luxembourg.

Willigis, born near Hanover, northern Germany, died Mainz, 1011. Chancellor of the empire from 971, archbishop of Mainz from 975, he was a statesman, working with three emperors, including Henry II. He was canonized for the life of prayer and charity sustained amid his political activity. Feast 23 February.

Willmer of Leaval, bl., seventh century. Feast 7 February.

Winefride (Welsh, Gwenfrew), patron of north Wales, seventh century. She was the daughter of a nobleman, and seems to have lived at Holywell, Flint (now Clwydd). Tradition has it that her head was cut off by a chieftain, Caradoc ap Alaric, or Alan, because she refused to marry him. Again according to legend, a well – St Winefride's Well at Holywell – sprang up where her head touched the ground. Her uncle and mentor, St **Beuno**, reunited her severed head to her body and Winefride was restored to life. She established a convent and became its abbess. Her relics were reburied in Shrewsbury in 1138. Feast 3 November.

Winnibald, abbot, born Hampshire, died Heidenheim, Wurtemberg, 18 December 761. The son of **Richard**, king of Wessex, he was brother of **Willibald** and **Walburga**. Richard and his sons set out for the Holy Land, but Richard is said to have died at Lucca. The brothers went on to Rome. There Willibald studied for seven years, and there he encountered **Boniface**. He joined Boniface in his missionary work, but eventually decided to found a double monastery on the Anglo-Saxon model at Heidenheim. He was assisted by his brother, who by this time was bishop of Eichstätt, and by his sister, who had experience of double monasteries in England. He had wanted to visit Monte Cassino to study the Benedictine Rule which he had adopted for his abbey, but ill-health prevented him.

Winnoc, abbot, born Britain (or possibly Brittany), died Wormhout, 6 November 716 or 717. He joined the abbey of St Peter in what is now St Omer, and then moved to a new foundation at Wormhout, near Dunkirk, in order to evangelize the surrounding region.

Winwaloe (Guénolé, Winnol, Onolaus), born Britanny, died Landévennec, sixth century. He lived for a time as a hermit on an island off the coast of Britanny, then founded Landévennec monastery, Britanny. This was destroyed by Vikings in 914, but was rebuilt. He is shown carrying a church, but sometimes with a goose, having, it is said, restored his sister's sight by ordering a goose to return her plucked-out eye. Feast 3 March.

Wiro of Utrecht, bishop, from Northumbria, died Holland, c. 753. A monk, he participated in the Anglo-Saxon mission to continental Europe, evangelizing in Frisia. He became bishop of Utrecht in 741 and built a church and monastery at Roermond. Feast 8 May.

Wistan (Wystan), king, died Wistow, Leicestershire, England, 850. He succeeded to the throne of Mercia in 840, but as he was still very young, his mother acted as regent. Wistan's godfather wanted to marry Wistan's mother, but Wistan refused to allow it – for which he was brutally murdered. Feast 1 June.

Wite, born England, died there. Nothing else is known of her (or possibly him, but it is more likely a woman), except that her shrine survives, apparently with relics, at Whitchurch Canonicorum in Dorset – the 'Whit' presumably taken from her name. Feast 1 June.

Withburga, born East Anglia, England, died East Dereham, 17 March 743. She was the daughter of King Anna of the East Angles, and sister of St **Etheldreda**. She lived as a hermit near Holkham, Norfolk, and later moved to East Dereham after her father's death. Her body was exhumed 50 years after her death and found to be incorrupt. Feast 8 July.

Wivina, abbess, born Oisy, Flanders, died Bigarden, c. 1170. Of noble birth, she determined at an early age to become a nun, and rejected all suitors. She became for a time a hermit, but too many people came to visit her, and eventually the count of Brabant offered her property at Bigarden, where she lived for the rest of her days. Feast 17 December.

Wolfgang of Regensburg, born Swabia, c. 924, died near Linz, 994. He was educated in the abbey of Reichenau, where he became friendly with a young nobleman called Henry and moved with him first to Würzburg, and then to Trier, when Henry became archbishop there. After Henry's death he became a monk at the abbey of Einsiedeln. There he was ordained priest, and sent as a missionary to the Magyars. In 972 he was appointed bishop of Regensburg, although he continued to wear his monastic habit, and there, apart from looking after his diocese and caring for the poor, he worked to restore religious life. He was responsible for the education of the future emperor and saint, **Henry II**. Feast 31 October.

Wolfhelm, bl., abbot, born Rhineland, died 22 April 109. He joined St Maximus abbey in Tier c. 1036, then moved to Cologne, later becoming abbot at Gladbach and Sieburg. A man of prayer and action and a renowned theologian, he was involved in controversies including the nature of the Eucharist. Feast 22 April (suppressed).

Wolfred, martyred 1029. He was an English missionary to Sweden. Feast 18 January.

Wulfhilda, abbess, born 940, died Barking, c. 1000. The daughter of a nobleman, she was educated by nuns, and became one herself. In 970 she was sent to Barking abbey as its abbess. Feast 9 September.

Wulfram, bishop, died Fontenelle, Normandy, seventh century. He was the son of an official at the court of King Dagobert, and was made bishop of Sens. After only two years, however, he left his see to evangelize the Frisians, visiting Fontenelle abbey to recruit some monks to help him. He had some success, and returned to Fontenelle after many years. Feast 20 March.

Wulfram of Córdoba, martyr, born France, died Córdoba, 931. He was a Frank who came to

Córdoba to preach and was arrested for this, since, while Christians were tolerated, public support for the faith was forbidden. He had met **Argentea** and they were executed and are commemorated together. Feast 13 May.

Wulfric (or Ulric or Ulfrick), born Somerset, *c.* 1080, died there, 20 February 1154. A parish priest, he became an anchorite, living for 30 years in a cell against the church wall. Many visited him, including the English sovereigns, to benefit from his reputed gifts of healing and second sight – not in the Roman martyrology.

Wulfrid, bl., monk, born Wales, died there, *c.* 1200. Feast 13 February.

Wulfsindis, died Reisbach, Bavaria, seventh century. Nothing is known of her, apart from a surviving cult. Feast 2 September.

Wulfstan, bishop of Worcester, and last of the Anglo-Saxon bishops, born Little Itchington, near Warwick, *c.* 1008, died 20 January 1095. Educated by Benedictines at Evesham and Peterborough, he became a monk at Worcester, and schoolmaster and prior in the cathedral monastery there. In 1062 he accepted with some reluctance the position of bishop of Worcester. He became famous for his continued monastic asceticism and personal sanctity. He had earlier been on friendly terms with Harold; he submitted to William I, the Conqueror, in 1066, and was very useful in checking the rebellious barons during the revolt of 1075. He was equally loyal to William II in his struggle with the Welsh. Wulfstan's relations with his superiors were not so harmonious, and both **Lanfranc** of Canterbury and Bayeux of York at one time unsuccessfully demanded his removal. By his preaching at Bristol, Wulfstan is said to have put an end to the kidnapping of English men and women and their sale as slaves. He wrote numerous homilies in Old English, including the famous *Lupi Sermo ad Anglos,* as well as works of political theory, notably his *Institutes of Polity, Civil and Ecclesiastical.* He also drafted a number of laws, including most of those promulgated by Ethelred II and **Canute**.

Wulsin (Wulfsin, Wulsige), bishop, born London, died there, 8 January 1002. A monk under **Dunstan** at Glastonbury, he was bishop of London, then abbot of Westminster and finally a reforming bishop of Sherborne – bringing in Benedictine monks and having his pastoral letters translated into English to ensure they were understood. Feast 8 January.

Xac'atur, martyr, died Tigranaakert, 20 August 1652. Armenian Church. A young man, he conceived the desire of undergoing martyrdom. He publicly insulted Islam, and was condemned to having his limbs cut off.

Xac'ik Vardapet, evangelist, fifth century. Armenian Church. He was a disciple of **Mesrop**, and continued his task of spreading Christianity in Armenia through knowledge of the Scriptures. The story was told of him that, in the village of Akori, he saw the souls of the dead being called to heaven – except for one man, named Lazarus, who was left behind because his family had not given alms to the poor in his memory. Xac'ik alerted Lazarus's relatives, and later saw his soul, also, taken up into heaven. Feast 30 May.

Xenia the Blessed of St Petersburg, Russian Orthodox, 'fool for Christ's sake', born 1732, died St Petersburg, 1803. She was married to an officer who died suddenly. Afterwards she took his name, dressed in his uniform and wandered the capital. She was revered as a healer and prophetess. She worked at night in all weathers helping to build the Smolenskoye Cemetery church, near which she was buried. Her grave was a place of pilgrimage even in the Soviet period. She was canonized in the emigration in 1978 and in Russia in 1988, and her shrine is now restored. Feast 24 January.

Xenophon, martyr, fourth century. Died with **Mary**, **John** and **Arcadius**. Feast 26 January.

Xystus, see **Sixtus**.

Yachard, bishop, born Kincardineshire, Scotland, fifth century. A missionary to the Picts. Feast 24 August.

Yafqeranna Egzi, monk, born Hamlo, Tigre, *c.* 1309, died 15 January 1372. Ethiopian Church. He was baptized with the name Afqaranna Egzi, meaning 'they have loved the Lord', but he later changed it to the above, which means 'he who loves the Lord'. He was ordained priest *c.* 1320, and became a monk soon afterwards. He worked for seven years on the island of Tana. He then became a hermit on Mount Ayfalba. When on one occasion he was sent for by the governor of Goggiam, he threw himself over a cliff rather than obey, but landed in a tree from which he had to be rescued. He lived in various places, eventually settling on Mount Guegueben. There he formed a community, writing for them a Rule which included manual labour, fasting, silence and numerous prostrations. Many miracles were attributed to him during his life.

Yam'ata, monk, born Qusyat, Syria (?), fifth/sixth century. Ethiopian Church. He founded the monastery of Guh in Tigre. Feast 8 November.

Yared Mahletawi, deacon, born near Axum, died Mount Semen, 19 May, in an unknown year, but sixth century. Ethiopian Church. He was ordained deaon, and became the first composer of sacred music in the Church of Ethiopia. He retired with some disciples to Mount Semen, and lived out his last years there.

Yaret, monk, third century (?). Syriac Church. He

was a monk of the monastery of Mar **Awgen** on Mount Izla. He later built a monastery inside a former pagan temple beside the river Sarya, where he lived with his disciple **Cyriac**, converting the pagans in the region by the power of his miracles. Feast 27 October.

Yasay, monk, fourteenth century. Ethiopian Church. A disciple of **Madhanina Egzi**.

Yawnan Rabban, monk, seventh century. Syriac Church. A follower of **Abraham the Great**, he was for a decade a monk at Bar Tura, just north of the modern city of Balad Singar. In 637, because of the Arab invasion, the monks moved east, to the Tigris, to the monastery of Mar Ba'ut, where he died, but when, after seven years, the monks moved back to their former home, they took his body with them.

Yawnan the Stranger, founder, died al-Anbar, fourth century. Syriac Church. He was born into a noble family. He moved to Cyprus, where he met Mar **Awgen** and became one of his followers, who persuaded him to settle in Persia, although only after a pilgrimage to Jerusalem and the desert of Scete, where he founded a monastery at Peroz Sapor (al-Anbar) on the Euphrates. According to later legends, he left his original foundation for some years, wandering around other monasteries in the region of Qatar.

Yazdandhot, born Erbil, died there, fourth century. A rich woman of Erbi (or Arbil, in Iraq) who cared for those about to be martyred, visiting them in prison and providing food and drink for them, and burying them after their execution. Feast 7 April.

Yazdapnah, bishop, died Kaskar, seventh century. Syriac Church. He was just possibly the founder of the monastery at Samarra, before becoming bishop of Kaskar.

Yazdapnah and Awid, martyrs, died Persia, fourth century. Syriac Church. Originally from Bet Huzaye in modern Iran, Yazdapnah spent five years in prison before being taken before King Chosroes at al-Anbar, where people offered to free him, but he refused. He was being sent to the capital when he was beheaded at the village of Taima. Awid, also from Bet Huzaye, had wished to join Yazdapnah in his martyrdom, but was unable to do so. Three years after the death of Yazdapnah, however, his nose and ears were cut off.

Yazdin, born Dawin, Iran, fifth century. Syriac Church. He and a brother converted to Christianity. He became a monk at the monastery of Karkha for 32 years, but then returned as a missionary to his native region, where he spread Christianity. Then, for a further 14 years, he became a hermit, living alone in a cell, with **Pethion** as his disciple. Feast 21 June.

Yemrehanna Krestos, king, twelfth century. Ethiopian Church. It is unclear when he ruled Ethiopia, after a bitter struggle for the throne, but he was remarkable in that he was the only ruler of Ethiopia who had been ordained priest, and apparently regularly celebrated the liturgy. (Most were, however, ordained deacons, so they might enter the sanctuary.) Feast 29 October.

Yerde'ana Krestos, abbot, born Bugena, died Dabra Libanos, 1268 (?). Ethiopian Church. He was head of the monastery of Dabra Libanos from 1225 to his death.

Yetbarak, king, thirteenth century. Ethiopian Church. He was the son of **Lalibala** and **Masqal Kebra**, although he did not succeed directly to the throne, because it was usurped by his cousin **Na'Akweto**.

Yimar, martyr, born Van, died there, 7 March 1416 (or 1418). Armenian Church. A widow, who had lost her husband in the invasion of Tamburlaine, then married a Muslim. They lived happily together, each following their own religion, but the husband's neighbours harassed her to become a Muslim, even persuading her finally to throw stones at a Christian church. Twenty years later, repenting of her action, she moved to a Christian city, but there was told she could only truly repent where her sin had been committed. She returned to Van, where she said to a mullah that the stones she had thrown at the church ought now to be thrown at her head. She was martyred by stoning. Feast 3 February.

Yohanni of Dabra Asa, hermit, born Tamben, thirteenth century. Ethiopian Church. He was the illegitimate son of the wife of a noble of Tamben, and was brought up by a monk named Ammoni, of the community at Dabra Asa – his mother having persuaded her husband on his return from war that the monk was the boy's father. He was ordained deacon when he was 12 years old. On the way to the ceremony Yohanni saw women for the first time, and was told by Ammoni that they were demons, and if he were to meet one he should throw himself into an abyss. Years later his mother came to see him, and he threw himself, as instructed, into an abyss, but by divine grace grew wings on his arms and was able to fly down into the land of the living, to be welcomed by the patriarch Enoch and the prophet Elias. The archangel Gabriel then instructed his spiritual director to write his life. Feast 14 November.

Yohanni of Dabra Damo, abbot, born Tigre, died there, thirteenth century. Ethiopian Church. A nobleman, he was seemingly governor of Tigre, having married the daughter of the king of Ethiopia. Later in life he decided to become a monk, and joined the community of the ancient monastery of Dabra Damo, of which he became abbot. He remained there for the rest of his life, but played a significant part not only in the spiritual guidance of, among others, **Takla Haymanot**, but also in the politics of the kingdom.

Yozadaq, monk, died Qardu, seventh century. Syriac Church. A companion of **Hormizd** on

Gabal Maqlub, he later went to Qardu and founded a monastery there, where he died aged 80.

Yuhanna Abu Nagah al-Kabir and Fahd, martyr, died Cairo, early eleventh century. Coptic Church. He was the head of the Coptic scribes during the caliphate of al-Hakim. Al-Hakim offered him the title of vizier if he would convert to Islam. He asked for time to decide, went home, told his relatives and friends of the proposition, but said he was going to die for the faith. When he returned, al-Hakim had him flogged to death. Al-Ra'is Fahd Ibn Ibrahim was made a similar offer, but also refused. He was killed by the sword, and his body burned, although the body remained untouched by the flames for three days, and Fahd's right hand, with which he had given money to the poor, survived longest. Another eight Copts were also asked to convert: four underwent martyrdom, one died under torture, the other three returned to Christianity once the persecution was over. Feast 14 April.

Yusab al-Abrahh, bishop, born al-Nuhaylah, Asyut, Egypt, 1735, died St Anthony's monastery on the Red Sea, 12 January 1826. Coptic Church. He was educated in the village school and, at the age of 25, resisting his parents' wish that he marry, he became a monk, first in the monastery of St Anthony at Bus (modern Nasir), then at St Anthony's monastery on the Red Sea, where he was ordained priest. In 1791 he was consecrated bishop of Girga and Ihmim, a see which had been vacant for some time after the conversion to Catholicism of its bishop. He then changed his name from his baptismal Yusuf to Yusab. It was Yusab who was chosen by the patriarch to answer letters from Rome about the theological position of the Coptic Church, and he left a number of other writings on theological, scriptural and liturgical topics. He retired from his post shortly before his death, going to live first in Cairo, then in his former monastery on the Red Sea.

Yusab I, patriarch, born Minuf al-Ulya, in the Delta, *c.* 769, died Alexandria, 20 October 849. He early decided he wanted to become a monk, and although his guardian attempted to dissuade him, he eventually did so in the monastery of St Macarius, of which he became the abbot. In 830, on the death of the patriarch **Simon of Alexandria II**, a number of the bishops chose a rich and married layman for the office, but other bishops, scandalized by this decision, chose Yusab, and went to his monastery to collect him, although he was unwilling to take up the post. It was a very difficult period. He had to face two revolts of the Copts against their Muslim overlords, troubles brought on by revolts of the faithful against some of their bishops, and an attempt to have him killed by the head of the army in Egypt. As a final humiliation he was turned out of his house in Alexandria by an Arab prince who slept with his concubine in the patriarch's bed. As a pastor, he travelled around Egypt, Nubia and Ethiopia supporting the bishops in those regions, and afterwards keeping contact with them by letter.

Z

Zachaeus, bishop, second century. The fourth bishop of Jerusalem, but little else is known of him. Feast 23 August.

Zachaeus, martyr, died Palestine, 303. Deacon in the church in Gadara, he was arrested and tortured during the persecution of Diocletian. He was beheaded with **Alphaeus**. Feast 17 November.

Zacharias, pope, born Calabria, pope from 3 December 741, died Rome, 15 March 752. Nothing is known of his early life other than that he was a Greek by birth in Calabria. He was the last Greek pope and appears to have been on intimate terms with Gregory III, whom he succeeded. A cultivated man, he translated Gregory's *Dialogues* into Greek, and was noted for his political adroitness and great personal persuasiveness. He reversed his predecessor's policy towards the Lombards, who were threatening Rome with invasion, and prevailed upon King Liutbrand and his successor, Rachis, to make peace with Rome and to restore four captured cities. It was largely through his tact in dealing with these princes in a variety of emergencies that the exarchate of Ravenna was rescued from becoming part of the Lombard kingdom. In 751 he sanctioned the deposition of the last Merovingian, Childeric III, in Pepin III's favour. He held synods at Rome in 743 and 745; the latter confirmed the condemnation of two heretics, Adalbert and Clement, by St **Boniface**. He sought to persuade the emperor in Byzantium to abandon his policy of supporting iconoclasm. Zacharias was an energetic and efficient administrator who, as well as controlling the militia and civil government of Rome, took an active interest in the papal patrimonies.

Zacharias, hermit, died *c.* 950. He was the master of **Nilus the Younger**. Feast 21 January.

Zacharias (Zachary), bishop, martyr, died Vienne, second century. He is said to have been the second bishop of Vienne, near Lyon. Feast 26 May.

Zacharias of Alexandria, patriarch, born Alexandria (?), died 9 November 1032. He was the priest of the church in which the electors gathered to find a successor to Patriarch Philotheus in 1003. When he fell from a ladder, but the jar of oil he was carrying remained intact, this was taken as a sign and he was himself chosen. Until 1010 his period of office was quiet, but then there arose accusations of simony within the Coptic Church, and the caliph al-Hakim made use of the unrest to close all churches and forbid the use of wine. Zacharias was arrested in November and was imprisoned for three months while al-Hakim tried to persuade him to abjure Christianity. Although a meek individual, and weak, he refused to abjure, although many members of his flock did so. Al-Hakim, however, suddenly changed tack, freed the patriarch, and allowed Christians freedom to worship. Zacharias, distrusting the caliph, retreated for the next nine years to the monastery of St Macarius. His last years passed peacefully.

Zacharais of Alt'amar, martyr, born Alt'amar (?), died Ostan, 1395. Armenian Church. He was elected catholicos of Alt'amar, an island on lake Van. Falsely accused of attacking a Persian, he went to see the emir at Ostan as the only way of defending himself. He was told by the emir that he had to convert to Islam, but he refused, and was lynched by the mob.

Zacharias of Arta, martyr, born Arta, died Patras, 1782. Byzantine Church. As a young man he became a Muslim and went to Patras, where he worked in the leather trade. He repented of his sin, and went before the judge saying that he now wished to abjure Islam. After various attempts to dissuade him, he died under torture. Feast 20 January.

Zacharias of Barbare, monk, fourteenth/fifteenth century. Ethiopian Church. A disciple of **Eustace of Sarabi**.

Zacharias of Corinth, bishop, born Corinth (?), died there, 30 March 1684. Byzantine Church. He was arrested on charges of conspiring with the Venetians to overthrow Muslim rule in Corinth, a charge which he denied. He was condemned to be impaled on a stake, then burned over a slow fire, but Christians in Corinth paid money for him to be executed by beheading.

Zacharias of Galila, monk, fourteenth century. Ethiopian Church. A disciple of **Philip of Dabra Libanos**. He founded a monastery on the island of Galila on lake Tana.

Zacharias of Gefa, monk, fourteenth century. Ethiopian Church. A disciple of **Madhanina Egzi**.

Zacharias of Jerusalem, patriarch, born Jerusalem, died there, 633. Byzantine Church. He was patriarch of Jerusalem from 609, and was therefore the bishop of the city when it was invaded by the Persian King Chosroes in 614. He was taken captive, but freed after the expedition of the Byzantine Emperor Heraclius in 628. Feast 21 February.

Zacharias of Nicomedia, martyr. Feast 10 June.

Zacharias of Prusa, martyr, born Prusa, Asia Minor, 1764, died there, 28 May 1802. Byzantine Church. He was ordained as a priest, but was too fond of alcohol and on one occasion, while drunk, declared himself a convert to Islam. He soon regretted what he had done, and decided to seek martyrdom. One day, when again drunk, he was persuaded to go before the judge to accuse a woman of refusing to return to him some money he had lent her. While in the court he was accused of criticizing Mohammed. He was imprisoned and, as he refused to abjure Christianity, was beheaded.

Zacharias of Sa, bishop, eighth/ninth centuries. Coptic Church. A disciple of **John of Scete**, he later became a bishop.

Zacharias of Saha, bishop, died Saha, 15 February 723 (or 730). Coptic Church. The son of a senior official in the Byzantine administration, he too became a civil servant, but then entered a monastery, and was later made bishop of Saha in the (modern) province of Kafr al-Sayh, which he ruled for 30 years. He produced a number of religious works, some of which survived.

Zacharias of Scete, monk, died Scete, Egypt, fourth century. He was brought up by his father who had left his wife, and settled as a hermit in Scete. This unusual situation caused much criticism both of Zacharias and his father. He was a friend of, among others, **Moses the Black**. Feast 5 December.

Zacharias of Senkursk, priest, died Senkursk, 1492 (?). Russian Church. Although he enjoys great veneration in northern Russia, where the city of Senkursk is located, nothing is known of this 'fool for Christ'.

Zacharias the Faster, monk, born Kiev, died there, eleventh/twelfth century. Russian Church. As a young boy he was left a large amount of money by a rich man of Kiev. It was left in the keeping of a friend of the rich man, Sergius, but when the time came to hand it over Sergius said that the money had been intended for the poor and the Kievan Cave monastery. Zacharias argued with him, and Sergius offered to swear upon an icon, but when he did so he was struck by a paralysis and Zacharias received the money, which he gave to the monastery, and then entered it himself. Feast 24 March.

Zacharias the Fool, priest, died Senkursk, 1325. Russian Church. A priest of Senkursk, he became a 'fool for Christ' and was renowned as a miracle worker.

Zacharias the Recluse, monk, born Egypt, died there. Although little is known of him, he had a reputation for generosity towards the poor and the outcasts. Feast 24 March.

Za'iyasus, abbot, thirteenth century. Ethiopian Church. The nephew of **Iyasus Mo'a**, he was brought up at Dabra Hayq, and assisted his uncle in the administration of its property. He eventually succeeded as head of the monastery, although he was married with children, and gave the monastery many precious gifts. Feast 24 July.

Za'iyasus, martyr, died sixteenth century. Ethiopian Church. A monk of Dabra Libanos, he died during an attack by pagan tribesmen.

Za'iyasus Buruk, monk, thirteenth century. Ethiopian Church. A monk of the monastery of Dabra Libanos. Feast 23 June.

Zakka, monk. Syriac Church. It is unclear who he was, although it seems possible that he was a disciple of Mar **Matta**, and is said to have lived in a small cell on Gabal Maqlub, north-east of Mosul. He later succeeded Mar Matta as head of the latter's monastery.

Zalibanos, monk, born Tamben, Tigre. Ethiopian Church. He founded Dabra Maryam Manawe.

Zamadhen, monk. Ethiopian Church. A disciple of **Takla Alfa**.

Zambdas, bishop, died Jerusalem, 304. Said to have been bishop of Jerusalem. Feast 19 February.

Zamik'ael Aragawi, monk, fifth/sixth century. Ethiopian Church. A late Life says he was related to the Byzantine imperial household, and became a monk through **Pachomius** when only 14. He lived with Pachomius in the Thebaid for a number of years, during which time his mother became a nun and joined him. After Pachomius's death he returned to Constantinople, then went to Axum with a group of monks. They lived for 12 years at the court, then spread out through Ethiopia

preaching the gospel. With his mother and a disciple called Matthew he went to Eggala, where, on Mount Damo, he established Dabra Damo.

Zanithas and Companions, martyrs, died Persia, 326. He was martyred with Lazarus, Nerses, Elias, Maris, Habibm Saba, Marutha and and Sembaytah. Feast 27 March.

Zanuphius, founder, died Marwayig. Coptic Church. He first founded a monastery for men near Marwayig, near Ihmim, and then, after a divine revelation, one for women.

Zar'a Abreham, monk, fifteenth century. Ethiopian Church. His father was commander of the royal guard, in which office Zar'a succeeded him. He was twice married, but both wives died without leaving him any children. He then became a monk at the monastery of Yelmatan. For some time he was an evangelist in Damot. He was particularly devoted to meditating on the passion of Christ, beating himself and wearing upon his head an imitation of the crown of thorns.

Zar'a Buruk, monk, born Sima, c. 1645, died 18 January 1700. Ethiopian Church. He lost his sight when only seven, but despite his many infirmities, he practised rigorous asceticism. He learned liturgical music, and was imprisoned for five years for his theological views. Much of his time he spent near the source of the Blue Nile, which is where he died.

Zar'a Endreyas, monk, born Eritrea. Ethiopian Church.

Zar'a Muse, monk. Ethiopian Church. An apostle of Tigre.

Zatra Wangel, monk, sixteenth/seventeenth centuries. Ethiopian Church. He was the sixteenth successor to **Takla Haymanot** as abbot of Dabra Libanos. Feast 28 May.

Za'ua, monk, born Palestine (?), fourth century. Assyrian Church. Of rich parents, he went to Jerusalem and there became a priest. With a disciple named **Tabor** he went about making many converts both from Jews and pagans, but then settled as a hermit in a cave on Mount Gara, north of Mosul, where he stayed for 40 years. Afterwards he moved to the mountains of Hakkari, where he built a church in a village which still bears his name. He lived to be 122.

Za'ura, hermit, died Thrace, sixth century. Syriac Church. He was forced to go to Constantinople by the Chalcedonians, but was given a house there on the Golden Horn by the Empress **Theodora**, who sympathized with the monophysites. He refused to take part in a debate organized by Justinian because it was to be held in Lent. When it finally took place Justinian was struck down by an illness because of his opposition to Za'ura, but the latter healed him. The Chalcedonian party now wanted to exile him from Constantinople, but the empress again found him safe refuge in Thrace. Feast 18 October.

Zayna, bishop and martyr, seventh century. Syriac Church. He was a monk, said to be the son of the king, around whom many legends have grown up, but it seems not unlikely that c. 620 he became bishop of Ba Rimmon near Tikrit, where he and his sister **Sarah** founded monasteries. Nothing is known of his death, beyond the fact that he was martyred.

Zayohannes, monk, born Marabete, fourteenth century. Ethiopian Church. At the age of seven he began to study the Scriptures, and was one day transported miraculously to Jerusalem, where he visited the bishop and was ordained. He returned home and lived with his parents, but resisted their attempts to arrange a marriage. After their deaths he gave away all his possessions and went to Dabra Libanos, where he became a monk. One day, while in church, he had a vision of Christ, who told him to go to Tigre, where again he was miraculously transported. He lived at Dara, on lake Tana, with a family of fishermen. They took him to the island of Kebran, where he freed the inhabitants from their worship of a serpent. He built a monastery there, which he governed until he was 95, when he handed over to his disciple **Melchisedech**. He died ten years later, on 18 July.

Zdislava Berka, born Krizanov, died Jabbone, Bohemia, 1252. A mother of four, she had an unhappy marriage, but her husband, count of Lemmbeck, allowed her to shelter those fleeing from the Tartars after seeing Christ crucified instead of the beggar he was evicting. She became the first Slavic Dominican Tertiary, and founded a Dominican convent at Jabbone, near her castle, where she died. Feast 1 January.

Zebinus, hermit, died Cyrrhus, fifth century. He was a hermit of Cyrrhus (Nabi Huri, some 40 miles north of Aleppo, Syria), and was the spiritual guide of, among others, St **Maro**. Feast 23 February.

Zenais, Cria, Valeria and Marcia, martyrs. Although celebrated together, Zenais, who died at Constantinople, is not linked to the others, who died at Caesarea in Palestine. Feast 5 June.

Zena Marqos, monk, thirteenth/fourteenth century (?). Ethiopian Church. Supposedly the cousin of **Takla Haymanot**, his birth and infancy are surrounded by miracle stories, including curing of his baldness the priest who baptized him. He was ordained deaon at the age of eight, and when on their way home he and his father were attacked by briagands, their staffs were turned into a serpent and a dragon, thus putting the brigands to flight. He married, but his wife immediately entered a convent while he was himself transported by the archangel Gabriel to Hagara Mehur, where he performed miracles and converted the pagan inhabitants. He was transported to Alexandria, where he was ordained priest, and then returned to Hagara Mehur to baptize the converts. With Takla Haymanot he entered the monastery of Dabra Besrat, but then went off to Muslim territory where again he converted the population, including the ruler, before setting of with his disciples preaching in various places. Feast 9 December.

Zena Maryam, nun, fourteenth century. Ethiopian Church. She was a very beautiful girl, with four brothers. When her mother died of plague she took her brothers and retreated to a cave, where one of them died. The others she entrusted to a friend, and then entered a convent. But she had already been betrothed, and her fiancé, who had paid much money for her, wanted to go ahead with the marriage. She returned to her father's house, but said she had already taken her vows and the money had to be repaid. A year later she went back to the convent. She later moved to Enfraz, near Gondar, where she remained for 20 years in prayer and fasting.

Zenas the Servant, see **Zeno and Zenas**.

Zeno, see also **Cosconius**.

Zeno, see also **Felicula**.

Zeno, hermit, died Antioch, c. 416. He was a disciple of **Basil the Great**, and served as a (military) imperial messenger at the court of the Emperor Valens. At the death of the emperor he left the court and settled in a cave near Antioch as a hermit, where he spent the rest of his life. Feast 10 February.

Zeno and Chariton, martyrs, died 303. Nothing is known of them. Feast 3 September.

Zeno and Zenas, martyrs, born Philadelphia, died there, 304 (?). Zeno was a rich man who gave away all his goods and freed all his slaves. Zenas was one of the slaves, but he chose to stay as a servant with Zeno, and was martyred – by beheading – alongside him. Feast 23 June.

Zeno, Cordius and Theodore, martyrs, died Nicomedia, 304 (?). A father and his two sons. Feast 2 September.

Zeno of Gaza, bishop, died Gaza, c. 399. He was one of the companions of **Eusebius, Nestabus and Companions** who were lynched for destroying a pagan temple. Zeno survived to become bishop of Gaza. Feast 26 December.

Zeno of Maiuma, bishop, fourth century. Maiuma is a bishopric near Gaza.

Zeno of Nicomedia, martyr, died Nicomedia, 303. He was a soldier, who laughed as the emperor offered sacrifice to the gods, and was beheaded for his blasphemy. Feast 22 December.

Zeno of Verona, bishop, born Africa, died Verona, Italy, c. 375. Little else is known of him. He was bishop from 362, and seems to have flourished

during the decade before his death, according to St **Ambrose**. As his own anti-Arian writings, which have affinities with African writers such as Tertullian and **Cyprian**, did not come into circulation until the earlier Middle Ages, they were unknown to St **Jerome**, in his *De Viris Illustribus*, and Grennadius. The sermons, and *Tractatus*, reveal a pastorally minded bishop intent on instilling a liturgical and sacramental life in his flock, insisting on liberality, hospitality and care for the poor. Ninety-three of his sermons survive; his teaching on the Trinity and the incarnation reveals the undeveloped status of theology in the West, but he insists on the absolute virginity of Mary, before, in and after giving birth. The miraculous preservation of Verona from flood in 598, attributed to Zeno's intercession, greatly increased his cult. Feast 12 April.

Zeno the Faster, monk, born Kiev (?), died there, fourteenth century. Russian Church. A monk of the Kievan Cave monastery, he is said to have been 'resplendent in fasting'. Feast 30 January.

Zenobia, see **Zenobius**.

Zenobius, martyr. A certain amount of confusion surrounds this saint. He may have been from Aegea (now Alexandretta), a physician and/or bishop, who with his sister **Zenobia** gave away everything to the poor and was later martyred, together with Zenobia. In which case they are reputed to have died c. 285, and their feast is celebrated 30 October. Or he may be a priest of Sidon, in the Lebanon, who was also a physician, and was martyred in Antioch in 310. The latter's feast is 29 October. They may, however, be the same person.

Zenobius of Florence, bishop, born Florence, c. 310, died there, 390. Apparently baptized and ordained by Theodore, whom he succeeded as bishop of Florence, he was a friend of **Ambrose**. Pope **Damasus** sent him to Constantinople in connection with the Arian controversies. He is a patron of Florence. Feast 25 May.

Zephyrinus, born the son of a Roman, Halrundius, pope from 199, died Rome, 217. Eusebius records that he reigned for 18 or 19 years, succeeding

Victor I. According to **Hippolytus**, who became an antipope, Zephyrinus had little intelligence (*aner idiotes kai agrammatos*) or strength of character, and the somewhat important controversies on doctrine and discipline that marked his pontificate are more appropriately associated with himself and **Callixtus**, his principal adviser and successor. Zephyrinus would not condemn monarchianism and patripassianism, as Hippolytus wished him to do. The statements Hippolytus attributes to him form, according to Harnach, the oldest recorded dogmatic definition of a Roman bishop. There is no proof of his alleged martyrdom in the martyrology of St **Jerome**, and his place of burial in the cemetery of Callixtus is uncertain. Feast 26 August (suppressed 1969).

Zikam, martyr. Coptic Church. Nothing is known of him. Feast 26 May.

Zinovius of Oten, monk, died 1571. Russian Church. Nothing is known of his life, except that he was a monk of the monastery at Oten, some 30 miles from Novgorod. He is known through his letters, which display a strong social conscience and a belief that all, and not just the learned, should have the Scriptures available to them. He blamed the fall of Constantinople in the fifteenth century on the decline in moral standards.

Zita, born Monsagrati, Tuscany, 1218, died Lucca, 27 April 1278. Patroness of domestic servants, at the age of 12 she entered the service of the Fratenelli family at Lucca and remained there until her death. Misunderstood and even maltreated at first, her piety, humility and exactitude in performing her domestic duties, in which she regarded herself, rather, as the servant of God, won the love and respect of her employers and fellow servants. She is especially venerated in Lucca, which Dante and Fazio degli Uberti called 'Santa Zita'. Her coffin was opened in 1446, 1581 and 1652, revealing her body intact, and she was canonized by Pope Innocent XII in 1696. Her relics lie in St Frigidian's church, Lucca. Feast 27 April.

Zoë, see **Hesperus**.

Zoëllus, martyr, died possibly Istria, Croatia, second/third century. He was put to death with Servilius, Felix, Silvanus and Diocles, with whom he is commemorated. Feast 24 May.

Zoerardus and Benedict, Slovak hermits of Zobor, late tenth, early eleventh century. Born in Silesia, Zoerardus came to Slovakia from Poland during the reign of King Stephen of Hungary (1002–03). He was also known as Andrew (Slovak name Svorad), and with his disciple Benedict (Stojislav) lived an eremitico-coenobitical life, combining aspects of the Camaldolese and the Benedictine traditions, in the cave of Shalka, diocese of Nitra. He excelled in mortification and penance; chains embedded in his flesh witnessed to his self-inflicted chastisement. The master died in 1009, and the disciple was martyred three years later by robbers and thrown into the river Vak in 1012. The relics of both are in the cathedral of Nitra; their cult was approved in 1083. St Svorad-Andrew is patron of some well-known Slovak institutions, e.g., St Andrew's Benedictine abbey in Cleveland, Ohio, spiritual centre of the Slovaks in North America. Feast 17 July.

Zoilus and Companions, martyrs, born Córdoba (?), died there, 304 (?) He is said to have died with 19 others during the persecution of Diocletian. Feast 27 June.

Zonus, Alexander, Dunus and Orion, martyrs, died Alexandria, third century (?). Zonus is said to have been the bishop of Alexandria, and the others deacons of his church.

Zosimas and Adrian, monks, died 15 August 1492. Russian Church. Zosimas was the religious name of Ignatius Eropkin, of Moscow, who embraced the religious life *c.* 1470. With Adrian he established a monastery in 1479 dedicated to the Dormition, apparently on property of the Eropkin family, close to the abbey of Volokolamsk.

Zosimas of Alexandrovsk, founder, born Smolensk, died Vladimir, *c.* 1715. Russian Church. Little is known of him, although he is thought to have come from a noble family. He established the hermitage at Alexandrovsk, which is near Vladimir. He is much venerated locally. Feast 24 October.

Zosimas of Vorbozom, hegumenos, died Vorbozom, 1550. Russian Church. A disciple of **Cornelius of Komel**, he came to the lake of Vorbozom, about 12 miles from Beloozersk, while on pilgrimage, and settled there, establishing a monastery dedicated to the Annunciation. Feast 4 April.

Zosimus, pope from 18 March 417, died Rome, 26 December 418. His pontificate was short and stormy. The *Liber Pontificalis* describes him as 'of Greek origin, his father was Abram'; this seems to indicate Jewish ancestry, although nothing else is known of his origins. He succeeded **Innocent I**, to whom he may have been recommended by **John Chrysostom**, and his election seems to have affronted a part of the Roman clergy. He figured in two incidents of note: (1) he granted to Patrocles, bishop of Arles, who voted for his election, the title of papal vicar in Gaul, and made him metropolitan of the provinces of Vienne and Narbonne. The bishops of Gaul resented this disturbance of their status quo. (2) In the Pelagian affair, **Augustine** had no sooner uttered at Carthage his famous words, '*Causa finita est*', approved by Innocent I, than Pelagius and Caelestius appealed to Zosimus, who absolved them as falsely accused. The African bishops were outraged, and so informed the pope, who was compelled to reverse his stand. He informed the Africans that he had not yet made up his mind, but that, meanwhile, the decision of his predecessor was to stand. He took the occasion to read the Africans a lecture on the Roman primacy, reaffirming the tradition that the judgement of the apostolic see must not be disputed. In the event, the Africans appealed to Emperor Honorius, who condemned Pelagius, and Zosimus was obliged to issue at Carthage (418) his *Epistola Tractoria* condemning Pelagianism. Zosimus's fractious temper coloured all the controversies in which he took part, in Gaul, Africa and Italy, including Rome, where part of the clergy appealed to the court at Ravenna against him. He excommunicated them and would have gone further, had he not died of a serious illness. The ninth-century *Martyrology of Ado* was the first to list him as a saint.

Zosimus, bishop, died Syracuse, Sicily, seventh century. Placed in the monastery of St Lucia near Syracuse at the age of seven, he spent 30 years as a monk there, became abbot, then bishop of Syracuse, and died aged 90. Feast 30 March.

Zosimus, hermit, born Palestine, died there, fifth century. He was placed in a monastery in Palestine when only five. Aged 35 he became a priest, and lived at the monastery of John the Baptist by the river Jordan. During Lent it was customary for the monks to live alone in the desert, and on one occasion by chance he encountered **Mary of Egypt**. Feast 4 April.

Zosimus, martyr, born Apollonia, died Antioch, c. 117. He was a soldier who converted to Christianity and, after refusing to sacrifice to idols, was tortured and then beheaded. Feast 19 June.

Zosimus and Athanasius, hermits. Zosimus was a hermit in Cilicia who was arrested and condemned to death in 303. His demeanour so impressed Athanasius, one of the spectators, that he, too, became a Christian and offered himself for martyrdom. However, it seems that both were released, and ended their days as hermits. Feast 3 January.

Zosimus, see also **Rufus and Zosimus**.

Zoticus and Companions, martyrs, died Rome, 120. These are ten soldiers, including Amantius, Hyacinth and Irenaeus, all buried in the Via Lavicana. Feast 10 February.

Zoticus of Constantinople, martyr, born Rome, died Constantinople, c. 350. He was a member of the Roman clergy who went to Constantinople when it was first established, and organized a hospital for orphans and for the poor in the imperial city, but was martyred under the Arian Emperor Constantius by being tied to wild horses. Feast 31 December.

Zoticus of Comana, bishop and martyr, died Comana, Cappodocia, 204 (?). Feast 21 July.

APPENDIX

Christian Traditions

Many of the entries in the *Dictionary* list the saint or blessed as belonging to a particular branch of Christianity – the Ethiopian Church, for example, or the Coptic Church. Some, however, have no tradition singled out. This may be because the saint is venerated across all, or at least several, of the traditions – this is particularly true for saints of the early Church – or it may be because they belong to the largest group of saints, those of the Western Church. The Western Church effectively means the Roman Catholic Church, because the Churches of the sixteenth-century Reform do not have a process of canonization, though some holy individuals have been accorded, as it were, an informal canonization. Apart from the Roman Catholic Church, the others are described below. It is necessary, however, to understand the various strands of the tradition, to know a little of the history of the early Church.

Christianity was probably never wholly united – even in the New Testament there is evidence of tension between Aramaic and Greek-speaking Christians in Jerusalem. In the course of time a number of sects developed, with a varied degree of relationship to the mainstream, but these have not survived down to modern times. In the fourth century, however, Arianism emerged, named after the priest Arius, who died in 336, which held that the Son of God was not eternal, in other words, in the Trinity the Son was subordinate to the Father. Although in various forms Arianism lasted a considerable time, again no permanent Arian community survived. It was different in the fifth century. In 428 Nestorius, a monk of Antioch, was appointed bishop, or Patriarch, of Constantinople.

A heresy has been named after him, the belief that in the incarnate Christ there were two quite separate persons, one human, the other divine. Whether Nestorius himself ever held the doctrine attributed to him is disputed, but Nestorianism became a significant strand in Christianity. The argument attributed to Nestorius was that Mary, Christ's mother, could not be called 'Theotokos' or Mother of God. This issue debated at the Council of Ephesus of 43, which affirmed the legitimacy of speaking of the 'Theotokos'.

This Council, however, left undefined the relationship between the divine and human in Christ. The Church returned to this topic in 451 at the Council of Chalcedon. Chalcedon determined that Christ is one person in two natures, his divine nature being of the same substance as the Father, while his human nature is of the same substance as other human beings, the two natures being united unconfusedly, unchangeably, indivisibly and inseparably – as the definition of the Council declared. Many in the East refused to accept the Chalcedonian formula, claiming instead that there was one nature out of two. They, the Monophysites (the term means 'one nature'), rejected Chalcedon because in their eyes it called into question the incarnation, that is, God becoming human in Christ, and it thus verged on Nestorianism. The upholders of Chalcedon, on the other hand, argued that the Monophysites absorbed the human nature of Christ into the divine. This was a crucial dividing line between Churches, as will be seen below.

The other major dividing line was that of 1054, when in Constantinople a cardinal representing the bishop of Rome, the Pope, excommunicated the patriarch of Constantinople, and the Pope was in turn excommunicated by the Patriarch. This had happened a number of times before, but on this occasion the breach never successfully healed, though there was a number of attempts to do so. The reasons for the division were many, both theological and political. The two Churches had grown apart for several hundred years, with different languages (Greek in Constantinople, Latin in Rome), which added to misunderstandings, different liturgical practices and different theological positions, especially on the Filioque, whether it was right to add to the Nicene creed the expression 'proceeds from the Father AND FROM THE SON' as was done in Rome.

The Churches listed below in alphabetical order reflect the divisions in Christianity. which have been briefly outlined above. They are given the titles which have been used in the Dictionary.

Assyrian Church, or Church of the East, often referred to as the Nestorian Church because its doctrine of Christ rejects the title of 'Theotokos' for Christ's mother. It lay outside the Roman Empire, in what is now Iraq, and its primatial see, that of its 'Catholicos' or leading bishop, was at Seleucia-Cctesiphon, the the capital of the Persian Empire. Its intellectual capital was at Nisibis (Nusaybin, now in Turkey), to which the famous theological school of Edessa (Urfa, also in Turkey) was transferred in 457. It was remarkable in establishing early missions in China, its missionaries following the Persian traders. Its liturgical language is Syriac.

Armenian Church: Armenia was converted by **Gregory the Illuminator**, who baptised King Tiridates III. For a time afterwards the patriarchate of Armenia was hereditary in the family of Gregory, and ots patriarchal see was at Etchmiadizin, near Mount Arat. In the fifth century its liturgy was translated into Armenian in the early fifth century (cf. Ss **Isaac the Great** and **Mesrob**). The Armenians rejected the Council of Chalcedon, and have since been regarded as Monophysites. Some Armenians united with Rome at the Council of Sis of 1307.

Bulgarian Church: the Bulgarian Prince Boris was baptized 864/.65, his territory having been evangelized by both Greek and Latin missionaries. He finally opted for Constantinople rather than Rome. In 917 he declared the Church self-governing, and a patriarchate, with the patriarchal see at Preslav. This see was later suppressed, to be replaced by Rome in 1204 by Trnovo. Under Ottoman domination Trnovo became increasingly dependent on Constantinople until eventually it again disappeared as a patriarchate. The metropolitan of Sofia again assumed the title of Patriarch, which in 1968 was recognized by Constantinople.

Byzantine Church, or the Greek Orthodox. The Greek-speaking Church of the former Eastern, or Byzantine, Empire, under the Patriarch of Constantinople, known as the Ecumenical Patriarch. The Patriarch of Constantinople has primacy of honour among other patriarchs, such as that of the Russian Church, as well as among the autocephalous, or self-governing Orthodox Churches. Constantinople was founded in 330 by the Emperor Constantine on the site of the ancient Greek city of Byzantium. Therefore it was not one of the earliest Churches, but it became more important when a number of other Churches, and particularly the ancient see of Alexandria, refused to accept the Chalcedonian definition.

Coptic Church, the Church of Egypt, which refused to accept the teaching of Chalcedon. It was the in the desert of Egypt that early monasticism flourished, and monastic life played an important part in the preservation of the Coptic tradition, under Muslim domination since 642. Coptic is the language used in the liturgy, derived from the ancient language of Egypt. There is a small Coptic Church in communion with Rome.

Cypriot Church: Cyprus was evangelized in New Testament times, and was recognized in 431 as an independent Church, governed by an exarch, or archbishop.

Ethiopian Church: the origins of Christianity in Ethiopia (Abyssinia) are unclear, but the first bishops seems to have been **Frumentius** who, after being taken prisoner by pirates, bcame advisor to the Ethiopian kings at Axum. He was consecrated bishop of Axum by St **Athanasius of Alexandria**, but Christianity really began to spread after the arrival of the a group of evangelists, probably

Syrian Monophysites fleeing the Byzantine Empire because of the persecution of their beliefs. The link with Egypts lasted until 1959. Up to that point the head of the Ethiopian Church, the Abuna, was a Copt appointed to his post by the patriarch of Alexandria. From 1959 it became independent under its own patriarch. Its liturgy uses Ge'ez, the ancient language of Ethiopia. There is a small Ethiopian Church in communion with Rome, as well as Latin-rite Catholics in the country.

Georgian Church: the conversion of Georgia to Christianity is traditionally attributed to St **Nino**, c. 350, and was originally dependent on the patriarchate of Antioch. In the eighth century it became self-governing. It was absorbed into the Russian Church in 1811, regaining its independence in 1917, though the Russian Church refused to recognize this until 1943. A patriarchate was established in 1918.

Melchites: the term means 'imperial' and is used of those Christians of Syria and Egypt who accepted the (imperial) Council of Chalcedon. The head of the Church, who resides in Damascus, is the Patriarch of Antioch. A large number of Melchites are in communion with Rome, under their own Patriarch, titled of Antioch and all the East, of Alexandria and Jerusalem.

Old Believers: members of the Russian Church who, led by the archprist **Avvakum**, refused to accept the liturgical reforms introduced by the Patriarch **Nikon**, and were excommunicated in 1667. This ban was removed in 1971, though the schism continues.

Romanian Church: the tradition of this Church was primarily Greek. In 1359 a patriarchate was established, first with its see at Targoviste, later in Bucharest. It became independent of Constinatinople lonly in 1885. In 1698 a number of Romanians entered communion in 1698. Under Communist domination they were forced to link to the Orthodox Church, but were re-established as a communion dependent on Rome in 1990.

Russian Church: Christian missionaries first came to what is now Russia in the ninth century and in 988 Prince (saint) **Vladimir** was baptized. The missionaries were Greek, and a Greek hierarchy was established, dependent on Constantinople, with Kiev as the metropolitan see. The metropolitan see was moved to Moscow in the fourteenth century, though in 1461 Kiev became a metropolitan see once again in addition to Moscow. The dependency on Constantinople lasted until, in 1589, the metropolitan archbishop in Moscow was raised to the rank of Patriarch.

Serbian Church: The first Christian prince was Muimir (860-91). The Serbs wavered between Constantinople and Rome before St **Saba** established an independent Church in 1219, under the Ecumenical Patriarch. The Serbian metropolitan took the title of Patriarch in 1346, with his see at Pec, and was recognized as such by the Patriarch of Constantinople in 1375. Ths patriarchate was suppressed in 1766, when under Ottoman rule, and only restored, with its patriarch in Belgrade, in 1920.

Ukrainian Church (Moscow Patriarchate): the history of this Church is extremely complicated. Originally the Church in Russia was under the jurisdiction of the metropolitan of Kiev, but Roman influence increased after the Ukraine became part of Poland. In 1595, by the Union of Brest-Litovsk, a number of bishoprics, including the metropolitan of Kiev, were united with Rome, and were joined by others including, in 1700, the bishop of Lvov. They were known as Ruthenians. However, much of the Ukraine being in Poland, the nobility of the country began increasingly to adopt the Latin – rather than the Greek – rite. When Poland was partitioned towards the end of the eighteenth century, the Greek-rite Catholics who now came within Russian territory were forced into union with the Orthodox. Lvov, however, fell under the control of (Catholic) Austria, and was raised to the rank of a metropolitan in 1807. In 1918 the Orthodox Church in the Ukraine became a self-governing exarchate of the Russian Orthodox Church. However, a separate autocephalous Church came into being in 1919. In 1946 the Greek-rite Catholic were forced to become part of the Russian Orthodox Church, but regained their independence of the Moscow patriarchate in 1989. It is the first of these three, the self-governing exarchate, which constitutes the Ukranian Church, Moscow Patriarchate, mentioned in the *Dictionary*.

Saints and *Beati* created under Pope Benedict XVI

The list which follows contains the names of those who have been made saints, or have been declared blessed (bl.) under Pope Benedict XVI. As in the main body of the Dictionary, first names have been anglicised wherever possible, though Maria (for Mary) has been allowed to remain

Albert Hurtado Cruchaga (1901–1952)

Anacletus González Flores (died 1927/1928) bl.

Andrew Solá Molist (1895–1927) bl.

Anne-Eugénie Milleret de Brou (1817–1898)

Anthony de Santa Ana (died 1822)

Ascension del Corazón de Jesú (1868–1940) bl.

Augustine Thevarparampil "Kunjachan" (1891–1973) bl.

Bronislaw Markiewicz 1842–1912) bl.

Charles de Foucauld (1858–1916) bl.

Charles of St Andrew *see* John Andrew Houben

Clement August Graf von Galen (1933–1946) bl.

Darius Acosta Zurita (1908–1931) bl.

Elias di San Clemente (1901–1927) bl.

Euphrasia of the Sacred Heart of Jesus Eluvathingal (1877–1972) bl.

Eurosia Fabris (1866–1932) bl.

Eustace von Lieshout (1890–1943) bl.

Felix of Nicosia (1715–1787)

Gaetano Catanoso (1879–1963)

George Preca (1880–1962)

Ignatius Klopotowski (1866–1931) bl.

John Andrew Houben (1821–1983)

Joseph Bilczewski (1860–1923)

Joseph Tàpies (1869–1936) bl.

Joseph Trinidad Rangel (1887–1927) bl.

Leonard Pérez (1883–1927) bl.

Louis Biraghi (1801–1879) bl.

Louis Monza (1898–1954) bl.

Margarita Maria López de Maturana (1884–1934) bl.

Maria Crocifissa Curcio (1877–1957) bl.

Maria Maddalena of the Passion (Costanza Starace) (1845–1921) bl.

MarÚa of the Angels Ginard Martí (1894–1936) bl.

Maria of the Passion (1866–1912) bl.

Maria Pia Mastena (1881–1951) bl.

Maria Rosa Pellesi (1917–1972) bl.

Maria Teresa of Jesus (1825–1889) bl.

Maria Teresa of Saint Joseph (1855–1938) bl.

Mary Eugenie de Jesus *see* Anne-Eugénie Milleret de Brou

Marianne Cope (1838–1918) bl.

Mariano de la Mata Aparicio (1905–1983) bl.

Moses Tovini (1877–1930) bl.

Paul Josef Nardini (1821–1862) bl.

Philip Smaldone (1848–1923)

Raphael Guízar Valencia (1878)

Rita Amada Of Jesus (1848–1913) bl.

Rosa Venerini (1656–1728)

Sara SalkahÃzi (1899–1944) bl.

Simon de Lipnica (c. 1437–1482)

Theodore Guérin (1798–1856)

Wladyslaw Findysz (1907–1964) bl.

Zygmunt Gorazdowski (1845–1920)